EVIDENCE LAW

A STUDENT'S GUIDE TO THE LAW OF EVIDENCE AS APPLIED IN AMERICAN TRIALS

Fifth Edition

Roger C. Park
James Edgar Hervey Professor of Law Emeritus
University of California—Hastings College of the Law

Aviva A. Orenstein
Professor of Law and Val Nolan Faculty Fellow
Indiana University Maurer School of Law

Dale A. Nance
Albert J. Weatherhead III & Richard W. Weatherhead Professor of Law
Case Western Reserve University School of Law

HORNBOOK SERIES®

WEST ACADEMIC PUBLISHING

444 Cedar Street, Suite 700
St. Paul, MN 55101
1-877-888-1330

Printed in the United States of America

ISBN: 978-1-63659-126-1

To Suzanne, always in my heart

R.C.P.

To David, Michael, and Ben, with whom this book could never have been written.

A.A.O.

To Melani, Michael, and Lyndlea,
and
In memory of Joyce Lynn

D.A.N.

Preface to the Fifth Edition

This fifth edition of EVIDENCE LAW: A STUDENT'S GUIDE TO THE LAW OF EVIDENCE AS APPLIED IN AMERICAN TRIALS maintains the book's original goal of serving as a succinct one-volume treatise on evidence, emphasizing practical courtroom application. As with the first four editions, we have attempted, wherever possible, to use the language of the courtroom and to provide examples and arguments that derive from trial practice. Our target audience is law students who need to learn evidence doctrine and policy, but who also wish to develop courtroom practice skills. Like the last edition, this edition expands discussion of the rationales underlying the rules and how the rules have developed, reflecting our conviction that evidence policy and history are indispensable to understanding the interpretation of those rules. Accordingly, we trust this treatise will continue to provide both a helpful review and a source of information and arguments for practitioners as well.

This edition retains the chapter reorganization introduced in the fourth edition. The twenty chapters fall into six parts: (I) Evidence in the Adversary System (three chapters that set the stage for the consideration of admissibility rules that form the bulk of evidence law); (II) An Overview of Privileges (one chapter); (III) Relevance and its Counterweights (three chapters); (IV) Specific Rules for Testimonial Evidence (four chapters); (V) Specific rules for Non-testimonial Evidence (two chapters); and (VI) Hearsay and Confrontation (seven chapters). As in the previous editions, the chapters are largely self-contained, allowing the student to read chapters in any order that corresponds to a plausible syllabus.

The new edition updates rules and case law. In particular, it reflects changes that have been made since the last edition in those parts of the Federal Rules of Evidence that govern character evidence and hearsay. It also adds a new section devoted entirely to corroboration requirements. Finally, it reflects a careful re-editing of every section to improve readability.

ROGER C. PARK
SAN FRANCISCO, CALIFORNIA

AVIVA A. ORENSTEIN
BLOOMINGTON, INDIANA

DALE A. NANCE
CLEVELAND, OHIO

August, 2021

Preface to the Fourth Edition

This fourth edition of EVIDENCE LAW: A STUDENT'S GUIDE TO THE LAW OF EVIDENCE AS APPLIED IN AMERICAN TRIALS maintains the book's goal of serving as a succinct one-volume treatise on evidence, emphasizing practical courtroom application. As with the first three editions, we have attempted, wherever possible, to use the language of the courtroom and to provide examples and arguments that derive from trial practice. Our target audience is law students who need to learn evidence doctrine and policy, but who also wish to develop courtroom practice skills. This edition expands discussion of the rationales underlying the rules and how the rules have developed, reflecting our conviction that evidence policy and history are indispensable to understanding the interpretation of those rules. Accordingly, we trust this treatise will provide both a helpful review and a source of information and arguments for practitioners as well.

The most conspicuous change from the third edition is the chapter reorganization. The rather long chapters on relevance and hearsay exceptions in the third edition have been separated into smaller chapters, and the original recording rule is distinguished from authentication and allotted a separate chapter. Also, the chapter on appellate review has been consolidated with the chapter on offering and opposing evidence, where it is naturally covered in most courses. The resulting twenty chapters have been reorganized into six parts: (I) Evidence in the Adversary System (three chapters that set the stage for the consideration of admissibility rules that form the bulk of evidence law); (II) An Overview of Privileges (one chapter); (III) Relevance and its Counterweights (three chapters); (IV) Specific Rules for Testimonial Evidence (four chapters); (V) Specific rules for Non-testimonial Evidence (two chapters); and (VI) Hearsay and Confrontation (seven chapters). As in the previous editions, however, the chapters are largely self-contained, allowing the student to read chapters in any order that corresponds to a plausible syllabus.

The new edition updates rules and case law. It also treats discrete new topics, including: evidence of defendant's flight from the crime scene, evidence of a party's withholding or destroying evidence, evidence of plea negotiations offered by the defense, and so-called "reverse 404(b)" evidence offered by the defense. It also adds brief discussions of the special constitutional right of the accused in a criminal case to present exculpatory evidence, a right that may override otherwise applicable exclusionary rules. Finally, the new edition reflects the continued development of the Sixth Amendment Confrontation Clause cases, discussed primarily in the final chapter. In light of disagreements that have emerged among the justices on the United States Supreme Court on this topic, there is reason to expect continued change in Confrontation doctrine, and our discussion attempts to suggest potential lines of future development.

The "restyled" Federal Rules of Evidence went into effect at the end of 2011. Enough time has passed that we do not think it necessary to include a full version of the pre-restyling rules, especially in light of the fact that some rules have been substantively revised since 2011 anyway. Thus, the appendix includes only the Rules as they read when this volume went to press, including the new rules expected to go into effect December 1, 2017. In the text and notes, however, we have tried to identify critical changes in language that the student may encounter when reading judicial opinions written before 2012 and to identify potential confusions arising from the restyling.

Dale Nance, the John Homer Kapp Professor at Case Western Reserve University School of Law, has joined as an author on the project. He wishes to express appreciation to his former students, Juliana Tindall and Paul Lubonovic, and his administrative assistant, Kimberly Peterson, for research and editing assistance.

ROGER C. PARK
SAN FRANCISCO, CALIFORNIA

AVIVA A. ORENSTEIN
BLOOMINGTON, INDIANA

DALE A. NANCE
CLEVELAND, OHIO

STEVEN H. GOLDBERG
WHITE PLAINS, NEW YORK

November 2017

Preface to the Third Edition

This third edition of EVIDENCE LAW: A STUDENT'S GUIDE TO THE LAW OF EVIDENCE AS APPLIED IN AMERICAN TRIALS maintains the book's goal of serving as a succinct one-volume treatise on evidence with an emphasis on practical courtroom application. As with the first two editions, we have attempted, wherever possible, to use the language of the courtroom and to provide examples and arguments that derive from trial practice. Our target audience is law students who need to learn evidence doctrine and policy, but also wish to develop courtroom practice skills. We trust this treatise will provide a helpful review and source of information for practitioners as well.

The new edition updates rules and case law. It reflects the 2006 amendments to the Federal Rules of Evidence (Rule 408 on compromises, Rule 404 on character, Rule 606 inquiry into validity of verdicts, Rule 609 on convictions). It also includes the new Rule 502 on waiver of attorney-client privilege added in 2008 and the amendment to Rule 803(b)(3) declarations against interest, which took effect December 1, 2010.

The continued development of the Sixth-Amendment Confrontation Clause cases mandated an expansion of the discussion of confrontation and the inclusion of a whole chapter (Chapter 11) dedicated to the subject. In addition to presenting the recent cases, it guides the reader through the many questions still left open by the new confrontation jurisprudence.

Additionally, the long chapter on hearsay and its exceptions in the previous editions has been divided into six smaller chapters for ease of reference. Discussion of rape shield (Rule 412) and sexual propensity rules (Rules 413–415) has been expanded. The entire treatise has been updated and revised for increased clarity and ease of use. New introductory sections have been added to give an overview of certain important subjects, such as hearsay and impeachment.

In December 2011, if the various proposed amendments stay on track, the restyled Federal Rules of Evidence will go into effect. Although this restyling affirmatively does not affect substance and is for clarity and form only, the numbering of some sub-parts of rules has changed, and much of the language has been altered slightly (almost always for the better). Consequently, this edition was written to be used with both the current rules and the new restyled rules. We have attempted to quote selectively from language that is common to both the current and restyled versions.

Aviva Orenstein, from the Indiana University Maurer School of Law, has joined as an author on the project. She wishes to express her appreciation to the team of dedicated and energetic law students who reviewed each chapter in form and content. For their excellent work, she would like to thank following students from the Indiana University Maurer School of Law: Jessica Bergman, Michelle Bird, Thomas Cameron, Michael Hulett, Elizabeth Ferrufino, Joshua Fix, Lydia Johns, Jacob Johnson, Jonathan Long, Caitlin Kerr, Larissa Koshatka, Aliina Kuismi, David Munkittrick, Judith Reckelhoff, Megan Shipley, Heather Shreve, and Ryan Yates.

Finally, it is with great sadness that we note the untimely passing of our friend, colleague, and co-author, David Leonard. Professor Leonard epitomized the qualities of a dedicated scholar and an excellent teacher. We will miss our collaboration with him. We will miss him.

ROGER C. PARK
SAN FRANCISCO, CALIFORNIA

AVIVA A. ORENSTEIN
BLOOMINGTON, INDIANA

STEVEN H. GOLDBERG
WHITE PLAINS, NEW YORK

December 2010

Preface to the Second Edition

In the six years since the first edition of this "lawyer's treatise designed specifically for law students," the law of evidence has continued to evolve. There have been changes in the Federal Rules of Evidence, some of substantial significance, others simply efforts at clarification. Judicial decisions have, as always, added nuance to already established doctrine. Those rule and interpretation changes pale, however, beside two blockbuster changes in the law of evidence.

First, there have been important developments in the treatment of expert testimony, as the courts and rule makers have wrestled with the revolution started by the Supreme Court's 1993 decision in *Daubert v. Merrell Dow Pharmaceuticals, Inc.* Some of the post-*Daubert* questions we anticipated in the first edition have been answered by Supreme Court decisions and by amendments to the Federal Rules of Evidence. Chapter Ten discusses these changes, highlights some of the specific areas of expert testimony that have been affected, anticipates some of the still unanswered questions raised by the *Daubert* approach, and compares that approach, as it has grown in the federal system, to the still important *Frye* approach to expert testimony.

The Court's 2004 decision in *Crawford v. Washington* made a sharp departure from earlier confrontation cases, holding that "testimonial" statements, even if they fall within firmly rooted exceptions to the hearsay rule, are inadmissible against criminal defendants unless the out-of-court declarant is unavailable and the defendant previously had an opportunity to cross-examine the declarant about the statement. The decision, discussed in Chapter Seven, may leave more questions than it answers. The Court leaves open the definition of a "testimonial" statement and suggests that in the future it may decide that "non-testimonial" statements do not implicate the confrontation clause, their admissibility depending solely upon the law of hearsay.

We have, in this edition, kept faith with the advocate's approach to evidence. As the first edition was an adaptation of the TRIAL OBJECTIONS HANDBOOK, this edition continues to rely for its approach on that practitioner manual's focus on the notion that evidence law is something lawyers must employ quickly and concisely in the courtroom. We have been gratified by our students' responses to learning the language of the courtroom from that perspective and have been reinforced in our resolve to present the law of evidence as much as possible through example and with a constant eye to context.

In addition to the debt we owe our Evidence and Trial Objections students for comments and suggestions that have made this edition closer to our ideal, we would not have been able to complete it without the hard work and dedication of our research assistants, Jone Tran and John-Paul Buchanan at University of California, Hastings, Sabrina Cao-Garcia at Loyola Law School, and Sarah Courtman at Pace Law School.

ROGER C. PARK
SAN FRANCISCO, CALIFORNIA

DAVID P. LEONARD
LOS ANGELES, CALIFORNIA

STEVEN H. GOLDBERG
WHITE PLAINS, NEW YORK

June 2004

Preface to the First Edition

This is a lawyer's treatise designed specifically for law students. It is an adaptation of the TRIAL OBJECTIONS HANDBOOK, a work for practitioners that provided a concise description of the law of evidence from the perspective of the advocate who had to offer and oppose it, rather than from the perspective of the judge who had to rule on it. Where possible, the HANDBOOK discussed evidence issues in the language of the courtroom—full of examples and arguments in context as spoken by trial lawyers. In preparing this version for students, we have kept the advocate's perspective and have tried to be true to the notion that lawyers must employ evidence rules quickly and concisely in the courtroom.

We have been mindful that law students do not have the courtroom experience of practicing lawyers. The first four chapters on the operation of the courtroom have been added to give law students a sense of the context and environment that has so much influence on individual evidence rulings. In addition, we have expanded discussions of major cases and doctrines beyond that presented in the Handbook.

We hope this approach will enhance the student's understanding of the law of evidence in action. Wherever possible, we have employed examples to give the student a feel for the context in which the particular evidence problem might arise and for the language used by lawyers and judges in resolving it. We have also discussed the rationales and purposes of particular rules, believing that effective advocacy often means persuading the decision-maker that the result sought is beneficial as a matter of policy.

If law students come away from this hornbook with a sense of how to speak the language of evidence in the courtroom, as well as with an understanding of the law of evidence, we will have fulfilled our desire to help beginning trial lawyers on their way.

For able research on the practitioner's edition, we wish to thank Mark Dunn, Julia Erickson, Tom Holm, and Brendan Randall, graduates of the University of Minnesota law school. Julia Erickson deserves special recognition for editorial contributions. Only her untimely death prevented us from inviting her to participate in this edition. Two trial lawyers, John Sands and Peter Wold, gave selflessly of their time and made perceptive comments on the practitioner's edition.

Students in the Trial Objections courses at Minnesota and Hastings and in Evidence classes at Pace offered helpful suggestions and spotted errors in earlier versions. Christine Cupino, Loyola Law School class of 1999, Gene Sitnitsky, Loyola Law School class of 2000, Melanie Slaughter, Pace University Law School Class of 1998, and Russell Stein, UC Hastings Class of 1999, provided helpful research assistance on the student edition. We also owe thanks to Stephen Lothrop, head of Faculty Support at UC Hastings, for his diligent and careful work.

Roger Park owes his largest debt to his wife and best friend, Suzanne Park—not only for her love and support and her large if not endless patience, but also for her tireless proofreading, editing, and counseling on both editions. Her organizational abilities alone made it possible to miss deadlines by much smaller margins than would otherwise have been the case.

ROGER C. PARK
SAN FRANCISCO, CALIFORNIA

DAVID P. LEONARD
LOS ANGELES, CALIFORNIA

STEVEN H. GOLDBERG
WHITE PLAINS, NEW YORK

June 1998

Summary of Contents

Table of Contents

EVIDENCE LAW

A STUDENT'S GUIDE TO THE LAW OF EVIDENCE AS APPLIED IN AMERICAN TRIALS

Fifth Edition

Part I

EVIDENCE IN THE ADVERSARY SYSTEM

Chapter 1

EVIDENCE AT TRIAL: AN OVERVIEW

Table of Sections

§ 1.01 The Adversarial Trial

The United States' system of justice is based on the common-law trial—a contest waged in court between at least two opposing parties before a neutral decision-maker. Inherited from the English common-law tradition, the trial is, theoretically, the centerpiece of adversary justice—a system of dispute resolution in which the parties gather, prepare, and present the evidence to a relatively passive and neutral decision-maker.

Despite its function at the heart of our system of justice, actual trials are rare. Few societal grievances ripen into legal disputes, and a small percentage of those disputes result in formal court filings.[1] Fewer than ten percent of court filings ever result in a full trial.[2] Nevertheless, adversarial justice pervades our dispute-resolution culture, even influencing some of the forms of Alternative Dispute Resolution. The prospect of trial casts a long shadow over the other stages of litigation and methods of dispute resolution because actors use potential trial outcomes as guides to settlement. Even for the lawyer who vows never to darken the door of a courtroom, knowledge of evidence rules is important to gauge the strength of a potential argument in court, to advise a client, or negotiate a claim.

Adversarial justice is at once more complex and more simple than finding the truth, or achieving results that seem "fair." It is a system of dispute resolution that helps order society, designed to keep us from resolving our differences by other less systematic, less

---

[1] *See* Richard E. Miller & Austin Sarat, *Grievances, Claims, and Disputes: Assessing the Adversary Culture*, 15 LAW & SOC'Y REV. 525, 541–43 (1980–81).

[2] These and other related statistics are available at the Department of Justice Website. Bureau of Justice Statistics, http://bjs.ojp.usdoj.gov (last visited January 10, 2021).

predictable, less reliable, and ultimately less peaceful methods. Although the validity of the system depends, at one level, upon a belief that a trial will help uncover what really happened, it depends equally upon a belief that this less-than-perfect process is the best available given the many conflicting societal, political, and administrative values.

We accept individual results that may less-than-perfectly reflect "the truth," not only because a perfect re-creation is impossible, but also because our dispute-resolution process incorporates other important values. For example, our interest in determining what really happened in a criminal matter coexists with our judgment that it is better to mistakenly let the guilty go free than to mistakenly incarcerate the innocent. In civil disputes, equity must coexist with society's interest in stability; our interest in maintaining the status quo (the possession of the property, the cost of repairing an injury, etc.) is balanced with the case for change in a particular dispute. In both kinds of cases, our interest in the truth must coexist with the desire to protect evidentiary privileges such as those that encourage privacy (communication between spouses) and confidential relations (such as those between a lawyer and client).

The idea that justice emerges when opposing parties gather, shape, and present information to a neutral decision-maker is not universally accepted. Predecessors to modern dispute resolution such as the ordeal and trial by battle depended, at least in theory, upon divine intervention. Today, so-called "inquisitorial" systems, such as those operating on the European continent and in much of Asia, reveal distrust for any process in which interested parties control the generation and presentation of evidence. For example, continental systems often depend more upon neutral persons than upon adversaries for the development of evidence and questioning of witnesses, especially in criminal cases. (Civil cases on the continent are often party-controlled.) Indeed, a lively dispute continues over whether control of evidence by partisans or by officially neutral (though perhaps still biased) persons is more likely to yield just results.[3]

To counteract adversarial bias in the selection and presentation of evidence, evidence rules seek to prevent adversaries from utilizing unreliable evidence when more trustworthy alternatives exist. For example, the hearsay rule partly serves to prevent adversaries from offering polished-up rumor reports in lieu of shakier live witnesses. When the adversarial system is coupled with the institution of the jury, the rules of evidence acquire increased significance. The supposed naïveté of the lay jury justifies many rules that seek to prevent unfair prejudice and misuse of evidence. Furthermore, exclusionary rules function better within a bifurcated system where judges screen evidence before it is presented to the jury.

§ 1.02 Stages of a Common-Law Trial

Reduced to its simplest form, the American trial provides a forum for resolution of an issue that the law is competent to decide and on which the parties do not agree. Usually, the party who wants to change the status quo brings the lawsuit, and that party bears the burden of persuasion on the contested issue. In civil cases, it is the plaintiff; in criminal cases, the prosecution.[4] (While trials today can involve multiple parties and

---

[3] *See, e.g.*, MIRJAN DAMAŠKA, EVIDENCE LAW ADRIFT, 74–124 (1997); Joan L. Dwyer, *Fair Play the Inquisitorial Way: A Review of the Administrative Appeals Tribunal's Use of Inquisitorial Procedures*, 22 J. NAT'L ASS'N ADMIN. L. JUDGES 81 (2002); Oscar G. Chase, *American "Exceptionalism" and Comparative Procedure*, 50 AM. J. COMP. L. 277 (2002).

[4] For a discussion of burdens and presumptions, see **§§ 2.01 et seq.**

become quite complex, in what follows we will employ a minimal model of two opposing parties and one cause of action for which the plaintiff (prosecution in criminal cases) bears the burden of persuasion, to further examine the conduct of American trials.)

Lawyers dominate the American trial process. Before trial, they interview witnesses and gather information, shape the client's legal posture, prepare the pleadings, conduct the formal discovery, prepare the witnesses, and oversee the production of exhibits that will convey information to the fact-finder. At trial, they participate in choosing the fact-finder, speak to the fact-finder about the case before the evidence is presented, and sum up the case afterwards. During presentation of evidence to the fact-finder, the lawyer examines the witnesses and limits the information that the opponent may present. Lawyers even assist the judge in determining the applicable law, especially when they propose jury instructions.

Rules and statutes governing the conduct of an American trial vary among jurisdictions, but the general structure is the same. The Federal Rules of Civil Procedure, Criminal Procedure, and Evidence provide an outline for the conduct of trials in the federal courts and in most states, though individual jurisdictions may have some variations.

Pretrial

In civil cases, pretrial discovery, motions, and hearings dominate our adversary system. There is often more adversarial activity before trial than during trial. Even in criminal cases, which provide for much less discovery, plea bargains resolve most disputes in the pretrial period. Although most pretrial rules and procedures are beyond the scope of this book, many important evidentiary issues are raised, considered, and sometimes decided during pretrial hearings.[5] In civil cases, for instance, motions for summary judgment require the parties to determine what, if any, evidence regarding a genuine material fact will be admissible at trial. Even though summary judgment motions often arise months or years before the trial, the rules of evidence play an essential role.

Jury Selection

Jurors play a crucial role in the trial process. Much of the law about the conduct of a trial, particularly the law of evidence, is based upon assumptions about how jurors think and act as fact-finders, even though many trials are conducted as "bench trials," with the judge as fact-finder.

When a party demands a jury trial, jury selection is the first trial activity. A group of prospective jurors, called the venire, comes to the courtroom, and members of the venire are questioned in court to determine their qualifications to sit as jurors in the particular case. This process is called voir dire. In most federal courtrooms, the judge does the questioning, and the lawyers may submit questions for the judge to ask. In many state courts, the lawyers question the prospective jurors directly, either as a group or individually.

After voir dire, the venire is reduced to the proper number of jurors and alternates through a series of challenges made by the lawyers. (A judge may remove a prospective juror sua sponte, but judges rarely do so.) Two types of challenges are available to a

---

[5] *See* **§ 3.02**.

party: challenge for cause and peremptory challenge. A challenge for cause may be asserted against any prospective juror. Such a challenge will be sustained if the judge finds that the juror does not meet the statutory qualifications for jury service or that the juror's responses during voir dire demonstrate that the person will not consider the matter impartially. A party may exercise a peremptory challenge for any reason and to any member of the venire. However, the right to exercise peremptory challenges is limited by the United States Constitution and attorneys cannot assert a challenge in order to discriminate because of race or gender in the selection of a jury.[6] The number of available preemptory challenges is regulated by statutes or rules of the various jurisdictions.

Opening Statements

Once the jurors and alternates have been sworn in, the lawyers have an opportunity to make opening statements. Often mischaracterized in the media as opening arguments, opening statements are limited to a description of the evidence the lawyer expects to present to the jury in support of the client's case. The lawyer can describe the evidence in a persuasive manner, but is prohibited from drawing inferences or asking the jury to reach conclusions about the described evidence. Although argument should be restricted to summation at the end of trial, many courts are less than strict in enforcing the prohibition against argument in an opening statement.[7]

The party with the burden of persuasion—the plaintiff or prosecutor—makes the first opening statement. In many jurisdictions, the defendant may reserve making an opening statement until after the plaintiff's case-in-chief. As a matter of practice, this is now rare, and most defendants seize the opportunity to address the jurors early in the trial. Given the non-linear way in which evidence is presented at trial, with witnesses often appearing out of chronological order and with cross-examination disrupting the flow of the narrative, the opening statement can be essential in organizing the evidence for the jury. Psychologists who study juries claim that many jurors, despite instructions to the contrary, make up their minds after opening statements.[8]

Witness Sequestration

Although it is not required, either party (or the court on its own initiative) may insist that anticipated witnesses be excluded from the courtroom (also known as "sequestration of witnesses") so that they do not hear the testimony of other witnesses.[9] This is designed to prevent a witness from falsely shaping testimony in response to what other witnesses have stated, and (in theory) it increases the credibility of corroborating

---

[6] *See, e.g.*, J.E.B. v. Alabama *ex rel.* T.B., 511 U.S. 127, 130–31 (1994) (restricting exercise of peremptory challenges based solely upon gender); Batson v. Kentucky, 476 U.S. 79, 96–100 (1986) (restricting exercise of peremptory challenges based solely upon race). Whether *Batson* applies to religious affiliation is still an unsettled, and complex, question. *See, e.g.*, United States v. DeJesus, 347 F.3d 500, 510 (3d Cir. 2003) ("Even assuming that the exercise of a peremptory strike on the basis of religious affiliation is unconstitutional, the exercise of a strike based on religious beliefs is not.").

[7] For the various objections to opening statements, *see* ROGER C. PARK, TRIAL OBJECTIONS HANDBOOK, ch. 10 (3d ed. 2017).

[8] *See* Gary L. Wells et al., *The Timing of the Defense Opening Statement: Don't Wait Until the Evidence Is In*, 15 J. APPLIED SOC. PSYCHOL. 758 (1985).

[9] *See, e.g.*, FED. R. EVID. 615. When witnesses are sequestered, the judge ordinarily will instruct the potential witnesses not to discuss their testimony with other witnesses. *See* United States v. Sepulveda, 15 F.3d 1161, 1176 (1st Cir. 1993).

witnesses.[10] There are, however, important exceptions to this practice, preventing the exclusion of the parties themselves and witnesses (such as experts) "whose presence a party shows to be essential to presenting the party's claim or defense."[11] In light of the extensive use of discovery, depositions, and witness preparation, especially in civil cases, it is not clear how effective this rule is in preventing witnesses from improperly molding their testimony, and use of sequestration varies by locale. But the option is there for the attorney who thinks it useful.

Plaintiff's Case-in-Chief

In the plaintiff's case-in-chief, the plaintiff calls witnesses to testify (subject to cross-examination) and produces tangible evidence in support of the plaintiff's cause of action. The plaintiff's attorney first examines the witnesses, who are then cross-examined by the defendant. When the plaintiff has produced all the evidence in support of the plaintiff's case, the plaintiff rests. For the trial to continue, the evidence from the plaintiff's witnesses and exhibits must be sufficient to support a jury finding in favor of the plaintiff for every proposition for which the plaintiff bears the burden of persuasion. If the evidence is insufficient, the judge will grant a defense motion for judgment as a matter of law on any claim for which the plaintiff has not met this burden. The plaintiff's obligation to produce sufficient evidence to avoid a judgment as a matter of law at the end of the plaintiff's case-in-chief (sometimes referred to as a prima facie case) is called the burden of production. It is sometimes also described as the burden of going forward or the burden of producing evidence.[12]

Defendant's Case-in-Chief

If the plaintiff has met the burden of production, the defendant proceeds with its case-in-chief.

Despite the judge's determination that the plaintiff has presented a prima facie case, the defendant might choose to present no evidence, believing that, while the evidence is sufficient to avoid a judgment as a matter of law, it is not sufficient to persuade the finder-of-fact. If the defendant believes it will prevail without presenting evidence of its own, the defendant may rest and argue to the jury based upon the evidence in the plaintiff's case-in-chief, including evidence elicited on cross-examination of the plaintiff's witnesses. This tactic—admittedly rare in civil cases—is possible because of the important difference between the burden of producing evidence and the burden of persuasion. The burden of producing evidence is satisfied if the plaintiff's evidence meets the minimum needed to support a jury verdict for the plaintiff, while the burden of persuasion is carried only when the evidence is powerful enough to actually persuade the jury to find for the plaintiff.

The defendant usually presents the testimony of witnesses and offers exhibits in roughly the same fashion as did the plaintiff. The defendant's evidence may be offered to establish the defendant's positive contentions (the defendant was somewhere else, the defendant has legal title to the property, etc.) or may be offered to discredit the plaintiff's

---

[10] *See* 6 WIGMORE ON EVIDENCE § 1838 (Chadbourn rev. 1976). If a witness violates the order of sequestration, the judge has discretion to fashion an appropriate remedy, typically including barring the witness from testifying. *See id.*, § 1841.

[11] *See, e.g.*, FED. R. EVID. 615(a)–(d).

[12] *See* **§ 2.06**.

witnesses or counter the plaintiff's evidence. When the defendant has presented all of the evidence relating to the plaintiff's claim, or any affirmative defenses the defendant may have to that claim, the defendant rests.

Plaintiff's Rebuttal and Defendant's Surrebuttal

After the defendant has rested, the plaintiff has an opportunity to offer witnesses and exhibits to rebut evidence or discredit witnesses put forth during the defendant's case-in-chief. The plaintiff may not, however, present evidence that does not in some way qualify or otherwise relate to the evidence or witnesses produced in the defendant's case-in-chief. For example, if the defendant presents testimony that tends to discredit the testimony of the plaintiff's second witness, the plaintiff may present rebuttal testimony that credits the plaintiff's second witness or that witness's testimony. The plaintiff may not present rebuttal testimony, however, that credits testimony given by the plaintiff's third witness if that witness or that witness's testimony was not attacked in the defendant's case-in-chief.[13]

When the plaintiff's rebuttal case is concluded, the defendant has an opportunity for surrebuttal (or rejoinder). The defendant's surrebuttal case is limited to qualifying or otherwise responding to the evidence produced in the plaintiff's rebuttal case.

If circumstances and fairness warrant, the trial judge may allow a departure from the ordinary practice of keeping rebuttal within the scope of the defendant's case and surrebuttal within the scope of rebuttal.

Motions for Preemptive Judgment

When both sides have completed any rebuttal testimony and both sides have rested, one or both parties in a civil action may move for a judgment as a matter of law. The motion asks the judge to rule that, based on all of the evidence presented in the trial, no reasonable jury could find in favor of the other party. The motion is often different from the defendant's motion for judgment as a matter of law at the end of the plaintiff's case-in-chief. Even if the plaintiff has met the burden of production, the judge may enter judgment for the defendant as a matter of law, if a reasonable jury could not conclude, based on all of the evidence from both sides, that the plaintiff has met the burden of persuasion. The judge will not grant the motion merely because the judge, in the absence of a jury, would find in favor of the moving party. Instead, the judge must be able to say that no reasonable jury could reach any other conclusion.

In criminal cases, only the defense may move the judge to take the decision away from the jurors and enter a judgment of acquittal. That motion may be made at the end of the prosecution's case-in-chief or at the end of the entire presentation of evidence.

Closing Arguments (Summation)

After all of the evidence has been presented to the jury, the lawyers have a final opportunity to address the jurors. Closing argument grants the lawyer an opportunity to sum up the case, explaining why the evidence presented to the jurors, combined with the law they will hear from the judge, mandates a verdict for the lawyer's client.

---

[13] Our discussion does not assume a counter-claim by the defendant. If the defendant asserts a counter-claim, the defendant presents that claim in the defendant's case-in-chief and the plaintiff presents evidence on that claim during the plaintiff's rebuttal case.

In both the federal system and many state jurisdictions, the party with the burden of persuasion has the first and last word to the jury. The plaintiff makes the first closing argument, the defendant makes the second, and the plaintiff may then rebut defendant's arguments. Various jurisdictions employ different rules concerning the order of summation. In criminal cases, the prosecution does not usually have the right to rebut the accused.

Jury Instructions

After the lawyers have made their closing arguments, the judge instructs the jurors on the applicable law. These instructions are usually worked out with the lawyers in an instruction conference held sometime before the closing arguments. This allows the lawyers to use the legal principles to frame their closing arguments. In a minority of jurisdictions, judges instruct juries on the law before the lawyers make their closing arguments.[14]

At common law, judges had the authority to summarize the evidence for the jury and even to comment on the credibility of witnesses and the weight of the evidence. After the American Revolution, in reaction to perceived abuses by judges appointed by the Crown, many of the new states rejected such judicial influence on juries. Although the federal courts retain this authority, judges use it sparingly.[15]

Jury Deliberations, Verdict Forms, and Verdicts

When the judge finishes instructing the jury, the jurors retire to the jury room where they are separated from contact with all outside influences. They will have a verdict form agreed to by the lawyers and the judge and, usually, all of the tangible evidence introduced at trial.

In most jurisdictions, the jurors' first task is to select a foreperson to lead the discussion and communicate, if necessary, with the court. In a few jurisdictions, the court appoints the jury foreperson before the beginning of testimony.

In the vast majority of jurisdictions, including federal court, a jury verdict in a criminal case must be unanimous.[16] Jurisdictions differ as to whether civil verdicts

---

[14] Our discussion does not include the situation in which the defendant asserts affirmative defenses for which the defendant carries the burden of production—insanity in a criminal case, for example. If there is an affirmative defense for which the defendant has the burden of producing evidence, the judge will include the law about the affirmative defense in the instructions only if the defendant has produced sufficient evidence to raise the issue with the jury.

[15] *See, e.g.*, Quercia v. United States, 289 U.S. 466, 469 (1933) (noting that a federal trial judge may "assist the jury in arriving at a just conclusion by explaining and commenting upon the evidence, by drawing their attention to the parts which he thinks important," and "he may express his opinion upon the facts, provided he makes it clear to the jury that all matters of fact are submitted to their determination"). When the Federal Rules of Evidence were adopted, Congress deleted a proposed rule that would have endorsed the court's authority to "impartially sum up the evidence and comment to the jury upon the weight of the evidence and the credibility of the witnesses." Proposed FED. R. EVID. 105. However, the deletion of this rule was not intended to remove federal courts' common-law authority. H.R. Rep. No. 650, 93d Cong., 1st Sess. (1973).

[16] *See* Burch v. Louisiana, 441 U.S. 130, 134 (1979) (nonunanimous conviction by jury of six or less jurors violated Sixth Amendment); Apodaca v. Oregon, 406 U.S. 404, 410–11 (1972) (plurality opinion) (state court conviction of crime by less than unanimous jury does not violate right to trial by jury in Sixth Amendment).

require unanimity or might be reached by some kind of a majority—often three-quarters or five-sixths of the jurors are required to join in the verdict.[17]

Verdict forms in criminal cases are general, giving the jurors options of "guilty" or "not guilty" on the various charges being considered. Verdict forms in civil cases vary. Many jurisdictions provide options of a general verdict form, a special verdict form, or a verdict form that requires the jurors to answer specific questions. If the jury reaches a verdict, the foreperson completes the verdict form, signs it, and delivers it to the judge.

After the verdict has been read, a party may request that the judge poll the jurors, asking each juror individually and in open court whether the verdict read is that juror's verdict. If the jurors affirm that the verdict read is their verdict, the judge enters judgment accordingly, unless the judge is asked to consider post-trial motions for judgment notwithstanding the verdict or for a new trial.[18]

§ 1.03 The Admissibility Filter

The term "evidence" has many meanings in common parlance and more than one meaning in legal jargon. We commonly say, in response to someone's assertion of a proposition, "show me the evidence." It is a way of saying "prove it." The great evidence professor Irving Younger was fond of using several of the various meanings lawyers employ for the word "evidence" all in one sentence: "Evidence is admissible in evidence in accordance with the law of evidence."

Younger's first "evidence" derives from the collection of available perceptions and objects regarding the event at issue—the totality of the information lawyers gather by interviewing witnesses and engaging in formal discovery. It includes all the information about what happened, whether it seems legally important or not. This is the starting point for the lawyers, the haystack of information in which lawyers may find the needle(s) of information that will support their clients' cause of action or defense. The process of finding everything that happened, without any prejudgment about its importance at trial, is a critical step for the lawyer. If the lawyer prejudges and screens pieces of information, something crucial almost always goes undiscovered. Still, not everything will be important enough to warrant presentation to the fact-finder. The lawyers cull through this body of information to arrive at Younger's first sense of "evidence," that which they will try to present to the fact-finder.

The second "evidence" represents perceptions about the events and objects from the events that support the clients' positions and that the lawyers present to the jury through witnesses and exhibits at trial. These are the needles of trial evidence that the lawyer found in the haystack of initial "evidence." The witnesses' testimony and the objects presented form the "evidence" that the jurors consider in reaching their verdict.[19]

---

[17] Federal courts require unanimity in civil cases unless the parties agree otherwise. FED. R. CIV. P. 48. Eighteen states require unanimity for civil jury trial; three others accept a non-unanimous verdict after six hours of deliberation. *See* Shari Seidman Diamond, Mary R. Rose & Beth Murphy, *Revisiting the Unanimity Requirement: The Behavior of the Non-Unanimous Civil Jury*, 100 NW. U. L. REV. 201, 203 (2006).

[18] In order to protect the defendant's rights to be tried by a jury and not to be tried twice for the same offence, these motions are not available to the government in a criminal case.

[19] To be sure, the evidence formally introduced is not the *only* thing that the jury considers. *See* Scott W. Howe, *Untangling Competing Conceptions of "Evidence,"* 30 LOY. L.A. L. REV. 1199, 1241 n.156 (1997) (stating that jurors consider substantially more than what judges instruct is "evidence"); *see also* Paul F. Kirgis, *The Problem of the Expert Juror*, 75 TEMPLE L. REV. 493 (2002).

Most of this evidence is oral testimony, and a substantial body of rules has evolved that specifically addresses such testimony. These are considered in Part IV of this book. But tangible evidence also plays a significant role in the decision-making process, and the rules specifically addressing the use of tangible evidence are considered in Part V.[20] Tangible evidence includes both "real" and "demonstrative" evidence. "Real" evidence is an object that played a role in the events at issue—for example, the knife found at a crime scene, a written contract, or nurses' notes about the progress of a hospital patient. "Demonstrative" evidence (primarily) is an object that played no role in the events at issue, but nevertheless illustrates something about those events. For example, demonstrative evidence could include a map, diagram, model, or photograph. If an object or a scene is too large or otherwise too inconvenient to be brought into the courtroom, the fact-finder may be taken to the object or scene to "view" it (a procedure accordingly called a "view"), provided that the relevant aspects of the object or scene cannot be satisfactorily reproduced in court by testimony, photographs, and so forth.

The third "evidence" to which Younger referred is the body of rules that determines which parts of the first kind of "evidence" may become the second kind of "evidence." This, the law of evidence, is a subset of the law of procedure. Unlike the law of property, torts, or contracts, evidence law does not define relationships or determine substantive rights.[21] The purpose of evidence law, in the words of the Federal Rules of Evidence, is "to administer every proceeding fairly, eliminate unjustifiable expense and delay, and promote the development of evidence law, to the end of ascertaining the truth and securing a just determination."[22]

A very important role for the trial judge—especially but not only in jury trials—is to rule on evidentiary questions. For every question of substantive law a judge must decide in a trial, there are numerous evidence questions presented.[23] Some important and foreseeable evidence issues will be resolved following written motions and briefs by the attorneys. Issues that can determine the outcome of the trial are often handled at pretrial hearings. Though civil procedure rules often require parties to submit witness and exhibit lists in advance of trial, many evidence questions arise unexpectedly during the heat of trial. A lawyer asks a question. Opposing counsel stands and says, "Objection," followed by a one-word or two-word label for the evidence issue, such as "leading," "hearsay," or "best evidence." The judge determines whether the objection is "sustained" or "overruled." In this way, a question of evidence law is often raised, discussed, and decided in approximately twenty seconds. Occasionally, a lawyer will ask permission to argue the matter to the judge, which may take a minute or two. Decisions

---

[20] Other groups of rules, including privileges (Part II), relevance (Part III), and hearsay (Part VI), apply to both testimonial and tangible evidence.

[21] An exception to this generalization is the law of privileges. Because privileges limit what can be introduced at trial, they are often considered together with other admissibility rules. But their impact extends beyond trials, and they give some definition to the general right of privacy. *See* **§§ 4.01 et seq.**

[22] FED. R. EVID. 102. For discussion of the many goals of the trial, see 1A WIGMORE ON EVIDENCE § 37.1 (Tillers rev. 1983); Milner S. Ball, *The Play's the Thing: An Unscientific Reflection on Courts Under the Rubric of Theater*, 28 STAN. L. REV. 81, 82 (1975); David P. Leonard, *The Use of Character to Prove Conduct: Rationality and Catharsis in the Law of Evidence*, 58 U. COLO. L. REV. 1 (1987); Charles R. Nesson, *The Evidence or the Event? On Judicial Proof and the Acceptability of Verdicts*, 98 HARV. L. REV. 1357, 1360 (1985); Laurence H. Tribe, *Trial by Mathematics: Precision and Ritual in the Legal Process*, 84 HARV. L. REV. 1329, 1376 (1971).

[23] Although there is no shortage of evidence case law in the appellate courts, the evidence questions raised on appeal represent a small percentage of the evidence issues decided by trial judges and an even smaller percentage of the evidence issues considered by trial lawyers in the heat of trial.

occur in the midst of an intellectual contest in which context is crucial. It is not surprising, then, that the common law of evidence gave the trial judge an uncommon amount of discretion, and that appellate courts afford substantial deference to the trial judge's evidence rulings.

The common law of evidence evolved over centuries.[24] It developed through lawyers' constant usage and through trial judges' evidence rulings. During this process of evolution, evidence law in the United States was relatively homogeneous, despite the plethora of jurisdictions and the lack of opportunity for appellate courts to decide the many and various evidence issues that arose in courtrooms around the country. The law of evidence evolved in the fashion of a language, influenced as much by the usage of lawyers and the on-the-spot rulings of judges in courtrooms as by appellate opinions.[25] As a result, the words that lawyers used in talking about evidence in the various jurisdictions were remarkably similar. A trial lawyer, familiar with one jurisdiction's law of evidence, might try a case in a different jurisdiction, confident that a general familiarity with the language of the courtroom would be sufficient to deal with most of the evidence questions that might arise during an average trial day. That is not to say that evidence law did not vary significantly among the jurisdictions, but those major areas of difference were often statutory or the subject of an important appellate decision in the jurisdiction, and were therefore relatively easy to find and assimilate.

Despite the many similarities, differences among jurisdictions were strongly held. Various attempts to codify evidence law were defeated by apathy and procedural conservatism[26] until the enactment of the Federal Rules of Evidence in 1975. The trial judge's considerable discretion at common law is continued under the Federal Rules. Indeed, the Federal Rules of Evidence codified the common law more than they changed it. Consequently, most evidentiary questions under the Rules still involve decisions that depend on context. In addition, some of the Rules place explicit discretion with the trial judge to determine specific issues.[27] In particular, Rule 611 grants the judge discretion to modify the order and the mode of interrogating witnesses and presenting evidence. This allows the judge to change even the normal conduct of the trial if the judge believes it will aid in ascertaining the truth, save time, or protect witnesses.

The common-law system of adversary justice and the Federal Rules depend upon the lawyers to find, produce, and refine the evidence.[28] An effective evidence advocate must have a firm grasp of the legal theory of the case, an ear for the nature of evidence being offered, and an easily retrieved understanding of the law of evidence—a speaking facility for the language of the courtroom. Yet knowing the law of evidence, or where to find it, is not enough to be an effective courtroom advocate. Evidence at trial comes as

---

[24] *See* John H. Langbein, *Historical Foundations of the Law of Evidence: A View from the Ryder Sources*, 96 COLUM. L. REV. 1168, 1169–72 (1996).

[25] *See* Ronald J. Allen, *The Simpson Affair, Reform of the Criminal Justice Process, and Magic Bullets*, 67 U. COLO. L. REV. 989, 995 (1996) (arguing that the law of evidence, like natural languages, resembles a grown order, developed spontaneously).

[26] *See* Roger C. Park, *A Subject Matter Approach to Hearsay Reform*, 86 MICH. L. REV. 52, 53 n.11–13 (1987) (concerning failure of 1942 Model Code of Evidence and 1953 Uniform Rules of Evidence to achieve significant support). The 1966 California Evidence Code was the first major enactment of an evidence code within the United States. *Id.*

[27] *See* Jon R. Waltz, *Judicial Discretion in the Admission of Evidence Under the Federal Rules of Evidence*, 79 NW. U. L. REV. 1097 (1984).

[28] Judges also have the power to call or interrogate witnesses on their own motion, but they rarely do so. *See* FED. R. EVID. 614.

fast as every question and answer. The lawyer's primary task is to pay careful attention to the substance of the testimony. To deal effectively with admissibility, the lawyer must be able to anticipate when a question is objectionable or an answer should be struck and make an instant fact-based legal argument for why evidence law does not allow the particular evidence. There is a rhythm to the admission and exclusion of evidence that the evidence advocate must master in order to make the law of evidence work for the lawyer's client.

§ 1.04 Sources of Modern American Evidence Law [FRE 402]

The Federal Rules of Evidence represent a comprehensive codification and, in some respects, rethinking of the common-law rules of evidence. The tendency of the Federal Rules of Evidence is towards admissibility. Where the Rules have deviated from common law, they have done so in the direction of admitting more evidence and letting the jury sort out credibility and weight, rather than excluding the evidence. The Rules also bestow tremendous discretion on the trial judge who makes many rulings, some of which are functionally unappealable.[29]

As with all procedural rules, the Federal Rules of Evidence inevitably affect substance and policy. Admission of key types of evidence and witnesses may determine outcomes. For instance, the ease with which expert testimony is received influences outcomes in products liability and toxic tort cases. The ease of admitting prior statements may affect the conviction rates of criminal defendants. In some cases, rulemaking debates have been highly polarized and political, with interests groups such as prosecutors, plaintiffs' lawyers, civil defense attorneys, and even evidence professors expressing keen interest in the results of the rulemaking process.[30]

Unlike the other Rules for federal courts (Civil Procedure, Appellate Procedure, Criminal Procedure, and Bankruptcy), the Rules of Evidence are at least in part statutory, which has implications for how they are interpreted and for choice of law issues when a case is in federal court because of diversity of citizenship of the parties.[31] Originally promulgated via the Rules Enabling Act,[32] the Rules as proposed were rejected by Congress. Congress was particularly concerned about some of the hearsay and privilege rules. Lack of a confidential communications privilege for spouses and an overly-protective executive privilege led Congress to reject the Rules.[33] In 1975, Congress passed the Evidence Rules as regular statutes, which explains why there is legislative history (House, Senate and Joint Committee reports) for the Evidence Rules. Since the Evidence Rules became law in 1975, alterations to the rules have been made via the regular rulemaking process (for example, changes to Rule 407, regarding remedial measures, and to Rule 702, regarding experts). Stylistic changes for gender neutrality

---

[29] *See* David P. Leonard, *Power and Responsibility in Evidence Law*, 63 S. CAL. L. REV. 937 (1990); Thomas M. Mengler, *The Theory of Discretion in the Federal Rules of Evidence*, 74 IOWA L. REV. 413 (1989).

[30] *See* Eileen A. Scallen, *Analyzing "The Politics of [Evidence] Rulemaking,"* 53 HASTINGS L.J. 843 (2002).

[31] *See* Flaminio v. Honda Motor Co., 733 F.2d 463 (7th Cir. 1984) (Judge Posner explains that Rules of Decision Act does not apply to Federal Rules of Evidence and explores choice of law issues under *Erie* doctrine, concluding that Fed. R. Evid. 407 trumps Wisconsin's version of Rule 407 in diversity case).

[32] 28 U.S.C. § 2072.

[33] Richard Nixon asserted an executive privilege during Watergate and Congress was deeply concerned about the extent of the privilege. *See* Jack H. Friedenthal, *The Rulemaking Power of the Supreme Court: A Contemporary Crisis*, 27 STAN L. REV. 673–685 (1975) (discussing Congress' rejection of Rules as presented by Judicial Conference).

and clarity were also made via rule promulgation from the Federal Judicial Center.[34] Congress has also amended the Rules by statute (for example Rules 413–415 were added to the Rules of Evidence as part of the Violence Against Women Act). As a result, the Federal Rules of Evidence are a mishmash of statutes and rules.

Although they constitute the law of evidence only in the federal system, the influence of the Federal Rules on the states and some administrative tribunals has been profound. Most jurisdictions have now codified their common law of evidence, and most of the codifications are similar in organization and substance to the Federal Rules of Evidence. In fact, the vast majority of states—forty-four at last count—have patterned their codes on the Federal Rules of Evidence, as has the military.[35] The way lawyers and judges talk about evidence crystallizes around the sixty relatively short rules that are the Federal Rules of Evidence. Even in New York, the largest remaining jurisdiction with a body of evidence law not patterned on the Federal Rules, the language of evidence spoken in state courtrooms is almost identical to that spoken in federal courtrooms. The Rules have been fairly stable since 1975, in part because a special Rules Committee for Evidence was not appointed until the mid-1990s and very few amendments were proposed until a separate committee was formed.[36]

The pivotal Rule 402 of the Federal Rule of Evidence specifies:

> All relevant evidence is admissible unless any of the following provides otherwise:
>
> - the United States Constitution;
> - a federal statute;
> - these rules; or
> - other rules prescribed by the Supreme Court.
>
> Irrelevant evidence is not admissible.[37]

Conspicuously and intentionally omitted from this list of exclusionary authorities is the category of "common-law exclusionary rules," the great body of (non-constitutional) exclusionary rules that developed almost entirely as a creature of common-law decision-making before the Rules' adoption. These common-law rules continue to exist only insofar as they are reflected in, or can be interpreted as part of, one of the indicated sources.[38] The drafters intended to eliminate such purely common-law barriers to the admission of evidence, which means that, at least in principle, a practitioner who wants

---

[34] For a description of the rulemaking process, *see* Brooke D. Coleman, *Recovering Access: Rethinking the Structure of Federal Rulemaking,* 39 N.M. L. REV. 261, 277–78 (2009).

[35] *See* 6 WEINSTEIN'S FEDERAL EVIDENCE ch. T (Mark S. Brodin ed., 2d ed. 2015) (Table of State and Military Adaptations of Federal Rules of Evidence).

[36] *See* Edward R. Becker & Aviva Orenstein, *The Federal Rules of Evidence After Sixteen Years: The Effect of "Plain Meaning" Jurisprudence, The Need for An Advisory Committee on the Rules of Evidence, and Suggestions for Selective Revision of The Rules,* 60 GEO. W. L. REV. 857 (1992) (arguing for appointment of advisory committee).

[37] FED. R. EVID. 402. Relevant evidence is evidence that is probative of some fact that is legitimately at issue in the case. FED. R. EVID. 401. Similar rules exist in the states. The subtleties of these rules are explored in **§§ 5.01 & 5.02**.

[38] *See* Edward W. Cleary, *Preliminary Notes on Reading the Rules of Evidence,* 57 NEB. L. REV. 908, 915 (1978) ("In principle, under the Federal Rules no common law of evidence remains. . . . In reality, of course, the body of common law knowledge continues to exist, though in the somewhat altered form of a source of guidance in the exercise of delegated powers.").

to exclude relevant evidence must be able to trace the authority for its exclusion to one of the sources on the list in Rule 402. This does not mean, however, that there is no common law of evidence, for the simple reason that there is an interpretive common law for each of the listed sources. But it does mean that no exclusion of evidence may rest on what is a purely common-law source.[39] That is the theory, at least, but as you will see, the common law has inertia, born of judicial habit, that keeps judges harkening back to pre-Rules case law. In any event, an understanding of the pre-Rules evidence law is often indispensable to an appreciation of what the drafters of the Rules were trying to achieve.

The bulk of the rest of the Rules of Evidence constitute exceptions to this default principle of the admissibility of relevant evidence. By its terms, Rule 402 allows for the exclusion of evidence by virtue of other provisions, such as the Federal Rules of Civil or Criminal Procedure, and also by virtue of statutes that cover very specific matters, such as providing for limited privileges against non-disclosure of certain public records. Although we will occasionally refer to such distinct authority, especially the Rules of Procedure, no comprehensive treatment is attempted here. Also generally beyond the scope of this text are the exclusionary rules developed to enforce principles of constitutional criminal procedure.[40] However, two particular constitutional principles will receive attention here. One is of relatively narrow scope, but considerable importance: the Confrontation Clause has been interpreted as limiting the admissibility of hearsay offered against the accused in criminal cases in ways that are sometimes more stringent than what is otherwise prescribed by the Rules. We address this after our examination of the non-constitutional hearsay rule.[41]

It was unnecessary (but harmless) to put "the United States Constitution" in the list of exclusionary authority: if the Constitution requires the exclusion of relevant evidence, the Federal Rules of Evidence have no authority to say otherwise. The opposite is also true (but seemingly *inconsistent* with the language of Rule 402): if the Constitution requires the *admission* of relevant evidence, neither the Rules nor any statute can require otherwise. In fact, the Supreme Court has recognized such an inclusionary principle. It is the right of the criminal defendant to present a defense, which is inherent in the "due process of law" guaranteed by the Fifth and Fourteenth Amendments and given somewhat greater concreteness by the explicit constitutional guarantees of the right to use compulsory process to present witnesses for the defense and the right to confront adverse witnesses.[42] In a series of decisions, the Court has given content to this right by holding that, in particular circumstances, otherwise valid rules that would block admission of evidence that the defense offers at trial must give way. Perhaps the most prominent case in which this occurred was *Chambers v. Mississippi*,[43] in which the constitutional right prevailed over objections raised by the state under the common-law voucher rule as well as the common-law hearsay rule, as these were then recognized in that state. The conditions under which this oft-called "*Chambers* doctrine" will come into play are not easy to encapsulate as a general proposition. Roughly, it protects the opportunity of the defense to present highly reliable evidence that is critical

---

[39] A quasi-exception is privilege law: by the explicit mandate of Rule 501, federal privilege claims are still governed largely by common law. *See* **§ 4.01**.

[40] *See, e.g.*, CHARLES H. WHITEBREAD & CHRISTOPHER SLOBOGIN, CRIMINAL PROCEDURE: AN ANALYSIS OF CASES AND CONCEPTS (5th ed. 2008).

[41] *See* **§§ 20.01 et seq.**

[42] U.S. CONST. Amend. VI.

[43] Chambers v. Mississippi, 410 U.S. 284 (1975). *Chambers* is discussed in **§ 18.04**.

to an effective defense. Some important instances of its application are noted where appropriate in the context of particular admissibility rules discussed later in the book. It is important to keep in mind, however, that this particular argument for introducing evidence is available to the defense in criminal cases, but it is not available to the prosecution, and there is only scant authority for a comparable right for a party in civil cases.[44]

§ 1.05 The Principle of Limited Admissibility [FRE 105]

Particular items of evidence can be relevant in more than one respect in a single case. For example, evidence about the high speed at which the defendant was driving can be relevant both to the question of whether the defendant was negligent and to the separate question of whether that negligence was the cause of the accident. It can also be relevant to the question of the extent of the damages suffered by the plaintiff.[45]

Many admissibility rules prevent the use of evidence only for certain purposes or only against certain parties. For example, an out-of-court statement may be hearsay if offered to prove the truth of what was stated, yet be nonhearsay and admissible to prove that the speaker was able to speak the English language at the time or to prove that some other person heard what the speaker said and reacted to it.[46] This means that evidence offered at trial can be admissible for one purpose (or against one party) but inadmissible for another purpose (or against another party).

When this happens, the law has three principal options: exclude the evidence for all purposes if there is any purpose for which it is inadmissible; admit it for all purposes if there is any purpose for which it is admissible; or, admit it only for the admissible purpose(s). Because one almost always can think of purposes as to which a given item of evidence would be inadmissible, the first option is unrealistic, at least as a general rule; it would involve the loss of far too much important information. The second is entirely feasible, but it would present too many opportunities for parties to introduce evidence that is technically admissible but of very little practical use for one purpose but that serves as a bootstrap to use of the evidence for other, ostensibly forbidden purposes.

Not surprisingly, the common law settled on the third alternative: admit the evidence, but only for its legitimate purposes. The Federal Rules of Evidence implicitly follow this common-law approach, as indicated by Rule 105:

> If the court admits evidence that is admissible against a party or for a purpose—but not against another party or for another purpose—the court, on timely request, must restrict the evidence to its proper scope and instruct the jury accordingly.[47]

As this rule explains, when evidence is limited in terms of its admissibility, the court will instruct the jury, if there is one, on its legitimate uses.[48] Even so, this option presents its own problems. There is a risk that the jury will either not understand or refuse to

---

[44] For a comprehensive treatment, *see* EDWARD J. IMWINKELRIED & NORMAN M. GARLAND, EXCULPATORY EVIDENCE: THE ACCUSED'S CONSTITUTIONAL RIGHT TO INTRODUCE FAVORABLE EVIDENCE (3d ed. 2004).

[45] *See* **§ 5.02**.

[46] *See* **§ 14.04**.

[47] FED. R. EVID. 105. The rule does not explicitly endorse the common-law approach because it does not assert that its "if" clause will ever be satisfied, but that is clearly the implicit assumption of the rule.

[48] *See* **§ 3.09**.

follow the court's guidance and use the evidence for the impermissible purpose. When the risk of this is too great, or the invitation to do it is too blatant, the court has discretion to exclude the evidence entirely, thus preventing its use for any purpose.[49]

§ 1.06 Presenting Testimony—the Form of Questions [FRE 611]

Common-law trials are largely oral events. Much of the evidence presented is the testimony of witnesses. Even when tangible evidence is used, the law almost always requires a sponsoring witness who will "lay the foundation" for admission of the object.[50] Testimony, therefore, is central. The lawyer's skill in asking questions can have as much influence on the evidence that is admitted as does the law of evidence. Moreover, the lawyer's skill in asking questions can significantly influence the jurors' assessment of the admitted evidence.

Rule 611(a) places the control of the mode and order of interrogation and presentation within the discretion of the trial judge, who must ensure the procedures are effective for determining truth, avoid waste of time, and protect witnesses from harassment and undue embarrassment. The trial judge's discretion is virtually never overturned on appeal.

The form of a question can vary from a completely open question that asks for a narrative response—"What happened next?"—to a completely closed question that leads the witness directly to the answer—"You next opened the window, didn't you?" Most of the questions that lawyers ask are in between—more directive than "what happened," but less suggestive than a question containing the answer. "What did you see?" is a less open question (more directive) than "What happened next?" because it limits the range of the witness's possible responses to visual cues excluding smells, thoughts, sounds, feelings, or information from other people. "What did you see behind the door?" is an even more direct question—narrowing the inquiry to a particular place—though still not so directive that it leads the witness to the answer, except insofar as it presupposes that the witness did see something behind the door. "Did you see a cat behind the door?" is so directive that it suggests the answer to the witness, even though the words of the question, alone, do not tell the witness what response the lawyer expects. "You saw a cat behind the door, didn't you?" is beyond suggestive, almost demanding a positive response from the witness.

Witnesses are more credible when important information comes from the witness's mouth, rather than from a mere affirmation by the witness of what the lawyer says. Conversely, a witness is more easily controlled and less likely to make a favorable impression on jurors when the witness is restricted to a one-word response—such as "yes" or "no." As a result, good trial lawyers ask mostly open questions on direct examination of friendly witnesses and mostly leading questions on cross-examination of witnesses called by the opponent.

A question is leading when its words or its context suggest the answer to the witness.

> "You knew why she was calling, didn't you?"
>
> "This is a leading question, isn't it?"

---

49 FED. R. EVID. 403. *See* **§ 5.03**.

50 *See* **§§ 12.01 et seq.**

A question is not leading just because it is one that can be answered "yes" or "no," though that is often a clue that the question may be leading. "Could you tell whether the driver was dead?" calls for a "yes" or a "no" answer, when asked of a person who saw an unconscious person pinned behind the steering wheel of a smashed car. It may not be leading, because the answer—the witness either could or could not tell—is not suggested by the words and may not be suggested by the context of the question.

Rule 611(c) establishes the norms of direct and cross-examination of witnesses at trial, instructing that "[l]eading questions should not be used on the direct examination of a witness except as may be necessary to develop the witness's testimony." The exceptions are for when a party calls a hostile witness, an adverse party, or a witness identified with an adverse party. Generally, leading questions may be employed in cross-examination.

By discouraging the use of leading questions during direct examination, the Rule forces the lawyer to ask questions that encourage the witness, rather than the lawyer, to tell the jurors what happened. This provides the jurors with a reasonable opportunity to assess the witness's credibility. By allowing leading questions on cross-examination, the Rule provides the cross-examiner, who is trying to identify specific weaknesses in the witness's testimony, with control of the organization and the flow of the inquiry. This provides the jurors with a reasonable opportunity to follow the inconsistencies the cross-examiner wants to explore.

The general rule is that a lawyer should not lead on direct examination, but may (and generally should) lead on cross-examination. Rule 611(c) has several exceptions. On direct examination, leading questions are permitted "as may be necessary to develop the witness's testimony." A child witness who freezes on the witness stand or who is merely not articulate is one example of when leading questions might be used.[51] If the normal direct examination method of examination proves ineffective in bringing the witness's testimony to the jurors, leading questions will often be permitted. The jurors will have seen that open-ended questions were ineffective in eliciting information from the witness and will, therefore, have the information necessary to evaluate the use of the leading questions by the examining party.

Transitional and preliminary questions are less dramatic, but more common examples of the permissible use of leading questions on direct examination. When such questions will elicit facts that are not in dispute, they allow the lawyer "to develop the witness's testimony" more expeditiously without the risk that the lawyer will suggest answers to the witness on anything of consequence.

Direct examination of witnesses who are not cooperative may often be conducted by using leading questions. This is most often the "adverse party, or a witness identified with an adverse party," though it may be a witness who is hostile without being necessarily aligned with the adverse party.[52] Conversely, leading questions may not be allowed on cross-examination if the witness is one who is likely to be favorable to the cross-examiner. The cross-examiner's client called for adverse testimony by the opponent

---

[51] *See, e.g.*, United States v. Wright, 119 F.3d 630 (8th Cir. 1997); Rotolo v. United States, 404 F.2d 316, 317 (5th Cir. 1968).

[52] FED. R. EVID. 611(c).

presents an obvious example. The category also includes a witness identified with the cross-examiner's client by employment or family relationship.[53]

The judge decides whether a witness is hostile, identified with the adverse party, or is for some other reason so situated that the normal method of examination should not be followed.[54] The various circumstances of examination cannot be conveniently categorized. For instance, a witness called by a party may not wish to testify because the witness has been threatened, because the witness is fearful that some interest of the witness's may be compromised, or because the witness simply does not like the party. Sometimes judges refuse the request to have a witness declared hostile or otherwise uncooperative,[55] and the lawyer must patiently try to extract the testimony with open-ended questions. Moreover, a lawyer who persists in asking improper leading questions in bad faith or in apparent defiance of the court is likely to find the examination terminated by the court.[56]

§ 1.07 Presenting Testimony—Direct Examination

Direct examination is the examination conducted by the party calling the witness, whether the witness is "friendly" or not. Most direct examinations are of friendly witnesses whom the lawyer would like the jurors to believe and who have more than one piece of information to share with the jury.

If a lawyer has a poised, articulate, and persuasive witness with knowledge of an important sequence of events, it can be tempting to give that witness an opportunity to tell the jurors their story without interruption. Whether such "narrative" testimony will be permitted depends on both the judge's discretion, as granted under Rule 611, and the nature of the evidence. A narrative response may be more expeditious, but it carries the potential for inadmissible evidence to the jurors. The lack of questions from the direct examiner makes it difficult for the opposing lawyer to object to the inadmissible material before the material has been presented to the jury. If the judge initially allows a narrative and inadmissible information is presented, the judge may require the direct examiner to direct the examination through more specific questions.

Lawyers often have difficulty conducting direct examination without using leading questions, in violation of Rule 611(c). Because direct examination is the lawyer's opportunity to present the client's story in as compelling a fashion as possible, the lawyer is eager to make sure the jurors hear all of the important details of the client's entire story in the most persuasive words possible. The poised, articulate, and persuasive witness who knows all about a sequence of events that we posited earlier is, in reality, quite rare. More often than not, the lawyer, who knows the story, the right words, and the courtroom, is tempted to tell the story through the questions rather than through

---

[53] *See* Deshpande v. Ferguson Bros. Constr. Co., 611 So. 2d 877, 878–79 (Miss. 1992) (noting that defense may ordinarily not ask leading questions in cross-examining witness called by plaintiff, but employed by defendant).

[54] *See* FED. R. EVID. 611(c). *See, e.g.;* United States v. Degraffenried, 339 F.3d 576, 581 (7th Cir. 2003); United States v. Collins, 321 F.3d 691, 695–96 (8th Cir. 2003).

[55] In the criminal trial of the Chicago Eight for conspiracy to riot during the 1968 Democratic National Convention, Judge Julius Hoffman refused to declare Mayor Richard Daly a hostile witness though it was clear he did not like nor did he wish to cooperate with the defendants. *See* DAVID DELLINGER, THE CONSPIRACY TRIAL 386–89 (J. Clavir & J. Spitzer eds., 1970).

[56] *See* United States v. Clinical Leasing Service, Inc., 982 F.2d 900, 905 (5th Cir. 1992) (holding that district court did not abuse discretion in terminating direct examination because of blatant and excessive leading questions).

the witness's answers. This temptation should be resisted because it will draw a sustained objection and because it is ineffective advocacy.

§ 1.08 Presenting Testimony—Refreshing Recollection [FRE 612]

Witnesses forget. It is often a long time between the witnessed event and the trial. For someone who is inexperienced in trials and unfamiliar with the courtroom, the witness box can be an intimidating place, not particularly conducive to recollection. Lawyers may refresh a witness's recollection, most often by showing the witness a document that reminds the witness of the forgotten information. Any question or device that will jog the witness's memory may be used, however, including a leading question. Rule 611(c) specifically provides for judicial discretion to allow leading questions on direct examination "to develop the witness's testimony."

Although memory failure can happen to any witness, it is, ironically, people familiar with trials and courtrooms that most often need to have their recollections refreshed. Witnesses who regularly perform similar tasks and testify in court about many of them often have difficulty sorting out the proper event months or years after it occurred. Police officers, who investigate hundreds of incidents and make written reports, are common examples. At trial, an investigating officer who arrives at the scene of an automobile accident is not likely to have a current detailed recollection of the event. If the direct examiner can establish the officer's lack of current recollection, the examiner will be able to use the officer's notes, leading questions, or any other device the judge will allow to refresh the officer's recollection.

The device used to refresh recollection need not be admissible evidence.[57] It must be shown to opposing counsel and may not be admitted into evidence by the party using it to refresh the witness's recollection.

Example

Direct Examiner: Officer, were you called to investigate an automobile collision between a Chevrolet and a Ford at the corner of Third and Sheridan on August 1st of last year?

Witness: Yes.

Direct Examiner: What did you find at the scene of the collision?

Witness: I'm sorry counsel. I investigate a lot of accidents in a year. I don't remember the details of this one.

Direct Examiner: Did you make a report of your investigation of the collision at Third and Sheridan on August 1 of last year?

Witness: Yes.

Direct Examiner: Would reviewing that report refresh your recollection about what you found at the scene of the collision?

Witness: Yes, I am sure that it would.

---

[57] *See, e.g.*, United States v. Weller, 238 F.3d 1215, 1221 (10th Cir. 2001); State v. Schultz, 392 N.W.2d 305, 307 (Minn. Ct. App. 1986).

Direct Examiner: Officer, does the report refresh your recollection about what you found at the scene of the collision?

Witness: Yes, it does.

The direct examiner has now completed the foundation needed to repeat the question about what was found at the scene of the collision. Before asking the question, the lawyer must retrieve the report from the officer. The report may be used to refresh the officer's recollection, but it may not, upon this foundation, be used as a substitute for the officer's current recollection.[58]

The same kind of foundation must be demonstrated regardless of the device being used to refresh the witness's recollection. Showing the officer glass collected from the intersection might refresh the officer's recollection as well. A leading question, "Did you find headlamp glass in the intersection?" might be equally as useful, and much quicker, than either the report or the glass. Just as with the use of the report, the object (the glass particles) or the leading question may only be presented after the direct examiner has shown that the officer cannot remember and that the device used will revive the memory. Some judges believe that the direct examiner should ask permission before using a leading question to refresh a witness's recollection, so that the opponent and the judge will have the same kind of notice as when the witness is shown the report.

The direct examiner may wish to use a leading question instead of a report if the report contains material that the direct examiner would rather not have before the jury. If the witness uses the report to refresh recollection during the trial, Rule 612 entitles the adverse party to have the report produced, to introduce into evidence those portions of the report that relate to the refreshed recollection, and to use the report to cross-examine the witness.

§ 1.09 Presenting Testimony—Cross-Examination

Cross-examination is the interrogation of a witness by a lawyer other than the lawyer who called the witness to testify. The usual purpose of cross-examination is to either discredit the witness or to diminish the impact of the witness's testimony. In most instances, a lawyer cross-examines a witness who has offered testimony harmful to the cause of the cross-examining lawyer's client and whom the other side prepared to testify. However, in order to constitute cross-examination, neither preparation by the other side nor harmful testimony is required. After one lawyer has called a witness and conducted direct examination, the subsequent examination is called cross-examination, even if the witness is friendly toward the cross-examiner.

To elicit facts that might diminish the weight the jury attributes to a witness's testimony, the cross-examiner usually employs leading questions. Such questions can focus the examination on aspects of potential concern in the witness's testimony, including the witness's uncertainty, a previous contrary statement made by the witness, additional facts that raise questions about the witness's direct testimony, or other factors that tend to either discredit the witness or raise questions about the direct testimony. The leading question ensures that the jurors hear the discrediting or doubt-raising information because it is built into the question and does not depend upon the witness's

[58] Use of the report itself, if it does not refresh the officer's current recollection, raises hearsay issues. The use of a report as a substitute for a witness's failure of current recollection is called "past recollection recorded." *See* **§ 16.06**.

willingness to volunteer it. Leading questions also help the lawyer control the witness and to limit the witness's response to an affirmation or denial of the cross-examiner's assertion.

Consider, again, the accident witness who, in the direct examination example, left the jurors with the impression that the witness clearly saw what happened. If, at the time of the collision, the witness was preoccupied, that is information the witness is unlikely to offer on direct examination. If the cross-examiner could not ask leading questions of the witness, the examination would probably not elicit the preoccupation and would prevent the lawyer from presenting information to the jurors that might cast doubt on the witness's direct testimony.

Examples

A non-leading examination would reveal only the following innocuous colloquy:

Cross-examiner: What were you doing just before seeing the accident?

Witness: Waiting for the bus.

If, on the other hand, the cross-examiner states the answer, which the witness does not want to offer, as a part of the question, the truthful witness will affirm the fact when confronted with it.

Cross-examiner: Just before seeing the accident, you were reading a memorandum for work, isn't that right?

Witness: Yes.

Cross-examiner: The memorandum was about a meeting to be held as soon as you arrived at work, wasn't it?

Witness: Yes.

Cross-examiner: That was an important meeting?

Witness: Yes.

Non-leading questions about the witness's estimate of the speed of the Chevrolet would be unlikely to elicit that the witness was not certain about the speed, was not experienced at judging the speed of cars, and was not in a position to see that the light for the Chevrolet was yellow.

Cross-examiner: How do you know the Chevrolet was going forty miles per hour?

Witness: It was right in front of me and going a lot faster than cars normally travel on this road.

Cross-examiner: How fast do cars normally travel on that road?

Witness: About the speed limit during rush hour.

Cross-examiner: How do you know what color the light was for the Chevrolet?

Witness: I could see it.

Leading questions, on the other hand, put the "answer" into the question. This allows the cross-examiner to "testify" (by asking the questions) to the witness's uncertainty about the exact speed, to the witness's lack of experience estimating the speed of passing cars, and to facts suggesting the witness did not actually see that the light was yellow for the Chevrolet.

Cross-examiner: You said that the Chevrolet was going forty miles per hour, isn't that right?

Witness: Yes.

Cross-examiner: Could have been thirty-eight, couldn't it?

Witness: Yes. [The Cross-examiner does not care what the witness answers. If the witness answers, "no," the Cross-examiner will argue that the witness is too precise to be credible on what is necessarily an estimate.]

Cross-examiner: You were not looking at the speedometer, were you?

Witness: No.

Cross-examiner: You did not have some other kind of timing device at the time?

Witness: No.

Cross-examiner: You have no experience watching cars pass by you at different speeds and then comparing their times against a timing device, do you?

Witness: No.

Cross-examiner: There were no other cars driving in the same direction as the Chevrolet, so you could draw a comparison when you estimated the Chevy's speed, were there?

Witness: No.

Cross-examiner: Now, you know the light for the Ford was green when it entered the intersection?

Witness: Yes.

Cross-examiner: The traffic lights at the intersection have those black hoods that shield the light color from cars approaching from the side, don't they?

Witness: Yes.

Cross-examiner: You were facing the Ford's light directly, weren't you?

Witness: Yes.

Cross-examiner: So that black hood that shields the light color from those approaching from the side didn't interfere with your ability to see that the Ford's light was green, did it?

Witness: No.

Leading questions may not be appropriate for every cross-examination. Rule 611 provides that "ordinarily leading questions should be permitted on cross-examination." When the witness is not prepared by and is not friendly to the direct examiner, the cross-examiner may be prohibited from leading the witness. This is the other side of the Rule 611(c) coin that allows a direct examiner to lead certain unfriendly witnesses. The judge has the discretion, but is not required, to prohibit leading questions if the examination is a cross-examination procedurally, but a direct examination in substance.

The common law attaches considerable importance to a party's right to cross-examine witnesses. It is a large part of the explanation of the hearsay rule and the criminal defendant's right to confront witnesses. Accordingly, common-law courts have been quite skeptical of situations in which a witness testifies on direct but is either not willing or not available to be cross-examined. Upon motion by the opponent, the usual judicial response is to strike the testimony given on direct or even to grant a mistrial. But some flexibility is shown when the loss of the opportunity to cross-examine is clearly not the fault of the witness or the party who called the witness, especially if cross-examination has been at least partially completed. In such cases, the trial court has discretion to leave the direct testimony in the record, perhaps coupled with an appropriate cautionary instruction to the jury.[59]

§ 1.10 Presenting Testimony—Scope of Cross-Examination and Other Subsequent Examinations [FRE 611(b)]

Rule 611(b), Scope of cross-examination, limits cross-examination to the subject matter of the direct examination and matters that affect the witness's credibility. This Rule is analogous to the rule that limits the plaintiff's rebuttal case to matters raised in the defendant's case-in-chief and the defendant's surrebuttal case to matters raised in the plaintiff's rebuttal case.

As a general proposition, each subsequent layer of examination must stick to the issues raised in the previous questioning, or raise issues of credibility. The direct examiner's subsequent examinations of the witness are called redirect examinations and the cross-examiner's subsequent examinations of the witness are called re-cross examinations. The number of redirect and re-cross examinations that are necessary to present the full testimony to the jurors is entirely within the discretion of the trial judge.

The language of Rule 611(b) addresses only cross-examination, but the principle expressed in the Rule—that the subsequent examination is limited to the subject matter of the preceding examination—usually applies to both redirect examinations and re-cross examinations. The judge possesses vast discretion to promote the orderly presentation of evidence, and may allow the proponent on redirect to repair omissions in direct examination by allowing questions that go beyond the scope of the cross-examination.

A few jurisdictions do not follow the principle that a subsequent examination must relate either to the subject matter of the preceding examination or to the credibility of the witness. Known as "wide open" cross-examination jurisdictions, they allow a cross-examiner to ask about any relevant matter within the witness's knowledge.[60] In most

---

[59] *See* 5 WIGMORE ON EVIDENCE §§ 1390–94 (Chadbourn rev. 1974); 1 MCCORMICK ON EVIDENCE § 19 at 157–58 (Kenneth S. Broun ed., 7th ed. 2013) (recommending the common-sense in recognizing that "the half-loaf of direct testimony is better than no bread at all.").

[60] *See, e.g.*, Dubreuil v. Witt, 781 A.2d 503, 508 (Conn. Ct. App. 2001) (cross is limited to scope of direct but "a question on cross-examination is within the scope of the direct examination if it is intended to rebut, impeach, modify, or explain any of the witness's direct testimony. A party who initiates discussion of an issue, whether on direct or cross-examination, is said to have opened the door to inquiry by the opposing party, and cannot later object when the opposing party so questions the witness."); Stotler v. State, 834 So. 2d 940, 943 (Fla. Dist. Ct. App. 2003) ("When the direct examination opens a general subject, the cross-examination may go into any phase, and may not be restricted to mere parts or to the specific facts developed by the direct examination. Cross-examination should always be allowed regarding the details of an event or transaction, a portion only of which has been testified to on direct examination. Cross-examination is not confined to the identical details testified to in chief, but extends to its entire subject matter, and to all matters that may modify, supplement, contradict, rebut or make clearer the facts testified to in chief."); People v. Milbratz, 751

jurisdictions, however, the lawyer must pay attention to the scope of examination in order to determine what questions they may ask in a subsequent examination.

Example

If the lawyer for the driver of the Ford calls the investigating officer to testify only about the location of the Chevrolet headlamp glass in the intersection, the Chevrolet driver's lawyer can cross-examine the officer on the time of their arrival at the scene; whether there was evidence that others had been in the intersection and moved the glass; whether the officer had accurately measured to locate the position of the glass; and the like. These are all within the scope of the direct.

If the officer happens to have more information—information the direct examiner elected not to present, for whatever reason—the cross-examiner might want to ask the following questions:

Q: Did the driver of the Ford say to you, "I should have been watching more carefully?"

Q: Isn't it true that the yellow light on the traffic signal at Third and Sheridan lasts for seven seconds?

Q: Officer, didn't you happen to see, quite by coincidence, the driver of the Ford about a month after the accident throwing a ball with the arm that was supposed to be broken?

If the direct examiner objects to these questions, which of them will be allowed will depend upon the judge's view of whether the question is within the subject matter of the direct examination.

It is difficult to state with precision a test for distinguishing between examination that does or does not go beyond the scope of the direct examination. A test sometimes cited says that in exercising discretion, the judge may permit cross-examination "as to all matters reasonably related to the issues put in dispute by . . . testimony on direct."[61]

If the judge believes that the subject matter of the direct examination, in the above example, was the location of broken headlamp glass, all of the additional questions are beyond the scope of the direct examination. If, on the other hand, the judge believes that the subject matter of the direct examination was the officer's investigation of the accident, some of the additional questions will be within the scope of the direct. The questions about the Ford driver's statement of fault and about the length of the yellow light at the intersection are probably part of the officer's investigation. The question about the officer's inadvertent observation of the plaintiff's use of a supposedly injured arm is probably beyond the scope of any characterization of the direct examination.

Even if the throwing incident is beyond the scope of the direct examination, the defendant's lawyer is not automatically prohibited from asking the officer about it. The scope of examination issue does not establish whether the cross-examiner may ask about

---

N.E.2d 650, 654 (Ill. App. Ct. 2001) ("Cross-examination is generally limited in scope to the subject matter of the direct examination of the witness and to matters affecting the credibility of the witness. However, courts should liberally construe this limitation to allow inquiry into whatever subject tends to explain, discredit, or destroy the witness's testimony."). *See also* State v. McCall, 549 N.W.2d 418 (Wis. 1996).

[61] United States v. Vasquez, 858 F.2d 1387, 1392 (9th Cir. 1988) (quoting United States v. Miranda-Uriarte, 649 F.2d 1345, 1353 (9th Cir. 1981)); United States v. Green, 648 F.2d 587, 594 (9th Cir. 1981).

the throwing incident, but rather when and how the examination may take place. Rule 611(b) provides that the court may permit inquiry into additional matters as if on direct examination. The judge has discretion to allow the question during cross-examination or to require the defendant to wait and present the officer during the cross-examiner's case-in-chief.

Judicial discretion on scope of the examination issues is likely to turn on questions of convenience for the witness, the length of the examination that the lawyer wants to conduct, how severely the examination will interfere with the orderly presentation of the proponent's case-in-chief, and similar factors that influence the orderly presentation of evidence—the flow of the trial. The scope of the trial court's discretion is broad and rarely reversed on appeal.[62]

§ 1.11 Opening the Door, Curative Admissibility, Fighting Fire with Fire

The theory of adversary justice and the notion that a trial should progress through a series of moves and related counter-moves explains the trial phenomena known alternatively as "opening the door," "curative admissibility," and "fighting fire with fire." These phrases are sometimes considered to be merely different colorful ways to express a single idea: that a party is allowed to do something or to present evidence that ordinarily would be improper, because the other party did so first. While each of the phrases describes a situation in which "evening up" is an important consideration, there are differences that affect the possible consequences when the action of one party, be it appropriate or inappropriate, opens the door to reaction by the opponent.

Curative admissibility, a term coined by Wigmore,[63] is the narrowest of the three terms. It applies only to the circumstance in which one party's presentation of inadmissible evidence causes a problem that the judge will cure by allowing the other party to present inadmissible evidence. Fighting fire with fire, a McCormick phrase,[64] is a broader concept. It includes curative admissibility, but it also includes an otherwise improper action—such as an argumentative opening statement—that a party might take in response to the other party's initial improper action. Opening the door is the broadest of the terms. It describes what the initial party does that leads to curative admissibility and that prompts the other party to fight fire with fire. But, it also describes what happens when the initiating party offers admissible evidence and, as a result, the other party may offer previously inadmissible evidence.

It is worth noting that the three terms describe different actors. The party who begins the process by doing something opens the door. In certain circumstances, that initial action will cause the judge to allow otherwise inadmissible evidence to go to the fact-finder as an act of curative admissibility. Fighting fire with fire describes what the responding party does in response to the initial action. The focus on the different actors can be helpful in sorting out the various situations that appear similar in some respects, but are analytically different.

---

[62] United States v. Speight, 75 Fed. Appx. 802, 806 (2d Cir. 2003); Martin v. State, 775 A.2d 385, 388 (Md. Ct. Spec. App. 2001).

[63] *See* DAVID LEONARD, THE NEW WIGMORE: RULES OF LIMITED ADMISSIBILITY § 6.7.4 (2000).

[64] *See* 1 MCCORMICK ON EVIDENCE § 57 (Kenneth S. Broun ed., 7th ed. 2013).

That one party's action opens the door to action by the other party—action that could not be taken but for the door opening—is a universal precondition to these forms of rebuttal. The action, however, may vary widely from offering competent, admissible evidence to making an improper argument to a jury. Whether and what kind of retaliation will be permitted depends in part on which door was opened, what was used to open the door, and what the opponent did to avoid the draft.

The following examples represent three different door openings: 1) presenting competent evidence that increases the issues before the jury and makes otherwise inadmissible counter evidence admissible, 2) presenting *inadmissible* evidence that creates a problem that can be cured only by allowing other inadmissible evidence, and 3) taking *inappropriate trial action* that justifies an opponent's otherwise inappropriate retaliatory action.

Example—Opening the door with admissible evidence

During a prosecution for possession and distribution of cocaine, the prosecution wants to elicit that the arresting agent set up the buy from the defendant because she had received word from U.S. Customs that he was a major drug dealer. Defendant's hearsay objection is sustained. The court rejects the prosecution's argument that the statement is offered to show the agent's state of mind, saying that the agent's state of mind is not relevant.[65]

In his case-in-chief, the defendant claims that the agent framed him, because she held a grudge against him. He produces evidence of the grudge.

In rebuttal, the prosecution should be able to call the agent and elicit the hearsay testimony that was not admissible in the government's case-in-chief. The defendant has opened the door to the testimony by making the agent's motive (state of mind) relevant.

Expanding the issues, as illustrated above, is a common explanation for the phenomenon of opening the door.[66] Notice that the defense opened the door without introducing inadmissible evidence or engaging in other improper conduct.

The following example illustrates the second kind of "opening the door."

Example—Opening the door with inadmissible evidence

The defendant presents a witness who testifies that the plaintiff has a reputation for being untruthful.

The plaintiff later calls a witness in the plaintiff's rebuttal case who is prepared to testify to three separate and compelling instances in which the plaintiff was truthful, in an attempt to undercut the untruthful reputation presented in the defendant's case-in-chief. Plaintiff objects.

Rule 608(b) specifically prohibits testimony about specific instances of conduct for the purpose of attacking or supporting a witness's credibility. The rebuttal

---

65 United States v. Hernandez, 750 F.2d 1256 (5th Cir. 1985).

66 *See* Clark v. State, 629 A.2d 1239 (Md. 1993) (discussing distinction between opening door and curative admissibility); State v. Lessley, 601 N.W.2d 521 (Neb. 1999); State v. Farthing, 751 A.2d 123 (N.J. Super. Ct. App. Div. 2000). Rules 404 and 608 present occasions for "opening the door" to otherwise inadmissible "character" evidence.

witness's testimony, therefore, will be inadmissible, if the defendant objects.

The defendant does not object to the rebuttal witness's testimony about the three specific instances of truthfulness, but during its surrebuttal case, calls a witness who will testify to two separate and compelling instances in which the plaintiff was untruthful.

The same provision of Rule 608(b) that would have prohibited the rebuttal witness's testimony, had the defendant objected, prohibits the surrebuttal witness's testimony, unless the plaintiff opened the door for the surrebuttal testimony by offering specific instances of truthful conduct during the rebuttal case. The trial judge is likely—but may not be required—to allow the defendant to present a witness who will "even up" the specific instance evidence available to the jury.

If the judge allows the defendant's inadmissible specific conduct evidence, it is because it is the only way to cure the problem caused by the plaintiff's inadmissible specific conduct evidence. The basis for the court's discretion to admit inadmissible evidence to cure other inadmissible evidence is not obvious. The early cases upholding trial court decisions to allow retaliatory inadmissible evidence consider it a matter of simple fairness.[67] This common-law rule that gives the judge discretion to use fairness as the standard for admitting inadmissible evidence to "cure" other inadmissible evidence apparently was not superseded by the Federal Rules of Evidence. The advisory committee's note to Rule 611(a) suggests that many of the common-law rules giving sufficient judicial discretion to make trials fair are embodied in the judge's obligation to "make the interrogation and presentation effective for the ascertainment of the truth."[68] When and under what circumstances the judge should use what one court has described as a "nebulous and nodous so-called doctrine"[69] to admit otherwise inadmissible evidence is not so clear from jurisdiction to jurisdiction. "Evening up" is the goal, and "fairness" the mechanism in almost every jurisdiction, but the methods for obtaining the goal and for being fair differ.

Waiver is another common explanation of the result. In *State v. Banks*,[70] a prosecution for child molestation, the defendant made an adamant and expansive denial: "As God is my witness, I have never had sexual contact with my daughter or with any child under the age of 18 years old." The portion of this statement referring to "any child" (other than the alleged victim in this case) was inadmissible character evidence for the defense. The *Banks* court held that the denial constituted a waiver of the jurisdiction's statute prohibiting evidence of specific instances of sexual activity (other than the charged incident) by either victims or defendants.[71] The defendant had opened the door

---

[67] *See, e.g.*, Bogk v. Gassert, 149 U.S. 17, 24 (1893) (it would be "manifestly unfair" to allow one party's inadmissible version of conversation without allowing other party to give its equally inadmissible version of conversation).

[68] The Advisory Committee's note on Rule 611(a) states that "[t]he ultimate responsibility for the effective working of the adversary system rests with the judge." It further notes that Rule 611(a)(1) "restates in broad terms the power and obligation of the judge as developed under common law principles. It covers . . . questions arising during the course of a trial which can be solved only by the judge's common sense and fairness in view of the particular circumstances."

[69] Daniels v. Dillinger, 445 S.W.2d 410, 415 (Mo. Ct. App. 1969).

[70] State v. Banks, 593 N.E.2d 346, 349 (Ohio Ct. App. 1991).

[71] For discussion of the rules regarding evidence of prior sexual misconduct by the accused, see **§ 7.06** & **§ 7.10** (subsection on "Other Acts of Sexual Misconduct").

to the prosecution's otherwise inadmissible evidence about prior sexual activity between the defendant and two minor girls.[72]

One federal court has stated succinctly the contours of the curative admissibility doctrine:

> Under the doctrine of curative admissibility "the introduction of inadmissible evidence by one party allows an opponent, in the court's discretion, to introduce evidence on the same issue to rebut any false impression that might have resulted from the earlier admission." However, the rule "does not permit the introduction of evidence that is related to a different issue or is irrelevant to the evidence previously admitted."[73]

Some jurisdictions enumerate circumstances under which the judge must allow curative admissibility.[74] Other jurisdictions leave curative admissibility to the discretion of the judge, if the proper circumstances exist. Some courts will not allow inadmissible "curative" evidence from a party who seeks "to introduce whatever incompetent evidence it desires by the simple expedient of failing to object to the introduction of incompetent evidence by the opposing party."[75]

McCormick used fighting fire with fire to describe what Wigmore called curative admissibility,[76] but the former phrase is useful to describe a kind of "evening up" that is common in trial courts, but that does not necessarily involve opening the door with inadmissible evidence or curing a problem with inadmissible evidence. This is the third kind of door opening. The closing arguments from *United States v. Young*[77] excerpted below, present a too common example of improper argument by counsel.

Example—Opening the door and fighting fire with fire through improper trial activity

> In a prosecution for mail fraud, the defendant's lawyer intimates that the prosecution deliberately withheld exculpatory evidence. He charges the prosecution with acting reprehensibly in attempting to cast a false light on respondent's activities, pointing to the prosecutor's table and saying: "I submit to you that there's not a person in this courtroom including those sitting at this table who think the defendant intended to defraud anyone." The defendant, he

---

[72] The extrinsic evidence regarding the other girls would not have been admissible absent this doctrine of waiver, even solely as impeachment, because it concerns a collateral matter. *See* **§ 11.06**.

[73] Nguyen v. Southwest Leasing & Rental, Inc., 282 F.3d 1061, 1067 (9th Cir. 2002) (internal citations and quotations omitted).

[74] *See, e.g.,* Busch v. Busch Const., Inc., 262 N.W.2d 377, 387 (Minn. 1977) (stating that, to be entitled as a matter of right to present rebutting evidence on an evidentiary fact: (a) the original evidence must be inadmissible and prejudicial, (b) the rebuttal evidence must be similarly inadmissible, and (c) the rebuttal evidence must be limited to the same evidentiary fact as the original inadmissible evidence); *see also* State v. Vandeweaghe, 827 A.2d 1028 (N.J. 2003).

[75] Busch v. Busch Const., Inc., 262 N.W.2d 377, 387 (Minn. 1977).

[76] 1 MCCORMICK ON EVIDENCE § 57 (Kenneth S. Broun ed., 7th ed. 2013).

[77] United States v. Young, 470 U.S. 1 (1985). *See also* United States v. Carter, 236 F.3d 777, 791 (6th Cir. 2001) (reversible error for prosecution to respond to defense counsel's improper argument with improper argument of his own, including repeatedly accusing defense attorney of lying and of telling "a colossal lie"); United States v. Brown, 327 F.3d 867 (9th Cir. 2003) (government's improper use of propensity evidence on closing argument coupled with trial court's failure to rule on defense's objection, offer curative instruction or admonish government was reversible error).

says, is "the only one in this whole affair that has acted with honor and with integrity."

The prosecutor does not object to defense counsel's summation, but rather improperly presents his own personal views about the guilt of the defendant, closing by giving his opinion about the defendant's honor and integrity. "I don't know whether you call it honor and integrity, I don't call it that. If you feel you should acquit him for that it's your pleasure. I don't think you're doing your job as jurors in finding facts as opposed to the law that this Judge is going to instruct you. If you think that's honor and integrity then stand up here in this courtroom and say that's honor and integrity. I don't believe it."

The *Young* Court expressed concern for the "all too common occurrence in criminal trials—the defense counsel argues improperly, provoking the prosecutor to respond in kind, and the trial judge takes no corrective action."[78] It asserted that "two improper arguments—two apparent wrongs—do not make for a right result" and clarified that courts "have not intended" by any means to encourage the practice of zealous counsel's going "out of bounds" as did defense counsel here, or to encourage prosecutors to respond to the "invitation."[79] The Court went on to say that the prosecutor should have objected, rather than fight fire with fire and that "invited responses" might be diminished if trial courts would take prompt action. But it let the conviction stand.

Misconduct in argument is not restricted to criminal cases.[80]

§ 1.12 The Doctrine of Verbal Completeness [FRE 106]

Unsurprisingly, a significant part of the evidence presented at trial concerns statements made or conversations that occurred out-of-court. Such statements include an admission of responsibility for a wrong; an offer to enter a contract and an acceptance thereof; a warning shouted to someone; and so forth. When an out-of-court verbal statement (whether oral or written) is evidenced in court, it is obviously important that the statement be fairly reported, that it not be distorted by the omission of details unfavorable to the proponent of the evidence. Much of the time, one can rely on the adversarial incentive of an opponent to make sure that missing portions of verbal utterances are added later to complete the picture, and that very potential operates as a countervailing disincentive: the proponent who distorts will be shown to have done so. But this mechanism is not always available. To address situations in which the usual adversarial counter is not practicable, common-law courts developed a set of rules known collectively as the doctrine of verbal completeness.[81]

---

[78] United States v. Young, 470 U.S. 1, 11 (1985).

[79] *Id.*

[80] *See, e.g.*, Harrison v. Purdy Bros. Trucking Co., 312 F.3d 346, 353–54 (8th Cir. 2002) (affirming trial court's use of curative instructions where plaintiff's attorney's closing argument stated that "the defendants in the case finally 'fessed up' " and "these defendants have not been willing to do [justice]"); Hemmings v. Tidyman's Inc., 285 F.3d 1174, 1192 (9th Cir. 2002) (holding that it was plain error for plaintiff's counsel to say in her closing argument that "[Tidyman's has] not corrected any of these discriminatory policies and they knew that they should because this is not the first time they have been sued. I have sued them before in 1994, so they had subjective policies which had disparate impact on all women, including plaintiffs, and that proves our case because they did not have a business necessity for doing it, and there were ways to fix it"); Findlay v. Griffin, 484 S.E.2d 80 (Ga. Ct. App. 1997); Amador v. Lea's Auto Sales & Leasing, Inc., 916 S.W.2d 845 (Mo. Ct. App. 1996).

[81] See 7 WIGMORE ON EVIDENCE § 2094 et seq. (Chadbourn rev. 1978).

The doctrine had two major strands, one dealing with *testimony* describing out-of-court verbal statements (oral or written); the other dealing with *documentary evidence* containing statements. As to the former, it sometimes happens that testimony reporting an out-of-court verbal statement is admissible when offered by one party but not when offered by the other. In these situations, one cannot count on the usual adversarial response at trial to counteract any distorting effects of an omission of part of the statement. The most commonly encountered example of this is the hearsay exemption for statements made by a party-opponent.[82] If, for example, the defendant made an out-of-court statement, the plaintiff may introduce testimony reporting it (to prove the truth of the statement) under this exemption, but the defendant may not introduce testimony reporting her own out-of-court statement (to prove its truth), at least not under this exemption (other exceptions to the hearsay rule might or might not apply). Such asymmetric rules create an incentive for the proponent (in this case, the plaintiff) to distort the content of the out-of-court statement, here the defendant's statement.

For example, suppose the defendant stated to a potential witness, "Yeah, I swerved and crossed the center line into the oncoming traffic. But I only did it because a child had jumped into the street to grab a ball." The plaintiff's attorney might then elicit the following testimony from the person who heard this statement by the defendant:

Direct-examiner: "What did the defendant say to you?"

Witness: "He said that he swerved and crossed the center line into the oncoming traffic."

Direct-examiner: "Thank you. No more questions."

If the defense counsel attempts to clarify on cross-examination, the plaintiff's response is predictable:

Cross-examiner: "What else did the defendant say to you?"

Direct-examiner: "Objection. Hearsay."

If the defense cannot offer some exception to the hearsay rule, the objection would seem to be proper; specifically, the exemption for statements of a party-opponent does not apply.[83] In situations like this, the doctrine of verbal completeness intervened to avoid the unfairness inherent in sustaining the plaintiff's objection. That doctrine would override, or "trump," the otherwise applicable exclusionary rule by permitting cross-examination regarding any other part of the out-of-court statement that the jury would need to place in context and thus properly understand the part originally introduced.[84]

---

[82] *See* **§ 15.06**.

[83] One option for a court in such circumstances would be to sustain an objection by the defense to the effect that the testimony elicited by the direct-examination is too misleading, but this objection may not be proper, *see* **§ 5.03**, and even it is, that could result in losing the testimony entirely, whereas the doctrine of verbal completeness accepts the testimony as useful, but only if fairly reproducing the out-of-court statement. Another option for a court would be to rule the misleading original portion inadmissible, *not* exclude it, and allow the opponent to invoke curative admissibility, *see* **§ 1.11**. This, however, assumes that curative admissibility is available in the particular jurisdiction and the particular context, and its use is limited to neutralizing the original inadmissible evidence. The common-law doctrine of verbal completeness simply and directly avoids these complexities and limitations.

[84] *See, e.g.*, Rokus v. Bridgeport, 463 A.2d 252, 256 (Conn. 1983) (applying completeness rule to witness's report of civil defendant's out-of-court statement); Commonwealth v. Britland, 15 N.E.2d 657, 658–59 (Mass. 1938) (applying completeness rule to witness's report of criminal defendant's out-of-court statement). For an exploration of the common-law doctrine, *see* Dale A. Nance, *A Theory of Verbal Completeness*, 80 IOWA L. REV. 825, 839–47 (1995). The author explains that this "trumping" function arises from the principle that

The other strand of the common-law doctrine applied only to documentary evidence. If a proponent tried to introduce only part of a document, this line of doctrine permitted an opponent to *require the proponent* to introduce other parts (or in some situations even other documents) necessary to place in context and thus understand the full import of the document introduced by the proponent. Under this part of the rule, the opponent did not have to wait to introduce the additional parts until cross-examination of a witness sponsoring the document or until the next opportunity for the opponent to present its evidence. The opponent could insist on simultaneous presentation of the relevant parts by the original proponent. This aspect of the rule involved a timing function, even when no asymmetric admissibility rules were implicated. This timing function was limited to documents, presumably because in that context the interruption of the original proponent's presentation could be kept (more easily) within reasonable bounds.[85] Obviously, both functions of the doctrine—the trumping function and the timing function—could be implicated in a particular case, as when a proponent only selectively introduced part of the written admission of an opponent and the doctrine was invoked to require the proponent to present additional portions of the written admission.[86]

Federal Rule of Evidence 106 only partially codifies the common-law rule of verbal completeness. It specifically covers "writings and recorded statements," and thus seems to be limited to the second strand of the common-law doctrine. It allows the judge, upon motion by the opposing party, to require the proponent of a portion of a document or recording to offer the remainder of the document or recording at the same time as a matter of fairness. Depositions are the most common document affected by this rule. For example, if a statement on page 3 of a deposition is qualified by another statement on page 100, the judge might not allow the statement from page 3 to be admitted without also admitting the qualifying statement from page 100. The Rule allows the same result when the proponent offers an entire document and its full context will not be understood without consideration of some other document, such as when a letter purporting to be an acceptance is offered. If determining whether the letter is really an acceptance requires that the jurors see the offering letter at the same time, the judge might require the offering letter to be admitted as well.

Like the common-law rule, Rule 106 does not mean that a party offering a portion of a document must always introduce the entire document or that all other related documents must necessarily be offered as well. For reasons of emphasis, admissibility, and economy of time, among other considerations, a party may introduce only a portion

---

the original proponent is required to present the utterance as a non-misleading whole, which means that the remainder, even when formally introduced by the opponent, should be considered *as if introduced by the proponent*, which means it is not barred by an admissibility rule that would not have been an obstacle to the proponent in the first place. In the example in the text, had the plaintiff elicited the defendant's explanation about the child running into the street, which the plaintiff *should* have done, such testimony would not have been barred by the hearsay rule, so it is not barred when offered by the defense to complete the verbal utterance.

85 *See id.*, at 847–52. The author also identifies a "discovery" function that was more important in the era of limited pre-trial discovery: if the opponent of the evidence did not have access to the completing portion of the verbal utterance, the rule could be invoked in order to force the proponent to provide it. *See id.*, at 852–855.

86 *See, e.g.*, Cody v. Louisville Nashville Ry Co., 535 So.2d 82, 85–86 (Ala. 1988) (applying common-law completeness doctrine to answers to interrogatories); People v. Gallo, 186 N.E.2d 399, 400–01 (N.Y. 1962) (applying common-law completeness doctrine to record of criminal defendant's out-of-court statement). *See also* State v. Mallar, 508 A.2d 1070, 107172 (N.H. 1986) (endorsing state's assertion of common-law completeness rule with regard to record of out-of-court statement introduced by defense as a declaration against interest).

of a document or only one of a series of documents. The opposing party is often (though not always) fully protected by the right to inquire about or offer the remainder of the document or related documents on cross-examination or through later examination of a different witness. Therefore, the judge is unlikely to interrupt the flow to compel a party to offer the entire document or related documents, if that can be accomplished later by the opposing party.

Despite the common-law background, federal circuits disagree as to whether Rule 106 is merely a rule about the order of proof,[87] or whether it also authorizes admission of otherwise inadmissible evidence in order to demonstrate the context of a document or a portion of a document and thereby avoid misleading the fact-finder.[88] Moreover, unlike the common-law doctrine, Rule 106 does not explicitly address *testimonial* evidence that misleadingly reports an out-of-court verbal statement (whether oral or written). The Advisory Committee Note to Rule 106 states, that "[f]or practical reasons, the rule is limited to writings and recorded statements and does not apply to conversations." But the drafters also write, rather ambiguously: "This rule does not in any way circumscribe the right of the adversary to develop the matter on cross-examination or as part of his own case." Of course, cross-examination (or later) is exactly where the first (and primary) strand of the common-law doctrine was invoked. Again, federal courts have not resolved how to handle this situation under the Rules when it is complicated by the effect of asymmetric admissibility rules.[89] Some state courts operating under similar rules have found authority to continue the common-law "trumping" principle in the general discretion of the trial court under Rule 611(a) to control the mode of presentation of evidence.[90] And several states have significantly modified their versions of Rule 106 in order to resolve this issue by specifically endorsing the common-law trumping function in this context.[91]

---

[87] *See, e.g.,* United States v. Terry, 702 F.2d 299 (2d Cir. 1983) (Rule 106 does not compel introduction of evidence otherwise inadmissible); United States Football League v. National Football League, 842 F.2d 1335, 1375–76 (2d Cir. 1988); United States v. Gallagher, 57 F. App'x 622, 629 (6th Cir. 2003) (holding that Rule 106 cannot be used to make otherwise inadmissible evidence admissible); United States v. Woolbright, 831 F.2d 1390, 1395 (8th Cir. 1987) (holding that Rule 106 addresses only order of proof). Both courts and commentators have sought to avoid this unfortunate conclusion by invoking the distinct concepts of curative or limited admissibility. *See, e.g.,* 1 MCCORMICK ON EVIDENCE § 56 (Kenneth S. Broun ed., 7th ed. 2013).

[88] *See* United States v. Sutton, 801 F.2d 1346, 1368–69 (D.C. Cir. 1986) (providing a thorough analysis and concluding that "[Rule 106] can adequately fulfill its function only by permitting the admission of some otherwise inadmissible evidence when the court finds in fairness that the proffered evidence should be considered contemporaneously. A contrary construction raises the specter of distorted and misleading trials, and creates difficulties for both litigants and the trial court."). *See also* United States v. Houlihan, 92 F.3d 1271 (1st Cir. 1996).

[89] *Compare* United States v. Harvey, 959 F.2d 1371, 1375–76 (7th Cir. 1992) *and* United States v. Gordon, 510 F.3d 811 (8th Cir. 2007) (rejecting a verbal completeness argument in the context of testimony about oral statements, citing Rule 106's limitation to writings), *with* United States v. Haddad, 10 F.3d 1252, 1258–59 (7th Cir. 1993) *and* United States v. Lopez-Medina, 596 F.3d 716, 734 (10th Cir. 2010) (recognizing authority under Rule 611(a) to enforce the principle of verbal completeness). For a thorough review of the conflict by a federal district court trying to prevent unfairness, *see* United States v. Bailey, 2017 WL 5126163 (D. Md. 2017) (concerning incomplete testimonial reports of defendant's oral, unrecorded interview with law enforcement agents).

[90] *See, e.g.,* State v. Eugenio, 579 N.W.2d 642 (Wis. 1998). In some states, the legislative history of the adoption of the state's version of the federal rule manifests an explicit intention to retain the common-law's trumping function. *See* ALA. R. EVID. 106 advisory committee note; FLA. EVID. CODE § 90.108 Law Revisions Council Note (1976); TEX. R. EVID. 106, notes and comments.

[91] *See, e.g.,* CONN. CODE EVID. § 1–5; IOWA R. EVID. 106; MONT. R. EVID. 106; NEB. REV. STAT. § 27–106; TEX. R. CRIM. EVID. 107. California's provision, CAL. EVID. CODE § 356, adopted before the federal rules, has also been interpreted to permit trumping of at least some otherwise applicable admissibility rules. *See, e.g.,*

In the 1988 case of *Beech Aircraft Corp. v. Rainey*,[92] the Supreme Court discussed the common-law rule of completeness in interpreting Rule 106. The Court's analysis suggests that the federal rules allow the admission of evidence of an otherwise inadmissible portion of an out-of-court verbal utterance if it is necessary to demonstrate the context of, and thereby render not misleading, the admissible portion evidenced by the opposing party. The case is complex, however, and it presents the situation in which no document was admitted, but rather testimony about what was previously written by the witness. Furthermore, there was no attempt to invoke the timing function expressed by Rule 106, because the party attempting to invoke the completeness doctrine waited until cross-examination of the witness to elicit testimony about the additional portions of the document. For both reasons, Rule 106 was not applicable on its face.

In *Rainey*, the defendant called the plaintiff, husband of the deceased Navy pilot, as an adverse witness and asked him about a portion of a letter he sent to the Navy concerning his wife's airplane accident. The plaintiff, a pilot himself, had written to the Navy expressing his opinion that the crash was a result of a power failure in the airplane. The portion of the letter that the defense elicited on direct examination of the adverse party made three points, suggesting the crash was the result of something other than a power failure. It said the plaintiff's wife had attempted to cancel the flight, partly because her student was tired and emotionally drained; that "unnecessary pressure" was placed on them to proceed with the flight; and that the plaintiff's wife or her student had abruptly initiated a hard right turn when the other aircraft unexpectedly came into view. On cross-examination, the plaintiff's lawyer attempted to ask about the remainder of the letter, which made clear the plaintiff's position that the crash was the result of power failure. The trial court would not allow the cross-examination because such testimony would constitute the opinion of a non-expert. His (out-of-court) opinion was admissible on behalf of the defense because of the asymmetry of the hearsay exemption for statements of a party opponent and the fact that the opinion rules are relaxed when that exemption is invoked.

The Court of Appeals reversed and remanded for new trial because the trial court's refusal to allow the plaintiff to testify to the rest of the letter misled the jury as to the plaintiff's position. Even though the letter itself had not been offered, the Court of Appeals held that the rule of completeness as to documents codified in Rule 106 applied. It held that the trial court had abused its discretion in not allowing examination about the remainder of the letter.

The United States Supreme Court found the "concerns underlying Rule 106" to be relevant and agreed with the Court of Appeals that the trial court abused its discretion in prohibiting questions about the remainder of the letter:

> The common-law "rule of completeness" which underlies Federal Rule of Evidence 106 was designed to prevent exactly the type of prejudice of which *Rainey* complains. In its aspect relevant to this litigation, the rule of completeness was stated succinctly by Wigmore: "[T]he opponent, against whom a part of an utterance has been put in, may in his turn complement it by

---

People v. Williams, 531 P.2d 778 (Cal. 1975) (en banc) (applying the completeness rule to evidence of a criminal defendant's out-of-court oral statement).

[92] Beech Aircraft Corp. v. Rainey, 488 U.S. 153 (1988).

putting in the remainder, in order to secure for the tribunal a complete understanding of the total tenor and effect of the utterance."[93]

[93] *Id.* at 171 (quoting 7 WIGMORE ON EVIDENCE § 2113 (Chadbourn rev. 1978)). For a detailed discussion of the federal rule, including an examination of the *Rainey* case and of the appropriate limits on the trumping function, *see* Dale A. Nance, *Verbal Completeness and Exclusionary Rules Under the Federal Rules of Evidence*, 75 TEX. L. REV. 51 (1996).

Chapter 2

BURDENS, PRESUMPTIONS, AND JUDICIAL NOTICE

Table of Sections

§ 2.01 Introduction

The great bulk of the law of evidence in Anglo-American courts concerns the admissibility of evidence, and most of this book is devoted to that topic. But to understand those issues, it is a good idea to understand the goal of this process of admitting evidence. Formally, that goal is to prove or disprove the elements of the cause(s) of action or affirmative defenses involved in the case. Certainty about the facts being rare, decisions must be made in the context of factual uncertainty, which poses the question of how strong the evidence must be to warrant a verdict. This is the general question of the burden of proof, which the present chapter addresses as background for the treatment of admissibility issues.

Unfortunately, few legal terms have engendered as much confusion as those considered in this brief chapter.[1] Indeed, the entire subject of burdens of proof and presumptions is not clearly associated with any particular area of law. As indicated, the lion's share of evidence law concerns the admissibility of particular classes of evidence, not with the effect evidence has under given circumstances. Thus, by one categorization, evidence law does not determine which party has a burden of proof with respect to a particular issue, nor is the stringency of that burden the type of rule normally associated with evidence law. These are, rather, matters of substantive law. The same might be

[1] Wigmore wrote of the "lamentable ambiguity of phrase and confusion of terminology under which our law has so long suffered." 9 WIGMORE ON EVIDENCE § 2485 at 283 (Chadbourn rev. 1981). McCormick's handbook calls the term *presumption* "the slipperiest member of the family of legal terms, except its first cousin, 'burden of proof.' " 2 MCCORMICK ON EVIDENCE § 342 at 675 (Kenneth S. Broun ed., 7th ed. 2013).

said for many presumptions, which concern not particular classes of evidence, but the effect evidence is to have if certain conditions are satisfied. The Federal Rules of Evidence contain no rules specifying the burdens of proof, though they do contain two rules related to presumptions in civil cases.[2]

It helps to understand three related aspects of the subject: (1) courts often describe issues involving burdens of proof and presumptions using ill-defined terms; (2) courts often use the same term to mean different things and do not indicate clearly which meaning is intended in a particular context; and (3) even where courts have reached consensus about the meaning of certain terms, some key questions remain unresolved. With these difficulties in mind, we approach this chapter with the modest goals of setting forth some basic principles and pointing out common pitfalls.

Although questions of "burden of proof" apply to bench trials as well as jury trials, throughout the discussion we will assume that the case is being tried to a jury.

§ 2.02 "Burden of Proof": Two Meanings

"Under our law, the term burden of proof has been used to express two rather different ideas, and as might be expected this usage has led to a jumble. Incisive thinkers have framed a more particularized vocabulary, duly segregating the ideas, but have not managed to get their vocabulary into universal use."[3] Specifically, the term "burden of proof" is an umbrella term that refers to both the burden of *persuasion* and the burden of *production*.[4]

The burden of persuasion concerns the final decision of the jury or other trier-of-fact, and involves two distinct components: the quantum of evidence (or standard of proof) required to establish an ultimate question of fact, and the allocation of the risk that the fact-finder will not be persuaded to that prescribed degree of certainty. The burden of persuasion is set by law, communicated to jurors by way of jury instructions, and applied by the fact-finder. Thus, *the fact-finder decides whether the burden of persuasion has been satisfied.*

The burden of production, on the other hand, concerns the role of the trial judge, and its force is usually expended before the case is submitted to the jury. Sometimes referred to as the burden of producing evidence or the burden of going forward, this burden comes into play when one party claims that the other party has not offered sufficient evidence even to merit continuing with the case as to that issue or claim, so that the judge must grant a preemptive motion at that point. Thus, *the trial judge decides whether the burden of production has been satisfied.*

These two burdens speak to different legal concerns. The burden of persuasion reflects how the law chooses to allocate the risk of error that remains at the end of the trial and deliberation. Criminal cases have a high burden of persuasion in order to allocate the risk of error so that the risk is borne disproportionately (though not completely) by the prosecution. Civil cases, on the other hand, generally treat the parties relatively equally in this regard. In contrast, the burden of production—which must be satisfied before the question of the satisfaction of the burden of persuasion can be posed—concerns the relationship between judge and jury and the adequacy of the

---

2 *See* **§ 2.13**.

3 JOHN M. MAGUIRE, EVIDENCE: COMMON SENSE AND COMMON LAW 175 (1947).

4 *See* JAMES B. THAYER, A PRELIMINARY TREATISE ON EVIDENCE AT THE COMMON LAW 355 (1898).

parties' efforts to provide the fact-finder with information on the basis of which to reach a verdict. Thus, the burden of production is focused on the regulation of the litigation process itself, as distinct from its outcomes. Its aim, generally speaking, is to balance the goals of maximizing accuracy against the pervasive need to minimize (and allocate) litigation costs, and its contours are not only related to the kind of case involved (for example, civil versus criminal) but also peculiar to the kind of adjudicative system that is being employed (here, the adversary system in general, and the jury trial in particular).[5]

The dual-burden description given above pertains to the burdens regarding proof of an actionable case—proof that the elements of a tort, crime, or breach of contract, etc. (or an affirmative defense) have been established. Once a cause of action is established, the matter of the measure of the appropriate remedy is governed by distinct proof requirements. In particular, once a plaintiff in a civil case establishes an entitlement to an award of damages (which requires proof of the existence of *recoverable* losses), the proof burden regarding the *amount* of damages is different. The assessment of damages is unlike the binary—liable or not liable—decision involved in regard to validity of the cause of action. Accordingly, most courts rightly do not use any of the familiar standards of proof discussed below—i.e., proof by preponderance of the evidence, proof by clear and convincing evidence, or proof beyond reasonable doubt—in stating what is required for proof of the amount of damages. Instead, the law requires simply as much precision in the proof of damages as it is reasonable to expect under the circumstances.[6] Aside from the minimal constraint that the amount cannot be too speculative, this burden is entirely a burden of production, and it requires no more than what the burdened party can reasonably be expected to provide.[7]

§ 2.03 Burden of Persuasion—Overview

The burden of persuasion concerns the ultimate question in the trial: legally satisfactory proof of all elements of a claim or defense.[8] Two key questions related to the "burden of persuasion" must be addressed as to any and all factual elements that the substantive law specifies as controlling. First, which party bears the burden of persuasion with regard to that element? That is, is that element part of plaintiff's (or prosecution's) claim or part of an affirmative defense? Second, to what level of confidence or degree of certainty must the fact-finder be persuaded for the burdened party to satisfy

---

[5] *See generally* DALE A. NANCE, THE BURDENS OF PROOF: DISCRIMINATORY POWER, WEIGHT OF EVIDENCE, AND TENACITY OF BELIEF (2016). Even a fully non-adversarial system of adjudication, one that did not allow parties to control what evidence is considered and did not use lay juries as fact-finders, would still be required to allocate the risk of error that results from unavoidable uncertainty, requiring resort to some kind of burden of persuasion. To the extent that a burden of production exists in non-adversarial systems of adjudication, it is a burden borne primarily by the investigating magistrate rather than the parties. *Id.* at 186–87.

[6] *See, e.g.*, Bigelow v. RKO Radio Pictures, 327 U.S. 251 (1946) (applying the principle that a wrongdoer must bear the risk of uncertainty in the amount of damages). For a recent case illustrating the idea, see Boyce v. Soundview Tech. Group, Inc. 464 F.3d 376, 391 (2d Cir. 2006).

[7] *See* DALE A. NANCE, THE BURDENS OF PROOF: DISCRIMINATORY POWER, WEIGHT OF EVIDENCE, AND TENACITY OF BELIEF 156–58 (2016).

[8] *See* CAL. EVID. CODE § 115 (using term "burden of proof" and stating that the concept "means the obligation of a party to establish by evidence a requisite degree of belief concerning a fact in the mind of the trier of fact or the court").

its burden? Both questions are matters of substantive law, not addressed (for example) by the Federal Rules of Evidence.[9]

Claims or defenses are only "proven" if the fact-finder believes that the party carrying the burden has established *each element* of the claim or defense by the requisite degree of proof. Thus, in a civil action for battery, the jury cannot find the defendant liable unless it believes that the plaintiff has established each element of the claim (volitional act, unlawful intent to contact, and harmful or offensive contact)[10] by the prescribed degree of proof (preponderance of the evidence). If the jury is sufficiently persuaded that the defendant acted volitionally and with unlawful intent, but concludes that no contact occurred, it must find for the defendant. The same principle holds in criminal cases, and indeed more strongly; before an accused may be convicted of a crime, the prosecution is constitutionally required to prove each element of the crime beyond a reasonable doubt.[11]

Most jury instructions regarding the burden of persuasion address only the *necessary* conditions for the jury to grant a verdict for the burdened party: they indicate what will prevent such a verdict, not what will warrant such a verdict. That is, they often neglect to specify what is logically *sufficient* proof for the jury to award a verdict against the burdened party. For example, they typically state that, if the burdened party does not prove each element to the requisite standard, that party should lose. But they only rarely state explicitly that, if each of the elements *is* proved to the requisite standard, then a verdict should be awarded to the burdened party. Moreover, some such instructions state that if *all* of the elements are proved (collectively) to the requisite standard, then a verdict should be awarded to the burdened party, which may not be the same thing.[12] But most frequently, jury instructions simply ignore the issue of what is sufficient proof. This reflects deep and unresolved controversies about the burden of persuasion—what it means, how it is set, and what it takes to satisfy it.[13]

---

9 While the distinction between "substance" and "procedure" is itself slippery, it is certainly the case that the burden of persuasion is considered "substantive" in the important sense that, under the *Erie* doctrine, a federal court adjudicating state-law claims employs state-law specifications regarding the burden of persuasion. *See* Cities Services Oil. Co. v. Dunlap, 308 U.S. 208 (1939). Although the matter is more contested in "horizontal" choice-of-law situations (when one state or national court is adjudicating rights arising under the "substantive" law of another state or nation), the trend is for the forum court to treat the burden of persuasion as substantive and adopt the burden of persuasion of the foreign state. *See* Dale A. Nance, *Choice of Law for Burdens of Proof*, 46 N.C. J. INT'L L. 227 (2021) (identifying, explaining, and endorsing the trend).

10 *See* RESTATEMENT (SECOND) OF TORTS § 18 (1965).

11 *In re* Winship, 397 U.S. 358, 364 (1970) ("[T]he Due Process clause protects the accused against conviction except upon proof beyond a reasonable doubt of every fact necessary to constitute the crime with which he is charged.").

12 For example, it is a simple proposition of ordinary probability theory that, just because the probability of A is greater than p and the probability of B is greater than p, it does not necessarily follow that the probability of the conjoint event, A&B, is greater than p. Thus, if the standard is interpreted probabilistically, one might satisfactorily prove A (in that the probability of A is greater than p) and satisfactorily prove B (in that the probability of B is greater than p) without satisfactorily proving A&B (because the probability of A&B is less than p). Of course, the law might contemplate a non-standard notion of probability that would not have these properties. *See, e.g.*, L. JONATHAN COHEN, THE PROBABLE AND THE PROVABLE (1977) (arguing for a notion of "inductive probability" that does not conform to the familiar axioms of mathematical probability and that, in Cohen's opinion, makes better sense of the legal standards of proof).

13 *See generally* DALE A. NANCE, THE BURDENS OF PROOF: DISCRIMINATORY POWER, WEIGHT OF EVIDENCE, AND TENACITY OF BELIEF 15–102 (2016) (exploring several proposed solutions to the controversies).

§ 2.04 Burden of Persuasion—Specifying the Standard of Proof

Standards of proof exist "to instruct the fact-finder concerning the degree of confidence our society thinks he should have in the correctness of factual conclusions for a particular type of adjudication."[14] The substantive law of particular subject matters prescribes the various levels of proof that must be offered to establish particular claims or defenses—levels of confidence the fact-finder must have in the correctness of the propositions at issue. Three degrees of proof are common: preponderance of the evidence, clear and convincing evidence, and beyond a reasonable doubt.

The lowest standard is most commonly referred to as "preponderance of the evidence," though the terms "greater weight of the evidence" and "more likely than not" are frequently used as well.[15] This is the least demanding burden to satisfy, as it requires the fact-finder's determination be tipped only slightly in favor of the party with the burden. The preponderance of the evidence standard applies to the vast majority of civil claims and defenses. Thus, in a negligence case, a plaintiff must offer enough evidence as to duty, breach, cause in fact, proximate cause, and compensable damages to cause the jurors' assessment to be tipped just slightly in favor of the existence of every element.

At the other end of the spectrum, the most onerous burden imposed by the law is that of proof "beyond a reasonable doubt," the standard constitutionally required for the prosecution to establish the offense in criminal cases.[16] Defining the term reasonable doubt is of course difficult, and there is debate about whether courts should even to attempt to define the concept in a jury instruction.[17] Although pattern instructions offer the flavor of "reasonable doubt,"[18] and jurisdictions have attempted to state their own definitions by statute,[19] in the end, the term is imprecise. Despite this lack of precision, courts scrutinize jury instructions on reasonable doubt with great care,[20] making it

---

14 *In re* Winship, 397 U.S. at 370 (Harlan, J., concurring).

15 *See* LARRY L. TEPLY & RALPH U. WHITTEN, CIVIL PROCEDURE 828 (1994) ("In civil actions, the burden of persuasion is usually described as a requirement that there must be a *preponderance of evidence*, or that the *greater weight of the evidence* must exist in favor of the party having the burden of persuasion . . .") (emphasis in original). These terms can be misleading because they suggest that the jury need only be convinced of the truth of a proposition by the greater weight of the *evidence actually produced at the trial*. This quantum of evidence might not be sufficient, however, to persuade the jurors that the proposition is "more likely than not" true. *See* Norman Dorsen & Daniel A. Rezneck, In re *Gault and the Future of Juvenile Law*, 1 FAM. L.Q. 1, 26–27 (Dec. 1967) (making a similar point), *quoted approvingly in In re* Winship, 397 U.S. 358, 367–68 (1970).

16 *In re* Winship, 397 U.S. 358, 364 (1970).

17 *See, e.g.*, Henry A. Diamond, Note, *Reasonable Doubt: To Define or Not to Define*, 90 COLUM. L. REV. 1716 (1990); Note, *Reasonable Doubt: An Argument Against Definition*, 108 HARV. L. REV. 1955 (1995).

18 *See, e.g.*, 1A KEVIN F. O'MALLEY ET AL., FEDERAL JURY PRACTICE AND INSTRUCTIONS § 12.10 (6th ed. 2008):

> It is not required that the government proves guilt beyond all possible doubt. The test is one of reasonable doubt. A reasonable doubt is a doubt based upon reason and common sense—the kind of doubt that would make a reasonable person hesitate to act. Proof beyond a reasonable doubt must, therefore, be proof of such a convincing character that a reasonable person would not hesitate to rely and act upon it in the most important of his or her own affairs.

19 *See, e.g.*, CAL. PENAL CODE § 1096 (Reasonable doubt "is not a mere possible doubt; because everything related to human affairs is open to some possible or imaginary doubt. It is that state of the case, which, after the entire comparison and consideration of all the evidence, leaves the minds of jurors in that condition that they cannot say they feel an abiding conviction of the truth of the charge.").

20 *See, e.g.*, United States v. Campbell, 874 F.2d 838, 842–43 (1st Cir. 1989) (stating that it was error to give instruction repeatedly using term "fair doubt," as such a term could impose a lower burden on the prosecution); Lanigan v. Maloney, 853 F.2d 40, 48 (1st Cir. 1988) (holding instruction stating that beyond a reasonable doubt meant "to a degree of moral certainty" constitutionally defective as potentially lightening prosecution's burden).

particularly important to frame instructions in accordance with existing statutory and judicial standards. In some jurisdictions, courts have approved of tendering no instruction defining reasonable doubt, or of instructions stating only a very general definition.[21] In *Victor v. Nebraska*,[22] the United States Supreme Court approved of such an approach, holding that the Constitution does not prohibit trial courts from defining reasonable doubt nor does it require them to do so. As long as the court instructs the jury of the necessity that the prosecution prove the defendant's guilt beyond a reasonable doubt, no particular form of instruction is required.[23]

A middle ground lies between "preponderance of the evidence" and "beyond a reasonable doubt." In some contexts, proof must be "clear and convincing." That term, of course, is no more easily defined than the others, but it certainly falls between mere preponderance and beyond a reasonable doubt.[24] This standard is encountered in regard to certain civil claims and defenses that are considered disfavored, such as claims of fraud or malice.[25] In some contexts, such a heightened standard is constitutionally required.[26]

At least in criminal cases, the usual standard of proof is sometimes made more demanding by the existence of "corroboration" requirements.[27]

§ 2.05 Burden of Persuasion—Allocating the Burden

In addition to the standard of proof, the law specifies who must "carry" the burden—which party must lose unless the jury finds that the burden has been met. In terms of the negligence example discussed in the previous section, if after considering all the evidence, the jurors either believe some element has not been proven to the requisite standard (here, a preponderance of the evidence), or are in "equipoise" (they cannot decide either way), then the party with the burden of persuasion (here, the plaintiff) must lose. This is why the burden of persuasion is sometimes referred to as the "risk of

---

[21] *See, e.g.*, United States v. Jorge, 865 F.2d 6, 10 (1st Cir. 1989) (affirming conviction even though defendant claimed error in not giving defendant's proposed jury instruction, which contained no definition of reasonable doubt; court stated that "it may be prudent on the part of a trial court to consider seriously a defendant's request to define the concept only minimally, or not at all").

[22] Victor v. Nebraska, 511 U.S. 1 (1994).

[23] *Id.* at 5.

[24] One state defines clear and convincing evidence as evidence that "leads you to a firm belief or conviction that the allegations are true. This is a higher standard of proof than proof by the greater weight of the evidence. The evidence presented need not be undisputed to be clear and convincing." N.D. Jury Instructions Civ. No. 1.41 (2004).

[25] For example, it is common for courts to hold that certain elements of a fraud case must be proved by clear and convincing evidence. *See, e.g.*, Kungys v. United States, 485 U.S. 759, 789 (1988) (requiring under statute applicable to naturalization of citizens, proof of materiality of a misrepresentation—that it was predictably capable of affecting decision to grant citizenship—be shown by clear, unequivocal, and convincing evidence). Some jurisdictions provide that punitive damages cannot be awarded unless the jury makes the requisite finding by clear and convincing evidence. *See, e.g.*, CAL. CIV. CODE § 3294 (stating that punitive damages are available if "it is proven by clear and convincing evidence that the defendant has been guilty of oppression, fraud, or malice . . .").

[26] *See, e.g.*, Gertz v. Robert Welch, Inc., 418 U.S. 323, 342 (1974) (applying heightened standard in context of actions for libel of public figures); Addington v. Texas, 441 U.S. 418, 431 (1979) (applying heightened standard to civil commitment determinations); Santosky v. Kramer, 455 U.S. 745, 748 (1982) (applying heightened standard to termination of parental rights).

[27] *See* **§ 2.07**.

nonpersuasion."[28] The choice of which party bears this burden is affected by several factors. As one commentator has written:

> (1) *Caution* and *convenience* often result in the burden of proof being placed upon the party seeking change. (2) *Policy* may dictate charging one side or the other with a particular element as a means of encouraging or discouraging a given kind of litigation. . . . (3) *Fairness* may suggest placing the burden of an element upon the party within whose control the evidence lies. . . . (4) *Probabilities* may be estimated and the burden placed upon the party who will benefit by a departure from the supposed norm.[29]

Though each of these factors affects the allocation of the burden of persuasion, no one factor controls the determination. Instead, the courts appear to accord the various factors different levels of importance in different situations.[30]

It is often said that the burden as to a particular ultimate fact or element is placed on the party to whose asserted claim or defense that element is essential.[31] That is true but misleading: the reason that the element is essential to a given party's asserted claim or defense is itself because a court or legislature at some point decided to allocate the burden on that element to that party.[32] As a justificatory matter, the court or legislature considers policies like those described above to determine whether something is assigned to be part of the plaintiff's claim for relief or, instead, to an affirmative defense. Thus, what is essential to the parties' claims is based on the legal allocation; the legal allocation is not based on what is essential to the parties' claims.[33] Nevertheless, as a matter of legal research—when a lawyer is simply inquiring as to the allocation of the burden, not attempting to discern its justification—the law's allocation is revealed by ascertaining whether it is part of the plaintiff's case or part of an affirmative defense.[34]

---

[28] *See, e.g.*, FED. R. EVID. 301 (referring to the "burden of proof in the sense of the risk of nonpersuasion"); 9 WIGMORE ON EVIDENCE § 2485 (Chadbourn rev. 1981).

[29] 1 MICHAEL H. GRAHAM, HANDBOOK OF FEDERAL EVIDENCE § 301.2 at 226–27 (6th ed. 2006) (emphasis in original). Wigmore listed several factors that courts consider in allocating burden of persuasion: (1) the burden is on the party having the burden of pleading; (2) the burden is on the party to whose case the fact is essential; (3) the burden is on the party assumed to have "*peculiar means of knowledge*" of the facts. 9 WIGMORE ON EVIDENCE § 2486 (Chadbourn rev. 1981). Morgan offered a similar list. Edmund M. Morgan, *Some Observations Concerning Presumptions*, 44 HARV. L. REV. 906, 910–11 (1931).

[30] 9 WIGMORE ON EVIDENCE § 2486 at 291 (Chadbourn rev. 1981) ("The truth is that there is not and cannot be any one general solvent for all cases. It is merely a question of policy and fairness based on experience in the different situations.").

[31] *See, e.g.*, CAL. EVID. CODE § 500 ("Except as otherwise provided by law, a party has the burden of proof as to each fact the existence or nonexistence of which is essential to the claim for relief or defense that he is asserting.").

[32] *See* Edward C. Cleary, *Presuming and Pleading: An Essay on Juristic Immaturity*, 1979 ARIZ. ST. L.J. 115, 120 (noting that the maxim in question "does no more than restate the question").

[33] Thus, in negligence cases one element (or collection of elements) that determines (or affects) liability is the existence of contributory negligence, and in earlier times some jurisdictions placed the burden of proving this element on the plaintiff, so that the plaintiff had to assert and prove that there was no contributory negligence. Under modern law, courts uniformly assign the defendant the burden of asserting and proving contributory negligence. *See* PROSSER AND KEETON ON THE LAW OF TORTS § 65 n.2 (W. Page Keeton gen. ed., 5th ed. 1984). For those jurisdictions that changed the allocation, this occurred only because policy-makers decided to move that element from being part of the plaintiff's case to being part of the defendant's case. They could not have based such a change on facts about what was "essential to a claim or defense," for that is what they were changing.

[34] One must be careful, however, to distinguish between the burden of pleading and the burden of proof because in a few contexts these are separated. In criminal cases, for example, a minority of jurisdictions place the burden to plead (and to produce some evidence on) the question of sanity on the defendant but, once the

These general principles apply regardless of the quantum of proof necessary to meet the burden of persuasion. In a criminal case, most of the essential facts that determine criminal liability are assigned to the prosecution's prima facie case. The prosecution bears the burden as to all these essential elements of the crime.[35] The constitutional law regarding affirmative defenses in criminal cases remains unclear. There is no absolute constitutional barrier against imposing a burden of persuasion on the defendant as to certain excuses or justifications, including insanity, intoxication, and self-defense.[36] However, it is likely that principles of due process impose some limits on the gravity of the burden the defendant must meet.[37]

Once the law places the burden of persuasion on a party, that burden rarely shifts during the trial. In criminal cases, even in the face of overwhelming evidence of guilt, the state may never shift the burden of persuasion to the defendant regarding to any element of the crime. The same is true in civil cases, with rare exceptions. One common exception holds that where two parties each acted negligently but only one caused the injury in question, the court may shift to each defendant the burden of showing that her conduct was not the cause-in-fact of the injury.[38] In some jurisdictions, the operation of a presumption can cause the burden of persuasion to shift.[39] With these few exceptions, however, the burden of persuasion stays put.[40]

§ 2.06 Burden of Production

The burden of production does not define or assign the ultimate burden of convincing the jury. Instead, it regulates the division of responsibilities between the judge and jury. If a motion for directed verdict, a motion for summary judgment, or a similar challenge is made, the party with the burden of production must convince the judge that the party has offered sufficient evidence to merit submission of the case to the

---

issue is thus raised, place the burden to prove sanity on the prosecution. *See* 1 WAYNE R. LAFAVE, SUBSTANTIVE CRIMINAL LAW § 8.3 (2d ed. 2003).

35 *In re* Winship, 397 U.S. 358 (1970). *See* 1 WAYNE R. LAFAVE, SUBSTANTIVE CRIMINAL LAW § 1.8(b) at 78 (2d ed. 2003).

36 1 WAYNE R. LAFAVE, SUBSTANTIVE CRIMINAL LAW § 1.8(b) at 86 (2d ed. 2003). *See also* Medina v. California, 505 U.S. 437 (1992) (concluding that the state may presume defendant competent to stand trial and require defendant to prove incompetence by preponderance of the evidence); Buzynski v. Oliver, 538 F.2d 6 (1st Cir. 1976) (applying Maine rule requiring defendant to persuade jury of insanity by preponderance of the evidence did not deny due process).

37 Although the Supreme Court held in Leland v. Oregon, 343 U.S. 790 (1952), that a state may require a defendant to prove insanity beyond a reasonable doubt, the continuing validity of the decision is unclear. In Mullaney v. Wilbur, 421 U.S. 684 (1975), the Court held that the prosecution has the burden of proving beyond a reasonable doubt the absence of heat of passion on sudden provocation when the issue is properly presented. And in Cooper v. Oklahoma, 517 U.S. 348 (1996), the Court held that an Oklahoma law providing that the defendant is presumed competent to stand trial unless the defendant proves incompetence by clear and convincing evidence violates due process.

38 *See, e.g.*, Summers v. Tice, 199 P.2d 1 (Cal. 1948) (holding that where two negligent hunters each fired the direction of the plaintiff but only one shot caused the significant harm, burden of proof shifted to each defendant to prove that his shot did not cause that harm).

39 *See* **§ 4.10**.

40 One should distinguish, however, the legal burden discussed in the text from what is sometimes called a "tactical" burden, a burden perceived by a party as a consequence of anticipating the likely verdict, but not formally imposed by law. For example, even though the burden of persuasion formally rests upon the prosecution to prove the elements of the crime, the proof provided by the prosecution may be so compelling that the defense anticipates a guilty verdict if the defense provides no exculpatory evidence. In such a case, a tactical burden may have shifted to the defense.

jury.[41] The party need not prove its case to the judge, but it must present sufficient evidence to demonstrate that a reasonable jury could find for it. If that party does not carry its burden of production with the judge, the judge will declare that party's claim or defense unproven, and will not allow that claim or defense to reach the jury. Generally speaking, the burden of producing evidence begins with the party on whom the burden of persuasion falls.[42]

Examples

P sues D for negligence following a collision between their two cars. At trial, P rests after producing evidence showing only that the two cars collided at an intersection, and that as a result of the collision, P suffered property damage and personal injury. D moves for a directed verdict. The court should grant the motion. In a negligence case, the plaintiff has the burden of persuasion as to all elements of the prima facie case (roughly speaking, duty, breach, cause in fact, proximate cause, and compensable damages). The plaintiff also has the initial burden of production as to each element. Because P failed to offer any evidence that the collision between the cars resulted from D's breach of a duty of reasonable care, P has not met the burden of production as to those elements.

If, instead, P offers evidence sufficient to meet the burden of producing evidence as to all elements of the prima facie negligence case, P meets his burden of production. If D's answer to P's complaint alleged that the accident was partly P's fault, and that accordingly, P's recovery, if any, should be reduced by the proportion of fault attributable to P's conduct, D will have the burden of production on that affirmative defense. At trial, if D offers no evidence to support the comparative negligence claim, and D did not produce any evidence to support the claim during cross-examination of P's witnesses, and P moves to dismiss D's comparative negligence defense, the court must grant P's motion. D had both a burden of persuasion and a burden of production as to the elements of the defense. Because D failed to produce any such evidence, the court must not permit the claim to go to the jury.

Following an art gallery heist, the state brings criminal charges against D for grand larceny (theft of property worth more than $1,000). At trial, the prosecution presents evidence that D did commit theft, but fails to call a witness to testify as to the value of the stolen property. If D moves for a directed verdict at the close of the prosecution's case-in-chief, the court will grant the motion on the grand larceny charge because the prosecution has failed to produce any evidence to support an element of the charge—property worth more than $1,000.

---

[41] *See, e.g.*, CAL. EVID. CODE § 110 (defining burden of producing evidence as "the obligation of a party to introduce evidence sufficient to avoid a ruling against him on the issue"). *See also* 9 WIGMORE ON EVIDENCE § 2487 at 293 (Chadbourn rev. 1981).

[42] *See* CAL. EVID. CODE § 550 ("The burden of producing evidence as to a particular fact is initially on the party with the burden of proof as to that fact."). That this generalization is not always true is illustrated by the rule in some states that a criminal defendant who wishes to rely on the defense of insanity must both plead and initially produce evidence tending to prove insanity, but that the prosecution bears the ultimate burden of persuading the jury that the defendant was sane. *See* 1 WAYNE R. LAFAVE, SUBSTANTIVE CRIMINAL LAW § 8.3 (2d ed. 2003).

Unlike the burden of persuasion, the burden of producing evidence can shift back and forth during the trial, at least in civil cases.[43] A party cannot shift the burden of production to the opponent merely by offering evidence sufficient to meet the burden. However, the burden will shift to the opponent if the party who had the burden offers evidence strong enough to require a peremptory finding in favor of that party.[44]

The operation of the burden of production can be illustrated graphically:[45]

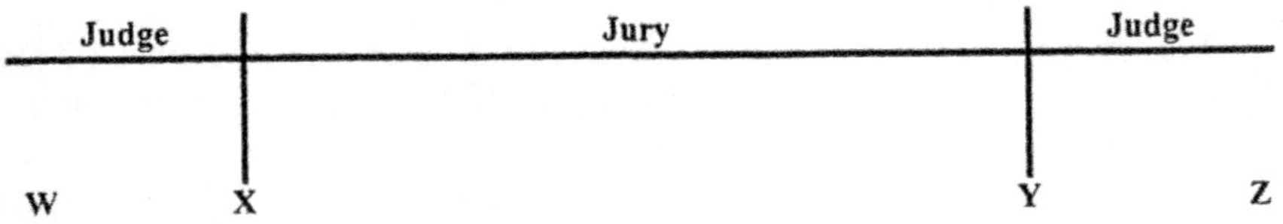

Imagine the following case: P brings a negligence action against D following an intersection collision between their two cars. P claims D ran a red light, causing the collision. P has the burden of production as to evidence of D's negligence. At the commencement of trial, consider P's evidence to be at point W. Were P to offer no evidence of the color of the light, the judge would grant D's motion for directed verdict. Because P has produced no basis for a jury finding that D was negligent, the judge must take the case from the jury.[46]

Suppose, however, that P and P's friend, who was a passenger in the car, testify that P had the green light. This will likely meet P's burden of production on that issue, which moves P's evidence into the points between X and Y in the diagram. Should D move for a directed verdict at the close of P's case, the court will deny the motion because P has presented a case sufficient to reach the jury. Note that at this point, P is entitled only to reach the jury. The burden of production has not shifted to D. Even if D rested without offering any evidence to rebut the inference of negligence created by P's

---

[43] As in civil cases, courts trying criminal cases may find that the government failed to meet its burden of production and acquit the accused. The reverse is not true in criminal cases however; the judge may not direct a conviction of a criminal defendant, so the government's burden of production is never formally shifted to the defense. *See* United States v. Martin Linen Supply, 430 U.S. 564, 572–73 (1977).

[44] *See* 2 MCCORMICK ON EVIDENCE § 338 at 657–58 (Kenneth S. Broun ed., 7th ed. 2013).

[45] This diagram can be found in RICHARD H. FIELD, BENJAMIN KAPLAN & KEVIN M. CLERMONT, CIVIL PROCEDURE: MATERIALS FOR A BASIC COURSE 672 (7th ed. 1997). It, in turn, is based on a diagram in 9 WIGMORE ON EVIDENCE § 2487 at 298 (Chadbourn rev. 1981).

[46] It is difficult (though not impossible) to resist the suggestion that evidentiary strength in favor of the plaintiff increases as one moves to the right along the horizontal line in the diagram. If this is the contemplated conception, then one could think of the horizontal scale as representing the probability that the plaintiff's claim is true according to the *trial court's* assessment, assuming that credibility determinations favor the burdened party as described in the text below. Then the bounds marked off by X and Y can be determined, in a simple model, by two parameters: (a) the tipping point, T, for proof under the burden of persuasion, and (b) the margin of a jury's reasonable divergence, m, from the judge's assessment. By that model, a reasonable verdict could go either way so long as the indicated probability lies between $T-m$ and $T+m$. If something like this is what one takes this picture to reflect, then there is no particular reason to think that the case would start to the left of X, and considerable reason to think it would not. (What would you, as a judge, think about the strength of a civil case that has not settled or been dismissed and is about to be tried, that is, before any formal evidence has been introduced?) Nevertheless, the law will treat the situation as starting to the left of X so that an initial burden of production falls on the party bearing the burden of persuasion on the issue. After all, someone must start the process of presenting evidence, and it is reasonable to assume that the party bearing the burden of persuasion has *some* evidence to present on the matter and that doing so is a reasonable condition on access to a public resolution of the dispute. This suggests that the burden of production does more work than simply monitoring the plausibility of the fact-finders' assessments of probability under the burden of persuasion. *See* DALE A. NANCE, THE BURDENS OF PROOF: DISCRIMINATORY POWER, WEIGHT OF EVIDENCE, AND TENACITY OF BELIEF 201–12 (2016).

evidence, the judge would still let the jury decide the negligence issue. This makes very good sense. Because P had an interest in the outcome, and because P's witness was an acquaintance who might have been biased in P's favor, the jury could rationally decide the case either way. This weighing of credibility is not for the judge; the judge's only role is to assess whether the evidence, if credible, could lead a rational jury to find for P on the negligence issue. If so, then the case goes to the jury. This is the most common situation; the burden of production has not shifted to D, but it has been discharged by P, so the burden of production disappears from the case (i.e., neither party is subject to an adverse directed verdict). P, of course, still must meet the burden of persuasion, which means convincing the jury that D was "more likely than not" negligent.[47]

Suppose, however, that in addition to the testimony noted above, P calls a police officer who lays the foundation for admission of a videotape produced by a police camera mounted near the intersection for monitoring of traffic. The tape displays the date and time of the accident, and clearly shows P and D entering the intersection simultaneously, with the green light in P's favor. At this point, P has most likely produced sufficient evidence to move the evidence past point Y, and the burden of production will shift to D. Unless D offers evidence refuting D's illegal entry into the intersection, the court would almost certainly grant a directed verdict for P on the issue of D's negligence. If D offers sufficient evidence to meet a burden of production on that issue, such evidence will have moved the case back between points X and Y, once again making a jury issue. On these facts, it is almost inconceivable that D could offer sufficient evidence to move the case back past point X; evidence already adduced by P is before the jury, along with D's evidence of non-negligence.

Failure to offer evidence sufficient to meet a burden of production will result in the granting of a motion generally leading to the dismissal of a claim or defense.[48] Such a move by the trial court is a decision as a matter of law, which is final (if no other claims remain) and reviewable de novo.[49] A decision *not* to dismiss on a peremptory motion is not final and can only be reviewed as a matter of law at the end of the proceedings. Of course, the trial court has discretion to grant the party's motion to reopen its case to offer additional evidence if the court believes that the interests of justice would be served by doing so.

What, then, is required to "meet" a burden of producing evidence? How much evidence is enough? No definitive answer can be given. To say that "more than a scintilla"

---

[47] Once again, the legal burden discussed in the text must be distinguished from what may be called a "tactical" burden, a burden perceived by a party as a consequence of anticipating the likely verdict, but not formally imposed by law. For example, if at the end of the plaintiff's case, the evidence nearly moves the case beyond Y, but not quite, then there is no legal burden on the defense to present evidence, precisely in the sense that no directed verdict will be imposed against the defense if the defense does not present counter-evidence. The jury will decide. But that does not mean the defendant will win. As a practical matter, the defense might well believe that, if no counter-evidence is presented, the jury will give a plaintiff's verdict. In that event, the defense might feel compelled to present evidence to avoid an adverse jury verdict. Though not imposed by law, such a tactical shift of the burden to produce evidence can be very real.

[48] The name and timing of the procedural motion used to test a party's satisfaction of the burden of production varies. In civil cases, it can be a summary judgment motion, a motion for a directed verdict (or nonsuit), or (in the language of the federal courts) a motion for involuntary dismissal (in bench trials) or for judgment as a matter of law (in jury trials). *See, e.g.*, FED. R. CIV. P. 41(b), 50(a). It can, however, also be raised after a jury verdict by a motion for a judgment *non obstante veredicto*. *See, e.g.*, FED. R. CIV. P. 50(b).

[49] *See* **§ 3.12**.

is required,[50] of course, is only to utter an abstract expression, and the same is true of other similar phrases that attempt to describe the standard.[51] More precision is rather difficult to find, though some guidance can be offered.

If a directed verdict or similar motion is made against a party who has the burden of production, the court will grant the motion if it finds that no reasonable jury could find in favor of the party with the burden.[52] For this purpose, even in criminal cases, the trial court may consider all evidence introduced at the time the motion is considered, regardless of which side presented it.[53] Whether this test is met depends on the burden of persuasion applicable in the case: what would be adequate to permit a reasonable jury to find fact X to be true by a preponderance of the evidence might not be adequate to permit a reasonable jury to find fact X to be true beyond a reasonable doubt.[54] Thus, the burden of production in a criminal case for which X is an essential element allocated to the government would require the introduction of evidence sufficient to permit a reasonable jury to find beyond a reasonable doubt that X is true.

Generally, courts require that the party with the burden of production must offer some *affirmative* evidence of the propositions it is burdened to prove. Reliance on the jury's disbelieving adverse witnesses is not enough even to permit the jury to find a fact governed by the weakest standard of proof, "preponderance of the evidence." In *Dyer v. MacDougall*,[55] the plaintiff brought a four-count complaint for libel and slander. The plaintiff could offer no affirmative evidence that the defendant had made the alleged statements, and the defendant moved for summary judgment, supporting the motion with several affidavits and a deposition, all of which denied that the statements were ever made. The plaintiff's response to the motion was supported by affidavits containing evidence that would be inadmissible at trial. Ultimately, the court granted summary judgment as to two counts on the ground that the plaintiff would have no evidence that the alleged statements were made, except the testimony of witnesses who would deny that they were made. On appeal from the dismissal of the two counts, the plaintiff argued

---

[50] *See* 2 MCCORMICK ON EVIDENCE § 338 at 654 (Kenneth S. Broun ed., 7th ed. 2013) ("A 'scintilla' of evidence will not suffice. The evidence must be such that a reasonable person could draw from it the inference of the existence of the particular fact to be proved . . .") (footnotes omitted). *See also* Rodney L. Bean & Sean P. McGinley, *West Virginia's Very Own* Celotex *Trilogy: A Series of Recent Opinions by the Supreme Court of Appeals of West Virginia Reveals that the Rumors of Rule 56's Death Were Greatly Exaggerated*, 98 W. VA. L. REV. 571, 596–97 (1996) (to defeat a motion for summary judgment, the party "must demonstrate the ability to produce enough competent evidence at trial to enable a finding in his or her favor. A mere 'scintilla of evidence' will not suffice, nor will evidence which is 'conjectural,' 'problematic,' 'merely colorable,' or 'not significantly probative' ") (footnotes omitted).

[51] *See* Laura G. Kniaz, *Animal Liberation and the Law: Animals Board the Underground Railroad*, 43 BUFF. L. REV. 765, 814 n.273 (1995) ("Across jurisdictions, the quantum of evidence required to satisfy a [criminal] defendant's burden of production have included the following standards: some evidence, more than a scintilla, slight evidence, evidence to support, some credible evidence, and evidence sufficient to raise a reasonable doubt.") (citing 1 PAUL H. ROBINSON, CRIMINAL LAW DEFENSES § 4(c) at 35–36 (1984)).

[52] One federal court wrote, in the similar context of a motion for judgment notwithstanding the verdict, that "if there is substantial evidence opposed to the [motion], that is, evidence of such quality and weight that reasonable and fair-minded men in the exercise of impartial judgment might reach different conclusions, the [motion] should be denied. . . ." Boeing Co. v. Shipman, 411 F.2d 365, 374 (5th Cir. 1969).

[53] By choosing to present evidence the defendant waives the right to appeal a denial of a motion for a directed verdict made at the end of the government's case-in-chief. *See, e.g.*, United States v. Keuylian, 602 F.2d 1033, 1040–41 (2d Cir. 1979). Of course, the defense may still appeal a denial of a similar motion made at the close of evidence, but for the latter motion the trial court properly considers evidence presented by the defense as well as that presented by the government.

[54] *See* James McNaughten, *Burdens of Production of Evidence: A Function of the Burden of Persuasion*, 68 HARV. L. REV. 1382 (1955).

[55] Dyer v. MacDougall, 201 F.2d 265 (2d Cir. 1952).

that he should be able to go to trial even without affirmative evidence because the jury would be entitled to disbelieve the defendant's evidence. The plaintiff wished to rely solely on the demeanor of adverse witnesses, and perhaps the inherent implausibility of their testimony, to establish the truth of his claims. The Court of Appeals for the Second Circuit, Judge Hand writing for the majority, affirmed. In the court's view, failure to grant summary judgment under these circumstances would eviscerate the effectiveness of such motions, because a party could always claim that a jury could find in her favor if it disbelieved the opposing witnesses. Thus, *Dyer* instructs us that satisfying a burden of production at trial means offering some affirmative evidence to support the allegations of the complaint.[56]

The rule in *Dyer* is followed by most courts.[57] Still, a few cases suggest that an adverse witness's demeanor and the content of that witness's testimony can, in some instances, suffice to meet a burden of production.[58] In *Dyer* itself, Judge Frank offered a persuasive argument that demeanor could, in some cases, suffice to allow a party to reach the jury:

> One can imagine a case in which a man would suffer a grave injustice, if it were the invariable rule that a plaintiff can never win a case when (1) he can offer only the oral testimony of the defendant, the one available witness, which is flatly and unswervingly against the plaintiff but (2) the jury (in a jury trial) or the judge (in a judge trial) is thoroughly convinced by the witness's demeanor that he is an unmitigated liar. On that account, I would oppose such a rule.[59]

---

[56] *See also* LARRY L. TEPLY & RALPH U. WHITTEN, CIVIL PROCEDURE 829 (1994) ("To satisfy the burden of production, a party must ordinarily introduce some affirmative evidence that the fact in question has occurred."). Although *Dyer* arose in the summary judgment context, rather than on a motion for directed verdict, the standards to be applied by the trial judge are essentially the same. *See Id.* at 786.

[57] "[T]here is virtual unanimity among the courts that have addressed the issue that a fact finder may not base its finding of fact on disbelief of a witness. The party with the burden of proof must introduce affirmative evidence to sustain its burden." J. Palmer Lockard, *Summary Judgment in Pennsylvania: Time for Another Look at Credibility Issues*, 35 DUQ. L. REV. 625, 656 n.216 (1997). Similarly, current practice often allows a party to call the fact-finder's attention to the fact that an opponent has not presented evidence that one might expect the opponent to present if it were favorable to the opponent. *See* **§ 5.05**. But such an "adverse inference" against the opponent from mere failure to present evidence cannot by itself satisfy the first party's burden of production. *See* 2 MCCORMICK ON EVIDENCE § 264 at 322 (Kenneth S. Broun ed., 7th ed. 2013).

[58] *See, e.g., In re* Melnick, 360 F.2d 918, 920 (2d Cir. 1966) (concluding that referee is entitled to disbelieve debtor's testimony in bankruptcy proceeding in which debtor had burden of proving he did not knowingly and fraudulently make a false oath as to a material matter); Morrison v. Lefevre, 592 F. Supp. 1052, 1065 (S.D.N.Y. 1984) (involving civil rights action against prison officials arising from alleged planting of contraband; three defendants who "found" contraband testified, and it was established that one of them planted it, even though defendants did not so testify; court held that "[t]he stories told by the three officers and their demeanor on the stand strongly support the inference that they were responsible for 'planting' and then 'discovering' the vial of florescent fluid."). Note that because neither of these cases involved jury trials, the propriety of directed verdicts was not in issue. Nevertheless, the courts' actions demonstrate a willingness to accept that a proposition may be sufficiently established even in the absence of affirmative evidence.

Some scholars have supported such an argument. *See, e.g.,* Richard D. Friedman, *Route Analysis of Credibility and Hearsay*, 96 YALE L.J. 667, 735 n.134 (1987) ("Indeed, it may be that in some cases a factfinder may find a proposition to be true solely on the basis of a witness's demeanor in testifying to the contrary of that proposition."); Edmund Morgan, *Admissions*, 12 WASH. L. REV. 181, 185–86 (1937). *See also* Olin Guy Wellborn, III, *Demeanor*, 76 CORNELL L. REV. 1075, 1102–03 (1991) (distinguishing between relying on demeanor and relying on the content of the testimony itself to establish facts contrary to the witness's testimony).

[59] Dyer v. MacDougall, 201 F.2d 265, 272 (2d Cir. 1952) (Frank, J., concurring). Judge Frank believed that *Dyer* was not such a case, because in the relevant counts plaintiff claimed to have been slandered in his absence and in the presence of only two other persons, both of whom would deny the slander. Thus, "only

Despite this possibility, the mere fact that the adverse witness is biased by virtue of association with the non-burdened party is not enough by itself to avoid the directed verdict. In *Chesapeake & O. Ry. Co. v. Martin*,[60] for example, the plaintiff brought an action to recover damages for alleged misdelivery of a carload of potatoes. A crucial issue concerned the reasonableness of an eight-day delay in delivery, which affected how long the plaintiff had to make its claim under the bill of lading. At trial, an experienced witness who worked for the defendant railroad testified that forty-eight hours was a reasonable time for delivery, and this witness's testimony stood unimpeached; if believed, this testimony implied that the claim was filed too late. Nevertheless, the trial court allowed this issue to go to the jury. The Supreme Court reversed, holding:

> We recognize the general rule . . . that the question of the credibility of witnesses is one for the jury alone; but this does not mean that the jury is at liberty, under the guise of passing upon the credibility of a witness, to disregard his testimony, when from no reasonable point of view is it open to doubt. The complete testimony of the agent . . . discloses no lack of candor on his part. It was not shaken by cross-examination; indeed, upon this point, there was no cross-examination. Its accuracy was not controverted by proof or circumstances, directly or inferentially; and it is difficult to see why, if inaccurate, it readily could not have been shown to be so.[61]

The Court acknowledged that the witness was an employee of the party that called him, but held that "[i]n the circumstances . . . we are of the opinion that this was not enough to take the question to the jury . . . ."[62]

Assuming the burdened party offers some affirmative evidence, will that be enough to reach the jury? American jurisdictions generally subscribe to the principle that the testimony of a single witness about a perceived event is sufficient to permit (though not require) the jury to find that an event occurred as the witness describes.[63] This "single witness" rule does not necessarily mean that such testimony is sufficient to permit the jury to find some *other* fact to be true, when that other fact is inferred from the event perceived. Thus, for example, a witness's testimony that he saw a man who looked like the defendant running from the scene of a crime is ordinarily sufficient to permit the jury to find (were they required to find it) that a man who looked like the defendant ran from the scene of the crime, but it is not automatically sufficient to permit the jury to make the further circumstantial inference that (a) the defendant ran from the scene of the crime, or (b) that the defendant committed the crime. On the other hand, if the witness makes a positive identification of the defendant as the man the witness saw

---

plaintiff's own suit serves to publicize the alleged slander." *Id.* In the majority opinion, Judge Hand also pointed out that plaintiff had failed to avail himself of the opportunity to depose the witnesses before trial. *Id.* at 267.

[60] Chesapeake & O. R. Co. v. Martin, 283 U.S. 209 (1931).

[61] 283 U.S. at 216.

[62] 283 U.S. at 216. In several opinions issued in 1986, the Supreme Court signaled its strong support for the judge's power to grant summary judgment against the party that had the burden of production. *See* Anderson v. Liberty Lobby, Inc., 477 U.S. 242 (1986) (libel action); Celotex Corp. v. Catrett, 477 U.S. 317 (1986) (wrongful death action alleging exposure to asbestos manufactured by defendant); Matsushita Elec. Indus. Co., Ltd. v. Zenith Radio Corp., 475 U.S. 574 (1986) (antitrust action). The cases demonstrate the Court's commitment to the trial court's close analysis of the allegations and proof, and the need for the plaintiff to rely on meaningful evidence to support its claims. Because of the similarity of the standard for granting summary judgment and directed verdict, these cases lend considerable support to the same conclusion regarding motions for directed verdict.

[63] *See, e.g.*, CAL. EVID. CODE § 411 ("Except where additional evidence is required by statute, the direct evidence of one witness who is entitled to full credit is sufficient for proof of any fact.").

plunging a knife into the victim's chest, then that would be sufficient to permit the jury to find that the defendant stabbed the victim.

Several caveats define and limit this single witness rule. First, and most important, the converse of the single witness rule is false: just because the burdened party does *not* have a witness who observed the very event or condition to be proved does not preclude a positive verdict. In most cases, circumstantial evidence can suffice.[64] For example, mental states constitute elements of most crimes, yet mental states cannot be directly observed by anyone, except perhaps the person who has them. Mental states are almost always proved by circumstantial evidence.[65] Second, special rules sometimes require corroboration of the testimony of a particular kind of witness or of a witness in a particular kind of case.[66] Third, in the rare case a judge may rule that the testimony of the single witness is so inherently implausible that a verdict cannot reasonably be based on believing it, as when the testimony contradicts indisputable physical laws.[67] Finally, some courts have made preemptive rulings against the burdened party apparently as a means of insisting on the presentation of available but missing evidence, even though the evidence already introduced should be sufficient to permit a reasonable jury to find for the burdened party under the applicable standard of proof.[68]

In addition to the foregoing, widely encountered principles, there are many subject-matter specific rules, often jurisdiction specific rules—"rules of thumb" might be a better descriptor—that have evolved from the process of appellate review of the countless trial court rulings on motions that test a party's satisfaction of the burden of production. The doctrine of *res ipsa loquitur* in the law of torts is a familiar example.[69] Sometimes these rules are sensible; sometimes not. One oft-encountered illustration of the latter: some appellate courts, in the course of affirming a trial court's directed verdict or reversing a refusal to direct such a verdict, have noted the weakness of the burdened party's evidence and then said something like, "an inference may not be based on an inference."[70] This

---

[64] On the distinction between direct and circumstantial evidence, see **§ 5.02**.

[65] *See, e.g.*, United States v. Tyler, 758 F.2d 66 (2d Cir. 1985) (holding circumstantial evidence sufficient to permit inference regarding mental state necessary for "aiding and abetting" offense, even in face of defendant's denial of such mental state).

[66] *See* **§ 2.07**.

[67] *See* 2 McCormick on Evidence § 338 at 655 n.9 (Kenneth S. Broun. ed., 7th ed. 2013).

[68] *See, e.g.*, United States v. Tornabene, 687 F.2d 312, 315–16 (9th Cir. 1982) (reversing a conviction because the government failed to take reasonable efforts to produce an informant whose presence had been requested by the defense); G.E.G. v. State, 417 So.2d 975 (Fla. 1982) (holding that, in prosecution for possession of controlled substance, that substance, if available, must be produced in court). To be sure, there are other ways to handle this kind of situation. One is to leave it to the opponent to procure and present the missing evidence, if that is possible. Another is to permit a party to inform the jury of the evidential omission and to invite the jury to draw an inference on the matter adverse to the other side. (*See* **§ 5.05**.) The question of what is the best tool to use in a given situation is not often considered explicitly in the case law. *See* Dale A. Nance, The Burdens of Proof: Discriminator Power, Weight of Evidence, and Tenacity of Belief 201–49 (2016) (discussing the factors that should guide the court's choice of an appropriate response in this and related contexts).

[69] By its more common interpretation, *res ipsa* operates as a permissive inference that precludes a directed verdict, but not as a presumption that would shift some aspect of the burden of proof. Whether or not the doctrine involves a shift in a formal burden, however, its application does entail satisfying the burden of production. *See generally* 9 Wigmore on Evidence § 2509 (Chadbourn rev. 1981). On the difference between a permissive inference and a presumption, *see* **§ 2.08.**

[70] *See, e.g.*, Sobolovitz v. Lubric Oil Co., 140 N.E.634, 635 (Ohio 1923) (reversing jury verdict for plaintiff and directing a verdict for the defense, and saying "an inference cannot be predicated upon an inference"); Industrial National Bank v. Dyer, 188 A.2d 909, 913 (R.I 1963) ("A conclusion reached by drawing inferences from inferences is never considered as being probative of an ultimate fact under any proper concept of juridical proof.").

language can get picked up by later advocates and judges and applied without regard to the specific context in which it was uttered, as if it were a valid general principle. As commentators have long observed, it is not, nor could it be,[71] and many courts reject it.[72] In those jurisdictions professing adherence to this limitation on inferences, it has been qualified to the point of virtual extinction, amounting to little more than a warning that multi-stage (or "catenated") inferences may become too attenuated to satisfy the production burden.[73]

§ 2.07 Corroboration Requirements

Medieval Roman-Canon law contained quantitative rules that required the testimony of more than one witness to support a claim.[74] In contrast, the traditional common-law rule is that the testimony of a single witness to a fact is, if believed by the fact-finder, sufficient to establish that fact.[75] And, as also explained in the previous section, circumstantial evidence may suffice to warrant a positive verdict, even in criminal cases. There are, however, exceptional situations in which corroborating evidence is required as a matter of law. The most conspicuous American example is the constitutional rule that precludes a conviction for treason "unless on the Testimony of two Witnesses to the same overt Act, or on Confession in open Court."[76] More commonly encountered examples are (a) the common-law rule that a criminal defendant may not be convicted solely on evidence of his or her uncorroborated, out-of-court confession,[77] and (b) the statutory rule, followed in more than a dozen states but not in federal practice, that a criminal conviction may not be based on the uncorroborated testimony

---

[71] *See* 1A WIGMORE ON EVIDENCE § 41 (Tillers rev. 1983). Wigmore developed a sophisticated approach to analyzing evidence that involved breaking down chains of inference that could be lengthy. *See* JOHN H. WIGMORE, THE SCIENCE OF JUDICIAL PROOF (3d ed. 1937). The idea is examined briefly below. *See* **§ 5.02**.

[72] *See, e.g.*, N.L.R.B. v. Camco, Inc., 340 F.2d 803, 811 (5th 1965) (addressing a challenge to the sufficiency of the evidence, and noting, "The so-called rule against pyramiding inferences, if there really is such a "rule" and if it is anything more than an empty pejorative, is simply legalese fustian to cover a clumsy exclusion of evidence having little or no probative value."); United States v. An Article of Device, 731 F.2d 1253, 1263 (7th Cir. 1984) (addressing a challenge to a jury instruction, expressing strong skepticism about a ban on inferences built on inferences, and stating, "We think it would be the better practice to avoid the "inference on inference" language and to concentrate instead on the jury's duty not to engage in speculation that is beyond the scope of the evidence."); Braun v. Roux Distributing Co., 312 S.W.2d 758 (Mo. 1958) (suggesting that any such rule, when it is invoked "is but a convenient way of guarding against what the court regards as 'attenuated reasoning' on the part of the jury, or evidence thought to be too remote or uncertain or lacking in probative force.").

[73] *See, e.g.*, Hurt v. Charles J. Rogers Transportation Co., 130 N.E.2d 820, 823 (Ohio 1955) (permitting "[a]n inference which is based in part upon another inference and in part upon factual support," provided it is a reasonable conclusion for the jury to deduce"); Motorists Mut. Ins. Co. v. Hamilton Twp. Trustees, 502 N.E. 2d 204, 207 (Ohio 1986) (permitting multiple inferences so long as later inferences are supported by "common human experience"). *Cf.* Waldman v. Shipyard Marina, Inc., 230 A.2d 841, 845 (R.I. 1967) ("[J]ustice may be promoted by the acceptance of an inference as having probative force which rests on another inference where that inference clearly excludes the drawing from the same fact of another reasonable inference. But an inference resting on an inference drawn from established facts must be rejected as being without probative force where the facts from which it is drawn are susceptible of another reasonable inference.").

[74] *See* MIRJAN DAMAŠKA, EVALUATION OF EVIDENCE: PRE-MODERN AND MODERN APPROACHES (2019).

[75] See the discussion of the "single witness" rule in **§ 2.06**. *See generally* 7 WIGMORE ON EVIDENCE §§ 2032–34 (Chadbourn rev. 1979).

[76] U.S. CONST., art. III, § 3.

[77] *See* 1 MCCORMICK ON EVIDENCE §§ 145–48 (Kenneth S, Broun, ed. 7th ed. 2013).

of an accomplice.[78] Other such requirements can be found, but they tend to be specific to particular kinds of cases.[79]

The cases implementing such doctrines exhibit considerable inconsistency about the status of the requirements. Specifically, there is little agreement about whether they modify the burden of persuasion—by creating a proof requirement that the jury must find to be satisfied *in addition* to the jury's finding beyond a reasonable doubt that the ultimate facts instantiating the elements of the crime are true—or they merely modify the burden of production—by altering the conditions under which the case is allowed to go to a jury—or they have some other function.[80]

With regard to treason cases, Wigmore explained that the two-witness rule arises from a desire to avoid the effects of political power in producing a false conviction in a context where acquitting the guilty is not too dangerous, an explanation that is consistent with taking the rule as a modification of the burden of persuasion in a manner favorable to the defense.[81] Wigmore opined that for the rule to be satisfied, the two witnesses "must *both be believed by the jury*."[82] That means that it is *not* enough that two witnesses give conflicting accounts of the same overt act, nor is it enough that they give varying accounts each of which, if believed, is inculpatory. If Wigmore's claim is sound, then conviction for treason requires more than the jury's determination that the proof of guilt is beyond a reasonable doubt.[83]

With respect to the second corroboration rule mentioned above, there is some agreement about the need to preclude conviction where the finding on an essential element is based only on the defendant's uncorroborated confession: it protects against false confessions arising from the accused's mental vulnerability or illness or desire to protect another.[84] But beyond that, consensus breaks down. There is conflicting case law

---

[78] The leading federal decision is Caminetti v. United States, 242 U.S. 470, 495 (1917) ("[T]here is no absolute rule of law preventing conviction on the testimony of accomplices if juries believe them.") *See generally* Christine J. Saverda, *Accomplices in Federal Court: A Case for Increased Evidentiary Standards*, 100 YALE. L.J. 785 (1990).

[79] For example, some jurisdictions apply the rule that, in order to convict the accused of perjury in having testified falsely that fact X occurred, the testimony of another person contradicting fact X is not sufficient to establish that the accused's testimony was false; the other person's testimony must be corroborated, at least by circumstantial evidence. *See* 7 WIGMORE ON EVIDENCE §§ 2040–43 (Chadbourn rev. 1979).

[80] When jurors are required to apply a corroboration test as well as the usual "beyond a reasonable doubt" test, one might argue that this does not involve a change in the standard, but merely a legal rule to the effect that reasonable doubt must be found in the absence of corroboration. Nevertheless, imposition of such a requirement means that *what the jury takes to be* beyond a reasonable doubt is not exclusively controlling for the jury's decision in such contexts.

[81] *See* 7 WIGMORE ON EVIDENCE § 2037, at 354 (Chadbourn rev. 1979) (arguing that "the harm of a real traitor escaping judicial punishment is relatively small, because treason, when it is confined to a few individuals, can never really endanger the State, and, when it represents a widespread opinion in the community, there will be ample array of witnesses to prove its acts.").

[82] *Id.* § 2038, at 357 (relying solely on opinions in Lord Castlemaine's Trial, 7 How. St. Tr. 1067 (1680)).

[83] To be sure, Wigmore argued as if this were a logical necessity: "If the testimony of one is rejected by the jury upon consideration, there remains but one witness—less than the rule requires." *Id.* That may reflect sound policy, but it does not follow literally: even if the jury rejects the testimony of one of two witnesses to the same act, there can still be two witnesses to the act; they simply are unlikely to agree in every respect. And that can be quite useful to the jury, for they have contrasting accounts out of which to reconstruct what happened. So the two witness rule, understood as a pure burden of production rule, would still serve a valuable purpose.

[84] *See, e.g.*, Opper v. United States, 348 U.S. 84, 89–90 (1954) (stating that "doubt persists that the zeal of the agencies of prosecution to protect the peace, the self-interest of the accomplice, the maliciousness of an

regarding what exactly satisfies the requirement: the traditional view requires the prosecution to present independent evidence of the commission of the alleged crime, whereas the more modern view (adopted by the federal courts) merely requires independent evidence corroborating the trustworthiness of the confession.[85] Courts do not even agree about whether the rule is a rule of admissibility—that is, imposing a condition on the admission of the confession—or a rule of sufficiency.[86] And among those courts that (rightly) understand the requirement as a rule of sufficiency, they disagree about whether the requirement is part of the burden of production, which is applied solely by the court, or part of the burden of persuasion, which is applied by the jury and thus requires instructions to the jury to the effect that they must determine whether the corroboration requirement has been met.[87] The view that the corroboration requirement is part of the burden of production rather than an additional component of the burden of persuasion does not, however, preclude *cautionary* instructions to the jury that they should be skeptical of confessions that are not supported by independent evidence, and this is a common practice.[88]

Similarly, fearing that an accomplice has much to gain by informing on the defendant in order to get a better deal from the prosecution, a number of states require corroboration of the testimony of an accomplice.[89] These states typically employ jury instructions requiring, for a guilty verdict, that the jury determine that any accomplice testimony upon which the jury relies is corroborated. This is in addition to its determination that the defendant's guilt is established beyond a reasonable doubt.[90] This effectively increases the stringency of the burden of persuasion and, of course, introduces an additional consideration for the trial court in ruling on defense motions testing whether the state has met its burden of production. The majority of states and federal courts, however, do not require such separate jury determinations of corroboration. In such states, the single witness rule generally will preclude directed verdicts for the defense based simply on the trial court's doubts about the accomplice's reliability. Instead, such courts typically give cautionary jury instructions informing the jurors that they should be careful about accepting the testimony of an accomplice, and in some

---

enemy or the aberration or weakness of the accused under the strain of suspicion may tinge or warp the facts of the confession.") *See generally* 1 MCCORMICK ON EVIDENCE § 145 (Kenneth S. Broun ed., 7th ed. 2013).

85 *See generally* David A. Moran, *In Defense of the Corpus Delicti Rule*, 64 OHIO ST. L.J. 817 (2003).

86 The authors believe that the rule is properly understood as a rule of sufficiency. It was initially so characterized. *See* SIMON GREENLEAF, A TREATISE ON THE LAW OF EVIDENCE § 217, at 301–02 (10th ed. 1860) ("In the United States, the prisoner's confession, when the corpus delicti is not otherwise proved, has been held insufficient for his conviction . . .") And a rule that, for good reason, says "evidence X is *insufficient* in the absence of other evidence" gains nothing by being converted into a rule *excluding* evidence X in the absence of other evidence. *Cf.* 7 WIGMORE ON EVIDENCE § 2030, at 323 (Chadbourn rev. 1979) (identifying the stringency standards for the burden of production with the sense of admissibility ("admissibility, in a broad but real sense") that is presented by corroboration requirements).

87 *See, e.g.*, Fowler v. United States, 31 A.3d 88 (D.C. 2011) (reviewing the discord in the case law and holding that the question of whether the confession is adequately corroborated is to be decided by the judge, not the jury, justifying this result, however, in part from the premise that the rule is a rule of admissibility of the confession).

88 *See, e.g.*, United States v. Singleterry, 29 F.3d. 733, 738–39 (1st Cir. 1994).

89 *See, e.g.*, ALA. CODE § 12–21–222; ALASKA STAT. § 12.45.020; CAL. PENAL CODE § 1111; MINN. STAT. § 634.04; N.Y. Crim Proc. L. § 60.22; ORE. REV. STAT. § 136.440. A few states have discarded the rule after gaining experience with it. *See, e.g.*, State v. Edwards, 665 P.2d 59, 66–68 (Ariz. 1983) (noting 1976 repeal of statutory rule); Martin v. Commonwealth, 409 S.W.3d 340, 344 n.1 (Ky. 2013) (noting 1980 repeal of statutory rule); State v. O'Dell, 543 N.E.2d 1220, 1225–26 (Ohio 1989) (noting 1986 repeal of statutory rule).

90 *See, e.g.*, People v. Chavez, 705 P.2d 372, 376–78 (Cal. 1985); People v. Sage, 11 N.E.3d 177 (N.Y. 2014).

situations such an instruction may be required.[91] However, some such states also require the trial court to consider the fact that an accomplice's testimony is uncorroborated in ruling on directed verdicts, thus augmenting the burden of production by qualifying the single witness rule.[92]

In civil cases, corroboration requirements are unusual, jurisdiction specific, and usually found only in certain substantive law contexts.[93]

§ 2.08 Presumptions—Presumptions Defined and Distinguished from Other Devices

Perhaps no evidentiary term has suffered from more incorrect and inconsistent use than the word "presumption." This and the next several sections distinguish true presumptions from other devices and concepts and then explain how presumptions operate. Despite arguments that no distinct law of presumptions is necessary,[94] courts and commentators continue to use the term, and the language of presumptions is likely to be with us for the foreseeable future.

A presumption is a rule providing that proof of a designated fact, or set of facts, has a predetermined effect in establishing the existence of another fact. It thus expresses a legal relationship between certain facts (what we will call the "foundational" or "basic" facts) proved by a party and a certain other fact (what we will call the "presumed fact").[95] Put simply, if X (the set of foundational or basic facts) is shown, Y (the presumed fact) will be assumed to be true.

A "true" presumption is rebuttable by evidence contradicting the presumed facts. When the presumption is not rebutted, it is deemed conclusive in the sense that the jury will be informed that the fact at issue is proven. The law may still demand that the

---

[91] *See, e.g.*, United States v. Davis, 439 F.2d 1105 (9th Cir. 1971) (holding failure to give cautionary instruction was prejudicial error under the circumstances). *See also* People v. Cobb, 455 N.E.2d 31, 35 (Ill. 1983); State v. Quintana, 621 N.W.2d 121, 139 (Neb. 2001); State v. Ferguson, 507 N.E.2d 388, 390–91 (Ohio 1986); Commonwealth v. Smith, 17 A.3d 873, 906–07 (Pa. 2011).

[92] *See, e.g.*, Washington v. State, 4 A.3d 375 (Del. 2015) (holding that trial judge must take case from the jury when the only evidence of defendant's guilt is uncorroborated testimonies of accomplices which present material conflicts).

[93] *See* 7 WIGMORE ON EVIDENCE §§ 2045–54, 2075 (Chadbourn rev. 1979).

[94] *See, e.g.*, Ronald J. Allen, *Presumptions, Inference and Burden of Proof in Federal Civil Actions—An Anatomy of Unnecessary Ambiguity and a Proposal for Reform*, 76 NW. U. L. REV. 892 (1982); Ronald J. Allen, *Presumptions in Civil Actions Reconsidered*, 66 IOWA L. REV. 843 (1981) (arguing that the presumption concept is artificial and should be replaced by a direct approach allocating burdens of proof and allowing careful judicial comment on evidence, and that where proof adduced at trial is sufficiently strong to require shifting or reassigning a burden of persuasion, this can be done by means of a "conditional imperative"); Edward W. Cleary, *Presuming and Pleading: An Essay on Juristic Immaturity*, 12 STAN. L. REV. 5 (1959) (suggesting elimination of concept of presumptions that transfer burden of proof). *But see* Kenneth S. Broun, *The Unfulfillable Promise of One Rule for All Presumptions*, 62 N.C. L. REV. 697 (1984) (recognizing validity of argument that courts should discuss propriety of allocating burdens rather than technical application of presumptions, but noting that presumption concept is unlikely to be displaced and that "conditional imperative" suffers from same difficulties as current presumption language).

[95] *See* CAL. EVID. CODE § 600(a) ("A presumption is an assumption of fact that the law requires to be made from another fact or group of facts found or otherwise established in the action."). McCormick's handbook states that "a presumption is a standardized practice, under which certain facts are held to call for uniform treatment with respect to their effect as proof of other facts." *See generally* 2 MCCORMICK ON EVIDENCE § 342 (Kenneth S. Broun ed., 7th ed. 2013).

underlying (presumed) fact be proven, but the presumed fact will be *deemed* proven in the absence of contrary evidence.[96]

Examples

A presumption states that a letter properly addressed, stamped, and deposited in an appropriate receptacle is presumed to have been received in the ordinary course of the mail.[97] Unless the presumption created by this rule is rebutted, the properly addressed, stamped, and deposited letter will be deemed to have been received in what is considered to be the ordinary amount of time needed in that delivery area.

A presumption states that money delivered to another person is presumed to have been due to that person.[98] Unless the presumption is rebutted, if delivery is proven, the money will be deemed to have been owed to the person to whom it was delivered.

A presumption provides that a writing is presumed to have been accurately dated.[99] Unless the presumption is rebutted, the writing in question will be deemed accurately dated.

If such true presumptions are not rebutted, they mandate a factual finding even though that finding may be contrary to reality or to what the fact-finder believes is true. For example, the properly addressed, stamped, and mailed letter might actually not have been received in what is considered to be the ordinary course of the mail. The money delivered might have been a gift rather than payment of a debt. The writing might have been dated incorrectly. Nevertheless, this mandatory effect is what separates them from mere inferences.

Presumptions are created for a variety of reasons.[100] Among them is fairness—to "correct an imbalance resulting from one party's superior access to the proof."[101] Some presumptions are supported by reasons of substantive policy—to encourage or discourage certain "primary" (non-litigation) behavior, or to effectuate a goal of the law.[102] Some presumptions are said to be created simply to resolve issues otherwise difficult to resolve because of the absence of proof.[103] The most common reason for creating presumptions, however, is simply the facilitation of the litigation process by resolving matters in accordance with what the presumption-creating authority believes to be high probability. This both streamlines the process of proof of the fact and avoids

---

[96] For detailed treatment of specific presumptions, see 1 & 2 JONES ON EVIDENCE: CIVIL AND CRIMINAL chs. 4–10 (Clifford S. Fishman ed., 7th ed. 1994).

[97] *See* Legille v. Dann, 544 F.2d 1 (D.C. Cir. 1976).

[98] *See* CAL. EVID. CODE § 631.

[99] *See* CAL. EVID. CODE § 640.

[100] 2 MCCORMICK ON EVIDENCE § 343 (Kenneth S. Broun ed., 7th ed. 2013).

[101] An example would be the presumption that as between connecting carriers of goods, damage occurred while the goods were in the possession of the last carrier. *Id.* at n.4. (citing Chicago & Nw. Ry. Co. v. C.C. Whitnack Produce Co., 258 U.S. 369 (1922)).

[102] A common example is the presumption of the death of a person not heard from for a specified period of years, which serves the goal of settling issues of title and of estates. *See, e.g.*, CAL. EVID. CODE § 667.

[103] 2 MCCORMICK ON EVIDENCE § 343 at 682 (Kenneth S. Broun ed., 7th ed. 2013) (giving as an example presumptions resolving questions of who survived longest in a common disaster). This explanation begs the question of why resolve these issues in accord with the choice made by the presumptions. *See* 9 WIGMORE ON EVIDENCE §§ 2532, 2532a (Chadbourn rev. 1981) (criticizing the artificiality of such presumptions and endorsing the use instead of substantive rules for the disposition of estates).

the fact-finding distortion that might occur were the jury to decide that the fact is not true.[104]

Individual presumptions often exist for a combination of reasons. For example, the common presumption that a person not heard from in a certain period of years is dead[105] does indeed facilitate proof of the person's death where the risk of error is slight. It also reflects a social policy that the affairs of people who have been missing for a period of years should be wrapped up without the necessity of burdensome (and often practically unavailable) proof. Similarly, the presumption that a ceremonial marriage is valid[106] both facilitates proof that a marriage is lawful and effectuates a policy that the marriage of people who go through a marriage ceremony should not be subject to question, except in unusual cases. Also, the common presumption that the official actions by public officers were regularly and legally performed[107] exists because the probability of regular and legal performance is high. It is often difficult for a public official who conducts a great deal of repetitive business to remember exactly how the act at issue was performed, and people should be confident that officials perform their duties correctly. Even the presumption of receipt of mail in the regular course is supported by more than probability; the presumption also facilities proof where, as is often true, the postal worker cannot be expected to remember delivering a particular piece of mail at a particular time.[108]

The multi-faceted rationale for presumptions is indicated by the use of presumptions in situations where a logical inference would be difficult to draw—or, more precisely, where the probative value of the evidence is very slight. For example, the presumption that the driver of an automobile was the agent of the owner reflects a rational inference, but the strength of the inference is often so slight that, in the absence of that agency presumption, the plaintiff will likely face dismissal of the claim against the owner. It is not logically necessary that a person driving a vehicle is an agent of the owner, nor is there a particularly high probability that the driver is an agent of the owner. The agency presumption is based on a combination of the factors noted above. The presumption of agency serves the substantive policy of encouraging owners to properly watch over their potentially dangerous vehicles, and it also serves fairness by putting the burden of showing agency or non-agency on the party with the best access to those facts—the owner.

True presumptions must be distinguished from other legal devices, including "permissive inferences" and "conclusive presumptions."[109] A permissive inference is a factual conclusion that the fact-finder *may*, but is not required to, draw from another

---

[104] For an illustrative list of such presumptions, see CAL. EVID. CODE §§ 630–647.

[105] *See, e.g.*, CAL. EVID. CODE § 667 (five years); Green v. Royal Neighbors of Am., 73 P.2d 1 (Kan. 1937) (seven years).

[106] *See, e.g.*, CAL. EVID. CODE § 663.

[107] *See* CAL. EVID. CODE § 664.

[108] Presumptions in Title VII employment discrimination cases provide an important example. *See, e.g.*, Price Waterhouse v. Hopkins, 490 U.S. 228 (1989) (holding that once plaintiff proved that firm's failure to promote her to partner was motivated in part by her gender, burden of persuasion was placed on defendant to demonstrate that the same hiring decision would have been made absent the discrimination). Such a presumption not only shifts the burden of production to the party more likely to have the necessary information, but also effectuates social policy in the absence of adequate proof.

[109] Another concept to be distinguished is the so-called "permissive presumption," a term the United States Supreme Court has used in the context of criminal cases, which raise special issues regarding presumptions. *See* **§ 2.12**.

fact or group of facts.[110] An inference is based on simple everyday logic—the fact-finder's application of everyday experience to determine the likelihood that a given fact is true. Thus, one may infer that a person whose usual practice is to fasten the automobile seat belt did so on the relevant occasion.[111] Similarly, one may infer that marks on a person's body matching the teeth of a particular dog living next door were made by that dog. Inferences, like presumptions, are not always accurate. The driver might not have worn the seat belt on the occasion in question; the dog might not have bitten the person. But in each case, it is logical to infer, given the facts stated, that the events happened as initially indicated. In each case, the court would not *require* the jury to reach a given conclusion; unless the evidence was so one-sided as to require the conclusion, the jury will be permitted to draw the inference but will not be compelled to do so.[112]

These types of inferences, then, are permissive as far as the jury is concerned. But they are mandatory as far as the trial court is concerned, because the court *must* allow the jury to draw such an inference if the jury chooses to do so. Sometimes such (mandatory-for-the-court but permissive-for-the-jury) inferences will be ad hoc assessments of the entire evidence on the point in a particular case, as when a trial court refuses to direct a verdict and explains this by saying that the jury could reasonably infer against the moving party and thus must be given the opportunity to do so. But other times such an inference is articulated as a general rule, often by an appellate court, applicable (and thus mandatory for the trial court) whenever certain foundation facts are present (and in that respect, like true presumptions). It can be difficult to tell the difference between the two, or between either and a true presumption.[113]

True presumptions must also be distinguished from so-called "conclusive presumptions" or "irrebuttable presumptions." These devices are not actually presumptions at all, even though they are mandatory and express a relationship between certain basic facts and a presumed fact. Instead, they are rules of law that change the nature of the facts to be proved. The following examples demonstrate the nature of "conclusive presumptions."

Examples

A statute states that except as provided in a separate statute, "the child of a wife cohabiting with her husband, who is not impotent or sterile, is conclusively presumed to be a child of the marriage."[114] This statute means that the biological facts are no longer important to the law. If a husband and wife are cohabiting, and if the husband is not impotent or sterile, the child is presumed to be the child of the marriage. Unless an exception applies (some states do

---

110 *See* CAL. EVID. CODE § 600(b) ("An inference is a deduction of fact that may logically and reasonably be drawn from another fact or group of facts found or otherwise established in the action.").

111 For more about this type of habit evidence, see **§ 7.15**.

112 A careful lawyer should not take at face value the legislative or judicial use of the term "presumption." To determine whether a true, rebuttable presumption is involved the attorney must focus on exactly how the legal device in question operates. Sometimes a court will use the term "presumption" in one opinion to describe a legal device only to recharacterize it in a later opinion as a permissive inference based on the actual function it serves. *See, e.g.*, *In re* Estate of McGowan, 250 N.W.2d 234 (Neb. 1977) (reinterpreting earlier rulings described in terms of presumptions of undue influence as really only permissive inferences).

113 Doctrines by the same name are sometimes treated differently in different jurisdictions. A good example is the doctrine of *res ipsa loquitur* in the law of torts. *Compare* CAL. EVID. CODE § 646 (treating *res ipsa loquitur* as a presumption) *with* DEL. UNIF. R. EVID. 304 (treating *res ipsa loquitur* as a permissive inference).

114 CAL. FAM. CODE § 7540 (1994). *See also In re* Findlay, 170 N.E. 471, 473 (N.Y. 1930).

consider the husband's paternity to be a rebuttable presumption that can be refuted by DNA evidence or a maternal affidavit), no evidence to the contrary is admissible.

A statute provides that "[t]he facts recited in a written instrument are conclusively presumed to be true as between the parties thereto, or their successors in interest; but this rule does not apply to the recital of a consideration."[115] What this rule means is that, in a dispute between the parties governed by the instrument, unless the issue concerns consideration, all facts recited in the written instrument are treated as true, and other evidence regarding those facts will not be heard.

A criminal statute provides that "[a] defendant who does not plead not guilty by reason of insanity shall be conclusively presumed to have been sane at the time of the commission of the offense charged. . . ."[116] As a result of this rule, even a person who meets the test for insanity under that state's law would be considered sane for purposes of the trial if she did not plead not guilty by reason of insanity.

"Conclusive presumptions" generate new rules of substantive law. They are not evidentiary devices. In virtually every case, they reflect policy-based judgments that the existence of certain facts should determine the dispute, that society would be ill-served by permitting contrary evidence. This is, perhaps, easiest to understand with respect to the presumption of paternity, which represents a legislative judgment that the legitimacy of children born under the specified circumstances should not be subject to challenge. This presumption was created to protect the inheritance right of children and to promote peace and tranquility in families.[117] The presumption thus establishes a new substantive rule of law: that a child born to a married woman cohabiting with her husband, who is not impotent or sterile, is entitled to inherit from the mother's husband whether or not the child is the biological child of the husband.[118]

Yet another use of the term "presumption" occurs when a court gives reasons for the *initial* allocation of the burden of persuasion on a particular issue to one party. For example, life insurance policies often contain exclusions from coverage for certain causes of death, such as suicide or death resulting from the insured's commission of a crime. When presented with the question of which party bears the burden of persuading the fact-finder regarding such facts, courts have sometimes said things like, "There is a presumption against suicide," and then allocated the burden of persuasion to the insurer to prove death by suicide.[119] Here, the initial burden of proving whether or not the

---

[115] CAL. EVID. CODE § 622.

[116] CAL. PENAL CODE § 1016.

[117] *See* Michael H. v. Gerald D., 491 U.S. 110, 125 (1989). At one time in the development of the common law, the state was especially worried that illegitimate children, for whom the father had no legal liability, would become wards of the state. *See id.*

[118] Even these "conclusive presumptions" are not completely irrebuttable. Instead, they operate to prevent a party from challenging the presumed facts. The party is still free to challenge the foundational (basic) facts. In the paternity example, where a conclusive presumption exists as to paternity, a party would not be allowed to challenge the presumed fact of legitimacy by showing DNA evidence that the husband is not the father of the child. However, he would be allowed to show that the man and woman were not married at the time (a foundational fact of the presumption), and therefore the presumption should not apply at all. For more on rebutting presumptions, *see* **§ 2.10**.

[119] *See, e.g.,* Life Ins. Co. of Va. V. Hairston, 62 S.E. 1057, 1066 (Va. 1908) (using the language of a "presumption of innocence" to assign the intermediate "clear and satisfactory proof" burden of persuasion to

exclusion applies does not rest on the insured, only to be "shifted" to the insurer upon the insured's proving some foundational facts, as would be the case with a true presumption. Rather, based on the various considerations courts have identified for allocating that initial burden, the burden is placed on the insurer *ab initio* to prove suicide as an affirmative defense, provided the defense is raised.[120]

§ 2.09 Presumptions—Invoking Presumptions

A presumption does not come into being until the party seeking to employ it has "proven" its foundational facts. This raises questions concerning proof of the foundational facts. Who decides them, and by what standard? As will be explained later, the principal impact of a presumption is to regulate the allocation of the burden of production or persuasion regarding the presumed fact. Because these allocation questions are ordinarily questions of law, one could conclude that the trial judge should decide whether the foundational facts have been proved, as least for this limited purpose, just as judges determine preliminary fact questions that determine admissibility.[121] If this approach were taken, the jury would hardly need to know that presumptions are involved: if a verdict is not directed, they would simply be told who has the burden of persuasion.[122] For whatever reason, however, the law has not taken this relatively simple path. Presumably, the close connection between presumptions and inferences on the merits is thought to make such a separation impracticable or undesirable. As a result, juries traditionally have participated in making findings about foundational facts. This entails predictable complexities, because the foundational facts must be determined before one can identify which party has the burden in question.

First, the party seeking to take advantage of the presumption must offer evidence sufficient to meet a burden of production as to each foundational fact. The trial court determines whether the party has met this burden. Unless the opponent offers evidence that overwhelmingly rebuts those facts, the party seeking to use the presumption is entitled to reach the jury for a determination of the existence of those facts. Second, the jury decides whether the foundational facts are indeed true. If the proponent passes both steps, the presumption comes into being. It will then have conclusive effect in the litigation unless the presumed fact is "rebutted."

Suppose P, a second-floor tenant in D's apartment building, suffers a fall on a dark stairway leading to the second floor. P sues D, the building's owner, claiming that D failed to maintain the stairway in a reasonably safe condition because several of its lights did not work. To prove notice to D of the stairway's condition, P wishes to prove that two weeks before the accident, she mailed a letter to D, who lived in the building, informing D that several of the lights in the stairway no longer worked. Notice to D of the defect would make D's failure to repair the condition more likely unreasonable. At trial, P testifies that she addressed the letter properly, placed a first-class stamp on it, and took

---

the insurer to prove exclusions from coverage involving acts of moral turpitude by the insured); Wellisch v. John Hancock, 56 N.E.2d 540, 543 (N.Y. 1944) (using a "presumption against suicide" to approve of the trial court's allocation of the burden of proof on the issue to the insurer, stating that the presumption "is one aspect of the broader rule that where evidence is susceptible of two constructions, the construction which does not imply criminality or moral turpitude is to be favored.").

[120] *See* **§ 2.05**.

[121] *See* **§ 3.11**.

[122] Thus, Professor Morgan argued that presumptions should be implemented so that juries need never hear about them. *See* Edmund M. Morgan, *Presumptions*, 12 WASH. L. REV. 255 (1937).

it to a United States Postal Service receptacle around the corner from the apartment building. P also offers testimony that letters sent from one address to another in the city normally arrive within two days.

As described, the testimony offered by P is sufficient to meet a burden of production as to each foundational fact necessary to raise the common presumption that a letter properly addressed, stamped, and mailed was received in the ordinary course of the mail. In the absence of substantial contrary evidence concerning those foundational facts, the court will instruct the jury that if it finds that those facts are true, it must find that D received the letter well before the accident, unless the presumed fact is rebutted. To prevent the issue from going to the jury, however, D will have to offer evidence not merely strong enough to meet a burden of production as to the nonexistence of the foundational facts, but strong enough to require that finding. This will not occur often.

§ 2.10 Presumptions—Rebutting Presumptions

How does one "rebut" a presumption? The obvious answer would seem to be by offering evidence attacking the presumed fact. As noted in the previous section, however, the opponent of a presumption may challenge the foundational (basic) facts in an effort to prevent the presumption from arising in the first place. And this is so even if the court has determined that sufficient evidence has been presented for the jury to find the foundational facts so as to create the presumption. Given this, a party against whom a presumption might operate actually has several choices. The party may:

1. offer no evidence challenging the existence of either the foundational facts or the presumed fact;
2. offer evidence challenging the existence of only the foundational fact;
3. offer evidence challenging the existence of only the presumed fact; or
4. offer evidence challenging the existence of both the foundational and presumed fact.

P's letter to D warning of the darkness of the stairway (introduced in the previous section) can be used to illustrate the consequences of these choices.[123]

Challenging Neither Foundational Nor Presumed Facts

Suppose that D chooses not to offer evidence challenging either the foundational facts (addressing, stamping, depositing) or the presumed fact (D's receipt of the letter well before the plaintiff's accident). In this situation, the court will simply instruct the jury that if it finds the foundational facts to be true, it *must* find that D received the letter in the ordinary course (about two days after P mailed it). As long as P's evidence is sufficient to meet her burden of production regarding the foundational facts, the question of the existence of the foundational facts will be for the jury. If the jury is more persuaded of the existence of the foundational facts than of their nonexistence, the presumption operates, and the jury must find that D received the letter well before the

---

[123] Thus, the following discussion assumes a civil case. For the treatment of presumptions in criminal cases, *see* **§ 2.12**.

accident (thus making it more likely than otherwise that D was negligent in failing to take precautionary steps).[124]

In the absence of evidence from D of the nonexistence of either the foundational or presumed facts, there are two possible outcomes: (1) In most instances, P will only have to meet a burden of production as to the existence of the foundational facts. This means that the court will merely leave the question of the foundational facts to the jury. This is the likely result in our hypothetical, where P's evidence, though compelling on the surface, comes from a witness with an interest in the outcome of the case, such as P. Thus, it would not be irrational for the jury to disbelieve P and find that the foundational facts are not true. (2) In some cases, the evidence of the existence of the foundational facts will be so strong as to compel a finding of their existence, and thus of the presumed fact. So, in the hypothetical case, assume that P's evidence of each of the foundational facts includes testimony from unimpeached, disinterested witnesses.[125] In such a case, P would be entitled either to a directed verdict as to an element of the case, or to a binding jury instruction requiring the jurors to make a certain factual finding.

Challenging Only Foundational Facts

If D chooses only to challenge the existence of the foundational (basic) facts, the consequences are similar. Suppose, then, that D testifies that there is no United States Postal Service mailbox around the corner from the apartment building, or that P was on vacation out of state for more than a week, beginning on the day P claims to have mailed the letter. In this instance, the court will almost certainly allow the jury to determine whether the foundational facts exist, and instruct the jury that if it finds that the facts do indeed exist, it *must* find that the letter was received in the ordinary course. Because D has done nothing to challenge the existence of the presumed fact—his receipt of the letter—the presumption will come into play and mandate a finding of receipt if proper addressing, stamping, and mailing are proven by the preponderance of the evidence.[126]

Challenging Only Presumed Fact

There is a long-standing debate about what happens when the party against whom the presumption operates challenges the existence of the presumed fact.[127] To take our hypothetical as the starting point, suppose D does not challenge P's proper addressing, stamping, and mailing of the letter, but offers testimony to support a contention that he never received the letter. For example, D might testify that he picked up and read his mail diligently each day from the date on which P claims to have mailed the letter until the date of the accident, and that he never saw the letter. There are two distinct views, each associated with respected evidence scholars, about what happens in this case.

---

[124] It may seem that choosing not to challenge the presumption is a tactical error on the part of D. However, there may be situations where allowing the presumption to stand either helps or is irrelevant to D's case. For example, if D's theory of the case is that the letter was received and he promptly replaced the lights, there would be no reason for D to contest the presumption.

[125] For example, suppose P claims to have sent the letter by registered mail. To establish mailing to the correct address, P offers in evidence a telephone book listing D's address and a postal receipt showing that the letter, addressed to the same address, was deposited in the post office on a date two weeks before the accident.

[126] In light of D's testimony attacking the foundational facts, there is virtually no chance that the court will instruct the jury to find that the foundational facts are true.

[127] "The problem of the effect of a presumption when met by proof rebutting the presumed fact has literally plagued the courts and legal scholars." 2 MCCORMICK ON EVIDENCE § 344 at 692 (Kenneth S. Broun ed., 7th ed. 2013).

(1) The Thayer-Wigmore "bursting bubble" theory. If presumptions are nothing more than devices that facilitate proof and help to ensure that the correct factual conclusions are reached,[128] presumptions should have no effect once "rebutted" with evidence challenging the presumed fact. This was the view of the Missouri Supreme Court, which in 1906 wrote that presumptions are "like bats of the law flitting in the twilight, but disappearing in the sunshine of actual facts."[129] This position also gave rise to the "bursting bubble" theory of presumptions, usually associated with Thayer,[130] and supported by Wigmore[131] (though the positions of both authors were actually somewhat different from the pure "bursting bubble" theory).[132] The theory holds that a presumption does no more than shift to the opponent the burden of producing evidence; it does not shift the burden of persuasion. When the opponent offers evidence sufficient to meet that burden of production, the presumption disappears from the case entirely.

Under the "bursting bubble" theory, the disappearance of the presumption means that the jury should not be instructed about the presumption.[133] However, as our hypothetical illustrates the presumption rests on logic and common sense. Even in the absence of a formal presumption, where P has offered evidence concerning proper addressing, stamping, and mailing of a warning letter, and D has offered evidence that he never received the letter, the jury would simply apply its sense of logic and experience to determine whether P mailed and D received the letter. The same inference process is

---

[128] For discussion of the purposes of presumptions, *see* **§ 2.08**.

[129] Mackowik v. Kansas City, St. Joseph & Council Bluffs R.R. Co., 94 S.W. 256, 262 (Mo. 1906).

[130] JAMES B. THAYER, A PRELIMINARY TREATISE ON EVIDENCE AT THE COMMON LAW 313–52 (1898).

[131] 9 WIGMORE ON EVIDENCE § 2491(2) (Chadbourn rev. 1981).

[132] Thayer was equivocal about the disappearance of presumptions upon the admission of evidence contradicting the presumed fact. *See* 2 MCCORMICK ON EVIDENCE § 344 at 692 n.7 (Kenneth S. Broun ed., 7th ed. 2013); 21 CHARLES A. WRIGHT & KENNETH W. GRAHAM, JR., FEDERAL PRACTICE AND PROCEDURE: EVIDENCE § 5122.2 (2005). As Wright and Graham state:

> [N]either Thayer nor Wigmore advocated the "bursting bubble" theory of presumptions, the notion that the judge was required to direct a verdict against the plaintiff once the presumption was rebutted, unless there was an underlying inference sufficient to take the case to the jury . . . In fact, what both Thayer and Wigmore seem to have believed was that a presumption had the effect of carrying the "third burden" of proof; i.e., it was the equivalent of evidence that would require a directed verdict on behalf of the proponent if it was not rebutted. The presumption vanished in the face of rebuttal only in the sense that the proponent was no longer entitled to a directed verdict; both Thayer and Wigmore seem to have assumed that the case would still go to the jury unless the evidence in rebuttal was such that no reasonable juror could find the nonexistence of the presumed fact.

Id. at 448 n.29 (citing JAMES B. THAYER, A PRELIMINARY TREATISE ON EVIDENCE AT THE COMMON LAW 336–37 (1898)); 9 WIGMORE ON EVIDENCE §§ 2487, 2491, 2493, 2494, 2498 (Chadbourn rev. 1981); James B. Thayer, *Presumptions and the Law of Evidence*, 3 HARV. L. REV. 141, 165 (1889).

[133] 2 MCCORMICK ON EVIDENCE § 344 at 692–93 (Kenneth S. Broun ed., 7th ed. 2013) (citing Orient Ins. Co. v. Cox, 238 S.W.2d 757 (Ark. 1951); Ammundson v. Tinholt, 36 N.W.2d 521 (Minn. 1949)). This might sound a bit perplexing. In the case of the ordinary burden of production (presumptions aside), the court determines whether evidence presented is "sufficient to support a finding" by the jury. But for the court to do this with regard to the burden that results from a presumption, the court would seem to have to know whether a presumption has arisen. Because, under conventional practice, this is a question ordinarily decided by the jury (see **§ 2.09**), the judge will not know whether the jury has determined the foundational facts so as to trigger a presumption in the first place. One option to deal with this would be to instruct the jurors that *they* must decide whether the counter-evidence is sufficient to support their own finding against the presumed fact and, if so, then to ignore the presumption. But to make this peculiar decision, the jury would have to be instructed about the presumption even when there is counter-evidence against the presumed fact. Fortunately, there is another option. The court can assume *arguendo* that the jury will find the foundational facts to be true and then determine itself whether the counter-evidence is sufficient to support a finding against the otherwise presumed fact. If so, then the court need not bother instructing the jury on the presumption at all. Not surprisingly, the latter approach seems to be the conventional practice.

involved under the "bursting bubble" theory; the question of D's receipt of a letter from P is simply left to the jury as a matter of logical inference. There is no more reason to instruct the jury about applying its reasoning powers to this evidence than there is with respect to any other disputed fact; the jury will simply decide, guided by argument of counsel.

Even under the "bursting bubble" theory of presumptions, it is possible that the evidence offered by the party against whom the presumption would operate is so strong as to require a directed verdict or partial directed verdict in the absence of further evidence from the opponent. Such a result would be rather unlikely in our hypothetical because the simple inference of receipt from proper mailing is so strong.[134] Suppose instead that the presumption on which a party seeks to rely is artificial, in the sense that it gives rise only to a weak logical inference. For example, suppose the jurisdiction in which the case is tried adheres to the presumption that the driver of a vehicle owned by another is the agent of the owner. P, a pedestrian, is struck in a crosswalk by a dry cleaning delivery truck driven by X. It is firmly established that D owns the dry cleaning business and the truck, and that X is employed by D as a delivery driver. Suppose, however, that D calls X, who testifies that she was on her way to a midnight poker game when the accident occurred, and that P is unable to do anything to impeach the witness. This evidence almost certainly exceeds the burden of production. Rather, it is likely so strong as to require a directed verdict for D. Thus, even under the "bursting bubble" theory of presumptions, it is possible for the party against whom the presumption operates to rebut the presumption with evidence sufficient to meet a burden of production (which would leave the factual matter for the jury), but it is also possible to rebut the presumption with evidence so compelling as to require a directed verdict for that party.

(2) The Morgan-McCormick theory. Morgan, McCormick, and some other legal scholars reject the notion that presumptions are so fragile as to disappear when evidence is offered to rebut the existence of the presumed fact. They have emphasized that presumptions are more than simple procedural devices for the facilitation of proof; sometimes they exist for reasons of policy.[135] As McCormick's handbook explains:

> Presumptions . . . have been created for policy reasons that are similar to and may be just as strong as those that govern the allocation of the burdens of proof prior to the introduction of evidence. These policy considerations may persist despite the existence of proof rebutting the presumed fact.[136]

Courts and scholars following this view believe that the "bursting bubble" theory gives too "slight and evanescent" an effect to presumptions.[137] Thus, they reject the view that presumptions disappear on the presentation of evidence sufficient to support the nonexistence of the presumed fact.[138] Instead, they maintain that once a presumption is

---

[134] One might imagine that if D succeeds in a motion for the court to take judicial notice that there was a nationwide postal strike stopping all mail delivery during the entire relevant period, the court would hold that D did not receive notice of the alleged defect in the manner claimed by P. *See* **§ 2.14**.

[135] *See* **§ 2.08**.

[136] 2 McCormick on Evidence § 344 at 694 (Kenneth S. Broun ed., 7th ed. 2013).

[137] Edmund M. Morgan & John M. Maguire, *Looking Backward and Forward at Evidence*, 50 Harv. L. Rev. 909, 913 (1937).

[138] *See* Edmund M. Morgan, Some Problems of Proof 74–81 (1956); Edward W. Cleary, *Presuming and Pleading: An Essay on Juristic Immaturity*, 12 Stan. L. Rev. 5, 18 (1959); Alfred L. Gausewitz,

raised by proof of the foundational facts, the *burden of persuasion* as to the existence of the presumed fact shifts to the opponent.[139] To use the landlord-tenant hypothetical, if the jury finds that P properly addressed, stamped, and mailed the letter sufficiently in advance of the accident, D must now prove it is more likely than not that he never received the letter or suffer a finding (by the jury) that he did.

Because the burden of persuasion can shift under the Morgan-McCormick theory, once the proponent offers sufficient evidence to meet a burden of production as to the existence of the foundational (basic) facts, a jury instruction is needed in most situations. There are several possibilities, each described below and then followed by an example of an instruction based on the hypothetical slip-and-fall case:[140]

Examples

Situation: If the proponent's evidence of the existence of the foundational facts is sufficient only to meet a burden of production, and the opponent's evidence of the nonexistence of the presumed fact is sufficient only to meet a burden of production, the court must instruct the jury that if it finds the foundational facts to be true, it must find the presumed fact to be true unless the opponent persuades the jury that it is more likely than not that the presumed fact is not true.

Instruction: If you find that the letter described by P was correctly addressed, stamped, and mailed two weeks before the accident, then you must find that D received the letter approximately two days after it was mailed unless D persuades you that it is more likely than not that he did not receive any such letter during the time in question.

Situation: If the proponent's evidence of the existence of the foundational facts compels a finding of their existence, but the opponent's evidence concerning the nonexistence of the presumed fact is only strong enough to meet a burden of production, the court must instruct the jury that it must find the presumed fact to be true unless the opponent persuades the jury that it is more likely than not that the presumed fact is not true.

Instruction: I instruct you to find that P correctly addressed, stamped, and mailed to D two weeks before to the accident a letter as described in P's testimony. You must therefore find that D received the letter approximately two days later unless D persuades you that it is more likely than not that he did not receive the letter during the time in question.

Presumptions in a One-Rule World, 5 VAND. L. REV. 324, 342 (1952); Edmund M. Morgan & John M. Maguire, *Looking Backward and Forward at Evidence*, 50 HARV. L. REV. 909, 913 (1937).

[139] McCormick agreed with Morgan in rejecting the Thayer-Wigmore theory, though he tended to emphasize the usefulness of jury instructions as a way to assure that presumptions retain their effectiveness even in the face of evidence challenging the presumed fact. He argued that the jury should be instructed about the existence of the presumption and about its power to make a factual finding consistent with the presumption even in the face of evidence challenging the presumed fact. CHARLES T. MCCORMICK, HANDBOOK ON THE LAW OF EVIDENCE §§ 311, 316 (1954).

[140] These examples do not directly mention the term "presumption" or instruct the jury to "presume" any facts. Other forms of instruction, including forms that address the matter in terms of presumptions, are possible. For discussion of alternative forms of jury instruction in the context of presumptions, *see* 2 MCCORMICK ON EVIDENCE § 344 at 698–702 (Kenneth S. Broun ed., 7th ed. 2013).

Situation: Regardless of whether the proponent's evidence of the existence of the foundational facts compels or merely allows a finding of its existence, if the opponent's evidence of the nonexistence of the presumed fact is so strong as to compel a finding of their nonexistence, the court need not mention a presumption, and need only instruct the jury that the presumed fact is not true.

Instruction: I instruct you to find that D never received from P during the time in question a letter describing the condition of the stairway.

(3) Compromise positions. As is often the case with long-standing academic debates, each position has merit. The reality is that most presumptions are overwhelmingly based in probability, and have little or no fairness or policy purpose; however, some have deeper substantive than probability-based roots, and some are almost entirely policy-based. Because of this, there is no reason to treat all presumptions equally. One approach that is theoretically simple, sensible, and adopted by the California Evidence Code,[141] is to treat probability-based presumptions under the Thayer-Wigmore theory, and to treat presumptions created largely for substantive reasons under the Morgan-McCormick view.[142] The problem with the California approach is that some presumptions are too difficult to categorize because they reflect a mixture of rationales. Different courts are likely to assign different levels of importance to the various factors, and thus treat the same presumptions differently.[143] Unless a legislature decides exactly how each presumption is to be treated, the risk of inconsistency among courts is unavoidable.[144]

If, then, the presumption is to be preserved as an evidentiary device, there does not appear to be a perfect solution to determining their effect where the opponent offers evidence contesting the existence of the presumed fact. Though neither the Thayer-Wigmore nor the Morgan-McCormick approach operates satisfactorily in all cases, these approaches at least offer some degree of consistency and predictability. Middle-ground approaches such as that of the California Evidence Code are more finely-tuned, but may lead to less consistent and predictable results.

Challenging Both the Foundational and the Presumed Facts

The party opposing the presumption could also attempt to rebut by challenging both the foundational (basic) facts and the presumed facts. Using the example from above, D could offer evidence that no mailbox exists at the location P claims to have mailed the

---

141 The California Evidence Code divides presumptions into those affecting only the burden of production (§§ 630–47), and those affecting the burden of persuasion (denoted burden of "proof") (§§ 660–70). A similar approach is taken in a few other states. *See* FLA. EVID. CODE §§ 90.302–90.304; HAW. R. EVID. 301–304; R.I. R. EVID. 301–305.

142 An approach based on similar principles, but which required the opposite conclusions, was that taken by the original version of the Uniform Rules of Evidence. Uniform Rule 14 (1953) provided that if a presumption has "probative value" (if it gives rise to a reasonable inference as to the presumed fact), it shifts the burden of persuasion, but that if the presumption does not have probative value, it shifts only the burden of production and disappears when sufficient contrary proof is offered. The drafters of the Uniform Rules eventually abandoned this approach in favor of a Morgan-McCormick position (all presumptions shift the burden of persuasion). UNIF. R. EVID. 301 (2004).

143 *See* 2 MCCORMICK ON EVIDENCE § 344 at 708–09 (Kenneth S. Broun ed., 7th ed. 2013).

144 Although the California Evidence Code divides presumptions into two categories, its list is hardly exhaustive of all presumptions that can be found in the massive California Code, many of which are stated in Codes other than the Evidence Code.

letter (a foundational fact) and that D diligently checks his mail and never received this notice (a presumed fact).

If the jurisdiction follows the "bursting bubble" theory of presumptions, this situation creates no additional complications. Once the opponent offers evidence sufficient to satisfy a burden of production as to the presumed fact, regardless of the evidence offered concerning the foundational (basic) facts, the presumption simply disappears, leaving the jury to decide the question as a matter of permissive inference.[145]

In a jurisdiction employing the Morgan-McCormick theory of presumptions, the matter is considerably more complicated. The court must consider the evidence offered on both sides concerning both the foundational (basic) facts and the presumed fact. A proposed but unadopted Federal Rule of Evidence attempted to set forth the possibilities, and what the trial court must communicate to the jury:

> When evidence as to the existence of the basic facts is such that reasonable minds would not necessarily agree whether their existence is more probable than not and evidence as to the nonexistence of the presumed fact is such that they would not necessarily agree that its nonexistence is more probable than not, the judge shall submit the matter to the jury with an instruction to find in favor of the existence of the presumed fact if they find from the evidence that the existence of the basic facts is more probable than not and unless they find the nonexistence of the presumed fact more probable than not, otherwise to find against the existence of the presumed fact.[146]

It is highly unlikely that jurors would understand the complex set of instructions mandated by this approach. As one author has written, the complexity of the proposed rule is "[t]he strongest single argument in favor of [the existing Federal Rule] and against the Morgan approach. . . . [T]here is not one juror in a hundred able to understand the instruction as presented at trial."[147]

§ 2.11 Presumptions—the Problem of Conflicting Presumptions

What should a court do when two presumptions appear to be raised by the facts of a case, and the presumptions would require inconsistent factual findings? *Atkinson v. Hall*,[148] a paternity case, provides an illustration. To summarize a complicated set of facts, the plaintiff claimed that the defendant was the father of her child, which the defendant denied. The child was born several months after the plaintiff married another man, though the couple divorced less than a year after the child was born.

Both parties relied on presumptions. Blood tests performed on the defendant showed a 98.27 percent probability that he was the father. A Maine statute provided that when blood tests show a 97 percent or higher probability of paternity, a presumption of paternity is created that can only be rebutted by "clear and convincing evidence." Plaintiff asked the court to instruct the jury in accordance with this presumption.[149]

---

[145] Of course, the opponent's evidence as to the nonexistence of the presumed fact might be so strong as to require a directed verdict or partial directed verdict.

[146] FED. R. EVID. 303(c), 46 F.R.D. 161, 214 (Preliminary Draft of Proposed Rules 1969).

[147] 1 MICHAEL H. GRAHAM, HANDBOOK OF FEDERAL EVIDENCE § 301.13 at 262–63 (6th ed. 2006).

[148] Atkinson v. Hall, 556 A.2d 651 (Me. 1989). This case arose before DNA testing was widely available.

[149] Actually, no blood test (or other forensics technique) can produce a result that establishes by itself that the probability the defendant is the father is 98.27 percent, or any other figure. This is because the blood test is not the only evidence to consider. What the result of the blood test can tell us is that 98.27 percent of all

Defendant relied on a different statutory presumption that a child born during a lawful marriage is presumed to be the child of the husband unless the party claiming otherwise proves the husband's nonpaternity beyond a reasonable doubt. The trial court ignored both presumptions and instructed the jury that plaintiff had the burden of proving paternity by a preponderance of the evidence.

The Maine Supreme Court affirmed. Maine evidence law provided that when two presumptions conflict, the court shall apply the presumption that is founded on weightier considerations of policy and logic, and that if neither satisfies this test, the court should disregard both presumptions. The Court examined the two presumptions raised by the facts and noted that the presumption of paternity from the blood tests was based on weightier considerations of logic, but that the presumption of legitimacy from marriage was supported by weightier considerations of policy ("to minimize official intrusion into marital and family relations"). The Court determined that the legitimacy presumption was at least as weighty as the paternity presumption, and hence that the trial judge did not prejudice the plaintiff's case by discarding both presumptions and sending the case to the jury with instructions that the plaintiff bore the standard burden of persuasion for civil cases.

Many cases of conflicting presumptions involve the validity of second marriages. One presumption is that a ceremonial marriage is valid; another is that a person's original married status continues. In these cases, a court could disregard both presumptions and leave the question of the validity of the second marriage to the jury. Apparently, however, many courts do not disregard the conflicting presumptions in these cases, but hold that the presumption of the validity of a marriage is stronger, and validate the second marriage.[150]

No single approach to conflicting presumptions serves all situations. Thayer believed that in such cases, both presumptions should be ignored and the jury should be left to weigh the logical inferences arising from the foundational facts.[151] In some circumstances, this seems to be the best course of action. In other cases, particularly where one of the presumptions is considerably more grounded in substantive policy than the other, perhaps it is better to give effect to the policy-based presumption, but to stress to the jury that it should examine the facts closely to determine whether the presumption has been rebutted.[152] Many courts have followed this approach, seeking to give effect to the "weightier" presumption.[153] Among the facts to be considered are the foundational facts supporting the other presumption, which may still be considered as a matter of

---

men are excluded from being the father by this test and that the defendant is *not* excluded by the test. In other words, it can tell us that the defendant is among the 1.73 percent of men who cannot be excluded by the test. That is not the same thing as saying that the test produces a probability of paternity of 98.27 percent. In fact, the test result information must be combined with other evidence, such as the witnesses' testimony, for the fact-finder to determine the probability that the defendant is the father. *See* 1 MCCORMICK ON EVIDENCE § 211 (Kenneth S. Broun ed., 7th ed. 2013). Nevertheless, the statutory presumption employed in the case and, therefore, the discussion in the opinion speak (misleadingly) in terms of the "probability of paternity" being generated by the result of the test alone, so it is discussed that way in the text.

[150] *See* 2 MCCORMICK ON EVIDENCE § 344 at 697 (Kenneth S. Broun ed., 7th ed. 2013).

[151] JAMES B. THAYER, A PRELIMINARY TREATISE ON EVIDENCE AT THE COMMON LAW 346 (1898). Wigmore agreed. 9 WIGMORE ON EVIDENCE § 2493 (Chadbourn rev. 1981).

[152] Morgan favored giving effect to the presumption founded on stronger considerations of policy. Edmund M. Morgan, *Some Observations Concerning Presumptions*, 44 HARV. L. REV. 906, 932 n.41 (1931).

[153] Other approaches to this difficult problem have also been considered, though none perfectly resolves all cases. *See* 2 MCCORMICK ON EVIDENCE § 344 at 697–98 (Kenneth S. Broun ed., 7th ed. 2013).

logical inference. Such an approach, however, suffers from the familiar problem of lack of predictability.

§ 2.12 Presumptions—Presumptions in Criminal Cases

In the landmark case of *In re Winship*,[154] the United States Supreme Court held that the Due Process Clause demands that a criminal defendant be convicted only "upon proof beyond a reasonable doubt of every fact necessary to constitute the crime with which he is charged."[155] In *Ulster County v. Allen*[156] and *Sandstrom v. Montana*,[157] the Court clarified that this requirement has left little or no room for the operation of true (mandatory) presumptions in criminal cases.

In *Ulster County*, four defendants were charged with illegal possession of handguns (among other items). Two of the handguns were found in the front of the car in a handbag belonging to one defendant, who was sixteen years old. A New York statute provided that a firearm in an automobile is presumed to be possessed illegally by all occupants. The Supreme Court attempted to set forth clearly the difference between permissive devices and mandatory devices, and their treatment under the Constitution:

> Inferences and presumptions are a staple of our adversary system of factfinding. It is often necessary for the trier of fact to determine the existence of an item of the crime—that is, an "ultimate" or "elemental" fact—from the existence of one or more "evidentiary" or "basic" facts. . . . The value of these evidentiary devices, and their validity under the Due Process Clause, vary from case to case, however, depending on the strength of the connection between the particular basic and elemental facts involved and on the degree to which the device curtails the factfinder's freedom to assess the evidence independently. Nonetheless, in criminal cases, the ultimate test of any device's constitutional validity in a given case remains constant: the device must not undermine the factfinder's responsibility at trial, based on evidence adduced by the State, to find the ultimate facts beyond a reasonable doubt.[158]

Thus, the key question is whether the device, as applied, undercut the fact-finder's role in determining guilt beyond a reasonable doubt based on the evidence. A mandatory device—one that *requires* the jury to reach a certain factual finding based on the presence of certain foundational facts—will usually do so, whereas a permissive device—one that allows the jury to reach conclusions it deems appropriate under the circumstances—will not. As the Court wrote:

> Because this permissive presumption leaves the trier of fact free to credit or reject the inference and does not shift the burden of proof, it affects the application of the "beyond a reasonable doubt" standard only if, under the facts of the case, there is no rational way the trier could make the connection permitted by the inference. For only in that situation is there any risk that an explanation of the permissible inference to a jury, or its use by a jury, has

---

[154] *In re* Winship, 397 U.S. 358 (1970).

[155] 397 U.S. at 364.

[156] County Court v. Allen, 442 U.S. 140 (1979).

[157] Sandstrom v. Montana, 442 U.S. 510 (1979). For a brief summary of the cases leading up to *Ulster County* and *Sandstrom*, see 2 MCCORMICK ON EVIDENCE § 347 (Kenneth S. Broun ed., 7th ed. 2013).

[158] Ulster County v. Allen, 442 U.S. 140, 156 (1979).

caused the presumptively rational factfinder to make an erroneous factual determination.[159]

The Court spoke in terms of "mandatory presumptions" and "permissive presumptions." This usage can easily confuse the reader accustomed to thinking of "presumptions" as mandatory devices and "inferences" as permissive devices. Nevertheless, for criminal cases, the Court has chosen this terminology, dividing presumptions into permissive and mandatory types, and holding that permissive presumptions are constitutional[160] while mandatory presumptions normally are not.[161] As applied to the facts of the case before it, the Court scrutinized not simply the language of the presumption, but also the way the trial court instructed the jury about the presumption. Analyzing the facts, the Court held that the device did not operate in a mandatory fashion because the court instructed the jury using permissive language.[162] This left only the question whether there was a rational basis for a finding of guilt beyond a reasonable doubt, which the Court held did exist.[163]

In *Sandstrom v. Montana*,[164] a homicide prosecution, the Court considered a presumption that a person intends the ordinary consequences of his voluntary acts. The defendant claimed that the degree of the offense should be reduced because he suffered from a personality disorder that was aggravated by his intoxication. The Supreme Court reversed the defendant's conviction, holding that as applied in jury instructions, the jury could have believed that the presumption was mandatory or shifted the burden of persuasion on the intent issue to the defendant. Even if the trial court's instruction could be understood as creating a permissive "presumption," the Court held that the instruction was unconstitutional because it could also have been interpreted as mandatory or as imposing on the defendant the burden of persuasion as to intent.[165]

In 1985, the Court revisited the subject in *Francis v. Franklin*.[166] The defendant, convicted of murder during a prison escape, sought federal habeas corpus relief. The only contested issue at trial was intent. The defendant claimed constitutional error in the trial court's jury instruction (1) that "[t]he acts of a person of sound mind and discretion are presumed to be the product of the person's will, but the presumption may be rebutted"; and (2) that a "person of sound mind and discretion is presumed to intend the natural and probable consequences of his acts but the presumption may be rebutted."[167]

---

159 442 U.S. at 157.

160 As the language quoted in text indicates, a permissive "presumption" will only be constitutionally infirm if the "presumption" allows a finding of fact where a rational inference is not even permissible. Such a situation would be unusual.

161 The Court's language left open the possibility that a mandatory presumption would be constitutional where the basic (foundational) facts, standing alone, would be sufficient to support the inference of guilt beyond a reasonable doubt. Ulster County v. Allen, 442 U.S. 140, 167 (1979). It has been suggested that such a presumption would always be unconstitutional. *See, e.g.*, Ronald L. Allen & Lee Ann DeGrazia, *The Constitutional Requirement of Proof Beyond Reasonable Doubt in Criminal Cases: A Comment Upon Incipient Chaos in the Lower Courts*, 20 AM. CRIM. L. REV. 1, 12–14 (1982). It is indeed difficult to visualize a mandatory presumption that could survive the *Ulster County* test.

162 Ulster County v. Allen, 442 U.S. 140, 160–65 (1979). The trial court instructed the jury about the presumption but stated that it "need not be rebutted by affirmative proof or affirmative evidence but may be rebutted by any evidence or lack of evidence in the case." *Id.* at 161 n.20.

163 442 U.S. at 167.

164 Sandstrom v. Montana, 442 U.S. 510 (1979).

165 442 U.S. at 516–19.

166 Francis v. Franklin, 471 U.S. 307 (1985).

167 471 U.S. at 309.

The Court held that the instructions were unconstitutional because they relieved the state of the burden of proving the defendant's guilt by creating a mandatory presumption of intent upon proof of other elements, and held that the instructions were in fact unconstitutional.

Even though the Georgia Supreme Court interpreted the offending language as creating no more than a permissive inference, the Court held that a reasonable juror could have understood the charge as creating a mandatory presumption shifting the burden of persuasion on the element of intent once the state had proved the underlying acts. The words of the charge were stated as a command; even though the Court instructed the jury that the presumption could be rebutted, the jurors reasonably could have understood that they must find intent unless defendant persuaded them to the contrary. As the United States Supreme Court explained, "a reasonable juror could . . . have thought that, although intent must be proved beyond a reasonable doubt, proof of the firing of the gun and its ordinary consequences constituted proof of intent beyond a reasonable doubt unless the defendant persuaded the jury otherwise."[168] Nor was the error cured by a later instruction that "[a] person will not be presumed to act with criminal intention," because a reasonable juror could have understood the instruction to refer to a different element of the crime than intent. Though any ambiguity in the instructions can be cured by the particular context, in this case neither the instruction concerning the presumption of innocence nor an instruction telling the jury that a person will not be presumed to act with criminal intention was sufficient. Even absent this interpretation of the instruction, the Court held that jurors might resolve the apparent conflict between this instruction and the invalid instructions "by choosing to abide by the mandatory presumption and ignore the prohibition of presumption."[169] Finally, while not addressing the question whether this type of error could ever be harmless, the Court let stand the court of appeals' determination that it was not harmless in this case.[170]

Although much uncertainty remains even after *Ulster County*, *Sandstrom*, and *Francis*,[171] the cases establish certain propositions. True (mandatory) presumptions are almost always unconstitutional as applied in criminal cases against the defendant. Counsel must scrutinize not only the language of the device itself, but the way in which it is explained to the jury and any other instructions that might have cured any defect, because even a presumption that appears mandatory on its face can be saved, under the circumstances, by an instruction that unambiguously leaves the matter to the jury's judgment as a matter of logical inference. A "permissive presumption," on the other hand, will be constitutional if a reasonable person could conclude that it is more likely than not that the "presumed" fact rationally follows from the foundational facts.[172]

---

[168] 471 U.S. at 319.

[169] 471 U.S. at 322.

[170] 471 U.S. at 325–26.

[171] *See* 1 MICHAEL H. GRAHAM, HANDBOOK OF FEDERAL EVIDENCE § 303.4 at 299–306 (6th ed. 2006). For discussion of the use of presumptions against the criminal defendant, see Ronald J. Allen, *Structuring Jury Decisionmaking in Criminal Cases: A Unified Constitutional Approach to Evidentiary Devices*, 94 HARV. L. REV. 321 (1980); Charles R. Nesson, *Rationality, Presumptions, and Judicial Comment: A Response to Professor Allen*, 94 HARV. L. REV. 1574 (1981); Stephen Saltzburg, *Burdens of Persuasion in Criminal Cases: Harmonizing the Views of the Justices*, 20 AM. CRIM. L. REV. 393 (1983).

[172] The use of affirmative defenses in criminal cases creates special problems. The Supreme Court has held that there are limits to the state's ability to create affirmative defenses, holding that such defenses are permissible as long as they do not simply negative an element of the crime. Patterson v. New York, 432 U.S. 197, 210 (1977) (noting that the legislature could not write the laws such that the defendant is automatically

§ 2.13 Presumptions—the Federal Rules of Evidence and Presumptions [FRE 301, 302]

The Federal Rules of Evidence address the subject of presumptions only in civil cases. Rule 301 provides the basic rule that, unless a federal statute provides otherwise, in civil cases "the party against whom a presumption is directed has the burden of producing evidence to rebut the presumption." However, the federal rule "does not shift the burden of persuasion, which remains on the party who had it originally."[173]

The first thing to notice about Rule 301, as well as similar state rules, is that it does not provide or endorse any particular presumption; it merely specifies the procedural effect of a true presumption when one is applicable in a case.[174] The existence and content of the presumption (its basic and presumed facts) are governed by legislation or common-law beyond the Rules. Moreover, Rule 301 is only a default rule: it specifies the procedural effect to be given a presumption when no such procedural effect is otherwise specified by a "federal statute or these rules." Sometimes, federal legislation creating substantive rights and duties will specify a presumption, and (more rarely) such legislation will specify what procedural effect the presumption has. When that happens, the legislation controls. But when the legislation does not speak to the procedural effect, then Rule 301 controls. Moreover, presumptions are often entirely creatures of common-law, even when the substantive right or duty to which they pertain is legislative in origin. In that situation as well, Rule 301 controls, and by its terms it overrides any contrary specification regarding the procedural effect of the presumption that may exist in the common law creating or applying the presumption. This is often overlooked in connection with common-law presumptions created prior to the effective date of Rule 301.[175]

The language of the rule appears to adopt the pure "bursting bubble" theory of presumptions, and some authorities have so stated.[176] Once a presumption goes into effect, it shifts to the opponent only the burden of going forward, not the burden of persuasion. However, the language and legislative history of Rule 301 leave some room for doubt as to the drafters' intent. While it is clear that the drafters rejected the Morgan-McCormick view, it is not so clear that they opted for full adoption of the "bursting bubble" theory either. At one point, for example, the Conference Committee report states that "[i]f the adverse party does offer evidence contradicting the presumed fact, the court cannot instruct the jury that it may *presume* the existence of the presumed fact from

presumed guilty, and then require the defendant to meet an affirmative defense of showing that some element of the crime was not present). Determining when that is the case is a difficult question of interpretation; the law needs further development. For further discussion of affirmative defenses in this context, see 2 McCORMICK ON EVIDENCE § 348 (Kenneth S. Broun ed., 7th ed. 2013).

173 FED. R. EVID. 301.

174 On the distinction between true evidentiary presumptions and other legal uses of the word "presumption," *see* **§ 2.08**.

175 Employment discrimination cases are illustrative. *Compare* Texas Dept. of Community Affairs v. Burdine, 450 U.S. 248 (1981) (alluding to, but not applying, Rule 301 in holding that presumption shifts only the burden of production), *and* St. Mary's Honor Center v. Hicks, 509 U.S. 502 (1993) (seemingly applying Rule 301 to limit presumption to shifting burden of production), *with* Price Waterhouse v. Hopkins, 450 U.S. 248 (1989) (articulating a shift in the burden of persuasion in certain circumstances, over dissent that invokes Rule 301).

176 *See, e.g.*, 1 MICHAEL H. GRAHAM, HANDBOOK OF FEDERAL EVIDENCE § 301.12 at 256 (6th ed. 2006). *See also In re* Yoder Co., 758 F.2d 1114, 1120 (6th Cir. 1985) (stating that most commentators take the position that Rule 301 embodies the "bursting bubble" approach).

proof of the basic facts. The court may, however, instruct the jury that it may infer the existence of the presumed fact from proof of the basic facts."[177] This appears to suggest that some remnant of the presumption may in fact outlive the admission of evidence contradicting the presumed fact. The authors of one treatise have argued that the Rule in fact adopts aspects of the Morgan-McCormick and "true" Thayer-Wigmore theories.[178]

Whatever the actual approach of Rule 301, it is limited to some degree by Rule 302, which provides that state law governs the effect of a presumption regarding a fact for which state law supplies the rule of decision. Thus, in cases brought in federal court by virtue of diversity jurisdiction, Rule 301 generally will not determine the effect of a presumption. Instead, the parties must look to the state's law. For civil cases arising out of federal questions, Rule 301 governs the presumptions.

As already discussed, many states have adopted versions of the federal evidence rules, and in that process some changes were made that created differences between the state rules and the federal rules. This is especially common in relation to Rule 301 and its state counterparts. Several states adopted a counterpart rule that shifts the burden of persuasion.[179] Again, this is only a default rule, and state courts have also wrestled with what to do with legal devices created before the adoption of their rules that use the term "presumption."[180] In addition, some states, following the guidance of the Uniform Rules of Evidence, have counterparts to federal Rule 302 that defer to federal law regarding presumptions when federal substantive law otherwise controls in the state court.[181]

As noted above, the Federal Rules do not address presumptions in criminal cases. The Advisory Committee proposed such a rule,[182] but Congress declined to adopt it. In federal criminal cases, therefore, the law of presumptions is based on criminal statutes and common law, as limited by judicial interpretation of the Constitution's demands, discussed in a previous section.[183]

---

[177] H.R. REP. NO. 93–1597 at 5 (1974) (Conf. Rep.); 1974 U.S. Code Cong. & Ad. News 7098, 7099 (emphasis in original).

[178] 21 CHARLES A. WRIGHT & KENNETH W. GRAHAM, JR., FEDERAL PRACTICE AND PROCEDURE (EVIDENCE) § 5122.2 (2005). The authors state:

> Rule 301 . . . attempts to walk "a narrow path between the so-called 'bursting bubble' theory of presumptions and the theory that a presumption permanently shifts the burden of persuasion regardless of the quantity of contradicting evidence." Courts and writers have embraced this view of Rule 301. Not surprisingly, Rule [301] resembles but still differs from other efforts to construct an intermediate route between the Thayer-Wigmore theory of presumptions and the Morgan-McCormick theory.

Id. at 449. For discussion the actual views of Thayer and Wigmore, *see* **§ 2.10**.

[179] In particular, several states adopted a version of Rule 301 that corresponds to that rule as it was originally proposed for the federal courts. That proposal would have created a default rule that would shift the burden of persuasion in accordance with the Morgan-McCormick view. See Fed. R. Evid. 301 advisory committee note.

[180] *Compare In re* Estate of Malnar, 243 N.W.2d 435 (Wis. 1976) (treating "presumption of undue influence" language of earlier cases as involving a true presumption governed by Wisconsin's default rule), *with In re* Estate of McGowan, 250 N.W.2d 234 (Neb. 1977) (treating "presumption of undue influence" language of earlier cases as merely involving permissible inferences not governed by Nebraska's new default rule).

[181] *See, e.g.*, N.C.R. EVID. 302 ("in civil actions and proceedings, the effect of a presumption respecting a fact which is an element of a claim or defense as to which federal law supplies the rules of decision is determined in accordance with federal law.").

[182] FED. R. EVID. 303, 46 F.R.D. 161 (Preliminary Draft of Proposed Rules 1969).

[183] *See* **§ 2.12**.

§ 2.14 Judicial Notice of Adjudicative Facts [FRE 201]

In one case, the witness testified that at eleven o'clock at night, by the light of a full moon, he saw the defendant kill a man in the middle of a field approximately 150 feet away. However, the moon was not full on that night—August 29, 1857. In fact, it was barely past the first quarter. How would Abraham Lincoln, the lawyer for the defendant, prove the moon was not full, so that he could argue to the jurors that the supposed eyewitness was not believable? Lincoln had several options. He might call a witness who remembered looking up at the moon at eleven on August 29, 1857 and who could recall it was barely past the first quarter. But who remembers the moon on a particular night? And moreover, why should the jurors believe one amateur stargazer over another? He might call an astronomer as an expert witness, if one were easily available in the pre-Civil War frontier of Illinois, and if the Court would recognize that area of expertise. Instead, Lincoln asked the sheriff to bring him a copy of the 1857 almanac. The Court took *judicial notice* of the moon phase information in the almanac.[184] By asking the Court to take judicial notice, Lincoln was taking advantage of a shortcut in proof that the common law had developed to reduce the time and expense required in proving something that is certain beyond argument.[185]

Rule 201 of the Federal Rule of Evidence permits a court to establish an "adjudicative fact" that is "not subject to reasonable dispute" merely by taking judicial notice of it; the fact must be one "generally known" within the trial court's territorial jurisdiction or one that can be accurately and readily determined from sources "whose accuracy cannot reasonably be questioned."[186] The judge may take judicial notice of it, even if no lawyer requests judicial notice.[187] If a lawyer does ask a court to take judicial notice and supplies the trial court with the "necessary information," the judge must take judicial notice of the fact.[188]

Rule 201 is limited to judicial notice of adjudicative facts as substitutes for presenting evidence to a fact-finder through witnesses and exhibits. "Adjudicative facts"—"simply the facts of the particular case"[189]—and "legislative facts" are two terms coined by Professor Kenneth Davis to help illustrate two different functions of the court—adjudication and law making.[190] "Adjudicative facts" are "facts that normally go to the jury in a jury case."[191] Professor Davis's definition is repeated with approval by the advisory committee:

> When a court or an agency finds facts concerning the immediate parties—who did what, where, when, how, and with what motive or intent—the court or agency is performing an adjudicative function, and the facts are conveniently called adjudicative facts. . . .[192]

---

[184] ALBERT A. WOLDMAN, LAWYER LINCOLN 123 (1996).

[185] For a thorough discussion of the history and rationale behind the development of common law judicial notice, *see* 2 MCCORMICK ON EVIDENCE § 328 (Kenneth S. Broun ed., 7th ed. 2013).

[186] FED. R. EVID. 201(b).

[187] FED. R. EVID. 201(c)(1).

[188] FED. R. EVID. 201(c)(2).

[189] FED. R. EVID. 201(a) advisory committee note.

[190] Kenneth C. Davis, *An Approach to Problems of Evidence in the Administrative Process*, 55 HARV. L. REV. 364, 404–07 (1942).

[191] FED. R. EVID. 201(a) advisory committee note (quoting Professor Davis).

[192] FED. R. EVID. 201(a) advisory committee note (quoting Professor Davis).

"Legislative facts," on the other hand, are those that a court uses in the law making process. Courts are often required to interpret a statute or to define the limits of a common-law rule. Such decisions often turn on policy, which in turn depends upon acceptance of some social, economic, or other hypothesis the court must adopt as "fact" to reach a decision.

The oldest and simplest basis for judicial notice is that the adjudicative fact to be established is so universally known that there can be no argument about it.[193] As Florida courts have said, "What everybody knows the courts are assumed to know. . . ."[194] For example, "everybody knows" that the Grand Canyon is in the United States; the Eiffel Tower is in Paris, France; and George Washington was the first President of the United States.

It is not actually a requirement that "everybody know" a fact in order for judicial notice to be available to the parties. A court may take judicial notice of a fact that is only "generally known" within the trial court's territorial jurisdiction. The facts that the Chicago Cubs did not win the World Series between 1908 and 2016 is probably not as well-known as the fact that George Washington was the first President of the United States. Nevertheless, the former fact might be the subject of judicial notice in a court sitting on Chicago's north side.

Even a fact that is *not* generally known within the court's territorial jurisdiction (or anywhere else, for that matter) may be judicially noticed. For example, a court in New Mexico might take judicial notice that the Cubs won the World Series in 1908—four years before New Mexico became a state—because the fact is capable of an accurate and ready determination via accurate sources.[195] Sometimes referred to as "almanac-type facts," these facts are often ones that "nobody knows" except after resorting to the "sources."[196]

Judicial notice of an adjudicative fact that is critically important to a case "may be taken at any stage of a proceeding."[197] even if no lawyer requests it. When the plaintiff in the often cited case of *Varcoe v. Lee*[198] forgot to prove that Mission Street was in a business district (in order to establish that speed in excess of fifteen miles per hour constituted negligence per se), the judge was free, nevertheless, to instruct the jury that Mission Street was in San Francisco's business district.

A party against whom a fact is judicially noticed is entitled "to be heard as to the propriety of taking judicial notice and the nature of the fact to be noticed."[199] While this

---

[193] 2 MCCORMICK ON EVIDENCE § 329 (Kenneth S. Broun ed., 7th ed. 2013).

[194] United States v. American Nat'l Bank, 255 F.2d 504, 507 (5th Cir. 1958); St. Lucie County Bank & Trust Co. v. Aylin, 114 So. 438, 440 (Fla. 1927). *See also In re* Buszta's Estate, 186 N.Y.S.2d 192, 193 (Sur. 1959).

[195] FED. R. EVID. 201(b)(2).

[196] *See* Smith v. Pro Football, Inc., 593 F.2d 1173 (D.C. Cir. 1978). In defending the use of the Encyclopedia of Pro Football to notice when the Minnesota Vikings selected a player in the pro football draft, MacKinnon, C.J., a former All-American football player at the University of Minnesota, said "The majority complains of reference to facts disclosed in the Encyclopedia of Pro Football and to matters of common knowledge that can be readily verified by reference to encyclopedias, books and other publications of established authenticity. This however is clearly permissible and may be done for the first time on appeal as is recognized by the Federal Rules of Evidence, Rule 201(f) which states: 'Judicial notice may be taken at any stage of the proceedings.' " *Id.* at 1213, n.71 (MacKinnon, C.J., concurring and dissenting).

[197] FED. R. EVID. 201(d).

[198] Varcoe v. Lee, 181 P. 223, 225 (Cal. 1919).

[199] FED. R. EVID. 201(e).

will often be easy to accommodate when one party asks for notice during a trial, it may not be so simple when the trial judge takes notice of a fact spontaneously, as in *Varcoe v. Lee*, or when it is an appellate court that takes the notice. The rule recognizes this problem and allows the party to be heard after judicial notice has been taken.[200]

In a civil case, a judicially noticed fact may be more powerful than a fact presented through the testimony of a witness. While jurors may refuse to accept what a witness says as fact, the judge instructs civil jurors that they *must* accept the judicially noticed fact as conclusive.[201] This avoids the necessity of proving that fact with witnesses and documents submitted in evidence in the usual way, subject to the many rules that constrain the introduction of such evidence.

In criminal cases, Rule 201 requires judges to instruct jurors that they *may* accept the judicially noticed fact, but are not required to do so.[202] Because the point of taking judicial notice is to avoid the necessity of taking formal evidence on the point, one may well question how a jury is supposed to decide whether to accept the noticed fact. And if the jury must have its say on the matter, then taking judicial notice at the appellate level, which is not uncommon in civil cases, would be impossible in criminal cases, at least when the fact noticed helps the government. These tensions have occasioned some difficulty in the courts.[203]

Judicial notice of such standard reference material as when the Cubs won the World Series is not particularly remarkable,[204] but what about Abraham Lincoln's use of the almanac to show that the moon was just past the first phase on August 29, 1857? The predicted phases of the moon were undoubtedly derived from the work of an astronomer who used a scientific principle to produce the information. In spite of the almanac, should the judge have required Lincoln to bring in the astronomer for cross-examination?

The first time expert opinion was offered in court about ballistics, radar, genetic testing, and the like, lawyers undoubtedly produced substantial testimony in an effort to persuade the judge of the validity of the underlying scientific principles.[205] As the

---

[200] FED. R. EVID. 201(e).

[201] FED. R. EVID. 201(f).

[202] FED. R. EVID. 201(f).

[203] *Compare, e.g.*, United States v. Jones, 580 F.2d 219, 223–29 (6th Cir. 1978) (holding that the appellate court may not take judicial notice that Southern Bell was an interstate communications company, which the prosecution had failed to evidence at trial in order to establish defendant's "unlawful interception of interstate telephonic communications"); *with* United States v. Piggie, 622 F.2d 486 (10th Cir. 1980) (affirming conviction despite the trial court's failure to instruct the jury, in accord with the Rule, that the jury was free to find that the crime committed in Leavenworth Penitentiary was not within the federal geographic jurisdiction, stating that "we cannot bring ourselves to give effect to [the predecessor of what is now Rule 201(f)]".).

[204] *See, e.g.*, Scotty's Contr. & Stone, Inc. v. United States, 326 F.3d 785, 789 n.1 (6th Cir. 2003) (page of brief submitted in different case); United States v. Coutchavlis, 260 F.3d 1149, 1153–54 (9th Cir. 2001) (judicial notice of map "in determining whether defendant known to have driven from one location to another passed through particular jurisdiction."); Hays v. National Elec. Contractors Ass'n, Inc., 781 F.2d 1321, 1324 n.2 (9th Cir. 1985) (judicial notice of American Automobile Association map of Alameda County); Ibarra v. Sunset Scavenger Co., 2003 WL 21244096 at *7 n.2 (N.D. Cal. 2003) ("statistics published by the Equal Employment Opportunity Commission which indicate the composition of the workforce in Oakland, San Jose and San Francisco by race and job category"); Estate of Torres v. Terhune, 2002 WL 32107987 at *2 (E.D. Cal. 2002) (records and reports of administrative body); Kraft Foods Holdings, Inc. v. Helm, 2002 WL 31473843 at *1 (N.D. Ill. 2002); George v. Hilaire Farm Nursing Home, 622 F. Supp. 1349, 1354 (S.D.N.Y. 1985) (judicial notice of dates from calendar); (copies of trademark registrations); *In re* Marriage of Aud, 491 N.E.2d 894, 897 (Ill. App. Ct. 1986) (statistics prepared by United States Bureau of Census were proper subject of judicial notice).

[205] *See* **§§ 10.03 et seq.**

underlying scientific principles became well accepted, trial courts no longer required elaborate proof of the validity of the science, but rather took judicial notice of the validity of the theory and required evidence only of the particular application or of the qualifications of the particular expert. Appellate courts in various jurisdictions have at one time or another decided that the forensic science of "ballistics" can assist in the identification of the gun from which a bullet was fired,[206] that the speed of an approaching car can be measured by a radar gun,[207] and that genetic markers can be used to establish parentage.[208] Although many scientific principles have become so well accepted that they are judicially noticed, the process to reach that status is often difficult during the period in which the science is being developed.[209]

It is sometimes difficult to draw the line between legislative and adjudicative facts. For example, when a court takes judicial notice of the scientific principle underlying radar it may not seem obvious whether that judicial notice is of an "adjudicative" or a "legislative fact." This distinction is of some consequence, because "legislative facts," are not governed by Rule 201.

"Legislative facts" are often central to a court's determination of a legal issue, but the "legislative fact" is not always identified as something of which the court takes judicial notice. A "legislative fact" need not be "generally known" and need not be found in a source "whose accuracy cannot reasonably be questioned," and is not something the parties necessarily have an opportunity to address.

The scientific principles underlying radar, ballistics, DNA and the like seem to be "adjudicative facts" to the extent that they constitute evidence that, without judicial notice, would normally go to a jury for its consideration. On the other hand, the scientific principle underlying radar is a hypothesis, not unlike the social or economic hypotheses that are usually characterized as "legislative facts." And they do not concern just the immediate parties—the who did what, when, where, and with what intentions. Nonetheless, what determines whether they should be treated as adjudicative facts or legislative facts is how these facts are used. Legislative facts inform the court's determination of the content of the law to be applied in the case, whether substantive or procedural. Adjudicative facts are those facts that must be determined in order to apply the law, the determination being made either by the fact-finder or, in the case of preliminary questions determining admissibility or preemptive rulings like directed verdicts, by the trial court.[210] Thus, the principles underlying the use of radar or

---

[206] DAVID FAIGMAN, ET AL., MODERN SCIENTIFIC EVIDENCE § 23–1.2 (1997) (crediting Oliver Wendell Holmes as being first judge to admit modern firearms identification in Commonwealth v. Best, 62 N.E. 748, 750 (Mass. 1902)).

[207] *See, e.g.*, People v. Knight, 530 N.E.2d 1273, 1275 (N.Y. 1988) (holding that it was no longer necessary to require expert testimony as to scientific principles underlying moving radar); People v. Magri, 147 N.E.2d 728, 730 (N.Y. 1958) (holding that it was no longer necessary to require expert testimony in each case as to nature, function, or scientific principles underlying stationary radar).

[208] *See, e.g.*, Clark v. Jeter, 486 U.S. 456, 458 (1988) (ordering blood test to determine parentage accepted as matter of course); United States v. Floyd, 81 F.3d 1517, 1521 (10th Cir. 1996) (trial court ordered blood test and used results to conclude that defendant was not biological father of child in question).

[209] For example, DNA testing is now widely accepted by courts. *See, e.g.*, Tuan Anh Nguyen v. INS, 533 U.S. 53, 80 (2001) ("Modern DNA testing, in addition to providing accuracy unmatched by other methods of establishing a biological link, essentially negates the evidentiary significance of the passage of time."); Henry Weinstein, *Death Penalty Foes Mark a Milestone*, L.A. TIMES, Apr. 10, 2002, at A16.

[210] Many essentially factual decisions made by judges, like rulings on directed verdict motions, are said to be decisions on (or as) "matters of law," not because they are not factual, but simply to distinguish them from factual decisions made by juries. Such decisions do not thereby become decisions on legislative facts.

ballistics should be treated as adjudicative facts in the context of admissibility determinations, because they are not used to determine the content of the rule that controls admissibility of such expertise, but rather they are used by the judge to decide how that rule applies to the case. Likewise, to the extent that they concern the weight the jury is to give to admissible expertise, they are clearly adjudicative facts separate from the substantive rules the jury is required to apply.

In re Sealed Case[211] presents a clear example of "legislative fact." In trying to secure notes of conversations between a White House aide and the aide's lawyer, a prosecutor argued that the lawyer-client privilege did not survive the death of the White House aide. While recognizing the Supreme Court's earlier finding of a "legislative fact"—that the provision of legal advice "can only be safely and readily availed of when free from the consequences or apprehension of disclosure"[212]—the District of Columbia Court of Appeals found its own "legislative fact," though it did not denominate it as such. To support departing from the long established rule that the client's need to be "free from the consequence or apprehension of disclosure" required that the privilege survive the death of the client, the court said: "[I]t is surely true that the risk of post-death revelation will typically trouble the client less than pre-death revelation."[213]

The "fact" that post-death disclosure of privileged information will trouble the client less than pre-death disclosure is as subject to quarrel as is the "fact" that legal advice cannot exist without confidentiality in the first instance.[214] Both propositions are more properly characterized as "hypotheses" than "fact," but they are noticed and treated as facts by courts that are engaged in the law making, as opposed to the fact-finding process.

While the individual judge's "knowledge" of a factual hypothesis that the judge will notice as a "legislative fact" in support of legal reasoning is inevitable, the individual judge's "knowledge" of an "adjudicative fact" is neither necessary nor sufficient for judicial notice under Rule 201. A judge who does not know the Chicago Cubs from the fuzzy, brown four-footed creatures in the zoo will take judicial notice of the last year the Chicago Cubs won the World Series when shown the Encyclopedia of Baseball. But if that same judge should happen to know the ages of the children of the Cubs' current manager, the judge is not entitled to take judicial notice of them.

The adjudicative facts most trial lawyers will be concerned about substituting for the testimony of witnesses may be called to the court's attention in any number of ways. The most common is: "Your honor, I ask the court to take judicial notice that the Chicago Cubs last won a World Series in 2016."

---

[211] *In re* Sealed Case, 124 F.3d 230 (D.C. Cir. 1997), *rev'd sub nom. See also* Swidler & Berlin v. United States, 524 U.S. 399, 407–08 (1998) (expressing doubt about validity of lower court's conclusions concerning likely effect of loss of privilege).

[212] Hunt v. Blackburn, 128 U.S. 464, 470 (1888).

[213] *In re* Sealed Case, 124 F.3d 230, 233 (D.C. Cir. 1997).

[214] *See* David W. Louisell, *Confidentiality, Conformity, and Confusion: Privileges in Federal Court Today,* 31 TUL. L. REV. 101, 112 (1956) (arguing that effect of disclosure is speculative and cannot be proven scientifically).

Chapter 3

PROCEDURES FOR OFFERING AND OPPOSING EVIDENCE

Table of Sections

§ 3.01 Lawyers as Evidence Police [FRE 103]

Lawyers are primarily responsible for the evidence presented at American trials. They have the privilege and the obligation, at least in the first instance, to determine which evidence rules will be enforced and which will not. The trial judge may, on rare occasions, exclude information sua sponte—when the United States Constitution prohibits the evidence, for example—but the lawyers are ordinarily responsible for rooting out inadmissible evidence.

Courts will usually admit information offered by a proponent that does not meet the requirements of the evidence rules, unless the opponent objects. Often the opponent knows the information is not admissible, but has no tactical or strategic reason to exclude it. Other times, both parties may have an equal interest in allowing excludable information to reach the jurors. Still other times, the opponent will be unaware that the information can be excluded. Finally, on occasion the opponent will not be quick enough with an objection to keep it from the jurors' ears, and the opponent will not ask the judge to strike it and to tell the jurors to disregard it for fear of further emphasizing the information.

Rule 103(a)(1) recognizes the importance of the lawyer as the enforcer of evidence law by requiring an objection before admission of evidence can be appealed, unless the admission amounts to plain error.[1] Conversely, Rule 103(a)(2) requires the proponent of excluded evidence to make clear to the trial court the nature of the evidence at issue before the exclusion can be appealed. These rules, and other parts of Rule 103, are elaborated in this chapter, together with the rules that govern the trial court's decision on admissibility, primarily Rule 104.

Lawyers enforce evidence law in various ways. The Federal Rules of Civil Procedure often require parties to list witnesses they plan to call and documents they plan to introduce in advance.[2] Failure to raise available objections to an opponent's evidence pretrial can waive those objections. Some evidence issues are sufficiently obvious before trial and critical enough to the way the trial will proceed to be researched, briefed, and argued to the judge. This method of enforcing evidence law demands the same skills and effort as the presentation of any other legal position. Most evidence issues, however, arise unexpectedly at trial. They require the trial lawyer to identify the issue in the examiner's question, recognize the applicable evidence law, gain the judge's attention while quieting the witness, object precisely, and prepare to argue evidence theory and its applicability to the facts presented, all in less than half a minute.

§ 3.02 Motions in Limine

A motion in limine is a common method for raising evidentiary issues the resolution of which will influence the conduct of the trial. This anticipatory motion, usually made in writing before the beginning of the trial, gives the lawyers an opportunity to ensure that objectionable and particularly prejudicial information will not be offered in front of the jurors. Although the motion is most often used to exclude evidence, it also can provide a mechanism for a lawyer planning to offer controversial evidence to obtain a pretrial ruling on its admissibility.

Lawyers should be sure to obtain a clear ruling from the judge on the motion in limine and ensure that the motion and the ruling are entered into the trial record. The record and the lawyer's understanding of the rationale for the judge's decision are important for the trial as well as for any possible appeal. Denial of a motion in limine does not necessarily mean that the judge has ruled finally on the evidence in question. In many cases, the judge will deny a motion in limine, not because the motion is wrong on the merits, but because a ruling is impossible without hearing the proffered evidence in the context of other evidence. For example, admission of a critical hearsay statement may depend upon the facts surrounding the utterance that are not apparent until the testimony of the person who heard the statement. Similarly, before trial, a judge may not know enough about the context in order to exclude evidence for which it is claimed the prejudicial effect substantially outweighs the probative value.[3]

If the judge merely postpones a final decision on the motion in limine, the moving lawyer will make the objection at trial. Similarly, when a judge postpones a motion in limine to admit evidence, the moving lawyer will offer the evidence at trial.

If the denial of a motion in limine to exclude evidence is not a postponement, but a ruling on the merits, the losing lawyer faces a quandary. The lawyer is tempted not to object at trial to avoid emphasizing the evidence in front of the jury. The problem is that

---

1 On plain error, *see* **§ 3.15**.

2 *See, e.g.,* FED. R. CIV. P. 26(a)(3).

3 **§ 5.03** (discussing FED. R. EVID. 403).

jurisdictions split on whether a matter determined on the merits in limine is preserved for appeal. The lawyer who fails to object again at trial runs a risk that the matter decided in limine will not be preserved.

A 2000 amendment to Rule 103 attempted to remove this risk in the Federal system by adding a provision that attorneys need not renew an objection or offer of proof once the court makes a definitive ruling on the record.[4] Courts have little trouble applying this principle, and most of the reported cases involve reminding parties that no renewed objection was necessary.[5] Where the district court has not ruled[6] or specifically reserved its ruling or indicated that the ruling is provisional,[7] the objection must be renewed. Potential problems arise where the nature of the ruling is unclear[8] or where the court indicates that the ruling is definitive but the record is ambiguous. The lawyer can attempt to ensure there are no unpleasant surprises by insisting upon a hearing record that includes the judge's specific ruling specifying whether it is definitive.[9] If the in limine ruling is definitive and the judge does not change course at trial on the issue as a result of a party's departure from the pretrial representations, the lawyer need not object to preserve the matter for appeal even in the face of the judge's invitation to renew the objection.[10] If, on the other hand, the court makes a definitive pretrial ruling, there is "nothing in the amendment [that] prohibits the court from revisiting its decision when the evidence is offered"; in that event, an "objection must be made when the evidence is offered to preserve the claim of error for appeal."[11]

Lawyers are sometimes forced to make hard choices at trial if the judge has made a pretrial ruling that evidence will be admissible to impeach their clients. The Supreme Court ruled in *Luce v. United States*[12] that, in the event of the denial of an in limine motion to prohibit the prosecution from impeaching the defendant with prior criminal convictions, the right to appeal the denial is forfeited unless the lawyer calls the defendant to testify and the defendant is impeached with the criminal convictions.[13] The high price for preserving the appeal—risking that the jury will be overly influenced by a

---

[4] FED. R. EVID. 103(b) ("Once the court rules definitively on the record—either before or at trial—a party need not renew an objection or offer of proof to preserve a claim of error for appeal.")

[5] *See, e.g.*, United States v. Collier, 527 F.3d 695, 699 (8th Cir. 2008); Wipf v. Kowalski, 519 F.3d 380, 385 (7th Cir. 2008); United States v. Mahone, 453 F.3d 68, 70 (1st Cir. 2006) (noting change after 2000 amendment).

[6] *See, e.g.*, Cohara v. CSX Transp. Inc., 2010 WL 1851370 (Ohio 2010).

[7] FED. R. EVID. 103 advisory committee's note, 2000 Amendment.

[8] Crowe v. Bolduc, 334 F.3d 124, 133 (1st Cir. 2003) (noting that burden is on counsel to clarify nature of ruling, but given district court's confusing comments about tentative nature of its in limine ruling, review should be for abuse of discretion or for plain error).

[9] Anticipating the problem, the Advisory Committee Note to the 2000 Amendment to Federal Rule of Evidence 103 suggests that the amendment "imposes the obligation on counsel to clarify whether an in limine . . . ruling is definitive when there is doubt on that point." Courts in ruling on motions in limine can make this task easier. *See, e.g.*, United States v. O'Neill, 680 F. Supp. 2d 255, 258 n.1 (D. Me. 2010) (trial court provided in its order: "To be clear, as there was no specific context set forth in the motion, the Court does not consider this Order to be definitive within the meaning of Rule 103(a) and the Government must make a timely objection at trial to any question that in its view elicits a response that in its view should be excluded.").

[10] United States v. Gajo, 290 F.3d 922 (7th Cir. 2002) (where definitive pretrial ruling admitted evidence if claimed foundation could be produced at trial and foundation was produced at trial, matter preserved for appeal even though defense counsel responded "no" when district judge inquired at trial whether defense wished to make objection).

[11] FED. R. EVID. 103 advisory committee's note, 2000 Amendment.

[12] 469 U.S. 38 (1984).

[13] The Advisory Committee, in discussing the 2000 amendment of Rule 103, specifically stated that the amendment was not "intended to affect the rule set forth in [*Luce*] and its progeny."

defendant's prior convictions—was made even higher by the Court's decision in *Ohler v. United States*.[14] Before *Ohler*, defense lawyers addressed the kind of dilemma involved in *Luce* by calling the defendant to testify, in order to preserve the appeal, and then eliciting such convictions during direct examination of the defendant. The idea was that, by having the defendant testify during direct examination about prior convictions that the prosecution was sure to ask about on cross-examination, the defendant could at least avoid the appearance of hiding something.[15] The *Ohler* Court held that the defendant waived her pretrial objection to the government's impeachment use of a prior drug conviction when she testified to the conviction on direct examination. Yet, *Luce* and *Ohler* are non-constitutional rulings and a number of state jurisdictions have agreed with the dissenting opinion in *Ohler* that these rulings are "unfair."[16]

§ 3.03 Objections and Motions to Strike at Trial

The lawyer's choices about the procedure for making objections at trial can significantly influence the outcome of the trial, as well as whether evidence issues are preserved for appeal. Lawyers' objections to evidence highlight the tension between effective trial tactics and the steps necessary to create a good record for appeal.

A lawyer can waive the ability to appeal an evidentiary ruling by any number of actions or failures to act. Failure to object constitutes a waiver.[17] Waiver also may result if an objection is untimely,[18] insufficiently specific,[19] or is made on the wrong ground.[20] Requiring a timely objection that states the proper specific ground gives the trial judge an opportunity to correct the error and prevents a wasted trial. Moreover, it gives the proponent an opportunity to withdraw the evidence and rely on other evidence, or to cure the problem by laying a further foundation.[21] The plain error rule occasionally preserves

---

[14] 529 U.S. 753, 754 (2000).

[15] The practice is sometimes called "removing the sting" of anticipated impeachment. *See* **§ 11.02**.

[16] *See, e.g.*, Cure v. State, 26 A.3d 899, 906–12 (Md. 2011) (recognizing in this situation an exception to the requirement of a contemporaneous objection); Zola v. Kelley, 826 A.2d 589, 592 (N.H. 2003) ("Because preservation is procedural issue, we are not bound by the Supreme Court's holding in *Ohler*" and "in general, a definitive ruling by the trial court on a motion in limine sufficiently preserves for appellate review the particular issue presented to the trial court. We concluded that this satisfies the requirement that a party must make a contemporaneous and specific objection at trial to preserve an issue for appellate review. . . ."); Vermont v. Keiser, 807 A.2d 378 (Vt. 2002); Washington v. Cross, 2002 WL 234832 at *2 (Wash. Ct. App. 2002) ("Even if we were inclined to agree with the general holding in *Ohler*, that rule is contrary to established precedent in this state."). *But see* Goodie v. State, 2005 WL 1508535 (Tex. Ct. App.) (following *Ohler*).

[17] Khanh Phuong Nguyen v. United States, 539 U.S. 69 (2003) (holding that failure to object at trial ordinarily constitutes waiver); Wilburn v. Mid-South Health Dev., Inc., 343 F.3d 1274, 1280 (10th Cir. 2003) ("An issue is waived if it was not raised below in the district court."). *See, e.g.*, Melendez-Diaz v. Massachusetts, 557 U.S. 305 (2009) (confrontation right may be waived if party fails to object to offending evidence); United States v. Wise, 588 F.3d 531, 537 n.5 (8th Cir. 2009) ("When a party fails to timely object to the [report and recommendation] of a magistrate judge, 'he waives his right to de novo review by district court of any portion of report and recommendation as well as his right to appeal from findings of fact contained therein.' ").

[18] In some courts, a timely objection requires objection during the opponent's opening statement if the proposed evidence is mentioned. *See* Diefenbach v. Sheridan Transp., 229 F.3d 27, 29–30 (1st Cir. 2000); Evans v. Andraschko, 70 Fed. Appx. 533, 535 (10th Cir. 2003); United States v. Carter, 42 Fed. Appx. 418, 425 (10th Cir. 2002); Bewley v. Allright Carpark, Inc., 617 S.W.2d 547, 552 (Mo. App. 1981).

[19] *See* **§ 3.04**; *see also* Diefenbach v. Sheridan Transp., 229 F.3d 27, 29 (1st Cir. 2000).

[20] International Land Acquisitions, Inc. v. Fausto, 39 Fed. Appx. 751, 756 (3d Cir. 2002); United States v. Causwell, 10 Fed. Appx. 80, 84 (4th Cir. 2001); United States v. Johnson, 722 F.2d 407, 409 (8th Cir. 1983); United States v. Farag, 41 Fed. Appx. 338, 344–45 (10th Cir. 2002); Ralston v. Plogger, 476 N.E.2d 1378, 1384 (Ill. App. 1985).

[21] *See* United States v. Del Llano, 354 F.2d 844, 847–48 (2d Cir. 1965); 1 WEINSTEIN'S FEDERAL EVIDENCE § 103.02[2] (Joseph M. McLaughlin ed., 2d ed. 2014).

an evidentiary matter for appeal, irrespective of anything that may have occurred at trial.[22] However, the trial lawyer cannot afford to rely on the remote chance that plain error will save a mistake in evidence advocacy. The effective evidence advocate must combine knowledge of the substance of the case with fluency in the language of the courtroom in order to make the most difficult judgment—whether to object to inadmissible evidence—and then to object in a timely and proper fashion.

Most accomplished trial lawyers object only when the question is objectionable *and* the answer will be harmful to the objecting party's case. The lawyer who makes too many objections may be perceived by the jury as obstructionist or having something to conceal. Moreover, overruled objections can be harmful to the case. The jurors may give the admitted evidence more weight than it would otherwise receive because the objection has drawn attention to it.

Sometimes failure to make a valid objection is sound because the opponent's evidence will open the door to admit devastating evidence that would not otherwise be admissible. This strategy, however, can be treacherous if the jurisdiction is restrictive in its allowance of curative admissibility.[23]

Technical objections to foundation can backfire. If the lawyer knows that the opposing party can lay the foundation, then the objection should ordinarily be withheld. Otherwise, the lawyer appears to be obstructing the trial for no reason. Moreover, the opponent's evidence may be more persuasive if the full foundation has been laid. The same principle applies to certain objections to the form of questions, such as objections to questions that are vague or overbroad. The rephrased question may elicit testimony that is more persuasive than what would have been elicited by the original testimony.

On the other hand, technical objections may also provide a strategic benefit by breaking the flow of a cross-examiner's examination and by giving the direct examiner's friendly witness time to think about what is coming next. Occasionally, a direct examiner will not be very adept. Posing technical objections may make it impossible for such an examiner to complete the direct examination, let alone make it persuasive.

The lawyer with a strong or sympathetic jury case should generally be less eager to make objections. The trial judge may err in sustaining the objection, thereby giving the opponent an appeal point with which to overturn the verdict.

Careful preparation and knowledge of the judge's individual predilections can help the lawyer prepare for the quick give-and-take of trial evidence. Judges have vastly different attitudes about the admission and exclusion of evidence. Some judges give lawyers much more leeway than others do. Since most of the Rules rest upon the judge's discretion, the lawyer must adjust to take into account whether the particular judge is free and easy in receiving evidence or extremely technical about excluding it. For example, some judges have a strict attitude toward asking questions in proper form, and frequently sustain objections to leading questions or to questions that call for a narrative response. Others are impatient with attorneys who make such objections and are likely to give the jury the impression that the objecting attorney is wasting time. Because a trial judge's rulings on matters of form almost never create reversible error, the individual judge's attitude is determinative.

---

22 *See* **§ 3.15**.

23 *See* **§ 1.11**.

A lawyer should anticipate and identify most of the opponent's damaging evidence before trial, outline the legal grounds for exclusion, and consider the language that will be most effective in persuading the judge without alienating the jurors. No lawyer, however, can anticipate every potential piece of damaging, but inadmissible, evidence that the opponent might offer. In the heat of trial, the jurors might hear such evidence because the witness responds to the question either before the objecting lawyer can object or before the judge can instruct the witness not to answer. If that happens, the objecting lawyer must immediately move to strike the question and answer from the record and the jurors should be instructed to disregard them in order to protect the record and preserve the matter for appeal. Care must be taken, however, not to draw too much attention to the inadmissible evidence.

Example

Proponent:	What happened next?
Witness:	My wife told me it was the same car that had been cruising around our house the day before.
Opponent:	Objection, hearsay, irrelevant and prejudicial. I move to strike the answer, your honor.
Judge:	Motion granted, the answer is stricken.
Opponent:	Move to instruct the jury to disregard.
Judge:	The jury will disregard the witness's answer to the question. Motion granted. The answer is stricken and the jury is instructed to disregard it.

The separate motion for an instruction may not be necessary. Judges will often anticipate and instruct the jurors to disregard at the same time as striking the testimony.

The same motion to strike will protect the record if a witness volunteers damaging, inadmissible information without a question being posed or if the witness makes a non-responsive answer to a proper question or testifies on direct but is unavailable for cross-examination for some reason.

Whether a lawyer should make the motion to strike and request an instruction to disregard is subject to the same tactical considerations as whether the lawyer should object to evidence in the first instance. When jurors have already heard the information, there is the added consideration that a motion to strike and an instruction from the judge to disregard will only emphasize the information and ensure that the jurors will not forget it. The more prejudicial the information, the more likely the lawyer will want to preserve the point for appeal and will move to strike and for an instruction to the jury to disregard.

In some cases, the information may be so prejudicial that the lawyer will consider moving for a mistrial. In deciding whether this is a wise course of action, the lawyer must analyze, among other things, whether the case will try better a second time, whether double jeopardy might bar a second trial in a criminal case, how the jurors are likely to decide the case if the judge instructs them to disregard the prejudicial evidence and they take it to heart, and the cost to the client of delay and appeal.

§ 3.04 How to Phrase an Objection

It is impossible to present a formula that will work in every courtroom for all objections. Much depends upon the particular judge. When preparing a case to be tried before an unfamiliar judge, the attorney should try to learn the unwritten customs of the trial judge by talking to other lawyers or by sitting in the courtroom. Knowing the judge informs the lawyer whether the judge is likely to rule on a general objection or will require articulation of a specific basis. If the judge requires a specific basis, the lawyer will learn whether the objection may be expressed by description or whether a rule number is required. In courts where the judge prefers a description, the lawyer will learn whether the judge expects a short legal description, such as "hearsay" or "document has not been properly authenticated," or will allow longer objections aimed at letting the jurors know why the particular question is "unfair."

For example, the phrase "Objection, Your Honor, the question calls for a hearsay response, depriving the jurors of the opportunity to hear the truth from the person who actually made the observation" tells the jurors more about the reason for the lawyer's objection than "Objection, hearsay." Some judges will not allow the lawyer to justify the objection to the jurors[24] for fear that the justification will persuade the jurors not to consider a type of evidence that the law of evidence entitles them to consider. The opposing view is that, without at least a brief explanation, the jurors may resent the objection itself because they think the lawyer is trying to hide something from them.[25] Although no two judges treat evidence issues in precisely the same fashion, the language of the courtroom has developed some general conventions of articulation that will work in most situations.

A lawyer who, upon hearing an objectionable question, stands and says, "Objection, Your Honor," and then states the precise reason for the objection, such as "hearsay," "leading," "calls for a narrative response," and the like will be on safe ground in most courtrooms. Anything less specific runs the risk of not preserving the objection for appeal. Rule 103 requires that if the ruling admits evidence, the objecting party must, on the record, make a timely objection or move to strike, and state the specific ground, unless the ground is apparent from the context. The requirement of more than a general objection to preserve the matter for appeal has nearly made extinct the old practice of forbidding lawyers to say anything more than "objection" unless asked to give a reason by the judge.[26] Because general objections will not preserve the issue for appeal, virtually all judges allow an objecting lawyer to articulate the specific reason.

Some reasons often used by lawyers are insufficient to preserve an issue for appeal. They are merely general objections, even though the lawyer has said something more than just "objection." The time-honored objection "irrelevant, immaterial and incompetent," despite its length, remains a general objection that is insufficient to

---

[24] *See* United States v. Galin, 222 F.3d 1123 (9th Cir. 2000); United States v. Valenzuela, 17 F.3d 397 (9th Cir. 1994); Auscape Int'l v. Nat'l Geographic Soc'y, 2002 WL 31014829 (S.D.N.Y. 2002); *see also* 1 McCormick on Evidence § 52 at 366 (Kenneth S. Broun ed., 7th ed. 2013) (noting that trial judges will accept "a short adjective, adverb, or phrase" which signals to the jury the substantive ground of the objection, but that lengthy explanations, called "speaking" objections, are not tolerated).

[25] *See* 1 McCormick on Evidence § 52 (Kenneth S. Broun gen ed., 7th ed. 2013).

[26] *See, e.g.,* United States v. Yeager, 331 F.3d 1216, 1223 (11th Cir. 2003).

preserve error, except when the only objection is that the evidence is irrelevant under Rule 402.[27]

Even though a general objection usually will not preserve a matter for appeal, this does not mean that a lawyer should never lodge a general objection. When a lawyer hears a question that leads to dubious evidence, but cannot think of the specific ground for objection, a general objection is better than nothing at all. "Objection" alone, or "objection" followed by a stock phrase such as "prejudicial," "no foundation," "not a proper question," or even "that can't be asked," will preserve the point for appeal if the appellate court finds that, in the language of Rule 103(a)(1)(B), the specific ground is "apparent from the context."[28] Moreover, the general objection may cause the evidence to be excluded at trial, because the trial judge may know the specific ground for the objection, even if the objecting lawyer does not. The judge's exclusion of the evidence will be upheld on appeal if there was any ground to support it.[29] Ironically, when the general objection is sustained at trial, the objecting lawyer may be in a better position on appeal than if a specific objection had been made on the wrong ground and sustained by the judge.[30]

When a general objection is made and sustained, the attorney offering the evidence should consider asking that the ground for objection be specified. This is particularly true when the lawyer is unsure how to proceed to get the testimony into evidence in the face of the objection. Many objections can be obviated by changing the form of the question or by bringing out the evidence in another fashion. Inexperienced lawyers, however, sometimes give up from confusion or embarrassment and lose the benefit of admissible testimony because of problems with the form in which it is being elicited. In such cases, the lawyer should *not* issue the request for clarification as a challenge to the trial judge ("Judge, why specifically did you sustain the objection?"), but should respectfully ask the court's help.

Example

Requesting that counsel give a specific ground.

Proponent: Dr. Green, when did you first see the patient?

Witness: [Refers to notes before answering.]

Opponent: Objection.

---

27 1 WEINSTEIN'S FEDERAL EVIDENCE § 103.12[1] (John M. McLaughlin ed., 2d ed. 2014); *see, e.g.*, United States v. Mejia, 909 F.2d 242, 246 (7th Cir. 1990).

28 *But see* United States v. Diaz, 300 F.3d 66, 75 (1st Cir. 2002) (holding "Objection, *Daubert*" insufficient to apprise District Court to which of "an array of expert witness issues" counsel was referring where "*Daubert*" requires court to look to Rule 702, which includes "qualifications of the witness, the relevance of the proffered testimony, the adequacy of the facts or data underlying an opinion, the scientific reliability of the witness's methodology, and the reliability of the witness's application of that methodology to the facts."); United States v. Moore, 923 F.2d 910, 914–15 (1st Cir. 1991) ("merely uttering word 'foundation' was insufficient objection to introduction of computer records that defendant contended on appeal were inadmissible under Fed. R. Evid. 803(6) because government's foundation evidence did not indicate sufficient trustworthiness.").

29 Jodoin v. Toyota Motor Corp., 284 F.3d 272 (1st Cir. 2002); Reddin v. Robinson Prop. Group, 239 F.3d 756 (5th Cir. 2001); Pittman v. ANR Freight Sys., 47 Fed. Appx. 266 (6th Cir. 2002); Gee v. Shepherd, 210 F.3d 389 (10th Cir. 2000); Killgore v. Agtrans, Inc., 208 F.3d 226 (10th Cir. 2000).

30 Although an objection sustained on the wrong ground, when a proper ground exists, will not be reversed on appeal in most cases, commentators have suggested the result might be different if the proponent of the evidence could have cured the problem upon a proper objection, had it been made. *See* EDMUND M. MORGAN, BASIC PROBLEMS OF STATE AND FEDERAL EVIDENCE 48 (5th ed. 1976); 1 MCCORMICK ON EVIDENCE § 52 at 363 (Kenneth S. Broun ed., 7th ed. 2013).

Judge: Sustained.

Proponent: [Confused] Your Honor, may I request that counsel state a specific ground for objection, so that I can ask the question in a proper form?

Judge: What is the basis for the objection?

Opponent: No foundation.

Proponent: Your Honor, that is still a general objection. Counsel should specify what type of foundational objection is being made.

Opponent: No foundation has been laid for the witness's use of the notes to refresh memory or as past recollection recorded.

Asking the trial judge for help.

Proponent: Mr. Green, would you indicate on the diagram where you were standing at the time of the collision?

Opponent: Objection, no foundation.

Judge: Sustained.

Proponent: [Having been stymied in this fashion on several similar questions] Your Honor, may I approach the bench?

Judge: Yes.

Proponent: Your Honor, I am having problems here. I think that the witness's testimony would be admissible if I could put the questions in the proper form. Could you give me some guidance about how to proceed? [Or simply, "Could you give me some help here, judge?"]

The best words to articulate various specific grounds for objections may not be susceptible to formula, but words should be chosen in light of the two rationales for requiring specificity. Specificity in the objection both allows the judge to make an intelligent ruling and provides the proponent of the evidence with an opportunity to cure the defect.

In jurisdictions in which the rules of evidence have been codified, the requirement of specificity can often be met by referring to rule numbers.[31] This is particularly true when there is no universally recognized catch phrase that describes the objection.

---

[31] *See* Jack Pope & Charles E. Hampton, *Presenting and Excluding Evidence*, 9 TEX. TECH L. REV. 403 (1978). Even when rule numbers would be more precise, use of them is not required to preserve error. "Any expression which pointedly discloses the vulnerable quality of the proof or the character of the incompetency is sufficient. . . . [However,] care must be taken that the objection strikes at the very heart of the infirmity." *Id.* at 445. *See also* Mason Ladd, *Objections, Motions and Foundation Testimony*, 43 CORNELL L. REV. 543, 550–51 (1958). *But see* United States v. David, 96 F.3d 1477, 1480 (D.C. Cir. 1996) (Federal rules "therefore, do not require a pinpoint citation to a provision of the Rules or relevant precedent for every objection; what they do require is enough specificity to alert the district court and opposing counsel to the basis for the objection.").

Examples

"Objection, the question asks about statements made during mediation designed to reach a compromised settlement. Those are excluded under Rule 408."

"Objection, Rule 407. That change was a subsequent remedial measure."

"Objection, Rule 403. Prejudicial, confusing, and a waste of time."

In other instances, the words describing the objection may be so familiar as to render reference to the rule number superfluous or pedantic.

"Objection, hearsay." [No need to refer to Rule 802.]

"Objection, attorney-client privilege." [No point in referring to Rule 501.]

When evidence is admissible in part and objectionable in part—for example, when the medical history portion of a hospital record is admissible, but the portion of the history that contains the plaintiff's description of the accident is not—the objecting lawyer must identify the portion of the offered or expected testimony that is objectionable. If the ground for objection is inapplicable to the entire statement or document, the court may overrule the objection.[32]

In many instances, multiple grounds for objection exist regarding a single item of evidence. The objecting lawyer should raise *all* legal grounds that apply. To make the grounds clear for the judge and to avoid confusion in the record, the grounds can be numbered as they are stated. Identifying multiple grounds not only avoids the risk of choosing the wrong ground, but may result in the judge being persuaded by one more than another.

A lawyer should enumerate all specific grounds to ensure preserving the objection on appeal. An objection that specifies the wrong ground is as bad as an insufficient general objection. If the trial judge overrules the objection on the specific ground stated, the appellate court will affirm, even if the evidence would be excludable on other grounds, unless that other ground is plain from the context.[33]

§ 3.05 Timing of Objections

The most perplexing problem for the lawyer who is learning the language of the courtroom is mastering the speed with which it must be spoken. If the lawyer does not spot the evidence issue as the question is asked and voice the objection in that brief pause between question and answer, the law of evidence might have little effect. Courts have held that objections raised after the answer is given are inadequate unless the answer came so quickly that an objection could not possibly be interposed.[34] Some trial judges are strict about requiring the objection before the answer, at least when the objection concerns a matter of form.

---

[32] *See, e.g.*, United States v. Ball, 35 F.3d 572 (9th Cir. 1994); United States v. Holland, 880 F.2d 1091, 1094 (9th Cir. 1989) (defendant's blanket objection to admission of tape, parts of which were admissible, does not preserve objection to court's failure to redact tape and admit only those parts which were relevant where defense had not made distinction).

[33] United States v. Evans, 883 F.2d 496, 499 (6th Cir. 1989); United States v. Sandifer, 188 F.3d 992, 995 (8th Cir. 1999); United States v. Johnson, 722 F.2d 407, 409 (8th Cir. 1983); Ralston v. Plogger, 476 N.E.2d 1378, 1384 (Ill. App. 1985). See **§ 3.15** (discussing "plain error").

[34] 1 McCormick on Evidence § 52 at 350 (Kenneth S. Broun ed., 7th ed. 2013).

Example

Proponent:	Did Mr. Brown's vehicle cross the centerline?
Witness:	Yes.
Opponent:	Objection, leading question.
Judge:	Asked and answered, counsel. Next question.

Despite the best efforts of the objecting lawyer and the judge, jurors may hear a witness's inadmissible testimony before the operation of the law of evidence can avoid the problem. The witness might offer testimony without a question being posed. The witness might answer so quickly that there is no time to interpose an objection. The basis for an objection might not be apparent in the question and become obvious only with the witness's answer. The witness might respond to an unobjectionable question with a non-responsive answer. The witness might respond to the question, despite a timely objection, before the judge has an opportunity to rule. The judge might sustain an objection, but the witness might answer anyway.

To preserve the point for appeal in any of these situations, the lawyer must make sure the objection is on the record and must move to strike the testimony and request an instruction to the jurors to disregard it. To be sure, the motion to strike and to give an instruction to disregard might not actually cure the harm. It might even aggravate it by calling attention to the matter. But if the lawyer believes that the client's cause will be better served by preserving the point for appeal, the lawyer must make the motion.

Occasionally, a lawyer anticipates objectionable evidence and wants to interpose the objection immediately to avoid any danger that the jurors will hear the prejudicial and inadmissible information. Some trial judges will treat objections to preliminary questions as premature. For instance, if the examiner asks whether the witness has an opinion and the other lawyer objects because the opinion will be inadmissible, the trial judge might treat the objection as untimely until the witness has actually been asked to state the opinion. Similarly, some trial judges treat objections to questions about conversations as premature until the witness has actually been asked to state the contents of the conversation. If the court takes this tack, the objecting lawyer should be careful to renew the objection in order to exclude the evidence. The problem might not be with the nature of the objection, but only with its timing.

Example

Prosecutor:	Did you have a conversation with the victim?
Defense lawyer:	Objection—hearsay.
Judge:	Overruled. He hasn't asked what was said.
Witness:	Yes.
Prosecutor:	What did the victim say?
Defense lawyer:	Objection, hearsay.
Judge:	Sustained.

The defense lawyer might make the early objection to avoid the common problem of a witness who does not respond to the first question with a "yes" or "no," but with a recitation of the conversation. If that is the case, the lawyer should ask the judge who overrules the objection to instruct the witness to answer precisely.

Example

Prosecutor:	Did you have a conversation with the victim?
Defense lawyer:	Objection, hearsay.
Judge:	Overruled. He hasn't asked what was said.
Defense lawyer:	Will Your Honor please caution the witness to answer "yes" or "no" and not to testify to the contents of the conversation?

A similar timing problem can arise when an exhibit is being marked, authenticated, and then offered into evidence. When the proponent begins the process by having the exhibit marked for identification, there is no question posed and, therefore, nothing about which to object. The handling of an exhibit can be cumbersome and can lead to the exhibit being seen by the jurors before it is admitted into evidence. If it is an exhibit the opponent expects to exclude, and even the mention of it might be prejudicial, the lawyer should raise the issue at the earliest possible time.

Example

Proponent:	Your Honor, may I have an exhibit marked for identification?
Judge:	[Assents by nodding the head and pointing toward the clerk who will mark the exhibit.]
Opponent:	May I approach the bench? [Alternatively—"Objection, may I approach?"]

The request for a sidebar conference without the objection is likely to alert the judge to an evidentiary issue surrounding the exhibit. The judge will probably respond by asking the lawyers to approach for a discussion outside the hearing of the jurors. If the judge does not understand or does not agree to the sidebar, the lawyer will have to expand the request and let the judge know specifically that the lawyer wishes to lodge an objection outside of the hearing of the jurors.

An objection to the marking of an exhibit cannot be sustained—even if the judge is not going to allow its admission—because the exhibit must be marked for the record to be complete. The judge may, nevertheless, entertain the argument over admission at the time the exhibit is being marked, particularly if the objection is one that can be settled without the judge first hearing the foundation testimony. By asking for the sidebar conference when the proponent first asks to have the exhibit marked, the objecting lawyer avoids making the objection in front of the jury, is not responsible for squelching the natural anticipation that jurors feel when they are about to see an exhibit, and avoids the jurors seeing the exhibit through inadvertent display.

§ 3.06 Sidebars (Bench Conferences); Excusing the Jury

Rule 103 explicitly encourages lawyers and judges, to the extent practicable, to conduct the trial in such a way as to prevent inadmissible evidence being "suggested to the jury by any means."[35]

Pretrial conferences, which occur even before the jurors are impaneled, and hearings conducted outside the presence of the jurors, which often employ lengthy offers of proof using the question and answer method, prevent jurors from learning information that, ultimately, will be ruled inadmissible. Although many judges try to encourage settling as many evidence issues as possible in pretrial conferences, particularly issues surrounding tangible exhibits, matters always arise at trial that should be discussed outside the presence of the jurors.

The sidebar (or bench) conference is still the most common device employed to further the ends of Rule 103. Lawyers may ask for a sidebar at any time, but granting the request is within the judge's discretion. Refusal to allow a sidebar is unlikely to be cause for a reversal unless a party is denied the opportunity to make an offer of proof or the jurors receive information so prejudicial that the party requesting the sidebar is denied a fair trial as a result.[36] When a lawyer wants a sidebar conference outside the hearing of the jurors to make an objection, to argue about an objection, or to make an offer of proof regarding evidence that the judge has ruled inadmissible, the lawyer requests a hearing. "Sidebar, Your Honor?" "May we approach?" "May we approach the bench, Your Honor?" "Bench conference, Your Honor?" are various ways a lawyer might signal the judge that the lawyer wishes to discuss a matter outside of the hearing of the jurors without excusing the jurors from the courtroom.

The sidebar can be an effective device for keeping matters from the jurors. The corresponding problem for the trial lawyer, and for the judge to some extent, is that the jurors sit around bored—and maybe resentful about being left out—while the lawyers and the judge hash out evidence law problems. Judges, aware of jurors' impatience with discussions in their presence to which they are not privy, do not grant every request for a sidebar. Generalization about how any individual judge will handle requests for a sidebar is impossible, but there are some general clues to the exercise of judicial discretion. Lawyers who wish to argue every objection, irrespective of the importance of the proposed evidence or the rectitude of the argument, are unlikely to be welcome at the bench when the pattern becomes apparent. When a real dispute about evidence is apparent, sidebars will almost always be granted.

"Offer of proof, Your Honor?" will almost always result in a sidebar conference, because it is specifically mentioned in Rule 103. If the offer is to be made by questioning a witness, the jurors will be excused, but often the offer can be made by narrative at the bench, without the disruption of removing the jurors from the courtroom.

When a question asks about character, criminal convictions, specific acts, or other matters that might have a prejudicial effect if even the nature of the objection is heard by the jurors, the court will likely grant a request for a sidebar following an objection that is made without stating a specific ground. Similarly, when the judge can tell from

---

[35] FED. R. EVID. 103(d).

[36] FED. R. EVID. 104(c) provides: "The court must conduct any hearing on a preliminary question so that the jury cannot hear it if: (1) the hearing involves the admissibility of a confession; (2) a defendant in a criminal case is a witness and so requests; or (3) justice so requires." *See* **§ 3.11**.

the context of a request for a sidebar that the articulation of an objection and a ruling might cause the jurors to give extraordinary weight to evidence they have heard or to speculate about excluded evidence, the request is likely to be granted.

During sidebar conferences, whether requested by the lawyers or initiated by the judge, the lawyer should be sure that the conference is conducted in the kind of hushed tones that will not be heard by the jurors *and that the conference is on the record*. Without the court reporter present to record the bench conference, anything said or done at the conference is beyond appellate review.

§ 3.07 Continuing Objections

The requirement that objections be specific, both as to the legal grounds and to the part of the evidence objected to, may require a lawyer to object to each one of a series of questions posed to a witness on the same topic. Because such repeated objections can antagonize both judge and jury, the objecting lawyer might want to request a continuing objection to a line of questioning.

When the objection is first raised and overruled by the judge, the lawyer may ask for a continuing objection that will obviate the constant need to interrupt the examination to preserve the issue for appeal.

Example

Proponent:	How many incidents did you discuss with the deceased?
Witness:	Seven.
Proponent:	Do you remember what the deceased said about the incident of March 2, 1998?
Witness:	Yes.
Proponent:	What did the deceased say about that incident?
Opponent:	Objection, hearsay.
Judge:	Overruled.
Opponent:	Your Honor, if counsel is going to ask what the deceased said about all seven encounters, may I have a continuing hearsay objection to what the deceased said?
Judge:	You may.

The lawyer asking for the continuing objection must obtain the judge's consent on the record in order for the continuing objection to preserve the issue for appeal.

If the testimony that is the subject of a continuing objection is likely to be crucial to the outcome, the lawyer should take care in relying upon a continuing objection. If the ground for objection to a later question differs from the ground upon which the continuing objection is granted, the issue for the later question will not be preserved because the continuing objection will not have stated the proper specific ground for exclusion.

It is often difficult to determine when the continuing objection should end, and differences of opinion on that point could result in the failure to preserve error. At the end of a witness's testimony for which a continuing objection has been taken, the objecting lawyer should renew the objection for the record, move to strike the entire line of testimony, and move to have the jurors instructed to disregard it.

§ 3.08 Voir Dire to Lay the Foundation for an Objection

There will be times when a lawyer believes that certain testimony will be improper, that the foundation is lacking for an exhibit, or that a witness is not qualified to testify, but that the basis for the objection is not apparent from the questions posed by the direct examiner. When such a circumstance first becomes apparent to the lawyer, it is appropriate to object and to ask permission of the court to "take the witness on voir dire." In doing so, the objecting lawyer asks the judge to interrupt the direct examination and to allow a limited cross-examination for the purpose of laying the foundation for the objection. Occasionally, the lawyer will ask or the judge may prefer that the voir dire is conducted outside the hearing of the jurors, but more often, the jurors will hear the examination. A typical example is when a proponent has apparently qualified a witness as an expert, and the objecting lawyer has additional information that might change the judge's willingness to accept the witness as an expert in the field designated by the direct examiner.

Example

Proponent:	Your Honor, the plaintiff submits that Dr. Wissard is qualified as an expert in the design and operation of radial tires.
Opponent:	Objection, Your Honor. May I take the witness on voir dire?
Judge:	You may.
Opponent:	Dr. Wissard, isn't it true that your Ph.D. is from Western Atlantic University?
Witness:	Yes.
Opponent:	Western Atlantic University is a correspondence school located above a hardware store, isn't that right?
Witness:	Well, yes. But it is a good school.
Opponent:	Dr. Wissard, you have never designed a radial tire, have you?
Witness:	No.
Opponent:	Dr. Wissard, you have never run tests comparing the operation of the defendant's radial tires to those of other manufacturers, have you?
Witness:	No. But I have read the literature.
Opponent:	Your Honor, the defense believes that Dr. Wissard is not qualified as an expert in the design and operation of radial tires and objects to the court accepting him as an expert witness in that field.

The judge might disqualify the witness, believing that the points raised in the voir dire disqualify the witness from testifying to an expert opinion. On the other hand, the judge might believe that the points raised on voir dire affect the weight of the expert's testimony but are insufficient to disqualify the witness as an expert. In the latter case, the judge is likely to say something like: "Counsel, the issues you have raised concerning the witness's education and experience go to weight. You may argue them to the jurors, but the court accepts Dr. Wissard as an expert in the design and operation of radial tires."

§ 3.09 Limiting Instructions [FRE 105]

Sometimes an out-of-court statement can be admissible for one purpose but not for another.[37] A portion of an exhibit may be admissible while other portions are not. Where there are multiple parties on one side, evidence may be admissible against one party, but not against another.[38] Valid objections to evidence will often be overruled because the evidence is admissible in part or for a limited purpose.[39] The proponent should be sure to state the admissible purpose for which such evidence is offered unless it is perfectly obvious.[40]

Likewise, the objecting lawyer often must take steps to prevent jurors from using the evidence improperly. A motion for a limiting instruction might be the only precaution available to the lawyer who is otherwise unable to persuade the judge to exclude the information.[41] The request for a limiting instruction must be timely and must specifically identify the portions of the testimony to be limited.[42] Failure to request the limiting instruction will result in forfeiture of the right to assert error in the instructions on appeal.[43] The court may also issue limiting instructions sua sponte when the judge finds them necessary.[44]

Many lawyers believe that an instruction to use something for one purpose and not for another is difficult to state and perhaps more difficult to follow. The lawyer who asks for a limiting instruction should be prepared to say something in closing argument to

---

[37] *See generally* DAVID P. LEONARD, THE NEW WIGMORE: SELECTED RULES OF LIMITED ADMISSIBILITY § 1.6.1 (rev. ed. 2002).

[38] *See id.*, § 1.6.4.

[39] *See* **§ 1.05**.

[40] *See* 1 MCCORMICK ON EVIDENCE § 59 at 407 n.3 (Kenneth S. Broun ed., 7th ed. 2013) ("It seems, however, that the proponent, to complain of the judge's exclusion of evidence inadmissible in one aspect, must have stated the purpose for which it is competent, unless the admissible purpose is plainly apparent") (citations omitted).

[41] Evidence that is admissible for one purpose, but not for another, may be excluded if the risk of unfair prejudice resulting from the inadmissible purpose substantially outweighs the probative value of the evidence for the admissible purpose. FED. R. EVID. 403. *See* **§ 5.03**. Some exhibits can have the inadmissible information redacted without ruining the proper use of the exhibit. When evidence is admissible against one party but not another, the evidence might be so prejudicial that the party against whom it is not admissible will be entitled to a severance, leading to separate trials.

[42] *See* FED. R. EVID. 103(a)(1); United States v. Dozier, 672 F.2d 531, 543 (5th Cir. 1982) ("If the defense, having lost the argument on general admissibility, desired a more precise limiting instruction on the extent to which the jury could consider such testimony, it could, and should, have requested one"); United States v. Thirion, 813 F.2d 146, 155–56 (8th Cir. 1987) (denying request where defendant did not specifically identify portion of testimony to be limited and where request was not specific or timely).

[43] Roth v. Black & Decker, United States, Inc., 737 F.2d 779, 782–83 (8th Cir. 1984) ("Black & Decker did not request a limiting instruction which may have been necessary under Rule 105 and 403 of the Federal Rules of Evidence. Not having requested such an instruction, Black & Decker cannot now claim that the district court erred") (citation omitted). Some courts have narrowed this requirement at times by finding that a failure to issue the requested limiting instruction was harmless error. *See, e.g.*, Lubbock Feed Lots, Inc. v. Iowa Beef Processors, 630 F.2d 250, 265–66 (5th Cir. 1980) (finding harmless error for court to have failed to give limiting instruction).

[44] *See* DAVID P. LEONARD, THE NEW WIGMORE: SELECTED RULES OF LIMITED ADMISSIBILITY § 1.11.1 (rev. ed. 2002).

turn the emphasis to the lawyer's advantage. If no such argument is apparent to the lawyer, a motion for a limiting instruction might hurt more than it will help. If the lawyer believes the jurors are more likely to heed the judge's instruction than to be influenced by the emphasis that the specific instruction might give to the evidence, the lawyer should make the motion as soon as the evidence is presented. The attorney should restate the motion at the completion of the case to insure inclusion of the instruction in the judge's instructions to the jurors.

Example

Cross-examiner:	Isn't it true that you previously said the light was green for the Chevrolet?
Direct examiner:	Objection, hearsay.
Cross-examiner:	I am not using the statement for its truth your Honor, only to impeach an inconsistent witness.
Judge:	Overruled.
Direct examiner:	Your Honor, I request an instruction to the jurors regarding the limited use of the witness's answer.
Judge:	Members of the jury: An out of court statement by a witness is not admissible in evidence to prove the truth of the statement. It may, however, be admitted as it bears on the credibility of the witness. You may consider the answer you hear from the witness only as it bears on the witness's credibility.
Cross-examiner:	You may answer.
Witness:	Yes.

The judge might well wait until after the witness's answer to give the limiting instruction. The instruction at the end of the trial might be a general admonition to use evidence only for the specific purpose for which it was admitted.

§ 3.10 Offers of Proof

Rule 103(a)(2) provides for offers of proof. When an objection to evidence is sustained, the issue will not be preserved for appeal by the proponent unless the proponent made the court aware of the substance of the evidence by offer or if the substance was apparent from the context. Rulings sustaining objections to the form of the question or lack of foundation do not call for an offer of proof, because the examiner should simply proceed by asking the question in a different fashion or by presenting (when possible) the additional information that will complete the foundation. An offer of proof is needed only when the judge sustains an objection excluding evidence and the lawyer cannot cure the problem.

An offer of proof furthers two of the examiner's goals. First, it complies with Rule 103(a)(2), making it possible for an appellate court to evaluate the effect of the exclusion of the evidence on the proponent's case and, therefore, may avoid the common appellate response that the trial judge's error does not justify reversal because the error was harmless.[45] Second, a solid demonstration of the importance of the evidence to the proponent's case may persuade the trial judge to reconsider the ruling and admit the evidence. Even if the context gives the trial judge sufficient knowledge of the substance of the evidence to preserve the point for appeal,[46] the proponent of the evidence might wish to make an offer of proof, in hopes that the judge will be persuaded to reverse the ruling and admit the evidence.

There are two usual forms of offer of proof that comply with the Rule 103(d) mandate to keep inadmissible evidence away from the jurors. First is the narrative form, in which the lawyer offering the evidence describes what the testimony would be, is usually conducted at sidebar. Second is the question and answer form, in which the proponent actually puts the witness on the stand and conducts the proposed examination, is usually conducted in the courtroom after the jurors have been excused.

Before making any offer of proof, the proponent should be certain of the grounds for the objection to ensure that they are addressed in the offer. If the specific ground is not clear, or if the court has sustained a general objection, the proponent should request the court to ask objecting counsel to state the specific grounds.[47]

The showing required in an offer of proof to persuade a trial judge to admit the evidence is the same as is needed to persuade an appellate court to reverse if the trial judge does not admit the evidence. The proponent must show:

That the examiner posed a pertinent question to a witness who could have provided an answer;

What the answer would have been;[48]

How the testimony would support the proponent's case; and

Why the evidence should be admitted notwithstanding the objection.[49]

The offer of proof must be precise. Where more than one piece of testimony or more than one tangible item are the subjects of an offer, the lawyer must handle each piece as if it were a separate offer of proof. If the lawyer does not differentiate the bases and arguments for each piece, there is a risk of losing the point on appeal, even though some of the evidence should have been admitted.[50]

When the proponent of excluded evidence makes an offer of proof at sidebar, ordinarily that lawyer should ask the judge to excuse the witness, and the opposing

---

45 *See* United States v. Jackson, 208 F.3d 633 (7th Cir. 2000); United States v. Peak, 856 F.2d 825 (7th Cir. 1988); United States v. Adams, 271 F.3d 1236, 1241–43 (10th Cir. 2001).

46 FED. R. EVID. 103 advisory committee's note. *See also* United States v. Rettenberger, 344 F.3d 702, 706 (7th Cir. 2003) ("An offer of proof is unnecessary if the substance of the excluded testimony may be found in the record.").

47 *See* **§ 3.04**.

48 *See, e.g.*, Phillips v. Hillcrest Med. Ctr., 244 F.3d 790 (10th Cir. 2001); Mason v. Southern Ill. Univ. at Carbondale, 233 F.3d 1036 (7th Cir. 2000).

49 The lawyer should state all grounds on which the evidence is admissible. This is particularly important when dealing with hearsay objections. *See* Huff v. White Motor Corp., 609 F.2d 286, 290 (7th Cir. 1979) (holding that, after hearsay objection, proponent should have alerted trial court to statement against interest exception in order to preserve error on that ground); *see also* Shepard v. United States, 290 U.S. 96 (1933) (leading case stating that all possible exceptions to hearsay doctrine should be interposed in defending against objection lest appellate court decline to review exceptions other than one argued at trial).

50 For a complete treatment of offers of proof for the trial lawyer, *see* ROGER C. PARK, TRIAL OBJECTIONS HANDBOOK 1.9–.14 (2d ed. 2009).

lawyer should insist on it. In the event the offer persuades the judge to admit the evidence, the witness will not have heard the offer and will not be able to tailor the testimony to be consistent with the offer. When a cross-examiner makes an offer of proof, it is even more important that the lawyers ensure that the witness is excused so that the offer does not tip the witness to the direction of the cross-examination.

Example

Defense lawyer:	What did she say she saw?
Plaintiff lawyer:	Objection, Your Honor, hearsay.
Judge:	Sustained.
Defense lawyer:	Offer of proof, Your Honor.
Judge:	Approach.
Defense lawyer:	[At sidebar, after the plaintiff's lawyer has requested that the judge ask the witness to stand down from the witness chair so the offer of proof is not overheard.] Your Honor, if allowed to answer the question about what she heard, the words used by the man who saw the accident will demonstrate why the testimony is admissible under two different exceptions to the rule against hearsay. If allowed, the witness will testify that the man said, "Oh my God, my God. Did you see that? Did you see that? That blue car sped right through that red light and slammed into the white car. Is anybody hurt? What should we do? Can we call someone? Oh my God." The words, themselves, indicate that the man was very excited and that the statement was made immediately after he saw the accident. That makes the statement admissible under two separate exceptions to the hearsay rule: the excited utterance exception and the present sense impression exception. This testimony is very probative in showing that the plaintiff here, not the defendant, caused this accident.[51]

In the rare case in which a trial judge will not allow an offer of proof to be made, error will be preserved if the lawyer puts the offer of proof in writing and requests that it be entered into the record before the close of trial.

---

[51] An advocate may be tempted to emphasize that party's *need* for the evidence. For example, the advocate in the example might say, "This testimony is the only available evidence we have to demonstrate that the plaintiff caused the accident." This might be rhetorically effective for some judges, but it is problematic in two respects: (1) admissibility rules generally do not have an exception for evidence that *a party needs in order to win*, which is entirely different from what the fact-finder needs to decide the case; and (2) by assumption, the judge has ruled against the offered evidence, so if the judge does not change that decision because of the offer of proof, the proponent's argument can backfire by inviting a motion from the opponent for a directed verdict.

§ 3.11 Preliminary Questions of Fact [FRE 104]

The trial judge, of course, must rule on objections to the admission of evidence. Often such objections raise only an issue of law. But what does the judge do when a lawyer raises an objection that poses a question of fact? Many rules excluding evidence and many exceptions to those rules depend on factual predicates. For example, an out-of-court non-verbal utterance is not hearsay, under the federal rules, unless the actor intended to assert something.[52] That intent is a question of fact. Similarly, the exception to the hearsay rule for "present sense impressions" depends on whether the out-of-court utterance was a "statement describing or explaining an event or condition, made while or immediately after the declarant perceived it."[53] The applicability of the exception can also raise questions of fact.

Rule 104(a): The Standard Framework

Rule 104(a) obligates the judge to decide whether evidence that is challenged by one of the lawyers is admissible, and this includes deciding factual questions that determine the applicability of some rule of exclusion or exception thereto. Rule 104(a) specifies that, in deciding such factual questions, the judge is not bound by the rules of evidence, except for privileges. Although Rule 104 is silent on the point, it is now established by common-law precedent interpreting Rule 104 that the "preponderance of the evidence" standard of proof applies to such factual questions.[54] For example, if the question is whether non-verbal conduct is hearsay, the judge determines, by a preponderance of the evidence, whether the actor intended to make an assertion.[55] And if the question is whether a witness is qualified to testify as an expert, the judge hears the qualifications of the witness, considers any discrediting or qualifying information from the opponent, and then decides whether the witness is more likely than not an expert. The qualification of witnesses, the existence of a privilege, the voluntariness of a confession, and the applicability of a hearsay exception are typical questions decided by the trial judge under Rule 104(a).

Example

The plaintiff sues the defendant for speeding, running a red light, and smashing his blue Miata sports car into the plaintiff's car. The defendant admits being involved in the accident, but denies speeding and running the red light. The plaintiff calls a witness who was a back seat passenger in another car driving along the same road the defendant was traveling. The plaintiff has just established that about two minutes before the accident, the passenger in the front seat of the car said something.

Plaintiff's lawyer: What did he say?

Defense lawyer: Objection, hearsay.

Plaintiff's lawyer: Your honor, may we approach?

---

[52] *See* FED. R. EVID. 801(a)–(c).

[53] *See* FED. R. EVID. 803(1).

[54] *See* Bourjaily v. United States, 483 U.S. 171 (1987).

[55] *See* **§ 14.02**.

> [At sidebar] The witness will say that the passenger in the front seat said: "That sports car just passed us going about 90." It is within the present sense impression exception to the rule against hearsay.

The passenger's statement is hearsay—an out-of-court statement offered to prove the truth of what is asserted in the statement—and is inadmissible unless it qualifies under the exception to the rule against hearsay for which the plaintiff's lawyer has argued. Under Rule 104(a), the judge determines whether the statement fits within the exception.

To admit the passenger's statement as a present sense impression, the judge must find as a preliminary fact that it was "a statement describing . . . an event . . . made while or immediately after the declarant perceived it."[56] Thus, when the judge is satisfied with what the parties have offered on the point, the judge will admit the statement upon finding it is more likely than not that the preliminary facts required for a present sense impression exist. The judge will exclude the statement upon finding it more likely than not that those preliminary facts do not exist. The judge, rather than the jury, decides these facts.

The judge finds a preliminary fact under Rule 104(a) even in cases where the jurors will ultimately consider the same question. Moreover, the judge applies the "more likely than not" standard even in those cases in which the jurors will decide the same question by applying a more rigorous standard. For example, in a criminal conspiracy prosecution the jury must decide beyond a reasonable doubt whether the defendant was a conspirator. The judge, however, must determine whether a conspiracy existed to decide whether a statement made by another constitutes an admission by a co-conspirator of a party. If the judge finds it more likely than not that the person making the statement was actually a co-conspirator,[57] then that statement will be admitted as part of the evidence for the jury's determination of whether a criminal conspiracy existed. The judge does not inform the jury of his determination and therefore avoids contaminating the jury's deliberation.

Why is the judge involved in this preliminary fact-finding under Rule 104(a)? In the car accident example, why should not the judge admit the statement and then instruct the jurors: "If you find that the passenger's statement was describing an event as it was happening, you may consider the statement in deciding the case; if you do not find this preliminary fact, you must decide the case without considering the passenger's statement"?

Rule 104(a) tasks this finding of preliminary facts to the judge to safeguard the operation of the rules of evidence. Many of these rules exist because we fear that jurors will not correctly process certain information or because we must supervise the parties' decisions about what to present. Asking the jurors to find such preliminary facts would place them in an untenable position. Jurors do they have the legal background to conduct

---

56 FED. R. EVID. 803(1). *See* **§ 16.03**.

57 FED. R. EVID. 801(d)(2)(E). *See, e.g.*, United States v. Barksdale-Contreras, 972 F.2d 111 (5th Cir. 1992) (holding that statements of co-conspirators were admissible even though defendant was acquitted of conspiracy, given different standards applicable to admissibility and guilt determinations); United States v. Elam, 678 F.2d 1234 (5th Cir. 1982) (noting that where trial judge determines that requisite foundation established for introduction of conspirator statements, no jury instruction is necessary and none should be given; jury should not know that judge has decided issue of conspiracy for purposes of evidence, lest jury think that issue has been finally decided for all other purposes as well).

such supervision of parties' choices. Moreover, if they found more likely than not that the preliminary facts did not exist, they would have to ignore relevant evidence they had already heard. Asking non-lawyers to compartmentalize their thinking in such a way asks too much. The rules of evidence are based on the assumption, in the example above, that jurors will have difficulty following the court's instruction to ignore the passenger's important out-of-court statement, even if they believe more likely than not that the passenger was not describing an ongoing event.

Moreover, Rule 104(a) contemplates that the judge may consider other inadmissible evidence in making the determination of whether the preliminary facts needed for admissibility exist. For instance, in determining whether a conspiracy existed as a preliminary question for the admission of a co-conspirator's statement, otherwise inadmissible evidence, such as hearsay and character evidence, could inform the judge's decision. Again, we hesitate to expose jurors to such inadmissible evidence, which they would then be expected to ignore in deciding the merits of the case.

Given that the judge decides the preliminary fact, the judge is permitted to assess the credibility of witnesses in making that determination. Once evidence has been admitted, however, the jurors alone determine whether the witnesses are credible and, therefore, how much weight, if any, to give to the witness's testimony.[58]

Rule 104(b): Conditional Relevance

Although Rule 104(a) designates the judge as the decision-maker regarding evidence rules, Rule 104(b) creates an exception for what is called "conditional relevance":

> When the relevance of evidence depends on whether a fact exists, proof must be introduced sufficient to support a finding that the fact does exist. The court may admit the proposed evidence on the condition that the proof be introduced later.[59]

In contexts to which this rule applies, the judge should send a question to the jury provided the proponent presents "proof" (that is, evidence) "sufficient to support a finding" of the conditioning fact. The incorporation of "sufficiency" ideas means that the judge must send such evidence to the jury if a reasonable juror could find the fact in question. Although the rule is silent on the point, the Supreme Court has ruled that the contemplated finding by the jury is to be made by the "preponderance of the evidence" standard, even in criminal cases.[60]

The theory underlying Rule 104(b) is that, when the relevance of the evidence depends on the existence of some other fact, the judge involves the jury because the preliminary fact-finding needed—i.e., to determine relevance—usually does not involve the jury in technical admissibility issues or require them to ignore clearly useful information they have already heard. Moreover, to do otherwise—to have the judge make the determination about such preliminary facts—would keep too much useful information from jurors.[61] Despite the plausibility of these points, conditional relevance

---

[58] *See* FED. R. EVID. 104(e).

[59] FED. R. EVID. 104(b).

[60] *See* Huddleston v. United States, 485 U.S. 681, 690 (1988).

[61] FED. R. EVID. 104(b) advisory committee note.

is a difficult concept. Several commentators have questioned its coherence.[62] Though the scholarship in the area is persuasive, it has yet to have much influence on the courts. The following explanation first presents the conventional analysis of conditional relevance as set forth in the Advisory Committee Note to Rule 104(b) and as typically used by the courts. The commentators' critique is then explained.

Example

Plaintiff's lawyer: What did he say?

Defense lawyer: Objection, hearsay.

[At sidebar] Plaintiff's lawyer: The witness will say that the passenger in the front seat said: "That sports car just passed us going about 90." It is admissible as a present sense impression.

Judge: The circumstances establish the preliminary fact that it is more likely than not that the passenger was describing an event as it was being perceived. Present sense impression. The hearsay objection is overruled.

Defense lawyer: It may be a present sense impression, your honor, but it isn't relevant. There is no evidence that the sports car the declarant saw was the defendant's.

The defense lawyer's relevance objection raises a question of "conditional relevance"; if the judge accepts it as presenting such a question, the judge will handle it under 104(b), rather than under 104(a).

The conventional analysis of this example identifies the fact that the speeding sports car belonged to the defendant as the "condition of fact" upon which the relevance of the passenger's statement depends. The thought here is that either (1) the sports car the declarant saw was the defendant's, in which case the testimony is relevant, or (2) the sports car the declarant saw was not the defendant's, in which case the testimony is irrelevant.[63] The jurors can decide which is true without being put in the untenable position of ignoring important information in the event that they do not find the preliminary fact that it was the defendant's sports car. If the jurors do not find that the speeding sports car was the defendant's, they will naturally ignore the passenger's statement. Accordingly, Rule 104(b) requires the judge to overrule the relevance objection and to let the jury decide the existence of the preliminary fact, unless no reasonable jury could (by a preponderance of the evidence) reach such a conclusion. If there is not enough evidence to support a jury finding that it was the defendant's sports

---

[62] *See, e.g.*, Vaughan C. Ball, *The Myth of Conditional Relevancy*, 14 GA. L. REV. 435 (1980); 1 WIGMORE ON EVIDENCE § 14.1 (Tillers rev., 1983). *See also* Ronald J. Allen, *The Myth of Conditional Relevancy*, 25 LOY. L.A. L. REV. 871 (1992). The upshot of this critique is that the doctrine permits judges to exclude evidence that is undeniably relevant and to do so with no coherent guiding principle. While endorsing the critique of the doctrine as articulated, other commentators have shown that the plausibly decided cases purportedly using the conditional relevance rationale can be better explained using other evidence principles, specifically the authority of trial courts to exclude evidence under FED. R. EVID. 403. *See* Dale A. Nance, *Conditional Relevance Reinterpreted*, 70 B.U. L. REV. 447 (1990); Richard D. Friedman, *Conditional Probative Value: Neoclassicism Without Myth*, 93 MICH. L. REV. 439 (1994).

[63] This way of thinking is confused. While it is the case that one or the other fact is true, does it follow that the relevance of the offered testimony depends on making a choice about which is true? If you see the point of that question, then you are on your way to understanding the critique of conditional relevance doctrine that will follow.

car that the passenger saw, the judge will sustain the objection and exclude the statement.

Example Continued

Defense lawyer: Judge, there is not enough evidence "to support a finding"[64] that the car the passenger saw belonged to the defendant.

Judge: I agree. The only evidence that the sports car belonged to the defendant is the coincidence that the accident and the sighting were on the same road. I need more to support a jury finding that it is more likely than not it was the defendant's car the passenger saw.

Plaintiff's lawyer: Your honor, I have another witness who saw the sports car. He was sitting right next to the declarant. Unfortunately, he cannot be here to testify for two days. When he testifies, he will say that the sports car was a blue Miata, driven by a big man with long black hair, both characteristics of the defendant. I ask that you allow the back seat passenger to testify to what the front seat passenger said and allow me to show the relevance—to "connect it up"—when the driver testifies.

Judge: Rules 104(b) and 611(a) give me discretion to allow this testimony now and to withdraw it from the jurors' consideration, if you do not connect it up. Given the flow of the case, I think it is important for this evidence to come out at this time.

[Two days later the driver testifies.]

Plaintiff's lawyer: Did you see the sports car that the passenger said was "going about 90?"

Witness: Yes.

Plaintiff's lawyer: Please describe it.

Witness: It was a blue Miata with a big guy behind the wheel.

Plaintiff's lawyer: Could you see the driver's face?

Witness: No, all I could see was that he was big man with long black hair.

Defense lawyer: Sidebar, your honor?

[At the sidebar]

Defense lawyer: Your honor, I renew my objection that the passenger's statement is not relevant because the fact has not been established that the car was the defendant's. I am prepared to bring in a witness who will testify that he was speeding in his blue Miata on the same road at the same time that the passenger saw the speeding sports car. My client will testify that he was not speeding.

Judge: Let me stop you, counsel. Even if you produce those witnesses, and even if I believe it is more likely than not that the speeding sports car the passenger saw belonged to the other witness, I have to admit the passenger's statement and leave it to the jury to decide whose sports car the passenger saw. There is

---

[64] FED. R. EVID. 104(b).

plenty of evidence to support a jury finding that the passenger saw the defendant's car. It was on the same road as the accident. The car was the same color and make as the defendant's and it was driven by someone the same size and with the same hair color and style as the defendant.

Defense lawyer: But your honor, what about my evidence that there was another car there and my client's testimony that he was not speeding?

Judge: Whether those witnesses—or any witnesses for that matter—are to be believed is the sole province of the jurors. There is enough evidence here, if the jurors believe it, and if they reject any evidence that might lead to a contrary judgment, for the jurors to conclude that it is more likely than not that the car the passenger saw belonged to the defendant. Your relevance objection is overruled. Argue it to the jury.

But what happens if the information suggesting that the car the passenger saw speeding belonged to the defendant was itself not admissible evidence? When the judge makes a 104(a) determination—such as whether the declarant spoke immediately upon perceiving the event so as to qualify for the hearsay exception—the judge can use inadmissible information to make the determination. When the judge is making a 104(b) judgment, the judge is not deciding whether the judge believes, based on whatever information the judge has, that the preliminary fact more likely than not exists. Under 104(b) the judge is deciding whether there is, or will be, evidence "*sufficient to support a finding*" by the jury. Both logic and authority suggest that the judge may *not* use inadmissible evidence in deciding whether there is sufficient evidence to support a jury finding.[65] The judge could not possibly use inadmissible information to make a decision that there is information to "support a jury finding" and then tell the plaintiff's lawyer, who must establish the preliminary fact that the car was the defendant's, to "argue it to the jury." There would be no evidence from which to argue.

That is the conventional analysis. Now consider the critique. First, was defense counsel correct in arguing, at the end of the first excerpt of the example, that there is "no evidence that the sports car the declarant saw was the defendant's"? Isn't the fact that it was a sports car on the same road in the relevant time-frame "some evidence" that it was the defendant's sports car? Not conclusive, for sure; maybe not enough by itself to prove the defendant was speeding. But does it need to be that strong for this line of inquiry to be relevant?[66] Thinking that it does conflates admissibility with sufficiency, does it not? Specifically, why does the jury need to make a "finding" that the two cars were the same? That is not one of the elements of the cause of action. Even if the jury concludes that it is more likely than not the two cars were *not* the same, so long as there is some probability (even if small) that they were the same, that fact is still relevant, so that this line of inquiry is evidence that, together with other evidence, might warrant a finding that defendant drove negligently. Isn't it enough, for this line of inquiry to be relevant, that the two cars *could* have been the same? Moreover, if the testimony at issue

---

[65] *In re* Japanese Elec. Prod. Antitrust Litig., 723 F.2d 238, 285 (3d Cir. 1983), *rev'd on other grounds*, 475 U.S. 574 (1986) ("[T]he evidence required to establish a prima facie case that the evidence is what the proponent claims it to be must itself be admissible."). *See* United States v. Casto, 889 F.2d 562 (5th Cir. 1989); United States v. Blackwell, 694 F.2d 1325 (D.C. Cir. 1982).

[66] A full understanding of the point of this question may not be possible without an appreciation of the generous concept of relevance mandated by the Rules: "Evidence is relevant if: (a) it has any tendency to make a fact more or less probable than it would be without the evidence; and (b) the fact is of consequence in determining the action." FED. R. EVID. 401. *See* **§ 5.01**.

is admissible only if the jury thinks that this probability is strong enough to make a finding that the two cars were the same, should the judge instruct the jury to ignore the testimony if it concludes (by a preponderance of the evidence) that the two cars were not the same? Doesn't that involve counter-intuitive "mental gymnastics" that the doctrine of conditional relevance was supposed to avoid, telling the jurors to ignore evidence that they may reasonably think is relevant? Wouldn't it be better just to say that a court should overrule a relevance objection if the court thinks a reasonable juror could consider the evidence relevant, thus dispensing entirely with the "sufficient to support a finding" idea?[67]

The import of the foregoing critique is that conditional relevance is an incoherent concept and that its invocation creates arbitrary obstacles to the admission of relevant evidence. Moreover, such obstacles can be invoked in virtually any context: one can "create" a conditional relevance problem in any situation merely by focusing on some proposition of fact that, if known to be true, would render proffered evidence irrelevant and then arguing that the proponent must disprove that fact.[68] In the foregoing example, it was the proposition that the two cars were not the same. It might also have been the proposition that the hearsay declarant was suffering from a form of mental disease that caused him to see speeding sports cars that are not there. The list of potential propositions that, if true, would render the evidence irrelevant is practically limitless.

The real question, then, is when and why do judges choose to invoke the doctrine. As to when, aside from the identification of persons and objects illustrated by the example above, the most commonly encountered situation is when proffered testimony tends to show notice to or knowledge by a person, in which case the "condition" considered is whether the person in question was aware of the event that would impart notice or knowledge.[69]

In addition, there are two specific rules (discussed elsewhere) that, according to the federal rules' drafters, instantiate conditional relevance. One is the requirement that a witness testify based on personal knowledge.[70] The other is the requirement that tangible evidence be authenticated or identified.[71] Whether that explanation of these requirements works is debatable, given the difficulties inherent in the logic of conditional relevance. Nevertheless, what is not debatable is that (1) these requirements existed at common law (for whatever reason) before this explanation for them was offered, and (2)

---

67 It is a different issue whether the inquiry about the speeding car is too weakly probative to be worth the time in court to explore it. That might indeed depend on how well the information tends to tie together the speeding car and the defendant's car. But that issue arises under a different rule, the rule that excludes evidence that *is* relevant but that is *insufficiently probative* to be worthwhile. *See* FED. R. EVID. 403, discussed *infra* **§ 5.03**.

68 *See* Dale A. Nance, *Conditional Relevance Reinterpreted*, 70 B.U. L. REV. 447, 449–56 (1990).

69 *See* Fed. R. Evid. 104(b) advisory committee note ("[W]hen a spoken statement is relied upon to prove notice to X, it is without probative value unless X heard it."); *see also* Cox v. State, 696 N.E.2d 853 (Ind. 1998) (applying Indiana Evidence Rule 104(b) to idea that relevance of testimony is conditional on whether the defendant became aware of certain events). The advisory committee's statement seems to suppose that there are two possibilities—either the statement was heard or it was not—and that the fact-finder cannot assess the significance of the spoken statement without making a finding about which is true and then treating it as certain. The point of the foregoing critique is that this assumption ignores the potential usefulness of such a spoken statement to the case when there is a relatively small (but non-trivial) probability that it was heard.

70 *See* **§ 8.07**.

71 *See* **§ 12.01**.

the same "sufficient to support a finding" standard appears in the federal version of those two common-law rules.

§ 3.12 Appeals—Trial Court Discretion and Standards of Review

As already discussed, to preserve an error for appeal, counsel generally must make a timely and specific objection, obtain a ruling from the court, and assure that the objection and ruling appear in the record.[72] This principle applies both to the erroneous admission and erroneous exclusion of evidence. Thus, if counsel believes the court has improperly admitted evidence, counsel must place on the record the reasons for the claimed error. If counsel believes the court has erroneously excluded evidence, counsel must make a record of precisely what the excluded evidence was in order to provide the appellate court with a basis for holding both that the trial court erred and that the error was prejudicial. Without a complete record, it is often very difficult for the appellate court to make the desired findings. Aside from cases of plain error,[73] courts will insist that the proper objection be made. Courts enforce the procedural requirements for preserving error for three reasons: (1) to preserve judicial resources; (2) to encourage lower courts to correct errors at the time they occur; and (3) to avoid unfairness to a prevailing party.[74]

In addition, counsel must successfully navigate the narrows of post-trial procedure to have an error reviewed. Failure to make post-trial motions for a new trial or for judgment as a matter of law may lead to forfeiture of claims of error otherwise properly preserved.[75] One's right to the correction of an error properly preserved at trial but not raised on appeal is generally considered waived or forfeited,[76] as is error from which an appeal is not timely filed.[77] The right to raise constitutional errors in a collateral proceeding such as habeas corpus may be forfeited by "procedural default," thus preventing the review of a federal constitutional claim by a federal court.[78]

Even if error is preserved, however, success on appeal of an evidentiary issue is a difficult task because appellate courts are reluctant to reverse trial courts' judgments on evidentiary matters. Appellate courts understand that trial judges must have a good deal of leeway in applying evidentiary rules. Many of the federal rules are not categorical but instead grant the trial court the authority—guided by the terms of the rules themselves—to reach an appropriate result in light of the context of the particular trial. The most obvious example of such flexibility and discretion is Rule 403, which allows the trial court to exclude otherwise admissible evidence when the court finds that its probative value is substantially outweighed by certain specified dangers.[79] Guided by

---

[72] *See* **§ 3.03**.

[73] *See* **§ 3.15**.

[74] Barry Sullivan, Barry Levenstam & David von Ebers, *Preserving Error in Civil Cases: Some Fundamental Principles*, 32 TRIAL LAW. GUIDE 1, 2 (1988).

[75] *Id.*, at 13–15.

[76] *See, e.g.*, United States v. Curtis, 380 F.3d 1308, 1310 (11th Cir. 2004); *see also* 5 Am. Jur. 2D *Appellate Review* § 577 (2007).

[77] *See* 5 AM. JUR. 2D *Appellate Review* § 269 (2007).

[78] Procedural default occurs when a defendant waives the right to state court review by procedural error. *See* United States v. Frady, 456 U.S. 152, 167–69 (1982) (stating that collateral attacks are reviewed under cause-and-prejudice test of Wainwright v. Sykes, 433 U.S. 72, 87 (1977)).

[79] *See* **§ 5.03**.

the terms of the Rule itself, as well as certain general provisions of the Federal Rules,[80] the court must make its Rule 403 rulings in the specific context of the trial. Many other provisions of the Federal Rules are similar, in whole or in part, and contain standards rather than categorical admission or exclusion rules.[81]

An evidence rule often grants discretion to the trial court because, in the particular context, an appellate court is not in as good a position as the trial court to determine the most appropriate ruling. The appellate court has only the cold, written record and cannot observe the demeanor of witnesses, the effect certain evidence appears to have on the jury, and other factors that one would have to "be there" to observe. Thus, it is said that the appellate court should only reverse the trial court's application of such rules if the trial court "abused its discretion," a standard rarely satisfied in actual practice.[82] The wisdom of this high degree of deference is debatable, but the fact remains that trial courts are granted a virtual shield from reversal based on error in applying discretionary rules. In addition to reliance on the trial judge's knowledge and discretion, the standard of review also reflects a desire for finality, concerns about judicial resources, and a need to grant the trial judge sufficient power to manage the courtroom.

Evidentiary rules differ in terms of the authority granted to trial judges. Some rules are categorical. The court has no authority, for example, to allow the plaintiff to offer evidence of the civil defendant's character to prove circumstantially that the defendant committed the tortious act.[83] Conversely, most courts hold that the trial court has no discretion to *exclude* evidence that a witness committed a crime involving dishonesty or false statement, when that evidence is offered to impeach the witness's credibility.[84] If the rule applied by the trial court does not confer discretion on the judge, the appellate court's standard of review is not abuse of discretion but a more searching, less deferential standard such as de novo review.[85] For example, if, in a murder prosecution, the trial court allowed the government to call a witness during its case-in-chief to testify to the defendant's prior acts of murder for the purpose of showing a character-based propensity to commit such crimes,[86] the appellate court should not review the trial court's ruling for

---

[80] *See, e.g.*, FED. R. EVID. 102 (requiring court to construe rules in such way as to achieve fairness, eliminate unjustifiable expenses, avoid delay, promote evidence law and its development, and seek ascertaining truth and just result); FED. R. EVID. 611(a) (requiring court to exercise reasonable control over mode and order of questioning witnesses and presenting evidence to (1) make process effective for ascertainment of truth, (2) avoid wasting time, and (3) protect witnesses from harassment or undue embarrassment).

[81] An important example of a hybrid rule is FED. R. EVID. 608(b), which absolutely forbids the use of extrinsic evidence of other misconduct of a witness to impeach the witness's credibility, but allows inquiry into such misconduct on cross-examination in the discretion of the court, if probative of truthfulness or untruthfulness. The Rule thus has both categorical and discretionary aspects.

[82] *See* Margaret A. Berger, *When, If Ever, Does Evidentiary Error Constitute Reversible Error?*, 25 LOY. L.A. L. REV. 893, 894 (1992) (finding only thirty officially reported decisions out of over 20,000 tried federal cases during 1990 in which federal appellate court reversed trial court for evidentiary error); David P. Leonard, *Appellate Review of Evidentiary Rulings*, 70 N.C. L. REV. 1155, 1212–29 (1992) (finding virtually no reversals for error in applying Rules 608(b) and 611 for ten-year period).

[83] *See* FED. R. EVID. 404(a); *see also* **§ 7.08**.

[84] *See* FED. R. EVID. 609(a)(2); *see also* **§ 11.10**.

[85] *Cf.* United States v. McConney, 728 F.2d 1195, 1199–1205 (9th Cir. 1984) (en banc) (reviewing possible standards of review of trial court's ruling on constitutionality of federal agents' entry into defendant's home with search warrant, and distinguishing situations in which review should be based on "clearly erroneous" standard and those in which appellate court should review "de novo").

[86] We are assuming, for purposes of this example, that the prosecution does not argue that the prior murders are admissible for some other purpose, such as to show motive for the charged offense. *See* FED. R. EVID. 404(b), discussed in **§ 7.09**.

"abuse of discretion." The trial court had no discretion to allow the government to offer such evidence.[87] Rather, the appellate court should simply find that the trial court erred as a matter of law.[88]

Unfortunately, appellate courts all too often fail to recognize that trial courts do not always have discretion in applying evidence rules. It is not uncommon for courts to state simply and generally that they review evidentiary rulings for abuse of discretion.[89] Holding that evidentiary rulings are reviewed on the basis of abuse of discretion virtually ensures that the trial court's rulings will not be disturbed on appeal.[90]

When arguing evidentiary issues on appeal, counsel should carefully review the nature of the rule in dispute and be prepared to argue for the appropriate standard of review. Though a finding that the trial court erred is only the first hurdle in winning reversal (such error must also be found prejudicial),[91] that hurdle must be overcome to have even a chance of reversal.

§ 3.13 Harmless Versus Prejudicial Error

Given the pace of trials and the fallibility of the judges and lawyers conducting them, there are bound to be evidentiary mistakes in every trial. Parties are not guaranteed perfect trials, and legitimate objections to errors in admitting evidence will not guarantee reversal on appeal. Generally, an appellate court will reverse because of an erroneous ruling on a proper objection only if the error was serious and prejudiced one of the parties.

Even if an objection was properly made, if the reviewing court finds that the error was "harmless"—that is, the error did not affect substantial rights of a party or did not significantly affect the outcome of the case—the error will not justify a reversal. Insisting on prejudicial error in this sense and deeming other error harmless avoids clogging the appellate courts with appeals from purely technical violations and avoids unnecessary reversals where no real injustice occurred.[92]

---

[87] *See* **§ 7.01**.

[88] The trial court's ruling would have constituted error for two reasons. First, the government would not be entitled to offer character evidence under these circumstances. *See* FED. R. EVID. 404(a). Second, even were character evidence admissible, it could not be offered in the form of specific instances of conduct during direct examination. *See* FED. R. EVID. 405(a).

[89] *See, e.g.*, Old Chief v. United States, 519 U.S. 172, 174 n.1 (1997) ("The standard of review applicable to the evidentiary rulings of the district court is abuse of discretion."); United States v. Suggs, 374 F.3d 508, 513 (7th Cir. 2004) ("Only where the district court has clearly abused its discretion, meaning that 'no reasonable person could take the view adopted by the trial court,' will we reverse an evidentiary ruling.").

In Gen. Elec. Co. v. Joiner, 522 U.S. 136 (1997), the Supreme Court held that the "abuse of discretion" standard applies even to the trial court's rulings on asserted expertise under Daubert v. Merrell Dow Pharmaceuticals, Inc., 509 U.S. 579 (1993). As a result of the Court's decision in *Joiner*, it is more apparent than ever that appellate oversight of trial court evidence rulings is quite limited. Applied to the *Daubert* context, one consequence will be that a type of forensic test found admissible in one courtroom may be found inadmissible in another.

[90] *See* Martin B. Louis, *Allocating Adjudicative Decision Making Authority Between Trial and Appellate Levels: A Unified View of the Scope of Review, the Judge/Jury Question, and Procedural Discretion*, 64 N.C. L. REV. 993 (1986).

[91] *See* **§ 3.13**.

[92] Historically, any error was ground for reversal. Statutory reform recognized that procedure is a means to an end, not an end in itself. *See* 11 CHARLES ALAN WRIGHT, ARTHUR R. MILLER & MARY KAY KANE, FEDERAL PRACTICE AND PROCEDURE § 2881 (2012).

The harmless error doctrine is codified in federal and state rules and has been expounded upon in numerous Supreme Court cases. This area is complicated for two reasons. First, it is governed by case law that varies among jurisdictions. Even within the various federal circuits, there are substantial differences in the standard for determining whether error is harmless. Second, the standards for determining harmless error depend on the nature of the case and the type of right involved.

The Federal Rules of Evidence,[93] Federal Rules of Civil Procedure,[94] and Federal Rules of Criminal Procedure[95] all mandate that courts disregard errors that do not affect a "substantial right" of a party." Thus, reversible or prejudicial errors are those that do affect the substantial rights of parties. The definition of substantial rights is vague, and prejudice is determined on a case-by-case basis.[96] Some generalizations emerge, however, from the case law, rules, and commentators. On the one hand, purely technical errors that do not affect the merits of the case are never prejudicial. On the other hand, "if the evidence is insufficient to support the verdict without the erroneously admitted evidence, the error must be held prejudicial."[97] In between these two extremes, courts look at the entire case to determine prejudice.[98] In civil cases, the party challenging an error has the burden of proving that the error was not harmless; in criminal cases, however, the burden of showing that an error was harmless will fall on the government.[99]

Most types of error are subject to a harmless error analysis, including most constitutional errors.[100] In nonconstitutional cases, the Supreme Court has held that substantial rights are affected if the error "substantially swayed" the jury's verdict.[101] Thus, if the error did not affect the jury deliberations or the outcome of the case, it will be harmless error. Courts differ on the degree of certainty required to find an error

---

93 *See* FED. R. EVID. 103(a).

94 *See* FED. R. CIV. P. 61.

95 *See* FED. R. CRIM. P. 52(a).

96 *See* Kotteakos v. United States, 328 U.S. 750, 760 (1946); 1 WEINSTEIN'S FEDERAL EVIDENCE § 103.41[1] (Joseph M. McLaughlin ed., 2d ed. 2014) ("Determining whether a substantial right has been affected is not susceptible to a mechanical analysis. The facts of each case are crucial. . . .").

97 11 CHARLES ALAN WRIGHT, ARTHUR R. MILLER & MARY KAY KANE, FEDERAL PRACTICE AND PROCEDURE § 2885 (2012); *see also* United States v. Silverman, 861 F.2d 571, 580 (9th Cir. 1988) (finding error prejudicial because it was "undoubtedly the bas[i]s for the jury's conclusion").

98 *See* Stockman v. Oakcrest Dental Ctr., P.C., 480 F.3d 791, 799 (6th Cir. 2007).

99 Shinseki v. Sanders, 556 U.S. 396, 129 S. Ct. 1696 (2009). Placing the burden on the government to show that an error is not prejudicial, which will likely make it more difficult for a reviewing court to find that an error is harmless, is justified because the government seeks to deprive an individual of his liberty and must prove its case beyond a reasonable doubt. 129 S. Ct. at 1706. Any discussion of burdens at the appeal level is somewhat misleading because determining whether an error is harmless does not involve a judge shifting "a 'burden' to help control the presentation of evidence at a trial, but rather involves a judge who applies a legal standard (harmlessness) to a record that the presentation of evidence is no longer likely to affect." O'Neal v. McAninch, 513 U.S. 432, 436–37 (1995) (finding that burden is on government for both nonconstitutional and constitutional errors); ROGER J. TRAYNOR, THE RIDDLE OF HARMLESS ERROR 26 (1970) ("Whether or not counsel are helpful, it is still the responsibility of the . . . court, once it concludes there was error, to determine whether the error affected the judgment. It must do so without benefit of such aids as presumptions or allocated burdens of proof that expedite fact-finding at the trial."). Rather than describing the challenging party or the government as having the burden, it may be appropriate to state that a party bears the "risk of nonpersuasion."

100 Some constitutional errors are always grounds for reversal. *See* **§ 3.14**.

101 *See* Kotteakos v. United States, 328 U.S. 750, 765 (1946); *see also* United States v. Lane, 474 U.S. 438, 449 (1986); Granfield v. CSX Transp. Inc., 597 F.3d 474, 488 (1st Cir. 2010).

harmless. The standard employed by courts ranges from "beyond a reasonable doubt"[102] to "more probable than not."[103]

The leading Supreme Court case articulating the harmless error doctrine is *Kotteakos v. United States*.[104] In *Kotteakos*, the Court interpreted § 269 of the Judicial Code of 1911, an early formulation of the harmless error rule. Despite its age, the decision's validity endures. The Court has cited the holding in more recent harmless error cases,[105] as have the lower courts.[106] In *Kotteakos* the Court stated:

> It comes down . . . to a very plain admonition: "Do not be technical, where technicality does not really hurt the party whose rights in the trial and in its outcome the technicality affects."[107]
>
> If, when all is said and done, the conviction is sure that the error did not influence the jury, or had but very slight effect, the verdict and the judgment should stand, except perhaps where the departure is from a constitutional norm or a specific command of Congress. . . . *But if one cannot say, with fair assurance, after pondering all that happened without stripping the erroneous action from the whole, that the judgment was not substantially swayed by the error, it is impossible to conclude that substantial rights were not affected.* The inquiry cannot be merely whether there was enough to support the result, apart from the phase affected by the error. It is rather, even so, whether the error itself had substantial influence. If so, or if one is left in grave doubt, the conviction cannot stand.[108]

Kotteakos holds that courts must base a finding of harmlessness on the error's probable effect on the jury's deliberation.[109] While the quantity of evidence cannot be ignored in evaluating whether the jury's determination was affected by an error, *Kotteakos* placed primary emphasis on the effect of the error on the jury's determination, not on the correctness of the result.[110] Despite the continuing vitality of *Kotteakos*, the Supreme Court has increasingly emphasized the existence of overwhelming evidence of guilt in its findings of harmless error.[111] When the evidence of guilt is overwhelming, courts often

---

[102] Goodwin v. State, 751 So. 2d 537, 543 (Fla. 1999) (reviewing both constitutional and nonconstitutional errors under "harmless beyond a reasonable doubt standard" because of difficulties of determining whether error is constitutional or nonconstitutional); State v. VanWagner, 504 N.W.2d 746, 750 (Minn. 1993) (prosecutor's pointed and persistent references to police interview with witness, which led police to charge defendant with drunk driving, improperly alluded to excluded hearsay statements, and, although misconduct was probably harmless beyond reasonable doubt, court reversed for "prophylactic reasons" and to protect "integrity of the fact-finding process"). Federal courts only use the standard "beyond a reasonable doubt" if the error is constitutional. *See* **§ 3.14**.

[103] *See* Obrey v. Johnson, 400 F.3d 691, 701 (9th Cir. 2005).

[104] 328 U.S. 750 (1946).

[105] *See* Shinseki v. Sanders, 556 U.S. 396, 129 S. Ct. 1696, 1705 (2009); Brecht v. Abrahamson, 507 U.S. 619 (1993).

[106] *See, e.g.*, United States v. Carrasco, 540 F.3d 43, 55 (1st Cir. 2008).

[107] 328 U.S. 750, 760 (1946) (citations omitted) (emphasis added).

[108] *Id.* at 764–65.

[109] *See* 1 WIGMORE ON EVIDENCE § 21 (Tillers rev. 1983).

[110] 328 U.S. 750, 761, 764–65 (1946).

[111] *See* Neder v. United States, 527 U.S. 1, 17 (1999); Darden v. Wainwright, 477 U.S. 168, 182 (1986); United States v. Young, 470 U.S. 1, 19 (1985); *see also* United States v. Simon, 995 F.2d 1236 (3d Cir. 1993) (holding trial court's "otherwise reversible error" in failing to give burden of proof jury instruction was harmless where government presented overwhelming evidence of defendant's guilt); United States v. Martinez, 588 F.3d 301, 313 (6th Cir. 2009) (finding any error in admitting inadmissible hearsay harmless in light of

disregard the effect of the error on the jury and find the error harmless, because the court below reached the "right" result.[112]

In reviewing the entire record to determine whether an error is harmless or prejudicial, courts consider several factors,[113] including: the number of errors in relation to the length of the trial, the closeness of factual disputes, whether the evidence related to a material consequential fact, the prejudicial effect of the evidence, the instructions given, whether the evidence was an important corroboration of other testimony, whether the evidence was cumulative,[114] and the amount of reliance counsel placed on the tainted evidence in their arguments. One factor conspicuously missing from the list, however, is the testimony of the jurors involved.[115]

Courts using the effect-on-the-jury analysis for harmlessness differ on how small the likelihood of the error affecting the jury deliberation must be to justify a finding of harmlessness.[116] For example, the Ninth Circuit uses a "more probably harmless than not" test for nonconstitutional errors.[117] The Third Circuit standard requires reversal unless it is "highly probable" that the verdict would have been the same if the error had not occurred.[118] In the Fifth Circuit, reversal is required unless the court is "sure, after reviewing the entire record, that the error did not influence the jury, or had but very slight effect on its verdict."[119]

"overwhelming evidence"); United States v. Hernandez, 476 F.3d 791, 797 (9th Cir. 2007) (examining whether there was "overwhelming evidence" of guilt in determination of whether error was harmless).

In objecting to this use of overwhelming evidence as the test for harmless error, Judge Clark of the Fifth Circuit wrote: "Unnecessary language seems to invite review of the sufficiency of the nonobjectionable [sic] evidence *alone*, even though our attention over and over again is *properly* called to the prejudicial impact of the objectionable evidence." Harryman v. Estelle, 616 F.2d 870, 885 (5th Cir. 1980) (Clark, J., concurring in part and dissenting in part) (emphasis added); *see also* United States v. Curbelo, 343 F.3d 273, 287 (4th Cir. 2003) (finding error prejudicial because could not say with fair assurance that error did not substantially sway jury despite substantial evidence being presented against defendant).

[112] This approach has been heavily criticized as displacing the role of the jury with the appeals court. *See* United States v. Hands, 184 F.3d 1322, 1329 (11th Cir. 1999) (discussing cases in which court had found prejudicial nonconstitutional errors to be harmless in criminal cases in which government had presented highly convincing, admissible evidence of defendant's guilt, such as confession); Roger A. Fairfax, Jr., *Harmless Constitutional Error and the Institutional Significance of the Jury*, 76 FORDHAM L. REV. 2027, 2048 (2008) ("Application of the traditional 'overwhelming evidence' test on harmless error review—a test that queries whether the untainted evidence is sufficient to support the conviction—places the appellate court into the jury's fact-finding role, a role it is neither intended nor competent to perform.").

[113] *See* 1 WEINSTEIN'S FEDERAL EVIDENCE § 103.41[5] (Joseph M. McLaughlin ed., 2d ed. 2014).

[114] *See* United States v. Austin, 823 F.2d 257, 260 (8th Cir. 1987).

[115] *See* Fed. R. Evid. 606(b) (prohibiting a juror from testifying with regard to the "effect of anything on that juror's or another juror's vote"). *See* **§ 8.05**.

[116] *See* United States v. Valle-Valdez, 554 F.2d 911, 914–15 (9th Cir. 1977) ("[S]tandards guiding appellate determination of harmless error are variable, often confusing and frequently left unarticulated . . . however, those standards are statements of the degree of certainty an appellate court must achieve regarding the effect of the error on the verdict.").

[117] *See* United States v. Freeman, 498 F.3d 893, 905 (9th Cir. 2007); *see also* United States v. Pursley, 577 F.3d 1204, 1227 (10th Cir. 2009) (finding by preponderance of evidence that an error did not have substantial influence on outcome); United States Indus., Inc. v. Touche Ross & Co., 854 F.2d 1223, 1252–53 (10th Cir. 1988) (applying "more probably harmless than not" standard in civil case).

[118] *See* United States v. Gambone, 314 F.3d 163, 177 (3d Cir. 2003) (" 'High probability' requires that the court possess a 'sure conviction that the error did not prejudice the defendant.' "); McQueeney v. Wilmington Trust Co., 779 F.2d 916, 924 (3d Cir. 1985).

[119] Price v. Rosiek Constr. Co., 509 F.3d 704, 707–08 (5th Cir. 2007). This standard is similar to the requirement that constitutional errors are prejudicial unless proven harmless "beyond a reasonable doubt." *See* Chapman v. California, 386 U.S. 18, 24 (1967).

Courts generally apply the same standard for harmlessness to nonconstitutional error in civil cases as in criminal cases,[120] although some courts argue that the standards should differ in accordance with the differing standards of proof applicable to civil and criminal cases.[121] State court standards for determining harmless error are similar to federal court standards.[122] In diversity cases, a federal court applies its own harmless error standard, rather than the state court standard.[123]

§ 3.14 Constitutional Error

Issues of constitutional error arise most frequently in criminal cases. These errors include violations of the Fourth Amendment, the Fifth Amendment's self-incrimination clause, due process rights under the Fifth and Fourteenth Amendments, the Sixth Amendment's right to counsel, right to an impartial tribunal, and right to confrontation, and the Eighth Amendment's protections against excessive punishment. In criminal cases, trial courts may also commit constitutional error when the trial court employs evidence rules to exclude crucial exculpatory evidence offered by the defendant. Cases so holding have spawned a body of law setting forth parameters for when exclusionary rules of evidence must give way to the defendant's constitutional rights, primarily under the due process clauses of the Fifth and Fourteenth Amendments and the Sixth Amendment right to present a defense.[124]

Before the Supreme Court's decision in *Chapman v. California*,[125] it was thought that constitutional errors were always grounds for reversal.[126] *Chapman* held, however, that the harmless error doctrine applies to most constitutional errors.[127] However, "before a federal constitutional error can be held harmless, the court must find that it was harmless *beyond a reasonable doubt*."[128] But if the improper evidence was merely cumulative of other properly admitted evidence, the error may be found harmless because the jury's judgment was not affected.[129]

For an influential discussion of the possible standards for determining whether an error is prejudicial, see ROGER TRAYNOR, THE RIDDLE OF HARMLESS ERROR 35 (1970).

[120] *Cf.* McDonough Power Equip., Inc. v. Greenwood, 464 U.S. 548, 553–54 (1984).

[121] *See* United States Indus., Inc. v. Touche Ross & Co., 854 F.2d 1223, 1252 n.39 (10th Cir. 1988) ("[I]t seems reasonable, absent some countervailing policy, that the harmless error standard should mirror the standard applied at trial"); *see also* Stephen A. Saltzburg, *The Harm of Harmless Error*, 59 VA. L. REV. 988, 988 (1973).

[122] *See, e.g.*, Carter v. State, 677 S.E.2d 71, 76 (Ga. 2009) (using "highly probable" standard); Supreme Pork, Inc. v. Master Blaster, Inc., 764 N.W.2d 474, 491 (S.D. 2009) (holding errors are prejudicial when "jury might and probably would have returned a different verdict if the alleged error had not occurred") (emphasis omitted). *But cf.* State v. VanWagner, 504 N.W.2d 746, 750 (Minn. 1993) (noting that harmless error rising from deliberate prosecutorial misconduct is still grounds for reversal as prophylactic measure against future prosecutorial misconduct).

[123] *See* 11 CHARLES ALAN WRIGHT, ARTHUR R. Miller & MARY KAY KANE, FEDERAL PRACTICE AND PROCEDURE § 2883 (2012).

[124] *See* **§ 1.04**.

[125] 386 U.S. 18 (1967).

[126] *See* 1 WIGMORE ON EVIDENCE § 21 (Tillers rev. 1983).

[127] 386 U.S. 18, 23 (1967).

[128] *Id.* at 24. *See, e.g.*, Earhart v. Konteh, 589 F.3d 337, 346 (6th Cir. 2009) (reversing for Confrontation Clause error); United States v. Gonzalez, 183 F.3d 1315, 1328 (11th Cir. 1999) (reversing for *Bruton* error).

[129] *See, e.g.*, Brown v. United States, 411 U.S. 223, 231 (1973); Ghent v. Woodford, 279 F.3d 1121, 1134 (9th Cir. 2002) (finding some claims of error harmless where evidence was cumulative and other errors prejudicial and reversing because wrongly admitted evidence was not cumulative).

Whether an error in a criminal trial rises to the level of constitutional error depends on the rights allegedly violated. If the error involves a violation of a specific provision of the Bill of Rights (e.g., the Sixth Amendment right to counsel or the Fifth Amendment privilege against self-incrimination), it will be deemed a constitutional error.[130] Because of the liberty interests at stake in a criminal trial, many errors that would affect the outcome of the case, and therefore are prejudicial but do not violate a specific provision of the Bill of Rights, may be raised on appeal as due process violations under the Fifth or Fourteenth Amendments. Errors in the prosecutor's closing argument often fall into this category. In these due process cases, the Supreme Court evaluates whether the error "so infected the trial with unfairness as to make the resulting conviction a denial of due process."[131] In the case of closing arguments, the Court often invokes the invited response doctrine—that the accused made an impermissible assertion to which the prosecution had to reply[132]—in concluding that no constitutional violation occurred.[133] Counsel appealing due process errors, therefore, should also challenge the error on nonconstitutional grounds. Because the entire proceeding is examined for unfairness, error that does not implicate a specific right will rarely be found to be constitutional error.[134] Even if a specific right is implicated, for instance, the right against self-incrimination, the Court may find that no constitutional error occurred based on the whole record.[135]

The burden of proving that a constitutional error was harmless is on the prosecution-appellee.[136] Courts consider the entire record in deciding whether a constitutional error was harmless[137] and the factors considered are the same as for nonconstitutional errors.[138] The plain error doctrine also applies to constitutional errors.[139]

Although *Chapman* required courts to focus on the possible impact of evidentiary error on the jurors' minds,[140] subsequent Supreme Court decisions have found constitutional errors harmless because the evidence of guilt was "overwhelming."[141] Commentators have criticized the *Chapman* harmless error rule as outcome-oriented[142]

---

130 *See* Donnelly v. DeChristoforo, 416 U.S. 637, 643 (1974).

131 *Id.*

132 *See* **§ 1.11**.

133 *See* United States v. Robinson, 485 U.S. 25, 33–34 (1988); Darden v. Wainwright, 477 U.S. 168, 182 (1986).

134 *See, e.g.*, Darden v. Wainwright, 477 U.S. 168, 182 (1986). *But see* Wainwright v. Greenfield, 474 U.S. 284, 295 (1986) (holding that use of *Miranda* silence as evidence of sanity rendered trial fundamentally unfair). Despite constitutional guarantees of due process, errors in criminal trial that do not involve violations of specific provisions of the Bill of Rights generally are not considered constitutional, because the "interests involved are not sufficiently important to merit explicit constitutional protection." United States v. Valle-Valdez, 554 F.2d 911, 916 (9th Cir. 1977).

135 *See* United States v. Robinson, 485 U.S. 25, 32–33 (1988).

136 United States v. Vonn, 535 U.S. 55, 62 (2002).

137 *See* United States v. Hasting, 461 U.S. 499, 509 (1983).

138 *See* **§ 3.13**.

139 *See, e.g.*, United States v. Morena, 547 F.3d 191, 197 (3d Cir. 2008).

140 United States v. McLaughlin, 386 F.3d 547, 555 (3d Cir. 2004) (citing Chapman v. California, 386 U.S. 18, 24 (1967)); 1 WEINSTEIN'S FEDERAL EVIDENCE § 103.43[3][b] (Joseph M. McLaughlin ed., 2d ed. 1997);

141 *See* Neder v. United States, 527 U.S. 1, 17 (1999); Milton v. Wainwright, 407 U.S. 371, 377 (1972). *Cf.* United States v. Pirovolos, 844 F.2d 415, 427 (7th Cir. 1988).

142 *See* Tom Stacy & Kim Dayton, *Rethinking Harmless Constitutional Error*, 88 COLUM. L. REV. 79, 84 (1988).

and without substantive doctrinal basis.[143] They note that the Court has been most concerned about the accuracy of the guilt determination rather than the protection of an individual's constitutional rights.

Some constitutional errors continue to be prejudicial per se because the rights affected are considered structural errors and "so basic to a fair trial that their infraction can never be treated as harmless error."[144] These errors include right to counsel violations,[145] absence of an impartial tribunal,[146] and complete denial of the opportunity to cross-examine.[147] Some constitutional errors, while not prejudicial per se, mandate reversal if the defendant can make a relatively low threshold showing. For example, the prosecution's failure to disclose material exculpatory evidence requires reversal if the defendant can demonstrate a "reasonable probability that, had the evidence been disclosed to the defense, the result of the proceeding would have been different."[148]

The *Chapman* standard does not apply to collateral attacks on constitutional error. In *Brecht v. Abrahamson*,[149] the Supreme Court reviewed a habeas case arising from a trial in which the prosecutor erroneously referred to the defendant's post-*Miranda* silence. The Court rejected the argument that the *Chapman* "harmless-beyond-reasonable-doubt standard" had to be satisfied to uphold the conviction. Instead, it held that when a conviction is collaterally attacked for constitutional error, the more lenient *Kotteakos* standard applies, so that the judgment will be upheld unless it is shown that the error "had substantial and injurious effect or influence in determining the jury's

---

[143] *See* Steven H. Goldberg, *Harmless Error: Constitutional Sneak Thief*, 71 J. CRIM. L. & CRIMINOLOGY 421, 427 (1980).

[144] Chapman v. California, 386 U.S. 18, 23 (1967); *see also* Sullivan v. Louisiana, 508 U.S. 275 (1993) (reversing conviction because trial court's incorrect definition of reasonable doubt in jury instructions deprived defendant of right to trial by jury; due to trial court's error, jury could not render verdict of guilty beyond reasonable doubt); Tom Stacy & Kim Dayton, *Rethinking Harmless Constitutional Error*, 88 COLUM. L. REV. 79, 87 (1988) (discussing Rose v. Clark, 478 U.S. 570, 577–78 (1986), in which Court stated these rights are so fundamental that in their absence "a criminal trial cannot reliably serve its function as a vehicle for determination of guilt or innocence . . . and no criminal punishment may be regarded as fundamentally fair"). *But see* Neder v. United States, 527 U.S. 1, 9–10 (1999) (holding that, when federal judge failed to submit to jury element of materiality in tax fraud prosecution, this was not "structural error" that defies ordinary harmless error analysis because trial was not fundamentally unfair as defendant was tried before impartial judge, under correct standard of proof and with assistance of counsel, and impartial jury was instructed to consider all evidence against him).

At one time, the Court considered the use of coerced confessions per se prejudicial, Chapman v. California, 386 U.S. 18, 23 (1967), but, in 1991, the Court reversed its treatment of coerced confessions, holding that harmless error analysis applies even to cases involving illegally coerced confessions. Arizona v. Fulminante, 499 U.S. 279 (1991) (a 5–4 decision). For criticism of that decision, see Charles J. Ogletree, Jr., Comment, *Arizona v. Fulminante: The Harm of Applying Harmless Error to Coerced Confessions*, 105 HARV. L. REV. 152 (1991). Similarly, receiving out-of-court statements as evidence in violation of the defendant's Sixth Amendment right to confrontation is not a ground for reversal unless the error was not harmless. Lilly v. Virginia, 527 U.S. 116, 139–40 (1999) (remanding for harmless error determination after finding violation of Confrontation Clause).

[145] Gideon v. Wainwright, 372 U.S. 335, 343 (1963).

[146] Tumey v. Ohio, 273 U.S. 510, 535 (1927).

[147] Davis v. Alaska, 415 U.S. 308, 318 (1974) (finding constitutional error in case involving complete denial of cross-examination). *Cf.* United States v. Owens, 484 U.S. 554, 560 (1988) (finding no Confrontation Clause violation where witness could not be thoroughly cross-examined about prior statement of which he had no memory due to brain damage); Delaware v. Van Arsdall, 475 U.S. 673, 684 (1986) (noting that unconstitutional restriction on defendant's right to cross-examine witness is subject to harmless error analysis).

[148] Kyles v. Whitley, 514 U.S. 419, 433 (1995) (quoting United States v. Bagley, 473 U.S. 667, 682 (1985)).

[149] 507 U.S. 619 (1993).

verdict."[150] This is so regardless of whether the state courts have already applied the Chapman test to the contested error.[151] However, the Supreme Court has cautioned that when a federal habeas court finds a constitutional trial error and is in grave doubt about whether the error had a "substantial and injurious effect or influence in determining the jury's verdict," the error is not harmless.[152]

§ 3.15 Plain Error

Despite the importance of making proper objections, federal courts and many state courts recognize that enforcing the rights of the parties and the public interest should occasionally trump enforcing legal technicalities.[153] Because trials are stressful and often fast-paced, even the most competent attorney may fail to object to improper evidence, comment, or argument or may omit one technical step in the procedure for properly preserving error. The "plain error" doctrine, as set out in the Federal Rules of Evidence,[154] the Federal Rules of Criminal Procedure,[155] and analogous state court rules, embodies an overriding concern for preserving important rights.[156] Federal courts and some state courts also apply the plain error doctrine in civil cases.[157] While there is no plain error rule in the Federal Rules of Civil Procedure, the rule is codified for evidential errors in Federal Rule of Evidence 103(e), and the circuit courts have recognized the doctrine as necessary for fairness and justice in some civil cases.[158]

A finding of plain error has the identical effect on a proceeding as a finding of preserved error—the lower court's decision will be reversed, and, in most situations, the case will be remanded, provided the error was prejudicial. Like the analysis for preserved

---

[150] Brecht v. Abrahamson, 507 U.S. 619, 622–23 (1993); *accord* California v. Roy, 519 U.S. 2, 5–6 (1996) (holding that *Kotteakos* "harmless error" standard applies where trial court failed to instruct jury that in order to find defendant guilty of murder committed by confederate, it must find that defendant had knowledge and intent or purpose of committing, encouraging, or facilitating killing; error was "trial error" rather than "structural error").

[151] Fry v. Pliler, 551 U.S. 112, 121 (2007).

[152] O'Neal v. McAninch, 513 U.S. 432, 436–43 (1995).

[153] *See* Hormel v. Helvering, 312 U.S. 552, 557 (1941).

[154] FED. R. EVID. 103(e) (providing for appellate review of plain errors affecting substantial rights regardless of whether they were properly preserved).

[155] FED. R. CRIM. P. 52(b) ("A plain error that affects substantial rights may be considered even although it was not brought to the court's attention.").

[156] *See* United States v. Atkinson, 297 U.S. 157, 160 (1936) (describing plain error). *See generally* 1 WEINSTEIN'S FEDERAL EVIDENCE § 103.42[3] (Joseph M. McLaughlin ed., 2d ed. 1997) ("[T]he doctrine should be applied only when the error is so obvious that a failure to notice it would seriously affect the fairness, integrity, and public reputation of the judicial proceeding").

[157] *See, e.g.*, Diaz-Seijo v. Fajardo-Velez, 397 F.3d 53, 56 (1st Cir. 2005) (finding that it is rare to find plain error in a civil case and that test is demanding); Teen-Ed, Inc. v. Kimball Int'l., Inc., 620 F.2d 399, 401–02 (3d Cir. 1980); Ammons-Lewis v. Metro. Water Reclamation Dist., 488 F.3d 739, 751 (7th Cir. 2007) (reviewing for plain error only in context of erroneous jury instructions); Cincinnati Ins. Co. v. Bluewood, Inc., 560 F.3d 798, 805 (8th Cir. 2009).

[158] *See* Teen-Ed, Inc. v. Kimball Int'l., Inc., 620 F.2d 399, 401–02 (3d. Cir. 1980). In addition to finding plain error in civil trial court rulings on evidentiary matters and arguments of counsel, appellate courts occasionally find plain error in trial court decisions on motions for directed verdict or summary judgment. One state court has explained that plain error "is reserved for situations where it is necessary to preserve confidence in the fairness and integrity of the adjudicative process, or where the issue is important to the development of the law." Beacon Falls v. Posick, 549 A.2d 656, 672 (Conn. App. Ct. 1988); *see also* Harper v. Landers, 348 S.E.2d 698, 701 (Ga. Ct. App. 1986) (finding plain error in grant of motion to dismiss in custody action).

judicial error, plain error analysis considers the impact of the error. In addition, plain error analysis addresses whether the error was obvious and important.[159]

Error in rulings on evidence can be prejudicial but not plain and vice versa. For example, suppose that, in response to an objection wrongly based on relevancy grounds, the trial judge admits devastating evidence that should have been excluded on hearsay grounds. This error would be prejudicial (because the jury heard very damaging evidence it should not have heard), but if the hearsay question was actually close, it would not likely be "plain." Reversal in such a case is highly unlikely. Similarly, it is also possible to have plain error that is not prejudicial. For example, if the trial judge erroneously excluded a lay opinion that the plaintiff was intoxicated, but admitted evidence of the person's specific behavior and symptoms of intoxication, the error might be "plain" (because the opinion should have been permitted), but harmless (because the testimony admitted by the court was most likely a reasonable substitute for the evidence wrongly excluded). In such a case, the appellate court will not reverse.

In interpreting language in the Federal Rules of Criminal Procedure that is similar to language in Federal Rule of Evidence 103, the Supreme Court clarified the scope of review for plain error. In *United States v. Olano*,[160] the leading case on plain error, the Court first held that the doctrine applies only to "forfeited" rights (rights lost by failure to assert them in a timely fashion), and not to "waived" rights (rights intentionally relinquished). Second, the error must be "plain" in that it was clear under current law. Third, the error must affect substantial rights. The defendant bears the burden of persuasion that the error was prejudicial by demonstrating that the error affected the outcome of the trial proceedings; normally, the defendant must make a specific showing of prejudice. If the forfeited error is plain and affects substantial rights, the appellate court may, but is not required to, exercise its discretion to remedy the error. The appellate court should exercise discretion when the error " 'seriously affect[s] the fairness, integrity or public reputation of judicial proceedings.' "[161]

Despite the Supreme Court's clarification in *United States v. Olano*, plain error is not easily defined and allows for substantial judicial discretion. The facts of the case, the gravity of the offense, and the probable effect of the error are factors considered by the

---

[159] *See* Permian Petroleum Co. v. Petroleos Mexicanos, 934 F.2d 635, 648 (5th Cir. 1991) (emphasizing that trial counsel did not object to admission of worksheet, admission of which was questioned on appeal, but did object to witness's description of part of worksheet; court stated that "[w]hen a party fails to object to the admission of evidence, we review for plain error. Plain error is error which . . . is so obvious and substantial that failure to notice and correct it would affect the fairness, integrity, or public reputation of judicial proceedings.") (citation omitted). However, plain error can also be found in cases where the error may not have been entirely apparent to counsel during the trial. New constitutional rules announced by the Supreme Court are applied retroactively to all convictions that are not yet final at the time the new constitutional rule decision is rendered. *See* Griffith v. Kentucky, 479 U.S. 314, 328 (1987); *see also* Teague v. Lane, 489 U.S. 288, 311 (1989). Though the new rules apply to this limited class of cases, the longstanding rule that legal issues will not be addressed for the first time on appeal still applies and so review is only for plain error. *See* Johnson v. United States, 520 U.S. 461, 467 (1997); United States v. Gonzales, 436 F.3d 560, 575–76 (5th Cir. 2006) (applying Crawford v. Washington, 541 U.S. 36 (2004), retroactively and reviewing for plain error).

[160] 507 U.S. 725 (1993).

[161] *Id.* at 736 (alteration in original) (quoting United States v. Atkinson, 297 U.S. 157, 160 (1936)); *see also* Johnson v. United States, 520 U.S. 461 (1997) (holding that, even if judge's error was obvious in sense of being departure from well-settled law, and hence was plain error, it was not "reversible" unless it seriously affected fairness, integrity, or public reputation of proceedings; trial judge's erroneous decision not to instruct jury on element of "materiality" in perjury prosecution hence was not plain error because no plausible argument could be made that defendant's false testimony was not material).

court in determining whether substantial rights have been violated.[162] Some courts require that the error be obvious in the record.[163]

As the drafters of the federal rules noted, "the application of the plain error rule will be more likely with respect to the admission of evidence than to exclusion, since failure to comply with normal requirements of offers of proof is likely to produce a record which simply does not disclose the error."[164] Plain error is invoked most often in criminal cases, such as when the defendant appeals from a conviction that infringes on some form of liberty.[165] The need for the plain error doctrine is especially great in the cases of children and criminal defendants who have court-appointed counsel.[166] Still, reversal for plain error is relatively rare.[167] Therefore, counsel should not rely on the discretion of appellate courts to find plain error. Trial counsel must present the client's case effectively and protect the client's rights by avoiding error and preserving error made by opposing counsel or the court.[168] If no objection was made, on appeal there is very little counsel can do even if the error was prejudicial.

In addition, when litigating under state law, counsel must research the case law and statutes to determine whether plain error analysis will be applied. Some states do not accept the plain error doctrine, holding instead that failure to object is an absolute forfeiture of the right to appeal.[169] Some states will find plain error when the court errs on issues of law such as instructions to the jury or rulings on motions to dismiss or for summary judgment but may not find plain error in relation to unpreserved errors in evidentiary rulings.[170]

---

[162] *See, e.g.*, United States v. Young, 470 U.S. 1, 12 (1985); United States v. Cedelle, 89 F.3d 181, 186 (4th Cir. 1996) (finding that central to plain error inquiry "is a determination of whether, based on the record in its entirety, the proceedings against the accused resulted in a fair and reliable determination of guilt"); United States v. John, 597 F.3d 263, 288 (5th Cir. 2010) (stating that ultimately whether error seriously affects fairness, integrity, or public reputation of judicial proceedings is dependent upon degree of error and particular facts of case).

[163] *See* Lowery v. State, 762 P.2d 457, 459 n.1 (Alaska Ct. App. 1988).

[164] FED. R. EVID. 103(d) advisory committee note.

[165] Under Rule 52(b) of the Federal Rules of Criminal Procedure, plain error applies to direct appeals and petitions for certiorari of criminal cases. It does not apply to habeas petitions by federal or state prisoners; those prisoners are required to meet the cause-and-prejudice test of Wainwright v. Sykes, 433 U.S. 72 (1977), before a waived or "defaulted" error will be reviewed by the federal courts. 28 MOORE'S FEDERAL PRACTICE § 652 (3d ed. 1997); *see also* United States v. Frady, 456 U.S. 152, 167–69 (1982).

[166] *See* Government of the Canal Zone v. P. (Pinto), 590 F.2d 1344, 1353 (5th Cir. 1979) (involving defendant who had a series of court-appointed attorneys).

[167] *See* United States v. Robinson, 485 U.S. 25, 35 (1988) (Blackmun, J., concurring in part and dissenting in part); United States v. Young, 470 U.S. 1, 15 (1985) (noting that plain error exception to contemporaneous objection rule is to be "used sparingly" (quoting United States v. Frady, 456 U.S. 152, 163 n.14 (1982))).

[168] *See* Sykes v. United States, 373 F.2d 607, 613 (5th Cir. 1966) ("Whether or not there was error was not visible because all of the circumstances of the arrest were not before the court. That which is not visible cannot be 'plain.' We are not equipped for divination.").

[169] *See, e.g.*, Calhoun v. State, 530 So. 2d 259, 262 (Ala. Crim. App. 1988) ("The plain error doctrine applies only to death cases."); Sales v. State, 289 S.W.3d 423, 429–30 (Ark. 2008) (rejecting plain error review except for four exceptions, which include "(1) a trial court, in a death-penalty case, fails to bring to the jury's attention a matter essential to its consideration of the death penalty itself; (2) a trial court errs at a time when defense counsel has no knowledge of the error and thus no opportunity to object; (3) a trial court should intervene on its own motion to correct a serious error; and (4) the admission or exclusion of evidence affects a defendant's substantial rights"); State v. Hernandez-Lopez, 639 N.W.2d 226, 234 (Iowa 2002).

[170] *Compare* State v. Patterson, 755 P.2d 551, 556 (Kan. 1988) (reviewing jury instruction for plain error) *with* State v. Bird, 708 P.2d 946, 961–62 (Kan. 1985) ("[F]ailure to comply with the contemporaneous objection rule bars a challenge to [the prosecutor's argument] in a state court.").

Part II

AN OVERVIEW OF PRIVILEGES

Chapter 4

EVIDENTIARY PRIVILEGES

Table of Sections

§ 4.01 The Origins and Policies of Privilege

Evidentiary privileges limit a party's ability to demand information about certain communications and to interrogate certain witnesses. These restrictions on otherwise admissible and sometimes vital evidence exist because maximizing accuracy and minimizing cost are not the only societal values cherished or promoted by our dispute resolution system. Moreover, the legal effect of privileges extends beyond the trial itself. They limit not only what can be introduced at trial, but also what can be discovered during pretrial procedures.[1]

[1] *See, e.g.*, FED. R. CIV. P. 26(b)(1) (limiting scope of discovery in civil cases to unprivileged information). Discovery in criminal cases is more limited, and the rules are usually written to avoid mandating discovery of privileged information. *See, e.g.*, FED. R. CRIM. P. 16. However, the limitations of privilege do surface explicitly in the context of pretrial depositions, when they are permitted. *See, e.g.*, FED. R. CRIM. P. § 15(e)(2). And subpoenas issued to non-party witnesses are generally subject to privilege claims. See 6 WAYNE R. LAFAVE, JEROLD H. ISRAEL, NANCY J. KING, & ORIN S. KERR, CRIMINAL PROCEDURE § 24.3(f) (4th ed. 2015).

The lawyer-client, doctor-patient, and spousal privileges, as well as the privilege against self-incrimination, are some of the more commonly known and more important evidentiary privileges. The holder of the privilege controls decisions about its use. Parties may suggest the existence of a privilege to a tribunal, but only the holder of the privilege may decide to claim or to waive it.[2] The focus on the privilege holder reflects the societal values underlying such protected conversations and relationships.

Privileges fall into two categories: those that focus on individual communications and those that entirely prohibit the testimony. Lawyer-client privileges and spousal privileges, the earliest recognized by common-law judges in England, represent each type.[3] The earliest lawyer-client privilege prevented testimony about confidential communications but did not bar testimony altogether, while the earliest spousal privilege prevented one spouse from testifying at all against the other spouse.[4]

Until the early part of the 19th century, all privilege law in the United States was judge-made and imported from the English common law. In 1828, the New York legislature passed the first statutory privilege, creating a privilege between doctor and patient.[5] From that time forward, the law of privilege has been a creature of the legislative process, except in the federal system, where the courts continue to create privilege via common law. The initial draft of the Federal Rules of Evidence attempted to codify the judicially created privileges applied in federal courts, but Congress rejected the proposed privilege rules, entrusting privilege law in the federal system to "reason and experience" as "interpreted by the courts." Therefore, federal privilege law is largely common law.[6]

Privilege law serves, in part, to define the contours of substantive privacy, so it is not surprising that *Erie* concerns would come into play.[7] Rule 501 provides that, when a federal court applies state substantive law (as in diversity cases), it must apply state privilege rules.[8] When applying federal substantive law, however, it must apply federal privilege law. Thus, when the federal district court tries a personal injury case under diversity of citizenship jurisdiction, it applies state privilege law; when it tries a federal antitrust case, it applies the general federal common law of privilege.[9] Sometimes a case

---

2 *See, e.g.*, Touma v. Touma, 357 A.2d 25 (N.J. Super. Ct. Ch. 1976) (marital communications privilege cannot be claimed by marriage counselor); Church of Jesus Christ of Latter Day Saints v. Superior Court of Arizona, 764 P.2d 759 (Ariz. Ct. App. 1988) (where penitent has waived clergymen/penitent privilege, priest cannot independently assert privilege). See 1 MCCORMICK ON EVIDENCE § 73.1 (Kenneth S. Broun gen. ed., 7th ed. 2013) (also discussing the question of who has standing to appeal rulings on privilege claims).

3 1 MCCORMICK ON EVIDENCE § 75 (Kenneth S. Broun ed., 7th ed. 2013).

4 As Wigmore observed, in roughly parallel timing, a rule of incompetency also developed that barred one spouse from testifying *in favor* of the other. 8 WIGMORE ON EVIDENCE § 2227 (McNaughton rev. 1961). For discussion of the competency rule, see **§ 8.01**.

5 N.Y. Rev. Stats. 1829, Vol. II, Part III, c. 7, tit. 3, art. 8, § 73.

6 Federal Rule 502, added in 2008, deals only with the waiver of attorney-client and work-product privileges, and was the first specific privilege rule to be added to the Federal Rules of Evidence.

7 Erie R. Co. v. Tompkins, 304 U.S. 64 (1938).

8 The matter was contested when the Federal Rules were proposed. The drafters of the proposed federal privileges argued against deference to state privileges—*see* Proposed Fed. R. Evid. 501 advisory committee note—but Congress rejected those arguments.

9 H.R. Conf. Rep. No. 93–1597 (1974). When state privilege law applies, the question can arise as to *which* state's privilege law should govern. This will come up only when the dispute implicates more than one state (or country). Under Klaxon v. Stentor Electric Manufacturing Co., 313 U.S. 487 (1941), the forum state's law of "conflicts" determines this matter. State law has traditionally resolved this "horizontal" choice-of-law issue by labeling privilege law "procedural" and applying the law of the state of the forum court. But this is

can involve both state and federal privileges, as when a state substantive claim is supplemental to a federal claim.[10]

Most modern privileges relate to professions and are justified by the utilitarian notion that the privilege facilitates communication between the person in need of help and the professional able to provide it. The goal of such privileges is to encourage open communication between the professional and the privilege holder so that the best advice can be rendered. Another purpose of protecting confidential communications is to respect the dignity of the individual who needs professional help; this objective argues in favor of protecting confidential communications. Even the marital privileges, which do not relate to professions, are usually justified by the instrumental concepts of preserving relationships and encouraging communication.

§ 4.02 General Principles Governing Privileges

There are a number of principles that govern all or most privileges and can be simply stated.

What rights does a privilege confer on its holder?

Except as authorized by a rule of privilege (including the "work product" doctrine), no person may:

(1) refuse to be a witness in response to a lawful subpoena;

(2) refuse to disclose any matter in response to a lawful discovery requests;

(3) refuse to produce any object or writing in response to a lawful process; or

(4) prevent another person from being a witness or disclosing any matter or producing any object or writing.[11]

Conversely, the holder of a privilege who validly exercises it generally may do these things.[12] If a potential witness has unprivileged information relevant to a case as well as privileged information, that person may not refuse a lawful subpoena, but must attend and testify; an objection may then be raised if and when the privilege is about to be violated.[13] The burden of establishing the facts showing the applicability of a privilege is on the person claiming the privilege.[14]

---

changing, with some courts applying the law of the state where the allegedly confidential communication occurred. *See, e.g.*, Ford Motor Co. v, Leggat, 904 S.W.2d 643 (Tex. 1995).

[10] *See, e.g.*, Hansen v. Allen Memorial Hosp., 141 F.R.D. 115, 121 (S.D. Iowa 1992) (where there is claim under both state and federal law, federal law of privilege controls, but court should give consideration to applicable state privilege).

[11] *See, e.g.*, United States v. Nixon, 418 U.S. 683, 709 (1974). *See also* CAL. EVID. CODE § 911; Proposed FED. R. EVID. 501.

[12] Within reason, of course. With respect to (4), for example, a privilege holder may not take steps that would otherwise be criminal or tortious in order to prevent a disclosure, but the holder might withhold consent that some other person (such as the holder's attorney) would require before disclosing material within the privilege.

[13] *See* PAUL F. ROTHSTEIN & SUSAN W. CRUMP, FEDERAL TESTIMONIAL PRIVILEGES § 2:4 (2d ed. 2015–16).

[14] *See* EDWARD J. IMWINKELRIED, THE NEW WIGMORE: EVIDENTIARY PRIVILEGES § 6.3.1 (2d ed. 2010). Under the federal rules, the determination of this issue, like other preliminary matters, is governed by FED. R. EVID. 104(a). *See* **§ 3.11**.

Are privileges coextensive with professional obligations of confidentiality?

The simple answer is, no. Some privileges, such as spousal privileges, are independent of any professional relationship. Even those evidentiary privileges for communications with professionals are distinct from professional ethical requirements to preserve confidentiality. Lawyers, doctors, and other professionals subscribe to self-regulating ethical codes that describe aspirations or propound rules to govern conduct. Such codes include confidentiality obligations, particularly in the three traditional robed professions: law, medicine, and clergy. Although the breach of ethical confidentiality obligations may lead to discipline or loss of license within the profession, these codes do not provide a legal basis to exclude evidence. Only the existence of a privilege will block otherwise lawful pretrial discovery or exclude a confidential communication from evidence.

The ethical obligations of confidentiality are usually broader than the privilege protecting communication between a professional and the client/patient/penitent. Such duties are not limited to confidential communications and are often designed to further goals beyond the utilitarian aim of the various privileges. The lawyer-client privilege, for example, only prohibits evidence in judicial or other formal proceedings such as depositions or police investigations. It only protects communication between the lawyer and the client. By contrast, the lawyer's ethical obligation of confidentiality applies in almost any situation and covers all information relating to the representation, regardless of source.[15] While the modern rationale for the privilege is to facilitate communication between client and lawyer, the ethical justification of the confidentiality requirement concerns the profession's high ethical aspirations of trust and loyalty.

How can a privilege be waived?

Generally speaking, a voluntary disclosure of privileged material by the holder of the privilege, or with his or her consent, or by his or her authorized agent constitutes a waiver of the privilege.[16] Moreover, as in most areas, ignorance of the law is no excuse: it does not matter that the holder was unaware of the existence of a privilege or the legal effect of the disclosure.[17] An important exception to the principle of waiver by voluntary disclosure is that no waiver occurs if the disclosure was made in the context of what is itself a privileged communication.[18] As an illustration, a privileged communication between husband and wife is not waived if the couple discloses the communication in the context of later consulting an attorney for legal advice. Otherwise, voluntary disclosure of any significant part of the privileged information generally effects a waiver of the privilege as to the entire subject matter.[19] The burden of establishing the facts showing waiver of a privilege is on the person claiming waiver, that is, the opponent of the claim

---

[15] ABA MODEL RULES OF PROFESSIONAL RESPONSIBILITY 1.6, comment 3.

[16] *See, e.g.,* Proposed FED. R. EVID. 511; CAL. EVID. CODE § 912. *See generally* EDWARD J. IMWINKELRIED, THE NEW WIGMORE: EVIDENTIARY PRIVILEGES § 6.12 (2d ed. 2010). Once waived, that privilege (as to that matter) cannot be claimed later. United States v. Suarez, 820 F.2d 1158, 1160 (11th Cir. 1987), *cert. denied*, 484 U.S. 987.

[17] *See* EDWARD J. IMWINKELRIED, THE NEW WIGMORE: EVIDENTIARY PRIVILEGES § 6.12.4 at 1084–86 (2d ed. 2010).

[18] *See, e.g.,* Proposed FED. R. EVID. 511 (providing that waiver by voluntary disclosure "does not apply if the disclosure is itself a privileged communication.").

[19] *See* EDWARD J. IMWINKELRIED, THE NEW WIGMORE: EVIDENTIARY PRIVILEGES § 6.12.4 at 1006–08, § 6.12.7 (2d ed. 2010).

of privilege.[20] Beyond these general points, however, waiver is a complex subject better addressed in the context of specific privileges.

Questions of waiver must be distinguished from questions about whether the privilege ever "attached" in the first place. If the privilege does not attach to particular information or a particular communication, then the issue of waiver is inapt. For example, if a communication with, say, an attorney or a spouse, is made in the presence of other people or overheard by such people, then it is possible that the privilege does not attach to the communication, in which case there is nothing to be waived. Sometimes, courts use the language of waiver in such contexts when what they should say is that the privilege never attached at all. The result is usually the same, but it might matter that the burden of persuasion regarding the attachment of the privilege differs from the burden of persuasion on the issue of waiver.[21]

What happens if privileged information is disclosed without the privilege holder's consent?

If, for example, an attorney has confidential communications with the client and then discloses the content of those communications without the client's knowledge or consent, what should happen if either the attorney or the person to whom the confidence was disclosed is called to testify about the communication? Clearly, the client did not waive the privilege, yet the information is now "out there"; it is no longer confidential. Should the privilege simply lapse or disappear? If it did, would any privilege ever be safe enough?

The drafters of the federal rules proposed a rule to deal with this kind of situation:

> Evidence of a statement or other disclosure of privileged matter is not admissible against the holder of the privilege if the disclosure was (a) compelled erroneously or (b) made without opportunity to claim the privilege.[22]

Like all the specific privilege rules, this one was not enacted, but it is thought to reflect the better view to be found in the case law.

May an opponent draw the attention of the fact-finder to the fact that a privilege has been invoked?

As a general matter, the common-law practice has allowed a party to invite the fact-finder to draw an adverse inference from an opponent's failure to provide evidence that is within the opponent's exclusive control.[23] If this idea is applied to privileges, there is a risk that the practice will undermine the value of the privilege to the public by discouraging the kind of information collection or communication that is covered by the privilege. At the same time, it invites jury speculation about the reasons for the privilege and the motives for its exercise. Consequently, much academic opinion supports the idea that, if a privilege is to be allowed, its exercise should be protected from adverse comment

---

[20] *Id.*, § 6.12.2.

[21] *See, e.g.*, Howell v. Jaffe, 483 F. Supp. 2d 659 (N.D. Ill. 2007) (applying Illinois law and concluding that there was no "waiver" when attorney's conversation with client was inadvertently recorded on opponent's telephone voicemail, but appearing to place the burden of persuasion on the issue on the holder of the privilege, which makes sense if the issue is actually whether the privilege attached).

[22] *See* Proposed FED. R. EVID. 512.

[23] *See* **§ 5.05** (subsection on "Evidence of a Party's Attempt to Withhold, Destroy, or Fabricate Evidence").

or inference; the cases, however, are in conflict on the question.[24] The drafters of the federal rules, following the California rule, proposed disallowing any such comment or inference, though the proposal, like the other specific rules regarding privilege, was not adopted.[25] That proposed rule (or the Uniform Rules' equivalent) was, however, adopted by several states, and this seems to reflect the trend in the case law.[26]

In one context, the accused's exercise of the privilege against self-incrimination, adverse inferences are prohibited as a matter of constitutional law.[27] The rationale of this no-inference rule, however, must be substantially different because the privilege against self-incrimination, unlike other privileges, is not intended to facilitate useful communication or to protect the process of collecting valuable information or to protect family integrity. A witness who is not the accused in a criminal case bears no risk that the jury will convict the witness. Accordingly, the courts have generally allowed the cross-examiner of a civil party or a non-party witness to invite an adverse inference from the witness's invocation of the privilege against self-incrimination.[28]

§ 4.03 The Lawyer-Client Privilege

Although many states have statutes that regulate the lawyer-client privilege, the surrounding case law often does not interpret the language of the statute precisely or technically.[29] State supreme courts tend to treat such statutes as merely announcing that the state has a lawyer-client privilege. The courts then derive the privilege's boundaries from case law and treatises, without paying much attention to the exact statutory language.[30] Thus, a statute that by its terms applies to all communications is likely to be interpreted to apply only to confidential communications. Common-law exceptions to the privilege, such as the exception for communications made in furtherance of fraud, are likely to be read into the statutes.[31]

---

[24] *See* 1 MCCORMICK ON EVIDENCE § 74.1 (Kenneth S. Broun gen ed., 7th ed. 2013); 2 CHRISTOPHER B. MUELLER & LAIRD C. KIRKPATRICK, EVIDENCE § 5.12 (4th ed. 2013).

[25] *See* CAL. EVID. CODE § 913 (rejecting comment on and adverse inferences from exercise of privilege); Proposed FED. R. EVID. 513.

[26] *See, e.g.*, United States v. Morris, 988 F.2d 1335, 1339 (4th Cir. 1993) (holding it improper for prosecution to question defendant's spouse, who had testified for the defense, about the witness's previous invocation of marital privilege at the grand jury); United States v. Chapman, 866 F.2d 1326 (11th Cir. 1989) (ruling it improper for the prosecutor to call the defendant's wife to the stand in order to force her to invoke a marital privilege in front of the jury). For illustrative state rules, *compare* and TEX. R. EVID. 513 (rejecting adverse inferences from exercise of privilege, except in civil cases with respect to the privilege against self-incrimination claimed by a party) *and* IND. R. EVID. 501(d) (to similar effect), *and* N.H. RULE EVID. 512 (to similar effect), *with* ALASKA R. EVID. 512 (rejecting adverse inferences in all contexts), *and with* ME. R. EVID. 512, 513 (rejecting adverse inferences in criminal cases but not in civil cases).

[27] *See* **§ 4.18.**

[28] *See, e.g.*, Baxter v. Palmigiano, 425 U.S. 308, 318 (1976) (inference against party in civil proceeding); United States v. Kaplan, 832 F.2d 676, 682–84 (1st Cir.1987), *cert. denied*, 485 U.S. 907 (1988) (inference against prosecution witness); High Fructose Corn Syrup Antitrust Litigation, 295 F.3d 651, 663–64 (7th Cir. 2002) (inference against non-party witness in civil case).

[29] *See* Gregory C. Sisk & Pamela J. Abbate, *The Dynamic Attorney-Client Privilege*, 23 GEO. J. LEGAL ETHICS 201 (2010).

[30] Note, *Developments in the Law-Privileged Communications*, 98 HARV. L. REV. 1450, 1458 (1985); RESTATEMENT (THIRD) OF THE LAW GOVERNING LAWYERS § 68 (2000) ("Most states whose law of the privilege is embodied in a statute or evidence code have not interpreted these narrowly or technically but have shown great flexibility of interpretation.").

[31] *See, e.g.*, State v. Montgomery, 499 So. 2d 709, 711 (La. Ct. App. 1986) (common-law rule that lawyer-client privilege extends to client's communications with lawyer's agents although statute only referred to communications with lawyer); Brown v. St. Paul City Ry. Co., 62 N.W.2d 688, 700–01 (Minn. 1954) (endorsing

Wigmore defined the attorney-client privilege as follows:

> (1) Where legal advice of any kind is sought (2) from a professional legal adviser in his capacity as such, (3) the communications relating to that purpose, (4) made in confidence (5) by the client, (6) are at his instance permanently protected (7) from disclosure by himself or by the legal adviser, (8) except the protection be waived.[32]

While this articulation accurately summarizes the modern privilege, three matters should be added. First, the privilege covers communications from the lawyer to the client, as well as those by the client to the lawyer.[33] Second, the privilege usually covers communications made through a representative of the lawyer or client.[34] Third, the privilege is subject to widely recognized exceptions, such as the exception for communications made in furtherance of crime or fraud.

Another frequently quoted formulation of the privilege appears in an opinion by Judge Wyzanski:

> The privilege applies only if (1) the asserted holder of the privilege is or sought to become a client; (2) the person to whom the communication was made (a) is a member of the bar of a court, or his subordinate and (b) in connection with this communication is acting as a lawyer; (3) the communication relates to a fact of which the attorney was informed (a) by his client (b) without the presence of strangers (c) for the purpose of securing primarily either (i) an opinion on law or (ii) legal services or (iii) assistance in some legal proceeding, and not (d) for the purpose of committing a crime or tort; and (4) the privilege has been (a) claimed and (b) not waived by the client.[35]

A more recent attempt to describe the privilege appears in an American Law Institute Restatement. Subject to exceptions, the Restatement's drafters provide that "[T]he attorney-client privilege may be invoked . . . with respect to (1) a communication (2) made between privileged persons (3) in confidence (4) for the purpose of obtaining or providing legal assistance for the client."[36] "Privileged persons" are elsewhere defined as "the client (including a prospective client), the client's lawyer, agents of either who facilitate communications between them, and agents of the lawyer who facilitate the representation. . . ."[37]

Originally, the lawyer-client privilege arose from the idea that the barrister was a gentleman of honor and that a gentleman should not be forced to betray confidences.[38]

Wigmore's definition of lawyer-client privilege, including requirement that communication be confidential, despite statute's unqualified language that appeared to apply to all communications).

[32] 8 WIGMORE ON EVIDENCE § 2292 (McNaughton rev. 1961).

[33] *See, e.g.*, Schwimmer v. United States, 232 F.2d 855, 863 (8th Cir. 1956) (purpose of lawyer-client privilege to promote communication by preventing disclosure of confidential information, requires protection of lawyer's communications to client); Natta v. Hogan, 392 F.2d 686, 692–93 (10th Cir. 1968) (lawyer's letters to client privileged); 8 JOHN H. WIGMORE, EVIDENCE IN TRIAL AT COMMON LAW § 2320 (McNaughton rev. 1961) (seldom questioned that lawyer's communications to client are privileged). *Cf.* Mead Data Central, Inc. v. United States Dep't of the Air Force, 566 F.2d 242, 254 (D.C. Cir. 1977) (privilege only extends to lawyer's communications to client if based on confidential information provided by client).

[34] *See* **§ 4.04 & § 4.05**.

[35] United States v. United Shoe Mach. Corp., 89 F. Supp. 357, 358–59 (D. Mass. 1950).

[36] RESTATEMENT (THIRD) OF THE LAW GOVERNING LAWYERS § 68 (2000).

[37] *Id.* § 70.

[38] 8 WIGMORE ON EVIDENCE § 2290 (McNaughton rev. 1961).

Under this concept, the privilege was for the benefit of the lawyer and the lawyer had the authority to waive it.[39] The utilitarian rationale for the privilege generally has replaced the original concept. Under the utilitarian rationale, the purpose of the privilege is to encourage clients to confide in lawyers, so that lawyers can provide full and frank advice.[40]

The legal philosopher Jeremy Bentham attacked the utilitarian theory, saying that its only effect was to help the guilty to receive better advice; the innocent did not need the protection of the privilege, since they had nothing to hide.[41] Bentham's scathing critique is too simplistic. It is rare for a client's case to be completely good or bad. Moreover, even people who have a "good" case may have something the lawyer should know but about which they are less than proud. The lawyer can give more realistic advice if the weak points of the client's case and situation are known. The more the lawyer knows of both the strengths and the weaknesses of the client's case, the more likely the matter is to be settled in a way that saves time and expense for both parties and society at large.

In any event, the abolition of the privilege would encourage misconduct. First, advocates would be more likely to call the opposing counsel to the stand as a litigation tactic, perhaps to sow dissension between lawyer and client or simply to disrupt the other party's case.[42] Second, a rule that allows the opponent to force testimony would place the lawyer in the trilemma of committing perjury, hurting the client, or being held in contempt. Dishonorable lawyers would prefer perjury, to keep the client's loyalty and business, and this would place honorable lawyers at a disadvantage. Despite these grounds for defending the privilege, even its supporters concede that the privilege can obstruct justice and that its benefits are conjectural and removed from the merits of the case.[43]

Communications, not acts and observations, are protected by the lawyer-client privilege. For example, suppose a client becomes a fugitive, and the lawyer is asked to provide evidence about the client's physical appearance to aid in apprehension. Information about the client's physical appearance is not privileged, because it was not acquired through a communication. The lawyer can be forced to testify about the client's physical characteristics, dress, bearing, sobriety, mannerisms, and other matters that are non-communicative.[44]

A controversial application of this concept occurs when the lawyer is required to testify about the mental competency of a client. For example, in *State v. Jensen*,[45] the prosecution called the defendant's lawyer in a prior trial to show that the defendant was mentally competent to stand trial. The defendant objected and the prior lawyer stated

---

39 *See id.* (Privilege was "consideration for the oath and the honor of the lawyer.").

40 Upjohn Co. v. United States, 449 U.S. 383, 389 (1981); 8 WIGMORE ON EVIDENCE § 2291 (McNaughton rev. 1961).

41 5 JEREMY BENTHAM, RATIONALE OF JUDICIAL EVIDENCE 302–04 (1827).

42 RESTATEMENT (THIRD) OF THE LAW GOVERNING LAWYERS § 68 (2000).

43 8 WIGMORE ON EVIDENCE § 2291 (McNaughton rev. 1961).

44 *See, e.g.*, United States v. Kendrick, 331 F.2d 110, 113–14 (4th Cir. 1964) (complexion, demeanor, bearing, sobriety, dress, matters "observable by anyone" not privileged); 8 WIGMORE ON EVIDENCE § 2306 (McNaughton rev. 1961) (facts that another person would observe if present and not intended as communication not privileged); *see also* EDWARD J. IMWINKELRIED, THE NEW WIGMORE: EVIDENTIARY PRIVILEGES § 6.7.1 (2d ed. 2010).

45 174 N.W.2d 226 (Minn. 1970).

that he would be unable to divorce confidential information from expressions and other behavioral manifestations of the defendant. The trial court required the lawyer to testify. He testified that the defendant appeared normal during the prior representation and that they had discussed trial tactics.[46] The Minnesota Supreme Court held that there was no error in admitting the testimony, saying that a lawyer's observations of his client are "simply not communications."[47] Though it would appear that the lawyer would base part of the assessment of competency on what the client communicated to the lawyer, the court ignored this aspect. The result (that lawyers may be required to testify about competency to stand trial) has been very widely accepted.[48] It has been suggested that these cases are really a special exception to the privilege founded on the necessity of getting testimony from the person best able to say whether the client was competent to cooperate in the client's defense.[49]

The Limited Protection for a Lawyer's Work Product

When material is sought from counsel during discovery, the claim of lawyer-client privilege is likely to be accompanied by a claim that the material is protected as the lawyer's "work product." Under Federal Rule of Civil Procedure 26(b)(3), a party may obtain discovery of documents and tangible things prepared "in anticipation of litigation" by a lawyer or other agent of the opposing party only by showing "substantial need" and that it is unable, without undue hardship, to obtain the substantial equivalent from other sources. Moreover, even if the party makes the requisite showing of need, the court must protect against disclosure of "the mental impressions, conclusions, opinions, or legal theories of a lawyer or other representative of a party concerning the litigation."[50] However, under the Federal Rules of Civil Procedure, a party or a witness is entitled to obtain from an opponent a copy of the party's own statement as a matter of course.[51]

---

[46] *See id.* at 228.

[47] *See id.* at 230.

[48] *See, e.g.*, United States v. Kendrick, 331 F.2d 110, 114 (4th Cir. 1964) (lawyer's testimony concerning client's cooperativeness and awareness at trial not privileged); Darrow v. Gunn, 594 F.2d 767, 774 (9th Cir. 1979) (state privilege protecting only "confidential communications" does not protect lawyer's observation and impressions of client's mental condition); Bishop v. Superior Court, 724 P.2d 23, 28–29 (Ariz. 1986) (lawyer's observations of defendant's ability to assist in defense not privileged); People v. Perry, 132 P.3d 235, 244 (Cal. 2006) ("An attorney's impression of his client's mental state is not protected by the attorney-client privilege."). *But see* Gunther v. United States, 230 F.2d 222, 223–24 (D.C. Cir. 1956) (lawyer's testimony concerning client's competency violates privilege because it would lead to examination of facts underlying opinion, thereby opening door to inquiry of entire lawyer-client relationship).

[49] RESTATEMENT (THIRD) OF THE LAW GOVERNING LAWYERS § 69 cmt. f (2000) (approach that would forbid defense attorney from testifying client's competency).

[50] FED. R. CIV. P. 26(b)(3), in relevant part, reads as follows:

> (A) Documents and Tangible Things. Ordinarily, a party may not discover documents and tangible things that are prepared in anticipation of litigation or for trial by or for another party or its representative (including the other party's attorney, consultant, surety, indemnitor, insurer, or agent). But, subject to Rule 26(b)(4), those materials may be discovered if:
>
> (i) they are otherwise discoverable under Rule 26(b)(1); and
>
> (ii) the party shows that it has substantial need for the materials to prepare its case and cannot, without undue hardship, obtain their substantial equivalent by other means.
>
> (B) Protection Against Disclosure. If the court orders discovery of those materials, it must protect against disclosure of the mental impressions, conclusions, opinions, or legal theories of a party's attorney or other representative concerning the litigation.

[51] Rule 26(b)(3)(C) provides that "Any party or other person may, on request and without the required showing, obtain the person's own previous statement about the action or its subject matter."

Both the work-product and the lawyer-client privilege rules protect material gathered for purposes of litigation. These two protections are distinct and there are several differences between them:

1. Material that is covered by the lawyer-client privilege cannot be discovered even upon a showing of special need.[52] Material that is covered by work-product protection can be discovered with such a showing, except for material that would reveal the mental impressions, etc., of the party's lawyer or other representative.[53]

2. Only confidential communications between the lawyer and client (or between the client and a representative of the lawyer) are covered by the lawyer-client privilege.[54] A much larger category of material is covered by the work-product protection. For example, a lawyer's memorandum about a statement made by a non-client to the lawyer falls within the work-product privilege.[55] In this case, a lawyer need not be involved at all for the work-product protection to take effect. Information gathered by the party or the party's agent (such as a claim adjuster) is covered by the work-product doctrine so long as the information is gathered in anticipation of litigation.[56]

3. The work-product protection applies only to information gathered in "anticipation of litigation."[57] The lawyer-client privilege covers confidential communications to the lawyer seeking legal advice or services, whether or not litigation is expected.[58]

§ 4.04 The Lawyer-Client Privilege—the Requirement of Confidentiality

The lawyer-client privilege applies to confidential communications only. A communication may be considered non-confidential because of a third party presence.[59]

---

52 *See, e.g.*, Diversified Indus., Inc. v. Meredith, 572 F.2d 596, 602 (8th Cir. 1977) (privilege is absolute where it exists); Ohl-Marsters v. Johnston, 2009 WL 3253866 (E.D. Mo. 2009).

53 FED. R. CIV. P. 26(b)(3)(B).

54 *See* **§ 4.04**.

55 *See, e.g.*, Upjohn Co. v. United States, 449 U.S. 383, 400 (1981) (purposes of F.R.C.P. 26 include protection of memoranda based on oral statements of witnesses); Hickman v. Taylor, 329 U.S. 495, 507–14 (1947) (lawyer could not be forced to disclose memoranda on statements of witnesses).

56 *See* FED. R. CIV. P. 26(b)(3)(A) (protected materials include those produced by "party's attorney, consultant, surety, indemnitor, insurer, or agent.").

57 *Id.*

58 *See* **§ 4.06**.

59 *See, e.g.*, United States v. Schussel, 291 Fed. Appx. 336, 347 (1st Cir. 2008) (information sent to individual's attorney with intent that information be conveyed to IRS was not protected by attorney-client privilege); Cavallaro v. United States, 284 F.3d 236, 249 (1st Cir. 2002) (attorney-client privilege could not be used to protect communications with accounting firm, where accounting firm was independently hired to provide tax advice and only later began coordinating with party's attorneys); United States v. Melvin, 650 F.2d 641, 645–46 (5th Cir. 1981) (third person not part of defense team); United States v. Landof, 591 F.2d 36, 39 (9th Cir. 1978) (second lawyer not representing client or acting as agent of client's lawyer); 8 WIGMORE ON EVIDENCE § 2311 (McNaughton rev. 1961) (presence of third person neither agent of client nor lawyer destroys privilege). *Cf.* United States v. Bigos, 459 F.2d 639, 643 (1st Cir. 1972) (presence of client's father did not destroy privilege when circumstances indicated that parties still viewed communications as confidential); *In re* Bieter Co., 16 F.3d 929 (8th Cir. 1994) (lawyer-client privilege applies to communications between independent consultant who was functional equivalent of client's employee and client's lawyer).

For example, if the client says something to the lawyer at an open shareholders' meeting, the communication is not privileged because it was not intended to be confidential.

Despite this rule, the presence of some third parties may not destroy the privilege. Courts universally allow the lawyer's secretary or clerk to be present without destroying the privilege.[60] Case law also allows the presence of persons who are necessary for communication, such as translators, without any effect on the privilege.[61] In some instances, this principle includes other persons helpful to communication, such as an accountant trusted by the client to interpret financial data or a close family member who aided the client.[62] The common-law cases are not wholly consistent on this point, but it seems that the privilege will be upheld if (1) the client reasonably believed that the discussion was confidential, and (2) the third person's presence was reasonably necessary in the furtherance of the consultation.[63] The ever-changing nature of the law and the chance that the third person will be found unnecessary make it dangerous to allow the client to bring third persons to an interview, unless a clear need exists. The risk that such an action will negate the privilege is substantial. However, if the third person also has a privileged relationship and communicates in furtherance of a service provided by both the third party and the lawyer, the circle of privilege remains unbroken.

Joint consultations present the possibility of unexpected loss of the privilege if the parties to the joint consultation become adverse.[64] Suppose that two business people consult a lawyer to form a corporation, have a falling out, and end up suing each other. Although their original consultation was privileged against any claim from others to produce its content in a judicial proceeding, neither party's communications with the lawyer are privileged in a dispute between the two clients. This result does not undermine the policy of encouraging disclosures to lawyers, because neither party would know who would profit or lose by later disclosure, and, hence, neither would be inhibited about making disclosures during the joint consultation. At any rate, the parties did not intend for the matter to be confidential between them, so the privilege fails.[65]

Historically, eavesdroppers have been permitted to testify, even if the client and the lawyer intended the communication to be confidential.[66] The client and lawyer are

---

60 *See, e.g.*, Taylor v. Taylor, 177 S.E. 582, 583 (Ga. 1934) (communications to lawyer's confidential secretary privileged); Sibley v. Waffle, 16 N.Y. 180, 183 (1857) (privilege protects communications to lawyer's clerk); 8 WIGMORE ON EVIDENCE § 2311 (McNaughton rev. 1961); EDWARD J. IMWINKELRIED, THE NEW WIGMORE: EVIDENTIARY PRIVILEGES § 6.8.1 (2d ed. 2010).

61 *See, e.g.*, United States v. Kovel, 296 F.2d 918, 921–22 (2d Cir. 1961) (privilege includes translators assisting lawyer to communicate with client).

62 *See, e.g.*, *Kovel*, 296 F.2d at 921–22 (analogizing accountant who helped client by interpreting data for lawyer to language translator; upholding privilege); *In re* Estate of Weinberg, 509 N.Y.S.2d 240, 242 (N.Y. Sup. Ct. 1986) (privilege covered daughter of client who aided in business).

63 *See, e.g.*, RESTATEMENT (THIRD) OF THE LAW GOVERNING LAWYERS § 70, cmt. f (2000) ("A person is a confidential agent for communication if the person's participation is reasonably necessary to facilitate the client's communication with a lawyer or another privileged person and if the client reasonably believes that the person will hold the communication in confidence.").

64 *See, e.g.*, Grand Trunk W. R.R. Co. v. H.W. Nelson Co., 116 F.2d 823, 835 (6th Cir. 1941) (communications made to lawyer when representing both parties not privileged in later dispute between parties); Emley v. Selepchak, 63 N.E.2d 919, 922 (Ohio Ct. App. 1945) (communications made to lawyer by two parties forming contract not privileged in suit for specific performance); 8 WIGMORE ON EVIDENCE § 2312 (McNaughton rev. 1961) (no privilege between joint clients because no secrecy existed between them at time of communication).

65 8 WIGMORE ON EVIDENCE § 2312 (McNaughton rev. 1961).

66 *See, e.g.*, Schwartz v. Wenger, 124 N.W.2d 489, 492 (Minn. 1963) (conversation admitted between lawyer and client overheard in hallway of courthouse).Clark v. State, 261 S.W.2d 339, 342 (Tex. Crim. App.

responsible for taking precautions to prevent such individuals from observing the content of the communication. If they try to do so, but do not succeed, the evidence is still admissible in some jurisdictions.[67] The law seems to be changing, however, and recent authority suggests that the privilege is not vitiated, so the privilege claim will be sustained, if the client and lawyer took reasonable precautions to keep the conversation confidential.[68] This is particularly true when the eavesdropper's conduct involves some degree of invasion of privacy, or is actually illegal, as in the case of an illegal wiretap.

Even if third parties are not present when the communication is made, a communication may fall outside the lawyer-client privilege because the client intended for the lawyer to make the communication public at some future time. For example, if the client gave the lawyer information to be included in a public document, the communication is not privileged.[69]

§ 4.05 The Lawyer-Client Privilege—the Requirement of Communication to a Proper Person

The lawyer-client privilege applies only to communications between the client and the lawyer or the lawyer's representative. A client who seeks legal advice from someone who is not a lawyer is not entitled to the lawyer-client privilege, unless the client reasonably believed that person to be a lawyer.[70] Confidential communications with the non-lawyers employed by the lawyer—such as secretaries, investigators, paralegals, and clerks—are usually covered by the privilege, even if the lawyer is not present at the time of the communication.[71]

Experts in various areas, such as doctors, engineers, accountants, and others with specialized knowledge, are often employed by a lawyer to assist in case preparation. Whether the lawyer-client privilege covers conversations between the lawyer's client and these experts usually depends upon the nature of the expert's work and who hired the expert. In many jurisdictions, if the lawyer hires the expert and the expert's sole

---

1953) (telephone operator who eavesdropped on conversation between lawyer and client could testify as to what she heard); 8 WIGMORE ON EVIDENCE § 2326 (McNaughton rev. 1961) (privilege does not cover third party overhearing communication with or without client's knowledge).

[67] *See, e.g.*, People v. Urbano, 26 Cal.Rptr.3d 871, 875–76 (Cal. Ct. App. 2005) (conversation overheard in courtroom during recess admitted).

[68] *See, e.g.*, *In re* Grand Jury Proceedings Involving Berkley & Co., 466 F. Supp. 863, 869 (D. Minn. 1979) (where employee retained documents without employer's consent and disclosed them modern trend preserves privilege when lawyer and client take reasonable precautions); *In re* Dayco Corp. Derivative Securities Litigation, 102 F.R.D. 468 (S.D. Ohio 1984) (sustaining privilege claim when intercepted communication was intended to be confidential and reasonable precautions were taken). *See generally* EDWARD J. IMWINKELRIED, THE NEW WIGMORE: EVIDENTIARY PRIVILEGES §§ 6.6.7, 6.8 (2d ed. 2010) (modern trend is not to allow unauthorized eavesdroppers to testify); PAUL F. ROTHSTEIN & SUSAN CRUMP, FEDERAL TESTIMONIAL PRIVILEGES § 2:16.

[69] *See* United States v. Naegele, 468 F. Supp. 2d 165, 170 (D.D.C. 2007) (draft bankruptcy filings are not protected by attorney-client privilege).

[70] *See, e.g.*, People v. Velasquez, 237 Cal. Rptr. 366, 371 (Cal. Ct. App. 1987) (client's communication not privileged because he did not talk to lawyer or person he reasonably believed to be lawyer); People v. Barker, 27 N.W. 539, 546 (Mich. 1886) (defendant's confession made to private detective falsely claiming to be lawyer privileged); 8 WIGMORE ON EVIDENCE § 2302 (McNaughton rev. 1961) (client entitled to peace of mind, should not bear risk of deception or defective professional title). *Cf.*, State v. Lender, 124 N.W.2d 355, 359 (Minn. 1963) (statements made to someone not yet admitted to bar not privileged).

[71] *See, e.g.*, Hillary v. Minneapolis St. Ry. Co., 116 N.W. 933, 934 (Minn. 1908).

responsibility is to assist the lawyer in preparing the case, the communication between the client and the expert will be covered by the lawyer-client privilege.[72]

There are two common circumstances in which the lawyer-client privilege may not cover the communication between the client and an expert assisting a lawyer to prepare the client's case. The first is when the expert is going to be a witness at trial. In such a case, the purpose of the communication between the client and the expert is to prepare the expert to testify, rather than to assist the lawyer in giving legal advice. The second is when the expert assisting the lawyer also has a separate professional relationship with the client. In that instance, there is some danger that the communication between client and expert will be viewed as one for the purpose of their professional relationship, rather than for the purpose of helping the lawyer to provide legal services. In that event, the communication is unlikely to be privileged, unless the relationship between the expert and the client is one that carries its own privilege. Therefore, a lawyer is well advised not to employ an expert who has either a mixed purpose or a dual relationship if the lawyer desires to ensure that communications between the lawyer's client and the expert are privileged.

Doctors present a common example. For example, in jurisdictions that do not recognize a doctor-patient privilege, communications between a client and a doctor hired by the lawyer for the sole purpose of assisting in case preparation are nonetheless covered by the lawyer-client privilege or work-product privilege.[73] However, even in jurisdictions that recognize a doctor-patient privilege, a communication between a doctor and a lawyer's client is not privileged if the doctor is a witness at trial.

The requirement that the client's communication be with the lawyer or lawyer's representative also means that the client's pre-existing documents do not become privileged when the client transfers them to the lawyer.[74] Therefore, the lawyer-client privilege does not cover documents prepared by the client for another purpose, even if transferred to the lawyer in preparation of the client's case or if created for a "secret" purpose. The original act of putting the thoughts or numbers on paper was not made for the purpose of communicating with a lawyer and, therefore, is not included in the lawyer-client privilege. In addition, many such documents were not intended to be confidential

---

[72] *See, e.g.*, United States v. Alvarez, 519 F.2d 1036, 1046 (3d Cir. 1975) (defendant's communications to psychiatrist retained privilege); City & County of San Francisco v. Superior Court, 231 P.2d 26, 31–32 (Cal. 1951) (client's communications to physician hired by attorney to help prepare for litigation privileged); RESTATEMENT (THIRD) OF THE LAW GOVERNING LAWYERS § 70, cmt. g (2000) ("The privilege also extends to communications to and from the client that are disclosed to independent contractors retained by a lawyer, such as an accountant or physician retained by the lawyer to assist in providing legal services to the client and not for the purpose of testifying."). *Cf.* United States *ex rel.* Edney v. Smith, 425 F. Supp. 1038, 1054–55 (E.D.N.Y. 1976), *aff'd*, 556 F.2d 556 (2d Cir. 1977) (under state law, defendant waived privilege in relation to communications to psychiatrist by raising insanity as defense).

[73] *In re* Grand Jury Proceedings v. United States, 947 F.2d 1188, 1190–91 (4th Cir. 1991) (client confers with accountant without consulting lawyer, no privilege attaches to matters discussed with accountant, even if lawyer is later consulted; but when accountant is used as client's agent in communicating with lawyer, lawyer-client privilege attaches as to matters that client discussed with accountant).

[74] *See, e.g.*, Colton v. United States, 306 F.2d 633, 639 (2d Cir. 1962) (pre-existing documents related to preparation and filing of tax returns, not prepared by client for purpose of communicating with lawyer not privileged); City of Philadelphia v. Westinghouse Elec. Corp., 205 F. Supp. 830, 831 (E.D. Pa. 1962) (client may not refuse to disclose relevant information merely because incorporated it into communication to lawyer); State *ex rel.* Dudek v. Circuit Court, 150 N.W.2d 387, 399 (Wis. 1967) (client cannot hide pre-existing document be merely giving it to lawyer).

when created,[75] and most were not created for the purpose of obtaining legal advice.[76] In contrast, if the client prepares a confidential document for his or her lawyer for the purpose of obtaining legal advice, that document is covered by the lawyer-client privilege whether the underlying information is secret or not.[77]

§ 4.06 The Lawyer-Client Privilege—the Requirement That the Purpose Be to Obtain Legal Advice or Service

The lawyer-client privilege applies only when the client seeks legal (as opposed to business, political, or personal) advice from the lawyer. Neither the formality of a lawyer-client retainer nor the condition of a professional environment is necessary to trigger the privilege.[78] For example, the communications of a person who seeks a preliminary discussion and decides not to hire the lawyer are covered to the same extent as the communication between the lawyer and a fee-paying client. Similarly, a communication about legal advice is covered to the same extent when conducted during a cocktail party as when conducted in the lawyer's office, so long as the person seeking the advice and the lawyer take measures to keep the communication confidential.

Another example is a communication made to a lawyer as a friend in her role as friend. This is not covered by the lawyer-client privilege, even if the friend is also a client.[79] For example, if a lawyer receives a phone call from a friend who is also a client about committing suicide, the conversation is not privileged if litigation later arises concerning whether that friend died a natural death.[80]

When a lawyer serves as an executive or business counselor and also provides legal advice, this can present difficult issues concerning the purpose of communication. Consider, for example, when a corporate vice president says in confidence to another corporate vice president who is also a lawyer, "We're thinking about acquiring Compaq Computer. What do you think?" If the question is asked to gain only business advice, it

---

75 *See* **§ 4.04**.

76 *See* **§ 4.06**.

77 *See, e.g.,* Upjohn Co. v. United States, 449 U.S. 383, 395 (1981) (responses to lawyers' questionnaires used for providing legal advice to corporation privileged); City of Philadelphia v. Westinghouse Elec. Corp., 205 F. Supp. 830, 831 (E.D. Pa. 1962) (client cannot be compelled to testify as to what she said or wrote to lawyer).

78 *See, e.g., In re* Dupont's Estate, 140 P.2d 866, 872–73 (Cal. Ct. App. 1943) (preliminary communications made by client seeking to contest will privileged, although lawyer refused employment; otherwise no person could safely consult lawyer for first time); Taylor v. Sheldon, 173 N.E.2d 892, 895 (Ohio 1961) (communications made to lawyer by client seeking preparation of will privileged, even though lawyer chose not to prepare will); 8 WIGMORE ON EVIDENCE § 2304 (McNaughton rev. 1961) (preliminary communications made by person seeking legal counsel privileged whether person does not hire lawyer or lawyer declines employment). *Cf.* McGrede v. Rembert Nat'l. Bank, 147 S.W.2d 580, 584 (Tex. Civ. App. 1941) (communications made after lawyer declines employment not privileged).

79 *See, e.g., In re* Lindsey, 158 F.3d 1263, 1270 (D.C. Cir. 1998) (White House Counsel's advice to President Clinton relating to "political, strategic, or policy issues" not privileged); G & S Investments v. Belman, 700 P.2d 1358, 1364–65 (Ariz. App. 1984) (speaker's conversation with lawyer-friend about nature of speaker's interest in business partnership not privileged where speaker's purpose was to inform lawyer-friend that he was going to receive bequest, rather than to get legal advice); 1 MCCORMICK ON EVIDENCE § 88 at 541 (Kenneth S. Broun ed., 7th ed. 2013) (noting that communications made to lawyer as friend not privileged).

80 *See, e.g.,* Modern Woodmen of America v. Watkins, 132 F.2d 352, 354 (5th Cir. 1942) (communication of suicidal intent made to lawyer as friend not privileged).

is not privileged.[81] However, if it is asked to gain legal advice, it is privileged, even if there is a secondary purpose to receive business advice.[82]

The context of a communication that might be business, legal, or both determines whether the lawyer-client privilege applies. If the question following the statement about acquiring Compaq had been, "Will this give us a great market share, or what?" the conversation probably seeks business, not legal, advice and, therefore, should not be privileged. If, on the other hand, the question had been, "Do we have an antitrust concern here?" there would be little doubt that the conversation was for the purpose of gaining legal advice and should be privileged. If the communication regarding antitrust problems is made in the presence of others, however, the privilege might not apply because the communication may not meet the confidentiality requirement of privilege.[83]

§ 4.07 The Lawyer-Client Privilege—Application to Fact of Employment, Identity of Client, and Payment of Fees

Information about the fact of employment and the identity of the client is generally not covered by the privilege.[84] Generally, no special principle is needed to reach this result. The client's name is likely to appear in correspondence to third parties from the lawyer, on bills from the lawyer that are sent through the mail, and perhaps on pleadings in litigation in which adversaries are entitled to know against whom they are contending.[85] Because clients rarely expect their name and the fact that they have retained a lawyer to be confidential, the general principle of the lawyer-client privilege, which only protects communications intended to be confidential, does not apply.[86]

A number of circumstances arise, however, in which a client might expect and even expressly request confidentiality. A whistle-blower with information about official corruption may want to hire a lawyer to convey the information to the proper authorities

---

[81] *See, e.g.*, United States v. Huberts, 637 F.2d 630, 640 (9th Cir. 1980) (lawyer who represented client in consignment sale of printing press served as business agent and may not assert privilege); *In re* Grand Jury Investigation, 842 F.2d 1223, 1224–25 (11th Cir. 1987) (communications about income to lawyer acting as tax return preparer not privileged because lawyer not giving legal advice; extensive citation of authority); 1 McCORMICK ON EVIDENCE § 88 at 541 (Kenneth S. Broun ed., 6th ed. 2006) (consultations with lawyer as business advisor, banker, negotiator, or accountant not privileged).

[82] *See, e.g.*, United States v. United Shoe Machinery Corp., 89 F. Supp. 357, 359 (D. Mass. 1950) (presence of relevant nonlegal considerations in communications primarily related to legal advice did not destroy privilege; "modern lawyer almost invariably advises his client upon not only what is permissible but also what is desirable"); *see also* Linde, P.C. v. Resolution Trust Corp., 5 F.3d 1508, 1514–15 (D.C. Cir. 1993) (attorney-client privilege does not apply to communications between law firm and its insurer); NXIVM Corp. v. O'Hara, 241 F.R.D. 109 (N.D.N.Y. 2007) (attorney-client privilege does not protect business or other non-legal advice).

[83] *See, e.g.*, Simon v. G.D. Searle & Co., 816 F.2d 397, 402–04 (8th Cir. 1987) (communication of data to lawyer not privileged, partly because data was business data, partly because it was shared with non-lawyer officers).

[84] *See, e.g.*, United States v. Legal Services for New York City, 249 F.3d 1077 (D.C. Cir. 2001) (no privilege for fact of representation for legal services grantee in governmental audit, even if government also sought information about general nature of cases that could be linked to clients' names); Alexiou v. United States, 39 F.3d 973, 976 (9th Cir. 1994) (attorney client privilege does not protect client from revelation of name, address, date, and amount of money paid to attorney in case in which client paid attorney with counterfeit $100 bill, as information would not constitute "last link" in chain of testimony necessary to convict client, and is therefore unprotected by privilege).

[85] *See* 1 McCormick ON EVIDENCE § 90 (Kenneth S. Broun ed., 7th ed. 2013); EDWARD J. IMWINKELRIED, THE NEW WIGMORE: EVIDENTIARY PRIVILEGES § 6.7.2 (2d ed. 2010) (citing 8 WIGMORE ON EVIDENCE § 2313 (McNaughton rev. 1961)).

[86] *See* 8 WIGMORE ON EVIDENCE § 2313 (McNaughton rev. 1961).

while keeping her identity confidential to reduce the likelihood of retaliation or legal consequence.[87] A client may wish to use a lawyer to accomplish some personal mission, such as the anonymous payment of taxes, hoping that this will provide a basis for arguing against penalties if the IRS ever discovers the client's failure to pay.[88] A client who has committed a crime, but who has not yet been identified by the authorities, may seek to have a lawyer engage in plea bargaining without revealing the client's identity.[89] Although courts commonly recognize a limited exception to the general rule that client identity is not privileged, they disagree over the exact nature of the exception.[90] The Restatement (Third) of the Law Governing Lawyers adopts the view that a client's identity is privileged whenever revealing the client's identity would necessarily disclose a confidential communication.[91]

The same general rule and exception that concerns the name of a client applies generally to information about a lawyer's fee. Information about a lawyer's fee is not privileged unless providing the fee information would divulge a confidential

---

[87] *See In re* Kozlov, 398 A.2d 882, 883 (N.J. 1979) (where client had information about juror on previous trial suggesting that juror misrepresented his impartiality, juror's presence on jury was violation of defendant's Sixth Amendment right to impartial jury; client shared this information with attorney but asked attorney to keep client's identity confidential when sharing this information with others). *See also* Stephan A. Saltzburg, *Communications Falling Within the Lawyer-Client Privilege*, 66 IOWA L. REV. 811, 822–23 (1981) (persuasive argument that if privilege does not protect client's identity in this situation, authorities may be denied information).

[88] The federal courts have divided over whether the attorney-client privilege and the attorney's ethical duty of confidentiality permit the attorney to refuse to disclose the client's identity when so required by IRS regulations. *See* Baird v. Koerner, 279 F.2d 623, 626–27 (9th Cir. 1960). *Compare* United States v. Leventhal, 961 F.2d 936, 940–41 (11th Cir. 1992) (no privilege in such circumstances), *with* United States v. Monnat, 853 F. Supp. 1301, 1302–04 (D. Kan. 1994) (privilege applicable).

[89] *See, e.g., Lawyer Refuses to Identify Hit-Run Driver*, 133 CHICAGO DAILY L. BULL., Nov. 11, 1987, at 1, col. 5.

[90] *See, e.g., In re* Grand Jury Subpoena, 204 F.3d 516, 520–21 (4th Cir. 2000) (identity of client privileged where it amounts to disclosure of otherwise confidential information); *In re* Grand Jury Subpoenas Duces Tecum, 695 F.2d 363, 365 (9th Cir. 1982) (identity of client privileged where it would implicate client in very matter for which client sought legal advice); *In re* Grand Jury Matter No. 91–01386, 969 F.2d 995, 997 (11th Cir. 1992) (identity of client privileged when "last link" of evidence necessary to incriminate client); *see also In re* Horn, 976 F.2d 1314, 1315–18 (9th Cir. 1992) (identity of clients ordinarily not protected, but letters of consultation and retainer agreements protected); *In re* Grand Jury Proceedings, 946 F.2d 746 (11th Cir. 1991) (attorney was not required to disclose client's identity, even though government already knew client's reason for seeking legal advice); D'Alessio v. Gilberg, 617 N.Y.S.2d 484 (App. Div. 1994) (name of hit-and-run driver represented by attorney in plea negotiations need not be revealed to civil litigant). *But see* United States v. Leventhal, 961 F.2d 936, 940–41 (11th Cir. 1992) (identity of client and fact of payment were not protected by attorney client privilege; court noted that these facts ordinarily have nothing to do with legal advice, and information was not protected by "last link" doctrine, which was said to apply to cases in which "disclosure of nonprivileged attorney-client communication also would reveal privileged information"; cash-reporting statute itself created exception to attorney-client privilege); United States v. Monnat, 853 F. Supp. 1301, 1303–04 (D. Kan. 1994) (attorney is bound to disclose client's identity in Form 8300 and may not advise client on how to avoid requirement, but should inform client regarding statutory disclosure requirement). *See generally In re* Grand Jury Investigation No. 83–2–35, 723 F.2d 447, 451–54 (6th Cir. 1983) (discussing various limited exceptions to general rule that identity of client not privileged).

[91] RESTATEMENT (THIRD) OF THE LAW GOVERNING LAWYERS § 69 cmt. g, illus. 6 (2000) (stating identity of client who anonymously paid back taxes through lawyer is privileged because it would reveal confidential communication).

communication[92] or providing the name of a third party who paid the fee would incriminate the client.[93]

§ 4.08 The Lawyer-Client Privilege—Duration of the Privilege Beyond the Life of the Client

Generally, the lawyer-client privilege survives the death of the client.[94] In the absence of implied or express consent from the client to reveal confidences after death, the lawyer should claim the privilege on behalf of the client, but the privilege is held by the client's estate or other legal successor in interest.[95] The principle of privilege survival does not apply, however, in disputes over the disposition of a client's estate. Those claiming an estate under the client's will and other claimants to an estate are entitled to have access to the confidential material; the privilege is impliedly waived in order to fulfill the client's testamentary intent.[96]

The long-standing principle of privilege survival came under attack in 1997, when an independent counsel appointed to investigate the President of the United States subpoenaed a lawyer's notes of a privileged communication between the lawyer and a former White House aide who had committed suicide shortly after the conversation. The trial court quashed the subpoena, but the appellate court reversed in a two to one panel decision, with the majority stating that the principle of privilege survival was presumed, rather than decided, under the common law.[97] Confronted with the United States Supreme Court's 1996 decision in *Jaffee v. Redmond*,[98] explicitly rejecting a balancing test for the newly recognized federal therapist-patient privilege, the majority tried to

---

[92] *See, e.g., In re* Shargel, 742 F.2d 61, 62–63 (2d Cir. 1984) (fee information that government sought as evidence of unexplained wealth potentially derived from criminal activity not privileged); *In re* Osterhoudt, 722 F.2d 591, 594 (9th Cir. 1983) (fee information not privileged unless it would reveal substance of confidential communication); *In re* Slaughter, 694 F.2d 1258, 1260 (11th Cir. 1982) (fee information not privileged unless it would reveal identity of previously undisclosed client/suspect).

[93] *See, e.g., In re* Grand Jury Subpoenas, 803 F.2d 493, 498 (9th Cir. 1986), *modified,* 817 F.2d 64 (9th Cir. 1987) (identity of third party who paid lawyer's fees for defendants in narcotics prosecution not privileged); Priest v. Hennessy, 409 N.E.2d 983, 986–87 (N.Y. 1980) (identity of third party who paid lawyer's fees for defendants charged with prostitution not privileged). *But see* Ralls v. United States, 52 F.3d 223, 226–27 (9th Cir. 1995) (identity of third party paying lawyer's fees for defendant in narcotics prosecution privileged where third party was also involved in crime and third party's identity was "intertwined" with privileged communications); *In re* Grand Jury Proceedings, 517 F.2d 666, 671–73 (5th Cir. 1975) (identity of third party paying lawyer's fees for defendants in narcotics prosecution privileged because it would incriminate client under circumstances); *In re* Grand Jury Subpoena c/d 91R0052–11, 142 F.R.D. 122, 128 (M.D.N.C. 1992) (where there is lawyer-client relationship between third party who paid lawyer's fees for defendants in drug conspiracy in which third party was also involved, third party's identity may be privileged).

[94] *See, e.g.,* United States v. Osborn, 561 F.2d 1334, 1340 (9th Cir. 1977) (privilege continues after client's death; remanded case for determination of whether communications privileged before death); 8 WIGMORE ON EVIDENCE § 2323 (McNaugton rev., 1961) (privilege continues even after death of client); 1 MCCORMICK ON EVIDENCE § 94 (Kenneth S. Broun ed., 7th ed. 2013) (privilege generally survives death of client).

[95] Many states by statute transfer the privilege to the deceased's personal representative. *See, e.g.,* Cal. Evid. Code § 953(c).

[96] Glover v. Patten, 165 U.S. 394, 406 (1897) (deceased's communications with lawyer concerning will not privileged in dispute between her daughters over construction of will); *see also* United States v. Osborn, 561 F.2d 1334, 1340 (9th Cir. 1977) (communications concerning will not privileged in dispute between testator's heirs, legatees, devisees, or other parties, all claiming under will); 1 MCCORMICK ON EVIDENCE § 94 (Kenneth S. Broun ed., 7th ed. 2013) (privilege does not apply in dispute between parties claiming under will); Wilcox v. Coons, 220 S.W.2d 15, 19 (Mo. 1949) (deceased client's privilege may be waived by either grantees under deed or devisees under will).

[97] *In re* Sealed Case, 124 F.3d 230 (D.C. Cir. 1997).

[98] 518 U.S. 1 (1996).

carve out a "discrete zone,"[99] in which a balancing test might be appropriate. The discrete zone chosen by the Court included all of criminal litigation.

In *Swidler & Berlin v. United States*,[100] the Supreme Court acknowledged that the principle of survival had been presumed as often as decided but rejected the appellate court's attempt to narrow the lawyer-client privilege by establishing a balancing test in criminal cases where the client was no longer alive. Proclaiming that "[k]nowing that communications will remain confidential even after death encourages the client to communicate fully and frankly with counsel,"[101] the Court refused to introduce "substantial uncertainty into the privilege's application."[102]

The Supreme Court's rejection of a balancing test must be understood in context. *Swidler & Berlin* involved an effort by counsel for the government to obtain information otherwise protected by the privilege. As the Court acknowledged, different principles apply in the very different context of an attempt by the accused in a criminal case to obtain information that is otherwise protected by the privilege.[103] In that context, most courts—including the Supreme Court—have employed an approach that balances the value of the privilege in context against the accused's need for the information.[104]

§ 4.09 The Lawyer-Client Privilege—Application of the Privilege to the Corporate Client

Any number of corporate employees, from the CEO to hourly workers, might have occasion to communicate with the corporation's lawyer. However, not all employees are entitled in their individual capacities to claim the protection of the lawyer-client privilege. The courts have held that a corporation may claim protection of the lawyer-client privilege for communications between corporate agents and its lawyers, but courts have not agreed as to which communications from which agents are covered by the privilege.

The "control group" test, first enunciated in *City of Philadelphia v. Westinghouse Electric Corporation*,[105] was at one time the majority rule in the federal courts.[106] It privileged communications from officers or employees in the upper echelon of the corporation, such as those employees in a position to control or take a substantial part in the decisions that the corporation might take upon the advice of the lawyer. The control group test was criticized for being too narrow and for failing to protect communications from lower-level employees who might possess information vital to the lawyer. Consequently, some courts accepted a broader view of the privilege under what became known as the "subject matter" test.

The subject matter test protected communications to a corporation's lawyers by persons who were not part of the control group if (1) the employee made the communication at the direction of superiors, and (2) the subject of the communication

---

99 *In re* Sealed Case, 124 F.3d 230 (D.C. Cir. 1997).

100 524 U.S. 399 (1998).

101 *Id.* at 407.

102 *Id.* at 409.

103 *Id.* at 409 n.3.

104 *See* **§ 4.21**.

105 210 F. Supp. 483, 485 (E.D. Pa. 1962).

106 *See* John E. Sexton, *A Post-Upjohn Consideration of the Corporate Lawyer-Client Privilege*, 57 N.Y.U. L. REV. 443, 451 (1982).

concerned a matter within the scope of the employee's duties.[107] In *Diversified Industry, Inc. v. Meredith*,[108] the Eighth Circuit added another requirement to the subject matter test, placing the burden on the corporation to show that the communication was made for the purpose of securing legal advice.[109] This was an attempt to narrow the "subject matter" test, so that it could prevent corporations from placing a protective shield over all employee communications, irrespective of the need for legal advice, by funneling them through the corporate lawyer to create the lawyer-client privilege.

When the United States Supreme Court granted certiorari in *Upjohn Co. v. United States*,[110] many observers expected it to establish a comprehensive approach to the lawyer-client privilege for corporate cases. Although the *Upjohn* Court rejected the control group test, it is difficult to say exactly what else it did.

In *Upjohn*, the Internal Revenue Service attempted to subpoena the results of an investigation conducted by the Upjohn Company's General Counsel aimed at discovering whether certain suspicious payments were illegal bribes to foreign officials. The internal investigation included a questionnaire transmitted to corporate managers by the Chairman of the corporation, stating that the General Counsel was conducting an investigation of questionable payments and sought detailed information about such payments. The recipients of the questionnaire were told to treat the investigation as "highly confidential" and not to discuss it with anyone other than with employees able to provide useful information. Responses were sent directly to the General Counsel. The General Counsel and outside counsel also interviewed the managers who received the questionnaire and thirty-three other officers and employees of Upjohn.

In March 1976, the company voluntarily submitted a report to the SEC and the IRS that disclosed certain questionable payments. The IRS began an investigation to determine the tax consequences of the payments and subpoenaed the questionnaire answers and the interview notes. The company refused to provide the material, citing the lawyer-client privilege and the work-product doctrine.

The Sixth Circuit Court of Appeals, applying the control group test, ruled in favor of the government,[111] but the Supreme Court disagreed. It rejected the control group test, stating that a broader privilege was needed to encourage communications to corporate lawyers. The narrow control group approach would "limit the valuable efforts of corporate counsel to ensure their client's compliance with the law."[112] The Court, however, declined to lay down a specific alternative rule. Instead, it simply held that,

---

107 *See, e.g.*, Harper & Row Publishers, Inc. v. Decker, 423 F.2d 487, 491–92 (7th Cir. 1970).

108 572 F.2d 596 (8th Cir. 1977) (en banc).

109 The *Diversified Industries* court defined the test as follows:

> The lawyer-client privilege is applicable to an employee's communication if (1) the communication was made for the purpose of securing legal advice; (2) the employee making the communication did so at the direction of his corporate superior; (3) the superior made the request so that the corporation could secure legal advice; (4) the subject matter of the communication is within the scope of the employee's corporate duties; and (5) the communication is not disseminated beyond those persons who, because of the corporate structure, need to know its contents.

Id.

110 449 U.S. 383 (1981).

111 United States v. Upjohn Co., 600 F.2d 1223, 1226 (6th Cir. 1979) ("only the senior management, guiding and integrating the several operations, . . . can be said to possess an identity analogous to the corporation as a whole."), *rev'd*, 449 U.S. 383 (1981).

112 *Upjohn*, 449 U.S. at 392.

under the circumstances of the case, the communications to the corporate lawyer were privileged and enumerated some circumstances that influenced its judgment:

1. "The communications at issue were made by Upjohn employees to counsel for Upjohn acting as such, at the direction of corporate superiors in order to secure legal advice from counsel."[113]

2. "The communications concerned matters within the scope of the employees' corporate duties, and the employees themselves were sufficiently aware that they were being questioned in order that the corporation could obtain legal advice."[114]

3. "Pursuant to explicit instructions from the Chairman of the Board, the communications were considered 'highly confidential' when made and have been kept confidential by the company."[115]

In addition, the Court may have been influenced by the fact that the information sought by the general counsel was not available from upper-level management.[116]

While *Upjohn* left open several issues (e.g., whether the privilege covers ex-employees whose information is sought by the lawyer), it suggests some guidelines that lawyers representing corporations should follow to ensure that information will be protected:

1. Ensure the corporation directs the employees to provide the information.
2. Ensure the employees know that the purpose of the inquiry is to obtain legal advice for the corporation.
3. Instruct the employees to keep the information strictly confidential.
4. Ask only for information that relates to matters within the scope of the employee's duties, as opposed to collecting information about unrelated matters.

The scope of the employee's duties appears to be the linchpin for the expansion of the group whose communication the court is willing to protect by the corporate lawyer-client privilege. For example, while a clerical employee who witnessed an accident involving a company vehicle would apparently not be covered under *Upjohn*, the driver of the vehicle might be.

Upjohn can lead to unintended mischief. For instance, the holding in *Baxter Travenol Laboratories, Inc. v. Lemay*[117] represents a remarkable and questionable extension of the *Upjohn* rationale. *Baxter* suggests that an outside witness's statement to corporate counsel may become privileged, simply by putting the witness on the payroll. Baxter hired a litigation consultant who had previously worked for Lemay. The litigation consultant's job was to provide Baxter's lawyer with information about Lemay's alleged misuse of Baxter's proprietary information. The United States District Court upheld Baxter's assertion that the confidential communications of the "litigation consultant" were protected by the privilege and found that nearly all features of *Upjohn* were

---

113 *Id.* at 394.

114 *Id.*

115 *Id.* at 395 (citation omitted).

116 *See id.* at 394.

117 89 F.R.D. 410 (S.D. Ohio 1981).

present. *Baxter* allows a corporation to hire an informant from the other side and then blanket the "espionage" with the lawyer-client privilege.

Upjohn does not demand the *Baxter* result. It could have been distinguished easily on grounds that the employees in *Upjohn* communicated about matters within the scope of the duties they performed for the corporation claiming the privilege. Baxter's "litigation consultant" communicated about matters concerning employment for Lemay, another corporation, one that had no interest in Baxter's privilege.

Although *Upjohn* and its progeny create a broad corporate lawyer-client privilege, they do not prevent the opposing party from seeking the same information from other sources. The lawyer-client privilege covers only confidential communications between lawyer and client, and not the underlying information upon which those communications are based. The IRS in *Upjohn*, for example, was free to depose Upjohn's employees to ask them what they knew about illegal payments; it was only precluded from gathering what employees told corporate counsel about illegal payments.[118]

The *Upjohn* case is not, of course, binding on state courts, and several refuse to follow it. Courts are free to follow the control group test or some other test for application of the privilege in the corporate context.[119]

The client of corporate counsel is, of course, the corporation, not any particular individual employee or officer. Officers and employees who provide information to corporate counsel normally are not protected if the corporation itself waives the privilege. Sometimes, however, counsel may work both for the corporation and for the employees as individual clients; this raises the issue of conflict of interest.[120]

In the absence of special circumstances, the default assumption is that only the corporation was the client. In *In re Grand Jury Subpoena (Newparent)*,[121] the First Circuit Court of Appeals reviewed the precedent on the subject and endorsed the position taken by the Third Circuit Court of Appeals in *Matter of Bevill, Bresler & Schulman Asset Management Corporation*,[122] that corporate employees must establish five elements in order to assert a personal claim of attorney-client privilege:

> First, they must show they approached [counsel] for the purpose of seeking legal advice. Second, they must demonstrate that when they approached [counsel] they made it clear that they were seeking legal advice in their individual rather than in their representative capacities. Third, they must demonstrate that the [counsel] saw fit to communicate with them in their

---

[118] Upjohn Co. v. United States, 449 U.S. 383, 395–96 (1981).

[119] *See, e.g.*, Alaska R. Evid. 503(a)(2) ("A representative of the client is one having authority to obtain professional legal services and to act on advice rendered pursuant thereto, on behalf of the client"); Nalian Truck Lines v. Nakano Warehouse & Transp. Corp., 8 Cal.Rptr.2d 467 (1992) (control group test maintained); Day v. Illinois Power Co., 199 N.E.2d 802, 806 (Ill. App. 1964) (employees' written reports to corporation's lawyer concerning investigation, repair or replacement of ruptured gas line not privileged because employees had no authority to determine corporate action based on lawyer's advice).

[120] *See* Kathryn W. Tate, *Lawyer Ethics and the Corporate Employee: Is the Employee Owed More Protection than the Model Rules Provide*, 23 IND. L. REV. 1 (1990) (conflicts that may arise where corporate counsel represents both corporate entity and individual employee); Nancy J. Moore, *Conflicts of Interest for In-House Counsel: Issues Emerging from the Expanding Role of the Attorney-Employee*, 39 S. TEX. L. REV. 497 (1998); *See also* Sarah Helene Duggin, *Internal Corporate Investigations: Legal Ethics, Professionalism and the Employee Interview*, 2003 COLUM. BUS. L. REV. 859 (2003) (ethical problems corporate counsel may encounter during internal investigations).

[121] 274 F.3d 563 (1st Cir. 2001).

[122] 805 F.2d 120 (3d Cir. 1986).

individual capacities, knowing that a possible conflict could arise. Fourth, they must prove that their conversations with [counsel] were confidential. And, fifth, they must show that the substance of their conversations with [counsel] did not concern matters within the company or the general affairs of the company.[123]

Newparent added its own gloss to the fifth prong of the *Bevill* test, stating that "if the communication between a corporate officer and corporate counsel specifically focuses upon the individual officer's personal rights and liabilities, then the fifth prong of *In Matter of Bevill* can be satisfied even though the general subject matter of the conversation pertains to matters within the general affairs of the company."[124] On the facts before it, however, the court held that the employees had not made an adequate showing to take advantage of an individual attorney-client privilege separate from that of the corporation.[125]

The attorney-client privilege for government entities may be narrower than what the law provides for corporations, at least where information is sought by another government entity in a grand jury investigation.[126]

§ 4.10 The Lawyer-Client Privilege—the Crime-Fraud Exception to the Privilege

The crime-fraud exception removes the mantle of privilege from confidential communications between lawyer and client. If a client seeks advice or aid from a lawyer to facilitate a crime or fraud, such communications are not protected.[127] This exception to the lawyer-client privilege only applies to communications made in furtherance of a

---

[123] *Id.* at 123 (brackets in original).

[124] 274 F.3d at 572.

[125] *Id.* at 574; *see also* United States v. Martin, 278 F.3d 988 (9th Cir. 2002) (where defendant's lawyer, hired to act as general counsel for sham corporation, reported fraud to government agents when he learned about it, attorney-client privilege did not apply, because lawyer was not defendant's personal counsel and crime-fraud exception would apply).

[126] *See In re* Lindsey, 158 F.3d 1263, 1282–83 (D.C. Cir. 1998) (where White House Counsel refused to answer certain questions in grand jury testimony on grounds of attorney-client privilege, privilege does not apply to communications between two federal officials when information is sought by another federal official, pursuant to grand jury subpoena); *In re* Witness Before Special Grand Jury 2000–2, 288 F.3d 289 (7th Cir. 2002) (although government agencies have attorney-client privilege, privilege did not apply to confidential communications made by former Illinois secretary of state to government counsel in case where former secretary was under bribery investigation and present secretary had waived department's attorney-client privilege); *In re* Grand Jury Subpoena Duces Tecum, 112 F.3d 910, 921 (8th Cir. 1997) (privilege does not cover consultation of public official with government attorney where information is sought by grand jury, stating that strong public interest in exposing wrongdoing by public officials would be "ill-served by recognition of a governmental attorney-client privilege applicable in criminal proceedings inquiring into the actions of public officials").

[127] *See, e.g.*, Clark v. United States, 289 U.S. 1, 15 (1933) (privilege does not protect communications in furtherance of crime or fraud regardless of lawyer's guilt); *In re* Doe, 551 F.2d 899, 900–01 (2d Cir. 1977) (client's revelation to lawyer that he planned to bribe juror not privileged); *In re* Grand Jury Proceedings, 680 F.2d 1026, 1028–29 (5th Cir. 1982) (privilege does not protect identity of third party who hired lawyer in course of drug smuggling conspiracy to defend clients charged with transporting narcotics even though lawyer did not know of illegal purpose); *In re* Grand Jury Proceedings, 87 F.3d 377, 381–82 (9th Cir. 1996) (client's intent to procure aid in crime or fraud is all that is needed to establish exception to privilege); United States v. Lentz, 419 F. Supp. 2d 820, 830 (E.D. Va. 2005) ("The attorney's knowledge and intent are not material to the operation of the crime fraud exception; only the client's knowledge and intent are material in this regard"); 1 MCCORMICK ON EVIDENCE § 95 (Kenneth S. Broun ed., 7th ed. 2013) (privilege does not apply where client seeks advice to further illegal or fraudulent scheme); 8 WIGMORE ON EVIDENCE § 2298 (McNaughton rev. 1961) (advice concerning criminal or fraudulent transaction is not privileged).

future or ongoing crime or fraud.[128] Although our system of justice protects a revelation of a past crime or fraud to a lawyer under lawyer-client communications, there is no rationale for protecting communication to facilitate crime or fraud in the future.[129]

The crime-fraud exception, while easy to state, is difficult to enforce. A client seeking advice in aid of submitting a false insurance claim, laundering money, or committing mail fraud is not entitled to the privilege. While courts determine if the exception applies based upon whether the communication was made in furtherance of crime or fraud, it must be known what was stated in the communication; yet, that communication may be privileged. Hence, the apparent paradox: to determine whether the privilege applies, one must breach the privilege.

The United States Supreme Court reached a typical solution to this problem in *United States v. Zolin*[130] by having the district court review the allegedly privileged materials in camera to determine whether the exception applied. This in camera review occurred only after the party seeking the evidence made a preliminary showing of crime or fraud.[131]

In *Zolin*, the Church of Scientology sought to prevent the IRS from obtaining access to tape recordings of meetings between Church representatives and legal counsel. The IRS argued that the tapes fell within the crime-fraud exception to the lawyer-client privilege. It urged the District Court to listen to the tapes in camera to determine whether the exception applied. In support of its position, it submitted affidavits from an undercover agent who gave reasons for believing that the tapes were relevant and who provided a partial transcript of the contents of the tapes.[132]

The Court held that, while fishing expeditions were not permissible, a judge could, upon a proper showing, examine allegedly privileged materials alone in chambers to determine whether the crime-fraud exception applied. The requisite showing is that of "a factual basis adequate to support a good faith belief by a reasonable person,"[133] and the standard permits, but does not require, a judge to review the materials in camera. Additional factors, such as the burden of reviewing voluminous materials, and the degree of need for the evidence in the litigation, should also be considered.[134] Further, the mere making of the showing does not mean that the privilege evaporates. It only means that

---

[128] *See, e.g., In re* John Doe Corp., 675 F.2d 482, 491 (2d Cir. 1982) (communication in furtherance of ongoing crime not privileged); United States v. Regan, 281 F. Supp. 2d 795, 802 (E.D. Va. 2002) (communication in furtherance of ongoing crime not privileged). *Cf. In re* Grand Jury Subpoenas, 926 F.2d 847 (9th Cir. 1991) (in case charging illegal export of goods to Iran, district court should not have examined in camera documents generated after completion of alleged crime, because crime-fraud exception does not cover communications about past or completed crimes where government had not alleged ongoing cover-up). In the authors' opinion, the court's holding is dubious, because communications made after the completion of a crime might throw light upon whether earlier consultations with counsel were made for purposes of obtaining aid in planning the crime; *see also* CHARLES WOLFRAM, MODERN LEGAL ETHICS § 6.4 at 281 (1986) (exception applies to crimes ongoing at time of consultation).

[129] *See, e.g., In re* Grand Jury Proceeding Impounded, 241 F.3d 308, 316–17 (3d Cir. 2001) (communications privileged if related to past crimes); *In re* Grand Jury Proceedings (Appeal of FMC Corp.), 604 F.2d 798, 803–04 (3d Cir. 1979) (communications privileged if crime completed before retention of counsel); 1 MCCORMICK ON EVIDENCE § 95 (Kenneth S. Broun ed., 7th ed. 2013) (advice concerning past crimes or misconduct privileged as opposed to advice in furtherance of crime or fraud, which is not).

[130] 491 U.S. 554 (1989).

[131] *See id.* at 571–72.

[132] *See id.* at 558–59.

[133] *Id.* at 572 (quoting Caldwell v. District Court, 644 P.2d 26, 33 (Colo. 1982)).

[134] *See id.*

the judge will examine the communications to determine whether the protection of the privilege should be stripped away.

Zolin also raised the issue of what materials could be used in making the preliminary showing. If an employee of the privileged party leaked privileged material to the opponent, or if an undercover agent acquired the material by participating in lawyer-client conferences, could that pilfered knowledge be used in making the preliminary showing? While purporting to recognize the dangers of abuse, the *Zolin* Court allowed that the showing could be made with knowledge acquired by subterfuge, so long as the information had not previously been adjudged to be privileged and so long as the leak or undercover work was not otherwise illegal.[135]

§ 4.11 The Lawyer-Client Privilege—Waiver

As with other objections, the privilege can be waived by failure to object at trial. A number of other acts can result in waiver of the privilege:

Putting privileged material in issue. The privilege can be waived by putting privileged material in issue.[136] A client, claiming to have believed a course of conduct to be legal because of a lawyer's advice, waives the right to claim the privilege as to that advice.[137] This does not mean that the privilege is waived merely because the subject matter of communications between the lawyer and client is the same as the subject matter of litigation. For example, the fact that lawyer and client discussed a contract does not mean the privilege is waived for those communications about the contract when the client later sues for its enforcement. Rather, the client must do something to put the confidential communications in issue in order waive the privilege.[138]

Intentional disclosure. As with all privileges, testimony about, or other intentional disclosure of, privileged material generally constitutes waiver.[139] Moreover, the party cannot be allowed to selectively disclose, or to reveal in a self-serving way, part of the privileged communication while withholding the rest, so intentional partial disclosure of a communication results in loss of the privilege regarding the remainder of that communication.[140] The wiser rule goes further: intentional partial disclosure results in

---

[135] *See id.* at 574. The Ninth Circuit Court of Appeals, interpreting *Zolin*, held that a past corporate employee's affidavit disclosing privileged material could not be considered in conjunction with a motion invoking the crime-fraud exception, until after the court had determined that there was a good faith basis to believe that an in camera review would show a crime or fraud. United States v. Chen, 99 F.3d 1495, 1503 (9th Cir. 1996).

[136] *Zolin*, 491 U.S. at 574.

[137] United States v. Miller, 600 F.2d 498, 501–02 (5th Cir. 1979).

[138] *See, e.g.*, Weizmann Inst. of Sci. v. Neschis, 2004 WL 540480 (S.D.N.Y. 2004) (party's defense placed in issue its attorney's advice about attending arbitration, so attorney's advice was discoverable); Pitney-Bowes, Inc. v. Mestre, 86 F.R.D. 444, 447 (S.D. Fla. 1980) (although party did not waive privilege by seeking arbitration in contract dispute, it did waive privilege by placing intent of parties in issue during subsequent litigation); Hearn v. Rhay, 68 F.R.D. 574, 581 (E.D. Wash. 1975) (party waives privilege where: (1) assertion of privilege resulted from party's affirmative act; (2) party placed information in issue; and (3) application of privilege would deny opposing party information required to respond effectively).

[139] See Westinghouse Electric Corp. v. Republic of the Philippines, 951 F.2d 1414 (3d Cir. 1991) (rejecting the idea that a holder might waive the privilege as to one potential litigant without waiving as to others).

[140] *See, e.g.*, Handgards, Inc. v. Johnson & Johnson, 413 F. Supp. 926, 929 (N.D. Cal. 1976) (holding that voluntary partial disclosure of communication waives privilege as to remainder of communication concerning same subject matter); 8 WIGMORE ON EVIDENCE § 2327 (McNaughton rev. 1961) (stating that offer of testimony as to any part of communication waives privilege as to whole communication).

loss of the privilege with regard to all communications on the same subject matter.[141] This rule is prescribed for disclosures made "in a federal proceeding or to a federal agency" by an amendment to the Rules in 2008.[142] However, insofar as this "subject matter" waiver is based on concerns about adjudicative fairness in preventing the privilege holder from misleading the fact-finder with a partial disclosure, arguably a different result should obtain when intentional disclosures are made extra-judicially so that the fact-finder is not exposed to the partial disclosure. In such situations, some courts have limited the scope of the waiver to the matter actually disclosed.[143]

Disclosure by mistake. Voluntary but inadvertent revelation of privileged material, such as mistakenly turning over a privileged document during discovery, traditionally resulted in waiver of the privilege.[144] There are signs of change in the case law, however, with some cases following the same principle encountered with regard to eavesdroppers, namely, that the taking of reasonable precautions by the lawyer and the client should preclude or at least limit the waiver of the privilege when privileged material is disclosed by mistake.[145] When waiver is found, some authorities extend the waiver of the privilege not only to the mistakenly disclosed document or conversation but also to the general subject matter covered by the mistaken disclosure.[146] If, however, the privileged party had taken reasonable precautions to protect the material, it would not be fair if the waiver extended beyond the particular document, at least so long as the privilege holder makes no attempt to use the disclosed information at trial.[147]

---

[141] *See, e.g., In re* Sealed Case, 676 F.2d 793, 824 (D.C. Cir. 1982) (holding that company's submission of report to Securities and Exchange Commission concerning bribes of foreign officials waived privilege as to any document necessary to evaluate report); Chinnici v. Central Dupage Hosp. Ass'n., 136 F.R.D. 464, 465 (N.D. Ill. 1991) (holding that condominium association's voluntary disclosure of meeting minutes summarizing attorney's advice waived attorney-client privilege with respect to all communications on same subject); Haymes v. Smith, 73 F.R.D. 572, 576–77 (W.D.N.Y. 1976) (client's disclosure of letter waived privilege as to all communication involving same subject matter). *See also* United States v. Thomas, 953 F.2d 107 (4th Cir. 1991) (holding that trial judge violated Confrontation Clause by excluding client and client's present attorney from in camera hearing in which former attorney was examined to determine whether privilege had been waived).

[142] *See* FED. R. EVID. 502(a).

[143] *See, e.g.,* Wi-Lan, Inc. v. Kilpatrick Townsend & Stockton LLP, 684 F.3d 1364 (Fed. Cir. 2012); *In re* von Bulow, 828 F.2d 94, 101–04 (2d Cir. 1987) (concerning privileged material disclosed to public by publication in book about criminal case arising out of same allegations). Such decisions have not come to grips fully with two difficult questions. First, there may be fairness concerns that warrant subject matter waiver in partial disclosures to persons other than the fact-finder. Second, if a concern about misleading the fact-finder is the only fairness concern, it makes sense to question why there should be a waiver even as to the information actually and intentionally disclosed, but not to the fact-finder.

[144] *See, e.g.,* 8 WIGMORE ON EVIDENCE § 2325 (McNaughton rev. 1961) (stating that privilege is waived as to any information attorney reveals in litigation because attorney acts on implied authority of client).

[145] *See* Hydraflow, Inc. v. Enidine, Inc., 145 F.R.D. 626, 638 (W.D.N.Y. 1993) (holding that inadvertent facsimile transmittal of documents for patent application did not waive privilege for documents to which privilege applied); Resolution Trust v. Dean, 813 F. Supp. 1426 (D. Ariz. 1993) (privilege not waived by publication of internal memo in unauthorized newspaper article); Martin v. Valley Nat'l Bank, 1992 WL 196798 (S.D.N.Y. 1992) (holding that plaintiff did not waive attorney-client privilege with respect to five inadvertently disclosed documents, where plaintiff took reasonable measures to avoid disclosure; plaintiff's attorneys screened 50,000 pages of documents produced, and plaintiff requested return of inadvertently disclosed documents in timely manner); SCM Corp. v. Xerox Corp., 70 F.R.D. 508, 519 (D. Conn. 1976) (holding that client did not waive privilege by inadvertently disclosing privileged information in transfer of voluminous unscreened documents; client would have waived privilege, however, if it had individually screened documents).

[146] This idea was reflected in Proposed FED. R. EVID. 511.

[147] *See In re* Keeper of Records, 348 F.3d 16, 23–25 (1st Cir. 2003) (rejecting subject matter waiver in absence of attempt by privilege holder to use disclosures in case); Gray v. Bicknell, 86 F.3d 1472, 1483–84 (8th Cir. 1996) (reviewing various approaches to the problem).

In 2008, Congress enacted Federal Rule of Evidence 502 to address the problem of inadvertent disclosure.[148] Rule 502 resolves the circuit court split on inadvertent disclosures[149] and addresses concerns about the costs of discovery.[150] It applies to disclosures of attorney-client privilege or work product[151] in all federal court proceedings or to federal agencies.[152] Under Rule 502, an inadvertent disclosure does not result in waiver of the attorney-client privilege if the disclosing party acted in accordance with two requirements outlined in 502(b). First, the privilege holder must have taken reasonable steps to *prevent* a disclosure.[153] Second, the privilege holder must have promptly taken reasonable steps to *rectify* the inadvertent disclosure.[154] The Committee Notes to Rule 502 suggest factors that may be relevant to a court's determination of whether a privilege holder took reasonable precautions to prevent disclosure and acted with reasonable prudence to address an inadvertent disclosure.[155] Those factors include "the reasonableness of precautions taken, the time taken to rectify the error, the scope of discovery, the extent of disclosure, the number of documents to be reviewed, and the time constraints for production."[156]

The protections offered by Rule 502 to inadvertent disclosures are seemingly broader than previous approaches. Under Rule 502, if a disclosure was inadvertent, it cannot result in a subject matter waiver.[157] Where there is a question of whether state or federal law should apply, the courts will apply the more protective rule.[158] Rule 502 goes even further, providing that a federal court's order that a disclosure did not result in a waiver of the privilege binds all other state or federal proceedings.[159] Rule 502 also recognizes that the parties themselves may reach an agreement limiting the effect of waiver on any inadvertent disclosures.[160] However, the rule may not extend to

---

[148] *See* Henry S. Noyes, *Federal Rule of Evidence 502: Stirring the State Law of Privilege and Professional Responsibility with a Federal Stick*, 66 WASH. & LEE L. REV. 673 (2009).

[149] *See* Gomez v. Vernon, 255 F.3d 1118, 1133 (9th Cir. 2001) (taking liberal approach in holding no waiver where privilege holder took reasonable measures to protect privileged information); *In re* Sealed Case, 877 F.2d 976, 980 (D.C. Cir. 1989) (taking strict approach in holding inadvertent disclosure constitutes waiver); Clady v. County of Los Angeles, 770 F.2d 1421, 1433 (9th Cir. 1985) (adopting compromise approach in holding that inadvertence of disclosure does not necessarily foreclose waiver, but it is one factor to consider in determining whether or not there was waiver).

[150] FED. R. EVID. 502 original committee note.

[151] FED. R. EVID. 502(g) original committee note.

[152] FED. R. EVID. 502(f) original committee note.

[153] FED. R. EVID. 502(b)(2).

[154] FED. R. EVID. 502(b)(3); *see also* United States v. Sensient Colors, Inc., 2009 WL 2905474, *6 (D.N.J. 2009) (disclosing party had duty to re-examine documents it had produced to check for inadvertent disclosures, because it had been alerted to flaws in its production).

[155] FED. R. EVID. 502(b) original committee note.

[156] *Id. See* Heriot v. Byrne, 257 F.R.D. 645, 655–660 (N.D. Ill. 2009) (using multi-factor balancing test to determine whether disclosure was inadvertent under Rule 502); Rhoads Indus., Inc. v. Building Materials Corp. of America, 254 F.R.D. 216 (E.D. Pa. 2008) (using five-factor test along with Fed. R. Evid. 502 determines whether inadvertent disclosure constituted waiver); *see also* Peterson v. Bernardi, 262 F.R.D. 424, 430 (D.N.J. 2009) (upholding privilege claim where attorney had not necessarily taken reasonable precautions to prevent disclosure; judging this to be a rare occasion where interests of fairness and justice weighed so heavily as to find no waiver).

[157] FED. R. EVID. 502(a)(1) and original advisory committee note.

[158] FED. R. EVID. 502(c) original advisory committee note.

[159] FED. R. EVID. 502(d).

[160] FED. R. EVID. 502(e).

disclosures made extrajudicially—such as disclosures made in anticipation of litigation—even if the litigation ends up in a federal court.[161]

Refreshing memory with a privileged document. Showing a privileged document to a witness on the witness stand, even if the witness is a client or lawyer, waives the privilege.[162] Some authorities find waiver when documents have been used before trial to refresh memory,[163] though the better view is that the privilege should ordinarily prevail.[164] This principle does not apply to expert testimony in civil cases. Federal Rule of Civil Procedure 26(a)(2) requires parties to provide the opposing party with a written statement prepared and signed by the expert witness, stating the opinions the expert witness will give at trial and the reasons for them. A testifying expert who relies on documents waives the privilege as to those documents.

Disclosure during negotiations. Disclosure of privileged matter during negotiations ordinarily does not waive the privilege as to undisclosed related matters. The policy of promoting settlement weighs in favor of the privilege and against treating this conduct as waiver.[165] However, authority exists to the contrary.[166] If necessary to reveal privileged matter during settlement negotiations, precautions, such as obtaining a confidentiality agreement from the opponent, should be taken.[167] Reliance on Rule 408, which excludes statements made by a lawyer during settlement negotiations, may not be sufficient to protect all privileged material. Rule 408 does not require the exclusion of evidence otherwise discoverable, merely because the existence or nature of the evidence is revealed during compromise negotiations.[168] Therefore, pre-existing documents containing privileged information disclosed during a settlement conference may not be protected, because the statements in them were made before, not during, the negotiations.

---

[161] See, e.g., Wi-Lan, Inc. v. Kilpatrick Townsend & Stockton LLP, 684 F.3d 1364 (Fed. Cir. 20120) (holding that Rule 502 does not cover a disclosure made prior to initiation of a federal proceeding).

[162] *See, e.g.*, Bailey v. Meister Brau, Inc., 57 F.R.D. 11, 13 (N.D. Ill. 1972) (holding that client waived privilege by viewing documents to refresh memory, because application of privilege would place unfair burden on cross-examiner); FED. R. EVID. 612 (requiring disclosure of document used to refresh memory while testifying).

[163] *See, e.g.*, People v. Scott, 193 N.E.2d 814, 821–22 (Ill. 1963) (requiring prosecution to produce documents that police officer testified he used to refresh memory before trial); 1 MCCORMICK ON EVIDENCE § 9 at 59 (Kenneth S. Broun ed., 7th ed. 2013) (witness's consultation of document before testifying generally should constitute waiver of privilege).; *see also* FED. R. EVID. 612 (confirming judicial discretion to require disclosure of document used to refresh memory before testifying).

[164] *See, e.g.*, Joseph Schlitz Brewing Co. v. Muller & Phipps (Hawaii), Ltd., 85 F.R.D. 118, 120 (W.D. Mo. 1980) (court should give privileged documents special discretionary safeguard against disclosure under Rule 612).

[165] *See, e.g.*, Sylgab Steel & Wire Corp. v. Imoco-Gateway Corp., 62 F.R.D. 454, 458 (N.D. Ill. 1974), *aff'd*, 534 F.2d 330 (7th Cir. 1976) (holding that lawyer did not waive privilege by incorporating certain legal conclusions from opinion letter to client into letter sent to opposing party); International Business Mach. Corp. v. Sperry Rand Corp., 44 F.R.D. 10, 13 (D. Del. 1968) (holding that disclosure during negotiations of privileged information concerning specific subject did not waive privilege as to all related information).

[166] R. J. Hereley & Son Co. v. Stotler & Co., 87 F.R.D. 358, 359 (N.D. Ill. 1980) (holding that partial disclosure of privileged memorandum from client to lawyer at settlement meeting waived privilege as to remainder of memorandum, and opponent is entitled to discovery of remainder of memorandum).

[167] SCOTT N. STONE & RONALD S. LIEBMAN, TESTIMONIAL PRIVILEGES § 1.51 (1983) (advising that lawyer should avoid reference to confidential information in negotiations and, when necessary, consider requesting opposing party to sign confidentiality agreement or moving for protective order).

[168] See **§ 6.10**.

§ 4.12 The Lawyer-Client Privilege—Disputes Between Client and Lawyer

When a lawyer and client litigate against each other, the privilege disappears. The lawyer may reveal confidential information necessary to establish a claim or defense.[169] For example, the lawyer may reveal client confidences when sued for malpractice[170] or to establish the lawyer's right to be paid a fee from the client.[171]

According to many courts, this exception to the privilege extends to disputes involving third persons. Some authority, for example, allows the lawyer to reveal confidences to defend the lawyer's reputation when the client criticizes the lawyer's competence, even in a suit in which the lawyer is not a party.[172]

§ 4.13 The Physician-Patient Privilege

The physician-patient privilege was not recognized at common law.[173] A physician is considered to be under a professional obligation to be discreet but, when called as a witness, could be compelled to disclose information related to the physician-patient relationship. Federal courts generally decline to recognize the physician-patient privilege as a matter of federal common law.[174]

Most state legislatures have sought to remedy this perceived defect in the common law by passing privilege statutes, usually at the behest of interest groups representing the medical profession.[175] These statutes, however, are diverse; some states recognize a

---

[169] *See, e.g.*, United States v. Ballard, 779 F.2d 287, 292 (5th Cir. 1986) (holding that lawyer-client privilege does not apply in dispute between client and lawyer over fees or improper conduct); 8 WIGMORE ON EVIDENCE §§ 2312(2), 2327(6) (McNaughton rev. 1961) (privilege does not apply in dispute over fees or claim of negligence, because client waives privilege by claiming breach of duty by lawyer); 1 MCCORMICK ON EVIDENCE § 91.1 (Kenneth S. Broun ed., 7th ed. 2013) (stating that privilege does not apply in dispute between lawyer and client or when client attacks lawyer indirectly in litigation between third persons).

[170] *See, e.g.*, Kracht v. Perrin, Gartland & Doyle, 268 Cal. Rptr. 637, 641 n.6 (Cal. Ct. App. 1990) (holding that client may not sue former lawyer for malpractice and simultaneously claim privilege to obstruct lawyer's defense).

[171] *See, e.g.*, Sokol v. Mortimer, 225 N.E.2d 496, 501 (Ill. App. Ct. 1967) (permitting lawyer to testify as to privileged and confidential communications with client in suit against client for fees).

[172] *See, e.g.*, Tasby v. United States, 504 F.2d 332, 336 (8th Cir. 1974) (holding lawyer permitted to testify when former client claimed ineffective assistance of counsel in habeas corpus proceeding, asserting that lawyer forced client to testify at trial); United States v. Weger, 709 F.2d 1151, 1156–57 (7th Cir. 1983) (in criminal prosecution against former client for making false statements to secure loan, allowing law firm to rebut client's implication that it was involved in producing fraudulent title opinion by giving prosecutor confidential letter from former client written on her typewriter to demonstrate that client forged title opinion on firm's letterhead).

[173] *See* Crow v. State, 230 S.W. 148 (Tex. Crim. App. 1921); 8 WIGMORE ON EVIDENCE § 2380 (McNaughton rev. 1961). *See generally* Daniel W. Shuman, *The Origins of the Physician-Patient Privilege and Professional Secret*, 39 SW. L.J. 661 (1985).

[174] *See* PAUL R. ROTHSTEIN & SUSAN W. CRUMP, FEDERAL TESTIMONIAL PRIVILEGES § 3:1 (2016–17 ed.). *But see* Mann v. University of Cincinnati, 824 F. Supp. 1190, 1196–98 (S.D. Ohio 1993) (recognizing existence of general physician-patient privilege under federal common law).

[175] 8 WIGMORE ON EVIDENCE § 2380 (McNaughton rev. 1961).

general physician-patient privilege,[176] while others restrict the privilege to therapists[177] or other specific health professionals.[178]

The strongest argument for the privilege is that the patient's privacy interest outweighs the contribution that the medical information would make to the judicial process. Sometimes a utilitarian rationale, similar to the argument for the lawyer-client privilege, is advanced, contending that potential patients would be deterred from seeking medical advice if the privilege did not exist. The self-interest in securing sound medical advice and treatment, however, probably outweighs the danger that the information would someday hurt the patient in court.[179]

Because of the great diversity among state statutes, it is difficult to generalize about medical privileges. The following features, however, are generally present:

1. A patient holds the privilege if a professional relationship exists between physician and patient and if the patient is consulting the doctor for medical treatment. Thus, when a court-appointed psychiatrist examines a patient for purposes of determining the patient's mental condition, no privilege exists because no professional relationship exists.[180] The same holds true when a doctor is paid by one side to examine an adverse party.[181] When a lawyer for the patient directs a doctor to examine the patient for an expert opinion, the better view is the lawyer-client privilege applies instead of the physician-patient privilege, because the doctor is acting as the lawyer's representative.[182] In most of these circumstances, however, either putting the patient's condition in issue or by offering the doctor's testimony waives the privilege.[183]

2. The privilege is not restricted to confidential communications; it covers other information acquired by the physician that is necessary to diagnosis or treatment. Even if the patient is in a coma when observed by the doctor, the

---

[176] *See, e.g.*, MICH. COMP. LAWS ANN. § 600.2157 (physicians); *Id.* at § 333.18237 (psychologists); TEXAS R. EVID. 509 (2009) (physicians); TEXAS R. EVID. 510 (mental health professionals).

[177] *See, e.g.*, FLA. STAT. ANN. § 90.503 (psychotherapists); MD. CODE ANN. [Cts. & Jud. Proc.] § 9–109 (psychiatrists and psychologists).

[178] *See, e.g.*, MINN. STAT. ANN. § 595.02 (physicians, psychologists, chiropractors, dentists, registered nurses, and sexual assault counselors); 42 PA. CONS. STAT. ANN. § 5929 (1982) (physicians); *id.* at § 5944 (psychologists); *id.* at § 5945 (school personnel); *id.* at § 5945.1 (sexual assault counselors).

[179] 8 WIGMORE ON EVIDENCE § 2380a (McNaughton rev. 1961); Zechariah Chafee, *Privileged Communications: Is Justice Served or Obstructed by Closing the Doctor's Mouth on the Witness Stand?*, 52 YALE L.J. 607, 609–10 (1943).

[180] People v. Primmer, 444 N.E.2d 829, 834 (Ill. App. Ct. 1983) (admitting state appointed psychiatrist's testimony over defendant's objection because state had defendant examined to prepare for defendant's possible insanity defense); State v. Jensen, 174 N.W.2d 226, 230 (Minn. 1970) (holding that defendant could not assert privilege to block psychiatrist's testimony about defendant's mental state because psychiatrist was appointed by court to judge defendant's competency to stand trial, not to offer diagnosis and treatment).

[181] VanSickle v. McHugh, 430 N.W.2d 799, 801–02 (Mich. Ct. App. 1988) (in action for injuries in auto accident, holding that plaintiff could not block testimony of physician employed by his no-fault insurance carrier since he lacked "reasonable expectation that the consultation [would be] cloaked with a veil of confidentiality" and examination was conducted by insurance company that could be adverse party if plaintiff disputed his insurance award).

[182] United States v. Alvarez, 519 F.2d 1036, 1046 (3d Cir. 1975) (in case where defense counsel retained psychiatrist to help prepare insanity defense, defendant's statements to psychiatrist are privileged because doctor was agent offering expert assistance to counsel).

[183] Mason v. Booker, 922 N.E.2d 1036, 1038–39 (Ohio Ct. App. 2009) (waiver of physician-patient privilege where patient's condition is in issue); Capps v. Lynch, 116 S.E.2d 137, 141 (N.C. 1960) (physician-patient privilege waived where patient permits physician to be witness).

privilege covers the facts learned by the doctor. In this respect, the physician-patient privilege is broader than the lawyer-client privilege, which generally does not include observations of physical condition.[184] In the case of the physician-patient relationship, the patient is entitled to protect information learned from examination and testing as well as information learned from patient communications.[185]

3. The privilege only covers statements to a physician that are pertinent to diagnosis or treatment. Thus, a patient's statement that the patient was wounded while trying to escape from police or that the patient was hit by a car going through a red light would not be covered.[186]

4. The privilege is riddled with exceptions. For example, some jurisdictions do not recognize it in criminal cases.[187] Others provide a more limited exception for treatment that is sought in furtherance of criminal activity, such as patching a wound incurred in escape from prison, or plastic surgery designed to change a fugitive's appearance.[188] Many states impose reporting requirements when necessary for the public health or safety, including mandatory reporting of sexually transmitted disease and child abuse.[189]

The privilege is waived easily. Most jurisdictions provide that once the party voluntarily places the party's mental or physical condition in controversy, the privilege is waived.[190] A party who brings a personal injury action, for example, waives the privilege with regard to information relevant to the injury evaluation.[191] The privilege

---

[184] In situations where something about the client's appearance, which is non-obvious to the casual observer, is deliberately shown to the lawyer, the lawyer-client privilege might cover what the lawyer observes. *Cf.* United States v. Kendrick, 331 F.2d 110, 113–14 (4th Cir. 1964) (holding matters "observable by anyone" *not* to be within attorney-client privilege).

[185] *See, e.g.*, State v. Santeyan, 664 P.2d 652, 654 (Ariz. 1983) (results of defendant's urinalysis privileged when test was made in course of his treatment for injuries sustained in car accident and request for treatment was made by defendant, not by law enforcement officer).

[186] State v. Sweet, 453 A.2d 1131, 1133 (Vt. 1982) (where defendant told nurse he was too drunk to sign consent-to-treatment form, that statement was not privileged because nurse did not need defendant's statement in order to render treatment) (citations omitted).

[187] *See, e.g.*, CAL. EVID. CODE § 998 (providing that physician-patient privilege does not apply in criminal trials); 42 PA. CONS. STAT. ANN. § 5929 (limiting privilege to civil cases).

[188] People v. Traylor, 377 N.W.2d 371, 372–73 (Mich. Ct. App. 1985) (holding that physician-patient privilege does not apply in case where physician testified in defendant's armed robbery trial about defendant's gunshot wound because MICH. COMP. LAWS ANN. § 750.411 requires that any wound inflicted by deadly weapon be reported to local authorities).

[189] *See, e.g.*, CAL. PENAL CODE § 11165.7 (creating affirmative duty to report all suspected cases of child abuse on both physicians and psychotherapists); CAL. EVID. CODE §§ 1006 and 1026 (providing that physician-patient and psychotherapist-patient privileges, respectively, do not apply where physician or psychotherapist is required to report to public employee).

[190] Leslie v. Brames, 682 F. Supp. 608 (D. Me. 1988) (where plaintiff claimed he suffered head and back injuries in accident with defendant, that plaintiff put his physical condition in issue, thus waiving physician-patient privilege).

[191] *See, e.g.*, MINN. R. CIV. P. 35.03.

may also be waived, in the same fashion as the lawyer-client privilege, by selective disclosure[192] or by the privilege holder calling the doctor to testify.[193]

§ 4.14 The Psychotherapist-Patient Privilege

The therapist-patient privilege is supported by stronger policy justifications than the physician-patient privilege. For example, a therapist is more likely to hear damaging, embarrassing, and personal information than an ordinary physician. As argued by the utilitarian deterrence hypothesis, some patients might not go to the therapist at all if they perceive that their communications would become public. Accordingly, even those states rejecting the doctor-patient privilege nevertheless recognize the therapist-patient privilege.[194]

The Supreme Court of the United States, settling a split in the circuits, interpreted the principles of the common law "in the light of reason and experience"[195] in *Jaffee v. Redmond*[196] to establish the federal therapist-patient privilege. The "reason" was the need for the privilege to encourage effective therapy. The "experience" was that of the fifty states, each of which have a therapist-patient privilege of some kind.

The Court determined that the therapist-patient privilege would serve a "public good transcending the normally predominant principle of utilizing all rational means for ascertaining truth."[197] It followed the lead of many states in expanding the privilege to cover licensed social workers, observing that "drawing a distinction between the counseling provided by costly psychotherapists and the counseling provided by more readily accessible social workers serves no discernible public purpose."[198] Though it accepted most of the lower court's decision, the Court disagreed with applying a balancing test to nullify the privilege in certain circumstances. In deciding to prohibit a trial judge from determining that the need for testimony might be greater in a particular case than a patient's interest in privacy, the Court observed that such a balancing test would "eviscerate the effectiveness of the privilege."[199]

The Court did not detail the scope and operation of the privilege. It noted that the federal courts would probably recognize exceptions to the privilege as they developed its scope and, as an example, gave the "dangerous patient" exception that many states apply

---

[192] *See, e.g., In re* Exxon Valdez, 270 F.3d 1215, 1249–50 (9th Cir. 2001) (in case where plaintiffs sought to prove failure to avoid danger resulting in oil spill was due to ship captain's alcoholism, holding that form sent by captain's doctor to company, for purpose of excusing absence from work, identifying captain as alcoholic was properly admitted); Jones v. Superior Court for County of Alameda, 174 Cal. Rptr. 148, 155 (Cal. Ct. App. 1981) (finding that plaintiff's mother waived physician-patient privilege because plaintiff's mother testified plaintiff ingested DES).

[193] People v. Newbury, 290 N.E.2d 592, 596 (Ill. 1972) (holding that defendant who voluntarily consults psychiatrist and offers psychiatrist's testimony waives psychiatrist-patient privilege); Matthews v. Commonwealth, 709 S.W.2d 414, 419 (Ky. 1985) (finding that psychiatrist-patient privilege was not violated in case where defendant had psychiatrist testify he acted under extreme emotional disturbance and prosecution cross-examined psychiatrist on same subject but asked more detailed questions about defendant's communications with him).

[194] *See* PAUL R. ROTHSTEIN & SUSAN W. CRUMP, FEDERAL TESTIMONIAL PRIVILEGES § 3:2 (2016–17 ed.) (noting that all states as well as the District of Columbia have enacted some type of psychotherapist-patient privilege).

[195] FED. R. EVID. 501.

[196] 518 U.S. 1 (1996).

[197] *Id.* at 15 (quoting Trammel v. United States, 445 U.S. 40, 50 (1980)).

[198] *Id.* at 17 (quoting Jaffee v. Redmond, 51 F.3d 1346, 1358 n.19 (7th Cir. 1995)).

[199] *Id.*

when the therapist reveals confidences to protect a third party.[200] The Court also cited the Supreme Court standard that had been originally submitted to Congress as Rule 504,[201] suggesting that the privilege detailed there might be influential in determining the nature of the privilege as it is drawn by future decision. The rejected standard, which applied to psychotherapists engaged in diagnosis or therapy,[202] accommodated the need for confidentiality in situations where third parties, such as family members or group therapy members, are present[203] and expanded it to include treating drug addiction.[204] It contained an exception for court ordered examinations, limited to the purpose of the examination,[205] and did not apply when the patient relied upon the condition as part of a claim or defense.[206] The standard did not address issues of confidentiality regarding the patient's name or permissible disclosure in the event of a dispute between therapist and patient. Although courts may be tempted to look at the lawyer-client privilege for guidance on these issues, disclosure of the identity of a person in therapy and the nature of communications during therapy may implicate more serious privacy concerns than in lawyer-client communications.[207]

§ 4.15 The Marital Privileges

There are two distinct spousal privileges. Some jurisdictions recognize one, but not the other, and some—including the federal courts—recognize both.[208]

The first is the absolute privilege against adverse spousal testimony. Designed to protect the peace and harmony of an existing marriage,[209] it prevents the spouse from testifying to any facts: the scope of its protection extends beyond confidential communications to all subject matter observed.[210] For example, the privilege could be invoked so that a wife could avoid testifying about her husband's reckless driving while

---

[200] For a post-*Jaffe* case discussing the dangerous patient exception, *see* United States v. Glass, 133 F.3d 1356 (10th Cir. 1998) (holding that a threat to the U.S. President communicated to psychotherapist is not automatically admissible, because trial judge must make findings about seriousness of threat and whether revelation was necessary to avoid harm); *see also* United States v. Hayes, 227 F.3d 578, 586 (6th Cir. 2000) (holding psychotherapist's testimony about patient's threats to kill postal supervisor inadmissible where patient asserted psychotherapist-patient privilege, reasoning that psychotherapist's professional and ethical duty to protect innocent third parties by disclosing threats does not include duty to testify against patient in criminal proceedings other than those related to patient's involuntary hospitalization); George C. Harris, *The Dangerous Patient Exception to the Psychotherapist-Patient Privilege: The* Tarasoff *Duty and the* Jaffe *Footnote*, 74 WASH. L. REV. 33 (1999) (duty to warn potential victims should be broader than exception to privilege, so that therapist might have duty to warn but still not be obliged to testify against patient in court proceeding).

[201] *Jaffee*, 518 U.S. at 8.

[202] FED. R. EVID. 504(a)(2) (Proposed draft 1972).

[203] FED. R. EVID. 504(a)(3) (Proposed draft 1972).

[204] *See* 42 U.S.C. § 290ee–3 (asserting confidentiality of drug abuse program patient records).

[205] FED. R. EVID. 504(d)(2) (Proposed draft 1972).

[206] FED. R. EVID. 504(d)(3) (Proposed draft 1972).

[207] *See generally* Deirdre M. Smith, *An Uncertain Privilege: Implied Waiver and the Evisceration of the Psychotherapist-Patient Privilege in the Federal Courts*, 58 DEPAUL L. REV. 79 (2008).

[208] The advisory committee for the federal rules originally recommended only one of these—the privilege against adverse spousal testimony—and specifically recommended abolition of the privilege for spousal communications. See Proposed FED. R. EVID. 505 advisory committee note. With the failure of Congress to pass Article V of the proposed rules, the matter was left to federal common law, which included both privileges.

[209] United States v. Byrd, 750 F.2d 585, 590 (7th Cir. 1984) (noting that privilege against adverse spousal testimony protects marriage from impact of negative testimony); *In re* Grand Jury Subpoena Koecher, 601 F. Supp. 385, 391 (S.D.N.Y. 1984) (stating that purpose of privilege is "prevention of dissension between spouses which might result from testimony of one against the other").

[210] *See* **§ 4.16**.

she was a passenger. Here, the privilege applies, even if the drive was public and the spouses did not speak while driving. However, the spouse's testimony is not privileged unless it is actually adverse to the other spouse, and courts sometimes have been willing to restrict the scope of the privilege by construing the answers to questions propounded to the witness as posing no significant risk of incriminating the witness's spouse, even when the witness's spouse is the target of the investigation.[211]

The second privilege is a privilege to prevent the disclosure of marital confidences. It applies only to confidences shared by marital partners.[212] It is often described as a privilege for confidential communications,[213] though some jurisdictions have extended it to acts that are performed in confidence before the spouse.[214]

Both spousal privileges require a legal marriage. Couples that live together without the benefit of marriage, including same-sex couples (even if they cannot legally marry), are not covered by the privilege. The legality of the marriage is not, however, the end of the inquiry, as various doctrines (to be discussed below) involve judicial assessment of the viability of the marriage.[215]

Although, like most privileges, spousal privileges are not codified in the Federal Rules of Evidence, they have been recognized in the federal system.[216] Many states have passed statutes governing spousal privilege,[217] though some have created the privilege through case law.

§ 4.16 The Marital Privileges—the Privilege Against Adverse Spousal Testimony

The adverse spousal testimony privilege protects the marriage against outsiders who seek to force testimony.[218] Although broader in subject matter coverage than the privilege for marital confidences, the adverse spousal testimony privilege does not apply unless the parties are actually married *at the time testimony is sought*. Because the adverse spousal testimony privilege is based on the notion that the "peace and harmony" of the marriage should not be endangered by forcing one spouse to testify against another, the privilege does not survive the end of the marriage by divorce or death.[219]

---

211 *See, e.g., In re* Grand Jury Proceedings, 664 F.2d 423, 430 (5th Cir. 1981), *cert. denied*, 455 U.S. 1000 (1982). A persuasive dissent in the case rejected the majority's narrow reading of what is "adverse" to the witness's spouse. 664 F.2d at 431–33 (arguing that spousal privilege should, at least in conspiracy cases, be extended to questions propounded to one spouse that, while seemingly calling for the acknowledgement of facts that are "innocuous," might nonetheless contain the potential for providing a link in a chain of inference that might be used to convict the other spouse).

212 United States v. Hamilton, 19 F.3d 350, 354 (7th Cir. 1994) (holding that, where defendant's wife had not been divorced from previous husband, there is no valid marriage and no privilege for marital confidences).

213 *See, e.g.*, 8 WIGMORE ON EVIDENCE §§ 2332–41 (McNaughton rev. 1961); 1 MCCORMICK ON EVIDENCE §§ 78–86 (Kenneth S. Broun ed., 7th ed. 2013).

214 *See* **§ 4.17**.

215 Steven N. Gofman, *"Honey, the Judge Says We're History": Abrogating the Marital Privileges Via Modern Doctrines of Marital Worthiness*, 77 CORNELL L. REV. 843 (1992).

216 *See* **§ 4.16** & **§ 4.17**.

217 *See, e.g.*, CONN. GEN. STAT. § 54–84a* (marital privilege in criminal cases); MINN. STAT. ANN. § 595.02(1)(a); N.C. GEN. STAT. § 8–57 (criminal); *id.* § 8–56 (civil).

218 If the *accused* calls his or her spouse to testify, there is no privilege because such testimony is not "adverse" to the accused and so is not within the scope of the privilege, regardless of who holds it.

219 *See* United States v. Bolzer, 556 F.2d 948, 951 (9th Cir. 1977) (holding testimony of defendant's ex-wife admissible because privilege does not continue after marriage is legally dissolved). *Cf.* Jurcoane v.

(As discussed below, this is *not* the case for the privilege for confidential marital communications.)

The traditional common-law rule gave control of the privilege to the defendant spouse, a rule confirmed in the 1958 case of *Hawkins v. United States.*[220] But when one spouse is ready and willing to testify against the other, the marriage is arguably already in ruins so that the adverse testimony will not do more damage. For that reason, in 1980 the Supreme Court changed the rule and held, in *Trammel v. United States,*[221] that it is the witness spouse, not the defendant spouse, who holds the privilege. Under *Trammel*, if the witness spouse chooses not to testify, the opponent cannot force the testimony, and if the witness spouse wishes to testify, then the defendant spouse cannot prevent it. Of course, it is possible that the witness spouse is willing to testify not because the "peace and harmony" of the marriage has been destroyed, but rather because the government has threatened to prosecute the witness spouse on the underlying crime if the privilege is claimed. Furthermore, particularly where there are children of the marriage, a spouse may agree to testify in return for immunity so that the testifying parent may continue to care for the children. Government pressure, not the deterioration of the marriage, may well have been the situation in *Trammel*, but the possibility did not seem to concern the Supreme Court. Evidently, the concern regarding the broad nature of the testimonial privilege and the cost of valuable lost testimony trumped concerns about family harmony.[222]

Not all states recognizing the adverse spousal testimony privilege have followed the *Trammel* doctrine. Some continue to make the defendant spouse the holder of the privilege.[223] Although some states allow the privilege in both civil and criminal cases,[224] it is limited to criminal cases in many jurisdictions.[225]

The adverse spousal testimony privilege does not apply when the spouses are themselves adversaries, such as a divorce action or an action in which one spouse is accused of a crime against the other.[226] It also does not apply in cases involving an

---

Superior Court, 113 Cal. Rptr. 2d 483 (Cal. Ct. App. 2001) (wife could claim marital privilege so that she need not testify against husband charged with murder even though she had had no contact with husband for 17 years, and magistrate erred in determining that marital privilege does not apply where viable marital relationship no longer exists). *But see In re* Witness Before Grand Jury, 791 F.2d 234, 238 (2d Cir. 1986) (holding woman unable to assert privilege because she had not lived with husband for eleven years and her husband lived with another woman); United States v. Singleton, 260 F.3d 1295, 1300–01 (11th Cir. 2001) (holding that marital privilege does not apply when couple was permanently separated without reasonable expectation of reconciliation).

220 358 U.S. 74 (1958).

221 445 U.S. 40 (1980).

222 *See* Louis W. Hensler III, *The Trammel Court's Hasty Rejection of Jerry Maguire's View of Marriage*, 23 GA. ST. U. L. Rev. 325 (2006).

223 *See, e.g.,* ARIZ. REV. STAT. ANN. § 13–4062(1) (criminal); *Id.* § 12–2231 (civil); MINN. STAT. ANN. § 595.02(1)(a); MONT. CODE ANN. § 26–1–802.

224 *See, e.g.,* ALASKA R. EVID. 505(a)(1); MINN. STAT. ANN. § 595.02(1)(a); MONT. CODE ANN. § 26–1–802. The precedent on the question whether the adverse spousal testimony privilege applies in federal civil cases is scant and unclear. *See* United States v. Yerardi, 192 F.3d 14, 19 (1st Cir. 1999) (privilege applies in criminal forfeiture case, absence of clear precedent on whether privilege applies in pure civil cases). For analysis, *see* Katherine O. Eldred, Comment, *"Every Spouse's Evidence": Availability of the Adverse Spousal Testimonial Privilege in Federal Civil Trials*, 69 U. CHI. L. REV. 1319 (2002).

225 *See, e.g.,* CONN. GEN. STAT. § 54–84a*; N.C. GEN. STAT. § 8–57; OHIO R. EVID. 601(B); OR. REV. STAT. § 40.255(3) (2009).

226 Brown v. Commonwealth, 292 S.E.2d 319, 323 (Va. 1982) (where husband allegedly shot his wife and her grandmother and trial court severed cases for trial, holding that wife may testify against defendant-husband in both trials); Hudson v. Commonwealth, 292 S.E.2d 317, 319 (Va. 1982) (holding spouse may testify

alleged crime by one spouse against a spouse's children.[227] There is a division of authority on whether the adverse spousal testimony privilege is available to married couples who jointly participate in crimes against third persons.[228] At least one state has created one exception for when the marriage occurs after a homicide.[229] Even when the crime is not as serious as homicide, the societal interest in hearing the testimony outweighs the benefits of preserving the harmony of a new marriage when it is likely that the marriage was consummated just to establish the privilege.[230]

As with other privileges, the adverse spousal testimony privilege can be waived. If a spouse testifies at trial at the request of the defendant-spouse, the privilege is waived regarding adverse testimony on the same subject matter.[231] The same may be true for spousal testimony given only in pretrial proceedings, such as a motion to suppress.[232]

The effect of *out-of-court* statements by the defendant's spouse is a more difficult matter and depends on which spouse holds the privilege and other circumstances surrounding the statement. Because such statements (at least those not made to police) are not ordinarily considered testimony, a *witness-spouse* holder (as under *Trammel*) ordinarily does not waive the privilege by speaking; accordingly, the spouse may still invoke the privilege if called to testify, but conversely, the prosecution may introduce evidence of the out-of-court statement without violating the privilege.[233] (Hearsay and confrontation clause restrictions may, of course, preclude this.) When the *defendant* is the holder of the privilege, one would think that the defendant may not invoke the privilege to prevent the other spouse from speaking when such a statement does not constitute testimony, and again, that would mean no waiver would be effected by the spouse's statement, and at the same time the prosecution would be free to use the out-of-court statement without violating the privilege.[234] However, in the context of

---

against defendant-husband regardless of whether offense is committed against spouse's person or her property).

[227] United States v. Allery, 526 F.2d 1362, 1367 (8th Cir. 1975) (in case where wife testified against husband accused of attempting to rape their daughter, privilege does not apply when spouse commits crime against child of either spouse).

[228] *Compare* United States v. Van Drunen, 501 F.2d 1393, 1396 (7th Cir. 1974) (*Hawkins* privilege not applicable); *with* United States v. Lilley, 581 F.2d 182, 189 (8th Cir. 1978) (*Hawkins* privilege applicable despite defendant's testimony implicating spouse), *and* Appeal of Malfitano, 633 F.2d 276 (3d Cir. 1980) (*Trammel* privilege applicable).

[229] MINN. STAT. ANN. § 595.02(1)(a).

[230] *See, e.g.,* United States v. Blair, 54 F.3d 639, 644–45 (10th Cir. 1995) (not only did "sham" marriage not immunize defendant's wife from testifying against defendant regarding his involvement in illegal wagering, but it also resulted in two-point sentence enhancement for obstruction of justice).

[231] *See, e.g.,* Donovan v. State, 584 P.2d 708, 710 (Nev. 1978) (holding prosecution's use of wife's prior statement to impeach her testimony not improper since defendant-husband waived right to assert privilege by calling wife as witness). *Cf.* State v. Walker, 403 A.2d 1, 4 (N.J. 1979) (holding that, where defendant testified at time of victim's rape that he was with his wife, who "conveyed the impression" at trial that she supported truth of his testimony, defendant thus made wife "crucial" witness and proper for prosecution to comment on defendant's failure to have his wife testify).

[232] *Compare* United States v. Lofton, 957 F2d 476, 477 (7th Cir. 1992) (holding that spouse, as holder of privilege, waived same by testifying at suppression hearing); *with* United States v. Mitchell, 2009 U.S. Dist. LEXIS 2978 (N.D. Iowa 2009) (holding that spouse, as holder of privilege, did not waive privilege by testifying before grand jury, when such testimony was "secret" and itself inadmissible at trial).

[233] *See* United States v. Archer, 733 F.2d 354 (5th Cir. 1984). In *Trammel,* the Court stated: "Neither *Hawkins,* nor any other privilege, prevents the Government from enlisting one spouse to give information concerning the other or to aid in the other's apprehension. It is only the spouse's testimony in the courtroom that is prohibited." *Trammel,* 445 U.S. at 52 n.12.

[234] *See, e.g.,* State v. Burden, 841 P.2d 758 (Wash. 1992). This had been the majority rule in the federal courts prior to *Trammel. See, e.g.,* United States v. Mackiewicz, 401 F.2d 219 (2d Cir.), *cert. denied,* 393 U.S.

statements made by a spouse to government agents without the defendant's consent, several courts have ruled that a defendant spouse who holds the privilege can use it to block the admission of evidence of such out-of-court statements, on the theory that to do otherwise would be tantamount to allowing the spouse to testify.[235] In any case, if the prosecution is free to use the out-of-court statement by the spouse without violating the privilege, then the defendant also ought to be able to use the spouse's out-of-court statement without effecting a waiver of the privilege, subject of course to other restrictions such as the hearsay rule.

§ 4.17 The Marital Privileges—the Privilege for Marital Confidences

The privilege for marital confidences[236] is rooted in the natural repugnance against the state's invasion of marital privacy. Although some jurists suggest that the marital confidences privilege exists to encourage spouses to share confidences in the fashion of the lawyer-client privilege,[237] it seems doubtful that the existence of the privilege affects marital intimacy. The privilege for marital confidences is more complex than the privilege against adverse spousal testimony.

The privilege for marital confidences differs from jurisdiction to jurisdiction, but generally has the following features:

(1) The privilege is applicable only to confidences that were made during the marriage. Confidential communications made after divorce are not covered. If the husband and wife are married but living separately, the applicability of the privilege is in doubt.[238] However, at least one case extended the privilege to

---

923 (1968); United States v. Tsinnijinnie, 601 F.2d 1035 (9th Cir. 1979). *But see* Ivey v. United States, 344 F.2d 770 (5th Cir. 1965).

[235] *See* United States v. Archer, 733 F.2d 354, 358 (5th Cir. 1984) (discussing precedents existing under the earlier federal rule placing the privilege in the hands of the defendant spouse). It is an open question whether courts will attempt to identify "testimony" for purposes of the privilege with "testimonial" for purposes of the Confrontation Clause. *Compare* State v. Crawford, 54 P.3d 656, 659–60 (Wash. 2002) (affirming conviction despite admission of evidence of out-of-court statements to police by wife of defendant privilege holder), reversed on Confrontation grounds by Crawford v. Washington, 541 U.S. 36 (2004) (holding that spouse's custodial statements to police were testimonial for purposes of Confrontation Clause and thus improperly admitted), *with* Peek v. United States, 321 F.2d 934 (9th Cir. 1963), *cert. denied*, 376 U.S. 954 (1964) (stating in dictum, in a case prior to *Trammel* and *Crawford*, that the privilege (then held by the defendant) would preclude testimony about what defendant's wife said to an FBI agent). Under *Crawford* the issue is unlikely to arise unless the Confrontation Clause objection is waived without there being a waiver of the defendant's spousal privilege.

[236] *See* Robert P. Mosteller & Kenneth S. Broun, *The Danger to Confidential Communications in the Mismatch Between the Fourth Amendment "Reasonable Expectation of Privacy" and the Confidentiality of Evidentiary Privileges*, 32 CAMPBELL L. REV. 147 (2010).

[237] *See, e.g.*, 8 WIGMORE ON EVIDENCE § 2332 (McNaughton rev. 1961).

[238] *See In re* Witness Before Grand Jury, 791 F.2d 234, 239 (2d Cir. 1986) (holding spouse could not claim marital communication privilege because she had lived apart from defendant-husband for four years when alleged communication occurred); United States v. Porter, 986 F.2d 1014, 1019 (6th Cir. 1993) (holding privilege does not apply to statements made by one spouse to other after spouses have permanently separated; whether permanent separation had occurred prior to statement is to be determined by district court); United States v. Fulk, 816 F.2d 1202, 1204–05 (7th Cir. 1987) (holding defendant could not assert communication privilege when communication was made at time when defendant-husband and wife were permanently separated); United States v. Jackson, 939 F.2d 625, 627 (8th Cir. 1991) (finding no error in admitting defendant's statement to wife made while couple was permanently separated without any semblance of marital relationship); State v. Hopkins 140 S.W.3d 143, 160–61 (Mo. Ct. App. 2004) (holding privilege does not apply where spouses are separated); *see also* 8 WIGMORE ON EVIDENCE § 2335 (McNaughton rev. 1961).

communications between separated spouses during an attempted reconciliation.[239]

(2) The privilege for confidences shared during the course of the marriage continues after the termination of the marriage.[240] This result reflect the policy of encouraging confidential communications during the marriage relationship and the concern that allowing divorce to vitiate the privilege might discourage spouses from sharing confidences.[241] However, a former spouse has no legal obligation to refrain from broadcasting marital confidences, so it is doubtful that the ordinary person considers the remote possibility of potential courtroom testimony when deciding whether to entrust confidences in a spouse. Despite this, the idea that the privilege protects pre-dissolution statements even after the marriage has ended is well-established.[242]

(3) In many jurisdictions, the privilege protects only confidences.[243] However, express requests for secrecy are uncommon in most marriages and in many jurisdictions, marital communications are presumed to be confidential unless demonstrated otherwise.[244] The confidentiality requirement means that the presence of a third person during a communication between marital partners destroys the privilege. Similarly, a spouse's intention that his or her communication be relayed to a third person also vitiates the privilege.[245] In jurisdictions that do not recognize a parent-child privilege, the presence of a child during the communication destroys confidentiality.[246]

(4) Although most jurisdictions limit the privilege to communications, some jurisdictions include testimony about conduct performed under circumstances suggesting reliance on the confidential nature of the marital relationship.[247] Therefore, the act of hiding something in the presence of one's spouse might be

---

[239] People v. Fediuk, 489 N.E.2d 732, 734 (N.Y. 1985) (husband's communication to wife was privileged though parties were separated at time of communication, because husband believed parties could reconcile).

[240] *See* 8 WIGMORE ON EVIDENCE § 2341 (McNaughton rev. 1961) (citations omitted).

[241] *See id.*

[242] *See, e.g.,* CAL. EVID. CODE § 980; Mich. Comp. Laws Ann. § 600.2162(4); MINN. STAT. ANN. § 595.02(1)(a); N.J. STAT. ANN. § 2A:84A–22.

[243] CAL. EVID. CODE § 980; FLA. STAT. ANN. § 90.504; *see also* 8 WIGMORE ON EVIDENCE § 2336 (McNaughton rev. 1961).

[244] *See, e.g.,* CAL. EVID. CODE § 917); 8 WIGMORE ON EVIDENCE § 2336 (McNaughton rev. 1961).

[245] *See* United States v. Madoch, 149 F.3d 596, 602 (7th Cir. 1998) (holding spousal communication privilege did not apply to tape-recorded phone conversations made while husband was calling wife from jail; spouses should have known that inmate conversations are monitored); United States v. Pensinger, 549 F.2d 1150, 1151–52 (8th Cir. 1977) (holding communication privilege did not apply because husband's conversation with wife about details of his bank robbery in presence of two other people destroyed confidential nature of communication); Resnover v. State, 372 N.E.2d 457, 459 (Ind. 1978) (finding that information in husband's letter to wife was intended to be given to third parties and thus could not be protected by communication privilege).

[246] People v. Sanders, 457 N.E.2d 1241, 1244 (Ill. 1983) ("presence of children of spouses destroys confidentiality unless they are too young to understand what is being said").

[247] Arnold v. State, 353 So. 2d 524, 527 (Ala. 1977) (holding that defendant-husband's act of driving by burned building with his wife is privileged communication because it was "performed with the confidence of the marriage in mind"); Commonwealth v. Byrd, 689 S.W.2d 618, 621 (Ky. Ct. App. 1985) (holding witness-spouse may not testify she saw her defendant-husband examine contents of stolen purse because husband did so in marital home and would not have done so if they had not been married). *See also* OHIO REV. CODE § 2317.02(D) (specifying that privilege extends to "any communication made by one to the other, or an act done by either in the presence of the other, during coverture, unless the communication was made, or act done, in the known presence or hearing of a third person competent to be a witness.").

covered by the privilege for marital confidences in some jurisdictions.[248] One can argue in favor of this extension on grounds that the security that the privilege is supposed to foster applies to conduct as well as words. However, this extension does not cover all acts observed by the spouse. If a spouse sees the other start a fight on the subway, the privilege does not apply because there is nothing confidential about the fighting spouse's public conduct.

(5) The spouse transmitting the confidence is the holder of the privilege in many jurisdictions, on the theory that the privilege is designed to encourage that spouse's communication or act.[249] The witness spouse cannot testify to confidences reposed during the marriage, even if the witness spouse is eager to testify.[250] Therefore, the wife who confides in her husband that she has committed a crime is able to invoke the privilege successfully, even if her husband wants to testify against her. Some jurisdictions require the consent of both spouses to waive the marital communications privilege.[251]

(6) If the holder of the privilege calls his or her spouse to testify about marital confidences, the privilege is waived and the content of the testimony no longer can be controlled.[252] In this respect, the privilege for marital confidences resembles the broader privilege against adverse spousal testimony. The privilege also can be waived by voluntary disclosure to a third person, as for example in a letter.[253] The marital confidences privilege is based on the confidentiality of the communication, so once the confidence is breached, there is no purpose to the marital confidences privilege.[254]

---

[248] 8 WIGMORE ON EVIDENCE § 2337 (McNaughton rev. 1961).

[249] *See, e.g.*, Kan. Stat. Ann. § 60–428 (2005); 8 WIGMORE ON EVIDENCE § 2340 (McNaughton rev. 1961); EDWARD J. IMWINKELRIED, THE NEW WIGMORE: EVIDENTIARY PRIVILEGES § 6.5.1 (2d ed. 2010).

[250] United States v. Neal, 532 F. Supp. 942, 947 (D. Colo. 1982); 8 WIGMORE ON EVIDENCE § 2340 (McNaughton rev. 1961).

[251] *See, e.g.*, NEB. REV. STAT. § 27–505 (2004) N.J. STAT. ANN. § 2A:84A–22, reprinted as N.J. R. EVID. 509. *See also* State v. Serrano, 210 P.3d 892, 902 (Or. 2009) (opining that OR. R. EVID. 505 recognizes both husband and wife as joint holders of privilege).

[252] However, the fact that a party calls the party's spouse to the witness stand does not mean that the opponent can cross-examine the spouse about prior invocations of the privilege. *See* United States v. Morris, 988 F.2d 1335, 1339–40 (4th Cir. 1993) (holding it reversible error for prosecutor to cross-examine defendant's wife and secretary of more than 20 years about her prior invocation of marital privilege during grand jury investigation preceding trial); *see also* United States v. Hall, 989 F.2d 711, 715–16 (4th Cir. 1993) (holding it reversible error for prosecutor during cross-examination of defendant to read from text of inculpatory statements made by defendant's wife when wife had invoked privilege after having made statements).

[253] *See, e.g.*, State v. Johnson, 643 P.2d 146, 152 (Kan. 1982) (holding common-law wife's daughter could testify about conversation she had with her mother that defendant-husband had shown his wife over $929 in cash because husband had shown both testifying daughter and another daughter money as well, in case where defendant-husband was on trial for first degree murder and aggravated robbery); *see also* Kan. Stat. Ann. § 60–437 (2005).

[254] For a case that stretches the concept of waiver to the breaking point, see United States v. Smith, 33 M.J. 114, 117–18 (C.M.A. 1991). The court held that a wife waived the privilege for marital confidences regarding a letter she wrote to her husband. In the letter, she urged him to testify that he had forced her to commit the crime with which she was currently charged, and to give other exculpatory testimony. The court held that she waived the privilege by testifying at trial to conversations with her husband in which he frightened her. She did not testify about the letter, but the court said that all the communications could properly be considered as one. Hence the holding suggests that revealing one communication with a spouse waives any objection to other communications at different times that touch on the same general subject matter. The court avoided basing its decision on the theory that the letter was an invitation to commit perjury, apparently because it was doubtful that the Military Rules of Evidence contained a crime-fraud exception to the marital confidences privilege. *See also* 8 WIGMORE ON EVIDENCE § 2340 (McNaughton rev. 1961).

(7) Sometimes accidental disclosure to persons outside the marriage can result in a waiver of the privilege. As in the case of the lawyer-client privilege, a third party can testify to matters otherwise covered by the marital confidences privilege if the conversation was legally overheard, at least if reasonable precautions were not taken by the spouses to maintain confidentiality.[255] The same result occurs when a holder-spouse accidentally discloses a writing, such as losing a letter.[256] However, a disclosure by a non-holder spouse without the holder spouse's consent does not destroy the privilege. For example, if a husband gossips about his wife's secrets, the privilege stops the recipient of the gossip from testifying about the confidential communication, even if there is a way around the hearsay problem.[257] Of course, if the wife discloses her secret conversations with her husband to a third person (with whom she is not also in a privileged relationship), she would be precluded from objecting to testimony by that third person.[258]

(8) The exceptions to the privilege for marital confidences are similar to those for the privilege against adverse spousal testimony. Generally, the privilege does not apply in suits between husband and wife, including marriage dissolution,[259] custody battles, criminal charges of assault on the spouse,[260] crimes against a child of either spouse, or other matters involving the child, as where the state seeks to terminate parental rights.[261] In addition, courts recognize a fraud exception to the application of the privilege.[262]

§ 4.18 The Privilege Against Self-Incrimination

The Fifth Amendment to the United States Constitution provides, in part, that "No person shall be . . . compelled in any criminal case to be a witness against himself. . . ."[263] In 1964, the Supreme Court held that the Fifth Amendment was incorporated by the Due Process Clause of the Fourteenth Amendment and applied to the states.[264] Various

---

[255] *See* State v. Summerlin, 675 P.2d 686, 694–95 (Ariz. 1983) (holding that defendant-husband could not claim communication privilege because prison guard in room could possibly overhear the conversation); Sumlin v. State, 617 S.W.2d 372, 376 (Ark. 1981) (holding that defendant-husband could not claim communication privilege because inmate overheard husband's conversation with his wife); *see also* 8 WIGMORE ON EVIDENCE § 2340 (McNaughton rev. 1961).

[256] 8 WIGMORE ON EVIDENCE § 2339 (McNaughton rev. 1961); *see also* Mikah K. Story, *Twenty-First Century Pillow-Talk: Applicability of the Marital Communications Privilege to Electronic Mail*, 58 S.C. L. REV. 275 (2006).

[257] United States v. Neal, 532 F. Supp. 942, 947 (D. Colo. 1982) (holding that neither FBI agent or defendant's wife could testify about content of phone conversation between defendant and his wife, because wife allowed FBI agent to monitor call and defendant did not know call was monitored and expected his call to be confidential); *see also* 8 WIGMORE ON EVIDENCE § 2339 (McNaughton rev. 1961).

[258] *See* State v. Johnson, 643 P.2d 146 (Kan. 1982).

[259] ARIZ. REV. STAT. ANN. § 12–2232; CAL. EVID. CODE § 984; MINN. STAT. ANN. § 595.02(1)(a).

[260] CAL. EVID. CODE § 985; MINN. STAT. ANN. § 595.02(1)(a).

[261] CAL. EVID. CODE § 985; MINN. STAT.§ 595.02(1)(a).

[262] *See In re* Donald Sheldon & Co, 191 B.R. 39, 48 (Bankr. S.D.N.Y. 1996) (holding privilege will not immunize spouse from disclosing marital communications where there was effort to conceal assets from creditors; New York courts do not recognize marital privilege when asserted to protect efforts to perpetrate fraud on third-party victims).

[263] *See* Marcy Strauss, *Silence*, 35 LOY. L.A. L. REV. 101 (2001).

[264] Malloy v. Hogan, 378 U.S. 1, 11 (1964).

state constitutional provisions that supplement the Fifth Amendment are interpreted more broadly than the Fifth Amendment.[265]

It is impossible to state a simple and satisfying rationale for the privilege against self-incrimination. It seems the privilege evolved as a reaction to the religious and political persecutions in England before the Restoration,[266] such as the practice of examining suspects under oath to determine whether they held forbidden beliefs.[267] At the time, the privilege was part of a larger privilege, the party-witness rule, which forbade parties from taking the witness stand even in their own defense.

Wigmore lists no fewer than a dozen policies that have been advanced in support of the privilege.[268] Perhaps the strongest are that the privilege prevents unreasonable pretrial interrogation methods and that it is inherently inhumane to confront an individual at trial with the trilemma of committing perjury, being held in contempt, or serving as the prosecution's witness.[269] When applied to crimes other than crimes of conscience, however, the famous legal philosopher Jeremy Bentham charged that the privilege benefits only the guilty, because the innocent will be eager to testify and promote their innocence.[270]

The privilege against self-incrimination is a personal privilege. It cannot be claimed on behalf of or used to protect another person, however unselfish one's motives may be.[271] A person can claim the privilege only when there is a danger of being subject to a criminal charge, not merely of humiliation or degradation. It is not necessary, however, to show that prosecution is probable as long as some danger of incrimination exists.[272] The privilege allows the witness to refuse to answer questions if the answers would directly incriminate the witness. But it goes further. It covers questions, the answers to which might provide an investigative lead for prosecuting the witness. For example, a witness is entitled to refuse to say whether she is acquainted with a certain person, if the information might provide the government with a lead.[273]

---

[265] *See, e.g.*, State v. Santiago, 492 P.2d 657 (Haw. 1971); Commonwealth v. Mavredakis, 725 N.E.2d 169, 177–78 (Mass. 2000).

[266] 8 WIGMORE ON EVIDENCE § 2250 (McNaughton rev. 1961).

[267] *See* Jan Martin Rybnicek, *Damned if You Do, Damned if You Don't?: The Absence of a Constitutional Protection Prohibiting the Admission of Post-Arrest, Pre-Miranda Silence*, 19 GEO. MASON U. CIV. RTS. L.J. 405, 409–11 (2009); *see also* John H. Langbein, *The Historical Origins of the Privilege Against Self Incrimination At Common Law*, 92 MICH. L. REV. 1047 (1994).

[268] 8 WIGMORE ON EVIDENCE § 2251 (McNaughton rev. 1961).

[269] *Id. See also* Murphy v. Waterfront Comm., 378 U.S. 52, 55 (1964) (quoting 8 WIGMORE ON EVIDENCE (McNaughton rev. 1961)):

> [The privilege] reflects many of our fundamental values and most noble aspirations: our unwillingness to subject those suspected of crime to the cruel trilemma of self-accusation, perjury or contempt; our preference for an accusatorial rather than an inquisitorial system of criminal justice; our fear that self-incriminating statements will be elicited by inhumane treatment and abuses; our sense of fair play which dictates "a fair state-individual balance by requiring the government to leave the individual alone until good cause is shown for disturbing him and by requiring the government in its contest with the individual to shoulder the entire load."

[270] JEREMY BENTHAM, RATIONALE OF JUDICIAL EVIDENCE (1827) (cited in 8 WIGMORE ON EVIDENCE § 2251 (McNaughton rev. 1961)).

[271] Rogers v. United States, 340 U.S. 367 (1951).

[272] Hoffman v. United States, 341 U.S. 479 (1951).

[273] *See id.* at 486 (witness may refuse to state whether knows alleged criminal and where alleged criminal is located if answers to those questions would "furnish a link in the chain of evidence needed to prosecute the claimant for a federal crime").

Although the court, not the witness, decides whether the privilege applies,[274] a witness's assertion that an answer raises a danger of incrimination will usually suffice. The Supreme Court has indicated that the claim of privilege should be sustained unless it is " 'perfectly clear, from a careful consideration of all the circumstances in the case, that the witness is mistaken, and that the answer(s) cannot possibly have [a] tendency' to incriminate."[275] This statement appears to place the burden on the government to show that the answers could not possibly incriminate the witness.

The privilege applies only to "testimonial" incrimination. So long as the government does not require a suspect to engage in communicative conduct that conveys factual assertions or information,[276] it can compel the suspect to commit affirmative acts that aid an investigation, even if those acts help incriminate the suspect.[277] For example, an investigative target may be compelled to sign a form permitting the government to examine foreign bank records,[278] to furnish handwriting and voice exemplars,[279] to appear in a lineup,[280] or to give a blood sample.[281] Subpoenas directed at the defendant present a special problem because the defendant's response often is communicative. While the information thus produced may be used against the suspect at trial (provided the information itself was not created under governmental compulsion), the suspect's compelled "act of production" may not be used at trial to identify the source of the produced thing if it entails the suspect's assertion that the thing is that which the government sought.[282]

The privilege belongs only to human beings. A corporation or other organization cannot claim the benefit of the privilege.[283]

A grant of immunity abrogates the privilege, even if the answers may cause the witness embarrassment or disgrace. Early precedent suggested that the immunity had to be transactional—that is, the immunity had to protect the witness against prosecution for the entire transaction about which testimony was being compelled. However, it is now clear that use immunity, which prohibits using the compelled testimony against the witness, is constitutionally sufficient.[284] If the government decides to prosecute the

---

274 Rogers v. United States, 340 U.S. 367 (1951).

275 Hoffman v. United States, 341 U.S. 479, 488 (1951) (quoting Temple v. Commonwealth, 75 Va. 892, 898 (Va. 1881)).

276 *See* Doe v. United States, 487 U.S. 201, 212 (1988).

277 Although there have been some indications of a willingness to remove this restriction, giving the accused broader protection against compelled production of evidence, so far it remains part of the doctrine. *See* United States v. Hubbell, 530 U.S. 27, 49 (2000) (Thomas, J., joined by Scalia, J., concurring) ("A substantial body of evidence suggests that the Fifth Amendment privilege protects against the compelled production not just of incriminating testimony, but of any incriminating evidence. In a future case, I would be willing to reconsider the scope and meaning of the Self-Incrimination Clause.").

278 *Id.* at 218.

279 United States v. Dionisio, 410 U.S. 1, 6–7 (1973); Gilbert v. California, 388 U.S. 263, 266–67 (1967).

280 United States v. Wade, 388 U.S. 218, 221–22 (1967).

281 Schmerber v. California, 384 U.S. 757, 765 (1966).

282 United States v. Doe, 465 U.S. 605, 612–14 (1984).

283 Bellis v. United States, 417 U.S. 85, 101 (1974); Hale v. Henkel, 201 U.S. 43, 75 (1906).

284 Kastigar v. United States, 406 U.S. 441 (1972).

witness, the government obviously cannot use the immunized testimony and has the burden of showing that the compelled testimony did not assist the prosecution.[285]

The witness may also lose the right to invoke the privilege because the danger of incrimination has been removed through acquittal, conviction, or application of double jeopardy to the underlying charge. If, however, the questioning about the adjudicated crime could lead to prosecution for other crimes, the witness may still invoke the privilege.[286]

The accused in a criminal case has a right not only to refuse answering self-incriminating questions but also to refuse taking the witness stand at all. Moreover, the prosecution may not allude to the defendant's failure to testify,[287] nor may it suggest in closing argument that the prosecution's evidence was not contradicted, if such argument implies that the defendant should have testified to provide such contradiction.[288] In a criminal case, when a witness other than the defendant who is identified with the defendant is likely to claim the privilege, the defense should move in limine to prohibit the government from calling the witness. This is because the jury may be confused or prejudiced against the defense by the witness's privilege claim and may not know how to interpret this conduct.[289]

Witnesses in civil cases may exercise the privilege to refuse to answer on grounds that their testimony could subject them to criminal charges. They must, however, take the stand to claim the privilege. In civil cases, he opposing party may ask the jury to draw an adverse inference from the witness's privilege claim.[290] If the person claiming the privilege is a litigant and not merely a witness, this may lead to other adverse consequences, including, in some jurisdictions, the dismissal of a plaintiff's case for withholding information.[291]

---

[285] *Id.* at 460 ("This burden of proof . . . imposes on the prosecution the affirmative duty to prove that the evidence it proposes to use is derived from a legitimate source wholly independent of the compelled testimony").

[286] Malloy v. Hogan, 378 U.S. 1, 13 (1964).

[287] Griffin v. California, 380 U.S. 609 (1965); *see also* Ted Sampsell-Jones, *Making Defendants Speak*, 93 MINN. L. REV. 1327 (2009) (wisdom of Supreme Court's holding in *Griffin* challenged).

[288] *Compare* Lindgren v. Lane, 925 F.2d 198 (7th Cir. 1991) (prosecutor argued that government witness was not contradicted because defense witness testified same point was not believable), *with* Lent v. Wells, 861 F.2d 972 (6th Cir. 1988) (where defendant was only one who could contradict).

[289] *See, e.g.*, Namet v. United States, 373 U.S. 179, 186 (1963) ("error may be based upon a concept of prosecutorial misconduct, when the Government makes a conscious and flagrant attempt to build its case out of inferences arising from [the witness'] use of the testimonial privilege"); Foster v. State, 687 S.W.2d 829, 832 (Ark. 1985) (reversible error for prosecution to call wife of deceased-whom prosecution knew would invoke her privilege against self-incrimination in defendant's murder trial because "there was an attempt by the prosecutor to build the state's case out of inferences arising from [the witness'] assertion of her fifth amendment privilege"). *See also* Clayton v. Commonwealth, 786 S.W.2d 866, 868 (Ky. 1990) (neither prosecution nor defense may call witness who they know would claim Fifth Amendment privilege).

[290] Curtis v. M & S Petroleum, Inc., 174 F.3d 661, 673–75 (5th Cir. 1999) (trial judge should have given instruction that adverse inference could be drawn from assertion of privilege by corporate president designated by corporation who took Fifth Amendment in individual capacity during deposition); Brink's Inc. v. City of New York, 717 F.2d 700, 710 (2d Cir. 1983); *see also* Robert Heidt, *The Conjurer's Circle—The Fifth Amendment Privilege in Civil Cases*, 91 YALE L. J. 1062, 1107–08 (1982).

[291] Lyons v. Johnson, 415 F.2d 540, 542 (9th Cir. 1969) (holding that plaintiff's suit was properly dismissed because plaintiff refused to answer interrogatories, despite fact plaintiff refused on Fifth Amendment grounds); Penn Commc'ns Specialties, Inc. v. Hess, 65 F.R.D. 510, 512 (E.D. Pa. 1975) (holding that plaintiff's suit may be dismissed unless plaintiff answers defendant's interrogatories, despite fact plaintiff refused on Fifth Amendment grounds); Master v. Savannah Surety Assoc., Inc., 252 S.E.2d 186, 187 (Ga. Ct. App. 1979) (dismissing suit).

A witness may waive the right against self-incrimination. A witness who has testified about part of a transaction cannot claim the right to self-incrimination when cross-examined about the remainder.[292] Testimony on a question of preliminary fact, however, such as testimony on a motion to suppress evidence resulting from an allegedly illegal search, does not waive a criminal defendant's ultimate right to assert the privilege.[293]

The right against self-incrimination applies to certain interrogations conducted by law enforcement officers before trial. In the celebrated case of *Miranda v. Arizona*, the Supreme Court held that statements made during custodial interrogation could not be used at trial, unless the person in custody had been given what have become known as the "*Miranda* warnings." The interrogation must be preceded by a warning that: (1) the suspect had a right to remain silent; (2) any statement made could be used against him in evidence; and (3) that the suspect had a right to counsel, either retained or appointed.[294] If the warnings are not given and if the suspect does not waive the rights, any statement obtained through custodial interrogation is inadmissible. Such a statement may be used, however, to impeach a defendant who testifies.[295]

Silence, too, may be used in some circumstances to impeach a criminal defendant. As a general rule, a defendant who remains silent after receiving *Miranda* warnings and then testifies to an alibi or some other explanation may not be impeached with the previous silence in response to police interrogation. In *Doyle v. Ohio*, the Supreme Court recognized that the silence was likely to be in response to the *Miranda* warning's reminder of the right to remain silent.[296] However, a defendant who testifies during trial and who did not tell law enforcement about the gist of her testimony before trial may be impeached by her silence where no *Miranda* warnings were issued[297] or where circumstances indicate that an innocent person would have spoken up, such as an accused's claim of self-defense that was impeached by a two week period in which the accused did not report the homicide.[298] The policy of impeachment based upon the silence of an arrested individual who, after not receiving proper *Miranda* warnings, exercised the right to remain silent, is questionable. Had the police followed the proper procedure and given the defendant *Miranda* warnings, no impeachment based on silence would be permissible. The Court's reasoning—that the lack of a warning avoided the risk that the silence might be a response to the warning's caution—is not terribly convincing; surely some defendants know their *Miranda* rights without being told. In ignoring the purpose and the spirit of *Miranda,* such decisions provide an incentive for police officers to forgo *Miranda* warnings after arrest as a way to ensure that a confused defendant will be limited in their ability to present exculpatory testimony at trial.

---

[292] Rogers v. United States, 340 U.S. 367, 372 (1951); United States v. Hearst, 563 F.2d 1331, 1341 (9th Cir. 1977).

[293] Simmons v. United States, 390 U.S. 377, 394 (1968).

[294] 384 U.S. 436, 467–73 (1966).

[295] Harris v. New York, 401 U.S. 222, 226 (1971) (holding defendant's statement to authorities, given without defendant having received proper Miranda warning, was admissible to impeach defendant's testimony even though statement was inadmissible in prosecution's case in chief).

[296] 426 U.S. 610 (1976).

[297] Jenkins v. Anderson, 447 U.S. 231 (1980).

[298] Fletcher v. Weir, 455 U.S. 603 (1982).

§ 4.19 The Government's Privileges

Military and state secrets are protected from compelled disclosure.[299] The privilege covers information that might harm the national defense or international relations if disclosed. The trial judge may make a limited in camera review to determine whether the privilege applies.[300] If the privilege applies, it is absolute and cannot be overcome by a showing of necessity.[301]

In *United States v. Nixon*[302] the Supreme Court recognized a qualified "executive privilege" for presidential communications made in confidence.[303] Unless military or state secrets are involved, the privilege is not absolute and may be overcome by a showing of specific need for information that will be key evidence in a criminal trial.[304] Absent such special circumstances, the president may be subpoenaed during federal and state criminal proceedings.[305] Moreover, while the president enjoys absolute immunity from a civil suit for damages based on official action,[306] the president does not have such immunity for civil actions based on non-official action, in the context of which the president is subject to appropriate discovery requests.[307]

A variety of other privileges for governmental information exist. Often the privileges are governed by statute and protect information that individuals or corporations must provide to the government.[308] They cover matters ranging from grand jury proceedings[309] to census information.[310]

The informer's privilege is often asserted in criminal cases. It allows the government to decline to identify informers, who, for obvious reasons, would rather not be known to those whom they have incriminated.[311] Where the identity of the informer is helpful to the defendant's case or is essential to a fair trial, the informer's identity must be revealed, or the case must be dismissed.[312] If, however, the informer was merely a

---

299 *See, e.g.*, United States v. Reynolds, 345 U.S. 1, 6–7 (1953) (holding privileged an Air Force accident report because it contained secret information that could not be disclosed without harming national security); *see also* Robert M. Chesney, *State Secrets and the Limits of National Security Litigation*, 75 GEO. WASH. L. REV. 1249 (2007).

300 *Reynolds*, 345 U.S. at 9–10.

301 *Id.* at 10–11.

302 418 U.S. 683 (1974).

303 *Id.* at 705–06.

304 *Id.* at 706–07. *See* Stephen C. N. Lilley, *Suboptimal Executive Privilege*, 2009 B.Y.U. L. REV. 1127 (2009).

305 Trump v. Vance, 140 S. Ct. 2412 (2020) (extending the long standing rule for federal proceedings to state proceedings).

306 Nixon v. Fitzgerald, 457 U.S. 731 (1982).

307 Clinton v. Jones, 520 U.S. 681 (1997).

308 *See* 2 CHRISTOPHER B. MUELLER & LAIRD C. KIRKPATRICK, FEDERAL EVIDENCE § 5:51 (4th ed. 2013).

309 *See, e.g.*, FED. R. CRIM. P. 6(e) (general rule imposing secrecy of grand jury proceedings).

310 *See, e.g.*, 13 U.S.C. §§ 8(b), 9(a) (limited access to and disclosure of census information to insure confidentiality).

311 *See, e.g.*, Roviaro v. United States, 353 U.S. 53, 59 (1957) (holding government not required to disclose communication that would reveal identity of person providing information concerning violation of law); *see also* Zathrina Zasell Gutierrez Perez, Note, *Piercing the Veil of Informant Confidentiality: The Role of In Camera Hearings in the Roviaro Determination*, 46 AM. CRIM. L. REV. 179 (2009).

312 *See, e.g.*, *Rovario*, 353 U.S. at 60–61 (holding identity of informer who witnessed crime not privileged because testimony might have been crucial to defense).

supplier of probable cause to arrest or search, then the informer's identity need not be revealed.[313]

§ 4.20 Other Privileges

Priest-penitent.[314] A privilege for confidential communications between parishioners and clergy is widely recognized.[315] Though early versions of the privilege applied only to religiously required communications,[316] such as confessions made by Roman Catholics, modern versions tend to include other communications made for spiritual guidance, comfort, or advice.[317] In a leading decision out of the Third Circuit, the court confirmed the existence of the privilege under federal common law, one that applies to protect "communications made (1) to a clergyperson (2) in his or her spiritual and professional capacity (3) with a reasonable expectation of confidentiality."[318] Further, the court held that the privilege is not vitiated by the presence of third persons whose presence is essential to and in furtherance of the communication, all of which may be determined by the trial judge by appropriately structured *in camera* proceedings.[319]

Journalists. Several jurisdictions recognize a privilege for journalists and other news gatherers.[320] The United States Supreme Court considered and rejected the argument that the First Amendment requires acceptance of a general privilege for journalists.[321] Some federal courts, nevertheless, recognize a qualified First Amendment journalists' privilege.[322]

The journalist's privilege differs significantly from all of the other privileges insofar as it is not aimed at keeping communications confidential. On the contrary, the whole idea is that it will facilitate communication of information that might not otherwise be

---

[313] *See, e.g.*, McCray v. Illinois, 386 U.S. 300, 312 (1967) (holding identity of informant who told police defendant was dealing drugs, pointed defendant out to police, and then left, privileged).

[314] Lennard K. Whittaker, *The Priest-Penitent Privilege: Its Constitutionality and Doctrine*, 13 REGENT U. L. REV. 145 (2000–2001).

[315] *See* 2 CHRISTOPHER B. MUELLER & LAIRD C. KIRKPATRICK, FEDERAL EVIDENCE § 5:44 (4th ed. 2013).

[316] *See* 8 WIGMORE ON EVIDENCE § 2395 (McNaughton rev. 1961) (privilege applies to communications made pursuant to church discipline); EDWARD J. IMWINKELRIED, THE NEW WIGMORE: EVIDENTIARY PRIVILEGES § 6.2.3 (2d ed. 2010) (many states limit privilege to religiously required communications).

[317] *See, e.g.*, MINN. STAT. ANN. § 595.02(1)(c) (including clergy's communications with "any person seeking religious or spiritual advice, aid, or comfort"); OHIO REV. CODE § 2317.02(C) (including any confidential communication made "directly" to a cleric "in the manner and context that places the cleric specifically and strictly under a level of confidentiality that is considered inviolate by canon law or church doctrine.").

[318] *In re* Grand Jury Investigation, 918 F.2d 374, 384 (3d Cir. 1990). In a footnote, the court endorsed the definition of clergyperson provided in the proposed federal rule on the subject: "a minister, priest, rabbi, or other similar functionary of a religious organization, or an individual reasonably believed so to be by the person consulting him." *Id.* at n. 13. The opinion continues with the following caution: "By endorsing this definition of a clergyperson, we do not intimate that the privilege should be interpreted to comprehend communications to and among members of sects that denominate each and every member as clergy, proclaim that all communications have spiritual significance, or dictate that all communications among members, whether essential to and infurtherance of the purportedly privileged communication or not, shall be confidential." *Id.*

[319] *Id.* at 385–88.

[320] *See* Markus E. Apelis, Note, *Fit to Print? Consequences of Implementing a Federal Reporter's Privilege*, 58 CASE W. RES. L. REV. 1369 (2008); 2 CHRISTOPHER B. MUELLER & LAIRD C. KIRKPATRICK, FEDERAL EVIDENCE § 5:46 (4th ed. 2013).

[321] Branzburg v. Hayes, 408 U.S. 665, 690 (1972).

[322] *Id. See, e.g.*, United States v. Sterling, 724 F.3d 482, 496 (4th Cir. 2013) (rejecting argument that, in a criminal case, the privilege can only be overcome by the government's satisfaction of a heavy, three-part, compelling-interest test, but recognizing that Fourth Circuit precedent provides for such a burden to override qualified privilege in civil cases).

available. The privilege generally protects a reporter from being required to reveal the identity of a confidential source of information.[323] In some jurisdictions, it covers unpublished notes and materials prepared by the news gatherer. The statutory privileges are not absolute and generally are governed by some sort of balancing test. For example, a statute might provide that the privilege must yield when there is a compelling reason for disclosure and no alternative means of obtaining the information.[324] Even where a statutory privilege purports to be absolute, an accused person's constitutional right to obtain witnesses may require that the privilege be abrogated when the reporter seeks to conceal information crucial to the defense.[325]

In re Farber[326] grew out of a homicide prosecution of a physician for a death in a New Jersey hospital. Farber, a reporter for the New York Times, had been deeply involved in investigative reporting about the case and may have been the driving force behind the prosecution. The trial judge held a hearing on the application of the privilege. At the hearing, the defendant showed that the main accuser had talked to Farber five times, that evidence suggested that Farber might be in possession of a prior inconsistent statement of a witness, that another important witness who Farber interviewed would not talk to the defense, and that another witness interviewed by Farber had died.[327] The New Jersey Supreme Court upheld a criminal contempt conviction imposed upon Farber for refusing to turn over his materials for in camera inspection by the trial court.[328]

Parent-child. Only a few jurisdictions recognize a parent-child privilege.[329] Where it exits, this privilege typically allows a parent to refuse to reveal confidential communications from a child. It is subject to the same exceptions applied to the marital

---

[323] *See, e.g.*, 735 ILL. COMP. STAT. ANN. § 5/8–901 (reporter generally cannot be compelled to disclose source of any information); Minn. Stat. Ann. §§ 595.021–595.024 (forced disclosure of confidential sources generally prohibited); N.J. Stat. Ann. § 2A:84A–21 (reporter has privilege to refuse to disclose source of information).

[324] *See, e.g.*, 735 Ill. Comp. Stat. Ann. § 5/8–907) (exception to basic privilege); MINN. STAT. ANN. § 595.024(2).

[325] *See In re* Farber (State v. Jascalevich), 394 A.2d 330, 337 (N.J. 1978) (holding criminal defendant's right under New Jersey Constitution to compel attendance of witness and production of documents prevails over facially absolute language of statute).

[326] 394 A.2d 330 (N.J. 1978).

[327] *Id.* at 340.

[328] *Id.* at 341.

[329] *See, e.g.*, MINN. STAT. ANN. § 595.02(1)(j) (providing that communications made in confidence by minor to minor's parent privileged); *In re* Grand Jury Proceedings, Unemancipated Minor Child, 949 F. Supp. 1487, 1494–95 (E.D. Wash.1996) (noting that, because it is supported by policy reasons similar to spousal privilege, recognition of federal parent-child privilege comports with reason and experience; in instant case, however, holding that grand jury subpoena to 17-year-old child would not be quashed because child failed to show either that confidential communications were sought or that testimony would be adverse to father's interests); People v. Fitzgerald, 422 N.Y.S.2d 309, 312, 317 (N.Y. 1979) (holding parent-child privilege flows directly from United States and New York Constitutions; adult child's confidential communication with parent concerning hit and run accident privileged in criminal prosecution). *But see In re* Grand Jury, 103 F.3d 1140, 1140–47 (3d Cir. 1997) (rejecting parent-child privilege after thoughtful discussion and extensive examination of authority); *In re* Erato, 2 F.3d 11, 16 (2d Cir. 1993) (refusing to recognize privilege in case where son residing in Netherlands was suspected of embezzling millions of dollars from United States citizens in fraudulent real estate scheme, and mother was allegedly benefiting from scheme; court suggested that privilege may not necessarily extend to protect adult child); United States v. Jones, 683 F.2d 817, 819 (4th Cir. 1982) (rejecting privilege where adult child was ordered to give testimony against father). *See generally* Catherine J. Ross, *Implementing Constitutional Rights for Juveniles: The Parent-Child Privilege in Context*, 14 STAN. L. & POL'Y REV. 85 (2003).

privileges; for example, it does not cover communications involving crimes against the family.[330]

Accountant-client. A few states recognize an accountant-client privilege,[331] but there is no such privilege under Federal law.[332] In *United States v. Arthur Young & Co.*,[333] the Supreme Court faced the issue whether an IRS subpoena for tax accrual work papers prepared by the corporation's independent CPA could be discovered pursuant to an IRS summons. The papers, which were prepared for a mandatory SEC filing, contained an evaluation of possible tax liability of the corporation that was based on information including "opinions, speculations, and projections of management with regard to unclear, aggressive, or questionable tax positions that may have been taken on prior tax returns."[334] Despite the sensitive nature of the information, the Supreme Court held that it was not protected either by privilege or by the work-product doctrine.[335]

§ 4.21 Privilege Claims Versus the Accused's Right to Present a Defense

The accused in a criminal case enjoys a right to present evidence that can, in special circumstances, override the exclusionary mandate of an otherwise valid rule.[336] The question arises whether this principle allows the accused to override an otherwise valid claim of privilege made by a witness, so that the witness can be compelled to testify.

Most of the leading Supreme Court cases on the constitutional right to present a defense have not arisen in the privilege context. In *Chambers v. Mississippi*,[337] for example, the Supreme Court held that the accused's constitutional rights were violated when he was prevented from presenting the highly reliable, well-corroborated confession of another person to the crime for which the accused was tried.[338] Critical to the Court's holding were the following points: (1) the hearsay rule prevented the accused from presenting crucial exculpatory evidence, (2) the hearsay rule is a rule designed to improve accuracy, and (3) the particular application of the hearsay rule in that case did not improve accuracy, so the hearsay rule had failed in its ultimate goal. As the Court there emphasized: "the hearsay rule may not be applied mechanistically to defeat the ends of justice."[339]

When a witness's otherwise legitimate claim of privilege prevents the defendant's presentation of evidence, the foregoing rationale does not directly apply; at least it is incomplete. Unlike the hearsay rule, as it is usually understood, privilege rules protect

---

[330] *See, e.g.*, MINN. STAT. ANN. § 595.02(1)(j) (providing that communications involving crimes against family members not privileged).

[331] *See, e.g.*, ARIZ. REV. STAT. ANN. § 32–749; 225 ILL. COMP. STAT. ANN. § 450/27 (confidential communications with accountant privileged). *See generally*, Thomas J. Molony, Note, *Is the Supreme Court Ready to Recognize Another Privilege? An Examination of the Accountant-Client Privilege in the Aftermath of Jaffee v. Redmond*, 55 WASH. & LEE L. REV. 247 (1998); Robert J. Tepper, *New Mexico's Accountant-Client Privilege*, 37 N.M. L. REV. 387 (2007).

[332] *See, e.g.*, Couch v. United States, 409 U.S. 322, 335 (1973) (tax records in possession of her accountant not privileged).

[333] 465 U.S. 805 (1984).

[334] *Id.* at 812.

[335] *Id.* at 817–18.

[336] *See* **§ 1.04**.

[337] 410 U.S. 284 (1973).

[338] *See* **§ 18.04**.

[339] 410 U.S. at 302.

values that go beyond, and often compete with, the law's interest in accuracy of adjudication.[340] The widely accepted view is that this fact requires that an additional test be met before a privilege is constitutionally overridden on constitutional grounds. The court must conduct a balancing test that compares the relative importance, in the particular context, of the interests protected by the privilege and the interests of the accused.[341]

Not surprisingly, the cases are split on how this balance plays out. Some lower courts have accepted claims that the defendant's right to present exculpatory evidence takes precedence over the interests protected by a communication privilege.[342] Other courts have disagreed.[343] In the context of one particular privilege, however—the witness's constitutionally based privilege against self-incrimination—the courts have consistently refused to compel the witness to testify to potentially self-incriminating facts.[344] This probably reflects the constitutional status of the privilege itself.[345]

Courts that are willing to override a witness's claim of privilege nonetheless emphasize the need to balance the importance of the two claims in context. For example, when the witness's privilege over a confidential communication is rendered less important because the witness has died (and the privilege is claimed by someone else on behalf of its now-deceased original holder), the interests of the accused in a fair trial and the public's interest in a correct result are more compelling.[346] And when the witness has been less than consistent in maintaining the confidentiality of the information that was the subject of his privileged communication, its importance declines, even if not so much as to constitute a waiver. On the other side of the balance, the court must consider how important the potential evidence is to the defense and whether its substance can be

---

[340] In the first case that saw the Compulsory Process Clause used to override a state exclusionary rule ostensibly designed to prevent perjury by co-defendants, the Supreme Court had stated, "Nothing in this opinion should be construed as disapproving testimonial privileges." Washington v. Texas, 388 U.S. 14, 23 n.21 (1967).

[341] For a thorough treatment of the issue, see EDWARD J. IMWINKELRIED, THE NEW WIGMORE: EVIDENTIARY PRIVILEGES §§ 11.1–11.4 (2d ed. 2010).

[342] *See, e.g.*, United States v. Alperin, 128 F. Supp. 2d 1251, 1253–55 (N.D. Cal. 2001) (addressing psychotherapist-patient privilege); United States v. Grace, 439 F. Supp. 2d 1125, 1142–43 (D. Mont. 2006) (addressing attorney-client privilege), *aff'd on other grounds*, 526 F.3d 499 (9th Cir. 2008); Salazar v. State, 559 P.2d 66, 79 (Alaska 1976) (addressing marital communication privilege).

[343] *See, e.g.*, Jenkins v. Wainwright, 763 F2d 1390 (11th Cir. 1985) (addressing attorney-client privilege), *cert. denied*, 476 U.S. 1164, United States v. Lea, 249 F.3d 632, 643 (7th Cir. 2001) (addressing marital communications privilege).

[344] *See, e.g.*, United States v. Khan, 728 F.2d 676, 678 (5th Cir. 1984); United States v. Highgate, 521 F.3d 590, 593 (6th Cir. 2008); United States v. Jones, 512 F.3d 1007, 1008–09 (8th Cir. 2008). Moreover, the defendant is usually not permitted, in an attempt to create reasonable doubt, to call the witness to the stand, force the witness to claim the privilege, and then invite the fact-finder to draw an adverse inference from the witness's invocation of the privilege. *See, e.g.*, United States v. Deutsch, 987 F2d 878, 883–84 (2d Cir. 1993).

[345] Many of the cases that pose this conflict involve a defendant accused of committing a crime that, according to the defendant, was committed by another person, who stated as much in the context of an otherwise privileged communication. Overriding the communication privilege in such contexts, arguably poses the risk of effectively overriding the communicator's privilege against self-incrimination. *See, e.g.*, Valdez v. Winans, 738 F.2d 1087, 1090 (10th Cir. 1984). This difficulty could be avoided by requiring disclosure of the communication as exculpatory evidence for the present defendant, but giving immunity against its use in a potential case against the communicator. However, such a solution presents obvious opportunities for multiple defendants to create reciprocating exculpatory evidence without having to testify.

[346] *See, e.g.*, *In re* Death of Eric Miller, 584 S.E.2d 772 (N.C. 2003).

placed before the fact-finder by other means or from other sources.[347] To make its assessment, the trial court may require a disclosure of the privileged material *in camera* to the extent necessary.[348]

A few Supreme Court decisions have resolved questions pitting the defendant's right to present evidence against privilege claims. *Davis v. Alaska*[349] involved a conflict between the defendant's right to confront an adverse witness and a statutory rule excluding evidence of the witness's juvenile criminal record. The exclusionary rule was clearly based on a governmental interest in protecting the confidentiality of juvenile court proceedings, not on any concern about the reliability or probative value of the information that was excluded. The defendant's right to confront a witness for the prosecution was held to take priority because of the importance of the defendant's interest in exploring the potential bias of the witness. And in an even earlier case, *Roviaro v. United States*,[350] the Court held that a defendant's right to disclosure of the name of a critical percipient witness whose identity was known to the government trumped the government's interest in maintaining the confidentiality of its informants. As a consequence of such a ruling, the government may choose to maintain that confidentiality only by dropping the prosecution. Both cases clearly manifest the need to balance the competing interests in the specific context of each case.

---

[347] All these factors are in play, for example, in the habeas proceeding, Morales v. Portuondo, 154 F. Supp. 2d 706, 730–31 (S.D.N.Y. 2001) (considering, inter alia, priest-penitent privilege and attorney-client privilege of deceased person who confessed to the crime for which defendant was convicted).

[348] *Cf.* United States v. Zolin, 491 U.S. 554 (1989) (permitting in camera review of allegedly privileged materials in order to make determination of the applicability of crime-fraud exception), discussed in **§ 4.10**.

[349] 415 U.S. 308 (1974).

[350] 353 U.S. 53 (1957).

Part III

RELEVANCE AND ITS COUNTERWEIGHTS

Chapter 5

RELEVANCE AND COUNTERWEIGHTS: GENERAL PRINCIPLES

Table of Sections

§ 5.01 Introduction to Relevance

Federal Rules of Evidence 401, 402, and 403 establish general principles of relevance, including general limits on the admission of relevant evidence. In many respects, these three rules form the core principles of modern evidence law, outlining the broad standards of admissibility under the modern rules. The rest of the evidence rules generally serve to narrow the admissibility of relevant evidence admitted under these three rules.

Rule 401 provides that an item of evidence is relevant if it has any tendency to make a fact of consequence to the determination of the action—that is to say a material fact—more probable or less probable than it would be without the evidence. Rule 402 sets forth the general rule that all relevant evidence is admissible except as otherwise provided by rule, statute, or constitution. Irrelevant evidence is inadmissible.[1]

Rule 401 adopts a very broad concept of relevance. Almost anything that a rational lawyer would attempt to offer into evidence would be relevant within the meaning of Rule 401 because it would have some minimal effect on the probability that a particular proposition of consequence to the case is true or false. The term *logically relevant* has sometimes been used to refer to evidence that meets the Rule 401 standard. Such logical relevance encompasses a tremendous amount of potential evidence.[2]

---

1 *See* **§ 1.04**.

2 *See* FED. R. EVID. 401 advisory committee note (explaining that evidence is relevant if it makes existence of fact "more probable or less probable than it would be without the evidence"). *See, e.g.*, United States v. Casares-Cardenas, 14 F.3d 1283, 1287 (8th Cir. 1994) (holding that evidence of woman with same surname as co-defendant captured with defendant during case-related illegal entry is relevant, even though it does not conclusively show link to co-defendant); Conway v. Chemical Leaman Tank Lines, Inc., 525 F.2d 927, 930 (5th Cir. 1976) (holding that Rule 401's definition of relevant evidence is "generous" and includes background information); International Merger & Acquisition Consultants, Inc. v. Armac Enters., 531 F.2d 821, 823 (7th Cir. 1976) (holding that Rule 401 provides "rather liberal standard" of relevance). *Compare* David Crump, *On the Uses of Irrelevant Evidence*, 34 HOUS. L. REV. 1, 6 (1997) ("the relevancy 'standard' in Rule 401 is no standard at all, because it indiscriminately admits every arguable proposition no matter how low its probative value"), with Richard D. Friedman, *Irrelevance, Minimial Relevance, and Meta-Relevance*, 34 HOUS. L. REV. 55, 67 (1997) (arguing that some evidence is rightly excluded for want of any probative value, but also suggesting that Rule 401 be amended so that Rule 402 would exclude evidence that does not have "significant probative value").

It would be impractical to admit all logically relevant evidence. Courts would be inundated with marginally useful, potentially confusing, and time-wasting evidence. From a practical perspective, the first and arguably most important rule of exclusion is Rule 403, which narrows the amount of evidence admitted to what is "legally" or practically relevant.[3] Rule 403 provides that even if evidence passes the relevance test of Rule 401, the trial court may exclude evidence if the probative value of the evidence is substantially outweighed by considerations of unfair prejudice, waste of time, or confusion of issues.[4]

For example, in a personal injury case, the fact that the defendant had a fight with his wife on the morning of the accident that is the subject of the suit might be minimally probative of a fact at issue (perhaps he was not paying attention to his driving because he was thinking about domestic problems). Though this fact is relevant within the broad scope of 401, the court would very likely exclude the evidence as a waste of time (and possibly for reasons of unfair prejudice) under Rule 403.[5]

§ 5.02 Relevance, Materiality, and Probative Value

Historically, the common law distinguished *relevance* from *materiality*. Evidence is irrelevant if it cannot logically help to establish the fact that the proponent asserts it will prove. Evidence is immaterial when, although it has a tendency in logic to establish the fact that it is offered to prove, that fact is not in issue.[6] For example, the fact that a worker drank on the assembly line while manufacturing a product is not material if the allegation regards faulty product design rather than negligence in the manufacturing process. As a second example, suppose the defendant, a physician, is on trial for murder. The defense would like to introduce evidence that the "victim" was slowly dying and in great pain and had requested the physician to end her life. The state recognizes no excuse or justification based on euthanasia, but the defense argues nonetheless that the jury should be aware of the context of the killing. The evidence likely would be excluded as immaterial.[7]

The Federal Rules generally avoid the term "material." Evidence that was previously described as "immaterial" is now "irrelevant" within the meaning of Rule 401 if, in the language of the Rule, it is not "of consequence" to the determination of the

---

3 The Federal Rules of Evidence do not use the terms "logical" and "legal" relevance, which sometimes appeared in case law, but the concept of "logical relevance" is, in effect, embodied in Rule 401, while evidence that previously might have been called "logically relevant but not legally relevant" can now be described as "relevant under Rule 401 but not admissible because of Rule 403."

4 *See, e.g.*, Cotton v. United States, 361 F.2d 673, 676 (8th Cir. 1966) (holding that, although evidence that some people who pass counterfeit bills are innocent is logically relevant in a counterfeiting trial, the evidence is not legally relevant because it is potentially confusing). *See also* 1A WIGMORE ON EVIDENCE § 28 (Tillers rev. 1983) (explaining that standard for "legal relevancy" is higher than that for logical relevance). To avoid creating confusion, we will eschew the term "legal relevancy" and instead discuss the precise principle under which logically relevant evidence might be excluded in a given situation.

5 *See* FED. R. EVID. 403 advisory committee note.

6 *See, e.g.*, 1 WIGMORE ON EVIDENCE § 2 at 18 (Tillers rev. 1983) (explaining distinction between materiality and relevance); United States v. Williams, 545 F.2d 47, 50 (8th Cir. 1976) (holding that evidence concerning state insurance statutes and regulations relevant to insurance agent's knowledge of law, but inadmissible in mail fraud prosecution against insurance purchaser because agent's knowledge of law is not material issue).

7 *See* People v. Kevorkian, 639 N.W.2d 291, 329–32 (Mich. App. 2001) (same result under state's version of Federal Rules).

action.[8] Suppose, for example, that in a prosecution for check forgery, the defendant admits signing another person's name to the check, but wishes to offer evidence that a week later, she covered the check with her own money. This evidence would be irrelevant—not of consequence—because it would not affect her guilt of the crime; evidence of later remorse has no bearing on the defendant's state of mind at the time she forged the check.[9]

Under the Federal Rules, when an opponent objects on grounds of relevance, the trial judge will look to the proponent to identify the "fact of consequence" toward which the evidence is directed and to explain how the evidence offered is probative of that fact. The evidence must be probative of some ultimate fact that determines whether an element of a claim or defense has been established, but a fact of consequence can also be some intermediate fact that the parties agree (at least for purposes of the objection) is itself relevant to such an ultimate fact.[10] Under the Federal Rules terminology, relevance is a binary attribute—something either is relevant or it is not. There are no degrees of relevance, so describing evidence as "very relevant" makes no sense, though it is an expression often heard. The term that is variable, that is a matter of degree, is *probative value*. Probative value, a concept that appears in Rule 403, is clearly gradational and it is appropriate to speak of evidence having "very high," "modest," or "very low" probative value.

As the foregoing suggests, identifying and assessing the relevance and probative value of a given item of evidence requires thinking about "chains of inference." Take as an example a murder case in which the defendant does not contest that the victim was murdered but claims he is not the murderer. The prosecution proposes testimony of a witness who will say that he observed the accused arguing angrily with the victim the day before the victim was found dead. The defense might object to the relevance of this testimony, and the prosecution might suggest that it tends to show motive. Motive is not an element of the crime of murder, but usually it will be conceded by the defense that the existence of a motive to kill would be a fact of consequence that is itself relevant to the question of the perpetrator's identity, and one of the elements of the alleged crime is that the defendant is the person who committed the homicide.[11] The evidence invites the fact-finder to infer hostility toward the deceased from the testimony (and perhaps other evidence) and to infer a motive to kill from that hostility (and perhaps other testimony), and then to infer the identity of the perpetrator from the motive to kill (and perhaps other evidence).[12]

---

[8] *See* FED. R. EVID. 401 advisory committee note; 2 WEINSTEIN'S FEDERAL EVIDENCE § 401.04[3] (Mark S. Brodin ed., 2d ed. 2015).

[9] Repayment is not a defense to a forgery charge. *See* United States v. Wilson, 28 C.M.R. 844, 850, 1959 WL 3562 (A.F.B.R. 1959) (military law); People v. Morris, 92 P.2d 644, 645 (Cal. Ct. App. 1939). *See also* 37 C.J.S., FORGERY § 41 (1943).

[10] Thus, the drafters of the federal rules wrote that a fact of consequence "may be ultimate, intermediate, or evidentiary; it matters not, so long as it is of consequence in the determination of the action." FED. R. EVID. 401, advisory committee note.

[11] *See* 2 WIGMORE ON EVIDENCE § 385 et seq., especially § 396 (Chadbourn rev. 1979) (discussing general receptiveness of courts to evidence offered to show motive, even though motive is usually not an essential element of a cause of action or defense).

[12] As the parentheticals indicate, this testimony may not be the only evidence on motive, and motive may not be the only indicator of identity. Thus, inference chains are not necessarily entirely separate from one another, but rather can form a "web" of interconnections. For the use of this idea to analyze the whole mass of evidence in a case, see JOHN H. WIGMORE, THE SCIENCE OF JUDICIAL Proof (3d ed. 1937); TERRENCE ANDERSON, DAVID SCHUM, & WILLIAM TWINING, THE ANALYSIS OF EVIDENCE (2d ed. 2005).

For the moment, focus on the second of these steps in the inference from this testimony:

If the fact-finder accepts that there was an angry argument, how does the fact-finder assess the strength of the inference to motive (and then to identity)? Inevitably, the fact-finder relies (at least in part) on his or her knowledge about the way the world works and what angry arguments between people indicate *in general*.[13] This background information is not knowledge about the particular parties involved (such knowledge would disqualify the person from acting as fact-finder under the American rules for adversarial trials).[14] Witnesses must provide the specific information about the conduct of the parties. But how the fact-finder will use that specific information depends on his or her background, knowledge, and experience.[15] If a trial judge believes that a rational juror, relying on commonly believed background information, could think anger makes the existence of a motive to kill more likely, as compared with the situation in which such anger was not present, then the proffered evidence will pass the relevance test, at least as far as this inference is concerned.

In assessing the relevance of the testimony about the argument, the fact-finder must consider not only the strength of the inference shown above, but also the strength of the inference from the evidence itself, which is the testimony of the witness, to the fact that an angry argument occurred, which we may represent thus:

Because we are supposing that the witness testified to observing that the defendant and the victim had the angry argument, the inference here involves simply the question of whether, or to what degree, to believe the witness. However, it would be a mistake to think this is actually "simple." A number of things can go wrong that would cause the witness to testify incorrectly: the witness might have perceived inaccurately in the first place; the witness might have inaccurately remembered what was perceived; the witness might fail to communicate accurately what is remembered; and the witness might be lying. So crediting the testimony involves a number of inferences imbedded in the foregoing representation: from the witness's testimony to the witness's present beliefs; from the witness's present beliefs to the witness's earlier beliefs; from the witness's earlier beliefs to the witness's earlier perceptions; from the witness's earlier perceptions

---

13 *See* EDMUND M. MORGAN, BASIC PROBLEMS OF EVIDENCE 183–88 (1962).

14 *See* **§ 8.05**.

15 The fact-finder's background knowledge need not be incontrovertible. Indeed, the fact-finder may be mistaken. In order to correct such mistaken ideas, the parties may resort to expert testimony (*see* **§ 10.03**), or, in appropriate cases, judicial notice (*see* **§ 2.14**). In some cases, if the matter is disclosed during voir dire, a prospective juror may be removed because of his or her views. *See* Paul F. Kirgis, *The Problem of the Expert Juror*, 75 TEMPLE L. REV. 493 (2002).

to the truth about the event observed.[16] Moreover, assessing these inferences involves the application of additional background generalizations by the fact-finder—generalizations about the ability of persons to perceive in the manner suggested by the testimony, the ability of persons to remember the details indicated for the time period involved, the likely behavior of persons placed under oath to testify, and so forth.[17]

The foregoing permits an explanation of the distinction between direct and circumstantial evidence. If the only inferences to be drawn from the testimony are those involved in deciding whether, or to what extent, to credit the witness's testimony, that is, to believe the facts that the witness asserts, then the evidence is called *direct* evidence. If additional inferences must be considered by the fact-finder to reach the fact of consequence in the case, then the testimony is called *circumstantial* evidence. Thus, in the example above, the testimony of the witness is direct evidence of the fact that there was an angry argument between the defendant and the victim the day before the crime, but the testimony is circumstantial evidence that the defendant had a motive to kill the victim or that the defendant was the perpetrator.[18] Although evidence rules rarely depend on the distinction, it is one commonly used by trial lawyers, as when a defense lawyer says, "All the evidence of my client's guilt is circumstantial." This just means, that the prosecution does not have an eye-witness to the crime. The distinction appears in the important "single witness" rule that is one of the principles of evidential sufficiency, and it marks off an important area of inference that is especially reserved for the fact-finder.[19] Because of this principle and the associated allocation of roles, some authorities assert that direct evidence of a fact of consequence cannot be excluded as irrelevant.[20]

In assessing the relevance and probative value of evidence, it is often difficult to think in straightforwardly causal terms, such as "anger tends to be a motive to kill" or "motive tends to cause killing," and a fact-finder is required to think in more indirect,

---

[16] Various legal rules, including placing the witness under oath and subjecting the witness to cross-examination, attempt to provide some assurance regarding the credibility of the witness. As explained in a later chapter, that these assurances are typically lacking in regard to out-of-court assertions is an important part of the rationale of the hearsay rule. *See* **§ 14.03**.

[17] The discussion in the text is careful to avoid suggesting that the fact-finder will or should reason in a series of binary, yes or no, steps, such as: (1) Do I believe the witness that there was a heated argument? If not, ignore the testimony. (2) If yes, do I believe that the defendant had a motive to kill? If not, ignore the testimony. (3) If yes, do I believe the defendant killed the victim? Such a mode of thinking would invite two kinds of errors. First, it would unreasonably ignore evidence that was probative but not strong enough to pass one of the tests along the way. Second, it could give too much weight to evidence that barely passed each of the tests along the way. These problems are closely related to the problems inherent in the concept of "conditional relevance." *See* **§ 3.11**. Also, we have focused on a single item of evidence. The empirical question of how fact-finders assess a mass of evidence presents complex and controversial issues beyond the scope of this text. For an introduction to contemporary thinking on the subject, see Mark Spottswood, *The Hidden Structure of Fact-finding*, 64 CASE W. RES. L. REV. 131 (2013).

[18] One statutory attempt to capture the distinction is the following:

> As used in this chapter, "direct evidence" means evidence that directly proves a fact, without an inference or presumption, and which in itself, if true, conclusively establishes that fact.

CAL. EVID. CODE § 410. A moment's reflection on the analysis in the text will reveal the defect in this definition: even direct evidence involves inferences, the various inferences involved in deciding whether and how much to credit the witness's testimony. The authors suggest that a better criterion of what lawyers have in mind, in the context of testimonial evidence, would be the following: "Direct testimonial evidence of a factual proposition, P, is a witness's testimony that he or she observed P." (For tangible evidence, "direct tangible evidence of a factual proposition, P, is tangible evidence from which the fact-finder can observe that P is true.")

[19] *See* **§ 2.06**.

[20] *See* 1 MCCORMICK ON EVIDENCE § 185 at 1000–01 (Kenneth S. Broun ed., 7th ed. 2013).

explanatory terms. That is, the fact-finder asks herself which party's theory of the case better or more easily accounts for the evidence.[21] Suppose, for example, that the victim dies in a knife attack and that evidence indicates finding blood at the scene that almost certainly belonged to the perpetrator. And suppose that there is expert testimony that a certain chemical compound, XYZ, is found in every small sample of that blood. Even if XYZ has no causal connection to violence, this evidence can be relevant. How would the fact-finder assess the relevance of expert testimony about whether or not XYZ is also found in the blood of the defendant? If it is not found in defendant's blood, then the hypothesis of guilt does not easily explain the presence of XYZ in the blood found at the scene, but the hypothesis of innocence can explain that fact even if XYX is only rarely to be found in anyone's blood. By contrast, if XYZ is found in the defendant's blood, then the guilt hypothesis easily accounts for the blood evidence found at the scene, whereas the hypothesis of innocence (i.e., that someone else is the perpetrator) presents more difficulty. The explanatory power of the hypothesis that someone else is the perpetrator depends on the chance that someone randomly selected from the population of potential perpetrators has XYZ in his or her blood. The smaller that chance—called the "random match probability" by forensic scientists—the harder it is for the hypothesis of innocence to explain the evidence found at the scene. Conversely, if XYZ is found in the blood of every person, then the two hypotheses are equally good explanations of the crime scene evidence and that evidence has no probative value.[22]

Another essential concept for understanding relevance is that a given item of evidence can have multiple modes of relevance. In the murder example just presented, suppose that the events described above all occurred in one city and that the defendant offers an alibi that he was in another city for several days leading up to and including the day that the victim was found dead. In that case, the proposed testimony about the argument between the defendant and the victim has two modes of relevance: it tends to show motive, and (quite apart from the anger of the conversation) it tends to show that the defendant was not in the city of his alibi. Even though the latter mode of relevance does not require an inference to the existence of a motive, it still requires intermediate inferences: the fact-finder must still infer that the witness is not lying and that the witness accurately observed and recalled the incident. But the inference process is not the same as the inference regarding motive.[23]

The materials that follow will show how, under many rules, evidence can be inadmissible for one purpose (usually, for one line of inference) and yet admissible for another purpose (i.e., a different line of inference). To understand such rules, one must

---

[21] *See generally* 1 MCCORMICK ON EVIDENCE § 185 at 996–98 (Kenneth S. Broun ed., 7th ed. 2013) (discussing what probability theorists call the *likelihood ratio* for the evidence). For a fuller discussion (by philosophers) of the relationship between the likelihood ratio and explanatory analysis, see PETER LIPTON, INFERENCE TO THE BEST EXPLANATION 103–20 (2004), and RICHARD S. SWINBURNE, EPISTEMIC JUSTIFICATION 102–07 (2001).

[22] The probative value of evidence of a "match" between the defendant's blood and the perpetrator's blood is also affected by factors such as (a) the probability that there was a laboratory error at some stage of the process and (b) the probability that the evidence of the match has been fabricated by the police or third parties. For an explanation and an empirical examination of how jurors react to such testimony, see Dale A. Nance & Scott B. Morris, *Juror Understanding of DNA Evidence: An Empirical Assessment of Presentation Formats for Trace Evidence with A Relatively Small Random-Match Probability*, 34 J. LEGAL STUD. 395 (2005).

[23] Multiple modes of relevance need not, of course, all end up at the same place, at the same ultimate fact. For example, if testimony is given, in a civil case concerning an automobile accident, that the defendant was going 90 m.p.h. in a 35 m.p.h. speed zone, this testimony will ordinarily be relevant in multiple ways: to show negligence, to help establish the extent of the damages, and to establish proximate cause.

be careful to identify exactly the line of inference that is prohibited by the rule. When such a rule applies, and when evidence is inadmissible for one line of inference under the rule but admissible for another line of inference, the general principle is that the evidence is admissible and that the opponent is entitled to a limiting instruction.[24] In some cases, limiting instructions may not be adequate to prevent jury confusion or unfair prejudice. Rule 403 then becomes important to the analysis.

§ 5.03 Rule 403: The (Almost) Universal Fall-Back Objection

Relevant evidence is not excluded by Rule 402, but it remains subject to the Rule 403 balancing test, and may be excluded if its reception would be too unfairly prejudicial, too misleading, or too wasteful of time.[25] The language of the rule—the court "may exclude"—places the decision within the discretion of the trial court, the exercise of which is reviewable on appeal only for "abuse of discretion."[26] Rule 403 applies in the background of almost every other evidence rule,[27] and thus provides an almost universal "fall back" argument for the attorney seeking the exclusion of evidence. The rule applies to all parties in both civil and criminal cases.[28] Rule 403 also serves a vital function in determining what to do with evidence admissible for one purpose but inadmissible for another. It provides authority for exclusion if the danger that the jury will misuse the evidence, even in the face of an appropriate limiting instruction, substantially outweighs the probative value of the evidence's permissible use.[29] Rule 403 operates only to *exclude* evidence; there is no discretion under the rule to *admit* evidence that is otherwise expressly excluded by a specific rule.[30]

The following are examples of Rule 403 in operation:

Emotional appeal. The plaintiff offers a day-in-the-life film that not only depicts the plaintiff's daily activities, but also shows the plaintiff in

---

[24] *See* **§ 1.05** & **§ 3.09**.

[25] *See generally* 2 WEINSTEIN'S FEDERAL EVIDENCE § 403 (Mark S. Brodin ed., 2d ed. 2015). *See, e.g.*, Trevino v. Gates, 99 F.3d 911, 922 (9th Cir. 1996) (though jury could consider suffering of plaintiff's child as element of damages in suit based on killing of father by Los Angeles Police Department officers, it was nonetheless proper to prevent five-year-old child from testifying; she had not been born at time of father's death and could contribute little to an understanding of her past or future suffering); *Cf.* United States v. Hicks, 103 F.3d 837, 842–44 (9th Cir. 1996) (holding that trial court did not abuse discretion in carjacking prosecution by admitting evidence of uncharged rape and murder of occupants; evidence went to "force and violence" element of carjacking offense).

[26] *See* Old Chief v. United States, 519 U.S. 172, 183 (1997); Sprint/United Management Co. v. Mendelsohn, 552 U.S. 379, 384, 387 (2008). *See* **§ 3.12**.

[27] The sole exception to the Rule 403 balancing test is the impeachment of a witness using evidence of conviction for a crime, in which context Rule 609 prescribes different balancing tests and, in one context, mandates admission without any discretionary balancing. *See* **§ 11.10**.

[28] One scholar has argued that in criminal cases, Rule 403 is unconstitutional because it prescribes a balancing test that places the major risk of erroneous decision making on the defendant; the author proposes revising the standard as applied to evidence offered against the defendant, requiring the prosecution to demonstrate that the probative value of its evidence substantially outweighs the danger of unfair prejudice (opposite of current standard). D. Craig Lewis, *Proof and Prejudice: A Constitutional Challenge to the Treatment of Prejudicial Evidence in Federal Criminal Cases*, 64 WASH. L. REV. 289 (1989).

[29] *See, e.g.*, United States v. Beasley, 809 F.2d 1273, 1278–80 (7th Cir. 1987) (holding that, while evidence of prior drug offenses is admissible to show intent in narcotics prosecution, trial court erred in admitting evidence without considering potential prejudice associated with the fact that the evidence was inadmissible to show defendant acted in conformity with a propensity shown by prior conduct). *See* **§ 3.09** (discussing limiting instructions).

[30] There are two different principles of much narrower applicability—curative admissibility and verbal completeness—that do give the court some discretion to admit evidence that is otherwise excluded by a specific rule. *See* **§ 1.11** (curative admissibility) and **§ 1.12** (verbal completeness).

sentimental scenes with the plaintiff's family. Rule 403 gives the trial judge discretion to edit out the portions of the film that are likely to have an undue emotional appeal.[31]

Waste of time, confusion. The plaintiff in a personal injury action offers evidence about defects in shotgun shells manufactured by the defendant, a corporation, at a plant other than the one that manufactured the shell that injured the plaintiff. The evidence has some probative value, but the evaluation requires extensive examination of differences between the two plants, which entails danger of confusing the jury and wasting resources. Rule 403 gives the trial judge authority to exclude.[32]

Confusion, ineffectiveness of limiting instruction. At a trial of D for murder by poison, where D claims that V, the alleged victim, took her own life, the prosecution offers evidence that before her death, V accused D of poisoning her. The prosecution claims that the statement, though inadmissible to prove the truth of what it asserted, should be admitted for the limited purpose of showing that V was not in a suicidal state of mind.[33] In this situation, an instruction to the jury to consider the evidence only to prove V's state of mind, and not to prove that D poisoned V, would almost certainly be ineffective. The low probative value of the evidence for this limited purpose, combined with the great potential for prejudice against D, calls for exclusion of the evidence under Rule 403.

The task of balancing probative value against the enumerated dangers in Rule 403 is hardly a precise one. Neither the rule itself nor its accompanying commentary offers specific guidelines for the judge. Certainly, the court must consider the dangers in the

---

31 *See* Grimes v. Employers Mut. Liab. Ins. Co., 73 F.R.D. 607, 610, 612 (D. Alaska 1977). *Cf.* Nichols v. Am. Nat. Ins. Co., 154 F.3d 875, 885 (8th Cir. 1998) (holding that where plaintiff claimed emotional distress from sexual harassment, court violated Rule 403 by admitting evidence that plaintiff had abortion eight years earlier, even if abortion could have provided alternative explanation for emotional distress because abortion was contrary to plaintiff's Catholic beliefs). *See also* State v. Smith, 857 S.W.2d 1 (Tenn. 1993) (finding no error in allowing witness to describe crime scene as victim lying in "pool of blood"); Moreno v. State, 858 S.W.2d 453, 465–66 (Tex. Crim. App. 1993) (holding that in murder prosecution, trial court erroneously admitted contents of deceased victim's wallet, including photographs of friends, and love poem written by his girlfriend; despite "infinitesimally incremental" probative value of evidence, admission constitutes harmless error due to overwhelming evidence of defendant's guilt).

32 *See* Classen v. Remington Arms Co., 379 N.W.2d 133, 136 (Minn. Ct. App. 1985) (interpreting MINN. R. EVID. 403, based on FED. R. EVID. 403). *See also* United States v. McVeigh, 153 F.3d 1166, 1189 (10th Cir. 1998) (holding that on review of conviction of Timothy McVeigh for bombing federal building in Oklahoma City, trial court did not err in excluding defense evidence that members of survivalist group had discussed bombing targets including federal building; probative value in suggesting possible alternative suspects was weak and evidence could have led to confusion and speculation); Strauss v. Springer, 817 F. Supp. 1211, 1222–23 (E.D. Pa. 1992) (in civil action for excessive use of force by police officer, other shootings evidence excluded as confusing to jury). *But cf.* United States v. Blackburn, 992 F.2d 666, 668–69 (7th Cir. 1993) (in prosecution for bank robbery, district court did not abuse its discretion by allowing government to introduce testimony of exotic dancer that defendant gave her approximately one hundred one-dollar bills as birthday present shortly after robbery, despite fact that government admitted to court that one-dollar bills were not same bills as those taken from bank; moreover, though defendant's character may have been impugned by evidence that he frequented bar where exotic dancer worked, testimony regarding defendant's patronage of bar supplied background narrative material linking him to dancer). *See generally* United States v. Thomas, 86 F.3d 647, 652–54 (7th Cir. 1996) (in cocaine conspiracy case, evidence that defendants belonged to same Mafia Insane Vice Lords gang admissible to illuminate relationship, but evidence of death threats by third parties should have been excluded as prejudicial).

33 *See* Shepard v. United States, 290 U.S. 96 (1933).

precise context of the case at hand.[34] And the court must give some explanation of the basis for its decision on the record.[35] Moreover, when assessing the probative value of evidence, for purposes of deciding a Rule 403 motion, the trial judge must respect the jury's role in assessing the credibility of witnesses and cannot exclude evidence on grounds that the testifying witness is unreliable. Weighing probative value against the various risks enumerated in Rule 403 means accepting the accuracy of the witness's testimony and then assessing the probative value of the inferences to be drawn from it; the judge may not decide whether or not the witness is believable.[36]

From the enumerated dangers, one can readily identify the two concerns that are typically controlling: verdict accuracy and judicial economy.[37] Appropriately, in our view, courts have not explored whether they may exclude relevant evidence in the service of other social goods.[38] It is fair to conclude that no other considerations are within the scope of the rule, besides the evenhandedness in the administration of justice that is stated as a general interpretive canon by Rule 102.[39]

Less clear is whether the balancing required by Rule 403 is *predictive* or *moral* in character. A predictive balancing would attempt to anticipate the *effect* of evidence and admit or exclude the evidence depending on whether the effect was salutary. Ordinarily, this would mean deciding based on whether admission will lead to a more accurate verdict, or to a verdict that is no less accurate but at less cost, than would exclusion. A moral balancing, on the other hand, would attempt to assess the proponent's conduct and its purpose, that is, whether the proponent is *attempting to elicit* one of the enumerated dangers. In particular, with regard to the idea of "unfair prejudice," the drafters of the rule stated, " 'unfair prejudice' within its context means an undue tendency to suggest decision on an improper basis, commonly, though not necessarily,

---

[34] For discussion of the meaning and operation of the rule, *see* Victor J. Gold, *Limiting Judicial Discretion to Exclude Prejudicial Evidence*, 18 U.C. DAVIS L. REV. 59 (1984); Victor J. Gold, *Federal Rule of Evidence 403: Observations on the Nature of Unfairly Prejudicial Evidence*, 58 WASH. L. REV. 497 (1983); Edward J. Imwinkelried, *The Meaning of Probative Value and Prejudice in Federal Rule of Evidence 403: Can Rule 403 Be Used to Resurrect the Common Law of Evidence?*, 41 VAND. L. REV. 879 (1988).

[35] *See* United States v. Sriyuth, 98 F.3d 739, 744 n.8 (3d Cir. 1996) ("We take this occasion, once again, to remind the district courts of their obligation to perform this weighing process on the record.") *See generally* 2 WEINSTEIN'S FEDERAL EVIDENCE § 403.02[1][b] (Mark S. Brodin ed., 2d ed. 2015).

[36] *See* Ballou v. Henri Studios, Inc., 656 F.2d 1147, 1154 (5th Cir. 1981) (holding that trial court erred in excluding results of blood alcohol test, on grounds that it did not find results credible).

[37] *See* FED. R. EVID. 403 advisory committee note:

> The case law recognizes that certain circumstances call for the exclusion of evidence which is of unquestioned relevance. These circumstances entail risks which range all the way from inducing decision on a purely emotional basis, at one extreme, to nothing more harmful than merely wasting time, at the other extreme.

[38] Standard accounts of the dangers enumerated in Rule 403 focus exclusively on various threats to verdict accuracy or judicial economy. *See, e.g.*, 1 CHRISTOPHER B. MUELLER & LAIRD C. KIRKPATRICK, FEDERAL EVIDENCE §§ 4.13–4.16 (4th ed. 2013). There is virtually no case law to suggest, for example, that the court may exclude evidence under Rule 403 because of substantive policy concerns, such as the risk that admitting testimony about the dangers of a product, or the resulting liability, might destroy an important industry, even though one might (with a straight face) call such a thing "unfairly prejudicial"—to society if not to the individual defendant. *Cf.* 2 WEINSTEIN'S FEDERAL EVIDENCE § 403.02[3] (Mark S. Brodin ed., 2d ed. 2015) (noting a pre-Rules case that suggests substantive legal policy might affect balancing of probative value with 403-dangers).

[39] FED. R. EVID. 102 provides:

> These rules should be construed so as to administer every proceeding fairly, eliminate unjustifiable expense and delay, and promote the development of evidence law, to the end of ascertaining the truth and securing a just determination.

an emotional one."[40] While this very brief explication is useful, it does not answer unambiguously the question posed here: "tendency" suggests a causal focus, whereas "to suggest decision" sounds like a moral focus. In particular, even if there is only a small chance that the jury will decide on an improper basis, the rule can be understood as articulating the moral norm that a proponent should not invite them to do so. Case law reveals a remarkable lack of judicial clarity on the issue.[41] About all that can be safely concluded is that both factors, causal and moral, seem to be pertinent to the decision. An anticipated high probability of bad effect (erroneous inference, waste of time) may warrant exclusion even if there is no purpose to induce such an effect, whereas a conspicuously improper purpose may warrant exclusion even if there is little likelihood of successfully generating the intended effect.[42]

Another analytical difficulty is raised by the Rule's use of the phrase "substantially outweighed." Suppose that the probative value of certain evidence is *outweighed* by the risk of the enumerated dangers, but not *substantially* so. Should that evidence be excluded? By the rule's explicit language, it would be improper to exclude such evidence under Rule 403. Yet, it is difficult to know what it could mean to accept that probative value is *outweighed* by the specified risks, other than that the good of admitting the evidence is dominated by the good of excluding it. That should indicate exclusion. Of course, in close cases, it may be difficult for the court to discern which way the balance tips, but that points to a separate consideration, namely, what to do in a context of judicial uncertainty.[43] As a consequence, one author believes that the drafters used the word "substantially" when they probably should have used a word like "clearly" or "unambiguously." For it makes perfect sense to say that, when there is *doubt* about whether the probative value is outweighed by the dangers, then the court should err on the side of admission, and that may be what was intended, rather than a requirement that the dangers outweigh the probative value by a wide but only vaguely specified margin. Another author believes that the drafters meant what they wrote and that the word "substantially" indicates a high level of imbalance between probative value and competing considerations, so that even where the dangers clearly outweigh the probative value, but not substantially so, evidence should be admitted in accordance with the pro-admissibility preference of the federal rules. Under either view, certain generalizations hold. First, the closer the competing considerations are, the less likely it is that a court

---

40 FED. R. EVID. 403 advisory committee note.

41 *See, e.g.*, State v. Bocharski, 22 P.3d 43, 49 ¶ 23 (Ariz. 2001) ("Under such circumstances, gruesome photographs may 'have little *use or purpose* except to inflame,' [citation omitted], and their prejudicial *effect* can be significant") (emphases added). In *Bocharski*, the Court further stated that judges have "an obligation to weigh the prejudice *caused* by a gruesome picture against its probative value," *id.* at ¶ 27, and that in the particular case, the court was "left to conclude that [certain photographs] were *introduced primarily to inflame* the jury," *id.* at ¶ 26 (emphases added). *See also* United States v. Ince, 21 F.3d 576, 578, 580–81 (4th Cir. 1994) (opining that '[f]ederal evidence law does not ask the judge, either at trial or upon appellate review, to crawl inside the prosecutor's head to divine his or her true motivation" but rather focuses on the "prejudicial impact" on the jury under Rule 403; reversing the conviction, however, "[b]ecause the United States' only *apparent purpose* for impeaching one of its own witnesses was to circumvent the hearsay rule and to expose the jury to otherwise inadmissible evidence" (emphasis added)).

42 In the latter context, error in admitting evidence may well be harmless. *See* **§ 3.13**.

43 One might be quite confident that probative value is outweighed by the dangers without its being substantially outweighed. Conversely, one might be in doubt about whether it is outweighed even when it is (truth be known) substantially outweighed. *See* Richard B. Kuhns, *The Propensity to Misunderstand the Character of Specific Acts Evidence*, 66 IOWA L. REV. 777, 808 (1981) (in the context of suggesting a balancing test that favors exclusion rather than inclusion, drawing the same distinction between the question of whether probative value outweighs countervailing factors and the question of how confident the trial judge is about the matter).

will exclude the evidence. Second, the greater the probative value of the challenged evidence, the more difficult it will be to exclude it under Rule 403.[44] And third, if the probative value of the evidence is slight, the degree of danger necessary to warrant exclusion need not be particularly great.

In assessing the probative value of challenged evidence, the trial judge should consider other evidence admitted (or expected to be introduced) on the same point because it is only the *marginal* contribution of the challenged evidence that matters. This is plainly indicated by that portion of the Rule that describes the danger of "needlessly presenting cumulative evidence."[45] But beyond that, the court should also consider *alternative ways* that the proponent could prove the fact without the proffered evidence, ways that the proponent will not choose without judicial intervention. As stated by the drafters of the rule, when deciding whether to exclude evidence that poses a risk of unfair prejudice, "the availability of other means of proof may be an appropriate factor" to consider.[46]

In *Old Chief v. United States*,[47] the Supreme Court attempted to clarify the trial court's task of applying Rule 403. The Court held that the trial judge should decide whether the questioned evidence raises the danger of unfair prejudice. If such a danger exists, the judge must "take account of the full evidentiary context of the case as the court understands it when the ruling must be made."[48] In particular, the judge should consider not just the offered evidence itself, even in the context of other admitted evidence, but also the probative value and risk of prejudice of any available substitutes for the proffered evidence. The Court continued:

> If an alternative were found to have substantially the same or greater probative value but a lower danger of unfair prejudice, sound judicial discretion would discount the value of the item first offered and exclude it if its discounted probative value were substantially outweighed by unfairly prejudicial risk. . . . The judge would have to make these calculations with an appreciation of the offering party's need for evidentiary richness and narrative integrity in presenting a case, and the mere fact that two pieces of evidence might go to the same point would not, of course, necessarily mean that only one of them might come in. It would only mean that a judge applying Rule 403 could reasonably apply some discount to the probative value of an item of evidence when faced with less risky alternative proof going to the same point.[49]

To do otherwise, the Court observed, would create perverse incentives. It would mean that, when a proponent has several options about how to prove a certain fact, each of which satisfies the Rule 403 balance if the others are not taken into account as options,

---

[44] *See, e.g.*, White v. Honeywell, 141 F.3d 1270, 1274–77 (8th Cir. 1988) (in racial harassment case, reversing as an abuse of discretion the trial court's Rule 403 exclusion, as unfairly prejudicial, of testimony about the statement of a deceased employee of defendant manifesting racial hostility, in context where trial court acknowledged the highly probative quality of the statement).

[45] FED. R. EVID. 403. Deciding whether evidence is "cumulative" necessarily involves reference to other evidence that has already been presented or can be expected to be presented on the same point.

[46] FED. R. EVID. 403, advisory committee note. *See* 1 CHRISTOPHER B. MUELLER & LAIRD C. KIRKPATRICK, FEDERAL EVIDENCE § 4.13 at 638–39 (4th ed. 2013) ("Need is affected by the strength of other evidence supporting the point to be proved and on the availability of other proof.").

[47] 519 U.S. 172 (1997).

[48] *Id.* at 182.

[49] *Id.* at 182–83.

the proponent would be free to choose the option that *maximizes* the risk of unfair prejudice to the opponent. The Court considered this an unacceptable interpretation of the Rules.[50]

Thus, a court may consider using verbal testimony in lieu of an exhibit, a stipulation in lieu of verbal testimony, pre-autopsy photos in lieu of post-autopsy photos, and still illustrations in lieu of computer animations. The court may also tell lawyers to instruct witnesses to avoid true but inflammatory characterizations, though this approach has obvious dangers of making witness testimony seem artificial and requiring witnesses to self-censor their most comfortable way of speaking.[51] Similarly, when part of a hearsay statement falls within a hearsay exception, but part does not, the inadmissible portion may be redacted. For example, the patient's account of who was at fault in an automobile accident can be removed from an otherwise admissible hospital record, and references to the guilt of a codefendant can be removed from an otherwise admissible confession.[52]

Old Chief shows that a reason to *exclude* evidence, one within the ambit of Rule 403, can be that the proponent does not "need" that particular evidence to put its legitimate probative value before the fact-finder. Proponents sometimes argue, however, that their need for the evidence is an affirmative reason to *admit* evidence that would otherwise fail the 403 analysis.[53] If the court determines that the marginal probative value of the evidence offered is substantially outweighed by the Rule 403 dangers, the fact that the proponent is unable to prove some fact without the proposed evidence, and may even suffer a directed verdict as a result, is not itself a reason to override the Rule 403 exclusion.[54] A party's need in this latter sense neither increases the probative value of the offered evidence nor decreases the dangers weighed against it.[55] Unfortunately, courts (and legislatures) sometimes are seduced by this affirmative argument from need.[56]

---

[50] *Id.* at 182–84.

[51] *See* United States v. Neill, 166 F.3d 943, 946 (9th Cir. 1999) (although defendant's residence in work-release center is relevant because he was absent from the center on the night of the crime, it was error to allow witnesses to refer to the work-release center in testimony because that reference revealed that defendant had a prior conviction; government should have prepared witnesses to testify using the phrase "Residential Program" instead of "Work Release Center"). In the authors' opinion, this decision might cause lawyers to rehearse their witnesses too much, overly reducing spontaneity and making it more difficult for the jury to judge demeanor. *Cf.* Bruce A. Green, *"The Whole Truth?": How Rules of Evidence Make Lawyers Deceitful*, 25 LOY. L.A. L. REV. 699 (1992).

[52] *See, e.g.*, Richardson v. Marsh, 481 U.S. 200, 206–208 (1987) (confession of codefendant held admissible where all references to defendant redacted); Ramrattan v. Burger King Corp., 656 F. Supp. 522, 530 (D. Md. 1987) (medical records admissible if plaintiff's statements regarding fault in an auto accident contained therein redacted). The court can, as in limiting instructions, order that information be redacted sua sponte. *See, e.g.*, Harris v. Upjohn Co., 115 F.R.D. 191, 192 (S.D. Ill. 1987) (court could invoke Illinois physician-patient privilege and order patient names redacted from report offered into evidence at its discretion).

[53] Ambiguous support for this is found in the drafters' comment that "[s]ituations in this area call for balancing the probative value of *and need for* the evidence against the harm likely to result from its admission. FED. R. EVID. 403 advisory committee note (emphasis added).

[54] This point applies even to criminal defendants, notwithstanding their Due Process right to present a defense. *See* **§ 1.04**. The Supreme Court has opined that a constitutionally appropriate application of the Rule 403 balancing test that yields an exclusion of defense evidence will not be subject to constitutional override because of the defendant's need for the evidence. *See* Holmes v. South Carolina, 547 U.S. 319 (2006) (reversing conviction on constitutional grounds because of particular rule used by South Carolina courts, but endorsing the applicability of the standard Rule 403 balancing text to evidence offered by the defense).

[55] Of course, the proponent who suffers such an adverse 403 ruling may be able to modify the proffer so that the balance of considerations is more favorable to admission.

[56] *See, e.g.* United States v. Woods, 484 F.2d 127, 134 (4th Cir. 1973) (recognizing prosecutorial need as an affirmative reason to admit evidence of prior crimes "in case of infanticide or other child abuse by suffocation

§ 5.04 Evidence Offered on an Uncontested Issue

Where a party offers evidence on an issue of consequence to the case, but one conceded or uncontested by the opponent, the Federal Rules generally deem such evidence relevant, taking a somewhat different position from that of the common law. For example, suppose that in a personal injury case, the plaintiff alleges that the defendant's negligent driving caused permanent disability. The plaintiff makes no claim for punitive damages; the defendant, knowing that the evidence of negligence is overwhelming, and wishing to avoid exposing the jury to damaging details of her conduct, admits negligence but disputes the amount of damages.[57] At trial, the plaintiff offers evidence that the defendant was intoxicated at the time of the accident. Assuming that the evidence of intoxication has no bearing on any issue other than that of liability, which has been conceded, some pre-Rules jurists would have excluded the evidence as immaterial or irrelevant,[58] and a number of states would do the same today under their own codes.[59] The Federal Rules, however, would treat such evidence as relevant, but exclude it as a waste of time or even unfairly prejudicial under Rule 403.[60]

Old Chief v. United States[61] clarified the importance of the Federal Rules' broad concept of relevance in relation to issues conceded by one party. In *Old Chief*, the defendant was charged with being a felon in possession of a firearm, assault with a deadly weapon, and using a firearm in connection with a crime. He had previously been convicted of assault causing serious bodily injury, a felony that put him within the scope of a federal statute prohibiting certain felons from possessing firearms. Before trial, the defendant moved to prevent the government from mentioning any details of the prior conviction, except to state that he had been convicted of a crime punishable by imprisonment in excess of a year. In return, defendant offered to stipulate to his status as a felon, without mentioning the details of the prior conviction. The prosecutor refused the stipulation, arguing that the government had a right to prove the essential facts of the case in its own way. The court denied the defendant's motion and, at trial, the prosecutor introduced the record of conviction, which revealed the defendant's prior conviction, including the nature of the crime and the sentence he received. Defendant

---

if the wrongdoer is to be apprehended"). *But see id.* at 141 (Widener, J., dissenting) (noting the proper role of "need" in regard to unfairly prejudicial evidence and arguing that majority's use of that factor "comes perilously close to a rule in the law of evidence that the end may justify the means"). Many post-Rules cases can be found that seem to endorse the broader role for need criticized here but on closer inspection usually turn out to be using the notion of need as merely a different way of saying *probative value taken in context*. *See, e.g.*, United States v. Trenkler, 61 F.3d 45, 56 (1st Cir. 1995) (explaining the government's need for the evidence in terms of its probative value in the context of other evidence in the case).

[57] *See* Jarvis v. Hall, 210 N.E.2d 414 (Ohio App. 1964) (evidence that the defendant drove drunk inadmissible where defendant admits liability).

[58] *See, e.g.*, 9 Wigmore on Evidence § 2591 at 824 (Chadbourn rev. 1981) ("A fact that is judicially admitted [e.g., by being admitted in the pleadings] *needs* no evidence from the party benefiting by the admission. But his evidence, if he chooses to offer it, *may* even be *excluded;* first, because it is now immaterial to the issues. . . .").

[59] *See, e.g.*, Cal. Evid. Code § 210 (" 'Relevant evidence' means evidence . . . having any tendency in reason to prove or disprove any *disputed fact* that is of consequence to the 'determination of the action' ") (emphasis added).

[60] Fed. R. Evid. 401 advisory committee note ("[T]he fact to which the evidence is directed need not be in dispute. While situations will arise which call for the exclusion of evidence offered to prove a point conceded by the opponent, the ruling should be made on the basis of such considerations as waste of time and undue prejudice . . ., rather than under any general requirement that evidence is admissible only if directed to matters in dispute.").

[61] Old Chief v. United States, 519 U.S. 172 (1997).

was convicted, and the Ninth Circuit affirmed. In a 5–4 decision, the Supreme Court reversed. Though the Court rejected the defendant's argument that the name of the prior offense was irrelevant under Rule 401,[62] it held that the trial court was obligated to grant defendant's motion pursuant to Rule 403.

In its discussion of relevance principles, the Court spoke broadly, emphasizing that in addition to supporting the parties contentions, evidence had to "give life to the moral underpinnings of law's claims."[63] To be effective, "there lies the need for evidence in all its particularity to satisfy the jurors' expectations about what proper proof should be."[64] As the Court explained:

> Unlike an abstract premise, whose force depends on going precisely to a particular step in a course of reasoning, a piece of evidence may address any number of separate elements, striking hard just because it shows so much at once; . . . Thus, the prosecution may fairly seek to place its evidence before the jurors, as much to tell a story of guiltiness as to support an inference of guilt, to convince the jurors that a guilty verdict would be morally reasonable, as much as to point to the discrete elements of a defendant's legal fault.[65]

In part, this reasoning gives supports the often expressed adage that the prosecution is entitled to prove its case by evidence of its own choice—that the defendant has no right to "stipulate or admit his way out of the full evidentiary force of the case as the government chooses to present it."[66] Asserting that "a syllogism is not a story," the Court wrote that the prosecution is entitled to the benefit of a colorful story with descriptive richness.[67] This led the Court to state a principle that, if carried to its logical extreme, would revolutionize the law of relevance: in ruling on the admissibility of evidence, the court should take into account the prosecution's need to establish the "human significance" of a crime and to awaken a juror's "obligation to sit in judgment."[68] This might suggest that the prosecution is entitled to offer evidence to show more than what is strictly necessary for logical inference when the extra evidence is needed to ensure that the jury does not nullify substantive law and does not require greater certainty than proof beyond a reasonable doubt. The Court also noted, less adventurously, that in some cases the absence of proof can cause the jury to draw unfair inferences unfavorable to the prosecution.[69]

---

[62] *Id.* at 178–79. The Court held that the nature of the conviction "was a step on one evidentiary route to the ultimate fact, since it served to place Old Chief within a particular subclass of offenders for whom firearms possession is outlawed by [the relevant federal statute]. A documentary record of the conviction for that named offense was thus relevant evidence in making Old Chief's . . . status more probable than it would have been without the evidence." *Id.* The Court made clear that the availability of alternative means of proving the prior crime did not render the proof offered by the prosecutor irrelevant. *Id.* at 179.

[63] *Id.* at 188.

[64] *Id.*

[65] *Id.* at 187–88.

[66] *Id.* at 186–87. For example, in a pornography case, the prosecution would ordinarily be entitled to display the allegedly pornographic material to the jury, even if the defendant was willing to concede that the material was pornographic and wanted merely to dispute the element of possession. *See* Parr v. United States, 255 F.2d 86, 88 (5th Cir. 1958) (cited favorably in *Old Chief*).

[67] 519 U.S. at 189 (1997). *See also* Blue Cross & Blue Shield of New Jersey, Inc. v. Philip Morris, Inc., 138 F. Supp. 2d 357, 369–70 (E.D.N.Y. 2001) (Weinstein, J.) (after *Old Chief*, relevance must be considered with an eye toward whether evidence contributes background to story of the case, not merely to whether it is logically relevant).

[68] 519 U.S. at 187–88 (1997).

[69] *Id.* at 188–89.

Nevertheless, the Court held that these principles had virtually no application in the case at bar. In *Old Chief*, the fact to be proved with the challenged evidence was the defendant's legal status, a matter standing apart from the concrete facts of the present case and based upon previously adjudicated events. As the Court stated, "[p]roving status without telling exactly why that status was imposed leaves no gap in the story of a defendant's subsequent criminality, and its demonstration by stipulation or admission neither displaces a chapter from a continuous sequence of conventional evidence nor comes across as an officious substitution, to confuse or offend or provoke reproach."[70] Here, then, the evidence the prosecution wished to offer carries the unfairly prejudicial risk that the jury will convict defendant because of his apparently bad character or simply to prevent him from committing future crimes, regardless of his guilt in the present case.[71] At the same time, the evidence has no greater probative value than the defendant's offered stipulation, which would have been "seemingly conclusive evidence" of this essential element of the crime.[72] Thus, in this situation, "the only reasonable conclusion was that the risk of unfair prejudice did substantially outweigh the discounted probative value of the record of conviction, and it was an abuse of discretion to admit the record when an admission was available."[73]

The foregoing analysis applies even when the uncontested fact is not an ultimate fact. Illustrative is the recurring controversy about whether the prosecution may introduce otherwise inadmissible evidence solely for the purpose of explaining the conduct of police during investigation of a possible crime. In many cases, it does not matter at trial what motivated an investigator to pursue some lead; what matters is the probative value of what was found. For example, if an officer decides to look for the perpetrator on 7th Street because 7 is her lucky number, that fact does not undermine the significance of finding (on 7th Street) a person with unexplained blood on his clothes the DNA of which matches the victim. The bad judgment or irrationality of the police officer in conducting her investigation ordinarily has little or no impact on the probative value of what she found, and the criminal trial ordinarily is not a trial of the investigating officer's rationality.[74] Conversely, no matter how sound were the reasons for the officer to look on 7th Street, those reasons are not properly put before the jury by the prosecution unless the evidence for those reasons is independently admissible to prove defendant's guilt. Thus, the fact that the officer reasonably relied upon statements made by an anonymous informer, for example—evidence that is hearsay and not independently admissible—has little or no permissible probative value at trial and may

---

[70] *Id.* at 190–91.

[71] *See generally* **§§ 7.01 et seq.**

[72] 519 U.S. at 186.

[73] *Id.* at 191. The Court left open the possibility that the error was harmless. *Id.* at 192 n.11. For a similar issue in a civil context, *see* Briggs v. Dalkon Shield, 174 F.R.D. 369, 375 (D. Md. 1997) (holding that in action against IUD manufacturer, plaintiff was not required to accept defendant's stipulation to all elements of her case except causation and damages; stipulation would change focus of trial from evidence against defendant's product to defendant's claim that plaintiff's injuries were caused by sexually transmitted disease rather than IUD).

[74] Matters are different, of course, if the defense makes a claim that there were no reasonable grounds for the officer's search that led to incriminating evidence. That might be the basis for a motion to suppress evidence derived from the search, and in the hearing on that motion, the officer's grounds for acting could be very probative. However, as a preliminary fact question regarding the admissibility of the evidence found during the search, this question would be decided by the trial court rather than the jury, in the context of which most admissibility rules do not apply. *See* **§ 3.11**.

be excluded under Rule 403.[75] Moreover, the officer's opinion about the collective importance of evidence known to her has little or no probative value independent of that evidence, except insofar as they constitute the basis of the officer's opinions about how to analyze the evidence. Such opinions are not themselves admissible, however, unless the officer is qualified as an expert on a particular topic.[76]

Still, the foregoing analysis rests on the assumption that *the defense does not contest certain facts*—specifically, it rests on the assumption that the defendant does not assert that he is being framed or that the police officer's behavior is so irrational as to cast doubt upon her credibility in reporting what she found. If the defense asserts at trial that the investigation was a sham and the defendant was framed, then the motives of the police become highly probative, and if the defense asserts a police officer acted quite irrationally and thus challenges the officer's credibility in reporting the evidence she did find, then the officer's credibility may be defended by the government.[77] But without such claims by the defense, the prosecution should not be allowed to introduce otherwise inadmissible evidence (such as hearsay) to "explain" the officer's investigative conduct or to give her "reasons for suspecting the defendant" just on the off chance that the jury might suspect a frame-up or doubt the officer's credibility on their own even though the defense has not raised such issues. Presentation of evidence explaining the police conduct is then unnecessary and poses the risk of its use for inadmissible purposes, such as inviting the jury to rely on inadmissible hearsay or inadmissible opinions by the investigating officer.[78]

---

[75] *See, e.g.,* United States v. Mancillas, 580 F.2d 1301, 1309–10 (7th Cir. 1978) (excluding for risk of unfair prejudice evidence of hearsay statement supposedly offered only as background for the investigation; error held harmless in context). Admission of such evidence may also violate the defendant's constitutional right to confront witnesses against him. *See, e.g.,* United States v. Jones, 930 F.3d 366, 375–78 (5th Cir. 2019) (rejecting argument that the evidence was needed for the nonhearsay purpose of explaining the arresting officer's conduct).

[76] *See* **§ 10.08**.

[77] *See, e.g.,* United States v. Cannon, 220 Fed. Appx. 104, 2007 WL 951407 (3d Cir. 2007) (holding report of out-of-court statement admissible for limited purpose of explaining officer's conduct in context where defendant challenged credibility of officer by questioning rationality of officer's actions). Similarly, evidence that police disregarded statements by out-of-court declarants that incriminated persons other than the accused will be admissible to show the state of mind of the police in "rushing to judgment" and twisting evidence to favor the hypothesis that the defendant was guilty. But where the evidence has only a weak bearing on the state of mind of the investigating officer, and where the most likely use of it would be for the truth of the matter asserted, in violation of the hearsay rule, it may be excluded, a principle that applies as well to evidence offered by the defense. In United States v. Sesay, 313 F.3d 591, 598–600 (D.C. Cir. 2002), the defendant wanted to put into evidence a police report that stated that witnesses had claimed someone else had been seen in possession of the gun in question at the time that defendant was later charged with possessing it. The government claimed it had checked with the witnesses and that the police report contained a mistaken rumor. The appellate court upheld the exclusion of the police report, saying that to use the report to support the defense's contention that the police had "lied and manipulated the evidence in a manner designed to strengthen the case against [defendant]" would have required that the jury rely upon the truth of the matter asserted in the report's double hearsay. *Id.* at 600.

[78] *See* United States v. Sallins, 993 F.2d 344, 346–47 (3d Cir. 1993) (police radio dispatch call alerting officers to whereabouts of black male suspect wearing black clothes and carrying gun was inadmissible hearsay, and should not have been admitted even when statement offered to explain officers' reasons for suspecting defendant and not for its truth; officers' conduct could be explained, to the extent that it needed to be explained, through "testimony that he acted 'upon information received' or words to that effect"); United States v. Mancillas, 580 F.2d 1301, 1309–10 (7th Cir. 1978) (excluding for risk of unfair prejudice evidence of hearsay statement supposedly offered only as background for the investigation; error held harmless in context). In *Mancillas*, the court opined:

> Viewed in the limited light necessary for admission despite the barrier of the hearsay rule, the tip evidence here would appear to make probable only one fact: that the law enforcement agents had a reason to be where they were at the pertinent times. But there was no suggestion here of any

§ 5.05 Some Recurring Examples of the Role of Rule 403

Many recurring issues call for the application of Rule 403. Some, such as evidencing remedial repair or the presence of liability insurance, have matured into specific rules of exclusion and are discussed in subsequent chapters. Other recurring questions are left entirely to ad hoc decisions by the trial court using 403-balancing. The following subsections illustrate the latter.

Evidence of Other Accidents

A personal injury plaintiff may seek to introduce evidence of similar accidents involving the defendant's property or product. For example, in a slip-and-fall case involving a fall on a carpet on the defendant's premises, the plaintiff might offer evidence that other customers had previously fallen on the same carpet, to support a claim that the carpet was loose.[79] Such evidence is relevant if the conditions under which the other accidents occurred were sufficiently similar to the accident at issue to make it more likely either that the prior accidents were caused by the same defect or that the prior accidents would have given a reasonable property owner notice of a possible defect. The opposing consideration, one to which trial courts are quite sensitive, is the fact that such evidence invites the parties to litigate an entirely separate incident involving other parties. That can be distracting and a waste of time. Whether the evidence will in fact be admissible in a given case turns on a Rule 403 balancing of probative value against confusion and waste of time (and sometimes unfair prejudice), with a measure of discretion accorded to the trial judge.[80]

In exercising discretion, the trial judge should consider whether a convincing showing of similar conditions has been made.[81] Also, the trial judge should consider whether the prior accidents are offered merely to show that a condition was dangerous—something that could be shown by other evidence with less waste of time or danger of unfair prejudice—or whether the evidence is also relevant to the issue whether the

---

> improper law enforcement purposes, and in any event the agents' reasons for investigation were most assuredly not something the Government had to prove to carry its burden.

Id. at 1310.

[79] *See, e.g.*, Beck v. City of Pittsburgh, 89 F.3d 966, 973–75 (3d Cir. 1996) (holding that court erred in excluding other complaints against police officer to show defendant city's tolerance of excessive force); Tait v. Armor Elevator Co., 958 F.2d 563, 568–69 (3d Cir. 1992) (excluding evidence of prior accidents in other elevators in same elevator bank, where plaintiff failed to substantiate argument that accidents arose from similar cause); Wyatt v. Otis Elevator Co., 921 F.2d 1224, 1228 (11th Cir. 1991) (allowing evidence of prior accidents involving failure of elevator doors to reverse and detract; discussion in court of other types of elevator accidents cured by jury instruction); Robitaille v. Netoco Community Theatres, 25 N.E.2d 749, 751 (Mass. 1940) (holding admission of evidence of other fall two or three weeks earlier in same spot reversible error because proponent provided insufficient showing of similar conditions or similar conduct by victims of fall); Gable v. Kroger Co., 410 S.E.2d 701 (W.Va. 1991) (excluding evidence of two previous slip-and-fall accidents, where neither accident occurred in same area of store or arose from a similar problem). *Cf.* Bitsos v. Red Owl Stores, Inc., 459 F.2d 656, 659–60 (8th Cir. 1972) (holding that earlier falls on steps admissible to demonstrate presence of foreign substance on steps).

[80] *See, e.g.*, Simon v. Kennebunkport, 417 A.2d 982, 986 (Me. 1980) (noting that ME. R. EVID. 403 abolishes former Maine rule of exclusion and leaves admissibility of prior falls on same sidewalk to discretion of trial judge).

[81] *See, e.g., id.* (error to exclude evidence of earlier falls; as many as one hundred people fell under similar circumstances). *See also* Drabik v. Stanley-Bostitch, Inc., 997 F.2d 496, 508 (8th Cir. 1993) ("[F]or other accidents evidence to be admissible, the proponent of the evidence must show that the facts and circumstances of the other incident are substantially similar to the case at bar."); Lolie v. Ohio Brass Co., 502 F.2d 741, 745 (7th Cir. 1974) (holding evidence that other metal clips failed inadmissible; no offer of proof that other clips were comparable to clips in issue.).

defendant was on notice of the existence of the dangerous condition. If the evidence is relevant to notice, then the requirement of similar conditions is applied less strictly. All that is required is that the prior accident be similar enough to alert the defendant to the danger.[82]

When the evidence of other accidents is offered to show the carelessness of a human being, rather than merely to show the dangerousness of a thing, then the rules against character evidence come into play. The evidence is admissible only if it can be received under Rule 404(b) as probative of something other than a propensity to be negligent.[83] This is the most common source of a risk of unfair prejudice in such cases.

Just as the plaintiff may wish to offer evidence of prior accidents to establish the dangerousness of a condition or notice to the defendant of possible danger, the defendant may wish to offer evidence that *no* accidents had occurred in the manner the plaintiff claimed, even though the conditions had remained essentially unchanged. While some jurisdictions forbid receipt of such evidence,[84] most appear to recognize that evidence of the absence of accidents can be relevant in various types of actions including basic negligence and product liability cases.[85] As with evidence of prior accidents, the issue is first one of relevance and then of balancing the probative value of the evidence against its potential to waste the court's time or to confuse the jury. The evidence should be excluded when its probative value is slight. In some cases, however, the evidence may have substantial probative value. Where, for example, a condition has remained static for a number of years and no one has suffered an injury, the plaintiff's claim that the condition represents an undue danger is particularly weak. Depriving the jury of the evidence of the lack of accidents in such a case would be misleading. The authorities have generally supported admission, and this appears to be the modern trend.[86] At least

---

[82] *See, e.g.,* Exum v. General Elec. Co., 819 F.2d 1158, 1159–60 (D.C. Cir. 1987) (holding that prior accident in which fast food employee was burned by appliance required higher degree of similarity when issue is dangerousness than when issue is notice); Gardner v. Southern Ry. Sys., 675 F.2d 949, 952 (7th Cir. 1982) (holding that it is appropriate to relax requirement of similar conditions to admit prior railroad collision to show notice of hazard at grade crossing; court indicates that); Taylorville v. Stafford, 63 N.E. 624–25 (Ill. 1902) (other people stumbled on sidewalk; admissible to show notice of dangerous condition). *See also* Four Corners Helicopters, Inc. v. Turbomeca, S.A., 979 F.2d 1434 (10th Cir. 1992) (holding that other failures of helicopter screws admissible to show notice where lesser showing of similarity is sufficient); Cooper v. Firestone Tire & Rubber Co., 945 F.2d 1103, 1105 (9th Cir. 1991) (noting that the circuits are split concerning whether evidence of similar accidents is admissible when relevant to witness's credibility).

[83] *See* **§ 7.08**.

[84] *See, e.g.,* Jones v. Pak-Mor Mfg. Co., 700 P.2d 819, 821 (Ariz. 1985) (categorical rule in Arizona forbidding receipt of evidence of absence of prior accidents to prove lack of defect, lack of danger, or similar issues); Paulison v. Chi., Milwaukee, St. Paul & Pac. R.R., Inc., 392 N.E.2d 960, 965–66 (Ill. App. 1979) (in wrongful death action against railroad for failure to provide automatic gates at crossing, evidence of only three minor accidents in prior fifteen years not admissible to prove lack of danger; prior Illinois authority held such evidence admissible only to prove lack of notice, which was not issue in case).

[85] *See, e.g.,* Benson v. Honda Motor Co., Ltd., 32 Cal. Rptr. 2d 322, 325–28 (Cal. Ct. App. 1994) (holding that manufacturer may offer evidence of absence of similar prior accidents in product liability action alleging both negligence and failure to warn); Carbin v. National Super Markets, Inc., 823 S.W.2d 93 (Mo. Ct. App. 1991) (holding that defendant may offer evidence that manager was not aware of any prior similar accidents in store to prove store lacked knowledge, or reason to know, of dangerous condition in negligence action by grocery store customer alleging injury from striking eye on display rack); Reiger v. Toby Enterprises, 609 P.2d 402, 404 (Or. Ct. App. 1980) (holding that in product liability action by employee of meat processing plant against manufacturer of meat slicer for hand injuries, evidence of absence of prior accidents admissible to prove product not unreasonably dangerous).

[86] *See, e.g.,* 1 MCCORMICK ON EVIDENCE § 200 at 1114–18 (Kenneth S. Broun ed., 7th ed. 2013); 2 WIGMORE ON EVIDENCE §§ 443–44 (Chadbourn rev. 1979).

one authority suggested, in fact, that evidence of favorable safety history carries more probative value than the plaintiff's evidence of prior accidents.[87]

Evidence of Flight and Similar Conduct

Evidence of a person's actions in the aftermath of some litigated event is often relevant to the person's state of mind regarding the event. Thus, prosecutors have offered evidence that the defendant fled the scene of a crime or the jurisdiction, assumed a false name, made a dramatic change in appearance, resisted arrest, and so forth. In all these contexts, the prosecution invites the inference from the evidenced post-event action to the defendant's consciousness of guilt regarding the crime.[88]

The traditional common-law view accepts such evidence as admissible and relegates to the opponent the task of providing an innocent explanation for the post-event conduct. However, modern commentators suggest, and some courts endorse, greater caution in admitting such evidence because of the often low probative value of the conduct in question and the potential risk of Rule-403 dangers.[89] Although some cases involve the question of the admissibility of the evidence of the conduct itself,[90] other cases involve the question of the appropriateness of the trial court's giving a jury instruction that would address the matter. The following is a typical jury instruction regarding the defendant's flight:

> Intentional flight of a person immediately after a crime has been committed is not, of course, sufficient in itself to establish his guilt but it is a fact which, if proved, may be considered by you, in the light of all the other evidence in the case, in determining guilt or innocence. Whether the defendant's conduct in this case constituted flight is exclusively for you to determine. And if you do so determine, whether or not that flight showed a consciousness of guilt on his part, and the significance to be attached to that evidence, are also matters exclusively within your province.
>
> In your consideration of any evidence of flight, if you should find that there was any flight, you should also consider that there may be reasons for this which are fully consistent with innocence. There may be many reasons for a person to be reluctant to be interviewed by law enforcement agents, which are perfectly innocent reasons, and which in no way show any consciousness of guilt on the part of that person. Also, a feeling of guilt does not necessarily reflect actual guilt of a crime you may be considering. You should always bear in mind that

---

[87] CLARENCE MORRIS, STUDIES IN THE LAW OF TORTS 87–89 (1952).

[88] *See* 2 WIGMORE ON EVIDENCE § 276 (Chadbourn rev. 1979). Of course, evidence of such conduct might be relevant quite apart from an inference to a consciousness of guilt. In the case of evidence of flight, for example, if the point of the testimony is solely to establish the defendant's presence at a particular place and time, such as the scene of a crime, then no inference to consciousness of guilt is required. In that case, no reference to "flight" would be required either, although it may be confusing to the fact-finder to ask a witness to testify that the defendant was seen without asking the witness to describe what the defendant was doing.

[89] *See* 2 MCCORMICK ON EVIDENCE § 263 (Kenneth S. Broun ed., 7th ed. 2013).

[90] *See, e.g.*, Jones v. State, 541 So.2d 1052 (Ala. 1989) (affirming admissibility, in robbery trial, of evidence of flight of defendant from officers seeking to arrest defendant for traffic violations five days after robbery).

> the law never imposes on a defendant in a criminal case the burden or duty of calling any witnesses or producing any evidence.[91]

On the probative value side of the balance, the opinion in one leading case observes that evidence of flight

> as circumstantial evidence of guilt depends upon the degree of confidence with which four inferences can be drawn: (1) from the defendant's behavior to flight; (2) from flight to consciousness of guilt; (3) from consciousness of guilt to consciousness of guilt concerning the crime charged; and (4) from consciousness of guilt concerning the crime charged to actual guilt of the crime charged.[92]

The inference from flight to guilt of the crime charged can go wrong at any of these steps. That does not mean the evidence of flight is not probative of guilt, but it potentially undermines the strength of the inference, depending on the specific circumstances of the case. With regard to the Rule-403 dangers, some courts express concern that jurors will not recognize the possible fragility of the line of inference described above and, as a consequence, will overvalue the evidence of flight.[93] This could be true, for example, if the person running had reason to fear the police because of his race.[94] Moreover, requiring the defendant to dispute some part of the inference chain described can be distracting, possibly even a waste of time.

Two additional sources of unfair prejudice have been suggested. First, it might be argued that the defendant would be required to forego his constitutional privilege to refuse to testify in order to counter the evidence of flight, because he might be the only source of evidence for an innocent explanation of his actions. This argument, however, proves too much, for it will often be the case, flight evidence aside, that the defendant is the only available source of counter-evidence about some material fact in a criminal trial, and the fact that the prosecution introduces evidence that places pressure on the defendant to testify cannot by itself constitute a violation of the privilege or be *unfairly* prejudicial. The second potential source of prejudice, however, presents a more serious argument, to which modern courts are sometimes receptive. Regardless of the source of the counter-evidence, the defendant might have to inform the jury of circumstances that would risk prejudicing the jury against the defendant, circumstances that the prosecution could not itself evidence because of Rule 403 or some other specific admissibility rule. For example, the real reason the defendant left the jurisdiction where a robbery occurred might be that he was in possession of drugs unrelated to the robbery, or that he wanted to avoid making child support payments, or that there was an arrest warrant for him in regard to a crime other than the one now being tried. Requiring the

---

91 United States v. Williams, 775 F.2d 1295, 1300 (5th Cir. 1985), *cert. denied*, 475 U.S. 1089 (1986) (affirming use of the instruction in the particular context).

92 United States v. Myers, 500 F.2d 1036, 1049 (5th Cir. 1977). This, of course, describes only the circumstantial evidence part of the inference, as the fact-finder must also assess its degree of confidence that the witness who describes the defendant's behavior is testifying accurately.

93 *See, e.g.*, Thompson v. State, 901 A.2d 208, 213–19 (Md. 2006) (emphasizing, however, that the use of the state's pattern jury instruction on flight actually encourages the jury to consider innocent explanations of the evidence of flight).

94 Dana Raigrodski, *Reasonableness and Objectivity: A Feminist Discourse of the Fourth Amendment*, 17 TEX. J. WOMEN & L. 153, 184 (2008) (discussing the relevance of unprovoked flight from the police in the case of Illinois v. Wardlow, 528 U.S. 119 (2000); arguing that ["t]his case exemplifies both the inherent subjectivity and positionality of common sense and the race and class biases that taint the concept of reasonableness. It is a particularly potent example because it demonstrates how our own experiences and identities influence even our perceptions of supposedly objective external facts").

defendant to place this information before the jury in order to avoid the misleading quality of the evidence of flight is plausibly considered unfairly prejudicial.[95]

Evidence of a Party's Attempt to Withhold, Destroy, or Fabricate Evidence

Notice that the word "evidence" appears twice in the title of this subsection. That reflects the unusual nature of this category of evidence: it is evidence about evidence. More specifically, it is evidence about how a party has mishandled what would otherwise be available as evidence by acts of suppression, destruction, alteration, or fabrication. In both civil and criminal cases, common-law courts have long accepted the general proposition that one party could draw the fact-finder's attention to the other party's handling of evidence if that conduct reflects on the facts in dispute. But there is enormous variation in the details of the courts' responses. In part, this is because there are several distinct tools available to a court for addressing such behavior, including: admitting evidence of the behavior at trial, with or without a jury instruction that would permit (or even encourage) the jury to draw an adverse inference against the party engaging in such behavior; excluding evidence offered by the party engaging in such behavior; granting monetary compensation to the adversely affected party; and granting a partial or complete preemptive determination on the merits of the case against the party engaging in such conduct. Some of these remedies are administered as discovery sanctions on appropriate pre-trial motion, remedies that did not exist when the early common-law doctrines evolved.[96] And sometimes this kind of conduct is prosecutable as a separate crime, such as obstruction of justice or subornation of perjury,[97] or actionable as a separate tort, the so-called "spoliation tort."[98] Unfortunately, the case law has not established a comprehensive framework for the choice of tools.[99] Pervasively important in this area is the general principle, explained in *Old Chief*, that unfair prejudice should be avoided when viable alternatives exist.[100]

Withholding of evidence. Many courts allow a proponent to evidence the opponent's peculiar access to certain evidence and argue that the opponent's failure to introduce such evidence reflects the opponent's awareness that the missing evidence would be

---

95 *See Myers*, 500 F.2d at 1048–51 (rejecting testimony regarding flight and use of jury instruction in particular context because of conflating influences of multiple crimes on defendant's behavior); *Thompson*, 901 A.2d at 219–22 (rejecting use of pattern flight instruction in context where defendant explained to police upon capture that he fled because he was in possession of illegal drugs).

96 *See, e.g.*, FED. R. CIV. PR. 37. *See generally* ROBERT WYNESS MILLAR, CIVIL PROCEDURE OF THE TRIAL COURT IN HISTORICAL PERSPECTIVE 201–28 (1952).

97 *See, e.g.*, 18 U.S.C. § 1501 et seq. (obstruction of justice); 18 U.S.C. § 1622 (subornation of perjury).

98 *See* JAMES S. GORELICK, STEPHEN MARZEN, & LAWRENCE SOLUM, DESTRUCTION OF EVIDENCE ch. 4 (2016), *at* https://1.next.westlaw.com (discussing the wide range of rules regarding the availability of a spoliation tort).

99 Unusual in this regard is Trevino v. Ortega, 969 S.W.2d 950, 955–61 (Tex. 1998) (rejecting the "spoliation tort" and canvassing the alternatives). For academic views on the spoliation tort, compare Ariel Porat & Alex Stein, *Liability for Uncertainty: Making Evidential Damage Actionable*, 18 CARDOZO L. REV. 1891 (1997) (advocating tort liability for damaging evidence); with Richard Friedman, *Dealing with Evidentiary Deficiency*, 18 CARDOZO L. REV. 1961, 1895–96 (1997) (arguing that remedies intrinsic to the litigation of the primary claim are more efficient that a distinct cause of action in tort, at least when the destruction is caused by a party to the litigation).

100 *See* **§ 5.03**.

unfavorable to the opponent.[101] Of course, the inference is not inevitably correct: a party might withhold evidence for a variety of reasons besides its being unfavorable—to avoid embarrassment, because retrieval is expensive, and so forth. Still, an awareness that the evidence would be unfavorable is one explanation for withholding, and the party against whom such an inference is suggested is free to provide alternative explanations.

Until fairly recently, this view had been nearly universal, with disputes focusing on the conditions that would undermine the inference, conditions that may need to be communicated to the jury. Generally speaking, the missing evidence had to be available to the opponent, usually unprivileged, admissible, and unavailable (or at least less easily available) to the proponent.[102] Courts have considered these factors extensively in deciding whether to encourage an "adverse inference" jury instruction against the opponent. A fairly typical jury instruction reads:

> If a party fails to produce evidence that is under that party's control and reasonably available to that party and not reasonably available to the adverse party, then you may infer that the evidence is unfavorable to the party who could have produced it and did not.[103]

However, a discernible modern trend rejects evidence of such withholding and the arguments and jury instructions that would supplement it. The main reasons given in judicial opinions for the trend are these: (1) modern discovery makes almost all evidence available to both sides; (2) the elimination of the "voucher" rule[104] means that the proponent of an adverse inference may instead introduce the evidence if the proponent expects it to be favorable, and may impeach it if it turns out not to be; (3) eliminating the practice of inviting such inferences eliminates the considerable expenditure of time and energy spent wrangling over whether to permit such arguments and to give a jury instruction; and (4) eliminating the practice reduces the need of parties to call unhelpful witnesses solely to avoid an anticipated adverse inference argument.[105]

Of course, cases can arise in which one party really does have exclusive access to an important witness, but in such cases, there remains the question whether an adverse inference is the best remedy for the problem. In criminal cases, for example, if the government withholds the identity of an informer even after the court determines that the identity is not privileged, then the remedy of choice is not simply to allow the defendant to invite an adverse inference by the jury; rather, it is to dismiss the case.[106]

---

[101] *See, e.g.,* United States v. Mahone, 537 F.2d 922, 926–28 (7th Cir. 1976) (approving the use of an adverse inference against the government from the government's failure to call an arresting officer as a witness). *See generally* 2 WIGMORE ON EVIDENCE § 285 (Chadbourn rev. 1979).

[102] *See* 2 WIGMORE ON EVIDENCE §§ 286–290 (Chadbourn rev. 1979).

[103] 3 KEVIN F. O'MALLEY, JAY E. GRENIG, & WILLIAM C. LEE, FEDERAL JURY PRACTICE AND INSTRUCTIONS § 104.26 (6th ed. 2006).

[104] *See* **§ 11.02**.

[105] *See, e.g.,* State v. Malave, 737 A.2d 442 (Conn. 1999) (discussing the statutory abolition of missing witness instructions in civil trials, abandoning such instructions in criminal trials, and discouraging prosecutorial arguments inviting such adverse inferences against the accused); State v. Brewer, 505 A.2d 774, 776–77 (Me. 1985) (abandoning missing witness inferences in criminal trials); Henderson v. State, 367 So.2d 1366, 1368 (Miss. 1979) (disallowing missing witness jury instructions from either party's failure to call a witness in criminal cases).

[106] *See, e.g.,* Roviaro v. United States, 353 U.S. 53, 60–61 (1957) (holding against the government's claim of privilege for an informer's identity and observing that, in the absence of a valid privilege, the prosecution must choose between disclosing the informer's identity and dismissing the prosecution); United States v. Tucker, 552 F.2d 202, 211 (7th Cir. 1977) (reversing conviction for failure to produce government informant despite trial court's employment of an adverse inference against the government).

Such an approach can be extended to other contexts.[107] In any case, if the court settles on what it considers an appropriate and exclusive remedy other than an adverse inference, and the matter nonetheless goes to verdict, the court may exclude evidence of, and argument from, the withholding of evidence under Rule 403 because it invites a confusion of the issues that the jury must decide.

Destruction or fabrication of evidence. Courts have responded similarly to allegations by a party that an opponent has intentionally destroyed or fabricated evidence: evidence of that fact is often admitted and sometimes supported by a jury instruction. A typical jury instruction reads:

> If you should find that a party willfully [*suppressed*][*hid*][*destroyed*] evidence in order to prevent its being presented in this trial, you may consider such [*suppression*][*hiding*][*destruction*] in determining what inferences to draw from the evidence of facts in the case.[108]

By comparing this instruction with the one for evidence withholding quoted above, one can see that in this context the evidence is admitted not simply to show that the destroyed evidence would have been unfavorable to the suppressing party or that the fabricated evidence is useless. In fact, courts traditionally permit the argument and inference that such party acted with a consciousness of a weak cause and from this the further inference that the party's cause is without merit.[109] Once again, the inference is not inevitable: destruction can be accidental or inadvertent—for example, the result of a general policy of destroying things to avoid storage costs[110]—and even a party's fabrication of evidence can be consistent with that party having a valid claim or defense.[111] Accordingly, the party against whom the inference is invited may attempt to explain its conduct in destroying or fabricating evidence.

Precisely because the inference is so broad, it presents the risk of improper character-based reasoning—e.g., a person who would suppress evidence is a bad person and should be punished, quite apart from whether that person is right on the merits of the complaint.[112] To be sure, the law is not averse to imposing sanctions for such conduct,

---

[107] *See* Dale A. Nance, *Adverse Inferences About Adverse Inferences: Restructuring Juridical Roles for Responding to Evidence Tampering by Parties to Litigation*, 90 B.U. L. REV. 1089 (2010) (arguing that the remedy of dismissal, directed verdict, or other preemptive ruling should be extended to all cases of unprivileged withholding of evidence by a party with exclusive control of the witness, except when the party is a criminal defendant, an exception necessary to protect the defendant's right to jury trial).

[108] 3 KEVIN F. O'MALLEY, JAY E. GRENIG, & WILLIAM C. LEE, FEDERAL JURY PRACTICE AND INSTRUCTIONS § 104.27 (6th ed. 2006).

[109] *See* 2 WIGMORE ON EVIDENCE § 278 (Chadbourn rev. 1979).

[110] *See, e.g.*, Lewy v. Remington Arms Co., 836 F.2d 1104 (8th Cir. 1988) (reversing judgment for plaintiff for failure of trial court to make preliminary determination concerning legitimacy of defendant's document retention policy before giving adverse inference instruction to jury).

[111] Sometimes the last inference—from *weak* case to *invalid* case—is not separately discussed. *See, e.g.*, McQueeney v. Wilmington Trust Co., 779 F.2d 916 (3d Cir. 1985) (reversing trial court's refusal of evidence of unsuccessful attempt to suborn perjury; appellate court's analysis ignores possibility that plaintiff may have had a valid case and acted only in response to defendant's improper withholding of evidence during discovery).

[112] *Cf.* 2 MCCORMICK ON EVIDENCE § 265 at 328 (Kenneth S. Broun ed., 7th ed. 2013):

> A question may well be raised whether the relatively modest probative value of this species of evidence is not often outweighed by its prejudicial aspects. The litigant who would not like to have a stronger case must indeed be a rarity. It may well be that the real underpinning of the rule of admissibility is a desire to impose swift punishment, with a certain poetic justice, rather than concern over the niceties of proof.

Id. at 328 (citations to cases excluding evidence omitted). On the character evidence rule, *see* **§§ 7.01 et seq.**

but it is not a part of the fact-finder's formal role, unless the destruction or fabrication is the very subject of the substantive claim, as in a prosecution for obstruction of justice or a tort claim for spoliation. Accordingly, some modern case law rejects the use of such adverse inferences in favor of judicially-administered remedies, sometimes involving harsher sanctions than merely permitting an adverse inference by the fact-finder.[113] For criminal cases in particular, when state actors have destroyed material evidence in violation of federal or state constitutional requirements, most courts tend to impose dismissal or the exclusion of related prosecution evidence, rather than limiting the defense to suggesting an adverse inference against the government, at least when the destruction was done in bad faith.[114]

The theory of relevance for admitting evidence of these acts depends on an inference from deliberate acts to consciousness of a weak cause, which would seem to preclude its use in cases of merely *negligent* destruction, a point long argued by commentators.[115] The case law, however, is in conflict: while most cases require bad faith—a fraudulent purpose or an intent to affect the evidence in the case—some cases, perhaps indicative of a trend, permit the use of evidence of negligent destruction of evidence to support an adverse inference.[116] The rationales for the latter result are (a) that requiring proof of bad faith or fraudulent intent would allow parties to conceal their intentions behind a false claim of accident, and (b) there should be some disciplinary consequences even for negligence in order to provide the necessary incentives for good conduct in relation to evidence. These rationales implicitly assume (a) that courts are unable to see through such artifices, an assumption belied by the common use of discovery sanctions, and (b) in cases where the courts are uncertain about intent or are clear that there is no intent to affect the evidence in the case, that no alternative remedy exists. In fact, there is a range of viable alternatives, including monetary sanctions and even preemptive judgments (dismissal or default), that can be deployed in cases of negligent destruction of evidence.[117] These alternatives have the advantage that they avoid involving the jury

---

113 *See, e.g.*, Telectron, Inc. v. Overhead Door Corp., 116 F.R.D. 107 (S.D. Fla. 1987) (imposing default judgment on defendant for deliberate destruction of evidence and specifically rejecting the use of evidence and argument for an adverse inference against the defense—an alternative suggested by the defense).

114 *See, e.g.*, United States v. Cooper, 983 F.2d 928, 931–32 (9th Cir. 1993) (holding that the appropriate remedy in a bad faith destruction case was dismissal of the indictment and specifically rejecting the prosecution's proposal to submit the matter to the jury with instruction to assume the truth of certain defense claims). *See also* California v. Trombetta, 467 U.S. 479, 486–91 (1984) (discussing appropriate remedies).

115 *See, e.g.*, John MacArthur Maguire & Robert C. Vincent, *Admissions Implied from Spoliation or Related Conduct*, 45 YALE L.J. 226, 231–35 (1935).

116 *See* JAMES S. GORELICK, STEPHEN MARZEN, & LAWRENCE SOLUM, DESTRUCTION OF EVIDENCE § 2.8 (2016), *at* https://1.next.westlaw.com. A 2015 amendment to the Federal Rules of Civil Procedure addressing the destruction of electronically stored information specifies that an adverse inference instruction may be given only if the court finds there was intent to deprive the opponent of the use of the destroyed evidence. *See* FED. R. CIV. P. 37(e)(2) 2015 advisory committee note (commenting that even gross negligence is not enough). Although the measure was adopted out of special concern regarding innocent destruction of electronic data, it remains to be seen how this will affect practice with respect to other kinds of evidence.

117 *See, e.g.*, Turner v. Hudson Transit Lines, Inc., 142 F.R.D. 68 (S.D.N.Y. 1991) (rejecting adverse inference without showing that records were deliberately destroyed to prevent their discovery, but imposing monetary sanctions for negligent destruction); Thiele v. Oddy's Auto & Marine, Inc., 906 F. Supp. 158, 1612–63 (W.D.N.Y. 1995) (confirming use of issue preclusion based on negligent destruction of key piece of evidence). *But see* FED. R. CIV. P. 37(e)(2)(C) (requiring, by 2015 amendment, an intent to deprive opponent of information before the sanction of dismissal or default can be used with regard to the destruction of electronically stored information). For the criminal trial context, *see* United States v. Ramirez, 174 F.3d 584, 589 (5th Cir. 1999) (holding that the proper remedy for the government's intentional or negligent destruction of material tape recordings must be dismissal of the indictment "because a new trial cannot remedy the government's nondisclosure," that is, even if an adverse inference were allowed at retrial).

in regulating the pretrial behavior of the parties in regard to evidence, a task that is quite distinct from their role as fact-finder and one for which lay jurors are arguably not well prepared.[118]

[118] *See* Dale A. Nance, *Adverse Inferences About Adverse Inferences: Restructuring Juridical Roles for Responding to Evidence Tampering by Parties to Litigation*, 90 B.U. L. REV. 1089 (2010) (arguing that various judicially administered remedies, distinct from the use of adverse inferences, are better tools for regulating party conduct in regard to destruction or fabrication of evidence, except when such conduct is that of the criminal defendant). *But see* Andrew S. Pollis, *Trying the Trial*, 84 GEO. WASH. L. REV. 55 (2016) (defending the role of the jury in disciplining litigation misconduct).

Chapter 6

RELEVANCE AND COUNTERWEIGHTS: APPLICATIONS

Table of Sections

---

§ 6.01 Introduction

As explained in Chapter 5, Federal Rules of Evidence 401, 402, and 403 articulate very general principles of admissibility. The specific rules discussed in this chapter provide, at least to some extent, concrete applications of those general principles. The drafters of these rules explained:

> The rules which follow in this Article [IV] are concrete applications evolved for particular situations. However, they reflect the policies underlying the present rule [403], which is designed as a guide for the handling of situations for which no specific rules have been formulated.[1]

Although it is true that the rules considered in this chapter reflect many of the principles and considerations presented summarily in Rule 403, they also reflect significant policies that are not a discernible part of the Rule 403 calculus. Specifically,

---

[1] FED. R. EVID. 403 advisory committee note.

they reflect policies designed to encourage certain kinds of out-of-court conduct, such as engaging in compromise, taking precautionary measures, or purchasing insurance. While susceptible to a Rule 403 analysis, these policies are probably better understood as attempts to influence events taking place outside the trial in order to effectuate certain social and economic policies. The considerations informing Rule 403 do not suggest any concern other than getting an accurate verdict, at no more than reasonably necessary cost,[2] but the rules discussed here often reflect additional policy concerns.[3]

A. EVIDENCE ABOUT A PARTY'S FINANCIAL RESOURCES

§ 6.02 Evidence of a Party's Wealth or Poverty—in General

Evidence of a party's wealth (or the parties' relative wealth) is usually ruled irrelevant. Ordinarily, no essential element of a claim or defense refers to the party's economic status.[4] One might suggest that a wealthy person is more inclined to commit torts, crimes, or breaches of contract because he has recourse to expensive lawyers who can protect him from the legal consequences. Alternatively, one could argue that the wealthy prefer to avoid conduct that imperils their wealth, and that, if anyone, the poor are more willing to commit delicts because they are "judgment proof." In any event, the weakness of such inferences suffices to cause courts to exclude evidence of wealth on the ground that admission of such evidence would tempt the fact-finder to make a decision on an improper basis—namely, the defendant's ability to pay or the plaintiff's financial needs.[5] Even if this concern is fanciful, and extant empirical evidence suggests it is,[6] the weakness and ambivalence of the evidence supports exclusion in most cases in order to avoid a waste of time. Similarly, courts preclude informing the jury that someone else, a

---

[2] *See* **§ 5.03**.

[3] Because of the contemplated effect on conduct outside the courtroom, an argument can be made, pursuant to the *Erie* doctrine, that federal courts sitting in diversity ought to defer to a state version of the relevant rule when it varies from the federal version. Unlike the rules for privileges (*see* FED. R. EVID. 501), this argument is not supported by an explicit rule in Article IV of the Federal Rules. It has, nonetheless, occasionally been accepted, particularly in the context of evidence of subsequent remedial measures. *See* 2 CHRISTOPHER B. MUELLER & LAIRD C. KIRKPATRICK, FEDERAL EVIDENCE § 4:55 (4th ed. 2013).

[4] *See, e.g.,* United States ex rel. Miller v. Bill Harbert International Construction, Inc., 608 F.3d 871, 896–98 (D.C. Cir. 2010); Brough v. Imperial Sterling Ltd., 297 F.3d 1172, 1178–90 (11th Cir. 2002). *See generally* 2 JONES ON EVIDENCE: CIVIL AND CRIMINAL § 13:25 (Clifford S. Fishman ed., 7th ed. 1994).

[5] *See, e.g.,* Koufakis v. Carvel, 425 F.2d 892, 902 (2d Cir. 1970) ("Remarks . . . which can be taken as suggesting that the defendant should respond in damages because he is rich and the plaintiff is poor, are grounds for a new trial."). The attitude of trial courts to evidence of the relative financial status of the parties is nicely revealed by the following *in limine* ruling in a breach of contract action between a physician (plaintiff Bhandari) and certain hospitals (defendants):

> The Defendants argue that the Court should preclude R. Bhandari, his counsel, and R. Bhandari's witnesses from commenting on or soliciting testimony concerning any comparison of wealth between R. Bhandari and the Defendants. They argue that the evidence is not relevant and that the danger of unfair prejudice outweighs any probative value. . . . [T]he Court will grant the Defendants' requests. . . Both parties must be careful, however, that they do not open the door at trial for evidence regarding their wealth. If one party starts to "poor boy" the other party, the Court will have to even the playing field. For example, if the Defendants start to present argument or evidence that they are just a poor community hospital, the Court may, upon request, level the playing field by allowing R. Bhandari to present evidence of the Defendants' assets.

Bhandari v. VHA Southwest Community Health Corp., 778 F. Supp. 2d 1155, 1163–64 (D. N.M. 2011). With regard to "opening the door" to otherwise inadmissible evidence, *see* **§ 1.01**.

[6] *See, e.g.,* Gregory Mitchell & Philip E. Tetlock, *An Empirical Inquiry into the Relation of Corrective Justice to Distributive Justice*, 3 J. EMPIRICAL LEG. STUD. 421 (2006) (reporting results of experiments indicating that people believe civil parties are entitled to equal consideration regardless of their surrounding circumstances, such as party wealth).

relative or employer, will pay for the defendant's liability.[7] No specific Federal Rule, other than the rule regarding liability insurance,[8] addresses this kind of issue, so the authority for exclusion, when courts even think it necessary to cite one, is Rule 403.

Exceptional situations arise in which financial status is relevant. Obviously, proof of solvency may be relevant in debtor-creditor law, and a commercial contract might make duties dependent upon financial status. Non-contractual examples also arise. In will disputes, for example, evidence about the estate's assets may be relevant in determining how it is to be distributed, but the assets of the contesting parties are generally irrelevant except to show that a natural potential beneficiary was deliberately omitted because that person already had adequate funds.[9] Other common exceptions concern damages. A plaintiff who claims "financial stress" as an element of compensatory damages, for example, may cause his financial status to be relevant, permitting the defendant to show that the plaintiff is actually well off.[10] And when there is a claim for punitive damages, the defendant's wealth becomes relevant to the measure of such damages, specifically what level of damages will be necessary and appropriate to deter the defendant (and other similarly situated individuals) from such conduct in the future.[11]

Similarly, evidence of a party's impoverishment is ordinarily immaterial because being poor is not a condition for any civil recovery for a wrong done to someone, nor is being impoverished (or becoming impoverished by having to pay the damage award) an affirmative defense to the imposition of liability.[12] In one case, plaintiffs sued for negligently inflicted personal injury and wanted to introduce evidence that they lacked medical insurance and otherwise could not afford medical treatment. The trial court excluded this evidence, a ruling affirmed on appeal.[13] The appellate court, however, also approved the trial court's admonition to the defense, that if the defense chose to elicit testimony about the plaintiffs not seeking medical attention for a considerable period of time after the injury, in order to suggest the absence of an injury, then plaintiffs would have been allowed to explain to the jury with evidence about their financial condition in order to counter this inference.[14]

Poverty can be relevant evidence of motive, especially for a crime or an intentional tort involving the acquisition of money or valuables. Thus, circumstances of need have long been admitted as evidence of motive for a property-related wrongdoing.[15] But when

---

[7] *See* Falkowski v. Johnson, 148 F.R.D. 132, 136 (D. Del.1993) (plaintiff's statements in closing argument implying that defendant's employer would pay personal injury damages constitutes reversible error).

[8] *See* **§ 6.03**.

[9] *See, e.g., In re* Estate of Smallman, 398 S.W.3d 134, 151–52 (Tenn. 2013).

[10] *See, e.g.*, Hayes v. Northern Hills General Hospital, 628 N.W.2d 739 (S.D. 2001).

[11] Even in such cases, courts often insist on admitting evidence of the defendant's wealth only after non-punitive liability has been determined or after the factual predicate for a punitive award has been established. *See, e.g.*, Hodges v. S.C. Toof & Co., 833 S.W.2d 896, 901 (Tenn. 1992); Campen v. Stone, 635 P.2d 1121 (Wyo. 1981) (including an extensive discussion of alternative approaches).

[12] *See, e.g.*, Rebolledo v. Herr-Voss Corporation, 101 F. Supp. 2d 1034, 1036–37 (N.D. Ill. 2000) (granting plaintiff's motion in products liability action to preclude defendant's argument that imposition of liability would impose financial hardship on defendant). *See also* Rodriguez v. Taylor, 468 So.2d 1186 (La. 1985) (abolishing Louisiana's rule allowing a defendant to show inability to pay as relevant to the measure of fair compensatory damages).

[13] Van Bumble v. Wal-Mart Stores, Inc., 407 F.3d 823, 826–27 (7th Cir. 2005).

[14] *Id.* This admonition will be understood as addressing an example of the defense "opening the door" to otherwise inadmissible evidence. *See supra*, **§ 1.11**.

[15] *See* 2 WIGMORE ON EVIDENCE § 392 (Chadbourn rev. 1979).

the allegation involves a property crime of violence, such as robbery, courts have shown some reluctance to admit evidence of lack of financial resources, without more, to show motive. The Supreme Court of New Jersey endorsed Wigmore's view, saying. "Undoubtedly a lack of money is logically connected with a crime involving financial gain. The trouble is that it would prove too much against too many."[16] This comment occurred in a case decided before the Federal Rules of Evidence were enacted, and it is not obvious that Rule 403 or any other federal rule contains an exclusion for evidence that "proves too much against too many." Perhaps the evidence is of too little probative value to be worth the court's time. In any event, courts continue to insist, as a condition on admitting such evidence, that some additional evidence be joined with it, such as evidence that the defendant had money or identifiable valuables in his possession after the crime, or that the defendant had some particular source of urgent financial need such as an expensive drug habit, or that the defendant possessed unexplained funds after the alleged crime.[17]

§ 6.03 Evidence of Liability Insurance [FRE 411]

Insurance, an important financial resource, can be involved in litigation in a variety of ways. Perhaps most commonly, tort defendants often have so-called "third-party" or "liability" insurance, which commits the insurer to pay damages to a third party for which the insured is liable.[18] In addition, a plaintiff may be the beneficiary under a so-called "first-party" insurance agreement, which provides for payments to cover losses without regard to liability, such as health insurance, fire insurance, or life insurance. This first-party insurance can be involved in litigation as well and is addressed in the next section. The present section addresses whether a court should admit evidence of the fact that a party has (or does not have) liability insurance.

Federal Rule of Evidence 411 prohibits evidence of the presence or absence of liability insurance, when offered on the issue whether the insured party acted negligently or wrongfully. The general rule is followed almost universally. Some states have adopted language identical or virtually identical to Federal Rule 411; others have codified somewhat different versions. The few remaining common-law states also tend to follow the general principles of Rule 411.[19]

The rule has three rationales. First, absent special circumstances, the relevance of insurance to the issue of liability is questionable. Although, conceivably, a person who buys insurance will act carelessly because there is less risk of economic loss, it is also possible that those who buy insurance are simply more careful by nature.[20] Second, the evidence about insurance has obvious potential for unfair prejudice. If the jury learns

---

[16] State v. Mathis, 221 A.2d 529, 538 (N.J. 1966).

[17] *See, e.g.,* United States v. Saniti, 604 F.2d 603 (9th Cir.), *cert. denied,* 444 U.S. 969 (1979) (permitting evidence that defendant had an expensive heroin and morphine habit to show motive for bank robbery); *but see* State v. LeFever, 690 P.2d 574 (Wash. 1984) (evidence of drug habit excluded in robbery case because of unfair prejudice). *See also* People v. Hogan, 647 P.2d 93, 115–16 (Cal. 1982); Vitek v. State, 453 A.2d 514, 517–20 (Md. 1982).

[18] The presence of this kind of insurance in litigation is not entirely coincidental in that potential plaintiffs after an event often look for someone to sue who has such insurance.

[19] For discussion of state law, see DAVID P. LEONARD, THE NEW WIGMORE: SELECTED RULES OF LIMITED ADMISSIBILITY § 6.6 (rev. ed. 2002). Interestingly, Louisiana appears to reject the general exclusionary rule. *See Id.* at 6:80. In light of Louisiana's "direct action" statute permitting the liability insurer to be made a party to the action, an exclusionary rule would serve little purpose.

[20] *See* FED. R. EVID. 411 advisory committee note.

that a defendant is insured, then it might be more likely to hold the party liable because of its deep pockets.[21] If the jury finds out that a defendant is uninsured, then the jury may find no liability because it fears that a contrary verdict will bring financial ruin upon the defendant.[22] Finally, the rule is occasionally supported by the rationale that excluding evidence of liability insurance encourages people to carry such insurance.[23]

Of course, in many situations jurors will assume that parties are insured in the absence of evidence. For example, jurors will ordinarily assume some level of insurance when a case involves an automobile accident or destruction of property by fire. In this situation, it can be argued that revealing the true state of affairs when there is no insurance merely counteracts unfair prejudice caused by this erroneous assumption. This argument, however, cannot be accepted in jurisdictions following the Federal Rules of Evidence, because it is contrary to the plain language of Rule 411. In other jurisdictions, the argument has had scant success.[24] The uninsured party can, however, request an instruction that at least suggests the possibility of no insurance. For example, the instruction could state:

> There has been no evidence in this case about whether [the party] was covered by liability insurance. The reason is that the law does not permit evidence of the absence or presence of liability insurance to be presented to you. The evidence is inadmissible because you are not supposed to consider insurance one way or the other in this case. When deciding the case, you should put out of your mind the possibility that the loss in this case was covered, or was not covered, by liability insurance.

Although evidence of liability insurance is inadmissible when offered to show negligence or wrongful conduct, it is admissible when offered for another purpose. For example, it is admissible to show agency, ownership, or control,[25] or to show the bias or prejudice of a witness.[26] Thus, when there is a dispute about whether landlord or tenant is responsible for the maintenance of an office building's elevator, evidence that the tenant maintained liability insurance on the elevator would be admissible. Similarly,

---

[21] Like so many judicial guesses about jury behavior, the risk of this may not be as great as has commonly been assumed. *See, e.g.*, NEIL VIDMAR, MEDICAL MALPRACTICE AND THE AMERICAN JURY: CONFRONTING THE MYTHS ABOUT JURY INCOMPETENCE, DEEP POCKETS, AND OUTRAGEOUS DAMAGE AWARDS pt. 4 (1995) (reporting results of experiments revealing verdict behavior inconsistent with a "deep pockets" hypothesis).

[22] On the other hand, there is the possibility that the jury might wish to punish a party who, contrary to law, fails to carry automobile liability insurance.

[23] *See, e.g.*, 2 WEINSTEIN'S FEDERAL EVIDENCE § 411.02[2] (Mark S. Brodin ed., 2d ed. 2015) (noting that the exclusionary rule "seeks to implement a general policy favoring insurance. Both insurers and insured are, in effect, encouraged to enter into contracts of insurance with the implied promise that they will not, as a result of their forethought, have what they believe to be the somewhat harmful inference of carelessness used against them").

[24] 1 MCCORMICK ON EVIDENCE § 201 at 1127 (Kenneth S. Broun ed., 7th ed. 2013) (stating that few courts will allow defendant to demonstrate lack of insurance; instruction on insurance suggested).

[25] *See, e.g.*, Hunziker v. Scheidemantle, 543 F.2d 489, 495 n.10 (3d Cir. 1976) (holding fact of insurance admissible to prove agency relationship between owner and pilot of crashed aircraft); Newell v. Harold Shaffer Leasing Co., 489 F.2d 103, 110 (5th Cir. 1974) (holding draft from insurance company to plaintiff for amount of damages naming defendant as insured, admissible to show defendant's ownership of truck in suit for accident); Dobbins v. Crain Bros., 432 F. Supp. 1060, 1069 (W.D. Pa. 1976) *aff'd in part, rev'd in part*, 567 F.2d 559 (3d Cir. 1977) (holding defendant's insurance coverage on barge admissible to prove ownership).

[26] *See, e.g.*, Charter v. Chleborad, 551 F.2d 246, 248 (8th Cir. 1977) (finding reversible error where plaintiff not permitted to show that impeachment witness for defense was employed by the same insurance company representing defendant).

when an insurance investigator testifies, evidence that the investigator works for the insurer of one of the parties is often admitted to show the witness's possible bias.[27] Some trial judges, however, will seek to eliminate possible prejudice by requiring that the reference to the insurer be removed. For example, the judge might require that the investigator be asked whether he or she is an investigator for the defense, without mention of the insurance company. Defense counsel should ask for a ruling before the question is asked.

Rule 411 sets forth certain purposes for which evidence of insurance may be received, such as agency, ownership, control, and bias or prejudice of a witness. This list, however, is not exclusive. Insurance evidence is admissible for any relevant purpose not specifically prohibited by Rule 411; that is, it is admissible on any issue other than showing whether the insured acted negligently or otherwise wrongfully.[28] Thus, for example, evidence of insurance sometimes is admitted incidentally in the impeachment of a witness's credibility, even if the impeachment is based on grounds other than the listed purpose of showing bias. If a witness files a claim of loss with her insurance company that is inconsistent with her in-court testimony, it is permissible to impeach the witness with the prior inconsistent statement.[29] Of course, if liability insurance is itself an essential element of a claim or defense, evidence of the insurance must be admitted.[30]

In the authors' view, the prohibition as stated in the first sentence of Rule 411 is overbroad. Some of the evidence supposedly permitted in the second sentence of the rule actually is used to show "whether the [insured] acted negligently or otherwise wrongfully." For example, if an insurance adjuster offers testimony that tends to prove that the defendant-insured was not negligent, and the relationship between the witness and the defendant's insurance company is offered to impeach the witness for bias, then by undermining the adjuster's testimony that the defendant was not negligent, the impeaching evidence tends to support the claim that the defendant was negligent. The purpose of such evidence is covered by the literal prohibition. Nevertheless, courts routinely admit such impeachment evidence, and rightly so. The apparent conflict is resolved by noting that only one line of inference to negligence is truly barred by the prohibition—the inference that the insured would act more (or less) carelessly *because* he or she was insured (or not).[31] Insightful judges understand this and decide objections

---

[27] *See, e.g.*, Conde v. Starlight I, Inc., 103 F.3d 210 (1st Cir. 1997) (finding no error in permitting the plaintiff to inform the jury that a witness for the defense was an adjuster for the defendant's insurance company); Ouachita Natl. Bank v. Tosco Corp., 686 F.2d 1291 (8th Cir. 1982), *modified on reh'g*, 716 F.2d 485 (8th Cir. 1983) (en banc) (holding that defendant could inform jury of insurance coverage when it intended to call insurance adjuster as witness); Filloon v. Stenseth, 498 N.W.2d 353, 355 (N.D. 1993) (finding reversible error in automatically barring evidence that key witness also worked for driver's insurance carrier; trial court should have admitted evidence under state's Rule 411, subject to probativeness versus prejudice balancing under state's Rule 403).

[28] For extended discussion of permissible uses of liability insurance evidence, *see* DAVID P. LEONARD, THE NEW WIGMORE: SELECTED RULES OF LIMITED ADMISSIBILITY §§ 6.9–6.15 (rev. ed. 2002).

[29] *See* Rozark Farms, Inc. v. Ozark Border Elec. Co-op., 849 F.2d 306, 309 & n.2 (8th Cir. 1988) (dictum) (stating that amount set forth on proof of loss form can be used to impeach testimony by insured that greater loss was suffered, and noting that it is not always possible to avoid reference to insurance in process of this impeachment).

[30] *See* DAVID P. LEONARD, THE NEW WIGMORE: SELECTED RULES OF LIMITED ADMISSIBILITY § 6.11 (rev. ed. 2002).

[31] *Id.* § 6.7 at 802 (noting that "the cases do not often state the proposition with much clarity" but "[o]nly when the liability insurance evidence is offered . . . as itself an indicator of the quality of a person's conduct, will it be excluded.").

accordingly.[32] Thus the implicit prohibition of the rule is this: Evidence that a person was (or was not) insured against liability is not admissible *to prove that the person's being insured (or not) affected whether the person acted negligently or otherwise wrongfully*.[33]

The fact that liability insurance evidence circumstantially tends to prove something other than the defendant's response to being insured does not automatically make it admissible. As with other evidence that is admissible for one purpose but not for another, the trial judge must, upon appropriate objection, weigh the danger of misuse of the evidence against its legitimate probative value in deciding whether to admit it under Rule 403.[34] When the court determines that admission is justified, it should issue a limiting instruction informing the jury of the limited purposes for which the evidence is admitted.

If the trial judge sustains an objection to the mention of insurance, counsel ordinarily should request a mistrial and then, if the request is denied, request a curative instruction telling the jury to ignore the evidence. These steps will protect the right to reversal on appeal. Of course, they may not be tactically wise in every situation. Getting a mistrial from the trial judge is no victory when the present jury is favorable.

In jurisdictions that allow substantial questioning of jurors on voir dire, insurance is sometimes brought in through the back door by questions to the jurors. For example, the plaintiff in a personal injury case might be permitted to ask jurors whether they work for an insurance company or whether they own stock in a liability insurance company.[35] In such jurisdictions, counsel may still be able to object successfully if the questions become too pointed. For example, one can argue that asking about employment with a specific insurance company is too suggestive, and that a question about general insurance employment is sufficient. Commentators have also suggested that the information about insurance be obtained from the venire by questionnaire prior to assignment to any particular case, but this solution does not appear to have been widely adopted.[36] In any event, the court must seek an appropriate balance between the

---

[32] This problem—that the drafters omitted a crucial intermediate proposition in the line of inference that is barred by the rule—recurs elsewhere in Article IV. The conspicuous exception is Rule 404, the rule regarding character evidence, which articulates more precisely the inference that is barred. *See* **§ 7.01**.

[33] The prohibited inference also seems to depend on the defendant being aware of his or her insured status, thus presenting a conditional relevance problem. *See* **§ 3.11**.

[34] *See, e.g.*, Posttape Assocs. v. Eastman Kodak Co., 537 F.2d 751, 757–58 (3d Cir. 1976) (holding that trial court erred in excluding as prejudicial otherwise admissible evidence of plaintiff's insurance; evidence not prejudicial).

[35] Drickersen v. Drickersen, 604 P.2d 1082, 1084–85 (Alaska 1979) (affirming that an attorney is entitled to ask prospective jurors if they had interest in, or connection with, any insurance company); 2 WEINSTEIN'S FEDERAL EVIDENCE § 411.04[4] (Mark S. Brodin ed., 2nd ed. 2015) (noting that jury panel may be questioned concerning interest in, or connection with, insurance company involved in litigation).

[36] *See* Edwin Boos, *Recent Decisions, Practice and Procedure—Under What Circumstances May Counsel Ask Jurors Regarding Their Interest in Insurance Companies on Trial of a Case Against an Insured Defendant*, 43 MICH. L. REV. 621, 623 (1944) (discussing the practice of giving every member of jury panel questionnaire concerning relations with insurance companies); *Recent Cases, Jury—Competency of Jurors—Questioning Jurors on Voir Dire as to Their Connections with Insurance Company*, 52 HARV. L. REV. 166, 166 (1938) (advocating examining entire jury panel concerning connections to insurance companies before trial of any cases during term).

conflicting rights to an unbiased jury and the avoidance of unfair prejudice to the insured party.[37]

§ 6.04 The Collateral Source Rule

A number of jurisdictions provide that the defendant's liability for damages caused by an injury is not diminished by the fact that the plaintiff has collected compensation for the same loss from a collateral source.[38] For example, under this rule, the plaintiff whose hospital bills were paid by health insurance is still entitled to recover the amount paid to the hospital from the party whose negligence caused the injury.[39] The rationale behind the collateral source rule is that the wrongdoer should not benefit from the injured person's expenditures or relationships.[40]

The collateral source rule is not a rule of evidence, but a rule of substantive law that renders certain evidence irrelevant.[41] If the substantive law does not allow collateral payments to diminish recovery, evidence of collateral payments should be excluded as irrelevant.[42] Of course, the absence of such a collateral source is irrelevant as well, and evidence showing absence of such sources could also be prejudicial, inviting the fact-finder to make an award that is legally unjustified. For example, if the jury finds out that a plaintiff is not insured for a loss such as destruction of property by fire, then the

---

[37] For further discussion of the problem of revealing evidence of liability insurance during jury selection, *see* DAVID P. LEONARD, THE NEW WIGMORE: SELECTED RULES OF LIMITED ADMISSIBILITY § 6.7.4 (rev. ed. 2002).

[38] *See, e.g.*, Gypsum Carrier, Inc. v. Handelsman, 307 F.2d 525, 535 (9th Cir. 1962) (benefits to injured seaman under compensation plan not deductible from Jones Act recovery; federal courts generally follow collateral source rule); Helfend v. Southern California Rapid Transit Dist., 465 P.2d 61, 63 (Cal. 1970) (compensation for injuries received from source independent of tortfeasor may not be deducted from damages injured party would otherwise recover); Wilson v. Hoffman Group, Inc., 546 N.E.2d 524, 530 (Ill. 1989) (benefits received by injured party from source independent of and collateral to tortfeasor will not diminish damages); RESTATEMENT (SECOND) OF TORTS § 920A (1979) ("Payments made to or benefits conferred on the injured party from other sources are not credited against the tortfeasor's liability although they cover all or a part of the harm for which the tortfeasor is liable.").

[39] The matter can be complicated when the source of the benefits and the tortfeasor are both the government. *Compare* Carter v. United States, 982 F.2d 1141, 1145 (7th Cir. 1992) (incremental veterans' benefits not considered collateral source payments and may be deducted from damages against federal government for medical malpractice at VA); *with* Berg v. United States, 806 F.2d 978, 985–86 (10th Cir. 1986) (Medicare benefits for injuries suffered at veterans' hospital could not be deducted from damages against federal government for medical malpractice).

[40] *See, e.g.*, *Wilson*, 546 N.E.2d at 524 (wrongdoer should not benefit from injured party's expenditures or take advantage of contacts or other relations between injured party and third parties); Greenwood v. Hildebrand, 515 A.2d 963, 968 (Pa. Super. 1986) (wrongdoer should not receive benefit of fortuitous existence of collateral remedy).

[41] As a rule of substantive law, one would expect that federal courts in diversity cases would be required to follow the state's collateral source rule. *See* Erie R. Co. v. Tompkins, 304 U.S. 64 (1938); Bradford v. Bruno's Inc., 94 F.3d 621 (11th Cir. 1996), (Alabama's statutory modification of its common law collateral source rule was substantive law that must be applied in federal diversity action); *In re* Air Crash Disaster Near Chicago, Illinois, on May 25, 1979, 803 F.2d 304, 308 (7th Cir. 1986) (federal court in diversity case must apply collateral source rule of state whose law governs case).

[42] *See, e.g.*, Rozark Farms, Inc. v. Ozark Border Elec. Coop., 849 F.2d 306, 309 (8th Cir. 1988) (finding reversible error where defendant's attorney asked plaintiff, "And was this property damage insured by you?", and trial judge did not rule on objection or give curative instruction). *See generally* JONES ON EVIDENCE: CIVIL AND CRIMINAL § 13:26 (Clifford S. Fishman ed., 7th ed. 1994) (evidence of plaintiff's financial condition including receipt of benefits from collateral sources inadmissible as irrelevant to issue of compensatory damages).

jury might make a lawless assignment of liability because of a defendant's greater resources.[43]

In considering the wisdom of the substantive rule and its exclusionary consequence, it is often supposed that the rule might permit a "double recovery" by the plaintiff, once from the plaintiff's insurance company and once from the defendant or the defendant's insurance company. Indeed, empirical study of jury deliberations reveals that jurors who are kept in the dark about insurance are more frequently concerned about such double recovery than about finding a "deep pocket" to pay for injuries regardless of fault.[44] Ordinarily, however, such double recovery is precluded by another substantive rule—called subrogation—that permits the plaintiff's insurance company to recover, out of the damage award, what it has paid to the plaintiff or to another party (e.g., a hospital) on the plaintiff's behalf. Double recovery can happen, to be sure, but only if neither the plaintiff's insurance agreement nor an independent equitable principle provides for the insurer's subrogation to plaintiff's recovery from the defendant or else the plaintiff's insurance company for some reason simply does not exercise its right to subrogation. The jury may not, however, be aware of such subrogation principles.[45] When the parties and the court do not explain the rules about collateral recoveries to the jury, jurors can be left to speculate about what is happening. We believe that addressing the matter openly with the jury would be a better practice.[46]

The collateral source rule has become controversial, with some scholars arguing that its rationale is outdated. Some have argued that the rule stymies what would otherwise be an economically sensible form of loss spreading.[47] In addition, the perceived proliferation of medical malpractice suits and the rising cost of insurance led the American Medical Association to campaign for a variety of tort reforms including abolition of the collateral source rule.[48] In recent years, several jurisdictions have modified or abolished the collateral source rule in medical malpractice cases.[49] Although

---

43 *See* **§ 6.02**.

44 *See* Shari Diamond & Neil Widmar, *Jury Room Ruminations on Forbidden Topics*, 87 VA. L. REV. 1857, 1888–89 (2001).

45 Subrogation rules and practices are complex and vary from state to state. *See, e.g.*, Drinkwater v. American Family Mutual Ins. Co., 714 N.W.2d 568 (Wis. 2006) (concerning an accident with connections to both Wisconsin and Iowa, where there was not enough payment by the defendant and defendant's liability insurance to cover all of plaintiff's damages; deciding whether to apply Iowa's rule that enforces health insurance contract giving insurance company priority under subrogation or to apply Wisconsin's rule that gives the insured plaintiff priority over subrogation rights of insurer).

46 *See* Shari Diamond & Neil Widmar, *Jury Room Ruminations on Forbidden Topics*, 87 VA. L. REV. 1857, 1907–14 (2001) (articulating suggested jury instruction and when to use it).

47 *See, e.g.*, John G. Fleming, *The Collateral Source Rule and Loss Allocation in Tort Law*, 54 CALIF. L. REV. 1478, 1547, 1547–48 (1966) (arguing that the collateral source rule is no longer justified in light of the high cost of shifting the loss to the tortfeasor from some form of collectivized risk-bearing regime that has already paid for the loss and could absorb it as well or even better than the tortfeasor; "question is not so much whether a wrongdoer deserves to be relieved as which of several competing 'risk communities' should bear the loss").

48 *See* Banks McDowell, *The Collateral Source Rule—The American Medical Association and Tort Reform*, 24 WASHBURN L.J. 205, 215–16 (1985). For a summary discussion of the accuracy and significance of such perceptions in the tort reform debate, see MAXWELL J. MEHLMAN & DALE A. NANCE, MEDICAL INJUSTICE: THE CASE AGAINST HEALTH COURTS 31–56 (2007) (noting, inter alia, the empirical evidence showing that the cost of the medical malpractice system has little impact on the overall cost of health care, physician income, or fluctuations in malpractice premiums).

49 *See* Bernier v. Burris, 497 N.E.2d 763, 774–75 (Ill. 1986) (listing state laws modifying or abrogating collateral source rule in medical malpractice cases permitting recovery to be reduced by amounts received from private or public sources).

such laws have been attacked on both equal protection and due process grounds, courts generally have held them constitutional.[50]

B. EVIDENCE OF VOLUNTARY COMPENSATION AND APOLOGIES

§ 6.05 Evidence of Payment of Medical and Similar Expenses [FRE 409]

Suppose that after a traffic accident, one of the parties offers to pay the hospital expenses of the other. If the offer is part of a settlement negotiation, then the evidence likely would be inadmissible under Rule 408.[51] But even if the offer or payment is made without settlement in mind, Rule 409 makes the evidence inadmissible. Under Rule 409, evidence of furnishing or offering or promising to pay medical, hospital, or similar expenses occasioned by an injury is not admissible to prove liability for the injury.

Rule 409 rests on several rationales.[52] One arises out of practical relevancy—that a payment of medical expenses is often not an expression of belief in fault, but merely an expression of human kindness, so the offer has weak probative value regarding fault.[53] The primary rationale, however, is one of policy—to encourage humane acts. Relatedly, there is the consideration of fairness—that it would be unfair to use a party's humanitarian behavior against her at trial.[54]

Though the general rule of exclusion is followed almost universally,[55] the rule has attracted little attention. Either it has rarely been invoked to exclude evidence, or the rule is so clear that it has not created the interpretive problems that beget reported decisions.

The rule covers just the fact of payment itself and does not apply to any statements made in conjunction with payment of medical expenses.[56] Thus, the party who pays medical expenses and apologizes for an accident is likely to have that apology admitted

---

[50] *See, e.g.*, Marsh v. Green, 782 So. 2d 223, 230–31 (Ala. 2000) (holding that statute abrogating collateral source rule does not violate equal protection or due process rights); Fein v. Permanente Med. Group, 695 P.2d 665, 685–86 (Cal. 1985) (holding that statute allowing defendant to introduce evidence of collateral payments to injured party in medical malpractice suit does not violate due process or equal protection); *Bernier*, 497 N.E.2d at 775 (provision allowing judgment in medical malpractice cases to be reduced by up to 50% for benefits received from collateral sources does not violate due process). *See generally*, Banks McDowell, *The Collateral Source Rule—The American Medical Association and Tort Reform*, 24 WASHBURN L.J. 205, 215–19 (1985) (discussing general reform movement and constitutional challenges to abrogation of rule).

[51] *See* **§ 6.10**.

[52] *See* DAVID P. LEONARD, THE NEW WIGMORE: SELECTED RULES OF LIMITED ADMISSIBILITY § 4.4 (rev. ed. 2002).

[53] FED. R. EVID. 409 advisory committee note. *See also* 2 WEINSTEIN'S FEDERAL EVIDENCE § 409.02 (Mark S. Brodin ed., 2d ed. 2015) (presenting traditional theory that offering to pay medical costs usually made from humane impulses "and is not meant as an admission of liability").

[54] *See* 2 CHRISTOPHER B. MUELLER & LAIRD C. KIRKPATRICK, FEDERAL EVIDENCE § 4:61 at 163 (4th ed. 2013) ("it would be unseemly to receive evidence that one who felt responsible had paid such expenses in a responsible manner, if he objected to the evidence"); 23 CHARLES A. WRIGHT & KENNETH W. GRAHAM, JR., FEDERAL PRACTICE AND PROCEDURE: EVIDENCE § 5321 at 298 (1980) (it is "considered unfair to pervert a generous act into a confession of fault").

[55] Nearly half of the states have adopted the language of Rule 409 verbatim, and several have adopted rules with only minor differences. Though other states have enacted rules somewhat less similar in structure to Rule 409, these rules are likely to have the same scope as Rule 409. *See* DAVID P. LEONARD, THE NEW WIGMORE: SELECTED RULES OF LIMITED ADMISSIBILITY § 4.7 (rev. ed. 2002).

[56] FED. R. EVID. 409 advisory committee note.

against him in court.[57] This aspect of the rule contrasts with Rule 408, which covers not only offers in compromise but statements in conjunction with the offers.[58] The rationale for the difference is that offers in compromise come as part of settlement negotiations and statements of fact are an indispensable part of such negotiations. The non-negotiator who does the good deed of paying medical expenses could do the deed just as effectively without commenting on the events that led to the injury, and hence does not receive the protection afforded to the negotiator on the ground that beneficial conduct is not being deterred by receiving evidence of the statements.[59]

The drafters of the rule provided no help in understanding its limitation to "medical, hospital, or similar expenses resulting from an injury." For example, it is not clear why an offer of financial assistance to soften the impact of a purely economic loss should not be treated the same way, but it is difficult to interpret the rule as protecting such offers. On the other hand, "similar expenses" can and should be interpreted to cover the provision of services with an economic value that are related to medical or hospital expenses. For example, a defendant who offers to take the plaintiff to the hospital would help defray the potential cost of an ambulance or other mode of transportation and should be within the scope of the rule.[60]

Unlike other prohibitions in Article IV, Rule 409 does not have an "other purposes" provision specifying that the evidence of payments is admissible for some purpose other than that which is specifically prohibited. In light of Rule 402, such "other purposes" provisions are not technically necessary; they merely restate the fact that relevant evidence not excluded by a given rule is admissible unless barred by some other rule. Nevertheless, lists of "other purposes," such as the one discussed above in connection with Rule 411, sometimes give helpful clues about the meaning and limits of the Rule.

In the case of Rule 409, some "other purposes" are obvious enough even without such a list. For example, because the rule only precludes the use of evidence of payment when offered "to prove liability for the injury," evidence of payment is admissible by the payor in order to mitigate damages.[61] Some candidates for "other purposes" are not so obvious, however, and the omission of an "other purposes" clause makes interpretation more difficult. It is nonetheless clear that the implicit prohibition is actually narrower than the prohibition as stated: the implicit rule is that evidence of offers or payments are inadmissible to prove the offeror's or payor's *belief* in his or her responsibility for the injury and thereby to help establish that responsibility.[62] Because there are few reported decisions interpreting the reach of Rule 409, it is unclear whether using the payor's

---

57 *See, e.g.*, Sims v. Sowle, 395 P.2d 133, 135 (Or. 1964) (defendant's apology to plaintiff accompanying offer to pay medical expenses admissible); 2 WEINSTEIN'S FEDERAL EVIDENCE, § 409.03[3] (Mark S. Brodin ed., 2d ed. 2015) (admissions of liability accompanying offer of assistance admissible if severable from offer).

58 *See* **§ 6.10**.

59 FED. R. EVID. 409 advisory committee note. For more detailed discussion of the admission of statements of fact made in connection with payment of medical expenses, *see* DAVID P. LEONARD, THE NEW WIGMORE: SELECTED RULES OF LIMITED ADMISSIBILITY § 4.6.2 (rev. ed. 2002).

60 *See* DAVID P. LEONARD, THE NEW WIGMORE: SELECTED RULES OF LIMITED ADMISSIBILITY § 4.8.3 (rev. ed. 2002).

61 *See, e.g.*, Williams v. Missouri Pac. R. Co., 11 F.3d 132, 135 (10th Cir. 1993) (noting that, on remand for reconsideration only of the amount of damages, "the jury should be advised that past medical expenses . . . have been paid and thus may not be estimated and added to the award.") *See also* 2 CHRISTOPHER B. MUELLER & LAIRD C. KIRKPATRICK, FEDERAL EVIDENCE § 4:61 at 163 (4th ed. 2013).

62 This may be inferred from the drafters' reference to the ambiguity of the inference from the evidence to an "admission of liability." *See* FED. R. EVID. 409 advisory committee note.

beliefs to infer something short of responsibility, but still forming part of what is required to establish liability, is allowed. Thus, evidence concerning payment of medical expenses might be admissible if offered to prove defendant's control of an instrumentality, the identity of the apparatus causing the injury, or the defendant's status as an employer or principal of the person who caused the injury,[63] at least if these matters are disputed.[64] Under such an interpretation, the evidence would be admissible even if these facts help to establish "liability for the injury," as they almost always do. Arguably, however, admission on these theories would undermine the purpose of the rule.

A Word of Warning About Imprecise Terminology. The kind of conduct at issue here is sometimes called an "admission by conduct" or an "implied admission." In discussing Rule 409, for example, the advisory committee referred to the possibility of an inference from the evidence to an "admission of liability."[65] This kind of language is also tempting in connection with the evidence covered by Rule 407 (discussed below) for subsequent remedial measures, as well as evidence of flight and evidence of tampering with evidence (both discussed in the previous chapter).[66] One might be tempted to think of all such conduct as "implied admissions of fault."[67] To be sure, when used in connection with Rule 409 or 407, this language at least attempts to get at something important—the missing premise of the prohibition as stated in the Rule—but it is misleading nonetheless, because the kinds of conduct at issue are (typically) neither admissions nor implied. First, the person whose action is the subject of the proposed evidence rarely intends to communicate anything about fault, in which case it is not an admission at all, whether express or implied.[68] In any event, the rules are concerned with the relevance of the actor's beliefs, not his or her communications. (One can admit something that one does not believe, and one can believe something that one does not admit.) Second, the prohibitions of these rules cover inferences, not implications: the proponent is barred from inviting the fact-finder to infer beliefs from actions and (sometimes) other actions from those beliefs. But neither what the actor implies, if anything, nor what the fact-finder implies, if anything, matters in the present analysis.[69] To be sure, the *proponent* might be said to invite the indicated inference only "impliedly" rather than explicitly. So what is sometimes in this context called an "implied admission of fault" is actually an

---

[63] *Cf.* **§ 6.08** (discussing permissible uses of evidence of subsequent remedial measures).

[64] *See* DAVID P. LEONARD, THE NEW WIGMORE: SELECTED RULES OF LIMITED ADMISSIBILITY § 4.13 (rev. ed. 2002). If such matters are not disputed, a Rule 403 analysis suggests exclusion lest the evidence be used to prove what is prohibited. *See id.* at 531.

[65] *See* FED. R. EVID. 409 advisory committee note.

[66] *See, e.g.*, 2 MCCORMICK ON EVIDENCE §§ 263–267 (Kenneth S. Broun ed., 7th ed. 2013) (describing various categories of "Admission by Conduct," including flight, failure to call witnesses, destruction of evidence, offers of compromise, subsequent remedial measures, and voluntary payments of medical expenses). To be sure, these sections appear in a part of the McCormick treatise addressing hearsay, where the concept of an implied admission has considerable importance.

[67] *See, e.g.*, DAVID P. LEONARD, THE NEW WIGMORE: SELECTED RULES OF LIMITED ADMISSIBILITY § 1.6.1 at 15 (rev. ed. 2002) (referring to "a sort of implied recognition of fault" and to an "implied admission of fault").

[68] An admission is a special kind of assertion. The concept of assertion plays a critical role in the law of hearsay, as does the concept of an "implied assertion." *See* **§ 14.01**. Statements made during compromise negotiations may be assertions. *See* **§§ 6.10 et seq.**

[69] "To imply is to express something indirectly. For example, you might imply that it's time for a guest to leave by saying that you are getting tired. To infer is to surmise or conclude, especially from indirect evidence. For example, if you were to tell a guest that you're getting tired, the guest might infer that it's time to leave." http://grammarist.com/usage/imply-infer/ (last visited, Oct. 6, 2016).

express (or implied) invitation to infer beliefs about fault, and the concept of an "admission" is nowhere to be found.[70]

§ 6.06 Evidence of Apologies

Rule 409 generally does not exclude statements of fact made in relation to payments offered or made. But research into the social value of apologies has led to a growing trend toward encouraging such expressions.[71] Concerned that current evidence rules discourage people from apologizing or expressing regret over accidents that injure others, at least thirty-seven states have enacted laws specifically forbidding the use of some such statements.[72] Some of these statutes cover only medical malpractice cases and are intended to encourage positive interaction between the patient and the doctor and to reduce the inclination of disappointed patients to sue. Others are worded more broadly to cover apologies in any context. As a separate distinguishing feature, some of these statutes cover only the speaker's statements of sympathy or compassion, while others more broadly cover the speaker's acknowledgment of fault as well.[73]

Massachusetts passed the first of these statutes in 1986. It provides that "[s]tatements, writings, or benevolent gestures expressing sympathy or a general sense of benevolence relating to the pain, suffering, or death of a person involved in an accident and made to such person or to the family of such person" are not admissible as admissions of liability as recognitions of responsibility in civil cases.[74] The statute is broad in that it covers speakers other than health care providers, but narrow in that it does not cover statements acknowledging fault.[75] It can be quite difficult, however, to distinguish between acknowledgements of fault and expressions of compassion.[76]

Connecticut's statute, passed in 2005, provides broader coverage for acknowledgments of fault and is an example of a statute aimed at issues of medical care:

> In any civil action brought by an alleged victim of an unanticipated outcome of medical care, or in any arbitration proceeding related to such civil action, any and all statements, affirmations, gestures or conduct expressing apology, fault, sympathy, commiseration, condolence, compassion or a general sense of benevolence that are made by a health care provider or an employee of a health care provider to the alleged victim, a relative of the alleged victim or a

---

[70] *See* DAVID P. LEONARD, THE NEW WIGMORE: SELECTED RULES OF LIMITED ADMISSIBILITY § 2.2 at 132 & § 4.2 at 453 n.1 (rev. ed. 2002) (making similar points in the contexts of evidence of subsequent remedial measures and evidence of payment of medical expenses).

[71] A great deal of "therapeutic jurisprudence" scholarship has been published in recent years. *See, e.g.*, THE PASSIONS OF THE LAW (Susan A. Bandes ed., 1999); PRACTICING THERAPEUTIC JURISPRUDENCE: LAW AS A HELPING PROFESSION (Dennis P. Stolle et al. ed., 2000); Laura E. Little, *Negotiating the Tangle of Law and Emotion*, 86 CORNELL L. REV. 974 (2001); Symposium, *The Role of Forgiveness in the Law*, 27 FORDHAM URB. L.J. 1351 (2000).

[72] *Apology Inadmissibility Laws: Summary of State Legislation*, American Medical Association Advocacy Resource Center (2012).

[73] For discussion of the various proposals, *see* Jonathan R. Cohen, *Legislating Apology: The Pros and Cons*, 70 U. CINN. L. REV. 819, 830–833 (2002). *See generally*, Aviva Orenstein, *Apology Excepted: Incorporating a Feminist Analysis into Evidence Policy Where You'd Least Expect It*, 28 SOUTHWESTERN L. REV. 221 (1999).

[74] MASS. ANN. LAWS ch. 233, § 23D. *See also* CAL. EVID. CODE § 1160; FLA. STAT. Ann. § 90.4026; TEX. CIV. PRAC. & REM. CODE § 18.061.

[75] *See, e.g.*, CAL. EVID. CODE § 1160 ("A statement of fault, however, which is part of, or in addition to, [the expression of sympathy or other benevolence] shall not be inadmissible pursuant to this section.").

[76] If an expression of fault is made in the context of an effort to compromise a disputed claim, it will be excluded by Rule 408, covering compromise negotiations. *See* **§ 6.10**.

representative of the alleged victim and that relate to the discomfort, pain, suffering, injury or death of the alleged victim as a result of the unanticipated outcome of medical care shall be inadmissible as evidence of an admission of liability or as evidence of an admission against interest.[77]

Research is being conducted to determine whether these relatively new statutes have the intended positive effects and whether they have unintended negative side effects.[78] To date, there is no federal rule protecting apologies unless such statements occur in the context of settlement negotiations.[79]

C. EVIDENCE OF SUBSEQUENT REMEDIAL MEASURES

§ 6.07 The Subsequent Remedial Measures Rule [FRE 407]

Under common-law doctrine, evidence that the defendant made repairs or took other remedial measures after an accident or incident that, if taken before the event, would have made the accident less likely to occur, is not admissible as evidence of a recognition of or belief in fault to prove negligence or other culpable conduct in regard to that accident or incident.[80]

Example

The plaintiff, who slipped and fell on the defendant's stairs, alleges that the defendant was negligent in not providing a handrail and in allowing the stairs to become slick and worn. After the accident, the defendant added an abrasive surface and a handrail to the stairs in question. Evidence of the defendant's subsequent improvements is not admissible to prove the defendant's recognition or awareness that he or she was negligent at the time of the accident.

Federal Rule of Evidence 407 provides a typical formulation of the subsequent remedial measures rule: "When measures are taken that would have made an earlier injury or harm less likely to occur, evidence of the subsequent measures is not admissible to prove: negligence; culpable conduct; a defect in a product or its design; or a need for a warning or instruction."[81] A majority of states have adopted rules based on Rule 407, and even those states that have yet to adopt an evidence code or have addressed the subsequent remedial measures problem with different statutory language usually follow the policy of the Federal Rule.[82]

The subsequent remedial measures rule often applies in cases in which a defendant made physical repairs after an accident. It is not, however, limited to evidence of repairs

---

77 CONN. GEN. STAT. § 52–184d.

78 *See, e.g.*, Jennifer Robbennolt, *Apologies and Legal Settlement: An Empirical Examination*, 102 MICH. L. REV. 460 (2003); Jennifer K. Robbennolt, *Apologies and Settlement Levers*, 3 J. EMPIRICAL L. STUD. 333 (2006); Richard C. Boothman, et al., *A Better Approach to Medical Malpractice Claims? The University of Michigan Experience*, 2 JOURNAL OF HEALTH & LIFE SCIENCES LAW 125 (2009); Gabriel H. Teninbaum, *How Medical Apology Programs Harm Patients*, 15 CHAPMAN L. REV. 307 (2011).

79 *See* **§ 6.10**.

80 *See* 2 WIGMORE ON EVIDENCE § 283 (Chadbourn rev. 1979).

81 FED. R. EVID. 407. Notice, however, that Rule 407 omits a crucial part of the common-law principle that specifies the prohibited line of inference. *See* **§ 6.08**.

82 Only Rhode Island has rejected the policy of the Federal Rule in favor of a rule freely admitting evidence of subsequent remedial measures. R.I. R. EVID. 407. For a review of the states' provisions, see DAVID P. LEONARD, THE NEW WIGMORE: SELECTED RULES OF LIMITED ADMISSIBILITY §§ 2.3.4, 2.5 (rev. ed. 2002).

or physical improvements. Any remedial measure that would have made the accident less likely to occur falls under the scope of the rule. For example, if a defendant fired a careless employee who caused an accident, the termination of the employee is a remedial measure that is inadmissible to prove the employer's recognition of the employee's negligence in causing the accident. A change in manufacturing procedures, in training of employees, or in the design of a product can also be a remedial measure within the meaning of the rule. A manufacturer's recall letter to product purchasers can qualify. So, too, can a hospital's post-accident self-evaluative study made to find ways to improve patient care.[83]

The rule applies to some conduct where the underlying claim was caused by a crime or an intentional tort by a third person and the defendant is being sued for breach of a duty to protect the plaintiff. For instance, in a sexual harassment case against an employer based on the conduct of a middle manager, evidence that senior management required the alleged perpetrator to attend sensitivity training would constitute a remedial measure. A store that erects bright lights in a parking lot after customers are mugged similarly engages in remedial measures. In neither case was the original problem an accident.

The primary purpose of the remedial measures rule is to encourage defendants to make needed improvements or repairs by removing the danger that evidence of improvements or repairs will be used against them in litigation. Though the real-world validity of this rationale has not been sufficiently tested, it is generally assumed that the absence of an exclusionary rule might discourage the taking of precautionary measures and thus increase overall societal harm.

The rule also has secondary purposes. One purpose is to exclude evidence with doubtful relevancy or that, even if relevant, has very low probative value. Even so, the conventional view is that subsequent remedial measures are relevant to infer the repairing party's recognition of responsibility or fault.[84] The need of a special rule arises precisely because relevance is plausible. Thus, in the example given above, it is likely that at least one motivation behind defendant's improvement of the stairway was the defendant's belief that the stairway was not sufficiently safe at the time of the accident. Because the defendant, as the owner of the stairs, is likely in a position to know whether the stairs are safe, the defendant's conduct is relevant.[85] But the fact that a defendant decided to take additional precautionary measures after the accident often does not provide the jury with much assistance in deciding whether the defendant was negligent

---

[83] *See id.*, § 2.3.4, *see also id.* at § 5.6.1.

[84] Wigmore wrote:

> The opponent's conduct in taking precautions to prevent an apprehended injury, or to remedy one already inflicted, may sometimes indicate a consciousness of wrong, in respect either to the party's identity as the wrongdoer or to his culpability in doing the act.

2 WIGMORE ON EVIDENCE § 282 at 146 (Chadbourn rev. 1979). It is often said that the conduct constitutes an "admission" of fault, *see* FED. R. EVID. 407 advisory committee note, but we do not use that term here because an admission is an intentional act, and intent to acknowledge is not essential to the exclusionary rule. *See* **§ 6.05** (paragraph entitled, "A Word of Warning About Imprecise Terminology").

[85] The existence of alternative explanations for the defendant's conduct (such as that defendant improved the stairs merely in order to make them more attractive) does not make the evidence irrelevant for its offered purpose unless under the circumstances it would be irrational for the jury to conclude that the defendant was motivated at least in part by a belief in the stairway's danger. *See* DAVID P. LEONARD, THE NEW WIGMORE: SELECTED RULES OF LIMITED ADMISSIBILITY § 2.2 (rev. ed., 2002).

at the time of the accident. As one court put it, it is fallacious to assume that "because the world gets wiser as it gets older, therefore it was foolish before."[86]

Another purpose of the rule is to promote fairness to the repairing party. It seems unfair to a party that engaged in useful, accident-preventing conduct to turn that conduct against the party in subsequent litigation.[87]

§ 6.08 Remedial Measures Evidence That Falls Outside the Prohibition

The subsequent remedial measures rule excludes evidence of safety measures only when the evidence is offered for the forbidden purpose of showing negligence (or culpable conduct, etc.) through an inference *that the conduct reflects the actor's belief that the previous condition was the result of negligence (or culpable conduct, etc.)*. To be sure, this is not what the rule says, but it is how it is rightly interpreted: only this particular line of inference is barred.[88] Therefore, subsequent remedial measures evidence is admissible, as far as Rule 407 is concerned, when offered for any purpose other than showing negligence, culpable conduct, or other fact specifically mentioned in the rule, by means of reasoning from such inferred belief of responsibility. As illustrations, the Rule lists using evidence of subsequent remedial measures to prove "ownership, control, or the feasibility of precautionary measures" as well as "impeachment."[89] These uses are discussed below.

If evidence of remedial measures is relevant both to the issue of the party's recognition of negligence, defect, etc., and to some other issue, such as whether the measures were feasible, then the trial judge must make a Rule 403 determination whether the probative value of the evidence when offered for its permissible purpose is substantially outweighed by its possible prejudicial effect. For this purpose, potential prejudice includes the possibility that the fact-finder will use the subsequent measures for the line of inference forbidden by Rule 407. If the trial judge admits the evidence, the objecting party has the right to a limiting instruction informing the jury that the testimony may not be used as evidence of the actor's belief that the previous condition was defective, negligently created, or negligently maintained, depending on the allegation in the case.[90]

Even if offered for a permissible purpose (other than impeachment), in federal court subsequent remedial measures evidence will only be admissible for these purposes if the

---

[86] Hart v. Lancashire & Yorkshire Ry. Co., 21 L.T.R. (N.S.) 261, 263 (1869).

[87] *See* 2 CHRISTOPHER B. MUELLER & LAIRD C. KIRKPATRICK, FEDERAL EVIDENCE § 4:49 (4th ed. 2013); 23 CHARLES A. WRIGHT & KENNETH W. GRAHAM, JR., FEDERAL PRACTICE AND PROCEDURE: EVIDENCE § 5282 at 96 (1980).

[88] The rule does not mention the particular prohibited line of inference to liability, but the missing content may be gleaned from the clarifications in the advisory committee note. *See* FED. R. EVID. 407 advisory committee note ("The rule incorporates conventional doctrine which excludes evidence of subsequent remedial measures as proof of an *admission* of fault. . . . In effect, it rejects the suggested inference that fault is *admitted*.") (emphasis supplied). To be sure, admitting something is an intentional communication, and it is rare that someone who makes such repairs actually intends to communicate anything by making the repairs, even if the party feels responsible for the previous injury. The actual prohibited inference is to the repairing party's belief in responsibility, and from that to a belief that the former condition was defective or negligently maintained.

[89] FED. R. EVID. 407.

[90] *See* FED. R. EVID. 105 (providing that on request, the court "shall restrict the evidence to its proper scope and instruct the jury accordingly"). *See generally* **§ 3.09**.

issue on which the evidence is offered is "disputed." Most states follow the same rule. Generally, courts have held that this requirement applies to all alternate uses of subsequent remedial measures evidence, whether or not the purpose at issue is listed in the rule, with the exception of impeachment. This is a wise position, as there is no principled reason to risk discouraging repair conduct and potential prejudice to the defendant when the evidence is offered on an undisputed point.[91]

Also, a question arises whether the subsequent remedial measures rule only excludes evidence of action taken *after* the accident at issue occurred. State rules that track the language of the original Federal Rule 407 provide for exclusion when measures are taken "after an event." Suppose the plaintiff is injured in an automobile accident and brings a product liability action against the automobile's manufacturer alleging defective design of the braking system. The plaintiff learns that after she bought the car, but *before* the accident occurred, the defendant altered the design of its braking system in a way that would have prevented the plaintiff's accident. The plaintiff argues that the exclusionary rule should not apply because the "event" at issue was the accident, and the design change was made before the accident. Although the literal language of the rule supports the plaintiff, some courts have held that the exclusionary rule applies, even if the remedial measure was not taken after the accident at issue.[92] Others, perhaps a majority, have held that for the exclusionary rule to apply, the remedial conduct must have been undertaken after the accident that gave rise to the action.[93]

If the primary purpose of the rule is to encourage remedial measures, thus reducing accidents, it is difficult to discern why it should matter whether or not the accident in question occurred after the remedial measure is taken. Especially if *some* accident has already occurred, or where the occurrence of accidents is a reasonably foreseeable event, application of the rule would encourage parties to take remedial measures without concern that doing so will be used against them. If the policy behind the rule is to prevail, it is difficult to identify a meaningful distinction between post-accident measures and pre-accident measures. On the other hand, if the accident happens after a repair has been initiated, there is no danger of deterring that repair because it already happened. Applying the rule to such cases will result in a windfall to the defendant and a loss of arguably relevant evidence. Moreover, there is little evidence that the exclusionary rule is needed in defective product cases as a means of encouraging the taking of remedial measures. It seems unlikely that a product manufacturer would forgo the remedial

---

[91] There is no requirement that the credibility of witnesses be "disputed." Whereas it is the choice of the party protected by the rule whether to dispute feasibility, ownership, or control, that party does not control the decision whether to impeach that party's witnesses. The party would not stipulate that its own witness is not credible.

[92] *See, e.g.*, Petree v. Victor Fluid Power, Inc., 831 F.2d 1191, 1197–98 (3d Cir. 1987) (in product liability action, trial court properly excluded evidence that after defendant sold machine at issue, but before plaintiff suffered injury, defendant added warning decal to machine; court rested decision on policy purpose of rule, holding that policy is "equally as supportive of exclusion of safety measures taken before someone is injured by a newly manufactured product. . . ."); Mills v. Beech Aircraft Corp., 886 F.2d 758, 763 (5th Cir. 1989) (claim that rule only applies to measures taken in response to accident at issue rejected).

[93] *See, e.g.*, Chase v. General Motors Corp., 856 F.2d 17, 21–22 (4th Cir. 1988) (holding rule inapplicable where automobile manufacturer changed brake design after sale of car at issue but before accident occurred); Roberts v. Harnischfeger Corp., 901 F.2d 42, 44 n.1 (5th Cir. 1989) (holding Rule 407 inapplicable where change in policy concerning equipment sold along with crane occurred one month before accident); Arceneaux v. Texaco, Inc., 623 F.2d 924, 928 (5th Cir. 1980) (holding Rule 407 inapplicable where accident occurred after design change; but trial court did not err in excluding evidence because it was irrelevant under circumstances of case).

measure solely to avoid liability in one case. More likely is that the manufacturer would take the measure in order to avoid future liability in many cases.[94]

In any event, a 1997 amendment to Federal Rule 407 attempted to clarify that the rule only applies to remedial measures taken after the event at issue in the case.[95] Even if this clarification is accepted by the courts, evidence that does not fit the temporal requirement might still be excluded under Rule 403.[96] This suggestion poses the difficult question whether the Rule 403 dangers embrace policy considerations such as encouraging desirable non-litigation activity. By the usual analysis of Rule 403, the dangers therein articulated relate to the truth-finding function of the court, not to the attainment of extraneous social policies that would compete with verdict accuracy (other than the conservation of litigation resources). Of course, the phrase "unfair prejudice" is sufficiently flexible that one could put almost any content into it—e.g., arguing that anything that is undesirable (for whatever reason) that adversely affects a party is unfairly prejudicial. But this would be a stretch, since the jury is not charged to pursue such policies.[97] Alternatively, a court could rely on the low probative value of the subsequent remedial measure to conclude that it is not worth the time and effort to sort out its implications.[98]

Evidence Offered to Show Ownership or Control

Evidence of subsequent remedial measures is admissible when it is offered to show that the defendant owned or controlled the instrument of injury rather than to show a belief that the prior condition was defective or the result of negligence, but only if the matter of ownership or control is disputed.

---

[94] For discussion of the lack of empirical support for the incentive effects of the exclusionary rule, see DAVID P. LEONARD, THE NEW WIGMORE: SELECTED RULES OF LIMITED ADMISSIBILITY § 2.4.1 (rev. ed. 2002).

[95] As amended in 1997, Rule 407 provided for exclusion only if the remedial measures were taken "after an injury or harm allegedly caused by an event." The rule, however, still does not say that the injury or harm after which the measures are taken must be the same injury or harm that is the subject of the present suit. That was, however, clearly the intention. See FED. R. EVID. 407 note re 1997 amendment ("[T]he words 'an injury or harm allegedly caused by' were added to clarify that the rule applies only to changes made after the occurrence that produced the damages giving rise to the action.") In the restyling, even the words "allegedly caused by an event" were dropped, but the intent remains unchanged. For detailed discussion of the "after an event" problem, *see* DAVID P. LEONARD, THE NEW WIGMORE: SELECTED RULES OF LIMITED ADMISSIBILITY § 2.6.4 (rev. ed. 2002).

[96] *See* Bogosian v. Mercedes-Benz of North America, Inc., 104 F.3d 472, 480–81 (1st Cir. 1997) (though Rule 407 does not apply to post-manufacture, pre-accident design modifications, such evidence may still be excluded under Rule 403).

[97] *See* FED. R. EVID. 403 advisory committee note (" 'Unfair prejudice' within its context means an undue tendency to suggest decision on an improper basis, commonly, though not necessarily, an emotional one.").

[98] A similar issue arises with respect to the question whether the Rule applies to measures taken by non-parties. Some courts have held that remedial measures by third parties fall outside the rule. *See* TLT-Babcock, Inc. v. Emerson Elec. Co., 33 F.3d 397, 399 (4th Cir. 1994) (evidence of subsequent remedial measures properly admitted when performed by third parties); Buchanna v. Diehl Machine, Inc., 98 F.3d 366, 370 (8th Cir. 1996) (Rule 407 does not preclude evidence of remedial measures by nonparties, since admitting such evidence does not deter safety measures); *But see In re* Air Crash Disaster, 86 F.3d 498, 528–30 (6th Cir. 1996) (defendant Northwest not entitled to put in evidence of its own safety improvements on aircraft to show that manufacturer's original version was unsafe; Rule 407 not limited to remedial measures by party who originally manufactured product). For discussion of whether the acts of non-parties are covered by the exclusionary principle, see DAVID P. LEONARD, THE NEW WIGMORE: SELECTED RULES OF LIMITED ADMISSIBILITY § 2.6.3 (rev. ed. 2002).

Example

Plaintiff is injured by a truck driven by a construction worker. A dispute arises about whether the truck was owned by the worker who was driving it or by the construction company that employed the worker. Evidence that the company subsequently had the truck repaired would be admissible to show the company's ownership and control of the truck.

Huxol v. Nickell[99] presents a typical case of the use of remedial measures to show control. The plaintiff sought to recover for injuries sustained when he fell into a hole at a construction site. The general contractor and the subcontractor each took the position that the other was responsible for safety measures at the site. This opened the door to the admission of evidence that the general contractor erected a barrier around the hole after the accident.[100] Because the evidence of the actor's conduct is not offered to prove that the actor's belief that the condition was unsafe, but only to prove that the condition was under the actor's control, the evidence is not excluded by the rule. In a case such as *Huxol*, the evidence is offered to prove the existence of a *duty*, not whether that duty was *breached*. Nevertheless, the permissible reasoning is only subtly different from the forbidden "negligence or culpable conduct" reasoning. Therefore, counsel should be prepared to request a limiting instruction or, in cases raising serious questions of unfair prejudice from the jury's improper use of the evidence, to ask that the evidence be excluded under Rule 403 or its state equivalent.

Evidence Offered to Explain Exhibit Illustrating Scene of Accident

In appropriate situations, evidence revealing that safety measures were taken after an accident will be admissible because it is offered, not to show a recognition of negligence, but to prevent the jury from being confused by an exhibit that depicts the scene of the accident after the measures were put into place.

Example

In an action to recover for injuries caused by falling down stairs, the plaintiff claims the defendant was negligent in maintaining stairs that were slick, worn, and had no handrail. At trial, the defendant introduces a photograph of the stairs to show that the stairs were not slick and worn. The photograph shows a handrail that was installed after the accident. The plaintiff is entitled to point out that the handrail was installed after the accident, in order to give the jury an accurate picture of the condition of the stairs at the time of the accident.[101]

---

[99] Huxol v. Nickell, 473 P.2d 90 (Kan. 1970). *See also* Clausen v. Sea-3, Inc., 21 F.3d 1181, 1191 (1st Cir. 1994) (holding that in personal injury suit, admission of evidence of subsequent remedial measures undertaken on ramp where plaintiff slipped and fell was not plain error because control over ramp was unresolved issue and evidence was admissible for limited purpose of showing that defendant controlled ramp area at time of accident); Eoff v. Hal & Charlie Peterson Found., 811 S.W.2d 187, 197 (Tex. App. 1991) (excluding evidence of sign subsequently placed in hospital emergency room notifying patients that physicians were not employees of hospital, where ownership of emergency room was uncontroverted, and where agency and control were issues in establishing liability).

[100] *See also* Wallner v. Kitchens of Sara Lee, Inc., 419 F.2d 1028 (7th Cir. 1969) (holding that evidence that after accident, defendant installed metal guard on conveyor, added drain lines, and took other steps that would have prevented injuries admissible to prove defendant was responsible for repair and daily maintenance of conveyor, where there was dispute concerning who was responsible for maintenance).

[101] The same principle would apply if the jury had taken a view of the scene of the accident. On jury views, *see* **§ 12.10**.

In such a case, the evidence that the handrail was installed after the accident is admissible on the theory that it is not being used to prove defendant's recognition of prior negligence or culpable conduct, but merely to prevent the jury from being misled or confused by the defendant's evidence about the condition of the stairs at the time of the accident. The defendant is entitled to a limiting instruction telling the jury not to use the testimony as evidence of a recognition of negligence.

This example illustrates a recurring phenomenon. Notice that the defendant, the party ostensibly protected by the rule in this context, introduces evidence that is misleading, thinking that the defendant can then object under the rule to the evidence that plaintiff must present in order to correct the misleading impression. This kind of deceptive use of the rule is called the (ostensibly protected) party's using the rule "as a sword rather than a shield." Courts are generally sensitive to such shenanigans and will deprive the party of the protection of the rule when necessary to avoid misleading the jury.[102]

May the plaintiff open this avenue of admissibility by offering a photograph that shows subsequent repairs and then offer evidence that the defendant made repairs after the accident? Clearly, this should not be permitted in cases in which the plaintiff's photograph does not serve to give the jury a clearer understanding of the physical facts at the time of the accident than could otherwise be obtained.[103] However, the issue should be resolved, not by an absolute rule excluding photographs showing repairs when they are offered by plaintiffs, but by a flexible rule that weighs whether the evidence is needed for some purpose other than showing defendant's recognition of negligence.

For example, if a photograph of the scene taken after the repairs were made is the only means available to help the jury visualize how the accident occurred, then the photograph should be admitted, with a limiting instruction, even if it unavoidably shows the existence of repairs.[104] If, however, the condition of the scene at the time of the accident can be satisfactorily illustrated in some other fashion, then the photograph should be excluded under Rule 403. For example, if the plaintiff has access to photographs or other evidence that adequately illustrates the scene without revealing that safety measures have been taken after the accident, then a photograph showing the safety measures should be excluded. Similarly, if, without distorting the condition of the scene at the time of the accident, the photograph could be cropped so that it does not show the subsequent repairs, then the photo should be cropped to avoid prejudice.[105]

Evidence Offered to Show Feasibility of Precautionary Measures

Although evidence of subsequent remedial measures is not admissible to show a recognition of prior negligence or culpable conduct, it is admissible to show that the remedial measures were feasible, if the defendant disputes feasibility.

---

[102] *See, e.g.*, Wood v. Morbark Industries, 70 F.3d 1201, 1208 (11th Cir. 1995) (holding that defendant took "unfair advantage" of an *in limine* ruling precluding evidence of subsequent remedies measures by introducing testimony suggesting that the product in question continues to be used unchanged, so that defendant opened the door to rebuttal evidence by plaintiff showing the changes).

[103] *See* Gignoux v. St. Louis Public Serv. Co., 180 S.W.2d 784, 785–87 (Mo. Ct. App. 1944), and cases cited therein.

[104] *See, e.g.*, Lebrecht v. Bethlehem Steel Corp., 402 F.2d 585, 592 (2d Cir. 1968) (plaintiff entitled to put in photo of site of accident, even though it showed planking added as safety improvement; photo illustrated conditions at time of accident and jury was instructed to ignore added planking).

[105] This is an application of the Rule 403 analysis prescribed in *Old Chief*. *See* **§ 5.03**.

Example

The plaintiff was injured while operating a drill press in the defendant's plant. The plaintiff claims that the drill press should have been protected by a finger guard. The defendant asserts that installing a finger guard was not feasible; the workers would not have been able to operate the drill press properly because a finger guard would have interfered with their access to it. Evidence that the defendant subsequently installed a finger guard would be admissible to show feasibility.

Most claims that remedial measures were infeasible do not involve assertions that it would have been physically impossible to take the proposed safety measure. Rather, the defendant concedes that safety measures were physically possible, but claims that they would be so costly or burdensome that they were not advisable or required by ordinary prudence. There is a thin line between offering evidence of the subsequent remedial measure to prove that it was feasible to take those steps (and thus that the defendant had a duty to consider taking them)—allowed under the rule—and offering the evidence to prove that the defendant was aware that there was a duty to correct it sooner—not allowed under the rule. Ultimately, the court must determine whether the evidence has sufficient probative value on the issue of feasibility, and whether the jury is likely to understand and abide by a limiting instruction.

Suppose the defendant claims that it was not negligent in failing to take remedial measures because such safety measures were so costly that no prudent person would undertake them. In that instance, one could argue that feasibility is controverted and the rule permits the admission of evidence to rebut the claim that the measures were impracticable because of cost. Some courts so hold. For example, in *Whitehead v. St. Joe Lead Co.*,[106] the court stated that evidence showing that, after the plaintiff's injury, the defendant had affixed warning labels to its product should be received as evidence that warnings were not too costly, and hence that precautions were feasible under the circumstances.

Even with such a broad conception of what it means to dispute "feasibility," it is possible to deny liability without controverting feasibility. For example, when the defendant claims that the lack of safety devices was not the cause of the plaintiff's injury, or that the need for safety devices could not have been foreseen at the time of the accident, then it is possible to defend against a negligence claim without controverting the feasibility of safety devices. The defendant should also be able to avoid controverting the issue of feasibility by conceding that additional safety measures were economically feasible, while maintaining that its original measures were adequate and acceptable.[107]

Some courts apply an even broader definition of "feasibility." For example, in *Anderson v. Malloy*,[108] the defendant did not contend that additional safety measures

---

[106] Whitehead v. St. Joe Lead Co., 729 F.2d 238, 247 n.6 (3d Cir. 1984).

[107] *See* Grenada Steel Indus. v. Alabama Oxygen Co., 695 F.2d 883, 888 (5th Cir. 1983)(noting that although feasibility may "almost always" be in question in design defect cases, a manufacturer does not necessarily have to claim that another design was impracticable, but "only that it adopted an acceptable one").

[108] Anderson v. Malloy, 700 F.2d 1208, 1213 (8th Cir. 1983). *See* Lewis v. Cotton Belt Route-Saint Louis Southwestern Ry., 576 N.E.2d 918, 929–30 (Ill. Ct. App. 1991) (allowing evidence that injured lone worker was replaced by worker plus spotter, to impeach and controvert defense witness's testimony that using spotter was not feasible, although witness apparently used word "feasible" to mean "not necessary under the circumstances" rather than "impossible"). *See also* Ross v. Black & Decker, Inc., 977 F.2d 1178, 1184 (7th Cir. 1992) (holding that defendant's "tactical error" in failing to stipulate feasibility of remedial measures makes

would have been too costly, but merely claimed that they would have been superfluous. The principal plaintiff had been raped by a stranger while alone in a room in a motel owned by the defendants. She had opened the door in response to a knock by the assailant, who spoke to her in a muffled voice that she thought was her husband's. She claimed that the motel should have installed peepholes and chain locks on the doors, and sought to introduce evidence that after the rape the defendants did install these devices. The trial judge excluded the evidence, and on appeal, the Eighth Circuit reversed, holding that the evidence was admissible.

The Eighth Circuit alluded to certain testimony by the defendant, Malloy, one of the owners of the motel whom the plaintiffs had called as an adverse witness. He testified that he had talked to the village police chief about security measures for the hotel. According to his testimony, the officer had told him that because the motel had six-foot picture windows right next to the doors (through which the guests could look to see who was knocking) peepholes were unnecessary and that chains would be "false security." In the view of the Eighth Circuit, this testimony raised an issue of the "feasibility" of peepholes and chains. The court held that "feasible" means not only "possible," but also "capable of being utilized . . . or dealt with successfully." For the defense witness to say that peepholes and chains would only provide a false sense of security was to say that they could not be "utilized successfully," and thus to challenge the feasibility of the security measure.

The dissenting opinion by Judge Gibson questioned the majority's definition of feasibility. In his opinion, a claim that a safety measure was infeasible had to be a claim that adopting the safety measure would be impossible or overly costly. Here, the defendants did not claim that the safety measures would not be feasible, only that they would not be desirable.[109]

The *Anderson* majority takes a very broad view of the concept of feasibility, making it more difficult for a defendant to claim that its failure to use certain safety measures was not negligent without simultaneously opening the door to an assertion that the defendant has challenged the feasibility of the safety measures. If the defendant claims that a reasonable person would not have used the safety measures because they were impracticable or too costly, then the defendant has challenged feasibility under the *Whitehead* line of cases. If the defendant claims that a reasonable person would not have used the safety measures because they were not necessary, then the defendant has challenged feasibility under the more debatable *Anderson* approach.

Other courts have taken a significantly narrower view of disputing feasibility, holding that a defendant can maintain that safety measures were not necessary without disputing feasibility. In *Tuer v. McDonald*,[110] an opinion that gives an extensive treatment of the problem, the highest court of Maryland noted the definition used in *Anderson v. Malloy* but preferred a different approach. The plaintiff sued for medical malpractice, alleging that the defendants should have continued administering Heparin,

post-manufacture remedial measures admissible); Wilkinson v. Hyatt Corp., 1993 WL 121287 at *2–3 (E.D. La. 1993) (holding that plaintiff may introduce evidence of subsequent security changes when report by defendant's expert witness stated defendant should not be expected to do what society itself cannot do, to prevent all crime). *See generally* Southland Enter., Inc. v. United States, 24 Cl. Ct. 596, 603 (1991) (discussing feasibility and allowing evidence that Park Service redesigned road well after plaintiff completed construction, where parties contested feasibility).

109 Anderson v. Malloy, 700 F.2d 1208, 215–16 (Gibson, dissenting).

110 Tuer v. McDonald, 701 A.2d 1101 (Md. 1997).

an anti-coagulant, in the hours before the decedent's scheduled surgery. The hospital changed its procedure after the surgery to mandate the administration of the drug when surgery was delayed. Despite defense testimony that it would have been "unsafe" to continue administering the anti-coagulant, the court held that "feasibility" had not been raised as an issue, noting that the testimony did not "constitute an assertion that restarting of the Heparin was not feasible. It was feasible but not advisable. Thus, in the Maryland court's view, the word "feasible" should be taken to refer not to whether a measure was advisable but to whether the measure was practicable. Under that approach, a defendant can contest the safety or wisdom of an improvement without raising an issue of "feasibility" that opens the door to subsequent remedial measures evidence.

Similarly, in *Gauthier v. AMF, Inc.*,[111] the defendant conceded that the safety devices in question were technologically and economically feasible, but argued it had been justified in deciding that the questionable benefit of the device did not outweigh such factors as the consumer frustration that would arise from the inconvenience it caused. The Ninth Circuit held that this position did not constitute a challenge to the feasibility of the safety devices, and hence did not open the door to evidence that they had been installed later.[112]

Evidence Offered to Show Causation of Accident

Some courts have allowed the plaintiff to offer evidence of subsequent remedial measures to prove that the defendant's negligence was a cause of the injury or harm. In *Kuhn v. Illinois C.R.R.*,[113] for example, the plaintiff alleged that his property was damaged by emissions from smokestacks on the defendant's roundhouse. To prove causation, the plaintiff was allowed to offer evidence that after the smokestacks were heightened, the damages ceased. Even though admission risked unfair prejudice to the defendant, the evidence in *Kuhn* appears to have been highly probative of causation.[114]

Evidence Offered to Support or Defend Against Award of Punitive Damages

In some circumstances, evidence of subsequent remedial measures can be relevant either to demonstrate the appropriateness of punitive damages or show that the party's behavior does not justify such an award. While the conduct that warrants punitive

---

[111] Gauthier v. AMF, Inc., 788 F.2d 634, 637–38 (9th Cir. 1986), *amended on denial of reh'g*, 805 F.2d 337 (9th Cir. 1986).

[112] *See also In re* Joint Eastern Dist. and Southern Dist. Asbestos Litigation, 995 F.2d 343, 345 (2d Cir. 1993) (observing that raising feasibility is "not an open sesame whose mere invocation parts Rule 407 and ushers in evidence of subsequent repairs and remedies. . . . [T]o read it that casually will cause the exception to engulf the rule . . ."); Flaminio v. Honda Motor Co., 733 F.2d 463, 468 (7th Cir. 1984) (noting that in product liability action against motorcycle manufacturer alleging that motorcycle was defective because of "wobble" at high speed, defendants did not controvert feasibility of eliminating wobble; "[t]heir argument was that there is a tradeoff between wobble and 'weave,' and that in designing the model on which Flaminio was injured Japanese Honda had decided that weave was the greater danger because it occurs at high speeds and because the Gold Wing model . . . was designed for high speeds. The feasibility, as distinct from the net advantages, of reducing the danger of wobble was not in issue"); Phar-Mor, Inc. v. Goff, 594 So. 2d 1213, 1218 (Ala. 1992) (excluding photographs of baskets in store, stacked different way after plaintiff's slip-and-fall accident; feasibility of stacking baskets different was not controverted).

[113] Kuhn v. Illinois C. R. Co., 111 Ill.App. 323 (1903).

[114] *See also* George v. Morgan Construction Co., 389 F. Supp. 253, 264 (D. Pa. 1975) (holding evidence of post-accident change in mill design admissible to prove, inter alia, that condition at time of accident was proximate cause of accident).

damages is invariably "culpable conduct" within the meaning of the Rule, some cases have nonetheless admitted evidence relevant to an award of punitive damages.

For example, in one case the plaintiff was permitted to present evidence of subsequent remedial measures when the subsequent measure itself constituted the predicate for an award of punitive damages. In *Northern Indiana Public Service Co. v. G.V.K. Corp.*,[115] for example, the plaintiffs brought suit against a public utility following an explosion that occurred while the utility was excavating property. While preparing to excavate, a government biologist with whom the plaintiffs were working, asked defendant NIPSCO where the utilities were located on the property. NIPSCO responded by placing yellow flags over an active gas line. The employee who did so knew there were actually four active pipelines, however. The plaintiffs avoided the flagged pipeline but caused an explosion when they struck an unmarked line. Aside from the basic damage claim, the plaintiffs sued NIPSCO for fraud, alleging that after the explosion, the company sent an employee back to the property to move the existing flags and place a second row of flags marking an active pipeline. Over the defendant's objection, the court permitted the plaintiffs to present evidence of this post-accident activity. Though the evidence would not be admissible to prove liability for the initial damage to the property, the measures were the very act that arguably justified an award of punitive damages.[116] Other courts, insisting that punitive damages may only be awarded to punish the acts that constitute the cause of action for compensatory damages, reject such reasoning.[117] This difference in judicial opinions, however, concerns not evidence law itself, but rather the substantive law regarding punitive damages and whether such awards may be grounded on conduct that is not the basis of the plaintiff's cause of action.[118]

The defendant, on the other hand, may wish to present evidence of subsequent remedial measures to support an argument against punitive damages. This might be appropriate when, for example, the defendant seeks to prove that it acted in good faith, corrected the problem as soon as it came to its attention and did not possess a state of mind that could support an award of punitive damages.[119]

Evidence Offered in Strict Liability Cases

Before the 1997 amendments, the applicability of Rule 407 in strict liability cases was a matter of dispute. By its terms, Rule 407 only prohibited the use of remedial measures to show "negligence or culpable conduct." A minority of the courts took the position that because "negligence or culpable conduct" is not an issue in a strict liability action, the rule did not apply.[120] They reasoned that the policy of Rule 407 did not require

---

[115] Northern Ind. Pub. Serv. Co. v. G.V.K. Corp., 713 N.E.2d 842 (Ind. Ct. App. 1999).

[116] *Id.* at 849–50. The court also held that the evidence was admissible to impeach NIPSCO's account of the events before the accident and to prove the feasibility of precautionary measures. *Id.* at 849.

[117] *See, e.g.*, Burke v. Deere & Co., 6 F.3d 497, 506–07 (8th Cir. 1993) (holding evidence of defendant's post-sale conduct may not be basis for punitive damages in defective design case; finding abuse of discretion in admitting evidence of subsequent remedial measures to show defendant's state of mind in order to support a punitive damage award).

[118] Post-accident behavior that tampers with the evidence also raises issues, addressed elsewhere, about alternatives to admitting such evidence. *See* **§ 5.05** (subsection on "Evidence of a Party's Attempt to Withhold, Destroy, or Fabricate Evidence").

[119] *See, e.g.*, Swinton v. Potomac Corp., 270 F.3d 794 (9th Cir. 2001) (general principle of admissibility for this purpose approved, but holding that trial court's exclusion was justified under circumstances).

[120] *See* Robbins v. Farmers Union Grain Terminal Assn., 552 F.2d 788, 792–93 (8th Cir. 1977). *Accord* Unterburger v. Snow Co., 630 F.2d 599, 603 (8th Cir. 1980); Herndon v. Seven Bar Flying Serv., 716 F.2d 1322, 1331 (10th Cir. 1983). *But see* DeLuryea v. Winthrop Labs., 697 F.2d 222, 227–28 (8th Cir. 1983) (finding that

that it be extended to strict liability cases because the typical defendant in a strict liability case is a mass producer of goods that will have independent incentive to make repairs. Mass producers will not forgo making improvements, and thereby risk innumerable future lawsuits, merely to prevent evidence from being introduced in a lawsuit over an injury that occurred prior to the improvement.[121]

Other courts disagreed, holding that Rule 407 applied to strict liability actions.[122] For example, in *Gauthier v. AMF, Inc.*,[123] the court took issue with the public policy basis for decisions holding that Rule 407 did not apply, saying that "it is precisely the large manufacturers who are defendants in many product liability suits who are most likely to know about Rule 407 and be affected by the decision whether to apply it."[124] The court also apparently considered a strict liability claim that the defendant had marketed a defective product to be a claim of "culpable conduct" that fell within the language of original Rule 407.[125] The court noted that nearly all the circuits that had reached the issue had decided that Rule 407 applies to strict liability cases.[126]

In 1997, Rule 407 was amended, clarifying that the exclusionary provision applies in all three main kinds of product liability cases (manufacturing defect, design defect, and failure to warn cases) not necessarily based on negligence.

Evidence Offered to Impeach a Witness

Evidence of subsequent remedial measures is sometimes admitted on the theory that it is offered not to show the repairing party's recognition of earlier negligence, defect, or inadequacy of warning, but rather to impeach a witness.[127]

Example

After falling down a flight of stairs, the plaintiff sues the owner of the stairs, claiming that the owner negligently maintained the stairs by allowing them to

---

change in warning label on medicine was similar to a negligence standard within the meaning of Rule 407, and should have been excluded; modifying position of the Eight Circuit); *see also* Werner v. Upjohn Co., 628 F.2d 848, 858 (4th Cir. 1980).

[121] *See* Robbins v. Farmers Union Grain Terminal Assn., 552 F.2d 788, 792–93 (8th Cir. 1977). The California Supreme Court reached the same conclusion in applying California's subsequent remedial measures rule. Ault v. International Harvester, 528 P.2d 1148 (Cal.1974).

[122] *See* Raymond v. Raymond Corp., 938 F.2d 1518, 1522 (1st Cir. 1991) (holding that Rule 407 applies to strict liability cases; noting that majority of sister circuits apply rule to strict liability cases); Cann v. Ford Motor Co., 658 F.2d 54 (2d Cir. 1981); Josephs v. Harris Corp., 677 F.2d 985, 990 (3d Cir. 1982); Werner v. Upjohn Co., 628 F.2d 848 (4th Cir. 1980); Grenada Steel Indus. v. Alabama Oxygen Co., 695 F.2d 883 (5th Cir. 1983); Bauman v. Volkswagenwerk Aktiengesellschaft, 621 F.2d 230 (6th Cir. 1980); Flaminio v. Honda Motor Co., 733 F.2d 463 (7th Cir. 1984); Gauthier v. AMF, Inc., 788 F.2d 634 (9th Cir. 1986), *amended on denial of reh'g*, 805 F.2d 337 (9th Cir. 1986); Wood v. Morbark Indus., Inc., 70 F.3d 1201, 1206–07 (11th Cir. 1995) (applying Rule 407 in strict products liability cases when plaintiff alleges that product is defective because design is unreasonably dangerous).

[123] Gauthier v. AMF, Inc., 788 F.2d 634 (9th Cir. 1986), *amended on denial of reh'g*, 805 F.2d 337 (9th Cir. 1986).

[124] *Id.* at 637.

[125] *Id.* at 636–37.

[126] *Id.* at 636, and authorities cited therein.

[127] *See, e.g.*, Dollar v. Long Mfg., N.C., Inc., 561 F.2d 613, 618 (5th Cir. 1977) (holding that, although letter warning of dangers of product was subsequent remedial measure, it should have been received to impeach trial testimony of expert who wrote it); Rimkus v. Northwest Colo. Ski Corp., 706 F.2d 1060, 1065 (10th Cir. 1983) (alternative holding) (evidence that rocks on which plaintiff was injured while skiing were subsequently marked with bamboo poles admissible to impeach defense witness who testified that rocks were visible for 200 feet).

become slick and worn. At trial, the defendant testifies that the stairs had an "excellent" surface at the time of the plaintiff's fall and that the surface would "never need to be replaced." This testimony opens the door to evidence that, shortly after the accident, the defendant covered the stairs with a more abrasive surface.[128] In theory, the testimony is offered not to show the defendant's recognition of negligence at the time of the injury but to impeach the defendant's credibility as a witness by showing that the defendant engaged in conduct that is inconsistent with her testimony or that the defendant attempted to mislead the jury with the testimony. Thus, the evidence impeaches the witness by contradiction; the witness's own prior behavior evidences facts different from those to which the witness has testified, casting doubt on the credibility of the witness's testimony.

The rule that evidence of subsequent remedial measures can be used for impeachment purposes opens large potential gaps in the exclusionary rule and, if interpreted too broadly, threatens to destroy the exclusionary principle. To be sure, the evidence should be admissible when the defendant has taken unfair advantage by presenting testimony that creates a misleading impression. That is true when the defendant testifies as in the example above, or has volunteered that she never made any changes to the instrumentality of the accident after its occurrence. In such instances, the plaintiff should be permitted to offer evidence to neutralize the defendant's unfair advantage.

If, however, the defendant merely testifies that the instrumentality was safe or in "normal condition" at the time of the accident, does this open the door to allowing evidence of the subsequent remedial measure? If it does, the exclusionary effect of the rule is narrow indeed, for one should expect just this kind of testimony from a party accused of negligence. Forcing the defendant to deny danger (and thus invite evidence of the subsequent remedial measure) or forgo evidence to support that defense (and risk an inference that her lack of denial is tantamount to an admission of danger), places defendant in an untenable position.[129] In the end, courts must decide the admissibility of the evidence under this kind of impeachment theory in the context of each case.

Another risk created by allowing impeachment use of subsequent remedial measures evidence concerns abuse by the plaintiff rather than the defendant. In some cases, the plaintiff's counsel might be able to maneuver the defendant's witnesses into saying something that could be "impeached" by evidence of subsequent measures when the main goal is to place the subsequent measures before the jury as evidence of the party's recognition of negligence. For example, in *Daggett v. Atchison, Topeka, & Santa Fe Ry. Co.*,[130] a case arising from a train-auto collision, the plaintiffs succeeded in

---

[128] *See* Pierce v. J.C. Penney Co., 334 P.2d 117 (Cal. Ct. App. 1959) (holding evidence that, after accident, manager authorized installation of new abrasive slips on stairs admissible to impeach manager's testimony that steps were neither worn nor slippery).

[129] *See* Kelly v. Crown Equipment Co., 970 F.2d 1273, 1278 (3d Cir. 1992) (holding that defendant's expert testimony that design of forklift was excellent and proper was not contradicted by design alteration made after accident because "alteration did not compel the conclusion that the first design was defective") *See also* Flaminio v. Honda Motor Co., Ltd., 733 F.2d 463, 468 (7th Cir. 1984) (making similar point).

[130] Daggett v. Atchison, T. & S. F. R. Co., 313 P.2d 557 (Cal. 1957). *See* Blythe v. Sears, Roebuck & Co., 586 So. 2d 861, 864–65 (Ala. 1991) (holding that evidence of subsequent remedial measures may be introduced to impeach testimony when witness testifies in superlative that condition was "the safest" or "the best"; but evidence is admissible to impeach only if it is initiated by defendant, witness authorized or directed remedial measures, evidence is offered for material purpose, evidence is relevant to issue at hand, and prejudicial effect does not substantially outweigh probative value). For a narrow interpretation of the impeachment exception

introducing evidence that the railroad had installed new signals after the accident and that the railroad had changed the speed limit for trains going through the intersection. The evidence of the new speed limit was introduced after the engineer who was operating the train at the time of the accident testified, during adverse examination by the plaintiff, that the speed limit "is 90" in the area. Over objection by the defense, the plaintiff was permitted to ask, "Well, Mr. Benton, the restriction now is 50 miles an hour, isn't it?" The California Supreme Court sustained this line of questioning on grounds that it impeached the credibility of the engineer. The court also sustained the reception of the evidence about the new signals on impeachment grounds. The evidence impeached the testimony of a defense expert that the signal in use at the time of the accident was the "safest type of signal."

Whenever subsequent remedial measures evidence is offered to impeach, the court should weigh the impeachment value of the evidence against its possible prejudicial effect (i.e., the possibility that the jury will use the testimony as evidence of the recognition of negligence). In some situations, the evidence should be excluded.[131]

Example

In a wrongful death action based upon a fall down a stairway, the defendant-landowner is questioned during a deposition about the condition of the stairway. In response to a question by the plaintiff's attorney, the owner answers that the stairway is now in the same condition that existed at the time of the accident. In fact, a handrail had been added after the plaintiff's fall. Subsequently, the defendant notifies the plaintiff that this answer was incorrect, claiming that the witness had misunderstood the question. In view of the negligible impeachment value of the witness's inaccurate deposition answer, the trial judge would have discretion to exclude evidence about the witness's inaccurate answer to the deposition question. The impeachment value of the evidence is substantially outweighed by the prejudice that would result from revealing the remedial measure.[132]

§ 6.09 Practice Considerations

The subsequent remedial measures rule has been characterized as ineffective because evidence of repairs is so commonly admissible for impeachment or to prove

to Rule 407, see Harrison v. Sears, Roebuck & Co., 981 F.2d 25 (1st Cir. 1992) (upholding trial judge's refusal to allow the plaintiff to impeach the witness with evidence that the witness had later made a design change that closed up the aperture through which the plaintiff's finger allegedly came into contact with the blade, where in-house expert testified for a defendant that there was no hazardous area on the joint-planer where the plaintiff's hand could unintentionally make contact with the cutter head; indicating that the impeachment use had to be strictly limited because of Rule 407).

[131] *See, e.g.*, Stecyk v. Bell Helicopter Textron, Inc., 295 F.3d 408 (3d Cir. 2002) (holding that admission of subsequent remedial measures evidence to impeach expert witnesses must be limited to prevent impeachment use of evidence from swallowing exclusionary rule; defense claim that improvement would have been difficult to install and was not suited to military environment was insufficient to justify admitting evidence that defendant later made improvement because other material was available with which to cross-examine witnesses).

[132] *See* Hanson v. Roe, 373 N.W.2d 366 (Minn. Ct. App. 1985). *See also* Agostinho v. Fairbanks Clinic Partnership, 821 P.2d 714, 716–17 (Alaska 1991) (holding that trial court committed reversible error by failing to balance probative value against potential prejudice before determining whether to admit evidence of subsequent sanding and salting to impeach defense witness's testimony that walks did not appear to be icy when plaintiff fell).

ownership, control, or feasibility. Nevertheless, defendants can take precautions to preserve the objection or to mitigate the effect of admission of the evidence.

Defense counsel should consider giving specific pretrial notice to the plaintiff that the feasibility of remedial measures is not controverted. Removing feasibility from contention eliminates one common way of placing into evidence the fact that defendant took remedial measures after an accident.

In preparing defense witnesses, counsel who wish to preserve the objection should bear in mind that testimony of defense witnesses may open the door to evidence of remedial measures to show feasibility or to impeach the witness. This can occur if the witness testifies that a given way of preventing an accident is not practical (even though the measure was later taken), if the witness states that the safety measures in effect at the time of the accident were the best available, or if the witness states or implies that conditions have not changed since the accident.

At trial, when opposing counsel asks a question or offers an exhibit that would reveal the existence of safety measures taken after an accident, the objection may be made as follows:

> Objection! Plaintiff is offering evidence of remedial measures taken after the accident.

Defense counsel should object to exhibits, such as photographs, that show the existence of remedial measures. The court should be asked to crop photographs so that repairs or safety measures are not shown. When this is impractical, counsel should point out that evidence about the condition of the premises could be presented in another fashion—for example, by use of drawings or diagrams or by oral testimony. If other evidence of the condition of the premises has already been introduced by the plaintiff, defense counsel should argue that reception of the photograph showing the safety measure is redundant and prejudicial.

Counsel should be prepared to argue that even if evidence of remedial measures fits one of the categories for which it is admissible, such as impeachment or showing feasibility, its value for this purpose is substantially outweighed by Rule 403 considerations—prejudice, confusion, and waste of time. In making this argument, it is helpful to point out that the fact the evidence is ostensibly offered to prove could be shown in some other fashion, or that other evidence on the point has been introduced and evidence showing safety measures is merely cumulative. When evidence is offered on a feasibility theory, counsel can point out that the defendant does not dispute the practicability of the safety measure, but only claims that the measures in effect at the time of the accident were adequate.

If the court overrules an objection to evidence of safety measures, defense counsel should request a limiting instruction.[133] The instruction will be most effective if it explains the policy of the rule to the jury:

> Your Honor, I request a limiting instruction telling the jury that evidence that [name of defendant] took additional precautions after the accident may not be used as evidence that the defendant realized that [he/she] was negligent at the time of the accident. The law provides that such measures cannot be used as

[133] Counsel should request a limiting instruction to preserve the issue for appeal, regardless of its practical value in convincing the jury.

> evidence against the defendant because the defendant might take such measures even if [he\she] had not been negligent and because taking such measures is something to be encouraged and supported.

If repairs appear on a photograph offered to show the condition of the premises, the defendant could request something like the following instruction:

> Members of the jury, you should disregard the fact that safety measures were taken after the accident. The law provides that such repairs cannot be used as evidence against the defendant, because the making of repairs and improvements is something to be encouraged and supported.

Even if an objection is made and sustained at trial, the jury may infer the existence of remedial measures from the nature of the questions asked by the plaintiff's counsel prior to the objection, and counsel should consider requesting a cautionary instruction explaining to the jury why such evidence is excluded.

If evidence of subsequent repairs has been offered and received, the defendant may wish to deal with the evidence in final argument. Defense counsel can point out that the law does not require perfection. The defendant's concern for safety caused it to make improvements after the accident, but the fact that improvements were made does not mean that the defendant was acting on the belief that it was careless before. Counsel should also request that the judge, in the final instructions, explain the reason for the remedial measures rule.

When evidence of remedial measures is likely to cause serious prejudice to the defendant, defense counsel should consider making a pretrial motion asking the court's assistance in preventing the jury from learning, directly or indirectly, of the remedial measures.

Example—Motion in Limine

> The defendant respectfully moves the Court to instruct the plaintiff's counsel to refrain from offering any evidence that, subsequent to the accident that is the subject of this suit, the defendant modified the design of any of its snow blower models or other products to incorporate control devices that would stop the engine from running when the user left the operator's position.
>
> The defendant also moves that the Court instruct plaintiff's counsel to refrain from asking any question, making any statement, offering any exhibit, or otherwise indicating to the jury, directly or by innuendo, that these design changes in the defendant's product were planned, discussed, or made after the accident in which the plaintiff was injured. The defendant further moves that the plaintiff's counsel be instructed to caution every witness called by her to refrain from any direct or indirect reference to design changes in the defendant's product after the accident.
>
> This motion is made on the ground that evidence of the design change would be evidence of a remedial measure offered in violation of Rule 407. The defendant concedes and will stipulate that the design change adding the above described control devices was feasible. Because feasibility is not controverted, there is no legitimate basis for offering evidence of the design change. If the design change becomes known to the jury, the defendant will be prejudiced

even if the court were to sustain an objection and instruct the jury not to consider the evidence.

If the trial judge denies the motion in limine on the ground that events at trial may open the door to remedial measures evidence, defense counsel may request that the court admonish the plaintiff not to introduce evidence of remedial measures without first clearing such evidence with the court in a conference held out of the hearing of the jury.[134]

D. EVIDENCE OF SETTLEMENT NEGOTIATIONS

§ 6.10 Exclusion of Evidence of Settlement Agreements and Settlement Offers [FRE 408]

Both at common law and under the Federal Rules of Evidence, a settlement offer or settlement agreement is generally inadmissible to prove the validity or invalidity of a claim or its value.[135] This exclusionary rule applies not only to offers of settlement between the parties to the litigation in which the evidence is offered but also to settlements between a party and a nonparty.

Examples

Offer of settlement to opposing party. The plaintiff, a condominium homeowners' association, sued the defendant, a general contractor, claiming damages for allegedly defective work on the condominium's heating system. The defendant offered a substantial settlement. The plaintiff declined the offer. At trial, the plaintiff seeks to introduce testimony about the defendant's offer, arguing that the size of the defendant's offer is evidence that the defendant was aware that the work was in fact defective. The evidence is inadmissible.

Completed settlement with a nonparty. The plaintiff, a motorcyclist, sues the defendant, a motorcycle manufacturer, after being injured in a motorcycle accident in which the plaintiff's motorcycle collided with a car. In a previous settlement, the plaintiff had received a payment from the driver of the car and released the driver from liability. At trial, the defendant offers the plaintiff's settlement agreement with the third party into evidence on the theory that the agreement is evidence that the plaintiff believed that the accident was caused by the car driver, not by any defect in the motorcycle. The agreement is inadmissible if offered solely to show the plaintiff's belief that the claim against the motorcycle manufacturer is invalid.[136]

Rule 408(a) excludes evidence of furnishing, offering, promising to furnish, accepting, offering, or promising to accept, a valuable consideration to compromise a claim that was disputed as to either validity or amount in order to prove liability for or invalidity of the claim or its amount. It also shields from admission any conduct or statement made during compromise negotiations. The 2006 amendment to Rule 408

[134] This was the procedure employed by the trial court, and noted with approval by the appellate court, in Rimkus v. Northwest Colo. Ski Corp., 706 F.2d 1060, 1065 (10th Cir. 1983).

[135] For a full discussion of common-law theories under which settlement evidence was excluded, *see* Esser v. Brophey, 3 N.W.2d 3 (Minn. 1942). *See also* DAVID P. LEONARD, THE NEW WIGMORE: SELECTED RULES OF LIMITED ADMISSIBILITY § 3.3 (rev. ed. 2002).

[136] *See* McInnis v. A.M.F., Inc., 765 F.2d 240 (1st Cir. 1985). The court in *McInnis* noted that the jury's verdict could be reduced by the amount of the payment received in the settlement.

clarifies that exclusion applies "even when a party seeks to admit its own settlement offer or statements made in settlement negotiations."[137]

As is apparent from the examples given above, the prohibition of Rule 408(a), like most of the rules in Article IV, is overbroad because it fails to identify the specific line of inference that is barred. The real, but implicit prohibition is that one may not introduce evidence of settlement negotiations to show that a party to the negotiations *had certain beliefs about the strength or validity of his or her case* and thereby to invite the fact-finder to infer from such beliefs something about the strength or validity of the claim. Other uses of evidence of settlement negotiations may be admissible, however, and they may indeed be used "to prove or disprove the validity or amount of a disputed claim." In the case of Rule 408, such other purposes include demonstrating witness bias, negating a claim of undue delay, and proving an effort to obstruct justice, according to Rule 408(b).[138] For example, in the second example stated above, if the driver testifies as a witness or remains as a party in the case under a so-called "Mary Carter" agreement, the prior settlement may be admissible to show the bias of the driver as a witness or to explain trial conduct.[139]

Rule 408 has proven very influential. Many states have adopted language substantively identical or nearly identical to the Federal Rule, and a number of others have followed most aspects of the rule. No state rejects the basic premise that evidence of compromises or compromise offers should be excluded when offered to prove validity or invalidity of a claim or defense.[140]

Several theories have been advanced in support of the exclusionary rule. One theory is that the evidence is simply irrelevant; an offer of settlement is not probative of the validity of the underlying claim, because the offeror may only have been seeking peace rather than revealing a belief that his or legal position was weak.[141] Although this theory may be valid in some situations, it does not explain a blanket rule of exclusion; an offer of settlement for more than the cost of litigation likely indicates something about the party's belief in the strength or weakness of its legal position. For example, an offer to settle for 90 percent of the other person's claim would certainly suggest that the offeror believed he or she had a weak case.

A policy of encouraging settlement provides a sounder basis for a blanket rule of exclusion and is the most commonly cited reason for the rule.[142] Settlement of disputes

---

[137] Rule 408 advisory committee note to amended rule.

[138] The restyling effort rather mysteriously changed the heading of Rule 408(b) from "Permitted uses" to "Exceptions." To the contrary, Rule 408(b) does not address *exceptions* to the prohibition in Rule 408(a); it addresses uses of evidence that do not come within the scope of the prohibition of Rule 408(a). "Permitted uses" was a more apt title. *Cf.* Rules 404(a)(2) and 404(b)(2).

[139] *See* General Motors Corp. v. Simmons, 558 S.W.2d 855, 857 (Tex. 1977) (evidence of agreement admissible because it gave settling parties interest in outcome that might affect their testimony or conduct). Mary Carter agreements arise when the plaintiff and one or more defendants settle, releasing the defendant(s) from liability in exchange for a specified sum and assistance with the trial. Settling defendant(s) remain in the case and retain a financial interest in the litigation and may receive a recovery from plaintiff's award from non-settling defendants. The name comes from Booth v. Mary Carter Paint Co., 202 So. 2d 8 (Fla. Dist. Ct. App. 1967). Extensive case law addresses both the validity and the admissibility of Mary Carter and similar types of agreements. For review of the problems raised by these agreements, *see* DAVID P. LEONARD, THE NEW WIGMORE: SELECTED RULES OF LIMITED ADMISSIBILITY §§ 3.7.4–3.7.5 (rev. ed. 2002).

[140] For examination of state provisions, *see* DAVID P. LEONARD, THE NEW WIGMORE: SELECTED RULES OF LIMITED ADMISSIBILITY § 3.6 (rev. ed. 2002).

[141] *See id.* § 3.3.2.

[142] For full discussion of the policy rationale, *see id.* §§ 3.3.3, 3.4.

serves the useful function of relieving court congestion and bringing peace to litigants. Whether the rule serves this purpose, or whether offers would be made even in the absence of an exclusionary rule, remains unclear. Still, the rule tends to discourage tricky pretrial tactics, such as inveigling the other party into making an offer solely for the purpose of acquiring evidence at trial.[143]

Finally, the rule arises from considerations of fairness and from a desire not to disadvantage a party who acts in a socially useful way by seeking to resolve disputes without the necessity of trial.[144]

Common Law and Federal Rule Approaches Compared

At common law, offers of settlement and settlement agreements were inadmissible, but statements made during settlement negotiations were admissible.[145] For example, if a party or a party's representative made an admission of fault during negotiations, that admission could be received into evidence, although the offer of settlement itself was inadmissible.[146] This result was consistent with the view advocated by Wigmore,[147] that the true reason for excluding settlement offers was that they were not probative of the fault of the offeror, who might be making an offer solely for the purpose of buying peace. A statement admitting fault was clearly relevant and hence was not excluded. Because statements in conjunction with settlement offers were often admitted at common law, counsel sought to protect clients by noting during settlement negotiations that all statements were made hypothetically, "without prejudice," or for purposes of discussion only.[148]

Contemporary law has taken the opposite position, holding that statements of fact made in connection with compromise discussions are generally inadmissible. This position is most consistent with the policy rationale of encouraging settlement. Achieving compromise requires candor; if parties were aware that their opponents could offer into evidence portions of the compromise discussions, they would be less likely to begin compromise discussions, or, even if they did enter into such discussions, they would certainly be less forthcoming. The fairness rationale for the compromise rule also demands exclusion of statements of fact made in the course of compromise discussions.

---

143 *See* FED. R. EVID. 408 advisory committee note; George M. Bell, *Admissions Arising Out of Compromise—Are They Irrelevant?* 31 TEX. L. REV. 239, 241–42 (1953). *See also* Pierce v. F.R. Tripler & Co., 955 F.2d 820 (2d Cir. 1992) (holding plaintiff in age discrimination case entitled, under circumstances, to have excluded evidence that defendant offered him job during subsequent settlement negotiations; rejecting argument that policy of Rule 408 does not support exclusion when offeror of settlement seeks to have evidence admitted, on grounds that free admission of such offers would result in rash of disqualification of counsel motions and that language of Rule 408 itself does not support exception for evidence proffered by maker of settlement offer).

144 *See* DAVID P. LEONARD, THE NEW WIGMORE: SELECTED RULES OF LIMITED ADMISSIBILITY § 3.3.4 (rev. ed. 2002).

145 For discussion of evolution in the treatment of statements of fact made in connection with compromise discussions, *see id.*, § 3.5.2.

146 *See* 2 MCCORMICK ON EVIDENCE § 266 at 334 (Kenneth S. Broun ed., 7th ed. 2013); Albert Hanson Lumber Co. v. United States, 261 U.S. 581, 588–89 (1923).

147 *See* 4 WIGMORE ON EVIDENCE § 1061 (Chadbourn rev. 1972).

148 By analogy to contract law, common-law courts were willing to treat an unaccepted offer as having no effect, evidential or otherwise, if it was made "without prejudice." *See id.* The contract rationale for the exclusionary rule never took hold in the United States. *See* DAVID P. LEONARD, THE NEW WIGMORE: SELECTED RULES OF LIMITED ADMISSIBILITY § 3.31 (rev. ed. 2002).

It is unfair to admit such statements made by a party in a candid effort to seek compromise.

The Federal Rules of Evidence follow this rationale, excluding both compromise offers and statements made during negotiations. Rule 408 expressly excludes evidence of conduct or statements made in compromise negotiations. The drafters of the Rules reasoned that uninhibited freedom of expression was necessary to facilitate settlement.

A good example of the operation of the Federal Rule may be found in *Ramada Development Co. v. Rauch*,[149] in which Ramada sued for the balance due under a construction contract with Rauch. Rauch claimed defects in Ramada's construction of the project. Ramada retained an architect to study the alleged defects and to prepare a report to be used as a tool in attempting settlement. The report was submitted to Rauch during settlement negotiations. There was no pretrial agreement between the parties about the admissibility of the report. At trial, Rauch offered the architect's report as evidence because it confirmed the existence of many of the alleged defects. The trial judge excluded it on grounds that it was inadmissible under Rule 408 and the Third Circuit upheld the exclusion.

Not all documentary evidence exchanged during compromise negotiations will be protected by Rule 408. Rule 408 at one time expressly provided that it did "not require the exclusion of any evidence otherwise discoverable merely because it is presented in the course of compromise negotiations." This phrasing was deemed superfluous and confusing and was therefore omitted in the revised 2006 version of the rule. Nevertheless, the expressed policy—preventing parties from immunizing pre-existing documents by turning them over to the opposing party during negotiations—remains in force. For example, a party cannot turn over its business records during negotiations and later claim that the opposing party may not use them at trial because of Rule 408. The opposing party would have been entitled to use the discovery rules to obtain the records and then to introduce them at trial. The case of *Ramada Development Co. v. Rauch* is distinguishable from the situation in which the party seeks to immunize pre-existing documents. As *Rauch* held, Rule 408's exception for documents "otherwise discoverable" does not apply to cases in which the document would *not have existed but for the negotiations*. In such cases, negotiations are not used to frustrate discovery by making existing documents unreachable.

Use as Impeachment

Until the 2006 amendment to Rule 408, courts disagreed over whether statements made in compromise negotiations could be used to impeach a witness with a prior inconsistent statement.[150] The theory was that such statements were not being offered

---

[149] Ramada Dev. Co. v. Rauch, 644 F.2d 1097, 1106 (5th Cir. 1981).

[150] *See* Stainton v. Tarantino, 637 F. Supp. 1051 (E.D. Pa.1986) (holding evidence admissible for impeachment); Wayne D. Brazil, *Protecting the Confidentiality of Settlement Negotiations*, 39 HASTINGS L.J. 955, 978 (1988) (advocating limited impeachment use because perfect consistency is almost impossible and allowing use of prior statements somewhat inconsistent with trial testimony would undercut exclusionary rule). *See also* Davidson v. Prince, 813 P.2d 1225, 1233 n.9 (Utah Ct. App. 1991) (holding that even if statements are part of offer in compromise, they are admissible to impeach maker's inconsistent trial testimony) (alternative holding). For a further analysis of inconsistent statements made during settlement negotiations for impeachment, see ABA SECTION ON LITIGATION, EMERGING PROBLEMS UNDER THE FEDERAL RULES OF EVIDENCE 61 (2d ed. 1991) (discussion of Rule 408, Appendix II of West's Federal Rules of Evidence pamphlet); MICHAEL H. GRAHAM, HANDBOOK OF FEDERAL EVIDENCE § 408.1 (4th ed. 1996); 1 STEPHEN A. SALTZBURG, MICHAEL M. MARTIN & DANIEL J. CAPRA, FEDERAL RULES OF EVIDENCE MANUAL 512–13 (6th ed. 1994). As these sources indicate, courts and commentators were divided on the appropriateness of allowing

for their truth, but to demonstrate the witness's inconsistency. The problem with this impeachment theory is that it potentially nullifies the effects of Rule 408's protection of statements made in compromise negotiations. The amended rule clarifies that statements made in settlement negotiations cannot be used to impeach a witness through a prior inconsistent statement[151] or impeachment by contradiction.[152]

§ 6.11 Uses of Evidence of Settlement and Compromise Efforts That Are Admissible Despite the Rule of Exclusion

The following sub-sections discuss both exceptions to Rule 408 and situations where the Rule simply does not apply. First, the amended rule explicitly creates an exception for statements made in negotiations with government agents in matters that later lead to criminal prosecution. Second, the rule of exclusion applies only to offers of compromise and statements made in seeking compromise of disputed claims.[153] If the context is not one of legal negotiations or the claim is not disputed as to liability or amount, then the rule does not apply. Third, the rule of exclusion does not apply when the evidence is offered for any purpose other than to prove the validity or invalidity of the claim at issue in the case. If offered for any other purpose, it is potentially admissible.

Exception for Compromise Negotiation Statements Made to Public Officials or Agents When Used in Subsequent Criminal Proceeding

A controversial 2006 amendment to Rule 408 permits admissions and conduct by parties during settlement negotiations with government regulators to be used against such parties in criminal investigations and prosecutions. It does not admit the fact of settlement,[154] but conduct or surrounding statements if made during negotiations related to government regulation, investigation, or enforcement are subsequently admissible in a criminal case.[155]

Example

A taxpayer negotiates with an agent of the Internal Revenue Service regarding a questionable tax shelter. The taxpayer immediately agrees to pay $100,000 in back taxes but wishes to negotiate other claims by the IRS. In a subsequent criminal actions for tax evasion, the fact of payment is not admissible, but statements made in compromise negotiations to the IRS agent are admissible.

This change was advocated by the United States Department of Justice and, not surprisingly, it is unpopular with the white-collar defense bar. The advisory committee note to the 2006 amendment states that: "Where an individual makes a statement in the presence of government agents, its subsequent admission in a criminal case should not

---

this use of statements made during settlement negotiations. For a more detailed examination of the strengths and weaknesses of the different impeachment theories under which compromise evidence might be offered. *See* DAVID P. LEONARD, THE NEW WIGMORE: SELECTED RULES OF LIMITED ADMISSIBILITY § 3.8.2 (rev. ed. 2002).

[151] *See* **§ 11.05**.

[152] *See* **§ 11.06**.

[153] Of course, the rule also applies to completed compromises, as the language of Rule 408 makes clear. *See also* DAVID P. LEONARD, THE NEW WIGMORE: SELECTED RULES OF LIMITED ADMISSIBILITY § 3.7.1(a) (rev. ed. 2002).

[154] *See* FED. R. EVID. 408(a)(1).

[155] FED. R. EVID. 408(a)(2).

be unexpected. The individual can seek to protect against subsequent disclosure through negotiation and agreement with the civil regulator, or an attorney for the government."

This exception is difficult to square with the goals of the rule. It puts a party disputing a civil claim with the government in much the same situation as litigants under the common-law prior to the adoption of Rule 408. The party must know the law sufficiently well to bargain for a privilege for his negotiations. Otherwise, the party risks the use of statements in negotiation against him in a later criminal prosecution.

Settlement of an Undisputed Claim

The purpose of Rule 408 and of many of its common-law analogs is to promote compromise when claims are genuinely disputed. The rulemakers did not intend to protect defendants who do not genuinely contest claims but who merely seek an extension of time or a discount for the nuisance value of litigation. Rule 408 provides no protection to the debtor who tells his creditor, "You'll have to take 50 cents on the dollar of what I owe you. If you don't like it, sue me." Such statements are admissible because they do not reveal any dispute; the debtor's reference to "what I owe you" demonstrates that she does not seek compromise, but instead seeks to avoid part of a rightful obligation. Rule 408 specifically provides that the rule of exclusion only applies to claims that are "disputed as to either validity or amount." The rulemakers reasoned that the policy considerations favoring settlement negotiations do not apply to a debtor who seeks settlement of an admittedly due amount for a lesser sum.

The rule applies if the claim is disputed as to *either* validity *or* amount. In tort actions, and in contract actions not involving a debt for a sum certain, the amount of the claim will almost always be disputed, even if its validity is not. Thus, if counsel for a personal injury defendant says "Okay, there's no doubt about liability, but your damages demand is too high. Let's try to arrive at a reasonable figure for damages," the statement is not admissible because, though liability is conceded, the plaintiff's damage claims are not.

The common-law rule about settlement offers is consistent with this aspect of Rule 408. To be affected by the rule of exclusion, the offer had to be an offer of compromise, not a concession that the full amount was due. Thus, for example, when the sales representative of an herbicide manufacturer told a farmer whose crop was damaged by the herbicide that the company would pay for the damage, the statement was held admissible on grounds that it was not an offer of compromise.[156] Of course, there is a gray area between offers of compromise and non-compromise offers, and an admission of liability accompanied by an offer to pay for damage can still be an offer of compromise if there is an express or implicit dispute about the amount of the damages.

Example

Demand for full payment of claim. Plaintiff, a retail store, brings a breach of contract action against a manufacturer for failure to deliver a popular toy in time for the holiday season. Plaintiff's letter to defendant setting forth its estimate of lost sales and demanding "full payment," though written after the scheduled delivery date had passed, is not an offer in compromise and is therefore not excluded by the compromise rule.

---

[156] Perzinski v. Chevron Chem. Co., 503 F.2d 654, 658 (7th Cir. 1974).

Discussions Constituting Business Negotiations Rather than Negotiations to Compromise a Legal Dispute

The compromise rule does not exclude evidence of discussions that took place in the context of business negotiations rather than in a legal dispute, nor does it apply to other situations that, in the court's view, fall short of "compromise negotiation."[157]

Sometimes, it is difficult to determine whether the parties actually disputed a question of liability or, rather, engaged in other types of communication, such as business negotiations. It is impossible to resolve such cases with a simple rule, but several factors can affect whether to treat such discussions as compromise negotiations.[158] The mere fact that all of the events that might give rise to liability have occurred prior to the discussions does not necessarily mean that the discussions fall within the rule and must be excluded. However, the timing of the discussions at issue is a primary factor. Certainly, communications can be excluded pursuant to the rule, even if no formal claim has been made at the time of the communications. However, if the discussions occurred before it was apparent to the parties that there was a genuine dispute, the discussions likely do not constitute an effort to compromise a disputed claim and are probably admissible.[159] Some courts have gone so far as to hold that discussions that transpire before litigation has been threatened constitute business communications,[160] though this is unlikely to become the majority position.[161]

The difficulty of distinguishing between business negotiations and compromise negotiations is illustrated by *Aaron v. Marcove*.[162] Aaron sued to partition property he and Marcove owned as tenants in common. A company formerly owned by Aaron and Marcove leased the property. Three years before the litigation commenced, Aaron sold his share of the company to Marcove. The issue was whether the company occupied the

---

157 *See* Sage Realty Corp. v. Insurance Co. of N. Am., 34 F.3d 124, 128 (2d Cir. 1994) (holding letter presenting party's version of obligations under lease not statement made in settlement negotiations and hence admissible); S.A. Healy Co. v. Milwaukee Metro. Sewerage Dist., 50 F.3d 476, 480 (7th Cir. 1995) (holding that a claim is not in dispute until rejected and that engineer's statement was properly admissible over Rule 408 objection because no dispute had arisen at time of statement); Davidson v. Prince, 813 P.2d 1225, 1232 (Utah Ct. App. 1991) (applying a narrow interpretation of rule and holding plaintiff's letter to defendant's insurance company describing circumstances of injury and demanding compensation not "offer in compromise").

158 For extended discussion of this issue, *see* DAVID P. LEONARD, THE NEW WIGMORE: SELECTED RULES OF LIMITED ADMISSIBILITY § 3.7.5 (rev. ed. 2002).

159 *See* Crues v. KFC Corp., 768 F.2d 230 (8th Cir. 1985) (holding that in fraud action by food franchisee, evidence that defendant offered to convert franchise from one type to another was properly admitted because, inter alia, conversation occurred more than three years before filing of action, when it was not clear that any disputed claim existed). *But see* Schlossman & Gunkelman, Inc. v. Tallman, 593 N.W.2d 374 (N.D. 1999) (holding that even though dispute was in its early stages, it was apparent to parties at time of their correspondence that potential dispute was brewing over what proved to be large real estate commission).

160 *See* Big O Tire Dealers, Inc. v. Goodyear Tire & Rubber Co., 561 F.2d 1365, 1368 (10th Cir. 1977) (holding that, because discussions took place before litigation had been threatened in trademark dispute, they were not subject to exclusion under Rule 408; decision might be justified on ground that circumstances indicated defendant was using negotiations to buy time and take advantage of trademark during pendency of talks and possible litigation).

161 *See* Affiliated Mfrs., Inc. v. Aluminum Co. of America, 56 F.3d 521, 526–27 (3d Cir. 1995) (arguing that for there to be a "dispute" within the meaning of Rule 408, there must have been at least "a threat or contemplation of litigation, that goes beyond conduct or statements made to resolve differences of opinion as to the validity or amount of a claim"; "Rule 408 is invoked "where an actual dispute or a difference of opinion exists, rather than when discussions crystallize to the point of threatened litigation"). *See also* Alpex Computer Corp. v. Nintendo Co., 770 F. Supp. 161 (S.D.N.Y. 1991) (rejecting narrow reading of exclusionary scope of Rule 408).

162 Aaron v. Marcove, 685 P.2d 268 (Colo. App. 1984).

premises under a long-term lease or as a tenant at will. Aaron and Marcove tried for some time to reach a compromise before giving up and turning to litigation. At trial, Aaron offered a letter Marcove wrote to Aaron's attorney denying the existence of a lease to the company. This position contradicted the position Marcove took at trial. On appeal, the court held that admission of the letter was proper because the letter was written during a period when the parties were negotiating a long-term lease, not the settlement of the controversy about whether a lease existed at all. In other words, the court characterized the letter as part of business discussions rather than discussions aimed at compromising the claim at issue in the trial. *Aaron* is a close call and certainly could have gone either way.

Example

Business discussions rather than negotiations to compromise disputed claim. The plaintiff and the defendant, two partners in a retail clothing business, disagree about whether their store should change its focus from middle-aged customers to younger buyers. As their differences increase, the partners begin to consider dissolving the partnership. At one point, the two discuss the value of the business, and agree that it is in the range of $2 million. A year later, the two partners end up in litigation. At trial, to prove the business was worth $2 million in total, the plaintiff wishes to present evidence of their prior discussion. The trial judge would be operating within her discretion in admitting the evidence on the ground that at the time of the prior discussion, the parties' differences probably did not reach the point of a "disputed claim" that would fall within the compromise rule.

Compromise or Behavior During Compromise Discussions as the Subject of the Action

The compromise rule does not apply in a suit enforcing the terms of the settlement contract itself. This result is required if the law is to be able to enforce the terms of agreements reached after an allegedly successful effort to compromise a disputed claim. Similarly, the exclusionary rule does not apply when the present action is based upon allegedly tortious conduct that occurred during discussions to compromise a disputed claim.

Examples

Compromise as subject of the action. The plaintiff, who suffered injuries when she was struck in a crosswalk by the defendant's vehicle, brings a breach of contract action against the defendant claiming that the defendant failed to pay damages agreed to pursuant to a compromise settlement of the claim. The compromise agreement is the subject of the action, and is therefore not excluded by the compromise rule.

Behavior during compromise negotiations as basis of action. The plaintiff brings a claim for intentional infliction of emotional distress against an insurance company after the insurance company, without a valid reason, threatens to withhold disability benefits. The insurance company's letters to the plaintiff containing those threats, written during discussions for compromise of the plaintiff's disability claim, were not offered to prove liability under the insurance policy, but as part of the conduct that caused emotional distress.[163] Therefore, they are not excluded by the compromise rule.

Evidence Offered for Other Purposes; Proving Bias or Delay

Rule 408 prohibits the use of statements made during compromise negotiations when the purpose is to show the validity or invalidity of a party's claim by way of what the negotiations reveal about the party's beliefs about the validity of the claim, but evidence of statements made during settlement negotiations may be introduced for a variety of other purposes that do not involve use of the evidence in the proscribed way. These include use of the evidence to negate a claim of unnecessary delay, to show that defendants engaged in dilatory negotiations that prevented plaintiffs from mitigating their damages,[164] to show that a party engaged in an unfair labor practice during the settlement negotiations, or to prove an effort to obstruct a criminal investigation or prosecution.[165]

Example

> *Showing witness bias.* The plaintiff and W, a passenger in the plaintiff's vehicle, are injured when the plaintiff's vehicle is involved in a collision with the defendant's vehicle. At trial, W testifies that the defendant's car ran the red light and struck the plaintiff's car. The defendant wishes to present evidence that previously, W had made a claim against the plaintiff, and that the plaintiff had paid W in settlement of the claim. This evidence is most likely admissible to demonstrate that W might have been biased toward the plaintiff, causing W to shade her testimony in the plaintiff's favor.[166]

Of course, the impeachment value of the evidence must be weighed against its prejudicial effect, and in cases where impeachment value is slight, counsel opposing the offer should argue that the evidence should be excluded on Rule 403 grounds. In addition, a fair settlement arguably has little impeachment value because the recipient of the settlement is not getting paid anything more than he or she lost.[167] In any event, the party objecting to the testimony is entitled to a limiting instruction to the effect that the evidence may only be used for its bearing on the credibility of the witness, not as evidence of the plaintiff's or the witness's beliefs about liability.

§ 6.12 Practice Considerations for Civil Cases

In the few jurisdictions that follow the common-law rule, statements of fact made during settlement negotiations are admissible when offered by the opposing party, though settlement offers are not. Counsel who wish to discuss the facts of a case during

---

[163] *See* Fletcher v. Western National Life Ins. Co., 89 Cal. Rptr. 78, 90 (1970).

[164] Urico v. Parnell Oil Co., 708 F.2d 852 (1st Cir. 1983).

[165] For discussion of alternate routes to admissibility, *see* DAVID P. LEONARD, THE NEW WIGMORE: SELECTED RULES OF LIMITED ADMISSIBILITY §§ 3.8.3–3.8.5 (rev. ed. 2002).

[166] *Cf.* John McShain, Inc. v. Cessna Aircraft Co., 563 F.2d 632 (3d Cir. 1977) (finding no error in admitting evidence of plaintiff's pretrial settlement with third party, where expert associated with third party testified in favor of plaintiff). *See also* Johnson v. Hugo's Skateway, 949 F.2d 1338, 1345–46 (4th Cir. 1991), *superseded on other grounds at* 974 F.2d 1408 (4th Cir. 1992) (holding evidence of prior consent decree admissible because evidence was not offered to show validity of claim that resulted in consent decree, but to prove subsequent acts of racial bias by showing that provisions of decree, such as posting sign on premises announcing policy of equal access to all races, were not followed); Reichenbach v. Smith, 528 F.2d 1072, 1075 (5th Cir. 1976).

[167] *Cf.* Paster v. Pennsylvania R.R., 43 F.2d 908, 911 (2d Cir. 1930) (Hand, J.).

negotiations should either make clear during settlement negotiations that any statements of fact are made without prejudice for the purpose of achieving settlement, or obtain an agreement with opposing counsel that statements made during negotiations will not be offered in evidence. In the absence of an express agreement, factual statements should be made hypothetically, or counsel should note that statements are being made "without prejudice."

Because the Federal Rules expressly provide protection for statements of fact as well as for offers, such precautions might seem unnecessary in jurisdictions that follow the Federal Rules. However, an express agreement not to offer statements during negotiations as evidence or a statement that negotiations are "without prejudice" does no harm and may serve a function even under the Federal Rules. For example, in *S. Leo Harmonay, Inc. v. Binks Mfg. Co.*,[168] the plaintiff's attorney sent the defendant a letter that stated: "In accordance with our prior discussions and without prejudice to our clients' respective legal positions, I am taking the liberty of setting forth below a summary of the damages suffered by Harmonay. . . ."

The defendant offered the letter in evidence at trial in order to impeach the testimony of one of plaintiff's witnesses. In deciding that Rule 408 barred admission of the letter, the court noted that the words *without prejudice* were no longer absolutely dispositive. However, it stated that the words "may still be evidence of the intent of the speaker which we may rely upon to determine whether the statement was made 'in compromise.' " Thus, use of the phrase *without prejudice,* which cost nothing, seems to have contributed to a decision in favor of excluding the evidence, even under the Federal Rules.

Because the exclusionary rule only applies to discussions aimed at compromising disputed claims, and because, in hindsight, it is sometimes questionable whether certain communications were of this type, counsel who wish to take advantage of Rule 408 should clarify the nature of the negotiation at the time the negotiation takes place in order to lay the foundation for invoking the rule.

At trial, the objection may be made as follows:

> Objection! The question calls for testimony about [a settlement offer] [an offer in compromise] [a statement made during settlement negotiations].

If the objection is overruled on grounds that the evidence is offered for some purpose other than showing the validity or invalidity of the claim, then the objecting party should request a limiting instruction. For example, in instances where the basis for admission is that the evidence shows the bias of a defense witness, defense counsel could request the following instruction:

> Your Honor, I request that a limiting instruction be given informing the jury that this evidence may be used only for the purpose of assessing credibility of the witness, and that it may not be used as evidence of the negotiating parties' beliefs in order to show that the plaintiff's claim is valid or that the defendant is liable.

---

[168] S. Leo Harmonay, Inc. v. Binks Mfg. Co., 597 F. Supp. 1014, 1023 (S.D.N.Y.1984), *aff'd,* 762 F.2d 990 (2d Cir. 1985).

If the evidence is admitted for a limited purpose, counsel should request a further instruction at the close of the case explaining the policy of the rule against use of settlement offers. For example, counsel might request the following instruction:

> Members of the jury, evidence that a settlement offer was made was admitted for the limited purpose of assisting you in assessing the credibility of a witness. You should not use this evidence as proof of the validity of the plaintiff's claim or as evidence that the defendant is liable. The settlement of cases before trial is something that the law seeks to encourage and promote. For that reason, the law protects persons who make settlement offers by providing that a settlement offer may not be used at trial as evidence that the person making the offer believes [he/she] is legally liable. Otherwise, people would hesitate to make offers and the chances of settlement would be reduced.

§ 6.13 Pleas and Plea Bargaining Statements Offered Against the Accused [FRE 410]

Under Rule 410, statements made during plea bargaining with an attorney for the prosecuting authority are inadmissible against the accused in any criminal or civil proceeding. The primary purpose of the rule is to encourage full disclosure during negotiations for a plea.[169] In this sense, the rule is analogous to the rule covering statements of fact made in the course of compromise discussions for civil disputes.[170]

A withdrawn guilty plea is also inadmissible.[171] The permission to withdraw must have been granted for a reason—such as involuntariness, lack of true understanding of the nature of the charges or the consequences of conviction, or the denial of assistance of counsel—and such a reason that is sufficient to permit the withdrawal is also sufficient to keep the plea out of the evidence.[172] The rule is thus based strongly in considerations of fairness.[173] Its primary purpose, however, is to encourage the settlement of criminal cases, which is necessary in order to prevent the criminal justice system from collapsing under the weight of contested trials.[174]

Like any other statement of a party, a guilty plea *not* withdrawn is admissible as an admission.[175] However, where the plea is to a minor traffic offense, especially where the "plea" is made by mail, the inference that the statement shows consciousness of guilt may be too weak to permit it to be received in evidence. Persons accused of traffic

---

[169] FED. R. EVID. 410 advisory committee note.

[170] *See* **§ 6.10**.

[171] *But cf.* United States v. Greene, 995 F.2d 793, 798 (8th Cir. 1993) (holding defendant, who argued that his rejection of agreement was evidence of "consciousness of innocence," not entitled to introduce evidence that he had rejected favorable plea agreement).

[172] FED. R. EVID. 410 advisory committee note (citing Kercheval v. United States, 274 U.S. 220 (1927)) (holding that admitting withdrawn guilty plea would undermine purpose of allowing defendant to withdraw plea); 2 MCCORMICK ON EVIDENCE § 257 273–74 (Kenneth S. Broun ed., 7th ed. 2013) (stating that, where plea withdrawn to correct injustice, admission would undermine effectiveness of remedy).

[173] *See* DAVID P. LEONARD, THE NEW WIGMORE: SELECTED RULES OF LIMITED ADMISSIBILITY § 5.4.2 (rev. ed. 2002). Another rationale for the exclusionary rule is to prevent unfair prejudice. *Id.* § 5.4.3.

[174] *See id.* § 5.4.4.

[175] *See, e.g.*, Taylor v. Whitley, 933 F.2d 325, 327 (5th Cir. 1991) (explaining that guilty plea is admission that defendant committed charged offense); Jacobs v. Goodspeed, 429 A.2d 915, 917 (Conn. 1980) (holding that plea of guilty for charge of following too closely was admissible as admission in negligence action); Teitelbaum Furs, Inc. v. Dominion Ins. Co., 375 P.2d 439, 441 (Cal. 1962) (holding guilty plea admissible in civil action as admission).

violations often make such pleas simply for convenience, to avoid going to court. Though such pleas are usually not excluded by the rule, their use as evidence of guilt may be misleading.[176] Nevertheless, the party pleading guilty will usually have the opportunity to explain to the fact finder why he or she did so, potentially minimizing the misunderstanding that could result from admission of the evidence.

A plea of nolo contendere is inadmissible in both civil and criminal suits.[177] The trial judge who allowed the plea, in which the defendant waives trial rights, determined in allowing the plea that this consequence should not attach to the conviction.[178] Indeed, in many cases the most compelling motivation to utilize the nolo contendere plea is precisely to dispose of the case without creating adverse evidence for subsequent civil or criminal litigation.[179]

Rule 410 generally does not allow the use of plea evidence to impeach the defendant at trial. Some state codes, however, expressly permit such use.

In *United States v. Mezzanatto*,[180] the Supreme Court issued an important decision holding that a person may waive protection of the rule. The defendant was arrested on narcotics charges. Shortly after his arrest, the defendant and his attorney met with the prosecutor to discuss cooperation. The prosecutor informed the defendant that he would not continue with the discussion unless the defendant agreed that any statements he made during the meeting could be used to impeach his testimony by contradiction should he testify at trial. After consultation with his attorney, the defendant agreed to the prosecutor's terms and then made evasive and false statements during the discussion. The prosecutor terminated the meeting on the basis that the defendant was not being truthful, and when the defendant testified inconsistently with certain statements he made during the session, the prosecutor offered the prior statements into evidence to impeach his credibility. The Supreme Court held that the trial court's admission of the evidence was proper, relying primarily on the theory that a criminal defendant may waive many rights by voluntary agreement. Defendant argued that the disparity of bargaining power makes such agreements "inherently unfair and coercive." In response, the Court acknowledged that the plea bargaining process exerts pressure on defendants to plead guilty and that there is potential for prosecutorial abuse. But, the Court wrote, such potential for abuse "is an insufficient basis for foreclosing negotiation altogether. . . . Instead, the appropriate response to [defendant's] predictions of abuse is

---

[176] *See, e.g.*, Hannah v. Ike Topper Structural Steel Co., 201 N.E.2d 63, 65 (Ohio Ct. App. 1963) (holding plea of guilty to failing to yield signed on form attached to traffic ticket inadmissible; cost of defense and inconvenience of court appearances compared to fine motivating factor for plea); 2 MCCORMICK ON EVIDENCE § 257 at 272 (Kenneth S. Broun ed., 7th ed. 2013) (recognition that collateral consequences as opposed to guilt often controlling factor in traffic violation guilty pleas led to some tendency to exclude plea); *But see* Duvall v. Borough of Oxford, 1992 WL 59163 at *4 n. 6 (E.D. Pa.1992) (rejecting argument that guilty plea to underage drinking charge should be inadmissible as admission because "like traffic violations, this charge is regularly 'admitted' even when false, because the costs of contest outweigh the punishment"); Ando v. Woodberry, 168 N.E.2d 520, 521, 203 N.Y.S.2d 74, 76 (N.Y. 1960) (holding plea of guilty to failing to signal and making improper turn admissible in negligence action; plea was made in court, so inconvenience explanation not available).

[177] FED. R. EVID. 410(a)(2).

[178] 1 MCCORMICK ON EVIDENCE § 257 at 273 & n.30 (Kenneth S. Broun ed., 7th ed. 2013) (stating that judge assumedly considers admissibility of plea as factor in deciding whether to permit plea of nolo contenders).

[179] For discussion of the application of the exclusionary rule to pleas of nolo contendere, *see* DAVID P. LEONARD, THE NEW WIGMORE: SELECTED RULES OF LIMITED ADMISSIBILITY § 5.8.3 (rev. ed. 2002). Many states do not permit the entry of nolo pleas. *See Id.* § 5.2.3.

[180] United States v. Mezzanatto, 513 U.S. 196 (1995).

to permit case-by-case inquiries into whether waiver agreements are the product of fraud or coercion."[181]

The scope of *Mezzanatto* is not fully clear.[182] Justice Thomas' opinion for the Court strongly hinted that *any* of the protections of Rule 410 could be waived, but three concurring justices distanced themselves from this position, and there were two dissenters. Certainly, any "waiver" of rights accorded by Rule 410 must be knowing and voluntary.[183] In addition, prosecutorial overreaching might invalidate an agreement.[184] But defense counsel should not underestimate the scope of waivers *Mezzanatto* will permit. Though the Supreme Court is unlikely to permit waiver of the defendant's constitutional right to exculpatory evidence relevant either to guilt or punishment under *Brady v. Maryland*,[185] many rights under Rule 410 are waivable. For example, the Supreme Court held that the Constitution does not require prosecutors to disclose information that would assist the defendant in impeaching the credibility of informants or other witnesses before entering into a binding plea agreement with a defendant.[186]

Even in the absence of waiver, statements made to prosecutors in hopes of obtaining lenience can fall outside the protection of the rule. The Eighth Circuit has held that revelations of incriminating information by the defendant, made during preliminary discussions with the prosecutor about the benefits of cooperation, did not occur during the "course of plea discussions" and hence did not qualify for protection.[187] Also, the rule does not exclude statements made to FBI or other law enforcement agents in the hope of obtaining leniency. The rule was amended in 1980 to limit its protection to discussion with "an attorney for the prosecuting authority." According to the legislative history, this was not intended to mean that plea negotiations conducted in good faith with a law enforcement officer (other than an attorney for the government) would necessarily be admissible.[188] Such an officer acting with authority explicitly delegated by an attorney for the prosecuting authority will be within the scope of the rule. Other principles of agency, such as agency by estoppel, may be available to bring particular discussions within the protection of the rule.[189]

---

[181] *Id.* at 210.

[182] Because *Mezzanatto* was decided largely as a matter of statutory interpretation, the states are free to interpret their own rules as they deem just.

[183] *See* United States v. Krilich, 159 F.3d 1020, 1021 (7th Cir. 1998) (holding that for waiver to be valid, party must be aware of right being abandoned as well as consequences of abandoning it).

[184] *See* United States v. Duffy, 133 F. Supp.2d 213 (E.D.N.Y. 2001) (holding that prosecutor's use of defendant's proffer statements at his trial violated his Sixth Amendment right to make defense and to effective assistance of counsel where prosecutor would not enter into plea discussions until defendant agreed to make proffer of facts, describe assistance he could provide in prosecution of other individuals, and sign standard, non-negotiable agreement providing, inter alia, that any statements he made in his proffer would be admissible "as substantive evidence to rebut any evidence offered or elicited, or factual assertions made, by or on behalf of [defendant] at any stage of a criminal prosecution" should plea negotiations not succeed; unlike waiver in *Mezzanatto*, the standard agreement essentially prevented defendant from making meaningful defense).

[185] Brady v. Maryland, 373 U.S. 83 (1963).

[186] United States v. Ruiz, 536 U.S. 622 (2002).

[187] United States v. Morgan, 91 F.3d 1193, 1196 (8th Cir. 1996) (interpreting Rule 410's counterpart in FED. R. CRIM. PROC. 11(e)(6)(D)).

[188] FED. R. EVID. 410 advisory committee note to 1980 amendment (deferring to "that body of law dealing with police interrogations"). Unless this refers to constitutional law, or other statutes that expressly supervene the Federal Rules of Evidence, this statement contradicts Rule 402.

[189] For a good discussion of the issue, *see* 2 CHRISTOPHER B. MUELLER & LAIRD C. KIRKPATRICK, FEDERAL EVIDENCE § 4:68 (4th ed. 2013).

§ 6.14 Using Plea Offers and Statements Against the Prosecution

Rule 408 protects civil litigants who attempt to negotiate a settlement. Rule 410 protects the criminal defendant who attempts to negotiate a plea. What about the prosecutor or law enforcement agent negotiating on behalf of the prosecutor? The prosecutor is clearly not covered by Rule 410.[190] Does this omission mean that the defense is free to use offers of pleas and statements made by way of concession during the plea negotiation as evidence to support the defendant's case at trial? May the defense argue, for example, that the prosecution's willingness to offer a plea agreement for a much lower charge than that in the indictment is evidence that the prosecutor is conscious of having a weak case, which could be used to infer that the prosecution's case is without merit? Alternatively, may the defense argue that the defendant's unwillingness to accept an offer indicates the defendant's consciousness of innocence?[191]

There are several reasons to think that Courts should bar this kind of evidence by the defense, just as a civil party's concessions and related statements may not be admitted under Rule 408 and the criminal defendant's concessions during plea negotiations may not be used against the defendant under Rule 410. The goal of encouraging plea bargains to resolve criminal cases is no less weighty in this context. The confusing and distracting nature of the offers and statements made in attempting to achieve a plea bargain present no less of a concern. And in one respect, the argument for excluding offers and statements by prosecutors is *stronger* than in the other contexts: a prosecutor—unlike a criminal defendant and most civil parties—does not have personal knowledge of relevant facts. If the prosecutor had such knowledge, then the prosecutor—like a lawyer for a private party—should be disqualified to act in that role; the person should instead be a witness. Likewise, the prosecutor's opinion about the strength of the admissible evidence is not properly introduced as evidence before the fact-finder, who is supposed to make its own, independent assessment of that evidence.[192] In contrast, the defendant's actions in rejecting an offer may at least communicate relevant information about the credibility of the defendant as a witness. (If the defendant does not testify at trial, it may communicate indirectly something about what the defendant knows from personal knowledge about the case, although the question may be raised whether the defendant should be allowed to effectively testify in this manner without taking the stand and being subject to cross-examination.)[193]

---

[190] Several parallel state rules provide protection to all parties to the plea discussion. *See, e.g.*, ALASKA R. EVID. 410; N.J. R. EVID. 410; TENN. R. EVID. 410; MINN. R. EVID. 410. *See also* CAL. EVID. CODE § 1153.

[191] Other issues arise from the narrow wording of Rule 410. One is whether one defendant may introduce evidence of another defendant's plea-related statement. *See, e.g.*, United States v. Rosario, 111 F.3d 293, 295–97 (2d Cir. 1997) (holding that redacted plea statement made by co-defendant was admissible to exculpate defendant, but not to inculpate co-defendant).

[192] A prosecutor sometimes is aware of inadmissible evidence. But that is all the more reason not to admit the prosecutor's opinion about the validity of the claim: in effect, to do so could smuggle into the trial the probative value of evidence the fact-finder is not supposed to consider. Insofar as the defense attempts to use statements acknowledging specific factual weaknesses in the prosecution's case, the defense also may have to get passed a hearsay objection. *See* **§ 15.08** (discussing whether statements of police and prosecutors, offered by defense, come within hearsay exception for statements of an agent or employee of a party opponent).

[193] Because of the hearsay rule, the defense may not introduce evidence of statements made by the defendant during plea negotiations to prove the truth of what the defendant asserted during such plea negotiations. *See* **§ 15.06**.

Perhaps such considerations lay behind the omission of the prosecutor from the protection of Rule 410. The drafters of the rule may have thought that Rules 402 and 403 adequately regulate such evidence. In fact, several courts have identified Rule 403 as the correct rule by which to determine the admissibility against the government of evidence concerning plea offers and the associated statements of the parties. Most courts confronting the issue have ruled that the defendant may not admit evidence of a plea offers, the prosecutor's statements in connection therewith, or the defendant's rejection of the offer,[194] whereas a defendant's refusal to accept an offer of *immunity* has been held admissible, at least in some contexts, to show the defendant's belief in innocence.[195]

It is difficult, though not impossible, to understand Rule 403 as capturing the policy of furthering settlement without trial, which is the core consideration animating Rules 408 and 410.[196] For this reason, some courts assert a broader protection for the prosecution based on the application of Rule 408, or at least its underlying rationale. Although the language of Rule 408 certainly suggests it was written primarily with settlement negotiations for civil suits in mind, that language is nonetheless broad enough to cover criminal cases as well.[197] The federal circuits are split on whether Rule 408 applies to negotiations taking place in the criminal context.[198]

---

194 *See* DAVID P. LEONARD, THE NEW WIGMORE: SELECTED RULES OF LIMITED ADMISSIBILITY § 5.9.6 at 703 n.178 (rev. ed. 2002) (citing cases).

195 *See, e.g.*, United States v. Biaggi, 909 F.2d 662 (2d Cir. 1990); United States v. Maloof, 205 F.3d 819 (5th Cir. 2001). *But see* United States v. Greene, 995 F.2d 793 (8th Cir. 1993) (rejecting, as inadmissible under Rule 408, defendant's evidence that defendant had rejected offer of immunity).

196 *See* **§ 5.03**.

197 *See* Mark T. Pavkov, Note, *Closing the Gap: Interpreting Federal Rule of Evidence 408 to Exclude Evidence of Offers and Statements Made by Prosecutors During Plea Negotiations*, 57 CASE W. RES. L. REV. 453 (2007).

198 *Compare* United States v. Alexander, 679 F.3d 721, 732 (8th Cir. 2012) (excluding defense evidence of rejected plea offer under precedent invoking the rationale of Rule 408), *with* United States v. Baker, 926 F.2d 179 (2d Cir. 1991) (holding Rule 408 inapplicable to exclude prosecution's evidence of defendant's statements made in effort to make a "deal" with FBI agents); *and* United States v. Graham, 91 F.3d 213 (D.C. Cir. 1996) (holding Rule 408 inapplicable to exclude prosecution's evidence of defendant's statements made during post-conviction bargaining with government). The earliest case endorsing the use of Rule 408 to protect the prosecution was United States v. Verdoorn, 528 F.2d 103 (8th Cir. 1976) (excluding defendant's evidence of plea offer by government by reference to the "rationale of Rule 408"). When Rule 410 was amended in 1980, the advisory committee stated that it intended "no disapproval" of that decision. FED. R. EVID. 410 advisory committee note (1980 revision).

Chapter 7

CHARACTER EVIDENCE

Table of Sections

§ 7.01 The Prohibition on Use of Character to Show Conforming Conduct [FRE 404]

In general, the rule against character evidence prohibits the admission of evidence that illuminates a person's general disposition when that evidence is offered to show action in conformity with that disposition on a particular occasion.[1] Thus, evidence of general character (i.e. someone tends to be violent or tends to be cautious) cannot be used as circumstantial evidence to prove that a person acted in character regarding the event in question. Although the rule is invoked most commonly in regard to evidence relating to the bad character of the accused in a criminal case, its prohibition extends to evidence of character—good or bad—of any person, whether or not a party to the litigation. For example, evidence that someone tends to be a careful driver cannot be used to prove he was not responsible for the accident in question, even if that person is not a party to the case.

Character evidence often has some probative value, passing the low threshold of Rule 401 relevance. However, that probative value tends to be low and, rather than

[1] FED. R. EVID. 404(a)(1); FED. R. EVID. 404(b)(1).

subject each case to a separate Rule 403 analysis and question whether such evidence creates unfair prejudice, danger of confusion, or waste of time, Rule 404 provides a general ban. The rule is subject to exceptions that will be discussed later. At this point, we will examine the contours and limits of the general prohibition itself.[2]

Surprisingly, neither the language of Rule 404 nor the official commentary to the rule defines the term "character."[3] However, in distinguishing "character" from "habit," the drafters wrote:

> Character is a generalized description of one's disposition, or of one's disposition in respect to a general trait, such as honesty, temperance, or peacefulness. . . . If we speak of character for care, we think of the person's tendency to act prudently in all the varying situations of life, in business, family life, in handling automobiles and in walking across the street.[4]

This description provides an incomplete definition of character. Not all general tendencies constitute character.[5] For example, a stroke victim's propensity to forget is considered a medical condition, rather than a trait of character.[6] To constitute a character trait, one would think (though this is not settled) that the tendency must arise in some reasonable degree from the person's *moral* being—from traits over which the person has a substantial element of choice, and which cause observers to regard the person more favorably or less favorably upon learning of the individual's behavior. This

---

[2] For general discussion of the character evidence rules, *see* H. Richard Uviller, *Evidence of Character to Prove Conduct: Illusion, Illogic, and Injustice in the Courtroom*, 130 U. PA. L. REV. 845 (1982); Richard C. Wydick, *Character Evidence: A Guided Tour of the Grotesque Structure*, 21 U.C. DAVIS L. REV. 123 (1987).

[3] Perhaps the only other rule of as much recurring importance in the law of evidence is the hearsay rule, as to which the Federal Rules give a comparatively precise definition of hearsay. See **§ 14.01**.

[4] FED. R. EVID. 406 advisory committee note (quoting CHARLES T. MCCORMICK, HANDBOOK OF THE LAW OF EVIDENCE § 162 at 340 (1954)). For discussion of the treatment of habit evidence, *see* **§ 7.15**.

[5] Unfortunately, the legal literature reflects little effort to define character. Wigmore defined character as "the actual moral or psychic disposition or sum of traits. . . ." 1A WIGMORE ON EVIDENCE § 52 at 1148 (Tillers rev. 1983). Elsewhere, however, he did not appear to confine the concept of character to aspects of the person that reflect her moral qualities. For example, he defined "character or disposition" as simply "a fixed trait or the sum of traits." *Id.* § 55 at 1159. The Model Code of Evidence offers a similarly broad definition of character as "the aggregate of a person's traits, including those relating to care or skill and their opposites." MODEL CODE OF EVIDENCE, R. 304 (1942). The authors of one treatise observe:

> The Evidence Rules do not define "character." That may seem quite justifiable; doesn't everyone know what the word means in this context? Perhaps. But suppose the prosecution in a criminal case offers evidence that the accused is a "professional gambler" or that the victim of an attempted rape was a "virgin." Is this evidence barred by Rule 404(a) when offered as circumstantial evidence of conduct? Or take a civil case in which it is proposed to prove that the defendant was "clumsy" or "colorblind" or "accident prone" or a "wealthy playboy." Are any or all of these evidence of "character"? Consider also testimony that the accused was "a member of the Mafia" or a "skillful practitioner of the martial arts" offered to show a motive for a murder or the ability to commit it or the identity of the perpetrator.

22 CHARLES A. WRIGHT & KENNETH W. GRAHAM, JR., FEDERAL PRACTICE AND PROCEDURE (EVIDENCE) § 5233 at 349–50 (1978).

[6] Despite the Advisory Committee's reference to "temperance" as a character trait, one could argue that intemperate use of alcohol is a medical condition rather than a character trait, though admittedly this view has not achieved acceptance. *See* Reyes v. Missouri Pacific R. Co., 589 F.2d 791, 794 (5th Cir. 1979) (holding evidence of plaintiff's "character trait of drinking to excess" to prove that he was drunk on night of accident inadmissible because it did not fall into any exception to the character evidence ban); 1 MCCORMICK ON EVIDENCE § 195 at 1083 n.11 (Kenneth S. Broun ed., 7th ed. 2013) (discussing "temperance" as character trait). *Cf.* Rowe v. United States, 167 Ct. Cl. 468 (1964) (noting Air Force regulation that apparently attempted to distinguish between character-based and medically-based causes of excessive alcohol consumption in granting authority to discharge personnel for "unfitness" on grounds including "evidence of habits or traits of character manifested by . . . chronic alcoholism" not caused by psychiatric disease).

principle becomes more obvious when one observes the examples listed in the drafters' notes to the Federal Rule. The drafters list "honesty, temperance, [and] peacefulness" in one place,[7] and use the terms "violent disposition" and "honesty" in another.[8]

Even more controversial is whether a behavioral propensity that is directed at a specific person should be considered a character trait. A history of domestic violence by the defendant invariably aimed at the same person is a recurring example. If this is too situationally specific to be regarded as a character trait, the prior acts of domestic violence would avoid the ban of the rule in a prosecution for a later act, even though these actions may be both voluntary and morally charged.[9]

However "character" is understood, the rule bans only character evidence that is offered to show action in conformity with character on a particular occasion—or, as it is sometimes put, character evidence is barred only when it is offered *circumstantially* to prove behavior.[10] When character is the ultimate issue, such as in a defamation case where truth is a defense or a parental termination case where parental fitness is the issue, the ban against character evidence does not operate because the evidence is offered to prove character as an end in itself, rather than to show action in conformity with character.[11]

The rule applies only if the evidence is being offered to show action in conformity with a general disposition. When evidence of a prior bad act is offered for another purpose, which may involve evidence of something like motive or opportunity to commit a crime, it does not run afoul of the propensity ban and the rule does not apply.[12] Rule 404(b)(2) governs when other crimes, wrongs, or acts are used for such other purposes.

One obvious way to prove the character of a person would be to call one or more witnesses who would testify to their familiarity with the person or the person's reputation regarding the character trait. The prohibition against character evidence, however, applies not just to evidence of the person's reputation and evidence of the opinion of others about the person's character, but to any evidence that illuminates character. Neither reputation nor opinion is itself character, but rather a way to show character. Likewise, evidence of a person's specific deeds, whether good or bad, can be character evidence if offered to show a person's general disposition as described above. These different ways of showing character are reflected in the rules discussed hereafter.

In fact, this difference—between a witness who provides opinion or reputation testimony about a person's character and a witness (or other evidence) that shows

---

7 FED. R. EVID. 406 advisory committee note.

8 FED. R. EVID. 404 advisory committee note.

9 *See, e.g.*, Myrna S. Raeder, *The Admissibility of Prior Acts of Domestic Violence: People v.* Simpson *and Beyond*, 69 S. CAL. L. REV. 1463, 1492 (1996) ("the defendant's specific conduct within a particular relationship educates us about his likely actions concerning the same person in the context of the same relationship.").

10 *See* FED. R. EVID. 404(a) advisory committee note. Although the drafters of the rule did not mention it, these modes of expression are not equivalent: a trait of character may be used circumstantially without being used to infer action in conformity with the character trait. For example, A's character trait—say, for aggressiveness or chronic drunkenness—might have been relied upon by B (outside of court) in deciding how to react to A. The evidence of the character trait would then be offered at trial to explain B's reaction or to increase the likelihood of a certain reaction by B, rather than to increase the likelihood that A acted in accordance with the trait. To avoid this confusion, we sometimes refer to the prohibited use as a propensity inference. In any event, the prohibition is limited to a particular kind of circumstantial use of character.

11 *See* **§ 7.14**.

12 *See* **§ 7.09**.

particular acts of a person reflecting on the person's character—helps to explain the peculiar structure of Rule 404. It contains two apparently distinct prohibitions, Rule 404(a)(1) and Rule 404(b)(1). The prohibition of Rule 404(b)(1) is not really necessary, given Rule 404(a)(1), because the prohibition on "specific act" evidence in 404(b)(1) is included in the prohibition in Rule 404(a)(1) of *any* evidence of character used in the prohibited way. To make sense of this, Rule 404 must be read in connection with Rule 405, which discusses permissible ways of proving character in the exceptional cases when character may be proved.[13] The drafters apparently contemplated that Rule 404(a) would govern when the character of a person is first broached by means of something *other than* evidence of that person's specific acts (i.e., reputation or opinion testimony), whereas Rule 404(b) would govern when the character of the person is first broached by means of evidence of that person's specific acts.[14]

Purposes of the Rule Excluding Character Evidence

It has long been accepted that character evidence is relevant in the minimal sense of having the tendency to make a fact of consequence more or less likely than without the evidence.[15] The fact that a defendant had previously robbed banks makes it somewhat more likely that the defendant is guilty of the bank robbery charged in the present case. Although the evidence is inconclusive, it possesses some probative value.

Similarly, the opinion testimony of a close acquaintance of the defendant that the defendant is the type of person who would rob banks is probative of the defendant's relevant character trait and is circumstantial evidence of behavior. The same can be said for testimony concerning the defendant's reputation as the kind of person who would rob banks. Yet, all these types of character evidence are inadmissible if offered to show that the defendant acted in conformity with such a general disposition.

The reason most commonly given for the character ban is that the trier-of-fact would be unduly prejudiced by the information,[16] and might either overestimate the value of

---

[13] *See* **§ 7.07**.

[14] Thinking about the Rule this way may help, but it is worth noting that this interpretive scheme does not carry through completely. For example, one of the exceptions to the prohibition of Rule 404(a)(1) is for the impeachment of witnesses under Rule 608 and 609, both of which allow the character of the witness for truthfulness to be first raised by the impeaching party's use of evidence of specific facts. *See* **§ 11.09–§ 11.11**.

[15] As Wigmore wrote, "[a] defendant's character, then, as indicating the probability of his doing or not doing the act charged, is essentially relevant." 1A WIGMORE ON EVIDENCE § 55 at 1157 (Tillers rev. 1983) (emphasis in original). *See also* JOHN JAY MCKELVEY, HANDBOOK OF THE LAW OF EVIDENCE § 108 at 149 (1898) ("Where the question is whether X. did or did not do a certain act, his character, if proved, might throw a strong light upon the issue, and justify an inference as to the act charged."); JAMES B. THAYER, A PRELIMINARY TREATISE ON EVIDENCE AT THE COMMON LAW 525 (1898) ("Undoubtedly, as a mere matter of reason, it often affords a good basis of inference.").

[16] *See, e.g.*, Michelson v. United States, 335 U.S. 469 (1948). Justice Jackson wrote:

> The inquiry [into character] is not rejected because character is irrelevant; on the contrary, it is said to weigh too much with the jury and to so overpersuade them as to prejudge one with a bad general record and deny him a fair opportunity to defend against a particular charge. The overriding policy of excluding such evidence, despite its admitted probative value, is the practical experience that its disallowance tends to prevent confusion of issues, unfair surprise, and undue prejudice.

Id. at 475–76 (footnote omitted). *See also* 1 WIGMORE ON EVIDENCE § 58.2 at 1212 (Tillers rev. 1983) (noting that evidence of other acts is excluded, "not because it has no appreciable probative value, but because it has too much. The natural and inevitable tendency of the tribunal—whether judge or jury—is to give excessive weight to the vicious record of crime thus exhibited, and either to allow it to bear too strongly on the present charge, or to take the proof of it as justifying a condemnation irrespective of guilt of the present charge").

the evidence as proof that the defendant committed the crime charged[17] or decide to punish the defendant for being a bad person (or for the past misconduct), even if the trier is not convinced that the defendant was guilty of the crime charged.

Unfair prejudice is not the only concern, however. Commentators have long stressed two other justifications for excluding evidence of other acts. The first reason is the supposed unfairness of surprising the actor with such evidence, potentially requiring the person to defend against allegations of the many events that collectively reveal character. This consideration overlaps with that of unfair prejudice, but encompasses procedural fairness as well. Though surprise is less of a concern under modern rules,[18] it can still be a factor in some situations.

The other commonly stressed reason for exclusion is the fear of over-complicating the issues of the trial, leading to confusion and distraction of the jury and undue lengthening of the trial. The danger of over-complication of issues is real. As one writer has noted, "particularly if there is a dispute about whether the defendant committed the other acts, introduction of evidence concerning those acts could be time-consuming and distract the fact-finder from the central issues in the case."[19] Thus, in some situations, the character evidence rule promotes adjudicative efficiency by preventing the tribunal from pursuing potentially confusing side issues about whether other crimes or acts were in fact committed.

A third possible justification for the character rule is aspirational. The principle that guards against trial by character represents a substantive value about how people *should* behave in relation to each other, the aspiration that people should be judged on their actions rather than their characters. When formal judgments affect a person's life or freedom, perhaps some otherwise rational considerations should be out of bounds. To be sure, we regularly use inferences from evidence of character in our daily lives when deciding diverse matters such as whom to hire as a babysitter or to entrust with a bank deposit. Nobody would deign to tell us we should not do so, and any effort to regulate our

---

[17] Empirical research suggests that "trait theory" is flawed. Trait theory relies on the notion that people possess relatively stable, general traits that manifest themselves consistently and predictably across situations. Today the more dominant theory, interactionism, posits that behavior in a given situation is governed both by a person's general tendencies and by the similarity of the situation to others the person has faced. Even with a large amount of data (an amount no trial court would presently allow), prediction is extremely difficult. For reviews of the psychological literature, *see* Susan M. Davies, *Evidence of Character to Prove Conduct: A Reassessment of Relevancy*, 27 CRIM. L. BULL. 504 (1991); David P. Leonard, *The Use of Character to Prove Conduct: Rationality and Catharsis in the Law of Evidence*, 58 U. COLO. L. REV. 1 (1986–87); Miguel Angel Mendez, *The Law of Evidence and the Search for a Stable Personality*, 45 EMORY L.J. 221 (1996); Miguel Angel Mendez, *California's New Law on Character Evidence: Evidence Code Section 352 and the Impact of Recent Psychological Studies*, 31 UCLA L. REV. 1003 (1984); Andrew E. Taslitz, *Myself Alone: Individualizing Justice Through Psychological Character Evidence*, 52 MD. L. REV. 1 (1993). *See also* MICHAEL R. GOTTFREDSON & TRAVIS HIRSCHI, A GENERAL THEORY OF CRIME 85–91 (1990) (propensity-based theory linking criminality to lack of self-control and appreciation for long-term consequences of committing crime; authors find much evidence of different crimes committed by criminals rather than specialization in particular crimes).

[18] The drafters of the Federal Rules of Evidence did not include "surprise" among the dangers against which probative value should be measured when determining whether to exclude relevant evidence. The Advisory Committee believed that any danger of surprise could be reduced by notice requirements and other procedural devices, and that its impact could be evaluated under the heading of "unfair prejudice." *See* FED. R. EVID. 403 advisory committee note. An amendment to Federal Rule 404(b), in fact, requires that in criminal cases, the prosecution provide the defendant notice of its intent to introduce evidence of the defendant's other acts, and of the general nature of the evidence it intends to offer. FED. R. EVID. 404(b)(2).

[19] Richard B. Kuhns, *The Propensity to Misunderstand the Character of Specific Acts Evidence*, 66 IOWA L. REV. 777 (1981).

behavior to prevent us from considering such qualities would necessarily fail. Moreover, we can reasonably accept more inaccuracy in such realms of private behavior. If it turns out that the information received about the person's past behavior or general character is simply wrong, the error will usually cause a relatively small degree of harm (though at times, the harm can be great, as in marriage or employment decisions). It would thus be impracticable, intrusive, and even counter-productive to try to regulate the use of character evidence in the private dealings of daily life. Indeed, at times the law holds individuals and companies liable for *not* taking character into account.[20] Decisions made in the courtroom, however, fundamentally differ from character assessments made in everyday life. In the courtroom, facts must be adjudicated; in doing so, we inevitably make concrete and largely final decisions about events. In this context, the harms that can be caused by character-based decision-making can be extremely costly.

How the Rules Address Character Evidence

The question of character evidence could be left to the discretion of the trial court, under the general guidelines provided by Rule 403. However, the common law establishes a specific rule structure to deal with this type of evidence and the drafters of the Federal Rules followed the common-law tradition in almost all respects. The result is a series of complicated and occasionally arbitrary rules governing reception of character evidence. In a leading case, the Supreme Court stated that much of the law is "archaic, paradoxical and full of compromises and compensations by which an irrational advantage to one side is offset by a poorly reasoned counter-privilege to the other."[21] Nonetheless, the Court observed, the system has proven workable if clumsy, and to "pull one misshapen stone out of the grotesque structure is more likely simply to upset its present balance between adverse interests than to establish a rational edifice."[22]

The choice to rely on a set of relatively specific rules does not mean, however, that judicial discretion under Rule 403 does not come into play. As discussed below, even if evidence does not violate the prohibitions of Rule 404, it may nonetheless be excluded under Rule 403 if there is too great a risk that the evidence will be used improperly, lead to confusion, or be a waste of time. And when the invocation of Rule 403 does not lead to exclusion, limiting instructions may help to prevent improper, character-based inferences.[23]

---

[20] A defendant's knowledge of a person's bad character trait of carelessness towards others may constitute part of the grounds for imposing liability on the defendant for negligent entrustment of dangerous instrumentalities. *See, e.g.,* Baltimore & Ohio R.R. C. v. Henthorne, 73 F. 634 (6th Cir. 1896) (evidence of defendant train engineer's repeated drunkenness used against defendant railroad to show negligent entrustment); Cullara v. Bldg. & Earth Scis., Inc., 794 S.E.2d 665 (Ga. Ct. App. 2016) (reversing summary judgment on negligent entrustment where employer knew of drunk-driving history of employee who injured plaintiff).

[21] Michelson v. United States, 335 U.S. 469, 486 (1948).

[22] *Id.*

[23] *See* **§ 7.16**. Problems of character evidence are especially likely to trigger the following reminder provided by the drafters of the Federal Rules: "In reaching a decision whether to exclude on grounds of unfair prejudice, consideration should be given to the probable effectively or lack of effectiveness of a limiting instruction." FED. R. EVID. 403 advisory committee note.

§ 7.02 Exceptions to the Character Evidence Prohibition—Overview

The rule against using character evidence circumstantially to prove conduct conforming to character on a particular occasion is subject to exceptions. Before examining these exceptions, however, it is helpful to recognize that most of the litigation concerning character evidence does not deal with the scope of the exceptions, but rather with whether the character evidence rule applies at all. The rule has limited scope, applying only to evidence of general disposition offered for the purpose of showing an action in conformity with that disposition. Evidence of other crimes, wrongs, and acts may be relevant and admissible on the theory that the character evidence prohibition simply does not apply, because no such inference from character is being invited. That possibility is taken up later in this chapter, after the discussion of exceptions to the character evidence prohibition.[24]

The prohibition on using character evidence to invite an inference that the person acted in conformity with a propensity is subject to five exceptions under the Federal Rules and similar state rules:

1. The defendant in a criminal case may offer pertinent character evidence about himself or herself. If the defendant opens the door by offering this evidence, the prosecution may rebut it with contradictory character evidence.[25]

2. Subject to the limit of the rape shield rule, the accused and the prosecution may offer pertinent evidence about the character of the victim of a crime. For example, in an assault case in which the defendant claims that the alleged victim was the first aggressor, the defendant may call witnesses to testify that the victim had a violent character. When the defendant makes this attack, the prosecution may rebut by supporting the victim's character or by attacking the defendant's character for the same trait.[26]

3. In a homicide case as to which the defense provides evidence (not necessarily character evidence) that the alleged victim was the first aggressor, the prosecutor may rebut with evidence that the victim had a peaceful disposition.[27]

4. In 1995, Congress added exceptions to the general rule against character to prove conduct. These rules allow evidence of the defendant's similar misconduct in prosecutions for sexual assault or child molestation. There is a similar exception for civil actions arising from such sexual misconduct.[28]

5. Any party in a civil or criminal case may attack the character of a witness for truthfulness.[29] After the witness's character for truthfulness has been

---

[24] *See* **§ 7.09–§ 7.14**.

[25] *See* **§ 7.03** & **§ 7.05**.

[26] *See* **§ 7.04** & **§ 7.05**.

[27] *See* **§ 7.05**.

[28] This controversial set of exceptions, which has also been enacted in some states, is discussed in **§ 7.06**.

[29] *See* FED. R. EVID. 404(a)(3).

attacked, it may be supported. This topic is addressed in a separate chapter in connection with impeachment of witnesses.[30]

§ 7.03 Exceptions to the Character Evidence Prohibition—Defendant's Evidence of Defendant's Good Character in Criminal Cases [FRE 404(a)(2)(A)]

Both the common law and the Federal Rules recognize an exception to the rules against character evidence for criminal defendants who wish to offer witnesses to attest to their good character.[31] In this respect, the defense possesses an advantage over the prosecution. The defense is entitled to offer character evidence as part of his or her case in chief. The prosecution, however, may offer character evidence only if the accused first "opens the door."[32] One possible explanation for this difference is that our system has a built-in preference for freeing the guilty over convicting the innocent. The inherent dangers in offering bad character against the criminal defendant are considerably greater than the possible inferential error by the use of good character evidence to prove innocence. Perhaps the exception is just a merciful courtesy to the defendant, or compensation for other features of a criminal trial that favor the prosecution. In any event, the danger that someone of good character may be falsely incriminated by circumstantial evidence leads to the desire to demonstrate the person's good character.

Although it is well established that the defendant in a criminal case may offer evidence of good character, the form of that evidence is limited. While evidence of specific good deeds by the defendant—for example, individual acts of honesty and kindness—might be the most persuasive evidence of character, such "specific act" evidence is universally excluded. Generally, evidence of specific acts is not admissible to show character, although the defendant's attorney may introduce some "background" about such matters as the defendant's occupation, education, family, and military service, at least when the defendant testifies.[33]

At common law, character evidence was limited to the rather colorless form of community reputation. Under the Federal Rules, the permissible form of evidence includes a knowledgeable witness's opinion of the defendant's character.[34] Originally, reputation in the community was considered more probative than specific acts, because

---

30 *See* **§ 11.07**.

31 *See* FED. R. EVID. 404(a); Michelson v. United States, 335 U.S. 469, 476 (1948) (common-law rule); David P. Leonard, *The Use of Character to Prove Conduct: Rationality and Catharsis in the Law of Evidence*, 58 U. COLO. L. REV. 1 (1986–87) (common law and Federal Rule); Richard Uviller, *Evidence of Character to Prove Conduct: Illusion, Illogic, and Injustice in the Courtroom*, 130 U. PA. L. REV. 845 (1982) (entire structure of character evidence rules); Richard C. Wydick, *Character Evidence: A Guided Tour of the Grotesque Structure*, 21 U.C. DAVIS L. REV. 123 (1987) (similar).

32 *See* **§ 7.05**.

33 *See* State v. Stokes, 523 P.2d 364, 366 (Kan. 1974) (holding that "background information" and "biographical data," such as "place of birth, education, length of residence in the community, length of marriage, size of family, occupation, place of employment, service in armed forces and receipt of honorable discharge," are not considered character evidence entitling prosecution to respond with evidence of bad character; defendant "entitled to let the jury know who he is"). In this respect, the criminal defendant is similar to other witnesses. *See* **§ 11.13**. The defendant may present at least a limited amount of information about his background through other witnesses without placing his character in issue and thus allowing the prosecution to respond with negative character evidence. *See* City of Topeka v. Harvey, 365 P.2d 1109 (Kan. 1961) (holding defendant's wife's testimony regarding length of marriage and number of children was not character evidence permitting the prosecution to introduce evidence of defendant's propensity for drunk driving).

34 *See* FED. R. EVID. 405(a). For further discussion, *see* **§ 7.07**.

it represented the community's collected wisdom about a lifetime of activity.[35] In modern society, where transient populations and breakdowns of community ties make it more difficult to derive reliable reputation testimony, evidence of specific acts is probably a better indicator of true character. Nonetheless, the limitation to reputation and opinion testimony remains a rational one, because restricting the testimony to that form saves time and avoids mini trials about whether conduct actually took place.

Testimony about the accused's character must concern a "pertinent" trait.[36] Thus, a defendant charged with a crime of dishonesty may not offer testimony about his character for peacefulness, but is limited to providing testimony about traits relating to honesty.[37] Regarding an extremely general trait, such as the defendant's proclivity to obey the law, some common law courts permitted witnesses to testify about the defendant's reputation as a law-abiding person; others have required more specificity.[38] The exception for defense character evidence in the Federal Rules of Evidence refers to the admissibility of a "pertinent trait of character" and the advisory committee's note states that proof is limited to "pertinent traits of character, rather than character generally."[39] Specific traits such as honesty and nonviolence are admissible, but general testimony that a person has "good character" is not. Many courts, however, have permitted opinion or reputation testimony to the effect that the defendant is a "law-abiding citizen."[40]

§ 7.04 Exceptions to the Character Evidence Prohibition—Defendant's Evidence of the Character of the Alleged Victim in Criminal Cases [FRE 404(a)(2)(B)]

Evidence about the character of the victim in a criminal case is not admissible to show the victim was a bad person who deserved to be a victim. However, the Federal Rules permit the accused in a criminal case to offer evidence of a "pertinent trait" of the victim's character to show that the victim acted in conformity with the pertinent character trait.[41] For example, suppose the accused is charged with assault and battery, and claims self-defense, asserting that the victim attacked first. The rule permits the accused to offer character evidence to show the victim's violent character, and thus, that the victim was likely the first aggressor.[42]

Generally, the accused is the one to get the ball rolling and must decide whether to offer evidence of the victim's character. If the accused does not offer evidence of the victim's character to invite a propensity inference about the victim's behavior on the

---

35 *See* 5 WIGMORE ON EVIDENCE § 1610 at 582 (Chadbourn rev. 1974).

36 *See* FED. R. EVID. 404(a)(2)(A).

37 *See* 22 CHARLES A. WRIGHT & KENNETH W. GRAHAM, JR., FEDERAL PRACTICE AND PROCEDURE: EVIDENCE § 5236 (1978).

38 *See* 1A WIGMORE ON EVIDENCE § 59 nn.1–2 (Tillers rev. 1983).

39 FED. R. EVID. 404 advisory committee note.

40 *See, e.g.*, United States v. Angelini, 678 F.2d 380 (1st Cir. 1982); United States v. Kellogg, 510 F.3d 188, 192 (3d Cir. 2007); United States v. Hewitt, 634 F.2d 277 (5th Cir. 1981).

41 This exception is limited to criminal cases and generally must be initiated by the accused.

42 *See, e.g.*, United States v. Perez-Casillas, 607 F. Supp. 88 (D.P.R. 1985) (in prosecution of police officers for perjury and conspiracy in killing two individuals, evidence that victims had reputation for violence and aggression to prove alleged victims were first aggressors in confrontation that led to their deaths).

occasion in question, the prosecution, with one limited exception, may not do so.[43] Of course, the rule permits the prosecution to rebut the accused's character evidence, as in those circumstances when the accused introduces character evidence about him or herself.[44]

Obviously, a general tendency toward violence would be pertinent to the accused's claim that the victim attacked first. But in many criminal cases, the victim's character simply will not be pertinent to any issue. It is difficult to imagine, for example, how the victim's character could be relevant in prosecutions for robbery, burglary, or fraud. Unless the accused can convince the court that a particular character trait is pertinent to her defense, this exception will not apply.

Crimes of personal violence present the most common situation in which the accused may seek to offer evidence of a victim's pertinent character trait. In those cases, the accused may offer evidence that the victim had a violent or turbulent character to support the claim that the alleged victim was the first aggressor, and hence that the accused should be acquitted on grounds of self-defense. To persuade the trier that the victim was not the first aggressor, the prosecution may seek to rebut such evidence by introducing evidence of the victim's peaceable character to show that the victim did not attack the accused.

When the victim's violent character was known to the accused, and is offered to show how the accused acted based on that knowledge, the rule against character evidence erects no obstacle, and no exception is needed to admit the evidence. The evidence would be admissible, even in the absence of an exception to the character evidence rule, because it is not offered to show action in conformity with character. Instead, it is used to show the reasonableness of the criminal accused's belief in the necessity for violent resistance. If the accused believed the victim had violent propensities, that belief might support a claim that the accused's conduct was reasonable, whether or not the victim actually possessed such a character trait or acted in conformity with it.[45] Moreover, if there is a question whether the accused was aware of the violent propensities of the victim, evidence of those violent propensities can support the accused's claim that he or she was aware of them, again without any propensity inference.[46] This constitutes a circumstantial use of (but not a propensity inference from) character.

An exception to the rule against character evidence is needed, however, when the accused offers evidence of the victim's violent character to show that the victim was the first aggressor. Most jurisdictions and the Federal Rules provide for such an exception.[47] By use of reputation evidence or, in jurisdictions following the Federal Rules, by use of

---

[43] In homicide cases the prosecutor may offer evidence of the victim's peaceableness where the victim is accused of being the first aggressor even if no character evidence was introduced. FED. R. EVID. 404(a)(2)(C).

[44] *See* **§ 7.05**.

[45] The admissibility of evidence of the victim's violent character, when that character was known to the defendant prior to the incident, is clearly established. 1A WIGMORE ON EVIDENCE § 63 at 1369 (Tillers rev. 1983); Smith v. State, 606 So. 2d 641, 642–43 (Fla. Dist. Ct. App. 1992) (holding that trial court erred by excluding evidence of victim's specific acts of violence against defendant, his family and others, when defendant knew about attacks and defendant pleaded self-defense); State v. Miranda, 405 A.2d 622 (Conn. 1978); People v. Lynch, 470 N.E.2d 1018 (Ill. 1984); State v. Jacoby, 260 N.W.2d 828 (Iowa 1977).

[46] *See, e.g.*, United States v. James, 169 F.3d 1210 (9th Cir. 1999) (holding it error to exclude evidence of the misconduct of a homicide victim to corroborate defendant's assertion that the victim had bragged about his violent past).

[47] *See* 1A WIGMORE ON EVIDENCE § 63 (Tillers rev. 1983).

opinion testimony as well, the accused may show that the victim possessed a violent character. In jurisdictions following the Federal Rules, specific instances of conduct are not admissible for this purpose if the sole reason is to show the victim had a general disposition toward violence.[48] Of course, specific acts of violence by the victim are admissible if they are relevant for some other, non-propensity inference, such as showing motive or a specific (and thus "non-character") disposition to act violently toward a specific person. Thus, a husband's prior acts of beating his wife while intoxicated are admissible when offered to show, not that the husband was a generally violent person, but that he had a specific propensity to beat his wife, and that his wife was aware of it, and hence she acted in self-defense.[49]

Rape Shield Limitation

At common law, courts construed the exception permitting a defendant to introduce evidence of a pertinent trait of character of the alleged victim to allow a particular kind of character evidence in sexual assault cases, particularly where the defendant asserted that the sex was consensual. Specifically, it permitted a defendant to present evidence of promiscuity on the part of the alleged victim on the theory that this indicated a propensity to consent. The defendant was permitted to invite the jury to infer that the alleged victim acted in conformity with this propensity by consenting to sex with the defendant. This use of evidence by the defense has been dramatically curtailed by rape shield laws, discussed later in this chapter.[50] Rule 404(a)(2)(B) specifically mentions the limitation of the federal version of this law, which appears as Rule 412. Because Rule 412 more broadly restricts the admission of evidence than being merely a limitation on Rule 404(a)(2)(B), we discuss it after a more complete presentation of the character evidence rules.

§ 7.05 Exceptions to the Character Evidence Prohibition—Rebuttal by the Government [FRE 404(a)(2)]

The criminal defendant may open the door to the prosecution's attack on his or her character in three ways. The first happens when the accused affirmatively presents favorable evidence about his or her own character and therefore places his or her character in controversy, pursuant to Rule 404(a)(2)(A). The second happens when the accused attacks the alleged victim's character, under Rule 404(a)(2)(B), which allows the prosecutor to attack the same trait of the accused.[51] Third, a criminal defendant can open the door to a character attack by taking the stand as a witness, pursuant to Rule 404(a)(3). As with any witness, testifying places his or her character as a witness in controversy, but the evidence is limited to character for honesty and trustworthiness. This last ground for the use of character evidence is addressed in another chapter,

---

48 FED. R. EVID. 405(a); *see* United States v. Waloke, 962 F.2d 824, 830 (8th Cir. 1992) (holding that although evidence of victim's reputation for violence after drinking was properly allowed, danger of unfair prejudice and "collateral mini trials" warrants excluding evidence in assault case of specific violent acts by victim); United States v. Keiser, 57 F.3d 847, 856–57 (9th Cir. 1995) (holding that evidence that victim pointed to defendant's brother and told his family and friends that he was "the fucker's brother" and to remember his face though relevant was properly excluded under Rule 405).

49 *See, e.g.*, United States v. McIntire, 461 F.2d 1092, 1092–93 (5th Cir. 1972); White v. State, 717 S.W.2d 784 (Ark. 1986); Worthington v. State, 405 N.E.2d 913 (Ind. 1980).

50 *See* **§ 7.13**.

51 In 2000, Rule 404 was amended to provide that if the accused offers evidence of a trait of the alleged victim's character, the prosecution may respond with evidence of the same trait of the accused. This is true even if the accused has not first offered evidence of her good character.

h other forms of impeachments.[52] The following paragraphs address the first
ıs other exceptional grounds for the prosecution's use of character evidence.

ʷʷnen the accused offers character witnesses who attest to the accused's good character, the accused opens the door to rebuttal by the prosecution. Although it is often said that by offering character evidence the defendant has put his or her "character in issue," this phrase can be confusing. Character does not become an ultimate issue, as Rule 405(b) uses the term,[53] merely because the defendant has offered character evidence. The ultimate issue remains whether the defendant committed the crime charged, not whether the defendant had a good or bad character. Character is merely an evidentiary fact that circumstantially bears upon the accused's guilt.

Once the accused opens the door, the prosecution may offer contrary evidence of the accused's character evidence in two ways. First, the prosecution may cross-examine the defendant's character witnesses, and such cross-examination may include questions about specific instances of the defendant's conduct that bear on the traits of character to which the witness testified on direct examination. Second, the prosecution may call its own witnesses to rebut the evidence of defendant's character. This rebuttal testimony must concern the same pertinent trait as that raised by the accused; such testimony must be in the form of reputation or opinion.[54]

This first form of attack is likely to be the most effective because, on cross-examination, the prosecution may elicit testimony about the accused's bad acts or prior crimes.[55] The prosecutor's questions about specific instances generally will be much more powerful than the evidence of the accused's character witnesses, who must testify in the form of opinion and reputation, and may not describe specific good deeds of the defendant. For example, in *Michelson v. United States*,[56] the defendant's character witnesses testified favorably about his reputation for honesty and truthfulness and for being a law-abiding citizen. On cross-examination, the prosecutor asked the character witnesses the following questions:

> "Did you ever hear that Mr. Michelson on March 4, 1927 was convicted of a violation of the trademark law in New York City in regard to watches?"

---

[52] *See* **§ 11.07**.

[53] *See* **§ 7.14**.

[54] *See* FED. R. EVID. 404(a)(2)(A). Rule 404(a)(2)(A) states that "if the [defendant's] evidence is admitted, the prosecutor may offer evidence to rebut it." One might be tempted to think that this refers to things it does not. Specifically, the prosecutor does not need the authority of this rule to *impeach* the defendant's character witness, and that is not what this provision is about. Rather, this provision authorizes the prosecution specifically to rebut the defendant's character evidence by offering contrary character evidence about the defendant, evidence that otherwise would be barred by Rule 404(a)(1). The form in which that rebuttal may occur is then governed by Rule 405(a).

[55] *See, e.g.*, United States v. Smith-Bowman, 76 F.3d 634, 636 (5th Cir. 1996) (permitting prosecution to ask accused's character witness whether he had heard that accused had used her Red Cross VISA card to pay for motel room for rendezvous with her boyfriend and to buy jewelry for herself); United States v. Holt, 170 F.3d 698, 701 (7th Cir. 1999) (holding that where part-time police officer charged with conspiring to transfer automatic weapon called character witness to testify about his good reputation for being law-abiding person, court did not err in allowing prosecution to ask witness about defendant's non-payment of child support and about sexual harassment allegations against him); SEC v. Peters, 978 F.2d 1162, 1171–73 (10th Cir. 1992) (holding that trial court committed reversible error by allowing defendant to present impressive array of "good character witnesses" while refusing to allow SEC to cross-examine witnesses about sworn charges and past lawsuits against defendant for fraud and insider trading).

[56] Michelson v. United States, 335 U.S. 469 (1948).

"Did you ever hear that on October 11th, 1920, the defendant, Solomon Michelson, was arrested for receiving stolen goods?"

One of these questions concerned a twenty-year-old conviction; the other concerned an arrest that did not result in conviction. Both involved specific acts, not general testimony about reputation or opinion. Nonetheless, the Supreme Court affirmed the conviction on the theory that they were pertinent to whether the character witnesses were in fact knowledgeable about the defendant's reputation (not to whether the defendant actually committed the prior acts). If the character witnesses had not heard about the arrest and conviction, they were not fully knowledgeable; if they had heard, then one might question their assessment of good reputation.

Thus, the presentation of character evidence by the defense opens the door to potentially damaging questioning of the character witnesses regarding specific prior bad acts. However, the rules place significant limitations upon the prosecutor's freedom to cross-examine a witness about specific instances. First, the prosecutor must accept the witness's answer. Extrinsic evidence (that is to say, evidence outside of cross-examination) of the defendant's prior conduct is inadmissible.[57] If the witness denies having heard of the prior conduct, the prosecution may not produce other witnesses to prove that the defendant in fact engaged in the character-destroying conduct.[58] Second, the prosecutor must have a good-faith basis for asking the question. That is, the prosecutor cannot simply manufacture questions about prior convictions, arrests, or bad acts, but must actually have information indicating that these events occurred.[59] Third, because the misconduct is only admissible to impeach the character witness, it cannot be secret misconduct known only to the prosecutor. In the case of an opinion character witness, it must be misconduct that the witness reasonably could be expected to know about; in the case of a reputation witness, it must be misconduct that would be known in the community.[60] Finally, the prosecution should refrain from asking hypothetical questions about whether the witness would testify differently if she assumed the defendant to be guilty of the charged crime.[61]

[57] Extrinsic evidence is any evidence outside of that derived from the witness currently being cross-examined. Extrinsic evidence is an important concept in the rules regarding impeachment of witnesses. *See* **§ 11.01**.

[58] *See* FED. R. EVID. 405(b) advisory committee note.

[59] United States v. Beno, 324 F.2d 582 (2d Cir. 1963); United States v. Wells, 525 F.2d 974 (5th Cir. 1976); State v. Keul, 5 N.W.2d 849 (Iowa 1942); 1 MCCORMICK ON EVIDENCE § 191 at 1065–66 (Kenneth S. Broun, 7th ed. 2013). Logically speaking, the prosecution should be permitted to ask defendant's reputation witnesses about the arrest as long as there is a good faith belief that rumors were circulating through the community that the arrest had occurred, even if such rumors were untrue. (If rumors were circulating, and the witnesses had not heard them, the jury might question the witnesses' knowledge; if the witnesses had heard the rumors but nevertheless testified favorably about defendant's reputation, the jury might question the witnesses' judgment.) The Supreme Court recognized this illogical aspect of the rule, but retained the common-law requirement of a good faith belief that the arrest actually occurred, in order to prevent undue prejudice to the defendant. Michelson v. United States, 335 U.S. 469, 481 n.18 (1948).

[60] *See* United States v. Monteleone, 77 F.3d 1086, 1090 (8th Cir. 1996) (question about whether character witness had heard that defendant perjured himself before grand jury improper since witness would not know what had happened in secret grand jury proceedings).

[61] United States v. Mason, 993 F.2d 406 (4th Cir. 1993) (court erred in allowing prosecutor to cross-examine character witness about whether witness would change mind if defendant was guilty of instant crime); United States v. Guzman, 167 F.3d 1350, 1352–53 (11th Cir. 1999) (error, although harmless, to allow prosecution to question character witness with hypothetical question asking whether witness's opinion would change if defendant was guilty of crime charged).

If the prosecutor questions character witnesses about prior acts of the accused, the defense is entitled to a limiting instruction describing how the jury should use the evidence.[62] Because the concept under which the evidence is admitted is a complicated one, the instruction is hard to understand and apply but should nevertheless be requested by the defense, if only to preserve the point on appeal. The instruction should state that the jury should not assume that the incidents asked about actually took place, but should instead use the evidence only to test the witness's knowledge of, or standard for evaluating, the reputation of the defendant.[63]

When the accused offers character evidence about the victim, under Rule 404(a)(2)(B), that also triggers rebuttal and cross-examination by the prosecution in regard to the same trait. Once the defendant opens the door by attacking the victim's character for peacefulness, or otherwise offers testimony to support the claim that the victim was the first aggressor, the prosecution may rebut with opinion and reputation evidence to support the victim's character with evidence that the victim had a peaceable disposition.

Under Rule 404(a)(2)(C), in a homicide case, the prosecution can also offer evidence of the peaceable character of the victim even if the defense did not introduce any character evidence against the victim, but merely asserted via eyewitness testimony that the victim struck first. The justification for allowing the prosecutor to initiate character evidence stems from the fact that it is a homicide case, and the victim is not available to tell her side of the story.

Finally, under the Federal Rules, if the accused introduces evidence about a particular trait of the victim, the prosecutor can challenge the character *of the accused* regarding that same trait. So if the accused argued that the victim tended to be violent and hence probably initiated the brawl, the prosecutor could rebut both with evidence of the victim's peaceableness as well as evidence of the accused's violent tendencies.

§ 7.06 Exceptions to the Character Evidence Prohibition—Character of Defendant in Sexual Assault and Child Molestation Cases [FRE 413–415]

In cases of alleged sex crime, evidence law faces a difficult issue of how to deal with an accused who has an alleged history of similar conduct. Evidence of similar sexual improprieties might be admitted on any of three bases. First, the prosecutor might offer such other crimes or acts for a non-propensity inference under Rule 404(b)(2), to show motive, plan, or preparation, or to show identity because "signature" crimes used the

---

[62] *See* FED. R. EVID. 105.

[63] One example of this instruction was given by the trial court in the *Michelson* case. The instruction stated:

> I instruct the jury that what is happening now is this: the defendant has called character witnesses, and the basis for the evidence given by those character witnesses is the reputation of the defendant in the community, and since the defendant tenders the issue of his reputation the prosecution may ask the witness if she has heard of various incidents in his career. I say to you that regardless of her answer you are not to assume that the incidents asked about actually took place. All that is happening is that this witness's standard of opinion of the character or reputation of the defendant is being tested.

Michelson v. United States, 335 U.S. 469, 472 n.3 (1948).

same modus operandi.[64] When offered on these grounds, the other act evidence is not prohibited character evidence, and no exception to the character ban is needed. Because the jury might use such evidence for impermissible purposes, however, admission is subject to Rule 403, whereby the judge weighs the danger that it will be used for the forbidden purpose against its probative value for the permitted purpose. If the judge admits the evidence, the defendant is also entitled to a limiting instruction.

Second, if the accused testifies, evidence that the defendant was *convicted* of a felony (even of a similar sex crime) might be offered to impeach the defendant's character for truthfulness as a witness under Rule 609.[65] As with the example of non-character purposes above, the evidence is not offered to prove propensity to commit a certain type of sex crime. Instead, evidence of prior convictions could be admissible solely on the issue of truthfulness and is subject to a special balancing test, weighing its probative value for this purpose against the risk of unfair prejudice to the accused, including the risk that it will be used to infer a propensity to commit sex crimes.

The foregoing possibilities are essentially the same as those for all alleged crimes. But there is a third possibility, an exception to the propensity ban that is available only in the context of sex crimes. In some jurisdictions, including the federal courts, prior sex offenses may be admissible as evidence of a propensity to commit sex crimes.[66] In 1995, Congress enacted new Federal Rules of Evidence specifically targeting crimes of rape and child molestation. Rule 413, concerning sexual assault, and Rule 414, concerning child molestation, allow prior sex offenses (of the same type) by the accused to be admitted for any relevant purpose, including the propensity to commit sex crimes.[67] Under Rule 415, the same types of misconduct are admissible in civil actions for alleged sexual assault or child molestation.[68] These rules obviously function as an exception to the traditional rule prohibiting circumstantial use of character evidence for a propensity

---

[64] *See* **§ 7.09** & **§ 7.10** (subsection on "Other Acts of Sexual Misconduct"); David P. Bryden & Roger C. Park, *"Other Crimes" Evidence in Sex Offense Cases*, 78 MINN. L. REV. 529, 540–56 (1994).

[65] *See* **§ 11.10**.

[66] Adoption of the rules by states has not been rapid, though it is still significant. Approximately fifteen states have adopted Rules 413–415, sometimes with interesting variations, including California, Florida, Arizona, Illinois and Alaska. *See, e.g.*, FLA. STAT. ANN. § 90.404; 725 ILL. COMP. STAT. ANN. § 5/115–7.3 (child molestation); ARIZ. REV. STAT. ANN. § 13–1420 (2008). For a review of state adoptions, see Joyce R. Lombardi, Comment, *Because Sex Crimes are Different: Why Maryland Should (Carefully) Adopt the Contested Federal Rules of Evidence 413 and 414 That Permit Propensity Evidence of a Criminal Defendant's Other Sex Offenses*, 34 U. BALT. L. REV. 103, 116 (2004). (Note, however, that Indiana courts, asserting control of the rules of evidence, have refused to accept a version of Rule 414 despite legislative action. *See, e.g.*, Brim v. State, 624 N.E.2d 27, 33 n.2 (Ind. App. 1993).)

[67] Rule 414 is identical to Rule 413 except that Rule 413 applies to rape, while Rule 414 applies to child molestation; the case law developed for one rule applies to the other. *See, e.g.*, United States v. Dewrell, 55 M.J. 131, 138 n.4 (C.A.A.F. 2001) ("As Rules 413 and 414 are essentially the same in substance, the analysis for proper admission of evidence under either should be the same.").

[68] FED. R. EVID. 415. The rule has been applied in sexual harassment cases, provided that the alleged conduct involves sexual assault as defined in Rule 413(d). *See, e.g.*, Boyce v. Weber, 2021 WL 2821154 at *8–*9 (S.D.N.Y., July 7, 2021).

inference.[69] Jurors may use this evidence to reason that the accused is more likely to be guilty of the crime charged because he committed similar wrongs in the past.[70]

To apply Rule 413 (or Rule 414), the prosecutor must demonstrate that (1) the defendant is accused of the offense of sexual assault (or, for Rule 414, child molestation); (2) the proffered evidence pertains to the accused's commission of another sexual assault (or child molestation); and (3) the evidence is relevant.[71] The accused need not take the stand for his prior bad sex acts to be admitted—these prior bad acts are admissible in the prosecutor's case-in-chief. Additionally, the accused's prior sex offenses need not have been the subject of a conviction, or even arrest.[72] There is no requirement of special similarity; the crime need only be of the same general type currently charged. Thus, even a dissimilar rape is admissible in a rape case, and a dissimilar act of child molestation is admissible in a child molestation case. The rules provide no time limit, and prior bad acts that occurred twenty to thirty years earlier are regularly admitted. To consider the propensity evidence, jurors need only reasonably believe that the asserted prior bad sex act occurred.[73]

As noted above, however, the rules limit the prosecution to evidence of the same type of misconduct. Thus, acts of child molestation (sometimes) will not be admissible in prosecutions for rape. However, if an act of child molestation also falls within the definition of sexual assault in Rule 413, then the former would be admissible in a trial for sexual assault.[74] A sexual assault involving a person under the age of 14 can come

---

[69] *See* United States v. Seymour, 468 F.3d 378, 386 (6th Cir. 2006) ("Rule 413 was enacted as an exception to the default position set forth in Rule 404(b) that propensity evidence is presumptively more prejudicial than probative."); United States v. Hawpetoss, 478 F.3d 820, 823 (7th Cir. 2007) ("[Rules 413–414] create an exception to the general prohibition against 'propensity evidence' found in Federal Rule of Evidence 404(b)."); United States v. Tyndall, 263 F.3d 848, 850 (8th Cir. 2001) ("Although Federal Rule of Evidence 404(b) generally excludes the admission of evidence of other crimes to show the propensity to commit a particular crime, Congress excepted sexual assault cases from this rule when it enacted Federal Rule of Evidence 413.").

[70] It is clear from the plain text of the rules and the few cases that have considered the issue, that uncharged offenses that occurred after the charged conduct are also admissible. *See* United States v. Sioux, 362 F.3d 1241, 1244–47 (9th Cir. 2004) (language and logic of rules apply to post-charged conduct); United States v. James, 60 M.J. 870, 873 (A.F. Ct. Crim. App. 2005) ("[T]he fact that propensity evidence occurs after the dates of the charged offenses is not a barrier to its admission."). *But see* United States v. Wright, 53 M.J. 476, 486 (C.A.A.F. 2000) (Sullivan, J., concurring) (majority's admission of conduct that occurred nearly six months after charged offense as inconsistent with Military Rules of Evidence questioned).

[71] *See* United States v. Stamper, 106 F. App'x 833, 835 (4th Cir. 2004); United States v. Fitzgerald, 80 Fed. Appx. 857, 863 (4th Cir. 2003); Doe v. Glanzer, 232 F.3d 1258, 1268 (9th Cir. 2000); United States v. Guardia, 135 F.3d 1326, 1328 (10th Cir. 1998).

[72] *See* United States v. Fitzgerald, 2003 WL 22700896 (4th Cir. 2003) ("The defendant does not have to have been convicted of, or even charged with, the prior act."). In some cases, prosecutors have even introduced previously acquitted conduct. *See* Hess v. State, 20 P.3d 1121, 1124, 1129 (Alaska 2001) (evidence of defendant's prior sexual assault admitted, but holding "that it was error not to inform the jury of [the accused's] acquittal"); People v. Mullens, 14 Cal. Rptr. 3d 534, 549–50 (Cal. Ct. App. 2004) (it was error to exclude evidence of acquittal of other sexual molestation offenses used for propensity purposes).

[73] This standard, that the jury could reasonably find by a preponderance of the evidence that the other acts had occurred, derives from Huddleston v. United States, 485 U.S. 681, 690 (1988), and is regularly applied in Rule 413–414 as well as 404(b) cases. *See* United States v. Norris, 428 F.3d 907, 913–14 (9th Cir. 2005) ("The Supreme Court's decision in Huddleston controls the standard of proof required to admit evidence under Rules 413–415."); United States v. Enjady, 134 F.3d 1427, 1433 (10th Cir. 1998) ("The district court must make a preliminary finding that a jury could reasonably find by a preponderance of the evidence that the 'other act' occurred."); United States v. Schroder, 65 M.J. 49, 54 n.2 (C.A.A.F. 2007) (military judge's instruction to jury "that 'the jury could reasonably find . . . by a preponderance of the evidence' that the other acts had occurred" did not suggest misapplication of the law).

[74] *See, e.g.*, United States v. Batton, 602 F.3d 1191, 1197 (10th Cir. 2010) (approving the use of Rule 413 under particular facts in a child molestation case).

within the scope of both Rule 413 and Rule 414. The principal difference between the criteria of the two rules is that child molestation under Rule 414, while narrower in the sense of covering only child victims, is broader in the sense that it includes various offenses related to child pornography under 18 U.S.C. ch. 110.[75] As a matter of trial strategy, of course, the two are very different because there is no consent defense to child molestation.

Only specific instances of conduct are allowed, and in this respect, this exceptional propensity use of evidence is quite different from that permitted under Rule 404(a)(2), discussed in the previous sections, whereby the defense initiates propensity inference evidence. The prosecutor invoking Rule 413 or 414 must give advance notice of his intent to admit such evidence, and failure to do so may lead to exclusion of the evidence.[76]

Application of Rule 403

While there was some initial confusion over the applicability of Rule 403, appellate courts uniformly have held that Rules 413–414 require an additional step of judicial balancing under Rule 403.[77] As a practical matter, however, in the context of Rules 413 and 414, Rule 403 is often transformed into "403-lite" and actually provides little real protection to the accused.[78] Rather than scrutinize the individual facts of the cases, courts tend to rely on the rules' legislative history to deem the probative value of the

---

[75] *See* FED. R. EVID. 413(d), 414(d). The definitions of "sexual assault" and "child molestation" are extremely broad, at least so long as the act in question occurred within the United States. *See* 2 CHRISTOPHER B. MUELLER & LAIRD C. KIRKPATRICK, FEDERAL EVIDENCE § 4:84 at 334–37 (4th ed. 2013). One very peculiar consequence of the drafting, however, is that evidence of other crimes that occur outside the United States do not seem to be treated the same way that the same crime would be treated if it occurred within the United States. Rule 413(d) and 414(d) define sexual assault and child molestation in terms of an act that is "a crime under federal law or under state law." While this might have been intended to protect defendants from bizarre definitions of criminal conduct used by other countries, such a possibility could easily have been avoided by defining these concepts in terms of what *would be* a sexual assault or child molestation had it occurred within federal geographical jurisdiction or by providing separate definitions of such acts for purposes of the rules of evidence.

[76] *See* United States v. LeCompte, 99 F.3d 274, 276 (8th Cir. 1996) (rejecting government admission of evidence under Rule 414 where notice was provided only "[o]n the eve of trial").

[77] Rules 413, 414, and 415, as originally enacted, stated that the evidence of prior acts "is admissible, and may be considered for its bearing on any matter to which it is relevant," a command that would seem to supersede all exclusionary rules other than Rule 402, thus permitting hearsay evidence of such prior acts, as well as evidence that cannot pass the Rule 403 balancing test. Based on the legislative history, the courts have clarified that the new rules function simply as exceptions to the character evidence prohibition of Rule 404. *See, e.g.*, United States v. Guardia, 135 F.3d 1326 (10th Cir. 1998). The restyling of the rules has made this only somewhat clearer by stating that "the court *may* admit" such prior act evidence. *See* FED. R. EVID. 413(a), 414(a), 415(a).

[78] *See* United States v. LeCompte, 131 F.3d 767, 768 (8th Cir. 1997) (Rule 403 must be read "to give effect to the decision of Congress, expressed in recently enacted Rule 414, to loosen to a substantial degree the restrictions of prior law on the admissibility of such evidence"); United States v. Meacham, 115 F.3d 1488, 1492 (10th Cir. 1997) ("[C]learly under Rule 414 the courts are to 'liberally' admit evidence of prior uncharged sex offenses."). *See generally* Aviva Orenstein, *Deviance, Due Process, and the False Promise of Federal Rule of Evidence 403*, 90 CORNELL L. REV. 1487 (2005) (coining term "403-lite"). Where the trial court fails to conduct a Rule 403 balancing test at all, however, the conviction will be reversed. *See* United States v. Velarde, 214 F.3d 1204, 1212 (10th Cir. 2000).

evidence high,[79] and denigrate any unfair prejudice as merely the dangers inherent in propensity evidence that are built into the rules' design.[80]

The new rules alter basic precepts about both sides of the Rule 403 balance—probativeness and unfair prejudice—but they especially change the understanding of the latter. The Eighth Circuit in *United States v. Gabe* emphasized that "[b]ecause propensity evidence is admissible under Rule 414, this is not unfair prejudice."[81] What once was considered one of the specific dangers of character evidence—a focus on the accused's propensities—is now a perfectly permissible inference.[82]

Although propensity itself is no longer unfair prejudice in the context of sex crimes, other unacceptable dangers exist that should lead to exclusion, even under this new regime. Rule 403 unfair prejudice may arise if the jurors become so horrified by the prior acts admitted under Rules 413–414 that they have an emotional reaction to the accused and desire to punish him for past deeds, even though they may not believe he committed the currently charged crime. More subtly, jurors could begin thinking of the accused as guilty, finessing the standard of proof, and convicting him because moral abhorrence of his guilty past assuages their reasonable doubts.[83] In addition, evidence of prior sex

---

[79] *See* United States v. Withorn, 204 F.3d 790, 794 (8th Cir. 2000). ("The district court was obligated to take into account Congress' policy judgment that Rule 413 was 'justified by the distinctive characteristics of the cases it will affect,' and that Rule 414 evidence is 'exceptionally probative' of a defendant's sexual interest in children.") (quoting United States v. Mound, 149 F.3d 799, 801 (8th Cir. 1998)); United States v. Benally, 500 F.3d 1085, 1090 (10th Cir. 2007) ("Consistent with congressional intent regarding the admission of evidence tending to show the defendant's propensity to commit sexual assault or child molestation, 'courts are to "liberally" admit evidence of prior uncharged sex offenses.' ") (quoting United States v. Meacham, 115 F.3d 1488, 1492 (10th Cir. 1997)).

[80] *See* United States v. Larson, 112 F.3d 600, 604 (2d Cir. 1997) (noting congressional sponsors' statements that "the presumption is that the evidence admissible pursuant to these rules is typically relevant and probative, and that its probative value is not outweighed by any risk of prejudice"); United States v. Horn, 523 F.3d 882, 888 (8th Cir. 2008) (testimony is prejudicial to accused "for the same reason it is probative—it tends to prove his propensity to commit sexual assaults on vulnerable female members of his family when presented with an opportunity to do so undetected"); United States v. Mound, 149 F.3d 799, 802 (8th Cir. 1998) ("There is no evidence that the prior conviction presented any danger of unfair prejudice beyond that which 'all propensity evidence in such trials presents,' but is now allowed by Rule 413.") (quoting United States v. LeCompte, 131 F.3d 767, 770 (8th Cir. 1997)).

[81] *See* United States v. Gabe, 237 F.3d 954, 960 (8th Cir. 2001) ("[The] testimony is prejudicial to Gabe for the same reason it is probative—it tends to prove his propensity to molest young children in his family when presented with an opportunity to do so undetected."); United States v. LeCompte, 131 F.3d 767, 769–70 (8th Cir. 1997) (reversing decision of trial court to exclude prior sexual offense evidence because " 'child sexual abuse deservedly carries a unique stigma in our society; such highly prejudicial evidence should therefore carry a very high degree of probative value if it is to be admitted' "; explaining that such "danger is one that all propensity evidence in such trials presents. It is for this reason that the evidence was previously excluded, and it is precisely such holdings that Congress intended to overrule") (citation omitted); United States v. Guardia, 135 F.3d 1326, 1330 (10th Cir. 1998) ("If Rule 413 evidence were always too prejudicial under 403, Rule 413 would never lead to the introduction of evidence. Therefore, Rule 413 only has effect if we interpret it in a way that leaves open the possibility of admission.").

[82] *Compare LeCompte*, 131 F.2d at 769–70 (noting highly prejudicial nature of prior offense evidence nonetheless admissible under Rule 413, even after performing Rule 403 balance), *with* United States v. Fawbush, 900 F.2d 150, 152 (8th Cir. 1990) (decided before adoption of the new rules) (holding that, even if prior sexual offense had been relevant to material issue in case, it still would not have survived Rule 403 balance because "the prejudicial effect of this evidence outweighed any legitimate probative value it may have had").

[83] The court in *Guardia*, one of the very few cases to affirm a denial of Rule 413 evidence under a Rule 403 balancing, expressed these concerns:

> While Rule 413 removes the per se exclusion of character evidence, courts should continue to consider the traditional reasons for the prohibition of character evidence as "risks of prejudice" weighing against admission. For example, a court should, in each 413 case, take into account the

crimes could trigger other Rule 403 dangers such as confusion and distraction. Where the prior crimes take up more court time than the crimes charged, the jurors could become confused as to the actual charges and what evidence supports which proposition.

Overwhelmingly, trial courts admit prior sex offenses under Rules 413 and 414, and appellate courts approve under a highly deferential abuse of discretion review. Furthermore, the appellate courts generally do not see the questions raised by Rules 413 and 414 as close, as long as the district court applied the correct standard and engaged in Rule 403 balancing.[84] Some courts exercise caution when determining whether to admit a defendant's prior sexual offenses, making sure that the prior offenses are substantially similar to the charged offense.[85] But not all cases involving prior bad acts apply the rules so scrupulously. Some courts have admitted evidence of prior bad acts even though the prior acts seem markedly different from the charged offense.[86]

Constitutional Challenges to Rules 413 & 414

Federal courts have rejected various constitutional challenges to Rules 413 and 414. Despite the historical ban on propensity evidence, all courts that have considered the question have determined that Rules 413 and 414 do not violate due process. In *United States v. Enjady*,[87] the Tenth Circuit, in holding Rule 413 constitutional, rejected a due process argument, observing that just because the traditional ban on propensity evidence "is ancient does not mean it is embodied in the Constitution."[88] The Supreme Courts of Iowa and Missouri, however, have held that provisions analogous to Rules 413–414 violate their state constitutions.[89]

> chance that "a jury will convict for crimes other than those charged—or that, uncertain of guilt, it will convict anyway because a bad person deserves punishment."

United States v. Guardia, 135 F.3d 1326, 1330–31 (10th Cir. 1998). *See also* D. Craig Lewis, *Proof and Prejudice: A Constitutional Challenge to the Treatment of Prejudicial Evidence in Federal Criminal Cases*, 64 WASH. L. REV. 289, 326 (1989) ("diminished regret about possible error in a determination of guilt when the fact finder learns that the accused is an evil person").

[84] *See, e.g.*, United States v. Hawpetoss, 478 F.3d 820, 827 (7th Cir. 2007) ("The district court very carefully considered the disputed evidence and determined it to be both relevant and non-violative of Federal Rule of Evidence 403. We certainly see no abuse of discretion in admitting evidence of Mr. Hawpetoss' molestation of both S.C. and M.W."); United States v. Benais, 460 F.3d 1059, 1063 (8th Cir. 2006) ("The evidence was probative and the only prejudice was that prejudice made admissible by Rule 413. There was no unfair prejudice as required for exclusion under Rule 403."); United States v. Benally, 500 F.3d 1085, 1092 (10th Cir. 2007) ("Considering the record as a whole, this court sees nothing to suggest the district court abused its discretion when ruling on the admissibility of Benally's four prior victims.").

[85] *See, e.g.*, United States v. McHorse, 179 F.3d 889, 899 (10th Cir. 1999) (district court's admission of similar acts by accused against other children approved, but not evidence of acts involving accused's half-sister because they were deemed too dissimilar, remote, and potentially confusing); *see also* Carpentino v. State, 38 P.3d 547, 553–54 (Alaska Ct. App. 2002) (trial court did not abuse its discretion when it excluded accused's prior sexual assault on victim's older brother because sexual abuse of eleven-year-old brother lacked sufficient similarity to abuse of eight-year-old sister).

[86] *See, e.g.*, United States v. Eagle, 137 F.3d 1011, 1013–16 (8th Cir. 1998). In *Eagle*, the defendant was accused of abusing his eight-year-old niece, and the government introduced evidence that the accused had "pleaded guilty in May of 1987 to a federal crime of 'carnal knowledge,' or 'engaging in sex with a child under sixteen.' " The fourteen-year-old victim of the prior offense was actually the defendant's common-law wife at the time of the trial. Although the court allowed the jury to learn about the subsequent marriage, it is still debatable whether the two crimes were sufficiently similar.

[87] United States v. Enjady, 134 F.3d 1427, 1430 (10th Cir. 1998).

[88] *Id. at* 1432.

[89] State v. Cox, 781 N.W.2d 757 (Iowa 2010) (admission of other wrong merely to show general sexual propensity violated due process clause of Iowa constitution); Missouri State v. Ellison, 239 S.W.3d 603, 607–08 (Mo. 2007) (sexual propensity rules were found to violate "the right to be tried only on the offense charged").

In addition, defendants have challenged Rules 413 and 414 on equal protection grounds. One version of the equal protection argument is that the rules treat sex offenders differently from those accused of other crimes.[90] Because sexual offenders are not a suspect class and discriminating against their particular crimes seems rational, such equal protection arguments have been essentially laughed out of court.[91] Another more persuasive variation of the equal protection argument arises from the fact that because rape and child molestation are primarily state crimes, Federal Rules 413 and 414 apply in only limited contexts, such as alleged crimes committed within military jurisdiction, in Indian territories, and cases involving interstate sex crimes. The new rules have a disproportionate effect on American Indians.[92]

Evaluating Rules 413 & 414

Much has been written on the wisdom of Rules 413 and 414. It is fair to say that the Rules are generally unpopular with evidence scholars.[93] Supporters of the Rules argue

---

[90] *See* United States v. Julian, 427 F.3d 471, 487 (7th Cir. 2005) ("Based on the special treatment that Rule 413 accords to prior sexual assault offenses in prosecutions charging a defendant with sexual assault, Julian suggests that the rule deprives him of equal protection of the law.").

[91] *See, e.g., id.* ("The more sweeping rule of admissibility that [Rule 413] creates for a defendant's prior acts in cases involving sexual assault does not violate equal protection principles so long as the rule has a rational basis."); United States v. Enjady, 134 F.3d 1427, 1435 (10th Cir. 1998); United States v. Mound, 149 F.3d 799, 801 (8th Cir. 1998) ("Because Rule 413 does not 'burden[ ] a fundamental right,' and because sex-offense defendants are not a 'suspect class,' we must 'uphold the legislative classification so long as it bears a rational relation to some legitimate end'. . . . Promoting the effective prosecution of sex offenses is a legitimate end.") (quoting Romer v. Evans, 517 U.S. 620, 631 (1996)).

[92] *See* Aviva Orenstein, *Propensity or Stereotype?: A Misguided Evidence Experiment in Indian Country*, 19 CORNELL J. L. & PUB. POL. 173 (2009) (concentration of cases in Indian country has reinforced stereotypes and eased the acceptance of radical departure of Rules 413–414 from general ban on character evidence). For instance, in United States v. LeMay, 260 F.3d 1018, 1030 (9th Cir. 2001), the Ninth Circuit acknowledged that such disproportion might exist (it seems incontrovertible), but viewed that disproportion merely as a quirk of federal jurisdiction. *See id.* The accused argued that Rule 414 "has a far greater impact on Native Americans because they are far more likely than members of other races to be prosecuted federally for child molestation. *LeMay* may be correct that a disproportionately large number of federal child molestation prosecutions involve Indian defendants. But this disproportion, if true, would arise simply because the federal government only has jurisdiction over crimes such as child molestation when they arise on Indian Reservations, military bases, or other federal enclaves." *Id.* The *LeMay* court noted that no evidence existed of any congressional intent to discriminate, and thus dismissed the claim as meritless. *See id.* (citing Washington v. Davis, 426 U.S. 229, 239 (1976) (discriminatory intent, not just effect, required to show violation of equal protection)).

[93] *See, e.g.,* David P. Leonard, *Perspectives on Proposed Federal Rules of Evidence 413–415: The Federal Rules of Evidence and the Political Process*, 22 FORDHAM URB. L. J. 305, 306 (1995) (although political process has always informed rules, these new amendments have "radically changed the shape of the rules" and to have created an exception to the principle that different types of cases and different types of litigants should be governed by the same evidence rules); *see also* James Joseph Duane, *The New Federal Rules of Evidence on Prior Acts of Accused Sex Offenders: A Poorly Drafted Version of a Very Bad Idea*, 157 F.R.D. 95, 125 (1994); Jeffrey G. Pickett, Note & Comment, *The Presumption of Innocence Imperiled; The New Federal Rules of Evidence 413–415 and the Use of Other Sexual-Offense Evidence*, 70 WASH. L. REV. 883, 883 (1995).

Technically, Rules 413 and 414, as part of the Federal Rules, will only apply to crimes committed on military bases and Indian Reservations. Yet the influence of the Federal Rules is so pervasive that its adoption is of vital importance. *See* Jeffrey G. Pickett, Note & Comment, *The Presumption of Innocence Imperiled; The New Federal Rules of Evidence 413–415 and the Use of Other Sexual-Offense Evidence*, 70 WASH. L. REV. 883, 893 (1995) ("lustful disposition"); Anne Elsberry Kyl, Note, *The Propriety of Propensity: The Effects and Operation of New Federal Rules of Evidence 413 and 414*, 37 ARIZ. L. REV. 659 (1995) (state adoption of Rule 413). The proposed rules do, however, effect a major change in the doctrine and tenor of character evidence. In a letter to Judge Ralph K. Winter, Jr., Chair of the Advisory Committee on Evidence Rules, a group of law professors expressed concern over numerous ambiguities that arise from the rules, including questions concerning the discretion of the trial judge and the interaction with other rules concerning hearsay, best evidence, and limitation on impeachment of witnesses. *See* David P. Leonard, *Perspectives on Proposed Federal Rules of Evidence 413–415: The Federal Rules of Evidence and the Political Process*, 22 FORDHAM URB. L.J. 305, 335 (1995) (quoting and discussing the letter).

that the probative value of the prior sex crimes is high because the sexual aggressiveness and proclivities of defendants are distinctive enough to warrant a propensity argument. Supporters also argue that the potential unfair prejudice is exaggerated,[94] and reflects the "anti-jury" assumption "that the ordinary people who serve on juries will behave unreasonably, if they are allowed to have this type of information and to accord it its natural probative value."[95]

The sexual propensity rules seem particularly appealing in cases of child molestation and in consent-defense rape cases.[96] These rules appear to address the phenomenon of sexual aggressors and abusers who commit repeat offenses but nevertheless manage to discredit each individual victim.[97] Supporters argue that evidencing the accused's similar prior bad acts will increase conviction rates.[98] In turn, the increased numbers of sex crimes that result in convictions will aid general deterrence and signal societal seriousness about these crimes. Rules 413 and 414 may also empower victims to speak out in confidence, knowing that they will be supported in their assertions and treated with respect by the jury.

Finally, courts, primarily through Rule 404(b)(2), but in some states also through common law "lustful disposition"[99] exceptions, sometimes admit evidence of prior sex crimes anyway.[100] It is questionable, however, whether this expansion is as prevalent in rape as in child molestation cases. Advocates of Rules 413–414 argue that the stretching of current doctrine proves the inadequacy of the character rules in dealing with the

---

94 David Karp's address to the Association of American Law Schools ("AALS") carried the weight, according to the sponsors of Rule 413. *See* David J. Karp, *Symposium on the Admission of Prior Offense Evidence of Propensity and Probability in Sex Offense Cases and Other Cases*, 70 CHI.-KENT L. REV. 15 (1994). Karp was senior counsel for the Office of Policy Development, United States Department of Justice. The ideas for new rules originated in the Department of Justice, and Karp was one of the original drafters.

95 *Id.* at 26–27 (quoting WIGMORE ON EVIDENCE § 62.2 (Tillers rev. 1983)).

96 *See* Roger Park, *Perspectives on Proposed Federal Rules of Evidence 413–415: The Crime Bill of 1994 and the Law of Character Evidence: Congress Was Right About Consent Defense Cases*, 22 FORDHAM URB. L.J. 271, 271–72 (1995) (arguing that where identification and sexual contact are admitted, but consent is in question, there is a strong policy argument in favor of admitting prior similar sexual attacks).

97 *See* Karen M. Fingar, *And Justice for All: The Admissibility of Uncharged Sexual Misconduct Evidence Under the Recent Amendment to the Federal Rules of Evidence*, 5 S. CAL. REV. L. & WOMEN'S STUD. 501 (1996); Debra Sherman Tedeschi, Comment, *Federal Rule of Evidence 413: Redistributing "The Credibility Quotient,"* 57 U. PITT. L. REV. 107 (1995).

98 Part of the justification of Rules 413 and 414 rests on unbridled need. As Representative Susan Molinari, the principal sponsor in the House of Representatives, explained: "The enactment of this reform is first and foremost a triumph for the public—for the women who will not be raped and the children who will not be molested because we have strengthened the legal system's tools for bringing the perpetrators of these atrocious crimes to justice." 140 CONG. REC. H8991 (daily ed. Aug. 21, 1994) (statement of Rep. Molinari). Senator Robert Dole explained the new rules: "evidence of this type is frequently of critical importance in establishing the guilt of a rapist or child molester, and that concealing it from the jury often carries a grave risk that such a criminal will be turned loose to claim other victims." 137 CONG. REC. S4925, S4927 (daily ed. Apr. 24, 1991) (statement of Sen. Dole).

99 Though they vary from state to state, lustful-disposition exceptions generally provide forthrightly that evidence of rape and sexual molestation are categorically different from other prior bad acts, much in the same way that Rule 413 does.

100 *See* **§ 7.10** (subsection on "Other Acts of Sexual Misconduct"). Critics and fans of Rules 413–415 alike have observed that courts seem to be more expansive in their application of Rule 404(b)(2) in sex abuse cases than in other areas of criminal law. Evidence of prior rapes and child molestations is sometimes inappropriately labeled as "other purposes" (besides propensity) listed in 404(b)(2), such as plan, intent, and identity. *See, e.g.*, Miguel A. Mendez & Edward J. Imwinkelried, People v. Ewoldt: *The California Supreme Court's About-Face on the Plan Theory for Admitting Evidence of an Accused Uncharged Misconduct*, 28 LOY. L.A. L. REV. 473, 473 (1995) (criticizing California Supreme Court's expansion of its interpretation of "plan" to allow prior bad acts to be admitted against defendant in child molestation cases).

unique principles of rape and child molestation. Rather than do violence to current character evidence rules, they support the frank exception for rape and child molestation.[101]

Opponents are troubled that Rules 413 and 414 contravene centuries of legal tradition prohibiting propensity evidence. The Rules depart from settled principles of evidence that focus on crimes charged, not past misdeeds or proclivities.[102] This may subtly reinforce and perpetuate biases and inaccurate stereotypes about rapists and child molesters, affect future cases and influence the quality of justice outside the courtroom.[103] It would seem especially difficult for jurors to maintain a presumption that the accused is innocent until proven guilty when he is presented as a serial sex offender. There is legitimate concern that the emotions these past offenses raise may overshadow the crimes charged and distract the jury. The jury may overvalue such evidence and desire to punish the accused for past crimes, ignoring the high threshold of reasonable doubt. Additionally, the jury's willingness to be swayed by evidence of prior sex crimes is heightened by its own misconceptions about the prevalence of rape. Once a jury is faced with a bona fide rapist (one who has been accused or convicted before), the temptation to demonize that person and ignore the depth and breadth of the problem of rape may be overwhelming.[104]

§ 7.07 Methods of Showing Character: Evidence of Reputation, Opinion, and Specific Acts

Admission of character evidence involves two, analytically distinct questions: whether evidence of character is admissible at all and, if so, what form such evidence may take. Though the rules governing the form of character evidence are technical, sometimes inconsistent across contexts, and occasionally arcane, lawyers must take care to offer character evidence in its permissible form. These specifications about how to admit character evidence, when it is allowed, are entirely distinct from the admissibility of specific act evidence under Rule 404(b)(2), which permits evidence to show something other than character. The rules governing form may be summarized as follows:

---

101 As then-Senator Robert Dole explained: "[I]f an exception admitting such evidence cannot be avowed openly and honestly, then the temptation is strong to achieve admission by manipulating other exception categories, and by applying evidentiary rules in a manner that is not consistent with their interpretation and application in non-sex offense cases. This state of affairs is undesirable because judges should not have to bend or break the law to do the right thing." 137 CONG. REC. S4925, S4927 (daily ed. Apr. 24, 1991) (statement of Sen. Dole).

102 Even before the adoption of Rules 413–415, the late Professor Peter Tillers compared the admissibility of prior sex offenses with the admissibility of other kinds of prior misconduct of the defendant and concluded: "If we wish to use sexual propensity evidence against an accused, consistency demands that we abolish the propensity rule in its entirety. However, we apparently lack the courage of our convictions." *See* 1A WIGMORE ON EVIDENCE § 62.2 at 1345 (Tillers rev. 1983).

103 Some have argued that Rules 413–415 are particularly unfair and unwise in rape cases where identification is an issue. In the case of stranger rape, where the search for the culprit begins with mug shots of known rapists, there is a significant possibility of false accusation built into the system. *See, e.g.* Katharine K. Baker, *Once a Rapist? Motivational Evidence and Relevancy in Rape Law*, 110 HARV. L. REV. 563, 592–97 (1997) (concern over wrongful convictions and perpetuation of criminal class drawn disproportionately from minorities and poor).

104 The probative value of past sex offenses may be overrated. For instance, Rule 413 assumes that some facet of a rapist's character exists that makes him not only a likely recidivist, but particularly aberrational and dangerous. Yet, rape, and acquaintance rape in particular, is widespread, occurring throughout all strata of society, and unfortunately are not the crimes of a perverted few. Aviva Orenstein, *No Bad Men!: A Feminist Analysis of Character Evidence in Rape Trials*, 49 HASTINGS L.J. 663, 692 (1998).

1. When character evidence is admissible because it falls within the exceptions specified in Rule 404(a)(2),[105] the initial proof (that is, what is presented by direct examination of character witnesses) is limited to evidence of reputation or opinion, whether the proponent is the accused or (by way of rebuttal) the prosecution. This rule is stated in Rule 405(a), which also permits inquiry into specific acts during cross-examination of the character witness.

2. When the evidence falls within Rules 413–415, pertaining to sexual assault or child molestation cases, *only* evidence of specific instances of conduct may be used to prove character.[106] Reputation and opinion evidence of character are not authorized by those rules and remain prohibited by Rule 404(a)(1).

3. When character is an ultimate issue in the case—an unusual situation—evidence of specific instances of conduct of the person may be used in addition to reputation and opinion testimony, as specified in Rule 405.[107]

4. When evidence of character is admissible because character is used circumstantially, but not to invite a propensity inference, proof of character may be made by evidence of reputation or opinion testimony, according to Rule 405(a). This usually occurs when what matters is the reaction of someone else because of that person's knowledge of the former person's character.[108]

5. When impeaching a witness with evidence related to the witness's character trait of truthfulness or honesty, Rules 608 and 609 allow reputation and opinion testimony as well as specific act evidence to a limited extent.[109]

While reputation and opinion testimony rarely impart as much flavor as specific act testimony, they are much less time-consuming and less likely to distract the jury with confusing collateral issues. The common-law rule restricted initial character witnesses to providing reputation evidence only, which was thought to represent the accumulated wisdom of the community, and hence to be more reliable than the mere opinion of a particular person. This restriction was found to be too hobbling; because of the transitory conditions of modern society, it is more difficult to acquire a broad, reliable reputation. At any rate, "reputation" evidence often merely represented the witness's opinion in disguise. The Federal Rules take a broader view, and allow the testimony in the form of either reputation or opinion.

---

[105] *See* **§§ 7.03–7.05**.

[106] *See* **§ 7.06**.

[107] *See* **§ 7.14**.

[108] Testimony about specific acts of the person are usually allowed as well, not under Rule 405(b) but rather under Rule 404(b)(2) to show how some other person reacted to those acts, if the latter person was present when those acts occurred, or to corroborate a person's testimonial assertion that they were aware of such acts. *See, e.g.*, United States v. James, 169 F.3d 1210 (9th Cir. 1999) (holding it error to exclude evidence of the specific acts of misconduct of a homicide victim in order to corroborate defendant's assertion that the victim had bragged to defendant about committing those acts).

[109] *See* **§ 11.07**.

The Personal Knowledge Requirement for Character Witnesses

A witness who offers character evidence in the form of reputation must have personal knowledge of reputation. The witness usually will also know the person whose reputation is the subject of testimony, but the rule requires personal knowledge of reputation, not direct knowledge of the person's character. The reputation knowledge must be acquired by having heard the reputation discussed with a sufficient number of people, though the number is not precisely quantifiable.[110] A witness who reports reputation secondhand (that is, who reports what one other person says about reputation) is reporting inadmissible hearsay.

Despite contrary early cases, the prevailing view appears to be that an investigator can acquire reputation knowledge for purposes of a particular case.[111] The partisanship of the investigator may cast doubt on the veracity of the evidence, but this is true of any facts discovered by an investigator, and, of course, the investigator is subject to cross-examination concerning his or her testimony about reputation. If the investigation was thorough and the investigator testifies truthfully, then the investigator's work product is as reliable as any testimony of a resident of the community.

When the witness offers opinion testimony concerning a person's character (as is permitted in jurisdictions following the Federal Rules), he or she must have personal knowledge of the subject and enough experience with the subject to justify forming an opinion; it is not necessary, however, for the opinion witness to know the reputation of the subject.

Reputation and Hearsay

Evidence of reputation, when used to show character, is evidence of out-of-court statements offered for the truth of the matter asserted, and hence is hearsay. Reputation, after all, is what the community *says* about a person. However, the Federal Rules provide a special hearsay exception for reputation testimony.[112]

Reputation in the Community or in the Workplace

Some common-law cases restricted reputation evidence to evidence about a person's reputation in the community in which he or she lived, thereby preventing testimony about the person's reputation in the place of work.[113] As a hard-and-fast rule, this view

---

[110] There is no precise number or percentage of people in a community who must discuss their opinion of a person for that opinion to be a "reputation." It is clear that it need not be a majority. *See* 5 WIGMORE ON EVIDENCE § 1613 (Chadbourn rev. 1974); Girch v. State, 177 N.W. 798 (Neb. 1920) (witness who heard 15 to 20 people in a community of 200 say that defendant had bad reputation for truth is competent to testify as to that reputation). *Cf.* United States v. Neff, 343 F. Supp. 978, 982 (E.D. Pa. 1972) (problem with testimony where witness talked to "seven or eight people" about defendant, was that they did not know defendant, rather than that number of people was insufficient).

[111] *See* 3 WIGMORE ON EVIDENCE § 692 (Chadbourn rev. 1970).

[112] FED. R. EVID. 803(21). This exception does not guarantee the admission of all reputation evidence that meets the requirements of the exception, but it does negate the hearsay objection. The reputation-for-character evidence, even though within a hearsay exception, must still fall into a category in which character evidence is admissible in order to be received. At common law, whether implicitly or explicitly, reputation for character was also treated as falling within a hearsay exception, so the question was not whether the evidence was hearsay, but whether it was admissible under the rules governing character evidence.

[113] *See* Williams v. United States, 168 U.S. 382 (1897) (reputation at place of work excluded on grounds that it existed only among limited number of people in particular building); *see also* United States v. Reveles, 1993 WL 135864 at *6 (A.F.C.M.R.1993), *aff'd.*, 41 M.J. 388 (1995) (holding that trial court properly excluded bartender's testimony as to victim's reputation for intemperance, because reputation based upon group of

never had much to recommend it; sometimes reputation at the place of work was more pertinent than reputation in the neighborhood. As one early source put it, when a schoolmaster is accused of beating schoolchildren, which reputation is more convincing, that of the schoolroom or that among his neighbors?[114] With the advent of suburbia and the apartment complex and the modern separation of job and home, the view has become even less defensible, since a person may often have closer acquaintances in the place of work than in the place of residence. The Federal Rules accordingly provide for the admission of reputation evidence either "in the community" or "among associates."[115]

Absence of Bad Reputation

A witness who testifies to being acquainted with people who know the defendant, and is in a position to hear derogatory statements if any were made, is permitted to testify about not having heard anything unfavorable. The mere fact that a person who was in a position to hear unfavorable comments has never heard them, despite having been privy to conversations concerning the person whose reputation is the subject of testimony, is itself evidence of good character. Acts of misconduct are more a topic of conversation among one's associates than acts of ordinary rectitude, and the law recognizes that the person who has led an unstained life may show that to be so through the testimony of a witness who has "never heard anything against" the person.[116]

Laying the Foundation for Character Evidence: Examples

Example (Reputation)

Q. Do you know Mr. Smith [the defendant]?

A. Yes

Q. Is he here in the courtroom today?

A. Yes.

Q. Where is he sitting?

A. Right next to you, on your left.

COUNSEL: Let the record reflect that the witness has identified Mr. Smith.

Q. How long have you known Mr. Smith?

A. Four years.

---

patrons at Officers' Club bar, not a "recognized community"; Rule 404(d) of Military Rules of Evidence defines reputation as the "estimation in which a person is generally held in the community").

[114] Keener v. State, 18 Ga. 194, 221 (1855), excerpted in 5 WIGMORE ON EVIDENCE § 1616 at 591 (Chadbourn rev. 1974).

[115] FED. R. EVID. 803(21).

[116] *See, e.g.*, Deschenes v. United States, 224 F.2d 688, 691 (10th Cir. 1955) ("silence speaks in his favor and the fact that a character witness has never heard ill said of the defendant is evidence within itself of a good reputation"); State v. Foster, 665 S.W.2d 348 (Mo. App. 1984); State v. Floyd, 289 S.E.2d 139 (N.C. App. 1982); 5 WIGMORE ON EVIDENCE § 1614 (Chadbourn rev. 1974). An interesting example of this problem arose in the celebrated murder trial of Harvard Medical College Professor John Webster in 1849. One of Webster's character witnesses testified that he had been defendant's neighbor for 15 years but had never heard his character for violence or inhumanity discussed. The neighbor was permitted to testify that he had "never heard any acts of violence, or inhumanity, imputed to him." Testimony of John G. Palfrey, Stone, Report of the Trial of Professor John W. Webster 145 (1850). *Cf.* SEC v. Peters, 978 F.2d 1162, 1171–73 (10th Cir. 1992) (holding that trial court erred by excluding "have you heard" cross-examination questions about defendant's prior misconduct to opinion character witness for defense).

Q. During that period, how often did you see him?

A. Every day during the weekends, then sometimes during the week.

Q. What is the nature of your association with him?

A. We are next-door neighbors.

Q. Anything else?

A. We served on the homeowners' association together, both on the Board of Directors for two years.

Q. Did you know other people who knew him?

A. Yes.

Q. How many?

A. Dozens. He is very well known.

Q. Did you discuss with these people, or hear discussed, the defendant's reputation for being a [law-abiding] [truthful] [peaceable and nonviolent] person?

A. Yes.

Q. What is his reputation for being a [law-abiding] [truthful] [peaceable and nonviolent] person?

A. It is excellent, the best.[117]

Example (Opinion)

Q. Do you know Mr. Smith [the defendant]?

A. Yes.

Q. Is he here in the courtroom today?

A. Yes.

Q. Where is he sitting?

A. Right next to you, on your left.

COUNSEL: Let the record reflect that the witness has identified Mr. Smith.

Q. How long have you known Mr. Smith?

A. Four years.

Q. During that period, how often did you see him?

A. Every day during the weekends, then sometimes during the week.

Q. What is the nature of your association with him?

A. We are next-door neighbors.

Q. Anything else?

---

[117] Note that in this example, the witness testifies to knowing Mr. Smith personally. This is not necessary for a reputation witness. It is common for such a witness to be quite familiar with a person's community reputation without knowing the individual personally.

A. We served on the homeowners' association together, both on the Board of Directors for two years.

Q. Did you know him well enough to form an opinion as to his character for [truth and veracity] [being a law-abiding person] [being a peaceable and nonviolent person]?

A. Yes, certainly.

Q. What is your opinion?

A. He is an extremely [truthful and honest] [law-abiding] [peaceable and nonviolent] person.

§ 7.08 Character Evidence in Civil Cases

The prohibition of using character evidence to invite propensity inferences applies even more broadly in civil cases than in criminal cases. Generally speaking, the Federal Rules of Evidence do not allow propensity evidence in civil cases, except insofar as such character evidence may be used to impeach the credibility of witnesses.[118] The Rules' drafters reasoned that character evidence is of slight probative value and may be very prejudicial or distracting. They recognized that the same could be said of character evidence in criminal cases, but stated the criminal rule, permitting the defense to raise the question of character, was "deeply imbedded in our jurisprudence," while the admissibility of character evidence in civil cases was not, and "those espousing change [in civil cases] have not met the burden of persuasion."[119]

The general rule against use of character evidence in civil cases must be understood in light of the limited nature of the character evidence ban. The ban applies only to evidence of general disposition, when offered to show conduct in conformity with that disposition.[120] It does not prohibit the use of habit evidence.[121] Nor does it prohibit the use of evidence of prior acts when offered for the purpose of showing something other than character, such as motive, opportunity, preparation, plan, or the like.[122] Also, it does not prohibit the use of evidence of character when the evidence is not used to show action in conformity with character, as in the rare case when character is the ultimate issue.[123] Moreover, the rule is subject to an exception, applicable in civil as well as criminal cases, permitting the impeachment of a witness by evidence of prior bad acts reflecting on the witness's honesty, by criminal convictions, or by opinion and reputation evidence concerning the witness's character for truthfulness.[124]

Aside from impeachment of witnesses, there is only one explicit exception in the Federal Rules that allows character evidence to be used to invite a propensity inference in a civil case. Rule 415 permits the civil plaintiff in a sexual assault or child molestation

---

[118] *See* FED. R. EVID. 404(a)(2) & (3), which create exceptions only for impeaching witnesses and for evidence offered for and against an accused in a criminal case.

[119] FED. R. EVID. 404 advisory committee note.

[120] *See, e.g.*, Bonilla v. Yamaha Motors Corp., 955 F.2d 150 (1st Cir. 1992) (in case where personal injury plaintiff sued for design defect in motorcycle, trial court committed reversible error by admitting evidence of prior speeding offenses in support of defendant's claim that speeding was cause of accident).

[121] *See* **§ 7.15**.

[122] *See* **§ 7.09**.

[123] *See* **§ 7.15**.

[124] *See* **§ 11.07**.

case to introduce evidence of the defendant's other instances of sexual assault or child molestation.[125] This exception unavailable to the defendant for the purpose of implicating someone else as the perpetrator. In addition, for civil cases in which the defendant asserts that the alleged wrongful act did not occur, the defendant has no recourse to provide evidence of his good character. The exception in Rule 404(a)(1)(A) is not available in civil cases.

Rule 412, the federal "rape shield" rule,[126] applies in modified form to civil cases. That rule generally excludes evidence offered to prove that an alleged victim engaged in other sexual behavior and the evidence of the alleged victim's sexual predisposition. The rule is worded broadly enough to preclude many uses of such evidence that might otherwise qualify as "other purposes" within the meaning of Rule 404(b)(2). Perhaps because of this, the rule further provides that, in civil cases, "evidence offered to prove the sexual behavior or sexual predisposition" of any alleged victim is admissible if "its probative value substantially outweighs the danger of harm to any victim and of unfair prejudice to any party."[127] Presumably, unfair prejudice would include a civil defendant's suggested propensity inference that the alleged victim consented to the sexual behavior. Further, evidence of an alleged victim's reputation is admissible only if the alleged victim has placed that reputation in controversy. This provision might cover, for example, a situation in which the plaintiff alleges injury to her reputation as an element of damages.

Not all jurisdictions follow the restrictive position of the Federal Rules concerning the use of character evidence in civil cases. In some jurisdictions, a party is permitted to offer evidence of good character in a civil case in response to an allegation of criminal conduct or conduct involving moral turpitude. Once this evidence has been offered and received, the opposing party may meet it with evidence of bad character.[128]

A character evidence problem can arise in civil cases where a litigant wishes to prove that a civil plaintiff is "claim-minded."[129] For example, a defendant in a personal injury case might offer evidence that on one or more other occasions the plaintiff claimed to have been injured in a similar manner. When offered to show that the plaintiff is litigious, it is character evidence that may prejudice the jury. Evidence of other claims is usually rejected.[130] However, courts have admitted such evidence if there is a showing of a distinct pattern of making false claims.[131] When such a showing is made, the evidence is not admitted as character evidence to show a general disposition to make such claims, but is admitted under Rule 404(b)(2) as evidence of intent, plan, or modus

---

125 FED. R. EVID. 415. Section (a) of the rule provides that "the evidence may be considered as provided in Rule 413 and 414," which govern criminal cases. *See* **§ 7.06**.

126 *See* **§ 7.13**.

127 FED. R. EVID. 412(b)(2).

128 *See generally* 1A WIGMORE ON EVIDENCE §§ 65–67 (Tillers rev. 1983).

129 *See generally* 3A WIGMORE ON EVIDENCE § 963 at 808 (Chadbourn rev. 1970) (noting that courts divided on admissibility of evidence); 1 MCCORMICK ON EVIDENCE § 196 (Kenneth S. Broun ed., 7th ed. 2013) (admissibility of party's prior actions or defenses).

130 *See, e.g.*, Lowenthal v. Mortimer, 270 P.2d 942, 945 (Cal. Ct. App. 1954) (holding plaintiff's fifteen prior lawsuits inadmissible, prejudicial); 1 MCCORMICK ON EVIDENCE § 196 at 1090 (Kenneth S. Broun ed., 7th ed. 2013) (evidence usually excluded when offered to show plaintiff is chronic litigant).

131 *See, e.g.*, Hemphill v. Washington Metropolitan Area Transit Authority, 982 F.2d 572 (D.C. Cir. 1993) (per curiam) (in personal injury action, trial court improperly gave "claims-minded plaintiff" instruction where defendant failed to show plaintiff's prior claims were false); Sessmer v. Commonwealth, 103 S.W.2d 647, 649 (Ky. 1937) (holding prior unfounded claims by attorneys admissible in disbarment proceeding for blackmailing physician with frivolous claim); 1 MCCORMICK ON EVIDENCE § 196 at 1089 (Kenneth S. Broun ed., 7th ed. 2013) (holding party's previous similar claims admissible if fraudulent).

operandi, though judicial opinions do not typically give as careful treatment to the question of whether such theories rightly apply as they do in criminal cases.

Civil cases in which a claim or defense turns on fraud can also raise potential character evidence problems. For example, the alleged victim of a misrepresentation by a real estate broker might wish to show that the broker made similar misrepresentations to other clients. In such instances, the party claiming fraud is usually allowed to admit evidence of similar past frauds by the opposing party.[132] This evidence would not be admissible if it were relevant only to show bad character. However, it usually comes in for its bearing on some other issue that is at least semantically distinct, such as intent, knowledge, or lack of mistake or accident.[133]

In terms of whether a forbidden propensity inference from character is involved, it is difficult to see how the inference from a history of false claims to a present false claim, or from a history of misrepresentations to the claimed misrepresentation, is substantially different from the inference from a history of criminal conduct to the charged criminal conduct. Rightly or wrongly, courts do not seem to be as discerning about the existence of an improper propensity inference in civil cases, at least when it is evidenced by specific acts. Instead, the concern about a propensity inference seems to be simply one of various factors considered in conducting a balancing under Rule 403.[134]

§ 7.09 Evidence of Other Crimes, Wrongs, or Acts Used for a Purpose Other than Showing Action in Conformity with Character—in General [FRE 404(b)(2)]

Suppose a defendant charged with bank robbery provides an alibi. As part of its proof, the prosecution seeks to show that the defendant robbed a convenience store a year before the bank robbery. The inferential process most likely set in motion by this evidence is the following:

PROPOSITION 1: The defendant committed one (other) armed robbery.

PROPOSITION 2: The defendant is, therefore, the type of person who commits armed robberies.

CONCLUSION: It is more likely that the defendant is guilty of the present crime than would otherwise be the case.

When offered on this reasoning, the evidence would be barred by the rule against character evidence.[135] It is evidence of a general disposition offered to show conduct in

---

[132] *See, e.g.*, Edgar v. Fred Jones Lincoln-Mercury, 524 F.2d 162, 167 (10th Cir. 1975) (holding that similar past tampering with odometer to falsify mileage on second-hand cars admissible to show knowledge or intent; oddly applying Oklahoma law); 1 McCormick on Evidence § 197 at 1095 (Kenneth S. Broun ed., 7th ed. 2013) (evidence of similar frauds frequently admitted).

[133] *See, e.g.*, Dial v. Travelers Indem. Co., 780 F.2d 520, 523–24 (5th Cir. 1986) (holding that plaintiff's association with two other intentionally set fires also destroying insured property admissible to show intent or plan); Edgar v. Fred Jones Lincoln-Mercury, 524 F.2d 162, 167 (10th Cir. 1975) ((holding that similar past tampering with odometer to falsify mileage on second-hand cars admissible to show knowledge or intent); 1 McCormick on Evidence § 197 (Kenneth S. Broun ed., 7th ed. 2013) (noting that past frauds admissible to demonstrate intent, knowledge, lack of accident, or plan or scheme).

[134] For a thorough discussion of the treatment of "similar events" evidence in civil cases, *see* David P. Leonard, The New Wigmore: Evidence of Other Misconduct and Similar Events § 14 (2009).

[135] *See, e.g.*, United States v. Brown, 71 F.3d 1158, 1162 (5th Cir. 1995) (holding that in drug sale case, error to admit, under Rule 404(b) evidence that defendant had previously been convicted of possession of cocaine with intent to distribute to show identity since prior conviction is only relevant to show bad character);

conformity with that disposition, and hence is barred by the general rule against character evidence.[136]

Nevertheless, in many instances, evidence of other conduct by the defendant (or by any person) may be admissible because these prior acts are not used to show character, but rather as evidence that is relevant in some other way. The Federal Rules provide that although evidence of crimes, wrongs, or acts—other than the crime or act that is the subject of the present trial—is not admissible to prove the character of a person in order to show that he acted in conformity therewith, such evidence may be admissible for other purposes. Rule 404(b)(2) lists some such other purposes: proof of motive, opportunity, intent, preparation, plan, knowledge, identity, or absence of mistake or accident.[137] This list is a time-honored (though non-exclusive) one. Similar lists appeared in decisions and treatises long before the adoption of the Federal Rules of Evidence.

As a convenient shorthand, this book will refer to evidence of such other crimes, wrongs, and acts as *uncharged misconduct* evidence.[138] The term *uncharged* refers to the fact that the other misconduct is not charged in the present case; it does not mean that the person was never charged with the misconduct; prior convictions can be one form of uncharged misconduct evidence, in this sense. The term *misconduct* correctly emphasizes that the evidence offered need not be evidence of a crime, but may be evidence of some form of non-criminal misconduct. The term is not absolutely precise, however; although the evidence will usually in practice be evidence of misconduct offered to show the commission of a crime, in theory (and occasionally also in practice) it might be evidence of a *good* act offered to show the defendant's innocence. The same principle applies to the latter as to the former; prior good acts are not admissible for an inference of good character en route to an inference of action in conformity with good character, but they may be admissible to show conduct if that can be done without relying upon an inference from character.[139]

Suppose, for instance, that in the previous bank robbery hypothetical, the evidence suggests that the crime was committed by an individual wearing a clown mask who handed the teller a note claiming to be Robin Hood, saying all the money would be given away to the "poor people on the streets," and instructing the teller to empty the drawer of all small bills. The prosecution wishes to prove that on at least one prior occasion, the defendant robbed a bank in the same town using precisely the same method. Though the

---

United States v. Phillips, 599 F.2d 134 (6th Cir. 1979) (holding that prior bank robberies inadmissible when no showing of similarity of plan). For a case that, in the authors' opinion, violates this principle, *see* State v. Smith, 707 P.2d 289, 297 (Ariz. 1985) (holding that robbery of other convenience stores in prosecution for robbing convenience store).

[136] *See* **§ 7.01**. The result would be the same if Proposition 1 were, instead, that the defendant committed five other armed robberies. While such a proposition, if true, would reveal a stronger propensity, the rule's prohibition is not limited to weak propensities.

[137] For an excellent analysis and critique of the rule, particularly noting that the rule does not avoid all propensity inferences, *see* Richard B. Kuhns, *The Propensity to Misunderstand the Character of Specific Acts Evidence*, 66 IOWA L. REV. 777 (1981).

[138] This follows the terminology of EDWARD J. IMWINKELRIED, UNCHANGED MISCONDUCT EVIDENCE (rev. ed. 2010).

[139] Of course, a "person" within the coverage of the character evidence prohibition in Rule 404(a)(1) need not be either a party or an alleged victim. The prohibition applies to proof of conduct by *any* person. There is a difference of opinion about whether the prohibition of Rule 404(b) applies to "neutral" acts, acts that are neither good nor bad. Practically speaking, neutral acts will not raise the concerns that motivate the rule. *See* DAVID P. LEONARD, THE NEW WIGMORE: EVIDENCE OF OTHER MISCONDUCT AND SIMILAR EVENTS § 4.6 (2009) (arguing that, in any event, the courts will need to assess the balance of probative value and competing concerns under Rule 403).

evidence would be inadmissible if offered to prove defendant's general character for unlawful behavior and thus her guilt of the present crime, it would likely be admissible to prove her identity as the bank robber on the following reasoning:

PROPOSITION 1: The same person robbed both banks, the one at issue in this case and one other bank.

PROPOSITION 2: The defendant robbed the bank that is not the one at issue in this case.

CONCLUSION: Defendant is the person who robbed the bank at issue in this case.

This reasoning (sometimes called "distinctive modus operandi") does not involve an inference to or from the accused's personality, general disposition to commit crime, or even tendency to rob banks or, more generally, to engage in illegal activity for monetary gain. It is offered to establish the defendant's identity as the bank robber solely through reasoning that does not require an inference that defendant possesses a general character trait. This does not mean the jury will not employ the forbidden reasoning. To be sure, all such admissions under Rule 404(b)(2) are subject to a Rule 403 balancing test. In this case, however, a limiting instruction, cautioning the jury as to the purpose for which the evidence may be used, would sufficiently address the danger, and the evidence would almost certainly be admissible.

The admissibility of other crimes and acts has been a hotly and exhaustively debated and litigated subject, and it is one of the most commonly asserted grounds for appeal in criminal cases. In such litigious terrain, one might expect to find well-trodden paths furnished with helpful guideposts, and perhaps even a paved way to the most common destinations. To the contrary—the terrain is so vast, inconsistent, and full of different starting points that judges who travel it must find a way to their destinations mainly through a sense of what is fit for the particular case, with the language of case law and treatises providing no more than a very generalized map.[140]

The decided cases do, however, provide some general guidelines. If the evidence is relevant only to invite an inference of conduct conforming to character, then its use is prohibited by Rule 404(b)(1). If the evidence is relevant for some other purpose—again, the list in 404(b)(2) is merely exemplary, not exhaustive—then the probative value of the evidence must be balanced against the risk of unfair prejudice, as well as the danger of waste of time and confusion.[141] In other words, even if the evidence does not fall within the prohibition of Rule 404(b)(1), it must still withstand scrutiny under Rule 403.

Among the considerations that bear upon the Rule 403 determination are:

- whether the uncharged misconduct has the capacity to arouse horror or to invoke a desire to punish;
- the remoteness in time of the evidence of other crimes and bad acts;
- whether the fact sought to be proven by the uncharged misconduct is really in dispute; and

---

[140] For a comprehensive treatment, *see* DAVID P. LEONARD, THE NEW WIGMORE: EVIDENCE OF OTHER MISCONDUCT AND SIMILAR EVENTS (2009).

[141] FED. R. EVID. 404 advisory committee note to subdivision (b).

- whether the alleged act might be proven with other evidence.[142]

Another factor mentioned by some courts is the strength of the evidence (aside from evidence of uncharged misconduct) that is available against the defendant. If the evidence directly concerning the charged crime is very powerful, then the incremental probative value of the other misconduct evidence is less, and therefore, (under this line of reasoning) there is less reason for admitting it.[143] As the Supreme Court made clear in *Old Chief v. United States*,[144] the trial court must consider the *context* in which evidence is offered, which includes the other evidence available to prove the fact.[145] The basic task is one of balancing, and as the advisory committee's note to Rule 404(b) states, the rule offers no mechanical solution.[146]

Admissible uncharged misconduct is not limited to that which evidences prior convictions. Other acts that did not result in conviction may be admissible if they are offered for a proper purpose. Indeed, most courts hold that even evidence of a crime that resulted in an acquittal may be admissible, provided that its commission is established in the present proceeding in accordance with the rules about quantum of proof that are in force in the jurisdiction. (To prove another wrong, crime, or act under Rule 404(b)(2), a party in federal court must offer evidence sufficient for a jury to find by a preponderance of the evidence that the defendant committed the act. Some states require a higher level of proof.[147]) In addition, uncharged misconduct that occurs *after* the events at issue may also be admissible; the rules do not require that the other crimes, wrongs, or acts have occurred prior to the events at issue in the case. For example, a defendant who allegedly used a distinctive modus operandi in a series of murders and is charged with the murder that was first in time, may be identified as the murderer partly by evidence that he is linked with subsequent murders having a similar method.

§ 7.10 Specific Purposes for Which Uncharged Misconduct Evidence May Be Offered

As the language of Rule 404(b)(2) suggests, the list of specific purposes for introducing evidence of uncharged misconduct is not exhaustive. For example, in "felon in possession" prosecutions, like the *Old Chief* case,[148] one use of prior misconduct evidence is simply to establish the defendant's status as a felon at the time he possessed the firearm. Hence, proof of a person's status as a convicted person may be an "other purpose" within the meaning of Rule 404(b)(2), because it does not involve a character

---

[142] *See* 1 MCCORMICK ON EVIDENCE § 190 (Kenneth S. Broun ed., 7th ed. 2013).

[143] United States v. Beechum, 582 F.2d 898 (5th Cir. 1978). One may question whether this is a proper consideration, since it seems to suggest that when proof of the charged crime is weak, evidence the prejudicial effect of which would otherwise outweigh its probative value should be admitted, thus putting the defendant with a good case on the facts of the particular crime charged in a worse position than one who is clearly guilty of the particular crime charged. Perhaps, however, in some cases the weighing of this factor can be justified on the ground that the other crimes evidence is simply a waste of time when the immediate evidence is overwhelming.

[144] Old Chief v. United States, 519 U.S. 172 (1997).

[145] *Id.* at 184 ("what counts as the Rule 403 'probative value' of an item of evidence, as distinct from its Rule 401 'relevance,' may be calculated by comparing evidentiary alternatives"). For discussion of *Old Chief*, *see* **§ 5.03**.

[146] *See* DAVID P. LEONARD, THE NEW WIGMORE: EVIDENCE OF OTHER MISCONDUCT AND SIMILAR EVENTS § 4.5 (2009).

[147] *See* **§ 7.11**.

[148] *See* **§ 5.04**.

propensity inference, but it is not listed in Rule 404(b)(2). In addition, the purposes listed below often overlap. For example, evidence that is offered to show intent may also show a common plan; evidence that is offered to show identity often does so by showing modus operandi. The proponent of the uncharged misconduct evidence must specify the 404(b)(2) purpose for which the evidence is offered.[149]

Not all of the various possible purposes for which the evidence might be offered are of the same evidentiary significance. A close examination of the list in Rule 404(b)(2) reveals that most of the potential uses of uncharged misconduct evidence are merely circumstantial evidence of other facts that must be proven to establish a claim or defense. For example, motive, opportunity, preparation, and plan are usually not ultimate facts, but only facts that, if shown to exist, offer circumstantial support to the existence or nonexistence of ultimate facts. On the other hand, intent, knowledge,[150] and identity are usually ultimate facts; unless these facts can be established, the facts necessary to sustain the charge are not proven. Because relevance issues often arise with respect to uncharged misconduct evidence, the proponent must not only identify the *immediate* purpose for which the evidence is offered, but also the *ultimate* fact such evidence tends to prove. While a person's conduct might well establish an evidentiary fact, unless that fact is relevant to an ultimate issue in the case, the evidence should be rejected.

Suppose, for example, that in a prosecution for knowingly receiving stolen goods, the defendant admits knowingly possessing the goods but claims they were not stolen. If the prosecution offers evidence of other instances in which the defendant received stolen goods, it is important to inquire why such evidence is relevant. If offered on a modus operandi theory to prove identity (that the defendant was the person who possessed the goods), the defendant can argue that the evidence should be rejected because identity is not a contested issue.[151] If offered to prove a plan as a means to show intent, the defendant should also argue for exclusion because the defendant admits to knowingly possessing the goods. Counsel should be prepared in advance to make and meet relevance arguments whenever the admissibility of uncharged misconduct evidence is at issue.

More generally, in thinking about what is contested in a criminal trial, it is helpful to distinguish among three typical components of the prosecution's affirmative case: actus reus (the criminal act), mens rea (the criminal state of mind), and identity (that the defendant is the perpetrator). Theoretically, a defendant may contest all three, but as a practical matter, a defendant who contests identity ("It wasn't me.") rarely contests that a crime occurred, and a defendant who contests mens rea or actus reus ("But I thought he was attacking me.") rarely contests identity. It matters greatly which aspect of the case the prosecution uses the uncharged misconduct to establish. If the defendant contests only identity, other act evidence offered on a theory that goes only to mens rea

---

[149] *See* United States v. Sampson, 980 F.2d 883, 888 (3d Cir. 1992) (holding that prosecution may not list "litany" of 404(b)(2) exceptions without specifying which one(s) apply).

[150] For example, in a prosecution for receiving stolen goods, it is insufficient that the prosecution prove that the defendant received goods and that the goods were stolen; the prosecution must also prove that the defendant *knew* the goods were stolen. Without proof of this fact, the defendant will prevail.

[151] Technically, the evidence would be relevant under Rule 401, but should be rejected under Rule 403. *See* **§ 5.04**. Some courts have held, however, that even if defendant does not contest the existence of an element of the crime, the prosecution may still offer evidence to prove that element. *See, e.g.*, United States v. Bastanipour, 41 F.3d 1178, 1183 (7th Cir. 1994); United States v. Gilliam, 994 F.2d 97, 102 (2d Cir. 1993). Even so, when an issue is undisputed, the defendant can argue that the probative value of the uncharged misconduct evidence is slight when compared with the danger of unfair prejudice.

has very low probative value and usually should fail the Rule 403 balance. Similarly, if the defendant contests only mens rea, other act evidence that goes only to identity should also be suspect.

Although most of the examples discussed and cases cited below involve prosecution evidence in criminal cases, civil litigants and the defense in criminal cases are also limited by the character evidence prohibition and sometimes invoke the theories here addressed to justify admission of evidence of uncharged misconduct. In particular, criminal defendants sometimes use these theories to implicate a third party as the perpetrator of the charged crime.[152]

Motive

The court may admit uncharged misconduct to show a motive for the charged crime. Though motive is not itself an ultimate issue in the usual criminal prosecution, motive can be relevant to an ultimate issue, such as criminal intent or the identity of the perpetrator. Motive can also be relevant in a civil case, for example, to prove the predicate for the award of punitive damages.

For instance, if a murder defendant and another person previously committed a crime together, and the defendant knew that the other person was prepared to testify against him in a prosecution for the other crime, then the defendant would have a motive for murdering the other person, and the prior crime—though perhaps not all of its details—would be admissible for that purpose.[153] In such a case, motive could be offered to prove that the defendant committed the crime (if the defendant denies involvement), or that the killing was intentional (if the defendant admits killing the victim but asserts lack of criminal intent).

Similarly, some courts have admitted evidence of a defendant's drug addiction as showing a motive for a crime of theft, on grounds that the addiction would create an extraordinary need for money.[154] This, in turn, would generally tend to establish the

---

[152] *See* **§ 7.12.**

[153] *See* United States v. Clark, 988 F.2d 1459, 1465 (6th Cir. 1993) (admitting evidence of defendant's car theft activities to show his motive for killing his brother-in-law and former employee, who told FBI about defendant's illegal acts); United States v. McKinney, 954 F.2d 471, 480–81 (7th Cir. 1992) (admitting evidence that victim had botched a drug transaction twenty months before to establish motive in charged conspiracy to commit murder); United States v. Dunn, 946 F.2d 615, 617–18 (9th Cir. 1991) (admitting evidence that defendant had been dealing cocaine on evening of gun offense to show defendant's motive for threatening security guard with gun); United States v. Felix-Gutierrez, 940 F.2d 1200, 1207 (9th Cir. 1991) (admitting prior drug trafficking offenses to prove motive for charged offense of accessory after fact to kidnapping, torture, and murder of DEA agent). *But see* United States v. Murray, 103 F.3d 310, 316–18 (3d Cir. 1997) (holding that it was reversible error to admit evidence of prior murder by defendant charged with drug-related murder; court noted lack of evidence that prior murder was part of some criminal scheme or committed in some distinctive fashion; dubious character of witness who purported to have knowledge of prior murder may have influenced court, though court did not expressly allude to that consideration as basis for its decision).

[154] United States v. Robinson, 956 F.2d 1388, 1396–97 (7th Cir. 1992) (holding that evidence of defendant's prior imprisonment admissible to show that raising money for his family was motive for charged cocaine distribution); United States v. Saniti, 604 F.2d 603 (9th Cir. 1979); Archie v. State, 224 S.E.2d 64 (Ga. Ct. App. 1976). *Cf.* United States v. Cunningham, 103 F.3d 553, 556–57 (7th Cir. 1996) (Posner, J.) (holding evidence of nurse's addiction admissible to show motive where nurse charged with replacing Demerol with saline solution in syringes and thus depriving patients of pain medication; conceding that "motive" overlaps with "propensity"). *But see* United States v. Swan, 250 F.3d 495, 501 (7th Cir. 2001) (holding that in RICO prosecution of city alderman who allegedly created "ghost jobs" for himself and others, trial court abused discretion by admitting evidence of defendant's gambling to show motive to steal; "most people want money for a variety of reasons"; case might have been different had prosecution been able to show large, pressing gambling debt; error not reversible because of strength of other evidence).

defendant's identity as the perpetrator. In an unusual case, the court admitted evidence that a doctor had patients perform fellatio while he wrote them prescriptions for Quaalude; the uncharged misconduct was received to show that the doctor was motivated by something other than a desire to provide legitimate medical treatment.[155] In a celebrated case growing out of the Watergate scandal, evidence of the break-in at the office of Daniel Ellsberg's psychiatrist was admitted to show a motive for a subsequent cover-up by Nixon administration officials Haldeman and Erlichman. Among other things, the court pointed out that the payment of money to one of the Watergate burglars, E. Howard Hunt, could have been motivated partly by a desire to conceal evidence of the Ellsberg break-in.[156]

Sometimes evidence of prior assaults is admitted in an assault case under the rubric of "motive." If the defendant has previously assaulted the same person, then these courts allow the prior assault to be used as evidence that the defendant disliked the person, providing a motive for a subsequent assault. Such evidence could be admissible to prove that defendant committed the crime,[157] or that the assault was intentional rather than the result of an accident.[158] Also, in an incest or statutory rape case, some courts admit the defendant's prior unlawful sex acts, when committed with the same person as the person involved in the charged crime, to show motive, on the theory that the prior acts show a passion for illicit relations with that particular person.[159] Courts also admit acts showing enmity toward a racial group as evidence of subsequent discrimination.[160]

Similarly, parties may prove enmity toward an opponent in corporate politics by introducing similar acts against another.[161] And some courts admit evidence of sexual misconduct toward a third person if it sprang from the same motive as the charged

---

[155] United States v. Potter, 616 F.2d 384 (9th Cir. 1979).

[156] United States v. Haldeman, 559 F.2d 31, 88–91 (D.C. Cir. 1976).

[157] *See* State v. Green, 652 P.2d 697, 700–01 (Kan. 1982) (holding that in prosecution for murdering wife, evidence of several prior violent altercations between defendant and wife, for one of which defendant had been convicted of battery, admissible to show relationship of parties giving rise to motive and intent and thus defendant's identity as killer). Normally, prior assaults upon the murder victim are admissible under Rule 404(b), for example to show hostility that gives a motive for the murder. Sometimes, however, the courts will exclude assaults that are remote in time. For an unusually restrictive attitude toward this sort of evidence, *see* Spencer v. State, 703 N.E.2d 1053, 1055–56 (Ind. 1999), where the court, while recognizing that normally the prior assaults would be admissible as showing something other than character, held that it was error, though harmless, to admit assaults occurring three years before the alleged murder because they were too remote. The court indicated, however, that the trial court acted properly in admitting evidence of an attack that occurred only two years before the murder.

[158] State v. Hedger, 811 P.2d 1170, 1173–74 (Kan. 1991) (holding that in prosecution for murdering wife where defendant claimed he shot her accidentally, evidence of two prior violent incidents between defendant and wife admissible to prove "ongoing relationship between the parties").

[159] *See* State v. DeLong, 505 A.2d 803 (Me. 1986) (holding that father's prior sexual relations with same daughter admissible in incest case); Commonwealth v. Machado, 162 N.E.2d 71, 72–73 (Mass. 1959) (holding that evidence of intercourse with same victim admissible if not too remote in time); Collins v. State, 669 S.W.2d 505 (Ark. Ct. App. 1984) (evidence of previous sexual overtures toward victim admissible in sexual abuse case). In jurisdictions that have adopted Rule 414, this use of Rule 404(b)(2) is not necessary. *See* **§ 7.06**.

[160] *See* Johnson v. Hugo's Skateway, 949 F.2d 1338, 1345–46 (4th Cir. 1991), *aff'd in relevant part*, 974 F.2d 1408 (4th Cir. 1992) (holding that failure to abide by prior consent decree's nondiscrimination requirements, including failure to obey requirement that sign be posted on premises stating policy of equal access to persons of all races, admissible in case alleging defendant caused racially biased arrest of plaintiff).

[161] Duckworth v. Ford, 83 F.3d 999, 1001–02 (8th Cir. 1996) (holding that in civil suit based on premise that superior retaliated against employee for supporting rival, judgment against same defendant in favor or another employee based on same theory admissible to show motive and intent).

misconduct.[162] Such cases blur the line between evidence offered to show a general bad character and evidence legitimately offered to show motive. Opponents of such evidence should be prepared to argue either that the line has been crossed, or that even if the evidence *in theory* is relevant to a purpose other than character, the jury is unlikely to use it in that permissible way, and Rule 403 should exclude the evidence.[163]

Opportunity

Evidence of uncharged misconduct may be used to show that the defendant had the opportunity to commit the charged offense. For example, evidence that the defendant had previously stolen a key to the premises that were later burglarized would be admissible, in a trial for the burglary, to show opportunity.[164] Other examples include evidence that the defendant escaped from prison shortly before a crime occurred in the vicinity,[165] which shows opportunity (the defendant was free in the area of the crime) as well as motive (a motive exists to commit crimes to obtain means of avoiding capture, as obtaining funds and transportation by legitimate means may be more difficult for a fugitive than for other people). The defendant's presence in an area where the defendant had no right to be also shows access and, therefore, opportunity.[166] Prior criminal activity that puts the defendant in contact with an organization or a mechanism for committing the prior crime may also be admissible to prove opportunity.[167]

Defense counsel faced with a claim that a prior crime is relevant to opportunity should seek to avoid prejudice by pointing out other ways in which the prosecution could prove that the defendant had access to the area in which the crime was committed, by stipulating to access, or by offering ways in which the evidence could be received in a redacted fashion. Doing so could prevent the prejudice likely to occur in situations such as that of the prison break just discussed; it is not very difficult to prove access to the area in which the crime was committed without mentioning that the defendant was present there as a result of an escape.

---

[162] *See* United States v. Aramony, 88 F.3d 1369, 1376–78 (4th Cir. 1996) (holding that in prosecution of former CEO of United Way of America, where prosecution's theory was that defendant had defrauded United Way in order to obtain sexual pleasure at no cost to himself, evidence of defendant's sexual advances and activities with other United Way employees was relevant and admissible to show motive for charged crimes, even though crimes involved expenditures on other women); Heyne v. Caruso, 69 F.3d 1475, 1478–81 (9th Cir. 1995) (defendant's acts of sexual harassment against other employees admissible to show that, in firing plaintiff, defendant was motivated by desire to retaliate because plaintiff had refused his sexual advance).

[163] For a general analysis of the "motive" theory for admission of uncharged misconduct evidence, with particular attention to the distinction, if any, between "motive" and "character" in particular types of cases, *see* David P. Leonard, *Character and Motive in Evidence Law*, 34 LOY. L.A. L. REV. 439 (2001).

[164] *See, e.g.*, State v. Uthe, 542 N.W.2d 810, 814 (Iowa 1996) (holding that in prosecution for forgery of checks from a stolen checkbook, evidence that defendant forged another check from same checkbook a few days later admissible to show possession of checkbook and therefore opportunity to commit earlier forgeries; opportunity tended to prove defendant's identity as perpetrator).

[165] United States v. Stover, 565 F.2d 1010 (8th Cir. 1977) (admitting escape from prison, to show presence in area).

[166] *See* United States v. DeJohn, 638 F.2d 1048 (7th Cir. 1981) (holding that testimony about defendant's presence and taking of checks at other times in mailbox area of YMCA admissible to show access).

[167] *See, e.g.*, United States v. Robinson, 956 F.2d 1388, 1395–96 (7th Cir. 1992) (holding that marijuana distribution conspiracy in the 1970s admissible to show opportunity in prosecution for cocaine distribution, where nearly identical organizational scheme was used for both offenses; prior offense evidence also relevant to establish intent and motive). *But see* United States v. Hill, 953 F.2d 452 (9th Cir. 1991) (holding evidence that co-conspirator used small amounts of cocaine five years earlier inadmissible even though it explained why co-conspirator approached defendant about financing drug transaction).

Knowledge

A court may admit uncharged crimes evidence to show guilty knowledge. In fact, this is one of the oldest uses of uncharged misconduct evidence.[168] One who tries to deduct a roommate as a dependent cannot claim good faith if the Internal Revenue Service warned her against doing the same thing in a previous year, and evidence of the spurious deduction that led to the warning would be admissible even though it necessarily suggests a predilection as a tax cheat.

Similarly, if a defendant found in possession of a quantity of heroin claimed that he did not know that the substance was heroin, evidence that he had previously used or sold heroin would be admissible to show guilty knowledge.[169] Even if the defendant previously was charged with possession of heroin and had been *acquitted*, evidence of the prior trial might be admissible on the theory that defendant became familiar with the appearance of heroin through the prior experience.[170] Similarly, where a person is charged with committing a crime using a sophisticated technique or device, evidence that the defendant previously had committed a similar crime using the same method would be admissible to prove defendant knew how to use such a device or method, and

---

[168] The most common use of other misconduct evidence in the English cases through the nineteenth century was to prove that a person possessed a particular kind of guilty knowledge that would constitute an element of a crime or tort. Many of the cases were prosecutions for forgery and uttering (putting into circulation) of forged instruments, where, to prove the uttering charge, it was necessary to demonstrate that the defendant knew the instrument was forged. *See, e.g.*, Rex v. Whiley, 168 Eng. Rep. 589 (1804), also reported at 127 Eng. Rep. 393 (1804) as Rex v. Wylie. Such evidence was also admitted in fraud cases, where it was necessary to demonstrate that the defendant knew the true nature of the item she sought to transfer to the alleged victim. *See, e.g.*, Regina v. Roebuck, 7 Cox C.C. 126 (1856). Courts also admitted evidence of other misconduct to prove guilty knowledge in prosecutions for receiving stolen goods, where defendant's knowledge that the goods in question were stolen was an essential element of the charge. *See, e.g.*, Rex v. Davis, 172 Eng. Rep. 1196 (1833). Early American case authority, which relied heavily on English law, was very similar. *See* SAMUEL MARCH PHILLIPPS, A TREATISE ON THE LAW OF EVIDENCE 137 (John A. Dunlap ed., 1816); THOMAS STARKIE, A PRACTICAL TREATISE ON THE LAW OF EVIDENCE 378 (Theron Metcalf ed., 1826). For a discussion of the reasoning behind and application of the "knowledge" theory for the admission of uncharged misconduct evidence, *see* David P. Leonard, *The Use of Uncharged Misconduct Evidence to Prove Knowledge*, 81 NEB. L. REV. 115 (2002).

[169] *See* United States v. Beckman, 298 F.3d 788, 794 (9th Cir. 2002) (holding that where self-proclaimed leader of drug smuggling ring testified as government witness against one of his couriers, evidence of courier's prior border crossing admissible to show that courier knew drugs were hidden on his vehicle and to show relationship of parties, explaining why courier was trusted with such a valuable load). *See also In re* Korean Air Lines Disaster of Sept. 1, 1983, 932 F.2d 1475, 1483–84 (D.C. Cir. 1991) (holding that in suit arising from shooting down of flight over Soviet airspace, evidence of prior instances of airline's commercial flights straying into Soviet airspace properly admitted to show knowledge of consequences of straying and to rebut certain defense evidence); United States v. Osum, 943 F.2d 1394, 1403–04 (5th Cir. 1991) (holding that subsequent fraudulent claims of injury from bus accidents admissible against bus driver charged with fraudulent claim, when bus driver claimed that he was genuinely injured and had not known that codefendants were making false claims); United States v. Obiuwevbi, 962 F.2d 1236, 1240–41 (7th Cir. 1992) (holding evidence that defendant withdrew large amounts of money five times in the previous five years before making trips to Nigeria admissible "other acts" evidence to show knowledge and intent failure to report currency charge).

[170] *See, e.g.,* United States v. Rocha, 553 F.2d 615 (9th Cir. 1977) (holding that where defendant was charged with possession of marijuana with intent to distribute and defendant claimed he thought sacks he loaded onto truck contained furniture, evidence of prior acquittal for possession of marijuana was properly admitted to prove knowledge).

thus, might have been involved in the crime.[171] In many cases, the evidence could also be characterized as proving opportunity; these categories overlap significantly.[172]

Not all cases in which evidence is ostensibly offered to show guilty knowledge are so easy. For example, suppose the search of a vehicle reveals a suitcase full of heroin in the trunk. The owner of the vehicle claims never to have seen the contents of the suitcase at all, asserting that the offending suitcase belonged to a passenger who told the vehicle owner nothing about its contents. Here, evidence that the vehicle owner had previous involvement in drug dealings would seem to be evidence of character; it shows "knowledge" only through the inferential route of demonstrating that the defendant has propensity to possess quantities of drugs, and hence that he is more likely to have been guilty on this particular occasion. The evidence does not show something narrower than character, such as familiarity with the physical characteristics of a drug. Nonetheless, courts have not always drawn such fine distinctions, particularly in drug cases, and the evidence is admitted occasionally to show knowledge of the presence of a drug even when there is no claim that the defendant was naïve about the drug's characteristics.[173] Such cases blur the line between character and non-character uses of uncharged misconduct evidence.

Preparation

Evidence of uncharged crimes may be admissible to show preparation for the charged crime. For example, the prosecution may show that the defendant stole a car (the uncharged crime) to use as a getaway car for the charged crime, or that the defendant broke into a store to steal tools to use in the charged burglary.[174] In these cases, preparation is offered to prove the ultimate fact of identity—that the defendant in

---

171 *See, e.g.*, United States v. Jones, 982 F.2d 380, 382 (9th Cir. 1992) (holding that where defendant charged with conspiracy involving large drug smuggling operation, evidence that defendant had been involved in similar operations in previous years was admissible to prove, *inter alia*, defendant's knowledge and intent with regard to present scheme).

172 *See, e.g.*, State v. Campbell, 367 N.W.2d 454 (Minn. 1985) (holding evidence of prior criminal act of using mace admissible to show defendant's knowledge of use of mace and to show that defendant had opportunity to use substance).

173 *See* State v. Garza, 735 P.2d 1089 (Idaho App. 1987) (holding that defendant's large money transactions with person shown to be drug dealer was evidence that he knew of existence of marijuana in residence he shared with his wife). *But see* United States v. Bakke, 942 F.2d 977, 980–83 (6th Cir. 1991) (holding that it was reversible error to admit evidence of unrelated subsequent drug transaction involving defendant accused of being member of drug conspiracy; only issue was membership in conspiracy, not knowledge or intent); United States v. Garcia-Orozco, 997 F.2d 1302, 1303–04 (9th Cir. 1993) (holding that prior incident in which defendant, passenger in car, fled car containing hidden drugs not admissible to show knowledge in subsequent case in which defendant prosecuted for importing drugs); United States v. Harrison-Philpot, 978 F.2d 1520, 1527 (9th Cir. 1992) (holding tape recording or drug negotiations between defendant and undercover agent admissible to show defendant's knowledge of drug distribution ring when defendant claimed drugs were for personal use only). *Cf.* United States v. Beasley, 809 F.2d 1273 (7th Cir. 1987) (Easterbrook, J.) (denying proposition that any drug offense can be used to show intent to commit another drug offense, and remanding for reconsideration of admission of other crimes evidence in case in which defendant was alleged to have fraudulently obtained prescriptions from physician to obtain drugs for sale).

174 *See* Lewis v. United States, 771 F.2d 454, 456 (10th Cir. 1985) (defendant broke into one establishment to steal cutting torch and oxygen for use in second burglary; prior crime admissible in trial for second). *But cf.* People v. Zackowitz, 172 N.E. 466 (N.Y. 1930) (Cardozo, J.), where the defendant whose wife had been insulted by a bystander, went home and returned with a pistol, which he used to shoot the bystander. The prosecution sought to introduce evidence that defendant had other weapons in his home, in rebuttal of defendant's claim that he shot the bystander in self-defense after an altercation started upon his return to the scene. In dictum, Justice Cardozo distinguished a hypothetical case in which the defendant purchased the weapons in preparation for the particular crime; had that been the case, the evidence would have been admissible.

fact participated in the charged crimes. Preparation can also be relevant to the ultimate issue of intent. For example, if, in a murder prosecution, the defendant claims lack of premeditation, evidence that she broke into a gun store prior to the killing and stole what would become the murder weapon would tend to prove premeditation. The "preparation" theory overlaps other categories including "plan" and "opportunity."

Modus Operandi

Evidence that the defendant was involved in prior crimes accomplished by a distinctively similar method is often admissible for several purposes. "Modus operandi" is not specifically listed in Rule 404(b)(2) as one of the "other purposes" for which evidence of uncharged crimes and acts may be admitted. This does not matter because the list of purposes in the rule is not exclusive. In any event, Rule 404(b)(2) does list "identity" as a purpose, and most often, evidence showing modus operandi is offered to identify the defendant as a perpetrator of the crime. At other times it may be relevant to matters such as intent, lack of mistake, or accident, which are also listed as permissible purposes in Rule 404(b)(2).[175]

An illustration of the use of modus operandi to show identity of the perpetrator is the Robin Hood example presented earlier.[176] Put in even more abstract form, the argument is this:

PROPOSITION 1: The same person (whoever that may be) committed two crimes, the one at issue in this case and one other.

PROPOSITION 2: The defendant committed the crime that is not the one at issue in this case.

CONCLUSION: Defendant is the person who committed the crime at issue in this case.

This theory rests on the fact that evidence shows that the same person—whoever it was—committed both the crime at issue and some other crime. There need not be many of these other crimes; a single crime besides the one involved in the present case will suffice.[177] The fact of a common perpetrator is inferred in part from the distinctive method of committing the crime, the "distinctive m.o."[178] To be sure, other evidence may help to establish Proposition 1, besides the distinctive m.o., such as the fact that the two crimes occurred in the same geographic area or the fact that the ill-gotten gains of the

---

[175] Modus operandi describes the nature of the circumstantial evidence (similarity of method) that causes us to infer guilt by inferring intent or identity, whereas intent and identity are not categories of evidence, but rather the ultimate inferences that are sought to be drawn from the evidence.

[176] *See* **§ 7.09**.

[177] *See, e.g.*, United States v. Trenkler, 61 F.3d 45 (1st Cir. 1995) (two bombs built and used in similar fashion; admitting evidence where defendant admitted that he had built the bomb that was not the one at issue in the case).

[178] *See, e.g.*, United States v. Hamilton, 684 F.2d 380, 384 (6th Cir. 1982) (prior crime with similar modus operandi admissible on issue of identity of defendant charged with circulating altered currency); Commonwealth v. Madyun, 458 N.E.2d 745 (Mass. Ct. App. 1983) (subsequent rapes by defendant admissible to prove identity, when there were "striking similarities in the unconnected crimes and the subject crime"); State v. Rehberg, 919 S.W.2d 543, 548–50 (Mo. Ct. App. 1995) (where defendant charged with stealing plumbing equipment by placing it in opened lamp box, sealing box with tape and later purchasing box, paying only for lamp, evidence that defendant had been stealing equipment in such a manner for past four years admissible since crimes were nearly identical and methodology so distinctive that it showed signature). *See also* State v. Williams, 670 P.2d 1348, 1352 (Kan. 1983).

two crimes reappear together at a later time in the same place.[179] Of course, the theory also presupposes that evidence supports Proposition 2, that the defendant committed the other, uncharged crime.

Courts tend to demand more than a superficial similarity between the current charge and the uncharged misconduct, although the degree of required similarity varies.[180] Sometimes uncharged crime evidence is admitted even though the degree of similarity is minimal—in one case, for example, the only similarity noted by the court between the uncharged crimes and the charged crime was that the crimes all involved robberies of similar convenience stores.[181] However, other courts require that evidence of modus operandi be extremely distinctive, amounting to the equivalent of the defendant's signature.[182] For example, the Fifth Circuit held that the similarities between two bank robberies were insufficient to justify admission of the second robbery in a trial for the first, despite similarities in time of day (late afternoon), disguise (gloves and stocking masks), weapons (revolvers), and location of bank (outlying, on a highway).[183] The court may have been influenced partly by the fact that the earlier robbery was committed by a single person, while the later one involved multiple robbers. Nevertheless, even the supposedly distinctive factors could describe many typical bank robberies. Another case displaying a strict attitude is *Sutphin v. Commonwealth*.[184] In *Sutphin*, the defendant was charged with burglary. A cinder block was thrown through the glass door to gain entry in the charged burglary. The trial court admitted evidence that earlier in the same day, the defendant had used a brick to break a glass door and enter another establishment. The appellate court reversed on grounds that the similarities between the two crimes were inadequate; breaking in with a cinder block, brick, or similar object was not distinctive enough to justify admission under a modus operandi rationale.

Two points are worth noting here. First, the less similar the uncharged misconduct and the charged crime are, the more likely the evidence will be rejected; even when the evidence is theoretically relevant for the non-character purpose, there is a greater risk that the defendant will be unfairly prejudiced by the jury's employing the evidence for its forbidden (character) purpose.[185] Second, the degree of similarity required depends,

---

[179] *See, e.g.,* Trenkler, 61 F.3d at 55 (noting importance of the fact that "both bombings occurred within a relatively close geographic proximity"); United States v. Stevens, 935 F.2d 1380, 1405 (3d Cir. 1991) (noting coincidence of eventual locations of robbery proceeds).

[180] *See* 1 CHRISTOPHER B. MUELLER & LAIRD C. KIRKPATRICK, FEDERAL EVIDENCE § 4:36 at 839–43 (4th ed. 2013).

[181] State v. Smith, 707 P.2d 289, 297 (Ariz. 1985). *See also* People v. Massey, 16 Cal. Rptr. 402 (Cal. Ct. App. 1961) (admitting evidence of similar burglary, though similarities hardly enough to justify analogy to "signature"); State v. Speer, 501 N.W.2d 429 434 (Wis. 1993) (in burglary prosecution, holding trial court properly admitted evidence of defendant's prior burglary conviction to establish identity; both burglaries occurred during daylight at houses with "For Sale" signs posted nearby).

[182] Allen v. State, 720 N.E.2d 707, 711 (Ind. 1999) ("The identity exception in Rule 404(b) was crafted primarily for crimes so nearly identical that the modus operandi is virtually a 'signature' ") (quoting Thompson v. State, 690 N.E.2d 224, 234 (Ind. 1997)).

[183] United States v. Myers, 550 F.2d 1036 (5th Cir. 1977).

[184] Sutphin v. Commonwealth, 337 S.E.2d 897 (Va. Ct. App. 1985).

[185] *See also* United States v. Murray, 103 F.3d 310, 316–18 (3d Cir. 1997) (holding trial court committed reversible error by admitting evidence of prior murder by defendant charged with drug-related murder; court noted lack of evidence that prior murder was part of same scheme or committed in same distinctive fashion; dubious character of witness who purported to have knowledge of prior murder might have influenced court as well, though court did not expressly allude to that consideration as basis for its decision); United States v. Carrillo, 981 F.2d 772 (5th Cir. 1993) (holding prior sales of drugs in balloon not sufficiently distinctive to satisfy modus operandi requirements in case where defendant charged with sale of drugs in balloon). *But see*

in part, on the strength of other, "non-m.o." evidence connecting the two crimes, such as their geographical proximity or investigators' finding the fruits of both crimes in the same location. The important requirement is that the evidence must support each of the two propositions; distinctive m.o. is just one way to establish Proposition 1.[186] Of course, if the probative value of the evidence under the modus operandi theory is substantially outweighed by the danger of unfair prejudice, the court should exclude the evidence.

The Doctrine of Chances

The "doctrine of chances" is a related theory for admitting uncharged misconduct evidence. As Wigmore described the theory, the relevance of similar misconduct

> derives purely from the point of view of the doctrine of chances—the instinctive recognition of that logical process which eliminates the element of innocent intent by multiplying instances of the same result until it is perceived that this element cannot explain them all. Without formulating any accurate test, and without attempting by numerous instances to secure absolute certainty of inference, the mind applies this rough and instinctive process of reasoning, namely that an unusual and abnormal element might perhaps be present in one instance, but that the oftener similar instances occur with similar results, the less likely is the abnormal element likely to be the true explanation of them.[187]

To put it more simply, the doctrine of chances requires an inquiry as to how likely it is that the defendant would be involved innocently in so many similar acts. Typically, in such cases, there is little doubt that the defendant is the one who committed the crime, assuming it was a crime. But the defendant asserts that the injury inflicted was accidental. Unlike the use of modus operandi to show identity, the doctrine of chances relies on a multiplicity of other events; the more such events there are, the less plausible is the claim of accident.[188]

In the "Brides in the Bath" case, one of the most celebrated examples of the use of uncharged misconduct evidence, the evidence was used both to show that a crime had been committed (in particular, that the death of the defendant's wife had been the result

---

United States v. Sanchez, 988 F.2d 1384, 1393–94 (5th Cir. 1993) (holding evidence of subsequent offense of drugs sold in pink balloons admissible to counter defendant's misidentification defense because act was sufficiently similar to charged crime to qualify as modus operandi evidence); United States v. Smith, 103 F.3d 600, 603–04 (7th Cir. 1996) holding similarities between two bank robberies justified admitting evidence of other robbery to show identity through modus operandi; court listed several similarities, most distinctive of which was that both robbers held knife vertically when entering bank) (authors' note: *query* appropriateness of court's listing fact that both robberies were "committed by young white males with slender builds"; such evidence goes only to whether defendant was guilty of other robbery, matter not in dispute, and not to *modus* of robberies); .

[186] From a conditional relevance standpoint, one could argue that Rule 104(b) provides the required degree of proof: evidence sufficient to support a finding (by a preponderance of the evidence) that both Proposition 1 and Proposition 2 are true. *See* United States v. Trenkler, 61 F.3d 45, 55 n.16 (1st Cir. 1995) (citing Huddleston v. United States, 485 U.S. 681, 690 (1988)). From a simple relevance standpoint, any evidence increasing the likelihood that these two propositions are true, should suffice to avoid the prohibition of Rule 404(b)(1). The greater degree of similarity often required by the cases has more to do with the question of whether the probative value is substantially outweighed by the risk of unfair prejudice under Rule 403, although the opinions do not often clearly recognize this distinction. *See* § **7.11**.

[187] 2 WIGMORE ON EVIDENCE § 302 (Chadbourn rev. 1979).

[188] *See, e.g.,* United States v. Woods, 484 F.2d 127 (4th Cir. 1973) (admitting evidence that nine other children in defendant's care had each suffered twenty or more episodes of cyanosis (blue coloration due to lack of oxygen) where defendant claimed her child's death was not homicide).

of a crime rather than an accident) and that the defendant was the perpetrator. The defendant, under a false name, married a woman who had inherited a small trust fund.[189] After the couple made out joint wills, the wife was found drowned in the bathtub. The defendant soon thereafter married another woman under another name in another county; she also made out a will to him (and named him the beneficiary of a life insurance policy), and drowned in the bathtub in similar circumstances. A third wife died in the same fashion, after devising her property and taking out insurance only one day after having married the defendant. In the trial for the murder of the first victim, the issue turned upon the admissibility of the second and third drownings. The evidence against the defendant was otherwise scant; there was no proof he was with the victim at the time of the drowning, the victim had previously consulted a doctor about seizures, which might account for an accidental drowning, and there was no sign of violence or of a struggle. The crucial issue concerned admissibility of the evidence of greatest importance to the prosecution: the strikingly similar other drownings.[190] The evidence was admitted, and the defendant, protesting to the end that he was an innocent victim of coincidence, was convicted and hanged.

The doctrine of chances has been applied in a wide variety of ways.[191] The reasoning behind the theory seems compelling.[192] Whereas modus operandi rests on the inferred proposition that it is extremely unlikely the two crimes were committed by different people, the doctrine of chances rests on the inferred proposition that it is extremely unlikely that multiple harms in a similar context would occur without criminal agency. But the reasoning can also be dangerously misleading and violate the character prohibition.[193] It tries to answer the question: "What is the best explanation of the evidence before the court?" Is it coincidence? Or is it something else? That something else appears to be a propensity to commit crime. Propensity comes in as the inferred explanation of the evidence, rather than as a means of inferring guilt from the evidence. That difference may matter so as to exempt these theories from the character evidence prohibition. Of course, the inference is not inevitably correct. For example, in the context of the modus operandi theory, where identity is the issue, one explanatory hypothesis that should be considered—besides coincidence, on the one hand, and guilt of the accused, on the other—is the possibility of a copy-cat criminal, someone who adopts the modus operandi of another. (Hence the common police practice of withholding from the public certain details about unsolved crimes.) If this possibility is ignored, the tendency

---

[189] Rex v. Smith, [1914–15] All E.R. Rep. 265. Technically, the defendant did not legally marry any of the victims with whom he went through the marriage ceremony; he was already married, a fact that, for obvious reasons, he did not reveal to the victims.

[190] One observer has written that "throughout the trial the atmosphere of the court was not, 'is this man innocent or guilty' but 'is there sufficient evidence in law to convict this undoubtedly guilty man.'" E. MARJORIBANKS, FOR THE DEFENSE: THE LIFE OF SIR EDWARD MARSHALL HALL 312 (1931).

[191] For a careful review of some of the many potential uses of "doctrine of chances" reasoning in a class of cases, *see* Mark Cammack, *Using the Doctrine of Chances to Prove Actus Reus in Child Abuse and Acquaintance Rape:* People v. Ewoldt *Reconsidered*, 29 U.C. DAVIS L. REV. 355 (1996).

[192] *See, e.g.*, Edward J. Imwinkelried, *The Evolution of the Use of the Doctrine of Chances as Theory of Admissibility for Similar Fact Evidence*, 22 ANGLO-AM. L. REV. 73 (1993).

[193] Paul F. Rothstein, *Intellectual Coherence in an Evidence Code*, 28 LOY. L.A. L. REV. 1259, 1260–64 (1995) (arguing that the doctrine relies on prohibited propensity reasoning). *But see* Edward J. Imwinkelried, *The Use of Evidence of an Accused's Uncharged Misconduct to Prove Mens Rea: The Doctrines that Threaten to Engulf the Character Evidence Prohibition*, 130 MIL. L. REV. 41, 54–56 (1990) (arguing that "doctrine of chances" reasoning is non-character reasoning).

to "round up the usual suspects"[194] can lead to undue suspicion of formerly guilty people who were uninvolved in the crime under consideration. Perhaps "it is not so unlikely that an innocent person would be repeatedly charged falsely."[195] Courts should use these doctrines with care to avoid possible inferential error.

Common Plan or Scheme

Evidence of uncharged misconduct may also be admissible to show a common plan or scheme leading to the charged crime. When it applies, the theory may help establish the defendant's identity as the perpetrator or the necessary mens rea or actus reus of the crime. Because of its potentially broad usefulness to the prosecution, this route to admission or exclusion of uncharged misconduct evidence is especially challenging for the courts, and diverse views prevail.

Where a person commits several acts in pursuit of a single, pre-established goal, the theory operates in a straightforward and uncontroversial manner. Thus, if the defendant is trying to reconstitute a gun collection previously owned by his father, evidence that the defendant committed one burglary in which one gun was recaptured would be admissible to show the defendant's involvement in another burglary in which another was recaptured.[196] Similarly, evidence that the accused secretly stole a car similar to that described by witnesses as the getaway car used in a daylight bank robbery that occurred soon afterwards would be admissible in the trial of the accused for the robbery.

It is important to distinguish the use of uncharged misconduct to prove a common plan or scheme from its use to prove modus operandi. Of course, the theories overlap somewhat, and some cases fall into both categories. The man who makes a preconceived practice of marrying women of means and then drowning them in the bathtub may be said to have a modus operandi (bathtub drowning) and a plan (to acquire wealth by marrying and murdering). In others, the plan theory applies though the modus operandi theory does not. That is true of the car theft and bank robbery plan, and it would be true of the gun collection case if the guns were obtained using different means. For example, the evidence would be admissible even if the first gun was obtained by using a passkey to obtain entry to an apartment, while the second was obtained by using a hatchet to break down the door of a house in broad daylight. Indeed, defendant need not have obtained the guns by means of burglary. If, for example, the first gun was obtained by burglary, and the charged crime involved alleged fraud, evidence of the burglary would likely still be admissible. Thus, under the common plan theory there is no need for a great degree of similarity in the *manner* in which the person committed the various acts.[197] In still other cases, modus operandi theory applies though there is no common scheme. A defendant may have committed multiple crimes with a distinctive method

---

194 For the most famous use of the phrase, *see Casablanca* (Warner Bros. 1942). In the movie's climactic scene, after the hero has killed a Nazi officer, a police officer lets the hero go and orders another officer to "round up the usual suspects" to hold responsible for the killing.

195 Paul F. Rothstein, *Intellectual Coherence in an Evidence Code*, 28 LOY. L.A. L. REV. 1259, 1263 (1995).

196 *See* State v. Wallace, 431 A.2d 613 (Me. 1981).

197 Another example of common plan or scheme that is distinct from modus operandi is provided by the film *Kind Hearts and Coronets* (Ealing Studios/General Film Distributors 1949), in which a character plotted to acquire a title by killing off the eight people with a superior claim. Each of the bizarre killings was different, but pursued the same goal. They showed a common plan but not a common method.

without planning more than one crime at a time. The actual Brides in the Bath case (discussed in the previous subsection) may have been such a case.[198]

The most controversial common scheme or plan cases are those in which the evidence fails to establish a single, persistent plan leading to a clear goal that covers both the uncharged acts and the crime for which the person is on trial. In such situations, the cases are most diverse and difficult to categorize. Some courts hold that the evidence is inadmissible unless a single plan linked the charged and uncharged acts.[199] Other courts are very expansive in finding a common plan in similar offenses. For example, prior acts of accepting kickbacks from different persons have been admitted to show a common scheme to use one's position to get kickbacks;[200] other activity involving drug offenses has been admitted liberally in some cases on the theory that selling drugs is a continuous business involving a common plan.[201] This very expansive interpretation of plan, a theory one commentator has called the "spurious plan,"[202] does not require a single, coherent scheme on the actor's part. Instead, the actor's thinking is "this worked before, therefore I'll do it again." This type of plan case threatens to undermine the character evidence ban because it relies on the same basic concept as the modus operandi cases, but without requiring proof of a distinctive method, even if it is offered to establish identity.[203] Under the more expansive approach to plan or scheme, virtually any time a person is charged with a crime, evidence that she has committed a similar type of crime on another occasion would be admissible, so long as she was not convicted of the first crime. It is difficult to square such an approach with the fundamental rule that forbids character evidence to prove conduct on a particular occasion.

The different approaches to these controversial cases are exemplified by a line of California cases. In a number of older cases, including *People v. Lisenba*,[204] decided in

---

[198] In fact, federal modus operandi cases sometimes use the phrase "common plan" because "plan" is listed as one of the specific purposes for which uncharged misconduct evidence may be offered, while "modus operandi" is not. There is no need to try to force the modus operandi cases into the common plan category, however, since the Rule 404(b)(2) list of permissible purposes for which other misconduct evidence may be offered is not exclusive, and hence modus operandi evidence may be admissible even though not specifically listed.

[199] *See* United States v. Varoudakis, 233 F.3d 113, 124 (1st Cir. 2000) (holding that evidence of car fire set by defendant was not admissible in case charging defendant with arson of restaurant; there was no link showing a common plan, and fact that both crimes arose from common motive of financial gain did not save evidence from exclusion as character evidence); United States v. Mejia-Uribe, 75 F.3d 395, 398–99 (8th Cir. 1996) (in trial for possession of cocaine with intent to distribute, holding that trial court erred in admitting evidence of defendant's 17-year-old drug conviction; two different crimes were not linked as such to be considered part of one common scheme, because earlier crime involved single sale whereas charged crime involved large scale, ongoing operations).

[200] Commonwealth v. Schoening, 396 N.E.2d 1004, 1009 (Mass. 1979) (holding that evidence that defendant took kickbacks on two other occasions, even if from different party, was admissible to show motive, plan, common scheme; "the defendant's use of his position to guarantee contracts to particular firms and thus to guarantee kickbacks to himself provided the common or general scheme underlying all three transactions"). *But see* United States v. O'Connor, 580 F.2d 38, 42 (2d Cir. 1978) (holding bribes taken from third parties insufficiently probative of "definite project" of committing present crime).

[201] *See* United States v. Carson, 702 F.2d 351, 368–69 (2d Cir. 1983). *But see* United States v. Beasley, 809 F.2d 1273 (7th Cir. 1987) (Easterbrook, J.) (rejecting proposition that any drug offense can be used to prove another drug offense).

[202] EDWARD J. IMWINKELRIED, UNCHARGED MISCONDUCT EVIDENCE § 3:24 (rev. ed. 1998).

[203] *See, e.g.*, United States v. Powers, 978 F.2d 354, 361–62 (7th Cir. 1992) (holding prior convictions for bank robbery and attempted bank robbery admissible as "plan" evidence when in all instances, perpetrator wore wide-brimmed hat, dark glasses, business suit, sported mustache, and carried briefcase; modus operandi concept could not have been used because of lack of sufficient distinctiveness).

[204] 94 P.2d 569 (Cal. 1939).

1939, the California Supreme Court had held that two sequential crimes (marrying two women in sequence, taking out life insurance on them, and then killing them in a way made to look accidental to collect life insurance) could form a common plan even though there was no evidence to show that the defendant had formed a single plan to kill both. But in 1984, in *People v. Tassell*,[205] the court held that the common design or plan idea could not fit evidence of even extremely similar misconduct unless all of the acts were part of a single, continuing conception or plot. A decade later, in *People v. Ewoldt*,[206] the court overruled *Tassell* and announced a new, less restrictive rule that "evidence of a defendant's uncharged misconduct is relevant where the uncharged misconduct and the charged offense are sufficiently similar to support the inference that they are manifestations of a common design or plan."[207] The idea seems to be something like the doctrine of chances. The validity of the respective views has been the subject of spirited debate.[208]

Intent; Absence of Mistake or Accident

Evidence of uncharged misconduct is sometimes relevant to show that the defendant possessed the requisite intent to commit the crime charged—for example, the intent to steal in a larceny case, or the intent to kill in a murder case. This use of evidence differs from showing motive, in that it seeks not to show the reason the defendant might have committed the crime, but instead to show directly a state of mind that is a prerequisite for the commission of the crime. (Motive can give rise to both a criminal intent and a criminal act, or to one without the other.) Also, the "intent" category overlaps with some of the other categories listed, since intent may be shown by evidence undermining the defendant's claim of mistake or accident.

Sometimes the use of uncharged misconduct evidence to show intent can be uncontroversial. The defendant's claim that he shot his wife on sudden impulse is less plausible if, on the way to shooting his wife, the defendant also shot his wife's lover.[209] Yet, in other circumstances, the showing of intent is very close to a showing of character. To show that a defendant intended to kill, one might argue that prior killings by the defendant of unrelated persons throw light upon intent. Prior killings do so, however, by showing that the defendant has a violent, murderous character—exactly the sort of inferential process that is prohibited by 404(b)(1), which forbids admission of uncharged misconduct to invite a propensity inference to conduct.[210] Some opinions recognize this

---

[205] 679 P.2d 1 (Cal. 1984).

[206] 867 P.2d 757 (Cal. 1994).

[207] *Id.* at 769.

[208] *See, e.g.*, Mark Cammack, *Using the Doctrine of Chances to Prove Actus Reus in Child Abuse and Acquaintance Rape:* People v. Ewoldt *Reconsidered*, 29 U.C. DAVIS L. REV. 355 (1996); Edward J. Imwinkelried, *Using a Contextual Construction to Resolve the Dispute Over the Meaning of the Term "Plan" in Federal Rule of Evidence 404(b)*, 43 U. KAN. L. REV. 1005 (1995); Miguel A. Mendez & Edward J. Imwinkelried, People v. Ewoldt*: The California Supreme Court's About-Face on the Plan Theory for Admitting Evidence of an Accused's Uncharged Misconduct*, 28 LOY. L. A. L. REV. 473 (1995); Jeannie Mayre Mar, Note and Comment, *Washington's Expansion of the "Plan" Exception After State v. Lough*, 71 WASH. L. REV. 845 (1996).

[209] *Cf.* State v. Shackford, 506 A.2d 315 (N.H. 1986) (admitting evidence that, shortly before he attacked victim, defendant accosted and threatened another woman was admissible on issues of premeditation and intent).

[210] *See* Chrysler Intern. Corp. v. Chemaly, 280 F.3d 1358 (11th Cir. 2002) (holding defendant's fraudulent alteration of bills of lading in way unrelated to fraud alleged in present action not admissible to show motive or intent; two frauds were significantly different).

principle and restrict the use of this type of evidence,[211] while others tend to ignore the principle or show a rather lenient attitude toward admitting evidence to show intent under Rule 404(b)(2).[212]

Because intent is often proved by showing the commission of similar crimes, one finds statements in court opinions that the similarities must be marked, or that the crimes must show the same intent, or even that they must show the same physical elements.[213] These requirements make sense if the only basis for showing intent is the inference that the defendant had the state of mind to commit that sort of crime—that is, if intent evidence is offered as a sort of narrow character evidence, in which the defendant has a behavioral tendency that is (somehow) deemed not to constitute a trait of character. Yet, in appropriate cases, intent may be shown even by producing evidence of a quite different crime. For example, if the defendant claims that he robbed a bank with X because of duress, proof that the defendant shortly afterward committed another crime with X under circumstances in which duress was obviously absent sheds light upon the claim of duress.[214]

---

[211] *See, e.g.*, Sparks v. Gilley Trucking Co., 992 F.2d 50, 52 (4th Cir. 1993). In *Sparks*, the plaintiff was injured when he lost control of his Corvette. He sued the defendant for negligence, alleging that its truck had run his car off the road. At trial, the defendant argued that the plaintiff had been racing another car and thus had been contributorily negligent. In support of this contention, the defendant offered evidence that the plaintiff had received six speeding tickets in the preceding three years. The district court admitted evidence of the speeding tickets "to show intent, preparation, plan or motive to race or speed on the day in question." The Fourth Circuit held that the evidence of the tickets virtually presented speeding as the plaintiff's character trait and, hence, was inadmissible. The court noted that the Circuit had approved the admission of such evidence when *intent to commit a crime* was at issue. However, in this case, the defendant merely sought to prove the plaintiff was negligent, and "proof of negligence does not require a showing of intent or plan." *See also* Hynes v. Coughlin, 79 F.3d 285, 290–92 (2d Cir. 1996) (holding that where prison inmate denied kicking guard, it was error to admit evidence of inmate's prior assaults and threats against prison staff because intent not in issue); State v. Robtoy, 653 P.2d 284, 292 (Wash. 1982) (holding prior unrelated murder inadmissible to show premeditation; jury "could well have interpreted the evidence of prior killing as proof that Robtoy acted in conformity therewith on this occasion"). The dangers of the "intent" theory of admissibility under Rule 404(b)(2) are discussed in Edward J. Imwinkelried, *The Use of Evidence of an Accused's Uncharged Misconduct to Prove Mens Rea: The Doctrines Which Threaten to Engulf the Character Evidence Prohibition*, 51 OHIO ST. L.J. 575 (1990).

[212] For a case that appears to ignore the principle, *see* State v. Harris, 726 P.2d 943 (Or. Ct. App. 1986) (holding prior assaultive behavior with rifle, unrelated to present incident, admissible to show intent to kill in murder case). For an example of a tendency towards admitting evidence to show intent, *see* United States v. Neely, 980 F.2d 1074 (7th Cir. 1992). The trial court admitted evidence of a prior insurance fraud scheme involving breaking up cars when the instant case involved faking automobile accidents. The Seventh Circuit held that the evidence was admissible even though the defendant claimed intent was not an issue. *See also* United States v. Long, 86 F.3d 81, 82–85 (7th Cir. 1996) (holding that evidence that defendant on another occasion had traded crack cocaine for goods admissible in case charging possession of crack cocaine with intent to distribute, where defendant claimed cocaine found in his car belonged to another person; stating that uncharged crime need not be a "duplicate" of charged crime to be admissible—an understatement in view of lack of similarity between two crimes).

[213] *See, e.g.*, United States v. Haywood, 280 F.3d 715, 721 (6th Cir. 2002) (holding, in 2–1 decision, that district court abused discretion in allowing evidence of subsequent offense of mere possession of cocaine to be introduced to show intent in case charging possession of cocaine with intent to distribute; "Haywood's possession of a small quantity of crack cocaine for personal use on one occasion, sheds no light on whether he intended to distribute crack cocaine in his possession on another occasion nearly five months earlier.").

[214] *See* United States v. Daniels, 948 F.2d 1033, 1035 (6th Cir. 1991) (holding that defendant's request to acquaintance to call in bomb threat against employer admissible against defendant charged with shooting at bus belonging to employer because prior act showed specific intent to harm employer during strike); United States v. Hearst, 563 F.2d 1331 (9th Cir. 1977) (holding subsequent criminal activity of Patricia Hearst admissible to show her intent at time of original bank robbery, thus rebutting duress defense). To be sure, the defense of duress may make the defendant's character trait an essential element in the case, because it asserts that the defendant is not the kind of person who would have committed the crime had the duress not been

United States v. Beechum[215] illustrates the difficulties inherent in the separation of intent and character evidence. Beechum, a substitute letter carrier, was accused of unlawfully possessing a silver dollar that he knew to be stolen from the mail. To establish that Beechum intentionally and unlawfully possessed the silver dollar, the prosecution introduced evidence that two Sears credit cards were found in Beechum's wallet when he was arrested, neither of which were issued to Beechum or signed; both were mailed some ten months earlier to addresses on Beechum's routes. Beechum claimed that the silver dollar fell out of the mailbox as he was raking out the mail and that he planned to turn it in. The fact that he kept the credit cards suggested he intended to keep the silver dollar. The crucial question was whether the inference of intent derived from a forbidden inference about character, or whether the evidence can be viewed as something other than character evidence. An en banc majority of the Fifth Circuit viewed the evidence as related to intent, not character, and held it admissible. According to the majority, the evidence shows a larcenous state of mind, even in the absence of proof that the credit cards had been stolen from the mail. A forceful dissent charged that the court's concept of intent was really propensity in disguise, and that the evidence was merely inadmissible character evidence. The case illustrates the very thin line between permissible and impermissible uses of uncharged misconduct evidence.

In addition to "intent," Rule 404(b)(2) lists "absence of mistake or accident" as one of the permissible purposes for which evidence of uncharged crimes may be offered. This seems to be a way of stating a subcategory of intent, since the defense of mistake or accident is a defense based on the absence of criminal intent.[216] Examples of using uncharged misconduct to rebut a claim of mistake or accident include cases in which the defendant claims that a death caused by him was accidental,[217] that sexual touching of a child was inadvertent,[218] that property was destroyed by accident, rather than by arson,[219] or that illegal dumping of waste was inadvertent.[220] Once again, such cases are often difficult to reconcile with the rule barring propensity inferences, unless special circumstances are present, such as the idea that a prior accident (even if accepted as such) should give the defendant a heightened awareness of certain risks and thus make

---

exerted. If this is correct, then Rule 405(b) applies, and specific act evidence is permissible to show intent by straightforwardly propensity inference. *See* **§ 7.14**.

[215] United States v. Beechum, 582 F.2d 898 (5th Cir. 1978).

[216] *See, e.g.*, United States v. Pless, 79 F.3d 1217, 1220 (D.C. Cir. 1996) (holding in bank fraud case that trial court properly received evidence of defendant's failure to pay corporate, employment withholding, and personal federal taxes to rebut defendant's claim that he believed that overdrafts would be treated as loans).

[217] *See* United States v. Harris, 661 F.2d 138 (10th Cir. 1981) (holding prior battering of child admissible to show death, which father claimed occurred because he tripped while holding child, was not accidental). *Cf.* Kopf v. Skyrm, 993 F.2d 374, 380–81 (4th Cir. 1993) (holding that in civil litigation claiming excessive force by defendant police officer, allegedly in retaliation for plaintiff's attack on defendant's police dog, trial court erred by excluding evidence of prior incident in which defendant shot and killed fleeing burglary suspect after suspect killed another police dog); United States v. Marion, 977 F.2d 1284, 1288 (8th Cir. 1992) (holding that prosecution may refute defendant's argument that failure to appear to serve sentence was mistake with evidence that defendant previously failed to appear in court and fled state).

[218] *Cf.* Findley v. State, 577 P.2d 867 (Nev. 1978).

[219] *See* Hammann v. Hartford Accident & Indem. Co., 620 F.2d 588 (6th Cir. 1980) (holding evidence of prior incendiary fires on plaintiff's property, in conjunction with evidence that plaintiff had concealed information about fires from insurance company, admissible to show arson).

[220] *See* United States v. Paccione, 949 F.2d 1183, 1198–99 (2d Cir. 1991) (holding evidence of attempt to bribe state officials who called buried garbage to defendant's attention, admissible in mail fraud RICO prosecution arising from illegal dumping of garbage in illicit landfill, to show that dumping was not accidental or mistaken).

the defendant's claim of accident in the present case less believable.[221] The probative value of such evidence rises significantly if the accused presents a defense of no knowledge, such as denying knowledge of what a certain illegal substance looks like.

Identity

Under Rule 404(b)(2), another stated purpose for which uncharged misconduct evidence may be offered is to show the identity of the person who committed a certain act. Like intent, identity is usually an ultimate fact rather than merely a fact offered to prove an ultimate fact. Sometimes, other misconduct evidence tends to prove another fact, and from that, identity. Most commonly, the uncharged misconduct evidence tends to prove identity by means of modus operandi. Alternatively, uncharged misconduct might be offered to prove that the defendant had a motive, and thus that she was the person who committed the crime.

Sometimes, the uncharged misconduct evidence proves identity more directly. For example, the fact that Lizzie Borden attempted, on a false pretense, to buy a deadly poison on the day before her parents were hacked to death with a hatchet was offered to identify her as the perpetrator on the theory that her original plan was to poison the parents.[222] That evidence, however, did not speak to her motive, nor did it involve a distinctive modus operandi. Similarly, evidence that the defendant threatened prospective prosecution witnesses or attempted to bribe a witness or juror tends to evidence a consciousness of guilt, which serves to identify the defendant as the perpetrator of the crime in question.[223]

Of course, there must be limits on the use of evidence of uncharged misconduct to prove identity. Otherwise, whenever there was an issue whether the defendant was the person who committed the crime charged, the door would open to evidence of other crimes by the defendant. The mere fact that the defendant committed prior robberies, for example, has some probative value in identifying the defendant as the one who committed the robbery involved in the instant case; all else being equal, a person who has robbed before is part of a population that is more likely to commit robbery than the general population. Yet, allowing that reasoning to prevail would open the floodgates to impermissible character evidence. While evidence of uncharged crimes is admissible to prove identity if the chain of reasoning can bypass inferences about the general character of the defendant, it is not admissible if identity is sought to be proven by showing the defendant to have a bad character and to have acted in conformity with that bad character. To hold otherwise would vitiate Rule 404(b)(1).

---

221 *See, e.g.*, United States v. Tan, 254 F.3d 1204, 1210–11 (10th Cir. 2001) (holding that, on remand, trial judge must conduct new Rule 403 balancing for admitting prior drunk driving convictions in drunk driving second degree murder case to show intent, because the jury could infer that because of prior convictions, defendant was "especially aware of the problems and risks associated with drunk driving" rather than for the "impermissible purpose of proving . . . a propensity to drive drunk").

222 In the actual Lizzie Borden case, the court excluded the evidence of her prior attempt to buy poison; this result, which was never the subject of appeal because Borden was acquitted, has been soundly criticized by Wigmore and other authorities. *See* ROBERT SULLIVAN, GOODBYE LIZZIE BORDEN 142–43, 194–98 (1974).

223 *See, e.g.*, United States v. Tai, 994 F.2d 1204, 1208 (7th Cir. 1993) (holding evidence of threats against others and assaults by defendant's employee admissible to show defendant's identity in prosecution of extortion scheme); United States v. Meling, 47 F.3d 1546, 1557 (9th Cir. 1995) (holding evidence that defendant threatened his father-in-law and uncle to intimidate them into withholding information from the FBI admissible to demonstrate consciousness of guilt in prosecution for product tampering).

Background; Complete Story Principle; "Intrinsic" Acts

Sometimes incidental crimes or acts are admitted simply because attempting to avoid reference to them in the testimony of witnesses would be unduly burdensome and the incidental crimes have no particular prejudicial effect. This would be true, for example, if a witness mentioned that the defendant and his cohorts smoked some marijuana while negotiating a cocaine sale, or that the defendant stole an uncharged item from B at the same time that a charged item was stolen from A. The concept behind admissibility is that the witness should be permitted to tell the story in a natural fashion. The trier should get the full flavor of the events that occurred at the time of the crime; it is for this reason that the evidence is admitted, not for the purpose of saying anything about the character of the defendant.[224] Though evidence often should be admitted under this theory if it provides the trier with a complete picture, it is also necessary to exercise great care to avoid prejudice. As the probative value in establishing the full story diminishes and the unfair prejudice increases, a point can be reached where the court should exclude the evidence under Rule 403.[225]

This theory is closely related to another, the theory that the act evidenced is "intrinsic" to the charged act. The prohibition of Rule 404(b)(1) reads as follows: "Evidence of any *other* crime, wrong, or act is not admissible to prove the character of a person in order to show that on a particular occasion the person acted in accordance with the character." (Emphasis supplied.) To fall within the scope of the prohibition, the act must be an "other" act, that is, *not* the act at issue in the case.[226] Courts have construed

---

[224] *See* United States v. Rivera (Reynaldo Vazquez), 83 F.3d 542, 546 (1st Cir. 1996) (Coffin, J.) (in case charging carjacking, not error to admit evidence that defendant raped victim during carjacking; might help explain, inter alia, why victim heard but did not see firearm); United States v. Dudley, 941 F.2d 260, 262–63 (4th Cir. 1991) (no error in allowing evidence of uncharged offense as part of res gestae; "The jury is entitled to know the setting of a case. It cannot be expected to make its decision in a void—without knowledge of the time, place and circumstances of the acts which form the basis of the charge"); United States v. Richards, 967 F.2d 1189, 1193–94 (8th Cir. 1992) (evidence of incriminating items seized from trunk at same time officers seized firearms is admissible as part of "res gestae" of firearms possession) (citing United States v. Moore, 735 F.2d 289, 292 (8th Cir. 1984) (per curiam) ("res gestae" exception to Rule 404(b) permits "introduction of evidence of other criminal activity" occurring at time and place of arrest "for the purpose of providing the context in which the crime occurred")); Atkins v. Singletary, 965 F.2d 952, 960 (11th Cir. 1992) (evidence of confession to uncharged sexual battery admissible as part of res gestae of charged homicide); State v. Price, 598 P.2d 985, 987 (Ariz. 1979) (in trial for aiding and abetting sale of heroin, evidence that defendant asked for "taste" of substance admissible, inter alia, under "complete story" theory); Hurns v. State, 616 So. 2d 313, 321 (Miss. 1993) (in prosecution for murder of inmate, evidence of sexual assaults admissible to show "complete story" of defendant's "total domination over all the inmates"). This route of admissibility is sometimes designated as res gestae, though perhaps it would be better to avoid the vagueness of the Latin term and refer to the "complete story" principle.

[225] *See* United States v. Hill, 953 F.2d 452, 457 (9th Cir. 1991) (doctrine allowing introduction of other crimes where inextricably intertwined with charged crime should be applied narrowly to avoid overly broad, so-called res gestae exception); United States v. Vizcarra-Martinez, 66 F.3d 1006, 1012–13 (9th Cir. 1995) (evidence of defendant's possession of small "personal-use" amount of methamphetamine when arrested should not have been admitted under aegis of complete story principle in case where defendant charged with more serious crime of possessing substance knowing it would be used to manufacture methamphetamine). *Cf.* United States v. Forcelle, 86 F.3d 838, 842 (8th Cir. 1996) (where defendant charged with illegally obtaining corporate funds to purchase drag racing chassis and make home improvements, trial court improperly admitted evidence that defendant stole platinum from corporation, since that alleged theft was distinct from charged crimes; however, trial court properly admitted evidence of defendant's home improvements since such activity could be construed to be intertwined with charged crimes). *See* 1 McCormick on Evidence § 190 at 1050–54 (Kenneth S. Broun ed., 7th ed. 2013).

[226] The restyling of the Rules in 2011 strangely moved the word "other," so that the prohibition applied to "evidence of a crime, wrong, or other act." This change had the unintended effect of undermining the distinction between extrinsic and intrinsic acts discussed in the text and (if read literally) greatly expanding the government's duty to provide notice of its intent to invoke 404(b)(1). The error was corrected, moving the

this to mean that acts *intrinsic* to the charged offense are not "other" acts; evidence is intrinsic to the charged offense "when the evidence of the other act and the evidence of the crime charged are 'inextricably intertwined' or both acts are part of a 'single criminal episode' or the other acts were 'necessary preliminaries' to the crime charged."[227]

In some contexts, this certainly seems plausible: a defendant accused of murdering Smith cannot plausibly assert that evidence that shows him preparing and executing the murder of Smith and breaking into a car to effect his escape is too unfairly prejudicial to be admitted because it invites a propensity inference from his bad character to the murder of Smith. "Felon-in-possession" cases are conspicuous examples, because being a convicted felon is an essential element of the crime prosecuted.[228] Many of the cases that address the intrinsic/extrinsic distinction involve ongoing conspiracies, in which a number of acts are part of the same overall conspiracy and thus qualify as acts intrinsic to the charged conspiracy.[229]

A difficult question arising from this observation concerns which evidentiary rules apply to evidence of acts characterized as intrinsic. To be sure, even intrinsic acts cannot be offered for a propensity inference; if they do not come within Rule 404(b)(1), they are still subject to the broader prohibition of propensity reasoning in Rule 404(a)(1). On the other hand, an act that is considered intrinsic to the charged offense may for that reason be evidenced without appealing to theories like knowledge or distinctive modus operandi. In principle, whether an act is extrinsic or intrinsic to the charged act should not determine whether Rule 403 balancing applies.[230] Rule 403 applies to either kind of act, although the differences between them may affect how that balance plays out because intrinsic acts will typically have higher probative value. As compared with the analysis of extrinsic acts, a review of the cases indicates that "courts tend to exhibit a considerably more relaxed attitude when determining the admissibility of 'inextricably

---

word "other" back to its original position, when the notice provision in the rule was modified at the end of 2020. *See* **§ 7.16**. The restyling was not intended to work any substantive change in the rules. *See* FED. R. EVID. 101 Restyled Rules Committee Note. And case law between 2011 and 2020 continued to apply the intrinsic/extrinsic distinction. *See, e.g.*, United States v. Heard, 709 F.3d 413 429–32 (5th Cir. 2013) (not commenting on the change in language).

[227] *See, e.g.*, United States v. Williams, 900 F.2d 823, 825–27 (5th Cir. 1990) (holding that previous instances of defendant's mailing from fictitious address were not intrinsic to the offense being tried—use of the mails to facilitate drug trafficking on specific occasion, but that the trial court nonetheless erred in excluding such evidence under the standards applicable to extrinsic act evidence). The court noted that "[t]he proper test to apply in deciding the admissibility of 'other acts' evidence depends upon whether the evidence in question is 'intrinsic' or 'extrinsic' evidence," *id.* at 825), but neglected to indicate what test should apply if the evidence is "intrinsic."

[228] *See* 1 CHRISTOPHER B. MUELLER & LAIRD C. KIRKPATRICK, FEDERAL EVIDENCE § 4:33 at 799 (4th ed. 2013):

> Felon-in-possession trials almost always involve proving other crimes, not merely because an element in the charged offense is a prior felony conviction (where a stipulation can reduce the problem of prejudice), but because felon-in-possession laws usually generate charges only when the defendant uses the gun in committing some other crime, which is for some reason not prosecuted, and proving that "other crime" helps explain why the defendant possessed the weapon.

(Footnote omitted.)

[229] *See* DAVID P. LEONARD, THE NEW WIGMORE: EVIDENCE OF OTHER MISCONDUCT AND SIMILAR EVENTS § 5.3.1 (2009).

[230] This is one of the lessons of *Old Chief*, a felon-in-possession case. *See* Old Chief v. United States, 519 U.S. 172 (1997), discussed in **§ 5.03** & **§ 5.04**.

intertwined' or 'intrinsic' [act] evidence."[231] For example, in *United States v. Summers,*[232] the defendant was convicted of conspiracy to distribute illegal drugs. On appeal he argued that the trial court erred in admitting evidence of a drug transaction that occurred before the start of the alleged conspiracy. Rather than analyzing the admissibility of this evidence under the principles associated with extrinsic act evidence, the court summarily rejected the argument on the ground that this was evidence of " 'bad acts that form the factual setting of the crime in issue . . .' which does not come within Rule 404(b)'s coverage at all."[233] Unfortunately, the court did not articulate what rules govern in that situation and thereby elided the issue whether the evidence should have been excluded under Rule 403.

Other Acts of Sexual Misconduct

The common law courts were often more receptive to evidence of the defendant's prior sexual misconduct than to other kinds of prior misconduct. To be sure, many cases applied the same principles discussed above.[234] But other cases stretched supposedly non-propensity theories beyond the breaking point in an effort to admit the evidence.[235] Rules 413–415 dramatically affected the admissibility of prior sex crimes in federal prosecutions. Under those rules, and similar state rules where they have been adopted, prior sex acts may be admissible as an *exception* to the ban against character evidence,[236] in which case no limiting instruction need be given and the proponent may argue that the subject has the character propensity of a rapist or a child molester.

In states not adopting the equivalent of Rules 413–415, but otherwise following the model of the Federal Rule 404, evidence of other sex offenses in cases involving charges of rape, sexual assault, child abuse, or incest may be admissible under the traditional non-propensity theories described above. Thus, prior sexual contact with a particular person may be received on the theory that it shows motive, because it shows sexual passion (however perverse) for that person. For example, when a defendant is accused of incest, other acts of incest with the same child are admissible, showing a desire to engage in sexual activity with that particular victim.[237] Where the defendant denies that any

---

[231] DAVID P. LEONARD, THE NEW WIGMORE: EVIDENCE OF OTHER MISCONDUCT AND SIMILAR EVENTS § 5.2 at 320 (2009). Professor Leonard's treatment of this subject is critical of this relaxed attitude. He concludes:

> It should make little or no difference, however, whether the court scrutinizes the evidence under the strictures of the "other crimes" rule or whether it views the evidence as part of the charged offenses and thus not "other." Either way, the court must determine whether the probative value of the evidence is substantially outweighed by the danger of unfair prejudice or that its admission would constitute a waste of time. Some courts seem to recognize this fact.

Id. § 5.3.1 at 336. (footnote omitted).

[232] United States v. Summers, 137 F.3d 597 (8th Cir. 1998).

[233] *Id.* at 602 (quoting United States v. Heidebur, 122 F.3d 577, 579 (8th Cir. 1997).

[234] *See, e.g.*, Commonwealth v. Machado, 162 N.E.2d 71, 73 (Mass. 1959) (broad statement that when defendant is charged with illicit sexual intercourse, evidence of similar crimes against the same victim, if not too remote in time, is admissible as "relevant to show the probable existence of the same passion or emotion at the time in issue").

[235] *See generally* IA WIGMORE ON EVIDENCE §§ 62.2, 62.3 (Tillers rev. 1993).

[236] *See* **§ 7.06**.

[237] *See, e.g.*, State v. DeLong, 505 A.2d 803 (Me. 1986) (father's prior acts with same daughter admissible in prosecution for incest); State v. Cameron, 349 S.E.2d 327, 331 (N.C. Ct. App. 1986) (trial court admitted evidence of prior sexual acts with same victim; on appeal, court notes that in sexual offense cases, state's courts have "liberally permitted the introduction of evidence of prior sexual acts committed by the defendant upon the same prosecuting witness"); Brown v. State, 736 P.2d 1110 (Wyo. 1987) (testimony of victim and her half-sister implicating defendant in prior sexual abuse was properly admitted).

crime occurred, evidence of other sexual misconduct with the same victim has been admitted to prove that the charged crime was, in fact, committed.[238] Prior rapes of other victims, committed in a particularly distinctive way may be admitted as evidence of a particular modus operandi.[239]

Nonetheless, sex crimes deserve special treatment here because some courts continue to show a greater willingness to admit evidence of uncharged misconduct in cases involving sexual offenses. Some courts have shown an inclination to admit, for example, prior acts of rape to rebut a consent defense, even when the only clear commonality between different incidents was alleged use of force. For example, in *Carey v. State*,[240] the court took a broad view of the admissibility of prior crimes in rape cases involving defense of consent. It held that two prior assaults (one sexual assault and one mugging) that resulted in acquittal and in dismissal of charges, were admissible on the issue of consent, stating that "in cases involving sexual misconduct prior conduct consisting of bad acts is of increased pertinency," and:

> In an instance such as this, when the accused denies the use of force and claims consent, evidence which contradicts his denials of previous use of force in sexual encounters is of assistance to the trier of fact in evaluating his testimony with respect to motive, knowledge and intent in resolving the issue of fact and in evaluating his credibility.

Similarly, some jurisdictions have admitted other acts of sexual misconduct under a common-law theory of showing "lustful disposition" or "depraved sexual instinct" in cases involving sex crimes against children.[241] The liberal admission of such evidence is a de facto exception to the general rule against character evidence.

Other courts have rejected such theories.[242] Often they interpret their states' versions of the Federal Rules of Evidence, which do not include equivalents of Rules 413–

[238] *See, e.g.*, People v. Ewoldt, 867 P.2d 757 (Cal. 1994) (in prosecution for child molestation, evidence of similar misconduct with victims was admissible to prove design or plan, which in turn is admissible to prove that defendant in fact engaged in alleged criminal conduct); Brown v. State, 817 P.2d 429, 433–35 (Wyo. 1991) (in prosecution for sexual abuse of two stepdaughters where defendant claimed the charges were fabricated, evidence of prior sexual misconduct between defendant and stepdaughters was admissible to prove course of conduct and motive; court held motive was important to case given defendant's claim of fabrication).

[239] State v. Coen, 382 N.W.2d 703, 705–08 (Iowa Ct. App. 1985) (prior offense admitted when similar modus operandi of flattening tire, then asking to fix it and get ride with woman in order to rape her); State v. Bennett, 672 P.2d 772 (Wash. Ct. App. 1983) (defendant had enticed teenage runaways into exchanging sex for food and shelter; prior conduct with unrelated runaways admitted in statutory rape case as showing plan to take advantage of runaways). *Cf.* State v. Kirsch, 662 A.2d 937 (N.H. 1995) (rejecting evidence of other assaults on minors by leader of activities of religious youth group, even though a similar pattern of alleged abuse existed, on ground that theories such as showing intent, motive, or common plan, were simply propensity evidence in disguise).

[240] 715 P.2d 244, 248 (Wyo. 1986). *See also* United States v. Sneezer, 983 F.2d 920, 924 (9th Cir. 1992) (applying a broad standard); State v. Crocker, 409 N.W.2d 840 (Minn. 1987) (upholding admission of other sexual assaults, including sex offense against seven-year-old girl, with no showing of similarity except that all the crimes were "opportunistic" assaults); State v. DeBaere, 356 N.W.2d 301, 305 (Minn. 1984) (enunciating and applying a broad test for admissibility).

[241] *See, e.g.*, State v. Raye, 326 S.E.2d 333, 335 (N.C. Ct. App. 1985) (admitting testimony of sister of alleged victim that defendant-stepfather had made sexual advances toward her; recognizing admissibility of evidence of "unusual or unnatural sexual impulses); .State v. Tobin, 602 A.2d 528 (R.I. 1992) (recognizing "lewd disposition" exception to rule against character evidence in case in which evidence of prior acts involved same victim); *See generally* EDWARD J. IMWINKELRIED, UNCHARGED MISCONDUCT EVIDENCE § 4:14 (rev ed. 1998).

[242] *See, e.g.*, Lannan v. State, 600 N.E.2d 1334 (Ind. 1992) (overruling Indiana "depraved sexual instinct" exception to character evidence rule). *See, e.g.*, Getz v. State, 538 A.2d 726, 733–34 (Del. 1988) ("[T]he sexual gratification exception proceeds upon the assumption that a defendant's propensity for satisfying sexual needs

415, as precluding the reception of evidence on a lustful disposition or depraved sexual instinct theory. In these jurisdictions, courts display somewhat more skepticism about prosecutors' use of uncharged sex crimes under state law equivalents of Rule 404(b)(2).[243]

§ 7.11 Quantum of Proof Required for Evidence of Uncharged Misconduct

Evidence of uncharged misconduct may include not only evidence of prior convictions, but also evidence of crimes or misconduct that did not result in conviction, including, in proper cases, crimes that resulted in an acquittal. This result is logical; the issue in the present case is not whether the person was guilty of the uncharged offense beyond a reasonable doubt, but whether all the evidence in the present case, including evidence of the uncharged offense, demonstrates proof of the *charged* offense beyond a reasonable doubt.[244] Some state courts require that the prosecution, as a preliminary matter, convince the judge by a preponderance of the evidence or even by clear and convincing evidence that the defendant committed the uncharged act or crime.[245] Pre-Rules federal practice varied on the issue until the Supreme Court resolved the issue in 1988.

In *Huddleston v. United States*[246] the Court unanimously held that the federal standard should be whether a jury could reasonably find that the uncharged conduct occurred.[247] In *Huddleston*, the defendant was accused of selling stolen goods in interstate commerce and the charge was based on the defendant's sale of 5,000 blank videocassette tapes at a price below the cost of manufacture. The defendant acknowledged selling the tapes, but denied knowing that they were stolen. As evidence of the defendant's guilty knowledge, the government offered, and the trial judge received, evidence that the defendant had, at other times, sold large quantities of stolen or apparently stolen consumer goods for extremely low prices.

The Court rejected the argument that the government must make a preliminary showing to the judge with proof by a preponderance of the evidence that the defendant committed the prior similar acts. Instead, it held that all that was required was a showing of evidence sufficient to allow a reasonable jury to conclude that the defendant

---

is so unique that it is relevant to his guilt. The exception thus equates character disposition with evidence of guilt contrary to the clear prohibition of DRE Rule 404(b).").

[243] *See, e.g.*, Lafayette v. State, 917 N.E.2d 660, 663 (Ind. 2009) ("Shortly after promulgating Evid. R. 404(b), we examined this subject in an appeal from a conviction for child molesting, Wickizer v. State, 626 N.E.2d 795 (Ind.1993). Our view was that an expansive reading of the intent exception would be inconsistent to the principal thrust of the rule itself."); State v. Saltarelli, 655 P.2d 697 (Wash. 1982) (in rape case with consent defense evidence of prior attempted rape of another woman four and a half years earlier was not admissible to show motive or intent to rape).

[244] *See* Dowling v. United States, 493 U.S. 342, 348–50 (1990) (holding admitting conduct resulting in acquittal not double jeopardy); People v. Massey, 16 Cal. Rptr. 402 (Cal. Ct. App. 1961) (admitting evidence about alleged burglary, of which defendant had been acquitted, to show similar modus operandi).

[245] Holmes v. State, 394 N.W.2d 818, 822 (Minn. Ct. App. 1986); Ali v. United States, 520 A.2d 306, 310 & n.4 (D.C. 1987).

[246] Huddleston v. United States, 485 U.S. 681 (1988). *See also* United States v. Anderson, 933 F.2d 1261, 1267–74 (5th Cir. 1991), *aff'd*, 976 F.2d 927 (5th Cir. 1992) (holding that proponent need show only that reasonable jury could conclude that defendant committed the prior acts; remanding for on-record determination of whether standard of proof for preliminary facts was met).

[247] Before *Huddleston*, several circuits followed rule that the trial court must find the uncharged conduct by a preponderance of the evidence. *See, e.g.*, United States v. Leight, 818 F.2d 1297, 1302 (7th Cir. 1987); United States v. Weber, 818 F.2d 14 (8th Cir. 1987); United States v. Vaccaro, 816 F.2d 443, 452 (9th Cir. 1987). For a summary of the pre-*Huddleston* practice in the various circuits, *see Huddleston* at 685 n. 2.

committed the prior acts. The Court concluded that the admissibility of the evidence was governed by the "conditional relevancy" theory embodied in Federal Rule of Evidence 104(b), which (at the time) provided that when "the relevancy of evidence depends upon the fulfillment of a condition of fact," the court must admit the evidence where there is sufficient evidence to support a jury finding that the condition has been fulfilled.[248] In sending the evidence to the jury, the court should inform the jury of its obligation to consider the evidence of the alleged commission of the other crime, wrong, or act only if it decides (by a preponderance of the evidence) that such an allegation is true.

In regard to concerns about the admission of evidence with prejudicial potential, the Court defended its holding with the following comment:

> We think . . . that the protection against such unfair prejudice emanates not from a requirement of a preliminary finding by the trial court, but rather from four other sources: first, from the requirement of Rule 404(b) that the evidence be offered for a proper purpose; second, from the relevancy requirement of Rule 402—as enforced through Rule 104(b); third, from the assessment the trial court must make under Rule 403 to determine whether the probative value of the similar acts evidence is substantially outweighed by its potential for unfair prejudice . . .; and fourth, from Federal Rule of Evidence 105, which provides that the trial court shall, upon request, instruct the jury that the similar acts evidence is to be considered only for the proper purpose for which it was admitted.[249]

In the opinion of some of the authors, Rule 104(b) does not answer the question confronted by the Court. In the first place, by referring to "sufficient" evidence that rule implicitly incorporates an unstated, externally established burden of persuasion; what is "sufficient" to support a reasonable verdict when the burden of persuasion is a mere preponderance of the evidence may not be sufficient when the burden is proof beyond a reasonable doubt. While Rule 104(b) suggests that the judge should defer to the jury in a jury trial, it does not state exactly what the level of deference should be. If common-law principles otherwise require that the jury be convinced by an extraordinary quantum of proof, then the judgment of what is sufficient should be altered accordingly.

In addition, the Court arguably did not adequately consider the problem of prejudice. Any time a jury is informed of a person's other misconduct—particularly serious criminal activities—a danger exists that the jury will employ the evidence for its improper character purpose and not for the narrower purpose for which it might properly be considered. The standard adopted by the Court takes a significant amount of filtering power out of the hands of the judge; it stands to reason that in the vast majority of cases, the prosecution can offer at least some evidence to support the defendant's participation in the uncharged misconduct, and that courts will generally find this evidence "sufficient to support a finding" that the defendant was in fact involved.[250] The court's ability to control the jury's natural (though impermissible) tendency to employ the evidence for

---

[248] *See* **§ 3.11**. Restyling has changed the wording but (supposedly) not the substance of Rule 104(b).

[249] Huddleston v. United States, 485 U.S. 681, 691–92 (1988) (footnote omitted).

[250] In a footnote, the Court rejected the defendant's contention that in performing the Rule 403 balance, the court must find that the prejudicial impact of the evidence outweighs its probative value unless the court concludes by a preponderance of the evidence that the defendant committed the uncharged act. The Court conceded, however, that "the strength of the evidence establishing the similar act is one of the factors the court may consider when conducting the Rule 403 balancing." Huddleston v. United States, 485 U.S. 681, 689 n.6 (1988).

the wrong reason is quite limited. Moreover, if the defendant decides seriously to contest her commission of the uncharged misconduct, the evidence of the uncharged activities will often sidetrack the trial on the charged activities. This, too, creates the risk of injustice.[251]

One of the authors, however, believes that the Court rightly attempted to follow the mandate of the Rules, especially Rule 402, in rejecting pre-Rules common-law restrictions on the admission of evidence. Rule 404(b)(1) bars evidence only when used for the propensity inference purpose; it presents no obstacle (other than the notice requirement) to the introduction of evidence of specific acts *not* barred by the propensity rule. Assuming that such evidence does not violate other rules, such as the requirement of personal knowledge and the prohibition on hearsay, it is admissible so long as relevant under Rule 402 and not unduly prejudicial under Rule 403. Under this view, the Court actually went further in restricting the prosecution than it probably should have by invoking the dubious concept of conditional relevance.[252] Insofar as the risk of unfair prejudice is concerned, Rule 403 is the right focus: it provides protection without any assistance from preliminary fact-finding about whether the prior acts occurred. Indeed, Rule 403 provides the right kind of flexibility for that protection, because it allows for the possibility that prior acts with a relatively low probability of occurrence can be admitted when the context indicates that the risk of unfair prejudice (or confusion or waste of time) is also low. In particular, Rule 404(b)(2) is not limited to prior "bad" acts,[253] acts that would potentially invoke unfair prejudice, and in contexts where no such potential exists, preliminary fact-finding by the court, even of the "sufficient to support a finding by a preponderance of the evidence" kind, is (like most invocations of "conditional relevance") an arbitrary restriction on the admission of relevant evidence.[254] The context-dependent, varying degree of unfair prejudice that courts encounter in the uncharged acts context requires a correspondingly varying threshold of minimum probative value, which is provided by Rule 403.[255]

---

[251] For a detailed discussion, *see* DAVID P. LEONARD, THE NEW WIGMORE: EVIDENCE OF OTHER MISCONDUCT AND SIMILAR EVENTS § 4.5 (2009).

[252] *See* Dale A. Nance, *Conditional Relevance Reinterpreted*, 70 B.U. L. REV. 447, 498–505 (1990). Given the Court's choice to invoke Rule 104(b), a meaning of "sufficient to support a finding" should be endorsed that keeps the test as close as possible to the meaning of relevance itself, as specified by Rule 401. When the issue is whether the defendant committed the prior act (not the act that is the subject of the present charge), "sufficient to support a finding by a preponderance of the evidence" is closer to that meaning than "sufficient to support a finding beyond reasonable doubt."

[253] It would be possible to construe the prohibition of Rule 404(b)(1) to apply only to "acts" that present a possible inference to a person's bad (or good) character, which tend to be acts with a negative (or positive) moral overtone, rather than "neutral" facts. *See* DAVID P. LEONARD, THE NEW WIGMORE: EVIDENCE OF OTHER MISCONDUCT AND SIMILAR EVENTS § 4.6 (2009) (exploring but not endorsing such a construction). But this would not eliminate the arbitrariness of pegging the minimum probative value required for admission to that probative value associated with alleged prior acts that happen to be more likely than not. As the drafters of Rule 404(b) stated: "No mechanical solution is offered. The determination must be made whether the danger of undue prejudice outweighs the probative value of the evidence in view of the availability of other means of proof and other factors appropriate for making decisions of this kind under Rule 403." FED. R. EVID. 404(b) advisory committee note.

[254] The "strength of the evidence as to the commission of the other crime" is one of the proper factors to consider in assessing probative value in this context. *See, e.g.*, State v. Castro, 756 P.2d 1033, 1041 (Haw. 1988).

[255] If judicial application of Rule 403 provides inadequate protection for defendants or other persons, the better solution is to modify that balancing test to favor exclusion for evidence of prior misconduct by requiring, for example, its probative value to outweigh the 403-dangers. *See, e.g.*, Richard B. Kuhns, *The Propensity to Misunderstand the Character of Specific Acts Evidence*, 66 IOWA L. REV. 777, 803–09 (1981).

In any event, the Supreme Court has spoken for the federal system. It is likely, though, that some states will continue to adhere to a stricter standard of proof, even where the Federal Rules of Evidence serve as a model for corresponding state rules. Even in jurisdictions that apply a more demanding standard, it is appropriate to consider all of the charged and uncharged misconduct together in deciding whether the standard has been met. Even if the defendant's commission of a prior crime, when considered by itself, has not been established by clear and convincing evidence, the suspicious prior circumstances, when taken together with the circumstances of the charged crime may be enough to prove the charged crime beyond a reasonable doubt. For example, it might be impossible to establish by clear and convincing evidence that the defendant had drowned his previous wife in the bathtub when the facts of that transaction are considered in isolation; however, when the facts are considered in conjunction with evidence that the defendant drowned his second wife in the bath, the two crimes corroborate each other and ought to be considered together.[256]

§ 7.12 "Reverse 404(b)" Evidence: Defendant's Use to Implicate Another

In criminal cases, problems of character evidence generally arise in connection with evidence offered by the prosecution. As already noted, however, the character evidence prohibition of Rule 404 is not limited to prosecution evidence. A defendant may not use reputation or opinion testimony to establish character in order to invite a propensity inference about another person unless it comes within the exception related to alleged victims, Rule 404(a)(2)(B), or within the exception for impeachment of witnesses, Rule 404(a)(3). The question naturally arises, however, whether the defendant may use Rule 404(b)(2) to present evidence of other specific acts by another person on a non-propensity theory. Occasional cases arise in which the defendant would like to use specific act evidence to show that some other person was the perpetrator of the crime for which the defendant is being tried. And the common law considered this permissible,[257] though subject to a traditional judicial skepticism about evidence used by the defense to cast suspicion on another party.[258]

---

[256] *Cf.* Rex v. Smith, [1914–15] All E.R. Rep. 265. For a case that apparently ignores this principle, *see* Tucker v. State, 412 P.2d 970 (Nev. 1966), which suggests, if nothing else, that the rules of character evidence are not just dressed-up common sense. In May, 1957, Tucker phoned the police station and asked someone to come to the Tucker home in North Las Vegas. When the police arrived, they noticed that Tucker had been drinking. Tucker led them to the dining room where Kaylor was lying dead on the floor, having been shot several times. Tucker explained that he had awakened and found Kaylor there. No one was ever charged with the crime. In October, 1963, Tucker again called the police. He had again been drinking. He led police to a dead man on the living room sofa. The man had been shot. Tucker explained that he had awakened and found the man dead on the couch. He was convicted of second-degree murder, with the evidence of the Kaylor killing admitted over objection. The Nevada Supreme Court reversed, reasoning that there was nothing in the record to establish that Tucker killed Kaylor. It announced a rule that before evidence of a collateral offense is admissible for any purpose, the prosecution must first establish by plain, clear, and convincing evidence that the defendant committed that offense.

[257] *See, e.g.,* Holt v. United States, 342 F.2d 163 (5th Cir. 1965) (reversing trial court's exclusion of defendant's misidentification in connection with two very similar crimes); Commonwealth v. Murphy, 185 N.E. 486 (Mass. 1933) (holding trial court erroneously excluded evidence of three other similar crimes and fact that defendant was in custody when one was committed and that one victim of such crimes admitted to erroneously identifying the defendant); State v. Bock, 39 N.W.2d 887 (Minn. 1949) (reversing trial court's exclusion of defendant's evidence that virtually identical crimes, uttering a forged check, were committed on the same day by someone else);. *See also* 2 WIGMORE ON EVIDENCE § 304 at 252 (Chadbourn rev. 1979).

[258] *See* David McCord, *"But Perry Mason Made It Look So* Easy*!": The Admissibility of Evidence Offered by a Criminal Defendant to Suggest that Someone Else is Guilty*, 63 TENN. L. REV. 917 (1996).

Although some opinions state that Rule 404(b) does not apply at all to evidence of other acts by a third person,[259] this contravenes the plain language of the Rule, which refers to "person," not just the "defendant" or "party." Neither the defendant nor the prosecution may use specific acts of a third person to invite a propensity inference about the actions of that third person. But the defendant may invoke Rule 404(b)(2) just as the prosecution invokes it against the defendant. Functionally, the defendant is then in the position of "prosecuting" the third party and must comply with the admissibility rules for "other act" evidence.[260] That is, upon objection by the prosecution under Rule 404(b)(1), the defendant must identify a non-propensity-inference form of relevance and, upon further objection, the evidence must survive a Rule 403 balancing test.[261] (Conditional relevance issues may also arise in connection with whether the third party committed the other acts.) Two differences emerge, however, in the assessment of the risk of unfair prejudice under Rule 403, both attributable to the fact that the person alleged by the accused to be the perpetrator is not before the court and cannot be convicted by the jury. First, a less strict standard of similarity between other acts and charged act is sometimes required. Second, the risk of unfair prejudice is usually muted: the jury is in no position to act on any unfair prejudice against a person not being tried. Consequently, the court's 403 decision should balance probative value against risks of confusion of the issues and waste of time.[262]

The picture is rather different regarding Rules 413 and 414, which concern evidence of other acts of sexual assault and child molestation.[263] Unlike Rule 404(b)(2), Rules 413 and 414 are written in a form that only benefits the prosecution. The latter rules do not authorize "reverse 413" or "reverse 414" evidence, whereby the defendant introduces evidence of other acts of sexual assault or child molestation to implicate a third party. This is a peculiar result that may not have been contemplated. All other things being equal, evidence (offered by the defendant) that a third person has a history of sexual assault or child molestation ought to be treated like evidence (offered by the prosecution) that the defendant has such a history. Moreover, like "reverse 404(b)" evidence, there is less risk of unfair prejudice when the person with the sordid history is not a party in the case. Together, these points make a strong argument for admitting "reverse 413" or "reverse 414" evidence, but there is no basis in the Rules for doing so. In this context, the only avenue available to the defendant is to invoke his constitutional right to present

---

[259] *See, e.g.*, United States v. Gonzalez-Sanchez, 825 F.2d 572, 582 n.25 (1st Cir.) ("Inasmuch as this evidence does not concern past criminal activity of [the defendant], Rule 404(b) is inapplicable."), *cert. denied*, 484 U.S. 989 (1987).

[260] *See* **§ 7.09–§ 7.11**. The defense is not, however, subject to the same notice requirement at the prosecution. *See* **§ 7.16**.

[261] *See* United States v. Williams, 458 F.3d 312 (3d Cir. 2006) (rejecting defendant's argument that he be allowed to invite a propensity-inference implicating an alternative perpetrator); United States v. Puckett, 692 F.2d 663, 671 (10th Cir.), *cert. denied*, 459 U.S. 1091 (1982) (same); United States v. McCourt, 925 F.2d 1229, 1232 (9th Cir. 1991) (same).

[262] *See* United States v. Stevens, 935 F.2d 1380, 1401–06 (3d Cir. 1991) (reversing for trial court's exclusion of defense evidence that similar crimes were committed by someone other than the defendant). For an interesting trial court opinion wrestling with these considerations, *see* United States v. Duran-Moreno, 616 F. Supp. 2d 1162 (D.N.M. 2009) (denying prosecution's motion to bar the defense from introducing evidence that the former owner of the car in which drugs were found, and attributed to the defendant, had been convicted of illegal drug distribution).

[263] *See* **§ 7.06**.

evidence. To date, however, there is little case law supporting such a constitutional override of the limits on propensity inferences under Rules 413 and 414.[264]

§ 7.13 Rape Shield Laws [FRE 412]

At common law, courts often admitted evidence of a woman's character for chastity in the form of either reputation or specific-acts testimony. Such evidence was traditionally considered relevant in two contexts. First, in cases of alleged rape in which the defense argued that the sexual interaction was consensual, promiscuity on the part of the victim indicated that she was willing to sacrifice her chastity or marriage vows (displaying a propensity to consent), thereby increasing the likelihood that she consented on the particular occasion.[265] Second—and applicable by some case law to any case in which a woman was a witness—prior sexual activity (outside the confines of marriage) constituted a character flaw that undermined the veracity of her testimony.[266]

The historical suspicion of women charging rape[267] and the subjection of women to invasion of privacy and degradation in the courtroom discouraged women from pursuing rape charges. In addition to presenting ethical concerns about maltreatment of rape victims and practical concerns about getting women to participate in the legal process, the evidentiary value of "character for chastity" evidence raised questions of logic and practical relevance. The effect on rape trials was disruptive and often disproportionate to any light it might have shed on the events of the case. Such character evidence drew upon the sexist presumption that once a woman consents on one occasion, she is unlikely to turn down another potential sexual partner.[268] This reasoning is untenable in a society that "presume[s] that a woman will freely choose her partners, picking some and

---

[264] *See* EDWARD J. IMWINKELRIED & NORMAN M. GARLAND, EXCULPATORY EVIDENCE § 9–3.b (3d ed. 2004). *But cf.* People v. Schwartz, 678 P.2d 1000, 1008–10 (Colo. 1984) (invoking Colorado and U.S. constitutional provisions in ruling that defendant's evidence of domestic violence and alleged child abuse by father may be admissible upon retrial of babysitter for acts leading to death of child; character evidence rules not mentioned).

[265] *See* 1A WIGMORE ON EVIDENCE § 62 at 1369 (Tillers rev. 1983); People v. Allen, 124 N.E. 329 (Ill. 1919); Graham v. State, 67 S.W.2d 296 (Tex. Crim. App. 1933); Fry v. Commonwealth, 177 S.E. 860 (Va. 1935). *See also* Heather D. Flowe, Ebbe B. Ebbesen & Anila Putcha-Bhagavatula, *Rape Shield Laws and Sexual Behavior Evidence: Effects of Consent Level and Women's Sexual History on Rape Allegations,* 31 LAW & HUM. BEHAV. 159 (2007) ("Many states, for example, once had cautionary instructions to the jury warning of women's propensity to make false charges of rape. Moreover, evidence of promiscuity was routinely admitted at trial to undermine the credibility of a complainant and to demonstrate to the jury that in all likelihood she consented on the occasion in question.") (citations omitted).

[266] *See, e.g.*, State v. Sibley, 131 Mo. 519 & 132 Mo. 102 (1895) (reversing conviction because trial court mistakenly allowed impeachment of male defendant as witness based on his unchaste character; dissenting opinion arguing to apply the same impeachment rule to male witnesses as applied to female witnesses). Even if not barred by rape shield provisions, such impeachment evidence would not pass the test of Rule 608 today. *See* **§ 11.07**.

[267] Sir Matthew Hale famously cautioned jurors in rape cases: "It must be remembered that this is an accusation easily to be made and hard to be proved, and harder to be defended by the party accused, tho' never so innocent." MATTHEW HALE, 1 HISTORY OF THE PLEAS OF THE CROWN 634 (Philadelphia, R.H. Small 1847).

[268] The logic of admitting character for chastity relies on rape myths, which are empirically untrue, but nevertheless firmly held notions about the incidence and nature of rape. Rape myths are defined as "prejudicial, stereotyped, or false beliefs about rape, rape victims, and rapists." Morrison Torrey, *When Will We be Believed? Rape Myths and the Idea of a Fair Trial in Rape Prosecutions,* 24 U.C. DAVIS L. REV. 1013, 1017–18 (1991) (citing work of psychologist Martha Burt). Such rape myths include the idea that women refusing sex secretly want it, that women who are promiscuous always consent to sex, and that women who dress provocatively are expressing consent to sex. By prohibiting inquiry into the victim's sexual history and proclivities, rape shield laws deprive the jury of precisely the type of information that feeds reliance upon rape myths. *See* Kim Lane Scheppele, *Just the Facts Ma'am: Sexualized Violence Evidentiary Habits and the Revision of Truth,* 37 N.Y.L. SCH. L. REV. 124, 154–55.

rejecting others, in line with highly personal standards not susceptible of generalization."[269] Evidence about the complainant's sexual history and proclivities is of low probative value and can lead to unfair prejudice and distraction. The victim's life and morals, not the nature of alleged rape, become the focus of the trial. Some jurors may even wish to punish the victim for being incautious or for behaving promiscuously.

As part of a reform effort supported by the women's movement and by law enforcement officials in the 1970s, state legislatures and Congress adopted "rape shield" legislation that limited the use of evidence of prior sexual conduct in sexual assault cases.[270] Rape shield was designed "to protect rape victims from the degrading and embarrassing disclosure of intimate details about their private lives, to encourage reporting of sexual assaults and to prevent wasting time on distractive collateral and irrelevant matters."[271] As a doctrinal matter, a major function of rape shield laws is to limit the defendant's use of the exception to the character evidence ban, provided by Rule 404(a)(2)(B) and similar state rules that permit the accused to raise pertinent traits of the victim.[272] Rape shield overrides Rule 404(a)(2)(B) and reverts to the general rule excluding character evidence used to invite a propensity inference.

Rape-shield legislation has been adopted by all fifty states and the District of Columbia and as part of the Federal Rules of Evidence[273] and the rules for military tribunals.[274] The provisions of rape shield vary significantly among jurisdictions, but all statutes in some way limit the use of evidence of sexual reputation, history, behavior, and proclivity to prove unchaste character or sexual proclivity.[275] Some jurisdictions do little more than provide a procedural mechanism for pretrial decision, calling attention to the potentially unfair prejudice and irrelevance of the victim's sexual history, and providing only some general standard of admissibility, such as weighing prejudice against probative value.[276] Other regimes, including the Federal Rules of Evidence, present a general rule of exclusion and admit specific instances of prior sexual behavior or proclivity only for limited purposes. Many rape-shield rules have the effect of

---

[269] Vivian Berger, *Man's Trial, Women's Tribulation: Rape Cases in the Courtroom*, 77 COLUM. L. REV. 1, 56 (1977). Such character evidence reinforced social norms whereby women who had consensual sex outside of marriage were in a vulnerable position if they suffered a sexual attack. Functionally, the law tended to privilege rape stories where a woman behaved within socially accepted norms and was attacked by a stranger; the law was significantly less helpful to a woman flouting social norms (out late, drinking, sexually active) who was attacked by someone she knew.

[270] For a thorough and insightful review of this legislation, *see* Harriett R. Galvin, *Shielding Rape Victims in the State and Federal Courts: A Proposal for the Second Decade,* 70 MINN. L. REV. 763 (1986). *See also* Ann Althouse, *Thelma and Louise and the Law: Do Rape Shield Rules Matter?*, 25 LOY. L.A. L. REV. 757 (1992).

[271] United States v. Torres, 937 F.2d 1469, 1472 (9th Cir. 1991).

[272] *See* **§ 7.04**.

[273] Rape shield was not included in the original Rules of Evidence that became law in 1975. However, Congress passed The Privacy Protection for Rape Victims Act of 1978, Pub. L. No. 95–540, 92 Stat. 2046 that became Federal Rule of Evidence 412.

[274] *See* American Prosecutors Research Institute, *Rape Shield Statutes, available at* http://www.arte-sana.com/articles/rape_shield_laws_us.pdf. (2003) (providing a state-by-state list).

[275] Another aspect of some rape-shield jurisdictions is a policy against naming the alleged victim. The prohibition on naming the victim often stems from self-imposed limits by the media, but some states have legal prohibitions on disclosure by the government and opposing counsel. *See* Daniel M. Murdock, *A Compelling State Interest: Constructing a Statutory Framework for Protecting the Identity of Rape Victims* 58 ALA. L. REV. 1177 n.102 (listing eleven states with such statutes, including New York and California). In many cases, judges will issue an order forbidding disclosure of the name, address, and likeness of the victim.

[276] *See, e.g.,* R.I. GEN. LAWS § 11–37–13 (providing for notice to court and discussion of admissibility "out of hearing of jury").

excluding evidence of the victim's dress[277] or her profession as an exotic dancer or a prostitute.[278] Rape-shield statutes also provide procedural protections, such as notice requirements, hearings in limine on the issue of admissibility, and, in some cases, in camera hearings to protect the woman's privacy.[279] The rape-shield statutes are gender neutral and apply to men who are victims of rape.

For federal criminal cases, the operative prohibition, subject to limited exceptions discussed below, is Rule 412(a):

> (a) *Prohibited Uses.* The following evidence is not admissible in a . . . criminal proceeding involving alleged sexual misconduct:
>
> > (1) evidence offered to prove that a victim engaged in other sexual behavior; or
> >
> > (2) evidence offered to prove a victim's sexual predisposition.

Notwithstanding the change of the title during restyling (from "Evidence Generally Inadmissible" to "Prohibited Uses"), the prohibition in this section is unusual in that it does *not* specify that evidence is inadmissible only for a particular "use" or "purpose." The prohibition sweeps more widely than a simple limitation on propensity inferences otherwise permitted under Rule 404(a)(2)(B).[280] Thus, on its face, the prohibition in Rule 412(a)(1) precludes the use of specific act evidence of sexual behavior for *non-propensity-inference* purposes under Rule 404(b)(2) as well as well as propensity inferences, and the prohibition in Rule 412(a)(2) bars a circumstantial use of evidence of character or propensity that is *not* offered to show action in conformity with the propensity or character.

According to the drafters, the term "sexual predisposition" is broad enough to include "evidence that does not directly refer to sexual activities or thoughts but that the proponent believes may have a sexual connotation for the factfinder," such as "the alleged victim's mode of dress, speech, or life-style."[281] On the other hand, evidence of the alleged victim's prior false claims of sexual assault or molestation is more concerned

---

[277] *See, e.g.*, N.Y. CRIM. PROC. LAW § 60.48 (Consol. 2007) ("Evidence of the manner in which the victim was dressed at the time of the commission of an offense may not be admitted in a prosecution for any [rape] offense . . .").

[278] *Compare* Collins v. State, 223 P.3d 1014 (Okla. Crim. App. 2009) (holding that fact that victim was prostitute is inadmissible under rape shield, did not demonstrate bias or propensity to lie, and exclusion does not violate accused's constitutional rights to confront witnesses); *with* People v. Chandler, 65 Cal.Rptr.2d 687, 690–91 (Cal. Ct. App. 1997) ("credibility exception" to California rape-shield statute "has been utilized sparingly," most often in cases where the victim's prior sexual history is one of prostitution); Drake v. State, 836 P.2d 52, 55 (Nev. 1992) (admitting victim's prior conviction for illegal prostitution where defense was that sex was consensual but complainant charged rape when she was not paid); N.Y. CRIM. PROC. LAW § 60.42(2) ("Evidence of a victim's sexual conduct shall not be admissible in a prosecution for an offense or an attempt to commit [a sex offense] . . . unless such evidence . . . proves or tends to prove that the victim has been convicted of [prostitution] . . . within three years prior to the sex offense which is the subject of the prosecution.").

[279] *See* 23 CHARLES A. WRIGHT & KENNETH W. GRAHAM, JR., FEDERAL PRACTICE AND PROCEDURE: EVIDENCE § 5391 (1980). *But cf.* United States v. Platero, 72 F.3d 806, 813 (10th Cir. 1995) (holding that issue whether rape victim had prior sexual relationship was for jury, not judge, to decide under amended Rule 412).

[280] Had the goal been merely to limit Rule 404(a)(2)(B), it would have sufficed to delete the prohibition in Rule 412(a)(1) entirely and to have stated the second prohibition instead as "evidence offered to prove a victim's sexual predisposition in order to invite an inference of action in conformity therewith." In that case, the exceptions stated in Rule 412(b)(1) would have been unnecessary. See FED. R. EVID. 412 advisory committee note ("Evidence, which might otherwise be admissible under Rules 402, 404(b), 405, 607, 608, 609, or some other evidence rule, must be excluded if Rule 412 so requires.").

[281] FED. R. EVID. 412 advisory committee notes (1994 amendment).

with claiming behavior than with sexual behavior or sexual predisposition, so it is admissible substantively if it falls within Rule 404(b)(2) or as impeachment of the alleged victim if she testifies and the evidence otherwise falls within Rule 608(b) or 609.[282]

Federal Rule 412(b)(1) and many state statutes recognize two exceptions to the broad prohibition of rape shield: (1) the complainant's prior sexual behavior with the defendant, when offered on the issue of consent (Rule 412(b)(1)(B), and (2) evidence of the complainant's sexual behavior with other persons, when offered to explain the physical consequences of the alleged rape (Rule 412(b)(1)(A)—e.g., injury, the presence of semen, pregnancy, or venereal disease.[283] The narrowness of these exceptions is illustrated by supposing a case in which the defendant offers evidence of prior sexual behavior between the defendant and the alleged victim that is offered not to show consent but rather to explain the existence of physical evidence that seems to implicate the defendant. This evidence falls into neither exception but is clearly within the purpose of the second, that is, to permit evidence that provides an innocent explanation of otherwise incriminating evidence.[284]

Another question that probes the limitations of these exceptions is whether the defense may introduce evidence concerning the complainant's behavior with others to support the defendant's claim that he believed the complainant consented, even if she did not in fact consent.[285] This use of evidence does not involve a propensity inference to show that the complainant consented, but once again Rule 412(a) sweeps more broadly than just propensity inferences: this evidence seems to fall squarely within the prohibition of Rule 412(a)(1). On the other hand, the evidence is not necessarily offered to show the *actual* sexual behavior or predisposition of the complainant, but rather to show only what the defendant *believed* about such matters.[286] Federal case law is split on the question, with the counter-argument being that it would be inconsistent with the purpose of the rule to suggest that the defendant could *reasonably* draw an inference of consent from what he had heard about the complainant's behavior with others.[287]

---

[282] *See* FED. R. EVID. 412 advisory committee notes (1994 amendment); State v. Smith, 743 So.2d 199 (La. 1999) (evidence of prior similar allegations by alleged victim, subsequently recanted, held admissible for impeachment purposes if rules other than rape shield provision satisfied).

[283] *See, e.g.,* MICH. COMP. LAWS ANN. § 750.520j; MASS. ANN. LAWS ch. 233, § 21B (1986); MINN. R. EVID. 404(c). If the prosecution seeks to prove rape by putting in evidence that, for example, the complainant became pregnant, it is only fair to allow the defense to rebut by showing that another man could have caused the pregnancy. But the defense is not entitled to introduce evidence of disease, pregnancy, or semen where the prosecution has not benefited from the evidence and has done nothing to open the door. *See* United States v. White Buffalo, 84 F.3d 1052, 1054 (8th Cir. 1996) (holding that where government made no effort to introduce semen evidence, defendant is not entitled to present evidence of rape complainant's prior consensual intercourse solely to impeach her by showing that she falsely told a hospital doctor that she had not had consensual intercourse within 72 hours of rape).

[284] Despite the clear language of the rule, such evidence has been held admissible. *See* United States v. Saunders, 943 F.2d 388, 392 (4th Cir. 1991).

[285] Whether this mistaken belief is relevant depends on the specific substantive rules concerning sexual assault in the jurisdiction. The current federal statute makes it relevant. *See* 18 U.S.C. § 2241(a) (defining aggravated sexual abuse in terms of specific intent).

[286] *See* 2 CHRISTOPHER B. MUELLER & LAIRD C. KIRKPATRICK, FEDERAL EVIDENCE § 4:78 at 271–73 (4th ed. 2013).

[287] *Compare* Doe v. United States, 666 F.2d 43 (4th Cir. 1981) (permitting defendant to introduce evidence of what he had heard about complainant to support his claim of reasonable mistake), *with* United States v. Saunders, 943 F.2d 388, 391–92 (4th Cir. 1991) (disapproving *Doe* as creating exception to the clear prohibition of Rule 412). *See also* People v. Guthreau, 102 Cal. App. 3d 436, 162 Cal. Rptr. 376, 380 (Cal. Ct. App. 1980) (holding evidence of complainant's sexual history inadmissible to show defendant's reasonable belief that she consented).

Depending on the specific wording of particular statutes, some jurisdictions admit evidence offered to show: (a) a motive for fabrication by the complainant;[288] (b) other behavior that constitutes a pattern of sexual conduct so nearly identical to the behavior on the occasion in question that it leads to a reliable inference of consent;[289] (c) the accused's reasonable but mistaken belief in the complainant's consent;[290] or (d) evidence of prior false accusations of sexual assault by the complainant.[291] A few states permit evidence of the complainant's sexual history as evidence to attack her credibility.[292] As an outlying example of an exception to rape shield, North Carolina Evidence Rule 412 permits "evidence of sexual behavior offered as the basis of expert psychological or psychiatric opinion that the complainant fantasized or invented the act or acts charged."[293]

Finally, the Federal Rules (and some state provisions) include an affirmative exception to the rape-shield rule where exclusion of the evidence would violate the accused's constitutional rights. Because this provision (added by a 1994 amendment) is, legally speaking, superfluous—the rule could not override the requirements of the constitution, even if that had been its intent—the inclusion of this special qualification, which appears as Rule 412(b)(1)(C) in the Federal Rules, can only be a signal that the drafters of Rule 412 were aware that the broad sweep of the prohibition would inevitably bring it into conflict with the defendant's constitutional rights.[294] Not surprisingly, rape-shield statutes have been challenged on the ground that they violate the accused's confrontation rights and right to compulsory process.[295]

In the principal case that motivated the 1994 amendment, *Olden v. Kentucky*,[296] the Supreme Court held that curtailing the defense's attempt to cross-examine the alleged victim about her affair with another witness violated the defendant's right to

---

[288] *See* MD. CODE ANN. art. 27, § 461A (1996).

[289] *See* MINN. R. EVID. 404(c).

[290] *See* NEV. REV. STAT. ANN. § 48.069 (accused may present "evidence of any previous sexual conduct of the victim of the crime to prove the victim's consent," in compliance with statutory procedures); WASH. REV. CODE ANN. § 9A.44.020(3) ("victim's past sexual behavior. . . is admissible on the issue of consent," in compliance with statutory procedures, including finding that exclusion of evidence "would result in denial of substantial justice to the defendant").

[291] *Compare* State v. Baker, 679 N.W.2d 7 (Iowa 2004) (reversing for error in excluding evidence that 13-year-old girl claimed, but later denied, that neighbor had raped her), *with* State v. Dorsey, 783 A.2d 947, 953 (R.I. 2001) (holding that evidence of false allegations of child abuse made by complainant 20 years previously was inadmissible in factually different sexual assault case).

[292] *See, e.g.*, CAL. EVID. CODE § 1103(a)(1) & (c)(5); DEL. CODE ANN. tit. 11 §§ 3508, 3509(d).

[293] N.C.R. EVID. 412(b)(4). This bizarre exception, which invites inquiry into the victim's mental health, harks back to Sigmund Freud's notion that women's charges of sexual abuse are often "hysterical" fabrications emanating from fantasies.

[294] *See* Daniel J. Capra & Liesa L. Richter, *Poetry in Motion: The Federal Rules of Evidence and Forward Progress as an Imperative*, 99 B.U. L. REV. 1873, 1880–81 (2019) ("[T]he amended language is useful for two reasons: (1) it avoids damage to the credibility of the Rules caused when a rule is subject to unconstitutional application; and (2) it operates as a red flag for unwary litigants, directing them to a source of law beyond the rule itself.").

[295] *See, e.g.*, State v. Garron, 827 A.2d 243 (N.J. 2003) (excluding victim's prior flirtations with the accused violated his constitutional rights to confront his accuser under both federal and New Jersey State constitutions). State v. Jalo, 557 P.2d 1359 (Or. Ct. App. 1976) (holding unconstitutional the exclusion of evidence of child complainant's prior sexual conduct when adult defendant claimed that she had falsely accused him because he told her that he was going to inform her parents of her sexual conduct with his son and others); Commonwealth v. Black, 487 A.2d 396 (Pa. Super. 1985) (holding unconstitutional the exclusion of sexual behavior evidence that shows bias). *See also* Clifford S. Fishman, *Consent, Credibility, and the Constitution: Evidence Relating to a Sex Offense Complainant's Past Sexual Behavior*, 44 CATH. U.L. REV. 709 (1995).

[296] Olden v. Kentucky, 488 U.S. 227 (1988).

confrontation. *Olden* was a sexual assault case in which the defendant claimed consent. After the incident, the defendant drove the complainant to the house of his half-brother, Bill Russell. The defense wished to cross-examine the complainant about an alleged affair she was having with Bill Russell on the theory that the complainant had fabricated her claim to protect her relationship with Bill Russell, who had seen her get out of defendant's car and may have been suspicious. The trial judge excluded the evidence concerning the affair. The Supreme Court held that the evidence was admissible.

Several factors favored admissibility in *Olden*. The complainant's alleged boyfriend saw her get out of the defendant's car. Her motive to fabricate a sexual assault to explain why she was with the defendant was greater than it would have been had she reported the assault to the police before her boyfriend knew about it. Also, although the court did not use this argument, the prosecution arguably lost its right to object to the evidence after it elicited from the complainant on direct examination that she lived with her mother, when in fact she lived with Bill Russell. These facts tend to make *Olden* somewhat special, though not unique. Normally, the court's refusal to allow free cross-examination of a rape victim about current sexual partners will not violate the defendant's constitutional right to confrontation. But *Olden* demonstrates that, at times, the Constitution requires that the court allow criminal defendants to offer evidence that otherwise would be excluded by rape-shield laws, especially when it shows a complainant's motive to fabricate.

The defendant's right to a jury trial may also limit the operation of rape-shield statutes. In *United States v. Platero*,[297] the trial judge excluded evidence on the ground that he did not believe an alleged affair between the victim and the defendant had occurred. The Tenth Circuit Court of Appeals held that the defendant's right to trial by jury guaranteed him the right to have a jury decide that factual issue. Under this approach, the rape-shield rule still has force, because the defendant must show that sexual conduct, if it occurred, fits one of the exceptions to the rule, but the testimony that the alleged victim did in fact engage in sexual conduct with another person must be assumed true in making that determination.

Rape shield has been criticized from all sides—as too permissive in admitting the sexual history of victims[298] and as too stringent in preventing the accused from mounting an effective cross-examination.[299] Examples can be found to support both positions.

---

[297] United States v. Platero, 72 F.3d 806 (10th Cir. 1995).

[298] *See* Elizabeth Kessler, *Pattern of Sexual Conduct Evidence and Present Consent: Limiting the Admissibility of Sexual History Evidence in Rape Prosecutions*, 14 WOMEN'S RTS. L. REP. 79 (1992) (arguing that pattern evidence is "poorly applied and frequently misused"); Ann Althouse, *Thelma and Louise and the Law: Do Rape Shield Rules Matter*, 25 LOY. L.A. L. REV. 757, 764 (1992) (arguing that rape shield law can be undermined by judges' and jurors' mistrust of rape survivor and that judges often apply "generous interpretation to the rape shield exceptions").

[299] *See, e.g.*, Merry C. Evans, *The Missouri Supreme Court confronts the Sixth Amendment in its Interpretation of the Rape Victim Shield Statute*, 52 MO. L. REV. 925, 926–27 (1987); Frank Tuerkheimer, *A Reassessment and Redefinition of Rape Shield Laws*, 50 OHIO ST. L. J. 1245, 1262–69 (1989); J. Alexander Tanford & Anthony J. Bocchino, *Rape Victim Shield Laws and the Sixth Amendment*, 128 U. PA. L. REV. 544, 582–83 (1980); David Haxton, Comment, *Rule 16.5.1.(a) Rape Shield Statutes: Constitutional Despite Unconstitutional Exclusions of Evidence*, 1985 WIS. L. REV. 1219, 1235–37 (arguing that an accused should be able to present a pattern of the woman's sexual activity under certain circumstances); Pamela J. Fisher, Comment, State v. Alvey: *Iowa's Victimization of Defendants Through the Overextension of Iowa's Rape Shield Law*, 76 IOWA L. REV. 835 (1990) (expressing concern over defendant who because of rape shield would not be allowed to bring up woman's past false charges of rape).

Many have questioned the efficacy of rape-shield rules, arguing that one cannot legislate around deeply entrenched biases.[300] Ideally, rape shield serves to focus the trial and to eliminate irrelevant, distracting, and potentially prejudicial information, thereby also promoting rape prosecutions. In practice, however, even with the formal protections of rape shield, victims are sometimes humiliated and harassed. When Kobe Bryant, the famous basketball player, was accused of rape, evidence that the victim had sex with three people in three days was introduced in a preliminary hearing to show other potential sources of injury, a recognized exception to rape shield. The practical effect, however, served to brand the complainant as promiscuous and to alert her to the defense's strategy of attacking her character.[301] This case also illustrates that, as a practical matter, in high-profile cases, publicity and information available over the Internet may provide such information to the public, influence the jury, and serve to deter women from pursuing charges.

Many jurisdictions provide a protection analogous to the rape-shield statutes for plaintiffs and others involved in civil sexual-harassment cases. For example, Federal Rule 412(a) excludes evidence of sexual predisposition or sexual behavior of an alleged victim offered in a civil case unless "its probative value substantially outweighs the danger of harm to any victim and of unfair prejudice to any party."[302]

§ 7.14 Character as an Ultimate Issue [FRE 405]

When character is used circumstantially to show propensity and then to argue that the party acted in conformity with that propensity, character is not the ultimate issue; it is merely an evidentiary fact that is offered to prove something else. Sometimes, however, character itself is an ultimate issue, or in the language of the Federal Rule 405(b), it is "an essential element of a charge, claim, or defense." This rule contemplates situations in which the substantive law renders a party's right or liability dependent on a trait of character. In such rare cases, character evidence is freely admissible. In fact, the character evidence need not be in the form of reputation or opinion testimony, authorized by Rule 405(a); under Rule 405(b), evidence of specific instances of conduct is also admissible.[303]

Examples

The fitness of a parent, in custody litigation. The criteria for awarding custody often refer to parental fitness, and a liberal attitude toward admissibility results.[304]

The relevant character trait that forms the basis for a defamation action, when truth is raised as a defense. For example, if the defendant called the plaintiff a thief, and in a defamation action admits making the statement but claims that it was true, the defendant may produce evidence showing the plaintiff to be a thief. The application of this principle is limited, however. For instance, where

---

[300] *See* Aya Gruber, *Rape, Feminism and the War on Crime,* 84 WASH. LAW. REV 581 (2009).

[301] *See* Tom Lininger, *Bearing the Cross,* 74 FORDHAM L. REV. 1353, 1376–79 (2005) (discussing the impotence of rape shield and the clear message that Bryant's attorneys would make trial about complainant's sexuality).

[302] FED. R. EVID. 412(b)(2). *See* **§ 7.08.**

[303] *See, e.g.,* United States v. Sonntag, 684 F.2d 781 (11th Cir. 1982); Crumpton v. Confederation Life Ins. Co., 672 F.2d 1248 (5th Cir. 1982).

[304] *See* 1A WIGMORE ON EVIDENCE § 69.1 (Tillers rev. 1983).

the defendant published an article that alleged that P stole a car on a certain date and D asserts truth as a defense, evidence to show that P stole the car would of course be admissible. However, evidence of P's general reputation as a car thief, or the opinion of one who knows P and that P is the kind of person who steals cars, would not be admissible to prove truth because, even though P's character trait (propensity) is relevant, it is not itself an "essential element" of the defense; the evidence would be offered as circumstantial evidence of P's conduct, for which purpose it is not admissible.

The fitness of a person to be entrusted with a dangerous instrumentality, such as an automobile. The injured party could sue the owner under a theory of negligent entrustment (rather than, say, respondeat superior). The character trait of the person to whom the instrumentality was entrusted—such as recklessness or chronic drunkenness—may indicate whether the defendant's entrustment was negligent, provided that the defendant was aware of the trait.[305]

The predisposition of a defendant, when the defendant relies on an entrapment defense. For example, if the defendant claims that he was entrapped by the government into selling drugs, the defendant effectively asserts that he is not the *kind* of person who would sell drugs absent the government's inducements. In that case, the government may freely introduce prior drug sales to show that the defendant was predisposed.[306]

After *Robinson v. California*,[307] modern legislators have avoided explicit attempts to make the possession of a trait of character itself a crime. But they do sometimes make a pattern of bad acts an element of an aggravated offense, as in enactments that make it an additional offense to commit crimes as part of racketeering enterprises or in furtherance of gang activities. Because the jury must determine whether the defendant is guilty of the offense, evidence of other crimes is freely admitted in cases in which the other crimes establish an element of a substantive offense. Such statutes may become as great a threat to traditional ideas about trying the defendant only for the offense charged as more overt assaults on the character evidence rule.[308]

§ 7.15 Character and Habit [FRE 406]

In most jurisdictions, character evidence is not admissible in civil cases as circumstantial evidence of conforming conduct,[309] and it is admissible in criminal cases

---

[305] *See* 3 JONES ON EVIDENCE §§ 15:5–15:8 (Clifford S. Fishman ed., 7th ed. 1998).

[306] *See* 1 CHRISTOPHER B. MUELLER & LAIRD C. KIRKPATRICK, FEDERAL EVIDENCE § 4:27 at 722–27 (4th ed. 2013).

[307] Robinson v. California, 370 U.S. 660 (1962) (unconstitutional to criminalize mere status of being addicted).

[308] *See* United States v. Tse, 135 F.3d 200 (1st Cir. 1998) (holding that trial court committed no error in admitting subsequent offense of attempting to smuggle aliens into the United States in charging attempted murder/conspiracy to commit murder in aid of a racketeering enterprise); People v. Gardeley, 927 P.2d 713, 722 (Cal. 1996), as modified *on denial of reh'g* (1997) (allowing testimony by an expert on "criminal gang activity" about pattern of criminal conduct in order to support "gang enhancement" of robbery and attempted murder charges). *Cf.* Old Chief v. United States, 519 U.S. 172 (1997) (holding that jury should not learn of nature of prior felony prosecution under federal "felon with a firearm" statute; though Court permitted jury to hear that defendant was convicted of unspecified qualifying felony in order to establish that element of offense).

[309] *See* § **7.08**.

only under prescribed exceptions.[310] However, evidence of *habit* is freely admissible. Federal Rule 406 states, in part, "Evidence of a person's habit, or an organization's routine practice may be admitted to prove that on a particular occasion the person or organization acted in accordance with the habit or routine practice." Given Rule 402, which specifies that all relevant evidence is admissible unless excluded by another rule, Rule 406 should seem odd, unnecessary. Its main purpose is simply to alert the user of the rules to the fact that habit is not caught by the prohibition of character evidence in Rule 404.

The distinction between character and habit is largely a matter of degree. In describing the distinction, the advisory committee to the Federal Rules of Evidence quoted McCormick's classic definition:

> Character and habit are close akin. Character is a generalized description of one's disposition, or of one's disposition in respect to a general trait, such as honesty, temperance, or peacefulness. "Habit," in modern usage, both lay and psychological, is more specific. It describes one's regular response to a repeated specific situation. If we speak of character for care, we think of the person's tendency to act prudently in all the varying situations of life, in business, family life, in handling automobiles and in walking across the street. A habit, on the other hand, is the person's regular practice of meeting a particular kind of situation with a specific type of conduct, such as the habit of going down a particular stairway two stairs at a time, or of giving the hand-signal for a left turn, or of alighting from railway cars while they are moving. The doing of the habitual acts may become semi-automatic.[311]

The Rules provide for the admission of habit evidence about human beings and for admission of evidence of the routine practice of a corporation or other organization. In contrast to the earlier practice of some jurisdictions, the Federal Rules do not require that habit or routine practice be corroborated by other evidence; the habit can by itself be admissible to prove the doing of an act. Nor is there any rule that habit evidence is allowed only in the absence of eyewitness testimony, another older common-law requirement. One's habit—say, a habit of using seat belts—is admissible under the Federal Rules whether or not eyewitnesses are also available who could testify that the person wore the seat belt on the occasion in question.[312]

Examples of habit or routine practice include: a doctor's regular practice of advising patients of the risks of joint replacement surgery, to show that the advice was given on

---

[310] *See* § **7.02**.

[311] FED. R. EVID. 406 advisory committee note (quoting CHARLES T. MCCORMICK, MCCORMICK ON EVIDENCE § 162 at 340 (1954)). *See also* Jones v. Southern Pac. R.R., 962 F.2d 447, 449 (5th Cir. 1992) (noting that habit evidence is superior to character evidence "because the uniformity of one's response to habit is far greater than the consistency with which one's conduct conforms to character"). *Cf.* Mobil Exploration & Producing U.S., Inc. v. Cajun Const. Servs., Inc., 45 F.3d 96, 100 (5th Cir. 1995) (holding that trial court erroneously excluded evidence of supplier's method of loading its trucks in suit claiming supplier had short-loaded its deliveries of limestone; supplier's method of loading amounted to habit under FED. R. EVID. 406 because same procedure was used with such regularity as to amount to routine business practice).

[312] The second sentence of Rule 406 states, "The court may admit this [habit] evidence regardless of whether it is corroborated or whether there was an eyewitness." FED. R. EVID. 406. Once again, given Rule 402, this statement seems superfluous, but it is intended to emphasize that the indicated common-law restrictions are eliminated. See FED. R. EVID. 406 advisory committee note and Reporter's Comment on Restyled Rule 406.

a particular occasion involving ankle replacement surgery;[313] a bar's regular practice of serving intoxicated persons, to support the inference that it did so on a particular occasion;[314] a drinker's habit of getting drunk at a particular social club nearly every weekend, to show intoxication at the time of a hit-and-run accident;[315] a railroad crew's practice of not blowing a whistle at a particular crossing,[316] or of operating a switch engine without a flagman in the street;[317] an undercover agent's routine practice of marking and sealing illicit drugs seized during an investigation, to show that the practice was followed on a particular occasion;[318] a nurse's routine practice of taking blood samples;[319] a business' routine practice of stamping mail with sufficient postage and sending it with a proper return address;[320] and a hospital's routine practices concerning the presentation and signing of medical malpractice arbitration forms.[321]

In general, habit evidence tends to be evidence of responses, often semi-automatic, to relatively narrow specific situations. The evidence is sometimes rejected on grounds that the conduct is not sufficiently regular or that the trait in question is actually a trait of character.[322] On the other hand, where the need is great enough and the testimony

---

[313] Bloskas v. Murray, 646 P.2d 907, 911 (Colo. 1982). *See also* Meyer v. United States, 464 F. Supp. 317, 321 (D. Colo. 1979) (admitting dentist's practice of informing patients of risks involved in extraction of third molars).

[314] Tommy's Elbow Room, Inc. v. Kavorkian, 727 P.2d 1038 (Alaska 1986).

[315] State v. Radziwil, 563 A.2d 856, 861 (N.J. Super. Ct. App. Div. 1989), *affirmed*, 582 A.2d 1003 (1990). *See also* Loughan v. Firestone Tire & Rubber Co., 749 F.2d 1519, 1522–24 (11th Cir. 1985) (holding worker's habit of bringing cooler of beer to work on back of truck and drinking from it while working admissible as evidence of drunkenness on a particular occasion).

[316] Bradfield v. Illinois Cent. Gulf R.R., 505 N.E.2d 331 (Ill. 1987).

[317] Williams v. Union Pac. R.R., 465 P.2d 975 (Kan. 1970).

[318] State v. Van Sickle, 434 A.2d 31 (Me. 1981).

[319] State v. Shelton, 176 N.W.2d 159, 161–62 (Iowa 1970).

[320] Swink & Co. v. Carroll McEntee & McGinley, Inc., 584 S.W.2d 393 (Ark. 1979).

[321] McKinstry v. Valley Obstetrics-Gynecology Clinic, P.C., 405 N.W.2d 88 (Mich. 1987).

[322] *See* Neuren v. Adduci, Mastriani, Meeks & Schill, 43 F.3d 1507 (D.C. Cir. 1995) (holding that evidence that plaintiff had experienced similar work-related problems, such as tardiness, on another job was inadmissible character evidence; court made no allusion to "habit" theory of admissibility); Jones v. Southern Pac. R.R., 962 F.2d 447, 450 (5th Cir. 1992) (holding evidence of nine violations in 29-year career as railroad engineer inadmissible to prove habit of driving negligently); Estate of Keys v. Harvey, 1996 WL 34422 at *2 (N.D. Ill. 1996) (holding records of sergeant's disciplinary and personnel files inadmissible under Fed. R. Evid. 406 in wrongful death action stemming from killing by police sergeant; records could only show tendency to react violently to challenges to his authority and did not reflect semi-automatic conduct; degree of "specificity and frequency" of action distinguishes habit evidence from impermissible character evidence); Smith v. State, 601 So. 2d 201 (Ala. Crim. App. 1992) (picking up prostitutes in certain area is not habit); Henry v. Cline, 626 S.W.2d 958 (Ark. 1982) (holding testimony that witness had seen party drive on road a dozen times and that party was speeding half of time not sufficient to establish habit; behavior not "nearly or completely involuntary"); Ritchey v. Murray, 625 S.W.2d 476 (Ark. 1981) (holding tendency of driver to weave across centerline when reaching for chewing tobacco or delivering newspapers not sufficiently regular to constitute habit; no evidence that driver was delivering newspapers on occasion in question); Stapleton v. Great Lakes Chem. Corp., 616 So. 2d 1311, 1317–18 (La. Ct. App.1993), *vacated in part on other grounds*, 627 So. 2d 1358 (1993) (holding that it was harmless error for trial court to admit testimony of defendant's good driving record and awards for safe driving as habit evidence); State v. Lagasse, 410 A.2d 537, 542 (Me. 1980) ("The tendency of a person to engage in violent acts while under the influence of intoxicating liquor does not establish 'the regular response to a repeated specific situation' necessary to constitute habit under M. R. Evid. 406."); DeMatteo v. Simon, 812 P.2d 361, 362–63 (N.M. Ct. App. 1991) (holding defendant's post-accident driving record inadmissible to show habit of negligence).

convincing, some courts treat rather broad traits as being "habit" traits.[323] There is much room for disagreement about just how much specificity is enough to establish habit.[324]

Habit evidence is often offered in civil cases to show carefulness or carelessness. In such instances, the evidence must actually demonstrate a habit, and not just a general tendency toward care or its opposite. It should be noted, however, that although use of the habit concept is one way of justifying the receipt of other acts evidence in civil cases, it is not the only way. As already discussed, in both civil and criminal cases, evidence of uncharged misconduct (or of good conduct) may be admitted for one of the other purposes listed in Rule 404(b)(2), as long as it is not offered for a propensity inference from character. Thus, in a civil case in which a fire insurance company offers a defense of arson, the company may wish to offer evidence that other property belonging to the defendant had been destroyed by the defendant's arson. Committing arson can hardly be regular enough to be considered a "habit," but if a distinctive modus operandi was involved, or if the arson was part of a common scheme or plan, it would be admissible under the principles of Rule 404(b)(2).[325]

§ 7.16 Procedural Aspects of Character and Other Crimes Evidence

Because character evidence is potentially inflammatory, procedural safeguards are sometimes used to prevent the jury from (1) learning about character evidence before it has been admitted formally; (2) using character evidence for an improper purpose; and (3) receiving more details than absolutely necessary.

The Notice Requirement

Since December 1991, the Federal Rules of Evidence have required that the prosecution provide notice of intent to offer evidence pursuant to what is now Rule 404(b)(2). Until the end of 2020, that rule had stated that, *upon request by the accused,* the prosecution was required to provide reasonable notice of the general nature of any evidence of acts falling within the scope of Rule 404(b)(2). This rule was amended in 2020 to make the notice provision, now Rule 404(b)(3), mandatory whether or not the defense requests it and to require the prosecution to identify the non-propensity theory on which its admission is grounded.[326] Reasonable notice must be given in writing before trial, or "in any form during trial if the court, for good cause, excuses lack of pretrial notice."[327]

---

[323] *See, e.g.,* Derring v. State, 619 S.W.2d 644 (Ark. 1981) (holding regularity, reliability, and promptness of supposed victim admissible as habit evidence to show he would not have disappeared without foul play). *Derring* arguably illustrates that some traits described as habit should really be considered character.

[324] *Compare* Loughan v. Firestone Tire & Rubber Co., 749 F.2d 1519, 1522–24 (11th Cir. 1985) (holding that evidence that employee regularly drank on job from cooler of beer he carried on his truck was admitted at trial for purposes of showing that employee was impaired at time of accident because regularity was sufficient to establish habit under Rule 406, despite absence of direct evidence that employee drank on day of accident) *with* Reyes v. Missouri Pac. R.R., 589 F.2d 791 (5th Cir. 1979) (holding four prior convictions for intoxication inadmissible character evidence, not habit, and hence forbidden). *See* 1 McCormick on Evidence § 195 at 1083 n.11 (Kenneth S. Broun ed., 7th ed. 2013) (probative force of habitual intoxication to prove intoxication on particular occasion depends on regularity of details of characteristic behavior).

[325] *See* **§ 7.10**. *Cf.* Hammann v. Hartford Accident & Indem. Co., 620 F.2d 588 (6th Cir. 1980) (holding prior incendiary fires on plaintiff's property admissible). *See also* Gail A. Randall, Note, *Product Liability Litigation: Impact of Federal Rule of Evidence 404(b) Upon Admissibility Standards of Prior Accident Evidence,* 61 Wash U. L. Rev. 799 (1983).

[326] Fed. R. Evid. 404(b)(3)(A), (B).

[327] Fed. R. Evid. 404(b)(3)(C).

The rules do not impose a notice requirement on the defendant in criminal cases, or on either party in civil actions.[328]

Similarly, some states require that the prosecutor notify defense counsel prior to trial of intent to use uncharged misconduct evidence. For example, the Minnesota Rules of Criminal Procedure require the prosecution to disclose any additional offenses that may be offered in evidence at trial,[329] and the admissibility of the prior offenses may be explored at the "omnibus hearing" prior to trial. Several states also provide for notice and pretrial hearings on uncharged misconduct evidence.[330]

Motions In Limine

The defendant, upon request, is entitled to a hearing outside the presence of the jury to determine the admissibility of other crimes evidence.[331] The hearing may occur prior to trial, during trial with the jury excused, at the sidebar, or in chambers.

When the defense learns before trial that the prosecution may use uncharged misconduct evidence, it should initiate a motion in limine to attempt to obtain a pretrial ruling on admissibility to plan an effective response against potentially very damaging evidence. The motion may be particularly useful, for example, when the prosecution does not plan to offer extrinsic evidence of other acts, but will cross-examine the defendant about them. The experience of testifying at the hearing on the motion may influence the defendant's decision whether to take the stand.[332] The trial judge is under no obligation, however, to decide the issue prior to trial, even where delaying a ruling until the issue arises during trial may put the defendant in a bind.[333]

---

[328] Between 2011 and 2020, there was a thorny issue concerning how far this notice requirement on the prosecution extended, an issue that was triggered by the restyling of the rule. Prior to the restyling in 2011, but after the notice provision was introduced, the notice requirement covered all "evidence of *other* crimes, wrongs, or acts" (emphasis supplied) that were offered for a purpose that did not fun afoul of the propensity prohibition of the rule, what is now Rule 404(b)(1). Most importantly, this meant that the notice requirement applied only to "extrinsic acts": according to the drafters of the amendment that added the requirement, it "does not extend to evidence of acts which are 'intrinsic' to the charged offense." *See* FED. R. EVID. 404 advisory committee note (1991 Amendment) (citation omitted). While that can present tricky questions about whether an act is "intrinsic" or "extrinsic" to the charged offense, drawing such a distinction was necessary to prevent the notice requirement being applied to any act by any person related to the charged offense, so long as no propensity argument was suggested. *See* DAVID P. LEONARD, THE NEW WIGMORE: EVIDENCE OF OTHER MISCONDUCT AND SIMILAR EVENTS § 5 (2009). Unfortunately, the restyling moved the location of the word "other," so that the prohibition applied to any "crime, wrong, or other act"—i.e., whether intrinsic or extrinsic—that is not used for a propensity inference, thus eliminating the textual basis for the intrinsic/extrinsic distinction. As a result, the notice provision seemed to apply to evidence of any act that is not used to invite a prohibited propensity inference, which would include almost any act by any person that the prosecution intends to show. The restyling was not intended to effect substantive change, however, and the courts continued to limit the notice requirement to extrinsic acts. *See, e.g.,* United States v. Heard, 709 F.3d 413, 429–32 (5th Cir. 2013) (applying the restyled rules and retaining the intrinsic/extrinsic distinction; holding that any deficiency in the notice provided by the government was harmless error because the defense should have expected the extrinsic acts in question to be evidenced based on the prosecution's disclosures). This problem was resolved by the 2020 amendment to Rule 404(b)(1), which returned the word "other" to its original location, thus limiting the reach of the notice requirement.

[329] MINN. R. CRIM. PROC. 7.05.

[330] *See* FLA. STAT. ANN. § 90.404; ALASKA R. EVID. 404; VT. R. CRIM. PROC. 26(c).

[331] *See* FED. R. EVID. 104(c); United States v. Beechum, 582 F.2d 898 (5th Cir. 1978).

[332] By testifying at the hearing the defendant does not waive his privilege not to testify at trial, nor may cross-examination at the hearing go beyond the admissibility issue at issue in the hearing. *See* FED. R. EVID. 104(d).

[333] *See* United States v. Lutz, 621 F.2d 940 (9th Cir. 1980).

Limiting Instructions

When evidence offered for a limited purpose, such as showing motive or intent, also reflects upon a defendant's character, the defendant is entitled to an instruction informing the jury of the limited purpose of the evidence. Often, the limiting instruction has little practical significance. An example of this sort of limiting instruction is contained in the account of the trial of Smith in the "Brides in the Bath" case. According to the account by Marjoribanks:

> The judge, however, admitted the evidence [that other wives of the defendant had been found drowned in the bath], warning the jury that they must not use it to infer that the prisoner was a man of bad character and infamous acts, likely to have committed the murder, but to help them to decide whether the death of Miss Mundy was accidental or designed by the prisoner.[334]

A juror, or anyone for that matter, would need a remarkably compartmentalized mind to be able to use the evidence solely on the issue of whether the defendant "designed" to kill his wife, and not whether the defendant was "likely to" have committed the murder. Yet even in these circumstances, it might be worthwhile to seek a limiting instruction, if only to preserve a point for appeal.

Limiting instructions can be made more effective than the one given in the "Brides" case, and counsel should be prepared to offer the court alternative language that more clearly communicates the permitted and prohibited uses of the evidence.[335] Where effective, limiting instructions may be worth reiteration in counsel's final argument. One such case was the Seddon trial, in which Mr. and Mrs. Seddon were accused of poisoning a lodger, Miss Barrow. One of the supposed motives was acquiring a sum of about £300 that Miss Barrow supposedly kept in a lockbox in the house, and which disappeared after her death. There was strong evidence that the Seddons took the money and other possessions of Miss Barrow, but the evidence that they had poisoned her was less convincing. The evidence that they stole her money was, of course, admissible as evidence providing a motive for the murder. Marshall Hall's closing argument pointed out the limited purpose for which the evidence could be used:

> [This] is one of those curious cases where, by reason of the fact that it is necessary in law to prove a motive for the poisoning, for the object of providing a motive, this man and this woman have been exposed to merciless cross-examination on the suggestion that they were thieves. In no other circumstances would that have been possible. If this man had been charged with any other crime, he could never have been cross-examined, nor could the woman have been cross-examined, as my learned friend the Attorney-General frankly admitted, to carry out the suggestion that they had robbed this woman. We are not trying these people on a charge of robbery. You will have to take the greatest care in this case that you do not allow the prejudice which has been brought into it to influence you unduly. . . . The only possible thing in which the matter might be dangerous, so far as your honest deliberations are

---

334 E. MARJORIBANKS, FOR THE DEFENSE: THE LIFE OF SIR EDWARD MARSHALL HALL 324 (1931).

335 For discussion of the factors that make jury instructions difficult to understand and of ways to improve their comprehensibility, *see* AMIRAM ELWORK, BRUCE D. SALES & JAMES J. ALFINI, MAKING JURY INSTRUCTIONS UNDERSTANDABLE (1983); Robert P. Charrow & Veda R. Charrow, *Making Legal Language Understandable: A Psycholinguistic Study of Jury Instructions*, 79 COLUM. L. REV. 1306 (1979); Peter Meijes Tiersma, *Reforming the Language of Jury Instructions*, 22 HOFSTRA L. REV. 37 (1993).

concerned, is that you might think that the proposition is, "We have cross-examined these people to show they are thieves. If you think they are thieves therefore you must think they are murderers." It is a fallacy. It is a proposition which will not hold water in a Court. It has nothing to do with the question we have to deal with.[336]

In general, a limiting instruction should inform the jury that the only purpose of the evidence is to shed light on the defendant's possible motive (or intent, or whatever forms the basis for admission), and that it may not be used as evidence that the defendant had a bad character and for that reason was likely to commit crimes of the nature charged.[337]

A limiting instruction is also appropriate when the prosecution has cross-examined a defense character witness about uncharged misconduct by the defendant to impeach the witness's knowledge of the defendant's reputation.[338] One form of limiting instruction, suggested by a well-known guide, reads as follows:

> The attorney for the government now proposes to ask certain questions on cross examination of this witness as to certain alleged events in the defendant's past.
>
> I caution you that these questions will be permitted solely for the limited purpose of testing the testimony of this witness that [*he*] [*she*] was familiar with the reputation of Defendant _______ in the community. The answers to these questions are to be considered by you only for the purpose of testing the credibility of this witness. The questions and answers in this area are not to be considered as any evidence that the defendant committed the crime[*s*] charged in this indictment.[339]

While the instruction is essentially accurate,[340] defense counsel should request that the forbidden purpose be more specifically described, by telling the jury that "[r]egardless of Mr. _______'s answer you are not to assume that the incidents asked about actually took place. All that is happening is that this witness's standard of opinion of the reputation of the defendant is being tested."[341]

Partial Exclusion; Redaction; Limited Inquiry

The fact that evidence of uncharged misconduct is relevant to some permissible purpose, such as demonstrating motive or opportunity, does not mean that the judge should admit the full facts concerning the uncharged misconduct. Courts can sometimes

---

336 F. YOUNG, TRIAL OF THE SEDDONS 281–82 (1914). Similarly, in the O.J. Simpson criminal trial, defense attorney Johnnie Cochran quoted the court's limiting instruction about the use of evidence of the defendant's prior physical abuse of one of the murder victims, and said, "So this isn't about character assassination of O.J. Simpson, as you might think at first blush. This is about Mr. Darden [one of the prosecutors] trying to conjure up a motive for you." State v. Simpson, 1995 WL 686429 at *35 (Cal. Super. Trans.).

337 *Cf.* United States v. Adcock, 558 F.2d 397, 401 (8th Cir. 1977).

338 *See* **§ 7.05**.

339 KEVIN F. O'MALLEY, FEDERAL JURY PRACTICE AND INSTRUCTIONS § 11.15 (5th ed. 2000).

340 A precise prosecutor might object that evidence that undermines the defendant's character witness thereby makes it more likely that the defendant committed the crime as alleged.

341 This was part of the instructions given by the trial judge, and implicitly approved by the Supreme Court, in Michelson v. United States, 335 U.S. 469, 473 n.3 (1948).

limit inquiry or exclude evidence in part to avoid prejudice. In *United States v. Sims*,[342] for example, the defendant's failure to return to a halfway house was offered to identify him as one of the robbers of a savings bank. The trial court admitted the evidence, but in neutered form. In affirming the conviction, the court noted approvingly the care with which the trial court had attempted to avoid prejudice:

> Sims is correct in his assertion that the jury may have inferred from his residency in the halfway house that he had previously been involved in some other criminal activity. However, the trial judge carefully confined the jury's consideration of this matter and thus mitigated any possible prejudice. The testimony was limited to a showing that Sims was a resident of the halfway house, was required to return, and had failed to return on the day of the robbery. There was absolutely no mention made of any of Sims' prior criminal activity. Additionally, there was no testimony that only convicted criminals resided at the halfway house.[343]

---

[342] 617 F.2d 1371, 1378–79 (9th Cir. 1980). *See also* United States v. Beasley, 809 F.2d 1273 (7th Cir. 1987) (Easterbrook, J.) (criticizing trial court for allowing evidence of missing witness's addiction and hospitalization, possibly because witness had obtained drugs from defendant; it would have been sufficient to tell jury that witness was missing through no fault of prosecution).

[343] United States v. Sims, 617 F.2d 1371, 1378–79 (9th Cir. 1980).

Part IV

SPECIFIC RULES FOR TESTIMONIAL EVIDENCE

Chapter 8

WITNESS COMPETENCY

Table of Sections

§ 8.01 Rules of Competency in General [FRE 601]

Rules of competency can disqualify a witness from testifying.[1] Usually the ground of disqualification is that the witness has some personal defect or characteristic that prevents the testimony from being helpful. However, some competency rules are based upon considerations of extrinsic policy. Rules rendering jurors incompetent to impeach their own verdicts, for example, are based on a desire for stability of verdicts and an end to litigation, not upon concerns about accuracy of testimony.[2]

The extensive common-law rules of incompetency, which persisted in many jurisdictions until the middle of the nineteenth century or later, seem bizarre and arbitrary to the modern lawyer. For instance, the party witness rule prohibited parties and others with a direct interest in the lawsuit from testifying, on the ground that interested parties were prone to perjury.[3] Similarly, a criminal defendant could not testify on his or her own behalf, though this rule was mitigated in many jurisdictions by allowing an unsworn statement that did not amount to "testimony."[4] Spouses could not testify on each other's behalf.[5] A convicted felon could not testify at all.[6]

By contrast, the modern approach to trials, generally speaking, is to admit evidence for what it is worth, trusting the trier-of-fact to recognize its weaknesses and to discern truthful and valuable information.[7] For the most part, the old rules of incompetency have

---

[1] Sometimes the term "incompetent" is used as a characterization of evidence, as in the phrase, "Objection, irrelevant, immaterial, and incompetent." When used in such general objections, the term "incompetent" means something like "inadmissible on some ground other than irrelevance," and may be intended to embrace a variety of objections such as hearsay. Such general objections may not preserve the right to appeal error. *See* **§ 3.04**. In any event, the use of the term "incompetent" in this chapter is much narrower, referring to specific grounds for barring a witness from testifying.

[2] *See* FED. R. EVID. 606(b) advisory committee's note.

[3] 2 WIGMORE ON EVIDENCE § 577 at 817 (Chadbourn rev. 1979).

[4] *See id.* § 579 at 826–27.

[5] *See id.* § 600 at 856.

[6] *See id.* § 519 at 725.

[7] The history of this change is told in Joel N. Bodansky, *The Abolition of the Party-Witness Disqualification: An Historical Survey*, 70 KY. L.J. 91 (1981). In the American context, the story includes a

given way to rules allowing witnesses to testify. Information that previously rendered a witness incompetent to take the stand now is used to impeach the witness instead.[8]

Some of the old rules of incompetency, however, persist in qualified form. Some states maintain rules prohibiting testimony by children or the insane, unless they can be shown to be of sufficient understanding.[9] Others maintain "dead man's statutes" that prevent interested survivors from testifying in their suits against a dead person's estate.[10] Some of the rules of competency—those prohibiting testimony by judges and jurors—have been sustained over time because they protect the distinctive roles that these persons play in the justice system, rather than because they shield against perjured or inaccurate evidence.[11] Additionally, a completely new type of incompetency rule has arisen in some states, barring the reception of testimony by a witness whose memory has been hypnotically refreshed.[12]

Rule 601 provides that every person is competent to be a witness except as otherwise provided by the Evidence Rules. The other evidence rules contain very few restrictions on witness competency aside from the requirement that a lay witness testify under oath[13] from personal knowledge[14] and various restrictions on the use of expert testimony.[15] The competency requirements for most lay witnesses are thus minimal. Considerations that might be thought to affect competency—a child's inability to distinguish between the truth and a lie, a person's impaired perception, a failure of memory, etc.—are more appropriately matters of weight and credibility for the jury.[16] When a party calls a witness of questionable competency, opposing counsel might be well advised to object even if the objection is likely to fail. The judge will allow the lawyer to conduct a voir dire examination on competency that may help the lawyer to develop facts to impeach the witness. In extreme cases testimony may be excluded as irrelevant under Rule 402 or as a waste of time under Rule 403.[17]

The Federal Rules of Evidence distinguish between federal questions and issues that are in federal court because of diversity of citizenship. Where the question is a federal one (either a federal crime or a federal civil cause of action), Rule 601, which presumes witness competence, applies. In civil cases where the claim arises out of state substantive law, state competence rules will apply. Although scholars might differ whether this result is commanded by principles of federalism and *Erie R. Co. v. Tompkins*,[18] it is a wise division of authority in that it respects states rules and deters

---

chapter during which states attempted to reconcile the trend to repeal party incompetence with the existence of rules making non-whites incompetent. *See* George Fisher, *The Jury's Rise as Lie Detector*, 107 YALE L.J. 575, 656–97 (1997).

[8] *See* FED. R. EVID. 601 advisory committee's note.

[9] *See* **§ 8.02, § 8.03**.

[10] *See* **§ 8.04**.

[11] *See* **§ 8.05**.

[12] *See* **§ 8.08**.

[13] *See* **§ 8.06**

[14] *See* **§ 8.07**.

[15] *See* **§§ 10.03 et seq.**

[16] FED. R. EVID. 601 advisory committee's note (citing 2 WIGMORE ON EVIDENCE §§ 501, 509 (Chadbourn rev. 1979)).

[17] *See* 3 CHRISTOPHER B. MUELLER & LAIRD KIRKPATRICK, FEDERAL EVIDENCE § 6.2 (4th ed. 2013).

[18] Erie R. Co. v. Tompkins, 304 U.S. 64 (1938). The *Erie* line of cases developed a choice-of-law doctrine devoted to figuring out when state law and rules apply in federal court. Aspects of the *Erie* decision do not apply to the Federal Rules of Evidence, which are statutory and not promulgated under the Rules Enabling

litigants from forum shopping based on the difference in the ability of witnesses to testify.[19]

Regardless of the source of a competency restriction, when it functions to exclude relevant evidence offered by the accused in a criminal case, there is a potential conflict with the accused's constitutional rights. The move away from incompetency rules based on concerns about witness perjury is reinforced by this constitutional consideration. In the pivotal case of *Washington v. Texas*,[20] the Supreme Court encountered a Texas competency-based restriction that prohibited an accused from calling as a defense witness any person charged or previously convicted as a principal, accomplice, or accessory in the same crime. This vestige of the common-law incompetency for interested witnesses might have served to prevent perjury in some cases. Nonetheless, the Court rejected it as an arbitrary limitation on the defendant's rights.[21]

§ 8.02 Mental Health and Mental Handicap as Grounds for Incompetency

The Federal Rules of Evidence do not disqualify anyone based on mental function or disease. Unless the insanity is so severe as to render the entire testimony irrelevant or a waste of time, insanity may be shown to impeach, but may not be used to keep the witness off the stand.[22] Some state jurisdictions still allow objections to testimony on the grounds of the witness's insanity.[23] Where incompetency by virtue of mental illness is a ground for objection, however, the objection will not succeed simply on a showing that the proposed witness is mentally ill. Typically, state rules provide that the insane person may testify if able to understand the duty to tell the truth, or able to express thought in an understandable manner, or both.[24]

Act, 28 U.S.C. § 2072. *See* Flaminio v. Honda Motor Co., 733 F.2d 463 (7th Cir. 1984). However, *Erie* also had constitutional dimensions, *id.*, and Rule 601 would arguably raise choice-of-law issues had it not explicitly provided for state competency law to apply when state law provides the substantive rule of decision.

[19] One difficulty is how to construe rules that states categorize as competency rules but that might be considered some other kind of rule by a federal court hearing the dispute. *See, e.g.*, OHIO R. EVID. 601(D) (imposing qualifications for expert witnesses in medical malpractice as part of the state's rules of witness competency, even though expert qualifications are addressed in Article 7 of both the Ohio and Federal Rules of Evidence). A federal court is not required by Rule 601 to honor a state evidence rule merely because the state labels that particular rule a rule of competency. *Cf.* Larca v. United States, 302 F.R.D. 148 (N.D. Ohio 2014) (addressing related question of whether Ohio's medical malpractice requirement that the plaintiff file an affidavit of merit, executed by an expert complying with OHIO R. EVID. 601(D), applies in medical malpractice cases filed in federal court under the Federal Tort Claims Act, when Ohio substantive tort law applies but federal procedural rules apply; noting split in rulings by federal courts in Ohio but holding the Ohio requirement is procedural and not controlling in federal court).

[20] Washington v. Texas, 388 U.S. 14 (1967) (holding that accused's Sixth Amendment right to present witnesses applies to the states under the Fourteenth Amendment's Due Process clause).

[21] *See generally* EDWARD J. IMWINKELRIED & NORMAN M. GARLAND, EXCULPATORY EVIDENCE: THE ACCUSED'S CONSTITUTIONAL RIGHT TO INTRODUCE FAVORABLE EVIDENCE § 4 (3d ed. 2004).

[22] FED. R. EVID. 601 advisory committee's note.

[23] *See, e.g.*, MICH. R. EVID. 601 (requiring a witness to have mental capacity or sense of obligation to testify truthfully and understandably); OHIO R. EVID. 601(A) (stating that persons of unsound mind, incapable of receiving just impressions or relating them truthfully, are not competent); TEX. R. EVID. 601(a)(1) (stating that persons insane at time offered as witness or when event occurred about which they are offered to testify are incompetent); GA. CODE ANN. § 24–9–7 (2002); ALA. CODE § 12–21–165 (2003). N.Y. CRIM. PROC. LAW § 60.20(1) (McKinney 2003) (permitting a person to testify in criminal proceeding unless he or she does not possess "sufficient intelligence or capacity to justify the reception of the evidence," based on young age or mental disability).

[24] *See, e.g.*, MICH. R. EVID. 601 (requiring witness to have mental capacity or sense of obligation to testify truthfully and understandably); MINN. STAT. ANN. § 595.02(1)(f) (stating that persons of unsound mind

§ 8.03 Incompetency of Children

The Federal Rules of Evidence do not categorically restrict testimony of child witnesses.[25] Many states, however, restrict, at least in theory, the testimony of children, and such rules apply in federal cases in which state law provides the substantive rule of decision.[26]

Typically, a state statute on incompetency of children will provide that a child under a certain age is presumed incompetent unless shown to understand the duty to tell the truth and to be of sufficient understanding to be able to testify accurately.[27] The relevant time for determining competency is the child's age is when the child's testimony is offered, not when the child observed the underlying events.[28]

In recent years, concern for prevention of child abuse has led to relaxation of competency requirements in some states.[29] Minnesota's statute, for example, now provides that a child under ten years is competent unless shown to lack the capacity to remember facts correctly or to testify truthfully, a reversal of the prior burden of persuasion on competency.[30]

§ 8.04 Dead Man's Statutes

The so-called "dead man's statute" is an evidence rule adopted by statute in many states when the general incompetency of parties was removed. Such statutes, broadly speaking, prohibit an adverse party from testifying against a dead person's estate about transactions or conversations with the dead person.[31] The theory behind the statute is that it is unfair to allow the party to give self-serving testimony when the lips of the dead person are sealed.[32] Not all states adopted a dead man's statute. Those jurisdictions with dead man's statutes have done so to counteract the risk that unscrupulous people will

---

not competent if they lack capacity to remember or to relate facts truthfully); N.C. R. EVID. 601(b) (disqualifying witness if incapable of testifying in understandable manner or incapable of understanding duty to tell truth).

25 *See* FED. R. EVID. 601; 3 WEINSTEIN'S FEDERAL EVIDENCE § 601 App.102[8] (Joseph M. McLaughlin ed., 2d ed. 1997) (noting the codified judicial practice in federal courts against indiscriminately disqualifying witnesses based on age).

26 FED. R. EVID. 601; State v. Warden, 891 P.2d 1074 (Kan. 1995) (ruling that trial court properly allowed autistic child witness to testify through a "facilitator" who guided witness's hands while he typed; but since child was capable of signing "yes" or "no," he should have been required to make those responses independently of facilitator; moreover, facilitator should generally be prevented from hearing questions asked to child to ensure that answer comes from child, not facilitator). *Cf.* People v. Montoya, 57 Cal. Rptr. 3d 770, 778 (Cal. Ct. App. 2007) (applying CAL. EVID. CODE §§ 700–701, which provides that regardless of age, a witness is competent as long as she is not incapable of understanding the witness's oath to tell the truth and is able to communicate in a way that she is understood on her own or by an interpreter); State v. Roman, 622 A.2d 96, 100 (Me. 1993) (holding that "[a] child of any age is presumed competent to testify as a witness unless disqualified under [Maine] Rule 601(b)" as incapable of expressing herself, of understanding duty to tell truth, or lacking "reasonable ability" to perceive or remember the issue).

27 *See, e.g.,* OHIO R. EVID. 601(A) (stating that children under ten years old, who appear incapable of perceiving facts correctly or of relating them truthfully, are incompetent); People v. Nisoff, 330 N.E.2d 638 (N.Y. 1975) (applying N.Y. CRIM. PROC. LAW § 60.20 (McKinney 2003), which states a witness under the age of nine may only testify if the court is satisfied that he or she understands the definition of an oath, through statement of definition, good grades, etc.).

28 *See, e.g.,* State v. Clark, 644 N.E.2d 331 (Ohio 1994).

29 JOHN E.B. MYERS, CHILD WITNESS LAW AND PRACTICE § 3.11 at 73–74 (1987).

30 MINN. STAT. ANN. § 595.02(1)(*l*).

31 *See* 1 MCCORMICK ON EVIDENCE § 65 (Kenneth S. Broun ed., 7th ed. 2012).

32 *See* Ed Wallis, *An Outdated Form of Evidentiary Law: A Survey of Dead Man's Statutes and a Proposal for Change,* 53 CLEV. ST. L. REV. 75, 105–07 (2005).

take advantage of the death of others to make false claims against their estates. Those jurisdictions that have not adopted (or since repealed) such statutes reflect concerns about the risk to honest creditors who will not be able to prove legitimate debts of the decedent.

The differences among dead man's statutes are so substantial that it is difficult to generalize about them, and it is essential to consult the local statute and case law.[33] One commonly recognized restriction on the disqualification, sometimes implied by judicial decision even when not apparent on the face of the statute, is that it covers only matters personally observed by the decedent, matters about which, had the decedent survived until the trial, he or she could have provided testimony that would contradict the opponent's account of events.[34] Also, as a compromise, some jurisdictions allow the interested party to testify but require corroboration[35] or a higher standard of proof,[36] or else seek to offset the admissibility of the interested party's testimony by permitting testimony about statements made by the deceased that would ordinarily not be admissible under the hearsay rule.[37]

The Federal Rules of Evidence do not contain any provision analogous to a dead man's statute.[38] There is no prohibition against the testimony of the surviving party in federal cases, unless state substantive law governs and the state maintains a dead man's statute. Under the federal rules, the danger of self-serving perjury is something that affects the weight of the testimony, not its admissibility.[39]

§ 8.05 Testimony by Judge or Juror [FRE 605, 606]

The Federal Rules of Evidence prohibit absolutely testimony by a judge in a case over which the judge is presiding.[40] No objection is necessary to preserve the error. To save the lawyer from the awkwardness of challenging the presiding judge, the rules provide for an automatic objection.[41] Occasionally, a judge will do the equivalent of testifying by commenting from the bench based on personal knowledge. Unless the statement concerns a matter that is an appropriate subject for judicial notice,[42] this conduct is objectionable.[43]

---

[33] Illinois has expanded the common-law rule to prevent an interested party from testifying about out-of-court communications with a descendant of someone deemed legally incompetent. *See* Kamberos v. Magnuson, 510 N.E.2d 112, 115 (Ill. App. Ct. 1987). North Carolina applies the statute to lunatics. N.C. R. EVID. 601(c).

[34] *See, e.g.*, Ziegler v. Moore, 335 P.2d 425 (Nev. 1959) (holding that bar of statute does not apply to party's testimony about events occurring before the accident and beyond the perception of the decedent, nor to testimony about plaintiff's medical expenses and other damages resulting from the accident).

[35] In Virginia, an interested witness may testify as to the statements of the deceased only if his or her testimony is corroborated by a disinterested witness. VA. CODE ANN. § 8.01–397.

[36] N.J. STAT. ANN. § 2A:81–2 (permitting interested witnesses to testify if clear and convincing proof exists to support the claim).

[37] *See, e.g.*, CAL. EVID. CODE § 1261; OHIO R. EVID. 804(B)(5).

[38] FED. R. EVID. 601 advisory committee's note.

[39] *Id.*

[40] FED. R. EVID. 605.

[41] FED. R. EVID. 605 advisory committee's note.

[42] *See* FED. R. EVID. 201(b) (permitting judicial notice of a fact when it is "not subject to reasonable dispute because it is either (1) generally known with the trial court's territorial jurisdiction; or (2) can be accurately and readily determined from sources whose accuracy cannot reasonably be questioned."). *See* **§ 2.14**.

[43] *See, e.g.*, United States v. Jones, 29 F.3d 1549, 1553 (11th Cir. 1994) (explaining that judicially noticing a fact is like precluding the opposing party from introducing evidence to the contrary and is essentially

The Federal Rules also provide that jurors may not testify in cases in which they are sitting.[44] When a juror is called to testify, a party must object to preserve error. The lawyer must be given an opportunity, however, to make the objection outside the hearing of the jury.[45]

The disqualification of the presiding judge and jurors from testifying at trial is usually unnecessary; it serves merely to reinforce the rules governing service in either capacity. If either judge or juror has personal knowledge that would otherwise qualify him or her as a witness, then that person should have been disqualified to serve as judge or juror in the first place. If an initial disqualification did not occur, then the person should be removed upon discovery that he or she possesses such relevant personal knowledge.[46]

But a distinct disqualification rule does serve an important practical purpose. After a verdict is entered, a juror might be called to testify after the trial about what happened during the trial. The desire to call a juror to testify usually arises when the losing party attempts to challenge the verdict based on what happened in jury deliberations. The long-respected doctrine that jurors may not be heard to "impeach" their verdict has been adopted for the federal courts as Rule 606(b). Case law provides many examples where jurors have been uncomfortable with the deliberation, such as where jurors felt bullied or when the jurors tossed a coin to decide the case. Jurors may not testify, however, about internal deliberation matters.[47] To challenge a verdict, such misconduct must be proved without the jurors' testimony. (For example, a bailiff may testify to what he or she saw.)

However, jurors may testify that there was a mistake in reporting the actual verdict.[48] The 2006 amendment to Rule 606(b) explicitly provides that post-verdict, jurors may testify that a mistake was made in entering the verdict onto the verdict form.[49] The advisory note to that same amendment rejects the view adopted by some courts that allows juror testimony to prove that the jurors operated under a misunderstanding of the consequences at their verdict.

---

a directed verdict against that party as to the noticed fact); Fox v. West Palm Beach, 383 F.2d 189, 191 (5th Cir. 1967) (holding that judge's frequent statements based on judge's own extrajudicial experience was reversible error); Fawcett v. State, 697 A.2d 385 (Del. 1997) (holding that judge may not take judicial notice of an element of the charged crime); 3 WEINSTEIN'S FEDERAL EVIDENCE § 605.07[1] (Joseph M. McLaughlin ed., 2d ed. 1997) (stating that judge may not introduce personal experience under guise of judicial notice).

[44] FED. R. EVID. 606(a).

[45] *Id.*

[46] See 3 CHRISTOPHER B. LAIRD C. KIRKPATRICK, FEDERAL EVIDENCE § 6.11 (4th ed. 2013) (addressing the judge as witness).

[47] *Id. See, e.g.*, Williams v. Price, 343 F.3d 223 (3d Cir. 2003) (explaining the "no impeachment" rule and its development); Solis v. Cockrell, 342 F.3d 392 (5th Cir. 2003) (concluding that juror's belief that inmate had reputation for stealing, learned while living near inmate, was not an extreme situation sufficient to presume bias); United States v. Straach, 987 F.2d 232, 242 (5th Cir. 1993) (holding that defendant was not entitled to mistrial when two jurors signed statements that they believed defendant's innocence throughout the jury deliberations, but were "pressured" into accepting a verdict of guilty); Dallas v. Arave, 984 F.2d 292, 296 (9th Cir. 1993) (holding that trial court properly denied defendant's motions to supplement the record with jurors' testimony that by finding the defendant guilty of voluntary manslaughter, they found the defendant initially acted in self-defense).

[48] *See, e.g.*, Latino v. Crane Rental Co., 630 N.E.2d 591 (Mass. 1994) (concluding that trial judge who suspected variation in verdicts properly inquired whether jury agreed on the special verdicts announced in open court by limiting questions to what jury decided, not why); State v. Williquette, 526 N.W.2d 144, 145 (Wis. 1995) (holding that after discharge, jurors were competent to testify as to clerical error in jury verdict).

[49] *See* FED. R. EVID. 606(b)(3).

Reflecting well developed common law, the Federal Rules also provide that jurors may testify about the introduction of extraneous prejudicial information or improper outside influence.[50] Thus, jurors may testify that one of the jurors brought a newspaper article describing the case into the jury room, or that a juror was bribed.[51] The Internet presents a more modern and perhaps more dangerous version of an external influence.[52] Antics, such a single juror's investigation or reenactment outside the jury room, also constitute an external influence on the deliberation.[53]

The Supreme Court has interpreted the exception for outside influence narrowly, holding in *Tanner v. United States*,[54] that jurors could not testify about other jurors' use of alcohol or drugs during the trial.[55] In *Tanner*, after the defendants in a mail fraud case were found guilty, but before sentencing, a juror approached a defense attorney, reporting the intoxication of several jurors throughout the course of the trial. Defense counsel requested permission from the trial judge to interview jurors, an evidentiary hearing on the matter, and a new trial.[56] The judge allowed the hearing, but pursuant to Rule 606(b), only permitted testimony from non-juror witnesses. As a result, the hearing did not persuade the judge of juror misconduct, and the new trial was denied.[57] The Supreme Court considered the advisory committee notes of Rule 606(b), and pointed to several strong policy considerations against hearing juror testimony, including the

---

[50] FED. R. EVID. 606(b); Fullwood v. Lee, 290 F.3d 663 (4th Cir. 2002) (requiring evidentiary hearing on whether juror had been improperly influenced by her husband and whether the jury improperly learned of a previous death sentence for the same murder); United States v. Walker, 1 F.3d 423 (6th Cir. 1993) (holding that the trial court erred in failing to hold hearing on impact on jurors of inadmissible taped depositions inadvertently sent to jury room with other exhibits); Hartley *ex rel.* Hartley v. Guthmann, 532 N.W.2d 331, 335–36 (Neb. 1995) (holding that brochure discussing detrimental effects of smoking on fetus in suit alleging malpractice during birth is sufficient evidence of juror misconduct; the jury's exposure suffices and proof that the brochure actually created prejudice is unnecessary); Castaneda *ex rel.* Correll v. Pederson, 518 N.W.2d 246, 252–253 (Wis. 1994) (concluding that juror's misconduct in researching and reporting average malpractice award was potentially prejudicial). *But see* Drew v. Collins, 964 F.2d 411 (5th Cir. 1992) (requiring that juror misconduct be so prejudicial as to have denied petitioner a fair trial in order to grant a new trial); United States v. Klee, 494 F.2d 394, 396 (9th Cir. 1974) (denying motion for new trial even though jurors discussed the case during breaks and expressed premature opinions about the defendant's guilt).

[51] FED. R. EVID. 606(b) advisory committee's note (citing Mattox v. United States, 146 U.S. 140 (1892)). *See also* United States v. Swinton, 75 F.3d 374, 381 (8th Cir. 1996) (concluding that juror revelation that defendant had a criminal record is extraneous prejudicial information); Haugh v. Jones & Laughlin Steel Corp., 949 F.2d 914, 916–919 (7th Cir. 1991) (holding that new trial was proper where marshal told jurors they would be locked up until they reached a verdict, but trial court was wrong to ask juror whether consent to verdict was result of agreement or desire to go home).

[52] *Cf.* John Schwartz, *As Jurors Turn to Google and Twitter, Mistrials Are Popping up*, N.Y. TIMES, Mar. 18, 2009.

[53] Doan v. Brigano, 237 F.3d 722 (6th Cir. 2001) (holding that juror engaged in misconduct and introduced external evidence to the jury when she conducted experiment at home to see if bruises would be visible in low lighting, and reported results to fellow jurors).

[54] 483 U.S. 107 (1987).

[55] *Id.* at 121–25. *See also* United States v. Griffith, 17 F.3d 865 (6th Cir. 1994) (holding that juror's attempt to discuss case with deputy marshal was not an extraneous influence); United States v. Martinez-Moncivais, 14 F.3d 1030, 1036 (5th Cir. 1994) (holding that statement by two jurors that if defendant were innocent he would have testified was not improper external influence); Sassounian v. Roe, 230 F.3d 1097 (9th Cir. 2000) (concluding that jurors' consideration of excluded evidence they overheard from sidebar of terrorist phone call claiming responsibility for assassination in question was misconduct having "substantial and injurious effect" on sentence); United States v. Davis, 177 F.3d 552 (6th Cir. 1999) (holding that there is no presumption of prejudice from the bare fact that improper contact with the jury occurred); State v. Cherry, 20 S.W.3d 354 (Ark. 2000) (noting that new first-degree murder trial was properly granted when jurors concluded appellee's guilt before deliberations and discussed those conclusions with other jurors).

[56] Tanner v. United States, 483 U.S. 107, 113 (1987).

[57] *Id.* at 110–115.

need for finality in a jury trial, the threat of parties harassing jurors after an unfavorable ruling, and the social benefit of having jurors feel free to speak and act during the deliberation process.[58]

One important and still largely unresolved question concerns the presence of overt racial, religious, or ethnic prejudice in jury deliberations.[59] Expressions of such prejudice as part of the deliberation process is clearly internal to the jury, and Rule 606(b) as well as *Tanner* would seem to prohibit juror testimony regarding such in the deliberation process. However, the presence of overt racial discrimination so subverts our goals for justice and equality before the law that some courts do permit inquiry into such matters to protect the integrity of the trial and due process of law.[60] In its 2017 decision in *Peña-Rodgriguez v. Colorado*,[61] the Supreme Court held that the criminal defendant's Sixth Amendment right to a fair trial took precedence over the confidentiality of deliberations articulated by Colorado's Rule 606(b) when racial discrimination infected the deliberation. According to two jurors in that case, during deliberations over harassment and sexual assault charges, another juror had said that he "believed the defendant was guilty because, in [his] experience as an ex-law enforcement officer, Mexican men had a bravado that caused them to believe they could do whatever they wanted with women," and that, in his opinion, Mexican men are physically controlling of women because of their sense of entitlement.[62] In this context, the Court held that:

> where a juror makes a clear statement that indicates he or she relied on racial stereotypes or animus to convict a criminal defendant, the Sixth Amendment requires that the no-impeachment rule give way in order to permit the trial court to consider the evidence of the juror's statement and any resulting denial of the jury trial guarantee.[63]

In an effort to allay concerns about the future stability of verdicts and about post-verdict harassment of jurors by defense counsel, the majority opinion, authored by Justice Kennedy, qualified the holding as follows:

---

[58] *Id.* at 120–121, 124.

[59] *See generally,* Colin Miller, *Dismissed with Prejudice: Why Application of the Anti-Jury Impeachment Rule to Allegations of Racial, Religious, or Other Bias Violates the Right to Present a Defense,* 61 BAYLOR L. REV. 872 (2009).

[60] *Compare,* United States v. Villar, 586 F.3d 76, 87 (1st Cir. 2009) ("While the issue is difficult and close, we believe that the rule against juror impeachment cannot be applied so inflexibly as to bar juror testimony in those rare and grave cases where claims of racial or ethnic bias during jury deliberations implicate a defendant's right to due process and an impartial jury"); *with* United States v. Benally, 546 F.3d 1230, 1231, 1234 (10th Cir. 2008) (noting "compelling interests for prohibiting testimony about what goes on in the jury room after a verdict has been rendered" and precluding inquiry into claims that racist statements during deliberations, where the foreman insisted that " '[w]hen Indians get alcohol, they all get drunk' and that when they get drunk, they get violent" in the trial of a Native American defendant). State law addresses this concern. *See* Powell v. Allstate Ins. Co., 652 So. 2d 354, 357 (Fla. 1995) (holding that all-white jury that allegedly made racial jokes about black plaintiffs during deliberations was a sufficient enough overt act that it could have prejudiced the jury as it reached its verdict). *Cf.* State v. Levitt, 176 A.2d 465 (N.J. 1961) (holding that it was not an abuse of discretion for trial judge to set aside verdict where anti-Semitism was expressed in deliberations).

[61] Peña-Rodriguez v. Colorado, 137 S. Ct. 855 (2017).

[62] 137 S. Ct. at 862.

[63] *Id.* at 869. As pointed out by Justice Thomas in dissent, the juror in question had said nothing about race; instead, he spoke about a cultural propensity associated with a nation of origin. *See id.* at 875 n.1 (Thomas, J., dissenting) (noting, however, that neither party "had suggested that these distinctions make a substantive difference" in the case).

> Not every offhand comment indicating racial bias or hostility will justify setting aside the no-impeachment bar to allow further judicial inquiry. For the inquiry to proceed, there must be a showing that one or more jurors made statements exhibiting overt racial bias that cast serious doubt on the fairness and impartiality of the jury's deliberations and resulting verdict. To qualify, the statement must tend to show that racial animus was a significant motivating factor in the juror's vote to convict.[64]

The majority also emphasized that jurors had come forth voluntarily to report the prejudiced statements made by another juror.[65] A dissenting opinion noted the careful balancing of considerations that went into the adoption of the federal rule and the similar Colorado rule as well as the substantial variety of tools available to ferret out juror bias short of using post-verdict juror testimony to impeach the verdict. The dissent thus questioned whether racial prejudice warrants a constitutionally mandated exception to the "no-impeachment" rule and, if so, doubted that such an exception could be limited to racial bias in the decision of criminal cases.[66]

Numerous subsequent cases have involved challenges to guilty verdicts based on the principle of *Peña-Rodriquez v. Colorado*, but few have been successful. Lower courts have resisted post-verdict requests to interrogate jurors based merely upon the defense's suspicion of racial bias in the deliberations.[67] And mere post-verdict allegations of juror bias made by another juror are not enough to trigger the exception when the allegation does not indicate specific statements or behavior manifesting such bias.[68] Nor are assertions of juror bias made by one juror against another juror during deliberations, unless they reveal that racial bias affected the decision in the case.[69] Even when specific bias-manifesting conduct by a juror during deliberation is alleged post-verdict by another juror, the Supreme Court's standard gives great discretion to the trial court in assessing its significance.[70] Thus, for example, one juror's post-verdict allegation that another juror said during deliberation that the latter knew the defendant was guilty the first time that juror saw the defendant (who appeared to be of a different race), did not require

---

64 *Id.* at 869.

65 *Id.* The Court seemed to be suggesting that judicial intervention would not be appropriate if at least one juror did not think the matter serious enough to warrant such intervention, but such a restriction would also mean that, if jurors keep quiet about it, overt racial discrimination in deliberations is to be ignored.

66 *Id.* at 874 (Alito, J., dissenting). One law review article soon argued that such an exception would be extended to civil cases and to other forms of bias representing denials of equal protection. Jarod S. Gonzalez, *The New* Batson*: Opening the Door of the Jury Deliberation Room after* Peña-Rodriguez v. Colorado, 62 ST. L. U. L.J. 397 (2018).

67 *See, e.g.*, United States v. Robinson, 917 F.3d 856 (5th Cir. 2019) (declining to allow "an improper fishing expedition in support of a hypothetical claim").

68 *See, e.g.*, Berardi v. Paramo, 705 Fed. App'x 517 (9th Cir. 2017) (holding that trial court did not err in ruling that juror's reported assertion—that defendant would have been convicted faster if the races of the defendant and the victim were switched—was insufficient to trigger an inquiry).

69 *Compare* United States v. Birchette, 908 F.3d 50 (4th Cir. 2018) (affirming conviction where white juror suggested African-American jurors were reluctant to convict African-American defendant); *and* United States v. Robinson, 872 F.3d 760 (6th Cir. 2017) (affirming conviction where a white foreperson told two African-American jurors that they were reluctant to convict because they felt they "owed something to their black brothers"), *with* State v. Berhe, 444 P.3d 1172 (Wash. 2019) (holding that evidentiary hearing must be held to determine whether racial bias affected the decision, where the sole African-American juror asserted that she was harassed into voting for a guilty verdict by other jurors who said she was partial to the defense because of her race; relying in part on state law principles not required by *Peña-Rodriguez*).

70 *See Peña-Rodriguez*, 137 S. Ct. at 869 ("Whether that threshold showing has been satisfied is a matter committed to the substantial discretion of the trial court in light of all the circumstances, including the content and timing of the alleged statements and the reliability of the proffered evidence.").

the trial court to undertake an inquiry under the *Peña-Rodriguez* exception.[71] In contrast, one juror's post-verdict report that another juror said something like, "You know he's just a banger from the hood, so he's got to be guilty," was enough to trigger an evidentiary hearing that resulted in the granting of a new trial.[72]

The difficulty of meaningfully capturing in a usable standard the Supreme Court's reasoning, together with the uncertainty of the Court's seeming attempt to limit its ruling to racial bias in criminal cases has so far caused the Advisory Committee on the Federal Rules of Evidence to forego an attempt to amend Rule 606(b) to reflect the *Peña-Rodriguez* exception.[73]

§ 8.06 The Requirement of Taking an Oath [FRE 603]

The purpose of the oath is to ensure truthfulness in those who give sworn testimony. Courts view the oath as providing an absolute declaration that any statement a witness gives is true.[74] Ideally, an oath or affirmation supports truth-telling and discourages a witness's natural inclination towards promoting self-interest.[75] Thus, an oath serves as a warranty on the truthfulness of a statement, and it is a practice that has existed throughout history.[76] The oath in American courts arose from Judeo-Christian historical roots, with the earliest recorded oath preserved in the Old Testament, and with other forms of a sworn oaths existing even earlier.[77] However, as with many other elements of law, the most direct influence for the modern American oath came from English law.[78] Early English law required jurors, judges, and witnesses to take an oath swearing to the Christian God. However, eventually, in the mid-1700s, the rule was revised and the oath became a general promise to God, with no specific religious requirements,[79] although belief in some kind of monotheism remained a requirement. It was not until as recently as 1975, with the passage of the Federal Rules of Evidence, that so-called "non-believers" were deemed competent to testify.[80] Today, Federal Rule of Evidence 601 stipulates that all persons are deemed competent regardless of religious affiliation (or lack thereof).[81] This rule is complemented by Rule 610, which prohibits the use of a witness's religious beliefs to attack or support the witness's credibility.[82]

Nevertheless, Rule 603 requires that all witnesses must provide an oath or affirmation promising to give truthful testimony.[83] A witness may refuse to swear under oath for various reasons. Some witnesses may refuse to take an oath on religious grounds. The Federal Rules and most state codes permit the witness to take either an

---

71 *See* United States v. Baker, 899 F.3d 124 (2d Cir. 2018).

72 *See* United States v. Smith, 2018 WL 1924454 (D. Minn. 2018).

73 *See* Daniel J. Capra & Liesa L Richter, *Poetry in Motion: The Federal Rules of Evidence and Forward Profess as an Imperative*, 99 B.U. L. REV. 1873, 1882–86 (2019).

74 Note, *A Reconsideration of the Sworn Testimony Requirement: Securing Truth in the Twentieth Century*. 75 MICH. L. REV. 1681, 1682 (1977).

75 Eugene R. Milhizer, *So Help Me Allah: An Historical and Prudential Analysis of Oaths as Applied to the Current Controversy of the Bible and Quran in Oath Practices in America*, 70 OHIO ST. L.J. 1, 4–5 (2009).

76 *Id.* at 6.

77 *Id.* at 7–8.

78 *Id.* at 19.

79 *Id.* at 23–25.

80 *Id.* at 33.

81 FED. R. EVID. 601.

82 FED. R. EVID. 610.

83 FED. R. EVID. 603.

oath or affirmation.[84] The affirmation omits the word "swear" and any references to "God." A witness might be asked, for example, "Do you affirm that the evidence you shall give is the truth, the whole truth, and nothing but the truth?" The trial judge should be willing to tailor the affirmation to avoid scruples of the witness, so long as the witness is willing to agree to tell the truth under penalty of perjury.[85]

Occasionally a witness who does not want to testify will simply refuse to take the oath. A witness who refuses to take the oath or affirmation may not testify.[86] When such a witness refuses to take an oath or affirmation, unless the refusal is on religious grounds, she may be held in contempt.[87]

§ 8.07 The Personal Knowledge Requirement [FRE 602]

The most important, broadly applicable competency rule remaining is the so-called "personal knowledge" requirement. Federal Rule of Evidence 602 prohibits a witness from testifying to a matter unless evidence is introduced sufficient to support a finding "that the witness has personal knowledge of that matter." This oddly worded rule leaves much to interpretation regarding what is "knowledge" and what kind of knowledge is "personal." The vast majority of a person's knowledge is obtained from one or more of three sources: (1) what one has observed oneself, that is, with one's own senses; (2) what one has been told by someone else; and (3) what one has acquired by religious revelation, clairvoyance, or mystical insight. At least the first and the third would seem to qualify as "personal." And, of course, one may plausibly (and "personally") infer knowledge from some combination of these sources. Fortunately, the drafters of Rule 602 left little doubt about what was intended:

> ". . . [T]he rule requiring that a witness who testifies to a fact which can be perceived by the senses must have had an opportunity to observe, and must have actually observed the fact" is a "most pervasive manifestation" of the common law insistence upon "the most reliable sources of information."[88]

---

84 *See id.*; see 6 WEINSTEIN'S FEDERAL EVIDENCE ch. T at T-89–T-94 (Mark S. Brodin ed., 2d ed. 2015) (indicating that overwhelming majority of states follow Rule 603 or comparable rule).

85 *See* FED. R. EVID. 603 advisory committee's note ("The rule is designed to afford the flexibility required in dealing with religious adults, atheists, conscientious objectors, mental defectives, and children. Affirmation is simply a solemn undertaking to tell the truth; no special verbal formula is required. As is true generally, affirmation is recognized by federal law."); United States v. Ward, 989 F.2d 1015, 1020 (9th Cir. 1993) (holding that witness should be allowed to replace the word "truth" with the phrase "fully integrated honesty" before taking the oath); Lawson v. Washington, 296 F.3d 799, 809 (9th Cir. 2002) (discussing oaths in general); Gordon v. Idaho, 778 F.2d 1397, 1400 (9th Cir. 1985) (concluding that any statement indicating that witness is impressed with duty to tell truth and understands that she is subject to penalty of perjury is sufficient).

86 *See* FED. R. EVID. 603; United States v. Fowler, 605 F.2d 181, 185 (5th Cir. 1979) (holding that lower court did not err in refusing to allow defendant to testify after he refused to swear or affirm that he would tell truth); United States v. Allen J., 127 F.3d 1292 (10th Cir. 1997) ("Fed. R. Evid. 603 requires every witness to declare he or she will testify truthfully. In addition to confirming for the court the victim understood the oath, the initial questioning of the victim also served 'to awaken the witness's conscience and impress the witness's mind with the duty to [testify truthfully as required by Rule 603.").

87 *See, e.g.*, IND. CODE § 34–47–2–2 (1999) (stating that witness who refuses to take an oath or affirmation is guilty of direct contempt of court); MO. REV. STAT. § 476.110 (2008) (stating that courts have power to find contempt in instances of "contumacious and unlawful" refusal to be sworn in before testimony); Commonwealth v. Stewart, 911 N.E.2d 161, 168 (Mass. 2009) (reversing decision of trial judge to waive the oath requirement for a witness for the prosecution, and holding that the witness should have instead been held in contempt, regardless of whether or not contempt would have persuaded witness to agree to take the oath).

88 FED. R. EVID. 602 advisory committee note (quoting MCCORMICK ON EVIDENCE § 10).

So the second and third sources listed above ostensibly are ruled out, manifesting the law's skeptical empiricism.[89] This comports with the historical practice of English courts, which prohibited witnesses from speculating about subjects they had not personally observed.[90] For example, a witness's opinion that the queen dressed in purple on her birthday was not admissible if the witness had not seen the queen on her birthday.

Regarding the second source—what one has been told by others—the rule might seem like a draconian restriction. After all, a great deal of what we think we know about the world we learned by being told, rather than by directly observing the fact. (Think of all the facts of history and science that you know, for example.) But the rule does not entirely preclude a witness from presenting knowledge acquired in this manner, because the witness observed *being told* of the fact. Suppose, for example, that D tells W that D saw the queen dressed in purple on her birthday. Rule 602 precludes W from simply testifying that the queen dressed in purple that day, because W did not observe what she wore, but it does not preclude W from testifying *that D told W* that the queen wore purple that day. Whether W will be allowed to report what D told W is regulated not by the personal knowledge rule but rather by the hearsay rule.[91]

The rule restricts sources of information, rather than the form of the testimony with which that "personal knowledge" is reported. The matter of form is governed by the rule regarding lay opinion testimony, Federal Rule of Evidence 701, which allows testimony in the form of an inference only under certain conditions.[92] The net effect requires lay witnesses to testify in the form of reports of what they have observed—i.e., with their ordinary senses—unless Rule 701 permits the witness to state an inference drawn from such perceptions. Both Rules 602 and 701 contain exceptions for expert witnesses, who are allowed to base their testimony on what they have learned from others in developing their expertise and who also are allowed to draw inferences from facts about the specific case that they have not personally observed.[93]

In questioning a lay witness, the direct examiner must therefore lay a foundation that the witness possesses such "personal knowledge" and did not merely gain the information second-hand or in some other unacceptable manner.

Example

Suppose at a trial it matters where Mr. Jones was at 8:00 p.m. on July 12. After calling a witness and eliciting the witness's identity, the direct examiner asks:

Direct examiner: Where was Mr. Jones at 8:00 p.m. on July 12?

Cross examiner: Objection, no showing of personal knowledge.

It may be that the witness did not observe where Jones was, though it is also possible that the witness did observe his whereabouts and that the lawyer simply failed to lay a proper foundation. Had the lawyer first laid a personal

---

89 Of course, even what one observes with the senses is filtered through a whole body of assumptions about the way the world works that incorporates other sources of knowledge, but that cannot be entirely avoided, and the law does not attempt to do so.

90 7 WIGMORE ON EVIDENCE § 1917 (Chadbourn rev. 1976).

91 1 MCCORMICK ON EVIDENCE § 10 at 62 (Kenneth S. Broun ed., 7th ed. 2013).

92 *See* **§ 10.02**.

93 *See* **§§ 10.03 et seq.**

knowledge foundation, there would have been no problem with the question. As the question stands, however, the judge should sustain the objection.

The requirement is not particularly demanding, as Rule 602 specifies that the evidence used to show personal knowledge may even be provided by the testimony of the same witness. This means that it is ordinarily "sufficient to support a finding" of personal knowledge if the witness asserts that he or she observed the event in question. Thus, the foundation in the example above might consist of an initial question such as, "Did you see Mr. Jones at 8:00 p.m. on July 12?" followed by a simple, "Yes, I did." Then, the witness would be permitted to identify Mr. Jones's location at the indicated time.

The drafters of Rule 602 stated that "the rule is in fact a specialized application of the provisions of Rule 104(b) on conditional relevancy."[94] Because Rule 104(b) is not an exclusionary rule, but rather is designed to work out the implications of the exclusion of irrelevant evidence by Rule 402, this seems to indicate that the personal knowledge requirement is simply an implication of the requirement that evidence be relevant. This supposition would only be correct if all testimony not based on personal knowledge (as explained above) were irrelevant. But that is quite implausible. Suppose, for example, that the testimony in the previous example went like this:

Direct examiner:	Do you know where Mr. Jones was at 8:00 p.m. on July 12?
Witness:	Yes, I do.
Direct examiner:	Where was he then?
Witness:	Mr. Jones was at the corner of Main Street and Fifth Boulevard.
Cross examiner:	Objection, irrelevant. Move to strike.

The testimony is hardly irrelevant. It surely invites inquiry into the source of the asserted knowledge, but that does not render it irrelevant. The (as yet unimpeached) witness's being willing to state under oath that the witness knows that Mr. Jones was at a certain place at a certain time must certainly increase the probability that Mr. Jones was there at that time.[95]

Though the rule cannot be an instantiation of conditional relevance, the rule is perfectly sensible nonetheless. Continuing the example, Jones's testimony might well be hearsay and excludable on that basis,[96] or it might be based on what the witness takes to be clairvoyance or mystical insight and thus excludable as irrelevant or a waste of time. But if a witness were not required to reveal his or her source(s) of asserted knowledge, the parties and the court would not have the information to invoke such exclusionary rules. Far from simply excluding irrelevant evidence, the personal knowledge requirement thus serves three distinct functions: (1) it reveals and facilitates the making of other potential objections, such as hearsay; (2) even if no other exclusionary rule is triggered, it facilitates the exploration of the witness's informational source(s), permitting the fact-finder to give them their proper weight; and (3) it requires the witness to reveal his or her sources "up front," which can facilitate the fact-finder's

---

94 FED. R. EVID. 602 advisory committee note.

95 Regarding the concept of conditional relevance, *see* **§ 3.11**.

96 Hearsay is not excluded merely because it is irrelevant. *See* **§ 14.03**.

assessment and also save considerable court time.[97] As to the last point, if personal knowledge did not have to be shown as a condition on testifying, a witness might, for example, testify for hours only to have the first question on cross-examination reveal that the entire direct testimony must be stricken as inadmissible hearsay.

§ 8.08 Hypnotically Refreshed Testimony

Investigators and therapists sometimes use hypnosis to gather information from witnesses when little other evidence is available.[98]. Though it is often useful in developing leads for investigation and offers the promise of otherwise unavailable testimony, it also presents great danger of inaccuracy. A hypnotized person is highly suggestible, can easily be influenced by unintentional cues from the hypnotist,[99] and is likely to manufacture false memory or confabulate true memory in a way that is undetectable either to the hypnotist or to the subject.[100] Moreover, the subject's memory tends to crystalize after hypnosis, creating an artificially high level of certainty.[101]

Courts have struggled with hypnotically refreshed testimony and disagree over what rules should be applied. Some courts treat the issue as one of witness competency, as it is treated here. Other courts consider the issue as one of expert testimony, because the use of hypnosis raises questions about the scientific validity and reliability of that technique. It does not make much difference which set of rules is applied, in terms of the results that are reached.[102]

The potential value and the potential danger of hypnotically refreshed testimony have led to varying judicial treatment. The testimony was considered per se inadmissible[103] until 1968, when, starting with the Maryland court's decision in *Harding v. State*,[104] many jurisdictions changed course and began to hold the testimony to be per

---

[97] *See* Dale A. Nance, *Conditional Relevance Reinterpreted,* 70 B.U. L. REV. 447, 488–92 (1990). Whether the "sufficient to support a finding" language makes sense in light of these functions is doubtful. *See* Richard D. Friedman, *Conditional Probative Value: Neoclassicism Without Myth,* 93 MICH. L. REV. 439 (1994); Dale A. Nance, *Conditional Probative Value and the Reconstruction of the Federal Rules of Evidence,* 94 MICH. L. REV. 419 (1995).

[98] *See* State *ex rel.* Collins v. Superior Court, 644 P.2d 1266, 1270 (Ariz. 1982).

[99] *See, e.g.,* State *ex rel.* Collins v. Superior Court, 644 P.2d at 1269–70 (Ariz. 1982) (noting that a common characteristic of subject under hypnosis is hyper-suggestibility); Emily E. Smith-Lee, Note, *Recovered Memories of Childhood Abuse: Should Long-Buried Memories Be Admissible Testimony?,* 37 B.C. L. REV. 91, 595–96 (1996) ("Courts have recognized three primary dangers associated with hypnosis: the danger of suggestibility; the possibility that the subject will 'confabulate,' or fill in the gaps of his or her story, in order to present a more coherent picture of an event; and the danger that the subject will experience an increased, often unjustified, confidence in the truth of his or her story"); Joseph A. Spadaro, Note, *An Elusive Search for the Truth: The Admissibility of Repressed and Recovered Memories in Light of* Daubert v. Merrell Dow Pharmaceuticals, Inc., 30 CONN. L. REV. 1147 (1998).

[100] *See, e.g.,* State v. Hurd, 432 A.2d 86, 92–93 (N.J. 1981) (quoting Martin T. Orne, *The Use and Misuse of Hypnosis in Court,* 27 INT'L J. CLINICAL & EXPERIMENTAL HYPNOSIS 311, 317–18 (1979)) (noting that a subject under hypnosis may create facts in order to fill gaps in memory; it is impossible to distinguish truth from fiction without independent verification); *see also* Rock v. Arkansas, 483 U.S. 44, 59–60 (1987).

[101] *Id.* at 93–94 (citing Martin T. Orne, *The Use and Misuse of Hypnosis in Court,* 27 INT'L J. CLINICAL & EXPERIMENTAL HYPNOSIS 311, 318–20 (1979)) (noting that a subject tends to be incapable of distinguishing prior memory from hypnotic recall; there may not be strong subjective confidence in validity of post-hypnotic recall); *see also* Rock v. Arkansas, 483 U.S. 44, 60 (1987); Alcala v. Woodford, 334 F.3d 862, 876 (9th Cir. 2003); Love v. Freeman, 1999 WL 671939 (4th Cir. 1999).

[102] *See* 2 FAIGMAN ET AL., MODERN SCIENTIFIC EVIDENCE: THE LAW AND SCIENCE OF EXPERT TESTIMONY § 18:2 (2015–16 ed.).

[103] People v. Ebanks, 49 P. 1049, 1053 (Cal. 1897) ("The law of the United States does not recognize hypnotism."), *overruled on other grounds,* People v. Flannelly, 60 P. 670 (Cal. 1900).

[104] 246 A.2d 302 (Md. Ct. Spec. App. 1968).

se admissible. Beginning in the 1980s, courts started to move back the other direction.[105] Today some courts consider the testimony per se admissible in at least some situations, leaving the opposing party to explore problems of hypnosis via impeachment.[106] While no jurisdiction considers the testimony per se inadmissible in all cases (in part because of constitutional constraints discussed below), most courts severely restrict such testimony.[107] Again, courts have based their decisions on various theories including witness competence (or lack thereof) following hypnosis,[108] the scientific validity (or invalidity) of hypnosis under the tests applicable to expertise,[109] and the defendant's Sixth Amendment confrontation right.[110]

Some jurisdictions admit hypnotically refreshed testimony if the proponent can establish that procedural safeguards were followed.[111] These safeguards can include a requirement that the hypnotist has certain qualifications, the witness's recollection of the event before hypnosis be recorded, the hypnotic sessions be recorded, and only the

---

[105] Roark v. Kentucky, 90 S.W.3d 24, 29–33 (Ky. 2002) (providing an exhaustive history of hypnotically refreshed testimony in the courts).

[106] *See* Borawick v. Shay, 68 F.3d 597, 604 (2d Cir. 1995) (describing the rule); State v. Brown, 337 N.W.2d 138 (N.D. 1983) (concluding that a previously hypnotized witness was not incompetent to testify; hypnotically refreshed recall is admissible with the jury determining the weight of that testimony); State v. Jorgensen, 492 P.2d 312 (Or. Ct. App. 1971); Haselhuhn v. State, 727 P.2d 280 (Wyo. 1986); State v. Glebock, 616 S.W.2d 897 (Tenn. Crim. App. 1981). *See also* OR. REV. STAT. § 136.675 (permitting hypnotically refreshed testimony to be offered in a criminal proceeding so long as the entire session was recorded and that recording made available to all parties).

[107] Mersch v. Dallas, 207 F.3d 732, 735, 736 (5th Cir. 2000) (holding testimony that is hypnotically refreshed per se inadmissible where "a hypnotized subject identifies for the first time a person he has reason to believe is already under suspicion" regardless of the procedural safeguards employed in the hypnotic session); Schall v. Lockheed Missiles & Space Co., 37 Cal.App.4th 1485 (Cal. Ct. App. 1995) (noting that in civil cases, refreshed testimony is per se inadmissible except for testimony about events recalled and related to others before hypnosis). Watson v. State, 604 S.E.2d 804, 813 (Ga. 2004) (stating that testimony derived from hypnosis is inadmissible); Thorp v. State, 777 So.2d 385, 393 n.8 (Fla. 2001) ("In Florida, statements elicited during and after hypnosis are considered unreliable and may not be admitted into evidence in a criminal trial"); Commonwealth v. Kater, 734 N.E.2d 1164, 1176–77 (Mass. 2000) (holding hypnotically aided testimony inadmissible); People v. Zayas, 546 N.E.2d 513 (Ill. 1989); State v. Tuttle, 780 P.2d 1203 (Utah 1989). *See generally* Daniel R. Webert, *Are the Courts in a Trance? Approaches to the Admissibility of Hypnotically Enhanced Witness Testimony in Light of Empirical Evidence*, 40 AM. CRIM. L. REV. 1301 (2003).

[108] *See, e.g.*, Franklin v. Stevenson, 987 P.2d 22 (Utah 1999).

[109] *See* **§ 10.04**. *See* State v. Coon, 974 P.2d 386 (Alaska 1999) (applying *Daubert* analysis in overruling Contreras v. State, 718 P.2d 129, in which court, based on *Frye* analysis, held testimony per se inadmissible); People v. Zayas, 546 N.E.2d 513 (Ill. 1989) (relying on *Frye*, holding testimony related to post-hypnotic recall per se inadmissible and requiring proponent of testimony of a previously hypnotized witness to bear the burden of proving that all testimony related to matters recalled *prior* to hypnosis).

[110] *See, e.g.*, Mancuso v. Olivarez, 292 F.3d 939 (9th Cir. 2002) (holding that hypnotically refreshed testimony for the prosecution does not violate confrontation clause). *See generally* **§ 20.09**.

[111] *See, e.g.*, White v. Ieyoub, 25 F.3d 245, 248 n.13 (5th Cir. 1994) (stating preference that hypnosis be performed by professional, independent hypnotist with little knowledge of case and that the session be recorded); Sprynczynatyk v. General Motors Corp., 771 F.2d 1112, 1122–23 & n.14 (8th Cir. 1985) (stating that hypnotically refreshed testimony admissible if certain safeguards followed); Borawick v. Shay, 842 F. Supp. 1501, 1505, 1508 (D. Conn. 1994) (excluding testimony on post-hypnotic memories where hypnotist held no educational degree, served apprenticeship abroad researching "faith healers," and spent time as a "stage hypnotist"); Haislip v. Roberts, 788 F. Supp. 482, 486 (D. Kan. 1992), *aff'd*, 992 F.2d 1085 (10th Cir. 1993) (holding that hypnotically refreshed testimony is not per se inadmissible, as long as proper safeguards protect the reliability of the testimony; opponent of testimony must show hypnosis accounts for differences in witness's pre- and post-hypnotic statements); State v. Lopez, 887 P.2d 538, 540 (Ariz. 1994) (holding that hypnotized police officers could not testify despite concurring pre-hypnosis reports where there were no records of safeguards used during hypnosis); State v. Evans, 450 S.E.2d 47, 51 (S.C. 1994) (concluding that post-hypnotic testimony is admissible if shown to be independent of the dangers associated with hypnosis, consistent with pre-hypnotic statements, and corroborated by circumstantial evidence).

hypnotist and the subject be present.[112] Other jurisdictions consider whether the "totality of the circumstances" suggest admitting the testimony.[113] The "totality of the circumstances" test has gained adherents in the federal circuits[114] even though there is no specific prohibition against hypnotically refreshed testimony in the Federal Rules of Evidence and prohibiting the testimony arguably conflicts with the spirit of the notion in Rule 601 that "[e]very person is competent." In applying the "totality of the circumstances" test, the courts often balance the probative value versus the prejudicial effect of hypnotic testimony.[115]

In *Borawick v. Shay*, the Second Circuit analyzed "the circumstances under which an alleged victim of sexual abuse may testify as to memories of abuse following therapeutic hypnosis"[116] using the principles for expert testimony in Rule 702 and *Daubert*.[117] Rejecting a per se rule for both admissibility and inadmissibility, it recommended that the trial court conduct a full pre-trial evidentiary hearing to weigh all of "the factors in favor and against the reliability of the hypnosis procedure in the exercise of its discretion whether to admit the post-hypnotic testimony."[118] The burden of proof should rest on the proponent of the refreshed testimony. Additionally, the trial court should consider: 1) "the purpose of the hypnosis," and even if the purpose was therapeutic, rather than investigative, to be wary of "the possibility that the subject may have received subtle suggestions from the therapist that abuse or trauma could be at the root" of the condition; 2) whether the witness received suggestions from the therapist or others before or during hypnosis; 3) the "presence or absence of a permanent record," with an audio or videotaped session being preferred; 4) whether the hypnotist was qualified in psychology or psychiatry; 5) whether corroborating evidence of the hypnotically refreshed memories existed; 6) how suggestible is the subject to hypnotic suggestions; and 7) expert evidence as to the reliability of the specific hypnosis procedures used in the case.[119]

Concern about the reliability of recovered memory has been sufficiently great that the United States Supreme Court has suggested that even a criminal defendant's constitutional right to testify might not include testimony based upon hypnotically refreshed testimony in some situations. In *Rock v. Arkansas*,[120] the accused in a murder

---

112 *See, e.g.*, Sprynczynatyk v. General Motors Corp., 771 F.2d 1112, 1123 n.14 (8th Cir. 1985); United States *ex rel.* Wilson v. Peters, 60 F. Supp.2d 777, 784 (N.D. Ill. 1999). *See also*, State v. Medrano, 86 S.W.3d 369 (Tex. App. 2002).

113 *See* Martin v. State, 839 So. 2d 665 (Ala. Crim. App. 2001) ("The fact that a witness has been hypnotized before testifying does not, per se, disqualify the witness. In considering hypnotically enhanced testimony, a court must conduct a balanced inquiry to determine if the testimony has a basis that is independent of the dangers associated with hypnosis. The inquiry should determine whether the witness's memory and ability to testify from it were distorted by an earlier hypnosis. The admissibility of such testimony is to be evaluated on a case-by-case basis, and the probative value of the testimony is to be weighed against its possible prejudicial effect."); Roark v. Commonwealth, 90 S.W.3d 24, 35 (Ky. 2002) (noting that the test analyzes "circumstances" including guidelines under which hypnosis must take place and balancing of probative value and prejudicial impact, with burden on proponent of testimony).

114 Borawick v. Shay, 68 F.3d 597, 598 (2d Cir. 1995); Mersch v. Dallas, 207 F.3d 732, 735, 736 (5th Cir. 2000); Armstrong v. Young, 34 F.3d 421 (7th Cir. 1994); *see, e.g.*, Lozado v. Superintendent, 2001 WL 1160592 (S.D.N.Y. 2001); Roark v. Commonwealth, 90 S.W.3d 24, 35 (Ky. 2002).

115 *See, e.g.*, Martin v. State, 839 So. 2d 665 (Ala. Crim. App. 2001).

116 68 F.3d 597, 598 (2d Cir. 1995).

117 *See* **§ 10.04**.

118 *Id.* at 608–09.

119 *Id.*

120 483 U.S. 44 (1987).

case had undergone hypnosis to help remember the events on the night of the fatal shooting. The trial judge excluded the hypnotically refreshed testimony. The Supreme Court held that the rigid Arkansas rule absolutely excluding such testimony violated the constitutional right to testify in one's own defense.[121] However, it left open the possibility that a more narrowly prescribed rule excluding hypnotically refreshed testimony taken without adequate precautions would be constitutional.[122]

The modern trend is toward something close to a per se rule of exclusion, admitting exceptions for pre-hypnosis recall and the refreshed testimony of the criminal defendant, at least to the extent required by constitutional law.[123] This is illustrated by the change in the rule in New Jersey. The New Jersey Supreme Court had been the first to adopt a procedural safeguards approach, in its 1981 decision in *State v. Hurd*.[124] But in 2006, the court rejected that approach in favor of a per se rule of inadmissibility (subject to the two exceptions) because of the inadequate scientific basis for believing that hypnosis improves recall, because there is no way to gauge the reliability of hypnotically refreshed testimony, and because there is a risk of instilling a false confidence in the witness.[125]

---

[121] *Id.* at 57–58.

[122] *Id.* at 61.

[123] *See* 2 FAIGMAN ET AL., MODERN SCIENTIFIC EVIDENCE: THE LAW AND SCIENCE OF EXPERT TESTIMONY § 18:6 (2015–16 ed.).

[124] State v. Hurd, 432 A.2d 86 (N.J. 1981).

[125] State v. Moore, 902 A.2d 1212 (N.J. 2006).

Chapter 9

THE LANGUAGE OF THE COURTROOM: COMMON OBJECTIONS TO TESTIMONIAL EVIDENCE

Table of Sections

---

§ 9.01 The Rules of the Game

This chapter presents a number of common evidence rules through the lens of objections to proposed testimony. Many of these objections relate to the "form" in which the testimony is given. Objections to the form of either the question or the answer stem from rules governing the conduct of the trial, rather than reflecting the usefulness of the underlying information. Put differently, these objections relate less to the content of the questions and answers and more to how they are presented. They reflect, in short, the rules of the testimonial game. As a result, most good trial lawyers avoid making such objections unless they believe that the objection will influence the relationship between the examiner and the witness or the examiner and the jurors. To be sure, how the information is presented to the jurors can often be as influential as what the information is. Trial lawyers use objections to the form of the question to influence the testimony's flow. The effectiveness of presentation (or lack of it) affects whether the information connects with the jurors. Just because a witness says something or a lawyer demonstrates a fact, does not mean that the jury has actually heard, seen, or understood it. The outcome of a trial turns on that ability to reach the jury.

Objections to the form of the question or answer generally invoke the judge's discretion under Rule 611 to control the mode of questioning witnesses. These objections rest on lawyers' and judges' understanding of the language of the courtroom. The particular dialect of the trial judge determines almost entirely whether objections to form are sustained or ignored, so the trial lawyer is well advised to be familiar with the judge's predilections about objections as to form. Except in the most egregious case (amounting to denial of a fair trial), the trial judge has the last word on how the evidence will be presented.

There are many objections to the form of testimony and more than a few ways to express each of them. This chapter presents some of the more common of these objections and the manner in which they are expressed. This is not intended, however, as a comprehensive list of objections to testimonial evidence. In particular, any of the specific admissibility rules discussed in previous chapters, and most of those in later chapters, can serve as the basis for an objection to testimony.

§ 9.02 "Objection. Leading the witness."

Leading questions are prohibited on direct examination, except for those questions that are preliminary, transitional, about non-controversial matters, or asked of an uncooperative witness or a witness listed in Rule 611(c).[1]

A question is leading when its words or its context suggest the answer to the witness:

Q: You were in the hallway when the shot was fired, weren't you?

This is an objection to "form" rather than "substance" of the question in the sense that the proponent usually can restate the question so as to elicit the same information. Thus:

Q: Where were you when the shot was fired?

Notice that even this question might be misleading if there were not already testimony from the witness indicating that the witness was aware that a shot was fired. In that case, the question suggests (implicitly assumes) that he *was* aware. Although this could be called leading the witness (by suggesting to the witness that he was aware), there is another objection that fits this issue more closely, namely, that the question "assumes facts not in evidence."[2]

Of course, to say that the same information *usually* can be obtained by changing the question is not to say that *invariably* it can be. In our example, the witness might not now remember where she was when the shot was fired. To get that information from the witness may require the questioner to refresh the witness's memory.[3] And even that may not work.

§ 9.03 "Objection. Calls for a narrative."

Judges prohibit questions that call for an extensive narrative response, particularly when they foresee that the narrative may make it impossible for the opponent to interpose timely objections. The inability to make an objection may result in the jurors hearing inadmissible and prejudicial evidence that an instruction to disregard will not cure. Although some judges are sticklers about the objection even in the absence of these dangers, narratives are tolerated, if not encouraged, in some courtrooms because they often speed up a trial. To be successful in objecting to a question that calls for a narrative

---

1 A discussion of the importance of leading questions in direct and cross-examination is found at **§ 1.06**.

2 *See* **§ 9.05**.

3 *See* **§ 1.08**.

response the lawyer should be prepared to illustrate the particular problem or the extremely prejudicial nature of the possible answer.

Some questions that call for a narrative are more dangerous than are others. "What happened next?" is a question without limitation, except for the starting point in time. "Will you please tell us how the collision occurred?" is limited to a specific event and asks for a description. Either question may be allowed or prohibited in the face of an objection that the question calls for a narrative, but the second question might carry less danger that the jurors will hear inadmissible evidence than the first because the subject matter of the second is known. "Will you please tell us what you know about the collision?" though limited to a specific event, might carry a greater danger that the opponent cannot interpose a timely objection concerning the source of the witness's knowledge. The answer might well contain inadmissible evidence, such as hearsay or opinion, that the opponent cannot reasonably anticipate.

§ 9.04 "Move to Strike. The answer is not responsive."

Witnesses often give narrative responses to questions that do not fairly call for a narrative and occasionally give answers that are simply not responsive to the question asked. The opposing lawyer should move to strike these answers and request an instruction to the jurors to disregard them. Although some judges maintain that the motion to strike a non-responsive answer belongs only to the lawyer asking the question, the better view is that either lawyer may make such a motion. The mistaken notion that the motion to strike as non-responsive belongs only to the questioner may originate in the fact that the cross-examiner almost always gets a non-responsive answer and wants it stricken.

The cross-examiner uses leading questions to control what the witness can tell the jurors. Witnesses often attempt to thwart that control and offer an excuse or an explanation with their answer to a cross-examination question that does not portray them or their testimony in a favorable light.

Example

Cross-examiner:	During your direct testimony you said that the Ford had the green light when it entered the intersection, didn't you?
Witness:	Yes.
Cross-examiner:	Two days after the accident you signed a statement under oath that the Chevrolet had the green light, didn't you?
Witness:	I was confused.
Cross-examiner:	Move to strike, Your Honor, as non-responsive, [and maybe add] and will Your Honor instruct the witness to answer the questions that are asked?
Judge:	The response is stricken; jurors, you are to disregard the witness's previous answer; [and maybe, if the witness has been evasive and non-responsive to a series of cross-examination questions] and, witness, you should listen to the question and answer only what is asked. If there are

explanations required, you may be asked about them on redirect examination.

In this example, the cross-examiner uses the motion to strike the non-responsive answer to control the witness and keep the witness's answers to one word ("yes" or "no"), rather than to withhold information from the jurors. Although the "explanation" will undoubtedly be part of the redirect examination, it may appear to be more of an after-the-fact excuse than an at-the-time reason for the difference between the testimony and the statement under oath.

A direct examiner may also receive non-responsive answers, but is less likely to want the non-responsive answer stricken. The non-responsive answer is likely to be the answer to the next question or inadmissible evidence that the direct examiner cannot otherwise present to the jurors. The opponent will probably not object if the non-responsive answer results from a witness's innocent anticipation of the next question, but will want the answer stricken if it is inadmissible evidence, constitutes a narrative, or requires further information to determine admissibility.

Example

Direct examiner:	Did you see what happened?
Witness:	I saw the Chevy speed into the intersection at the end of a yellow light and smash into the Ford.

The responsive answer to the question, "Did you see what happened," would be "yes." Neither lawyer, however, is likely to object that the answer is non-responsive, because it is a proper answer to the next question: "What did you see?"

Example

Direct examiner:	What happened at the intersection of Third and Sheridan?
Witness:	The Chevy sped into the intersection on a yellow light and smashed into the Ford. The driver of the Chevy was drunk.
Opponent:	Move to strike that portion of the answer following "smashed into the Ford" as non-responsive and for an instruction to the jurors to disregard it.

Here, the question did not ask for the witness's opinion about the condition of the driver of the Chevy. Thus, that part of the response is non-responsive. The witness's opinion that the Chevy driver was drunk may be admissible if the direct examiner can demonstrate that the opinion is the result of the witness's rational perception, but the opponent should be entitled to strike the testimony until the foundation for the opinion has been shown. The judge should (and most judges will) strike the non-responsive testimony, even though it is the opponent, not the questioner, making the motion.

§ 9.05 "Objection. Assumes facts not in evidence."

The question, "When did you stop embezzling from your corporation?", when posed as the first question to a witness on cross-examination, is the classic example of a question that assumes facts not in evidence. The first assumed fact is that the witness embezzled from his corporation. The second assumed fact is that he stopped.

A question that assumes facts not in evidence is particularly unfair on cross-examination because the assumed fact is usually inadmissible or unavailable. The cross-examiner can place the fact into a leading question, creating the danger that the jurors will remember the information, but not the source. To answer properly, the witness must explain why the assumed fact is untrue, though the form of the question does not generally allow for an explanation. The process may make the witness appear evasive, when the witness seems to qualify his answers or refuses to answer directly. If the direct examiner does not protect the witness by objecting to the question that assumes a fact not in evidence, the witness may seem less credible to the jurors.

Example

The plaintiff's witness in a wrongful death action came upon the accident at 12:30 in the morning. The witness was driving home from a dinner club after seeing a late show. There has been no evidence that the witness was drunk, or had even been drinking.

Cross-examiner:	What time was it when you were driving drunk on the loop highway?
Witness:	I wasn't drunk.
Cross-examiner:	You don't know what time it was?
Witness:	Yes, but I wasn't drunk.
Cross-examiner:	You had been drinking, isn't that right?
Witness:	No.
Cross-examiner:	You didn't have wine with dinner?
Witness:	Well, yes, but that was one glass at 7:30 in the evening.
Cross-examiner:	What time was it when you were driving drunk on the loop highway?
Direct examiner:	Objection, Your Honor. The question assumes a fact not in evidence.
Judge:	Sustained.
Direct examiner:	Will Your Honor instruct the jury that there is no basis in fact for the cross-examiner's assertion that the witness was drunk?
Judge:	Yes. Members of the jury, there has been no showing that this witness was under the influence of alcohol.

Sometimes the assumed facts may actually be evidenced, though not from the mouth of this particular witness. Thus, in the example posed in the first sentence of this section, suppose the prosecution had introduced evidence that the defendant did embezzle funds from the corporation. (Indeed, without such evidence, a motion to dismiss might have been in order.) The awkwardness for the witness remains, however, if the witness had testified on direct that no embezzlement occurred.

The direct examiner might also ask questions that assume facts not in evidence, though the opponent may not be as eager to object as when such a question is asked on cross-examination. When the direct examiner asks a question that assumes a fact not in evidence, the jurors, who have not heard the assumed fact, may be confused by the question and may not understand the answer. In that circumstance, the opponent is unlikely to object and give the direct examiner an opportunity to dispel the confusion.

Example

The plaintiff's first witness saw the collision between the Ford and the Chevrolet. The person is called to the witness stand, takes the oath, and then gives his name, address, and occupation.

Plaintiff's lawyer:	Where were you when the collision occurred?
Witness:	On the corner of Third and Sheridan.
Jurors:	[What collision? When? How many cars? Not much chance they will hear the witness's answer while they are trying to figure out what this is all about.]
Defense lawyer:	[Does nothing and hopes the direct examiner does not remember to get back to the collision so that the jurors know what the witness is talking about.]

A direct examination question that assumes facts not in evidence is sometimes used to lead a witness or fill in facts not otherwise available. The opponent will object if the evidence is important and unavailable.

Example

A police officer-witness testifies to arriving at the scene of a shooting and conducting an investigation, including taking photographs of the scene after the body had been removed. The pictures show the locations of some objects that suggest the defendant was the shooter.

Prosecutor:	After the body had been removed and everything was put back in place, did you take pictures?
Defense lawyer:	Objection, Your Honor, assumes facts not in evidence.

Because the objects and their locations are important in this case, the picture will not be admitted unless the prosecution can show that the objects were moved and replaced with great precision after the body was moved. If care was not taken or if officers moved the objects so that no one person could say where all the objects were originally located, the prosecution will be unable to make this necessary showing. If the defense lawyer fails to object to the question that assumes the fact that "everything was put back in place," the prosecution will put valuable evidence before the jurors that would be unavailable otherwise.

Some questions that assume facts not in evidence are permissible on direct. If the fact assumed is a natural consequence of a previous answer, most judges will allow the question as a convenient way to move the testimony along.

Example

Direct examiner:	Where did you go?
Witness:	Into the bedroom.
Direct examiner:	What did you see?
Witness:	There was a body on the bed.

The question, "What did you see?" assumes a fact not in evidence—that the witness saw something. Seeing something when one enters a room is a natural consequence of being in the room, absent some additional evidence that the room was dark, the witness was blind, or the witness's eyes were shut.

Direct examiners, unaware that most judges will allow a question that assumes a fact of natural consequence, often try to cure the problem by adding an awkward and disingenuous "if anything" somewhere in the question. For example, "What did you see, if anything" or "what, if anything, did you see." These questions still assume that people see things wherever they are. For those concerned that a judge may disfavor a question that assumes a fact of natural consequence, an easier and less awkward sounding approach is to lead the witness with a transition question.

Example

Direct examiner:	Did you see anything when you went into the bedroom? [Mildly leading, but transitional or preliminary.]
Witness:	Yes.
Direct examiner:	What did you see? [No longer assumes a fact not in evidence.]

It is important to distinguish the objection that a question assumes a fact not in evidence from the objection that a question on cross-examination asks about a specific fact not brought out during direct examination. If a question on cross-examination is within the scope of direct, it is proper even if it elicits new facts. Indeed, a cross-examination that brings out new facts is both proper and common.

Example

A police officer testifies on direct examination about the investigation conducted at the crime scene, but says nothing about fingerprints because none were found. The defense wishes the jury to know that the police did check for fingerprints and that the defendant's prints were not found at the scene.

Defense lawyer:	You checked for fingerprints at the scene, didn't you?
Prosecutor:	Objection, assumes a fact not in evidence.
Judge:	Overruled. You may answer.
Police officer:	Yes.

Defense lawyer:	When you checked for prints, you did not find my client's fingerprints at the scene of the crime did you?
Prosecutor:	Objection, assumes a fact not in evidence.
Judge:	Overruled. You may answer.
Police officer:	No.

Notice that had the second question, "When you checked for prints, you did not find my client's fingerprints at the scene of the crime did you?" been asked first, it would have improperly assumed a fact not in evidence. It would have *assumed* that the police "checked for prints"—a fact not brought out during direct examination and, without the first question, not brought out during cross-examination, either.

§ 9.06 "Objection. Argumentative."

An argumentative question is one that makes an argument to the jurors rather than posing a question to the witness.

Example

Cross-examiner:	Isn't that preposterous?
or	
Cross-examiner:	Do you expect the jury to believe that you drove twenty miles home and back during the most important business day of the year solely to get your handkerchief?

"Objection, argumentative," is the direct examiner's proper response to both questions.

The argumentative objection often is made when counsel harasses a witness. The harassment, however, is not the basis for the argumentative objection. The essential feature of the objection is that counsel is making an argument that should be saved for the summation. In the summation, counsel may draw inferences from the testimony, characterize it as believable or ridiculous, and demonstrate inconsistencies and improbabilities. Ordinarily, counsel should limit questions to drawing information from the witnesses about what they observed or know. Questioning is not the time to argue regarding the testimony's credibility or the propriety of drawing inferences from it.

§ 9.07 "Objection. Counsel is harassing the witness."

This objection is not really about a particular question, but rather, about the cross-examiner's approach to the witness. Cross-examination can be embarrassing, insulting, and unpleasant for the witness and still be permissible if the questions are pertinent and non-cumulative. But the cross-examiner may not make it unnecessarily ugly. Rule 611 instructs the trial court to "protect witnesses from harassment or undue embarrassment."[4] In addition to posing questions in an unfair form—argumentative, assuming facts, and the like—harassment might include yelling at a witness, cutting off the witness's answer unreasonably, and impinging on the witness's personal space. The objection that counsel is harassing the witness says to the judge: "Please stop that lawyer

[4] FED. R. EVID. 611(a)(3).

from beating up my witness; enough is enough." Whether the objection is sustained will depend upon the judge.

§ 9.08 "Objection. Compound question."

The objection for compound questions is meant to avoid confusion and trapping the witness into saying something she did not mean.

Example

Cross-examiner:	As you approached the intersection, did you look down, change the radio station, and then look up and for the first time notice the oncoming car?
Opponent:	Objection, compound question.

§ 9.09 "Objection. The question is vague (or ambiguous or confusing)."

Vague questions or those that misstate the evidence can confuse the witness and produce answers that do not reflect what the witness knows or wants to say. While any such questions might be asked on direct examination, they are most likely to draw objection on cross-examination. The direct examiner, who called the witness, makes the objection during cross-examination to protect the witness from appearing less than fully credible. The cross-examiner, upon hearing a confusing direct examination question is usually pleased and unlikely to object. The unintelligible question on direct examination carries its own penalty.

Ambiguity illustrated:

Examiner:	Your wife works downtown?
Witness:	Yes.
Examiner:	When does she get home?
Opponent:	Objection, vague as to date.

Confusing question illustrated:

Direct examiner:	Did you turn left or right or not?
Opponent:	Objection, confusing.

Occasionally a question is so incomprehensible that a mere objection that the question is vague does not do the situation justice. Consider the following question and imaginative objection taken from an actual trial transcript:

Direct examiner:	When he went, had you gone and she, if she wanted to and were able, for the time being excluding all the restraints on her not to go, gone also, would he have brought you, meaning you and she, with him to the station?
Opponent:	Objection, that question should be taken out and shot.

§ 9.10 "Objection. Misstates the evidence."

On cross-examination, a question that misstates the evidence can operate in the same fashion and may pose the same dangers as the question that assumes a fact not in evidence.

Example

After a witness testifies on direct examination to hearing the fire truck make a noise like a foghorn, the following cross-examination occurs:

Cross-examiner:	When you first heard the fire truck siren, where were you?
Opponent:	Objection, misstates the evidence.

§ 9.11 "Objection. Asked and answered."; "Objection. Cumulative."

Both these objections invoke the judge's discretion to prohibit questions that waste time or needlessly present cumulative evidence. However, the two objections usually arise in different circumstances.

The "asked and answered" objection is usually made by the direct examiner when a cross-examiner has asked the same question or different questions about the same subject, a number of times. It is one of a number of objections that a direct-examiner uses to protect the witness from an unfair cross-examination.

Example

Cross-examiner:	You were drunk when you walked into that room, weren't you?
Witness:	No.
Cross-examiner:	You had consumed so much alcohol you didn't know where you were, isn't that right?
Direct examiner:	Objection, Your Honor, asked and answered.
Judge:	This is cross-examination, counselor. Overruled.
Witness:	No.
Cross-examiner:	Isn't it true that you had so much to drink that you were not even aware of what was going on?
Direct examiner:	Objection, Your Honor, asked and answered.
Judge:	Sustained. Move along, counselor.

The "cumulative" objection is usually made by the cross-examiner when a direct examiner has tried to drive a point home by having the witness or a succession of witnesses testify to the same thing a number of different times.

Example

Direct examiner:	What did you see at the intersection?
Witness:	I saw the Chevrolet speed into the intersection and slam into a Ford that was entering the intersection on a green light.
Direct examiner:	What color was the light for the Ford when it was entering the intersection?
Cross-examiner:	Objection, cumulative.
Judge:	Overruled.
Witness:	It was green.

[A number of intervening questions about other observations during the collision and the aftermath.]

Direct examiner:	Now what color was the light for the Ford when it entered the intersection?
Cross-examiner:	Objection, cumulative.
Judge:	Sustained.

Repeating questions on both cross-and direct examinations is subject to the judge's tolerance for allowing lawyers to do things that they believe will help persuade the jurors and to extend the judge's patience with the pace of the trial at the time the objection is made. As a result, cross-examiners may often be allowed a couple of questions on the same subject and direct examiners are likely to be able to present important facts at least twice. When the repetition becomes obvious or the judge becomes irritated, the objection will be sustained.

§ 9.12 "Objection. Calls for speculation."

In the courtroom, "speculation" is a rather value laden term: it suggests something improper, as in, "That is mere speculation." In truth, fact-finding always involves a degree of speculation, if that means reaching conclusions one is not certain about, because the fact-finder was not a percipient witness to the litigated events.[5] The rules of adjudication attempt to keep speculation to a minimum, however, and to subject it to certain regulatory controls. That is all that can be expected. Generally speaking, it is not the province of *witnesses* to do the speculating, to the extent it can be avoided. Expert opinions and even lay opinions are often admissible, to be sure, but that does not mean that all opinions are admissible. The objection that a question "calls for speculation" is usually an imprecise way of objecting to the admissibility of an opinion under the rules governing either expert or lay witnesses.[6] In that case, "improper opinion" would be the better form of the objection: it encourages the parties to address in what particular the rules governing opinion testimony would be violated by the proposed testimony. On the other hand, the "speculation" objection might also be a clumsy way of objecting that the witness's testimony is not based on personal knowledge, and in fact is outside what the

---

5 *See* **§ 8.05**.

6 *See* **§§ 10.01 et seq.**

witness could perceive, such as suppositions about a party's motive or understanding.[7] Without some clarification, it is difficult to know.

§ 9.13 "Objection. No foundation."

One often hears the objection, "No foundation." This is *not* just an objection to the form of the evidence. But it is problematic as an objection because it is imprecise. The foundation required depends on the rule of exclusion, or the exception to such a rule, that is invoked. Each rule and each exception has distinct foundation requirements.[8] Thus, testimonial evidence requires a foundational showing of personal knowledge (for a lay witness) or expertise (for an expert witness). As discussed in later chapters, tangible evidence, like a document or a knife, requires foundation by way of authentication. Similarly, a foundation also must be established to show the existence of a valid excuse to present evidence of the contents of an original document other than by introducing the original itself, and a foundation must be introduced to warrant the application of most exceptions to the hearsay rule.

Unless the context makes it obvious for which rule the foundation (allegedly) has not been laid, the objecting party needs to clarify by so stating. Thus, the objecting party might say, "Objection, your honor. No foundation has been laid for the authenticity of this document." Or, "No foundation has been laid to warrant the acceptance of secondary evidence of the contents of the document." Of course, if you as the objecting lawyer are confident that some foundation is missing, but not sure exactly which one, an objection that the evidence "lacks foundation" may at least give you some time to think. From the proponent's point of view, however, one is entitled to meet the "no foundation" objection with a request that the objecting party specify the admissibility rule with respect to which the foundation is inadequate.

---

7 *See* **§ 8.07**.

8 *See generally* EDWARD J. IMWINKELRIED, EVIDENTIARY FOUNDATIONS (9th ed. 2014).

Chapter 10

OPINION EVIDENCE AND EXPERT TESTIMONY

Table of Sections

§ 10.01 The Common-Law Rule Against Lay Opinion Testimony

A primary goal of the common-law system of proof is ensuring that only trustworthy evidence is presented to the fact-finder, or at least ensuring that the evidence is as trustworthy as possible. One indication of this goal is the requirement that witnesses testify only on the basis of their first-hand observations.[1] The fact-finder decides whether to credit such testimony and what inferences to draw from it.

Until the twentieth century, American courts went well beyond this, purporting to apply a strict rule against opinion testimony by witnesses. Nineteenth century American courts endorsed the English rule requiring personal knowledge but they went further, prohibiting witnesses from testifying to inferences or conclusions even when based on their personal observations.[2] Thus, the historical American rule drew a line between "fact" and "opinion." This rule allowed a witness to testify about facts only and left matters of opinion for the jury. Under this approach, a witness could testify that an individual had bloodshot eyes, slurred speech, poor motor control, and breath that smelled of alcohol, but it was left for the jury, not the witness, to conclude that the individual was drunk.[3] The net effect was to require the witness to testify to the facts of which the witness had personal (i.e., direct observational) knowledge.

This rule was unwieldy because the dividing line between fact and opinion is often blurry. In many situations, testimony that might be characterized as "opinion" is actually a more general articulation of a set of "facts." In the previous example of testimony as to an individual's drunkenness, the "opinion" that the individual was drunk generally articulates the particular set of observed "facts." Further, the discrete "facts" upon which that "opinion" was based are themselves actually "opinions" about more

---

[1] A witness may only testify if "evidence is introduced sufficient to support a finding that the witness has personal knowledge of the matter." FED. R. EVID. 602. *See* **§ 8.07**.

[2] 7 WIGMORE ON EVIDENCE § 1917 (Chadbourn rev. 1976).

[3] Even during the heyday of the orthodox rule, however, courts found it hard to resist common sense, and often admitted lay opinion about drunkenness. *See id.* at § 1974 n.1 (collecting authorities).

discrete "facts." For example, testimony that the individual had poor motor control is arguably an "opinion" based on the "fact" that the individual moved hesitantly and needed several attempts to accomplish common tasks. These "facts" could likewise be recharacterized as "opinions" and subdivided accordingly. Were the historical rule against opinion testimony applied rigorously, it would have made jury trials tedious to the point of absurdity.

Critical of many arbitrary common-law rulings applying the distinction, Wigmore recommended a flexible test that anticipates the liberal federal standard:

> Such a [lay] witness' inferences are inadmissible when the jury can be put into a position of equal vantage for drawing them—in other words, when *by the mere words and gestures of the witness the data he has observed can be so reproduced that the jurors have those data as fully and exactly as the witness had them at the time he formed his opinion.*[4]

Today, the Federal Rules allow for lay opinion testimony, with certain restrictions. The next section of this chapter is devoted to those restrictions.

§ 10.02 Lay Opinion Testimony Under the Federal Rules [FRE 701]

Any witness may offer his or her opinion or inference as testimony under Rule 701, subject to three requirements:

(a) The opinion must be rationally based on the witness's perceptions;

(b) The opinion must be helpful to the finder of fact by either clarifying the witness's testimony or aiding in the determination of a fact in dispute; and

(c) The opinion must not rely on expertise, scientific, technical, or other specialized knowledge that may only be offered under Rule 702.

The judge's decision to allow or disallow lay opinion testimony will not be overturned on appeal absent a clear abuse of discretion.[5] This makes the prospect of having a Rule 701 matter overturned on appeal highly unlikely, placing a premium on good advocacy at trial.

Rationally Based on Perception

The first requirement under Rule 701, that the opinion be rationally based on the witness's perceptions, has two parts: (1) that the opinion must be based on the witness's perception (which simply restates the personal knowledge requirement), and, (2) that the opinion must be *rationally* based on those perceptions. The requirement that an opinion be rationally based on the witness's perceptions invokes the common sense of the matter. When this requirement is applied to testimony about an apparently drunk individual, for example, it does not matter whether testimony that the individual "had poor motor control" is a considered a fact or an opinion, as long as it is rationally based on the perceptions of the witness.

---

4 *See id.* § 1924 at 32 (emphasis in original). *See also id.* § 1926.

5 Nationwide Transp. Fin. v. Cass Info. Sys., 523 F.3d 1051, 1058 (9th Cir. 2008) ("The admissibility of lay opinion testimony under Rule 701 is committed to the sound discretion of the trial judge and his decision will be overturned only if it constitutes a clear abuse of discretion." (quoting United States v. Yazzie, 976 F.2d 1252, 1255 (9th Cir. 1992))).

Example

Direct examiner:	Where was the cow when you arrived?
Witness:	On the roof of the building.
Direct examiner:	How did it get there?
Cross-examiner:	Objection, there has been no showing that the witness could have personal knowledge of that.
Judge:	Sustained.

Example

Direct examiner:	What was his condition when you first saw him?
Witness:	He was stoned on marijuana.
Cross-examiner:	Objection, improper opinion. Not rationally based on perception.
Judge:	Sustained. The answer will be stricken from the record.
Cross-examiner:	Move to strike.

The more perceived facts to which the witness testifies in support of his or her eventual opinion, the stronger the rational basis of that opinion becomes. An opinion indicating spaciness, red-rimmed eyes and a penchant for Doritos might serve as the basis for an opinion that someone was stoned on marijuana.

Helpful

The second requirement under Rule 701 is that the opinion must be helpful to the finder of fact. Opinion testimony is arguably most helpful when the facts underlying the opinion do not adequately convey the perception of the witness. In such situations, lay opinion testimony is helpful because the whole of the witness's perception is greater than the sum of its parts. Testimony that "I felt fine" or "He looked angry" is a general opinion that almost everyone would recognize and understand, but the witness might be hard pressed to articulate in discrete components. "I was not coughing, not feverish, not debilitated, not crying, and not sneezing," might begin to convey the concept "I felt fine" but does not convey the full meaning of "I felt fine." The opinion "he looked angry" might be broken down into features, including a knitting of the brow, narrowing of the eyes, and hardening of the mouth, but describing those features alone may not convey the full gravity of the simple opinion "he looked angry."

The perception that an individual "had slurred speech" can rationally lead to the opinion that the individual was drunk, because drunkenness is a common cause of slurred speech. Thus, such an opinion should not be prohibited as irrational. It may, however, be prohibited as unhelpful because the opinion that the cause of slurred speech was drunkenness arguably adds nothing to the testimony as the jury is theoretically just as capable of inferring the cause of the slurred speech as the witness. Practically, though, almost no observation is made in true isolation. Virtually any event includes innumerable contextual factors and minute observations that, while difficult to articulate, allow a direct witness of the event to evaluate the observed phenomenon better than could a third party to whom the event is later related.

The helpfulness requirement is essentially an invitation for the trial judge to exercise broad discretion to prohibit opinions that are either unduly general, conclusive,[6] or too obvious, and potentially subvert the fact-finding role of the jury.[7]

Example

Direct examiner:	What was he doing?
Witness:	He was acting silly.
Cross-examiner:	Objection, this lay opinion is too unspecific to help the jury.
Judge:	Sustained.
Cross-examiner:	Move to strike.

The trial court may insist that the opinion is not helpful without some specification of the perceptual data upon which it is based. The necessity of testifying to additional facts to support an eventual opinion obviously varies with the facts involved. There is some tension in these requirements, as a witness who lays a strong foundation for his or her opinion in order to show that it is rationally based on perception and to prevent the opinion from being held too general or conclusive may make the witness's ultimate opinion so obvious as to be superfluous.

Although Rule 704 rejects the common-law prohibition on witnesses offering opinions on the ultimate question,[8] the refusal to admit certain characterizations by a witness as superfluous shows a lingering concern about preserving the independent fact-finding role of the jury.[9] A judge is more likely to prohibit a witness from offering an opinion relating to a key question the jury must decide than to prohibit an opinion about something tangential to the case.[10] If the issue for the jury is whether a driver was negligent, a witness's opinion that the driver "drove negligently" is unlikely to be allowed. In such a case, the judge will likely require a description of the driver's conduct in less legally charged terms, such as: "the driver was weaving in and out of traffic without using a turn signal while drinking coffee and texting on a cell phone." As a practical matter, the more important the opinion, the more scrutiny the judge will give to whether the general opinion is "helpful."

---

[6] *See* United States v. Garcia, 413 F.3d 201, 213–14 (2d Cir. 2005) (holding that summary opinion of witness that defendant was culpable member of conspiracy was not helpful, inter alia, because it was based on witness's "total investigation" and not based on discrete observations witness otherwise testified to).

[7] *See* United States v. Skeet, 665 F.2d 983, 985 (9th Cir. 1982) ("If it is impossible or difficult to reproduce the data observed . . . the witness may state . . . opinions. . . . If the jury can be put into a position of equal vantage with the witness for drawing the opinion, then the witness may not give an opinion.").

[8] *See* **§ 10.06**.

[9] *See, e.g.*, Torres v. County of Oakland, 758 F.2d 147, 150 (6th Cir. 1985) (stating that legal conclusion of lay witness was not "helpful" within the meaning of Rule 701).

[10] In fact, the advisory committee note advocates this practice:

> The abolition of the ultimate issue rule does not lower the bars so as to admit all opinions. Under Rules 701 and 702, opinions must be helpful to the trier of fact, and Rule 403 provides for exclusion of evidence which wastes time. These provisions afford ample assurances against the admission of opinions which would merely tell the jury what result to reach, somewhat in the manner of the oath-helpers of an earlier day.

FED. R. EVID. 704 advisory committee note.

Although a persuasive advocate may be able to have a lay opinion excluded at trial as either not rationally based on the witness's perceptions or as unhelpful, it is not always a good tactic to do so. In some situations, it may be more damaging to have a witness relate many discrete facts to the jury than to have the witness draw a summary conclusion. In the example above about an allegedly careless driver, the attorney representing that driver may not wish to object to a proffered opinion that the driver "drove negligently" because such an objection would prompt the opposing counsel to elicit more vivid and particularized testimony (the witness's damaging detailed perceptions about the driver's weaving and failing to signal, etc.), which is arguably more compelling and effective.

Whenever possible, it is probably advantageous to elicit on direct both discrete facts and opinions based on those facts. Summary opinions, as opposed to a recitation of discrete facts, are vulnerable to attack on cross-examination. If only a summary opinion were given by the witness above, the cross-examiner might ask leading questions to highlight all the facts that run contrary to the opinion that the driver "drove negligently."

Q: "The driver wasn't speeding, was he?"

A: "No."

Q: "He never drove on the shoulder, did he?"

A: "No."

Q: "Isn't it true that your opinion is only based on a few seconds of observation?"

A: "Yes."

Q: "And you had to pay attention to all the other traffic around you at the same time as you observed the driver, didn't you?"

A: "Yes."

Such a cross-examination might open the door for a redirect to elicit the specific details that were omitted from the witness's summary opinion, but it would be less persuasive than painting a vivid picture for the jury to begin with.

Non-Expert

The final restriction under Rule 701 is that lay opinion must not be based on scientific, technical, or specialized knowledge within the scope of Rule 702. This restriction was not part of the original rule but was added in the 2000 amendments as a reaction to the strategic behavior of litigants. Rule 701(c) is intended to ensure that a party will not "evade the expert witness disclosure requirements" of the Federal Rules of Civil or Criminal Procedure[11] "through the simple expedient of proffering an expert in lay witness clothing."[12] The disclosure rules for expert testimony are designed to prevent surprise opinions and to allow the opposing party to develop alternative expert opinions based on the same facts. Lay witnesses are subject to far less exacting disclosure requirements. Allowing functionally expert testimony without proper expert disclosure would be unfair to the opposing party in the modern litigation environment.

---

11 FED. R. EVID. 701 advisory committee note.

12 *Id.*

Another reason for prohibiting expert testimony in the guise of lay opinion is that, unlike lay opinion, expert testimony is subject to the reliability requirements of Rule 702. If expert testimony does not meet the reliability requirements of Rule 702, it cannot simply be offered under Rule 701 instead. For example, an undercover police officer might be qualified under Rule 702 to give an expert opinion concerning whether a defendant's conduct was consistent with that of a drug trafficker. If, however, the proffered testimony does not meet the reliability requirements of Rule 702, the prosecution cannot instead treat the officer as a lay witness who testifies to having seen both drug trafficking and the conduct of the defendant, and then offer the lay opinion that they are the same.[13] Rule 702's requirements regarding expert testimony cannot be subverted by a retreat to lay opinion under Rule 701.

The 2000 amendment identifies but does not fully resolve the difficult problem of distinguishing between lay and expert witnesses. Formally, the question is whether the witness must, in giving his or her opinion, rely on "scientific, technical, or other specialized knowledge." Because "scientific knowledge" and "technical knowledge" are clearly intended as two illustrations of the broader and determinative genus, "specialized knowledge," Rule 701 (like Rule 702) contemplates that a witness can have specialized knowledge that is neither scientific nor technical and that, to use that kind of knowledge at a trial, the witness and the testimony still must be qualified under the rules for experts.[14] The usual illustration of such a residual category is "experiential knowledge," as might be possessed by a self-taught carpenter or mechanic or the experiential knowledge developed by a police officer. There is no doubt that such individuals can and sometimes do testify *qua* experts, if they can meet the requirements discussed in the following sections. Alternatively, at least before the 2000 amendment, such witnesses sometimes were admitted under the rubric of "skilled lay witnesses," without the necessity of complying with the rules for experts.[15] The amendment seems to foreclose that option.[16] Accordingly, some judicial opinions address directly the role of an expert that determines what "specialized" means in this context, namely, assisting the fact-finder by providing or applying general information about how the world works that is not otherwise available to the ordinary person (whether juror or trial judge) serving as fact-finder.[17] This is the proper framework for analysis. While it may seem to pose a risk

---

[13] *Id.* (citing United States v. Figueroa-Lopez, 125 F.3d 1241, 1246 (9th Cir. 1997)).

[14] *See* **§ 10.03**.

[15] *See* RONALD L. CARLSON, EDWARD J. IMWINKELRIED, JULIE SEASMAN, & ERICA MEECHER-MONAS, EVIDENCE: TEACHING MATERIALS FOR AN AGE OF SCIENCE AND STATUTES 585–87 (7th ed. 2012).

[16] It is entirely possible, to be sure, for a single witness to testify both as a lay witness and as an expert in the same case, though that can cause confusion. Someone who personally observes case-specific events, and may thus testify to those events from personal knowledge, may also have expertise that can be used to draw inferences from those events. This happens frequently with police officers. *See, e.g.,* United States v. Freeman, 498 F.3d 893, 904–07 (9th Cir. 2007) (holding that detective could testify both as an expert interpreting coded drug jargon (based on information acquired prior to investigation of particular case) and as a lay witness reporting uncoded conversations and interpreting the latter within the confines of Rule 701).

[17] *See, e.g.,* United States v. Smith, 640 F.3d 358, 364–65 (D.C. Cir. 2011) (holding FBI agent's testimony about meaning of slang words in drug case improperly admitted as lay testimony because it relied on agent's experience as law enforcement officer, noting that "knowledge derived from previous professional experience falls squarely 'within the scope of Rule 702' and thus by definition outside of Rule 701," citing Rule 701(c)); Williams v. Mast Biosurgery USA, Inc., 644 F.3d 1312 (11th Cir. 2011) (distinguishing those aspects of treating physician's testimony that are permissible lay testimony and those that cross over into expert testimony). Many of the better reasoned cases are state cases decided without the benefit of an amendment equivalent to FRE 701(c). *See, e.g.,* Ragland v. State, 870 A.2d 609 (Md. 2005) (holding erroneous the admission, as lay opinion, of testimony by police officers, based on their training and experience, that a series of events observed constituted a drug transaction); Palmer v. Volkswagen of Am., Inc., 904 So. 2d 1077, 1089–93 (Miss.

of excluding too much by sweeping what has been thought to be admissible into the category of expertise, the better solution to that problem is greater flexibility in the admission of experts.[18]

Unfortunately, the advisory committee note regarding the 2000 amendment raised more questions than it answered in this regard. It states:

> For example, most courts have permitted the owner or officer of a business to testify to the value or projected profits of the business, without the necessity of qualifying the witness as an accountant, appraiser, or similar expert. [citation omitted] Such opinion testimony is admitted not because of experience, training or specialized knowledge within the realm of an expert, but because of the particularized knowledge that the witness has by virtue of his or her position in the business. The amendment does not purport to change this analysis. Similarly, courts have permitted lay witnesses to testify that a substance appeared to be a narcotic, so long as a foundation of familiarity with the substance is established. [citation omitted] Such testimony is not based on specialized knowledge within the scope of Rule 702, but rather is based upon a layperson's personal knowledge.[19]

This is not helpful. With regard to the first illustration, such "particularized knowledge" gained from experience clearly falls within the category of specialized knowledge that can be the subject of expert testimony, if suitably qualified, so the comment suggests that the proponent can obtain admission of the opinion as lay opinion if it fails to satisfy the requirements for expertise, contrary to the explicit purpose of Rule 701(c). With regard to the second illustration, if "personal knowledge" in this context means the same as the personal knowledge required by Rule 602, then any lay witness who satisfies Rule 701(a) will automatically satisfy Rule 701(c), rendering Rule 701(c) ineffectual. Alternatively, if this sense of "personal knowledge" extends to more general background information acquired by direct personal experience, then it would create an overlap in the categories of lay and expert opinion because (at least) experiential expertise could ground either kind of opinion, thus defeating the very purpose of the amendment.

Relying on the advisory committee's note, some courts continue to wrestle with the supposed distinction between "specialized" knowledge, on the one hand, and "particularized" or "personal" knowledge, on the other.[20] Such rulings sometimes allow

---

2005) (rejecting lay testimony by engineer employed by defendant, noting that testimony relying on knowledge "beyond that of the randomly selected adult" must qualify as expert testimony); Christofferson v. City of Great Falls, 74 P.3d 1021 (Mont. 2003) (rejecting as lay testimony the opinion of paramedics about the prospects for success of an earlier intubation); State v. McClean, 16 A.3d 332 (N.J. 2011) (holding that questioning police officer regarding the officer's training and experience to interpret defendant's conduct in hand-to-hand drug transaction called for impermissible lay opinion). *See generally* DAVID H. KAYE, DAVID E. BERNSTEIN, & JENNIFER L. MNOOKIN, THE NEW WIGMORE: EXPERT EVIDENCE § 2.6 (2d ed. 2011).

[18] *See, e.g.*, United States v. Conn, 297 F.3d 548, 554 (7th Cir. 2002) (holding that ATF Agent's testimony, based on experience, that firearms possessed by defendant were not collectors' items was inadmissible as lay opinion, but that adequate foundation was presented to admit as expert testimony even though not offered as such; stating that "[l]ay opinion testimony is admissible only to help the jury or the court to understand the facts about which the witness is testifying and not to provide specialized explanations or interpretations that an untrained layman could not make if perceiving the same acts or events").

[19] FED. R. EVID. 701 advisory committee note (2000 amendment).

[20] *See* 3 CHRISTOPHER B. MUELLER & LAIRD C. KIRKPATRICK, FEDERAL EVIDENCE § 7:6 (4th ed. 2013). These commentators suggest that, in making the categorization, courts focus on factors such as the extent of formal training of the proposed witness and the degree of professionalization of the asserted knowledge. *Id.* at 745–46.

witnesses to use certain kinds of general knowledge that are unavailable to the ordinary fact-finder in giving their "lay" opinions.[21] It is difficult to reconcile these rulings with the language or purpose of Rule 701(c). To fully appreciate the issue, however, one must also consider in greater detail the rules that apply to experts, because that understanding informs a purposive decision. That is, whether one should categorize a particular witness as offering a lay opinion or an expert opinion may depend on whether one thinks the panoply of expert witness rules ought to apply to the witness in question.[22] The following sections address those rules.

§ 10.03 Expert Testimony: A Brief Analytical and Historical Introduction

What Experts Do

To understand the limits placed on expert testimony, it is useful to analyze exactly how *admissible* expertise can help the fact-finder. And to do that, it is necessary to think about how fact-finders draw inferences from evidence.[23]

Consider a simple example: a witness reports seeing the criminal defendant running from the scene of a crime. The fact-finder must assess how credible the witness is and also must assess how probative the accused's flight would be. (This assessment, of course, is made in the context of all the other evidence in the case, but we will focus on this one line of inference.) At least three distinct inferences are involved here: (1) an inference from the testimony that the defendant was running from the scene to the proposition that the defendant was in fact running from the scene; (2) an inference from the fact that the defendant was running from the scene to the fact that he was doing so out of a consciousness of guilt; and (3) an inference from a consciousness of guilt to actual guilt of the crime of the alleged crime. For present purposes, focus on just the second of these inferences:

---

[21] *See, e.g.,* United States v. Roe, 606 F.3d 180 (4th Cir. 2010) (permitting police sergeant to testify as lay witness, based on personal knowledge, to the legal authority conferred by issuance of handgun permits and private detective certifications); JGR, Inc. v. Thomasville Furniture Industries, 370 F.3d 519, 524–26 (6th Cir. 2004) (rejecting testimony of CPA regarding plaintiff's lost profits because witness was not owner or employee of plaintiff); Tampa Bay Shipbuilding & Repair Co. v. Cedar Shipping Co., 320 F.3d 1213 (11th Cir. 2003) (admitting as lay opinion testimony by ship repairer's employees that charges were fair and reasonable and in line with similar services provided by other companies). For courts that adopt this approach, the authors suggest another factor affecting courts' decisions—necessity. It may be necessary to allow a lay witness to present an opinion on a matter as to which no other helpful opinion of superior expertise is available. This idea finds support in cases decided before the 2000 amendment. *Compare* United States v. Paiva, 892 F.2d 148, 156 (1st Cir. 1989) (lay witness allowed to offer opinion that substance was cocaine in context where witness had familiarity with characteristics of cocaine and the substance was not available for subsequent chemical testing before trial), *with* People v. Park, 380 N.E.2d 795 (Ill. 1980) (holding sheriff's testimony identifying seized substance as marijuana by "feel, smell, texture, and looks" inadmissible in light of readily availability chemical tests of superior reliability).

[22] Taking the broad view of expertise suggested in the text mutes controversies about which rules—those for lay witnesses or those for experts—apply to so-called "skilled lay" witnesses. *See, e.g.,* United States v. Oschatz, 912 F.2d 534 (2d Cir. 1990) (addressing the question whether to distinguish between lay character witnesses and expert character witnesses in terms of the use of hypothetical questions). This problem becomes a non-issue if the foundational skills necessary for a character witness or other "skilled lay" witness necessarily invoke specialized knowledge that imposes on the witness the rules for an expert. *Cf.* United States v. Kellogg, 510 F.3d 188 (3d Cir. 2007) (permitting use of hypothetical questions with an opinion character witness).

[23] *See also* **§ 5.02.**

In assessing the strength of this inference, and many others that are presented to a fact-finder in the course of a particular trial, the fact-finder ordinarily resorts to generalizations about the way the world works, such as: "People who run from the scene of a crime probably feel a consciousness of guilt for the crime." The fact-finder will have his or her own sense, based on accumulated experience, about how "probable" the inference is.[24]

A suitably qualified expert might assist the fact-finder in making this assessment in at least three distinct ways. First, an expert might help by simply giving testimony that provides the fact-finder information about people who flee from crime scenes, assuming such information is available. That is, the expert provides information that could affect the strength of the generalization about the way the world works that connects the first proposition to the second. For example, an expert might testify (if the necessary knowledge base exists in the expert's field) that "most people who run from the scene of a crime are not fleeing because of consciousness of guilt of that crime, but for some other reason." That might very well affect the fact-finder's thinking; depending on how credible the expert is, it might change how "probably" the fact-finder thinks that the consciousness of guilt follows from flight. Note, however, that the expert on this assumption has not testified to an opinion about *this* defendant, only about what happens generally.[25] This kind of expert testimony can be called "informational."[26]

Second, an expert might assist the fact-finder by providing such general informational testimony and then using it to offer and explain an opinion about whether this particular defendant was conscious of guilt. This kind of expert testimony can be called "advisory." Notice that the expertise does not extend to answering the question of whether the defendant did run from the scene. Indeed, there may well be other case-specific facts that will have to be assumed for the expert to give this kind of opinion.

Finally, an expert might assist the fact-finder by skipping the informational aspect of the testimony and simply giving the expert's opinion about whether, on the assumption that this defendant was running from the scene, this defendant was conscious of guilt. This kind of expert testimony can be called "directive." The difference between an advisory opinion and a directive opinion is that the advisory expert explains why the expert has reached the opinion given, whereas the directive expert omits the explanation, at least initially.[27]

[24] *See* **§ 5.02**. The reasonableness of an inference reflects the life experiences, biases, and world view of the fact-finder. Experience with police, for example, varies with race, social class, and geography.

[25] If particular facts are evidenced about the defendant that place him in a smaller class of individuals about which a knowledge base exists in the field, and as to which there is a heightened or lowered tendency for flight to reflect consciousness of guilt, then the expert might testify about the tendencies of that smaller class, but it would still be testimony about a class to which the defendant belongs, not testimony about this particular defendant.

[26] One commentator calls this "summarizational" expertise, because it summarizes the expert's relevant knowledge. *See* D. Michael Risinger, *Preliminary Thoughts on a Functional Taxonomy of Expertise for the Post-*Kumho *World*, 31 SETON HALL L.J. 508 (2000).

[27] Professor Risinger calls the second and third modalities "translational" expertise. Other commentators emphasize the difference between the second and third modes by calling it a difference between "education" and "deference," between the fact-finder being educated to understand why the expert's opinion is true and the fact-finder being asked to defer to the expert's opinion without necessarily understanding why

All three of these modalities involve the expert using general information about the way the world works, information that is part of the field of claimed expertise. This is the core feature of expert testimony. The adequacy of the expertise, of the expert to provide it, and of the application of the expertise to the particular case are all governed by Rule 702 in the Federal Rules and state counterparts. Only the second and the third modalities involve the expert using that knowledge to give an opinion about the particular case by applying those generalizations to draw inferences from case-specific facts. When an expert does so, the question of where the expert obtains the case-specific facts upon which to base an opinion is especially important, and the rules vary among jurisdictions about which sources of factual information they permit the expert to use. Among the possibilities are: (a) facts not controverted by the parties, (b) facts evidenced by the testimony of other witnesses and *assumed* to be true by the expert for the purpose of giving an opinion, even if they are controverted; (c) facts personally observed by the expert, whether or not reported in the expert's testimony; and (d) facts not personally observed by the expert but observed by someone else and communicated, directly or indirectly, to the expert outside of the courtroom. The question of what sources of case-specific facts may be used by an expert is governed by Rule 703 and state counterparts.[28]

The category of facts personally observed by the expert does not appear in the hypothetical presented above about the defendant running from the scene, but some experts, such as emergency room doctors and other treating physicians, often also have personal knowledge of case-specific facts. Such experts are sometimes called "percipient" experts.[29] Percipient experts cannot be fully replaced by bringing in another expert who did not observe the case-specific facts. By contrast, non-percipient experts are almost always replaceable. In the example, if the social-psychologist who is prepared to provide the expertise about consciousness-of-guilt inferences were to become unavailable before trial, another expert ordinarily could be found to testify on the matter. This difference can have a significant impact on admissibility decisions.[30]

All three kinds of expert testimony—informational, advisory, and directive—appear in American courts in varying degrees and subject to varying limitations.[31] Experts perform some of the inferential work usually allocated to the fact-finder, and (in the

---

the expert thinks it is true. *See* Ronald J. Allen & Joseph S. Miller, *The Common Law Theory of Experts: Deference or Education?*, 87 NW. U. L. REV.1131 (1993).

[28] *See* **§ 10.05**. On the distinction between the scope of Rule 702 and that of Rule 703, see Edward J. Imwinkelried, *The Bases of Expert Testimony: The Syllogistic Structure of Scientific Testimony*, 67 N. C. L. REV. 1 (1988). *Cf.* 3 CHRISTOPHER B. MUELLER & LAIRD C. KIRKPATRICK, FEDERAL EVIDENCE § 7:13 (4th ed. 2013) (arguing that Rule 703 requires not only that the expert rely on particular kinds of facts and data but that the reliance on them be reasonable and that, therefore, "the coming of *Daubert*, and the later amendment to Rule 702, largely expanded and essentially duplicated the standard that had previously been expressed only in Rule 703.") In the authors' view, Professor Imwinkelried is correct: Professors Mueller and Kirkpatrick echo the error of some courts in reading a requirement into Rule 703 that is not there.

[29] Percipient experts are the source of much of the confusion that led to the adoption of Rule 701(c) because and when the proponent attempts to elicit the inferential aspect of the testimony as lay opinion. *See, e.g.*, Weese v. Schukman, 98 F.3d 542, 549 (10th Cir. 1996) (permitting defendant in medical malpractice case to give "lay" opinion on the standard of care and causation; case decided before 2000 amendment). *See* **§ 10.02**.

[30] For example, in Williams v. Mast Biosurgery USA, Inc., 644 F.3d 1312 (11th Cir. 2011), the appellate court affirmed the exclusion of plaintiff's treating physicians on the identity of a foreign object removed from the plaintiff during surgery, which she alleged was defectively functioning SurgiWrap manufactured by the defendant. The physicians had not been qualified as experts on SurgiWrap and therefore were offered as lay witnesses. The court held that the witnesses could not testify as lay witnesses, and the plaintiff did not appeal their exclusion as experts. Significantly, these witnesses could not be replaced with (other) experts because the foreign object was not preserved after plaintiff's surgery.

[31] *See* **§§ 10.06–10.08**.

context of percipient experts) they also do some of the work usually allocated to fact-witnesses. As one moves from the informational to the advisory, and from the advisory to the directive, the expert increasingly risks invading, perhaps "usurping," the role of the jury. This mixture of roles accounts for the controversy that has long accompanied their use in court.

Early Judicial Response to Experts

Openness to expertise is a relatively modern phenomenon. Opinions from expert witnesses were not much more welcome in nineteenth and early twentieth century American courts than were inferences drawn by lay witnesses. Before the enactment of the Federal Rules, expert testimony was relatively rare and the scope of testimony comparatively limited. There was little need to categorize expert testimony. Indeed, in the nineteenth and early twentieth centuries, courts did not examine the nature of the expertise but rather merely inquired whether the proposed witness qualified as an expert.[32] The primary inquiry of a court ruling on the admissibility of expert testimony was whether the testimony provided information beyond the knowledge of the average juror. Successful professional experience was usually determinative.[33] Medical testimony by doctors was among the earliest forms of expert testimony.[34] Doctors were respected and well-educated as to the mysteries of medicine, a subject about which most jurors knew almost nothing.

During this period, rules curtailed the influence that an expert might have on the trial. For example, common-law courts often required that the case-specific factual basis of expert testimony be available to the fact-finder, meaning that the case-specific factual basis for the expert testimony had to be put into evidence by other witnesses, except in the case of percipient experts, and that lawyers had to use hypothetical questions in examining non-percipient experts. This also meant that the facts upon which the expert relied had to pass the hurdles of the admissibility rules, most notably the hearsay rule. Some courts prohibited experts from testifying to the ultimate issue, and virtually all courts frowned upon directive experts.[35]

Toward the end of the nineteenth century, various techniques began to develop that engendered modern forensic science, techniques such as handwriting and fingerprint analysis. Unlike expertise grounded in professional practice that existed independent of the courts, such as medicine and engineering, these new forensic techniques were primarily intended for investigatory and courtroom application. The assurance of practical reliability associated with successful professional application in the marketplace outside the courtroom was greatly diminished in the context of these new forensic techniques.[36] While often accepted with little thought, occasionally courts gave serious consideration to the validity of the expertise offered. One such occasion produced a still commonly encountered test for the admissibility of expertise, called the *Frye* test.

---

[32] 1 DAVID L. FAIGMAN ET AL., MODERN SCIENTIFIC EVIDENCE: THE LAW AND SCIENCE OF EXPERT TESTIMONY § 1:2 (2016–17 ed.).

[33] *See* 7 WIGMORE ON EVIDENCE § 1923 (Chadbourn rev. 1978).

[34] Stephan Landsman, *Of Witches, Madmen, and Products Liability: An Historical Survey of the Use of Expert Testimony,* 13 BEHAV. SCI. & L. 131 (1995).

[35] *See* **§ 10.05 & § 10.06**.

[36] *See* Michael J. Saks, *Merlin and Solomon: Lessons from the Law's Formative Encounters with Forensic Identification Science*, 49 HASTINGS L. J. 1069, 1076 (1998).

The Frye *Test*

In 1923, a trial court rejected the expert testimony of an attorney and research psychologist[37] who was prepared to testify that James Frye, a criminal defendant claiming innocence, had passed the "systolic blood pressure deception test," an early form of the "lie detector." Although he seemed to bring to the trial something beyond the knowledge of the average juror, the trial judge's ruling was affirmed with a brief comment that has become the basis of one test of expertise:

> Just when a scientific principle or discovery crosses the line between the experimental and demonstrable stages is difficult to define. Somewhere in this twilight zone the evidential force of the principle must be recognized, and while courts will go a long way in admitting expert testimony deduced from a well-recognized scientific principle or discovery, the thing from which the deduction is made must be sufficiently established to have gained general acceptance in the particular field in which it belongs.[38]

This "general acceptance" test, originally devised to determine the admissibility of testimony about a novel scientific principle, became the dominant standard by which scientific expert testimony would be measured for more than half a century.

Frye's basic rationale rested on the assumption that the scientific community, not judges, should decide when a particular theory or principle is sufficiently reliable to offer it as fact at trial. This method of ruling on the admissibility of expert testimony has an appealing simplicity and likely results in appropriate rulings more often than not, while preserving judicial economy. However, as later courts and commentators explained, the *Frye* test has several drawbacks, not the least of which is that it substitutes the prevailing vogue of the scientific community for judicial oversight.

Enactment of the Federal Rules

The Federal Rules of Evidence codified a sea change in American courts' approach to opinion evidence. Overall, the Federal Rules take a liberal approach to the admission of evidence, and that liberalization is evident in the expanded admissibility of expert testimony. Testimony by experts, once rare, has become commonplace, if not overbearing, in courts of every jurisdiction, and the limitations on their testimony have been relaxed substantially.[39] Expert testimony, be it general background information or an opinion central to the resolution of the particular case, has become a staple of the American trial. It is obvious that the Federal Rules substantially changed the landscape of expert testimony.[40]

Rule 702 defines expertise broadly, extending to "scientific, technical, or other specialized knowledge." Qualification as an expert can stem from knowledge, skill, experience, training, or education. Under Rule 702, expert testimony is no longer limited

---

[37] Marston was also the creator of the comic book super heroine, Wonder Woman. Stephen J. Lyons, *Making a Living out of Looking for Liars; Book Helps Uncover Truth About Polygraph*, CHI. TRIB., April 22, 2007, at C5.

[38] Frye v. United States, 293 F. 1013, 1014 (D.C. Cir. 1923).

[39] *See, e.g.*, Barry J. Brett, *Expanded Use of Expert Witnesses Poses New Problems for Counsel*, NAT'L L.J., Dec. 31, 1979, p. 22; Walter Olson, *The Case Against Expert Witnesses*, FORTUNE, Sept. 15, 1989 at 133.

[40] *See* David Faigman et al., *Check Your Crystal Ball at the Courthouse Door, Please: Exploring the Past, Understanding the Present, and Worrying about the Future of Scientific Evidence*, 15 CARDOZO L. REV. 1799, 1808 (1994).

to information about a subject matter that is beyond the knowledge of the jurors. It is sufficient that the testimony will help the jurors, which presupposes only that the average juror is not as knowledgeable about the subject as the proposed expert.[41] The subjects on which experts can be helpful are many and varied, but recurring examples include: common business practices in a given industry; values of property or businesses; dangerousness of conditions; injury causation; lost earnings; and conventions regarding communication among those in a particular industry, legal or illegal.[42]

As detailed in later sections of this chapter, under the Federal Rules and similar state rules attorneys may solicit expert opinions about specific issues in the case without resort to hypothetical questions. Experts sometimes may offer opinions about the ultimate issue for the jurors' consideration. Finally, expert opinions may be based on case-specific factual materials—documents, out-of-court statements—that are not and could not be admitted into evidence.

The Daubert *Revolution*

The *Frye* test, though not followed in all jurisdictions or supported by all commentators, dominated the admissibility of expert testimony for half a century, including the first two decades under the Federal Rules. Those who opposed the *Frye* test argued that it created a lag period, during which reliable evidence was excluded while the scientific community evaluated a new technique.[43] Proponents of the *Frye* test advocated it as a bulwark against "junk science."[44]

The original version of Rule 702 of the Federal Rules of Evidence required only that the judge decide whether the "scientific, technical, or other specialized knowledge will assist the trier of fact to understand the evidence or to determine a fact in issue" and whether the witness was "qualified as an expert by knowledge, skill, experience, training, or education."[45] Federal courts divided over whether the "general acceptance" test survived enactment of the Rules.[46] In 1993, the Supreme Court settled the issue in *Daubert v. Merrell Dow Pharmaceuticals, Inc.*,[47] holding that the *Frye* test was "incompatible with the Federal Rules and should not be applied in federal trials."[48]

Daubert concerned a claim that the anti-nausea drug, Bendectin, caused birth defects. Bendectin had been the subject of more than thirty published epidemiological studies, covering over a hundred thousand patients, none of which concluded that Bendectin causes birth defects. Nevertheless, eight plaintiff experts were prepared to

---

41 Under modern practice, however, if the subject matter really is "beyond the ken" of lay fact-finders, then expert testimony may not only be permitted; it may be *required*. The most common instances of such requirements are professional malpractice claims, toxic tort causation issues, and actions for institutionalization for mental incompetence. *See* DAVID H. KAYE, DAVID E. BERNSTEIN, & JENNIFER L. MNOOKIN, THE NEW WIGMORE: EXPERT EVIDENCE § 2.5 (2d ed. 2011).

42 *See* 3 CHRISTOPHER B. MUELLER & LAIRD C. KIRKPATRICK, FEDERAL EVIDENCE § 7:10 (4th ed. 2013).

43 *See, e.g.*, Paul C. Giannelli, *The Admissibility of Novel Scientific Evidence: Frye v. United States, a Half-Century Later*, 80 COLUM. L. REV. 1197 (1980).

44 *See, e.g.*, PETER HUBER, GALILEO'S REVENGE: JUNK SCIENCE IN THE COURTROOM (1991); Kenneth J. Chesebro, *Galileo's Retort: Peter Huber's Junk Scholarship*, 42 AM. U. L. REV. 1637 (1993).

45 FED. R. EVID. 702 (emphasis added).

46 *Compare, e.g.*, United States v. Shorter, 809 F.2d 54 (D.C. Cir. 1987) (applying "general acceptance" standard), *with* DeLuca v. Merrell Dow Pharmaceuticals, Inc., 911 F.2d 941 (3d Cir. 1990) (rejecting "general acceptance" standard).

47 509 U.S. 579 (1993).

48 *Id.* at 589.

testify—based on test tube and animal studies, and on re-analysis of prior epidemiological studies—that Bendectin can cause birth defects.[49] The trial court ruled that the opinions of the plaintiffs' experts were inadmissible.[50] Consequently, it granted the defendant's motion for summary judgment because the plaintiffs presented no other evidence of causation. The Ninth Circuit Court of Appeals affirmed, citing *Frye* and stressing the importance of the "general acceptance" standard.[51] The Ninth Circuit Court of Appeals explained: "We impose this requirement because such evidence 'create[s] a substantial danger of undue prejudice or of confusing the issues or of misleading the jury . . . because of its aura of special reliability and trustworthiness.' "[52]

The Supreme Court reversed, holding that after the enactment of Rule 702:

> "General acceptance" is not a necessary precondition to the admissibility of scientific evidence under the Federal Rules of Evidence, but the Rules of Evidence—especially Rule 702—do assign to the trial judge the task of ensuring that an expert's testimony both rests on a reliable foundation and is relevant to the task at hand.[53]

The *Daubert* opinion listed five non-exclusive factors that might assist lower courts in determining whether a claim of scientific knowledge is reliable and thus an appropriate subject for expert testimony:

(1) whether a particular theory or technique can be and has been tested;

(2) whether controls and standards were maintained;

(3) whether the theory has been subject to peer review and publication;

(4) whether there is a known error rate; and

(5) whether the theory has acceptance within the scientific community (similar to *Frye*).[54]

The Court further directed judges to focus "solely on principles and methodology, not on the conclusions that they generate."[55] This portion of the opinion was later legislatively overruled by amendments to Rule 702. Trial courts now must evaluate not only the methodology, but also the conclusions of a proffered expert before allowing him or her to testify under Rule 702.[56]

One other feature of the *Daubert* decision is worth highlighting. Despite the frequent complaints around the time of the decision—in articles, books, and even judicial opinions—about the "aura of infallibility" of experts that might baffle jurors, the Supreme Court's decision did *not* rely upon any such stated concern. Quite the contrary. The Court's only reference to the risk of jury misunderstanding concerned arguments in

---

49 *See* Daubert v. Merrell Dow Pharmaceuticals, Inc., 727 F. Supp. 570 (S.D. Cal. 1989).

50 *Id.* at 575.

51 Daubert v. Merrell Dow Pharmaceuticals, Inc., 951 F.2d 1128, 1129–30 (9th Cir. 1991) (citations omitted).

52 *Id.*

53 *Daubert*, 509 U.S. at 597.

54 *Id.* at 593–94.

55 *Id.* at 595.

56 FED. R. EVID. 702 advisory committee note.

favor of retaining the *Frye* rule in order to reduce that risk. Regarding this argument, the Court stated:

> In this regard respondent seems to us to be overly pessimistic about the capabilities of the jury and of the adversary system generally. Vigorous cross-examination, presentation of contrary evidence, and careful instruction on the burden of proof are the traditional and appropriate means of attacking shaky but admissible evidence.[57]

Elsewhere, the Court noted the availability of Rule 403 to deal with problems of jury misuse.[58] Unfortunately, the Court said virtually nothing affirmative about the purpose of the requirement it imposed. Instead, the Court reasoned in a quite formalistic manner, saying that the requirement of reliability, as a condition on admissibility, simply follows from the requirement that the expertise reflect "scientific knowledge."[59]

In any event, under *Daubert*, trial judges became the gatekeepers of expert testimony, responsible for independent screening of purported science and the reliability of expert witnesses. But *Daubert* left open many questions, including its applicability to non-scientific expert testimony, and the standard of appellate review applicable to trial court rulings on expert testimony.

General Electric Co. v. Joiner,[60] decided four years after *Daubert*, clarified the standard of review. The plaintiff claimed that his small cell lung cancer resulted from exposure to PCBs while working for General Electric. The District Court ruled the testimony of the plaintiff's experts inadmissible and, as a result, granted summary judgment for the defendant. The Eleventh Circuit reversed, applying "a particularly stringent standard of review to the trial judge's exclusion of expert testimony."[61] The Supreme Court overruled the Eleventh Circuit, holding that "abuse of discretion," the least stringent standard of review, is the proper standard of review for a lower court's admission or exclusion of expert testimony, even when such exclusion is outcome determinative.[62]

Two years after *Joiner*, *Kumho Tire Co. v. Carmichael*[63] addressed whether *Daubert* applied to non-scientific expert testimony. The district court granted summary judgment for the defendant tire company after excluding the testimony of the plaintiff's tire expert, who could not show, through publications or otherwise, support for his views about detecting tire abuse. In holding that the exclusion was justified, the Supreme Court said that, although experts who base their testimony on specialized experience rather than formal scientific training need not meet the requirements that might be imposed on

---

[57] *Daubert*, 509 U.S. at 595–96. The Court did not pause to explain how expertise that is admissible, and thus by hypothesis has passed its reliability test, can still be "shaky."

[58] *Id.* at 595. Some lower courts continue to talk about jury misuse of expertise as the rationale underlying the reliability requirement of *Daubert*. *See, e.g.*, SmithKline Beecham Corp. v. Apotex Corp., 247 F. Supp. 2d 1011, 1042 (N.D. Ill. 2003) ("The primary purpose of the *Daubert* filter is to protect juries from being bamboozled by technical evidence of dubious merit.") But more perceptive judges have realized the contrary implications of the Court's opinion. *See, e.g.*, *In re* Paoli R.R. Yard PCB Litig., 35 F.3d 717, 746–47 (3d Cir. 1994) (per Becker, J.) (noting that *Daubert* took the dangers of confusing or overwhelming the jury out of the reliability test of Rule 702 and committed them to analysis under Rule 403).

[59] *Daubert*, 509 U.S. at 589–90.

[60] 522 U.S. 136 (1997).

[61] *Id.* at 140 (citing Joiner v. General Elec. Co., 78 F.3d 524, 529 (11th Cir. 1996)).

[62] *Id.* at 142–43.

[63] 526 U.S. 137 (1999).

scientific testimony, they must nevertheless use a demonstrably valid methodology. The Court agreed with the trial judge that the expert's theory, in addition to having no demonstrable support from others in the field, was not supported by adequate data or other explanation. In addition to refuting those cases that had drawn a sharp distinction between "specialized" knowledge and "scientific" knowledge,[64] *Kumho* emphasized the flexibility and discretion exercised by a trial judge by holding that the helpfulness of the expert "depends upon the particular circumstances of the particular case at issue."[65] The list of *Daubert* factors "was meant to be helpful, not definitive," and not all of the factors will necessarily apply.

Although in some ways the *Daubert* approach expands the admissibility of expert testimony, it also limits evidence that would have been unthinkingly admitted under *Frye*. As the Court in *Kumho* noted, the presence of general acceptance cannot render an expert's testimony reliable "where the discipline itself lacks reliability."[66] Examples may include handwriting[67] and fiber[68] analyses, which do not (currently) seem very reliable but have been traditionally accepted by the courts. Post-*Daubert* courts have even re-examined the reliability of fingerprint identification.[69] As a general rule, courts still routinely allow expert testimony on handwriting and fiber analysis, but the door is now open to challenge such testimony under the proper circumstances.[70] It is highly unlikely, however, that testimony as to fingerprint identification will be categorically excluded anytime soon.[71] The *Daubert* opinion advises courts that "vigorous cross-examination, presentation of contrary evidence, and careful instruction on the burden of proof are the traditional and appropriate means of attacking shaky but admissible evidence."[72] Hence, future studies casting doubt on venerated areas of expert testimony are likely to go to the weight of such testimony, not the admissibility.

To complicate matters, although the rule is written to apply equally in civil and criminal cases, in practice it has been applied more rigorously in civil tort cases,

---

64 *See, e.g.*, McKendall v. Crown Control Corp., 122 F.3d 803, 807 (9th Cir. 1997).

65 *Kumho,* 526 U.S. at 150.

66 *Id.* at 150–51.

67 *See* NATIONAL RESEARCH COUNCIL, STRENGTHENING FORENSIC SCIENCE IN THE UNITED STATES: A PATH FORWARD 163–67 (2009).

68 *Id.* at 161–63.

69 United States v. Crisp, 324 F.3d 261, 268–69 (4th Cir. 2003); United States v. Havvard, 260 F.3d 597, 600–01 (7th Cir. 2001).

70 *See Crisp*, 324 F.3d at 269 ("While Crisp may be correct that further research, more searching scholarly review, and the development of even more consistent professional standards is desirable, he has offered us no reason to reject outright a form of evidence that has so ably withstood the test of time."). On handwriting identification testimony, *see* **§ 10.08**.

71 As a practical matter, fingerprint identification evidence has been allowed post-*Daubert* by every circuit court to consider the issue. *See* United States v. Pena, 586 F.3d 105, 110–111 (1st Cir. 2009) (affirming trial court's admission of fingerprint evidence without holding a *Daubert* hearing); United States v. Stevens, 219 Fed. Appx. 108, 109 (2d Cir. 2007) (same); United States v. Mitchell, 365 F.3d 215, 221 (3d Cir. 2004) (applying thoroughly *Daubert* factors point-by-point to latent fingerprint identification evidence); United States v. John, 597 F.3d 263, 274–75 (5th Cir. 2010) (suggesting reliability of fingerprint identification is so well-known that individualized *Daubert* inquiry is not necessary "absent novel challenges"); United States v. Stone, 218 Fed. Appx. 425, 442 (6th Cir. 2007) (affirming admission of fingerprint identification evidence); United States v. Havvard, 260 F.3d 597, 601 (7th Cir. 2001) (same); United States v. Spotted Elk, 548 F.3d 641, 663 (8th Cir. 2008) (same); United States v. Calderon-Segura, 512 F.3d 1104, 1110 (9th Cir. 2008) (same); United States v. Baines, 573 F.3d 979, 991–92 (10th Cir. 2009) (same); United States v. Douglas, 489 F.3d 1117, 1124–25 (11th Cir. 2007) (affirming introduction of evidence of age of fingerprint).

72 Daubert v. Merrell Dow Pharmaceuticals, Inc., 509 U.S. 579, 596 (1993), *quoted in Crisp*, 324 F.3d at 270.

screening out the plaintiff's experts, and less rigorously in criminal cases, involving prosecution experts testifying on dubious forensic science techniques.[73]

The 2000 Amendments to Rule 702

The 2000 Amendments to Rule 702 codified *Daubert* and *Kumho* and provided general standards for the trial court to assess the reliability and helpfulness of proffered expert testimony. It did not give the trial judge much more to go on. Since 2000, Rule 702 now requires the Court to make three additional specific findings:

(1) the testimony is based upon sufficient facts or data;

(2) the testimony is the product of reliable principles and methods; and

(3) the witness has applied the principles and methods reliably to the facts of the case.

While the 2000 amendments partially codified *Daubert* and *Kumho*,[74] the third requirement in the rule, that the witness applied the underlying principles reliably to the facts of the case, is contrary to the portion of *Daubert* that directs trial judges to focus only on the methods and not on the results of the proffered expert.[75] Whether this was a misreading of *Daubert* or a minor correction of an opinion lawmakers otherwise approved of is unclear and, ultimately, unimportant.[76] The 2000 amendments clearly allow a trial judge to exclude the opinion of a purported expert if the court finds the conclusion of that opinion inconsistent with the application of reliable principles.

Which Test Should States Adopt—**Daubert** *or* **Frye?**

While everyone agrees that judges must play some role in screening out "junk science" and other deficient claims of expertise, scholars and practitioners do not agree as to when and how much judges should defer to the community of experts in screening evidence.

Daubert (as codified in the 2000 amendment to Rule 702) binds federal courts but not necessarily state courts, even those that have adopted rules on experts that are equivalent to the Federal Rules. A state's highest court is free to interpret state rules as it sees fit, notwithstanding the fact that federal courts interpret identical Federal Rules differently. The language of the rule prior to the 2000 amendment, requiring simply that scientific, technical, or other specialized knowledge must assist the trier of fact, hardly requires the adoption of the *Daubert* test, and several state supreme courts have had little difficulty finding in these same words rather different requirements.[77] If *Frye* is better than *Daubert* on policy grounds, then it presents a better way of deciding what

---

[73] Erica Beecher-Monas, *Reality Bites: The Illusion of Science in Bite-Mark Evidence*, 30 CARDOZO L. REV. 1369, 1371 (2009).

[74] The advisory committee note to Rule 702 states that the purpose of the amendment is to codify *Daubert* and *Kumho* and to provide "some general standards that the trial court must use to assess the reliability and helpfulness of proffered expert testimony."

[75] *See Daubert*, 509 U.S. at 597.

[76] *Cf.* FED. R. EVID. 702 advisory committee note ("Under the amendment, as under *Daubert*, when an expert purports to apply principles and methods in accordance with professional standards, and yet reaches a conclusion that other experts in the field would not reach, the trial court may fairly suspect that the principles and methods have not been faithfully applied.").

[77] *See, e.g.*, Marron v. Stromstad, 123 P.3d 992 (Alaska 2005); Searles v. Fleetwood Homes of Pennsylvania, Inc., 878 A.2d 509 (Me. 2005); and Higgs v. State, 222 P.3d 648 (Nev. 2010); Grady v. Frito-Lay, Inc., 839 A.2d 1038 (Pa. 2003).

will "assist" under the rule and vice-versa.[78] A number of states, including the influential jurisdictions of California[79] and New York,[80] still use the *Frye* test or some version of it.

The *Frye* test promotes judicial economy whereby judges defer to the scientific community. If scientists in the field believe that a principle is valid, then judges should admit expert testimony as to that principle. If scientists in the field do not accept the principle—if, for example, they believe that the polygraph test is not reliable—then judges should exclude the evidence. Supporters of *Frye* would argue that experts are best qualified to determine which principles and methods are reliable. Judges should not try to become amateur scientists. Experts are better qualified to make such judgments, and it is a better use of everyone's time.

The *Frye* approach also seems consistent with the day-to-day reality that deference to expert authority is the norm. For instance, the only way that the informed lay-person knows that the earth goes around the sun is by trust of authority: the Copernican conclusion cannot be reached by lay observation or by lay evaluation of the raw data.[81]

Even if judges are capable of doing the job assigned by *Daubert*, a cost-benefit analysis might call for a less onerous approach. Is learning the basics of the scientific method the best use of judges' time? Study of the scientific method will come at the cost of the study of something else. Perhaps judges would be better off reading Holmes, Cardozo, or Wigmore, or merely studying with greater care the facts and law in the cases pending before them. But supporters of *Daubert* insist that scientific literacy is a necessity in contemporary life, and time may prove them right.

If the core value of *Frye* is judicial economy, it might be said that the core value *Daubert* promotes is judicial integrity. Under *Daubert*, a judge has broad discretion in deciding how much weight to place on the view of the expert community. Judges may also appoint third-party experts to aid in determining difficult evidentiary questions.[82] Federal judges are public officials with authority vested in them by the Constitution of the United States. *Daubert* resists the replacement of the judgment of trusted public officials with the say-so of privately employed professionals from various non-legal fields.

A rigid application of *Frye* might hold courts hostage to industry dogma or vogue. Distinguished jurists have pointed out that even industry-wide custom may follow logically indefensible or legally negligent custom.[83] Similarly, courts may rightly balk at the logical conclusion of *Frye* that not only should the consensus opinion of a particular science or industry be *per se* admissible, but also all other coherent theories should be

---

[78] In analyzing Rule 702, the Supreme Court merely observed that "[n]othing in the text of this Rule establishes 'general acceptance' as an absolute prerequisite to admissibility." Daubert v. Merrell Dow Pharm., Inc., 509 U.S. 579, 588 (1993). Arguably, this is a pretty weak reed on which to base a conclusion that the *Daubert* approach is required by the Federal Rules of Evidence. Deference to authority is one of the background assumptions of the legal system. The judge has to find some way to determine whether the evidence is helpful science or whether it is junk science that will only do harm. The judge cannot become a true scientist—a population geneticist one week and an epidemiologist the next—so some shortcut is necessary to implement the requirement that the testimony assist the trier of fact. *Frye* is one shortcut, *Daubert* another; the original text of the rule provided no guidance about which to use beyond what one would get by deciding which is better as a matter of policy.

[79] *See* People v. Kelly, 549 P.2d 1240 (Cal. 1976).

[80] *See* People v. Wesley, 633 N.E.2d 451 (N.Y. 1994).

[81] *See* RICHARD A. POSNER, THE PROBLEMS OF JURISPRUDENCE 79 (1990). Ironically, however, a *Frye*-type deference in Copernicus' time would have excluded his claims as not generally accepted.

[82] Rule 706 provides for court-appointed experts, but this authority is rarely invoked.

[83] *See* The T. J. Hooper, 60 F.2d 737, 740 (2d Cir. 1932) (opinion by Learned Hand).

excluded. Moreover, the application of *Frye* can present serious difficulties of defining the relevant scientific or professional community in which to assess consensus as well as the percentage of the community (or other measure) that determines whether a consensus exists. Arguably, it is healthy to have judges adopt a scientific perspective and ask, "Can this be tested?" "Where are your data?" Some fields, including ones whose practitioners have traditionally been allowed to testify, do not have a strong tradition of data collection and impartial testing. This is true of many areas of forensic science, such as handwriting and hair analysis.[84]

Aside from these competing policy perspectives, *Frye* has one distinct conceptual advantage over *Daubert*. The opinion in *Frye* explicitly (and rightly) recognized that reliability or trustworthiness is a gradational attribute—a matter of more or less. In contrast, *Daubert* spoke as if trial courts make findings, by a preponderance of the evidence, about a dichotomous attribute: reliable or not. Recognizing the gradational quality of reliability leads to the inevitable, more nuanced and appropriate question: How reliable is reliable enough for the particular purpose of admitting the proposed testimony?[85] *Frye*'s answer was simple to state, if difficult to apply: as soon as the technique is reliable enough to gain general acceptance among the relevant community of experts. As detailed in the following section, neither *Daubert* nor its codification in Rule 702 gives any answer to this question at all. Not surprisingly, there continues to be support for some version of the *Frye* approach that relies upon the consensus of experts in the field.[86]

§ 10.04 Admissible Expertise [FRE 702]

Under the federal and comparable state rules, Rule 702 is the primary regulator of expert testimony at trial. It specifies when claimed expertise is admissible. Before an expert may present testimony to the jury, the trial judge, as gatekeeper of the evidence, evaluates the expert testimony based on the requirements of Rule 702 and the guidance of *Daubert*. As one commentator has written, "[t]he single most important 'guidepost' contained in *Daubert* is the Court's directive to judges to actively evaluate scientific evidence."[87]

Testimony is admissible under amended Rule 702 only if the court finds:

(1) the testimony consists of scientific, technical, or other specialized knowledge;

(2) the testimony will assist the trier of fact to understand evidence or to determine a fact in issue;

(3) the witness offering such testimony is qualified as an expert by knowledge, skill, experience, training, or education;

(4) the testimony is based on sufficient facts or data;

---

[84] 4 DAVID L. FAIGMAN ET AL., MODERN SCIENTIFIC EVIDENCE: THE LAW AND SCIENCE OF EXPERT TESTIMONY §§ 29:53, 29:58 (2016–17 ed.) (finding handwriting identification and hair identification highly vulnerable to attack on *Daubert* grounds).

[85] *See* Dale A. Nance, *Reliability and the Admissibility of Experts,* 34 SETON HALL L. REV. 191 (2003).

[86] *See, e.g.,* Edward K. Cheng, *The Consensus Rule: A New Approach to Scientific Evidence*, 75 VAND. L. REV. (forthcoming, 2022) (arguing that the jury, rather than judge, should determine and rely on the consensus of the scientific community in resolving issues for which expertise exists).

[87] David L. Faigman, *Mapping the Labyrinth of Scientific Evidence*, 46 HASTINGS L.J. 555 (1995).

(5) the testimony is the product of reliable principles and methods; and

(6) the witness has applied the principles and methods reliably to the facts of the case.

Each of these conditions is considered in the following paragraphs.

Does the testimony consist of scientific, technical, or other specialized knowledge?

While it is possible to debate the vagaries of whether a given discipline reflects "scientific" "technical," or some "other specialized" knowledge, the preliminary criterion of Rule 702 requires only that the proffered testimony fit any one of these categories. The court need not select which category the testimony most properly occupies. The difference among "scientific" and "technical" and "other specialized" knowledge may be important when determining whether proffered testimony is based on reliable principles or methods,[88] but the scope of Rule 702 is quite broad.[89]

The breadth of the notion of specialized knowledge is suggested by the reference in the rule to those qualified by "knowledge, skill, experience, training, or education." For example, one federal court allowed the testimony of a frequent marijuana user as to the quality and origin of certain marijuana the "expert" smoked. The specialized knowledge here is the ability to identify marijuana by smoking it.[90]

Will the testimony assist the trier of fact to understand evidence or determine a fact in issue?

Pre-Rules common-law courts sometimes excluded testimony unless the subject matter was entirely "beyond the ken" of lay fact-finders. The Federal Rules approach is less demanding: even if lay fact-finders can be assumed to have some knowledge of the matter, courts permit expert testimony if it would be helpful, that is, if it would improve, qualify, or even negate the background knowledge that fact-finders bring to the case.[91] Helpfulness is the most important requirement for expert testimony and usually presents a very context specific inquiry.[92]

Testimony might fail the requirement to assist the trier of fact in two primary ways: first, the testimony might "merely put an expert gloss on a conclusion the jury should draw."[93] For example, an expert opinion on drug dealer lingo will not assist the jury in interpreting a recording where the accused clearly states, "I will sell you one gram of my finest cocaine for one hundred dollars," because the meaning of the statement is

---

[88] *See* Kumho v. Carmichael, 526 U.S. 137, 150–151 (1999); First Tenn. Bank Nat'l Ass'n v. Barreto, 268 F.3d 319, 332 (6th Cir. 2001).

[89] *See Barreto*, 268 F.3d at 332.

[90] United States v. Johnson, 575 F.2d 1347, 1362 (5th Cir. 1978), *cert. denied*, 440 U.S. 907 (1979). It is unclear whether this issue would be resolved similarly under *Daubert*. The liberality in the breadth of permissible expertise should inherently constrain the scope of lay opinion under Rule 701(c). *See* **§ 10.02**. By contrast, in United States v. Westbrook, 896 F.2d 330 (8th Cir. 1990), two "lay" witnesses who were heavy users of amphetamine were permitted to testify that a substance was amphetamine. Both cases pre-date the amendment to Rule 701, which added the explicit restriction of 701(c). However, *Westbrook* is cited approvingly by the drafters of that amendment without any effort to account for cases like *Johnson*. See FED. R. EVID. 701 advisory committee note for 2000 amendment.

[91] *See* DAVID H. KAYE, DAVID E. BERNSTEIN, & JENNIFER L. MNOOKIN, THE NEW WIGMORE: EXPERT EVIDENCE § 2.1 (2d ed. 2011).

[92] *See* 7 WIGMORE ON EVIDENCE § 1923 at 29 (Chadbourn rev. 1978) (observing that the proper question is: "On *this subject* can a jury receive from *this person* appreciable help?").

[93] United States v. York, 572 F.3d 415, 423 (7th Cir. 2009) (" 'Interpretations' of unambiguous words or phrases that are plainly within the jury's understanding are unlikely to be admissible under Rule 702.").

unambiguous. Similarly, a sociologist's opinion is not helpful to a jury's assessment of whether a police officer's use of derogatory terms, like "bitch" and "fucking idiot," in reference to a woman seeking police protection represents gender discrimination.[94] This aspect of the requirement is the source of many rulings limiting the use of expert testimony.[95]

Second, the testimony might not sufficiently inform the jury regarding any fact in issue. For example, if a criminal defendant claims self-defense after being charged with killing a police officer, a court might exclude expert testimony that the slain officer improperly served a search warrant on the defendant, because whether the officer's objective actions followed proper procedure is not sufficiently related to whether those objective actions conveyed the fact that the officer was in fact law enforcement.[96] This requirement is very similar, but is not necessarily identical, to the relevancy standard.

Is the witness who is offering testimony qualified as an expert by knowledge, skill, training, experience, or education?

Rule 702 allows an expert to be qualified through both formal education and training and informal experience. At least in theory, no matter how someone gained scientific, technical, or other specialized knowledge, he or she may convey that knowledge to jurors. Under Rule 702, both an academic with a PhD in botany, and a lifelong farmer with a high school education should be allowed to explain the lifecycle of crops to jurors. Indeed, a carpenter, plumber, or other skilled worker, even one without a day of formal education, can qualify as an expert if the person's experience provides specialized knowledge.[97]

A proffered expert may not be qualified within the meaning of Rule 702 if he or she has been long absent from the field of purported expertise,[98] or if his or her field of expertise is significantly different from the necessary expertise. The simple fact that a witness is qualified as an expert in one discipline does not mean he or she is qualified as an expert in other disciplines. For example, an orthopedic surgeon may not be qualified to opine that an injury was caused by the ingestion of a pharmaceutical.[99] The more complex the area of claimed expertise, the greater the qualifications required, so that experience alone may not be enough to qualify a witness to testify to complex sociological phenomena.[100]

---

[94] Cooper v. City of Chicago Heights, 85 Fed. R. Evid. Serv. 554, 2011 WL 2116394 (N.D. Ill. 2011).

[95] *See* **§ 10.06**.

[96] *See* United States v. Wilk, 572 F.3d 1229, 1235 (11th Cir. 2009) (finding that fact that victim-officer was dressed in civilian clothes was admissible, but whether this violated internal police standards was not related to the perception of defendant at time he shot victim and was therefore inadmissible).

[97] *See, e.g.*, FED. R. EVID. 702, advisory committee note; *see also* United States v. Frazier, 322 F.3d 1262, 1267 (11th Cir. 2003) (explaining admission of expert testimony in *Maiz* and similar cases); Maiz v. Virani, 253 F.3d 641, 668–69 (11th Cir. 2001) (affirming admission of expert testimony as to immigration practices based on personal experience and not on formal training).

[98] *See* Ronwin v. Bayer Corp., 332 Fed. Appx. 508, 512–13 (10th Cir. 2009) (upholding exclusion of one expert's opinion do to "lengthy departure from active research, publication, and teaching").

[99] *See id.* (upholding exclusion of orthopedic surgeon's opinion that rotator cuff tear was due to drug Baycol despite surgeon never having dealt with that drug before).

[100] *See*, e.g., Jinro America, Inc. v. Secure Investments, Inc., 266 F.3d 993 (9th Cir. 2001) (rejecting, over concurring opinion, the admissibility of testimony of experienced commercial security investigator regarding the reliability of Korean business commitments).

Is the testimony based on sufficient facts or data?

Whether testimony is based on sufficient facts or data depends significantly on the nature of the testimony. An expert may be allowed to testify about general principles of his or her field of expertise based on nothing more than his or her qualifying experience. For example, a doctor may be allowed to testify about heart attack risk factors based on nothing more than his or her medical training. However, to testify that a specific individual had risk factors for a heart attack, that same doctor must base his or her opinion on more specific information. The body of knowledge constituting the expertise will determine which case-specific facts or data must be present in order to warrant a particular opinion.

Expert opinions regarding the facts of the case, such as whether a defendant's conduct caused the plaintiff's loss, should be supported by the study of case-specific information, not just general principles or common sense.[101] If a conclusion naturally follows from general principles of an expert's discipline, the expert may (but is not usually required to) simply testify as to those general principles and allow the jury to reach the proper conclusion on its own. (If a particular conclusion naturally follows from the facts of the case based on common sense alone, expert testimony is superfluous because the jury will reach the proper conclusion without expert assistance.)

Is the testimony the result of reliable principles and methods?

Whether proffered expert testimony is the product of reliable principles or methods is probably the most fiercely litigated aspect of Rule 702. As discussed above, the *Daubert* opinion gives some guidance as to what factors a trial court should consider in resolving this question. The five non-exclusive factors listed in *Daubert* are whether:

(1) a particular theory or technique can be and has been tested;

(2) controls and standards were maintained;

(3) the theory has been subject to peer review and publication;

(4) there is a known error rate; and

(5) the theory has acceptance within the scientific community.[102]

These *Daubert* factors were never intended to be mandatory or exclusive, and lower courts have added to the list. The Advisory Committee Note to the 2000 amendment of Rule 702 acknowledges and approves of some of additional factors including whether:

- experts are "proposing to testify about matters growing naturally and directly out of research they have conducted independent of the litigation, or whether they have developed their opinions expressly for purposes of testifying;"[103]

---

[101] *See* IQ Prods. Co. v. Pennzoil Prods. Co., 305 F.3d 368, 376–77 (5th Cir. 2002) (finding that market analyst was not allowed to testify that defendant's misleading statements caused consumers to purchase defendant's product rather than plaintiff's when analyst had done no market surveys or similar research related to those statements).

[102] *See* Daubert v. Merrell Dow Pharm., Inc., 509 U.S. 579, 593–94 (1993).

[103] Daubert v. Merrell Dow Pharm., Inc., 43 F.3d 1311, 1317 (9th Cir. 1995), *cited with approval in* FED. R. EVID. 702 advisory committee note.

- the expert has adequately accounted for obvious alternative explanations;[104] and
- the field of expertise claimed by the expert is known to reach reliable results for the type of opinion the expert would give.[105]

Although *Kumho* and the 2000 amendment to the Rule make clear that *Daubert's* gatekeeper-reliability approach applies irrespective of the category, it is equally clear that the judge's task and the standards by which the judge determines whether the "testimony is the product of reliable principles and methods" will differ depending upon the category. Painstaking analysis of reliability factors is not appropriate in every situation. The Court in *Kumho* suggested that trial judges have the proper authority "to avoid unnecessary 'reliability' proceedings in ordinary cases where the reliability of an expert's methods is properly taken for granted."[106]

Furthermore, categorization is not always so obvious. Some enterprises are easy to categorize—the existence and structure of the atom is "scientific," the diagram for putting together a computer is "technical," and the best apple shape for shipping purposes might be considered "other specialized knowledge"—but not every example is so simple. Is how a cyclotron smashes atoms scientific or technical? Is how a computer processes information technical or scientific? What category is handicapping racehorses or predicting future earning potential?

It is difficult to overemphasize the discretion afforded trial courts in determining whether proffered testimony is reliably founded. As the Court stated in *Kumho*, "the trial judge must have considerable leeway in deciding in a particular case how to go about determining whether particular expert testimony is reliable."[107] Thus, the unspoken but potentially dispositive factor in resolving reliability for the purposes of Rule 702 is the experience, research, and discretion of the trial court judge.

Has the witness reliably applied the principles and methods to the facts of the case?

Even if it is established that an expert witness's testimony is the result of (sufficiently) reliable principles and methods, the court can still exclude the testimony if it finds that those principles and methods were not correctly applied to the facts of the case. It is rare for a court to exclude testimony for this reason alone. Usually an expert will testify as to the actual methods that he or she employed. Unless the witness states a conclusion that is clearly inconsistent with the methods he or she claims to have followed, or there are conspicuous holes in the expert's logic,[108] there is little room to object that the witness has not reliably applied the methods that he or she has already testified to applying.

For example, suppose that a witness testifies that he has applied a method of fingerprint analysis that requires eight matching points between two samples of fingerprints to determine that the fingerprints come from the same person, but the witness later testifies that he concluded that two sets of fingerprints are from the same

---

[104] FED. R. EVID. 702 advisory committee note.

[105] *Id.* Admittedly, this factor borders on tautology.

[106] Kumho Tire Co. v. Carmichael, 526 U.S. 137, 152 (1999), *cited with approval in* FED. R. EVID. 702 advisory committee note.

[107] *Id.*

[108] *See, e.g.*, Fireman Fund Ins. Co. v. Canon, 394 F.3d 1054 (8th Cir. 2005) (expert's testimony on cause of fire rejected because of faulty logic).

person based on only five points of similarity. The court may find that although the witness's principles—requiring eight points of similarity—were reliable, the witness did not employ those principles reliably because he based his conclusion on only five points of similarity.[109] It is very unusual for an expert witness to make such an obvious mistake. Hence, it is far more likely that a court will exclude testimony based on the application of unreliable principles rather than based on the unreliable application of reliable principles. Generally, courts encourage adversaries to challenge the way an expert has applied his or her methods through cross-examination and through the proffer of opposing experts who may explain flaws in the first expert's conclusions.[110]

Has the proponent met its burden of establishing the foregoing requirements?

Generally, the proponent of an expert witness has the burden of establishing, by a preponderance of the evidence, the requirements that the expert is qualified and that the expertise supporting the testimony is reliable and reliably applied.[111] Drawing on Rule 104(a), which governs preliminary determinations, that sounds simple enough, but such preliminary judicial fact-finding is much more complicated. As noted at the end of the previous section, reliability of expertise is a matter of degree, falling on a continuum from extremely reliable to worthless. The same is true of the qualifications of an expert. The real questions, therefore, are whether the expertise is *sufficiently* reliable and whether the particular expert is *sufficiently* qualified. Without more, it is difficult to squeeze such determinations into a binary model of a fact to be found either true or false by a preponderance of the evidence.[112]

In particular, neither the Supreme Court case law nor the codification of the reliability requirement in Rule 702 provides guidance about the following:

(a) how to prioritize the various factors affecting reliability or to synthesize the degree of success of proposed expertise regarding the various factors into an overall assessment of reliability;

(b) the purposes to be achieved by the admissibility ruling in this context; or

(c) how to use the assessment in (a) to achieve the purpose(s) in (b).

As a result, Rule 702 does not provide a coherent rule of decision. The norm expressed in both *Daubert* and Rule 702 is, in this respect, analogous to a hypothetical version of Rule 403 that would read simply: "The court may exclude relevant evidence if its probative value is substantially outweighed." Even with detailed instruction on how to assess "probative value," including a detailed specification of the factors that affect it, this directive begs the central question: "Outweighed by what?"[113] At best, the Court's

---

[109] *Cf.* United States v. Vargas, 471 F.3d 255, 265–66 (1st Cir. 2006) (finding no error where trial court admitted testimony of fingerprint expert who applied method requiring eight points of matching, and found twenty, but only demonstrated five to jury as examples).

[110] *See* Ruiz-Troche v. Pepsi Cola of P.R. Bottling Co., 161 F.3d 77, 85 (1st Cir. 1998) ("As long as an expert's scientific testimony rests upon 'good grounds, based on what is known,' it should be tested by the adversary process—competing expert testimony and active cross-examination—rather than excluded from jurors' scrutiny for fear that they will not grasp its complexities or satisfactorily weigh its inadequacies.").

[111] *See* 1 DAVID L. FAIGMAN ET AL., MODERN SCIENTIFIC EVIDENCE: THE LAW AND SCIENCE OF EXPERT TESTIMONY §§ 1:8, 1:9 (2016–17 ed.).

[112] See DAVID H. KAYE, DAVID E. BERNSTEIN, & JENNIFER L. MNOOKIN, THE NEW WIGMORE: EXPERT EVIDENCE § 7.5.3 at 347 (2d ed. 2011) (concluding for this reason that "it seems sensible to adjust the requisite degree of validity to the specific use to which the evidence is put").

[113] Interestingly, one of the first post-*Daubert* efforts at codifying a reliability requirement, put forward by House Republicans in 1995 as part of their "Contract with America," included a test that the opinion be

Daubert decision and Rule 702 simply direct lower courts to pay attention to reliability (again, without simply deferring to the opinions of experts in the relevant field). At worst, it invites courts to make decisions about the sufficiency of the evidence offered by the proponent of the expert in the guise of making admissibility rulings.[114] To the extent that the new rule's directive effects an improvement, it is because courts have found, albeit implicitly, helpful ways to fill out this starkly incomplete reliability requirement.[115]

§ 10.05 The Case-Specific Factual Basis of Opinion Testimony by Experts [FRE 703, 705]

An expert necessarily testifies based on general factual information that is part of her expertise, that is, part of her "scientific, technical, or other specialized knowledge." But to give an opinion about the case being litigated, the expert must apply that expertise to the particular facts of the case. Common law carefully regulated this case-specific factual basis for an expert opinion, limiting experts to opinions based on case-specific facts that are evidenced in court or uncontested. The evidenced facts could be provided by the testimony of other witnesses, or by admitted documents, or case-specific facts observed by the expert and reported as part of the expert's testimony. Suppose a doctor was called to testify at a murder trial that, in her opinion, the victim died from a blow to the back of the head. Before the doctor could give such opinion testimony at common law, the facts underlying that opinion must have already been presented to the jury. Such facts might include the location of the victim's body when the skull fractured and internal bleeding began. If the facts are evidenced, but controverted, the proponent of the expert could elicit the testimony of the expert by asking the expert to assume, hypothetically, the facts to be resolved in a certain way by the fact-finder and indicate the expert's opinion on that assumption.

Such rules still prevail in some jurisdictions, even those that have otherwise adopted much of the Federal Rules.[116] But a substantial and controversial liberalization

---

"sufficiently reliable so that the probative value of such evidence outweighs the dangers specified in rule 403." *See* Attorney Accountability Act of 1995, HR. 998, 104th Cong. § 3. Unfortunately, nothing as concrete as that language, which would have created a "reverse-403" test, was ultimately adopted by Congress.

114 *See* Dale A. Nance, *Reliability and the Admissibility of Experts,* 34 SETON HALL L. REV. 191, 193–219 (2003).

115 *See id.* at 220–52 (identifying three seemingly plausible purposes of the reliability requirement—offsetting jury incompetence, avoiding the expense of considering minimally useful expertise, and encouraging parties to present the most reliable expertise practically available—and concluding that only the last two are compatible with either the *Daubert* opinion or what is known about jury behavior). Interestingly, most courts and commentators pause to consider the specific purposes of the *Daubert* rule only in the context of deciding whether it applies in bench trials. In that context, for example, one treatise defends its application in bench trials by explaining that:

> The *Daubert* gate not only blocks the entry of unreliable expert testimony in order to protect jurors from being bamboozled, it also protects: (1) opponents from having to muster evidence and resources to counter junk expertise; (2) the judicial system from wasting time and resources; and (3) the integrity of the system from seeming reliance on (or countenance of) bad science.

1 DAVID L. FAIGMAN ET AL., MODERN SCIENTIFIC EVIDENCE: THE LAW AND SCIENCE OF EXPERT TESTIMONY § 1:10 at 37–38 (2016–17 ed.). Commentators frustrated with judicial recalcitrance in implementing the demands of *Daubert* might do well to focus on the current incompleteness of its decision rule. *Cf.* David E. Bernstein & Eric G. Lasker, *Defending* Daubert*: It's Time to Amend Federal Rule of Evidence* 702, 57 WM. & MARY L. REV. 1 (2015) (suggesting amendatory language to further encourage rigorous judicial scrutiny of expert testimony but neglecting to incorporate a decision rule that would specify how reliable is reliable enough for admission).

116 *See, e.g.,* OHIO R. EVID. 703, 705.

in the Federal Rules expands the range of case-specific information upon which experts may rely. Rule 703 clarifies that an expert's opinion testimony may be based on information the expert has personally observed or information "the expert has been made aware of." Essentially, as long as the expert's opinion passes Rule 702 muster, it can be based on virtually any case-specific information available to the expert in any way. For example, in the previous example, under the Federal Rules, the doctor may be able to give her opinion even if none of the facts underlying her opinion about the cause of death are presented to the jury.

In fact, Rule 703 clarifies that the information used to form the testifying expert's opinion need not be otherwise *admissible* as evidence at trial as long as experts in the same field reasonably rely upon information of the same type. This means that the Rules largely cede to experts the discretion to make conclusions the way they normally would in their field. Experts may rely on hearsay, character evidence, and unauthenticated documents if this is the accepted method of gathering information in their fields. For instance, an expert testifying as to why a plane crashed may rely on out-of-court statements of eyewitnesses whose statements are not admitted in court and might not be admissible. Or, a doctor may give her opinion even if it is based on a nurse's report that is otherwise inadmissible.[117]

The point of this liberalization in Rule 703 is to "bring judicial practice into line with the practice of the experts themselves when not in court."[118] The Advisory Committee Note focuses on the circumstances of medical experts, noting that physicians rely upon "statements by patients and relatives, reports and opinions from nurses, technicians, and other doctors, hospital records and x-rays" to make "life-and-death decisions." The Committee proposes that those opinions and hearsay "ought to suffice for judicial purposes." Despite the "life-and-death" rationale, the Rule is not so restricted.[119] Experts testifying about everything from product liability[120] to land value[121] to chemical composition[122] have relied upon hearsay and the opinions of others in presenting their testimony.[123] But there are certainly cases in which hearsay has been rejected as a basis

[117] The language of the rule leaves open the possible interpretation that an expert may base his or her opinion on facts or data *not* relied upon by other experts in the field so long as those facts or data are also admissible as evidence. This would seem to pose not a question of compliance with Rule 703, but rather a question of the adequacy of the expert's opinion under Rule 702.

[118] FED. R. EVID. 703 advisory committee note.

[119] Even in the case of life and death decisions by medical personnel, the rationale for the rule takes a rather naïve mid-twentieth century attitude toward the reliability of medical decision-making. *See, e.g.,* Martin Makary & Michael Daniel, *Medical Error—The Third Leading Cause of Death in the U.S.,* 353 BRIT. MED. J. i2139 (2016).

[120] *See, e.g.,* Lewis v. Rego Co., 757 F.2d 66 (3d Cir. 1985).

[121] *See, e.g.,* United States v. 1,014.16 Acres, 558 F. Supp. 1238 (W.D. Mo.1983).

[122] *See, e.g.,* United States v. Smith, 964 F.2d 885 (9th Cir. 1992).

[123] For other cases admitting opinions based at least partly upon hearsay reports of others, see First Nat'l Bank of Louisville v. Lustig, 96 F.3d 1554, 1575 (5th Cir. 1996) (allowing "expert in civil fraud detection and investigation" to testify for bank that bank relied on loan officer's misrepresentations in approving loans even though witness had no personal knowledge of this fact; "experts may rely on hearsay evidence in forming their opinions"); Nachtsheim v. Beech Aircraft Corp., 847 F.2d 1261, 1270 (7th Cir. 1988) (finding admissible expert opinion relying on hearsay); United States v. Rollins, 862 F.2d 1282, 1293 (7th Cir. 1988) (finding expert testimony properly admitted even though based partially on word meanings supplied by informant); United States v. Lundy, 809 F.2d 392, 395 (7th Cir. 1987) (finding expert's testimony based partially upon hearsay and third-party observations was properly admitted); United States v. Posey, 647 F.2d 1048 (10th Cir. 1981).

of the expert's opinion.[124] In any event, the "reasonably relied upon" element of Rule 703 should not be read as a higher standard than that set forth in Rule 702.[125]

Although Rule 703 offers remarkable flexibility in allowing experts to rely on inadmissible evidence, it does not provide automatic license to admit the evidence itself. Generally, the expert cannot become a mere conduit for hearsay and other inadmissible evidence and may not testify on direct examination as to any inadmissible evidence on which she relies.[126] This limitation, however, applies only to the proponent of the expert.[127] The Rules place no restriction on the opposing party eliciting any and all underlying facts or data on cross-examination, and, in fact, such efforts are directly supported by Rule 705, discussed below.

The 2000 amendment to Rule 703 allows the proponent of the expert to present otherwise inadmissible facts or data underlying the expert's opinion only if, in the discretion of the court, the probative value of those facts or data in helping the jury evaluate the expert opinion substantially outweighs the risk of prejudice to the opposing

---

124 *See, e.g., In re* Air Crash Disaster, 86 F.3d 498, 537 (6th Cir. 1996) (finding that, in forming opinion, expert could not reasonably rely upon second-hand report about criticism of airline crew by expert employee of opposing party); *see also* Dallas & Mavis Forwarding Co., Inc. v. Stegall, 659 F.2d 721 (6th Cir. 1981).

125 *In re* Agent Orange Product Liability Litigation, 611 F. Supp. 1267 (E.D.N.Y. 1985), *aff'd*, 818 F.2d 187 (2d Cir. 1987) is a pre-*Daubert* case illustrating some boundaries on the types of inadmissible information upon which an expert may rely under Rule 703. At the summary judgment stage, the court had to determine if any evidence existed to support a link between the deceased's terminal cancer and his Agent Orange exposure. The plaintiff offered the affidavit of a medical expert that exposure to Agent Orange had caused the cancer and death of the plaintiff's husband. The trial judge ruled that the expert's opinion would be inadmissible, based on Rule 703, because the expert relied on inconsistent interviews with the plaintiff, the deceased's widow, and drew tenuous causal conclusions from otherwise reliable epidemiological studies. *Id.* at 1283.

While the trial judge's ruling in *Agent Orange* is probably supportable based on a Rule 702 theory to the effect that the expert's methodology was unreliable, the ruling's basis in Rule 703 reflects a pre-*Daubert* approach. Doctors routinely rely on the report of family members to diagnose the cause of poisoning or disease when a patient cannot speak for himself. The Advisory Committee Note to Rule 703 clearly anticipates the use of such interview evidence, providing: "Thus a physician in his own practice bases his diagnosis on information from numerous sources and of considerable variety, including statements by patients and relatives, reports and opinions from nurses, technicians and other doctors, hospital records, and X rays." There is also no principled distinction under Rule 703 between interviews conducted when the patient is dead or alive. The posthumous nature of the interview should go to the veracity of the expert's opinion, not its admissibility. The judge in the *Agent Orange* case may still have reached the correct (post-*Daubert*) result, however, because contradictory interviews and inapposite epidemiological studies hardly satisfy the standard of an opinion that is to be based on (1) *sufficient* facts or data, (2) *reliable* principles, and (3) *reliable* application of those principles. These are Rule 702 factors, not Rule 703 factors.

126 *See, e.g.*, Rose Hall, Ltd. v. Chase Manhattan Overseas Banking Corp., 576 F. Supp. 107, 158 (D. Del. 1983), *aff'd*, 740 F.2d 958 (3d Cir. 1984) (holding that, while expert on value of land could base opinion partly on information gleaned from telephone conversation with surveyor, the expert could not repeat the contents of the conversation); Carignan v. New Hampshire Int'l Speedway, Inc., 858 A.2d 536, 544 (N.H. 2004) (holding that trial court did not err in not allowing the accident reconstruction expert to testify about a police report that he relied on in reaching his opinion); State v. Towne, 453 A.2d 1133 (Vt. 1982) (excluding testimony by expert witness that he had talked to author of learned treatise and that author agreed with him); *see also* Gacy v. Welborn, 994 F.2d 305, 315–16 (7th Cir. 1993) (holding that trial court properly excluded as hearsay testimony by psychiatrists and psychologists repeating murder defendant's comments, but allowing experts to paraphrase defendant's remarks). *See generally* Ronald L. Carlson, *Experts, Judges, and Commentators: The Underlying Debate About an Expert's Underlying Data*, 47 MERCER L. REV. 481 (1996); Ronald L. Carlson, *Policing the Bases of Modern Expert Testimony*, 39 VAND. L. REV. 577, 584 & n.23 (1986); Ronald L. Carlson, *Collision Course in Expert Testimony: Limitations on Affirmative Introduction of Underlying Data*, 36 U. FLA. L. REV. 234 (1984).

127 The advisory committee stated, "In a multi-party case, where one party proffers an expert whose testimony is also beneficial to other parties, each such party should be deemed a 'proponent' within the meaning of the amendment." FED. R. EVID. 703 advisory committee note (2000 amendment).

party in making those facts or data known to the jury. This is a high standard and will not often be met.[128] Admission of otherwise inadmissible facts underlying an expert opinion is unusual in jury trials.[129] Following the lead of the advisory committee, one court has stated that Rule 703 "clearly establishes a presumption against disclosure to the jury of otherwise inadmissible evidence."[130] Although Rule 703 explicitly restricts presenting otherwise inadmissible material to a *jury*, the plain language of the rule does not restrict presenting such underlying material to a *judge* sitting as finder of fact.[131]

The presumption against admission of facts and data underlying expert opinions only pertains to otherwise inadmissible facts and data. If facts or data relied upon by an expert are otherwise admissible, the expert may testify as to those facts or data unimpeded by Rule 703's balancing test. For example, in *United States v. Ward,*[132] the court upheld the admission of expert testimony as to lab reports that were admissible under the business records exception to the hearsay rule but deemed improper the same expert's testimony as to conversations he had with an on-scene fire investigator that did not fall into a hearsay exception.[133]

Rule 705 complements Rule 703 and has two functions. First, the Rule expressly affirms the strong implication of Rule 703 that an expert may offer an opinion without testifying to all the facts or data (case-specific or otherwise) underlying that opinion. This is an unavoidable consequence of Rule 703, which allows experts to offer opinions based on facts or data that are otherwise inadmissible as evidence. Second, Rule 705 provides that on cross-examination, the opposing party may inquire into the facts or data forming the basis of the expert witness's opinion regardless of whether such facts or data are otherwise admissible.

The main import of Rule 705 is that an expert can always be asked about the facts or data underlying his or her opinion by the opposing counsel on cross-examination.[134] This can be a very useful way for the opponent to introduce facts that are otherwise inadmissible at trial. While such facts are technically only admissible for the purpose of allowing the jury to evaluate the basis for the expert's opinion, the overall effect they may have on the jury is probably greater than that for which the facts are technically intended.

The downside of eliciting otherwise inadmissible facts or data during the cross-examination of an expert is that it may open the door for the party offering the expert's

---

[128] *See, e.g.*, Mike's Train House, Inc. v. Lionel, L.L.C., 472 F.3d 398, 409 (6th Cir. 2006) (finding admission of hearsay opinion of consultant relied upon by expert witness improper); United States v. Ward, 182 Fed. Appx. 779, 792–93 (10th Cir. 2006) (finding admission of hearsay relied upon by expert improper).

[129] *But see* Young v. County of Cook, 2009 WL 2231782 (N.D. Ill. 2009) (allowing expert to state that he relied on affidavits in reaching opinion, but not allowing expert to state content of those affidavits).

[130] Pineda v. Ford Motor Co., 520 F.3d 237, 247 (3d Cir. 2008). *See also* FED. R. EVID. 703 advisory committee note (2000 amendment).

[131] *See* Johnson v. Big Lots Stores, Inc., 2008 WL 1930681 (E.D. La. 2008) (allowing admission of data and facts underlying expert opinion at bench trial in order to allow judge to weigh value of expert opinion).

[132] 182 Fed. Appx. 779 (10th Cir. 2006).

[133] *Id.* at 792–93. Note, however, that admission of both the out-of-court statements and the expert's testimony in reliance on them have been affected by subsequent developments in the law of the Confrontation Clause. *See* **§ 20.06**.

[134] *See also* FED. R. EVID. 703 advisory committee note ("Nothing in this Rule restricts the presentation of underlying expert facts or data when offered by an adverse party. See Rule 705.").

testimony to elicit further facts that would be otherwise inadmissible.[135] To prevent a lengthy back-and-forth of otherwise inadmissible facts and data on cross-examination and re-direct, the trial judge may rule in advance to allow the presentation of certain facts and data underlying the expert's opinion during direct examination under the Rule 703 balancing test. In close cases, the best practice is probably for the parties to proceed by way of stipulation made in advance of the testimony.

§ 10.06 Opinions on the Ultimate Issue and Other Disfavored Opinions

Opinions on the Ultimate Issue [FRE 704]

The common-law courts developed a number of restrictions on particular opinions. Perhaps the most widely recognized was the rule prohibiting testimony on the ultimate issue at trial.[136] For example, a psychiatrist testifying in an insanity defense case might be precluded from testifying that the defendant could not distinguish right from wrong because (under the prevailing test) that was the ultimate issue to be decided by the jurors. Similarly, an actuarial expert could not testify as to the financial loss to the family caused by the breadwinner's wrongful death.[137] Exclusion of such testimony was justified on the ground that it concerned the "very issue before the jury"[138] and, by giving such testimony, the witness would be "usurping the function of the jury."[139] Critics of the rule against testimony on the ultimate issue observed that the jury could always reject the witness's opinion.[140] In addition, the rule often made the testimony stilted and artificial.

When the Federal Rules of Evidence were originally enacted in 1975, Rule 704 abolished the ultimate issue objection completely.[141] The drafters were clear, however, that Rule 704 cannot render admissible an expert opinion that is not otherwise admissible under Rule 701 or Rule 702.[142] In fact, opinions on the ultimate issue may be more likely to be excluded than other opinions because they are not "helpful" under Rule 701 or do not "help the trier of fact" under Rule 702. Furthermore, opinions appearing to direct a finding of fact may also be excluded as confusing under Rule 403.

In the wake of controversy over expert testimony on insanity regarding John Hinckley's shooting President Reagan, Congress partially resurrected the prohibition in 1984. In Rule 704(b), Congress prohibited expert testimony about a criminal defendant's

---

[135] *See id.* ("Of course, an adversary's attack on an expert's basis will often open the door to a proponent's rebuttal with information that was reasonably relied upon by the expert, even if that information would not have been discloseable [sic] initially under the balancing test provided by [Rule 703].").

[136] 1 MCCORMICK ON EVIDENCE § 12 (Kenneth S. Broun ed., 7th ed. 2013).

[137] *See also* State v. Boyles, 60 S.E. 233, 234 (S.C.1908) (holding that negative answer to question of whether defendant was connected to crime was properly excluded because it went to "issue before the jury").

[138] 7 WIGMORE ON EVIDENCE § 1921 (Chadbourn rev. 1976).

[139] *Id.* at § 1920.

[140] *Id.* at § 1920–21. *See also* Stoebuck, *Opinions on Ultimate Facts: Status, Trends, and a Note of Caution*, 41 DEN. L. C. J. 226 (1964).

[141] *See, e.g.* United States v. Sheffey, 57 F.3d 1419, 1426 (6th Cir. 1995) (permissible to ask witnesses whether defendant drove "recklessly and in extreme disregard of human life" even though that was ultimate issue).

[142] As the advisory committee note explains: "The abolition of the ultimate issue rule does not lower the bars so as to admit all opinions."

mental state or condition at issue.[143] While the purpose of Rule 704(b) was to prevent expert testimony regarding insanity and similar defenses, the Rule is broad enough to prohibit any expert testimony as to the mens rea of a criminal defendant. In fact, a review of Rule 704 cases suggests the most common area where this rule is invoked is in the prosecution of drug couriers who claim no knowledge of the contraband they were carrying.

Rule 704(b) permits expert testimony that is highly suggestive of the mental state of a criminal defendant, but an expert may not offer an opinion explicitly as to that mental state.[144] The closer an expert comes to stating an unambiguous opinion as to the relevant mental state of an accused, the greater the chance that a persuasive advocate can successfully challenge the testimony as violating Rule 704. For example, a Drug Enforcement Administration expert may testify that "the presence of crew members unaware that [a] smuggling vessel carried large quantities of drugs would jeopardize the criminal operation."[145] While the quoted statement clearly suggests that, in the expert's opinion, the crewmembers on trial had knowledge of the drugs they carried, the testimony was allowed. "The obvious inference of this is that the defendants in this case were aware of contraband aboard the vessel. Nevertheless, the expert left this inference for the jury to draw. He did not expressly 'state [the] inference.' Therefore, his testimony did not violate Rule 704(b)."[146]

Opinions on the Law and on the Application of the Law to the Facts

Generally, expert testimony on a point of domestic law is inadmissible.[147] Such testimony is unhelpful in light of the trial judge's presumed expertise, at least when the court is informed by briefs and arguments of counsel.[148] In some contexts, the content of

---

143 United States v. Blumberg, 961 F.2d 787 (8th Cir. 1992) (exclusion of defense expert's ultimate opinion about whether defendant appreciated the nature and wrongfulness of his acts was appropriate under Rule 704(b)).

144 *See* United States v. Reno, 992 F.2d 739, 743 (7th Cir. 1993) (psychiatrist's testimony as to effect of paranoid schizophrenic's delusions on ability to appreciate wrongfulness of his acts did not violate Rule 704 because testimony aided jury by describing presence of mental disorder and its behavioral characteristics); United States v. Kristiansen, 901 F.2d 1463, 1466 (8th Cir. 1990) (following question should have been allowed: "would this severe mental disease or defect, which you've testified [the defendant] has, if an individual has that, affect the individual's ability to appreciate the nature and quality of the wrongfulness of his acts?").

145 United States v. Alvarez, 837 F.2d 1024, 1031 (11th Cir. 1988).

146 *Id.* The Ninth Circuit has explained: "A prohibited 'opinion or inference' under Rule 704(b) is testimony from which it necessarily follows, if the testimony is credited, that the defendant did or did not possess the requisite *mens rea*." United States v. Morales, 108 F.3d 1031, 1037 (9th Cir. 1997). This formulation has been adopted by the Third and Tenth Circuits, but rejected by the Seventh Circuit. *See* United States v. Bennett, 161 F.3d 171, 183 (3d Cir. 1998); United States v. Are, 590 F.3d 499, 512 (7th Cir. 2009); United States v. Reyes, 183 Fed. Appx. 755, 759 (10th Cir. 2006). *See generally* Deon J. Nossel, Note, *The Admissibility of Ultimate Issue Expert Testimony by Law Enforcement Officers in Criminal Trials*, 93 COLUM. L. REV. 231 (1993).

147 *See* 1 MCCORMICK ON EVIDENCE § 12 at 83 (Kenneth S. Broun ed., 7th ed. 2013).

148 *See* United States v. Wilson, 133 F.3d 251 (4th Cir. 1997) (noting, in prosecution for violation of Clean Water Act, that district court should not have permitted experts to "give opinions on what the law means or how it is to be interpreted;" though government witnesses administering complex regulations understandably refer to those regulations in describing their actions and motives, their testimony should have been limited to "facts of history, practices and procedures followed by them in their work" and to matters in which they had "demonstrated expertise"); CMI-Trading, Inc. v. Quantum Air, Inc., 98 F.3d 887, 890 (6th Cir. 1996) (finding inadmissible opinion of expert, who was specialist in private equity transactions, that transaction was intended as joint venture, not as loan, because it trespassed on jury's territory to extent it unhelpfully drew conclusions on intent and on court's territory to the extent that it defined legal concepts); Estes v. Moore, 993 F.2d 161, 163 (8th Cir. 1993) (finding, in action for deprivation of civil rights, trial court properly excluded testimony

foreign law that must be applied by an American court is considered subject to proof by testimony, which will inevitably mean testimony by experts in foreign law. Under modern procedures, this process is not subject to the usual rules of evidence at all. Even when such testimony is received in a jury trial, it is directed to a pure question of law and determined by the judge. The experts help inform the trial judge so that the latter can instruct the jury.[149]

Often troublesome are opinions on mixed questions of law and fact, that is, of the application of law to fact. Historically, such opinions were prohibited at common law.[150] For example, a witness could not testify that the conduct of the parties resulted in the formation of a legally enforceable contract. In jury trials, conflicting opinions could confuse the jury and undermine the authority of the judge. In bench trials, the judge's specialized knowledge made the testimony superfluous.[151] There is some question as to whether the common-law rule against opinion testimony in the form of legal conclusions survived enactment of Rule 704. The Federal Rules contain no express prohibition of expert testimony regarding legal conclusions.[152] Some have argued, therefore, that the admissibility of expert testimony as to a legal conclusion should be judged by the general criteria of helpfulness set forth in Rule 702.[153] In fact, courts rightly disfavor such testimony and are quick to reject conclusory legal opinions as not satisfying the threshold helpfulness requirement of Rule 702.[154]

---

from plaintiff's expert as to whether police officer had probable cause to arrest plaintiff; although probable cause involves both legal and factual issues, "ultimate concern is a question of law").

Courts sometimes handle the issue of legal expert opinion on domestic law testimony differently in jury trials than in bench trials. If a judge conducting a bench trial believes that he or she will benefit from expert testimony about legal conclusions, as opposed to having a legal expert brief or argue the issue, then there seems to be little potential for harm in allowing the testimony. In a jury trial, however, there is a danger that the jury might become confused or that it might follow the expert's view of the law instead of the judge's view. *Compare* Knisley v. United States, 817 F. Supp. 680, 690 (S.D. Ohio 1993) (finding legal expert testimony admissible in bench trial of legal malpractice action because judge might "frequently find help in expert legal opinion orally delivered, as opposed to being found in books"), *with* Willette v. Finn, 778 F. Supp. 10 (E.D. La. 1991) (finding expert testimony on law of informed consent to medical procedures inadmissible, at least in jury trial).

149 *See* ROBERT L. FELIX & RALPH U. WHITTEN, AMERICAN CONFLICTS LAW §§ 83, 84 (6th ed. 2011).

150 *See* Adalman v. Baker, Watts & Co., 807 F.2d 359, 366 (4th Cir. 1986), *rev'd in part on other grounds*, Baker, Watts & Co. v. Miles & Stockbridge, 876 F.2d 1101 (4th Cir. 1989); Specht v. Jensen, 853 F.2d 805, 808 (10th Cir. 1988), *cert. denied*, 488 U.S. 1008 (1989) (finding that expert testimony of lawyer in § 1983 case as to whether search occurred and whether plaintiffs consented was improperly admitted because testimony concerned a broad array of legal conclusions, not ultimate issue of fact). *See generally* 1 MCCORMICK ON EVIDENCE § 12 at 84 (Kenneth S. Broun ed., 7th ed. 2013).

151 *See* 7 WIGMORE ON EVIDENCE § 1952 (Chadbourn rev. 1976).

152 The advisory committee note for Rule 704, which permits expert testimony to embrace the ultimate issue, suggests that ultimate issue testimony involving the application of law to fact, while not per se inadmissible, should be excluded when it might be misleading. The note states that under Rule 702, which requires that opinions must be helpful to the trier of fact, and Rule 403, which provides for exclusion of evidence which wastes time, the trial court could exclude "opinions phrased in terms of inadequately explored legal criteria." Thus, in the advisory committee's view, an objection to the question, "Did T have capacity to make a will?" should be sustained, while the question, "Did T have sufficient mental capacity to know the nature and extent of his property and the natural objects of his bounty and to formulate a rationale scheme of distribution?" should be permitted.

153 *See* Note, *Expert Legal Testimony*, 97 HARV. L. REV. 797 (1984). For other useful commentary see Thomas E. Baker, *The Impropriety of Expert Witness Testimony on the Law*, 10 KAN. L. REV. 325 (1992), and Howard G. Pollack, *The Admissibility and Utility of Expert Legal Testimony in Patent Litigation*, 32 IDEA 361–381 (1992).

154 *See, e.g.*, United States v. Scop, 846 F.2d 135, 140 (2d Cir. 1988) (finding that it was error to admit testimony by securities trading expert that defendant committed securities fraud, because testimony embodied legal conclusions and used language from statute); United States v. Barile, 286 F.3d 749, 760 (4th Cir. 2002)

Professional malpractice is a context with conspicuous tensions, because expertise is often required to articulate the standard of professional care.[155] And Rule 704 permits the expert to offer an opinion about whether the defendant met that standard. For example, a medical expert may be allowed to opine that a physician did not meet the standard of care expected of a reasonable physician. But the same expert may not testify to the legal opinion that the physician acted "negligently."[156]

The legal opinion restriction and (where still applicable) the ultimate issue restriction can usually be overcome through artful examination. The Advisory Committee Note provides an example: The question "Did the testator have the capacity to make a will?" is about the ultimate issue, but it is excludable because it asks for an opinion about "inadequately explored legal criteria." The question "Did the testator have sufficient mental capacity to know the nature and extent of his property and the natural objects of his bounty and to formulate a rational scheme of distribution?" is about the same ultimate issue, but it would be allowed because the legal criteria are spelled out.

Opinions on the Credibility of a Witness

Opinions on the truthfulness or untruthfulness of a witness are also treated by courts as highly suspect and inappropriate.[157] Traditionally, such evidence was simply considered unhelpful because it was a matter about which the fact-finder could judge equally well.[158] Of course, expert testimony about mental defects of a witness—concerning problems with perception, memory, and so forth—are admissible even though they affect credibility.[159] Similarly, expert testimony may be helpful on matters of bias, for example, by unraveling a complex financial transaction that would reveal a witness's financial interest.[160] The courts' crucial concern focuses on expert testimony that a particular witness is either lying or speaking truthfully in testimony.[161] Even when no

---

("Expert testimony that merely states a legal conclusion is less likely to assist the jury in its determination."). *But see* United States v. Barile, 286 F.3d 749, 760 n.7 (4th Cir. 2002) ("We note, however, that 'in some circumstances, opinion testimony that arguably states a legal conclusion is helpful to the jury, and thus, admissible.' 'For example, the testimony may be helpful if the case involves a specialized industry such as insurance.' " (quoting WEINSTEIN'S FEDERAL EVIDENCE § 704.04[2][a] (2d ed. 2001))).

[155] *See* DAVID H. KAYE, DAVID E. BERNSTEIN, & JENNIFER L. MNOOKIN, THE NEW WIGMORE: EXPERT EVIDENCE § 2.5 (2d ed. 2011).

[156] *See* Davidson v. Prince, 813 P.2d 1225, 1230–31 (Utah Ct. App. 1991) (finding, in action for negligence, trial court properly prevented plaintiff's accident reconstruction expert to state opinion on whether defendant was "negligent" because such opinion would be "legal conclusion"; although state has adopted its own version of Rule 704, ultimate issue testimony in form of legal conclusion is still not admissible); Vanderpool v. Edmondson, 2005 WL 5164857 (E.D. Tenn. 2005) ("The terms 'negligent' and 'negligence' have a distinct and specialized meaning in the law different from that present in the common vernacular."); Hermitage Indus. v. Schwerman Trucking Co., 814 F. Supp. 484, 487 (D.S.C. 1993) (excluding testimony from defense expert that plaintiff was "negligent" and was "direct, proximate and efficient cause" of accident because both phrases have "a clear legal meaning which is distinct from the common vernacular").

[157] *See generally* DAVID H. KAYE, DAVID E. BERNSTEIN, & JENNIFER L. MNOOKIN, THE NEW WIGMORE: EXPERT EVIDENCE § 2.4 (2d ed. 2011).

[158] *See, e.g.*, United States v. Benson, 941 F.2d 598, 605 (7th Cir. 1991).

[159] *See, e.g.,* State v. Parks, 359 N.E.2d 358, 367 (N.Y. 1976) (admitting testimony by teacher of complainant that complainant, though 16 years old, had the mental capacity of a 12-year-old). *See* DAVID H. KAYE, DAVID E. BERNSTEIN, & JENNIFER L. MNOOKIN, THE NEW WIGMORE: EXPERT EVIDENCE § 2.4.3 (2d ed. 2011).

[160] *See* **§ 11.04**.

[161] *See, e.g.,* United States v. Masat, 896 F.2d 88, 93–94 (5th Cir. 1990) (affirming trial court's exclusion, in tax evasion prosecution, of expert testimony to the effect that defendant's beliefs were strongly and sincerely held). *See generally* 3 CHRISTOPHER B. MUELLER & LAIRD C. KIRKPATRICK, FEDERAL EVIDENCE § 6:32 (4th ed. 2013).

such explicit opinion is provided, expert testimony that has the effect merely of declaring the expert's belief or disbelief of a witness's testimony has been rejected.[162] As psychological sciences have advanced, it is more likely that lay fact-finders (whether juries or judges) can be assisted by relevant expertise even on the question of sincerity. Courts nevertheless continue to express significant concern that the jury may abdicate its role by deferring to the expert. In many contexts, however, this concern can be assuaged, and the testimony accepted, if it is limited to providing relevant (and sufficiently reliable) general information about behavior that would inform the fact-finder's assessment of credibility. This can be presented without offering a direct opinion on the credibility of the witness.[163]

Other Suspect Opinions

The common law on expert testimony has generated a variety of other doctrines that are reflected, if at all, in the helpfulness requirement of Rule 702. For example, one bit of common-law lore sometimes encountered is the idea that an inference may not be based on an inference.[164] Because expert opinions often endorse inferences, this (dubious) principle about the sufficiency of the evidence can get transformed into an admissibility idea, the idea that an expert may not give an opinion based on another opinion. In modern case law, however, this amounts to little more than a warning that complex, multi-stage inferences may become too attenuated to be helpful.[165]

§ 10.07 Practical Considerations Regarding Expert Testimony

The Daubert *Hearing and Expert Qualification*

What is now known as a *Daubert* hearing has become common practice in trials involving experts. Although a hearing is not needed in all cases, failure to perform proper *Daubert* scrutiny can itself be grounds for appeal.[166] Many trials will be won or lost based

---

[162] *See, e.g.*, Commonwealth v. Mantanino, 567 N.E.2d 1212 (Mass. 1991) (rejecting testimony of police officer that, in his experience, sexual assault victims provide greater details about the assault as time goes on, offered to explain inconsistencies between early reports and later testimony by the alleged victim); State v. Haslam, 663 A.2d 902, 904–07 (R.I. 1995) (rejecting therapist's testimony that she was meeting the complaining witness over an extended period of time for "sexual-abuse-recovery counseling," which would be seen by the jury as endorsing the truthfulness of the complainant's testimony; similarly rejecting testimony by child-protective investigator that defendant's claim that alleged victim had been molested by her older brother was "unfounded").

[163] *See* **§ 10.03** (discussing informational expert testimony). *See also* State v. Batangan, 799 P.2d 48 (Hawaii 1990) (applying Hawaii's version of 702 and concluding that "while expert testimony explaining 'seemingly bizarre' behavior of child sex abuse victims is helpful to the jury and should be admitted, conclusory opinions that abuse did occur and that the child victim's report of abuse is truthful and believable is of no assistance to the jury, and therefore, should not be admitted").

[164] *See* **§ 2.06**.

[165] *See, e.g.*, Donaldson v. Northern Trading Co., 612 N.E.2d 754 (Ohio App. 1992) (allowing multistage inferences to the cause of an injury).

[166] Some appellate courts applying *Daubert* have reversed trial court rulings on expert testimony, not because the district judge made a demonstrable mistake in assessing the scientific validity of a theory or application, but because the district court did not make a *Daubert* inquiry at all. *See, e.g.*, Tyus v. Urban Search Mgmt., 102 F.3d 256, 263–64 (7th Cir. 1996) (holding that, in housing discrimination action, district court erred in failing to apply *Daubert* when it excluded testimony of a well-qualified expert in marketing communication about how advertising sends message to its target market and how all-white advertising campaign affects African-Americans); United States v. Hall, 93 F.3d 1337, 1345 (7th Cir. 1996) (finding that it was reversible error to fail to make full *Daubert* inquiry before excluding crucial testimony (1) by defense psychiatrist that defendant confessed because he had personality disorder making him abnormally suggestible and eager to please and (2) testimony of another defense expert about conditions under which false confessions are made).

on what testimony is allowed as a result of a *Daubert* hearing, and such hearings can become more complicated than some trials. In conducting the Rule 702 analysis, some judges have even used court-appointed experts to help them,[167] a practice encouraged by Justice Breyer in his *Joiner* concurrence.[168]

Because expert qualification will be part of a *Daubert* hearing, and because many experts will be unquestionably qualified in their field, the party opposing the expert may offer to stipulate that the witness is qualified as an expert. Even if the *Daubert* hearing occurs pre-trial, as they often do, the opposing party may do this in an attempt to avoid having the expert's impressive credentials later paraded before the jury. At trial, the party opposing the expert may object to testimony about the witness's background, education, and achievements on the grounds that such testimony is a waste of time because the witness's competence to testify as an expert is not in dispute. However, that objection should be overruled.[169] The testimony is relevant because the jurors must still assess the credibility of the expert. The jurors are entitled to know the witness's background and achievements in order to assess credibility. Nonetheless, the lawyer making this objection may succeed in limiting the duration of the direct examination, because extended and detailed review of qualifications may be a waste of time when the witness's competence to testify as an expert is not in dispute.

The Use of Hypothetical Questions

Historically, the common law required rigid, formalistic examination of an expert witness. An expert was not allowed to offer an opinion unless it was based upon personal knowledge of the underlying information (a relatively rare occurrence) or upon case-specific facts that had already been admitted into evidence.[170] Moreover, the opinion had to specify on which facts it was based so that the trier of fact could reject the opinion if it rejected its factual basis. To assure that the underlying facts and data were before the witness and the jury, the common law developed the hypothetical question as the universally accepted device for eliciting expert testimony. The examining lawyer would ask the expert to assume the existence of certain specified facts and then to give an opinion based upon those facts. Alternatively, if the expert had been in the courtroom and heard previous testimony, the examining lawyer could ask the expert to assume the truthfulness of specified testimony and to give an opinion based upon the facts from the testimony. Often the examining lawyer would ask a hypothetical that combined the two approaches.[171]

---

167 *See* Hall v. Baxter Healthcare Corp., 947 F. Supp. 1387, 1413 (D. Or. 1996) (discussing how court appointed four "technical advisors" to assist in four-day Rule 104(a) hearing in consolidated breast implant cases; technical advisors participated in questioning of parties' experts and issued reports).

168 General Elec. Co. v. Joiner, 522 U.S. 136, 149–50 (1997) (concurring opinion).

169 Murphy v. National R.R. Passenger Corp., 547 F.2d 816, 817 (4th Cir. 1977) (holding that, despite stipulation of the witness's expertise, "a jury can better assess the weight to be accorded an expert's opinion if the witness is permitted to explain his qualifications).

170 *See, e.g.,* Stanley Co. of Am. v. Hercules Powder Co., 108 A.2d 616, 621 (N.J. 1954) ("The opinions of experts must be based either upon facts within their own knowledge which they detail to the jury or upon hypothetical questions embracing facts supported by the evidence upon which the expert opinion is sought.").

171 2 WIGMORE ON EVIDENCE §§ 672–84 (Chadbourn rev. 1976). A hypothetical question is not misleading if it merely fails to include the opponent's version of disputed facts. *See* Johns-Manville Prod. Corp. v. Industrial Comm., 399 N.E.2d 606, 611 (Ill.1979). On the other hand, if certain facts are not in dispute, they must be incorporated in the hypothetical question if the question would be misleading without them. *See, e.g.,* De Donato v. Wells, 41 S.W.2d 184 (Mo.1931). For example, if one witness testifies that the plaintiff was exposed to a toxic chemical and others testify that the plaintiff was not exposed, it is permissible to ask the

The Federal Rules neither require nor prohibit the use of hypothetical questions in the examination of expert witnesses. One common form of direct examination without using hypothetical questions now tracks the language of Rule 702 by first qualifying the witness as an expert and then asking:

(1) whether the expert has formed an opinion as to an issue in the case at trial;

(2) what facts or data the expert relied upon to form his or her opinion;

(3) what principles or methods the expert applied to form his or her opinion; and

(4) what the expert's opinion is.

The party offering the expert witness will then further explore the reasons underlying the expert's opinion and why the expert rejects contrary possibilities.[172]

Still, hypothetical questions can be useful in the right situations. Some lawyers in Federal Rules jurisdictions continue to use the hypothetical question, believing that the form provides an opportunity to control and focus the expert and allow the attorney to sum up damaging testimony in the middle of trial. The hypothetical question is also a useful way of exploring "what if" questions regarding alternative actions a party could have taken regarding an issue at trial.

Some states prefer experts in criminal trials to testify in the form of answers to hypothetical questions mirroring the facts of the case.[173] In such jurisdictions, the hypothetical question may be the only way of skirting the common-law rule against opinions on the ultimate issue.[174] For example, a prosecutor offering a police investigator as an expert with an opinion about whether the defendant possessed drugs for distribution or for personal use might use hypothetical questions, asking the witness to assume the presence of a certain quantity of drugs and certain paraphernalia, as opposed to testifying that on the basis of his investigation he believes that this defendant possessed drugs for distribution.[175]

---

expert to assume the plaintiff was exposed to the chemical and to base an opinion on that assumption. *See, e.g.*, Taylor v. Reo Motors, 275 F.2d 699 (10th Cir. 1960).

[172] This is merely an example of a common method of direct examination of an expert witness. There are innumerable variations of direct examination that are equally valid under the Federal Rules.

[173] *See, e.g.*, Commonwealth v. Avila, 912 N.E.2d 1014, 1028 (Mass. 2009) (finding that expert with no first-hand knowledge of facts must testify based on hypothetical questions assuming facts in evidence); Simpson v. Commonwealth, S.E.2d 386, 391 (Va. 1984) (finding that expert in criminal case may either testify based on personal knowledge of facts disclosed in his or her testimony or based on facts in evidence and assumed in hypothetical question). *But see* State v. Collins, 12 So.3d 1069, 1081 (La. Ct. App. 2009) ("Louisiana jurisprudence has condemned the use of hypothetical questions that parallel the actual fact situation of the case.").

[174] *See* State v. Yarbrough, 210 P.3d 1029, 1042–43 (Wash. Ct. App. 2009) (finding that, under Washington law, no witness may give opinion testimony as to guilt of defendant in criminal case, but hypothetical question assuming facts that jury may or may not accept from evidence presented at trial is permitted).

[175] *See* Commonwealth v. Wilson, 805 N.E.2d 968, 978–79 (Mass. 2004) (allowing police expert to testify in hypothetical that person with 20 bags of marijuana, $476 dollar in cash, cell phone, and pager, but no marijuana smoking paraphernalia was consistent with profile of person intent on street distribution and not personal use of drug); State v. Odom, 560 A.2d 1198 (N.J. 1989) (holding that, in Federal Rules state, police offer testifying about whether defendant possessed crack for his own use or with intent to distribute must testify in response to hypothetical questions that do not use defendant's name and that are based on facts admitted in evidence). *But cf.* People v. Gardeley, 927 P.2d 713, 721 (Cal.1996) (allowing, under provision

Hypothetical questions present a particular challenge to the examiner and the opponent because they usually involve an extended recitation of facts upon which the expert is expected to base an opinion. If the hypothetical omits material undisputed facts, misstates facts, or includes prejudicial facts, it may be misleading, confusing, or prejudicial and therefore improper under Rule 403. To preserve rights on appeal, the objecting party should be careful to specify omitted, misstated, or prejudicial facts that make the hypothetical objectionable.[176] Courts have displayed varying degrees of flexibility in allowing the omission of undisputed facts from hypothetical questions, depending mostly upon the importance of the fact. A certain amount of leeway is given when the omission is not materially misleading and may be subject to correction by an alert cross-examiner.[177] However, when the omission of an undisputed fact reduces the value of the resulting opinion to a point where its probative value is outweighed by dangers of prejudice or of misleading the trier of fact, the question will not be allowed.[178]

A recurring criticism of the hypothetical centers on lawyers' use of such questions to inject or unduly emphasize case facts unrelated to anything the expert needed as a basis for an opinion. In the hands of a skilled practitioner, the hypothetical question could be transformed into a final argument. *Ingram v. McCuiston*[179] is a pre-Rules example. The plaintiff's lawyer asked the expert a twenty-three-paragraph question, purportedly to elicit the expert's opinion as to whether the plaintiff had been disabled by her injury. The question was replete with facts relevant to liability but not to damages. For example, the lawyer included in the question that the plaintiff had been hit from behind while stopped "in obedience to a traffic control device."[180] The lawyer also asserted in the question that the plaintiff had slowed down because "she saw, and anyone who was properly observant could and should have seen"[181] that the traffic ahead was slowing down. In holding that the hypothetical question was improperly prejudicial

---

similar to Federal Rules, expert to base testimony about criminal gang activity on interviews with gang members, not strictly on facts in evidence that were incorporated into hypothetical questions).

[176] *See* First Nat'l Bank of Dunmore v. WCAB, 532 A.2d 526, 528 (Pa. Commw. Ct. 1987); Serafin v. Workmen's Compensation Appeal Bd., 436 A.2d 1239, 1241–42 (Pa. Commw. Ct. 1981).

[177] *See* WIGMORE ON EVIDENCE § 6782 (Chadbourn rev. 1976).

[178] *See, e.g.*, Podedworny v. Harris, 745 F.2d 210, 218–19 (3d Cir. 1984) (finding defective hypothetical question about claimant's disability because it failed to mention claimant's dizziness and blurred vision). *See also* Stumpf v. State Farm Mutual, 251 A.2d 362 (Md. 1969), concerning whether the insured had made an intentionally false statement on an automobile insurance application in denying that his epilepsy constituted a mental or physical disability. His lawyer asked the following question to a specialist in internal medicine who had been called as an expert witness:

> Doctor, assuming that you have a patient who is gainfully employed and has a history of infrequent epileptic seizures of the grand mal type over a period of years, takes regular oral medication for his epileptic condition three times daily, assume further that the patient, before suffering an epileptic seizure gets warning of the impending seizure sufficient to allow him to sit down and make adjustments, do you have an opinion, based on reasonable medical probability, whether that patient has a mental or physical disability?

Id. at 372. State Farm's objection that the question omitted several material facts was sustained by the trial court and affirmed on appeal. The question omitted that the insured had also suffered petit mal seizures (which, unlike grand mal seizures, came upon him without warning) and that he had been discharged from the Marine Corps with a 30% disability because of epilepsy. *Id.* at 372–73. The court of appeals said that the omissions caused the question to fall short of the standard that a hypothetical question "should contain a fair summary of the material facts in evidence essential to the formulation of a rational opinion concerning the matter to which it relates." *Id.* at 372 (quoting Wolfinger v. Frey, 162 A.2d 745, 749 (Md. 1960)).

[179] 134 S.E.2d 705 (1964) The hypothetical at issue consisted of more than 1,800 words, approximately the same as four printed pages of this treatise, including footnotes.

[180] *Id.* at 708.

[181] *Id.*

because it was "slanted and argumentative," the court stated, "it was no part of the legitimate purpose of the hypothetical question under consideration to establish defendants' negligence."[182] Under the Federal Rules, the court might also add that such a question is unduly prejudicial and confusing under Rule 403.

The Required Degree of Certainty of the Opinion

A number of common-law courts have endorsed the idea that an expert's opinion must be stated with a minimum degree of certainty, commonly that the opinion must be given "to a reasonable degree of certainty."[183] Thus, some courts insist that, to be admitted, expert testimony about causation must state that some agent or event was the cause with a reasonable degree of scientific, medical, engineering, or other professional certainty.[184] This requirement does not appear in the Federal Rules, yet some jurisdictions applying a version of those rules still invoke the requirement.[185] Some courts have been even more exacting, requiring that the expert's opinion must not merely state that something is "possible," but must state that it is "probable," meaning more likely than not.[186]

The story behind this requirement is a classic example of a sensible holding that is generalized into a rule that makes no sense when applied in other contexts.[187] The requirement originated in cases that imposed an evidential sufficiency (burden of proof) requirement that dealt with the narrow issue of the degree of precision required for proof of future damages, where the only evidence on the matter was expert testimony. Although proof of the damages already incurred has generally been subject to a very liberal standard—as much precision as the nature of the case admits[188]—proof of future losses sometimes has been subjected to a reasonable certainty standard, supposedly to deter fraudulent claims. From that humble beginning, the rule evolved from a rule of sufficiency to a rule of admissibility; from a rule concerning future damages to one that encompassed causation and other issues. This development was strongly criticized by Wigmore,[189] but it lingers in the case law nonetheless.

The rule does little harm where the expert's opinion is the only basis for an inference to a factual proposition that itself must be established by a preponderance of the evidence. If the expert is unwilling to commit to proof by such a standard, then why should the fact-finder be allowed to find by such a standard? But in a great many cases, the expert's opinion is not the only evidence with which to support an inference, and then the requirement is too strong, particularly when applied to a party who does not bear

---

182 *Id.* at 712.

183 *See* 1 PAUL C. GIANNELLI & EDWARD J. IMWINKELRIED, SCIENTIFIC EVIDENCE § 5.06 (4th ed. 2007).

184 *See, e.g.*, Cohen v. Albert Einstein Medical Center, 592 A.2d 720, 723 (Pa. Super. 1991) ("When a party must prove causation through expert testimony the expert must testify with 'reasonable certainty' that in his 'professional opinion, the results in question did come from the cause alleged'.").

185 *See* STEVEN LUBET & ELIZABETH BOALS, EXPERT TESTIMONY 8 (2d ed. 2009) ("Although not mentioned specifically by the Federal Rules of Evidence, most jurisdictions require that an expert's opinion be stated, within the standards of the relevant field, 'to a reasonable degree of certainty'.").

186 *See, e.g.*, Shumaker v. Oliver B. Cannon & Sons, Inc., 504 N.E.2d 44 (Ohio 1986). However, the Ohio courts have abandoned the rule in criminal cases. *See, e.g.*, State v. D'Ambrosio, 616 N.E.2d 909 (Ohio 1993) (permitting coroner's testimony that wound was merely consistent with having been inflicted by a certain knife).

187 *See* Jeff L. Lewin, *The Genesis and Evolution of Legal Uncertainty about "Reasonable Medical Certainty,"* 57 MD. L. REV. 381 (1998).

188 *See* **§ 2.02**.

189 *See* 7 WIGMORE ON EVIDENCE § 1976 (Chadbourn rev. 1978).

the burden of persuasion. But once stated as a competency rule, courts naturally apply it even to a party who does not bear the burden.[190]

The better approach is to treat any "reasonable certainty" requirement as relating to the grounds for the opinion—i.e., whether it satisfies reliability requirements—rather than to the degree of probability associated with the conclusion. For example, one can have reasonable certainty that the probability of something is 25%. And one can have reasonable certainty that the probability of something is substantial even if not "more likely than not" or "beyond reasonable doubt." Many courts have expressed conclusions that reflect this point, allowing expert opinions expressed as possibilities, such as the conclusion that certain signatures "may" be those of the defendant or that the shoes the defendant was wearing "could have made" the impressions found.[191] The better view is that the fact that an opinion is offered as less than certain, or less than the standard required by the burden of persuasion, goes to its weight rather than its admissibility.[192]

§ 10.08 Examples of Controversial Expert Testimony

In the wake of *Daubert*, both advocates and commentators have reexamined whether various areas of expert testimony are admissible. As noted above, *Daubert* was perceived at the time of its decision as a liberalizing force. However, *Daubert*'s focus on reliability may indeed constrict admissibility of expert testimony previously accepted under the *Frye* regime.

In 2009, a groundbreaking report commissioned by Congress entitled, *Strengthening Forensic Science in the United States: A Path Forward*, reexamined the validity of numerous forms of forensic evidence routinely held admissible in American courts.[193] Shortly thereafter, the report was cited by the Supreme Court, which noted that "[s]erious deficiencies have been found in the forensic evidence used in criminal trials" and "[f]orensic evidence is not uniquely immune from the risk of manipulation."[194] A reevaluation of the methods behind expert testimony that are routinely relied upon in criminal cases was warranted. According to the Innocence Project, data from post-conviction DNA exonerations in the United States shows that a substantial portion of the erroneous convictions involve faulty forensic science.[195]

---

190 *See, e.g.*, Stinson v. England, 633 N.E.2d 532 (Ohio 1994) (applying the requirement as a competency rule to an expert offered by the party not bearing the burden of persuasion).

191 *See, e.g.*, United States v. Hardrich, 707 F.2d 992, 994 (8th Cir. 1983) (handwriting expert testimony); United States v. Allen, 390 F.3d 944, 949 (7th Cir.2004) (shoe print expert).

192 *See, e.g.*, Stutzman v. CRST, Inc., 997 F.2d 291, 296 (7th Cir. 1993). *See generally* 3 CHRISTOPHER B. MUELLER & LAIRD C. KIRKPATRICK, FEDERAL EVIDENCE § 7:9 at 777–78 (4th ed. 2013):

> Where reasons for reservations can be made intelligible to a lay jury, it is entirely appropriate to let the expert lay them out, so the jury may better evaluate his testimony and reach its own conclusions on its worth. On the other hand, uncertainty that is so acute that the testimony would amount to little more than a guess or a shrug does implicate the helpfulness criterion, and such testimony may properly be excluded as unhelpful.

193 NATIONAL RESEARCH COUNCIL, STRENGTHENING FORENSIC SCIENCE IN THE UNITED STATES: A PATH FORWARD (2009); *see also* Paul C. Giannelli & Susan Friedman, The National Academy of Sciences' Forensic Report, 45 CRIM. L. BULL. 6 (2009) (examining report's recommendations and statements concerning forensic techniques, including fingerprint examination, handwriting comparison, firearms (ballistics) identification, bite mark analysis, and hair comparison).

194 Melendez-Diaz v. Massachusetts, 557 U.S. 305, 318–19 (2009).

195 NATIONAL RESEARCH COUNCIL, STRENGTHENING FORENSIC SCIENCE IN THE UNITED STATES: A PATH FORWARD 100 (2009) (discussing Innocence Project); Brandon L. Garrett & Peter J. Neufeld, *Invalid Forensic Science Testimony and Wrongful Convictions*, 95 VA. L. REV. 1, 14 (2009).

Although several disciplines have been generally called into question, *Daubert* mandates an independent inquiry into the admissibility of testimony by individual experts. Thus, the following discussion of selected area of expertise is only intended to help frame the issues likely to arise for different kinds of experts. The elements of admissibility must still be established independently for each proffered witness and the testimony he or she offers. The topics considered below provide a sampling of current issues.[196]

Handwriting Analysis

Experts in handwriting analysis have long been allowed to testify as to the authorship or authenticity of a document.[197] Under *Frye*, there was little inquiry into the reliability of such expert opinion; so long as the proffered expert had the requisite qualifications and followed procedures generally accepted in the document examiner community, the testimony was admissible.[198] *Daubert* created an avenue of attack upon such evidence that many argue was long overdue.

Debunkers of handwriting identification maintain that no proof exists that document examiners can distinguish between forgeries and authentic documents by handwriting analysis. Such so-called expertise has been attacked because its foundational assumptions are unproven and because the error rate as measured by proficiency testing is unacceptably high.[199]

An influential, pre-*Daubert* article, undertook a comprehensive examination of then available studies quantifying the proficiency of handwriting experts in controlled settings. The authors concluded "[a] rather generous reading of the data would be that in 45% of the reports forensic document examiners reached the correct finding, in 36% they erred partially or completely, and in 19% they were unable to draw a conclusion."[200] In tests where handwriting exemplars contained attempts to forge documents the accuracy levels were even lower. Subsequent research supports the proposition that document examiners are subject to a high error rate. A controversial study conducted for the FBI indicates that document examiners do somewhat better than lay people[201] but that result may be due to the greater motivation of document examiners to perform well in tests upon which their livelihood depends.

Despite the potential error rate, the Federal Rules (adopted long before *Daubert* was decided or these proficiency results were available) seemingly endorse the use of

---

196 For more extensive casebook treatment, see JOHN M CONLEY & JANE CAMPBELL MORIARTY, SCIENTIFIC AND EXPERT EVIDENCE (2007). For treatise coverage, with additional topics, see PAUL C. GIANNELLI & EDWARD J. IMWINKELRIED, SCIENTIFIC EVIDENCE (4th ed. 2007), and DAVID L. FAIGMAN ET AL, MODERN SCIENTIFIC EVIDENCE: THE LAW AND SCIENCE OF EXPERT TESTIMONY (2015–16 ed.).

197 *See generally* Jennifer L. Mnookin, *Scripting Expertise: The History of Handwriting Identification Evidence and the Judicial Construction of Reliability,* 87 VA. L. REV. 1723 (2001).

198 The rationale for doing so is revealed starkly by one of the earliest decisions to admit such expertise. In Moody v. Rowell, 34 Mass 490 (1835), the court held that putative expertise was admissible in light of the traditional rule allowing lay persons familiar with a person's handwriting to identify the authorship of a writing. The court reasoned that the putative expertise could not be worse than the dubious lay testimony already allowed.

199 *See, e.g.,* D. Michael Risinger & Michael J. Saks, *Science and Nonscience in the Courts: Daubert Meets Handwriting Identification Expertise,* 82 IOWA L. REV. 21 (1996).

200 D. Michael Risinger et al., *Exorcism of Ignorance as a Proxy for Rational Knowledge: The Lessons of Handwriting Identification "Expertise",* 137 U. PA. L. REV. 731, 747 (1989).

201 Moshe Kam et al., *Proficiency of Document Examiners in Writer Identification,* 39 J. FORENSIC SCI. 5 (1994).

document examiners for the purpose of authenticating documents under Rule 901.[202] While this provision of Rule 901 does not necessarily mean that document examiners should be allowed to testify as expert witnesses for all document-related purposes, it is difficult to conceive of a principled distinction between the use of an expert to authenticate a document under Rule 901, and the use of an expert to identify forgery or general authorship under Rule 702. On the other hand, courts who have addressed the matter have noted that Rule 901 does not address the question whether a given expert qualifies under the rules for expert testimony.[203]

Some trial courts, invoking *Daubert*, have limited examiners to testimony about similarities between known samples and the questioned document but do not allow examiners to state a conclusion about whether the samples were in fact written by the same person.[204] Other trial courts have gone further, excluding such expert testimony entirely.[205] Such total exclusion is rare, however, and as long as the trial court has conducted a thorough *Daubert* analysis, every federal appellate court to consider the issue has affirmed the admissibility of expert testimony as to handwriting identification under *Daubert*.[206]

Polygraph Evidence

In the years following the holding in *Frye*, some courts revisited the issue of whether experts may testify as to polygraph test results. At least one circuit eventually concluded that advances in technology and industry practices rendered polygraph evidence admissible under the "general acceptance" standard of *Frye*.[207] Today, federal courts are, of course, subject to the *Daubert* standard.

The Fourth Circuit as well as a number of state courts maintain a *per se* ban on polygraph evidence.[208] All other circuit courts to consider the issue after *Daubert* agree

---

202 *See* FED. R. EVID. 901(b)(3). *See, e.g.*, United States v. Blackwood, 878 F.2d 1200, 1202 (9th Cir. 1989) (approving expert testimony authentication).

203 *See, e.g.*, United States v. Saelee, 162 F. Supp. 2d 1097, 1106 (D. Alaska 2001) ("Rule 901(b)(3) contemplates testimony by an expert—but before an expert's testimony can be admitted, it must past through the gates of Rule 702."); United States v. Greco, 2002 WL 746037 (E.D. Pa. 2002) (admitting qualified handwriting expert testimony comparing handwriting after passing muster under *Daubert*).

204 *See, e.g.*, United States v. Hernandez, 42 Fed. Appx. 173 (10th Cir. 2002) (holding such an approach is not an abuse of discretion); United States v. Hines, 55 F. Supp. 2d 62, 70–71 (D. Mass. 1999); United States v. Rutherford, 104 F. Supp. 2d 1190, 1194 (D. Neb. 2000); United States v. Van Wyk, 83 F. Supp. 2d 515, 524 (D. N.J. 2000); United States v. Oskowitz, 294 F. Supp. 2d 379 (E.D.N.Y. 2003). *But see* Taylor v. Abernethy, 560 S.E. 2d 233 (N.C. App. 2002) (reversing such a limitation imposed by the trial court).

205 *See, e.g.*, United States v. Fujii, 152 F. Supp 2d 939 (N.D. Ill. 2000) and United States v. Saelee, 162 F. Supp. 2d 1097 (D. Alaska 2001) (excluding, in its entirety, testimony of forensic documents examiner as failing *Daubert* test).

206 United States v. Adeyi, 165 Fed. Appx. 944, 946 n.1 (2d Cir. 2006) (stating explicitly this proposition and conducting brief survey of such decisions, including citation to rare district court case to contrary); *see also* United States v. Mooney, 315 F.3d 54, 62–63 (1st Cir. 2002) (citing Rule 901(b)(3)); United States v. Brown, 152 Fed. Appx. 59, 62–63 (2d Cir. 2005); United States v. Mornan, 413 F.3d 372, 380–381 (3d Cir. 2005); United States v. Crisp, 324 F.3d 261, 270–71 (4th Cir. 2003); United States v. Jones, 107 F.3d 1147, 1156 (6th Cir. 1997); United States v. Jolivet, 224 F.3d 902, 906 (8th Cir. 2000); United States v. Mitchell, 346 Fed. Appx. 281, 283 (9th Cir. 2009); United States v. Paul, 175 F.3d 906, 911 (11th Cir. 1999). *Cf.* Deputy v. Lehman Bros., Inc., 345 F.3d 494, 508 (7th Cir. 2003) (remanding to trial court for proper *Daubert* analysis, but implicitly stating that handwriting analysis in general is admissible so long as *Daubert* standard is satisfied for specific testimony at issue).

207 United States v. Piccinonna, 885 F.2d 1529, 1536–37 (11th Cir. 1989).

208 Surprisingly, the Fourth Circuit maintains a *per se* ban on polygraph evidence without applying the *Daubert* test to reach such a result. United States v. Prince-Oyibo, 320 F.3d 494, 501 (4th Cir. 2003). Illustrative state cases include: State v. Porter, 698 A.2d 739 (Conn. 1997); State v. Shively, 999 P.2d 952 (Kan.

trial courts must conduct an individualized *Daubert* analysis before allowing the admission of polygraph evidence.[209] For example, the Fifth Circuit held that its former *per se* ban of polygraph evidence did not survive the move to the *Daubert* standard.[210] Several circuits note that Rule 403 may prohibit the admission of such evidence even if it otherwise meets the requirements of *Daubert*.[211]

The judicial trend appears to be toward making Rule 403 the primary gate-keeping test for polygraph evidence. This is partly due to the "special risk that the jury might give excessive weight to the polygrapher's conclusions."[212] In many criminal cases, intent is an element of the charged offense, and polygraph evidence may be explicitly barred by Rule 704, which prohibits expert opinions on the issue of a criminal defendant's mental state.[213]

Military courts have an extra rule prohibiting polygraph evidence in its entirety.[214] The Supreme Court has upheld this exclusion against Sixth Amendment challenge, foreclosing any argument that there is a constitutional right of the defendant to present polygraph evidence in criminal trials.[215]

2000); State v. Robertson, 712 So.2d 8 (La. 1998); Tavares v. State, 725 So. 2d 803 (Miss. 1998); and State v. Hall, 955 S.W. 2d 198 (Mo. 1997). The Sixth Circuit may also have a *per se* exclusionary rule but appears to concede that *Daubert* applies to polygraph experts. The Sixth Circuit rule is currently predicated on Rule 403, rather than Rule 702. *See* United States v. Thomas, 167 F.3d 299, 309 (6th Cir. 1999) (preserving Rule 702 analysis for another case).

209 *See* United States v. Rouse, 410 F.3d 1005, 1011 (8th Cir. 2005) (finding that *Daubert* was correctly applied to exclude polygraph evidence); United States v. Henderson, 409 F.3d 1293, 1302 (11th Cir. 2005) (finding that trial court properly excluded polygraph evidence under *Daubert*); . Cf. Nawrocki v. Township of Coolbaugh, 34 Fed. Appx. 832, 838 (3d Cir. 2002) (acknowledging applicability of *Daubert* to admissibility of polygraph evidence in general, but holding that is does not necessarily extend to evidence presented to show probable cause, rather than to prove the truth of the results of the test).

210 United States v. Pasado, 57 F.3d 428 (5th Cir. 1995). *See also* Gibbs v. Gibbs, 210 F.3d 491, 500 (5th Cir. 2000) (affirming admission of polygraph evidence under *Daubert*).

211 See United States v. Kwong, 69 F.3d 663, 668 (2d Cir. 1995) (acknowledging that *Daubert* now controls admissibility of polygraph evidence but not reaching issue of Rule 702 admissibility because Rule 403 rendered polygraph evidence in issue inadmissible); United States v. Thomas, 167 F.3d 299, 309 (6th Cir. 1999) (suggesting that *Daubert* controls admissibility of polygraph evidence but finding that Rule 403 rendered evidence inadmissible; preserving possibility that polygraph evidence is *per se* inadmissible, even under *Daubert*); United States v. Lea, 249 F.3d 632, 639–40 (7th Cir. 2001) (requiring both *Daubert* analysis and Rule 403 balancing, where reliability under *Daubert* weighs in favor of admission under Rule 403); United States v. Waters, 194 F.3d 926, 928 (8th Cir. 1999) (holding polygraph evidence offered by defense properly excluded under Rule 403 without reaching the *Daubert* issue); United States v. Ramirez-Robles, 386 F.3d 1234, 1245–46 (9th Cir. 2004) (finding that, in order to be admitted, polygraph evidence must pass *Daubert* test, but if evidence fails Rule 403 balancing it is inadmissible regardless of whether it would pass *Daubert*); United States v. Call, 129 F.3d 1402, 1404–05 (10th Cir. 1997) (finding that *Daubert* analysis required for admissibility, but Rule 403 may still prevent admission). *See also* United States v. Mare, 668 F.3d 35, 41–42 (1st Cir. 2012) (finding no error in trial court's refusal of mistrial when prosecutor attempted to ask if witness had been willing to take a polygraph test; trial court's sustaining of defense objection and giving of cautionary instruction to jury held adequate, court stating that "polygraph evidence, even that dealing with matters other than the actual results of an examination, is usually more trouble that it is worth.").

212 United States v. Benavidez-Benavidez, 217 F.3d 720, 725 (9th Cir. 2000).

213 *See id.*; *see also* FED. R. EVID. 704(b).

214 MIL. R. EVID. 707(a) ("Notwithstanding any other provision of law, the results of a polygraph examination, the opinion of a polygraph examiner, or any reference to an offer to take, failure to take, or taking of a polygraph examination, shall not be admitted into evidence.").

215 United States v. Scheffer, 523 U.S. 303, 312 (1998) ("Although the degree of reliability of polygraph evidence may depend upon a variety of identifiable factors, there is simply no way to know in a particular case whether a polygraph examiner's conclusion is accurate, because certain doubts and uncertainties plague even the best polygraph exams. Individual jurisdictions therefore may reasonably reach differing conclusions as to whether polygraph evidence should be admitted.").

Evidence About Eyewitness and Cross-Racial Identification

One fairly controversial area of expert testimony is that of experts testifying to the problems surrounding eyewitness identification and the special issues surrounding cross-racial eyewitness identification. The main import of such expert testimony is to explain to the jury that eyewitnesses to a crime are not as good at correctly identifying perpetrators as is commonly believed and that individuals are even less proficient at correctly identifying persons of races other than their own.[216] In reviewing exonerations of false convictions, scholars have found that mistaken but sincere eyewitness testimony, false confessions, and prosecutorial failure to turn over exculpatory material are the leading reasons for innocent people being convicted of crimes.[217] In addition, it can fairly be said that the science behind expert testimony about the reliability of eyewitness testimony "is of relatively high quality" as compared to other types of social science.[218]

Of course, for federal courts the admissibility of such testimony must be evaluated under Rule 702 and *Daubert*.[219] What little judicial consensus exists with respect to expert testimony on eyewitness identification is that the trial court has wide discretion in deciding whether to admit such testimony.[220] Common criticisms of expert testimony on the reliability of eyewitness identification include that such testimony impermissibly encroaches on the jury's role of weighing witness credibility and is unhelpful in that it merely adds an expert gloss to the common-sense phenomenon that witnesses can falsely identify defendants.[221] Accordingly, many courts refuse to admit such testimony on the grounds that mistaken identifications are fully within the ken of a lay jury.[222]

There has been a gradual but discernible increase in the willingness of courts to consider such expert testimony. Courts are more likely to admit expert testimony on particular problems in eyewitness identification, such as cross-racial identification and weapon-focus, than on more general issues of eyewitness accuracy.[223] Courts are also

---

[216] *See generally* John P. Rutledge, *They All Look Alike: The Inaccuracy of Cross-Racial Identifications*, 28 AM. J. CRIM. L. 207 (2001). It is worth noting that this effect is thought to originate from increased exposure to certain ethnic characteristics, and therefore should, *in theory*, be less pronounced in persons living or raised in multi-ethnic households or neighborhoods. *See, e.g.*, Nathan Daniel Doty, *The Influence of Nationality on the Accuracy of Fact and Voice Recognition*, 111 AM. J. OF PSYCHOLOGY 191, 193–95 (1998) (noting difficulty in showing consistent improvement in cross-racial identification via casual cross-racial contact, and reporting analogous problem in same ethnicity, cross-national identification).

[217] *See* Brandon L. Garrett, *Judging Innocence*, 108 COLUM. L. REV. 55, 76 (2008) (finding erroneous eyewitness testimony in seventy-nine percent of cases).

[218] 2 FAIGMAN ET AL., MODERN SCIENTIFIC EVIDENCE: THE LAW AND SCIENCE OF EXPERT TESTIMONY § 15:1 at 575 (2015–16 ed.).

[219] United States v. Smithers, 212 F.3d 306, 313 (6th Cir. 2000) (reversing trial court's exclusion of expert testimony on eyewitness identification for failure to conduct *Daubert* analysis).

[220] *See, e.g.*, United States v. Langan, 263 F.3d 613, 621–22 (6th Cir. 2001) (concluding, after conducting a survey of recent cases on issue, that "the district court has broad discretion in, first, determining the reliability of the particular testimony, and, second, balancing its probative value against its prejudicial effect").

[221] *See id.* at 621. *But see* Rudolf Koch, Note, *Process v. Outcome: The Proper Role of Corroborative Evidence in Due Process Analysis of Eyewitness Identification Testimony*, 88 CORNELL L. REV. 1097, 1099 n.7 (2003).

[222] *See, e.g.*, United States v. Baylor, 537 Fed. Appx. 149, 159 (4th Cir. 2013), *cert. denied*, 134 S. Ct. 717 (2013); United States v. McGinnis, 201 Fed. Appx. 246, 252 (5th Cir. 2006) (finding that expert testimony on flaws in eyewitness identification was properly excluded because jury could still choose to disbelieve eyewitness's testimony as to identification of defendant without aid of expert testimony); United States v. Holloway, 971 F.2d 675 (11th Cir. 1992) (adopting a *per se* rule of exclusion for want of helpfulness).

[223] *See, e.g.*, United States v. Brownlee, 454 F.3d 131, 136–37 (3d Cir. 2006) (noting that trial court admitted expert testimony on cross-racial identification, weapon-focus, and hair-covering, but excluded testimony on other factors); United States v. Smithers, 212 F.3d 306, 313 (6th Cir. 2000) (noting "inherent

more likely to admit expert testimony on eyewitness identification when such identification is the primary, or only, evidence against the defendant,[224] and when the witness was not previously acquainted with the person identified.[225] The admission or exclusion of expert testimony based on the importance of eyewitness identification to the case at trial is supported by the Rule 702 requirement that testimony "assist the trier of fact." Alternatively, the importance of eyewitness testimony to the case at bar should be considered with respect to whether Rule 403 limits such testimony as confusing or a waste of time.

Jury instructions are often used to warn jurors about the dangers of relying on eyewitness identification, and the courts have taken various attitudes about whether to use such instructions instead of, or in addition to, live testimony by an expert.[226]

So far, the courts have not been willing to consider the use of such expertise as falling within the criminal defendant's Due Process/Compulsory Process right to present exculpatory evidence.[227] Nor have they generally been receptive to the claim that a defendant is entitled to court appointed experts on this issue.[228]

Evidence About Rape Trauma Syndrome and Related Issues

Expert testimony on rape trauma syndrome can assist the jury to understand the victim's behavior in a rape case. Rape trauma syndrome evidence explains the psychological reasons for delayed reporting, attempts by the victim to cover-up the rape, and the loss of material evidence (through the washing of clothes, etc.). Such explanations can help rebut the defendant's claim of consent, fabrication, or mental illness on the part of the alleged victim. Expert testimony on rape trauma syndrome can be vital to an effective prosecution because of the enduring prevalence of rape-myths in society.[229]

Because most rapes are prosecuted under state law rather than federal law, the majority of federal precedent for the application of *Daubert* to rape trauma testimony comes from military appellate courts,[230] reviewing the admission of expert testimony in

---

unreliability of cross-racial identifications"); United States v. Smith, 156 F.3d 1046, 1053 (10th Cir. 1998) (noting that cross-racial identification is one of "narrow circumstances" where expert testimony is helpful).

[224] *See, e.g.*, Johnson v. State, 526 S.E.2d 549, 552–53 (Ga. 2000); People v. McDonald, 690 P.2d 709 (Cal. 1984), *overruled on other grounds by* People v. Mendoza, 4 P.3d 265 (Cal. 2000).

[225] *See, e.g.*, State v. Guilbert, 49 A.3d 705 (Conn. 2012) (overruling earlier case law).

[226] 2 FAIGMAN ET AL., MODERN SCIENTIFIC EVIDENCE: THE LAW AND SCIENCE OF EXPERT TESTIMONY § 15:7 (2015–16 ed.).

[227] *See, e.g.*, Johnson v. Wainwright, 806 F.2d 1479, 1485 (11th Cir. 1986).

[228] *See, e.g.*, Barker v. Fleming, 423 F.3d 1085, 1089 n.1 (9th Cir. 2005). *But see* State v. Bradley, 907 N.E.2d 1205 (Ohio Ct. App. 2009) (holding that failure to provide eyewitness expert violated due process where identification was central issue in case).

[229] United States v. Cox, 23 M.J. 808, 815 (N.M.C.M.R. 1986) ("We find that evidence of rape trauma syndrome is relevant and of particular assistance to the trier of fact under Military Rule of Evidence 702 where it helps to dispel some of the popular myths concerning rape—especially in a case, such as the instant case, where the very crux of the defense depends upon the pervasiveness of the common man's belief in those myths."). For an overview of the pervasiveness of rape-myths, *see generally* Mary I. Coombs, *Telling the Victim's Story*, 2 TEX. J. WOMEN & L. 277 (1993).

[230] What little can be found in the way of non-military courts' consideration of rape trauma testimony also trends toward admission of such evidence. *See* Hirst v. Inverness Hotel Corp., 544 F.3d 221, 225 (3d Cir. 2008) (noting that rape trauma expert testified, but not directly addressing Rule 702 issue as it was not part of appeal); Jenkins v. McCoy, 1994 WL 501983, at *4 (4th Cir. 1994).

the trial of an accused rapist who was thereby convicted. Military appellate opinions routinely affirm the admission of expert testimony regarding rape trauma syndrome.[231]

Numerous state courts have held, however, that expert testimony regarding rape trauma syndrome should only be offered to dispel rape myths and not to serve as affirmative evidence that, in the expert's opinion, the victim was raped,[232] or to bolster the credibility of the complaining witness,[233] though the line between permissible and impermissible testimony can become quite thin. Reluctant to allow a psychological expert witness to opine about witness credibility or whether a sexual crime took place, courts limit the expert to testifying as to common, but perhaps unknown and counterintuitive reactions to sex crimes, such as delay in reporting, disassociation, and withdrawal.[234]

Similarly, in child molestation cases, courts will permit a description of how abused children behave (including sexual acting out, delayed reporting, and recantation of

---

[231] *See* United States v. Houser, 36 M.J. 392, 398 (C.M.A. 1993) (conducting survey of cases admitting rape-trauma testimony and concluding " 'The plain rule of law is that an expert's testimony concerning rape-trauma syndrome' [is] admissible" (quoting United States v. Reynolds, 29 M.J. 105, 111 (C.M.A. 1989))). While many of the military cases on rape trauma syndrome were decided pre-*Daubert*, the Court of Appeals for the Armed Forces has noted that the framework military courts were applying to such evidence pre-*Daubert* was remarkably similar to the *Daubert* standard, and that such cases maintain their precedential weight in the *Daubert* era. *See* United States v. Griffin, 50 M.J. 278, 284 (C.A.A.F. 1999). To its credit, the Court of Appeals for the Armed Forces laid down the following factors that must be established before expert testimony is admitted before the *Daubert* opinion came down from the Supreme Court: (A) the qualifications of the expert, (B) the subject matter of the expert testimony, (C) the basis for the expert testimony, (D) the legal relevance of the evidence, (E) the reliability of the evidence, and (F) whether the "probative value" of the testimony outweighs other considerations under Rule 403. United States v. Houser, 36 M.J. 392, 397 (C.M.A. 1993).

[232] *See, e.g.*, People v. Bledsoe, 681 P.2d 291, 298, 301 (Cal.1984) (surveying other jurisdictions, and coming to same conclusion). It is worth quoting the reasoning of the court in *Bledsoe* at length:

> Unlike fingerprints, blood tests, lie detector tests, voiceprints or the battered child syndrome, rape trauma syndrome was not devised to determine the "truth" or "accuracy" of a particular past event—i.e., whether, in fact, a rape in the legal sense occurred—but rather was developed by professional rape counselors as a therapeutic tool, to help identify, predict and treat emotional problems experienced by the counselors' clients or patients. As the professional literature makes clear—and as the expert testimony in this case also reveals—because in the past women who have brought charges of rape have traditionally had their credibility or motives questioned by the police and others, rape counselors are taught to make a conscious effort to avoid judging the credibility of their clients. * * *
>
> We emphasize that our conclusion in this regard is not intended to suggest that rape trauma syndrome is not generally recognized or used in the general scientific community from which it arose, but only that it is not relied on in that community for the purpose for which the prosecution sought to use it in this case, namely, to prove that a rape in fact occurred. Because the literature does not even purport to claim that the syndrome is a scientifically reliable means of proving that a rape occurred, we conclude that it may not properly be used for that purpose in a criminal trial.

Id. at 300–01. While the *Bledsoe* analysis is not illogical, it does question whether a victim would seek rape trauma counseling if he or she had not been raped. The opinion also may shortchange the ability of a clinical psychologist to discern the client's underlying problems. *Cf.* Townsend v. State, 734 P.2d 705, 707–09 (Nev. 1987) (extending permissible scope of testimony to the fact that the complaining witness had been sexually assaulted, but not to the identification of the perpetrator).

[233] *See, e.g.*, State v. Kinney, 762 A.2d 833, 844 (Vt. 2000) (rejecting expert testimony regarding the percentage of rape complaints that are false). *See also* Commonwealth v. Balodis, 747 A.2d 341, 344 (Pa. 2000); Commonwealth v. Federico, 683 N.E.2d 1035, 1039 (Mass. 1997); State v. Alberico, 861 P.2d 192 (N.M. 1993); State v. Taylor, 663 S.W.2d 235, 241 (Mo. 1984).

[234] *See, e.g.*, State v. Taylor, 552 N.E.2d 131 (N.Y. 1990); State v. Hall, 412 S.E.2d 883 (N.C. 1992); State v. Middleton, 657 P.2d 1215, 1217–21 (Or. 1983); State v. Jensen, 432 N.W.2d 913 (Wis. 1988).

abuse) but typically will not permit the expert to testify that the child was actually abused or to identify the abuser.[235]

Police Experts

Testimony by police offers and other law enforcement agents is common in both criminal and civil trials. Officers may be able to qualify as experts when issues of appropriate police conduct are at stake, such as another officer's need to use force.[236] Such testimony becomes more problematic when officers are called to testify as experts in other civil or criminal matters. Obviously, police officers can report, as *lay* witnesses, facts they observe and lay opinions based on their observations, such as the location and condition of a body, the state of intoxication of a suspect when arrested, or the location of automobiles at the scene of an accident. But the extent to which they can serve as experts is more controversial.

One area where expert testimony by police continues to be common is in regard to the method of operation of criminal enterprises.[237] Although, after *Kumho*, all expertise falls within the purview of *Daubert*, the expertise may be judged valid by use of criteria other than scientific testing, peer review and publication, or assessment of an error rate. The fact that all expertise must be screened certainly indicates that it is appropriate for trial judges to ask police experts about the basis for their opinions and to exclude the opinions if they are not based on reliable data and methodology in view of the subject matter and the practical alternatives.[238]

The most troublesome cases involve investigating agents who attempt to explain why they think the defendant is guilty. While it is true that those who investigate crime may develop an expertise in the assessment of evidence in criminal cases, allowing such investigators to testify to their conclusions, even if it would (in some sense) help the fact-finder, treads on important constitutional norms. Perhaps the most important function of the presumption of innocence is to remind fact-finders that they are to assess the evidence for themselves and not to take, as evidence against the accused, the fact that investigators think the defendant is guilty.[239] This practice is surprisingly common, however, and it is hard to distinguish between legitimate expertise on discrete topics

---

[235] *See, e.g.*, State v. Batangan, 799 P.2d 48, 49 (Hawaii 1990) (applying Hawaii's version of 702 and concluding that "while expert testimony explaining 'seemingly bizarre' behavior of child sex abuse victims is helpful to the jury and should be admitted, conclusory opinions that abuse did occur and that the child victim's report of abuse is truthful and believable is of no assistance to the jury, and therefore, should not be admitted."); People v. Beckley, 456 N.W.2d 391 (Mich. 1990); State v. Spigarolo, 556 A.2d 112, 122–24 (Conn. 1989); State v. Moran, 728 P.2d 248 (Ariz. 1986).

[236] *See, e.g.*, Kopf v. Skyrm, 993 F.2d 374, 377–79 (4th Cir. 1993) (reversing trial court's exclusion of plaintiff's experts with police experience). *See generally* STEPHEN M. RYALS, DISCOVERY AND PROOF IN POLICE MISCONDUCT CASES §§ 7.6–7.15 (1995).

[237] *See, e.g.*, United States v. Dukagjini, 326 F.3d 45 (2d Cir. 2003) (permitting prosecution to use case agent as expert to interpret coded language of drug trafficking; finding harmless error in allowing hearsay through the expert); United States v. Are, 590 F.3d 499, 512 (7th Cir. 2009) ("This circuit has routinely upheld the admission of expert testimony from law enforcement purporting to translate 'code words' used by conspirators during intercepted phone calls."). In some cases, it may be permissible for an investigating agent to testify as a *lay* witness to the meaning of code words used by the targets of an investigation, provided that the opinion is based entirely on the agent's own observation of this particular target's behavior in the transaction that is the subject of the charge and not on background training or experience with drug trafficking more generally. *See, e.g.*, United States v. Santiago, 560 F.3d 62, 66–67 (1st Cir. 2009). *See* **§ 10.02**.

[238] *See* Joëlle Anne Moreno, *What Happens When Dirty Harry Becomes an (Expert) Witness for the Prosecution?*, 79 TUL. L. REV. 1 (2004).

[239] *See* 9 WIGMORE ON EVIDENCE § 2511 at 530 (Chadbourn rev. 1981); 2 MCCORMICK ON EVIDENCE § 342 at 681 (Kenneth S. Broun ed., 7th ed. 2013).

and impermissible opinion testimony that belongs instead in an attorney's closing arguments.[240]

Field Sobriety Tests

For several decades, it has been common for police officers to administer a series of "field sobriety tests" (FSTs) to drivers they suspect of being under the influence of alcohol. Developed for the National Highway Traffic Safety Administration in the 1970s, there are three main tests.[241] The test that has the best claim to a scientific basis is the Horizontal Gaze Nystagmus Test (HGN). Nystagmus is the involuntary jerking of the eyes as a person gazes to the side. It is a natural phenomenon, but alcohol and certain other drugs are thought to magnify it.[242] Because the HGN test requires the administering officer to make visual measurements based on the motorist's eye movements, the validity of the test depends on the officer's accuracy.

The other FSTs are more subjective and based less on scientifically observed phenomena. They include the "Walk and Turn" test[243] and the One Leg Stand, both of which are performed in the manner their name suggests. Again, the officer monitors the subject's performance using certain "clues" and is purported to be able to make a judgment with reasonable accuracy that a given subject has a blood alcohol content of over 0.10. Other tests include a "finger-count" test, and a test in which the subject is asked to write the letters of the alphabet.

Prosecutors of drunk driving cases have offered FST evidence for two principal purposes: (1) to demonstrate the existence of probable cause to charge a driver with driving under the influence of alcohol and (2) to prove a subject's actual blood alcohol content.

Beginning in the 1980s, state courts began to evaluate the admissibility of FST evidence.[244] Many courts distinguish the HGN test from the other less "scientific" FSTs.

---

[240] Because the expertise is often largely experience-based and used to interpret case-specific facts observed by the officer, it is not uncommon for this kind of specialized knowledge to be offered and (erroneously) admitted as lay testimony. *See* **§ 10.02**; United States v. Garcia, 413 F.3d 201 (2d Cir. 2005) (finding harmless error in admission as lay testimony of investigating agent's summary of evidence to come and conclusions he inferred from that evidence based on his experience; court noting that the agent's testimony was an improper substitute for opening statement); United States v. Cano, 289 F.3d 1354 (11th Cir. 2002), *cert. denied*, 540 U.S. 985 (2003) (rejecting defendant's argument on appeal that detective's testimony analyzing facts was expert testimony not in compliance with rules for experts but opining that detective's testimony analyzing the facts was improper lay opinion introduced as a substitute for argument of government counsel; error held to be harmless).

[241] For a detailed discussion of the various tests, *see* United States v. Horn, 185 F. Supp. 2d 530, 535–38 (D. Md. 2002).

[242] The officer administering the test looks for three "clues" to exaggerated nystagmus: the subject's inability to follow a slowly moving stimulus smoothly; a more distinct nystagmus when the subject has moved the eyes as far as possible to the left or right and held them in that position for several seconds; and the presence of nystagmus before the eyes have moved 45 degrees to the left or right. NHTSA publications, which are cited repeatedly in judicial opinions, take the position that, if a subject exhibits nystagmus before moving the eyes 45 degrees to the right or left, the subject normally has a blood alcohol content above 0.10, which is above the legal limit in most states.

[243] This test requires the subject to walk a straight line in the heel-to-toe position for a set number of paces and then to turn and walk back in the same manner, all the while holding his hands to the side, watching his feet, and counting his steps out loud. As with the HGN test, NHSTA publications assert that the officer should watch for certain "clues," and that the subject's performance can indicate a blood alcohol content above 0.10. The NHTSA asserts that when the results of the HGN and WAT tests are combined, the officer can achieve 80 percent accuracy in judging that the subject's blood alcohol content exceeds 0.10.

[244] Apparently the first reported opinion is State v. Superior Court, 718 P.2d 171 (Ariz. 1986), where the Arizona Supreme Court held the results of the HGN test sufficiently trustworthy to establish probable cause

These courts have generally evaluated the HGN test under the applicable standard for scientific evidence, while viewing the other tests as involving the kinds of common sense observations within the general knowledge of laypersons and thus not requiring expert testimony.[245] Often, courts admit this evidence simply as a police officer's lay observation that can be helpful in determining whether the subject was intoxicated.[246] Most courts allow the evidence only as circumstantial evidence of intoxication, and not as proof of the defendant's specific blood alcohol content.[247]

The most searching analysis to date of FST evidence under the Federal Rules was conducted by the district court in *United States v. Horn*,[248] which held a two-day hearing on the admissibility of FSTs. The court considered the affidavits of four defense experts as well as the arresting officer. The government also introduced a number of "validation studies." The defense experts criticized these studies on many grounds. Among the more important criticisms were that some studies were conducted under laboratory conditions that facilitated observation that would not be duplicated in the field; that the officers who submitted to some tests were self-selected and might not have been representative; that some estimates of accuracy were artificially inflated by the test methodology; that some data was described incompletely or in a manner that cannot be evaluated adequately; that certain studies reported misleadingly high accuracy rates; and that the results of the studies were not published in peer reviewed journals.[249] The court ultimately concluded that the results of the tests would only be admissible to determine whether probable cause exists to charge a driver with driving while intoxicated; that the test results, whether taken individually or combined, are not admissible to prove the specific blood alcohol content of a subject; and that while a police officer trained in FSTs may testify about her observations of a subject's performance on properly administered tests, the officer may not use "value-added descriptive language to characterize the subject's performance." In addition, the court held that although the officer may offer an opinion as a lay witness that the defendant was driving while intoxicated, she may not bolster that opinion by referring to any scientific, technical, or specialized information gleaned from law enforcement instruction.[250]

---

for arrest. The court also held that the HGN test had achieved general acceptance among behavioral psychologists, highway safety experts, neurologists, and law enforcement agencies.

[245] *See, e.g.*, State v. Witte, 836 P.2d 1110, 1111 (Kan. 1992) ("The horizontal gaze nystagmus test is distinguished from other field sobriety tests in that science, rather than common knowledge, provides the legitimacy for horizontal gaze nystagmus testing.") State v. Cissne, 865 P.2d 564, 568 (Wash. Ct. App. 1994) ("The HGN test is a different type of test from balancing on one leg or walking a straight line because it rests almost entirely upon an assertion of scientific legitimacy rather than a basis of common knowledge");. *But see* State v. Bresson, 554 N.E.2d 1330 (Ohio 1990) (finding that HGN test is no different from any other FST).

[246] *See, e.g.*, State v. Meador, 674 So. 2d 826, 832 (Fla. Ct. App. 1996) (holding "psychomotor FSTs" admissible to show intoxication, but holding that officer should avoid referring to observations as "tests" or suggesting that subject "failed" or received certain number of "points").

[247] *See, e.g.*, Ballard v. State, 955 P.2d 931 (Alaska Ct. App. 1998); State v. Superior Court, 718 P.2d 171 (Ariz. 1986); State v. Taylor, 694 A.2d 907 (Me. 1997); State v. Baue, 607 N.W.2d 191 (Neb. 2000); State v. Yuel, 840 N.W.2d 680 (S.D. 2013); White v. Miller, 724 S.E.2d 768 (W. Va. 2012). Though research appears to support the validity of the assumptions underlying the HGN test (that an intoxicated person exhibits exaggerated nystagmus), neither that test nor any of the more subjective FSTs are likely to be sufficiently trustworthy to justify an estimate of a subject's actual blood alcohol content. In fact, the data supporting FSTs is rather thin, and the error rates are relatively high. *See* Steven J. Rubenzer, *The Standardized Field Sobriety Tests: A Review of Scientific and Legal Issues*, 32 LAW & HUM. BEHAV. 293 (2008).

[248] 185 F. Supp. 2d 530 (D. Md. 2002).

[249] *Id.* at 539–46.

[250] *Id.* at 532–34.

Though some courts applying the *Daubert* standards have been more generous toward admission of FST evidence,[251] the direction suggested by the *Horn* court seems most appropriate under the modern Federal Rules. In light of the ready availability of more reliable chemical tests,[252] there is little reason to permit such FST evidence at trial when the issue is whether the defendant's blood alcohol level exceeded some specific legal limit.

---

[251] *See, e.g.*, Volk v. United States, 57 F. Supp. 2d 888 (N.D. Cal. 1999) (holding that *Kumho* standard applies, and that courts have broad discretion within that standard).

[252] *See generally* 5 David L. Faigman et al., Modern Scientific Evidence: The Law and Science of Expert Testimony § 39 (2016–17 ed.).

Chapter 11

IMPEACHMENT AND REHABILITATION OF WITNESSES

Table of Sections

§ 11.01 Introduction to Impeachment

Impeaching a witness means discrediting that witness's testimony by presenting flaws in the witness's credibility. Such flaws can be demonstrated on cross-examination and sometimes by extrinsic evidence. Witness impeachment rules require that a witness actually testify and can only be triggered by a witness on the stand.[1] This is especially significant in criminal prosecutions, because some evidence that is admissible for impeachment only (such as the accused's conviction for a prior felony) will not come in at all if the accused invokes her Fifth-Amendment right against self-incrimination and declines to testify.[2]

A witness may be impeached in many different ways. Although old movies give us a picture of a tearful witness badgered into honesty by an angry, probing cross-examiner, it is the rare case that impeachment changes a witness's story entirely. Instead, the

---

[1] There is one exception to this principle: When hearsay is admitted by way of a hearsay exception, the hearsay declarant is, for many purposes, treated as a witness and is subject to impeachment even if the declarant never takes the stand. *See* **§ 14.09**.

[2] *See* **§ 4.18**.

purpose of impeachment is to alert the finder-of-fact to potential problems with the testimony and the witness. Forms of impeachment include:[3]

- a showing of bias or interest;
- a showing that the witness made a prior inconsistent statement;
- contradiction through another witness;
- an attack on character for truthfulness;
- a showing of defects in the witness's perception or ability to observe; and
- a showing of a mental disease or defect of the witness.

Trial judges have leeway to regulate cross-examination on these and other subjects, and many allow fairly free-ranging cross-examination.[4]

The common impeachment modalities listed above fall into two rather distinct categories. Impeachment by showing a bias, a dishonest character, or a sensory or cognitive defect in the witness all attempt to explain why the witness is testifying the way he is. The impeaching party wants the fact-finder to think: "The witness is only saying that because he is biased/dishonest/blind/insane/etc." The other two common impeachment techniques—impeachment by showing prior inconsistent statements and impeachment by contradicting the witness—operate more indirectly: they do not attempt to explain why the witness is testifying as he is, but only raise questions about it. For example, that the witness previously said something different from his testimony does not tell the fact-finder why the change occurred. Was it because the witness was bribed to change his tune (bias)? Was it because he does not respect the difference between telling the truth and lying (a character flaw)? Was it because his memory has faded (a cognitive problem)? Or did he just think more carefully about what he was saying when he testified under oath (as, indeed, one would hope). And so forth.[5]

In addition, there are two distinct ways that impeachment may be conducted. The obvious way is through cross-examination. But when the impeacher is dissatisfied with a witness's answers during cross-examination, the impeacher may wish to introduce extrinsic evidence to further the attack on the witness's credibility. For this purpose, "extrinsic evidence" is any testimony other than testimony from the mouth of the witness during cross-examination.[6] Therefore, testimony of another witness would be extrinsic. Likewise, a document introduced to impeach a witness is also extrinsic evidence, at least when it is necessary to call another witness to authenticate the document. The common law did not admit extrinsic evidence for some types of impeachment but did for others.

---

[3] *See* ROGER PARK & TOM LININGER, THE NEW WIGMORE: IMPEACHMENT AND REHABILITATION § 2.1 (2012); 27 CHARLES A. WRIGHT & VICTOR J. GOLD, FEDERAL PRACTICE AND PROCEDURE (EVIDENCE) § 6094 (2007). The credibility of a witness may also be attacked in other ways, such as by demonstrating the implausibility of the witness's story and by observing the demeanor of the witness while testifying. For a useful list of factors affecting the credibility of a witness, see CAL. EVID. CODE § 780. These additional ways of attacking credibility are typically not subject to special evidentiary rules.

[4] United States v. Phelps, 733 F.2d 1464, 1472 (11th Cir. 1984) (holding that trial court has discretion about scope and extent of cross-examination, and "presumption favors free ranging cross-examination on possible bias, motive, ability to perceive and remember, and general character for truthfulness").

[5] *See* 3A WIGMORE ON EVIDENCE §§ 1000, 1017 (Chadbourn rev. 1970).

[6] *See* ROGER PARK & TOM LININGER, THE NEW WIGMORE: IMPEACHMENT AND REHABILITATION § 2.2 (2012).

The same is true of the Federal Rules.[7] In determining the propriety of offering evidence to impeach a witness, it is crucial to identify not only the mode of relevance of the impeachment, but also the precise tool by which such impeachment can be accomplished.

§ 11.02 Impeaching One's Own Witness [FRE 607]

The common law prohibited impeaching one's own witness.[8] The historical roots and policy basis for the common-law rule forbidding impeachment of one's own witness are unclear. Wigmore thought that the rule probably arose from an ancient form of trial known as compurgation, in which a party's witnesses were called not for their personal knowledge of the facts of the case (in fact, they likely had no such knowledge), but rather for their belief in the party's truthfulness and general good character. Under such a system, it would be illogical to impeach one's own oath-helper. Instead, the party vouched for the credibility of the witnesses the party called.[9]

Another prominent commentator believed this voucher rule arose from the transition from an inquisitorial to an adversarial system of trial. Under the inquisitorial system, jurors decided the case based on their personal knowledge of the facts, and there was simply no opportunity to call witnesses on one's own behalf.[10] At least for occurrence witnesses (as opposed to character and expert witnesses), the rationale that one vouches for one's witnesses ceased to have a sensible basis centuries ago.[11] A modern litigant must take occurrence witnesses where they can be found and has no control over the character and credibility of those who happen to possess personal knowledge of relevant events.

Another justification for the rule against impeaching one's own witness is that it allows the proponent an opportunity for blackmail. The proponent could put the witness on the stand under the threat of revealing dark secrets about the witness's past if the witness did not testify favorably for the proponent.[12] Blackmail would only pose an actual danger in cases in which the proponent had character-smearing evidence that was not available to the opponent, who might use it to attack the witness's credibility. In any event, this theory does not explain the broad applicability of the anti-impeachment rule,

---

7 There is very little in the Rules explicitly addressing the issue of impeachment on collateral matters with extrinsic evidence. Only Rule 608(b) articulates such an idea. *See* **§ 11.09**. While the wording of that rule caused some confusion before 2004, the rule was amended to clarify that its "absolute prohibition on extrinsic evidence applies only when the sole reason for proffering that evidence is to attack or support the witness' [sic] character for truthfulness" and that "the amendment leaves the admissibility of extrinsic evidence offered for other grounds of impeachment (such as contradiction, prior inconsistent statement, bias, and mental capacity) to Rules 402 and 403." FED. R. EVID. 608(b) advisory committee note (2003 amendment).

8 *See In re* San Miguel Gold Mining Co., 197 F. 126, 127 (W.D. Pa. 1912) (holding that party who called witness vouched for witness's credibility by putting him on stand and therefore may not impeach his testimony); *In re* Calvi, 185 F. 642, 652 (N.D.N.Y.1911) ("when a party calls a witness, he represents him as worthy of credit, and cannot impeach him in any way"); 3A WIGMORE ON EVIDENCE § 896 (Chadbourn rev. 1970).

9 Wigmore wrote that the voucher rule may have been based on "[t]he primitive notion, that a party is morally bound by the statements of his witnesses." 3A WIGMORE ON EVIDENCE § 899 (Chadbourn rev. 1970).

10 Mason Ladd, *Impeachment of One's Own Witness—New Developments*, 4 U. CHI. L. REV. 69, 72 (1936) ("Until there were witnesses in the modern sense, there could be no reason for the idea that a party was bound by his witness or that he could not impeach him."). *See* Don Johnsen, Note, *Impeachment With an Unsworn Prior Inconsistent Statement as Subterfuge*, 28 WM. & MARY L. REV. 295, 296 n.1 (1987) (discussing Wigmore's and Ladd's views).

11 Wigmore wrote that the "traditional notion of a witness, that of a person 'ex officio' a partisan pure and simple, persisted as a tradition long past the time when their function had ceased to be that of a mere oath-taker and had become that of a testifier to facts." 3A WIGMORE ON EVIDENCE § 896 (Chadbourn rev. 1970).

12 *See, e.g., id.* § 899.

given that the limitation could have been restricted to prevent impeaching the character of one's own witness.

Finally, the anti-impeachment rule may have served to prevent a proponent from calling an unfavorable witness solely to introduce a prior inconsistent statement, in hopes that the jury would disregard instructions to limit the statement to its impeachment value, and instead use the statement for its truth. Although this danger is real and worthy of consideration,[13] it does not justify a broad rule prohibiting any impeachment of one's own witness.

However justified, the common-law prohibition applied to all methods of impeachment.[14] However, in the case of impeachment by prior inconsistent statement, the common law developed a two-part exception to aid the attorney whose witness had unexpectedly become hostile. First, the "turncoat" witness's testimony had to be actually harmful;[15] it was not enough for the witness merely to testify "I don't know" or "I don't recall." Second, the attorney had to be surprised by the witness's harmful testimony.[16] When the attorney knew beforehand that the witness was going to offer harmful testimony, the attorney was supposed to refrain from calling the witness, rather than calling the witness and then impeaching him or her.

Federal Rule of Evidence 607 provides that the credibility of a witness may be impeached by any party. This brief rule abolishes the troublesome and outdated common-law rule. Overturning the common-law rule helps to secure accurate fact-finding by increasing the admissibility of relevant evidence—in this case, evidence concerning a witness's credibility.[17]

The codified rule has caused little difficulty, except in cases involving allegations that the proponent has called a witness solely to create a pretext to introduce other evidence that is admissible only for impeachment purposes. Imagine that a prosecutor wishes to call W to the stand to testify that he had been at D's house and that D had shown W $100,000 in currency. W gave a police investigator a written statement about seeing the $100,000. Subsequently, W recanted and now maintains that, although W was present at D's house on the day in question, D did not show W any currency. Suppose the prosecutor is certain that the witness will testify that nothing happened at D's

---

[13] *See, e.g.*, 1 MICHAEL H. GRAHAM, HANDBOOK OF FEDERAL EVIDENCE § 609.3at 680–81 (4th ed. 1996); Randolph N. Jonakait, *The Supreme Court, Plain Meaning and the Changed Rules of Evidence*, 68 TEX. L. REV. 745 (1990).

[14] *See* 3A WIGMORE ON EVIDENCE §§ 896–99 (Chadbourn rev. 1970).

[15] Mitchell v. Swift & Co., 151 F.2d 770, 772 (5th Cir. 1945) (holding that plaintiff may not introduce ex parte statement of witness called by him solely because witness's testimony was not favorable to plaintiff's case); Arine v. United States, 10 F.2d 778, 780 (9th Cir. 1926) (holding impeachment attempts by prosecutor improper in case where testimony is immaterial but not harmful). *See, e.g.*, State v. Perez, 594 N.E.2d 1041, 1045–46 (Ohio Ct. App. 1991) (trial court committed reversible error by declaring state's witness hostile and allowing impeachment by leading questions about prior inconsistent statement; Ohio R. Evid. 607 allows impeachment of own witness only on showing of "surprise and affirmative damage," elements not shown by the state).

[16] Bedell v. United States, 68 F.2d 776, 777 (D.C. Cir. 1934) (holding that prosecutor may impeach witness with prior written statement because he was genuinely surprised by witness's testimony, but prior statement may only be used for impeachment, not substantive purposes); Sullivan v. United States, 28 F.2d 147, 149 (9th Cir. 1928) (holding that in case where three convicts had signed joint statement implicating defendant, failure of first witness to testify he saw defendant at robbery gave "fair warning" to government that other two convicts would very likely not testify against defendant; therefore, government could not impeach latter two witnesses because it could not claim it was surprised by their statements).

[17] *See* 27 CHARLES A. WRIGHT & VICTOR J. GOLD, FEDERAL PRACTICE AND PROCEDURE (EVIDENCE) § 6092 (2007).

house—(the defense counsel even conducted a voir dire of the witness at this very trial and the witness testified that nothing happened at D's house). Nevertheless, the prosecutor seeks to put W on the stand before the jury. The witness offers no affirmative testimony that helps the prosecution. And because of the hearsay rule, W's prior statement to the investigator concerning the currency is not admissible for the truth of the matter asserted.[18] The prosecutor offers the prior statement to "impeach" W in the hope that, instead of following a limiting instruction, the jury will nevertheless use the statement for its truth. Otherwise, there is no reason to call the witness; testimony that merely demonstrates that an unhelpful witness is unreliable proves nothing in the prosecutor's case.

In this situation, a number of courts have held that the prosecution may not impeach its own witness.[19] The same principle applies to other proponents who would call a witness solely for the purpose of impeachment. To hold otherwise invites parties to call witnesses and offer evidence solely in hopes that the jurors will disregard the limiting instructions and use the evidence for an improper purpose.[20] However, as at common-law, the party who called the witness may still impeach the witness if the witness had some useful information, there was some legitimate question as to how the witness might testify, or if the turnabout in testimony was a surprise.[21]

Although most cases concerning the improper calling of a witness solely to impeach with otherwise inadmissible evidence involve prior inconsistent statements, not all arise in that context. For example, in *United States v. Gomez-Gallardo*[22] the government called Gutierrez, who had previously pleaded guilty to participation in the charged conspiracy. Gutierrez testified that he had participated in a cocaine deal with another

---

[18] Had the statement been made under oath in a grand jury or other proceeding, it would have been admissible for the truth of what it asserts under FED. R. EVID. 801(d)(2)(A). *See* **§ 15.03**.

[19] United States v. Hogan, 763 F.2d 697, 702 (5th Cir. 1985), *opinion withdrawn in part on other grounds*, 771 F.2d 82 (5th Cir. 1985) ("prosecution . . . may not call a witness it knows to be hostile for the primary purpose of eliciting otherwise inadmissible impeachment testimony, for such a scheme merely serves as a subterfuge to avoid the hearsay rule"); United States v. Crouch, 731 F.2d 621, 624 (9th Cir. 1984) (holding it improper for prosecution to call witness to testify to get her previous statement into evidence under guise of impeachment, but not reversible error because defendant's guilt clearly demonstrated by admissible evidence).

[20] United States v. Pollard, 38 M.J. 41, 50 (C.M.A. 1993) (holding that trial court committed reversible error by allowing trial counsel to read, under guise of impeachment, pretrial statements of 13-year-old alleged, sexual assault victim despite her subsequent recantation of those statements); Whitehurst v. Wright, 592 F.2d 834, 840 (5th Cir. 1979) (holding it proper for court to exclude use of witness's prior inconsistent statement for impeachment purposes when plaintiff knew witness would deny the facts asserted in previous statement during his testimony, because use of impeachment merely a ploy to "use hearsay evidence for substantive purposes").

Some authority supports the proposition that the judge should disregard the prosecutor's motive in deciding whether to exclude the evidence. *See* United States v. Logan, 121 F.3d 1172, 1175–76 (8th Cir. 1997) (holding that government's motive in calling witness was irrelevant and sole issue was whether evidence was prejudicial under Rule 403; here, where value of evidence for impeachment was minimal and danger of prejudice high, it was error to admit). In the authors' opinion, a test that completely disregards motive risks injustice, because the prosecution should be allowed to impeach an unexpected turncoat but not to impeach a witness called solely with the motive of offering otherwise inadmissible evidence. Consideration of motive has the beneficial effect of discouraging adversaries from offering unnecessary evidence in hopes of benefiting from prejudicial effect, while still safeguarding against the injustice that can occur when a party who is genuinely surprised by a change in testimony is deprived of the opportunity to put in the witness's inconsistent statements.

[21] *See* United States v. Johnson, 977 F.2d 1360, 1381–82 (10th Cir. 1992) (holding that trial court may allow prosecutor to question federal marshal about prior, inconsistent statements made by government witness when prosecutor expected witness to testify that defendant fired on law enforcement officials with an automatic weapon, but witness testified he saw and recalled no weapons).

[22] United States v. Gomez-Gallardo, 915 F.2d 553 (9th Cir. 1990).

individual and he knew the defendant but he had never participated in any drug transactions with him. Gutierrez also testified that the defendant was at the home of another alleged drug dealer, but that he was there for innocuous purposes only. The government then called three witnesses to impeach Gutierrez by contradiction and by showing Guttierez's bad character. In its closing argument, the government urged the jury to reject Gutierrez's testimony. On appeal of the defendant's guilty verdict, the court reversed, ruling that none of the contradiction evidence was properly admissible as substantive evidence of the defendant's guilt and that the evidence suggesting Gutierrez's bad character was only admissible to impeach Gutierrez, not the defendant. Thus, the appellate court held that "the government called Gutierrez for the primary purpose of impeaching Gutierrez's credibility to prove the substance of the charges against Gallardo,"[23] and such testimony was impermissible.

A special kind of impeachment of one's own witness is the generally accepted practice of *anticipating* an opponent's impeachment, known as "removing the sting" of such impeachment.[24] If the direct examiner anticipates that the opponent will impeach the witness, then the direct examiner may choose to bring out the impeaching facts on direct examination in order to avoid the appearance of hiding something from the fact-finder—or to put the matter positively, in order to be fully forthcoming with useful information. It can be difficult to discern when this practice has crossed over the line into the prohibited practice of bolstering the credibility of a witness before it has been attacked,[25] especially when the opponent is willing to agree *not* to engage in the anticipated impeachment.[26]

§ 11.03 Good Faith Basis for Cross-Examination

Trial courts have authority to prevent or curtail any impeachment or cross-examination that risks exposing the jury to potentially unfair prejudicial innuendo. In particular, counsel may not pose any question without possessing a good faith basis to believe the matters raised by the question.[27] Though the application of this rule is highly fact-sensitive, some general guidelines exist. Counsel need not know the answer to every

---

23 *Id.* at 556.

24 See, e.g., Ohler v. United States, 529 U.S. 753, 758 (2000) ("The defendant must choose whether to introduce the conviction on direct examination and remove the sting or to take her chances with the prosecutor's possible elicitation of the conviction on cross-examination.") The *Ohler* decision held, however, that this practice may effect a waiver of the right to appeal an in limine ruling that had declined to preclude impeachment by the opponent). *See* **§ 3.02**.

25 *See* **§ 11.13**.

26 See, *e.g.*, United States v. Universal Rehabilitation Services (PA), Inc., 205 F.3d 657 (3d Cir. 2000) (en banc) (holding, over strong dissents, that the prosecution may introduce evidence of plea agreements with witnesses who were alleged co-conspirators of the defendants in order to offset potential jury speculation that the witnesses were biased by plea agreements, even though the defendants agreed not to attack the witnesses credibility on such grounds.).

27 *See* United States v. Sampol, 636 F.2d 621, 658 (D.C. Cir. 1980) ("It is true, of course, that defense counsel need not proffer a factual foundation for all questions asked on cross-examination. A well-reasoned suspicion that a circumstance is true is sufficient. . . . On the other hand, counsel must have a reasonable basis for asking questions on cross-examination which tend to incriminate or degrade the witness and thereby create an unfounded bias which subsequent testimony cannot fully dispel. . . . The general rule in such situations is that 'the questioner must be in possession of some facts which support a genuine belief that the witness committed the offense or the degrading act to which the questioning relates.' ") (quoting United States v. Fowler, 465 F.2d 664, 666 (D.C. Cir. 1972)). *See also* United States v. Katsougrakis, 715 F.2d 769, 778–79 (2d Cir. 1983) ("Although counsel may explore certain areas of inquiry in a criminal trial without full knowledge of the answer to anticipated questions, he must, when confronted with a demand for an offer of proof, provide some good faith basis for questioning that alleges adverse facts.").

question before asking nor demonstrate to the court a factual basis for every question posed. Courts have suggested that it is sufficient for counsel to possess a "well-reasoned suspicion that a circumstance is true."[28] "[A]lthough counsel may explore certain areas of inquiry in a criminal trial without full knowledge of the answer to anticipated questions, [counsel] must, when confronted with a demand for an offer of proof, provide some good faith basis for questioning that alleges adverse facts."[29] When counsel inquires about the witness's criminal or otherwise bad conduct, "the questioner must be in possession of some facts which support a genuine belief that the witness committed the offense or the degrading act to which the questioning relates."[30] Although these standards are particularly important in the government's cross-examination of the criminal defendant, they apply to other witnesses as well. Thus, if it would be improper for the government to ask an accused's witness whether the witness was having an affair with the accused in the absence of a good faith belief that the fact is true, it would be equally improper to ask the question of a party's witness in a civil case. Although generally the good faith basis need not be admissible evidence, the trial court has discretion to reject a claim of a good faith basis that derives from a dubious source, such as an obviously biased, hearsay assertion made by the client to the impeaching lawyer, at least when the proposed cross-examination poses a risk of unfair prejudice.[31]

Although the court must exercise control over improper cross-examination, the Supreme Court has clarified that trial courts must permit the parties to conduct probing cross-examination:

> Cross-examination is the principal means by which the believability of a witness and the truth of his testimony are tested. Subject always to the broad discretion of a trial judge to preclude repetitive and unduly harassing interrogation, the cross-examiner is not only permitted to delve into the witness's story to test the witness's perceptions and memory, but the cross-examiner has traditionally been allowed to impeach, i.e., discredit, the witness.[32]

While courts may, and indeed should, curtail fishing expeditions that consume too much time and raise too great a danger of unfair prejudice, courts must also allow sufficient leeway for probing cross-examination of adverse or reluctant witnesses. The balance is a delicate one and must be struck on a case-by-case basis.

§ 11.04 Impeachment with Evidence of Bias

Early nineteenth century common law excluded a great many categories of witnesses on account of identifiable sources of bias.[33] When courts eliminated these restrictions they substituted a generous attitude toward impeachment for bias, which

---

28 United States v. Sampol, 636 F.2d 621, 658 (D.C. Cir. 1980).

29 United States v. Katsougrakis, 715 F.2d 769, 779 (2d Cir. 1983).

30 United States v. Lin, 101 F.3d 760, 768 (D.C. Cir. 1996) (quoting United States v. Fowler, 465 F.2d 664, 666 (D.C. Cir. 1972)).

31 *See, e.g.*, United States v. Lin, 101 F.3d 760, 767–68 (D.C. Cir. 1996) (affirming trial court's rejection of good faith basis consisting solely of criminal defendant's out-of-court assertion to defense counsel that government witness was biased by his involvement with a gambling parlor in competition with that of the defendant, noting the risk of unfair prejudice arising from the proposed line of inquiry; rejecting challenge that such restriction of cross-examination violates defendant's right to confront adverse witnesses).

32 Davis v. Alaska, 415 U.S. 308, 315 (1974).

33 *See* **§ 8.01**.

continues to the present day. The Federal Rules of Evidence do not treat impeachment for bias directly, though uncovering bias is mentioned as a permitted purpose for introducing offers to compromise under Rule 408.[34] Rule 402 provides ample authority to admit such evidence, and opponents may freely attack the credibility of a witness with evidence of bias or interest.

Admissible evidence of bias includes evidence that a witness:

1. is a friend or relative of a party;[35]
2. is in a sexual or romantic relationship with a party;[36]
3. bears a grudge against a party or a party's witness;[37]
4. has a business relationship with a party;[38]
5. has hopes of leniency in a criminal case pending against him and is testifying for the government;[39]
6. has expenses or fees paid by a party;[40] or
7. is a member of an organization that is interested in the lawsuit.[41]

As these examples suggest, witnesses often have identifiable connections to the parties. Even when no direct connection exists, impeachment for more general forms of bias is possible, including racism or religious antagonism.[42]

Several criminal cases emphasize the vital importance of exposing witness bias. The accused's interest in impeaching a witness for bias has been the basis for invoking the

---

[34] *See* **§ 6.11**. *Cf.* UNIF. R. EVID. 616 (1986) (providing that "for the purpose of attacking the credibility of a witness, evidence of bias, prejudice, or interest of the witness for or against any party to the case is admissible").

[35] *See* ROGER PARK & TOM LININGER, THE NEW WIGMORE: IMPEACHMENT AND REHABILITATION § 6.3.1 (2012).

[36] *See id.*, § 6.3.2.

[37] *See id.*, § 6.3.3. *See also* State v. Sweeney, 443 So. 2d 522, 529–30 (La. 1983) (holding that, where government's two key witnesses had arrested one of defendant's proffered witnesses, prosecution may cross-examine defense witness about his previous arrest by those officers to explore defendant's witness's bias towards two officers).

[38] *See* ROGER PARK & TOM LININGER, THE NEW WIGMORE: IMPEACHMENT AND REHABILITATION § 6.3.6 (2012).

[39] *See id.*, § 6.3.9.

[40] *See id.*, § 6.3.7.

[41] *See id.*, § 6.3.5. Where the organization is faith-based, the value of bias impeachment will normally outweigh even the policies served by FED. R. EVID. 610, which provides that beliefs about religion are not admissible for purposes of showing that "by reason of their nature the witness's credibility is impaired or enhanced." The purpose of the church membership evidence would not be to impeach by showing illogical or evil belief, but by showing bias due to loyalty to the institution, and the Advisory Committee's Note to Rule 610 states that "disclosure of affiliation with a church which is a party to the litigation would be allowable under the rule." Of course, courts must exercise care to avoid prejudicial evidence where its relevance to bias is remote. *See* Malek v. Federal Ins. Co., 994 F.2d 49, 54 (2d Cir. 1993) (holding that, in property owners' suit to recover proceeds from fire insurance policy, improper under Rule 610 for district court to permit defendants to impeach plaintiffs' expert witness on cross-examination with evidence that plaintiffs were members of Hasidic Jewish community, that witness was also Jewish, and that witness had other Hasidic clients; dissent argued that evidence was properly admitted as evidence of bias because it demonstrated that witness depended in part on Hasidic community for his livelihood).

[42] *See* ROGER PARK & TOM LININGER, THE NEW WIGMORE: IMPEACHMENT AND REHABILITATION § 6.2 (2012).

criminal defendant's constitutional right to present evidence that can override otherwise valid exclusionary rules.[43]

Evidence of bias and interest has never been subject to the common-law principle against the use of extrinsic evidence to impeach a witness on a collateral matter.[44] The cross-examiner is not obliged to "take the answer" of the witness regarding matters affecting bias. For example, if the witness is asked about fighting with the defendant, and the witness denies the fight, the opponent is entitled to call another witness to introduce evidence that the fight took place.[45] The Supreme Court endorsed the view that extrinsic evidence of bias is admissible in the case of *United States v. Abel*.[46] In that case, the government offered a witness who would testify that a defense witness belonged to the same prison gang as the defendant and that the gang required its members to commit perjury, theft, and murder for each other. The Court upheld the admission of this evidence, noting that the common law permitted extrinsic evidence of bias, while requiring the cross-examiner to "take the witness's answer" with regard to less favored forms of impeachment evidence. The Supreme Court decided that the Federal Rules of Evidence did not change this common-law rule.

While extrinsic evidence of specific conduct is admissible to show bias, it is generally not admissible to attack the witness's character for truthfulness.[47] Sometimes the border between bad acts that show character and bad acts that show bias is unclear. For example, in a criminal case the defense might claim that uncharged misconduct by a prosecution witness demonstrates bias because the witness is motivated by a desire to avoid being prosecuted. However, the existence of this conceivable motive does not grant defense counsel license to bring in evidence of every bad act of the witness. A foundation must be laid showing that there is a basis for believing that the witness is influenced by fear of prosecution. Some cases have required a showing of a deal between the government and the witness before the extrinsic evidence may be admitted.[48] For

---

[43] *See, e.g.*, Davis v. Alaska, 415 U.S. 308, 317–18 (1974) (holding defendant had constitutional right to explore bias of prosecution's witness associated with witness's pending probation, overriding rule requiring privacy of witness's juvenile record); Olden v. Kentucky, 488 U.S. 227 (1988) (holding defendant had constitutional right to explore romantic relationship between witness and alleged victim, notwithstanding privacy accorded witness by state's "Rape Shield" law).

[44] *See* Commonwealth v. Moorer, 728 N.E.2d 288, 291 (Mass. 200) ("If, on the facts, there is a possibility of bias, even a remote one, the judge has no discretion to bar all inquiry into the subject.) It is not difficult to imagine a matter that is so tangential to the material facts being tried that a witness's bias with respect *only* to that matter plausibly can be called collateral, but in that case neither intrinsic nor extrinsic evidence of bias would be admissible.

[45] United States v. Keys, 899 F.2d 983, 986 n.2 (10th Cir. 1990) (holding that bias is never classified as a collateral matter that lies beyond the scope of inquiry, nor as a matter on which an examiner is required to take a witness's answer; "[b]ias may be proved by extrinsic evidence even after a witness's disavowal of partiality.") (citation omitted); United States v. Anderson, 881 F.2d 1128, 1139 (D.C. Cir. 1989); United States v. Robinson, 530 F.2d 1076, 1079 (D.C. Cir. 1976). *See also* United States v. Harvey, 547 F.2d 720, 723 (2d Cir. 1976) (reversible error to exclude extrinsic evidence that witness had bias against defendant, consisting of witness's accusation charging defendant with fathering her child and refusing to take responsibility for it).

[46] United States v. Abel, 469 U.S. 45, 52 (1984).

[47] *See* **§ 11.09** & **§ 11.10**.

[48] United States v. Capozzi, 883 F.2d 608, 616 (8th Cir. 1989) (recognizing that extrinsic evidence that government witness testified for government to avoid prosecution would be admissible to show bias but upholding exclusion in this case because "[t]he record . . . reveals no evidence of any arrangement or deal between the government and [the witness]"). *But see* United States v. Lankford, 955 F.2d 1545, 1548–49 (11th Cir. 1992) (holding that trial court violated defendant's Sixth Amendment right to cross-examine witnesses for possible bias by excluding evidence that two sons of prosecution's key witness were on probation for state court drug distribution convictions, even though witness had made no deal precluding federal investigation of his sons in exchange for the witness's testimony).

example, in *United States v. West*,[49] the Seventh Circuit described a fairly elaborate requirement of foundation, stating that before the defense could question a prosecution witness about prior misconduct in order to establish bias and motive to fabricate, a foundation had to be laid establishing (1) the bad act; (2) the government's knowledge of the bad act; (3) the lack of any prosecution of the bad act; and (4) the existence of a promise not to prosecute the bad act.[50] The authors believe that this standard is too high in light of the fact that the witness might well be influenced by a fear of the government, even in the absence of any explicit threat or promise. On the other hand, some foundational requirement is needed to keep the defense from bringing in witnesses to testify about collateral bad acts that would be inadmissible against any nongovernment witness and that serve only to destroy the character of a witness who may not be prepared to defend an entire lifetime of activity. A showing that the bad acts were known to the government under circumstances that would give rise to a reasonable fear of prosecution should be considered a sufficient foundation.[51]

Must the witness being impeached be asked about the source of the bias or the potential evidence indicating bias *before* extrinsic evidence is admitted? Such a "foundation" requirement would give the witness being impeached a fair chance to admit, explain, or deny the bias-exhibiting fact or statement. The Federal Rules of Evidence expressly impose a foundation requirement for prior inconsistent statements, but the Rules are silent about a foundation for bias impeachment. Nonetheless, authority

---

[49] United States v. West, 670 F.2d 675, 683 (7th Cir. 1982). *See* United States v. Parker, 133 F.3d 322, 327 (5th Cir. 1998) (holding that because defense failed to present evidence that federal prosecutors had agreed to help witness in state murder case, trial court's refusal to allow cross-examination of witness about state charges pending against witness for murder of witness's husband was harmless error); United States v. Triplett, 104 F.3d 1074, 1079 (8th Cir. 1997) (holding no error to exclude testimony that police search found possible controlled substance in home of prosecution witness, despite possible bias due to witness's hope of leniency; court noted that "the confiscated substance was never tested or positively identified as a controlled substance" and that witness was never charged); United States v. Matthews, 168 F.3d 1234, 1243 (11th Cir. 1999), *opinion amended on denial of reh'g*, 181 F.3d 1205 (11th Cir. 1999) (holding that evidence of government witness's arrest for vehicle theft, allegedly providing motive for her to testify for the government, was properly excluded because theory that charges had been brought and dropped in exchange for cooperation were speculative and unsupported by evidence).

[50] *Cf.* United States v. Rovetuso, 768 F.2d 809, 817 (7th Cir. 1985) (holding that defendant-appellant may not offer evidence about witness's activities in Panama, based on theory that witness was afraid of being deported to Panama, on grounds that defendant had neither argued bias at trial nor laid a factual foundation).

[51] Even when the evidence goes to bias rather than character, the trial judge has leeway under Rule 403 to exclude details that are cumulative, a waste of time, or prejudicial. *See* United States v. Phillips, 888 F.2d 38, 42 (6th Cir. 1989) (holding that in trial for unlawful cocaine distribution, defendant cannot offer extrinsic evidence about government witnesses using drugs at a party after witnesses denied accusation because the only bias that could possibly exist were government witnesses lying about a "remote matter" in order to save their jobs; trial court acted within its discretion because information "might be more damaging than probative"); United States v. Williamson, 202 F.3d 974 (7th Cir. 2000) (finding no abuse of discretion to restrict cross-examination to exclude alleged nature of crimes committed by informant who was working for government in return for leniency); United States v. Ferrell, 625 F. Supp. 41, 46–47 (E.D. Pa. 1985) (holding that, where government witness testified he had not sold drugs in the past, defendant could not offer extrinsic evidence that witness had sold drugs because defendant could offer no theory on why evidence was probative of bias). *See also* Cummings v. Malone, 995 F.2d 817, 827 (8th Cir. 1993) (holding that, in inmate's Eighth Amendment action for excessive force by prison officers, trial court property excluded testimony that two of the defendants testified in inmate's attempted rape prosecution, resulting in additional 15 years of imprisonment, when record already contained indications of inmate's bias against defendants); United States v. Morrison, 98 F.3d 619, 627–28 (D.C. Cir. 1996) (finding no abuse of discretion where trial judge cut off questioning of witness about whether she was testifying against defendant to get lower sentence and thus avoid losing children; question called for "speculative answer" by witness); State v. McCall, 549 N.W.2d 418, 422 (Wis. 1996) (finding no error in excluding evidence that prosecutor had dismissed two pending charges against alleged victim and sole prosecution witness in prosecution growing out of shooting in which the victim was rendered quadriplegic).

for requiring a foundation can be grounded on the trial judge's general authority to control the "mode and order of interrogating witnesses and presenting evidence" under Rule 611(a). There is a division of authority on the question of whether a foundation is required.[52] If foundation is required, it should not be treated as a rigid, technical requirement. In any event, some cases hold that once a witness has admitted a possible ground of bias, the impeaching attorney may not introduce extrinsic evidence of it.[53]

Prior statements by the witness are one common form of extrinsic evidence of bias. For example, a witness might have previously stated out of court that he hated the defendant. A plausible objection can be made if the cross-examiner fails to lay a foundation before admitting the extrinsic evidence of the statement. In addition, if (as in the example) the prior statement constitutes hearsay, the court must exclude it unless it is covered by an exemption or exception to the hearsay rule.[54]

§ 11.05 Impeachment by Prior Inconsistent Statement [FRE 613]

Witnesses are often impeached with out-of-court statements that are inconsistent with testimony at trial. Evidence that the witness said different things at different times casts doubt upon the witness's overall credibility, regardless of which statement the jury ultimately believes, if either.[55] Perhaps because of the popularity of this method of impeachment, many rules have been developed to govern it. This section approaches the subject by addressing the most common objections to attempts to impeach witnesses with prior inconsistent statements.[56] (A similar approach could be taken to any of the impeachment techniques.) The Federal Rules provide only meager guidance—in Rule 613—regarding the use of prior inconsistent statements. Much of the court's decision-making is governed by the standards of Rules 402, 403, and 611(a).[57]

---

[52] *Compare* United States v. DiNapoli, 557 F.2d 962, 965 (2d Cir. 1977) (holding extrinsic evidence of prior statement showing bias inadmissible unless witness allowed to explain or deny statement); United States v. Marzano, 537 F.2d 257, 265 (7th Cir. 1976) (holding that foundation required when witness's prior statement offered to prove bias) *with* State v. Kehn, 361 N.E.2d 1330, 1335 (Ohio 1977) (holding that no foundation required before offering extrinsic evidence showing bias); State v. Carlson, 508 N.E.2d 999, 1002 (Ohio App. 1986) (holding that where victim of assault had civil suit filed against defendant, evidence of victim/witness's suit admissible to show bias even though witness was not given opportunity to explain or deny alleged bias). *See also* United States v. Hudson, 970 F.2d 948 (1st Cir. 1992) (holding that foundation for admission of prior inconsistent statement to show witness's bias requires only that witness be available to be recalled to explain or deny the prior inconsistent statement; trial court's exclusion of evidence of prior statement reversed on other grounds; concurring opinion urged court to reconsider rule en banc at earliest opportunity and to join majority of circuits in requiring that witness first be given opportunity to explain or deny prior inconsistent statement).

[53] *See* ROGER PARK & TOM LININGER, THE NEW WIGMORE: IMPEACHMENT AND REHABILITATION § 6.4.2 (2012).

[54] Often such statements of then-existing states of mind will be admissible under a hearsay exception. *See* FED. R. EVID. 803(3); **§ 16.04**.

[55] *See* 28 CHARLES A. WRIGHT & VICTOR J. GOLD, FEDERAL PRACTICE AND PROCEDURE (EVIDENCE) § 6206 at 592 (2012) ("Evidence that a witness has told one story on the stand and a conflicting story at an earlier time suggests that the witness has lied or was mistaken when he made the prior statement or when he testified or both."). The effect may extend beyond casting doubt on the specific testimony with which the prior statement is inconsistent. The theory is that inconsistency as to one fact casts a shadow over the witness's reliability as to other facts. The validity of this assumption has been challenged. *See Id.* at 595 (challenging the assumption that evidence of prior inconsistent statement carries much value for impeachment purposes, stating that "it usually is not fair to conclude that, because a person errs or even lies as to one matter, he is more likely to err or lie as to all other matters.").

[56] *See also* **§ 15.03** (discussing treatment of prior inconsistent statements under hearsay rule).

[57] Sometimes a witness will have acted in a non-assertive manner that nonetheless indicates a belief inconsistent with the witness's later testimony, what might be called *prior inconsistent conduct*. Evidence of

Objection—Prior Statement Is Consistent with Trial Testimony

A party may object to impeachment of its witness on the ground that the witness's out-of-court statement is actually consistent with the witness's in-court testimony. Suppose, for example, that the witness testifies in court that the witness has forgotten an event while a prior statement by the witness describes the event. Arguably, the two statements are consistent. It is possible that the witness remembered the event when the prior out-of-court statement was made but has forgotten the event at the time of testimony.

In considering an objection that the out-of-court statement is actually consistent, however, the court should keep the purpose of impeachment in mind. The cross-examiner is trying to cast doubt on credibility. The ultimate question is whether the prior statement actually sheds light on the witness's believability. In this instance, it throws enough light on the witness's believability to justify receiving it. Although the witness might have remembered at a previous juncture and forgotten the event at the time of testifying, it is also possible that the witness remembers and is lying. The jury must determine which of these inferences is correct. The test of admissibility is whether the statement provides insight into the witness's credibility, not whether the statement is inconsistent in the technical sense that the two statements cannot possibly both be true.[58]

A similar question arises when the witness testifies in detail about an event and adds testimony about a fact that the witness did not mention in a prior statement or report about the event. If the fact was one that would naturally have been mentioned, then courts generally allow the statement or report to be treated as a prior inconsistent statement.[59]

---

such conduct may be relevant for impeachment purposes, but such evidence is not governed by Rule 613, which only concerns prior statements. *See* FED. R. EVID. 613 advisory committee note ("the rule does not apply to impeachment by evidence of prior inconsistent conduct").

[58] United States v. Stock, 948 F.2d 1299, 1300–01 (D.C. Cir. 1991) (finding error, though harmless, to exclude evidence that officer's police report omitted statement allegedly made by defendant; police officer testified that defendant said "I don't have anything" as defendant pulled his hand out of dumpster in which drugs were later found); United States v. Malik, 928 F.2d 17, 22–23 (1st Cir. 1991) (finding no error in admitting evidence of defendant's prior statements about heroin-smuggling after defendant's testimony, "We don't believe in heroin because we don't like it. And we don't do it;" contradiction need not be in "plain terms"); United States v. Causey, 834 F.2d 1277, 1283 (6th Cir. 1987) (holding that trial court did not abuse discretion in allowing prosecution to impeach witness with prior statement where witness testified she did not remember conversation with her husband but had in fact called FBI agent about the conversation previously); United States v. Gajo, 290 F.3d 922 (7th Cir. 2002) (holding that prosecution may present forgetful witness's prior grand jury testimony as substantive evidence under Rule 801(d)(1)(A); inconsistency does not necessarily mean logical incompatibility, but includes changes of position, silence, or evasive answers); United States v. Rogers, 549 F.2d 490, 496 (8th Cir. 1976) ("A statement's inconsistency may be determined from the circumstances and is not limited to cases in which diametrically opposite assertions have been made. Thus inconsistencies may be found in changes in position; they may be implied through silence; and they may also be found in denial of recollection."); United States v. Jackson, 748 F.2d 1535 (11th Cir. 1984) (allowing impeachment with prior statement because testimony that witness was supposed to receive football tickets and video game passes was inconsistent with earlier statement that he did not know what was in envelope he received). *But see* United States v. Devine, 934 F.2d 1325, 1344–45 (5th Cir. 1991) (witness's prior conversation about defendant's role in conspiracy was not inconsistent with trial testimony that he could not remember conversation); United States v. Poindexter, 942 F.2d 354, 361 (6th Cir. 1991) (testimony, in response to cross-examination questions, denying that drug use caused her to have memory loss, was not inconsistent with trial testimony that she was not using drugs).

[59] *See, e.g.*, State v. Irving, 555 A.2d 575, 581 (N.J. 1989) (holding that where defendant testified his roommate was with him at time of alleged crime but did not name his roommate as a possible witness when

Objection—Document Should Be Shown to Witness Before Using It to Impeach

In *Queen Caroline's Case,* a spectacular contested divorce action that initiated the era of the tabloid press, George IV, King of England, accused his wife, Caroline, of adultery. The Queen resisted, and the case was dropped after a hearing in the House of Lords.[60] The case is important to evidence scholars for the "Rule in the Queen's Case," which governs the foundational requirements for impeachment by prior inconsistent statements. Under that rule, announced by the Law Lords in response to a question from the House of Lords, a witness could not be cross-examined about a document written by the witness unless the document was first shown to the witness.[61]

The requirement that a document be shown to the witness first can sometimes impede cross-examination, especially when the cross-examiner is trying to undermine the witness, rather than to get the witness to qualify unhelpful testimony. Suppose, for instance, the cross-examiner's theory is that the witness has taken an illicit payment. Cross-examination will be more effective if the cross-examiner conceals from the witness the fact that the cross-examiner has, in hand, a letter by the witness in which the witness describes receiving the illicit payment. If the witness denies ever having received money, then the letter can be a bombshell. If the witness is allowed to view the letter first before being asked about transactions with the person who allegedly gave the money, then the witness might manufacture some relatively benign explanation, such as the money was payment for legal services.[62] To prevent this blunting of cross-examination, the Federal Rules abolished the Rule in the Queen's Case.[63] Rule 613(a) now provides that, when examining a witness about the witness's prior statement (whether that statement is written or oral), the statement need not first be disclosed to the witness.[64]

When the cross-examiner uses a document that has not been placed in evidence to impeach a witness with a prior statement, Rule 613(a) expressly provides that the opposing counsel has the right to see the document. This rule is designed to prevent misquoting or misuse of the document. In addition, if the cross-examiner purports to read from the document, some judges will require that it be shown to the witness, despite the express language of Rule 613(a). This reflects a fairness concern in that the cross-

---

he filed his original notice-of-alibi statement with court, omission of roommate's name was inconsistent with defendant's testimony).

[60] Caroline had gone abroad after being excluded from court by her husband during his regency. When her husband ascended to the throne in 1820, she returned and claimed her rights as Queen. Her husband claimed that she had committed adultery with an Italian lover while abroad. A bill was brought in the House of Lords seeking to deny the Queen all rights associated with her title and to grant the King a divorce, based on the alleged adultery—the only available grounds for divorce. After a hearing, the bill was abandoned for lack of support, even though it had passed the House of Lords by a slim margin on the third reading. Though she never regained admission to court, Caroline lived out her few remaining days as titular Queen of England with an annuity of 50,000 pounds. For a vivid account of the facts of the case, *see* Richard H. Underwood, *Perjury: An Anthology*, 13 ARIZ. J. INT'L & COMP. L. 307, 323–28 (1996).

[61] The Queen's Case, 2 Br. & B. 284, 286–90, 129 Eng. Rep. 976, 11 Eng. R.C. 183 (1820); 4 WIGMORE ON EVIDENCE §§ 1259–60.

[62] Examples of crushing cross-examination in which the cross-examiner's knowledge was concealed from the witness are collected in 4 WIGMORE ON EVIDENCE § 1260 (Chadbourn rev. 1972).

[63] *See* 28 CHARLES A. WRIGHT & VICTOR J. GOLD, FEDERAL PRACTICE AND PROCEDURE (EVIDENCE) § 6202 (2012).

[64] Of course, the opportunity for a devastating confrontation has been somewhat diminished in the modern era of civil discovery, although it sometimes arises. When it does, the witness's normal right under the rules of discovery to see the witness's own statement would be suspended temporarily until the end of cross-examination. *See* FED. R. EVID. 613(a) advisory committee note.

examiner might be distorting the document or reading it out of context. In this respect, the plain language of 613(a) seems at odds with the general power of the judge under Rule 611(a) to control the mode of interrogation of witnesses.[65]

Objection—No Foundation for Extrinsic Evidence

Under the traditional common-law rules, a party also had to lay a foundation in order to impeach a witness by introducing extrinsic evidence of the witness's prior inconsistent statement. The impeaching attorney was free to ask the witness who made the statement about it without any foundation.[66] However, if the attorney wanted to call another witness to describe the statement (this other witness would provide extrinsic evidence), then the attorney must lay a foundation by giving the witness who made the statement the opportunity to explain or deny the statement on the witness stand. This was accomplished by calling the statement and the surrounding circumstance to the witness's attention. A typical formulation of the foundation requirement provided that "the [impeaching] statements must be related to him, with the circumstances of times, places, and persons present; and he shall be asked whether he has made such statements, and if so, allowed to explain them."[67]

The foundation requirement was designed to give the witness a fair chance to explain any circumstances, such as duress or influence, that might excuse or explain the inconsistency; to reconcile the statements by explaining why they were not really inconsistent; or to deny having made the statement at all. The foundation requirement was also intended to require that the impeacher seek first to authenticate the inconsistent statement using the witness who made it. Where the witness being impeached admitted making the prior inconsistent statement, there was no need to call an additional witness to authenticate the statement.

Unlike their rejection of the Rule in the Queen's Case, the Federal Rules of Evidence retain the common-law foundation requirement for the use of extrinsic evidence but relax the common-law approach somewhat. Rule 613(b) provides that to admit extrinsic evidence of a prior inconsistent statement, either (1) the witness must be provided an opportunity to "explain or deny" the statement and the party who called the witness must be given an opportunity to question the witness about the statement; or (2) the interests of justice require admission of the extrinsic evidence. Although Rule 613(b) might appear merely to codify the common-law rule, it does not specify the time at which the witness must be given the opportunity to explain or deny. This was an intentional change.[68] With this difference in mind, some courts have held that the rule is satisfied even if the witness is not asked about the prior statement on the stand, as long as the witness remains available.[69] This position is justified by reasoning that the witness has

---

[65] The authors of one treatise argue that the policy justification for abandoning the common-law rule is weak, and that when the justifications for the old rule are particularly strong, courts should have the power under Rule 611(a) to require the impeaching party to adhere to the common-law rule by showing the statement to the witness before cross-examination. 28 CHARLES A. WRIGHT & VICTOR J. GOLD, FEDERAL PRACTICE AND PROCEDURE (EVIDENCE) § 6204 (2012).

[66] Of course, the cross-examiner must be prepared to respond to a request to provide the good faith basis for the question. *See* **§ 11.03**.

[67] Coles v. Harsch, 276 P. 248, 250 (Or. 1929) (quoting 1920 OR. LAWS § 864).

[68] *See* FED. R. EVID. 613(b) advisory committee note (noting that the rule allows several "collusive witnesses" to be examined "before disclosure of a joint prior inconsistent statement").

[69] Theriot v. Bay Drilling Corp., 783 F.2d 527, 533 (5th Cir. 1986) (holding that Rule 613 only requires that witness have chance to deny or explain inconsistent statement at some point in proceedings, it does not

the opportunity to explain or deny as long as the witness *could* be recalled for additional testimony. Not all states that use the Federal Rules as a model have accepted this federal liberalization.[70]

The foundation requirement, whether under federal or common-law, does not apply to statements of a party-opponent. Such statements are admissible whether or not a foundation has been laid.[71]

Objection—Collateral Impeachment with Extrinsic Evidence

The common-law rule, which continues to be enforced as a general principle under the Federal Rules, is that a prior inconsistent statement may not be proved with extrinsic evidence when the statement is being offered solely for impeachment on a collateral matter.[72] The impeachment is collateral when the statement is not independently relevant to some issue other than impeachment by inconsistency.[73] Collateral impeachment out of the witness's own mouth—that is, elicited by cross-examination—is distinct from collateral impeachment with extrinsic evidence. An objection can still be made, but trial judges have wide discretion to allow collateral impeachment by cross-examination. When collateral questioning about a prior inconsistent statement is allowed by the trial judge, the questioner is bound by the witness's answer. The questioner may not bring in another witness or document to prove that the out-of-court statement was made.[74]

---

require that the witness have that chance prior to introduction of extrinsic evidence); Wammock v. Celotex Corp., 793 F.2d 1518, 1521–22 (11th Cir. 1986) (holding that Rule 613(b) does not require that witness be confronted with inconsistent statement before extrinsic evidence is introduced, but traditional method is still preferred especially if witness might be unavailable later).

[70] *See, e.g.*, ALASKA R. EVID. 613(b) ("before extrinsic evidence of a prior contradictory statement. . . may be admitted, the examiner shall lay a foundation for impeachment by affording the witness an opportunity, while testifying, to explain or deny any prior statement."); MINN. R. EVID. 613(b) ("Extrinsic evidence of a prior inconsistent statement by a witness is not admissible unless the witness is afforded a prior opportunity to explain or deny the same."). *See also* State v. Martin, 964 S.W.2d 564, 568 (Tenn. 1998) (applying state rule identical to FED. R. EVID. 613(b), court held that it was error, though harmless, to admit extrinsic evidence of prior inconsistent statement without requiring impeaching party to lay traditional foundation under which witness being impeached is given prior opportunity to explain or deny statement).

[71] *See* FED. R. EVID. 613(b); 4 WIGMORE ON EVIDENCE § 1051 (Chadbourn rev. 1972).

[72] 28 CHARLES A. WRIGHT & VICTOR J. GOLD, FEDERAL PRACTICE AND PROCEDURE (EVIDENCE) § 6206 (2012). For a discussion of collateral impeachment in the context of impeachment by contradiction, *see* **§ 11.06**.

[73] United States v. Roulette, 75 F.3d 418, 423 (8th Cir. 1996) (endorsing independent relevance test and finding it satisfied under facts of case); United States v. Laughlin, 772 F.2d 1382, 1393–94 (7th Cir. 1985) (holding that extrinsic evidence witness previously told FBI agent that her husband had "source" for drugs was independently relevant in case where defendant was charged with possession of cocaine with intent to distribute and witness testified her defendant-husband only used drugs if his friends brought drugs to his house); United States v. Nace, 561 F.2d 763, 771 (9th Cir. 1977) (holding that defendant could not impeach witness with his bankruptcy petition statement where witness testified that he did not owe defendant any money but had listed loan as liability in his bankruptcy petition because issue was whether defendant used extortion to get repayment of alleged loan, not whether witness had in fact borrowed money from the defendant); *cf.* United States v. Nazarenus, 983 F.2d 1480, 1485 (8th Cir. 1993) (holding it improper to impeach defendant who told police officer on night of alleged sex crime that he had sped only to test car's alignment with evidence that defendant frequently drove fast); *see also* 3A WIGMORE ON EVIDENCE § 1020 (Chadbourn rev. 1970).

[74] *See, e.g.*, State v. Mangrum, 403 P.2d 925, 929 (Ariz. 1965) (holding that opponent could inquire on cross-examination about witness's alleged statement that witness had testified falsely in unconnected case but could not bring in extrinsic evidence about alleged statement); 3A WIGMORE ON EVIDENCE §§ 1020–23 (Chadbourn rev. 1970). *See also* United States v. Grooms, 978 F.2d 425, 428–29 (8th Cir. 1992) (holding that in prosecution for child sex abuse, where victims' mother denied stating that victims' father coached their testimony, defendant could not call witness to testify that mother made statement because issue was collateral;

For example, suppose that, in a sexual harassment case, the witness denies that anything improper happened at the office picnic. On cross-examination the witness is questioned about the witness's prior inconsistent statements about (a) what food was served at the picnic and (b) whether the defendant tried to kiss the plaintiff. The trial judge would have discretion to allow cross-examination about both issues. The question about what food was served deals with a collateral matter of no importance to the substance of the case, but so long as the cross-examiner is content merely to ask questions of the witness being impeached, not much time is wasted. The answers may reveal a confused or forgetful witness. However, if the witness denies making an inconsistent statement about what food was served, then the cross-examiner cannot bring in another witness (which would constitute extrinsic evidence) to prove the making of the statement because an additional witness would be a waste of time. In contrast, if the prior inconsistent statement concerned something independently relevant—such as whether the defendant tried to kiss the plaintiff—then the extrinsic evidence would be admissible. It has relevance quite apart from its tendency to impeach the first witness.

A prior inconsistent statement can be independently relevant because it addresses one of the substantive issues of the lawsuit, as in the example of the attempted kiss at the picnic.[75] Alternatively, a prior inconsistent statement can be independently relevant because it goes to bias (e.g., the witness denies making a prior statement that he was paid for testimony) or perception (the witness denies having made a prior statement saying that he was drunk at the picnic).[76]

§ 11.06 Impeachment by Contradiction

Perhaps the simplest way for a witness to be impeached is by means of introducing contradictory testimony by another witness. If witness X testifies that the light was red, and witness Y testifies that it was green, then witness X has been impeached by contradiction. This type of impeachment is distinguished from impeachment by prior inconsistent statement, which involves self-contradiction. Impeachment by contradiction challenges a witness with contrary evidence about the underlying facts. Impeachment by prior inconsistent statement challenges the witness with the witness's own prior inconsistent statement. By its very nature, impeachment by contradiction involves extrinsic evidence. It is also reciprocal: if Y's testimony impeaches X's, then X's testimony impeaches Y's.

Impeachment by contradiction is usually a by-product of the parties' introducing conflicting evidence to prove a substantive issue in the case, such as the color of the traffic light. However, a party might want to impeach the witness by contradicting some fact about which that witness has testified that is not itself relevant aside from its impeaching effect. A common-law rule, however, bars a party from calling another witness for this purpose. The rule excludes extrinsic evidence offered to contradict the witness on a "collateral" matter.[77]

---

in the authors' opinion, the court's conclusion is questionable because the prior statement was relevant not only to the mother's credibility but also to the bias of the child witness).

[75] 3A WIGMORE ON EVIDENCE § 1021 (Chadbourn rev. 1970).

[76] *Id.* § 1022.

[77] *See* 3A WIGMORE ON EVIDENCE §§ 1000–1003 (Chadbourn rev. 1970).

State v. Oswalt presents an example of this type of forbidden impeachment.[78] In *Oswalt*, an alibi witness for the defendant, who was accused of robbing a house in Seattle, testified that the defendant had been at the witness's restaurant in Portland on the day in question. On cross-examination, the witness also testified that the defendant had been in the restaurant in Portland every day for a period of two months before the robbery. The prosecution then offered in evidence the testimony of a police officer that he had seen the defendant in Seattle on a date about a month before the robbery. One theory of admissibility was that this testimony impeached the alibi witness by contradiction. The alibi witness had testified that the defendant had been in a restaurant in Portland on that day; the police witness indirectly contradicted this testimony because it was unlikely that the defendant would be in the restaurant in Portland and also in Seattle on the same day. The court held that the evidence should have been excluded at trial. In doing so, it endorsed the often-stated test: the contradicting evidence is inadmissible if it is put forward on a "collateral" matter. The court stated that the test for determining whether a matter is collateral is this: "Could the fact, as to which error is predicated, have been shown in evidence for any purpose independently of the contradiction?"[79] Because the officer's testimony was only relevant to impeach the alibi witness by contradicting the witness's testimony about the defendant's whereabouts a month before the robbery, the evidence was collateral. Since the evidence was offered at a time other than during cross-examination of the defendant's alibi witness, it was "extrinsic" evidence and thus inadmissible.[80]

Examples

A witness shown by other evidence to have observed the accident in question testifies to seeing the accident while on the way home. In reality, the witness was on his way to a poker game. Extrinsic evidence that the witness lied when he said he was on the way home is not admissible, because the evidence has no relevance to the case except to impeach the witness by contradiction. The witness could be challenged about his destination on cross-examination, but the questioner would have to accept the answer and could not follow up a denial with extrinsic evidence that the witness went to a poker game.

A witness for the plaintiff testifies that he had never met the plaintiff before the litigation. Actually, the witness was involved in a business deal with the plaintiff. Extrinsic evidence of the prior relationship is admissible because it is relevant to the bias or interest of the witness, and thus would be otherwise admissible. The business relationship between the plaintiff and the witness may bias the witness in the plaintiff's favor.

A witness for the plaintiff testifies that he was on the way home from a school meeting at the time of the accident. In fact, the witness had been drinking in a

---

[78] State v. Oswalt, 381 P.2d 617 (Wash. 1963).

[79] *Id.* at 619, quoting 3A WIGMORE ON EVIDENCE § 1003 (Chadbourn rev. 1970). This standard suggests a relevancy basis for determining whether evidence is "collateral." The principle is probably more complicated, however. *See* 27 CHARLES A. WRIGHT & VICTOR J. GOLD, FEDERAL PRACTICE AND PROCEDURE (EVIDENCE) § 6096 (2007) (suggesting that Wigmore test is underinclusive, encompassing only two of three types of non-collateral evidence that commentators have identified).

[80] Of course, the trial judge retains the power to exclude the impeaching evidence even if offered during cross-examination. If, for example, the judge finds that the evidence is of infinitesimal probative value for impeachment purposes, and the time required to offer the evidence (even on cross-examination) would not justify its presentation, the judge may exclude it on Rule 403 grounds.

bar all night long. Extrinsic evidence of the drinking is admissible because it is relevant to the witness's perception, and not merely to contradict the witness's testimony.

The second and third illustrations demonstrate why it is important to identify not only whether evidence is offered to impeach the witness but also the precise means by which it does so. In the second example, the testimony tends to impeach both by contradiction and by showing bias. Because extrinsic evidence is permitted in impeachment for bias,[81] the party is permitted to call the witness to offer the impeaching evidence. The same is true in the third illustration. While the evidence does tend to impeach by contradiction, it also impeaches by showing the possibility of impaired perception, a form of impeachment that is not limited by the collateral issue-extrinsic evidence rule.[82]

The principal purpose of the rule prohibiting extrinsic evidence to impeach when the evidence concerns a collateral matter is to prevent confusion and waste of time.[83] It is rarely useful to receive testimony from both sides about a collateral issue when the only relevance of the evidence would be whether the witness gave inaccurate testimony about a matter irrelevant to the lawsuit. Contradicting on an irrelevant matter has some probative value in demonstrating that a person is wrong about one fact and thus might be wrong about other, relevant facts. It is not probative enough, however, to justify the consumption of trial time. The rule prohibiting extrinsic evidence of collateral matters is also supported by the danger that the jury may misuse the evidence when it involves information prejudicial to the witness or the party who called the witness.[84] This danger is particularly great when the witness is a party.[85]

Did the rule against using extrinsic evidence to impeach on collateral matters survive the adoption of the Federal Rules of Evidence? The Rules are silent on the matter.[86] Many courts in Federal Rules jurisdictions have continued to follow the

---

[81] *See* **§ 11.10**.

[82] In each case, because the extrinsic evidence would be admissible for a purpose independent of contradicting the witness, it is *also* admissible to contradict the witness. The rule does not bar extrinsic impeachment by contradiction on a non-collateral matter. Thus, a limiting instruction—such as one telling the jury that they may use the evidence to infer bias, but not to impeach by contradiction—is neither necessary nor appropriate. The main point of the rule is conserve court time, not to limit inferences, and that goal would hardly be served by adding the complication of a limiting instruction.

[83] *See* 27 CHARLES A. WRIGHT & VICTOR J. GOLD, FEDERAL PRACTICE AND PROCEDURE (EVIDENCE) § 6096 at 658 (2007).

[84] *Id.*

[85] When there is a problem of potential prejudice to a party, as when the extrinsic evidence reflects poorly on the party's character, but the extrinsic evidence is admitted nonetheless because it relates to a non-collateral matter without using a forbidden propensity inference, a limiting instruction might be appropriate. *See* **§ 3.09**, **§ 7.01**, & **§ 7.16**.

[86] The only rule that even plausibly addressed this issue was Rule 608(b), before it was amended in 2003, but better reasoned opinions even before the amendment had held that Rule 608(b) dealt only with character impeachment. *See* United States v. Tarantino, 846 F.2d 1384, 1409 (D.C. Cir. 1988) (holding that Rule 608(b) inapplicable to impeachment by contradiction); Bufford v. Rowan Companies, Inc., 994 F.2d 155, 159–60 (5th Cir. 1993) (Rule 608(b) does not bar extrinsic evidence offered to contradict witness's testimony concerning material issue); United States v. Chu, 5 F.3d 1244, 1249 (9th Cir. 1993) (holding that Rule 608(b) does not address whether extrinsic evidence is admissible to impeach by contradiction); Boutros v. Canton Regional Transit Authority, 997 F.2d 198, 205 (6th Cir. 1993) (holding that Rule 608(b) ban on extrinsic evidence not applicable to use of such evidence to contradict witness as to material issue); United States v. Fleming, 19 F.3d 1325, 1331 (10th Cir. 1994) (holding that Rule 608(b) inapplicable when extrinsic evidence offered to show statement made by defendant on direct examination is untrue, even if statement concerns collateral issue). In the wake of the 2003 amendment to Rule 608(b), it is clear that exclusion of collateral matters should be handled under the balancing test of Rule 403. The advisory committee note to the 2003

common-law collateral impeachment rule regarding impeachment by contradiction.[87] Most often, evidence that contradicts a witness concerning a collateral issue will be of only marginal value in evaluating the witness's credibility and it usually will not be worthwhile to call another witness to provide the impeaching testimony. Thus, the court often should grant a Rule 403 motion to exclude the evidence. Of course, this assessment will not always be correct. If the case is very close and will be decided largely on the basis of the jury's determination of the credibility of opposing witnesses, the court would be justified in permitting the opponent to call the impeaching witness.[88]

§ 11.07 Showing Untruthful Character of Witness—in General

A witness may be impeached by showing that the witness has a bad character for truthfulness. This evidence is admissible under an exception to the general rule prohibiting the use of character evidence to prove conduct and applies to both civil and criminal trials.[89]

Impeachment for untruthful character may take one of three forms. First, the impeaching party can attack by offering generalities about the witness's character for truthfulness via character witnesses. This can take the form of showing that the witness has a bad reputation for truthfulness or veracity. The Federal Rules of Evidence also permit opinion testimony to the same effect. Second, the impeaching party may cross-examine the witness regarding specific misconduct of the witness that reflects on truthfulness. Third, the impeaching party may offer evidence of a prior criminal conviction of the witness to show that the witness is untruthful.

Each of these methods of attacking character is subject to fairly strict limits. Consequently, it is important to be precise about whether a particular impeachment effort attacks character. The limits described in the following sections only apply when the attack is on the witness's character. If the witness is impeached via some other method (such as bias or defects in perception), then these limits do not apply.[90] This is

---

amendment of Rule 608(b) states that "the absolute prohibition on extrinsic evidence applies only when the sole reason for proffering that evidence is to attack or support the witness' character for truthfulness," and that "the amendment leaves the admissibility of extrinsic evidence offered for other grounds of impeachment (such as contradiction, prior inconsistent statement, bias and mental capacity) to Rules 402 and 403."

[87] *See, e.g.*, United States v. Cruz-Rodriguez, 541 F.3d 19, 29–30 (1st Cir. 2008) (holding that party may not present extrinsic evidence to impeach witness by contradiction on a collateral matter); United States v. Payne, 102 F.3d 289, 294 (7th Cir. 1996) (invoking collateral evidence rule in excluding evidence relevant only to impeach a witness's assertion on cross-examination that his girlfriend did not know of his criminal activity); United States v. Edwards, 696 F.2d 1277, 1281 (11th Cir. 1983) (holding extrinsic evidence that government witness was drug dealer inadmissible to impeach by contradiction); United States v. Terebecki, 692 F.2d 1345, 1351 (11th Cir. 1982) ("Since the statement did not concern a major issue in the case, impeachment would have been on a collateral issue and was properly excluded.").

[88] *See* ROGER PARK & TOM LININGER, THE NEW WIGMORE: IMPEACHMENT AND REHABILITATION § 4.2 at 204 (2012). One view is that, for ease of administration, extrinsic contradicting evidence on a collateral matter ought to be considered a waste of time without inquiring in each case whether it is. Thus, the collateral impeachment rule could be regarded as a useful elaboration of Rule 403. For a contrary view, see Edward J. Imwinkelried, *Federal Rule of Evidence 402: The Second Revolution*, 6 REV. LITIG. 129 (1987), arguing that "Rule 402 permits trial judges to exclude relevant evidence only on grounds recognized in the Constitution, by statute, or by court rule . . . Rule 402 impliedly abolishes all common-law evidentiary rules that have not been codified." A compromise view would take the common-law rule as a "rule of thumb" that creates a predisposition (i.e., a rebuttable presumption applied only by the court) against the use of extrinsic evidence to contradict a witness on a collateral matter.

[89] *See* FED. R. EVID. 404(a)(3).

[90] An amendment to FED. R. EVID. 608(b), which went effect on December 1, 2003, clarified the rule by adding explicit language stating that its prohibition on the use of extrinsic evidence of specific instances of

true even if the other types of impeachment evidence also reflect poorly on character, such as impeachment for bias where the witness took a bribe to testify falsely, indicating both bias and lack of trustworthiness.

In addition, because the three different ways of attacking character listed above are subject to different restrictions, one must be clear about which kind of attack is involved. Reputation or opinion witnesses are easily distinguished from cross-examination about specific acts of dishonesty and criminal convictions. Creating more confusion, however, is the fact that the use of convictions to attack character is one way of using the witness's misconduct to prove character, so that cross-examination as to specific acts and impeachment with convictions are overlapping categories. For clarity, we cover these topics in four sections. First, we address character witnesses, who provide testimony in the form of opinions and reports of reputation regarding the truthfulness of the witness being impeached.[91] Second, we consider the use of evidence of specific misconduct by the witness that does not end in conviction.[92] Third, we consider the use of evidence of the witness's conviction for misconduct.[93] Finally, we consider the use of evidence of misconduct that results in a conviction but where the impeacher does not attempt to introduce evidence of the conviction itself.[94]

§ 11.08 Showing Untruthful Character of Witness—Reputation and Opinion Testimony [FRE 608(a)]

A party may impeach a witness by calling another witness (a "character witness") who testifies to the first witness's reputation or, in jurisdictions following the Federal Rules, opinion as to character.[95] The character testimony must be restricted to the character trait of truthfulness. As with other reputation and opinion testimony, the testimony is supposed to be extremely general in form. A minimalist examination of such a character witness follows:

Q. Do you know the witness, Mr. X?

A. Yes.

Q. Do you know other persons in the community who know Mr. X?

A. Yes.

Q. Have you had occasion to hear Mr. X's reputation for truth and veracity discussed among those persons?

A. Yes, many times.

Q. Do you know Mr. X's reputation for truth and veracity?

A. Yes.

---

conduct applies to evidence offered to attack or support "character for truthfulness," not to all evidence offered to attack or support credibility.

[91] *See* **§ 11.08**.

[92] *See* **§ 11.09**.

[93] *See* **§ 11.10**.

[94] *See* **§ 11.11**.

[95] *See* FED. R. EVID. 608(a); *see also* State v. Lewis, 847 P.2d 690, 690–94 (Kan. 1993) (in prosecution for attempted rape, holding it reversible error for trial court to exclude four witnesses' testimony about victim's reputation for lack of veracity).

Q. What is that reputation?

A. It is very bad. He has the reputation of being a terrible liar.

Tradition allows the direct-examiner to add the following question:

Q. Based on that reputation, would you believe Mr. X when he testified under oath?

A. No.[96]

Although the testimony about reputation is admissible, testimony about the specific acts of lying upon which the testimony was based is not admissible. Some courts nowadays might require something more specific than "the community," as people participate in various communities in their lives—professional, residential, recreational, and so forth.[97]

The Federal Rules also permit the character witness to be questioned about his or her opinion of the truthfulness of the first witness. The stated reason for this addition is that much reputation testimony is actually opinion testimony in disguise and that, at any rate, in a modern, disconnected society a person who knows character may not know reputation for character. Thus, if an adequate foundation is shown establishing the character witness's familiarity with the initial witness, then the character witness may give an opinion about the first witness's character for truthfulness.[98] The character witness may not, however, go so far as to opine on whether the first witness is telling the truth in the testimony in the present case.[99]

Such opinion testimony can lead to the danger of admitting specific-act testimony, allowing the jury to infer specific acts of dishonesty. Consider the following hypothetical examination:

Q. Do you know Mr. X?

A. Yes.

Q. How do you know him?

A. We work for the same company.

Q. What is your position with that company?

A. I am the comptroller.

---

[96] This is technically opinion and not reputation evidence. In theory, it would not be admissible at common law, where only reputation testimony was permitted. But custom sanctioned its reception even at common law. *See* 7 WIGMORE ON EVIDENCE § 1982 (Chadbourn rev. 1978). The Federal Rules permit opinion testimony, though a technical objection could be made to the question in text on grounds that there is insufficient foundation to show a basis for a personal opinion of character. It is not clear how long or how well the testifying witness has known the witness whose character is being attacked.

[97] For a useful discussion of the required community, see State v. Kalex, 789 A.2d 1286 (Me. 2002). Evidence of reputation is hearsay, but a hearsay exception provides for the admissibility of evidence of "reputation among a person's associates or in the community concerning the person's character." FED. R. EVID. 803(21).

[98] Technically, familiarity with the person (in order to give an opinion) is not the same as familiarity with the person's reputation (in order to report reputation); one can have knowledge of one without knowledge of the other. See 3 CHRISTOPHER B. MUELLER & LAIRD C. KIRKPATRICK, FEDERAL EVIDENCE § 6:30 at 178–82 (4th ed. 2013).

[99] *See* ROGER PARK & TOM LININGER, THE NEW WIGMORE: IMPEACHMENT AND ACCREDITATION § 3.2 at 105 (2012).

Q. Do your duties as comptroller include the review of expense accounts?

A. Yes.

Q. Have you reviewed Mr. X's expense account?

A. Yes.

Q. Do you have an opinion about Mr. X's character for truthfulness?

A. Yes.

Q. What is that opinion?

A. He is extremely untruthful.

The examination above borders on putting in specific instances of conduct by extrinsic evidence, a form of impeachment prohibited by the Federal Rules and common-law.[100] The examination carries with it the strong implication that the testifying witness examined Mr. X's expense account and found that it contained falsehoods. The examiner's conduct warrants an objection or, if the problem is foreseeable, a motion in limine.[101]

Another possible abuse arises from testimony by persons who acquire knowledge of a witness's character trait only in anticipation of litigation. The most common example is police agents who testify about the character of investigative targets. For example, in *United States v. Dotson,*[102] the government called an FBI agent to the stand and elicited the following testimony:

Q. Have you had occasion to conduct an investigation into the activities of the defendant, Fred Dotson, and his associates?

A. Yes, sir, I have.

Q. As a result of this investigation and what you have learned and all that you have seen in this case, have you formed an opinion as to the truthfulness of the defendant, Frederick Leon Dotson?

A. Yes, sir, I have.

Q. Is that opinion of his truthfulness good or bad?

A. Bad.

Q. Would you believe Frederick Leon Dotson under oath?

A. No, sir, I would not.

---

[100] See **§ 11.09**. *See, e.g.*, United States v. Perez-Perez, 72 F.3d 224, 227 (1st Cir. 1995) (holding that complaints by other police officers about the witness's misconduct were properly excluded under Rule 608(B); while certain prior good or bad acts of a witness may constitute character evidence bearing on veracity, they are not evidence of enough force to justify admitting extrinsic proof).

[101] For a case in which such testimony was approved, see United States v. Dotson, 799 F.2d 189, 193 (5th Cir. 1986) (holding IRS agent's opinion about lack of financial truthfulness of witness, based on interviews, examination of tax returns, and study of witness's testimony before grand jury, noted approvingly in dictum as example of character opinion based on proper and sufficient foundation). *See also* People v. Bieri, 396 N.W.2d 506, 513 (Mich. Ct. App. 1986) (holding that prison guard may testify about witness's reputation for untruthfulness because he had known witness for five months and had discussed witness's reputation with other correctional officers).

[102] United States v. Dotson, 799 F.2d 189, 191 (5th Cir. 1986).

Although the appellate court held that this evidence should have been excluded at trial, it did not forbid government agents from testifying to their opinions about the defendant's character that were formed during the investigation. The court merely held that the foundation was insufficient in the case before it, because the agent had not described anything more than minimal contact with the defendant.[103]

Because of the potential dangers of character-based impeachment, the trial court has discretion to forbid or limit such impeachment. The trial court may exclude such evidence when it finds that its value for impeachment purposes is substantially outweighed by any of the dangers listed in Rule 403.[104] In addition, the court may limit the number of witnesses who may be called to attack the character of a witness. Where testimony would be duplicative, limiting a party to only one attacking witness has been upheld as a reasonable exercise of judicial discretion under Rule 403, which governs the introduction of cumulative evidence.[105]

§ 11.09 Showing Untruthful Character of Witness—Evidence of Witness's Misconduct Not Leading to Conviction [FRE 608(b)]

Common-law courts have looked with disfavor upon extrinsic evidence offered to show specific conduct that reflects badly on the character of the witness and that is not otherwise relevant to the case.[106] The principal concerns have been to avoid (a) confusion of the issues that distracts the fact-finder from the material events of the case, and (b) unfair surprise where the party resisting impeachment of its witness cannot anticipate all such challenges regarding the witness's past. These reasons do not apply as strongly to impeachment with a conviction (addressed in the following section) or to impeachment by proof of misconduct elicited during cross-examination of the witness being impeached. Accordingly, most common-law courts allowed inquiry into specific acts of past misconduct when limited to cross-examination of the witness being impeached.[107] Nevertheless, some pre-Rules jurisdictions precluded even cross-examination about such collateral events, and courts permitting such cross-examination have differed about its scope.[108]

Under Federal Rule 608(b), the trial judge has discretion to permit a witness to be questioned about conduct that has not resulted in conviction for the purpose of

---

[103] *See also* United States v. Williams, 822 F.2d 512, 516 (5th Cir. 1987) (prosecution laid adequate foundation for opinion testimony by government agents about witness's character for truthfulness by showing both had learned about witness through surveillance and by interviewing his acquaintances [note: court used the plain error standard to review issue because defendant did not make proper objection during his trial); United States v. Cortez, 935 F.2d 135, 139–40 (8th Cir. 1991) (error, though harmless, to admit testimony of two law enforcement officers who spent less than one day each interviewing defendant about his conversations with a third person and who spoke only of their belief in particular story rather than of defendant's general character for truthfulness).

[104] *See, e.g.*, Polanco v. City of Austin, Tex., 78 F.3d 968, 981 (5th Cir. 1996) (excluding character testimony by ex-mistress of witness as "imbued with her frustrations" on their failed relationship).

[105] *See* United States v. Haynes, 554 F.2d 231 (5th Cir. 1977). *See* **§ 5.03**.

[106] *See* 3A WIGMORE ON EVIDENCE § 977 (Chadbourn rev. 1970).

[107] *Id.* § 978.

[108] *Id.* § 979. Today, some jurisdictions, even some otherwise following the model of the Federal Rules, do not permit cross-examination about specific acts to prove untruthfulness, except insofar as this cross-examination concerns conviction of a qualifying crime. *See* ROGER PARK & TOM LININGER, THE NEW WIGMORE: IMPEACHMENT AND ACCREDITATION § 3.3 at 114 n.5 (2012) (citing CAL. EVID. C. § 787 (applicable in civil cases), ALA. R. EVID. 608, IND. R. EVID. 608, OR. REV. STAT. § 40.350 (Rule 608), and TEX. R. EVID. 608).

supporting or attacking the truthfulness of the witness. The conduct must relate to truthfulness, however, and not to some other character trait.[109] Thus, a witness may be questioned about the witness's dishonesty in falsifying an academic record on an employment application but not about sexual misconduct or cruelty to animals.[110] Harder cases involve questions about dishonest acts that do not involve lying, such as threatening witnesses, thefts by stealth, or failure to make required disclosures or reports, where some cases permit inquiry.[111]

If the witness denies the misconduct, then the cross-examiner must "take the answer."[112] This does not mean that the cross-examiner is prohibited from further cross-examination to get the witness to admit the misconduct,[113] but it does mean that extrinsic evidence of the misconduct is not admissible, even though it contradicts the witness's denial.[114] Again, the main purpose of this ban on extrinsic evidence is to prevent the waste of time, confusion of the issues, and unfair surprise that would occur

---

[109] *See* 28 CHARLES A. WRIGHT & VICTOR J. GOLD, FEDERAL PRACTICE AND PROCEDURE (EVIDENCE) § 6115 (2012).

[110] *See* United States v. McMillon, 14 F.3d 948, 955–56 (4th Cir. 1994) (holding defendant in conspiracy prosecution not entitled to cross-examine government's witness regarding witness's prior homosexual activities); United States v. Blake, 941 F.2d 334, 339–41 (5th Cir. 1991) (finding harmless error in impeachment of narcotics defendant with questions about whether he had ever killed anyone and whether he had told police officer that he had killed 10 people); United States v. Parker, 133 F.3d 322, 326–27 (5th Cir. 1998) (finding no abuse of discretion in denying cross-examination of government witness in bribery case about witness's alleged murder of witness's husband because acts of violence do not reflect on character for truthfulness); Mason v. Texaco, Inc., 948 F.2d 1546, 1555–56 (10th Cir. 1991) (holding that district court was within discretion in ruling that plaintiff's expert witnesses could not be cross-examined about allegedly biased study they prepared on subject unrelated to instant suit; such impeachment is barred on ground, among others, that cross-examination would not have challenged character for truthfulness but merely objectivity on particular study; authors believe court erred in stating that evidence did not reflect on character, though its overall ruling that exclusion was within district court's discretion is supportable); Wanke v. Lynn's Transp. Co., 836 F. Supp. 587, 597 (N.D. Ind. 1993) (in wrongful death action against trucking company, holding evidence of truck driver's prior arrests for disorderly conduct not admissible under Rule 608(b) because not probative of veracity); People v. Chaplin, 313 N.W.2d 899, 902 (Mich. 1981) (finding it reversible error to permit cross-examination suggesting witness was prostitute and defendant may have been her pimp); Heshelman v. Lombardi, 454 N.W.2d 603 (Mich. Ct. App. 1990) (finding error to allow cross-examination of doctor about prior malpractice action); Unmack v. Deaconess Medical Center, 967 P.2d 783, 785–86 (Mont. 1998) (finding reversible error to allow impeachment of expert medical witness who was also lawyer with evidence of improper solicitation of clients; bar discipline was not based on imputation of dishonesty).

For examples of cross-examination deemed permissible see Vichare v. AMBAC Inc. 106 F.3d 457, 468 (2d Cir. 1996) (holding that employment discrimination plaintiff could be impeached under Rule 608(b) by cross-examination about taking kickbacks; after-acquired evidence of misconduct can be used to impeach even though it does not automatically bar substantive recovery by providing grounds for discharge); United States v. Waldrip, 981 F.2d 799, 802–03 (5th Cir. 1993) (holding that government may cross-examine defendant about incident in which defendant signed another's name to document without authorization, even though incident resembled crime charged).

[111] *See, e.g.*, United States v. Manske, 186 F.3d 770, 774 (7th Cir. 1999) (opining that conduct need not involve lying to be probative of untruthfulness; concluding that the act of threatening a witness is within the scope of Rule 608(b)). *See generally* 3 CHRISTOPHER B MUELLER & LAIRD C. KIRKPATRICK, FEDERAL EVIDENCE § 6:33 (4th ed. 2013) (endorsing view that "behavior seeking personal advantage by taking from others in violation of their rights reflects on veracity").

[112] *See, e.g.*, United States v. Perez-Perez, 72 F.3d 224, 227 (1st Cir. 1995) (holding that complaints by other police officers about the witness's misconduct were properly excluded under Rule 608(b); "while certain prior good or bad acts of a witness may constitute character evidence bearing on veracity, they are not evidence of enough force to justify the detour of extrinsic proof"); Lambert v. Commonwealth, 383 S.E.2d 752, 754 (Va. Ct. App. 1989).

[113] *See* 4 WEINSTEIN'S FEDERAL EVIDENCE § 608.22[1] (Mark S. Brodin ed., 2d ed. 2015).

[114] FED. R. EVID. 608(b).

if mini-trials were held about blemishes in each witness's past.[115] Again, testimony from the mouth of the witness during cross-examination is not extrinsic for this purpose. Just as clearly, testimony of another witness would be extrinsic.[116]

The rule forbids the use of documents to impeach when it is necessary to call another witness to authenticate those documents.[117] Therefore, if on cross-examination counsel asks the witness to admit that she once lied about her age in an effort to enter an adults-only bar, in its discretion, the court could allow this question because it concerns conduct reflecting on the witness's truthfulness. If the witness refuses to admit that the event occurred, the opponent would not be permitted to call a friend to testify that she was with the witness when this event occurred, nor would the opponent be permitted to call an employee of the bar to authenticate a document reporting on the incident.

Suppose, however, that during cross-examination the witness denies engaging in the conduct but admits the authenticity of a document reporting the conduct. Would introduction of the document still violate the extrinsic evidence rule? The courts are divided on this question. Some courts hold that the document still constitutes extrinsic evidence.[118] Others, however, hold that the extrinsic evidence rule would not be violated by its admission.[119] The latter courts appear to have the better argument. As one court stated, "[w]hen . . . the extrinsic evidence is obtained from and through examination of the very witness whose credibility is under attack, . . . [Rule 608(b)'s] core concerns are not implicated."[120] Because no other witness is involved, no extra time is spent inquiring

---

[115] *See* United States v. Martz, 964 F.2d 787, 789 (8th Cir. 1992) (explaining that reason for barring extrinsic evidence "is to avoid holding mini-trials on peripherally related or irrelevant matters"). *See* Frederick C. Moss, *The Sweeping-Claims Exception and the Federal Rules of Evidence*, 1982 DUKE L.J. 61, 70 ("The policy reasons for excluding extrinsic evidence are the avoidance of undue prolongation of the trial, confusion of the issues, and unfair surprise to the witness.").

[116] *See* United States v. McNeill, 887 F.2d 448, 453 (3d Cir. 1989) ("Extrinsic evidence is evidence offered through other witnesses, rather than through cross-examination of the witness himself or herself."); 28 CHARLES A. WRIGHT & VICTOR J. GOLD, FEDERAL PRACTICE AND PROCEDURE (EVIDENCE) § 6117 at 94 (2012). Wigmore found this limitation to be entirely consistent with the underlying purposes of the rule forbidding extrinsic evidence. 3A WIGMORE ON EVIDENCE § 979 at 826 (Chadbourn rev. 1970).

[117] *See* United States v. Peterson, 808 F.2d 969, 972–74 (2d Cir. 1987) (holding that, where witness denied forging endorsement on check, party could not introduce check); United States v. Lashmett, 965 F.2d 179, 181–82 (7th Cir. 1992) (holding court filings in related civil action inadmissible under Rule 613, which contains same extrinsic evidence limitation); *Cf.* United States v. Elliott, 89 F.3d 1360 (8th Cir. 1996) (finding that trial court did not err when it refused to allow defendant to use documentary exhibits during cross-examination of government witness in an effort to impeach witness by showing that she misrepresented her educational and work experience on her resume; though court based decision on Rule 608(b), defendant also appeared to have offered evidence substantively to prove a defense, for which purpose Rule 608(b) would not have applied).

[118] *See* United States v. Elliott, 89 F.3d 1360, 1368 (8th Cir. 1996) (upholding trial court's decision to bar use of witness's allegedly false resume to attack her credibility on cross-examination; exact nature of attempted use unclear from opinion). *Cf.* United States v. Whitehead, 618 F.2d 523, 529 (4th Cir. 1980) (refusing to admit document even if witness admits engaging in conduct).

[119] *See, e.g.*, Carter v. Hewitt, 617 F.2d 961, 969–70 (3d Cir. 1980) (holding that extrinsic evidence rule not violated when, during cross-examination of witness, letter that witness admittedly had written and which evidenced his character for truthfulness was admitted into evidence). United States v. Jackson, 882 F.2d 1444, 1448 (9th Cir. 1989) (affirming the admission of letter that witness admitted signing and that included confession to misappropriating client's funds).

[120] Carter v. Hewitt, 617 F.2d 961, 970 (3d Cir. 1980).

into the credibility of yet another person.[121] The jury is less likely to be confused, and the witness is unlikely to be surprised by the document.[122]

Even if the witness denies the conduct or the authenticity of the document, the extrinsic evidence rule does not bar the attorney from using the document solely to attempt to refresh the witness's recollection.[123] Under those circumstances, any testimony still comes from the mouth of the witness; the document is not offered as evidence.[124]

One approach to avoiding the impact of the extrinsic evidence rule as applied to documents is to send the inculpating documentation to the witness and counsel before trial. While this will tip off the witness about the nature of the expected cross-examination, it will put the witness on notice before trial, so that the witness may feel obliged to tell the truth.[125]

Sometimes a witness will open the door to a counter-attack that otherwise would be impermissible by voluntarily injecting an assertion about specific instances into his or her testimony. For example, a witness who proclaims never to have been suspected of involvement with drugs opens the door to counter-evidence showing a prior drug arrest.[126] Of course, the information must first be elicited on direct examination or volunteered in a non-responsive answer; the cross-examiner cannot force the witness into making the avowal just to contradict it. This rule seems to be based on application of the general principles of waiver.[127]

---

[121] Of course, even asking additional questions of a witness consumes a small amount of time, and, where the witness has actually admitted the conduct, the court may well exclude the document as cumulative and a waste of time. 28 CHARLES A. WRIGHT & VICTOR J. GOLD, FEDERAL PRACTICE AND PROCEDURE (EVIDENCE) § 6117 at 97 (2012); *see also* Carter v. Hewitt, 617 F.2d 961, 970–71 (3d Cir. 1980) (noting that where witness admits conduct, court may exclude evidence under Rule 403 as cumulative).

[122] Commentators have approved of the practice of allowing the use of a document on cross-examination when the witness either admits the conduct or the authenticity of the document. *See, e.g.*, 28 CHARLES A. WRIGHT & VICTOR J. GOLD, FEDERAL PRACTICE AND PROCEDURE (EVIDENCE) § 6117 at 97 (2012); Frederick C. Moss, *The Sweeping-Claims Exception and the Federal Rules of Evidence*, 1982 DUKE L. J. 61, 70 (noting that in context of common-law rule governing impeachment by contradiction, which also contains an extrinsic evidence limitation, "[n]one of [the] policies [underlying the extrinsic evidence rule] is necessarily violated when a witness is confronted with nontestimonial evidence on cross-examination. If he is confronted with a document and admits its authenticity, the contradiction is completed, swiftly and clearly"). *But see* 3 CHRISTOPHER B. MUELLER & LAIRD C. KIRKPATRICK, FEDERAL EVIDENCE § 6:36 at 227 (4th ed. 2013) (endorsing questioning of the witness regarding the document but not introduction thereof).

It is unclear whether the reasoning described above approving the use of documents during cross-examination would support the use of self-authenticating documents in the face of the witness's refusal to admit the conduct or authenticate the document. Time is not of particular concern, as no additional witnesses need be called. However, issues of harassment and surprise might be implicated in some circumstances, counseling against admission.

[123] *See* United States v. Chevalier, 1 F.3d 581, 584 n.1 (7th Cir. 1993) (holding that court properly allowed prosecution to use loan document to refresh recollection concerning statement defendant had made in effort to convince defendant-witness to admit bank fraud).

[124] *See* **§ 16.06**.

[125] *See* B. HOUSE, GREAT TRIALS OF FAMOUS LAWYERS 180–81 (1962) (describing counsel's preparation for cross-examination of witness who was a member of Congress; counsel sent witness letter asking witness to refresh memory on subjects so that witness would not claim to have forgotten facts surrounding prior falsifications).

[126] *See* United States v. Garcia, 900 F.2d 571 (2d Cir. 1990). *See also* State v. Syriani, 428 S.E.2d 118, 135 (N.C. 1993) (admitting evidence of prior threats and specific acts of violence by defendant against his wife and children in prosecution for first-degree murder of defendant's wife, when defendant testified he was a "loving and supportive husband and father").

[127] *See* **§ 1.11**.

Again, it is important to remember that extrinsic evidence of a witness's particular dishonest behavior may fall outside the ban of Rule 608(b). For example, evidence that a witness engaged in a distinctively similar type of lying on different occasions may be admissible not as character evidence to impeach the witness, but as non-character evidence. Thus, evidence that a witness has made prior false accusations of the same crime in the same circumstances may be admissible to show motive or common plan.[128] Of course, if the evidence of a witness's bad acts independently supports a claim or defense, then the evidence is admissible, regardless of whether it impeaches the witness.[129] This would be the case, for example, when the witness's prior acts included concealing from the defendant criminal activity of the type that the defendant is now alleged to have committed in concert with the witness. In these cases, even if the evidence is independently admissible for a non-impeachment purpose, the court should examine carefully whether the evidence should be excluded as unfairly prejudicial under Rule 403.[130]

In reading cases decided before 2004, one should bear in mind that the inartfully broad wording of Rule 608(b), as it then read, occasionally misled some courts into thinking that it imposed limits on extrinsic evidence offered to impeach a witness in a wide variety of ways.[131] Rule 608(b), however, concerns only impeachment by an attack on the *character* of a witness for truthfulness, and better reasoned decisions so held.[132] The point was confirmed by an amendment to Rule 608(b), which took effect on December 1, 2003. The advisory committee explained the amendment, noting that "the absolute prohibition on extrinsic evidence applies only when the sole reason for proffering that evidence is to attack or support the witness' [sic] character for truthfulness," and that "the amendment leaves the admissibility of extrinsic evidence offered for other grounds of impeachment (such as contradiction, prior inconsistent statement, bias and mental capacity) to Rules 402 and 403."[133]

---

[128] *See* FED. R. EVID. 404(b)(2). *See, e.g.*, United States v. Stamper, 766 F. Supp. 1396 (W.D.N.C. 1991), *aff'd, In re* One Female Juvenile Victim, 959 F.2d 231 (4th Cir. 1992) (holding complainant's previous allegedly false allegations of sexual abuse by three other men admissible to show motive of manipulating complainant's custodians).

[129] *See* United States v. Costa, 947 F.2d 919, 925–26 (11th Cir. 1991) (holding that, while Rule 608(b) prohibits use of extrinsic evidence of bad acts solely to impeach character, it does not prohibit extrinsic evidence that is independently relevant to defendant's defense that he was not involved in the drug ring which was subject of testimony of government witnesses).

[130] *Cf.* United States v. Smith, 80 F.3d 1188, 1193 (7th Cir. 1996) (finding no plain error where defendant, charged with cargo theft was cross-examined about uncharged cargo thefts for purposes of impeachment under Fed. R. Evid. 608(b); "Prior acts of theft or receipt of stolen property are, like acts of fraud or deceit, probative of a witness's truthfulness or untruthfulness under Rule 608(b)"). It is questionable whether any jury could be expected to use the fruits of such a cross-examination solely for the permitted purpose of impeaching credibility while ignoring its natural probative force in showing propensity to commit cargo theft but that is a matter for the judge to determine under Rule 403, and the objection was not raised in this case.

[131] *See* American Bar Association Section of Litigation, EMERGING PROBLEMS UNDER THE FEDERAL RULES OF EVIDENCE 161 (3d ed. 1998).

[132] *See also* United States v. Whiting, 28 F.3d 1296, 1301 (1st Cir. 1994) (Rule 608(b) does not exclude evidence offered for non-character purpose). The Uniform Rules, UNIF. R. EVID. 616 (1986), were amended in 1986 to make explicit that extrinsic evidence attacking credibility with evidence of bias, prejudice, or interest is admissible. For an example of state adoption of this rule, see MINN. R. EVID. 616 (as amended Jan. 1, 1990).

[133] FED. R. EVID. 608(b) advisory committee note to proposed amendment.

§ 11.10 Showing Untruthful Character of Witness—Evidence of Prior Convictions of Witness [FRE 609]

Rule 609 allows impeachment of witnesses with evidence of their prior crimes in many instances. The admissibility of a witness's convictions for serious crimes has a history that is tied to the common-law incompetency of such convicts.[134] When incompetency was removed, and convicts were permitted to testify, impeachment for bad character of the witness replaced incompetency even though the logical grounds for incompetency are not necessarily the same as those for impeachment.[135] Given the availability of an official record, evidence of a conviction can be presented with minimal distraction, and the witness is hard pressed to deny he did the act for which he was convicted. Therefore, the restriction on extrinsic evidence regarding this collateral fact has traditionally not applied.[136]

Courts and scholars have long debated the extent of and justification for admitting prior convictions to show a dishonest or untruthful character. Some jurists have argued that only crimes of falsehood should be admitted to impeach a witness in this way, because crimes of violence (for example) are likely to prejudice the jury without providing insight into the witness's credibility.[137] Other jurists have argued that all prior crimes, or at least all serious ones, are relevant to truthfulness. The theory is that someone who would flout social norms by committing felonies might also be more likely to lie; the same anti-social tendency that led to criminal conduct could lead to perjury.[138]

These conflicting viewpoints have led to a variety of approaches to using prior convictions as impeachment. Some states follow the *crimen falsi* approach, admitting only crimes of dishonesty or false statement.[139] Other states adopt a broader approach,

---

[134] *See* **§ 8.01**.

[135] *See* ROGER PARK & TOM LININGER, THE NEW WIGMORE: IMPEACHMENT AND ACCREDITATION § 3.4.2 (2012).

[136] *See* 3A WIGMORE ON EVIDENCE § 980 (Chadbourn Rev. 1970).

[137] *See, e.g.*, United States v. Fountain, 768 F.2d 790 (7th Cir. 1985) (Posner, J.) ("Violent men are not necessarily liars, and indeed one class of violent men consists of those with an exaggerated sense of honor"); Mason Ladd, *Credibility Tests-Current Trends*, 89 U. PA. L. REV. 180–82 (1940) (quoting 7 Jeremy Bentham, Rationale of Judicial Evidence 407 (Bowrings ed. 1827)):

> Take homicide in the way of dueling. Two men quarrel; one of them calls the other a liar. So highly does he prize the reputation of veracity, that, rather than suffer a stain to remain upon it, he determines to risk his life, challenges his adversary to fight, and kills him. Jurisprudence, in its sapience, knowing no difference between homicide by consent, by which no other human being is put in fear—and homicide in pursuit of a scheme of highway robbery, of nocturnal housebreaking, by which every man who has a life is put in fear of it—has made the one and the other murder, and consequently felony. The man prefers death to the imputation of a lie—and the inference of the law is, that he cannot open his mouth but lies will issue from it. Such are the inconsistencies which are unavoidable in the application of any rule which takes improbity for a ground of exclusion.

[138] This theory was articulated by Oliver Wendell Holmes, who, as a Justice on the Supreme Judicial Court of Massachusetts, wrote in a civil case:

> [W]hen it is proved that a witness has been convicted of a crime, the only ground for disbelieving him which such proof affords is the general readiness to do evil which the conviction may be supposed to show. It is from that general disposition alone that the jury is asked to infer a readiness to lie in the particular case, and thence that he has lied in fact. The evidence has no tendency to prove that he was mistaken, but only that he has perjured himself, and it reaches that conclusion solely through the general proposition that he is of bad character and unworthy of credit.

Gertz v. Fitchburg Railroad Co., 137 Mass. 77, 78 (1884). *See also* 3A WIGMORE ON EVIDENCE § 982 (Chadbourn rev. 1970).

[139] See PA. R. EVID. 609(a); ALASKA R. EVID. 609(a); IOWA R. EVID. 609(a).

either mandating or allowing judges to receive evidence of other crimes.[140] And at least one state takes an extremely restrictive approach, barring use of any convictions for this purpose.[141]

The federal rulemakers reached a compromise.[142] Convictions for crimes of dishonesty or false statement are generously admissible to impeach a witness, regardless of the seriousness of the crime as reflected in the possible punishment. At the other extreme, crimes that do not involve dishonesty or false statement, for which the maximum sentence is one year or less (typically misdemeanors) are not admissible to impeach a witness under the Rule. The most challenging policy questions concern evidence of conviction for crimes punishable by death or imprisonment in excess of a year that do not involve dishonesty or false statement. Whether such evidence is admissible depends, in part, on the witness being impeached (whether it is the criminal defendant or some other witness).[143]

Rule 609(b): Ten-Year Time Limit

Rule 609(b) provides a time limit on the use of all types of convictions to impeach witnesses under Rule 609(a). If more than ten years have passed since the conviction or release from confinement (whichever is later), the Rule requires an extremely strong showing of probative value to admit the conviction, even if it otherwise qualifies under Rule 609(a).[144] A conviction offered after the ten-year limit will be admitted only if its probative value, "supported by specific facts and circumstances, substantially outweighs its prejudicial effect." This showing should not be confused with that required for exclusion under Rule 403. In fact, the standard of proof is the mirror opposite of that found in Rule 403 and highly favors exclusion of the evidence. In addition, Rule 609 requires that the proponent give the adverse party advance written notice of an intention to introduce a conviction of any type that will be beyond the ten-year limit.[145]

Rule 609(a)(1): Crimes Punishable for More than One Year

Rule 609(a)(1) deals with serious crimes—those punishable by death or imprisonment for more than one year—that do not fall within the more generous admissibility rule for crimes involving dishonesty or false statement in Rule 609(a)(2). It establishes two balancing tests, one for the accused in a criminal case and the other for all other witnesses in both criminal and civil cases. For the accused, impeachment with

---

140 *See* CAL. EVID. CODE § 788; IDAHO R. EVID. 609(a).

141 *See* MONT. R. EVID. 609.

142 For a detailed examination of the legislative history of Rule 609 and of the compromise represented by the rule that emerged from the debates, *see* 28 CHARLES A. WRIGHT & VICTOR J. GOLD, FEDERAL PRACTICE AND PROCEDURE (EVIDENCE) §§ 6131–6132 (2012). *See also* Victor J. Gold, *Impeachment by Conviction Evidence: Judicial Discretion and the Politics of Rule 609*, 15 CARDOZO L. REV. 2295 (1994).

143 In each context, the rule reads as follows: "[E]vidence of a criminal conviction . . . must be admitted" under the stated conditions. Read literally, this entails that evidence of the fact of such a conviction is to be admitted under the indicated conditions even if it would be barred by some other rule, such as the hearsay rule, the original recording rule, or the authentication requirement. In the context of the structure of the rule, however, it is clear that the purpose of this language was only to modify trial judges' usual residual authority under Rule 403.

144 FED. R. EVID. 609(b). Courts occasionally will have to rule on measuring the ten-year time period. If confinement is imposed, the ten-year period does not start running until release. *Id.*

145 If a mistrial is offered and refused by the opponent, that refusal may be deemed a waiver of the objection to lack of notice. *See* Zinman v. Black & Decker (U.S.), Inc., 983 F.2d 431, 434–35 (2d Cir. 1993) (in 1992 civil trial that admitted 1975 conviction for Medicaid fraud as impeachment, holding that plaintiff waived objection to sufficiency of notice by twice declining mistrial).

a conviction punishable by more than a one-year sentence is admissible only where the probative value of the evidence outweighs its prejudicial effect. For all other witnesses, impeachment with a conviction punishable by more than a one-year sentence must be admitted subject to a Rule 403 balancing test.

Although both tests use the familiar terms of the Rule 403 balance, their outcomes are quite different. For all witnesses except the criminal defendant, the prior serious crime comes in unless the unfair prejudice substantially outweighs the probative value of the evidence. This places the burden on the objecting party to demonstrate that the probative value of the evidence for impeachment purposes is substantially outweighed by the unfair prejudicial effect (or other dangers listed in Rule 403), a showing that will be very difficult to make in most cases. In other words, evidence of the prior conviction has to be seriously prejudicial to exclude such impeachment. For the criminal defendant, however, the court must affirmatively determine that the probative value of the conviction outweighs its prejudicial effect to the accused. This test provides greater protection for the accused than the normal Rule 403 balancing test, because it places the burden on the proponent to show probative value and does not require that prejudice "substantially outweigh" probative value.

Neither the language of Rule 609 nor the advisory committee note provides meaningful assistance in understanding the nature of the balance the court must strike between probative value and prejudicial impact in either context.[146] When a witness is not a party or closely aligned with one, unfair prejudice poses a less significant issue than concerns about distraction and waste of time. But when the witness is the accused, the risk of unfair prejudice is more serious, a fact reflected in the different balancing tests employed.[147] In deciding whether a conviction should be admitted under Rule 609(a)(1), the courts have identified a number of factors, some of which specifically address the situation when the accused is the witness who is being impeached:[148]

1. *The degree to which the crime reflects on credibility.* For example, a sex crime may not reflect on credibility to the same extent as a robbery conviction.[149]

2. *The nearness or remoteness in time of the prior conviction and the witness's subsequent history.* If a person has led a blameless life for many years after a

---

[146] *See* 28 CHARLES A. WRIGHT & VICTOR J. GOLD, FEDERAL PRACTICE AND PROCEDURE (EVIDENCE) § 6134 (2012).

[147] Sometimes, the same case will see the two standards employed such that the same type of criminality that should be permitted to impeach a witness for the prosecution should not be permitted to impeach the accused. See, e.g., United States v. Tse, 375 F.3d 148 (1st Cir. 2004), discussed in ROGER PARK & TOM LININGER, THE NEW WIGMORE: IMPEACHMENT AND ACCREDITATION § 3.4.4.1.2 (2012).

[148] For a thorough discussion, see ROGER PARK & TOM LININGER, THE NEW WIGMORE: IMPEACHMENT AND ACCREDITATION § 3.4.4.1.1 (2012).

[149] United States v. Larsen, 596 F.2d 347, 348 (9th Cir. 1979) (finding harmless error for trial court to admit defendant's two prior felony convictions for child molestation since crime "bears only nominally on credibility;" not reversible error because court "relied exclusively" on prosecution's case-in-chief in defendant's trial for uttering counterfeit government obligations); *see also* United States v. Lugo, 170 F.3d 996 (10th Cir. 1999) (holding that defendant charged with drug offense who disclaimed any involvement whatever with drugs, invoking anti-drug education by his father, could properly be impeached under Rule 609 with prior drug possession conviction). In the authors' opinion the principle that a defendant who volunteers a sweeping claim of lifelong innocence has forfeited the right to object to evidence contradicting the claim might have been a better basis for the decision than Rule 609; in the absence of such a claim, the probative value of a prior drug offense in impeaching veracity would have been outweighed by the danger that the jury would misuse it as evidence of a propensity to be involved with drugs.

conviction, that should be considered in assessing the probative value (although the lack of criminal activity is not particularly impressive if the person has been incarcerated the whole time and unable to commit another crime). Conversely, courts are more likely to admit recent convictions in impeaching a witness.[150]

3. *The similarity of the prior offense to the offense charged*. While it may seem odd, greater similarity actually weighs against admissibility when the witness is the accused and the only theory of admission is impeachment of the accused as a witness. The concern is that the jury may use the evidence not for its bearing upon the credibility of the witness but for a different, forbidden, character inference that "because she did it before she probably did it again." Thus, a stronger case can be made for receiving a prior auto theft conviction in a bank robbery case than in an auto theft case.[151] Of course, if the two auto thefts were so similar that the first one is admissible under Rule 404(b) to show plan, intent, modus operandi, or the like, then the evidence should not be excluded on this ground. But when the only basis for receiving the prior offense is to impeach credibility, similarity between the two crimes is a factor disfavoring admission.

4. *The extent to which accused's testimony is needed for a fair adjudication*. If that testimony is crucial, this fact weighs against the admissibility of the prior convictions,[152] because, if the evidence will be admissible, it is less likely the accused will elect to testify.

5. *Whether the witness's credibility is central to the case*. If so, that argues in favor of admission.[153]

Some courts will also consider whether the witness's credibility can be explored adequately without using evidence of the witness's prior conviction. If the witness can be impeached convincingly using other means (e.g., bias, prior inconsistent statement),

---

150 United States v. Rein, 848 F.2d 777, 782 (7th Cir. 1988) (holding that time of witness's prior conviction and her post-conviction behavior are factors to consider when evaluating probative value of conviction); *see also* People v. Allen, 420 N.W.2d 499, 522 (Mich. 1988) (when determining probative value of conviction, trial court must consider recency of the conviction).

151 *See, e.g.*, People v. Barrick, 187 Cal. Rptr. 716, 722, 654 P.2d 1243, 1250 (Cal. 1982) (en banc) (holding that it was error, under circumstances, to impeach defendant with prior conviction for offense identical to one charged). Though *Barrick* was not a Federal Rules case, it illustrates a principle that is equally applicable under the Federal Rules. For federal case examples, *see* United States v. Wallace, 848 F.2d 1464, 1473 (9th Cir. 1988) (finding error for trial court to admit defendant's prior conviction for heroin trafficking in defendant's trial for possession with intent to distribute heroin, especially since prosecution could also use his prior conviction for perjury for impeachment purposes); United States v. Field, 625 F.2d 862, 872 (9th Cir. 1980) (holding that defendant's prior conviction for receiving stolen property was sufficiently different from his alleged armed bank robbery that it was admissible for impeachment purposes).

152 *See* United States v. Rein, 848 F.2d 777, 782 (7th Cir. 1988).

153 United States v. DeVore, 839 F.2d 1330, 1333 (8th Cir. 1988) (holding that evidence of defendant's prior weapons conviction was properly admitted because his credibility was central to jury's decision of his guilt/innocence, in case where defendant offered alibi to his alleged robbery that was contradicted by other witnesses); United States v. Johnson, 720 F.2d 519, 522 (8th Cir. 1983) (holding defendant's prior felony convictions properly admitted in case where he testified he lacked intent to sell cocaine in his trial for cocaine distribution).

the existence of such alternative impeachment methods is a factor weighing against allowing use of the prior conviction.[154]

There is an obvious tension between factors 4 and 5 above, when applied to the testimony of the accused: the credibility of the accused is likely to be central (calling for full exploration of credibility) when the accused's testimony is needed for a fair adjudication (calling for restraint on impeachment). One possible resolution to this is to emphasize full exploration of credibility in cases where there is a direct conflict in the testimony between the accused and a victim, but to emphasize the need to hear from the accused when the evidence against the accused is largely circumstantial.[155]

Rule 609(a)(1) has been severely criticized, especially in its application to the accused as a witness.[156] The impeachment value of a prior crime that has nothing to do with honesty is low; at best it offers a weak inference about the witness's credibility. Because of the extreme prejudice of such prior convictions, however, some criminal defendants with past convictions choose not to take the stand at all. By doing so, the accused avoids the impeachment but also limits his or her ability to offer a convincing defense. Admission of prior convictions under Rule 609(a)(1) is a major factor in criminal trials, and troubling evidence exists that most defendants do not take the stand primarily to avoid triggering this form of impeachment.[157] One reason why an *innocent* defendant would not take the witness stand in her own defense is that the defendant is afraid of the effects of being impeached by a prior conviction.[158]

Furthermore, as a functional matter, courts regularly misapply Rule 609(a)(1) by allowing prosecutors to impeach the accused with felonies in ways that conflict directly with the letter, spirit, and history of the Rule.[159] Courts do, however, tend to take seriously the factor concerning the similarity between the past conviction and the

---

[154] United States v. Reeves, 730 F.2d 1189, 1196 (8th Cir. 1984) (holding evidence of witness's prior conviction for breaking and entering properly excluded because defendant offered several character witnesses and proof of witness's more recent conviction for selling controlled substances).

[155] See ROGER PARK & TOM LININGER, THE NEW WIGMORE: IMPEACHMENT AND ACCREDITATION § 3.4.4.1.1.4 at 149 (2012).

[156] *See generally* Richard D. Friedman, *Character Impeachment Evidence: Psycho-Bayesian [!?] Analysis and a Proposed Overhaul,* 38 U.C.L.A. L. REV. 637 (1991) (arguing that impeachment for character for truthfulness or prior convictions should never be allowed against criminal defendant and explaining limited probative value of such impeachment where accused is witness).

[157] *See* John H. Blume, *The Dilemma of the Criminal Defendant with a Prior Record—Lessons from the Wrongfully Convicted,* 5 J. EMPIRICAL LEGAL STUD. 477 (2008) (documenting that, of factually innocent accused in his data set who failed to take the witness stand, 91% had prior convictions and "[i]n almost all instances, counsel for the wrongfully convicted defendant indicated that avoiding impeachment was the principal reason the defendant did not take the stand.").

[158] To be sure, a defendant (or any other party) who testifies and is impeached by evidence of a prior conviction admissible only as evidence of bad character for truthfulness is entitled to a limiting instruction. *See* **§ 3.09**. The effectiveness of such an instruction is doubtful. *See* Roselle L. Wissler & Michael J. Saks, *On the Inefficacy of Limiting Instructions: When Jurors Use Prior Conviction Evidence to Decide on Guilt,* 9 LAW & HUM. BEHAV. 37 (1985).

[159] One commentator has criticized the federal courts' "routine admission of defendants' prior convictions" under Rule 609(a)(1) as contravening congressional intent. Jeffery Bellin, *Circumventing Congress: How The Federal Courts Opened The Door To Impeaching Criminal Defendants With Prior Convictions,* 42 U.C. DAVIS L. REV. 289, 293 (2008). Such a framework is the intellectual descendant of the old English common-law tradition barring felons from testifying at all. *See id.* at 296–97 nn. 21, 23–24. Bellin outlined the "decidedly pro-impeachment," five-factor analytical framework that "places an almost insurmountable burden on defendants attempting to exclude prior convictions." *Id.* at 293.

charged crime, excluding evidence of prior felonies to the extent that they resemble the crime charged.[160]

Rule 609(a)(2): Crimes of Dishonesty or False Statement

Under Federal Rule 609(a)(2), crimes of dishonesty or false statement must be received regardless of the punishment if the "the court can readily determine that establishing the elements of the crime required proving—or the witness's admitting" the "dishonest act or false statement." The Rule was amended in 2006 to "give effect to the legislative intent to limit the convictions that are to be automatically admitted under subdivision (a)(2)" to such cases where the act of falsity or dishonesty is obvious from the nature of the crime charged.[161]

The judge has no residual discretion under this part of the Rule to admit or reject the evidence; there is no balancing of probative value against undue prejudice under Rule 403 or any other balancing formula.[162] Courts may, however, exclude such convictions if they fall within the Rule 609's limitation regarding old convictions (Rule 609(b)), pardons (609(c)), or juvenile adjudications (609(d)).

Some crimes are clearly crimes of dishonesty or false statement. The archetype example is perjury. Other core examples of such crimes include fraud, tax evasion, and forgery. The original Conference Committee note provides guidance by saying the relevant category includes "crimes such as perjury or subornation of perjury, false statement, criminal fraud, embezzlement, or false pretenses, or any other offense in the nature of crimen falsi, the commission of which involves some element of deceit, untruthfulness, or falsification."[163] Nevertheless, scholars, rulemakers, and courts have disagreed about what types of crimes fall into this special category regarding dishonesty and false statement, with theft and receipt of stolen property being areas of particular contention.[164] Moreover, before the 2006 amendment, some courts looked beyond the

---

[160] *See, e.g.*, United States v. Bagley, 772 F.2d 482, 488 (9th Cir. 1985) (prior conviction for bank robbery excluded as impeachment of accused in current bank robbery charge because "there is substantial risk that all exculpatory evidence will be overwhelmed by a jury's fixation on the human tendency to draw a conclusion which is impermissible in law; because he did it before, he must have done it again"); United States v. Joe, 2008 WL 2810169 (S.D.N.Y. 2008) (excluding prior conviction because "the prior conviction for firearms possession is nearly identical to the conduct charged in Count One, the jury may infer unfairly that Defendant has a propensity to commit firearms offenses"); United States v. Jaramillo, 2007 WL 1556844 (D. Utah 2007) (accused's prior convictions for possession of controlled substances would not be admissible because their probative value "would be outweighed by their prejudicial effect because the jury may consider them to be evidence that he committed the possession crimes charged rather than merely probative of his character for truthfulness").

[161] FED. R. EVID. 609 advisory committee note.

[162] *See* United States v. Wong, 703 F.2d 65, 68 (3d Cir. 1983). *See* ROGER PARK & TOM LININGER, THE NEW WIGMORE: IMPEACHMENT AND ACCREDITATION § 3.4.4.2(a) (2012). For a contrary minority view held by one of the authors, *see* Aviva Orenstein, *Honoring Margaret Berger with a Sensible Idea: Insisting that Judges Employ a Balancing Test before Admitting the Accused's Convictions under Federal Rule of Evidence 609(a)(2)*, 75 BROOKLYN L. REV. 1291 (2010) (arguing for the use of a balancing test when the witness is the accused).

[163] FED. R. EVID. 609(a), H.R. Conf. Rep. 93–1597 (1974).

[164] Many courts treat theft as a crime of dishonesty. *See* United States v. Del Toro Soto, 676 F.2d 13, 18 (1st Cir. 1982) (holding that grand larceny is crime of dishonesty under Fed. R. Evid. 609(a)(2)); United States v. Gunter, 551 F.3d 472, 483 (6th Cir. 2009) (refusing to consider trial court ruling "that because theft is an offense involving dishonesty under Tennessee state law, the convictions could be used for impeachment purposes under Rule 609(a)(2)" where defendant chose not to testify in light of trial court's ruling and therefore waived his right to appeal the ruling); United States Xpress Enters. v. J.B. Hunt Transp., 320 F.3d 809, 816–817 (8th Cir. 2003) (finding that trial court did not abuse discretion in finding receiving stolen property was crime involving dishonesty within meaning of Rule 609(a)(2); *see also* Wal-Mart Stores, Inc. v. Regions Bank

definition of the crime to see whether, under the particular facts, the crime was carried out in a deceitful way. Under such an expansive approach, if the witness did anything dishonest in the course of committing the crime, even if the dishonest act was not itself criminal, the mandatory admission rule might be triggered.[165] This approach raised dangers of collateral disputes and waste of time. The recent amendment, with its focus on what the court can "readily determine," rejects that approach. Instead, the current rule permits impeachment when either (1) the statutory elements specify an act of dishonesty or false statement or (2) it is otherwise "readily determinable" that the fact-finder could not have convicted the witness without having found that he committed such acts. One commentary explains:

> Under the amended rule, it appears that the prosecution may not call eyewitnesses to the prior crime to testify about what occurred. Instead, the subsequent court is restricted to examining documents such as the indictment or jury charge. Moreover, under the text of the rule, those documents support categorizing the prior crime as one of deceit only when they show that the prior fact-finder was "*required*" to make a finding of deceit in order to convict the defendant in the prior case.[166]

Summary of Admissibility of Convictions Under Rule 609(a)

The operation of Rule 609(a) is summarized in the following chart. The term "Serious" refers to crimes punishable by death or by imprisonment for more than one year. In all cases, the indicated result will occur unless other parts of Rule 609 require otherwise.[167]

Trust Dept., 69 S.W.3d 20 (Ark. 2002) (holding that "check-kiting" is crime of dishonesty under state equivalent of FED. R. EVID. 609(a)(2), even though definition of crime did not require intent to defraud).

The majority and, in our opinion, better view, however, goes the other way. *See* United States v. Pruett, 681 F.3d 232, 245–46 (5th Cir. 2012) (emphasizing the requirement of a false statement or deceitful act, holding that larceny does not necessarily fall within 609(a)(2)); United States v. Yeo, 739 F.2d 385, 388 (8th Cir. 1984) (holding that theft is not crime of dishonesty or false statement within meaning of FED. R. EVID. 609(a)(2)); United States v. Foster, 227 F.3d 1096, 1100 (9th Cir. 2000) ("We therefore hold that receipt of stolen property is not per se a crime of dishonesty for purposes of Rule 609(a)(2), and conclude that the district court erred in treating it as such."). United States v. Brackeen, 969 F.2d 827, 827–31 (9th Cir. 1992) (en banc) (holding that bank robbery is not necessarily crime of dishonesty under Rule 609(a)(2)); United States v. Glenn, 667 F.2d 1269, 1273 (9th Cir. 1982) ("Generally, crimes of violence, theft crimes, and crimes of stealth do not involve 'dishonesty or false statement' within the meaning of rule 609(a)(2).").

[165] *See, e.g.*, Altobello v. Borden Confectionary Prods., Inc., 872 F.2d 215, 217 (7th Cir. 1989) (holding that, if trial court determines that method used to commit misdemeanor crime of tampering with electric meters involved use of deceit, prior conviction for that offense is admissible under Fed. R. Evid. 609(a)(2), even if deceit is not element of crime).

[166] ROGER PARK & TOM LININGER, THE NEW WIGMORE: IMPEACHMENT AND ACCREDITATION § 3.4.4.2.at 163 (2012).

[167] For example, Rule 609(b) may require the exclusion of convictions over ten years old.

Conviction Offered to Impeach Witness's Truthfulness	Accused as Witness	Any Other Witness
Involves Dishonesty/False Statement (potential punishment immaterial)	Always admissible	Always admissible
Serious but No Dishonesty/False Statement	Only admissible if probative value exceeds unfair prejudice	Admissible unless probative value is substantially outweighed by a 403 danger
Minor and No Dishonesty/ False Statement	Never admissible	Never admissible

Eliciting the Prior Conviction

Often the qualifying conviction will be elicited during cross-examination of the witness being impeached; Rule 609 does not require the use of extrinsic evidence, and if the witness admits the conviction, then extrinsic evidence is usually unnecessary. On the other hand, the cross-examiner is not bound by the witness's denial of the prior conviction and instead may prove its existence by public record. The party supporting the witness, knowing that the conviction will ultimately be admissible, will often choose to bring out the prior conviction on direct examination to blunt its impact.

Sometimes a party will want to go into the details of the prior conviction or present facts that are not on the face of the document constituting the certified conviction. The impeached witness may want to say that the guilty plea was entered to protect a loved one, or the witness may wish to claim intoxication at the time of the crime. The impeacher may want to show that the crime was committed in a cruel and barbarous fashion or parade before the jury other details that demonstrate poor character. The courts have not settled on a single approach regarding the degree of detail that may be elicited about the prior conviction.[168]

Regarding the rights of the impeacher to elicit additional details about the prior conviction, some cases set forth fairly strict limits. One formulation of these limits restricts the impeacher to asking about (1) the existence of prior conviction(s); (2) the name of the crime(s); and (3) when the conviction(s) occurred.[169] Another common

---

[168] *See generally* ROGER PARK & TOM LININGER, THE NEW WIGMORE: IMPEACHMENT AND ACCREDITATION § 3.4.4.5 (2012); 28 CHARLES A. WRIGHT & VICTOR J. GOLD, FEDERAL PRACTICE AND PROCEDURE (EVIDENCE) § 6134 (2012).

[169] *See, e.g.*, United States v. Sampol, 636 F.2d 621, 670 (D.C. Cir. 1980) (holding that court properly prevented defendants from cross-examining witness about the length of his confinement in prison when the prosecution had already established his criminal record and dates of his convictions); Shows v. M/V Red Eagle, 695 F.2d 114 (5th Cir. 1983) (stating in dicta that inquiry into witness's length of confinement for robbery conviction is impermissible even when impeachment is permissible under FED. R. EVID. 609); United States v. Tumblin, 551 F.2d 1001, 1004 (5th Cir. 1977) (holding it improper to inquire about matters such as length of time spent in prison and length of time between release from prison and arrest for current offense); United States v. Williams, 272 F.3d 845, 860 (7th Cir. 2001) ("[o]rdinarily . . . the details of the prior convictions should not be exposed to the jury. However, where a defendant attempts to explain away the prior conviction during direct examination by giving his own version of events, he has 'opened the door.' "); Foulk v. Charrier, 262 F.3d 687 (8th Cir. 2001) (holding that trial court has discretion to exclude details of prior convictions if it determines convictions might inflame jury; here, trial judge acted within discretion in excluding fact that convictions were for sex crimes; trial judge did allow in evidence that plaintiff had been convicted of two felonies and sentenced to 20 years imprisonment). *Cf.* United States v. Howell, 285 F.3d 1263, 1270 (10th Cir. 2002) (holding that,

formulation allows inquiry into the length of the punishment imposed.[170] However, the impeaching party may elicit details of the witness's conviction if the witness attempts to "explain away" the convictions.[171] In addition, if the facts underlying the conviction are probative of untruthfulness, it may be permissible to inquire about them on cross-examination of the witness being impeached, pursuant to Rule 608(b).[172]

The party anticipating impeachment will often choose to elicit the fact of the conviction during direct examination to blunt its effect on cross-examination.[173] Also, counsel expecting the opponent to impeach the witness with prior convictions may wish to elicit sufficient detail during direct examination to demonstrate that the convictions were minor, that the punishment was slight, or that other salient details of the convictions suggest that the convictions do not affect the witness's credibility.

If the party calling a witness chooses to elicit testimony concerning prior convictions of a witness, the cross-examiner still has the right to fill in details to the extent allowed by the governing law of the jurisdiction. For example, the cross-examiner could ask when the conviction occurred and what the punishment was.[174] Though limits on eliciting the details of prior convictions are sensible when the prior conviction goes to impeachment only, the impeacher may be able to find another theory under which the details of a crime can be admitted into evidence. For instance, the details would be admissible if the witness being impeached were the criminal defendant and the details revealed that the defendant had used the same modus operandi in the prior crime as in the current one. In that case, the prior crime is not being used solely to impeach but also to show a common pattern of behavior, which is admissible under Rule 404(b)(2).[175] Yet, the similarity of the prior crime can cut both ways. When the prior crime is not quite similar enough to qualify under Rule 404(b)(2), then sometimes judges rule that similarity increases the prejudice of going into the details, because the jury is more likely to use

---

where inmates testified against correctional officer and were impeached with prior convictions, it was abuse of discretion for trial judge to adopt blanket rule, without Fed. R. Evid. 403 balancing, that while prior felony convictions not involving fraud or dishonesty could be used to impeach, nature of such convictions could not be revealed).

170 State v. Amburgey, 515 N.E.2d 925, 927 (Ohio 1987) ("a trial court has broad discretion to limit any questioning of a witness on cross-examination which asks more than the name of the crime, the time and place of conviction and the punishment imposed, when the conviction is admissible solely to impeach general credibility."); 1 MCCORMICK ON EVIDENCE § 42 at 273–74 (Kenneth S. Broun ed., 7th ed. 2013).

171 *See* United States v. Amahia, 825 F.2d 177, 181 (8th Cir. 1987) (holding that prosecution may cross-examine witness about details of prior conviction where defendant testified he only pleaded guilty to four felony counts because he was assured he would only receive probation and because of strain of working and going to school); United States v. Wolf, 561 F.2d 1376, 1381 (10th Cir. 1977) (holding that defendant may be cross-examined about facts underlying his conviction for making false claims to federal government in case where defendant claimed he agreed to plead guilty because he did not have money to defend charges).

172 *See* **§ 11.11.**

173 *See, e.g.*, Michelson v. United States, 335 U.S. 469, 471 (1948) (allowing defendant, in prosecution for bribing federal revenue agent, to testify on direct examination concerning old misdemeanor conviction dealing with trading in counterfeit watch dials); Gill v. Thomas, 83 F.3d 537 (1st Cir. 1996) (allowing plaintiff in federal civil rights action to discuss past crimes "preemptively to 'remove the sting' from [the] anticipated impeachment"); United States v. Berry, 661 F.2d 618, 621 (7th Cir. 1981) (noting that "defense counsel often uses this trial tactic to preclude the Government from first bringing out a defendant's prior criminal record.").

174 This, of course, assumes that, as seems to be commonly the case, the jurisdiction allows questions about punishment. *See* State v. Amburgey, 515 N.E.2d 925, 926–27 (Ohio 1987).

175 *See* United States v. Fountain, 768 F.2d 790, 796 (7th Cir. 1985) (Posner, J.) (murder of prison guard; defendant's prior use of knife in stabbing other inmate 57 times admissible on grounds that it would illuminate intent and modus operandi under Rule 404(b); strong dissent by Swygert, J.).

the prior crime as evidence of propensity to commit the type of offense rather than limiting its use purely to assessing credibility.[176]

Pardons; Juvenile Adjudications

Crimes that have been pardoned and juvenile adjudications are generally not admissible. However, Rule 609(c) provides that evidence of pardoned offenses may be received if the person was convicted of a subsequent crime and the pardon was grounded upon a basis other than a finding of innocence. Under Rule 609(d), Juvenile convictions may be received if the convicted witness is someone other than the accused and the judge decides that justice requires the impeachment.[177]

§ 11.11 Showing Untruthful Character of Witness—Evidence of Witness's Misconduct Leading to Conviction with or Without Evidence of the Conviction Itself

Many analyses of character evidence recognize only two categories of specific act evidence offered to prove a dishonest character: (1) evidence of (alleged) misconduct not leading to a conviction, governed by Rule 608(b); and (2) evidence of a conviction, governed by Rule 609.[178] This categorization, however, omits an important class of evidence: evidence of (alleged) misconduct that leads to a conviction when no attempt is made to introduce the fact of conviction. The problem can also arise when the proponent wants to use *both* conviction evidence satisfying Rule 609 *and* evidence of the specific acts that led to that conviction under Rule 608(b).[179] Suppose, for example, that a witness was convicted of impersonating John Q. Smith, and suppose the cross-examiner attempts to impeach the witness's truthfulness by asking: "Did you impersonate John Q. Smith?" This question does not ask about conviction. The implicit assumption of many analyses, however, is that (alleged) misconduct that *results in* a conviction must be evidenced *by* the conviction or not at all, at least not for this impeachment purpose.

But that is not the only possibility. Indeed, it is not the obvious reading of the plain language of the rules. Because the illustrative question posed above does not attempt to evidence the conviction, Rule 609 does not apply on its face. That rule governs when "attacking a witness's character for truthfulness by evidence of a criminal conviction."[180] Instead, the question asks about specific misconduct, and if offered to prove a dishonest character, it seems to be governed by Rule 608(b) and would not violate the extrinsic evidence ban of that rule. This issue matters because some misconduct that is otherwise admissible under Rule 608(b) and results in a conviction may not involve convictions

---

[176] *Cf.* United States v. Harding, 525 F.2d 84, 91 (7th Cir. 1975) (improper to go into details of marijuana conviction in cocaine prosecution; similarity of crimes considered a factor weighing against going into details). Although it does not deal with receiving the details of the conviction, United States v. Wallace, 848 F.2d 1464, 1473 (9th Cir. 1988) suggests the duality of courts' attitudes toward similarity of crimes. There, the court said that an old conviction for heroin distribution should have been barred in a prosecution for the same crime, saying that similarity weighs against receiving the evidence, not in favor of receiving it. Had the crime been more similar—say, heroin distribution using the same highly unusual method, then the prior conviction would have been admissible under 404(b).

[177] *Cf.* Davis v. Alaska, 415 U.S. 308 (1974) (unconstitutional to exclude juvenile record of witness under circumstances).

[178] *See, e.g.*, 1 MCCORMICK ON EVIDENCE §§ 41, 42 (Kenneth S. Broun ed., 7th ed. 2013); ROGER PARK & TOM LININGER, THE NEW WIGMORE: IMPEACHMENT AND REHABILITATION §§ 2.1.3, 3.3, & 3.4 (2012).

[179] *See, e.g.*, State v. Hoverson, 710 N.W.2d 890, 895–901 (N.D. 2006).

[180] FED. R. EVID. 609(a).

that are admissible under Rule 609. The plain meaning approach to the Rules thus presents the possibility that the cross-examiner can avoid the strictures of Rule 609 by asking directly about the misconduct, rather than about the conviction.

A revealing illustration of this occurred in a Montana case, applying that state's version of Rule 609, which bars the use of *all* conviction evidence for impeachment of truthfulness.[181] In *State v. Martin*,[182] the Supreme Court of Montana held that the lower court did not abuse its discretion under Montana's version of Rule 608(b), which is similar to the federal rule, when the trial court permitted cross-examination on the witness's previous act of giving false alibi information, an act that led to conviction of the defendant's witness. Responding to the defendant's argument that this contravenes the policy of Montana's Rule 609, the court held that the witness may be asked about the acts of misconduct, but not about whether the witness has been convicted of a crime based on them, and no extrinsic evidence on the matter is allowed in accordance with the limits of Rule 608(b).[183] A more restrictive reading of that state's Rule 608(b) would have generated a transparently perverse result. Had the defendant's argument been accepted, and the impeachment of the witness been barred simply because her misconduct had resulted in a conviction, then a witness would be *more* immune from impeachment (by inquiry into misconduct) when her misconduct resulted in a conviction than when it did not.

Somewhat more complex illustrations arise under the Federal Rules, where considerable conviction evidence is admissible under Rule 609. For example, suppose the cross-examiner proposes to ask the witness about committing a fraudulent act, one that resulted in a conviction that is old enough such that it falls within the 10-year rule of Rule 609(b). That rule places a heavy burden on the proponent, which we may suppose cannot be met. But the cross-examiner does not propose to ask about the conviction, only about the fraudulent act. If the question is considered under Rule 608(b), the relevant standard—probative of character for untruthfulness and not excluded by the pro-admissibility standard of Rule 403—may well be met.[184]

The legislative history suggests the drafters did not consider this kind of issue, and the plain meaning of Rule 608(b) may not be a very accurate guide to legislative purpose. Given this inadvertence, consider the policy question: When the witness's conduct led to a conviction, should the cross-examiner be permitted to inquire into the witness's underlying conduct, subject to the standards of Rules 608(b) and 403, or should the cross-examiner be limited to inquiring about the fact of conviction itself and then only when the conviction itself passes the hurdles of Rule 609? Arguments can be marshalled for

---

[181] *See* MONT. R. EVID. 609: "For the purpose of attacking the credibility of a witness, evidence that the witness has been convicted of a crime is not admissible."

[182] 926 P.2d 1380 (Mont. 1996).

[183] *Id.* at 1389.

[184] *Cf.* Hampton v. Dillard Dept. Stores, Inc., 18 F. Supp. 2d 1256 (D. Kan. 1998) (permitting impeachment by inquiry regarding untruthful conduct going back over 20 years). Because of the limits on admissibility under Rule 608(b), most of the situations that raise the problem addressed in this section would involve conduct leading to conviction for dishonesty or false statement within the meaning of Rule 609(a)(2) but barred by some other provision of Rule 609, such as the ten-year rule of 609(b). However, given the narrowness of Rule 609(a)(2), the problem might arise in situations where the conduct leads to (i) a conviction for a minor offense that that does not fall within any part of Rule 609(a), (ii) a conviction that falls within Rule 609(a)(1)(B), which is applicable when the accused is a witness and imposes a balancing test more stringent than Rule 403, or (iii) a conviction that falls within Rule 609(a)(1)(A) but is barred by a subsequent provision in Rule 609, such as the ten-year rule of 609(b).

both positions, and courts are split on the question.[185] Pending an authoritative resolution by the Supreme Court, or by rule-making or legislation, it is important to understand those arguments.

Favoring a narrow reading of Rule 608(b)—precluding cross-examination about the misconduct when the resulting conviction does not pass the tests of Rule 609—is the fact that it reduces the number of reasonably disputable but tangential facts that must be considered by the fact-finder. If the misconduct itself is the subject of the cross-examination, a denial by the witness will leave the fact-finder to ponder the suggestion of the cross-examiner without much assistance because of the ban on extrinsic evidence. To be sure, this problem attends misconduct that does *not* lead to a conviction as well, but the question may still be asked: Why add to that problem? Additionally, not mentioning the conviction, when there is one, might be prejudicial, especially when the witness is a party, because the fact-finder might speculate that the witness escaped punishment for the prior wrongdoing. Finally, in the context of the specific illustration given above, the ten-year cutoff imposed by 609(b) arguably was intended to provide convicted persons with a "clean slate," something that would be undermined if the witness can be impeached with the same behavior under another rule.

Favoring the plain meaning approach is the fact that the specific act itself is more probative of truthfulness than a conviction for it, which after all merely evidences that act, and does so in an abstract manner. Moreover, avoiding the topic of conviction may reduce the potential for prejudice associated with a public denunciation of the conduct. Finally, but most importantly, adopting the approach of allowing the cross-examiner to inquire about the misconduct without mentioning the conviction would avoid the disturbing possibility that the same act would be cross-examinable if it did *not* result in a conviction but would be out of bounds if it *did* result in a conviction. If anything, the fact of conviction means that the witness is less likely to be surprised by inquiry into the prior conduct. Such an approach still allows the trial court to consider the lines drawn in Rule 609, between permissible and impermissible subjects of inquiry, as guidance in exercising discretion under Rule 608(b). For example, the court would view evidence of misconduct that occurred more than ten years before the trial with greater skepticism than evidence of misconduct that occurred three years ago, but that would not depend on the happenstance that the misconduct resulted in a conviction, nor would there be a discontinuity between the assessment of conduct that is just under ten years in the past and conduct that is just over ten years in the past.

On balance, if one had to choose between them, the plain meaning of the rules should probably be followed here. Yet there seems to be something to the argument that

---

[185] *Compare* United States v. Barnhart, 599 F.3d 737, 747 (7th Cir. 2010) (allowing impeachment with conviction under Rule 609 and inquiry into specific acts leading to the conviction, if probative of untruthfulness, under Rule 608(b); and State v. Hoverson, 710 N.W.2d 890, 897 (N.D. 2006) (same); *with* United States v. Osazuwa, 564 F.3d 1169, 1173–75 (9th Cir. 2009) (Rule 608(b) "permits impeachment only by specific acts that have not resulted in a criminal conviction"). Kentucky, which does not allow character impeachment using evidence of misdemeanor convictions, at one time followed the latter rule, limiting Rule 608(b) to inquiries about conduct that did not result in a conviction. *See* Childers v. Commonwealth, 332 S.W.3d 64, 67–73 (Ky. 2010). But that position was later rejected. *See* Allen v. Commonwealth, 395 S.W.3d 451, 461–67 (Ky. 2013) (noting, at p. 463, that "*Childers* allows the absurd result that misdemeanor-level dishonest conduct is admissible under KRE 608(b) if a person were simply lucky enough not to have been convicted (whether because the crime was never charged or the charge was dismissed), but that a person who has actually been convicted of a misdemeanor involving a crime of dishonesty could avoid impeachment.") The reasoning in *Allen* does, however, also emphasize the difference between the federal rules and the Kentucky rules regarding impeachment with misdemeanor convictions for dishonesty or false statement.

permitting use of Rule 608(b) allows an improper circumvention of the policies of Rule 609. This arises not from the circumvention of the standards of Rule 609 but rather from the circumvention of the efficiency and avoidance of distraction associated with proceeding via Rule 609 *when that option is available*. Thus, a compromise position is worth considering. It would allow inquiry on cross-examination into the misconduct under the standards of Rule 608(b), with appropriate (but not necessarily determinative) guidance from the detailed provisions of 609, *except* when (a) the misconduct resulted in a conviction *and* (b) evidence of the conviction *is admissible* under Rule 609. When the exception applies, the efficiency associated with using the conviction tips the balance in favor of a rule preferring that mode of impeachment. It also harmonizes with the restriction on questioning about the details of the underlying conduct when the witness is impeached with the fact of conviction. When, however, the conviction is inadmissible under Rule 609, inquiry into the misconduct would still be permissible on cross-examination if it otherwise meets the standards of Rule 608(b).

§ 11.12 Impeachment with Evidence of Defects in Perception, Memory, or Mental Health

One potentially powerful form of impeachment is to attack the witness's capacity to perceive, recollect, or narrate.[186] Defects in the witness's capacity may be shown on cross-examination or by the production of extrinsic testimony.[187] Much, however, depends on the nature of the particular defect and the attendant likelihood of prejudice.

Defects in the Five Senses

Such defects may be freely shown to cast doubt upon the witness's ability to perceive the events that were the subject of the witness's testimony.[188] Most commonly, the evidence concerns the witness's eyesight or hearing, although questioning about the sense of touch, smell, or taste would be permitted when relevant. Impeaching counsel may cross-examine on these subjects but is not bound by the witness's answer, as extrinsic evidence is freely admissible.[189]

Alcohol Intoxication and Alcoholism

Admitting evidence of a witness's alcohol intoxication or alcoholism to impeach the witness presents a complicated question. There is no doubt that counsel can show, by evidence of drinking on the occasion in question, that the witness's capacity to observe

---

[186] *See* 27 CHARLES A. WRIGHT & VICTOR J. GOLD, FEDERAL PRACTICE AND PROCEDURE (EVIDENCE) § 6097 at 672 (2007) (noting that attack on capacity "undermines credibility by showing that the witness lacks the perceptual, recall, or narrative abilities presupposed by his testimony").

[187] *See, e.g.*, 1 MCCORMICK ON EVIDENCE § 44 (Kenneth S. Broun ed., 7th ed. 2013) (stating that witness may be impeached by eliciting facts discrediting witness through cross-examination or by proving facts discrediting witness through extrinsic evidence); 3A WIGMORE ON EVIDENCE § 931 at 758–59 (Chadbourn rev. 1970) (stating that extrinsic evidence is admissible to prove defective power of observation, recollection, or communication).

[188] *See, e.g.*, 1 MCCORMICK ON EVIDENCE § 44 at 286 (Kenneth S. Broun ed., 7th ed. 2013) (stating that any deficiency of senses substantially lessening witness's ability to perceive facts to which witness testified is provable to attack that witness's credibility).

[189] *See id.* (stating that defects in witness's sense may be proved by producing other witnesses); 3A WIGMORE ON EVIDENCE § 931 at 758 n.152 (Chadbourn rev. 1970) (stating that extrinsic evidence demonstrating defective power of observation of events to which witness testifies admissible).

was impaired.[190] The answer becomes more difficult when the attempt is to attack credibility by showing chronic alcoholism or when evidence of chronic alcoholism is offered for the purpose of inviting the inference that the witness was intoxicated on the occasion in question. The traditional approach has been to exclude such evidence of alcoholism as overly prejudicial.[191] If counsel is able to lay the foundation for a more specific showing that the witness habitually became intoxicated on a certain occasion or at a certain place, however, then the evidence may be admissible.[192] Thus, if the witness invariably joined friends after work in a certain bar and drank excessively, the proponent of the impeachment evidence has a better chance to be admitted than if the evidence took the form of testimony that the witness had been drunk on several occasions at different places and times.

Drug Use and Drug Addiction

Drug use and addiction traditionally have been treated differently from alcohol intoxication and alcoholism. The witness who is a heavy drinker has been treated with more delicacy and regard than the witness who is a heavy, or even occasional, user of illicit drugs. Of course, evidence of drug use on the day that the witness made the observations recounted in the witness's testimony is admitted freely,[193] just as in the case of alcohol use. Some older cases went much further and were receptive to the idea that drug abuse on other occasions is admissible for impeachment purposes on general credibility grounds.[194] A broad acceptance of this approach is unjustified, given the varied effects of different drugs and the prejudicial impact of evidence of a witness's use of forbidden drugs. Accordingly, a trend developed toward excluding evidence that the witness used drugs on occasions other than the one that was the subject of witness's testimony, unless evidence of habitual, memory- or communication-impairing drug use exists.[195] One plausible rule allows impeachment by evidence of drug abuse only if it is

---

[190] *See, e.g.*, Rheaume v. Patterson, 289 F.2d 611, 614 (2d Cir. 1961) (holding testimony that driver had been drinking before accident admissible to impeach credibility of driver's version of how accident happened); United States v. Infelise, 1992 WL 7837 (N.D. Ill. 1992) (prohibiting inquiry into witness's pattern of drinking during any particular period, but allowing inquiry into whether he had had drink on particular day about which he testified) People v. McGuire, 163 N.E.2d 832, 833 (Ill. 1960) (admitting evidence indicating intoxication of witness at time of event to which witness testifies).

[191] *See, e.g.*, United States v. DiPaolo, 804 F.2d 225, 229–30 (2d Cir. 1986) (holding that trial court properly refused to permit defendant to impeach prosecution witness on basis of drinking problem); Springer v. Reimers, 84 Cal. Rptr. 486, 494–95 (Cal. Ct. App. 1970) (holding that trial court erred in admitting evidence that witness had drinking problem where impeaching party did not show witness intoxicated when observing events about which he testified or when testifying); Smith v. State, 644 S.W.2d 500, 502 (Tex. Ct. App. 1982) (holding that trial court properly excluded evidence of general habit of intoxication to prove witnesses were drunk at time they observed events about which they testified); 3A WIGMORE ON EVIDENCE § 933 at 767 (Chadbourn rev. 1970) (noting that general habit of intemperance usually inadmissible because it reveals nothing about witness's testimonial capacity unless it indicates intoxication at time event observed or when testifying).

[192] *See* **§ 7.15**.

[193] *See, e.g.*, United States v. Fowler, 465 F.2d 664, 665–66 (D.C. Cir. 1972) (holding that trial court erred in not allowing defendant to cross-examine prosecution witness as to whether he was using narcotics at time he observed defendant commit alleged offense).

[194] *See, e.g.*, People v. Strother, 290 N.E.2d 201 (Ill. 1972) (admitting evidence of narcotics addiction to impeach witness's general credibility because addicts are notorious liars); 3A WIGMORE ON EVIDENCE § 934at 763 (Chadbourn rev. 1970) (evidence of drug habit should be admissible).

[195] *See, e.g.*, United States v. Gallardo, 497 F3d 727 (7th Cir. 2007) (holding that expert testimony about witness's past drug use was properly excluded by the trial court because it was proffered as general character evidence and did not reflect any impairment at the time of relevant events); United States v. Cameron, 814 F.2d 403, 405 (7th Cir. 1987) (holding that trial court properly excluded evidence of witness's drug use to attack general character; evidence of drug use admissible only when probative to witness's inability to recollect and

accompanied by expert testimony or proof from reliable scientific literature about the effects of the particular drug.[196]

Mental Defect, Abnormality, or Disease

Many states have competency rules that prohibit testimony by witnesses whose mental state prevents them from accurately relating facts.[197] This section deals with use of such evidence for impeachment purposes, not to prevent the witness from testifying altogether under the rules of competency.[198]

When offered for impeachment, evidence of low intelligence or developmental delay is admissible unless its value is substantially outweighed by other considerations such as waste of time. Thus, evidence about how the witness did in school would ordinarily be excluded, though evidence of severe cognitive disability would be admissible.[199]

Evidence of mental disease is admissible if it is relevant to the witness's ability to accurately perceive, recollect, or communicate information.[200] Its admissibility, however, is subject to Rule 403 considerations, such as prejudice or confusion of the issues.[201] Considerations of embarrassing the witness are not often mentioned but undoubtedly

---

relate); Gonzalez v. Van Zandt, 1992 WL 30616 (S.D.N.Y. 1992) (holding that trial court did not violate defendant's Sixth Amendment confrontation right by limiting cross-examination of state's key witness about drug use history, where witness testified that he "felt all right" on the day in question and that his heroin habit hadn't "interfere[d] with anything" even though he had been without heroin for a few days); Lusher v. State, 390 N.E.2d 702, 704 (Ind. Ct. App. 1979) (holding that trial court erred in refusing to permit cross-examination of witness's use of different drugs causing problems with hallucinations; evidence of drug use admissible where it may have substantially affected witness's ability to perceive, remember, and testify).

[196] *See* People v. Balderas, 711 P.2d 480, 507 (Cal. 1985) (holding that trial court properly refused to permit inquiry into prosecution witness's use of narcotics on days other than day to which he testified where defendant failed to offer expert testimony on probable effect of such use on general recall and perceptive abilities).

[197] *See* **§ 8.02**. The Federal Rules of Evidence, however, have no such competency requirement. FED. R. EVID. 601.

[198] Although an attack on competency will not usually result in keeping the witness off the stand, it may provide a chance to acquire information about the witness's mental condition or obtain a mental exam, which, can be used for impeachment purposes if the incompetency attack fails.

[199] *Compare* Polson v. State, 207 N.E.2d 638 (Ind. 1965) (holding that trial court abused discretion in sustaining objection to defendant's question as to whether witness was "a little behind in school") *with* State v. Armstrong, 62 S.E.2d 50, 51 (N.C. 1950) (holding that trial court erred in refusing to permit physician and another witness to testify that prosecution witness was retarded, having the mind of a child 9 to 12 years old).

[200] *See, e.g.*, United States v. Diecidue, 603 F.2d 535, 551 (5th Cir. 1979) (holding that trial court did not err in refusing to admit witness's psychiatric records where witness's treatment had occurred 12 years before event to which he testified and records were not probative of his ability to testify accurately); United States v. Partin, 493 F.2d 750, 763 (5th Cir. 1974) (finding reversible error in refusal to admit evidence concerning witness's mental condition and treatment where witness entered hospital five months before events to which he testified occurred, complaining of auditory hallucinations and belief that he was some other person); People v. Cooks, 190 Cal. Rptr. 211, 268 (Cal. App. 1983) (finding that trial court did not abuse discretion in refusing to allow defendant to cross-examine witness as to psychiatric treatment where no evidence demonstrated that witness's mental condition impaired his ability to accurately perceive, recollect, or communicate); United States v. Pryce, 938 F.2d 1343, 1345–50 (D.C. Cir. 1991) (holding that trial court committed reversible error in refusing to allow cross-examination about witness's hallucinations, which occurred four months before events to which witness testified). *See generally* 3A WIGMORE ON EVIDENCE § 932 at 759 (Chadbourn rev. 1970) (stating that evidence of insanity is admissible to discredit witness, if mental condition affected witness at the time of the event, while testifying, or during the time in between, so as to impair the witness's ability to recollect).

[201] *See, e.g.*, United States v. Rivera-Santiago, 872 F.2d 1073, 1084–85 (1st Cir. 1989) (trial court properly refused to permit counsel to question witness as to court-ordered referral for psychiatric evaluation, because jury could improperly infer that witness needed psychiatric treatment); United States v. Lopez, 611 F.2d 44, 45–46 (4th Cir. 1979) (cross-examination concerning witness's mental condition subject to Rule 403 limitations; must not introduce collateral issue which would confuse jury).

are considered.[202] Some conditions, such as schizophrenia, clearly have more probative value in showing that the witness's testimony may have been deluded than do other conditions, such as depression in reaction to a life crisis.[203]

If expert testimony is offered regarding a witness's mental impairment, an objection can sometimes be based on the expert's lack of opportunity to acquire information necessary for the diagnosis. If the expert did not perform a clinical examination of the witness, some courts will automatically exclude the expert's testimony or use the absence of the clinical examination as a factor in excluding the expert's testimony.[204]

Expert testimony that the witness has an emotional condition that makes the witness a liar is often objectionable. Such evidence may be unhelpful to the jury in its special province of determining truthfulness, as its scientific basis is often questionable, and it can amount to making a character attack under the guise of medical testimony.[205]

§ 11.13 Bolstering and Rehabilitation

The common law accepted a principle, which continues under the Federal Rules, that "every witness may be assumed to be of normal moral character for veracity."[206] From this principle, another is held to follow: there can be no support of a witness's credibility in the absence of an attack on it.[207] The witness whose credibility has not been

---

202 United States v. Lopez, 611 F.2d 44, 45 (4th Cir. 1979) (trial court did not err in refusing to permit defendant to cross-examine prosecution witness as to psychiatric examination where examination had no relevance to witness's qualification and was merely attempt to stigmatize witness). The trial judge is empowered under Rule 611(a)(3) to "protect witnesses from harassment or undue embarrassment."

203 *Compare* United States v. Lindstrom, 698 F.2d 1154, 1163 (11th Cir. 1983) (holding that trial court erred in refusing to permit defendant to cross-examine prosecution witness as to her mental condition, to support theory of vendetta against defendant, where witness's medical records suggested history of psychiatric disorders, including schizophrenia, manifesting themselves in violent threats and manipulative and destructive conduct) *with* United States v. Brumbaugh, 471 F.2d 1128, 1129 (6th Cir. 1973) (holding that trial court did not err in refusing to permit defendant to introduce hospital report concerning witness's treatment for depression into evidence to impeach witness).

204 *See, e.g.*, United States v. Riley, 657 F.2d 1377, 1387 (8th Cir. 1981) (holding that trial court did not err in excluding expert testimony as to witness's mental condition and her capacity for telling truth where expert's opinion was based only on in-court observations of witness); United States v. Daileda, 229 F. Supp. 148, 153–54 (M.D. Pa. 1964) (holding that trial court properly excluded expert testimony concerning witness's capacity to tell the truth where expert did not treat or examine witness but only observed witness testify).

205 *See, e.g.*, People v. Ainsworth, 755 P.2d 1017, 1033–34, 248 Cal. Rptr. 568, 583–85 (Cal. 1988) (stating in dicta that psychiatrist may not testify as to whether witness is telling truth on particular occasion where only purpose of testimony is to impeach witness's credibility); State v. Munro, 680 P.2d 708, 710 (Or. Ct. App. 1984) (holding that trial court properly excluded expert testimony concerning victim's emotional disturbance and effect on her perceptions and veracity; experts cannot testify as to veracity of particular witness). *Cf.* Westcott v. Crinklaw, 68 F.3d 1073, 1076–77 (8th Cir. 1995) (holding that trial court erroneously admitted testimony of expert that police officer suffered from post-traumatic stress disorder in civil action alleging excessive force by a police officer to explain officer's incomplete and inaccurate statements after shooting; expert testimony usurped the jury's role to determine credibility); United States v. Shay, 57 F.3d 126, 129–34 (1st Cir. 1995) (finding abuse of discretion when trial judge prevented defense from explaining defendant's self-incriminating statements with expert psychiatric testimony that defendant suffered from "pseudologia fantastica").

206 *See* 4 WIGMORE ON EVIDENCE § 1104 (Chadbourn rev. 1972).

207 *See* United States v. Binker, 795 F.2d 1218, 1223 (5th Cir. 1986) (holding that prosecutor on redirect may ask witness to testify that his plea agreement required him to testify truthfully after defendant cross-examined witness for bias due to plea agreement); United States v. Jackson, 588 F.2d 1046, 1055 (5th Cir. 1979) (holding that defendant who takes stand to testify does not, as a matter of course, have right to support his testimony; however, if his credibility is attacked, defendant may introduce evidence of good character for truthfulness). *See also* 27 CHARLES A. WRIGHT & VICTOR J. GOLD, FEDERAL PRACTICE AND PROCEDURE (EVIDENCE) § 6098 (2007) (describing common-law principle "that evidence supporting credibility is admissible only if credibility has been or certainly will be attacked") (footnotes omitted).

attacked cannot have their testimony "bolstered," whether by character evidence, prior consistent statements, or other support.[208] (For this purpose, offering separate testimony that merely corroborates a witness on a non-collateral matter is not considered "bolstering," even though it does support the first witness's credibility.[209]) To be sure, courts allow direct examiner's some leeway in developing a modest amount of "backgoround" information about the witness, though this has the likely effect of increasing the witness's credibility.[210] Rulings on such matters are mostly resolved by application of Rule 403.[211] Similarly, an expert's qualifications can serve to establish credibility, but the presentation of such qualifications to the jury is regularly allowed even on direct.[212]

Another implication of the principle against bolstering is that, when a witness's credibility is attacked on one ground, such as being biased, that does not permit the proponent of the witness to rehabilitate the witness by offering evidence that supports the witness's credibility in some other way, such as showing that the witness has a good memory. Rehabilitation must address the opponent's specific form of attack.[213]

One specific application of these principles, which appears in Rule 608(a), is that rehabilitation with evidence of good character for truthfulness is not permitted unless the witness's character for truthfulness has been attacked.[214] When character for truthfulness has been attacked in any fashion, the witness can be rehabilitated with

---

[208] A long recognized exception was made for evidence of a "prompt complaint" of rape, the theory being that a jury that is not informed that the alleged victim made such a complaint might draw an inference against the complainant's credibility even without an attack by opposing counsel. *See* Kathryn M. Stanchi, *The Paradox of the Fresh Complaint Rule*, 37 B.C.L. REV. 441 (1996).

[209] 1 MCCORMICK ON EVIDENCE § 47 at 307 (Kenneth S. Broun ed., 7th ed. 2013).

[210] *See, e.g.*, State v. Stokes, 523 P.2d 364, 366 (Kan. 1974) (holding that "background information" and "biographical data" such as "place of birth, education, length of residence in the community, length of marriage, size of family, occupation, place of employment, service in armed forces and receipt of honorable discharge" not considered character evidence entitling prosecution to respond with evidence of bad character; defendant "entitled to let the jury know who he is").

[211] One controversial application concerns whether the prosecution may elicit, during direction examination of a government witness, that the witness is testifying pursuant to a cooperation agreement that is part of a plea deal. *See, e.g.*, United States v. Spriggs, 996 F.2d 320, 323–24 (D.C. Cir. 1993) (describing conflict in the circuits and holding that introduction of evidence of cooperation agreement on direct was acceptable in the context).

[212] *See, e.g.*, Murphy v. National R.R. Passenger Corp., 547 F.2d 816, 817 (4th Cir. 1977) (holding that, despite stipulation of the witness's expertise, "a jury can better assess the weight to be accorded an expert's opinion if the witness is permitted to explain his qualifications).

[213] *See, e.g.*, United States v. Bermudez, 529 F.3d 158, 167–68 (2d Cir. 2008) (explaining general principle). *See generally* ROGER PARK & TOM LININGER, THE NEW WIGMORE: IMPEACHMENT AND REHABILITATION § 9.9 (2012).

[214] FED. R. EVID. 608(a). *See also* United States v. Dring, 930 F.2d 687, 690–95 (9th Cir. 1991) (finding no error in exclusion of rehabilitative evidence of defendant's truthful character, where prosecution merely emphasized inconsistency between defendant's testimony and that of other witnesses and noted defendant's interest in the outcome of the case but did not offer evidence of defendant's general character for untruthfulness); United States v. Jackson, 588 F.2d 1046, 1055 (5th Cir. 1979) (holding that mere fact that prosecution pointed out defendant's version of facts was different from those of other witnesses was not attack on defendant's character and defendant could not bolster his credibility by offering evidence of defendant's character for veracity).

Even where the defendant testifies, issues can arise about whether it is proper to admit consistent statements in anticipation of impeachment. *See* Ross v. Saint Augustine's College, 103 F.3d 338, 342 (4th Cir. 1996) (no error to allow plaintiff to put in her consistent statements prior to her testimony; evidence was linked up to later impeachment efforts by defendant when she did testify; court distinguished United States v. Bolick, 917 F.2d 135, 138–39 (4th Cir. 1990), a case where government pursued deliberate strategy of attempting to minimize the problems of its witnesses by admitting their statements through federal agent first).

reputation or opinion testimony about character for truthfulness.[215] Because impeachment for bias is not normally a character attack, the witness impeached with evidence of bias cannot be rehabilitated with testimony about character for truthfulness.[216] Other types of impeachment, however, may be considered attacks on character. If the facts of the case show the impeachment to involve an attack on character for truthfulness (as may be the case when the witness is impeached by contradiction or with a prior inconsistent statement), evidence showing good character for truthfulness should be admissible.[217] Rehabilitation of a witness with character evidence is subject to the Rule 608(b) prohibition against extrinsic evidence of specific acts. Just as the party impeaching the witness may not offer extrinsic evidence of specific acts to show the target witness's bad character for truthfulness, the party rehabilitating the witness may not call other witnesses to tell of the target witness's honest deeds.[218] This prohibition against extrinsic evidence of specific acts does not apply if the rehabilitation addresses a charge of bias, as opposed to an attack on character. Thus, evidence of bad deeds that show bias may be rebutted with extrinsic evidence of specific acts.[219]

Rehabilitation with evidence of prior consistent statements is permitted in response to an attack based on fabrication or other improper influence.[220] Under the majority view, to be admissible, the consistent statement must have been made before the alleged motive for fabrication or improper influence arose.[221] Thus, if a prosecution witness is attacked for bias arising from a deal with the prosecution after the witness's arrest on a criminal charge, consistent statements by the witness made before the arrest would be admissible, but statements made after the motive to cooperate with the prosecution arose would not.

Prior consistent statements are also relevant to rehabilitate the credibility of a witness about whom it has been asserted or suggested that the witness's memory is

---

[215] Beard v. Mitchell, 604 F.2d 485, 503 (7th Cir. 1979) (holding that defendant may offer proof of reputation for truthfulness after plaintiff introduced prior inconsistent statement by defendant in order to attack defendant's credibility). *See also* FED. R. EVID. 608(a)(2); 4 WIGMORE ON EVIDENCE § 1105 (Chadbourn rev. 1972).

[216] FED. R. EVID. 608 advisory committee note.

[217] *Id.* (recognizing that whether impeachment by contradiction constitutes character attack must depend on circumstances); 1 MCCORMICK ON EVIDENCE § 47 at 311 (Kenneth S. Broun ed., 7th ed. 2013) (cautioning against categorical rules and stating that "in each case the judge should consider whether a particular impeachment for inconsistency or a conflict in testimony amounts in effect to an attack on character for truthfulness") (footnotes omitted).

[218] *See* United States v. Taylor, 900 F.2d 779 (4th Cir. 1990) and cases cited therein.

[219] *See* United States v. Lindemann, 85 F.3d 1232, 1243 (7th Cir. 1996) (holding that, because Rule 608 does not limit rehabilitation of witness attacked for bias, government could show via extrinsic evidence that prosecution witness had incriminated other persons who had pled guilty, thus refuting defense contention that witness was fabricating case against defendant to save himself; evidence showed that witness had many "bargaining chips," hence reducing his need to fabricate case against the defendant).

[220] *See* United States v. Montague, 958 F.2d 1094, 1096 (D.C. Cir. 1992) (holding that trial court did not abuse discretion in allowing government to rehabilitate witness by introducing prior consistent statement, where defense's cross-examination of witness about terms of plea agreement was at least "implied charge of improper motive"); United States v. Duncan, 693 F.2d 971, 980 (9th Cir. 1982) (holding that where customs agent testified that defendant made admission to him but did not include admission in his notes from interview, government could introduce three prior consistent statements by agent to rebut defendant's claim that agent fabricated admission); United States v. Allen, 579 F.2d 531 (9th Cir. 1978) (holding that government may offer witness's prior consistent statement after defendant argued that witness's testimony was based on fear of being prosecuted herself). *See also* FED. R. EVID. 801(d)(1)(B); *compare to* MINN. R. EVID. 801(d)(1)(B) (consistent statement may be admitted if it is helpful to trier-of-fact in evaluating witness's credibility; consistent statement admissible even if witness is not charged with a recent fabrication).

[221] 4 WIGMORE ON EVIDENCE § 1128 (Chadbourn rev. 1972).

faulty. That the witness made essentially the same assertions when they were fresher in memory supports the proponent's position that the witness's present testimony is still based on sound memory. Until 2014, however, there was some dispute about the admissibility of prior consistent statements on this theory as a result of the Supreme Court's 1995 decision in *Tome v. United States.*[222] Though this decision arose under the hearsay rules, it had arguable implications for purely rehabilitative uses.[223] That dispute has now been resolved by an amendment to the hearsay rules that recognizes the possibility of rehabilitating the credibility of a witness with prior consistent statements when the attack on credibility does not take the form of a charge of recent fabrication or improper influence that entails dishonesty.[224]

When prior consistent statements are admissible solely to rehabilitate a witness, formally it may not be used to prove the truth of the matter asserted, at least not by virtue of the credibility of the prior statement, unless some exception to the hearsay rule is available. This limitation on its use has relatively trivial consequences. But it can lead to truly unintelligible limiting instructions, telling the jury, for example, not to use the prior statement that the light was red as evidence of the truth of the matter asserted (that the light was red), but only for its bearing on the witness's credibility (in testifying that the light was red). For this reason, the Federal Rules contain a hearsay exemption that admits such prior consistent statement as "substantive" evidence as well, thereby eliminating the need for such limiting instructions.[225]

---

[222] *See* Tome v. United States, 513 U.S. 150 (1995).

[223] Though *Tome* does not directly address this issue, some of the language in the case suggests that the Court assumed that Rule 801(d)(1)(B) was the only route through which evidence of a prior consistent statement could be received to counter impeachment of a witness. *See generally* Norman M. Garland & Romy Schneider, *Prior Consistent Statements As Evidence in the United States and Canada*, 2 S.W.U. J.L. & TRADE IN THE AMERICAS 451 (1995). Some courts clearly distinguished the permissible scope of rehabilitation from the permissible scope of the hearsay exemption. *See, e.g.*, United States v. Gluzman, 154 F.3d 49, 51 (2d Cir. 1998) (holding that prior consistent statements may be admissible for rehabilitation without making use of Rule 801(d)(1)(B) and without making *Tome* showing that statement was made prior to motive to fabricate).

[224] For further discussion of *Tome* and the 2014 amendment, see **§ 15.04**.

[225] *See* **§ 15.04**.

Part V

SPECIFIC RULES FOR NON-TESTIMONIAL EVIDENCE

Chapter 12

AUTHENTICATION AND IDENTIFICATION OF TANGIBLE EVIDENCE

Table of Sections

§ 12.01 Authentication and Identification at Common Law and Under the Rules [FRE 901]

Although most evidence produced in court consists of witness testimony, a considerable amount of evidence involves the presentation of physical objects, such as documents, knives, packets of drugs, and even displays of bodily injuries. The common-law courts required a proponent of such evidence to provide a "foundation" as a condition of admission.[1] This foundation consisted of "extrinsic" evidence—evidence beyond what the fact-finder could observe by simply inspecting the object—that would support the proponent's claim that the tangible object was connected to the events being litigated. The nature of the required foundation, which was almost always testimony by a sponsoring witness, depended on the nature of the claimed connection.

In the special, but important case when a document purported its own authorship, by a signature for example, and the proponent endorsed that authorship, this foundation was called "authentication." The proponent was then expected to offer supporting evidence that the document was "authentic," that it really was signed or published by the person or organization whose name appeared on it.[2] When a non-documentary object was offered, or when a document was offered as to which the proponent did not endorse any purported authorship, or when the proponent advanced some connection with the parties aside from a claim of authorship, the process was called "identification."[3] Unfortunately, this distinction is often lost in modern discussions, and both kinds of

[1] *See* 7 WIGMORE ON EVIDENCE § 2129 (Chadbourn rev. 1978).

[2] This requirement was codified in California before adoption of the Federal Rules. *See* CAL. EVID. CODE § 1401(a) ("Authentication of a writing is required before it may be received in evidence.").

[3] *See* 7 WIGMORE ON EVIDENCE § 2129 at 709 (Chadbourn rev. 1978) (distinguishing authentication from identification).

foundation have come to be known generically as "authentication."[4] Because of its widespread acceptance, we follow this practice, except where it leads to confusion.[5]

Practice under the Federal Rules is not much different from practice under the common law. But the formal rule is rather cryptic. Rule 901(a), the only rule that speaks directly to this authentication requirement, provides as follows:

> To satisfy the requirement of authenticating or identifying an item of evidence, the proponent must produce evidence sufficient to support a finding that the item is what the proponent claims it is.

This rule *assumes* that a requirement "of authentication or identification" exists and instructs on what it takes to satisfy it. It does not, however, state the requirement itself or indicate to what kinds of evidence it applies. Nevertheless, practice under the Rules follows the common law in the following respects: (1) courts impose an authentication or identification requirement on all proffers of tangible evidence; (2) generally courts do *not* impose such a requirement on testimonial evidence (with one amorphous but potentially enormous exception); and (3) when it applies, the requirement generally requires extrinsic evidence.[6]

Regarding (1), the drafters of the Rules apparently did not think that the authentication requirement needed to be stated separately because they considered it to be a direct outgrowth of the relevance requirement, Rule 402. Specifically, the drafters thought that the authentication requirement was an example of "conditional relevance."[7] This is the source of the "sufficient to support a finding" language in Rule 901(a), which mirrors the language of Rule 104(b): the rule requires the proponent to present evidence "sufficient to support a finding" that the item is what its proponent claims it to be.

Regarding (2), the authentication requirement is generally thought to apply to testimonial evidence relating a live conversation with a person whose identity matters, at least when the speaker is not visible to the witness. But the reach of this requirement is unclear.[8]

Regarding (3), the general requirement of extrinsic evidence can be inferred from Rule 902, which lists various exceptional types of documents that will be admitted without any "extrinsic evidence of authenticity."[9] This exception suggests the rule: most items do require extrinsic evidence of authenticity or identity, which will almost always involve testimony. Rule 901(b) provides ten illustrations (the list is not exclusive) of the kind of extrinsic evidence that meets the rule's requirement. Examples include opinion testimony about the similarity of two instances of handwriting, distinctive characteristics of an item when taken together with attendant circumstances (evidenced

---

4 *See, e.g.*, 2 MCCORMICK ON EVIDENCE § 212 at 4 (Kenneth S. Broun ed., 7th ed. 2013).

5 For example, under prevailing modern usage, if a proponent wants to introduce a rock that is allegedly the murder weapon, the proponent is required to "authenticate" the rock even though the rock does not *purport to be* anything. (It just *is* a rock.) This does not mean, as you might expect from the language, that the proponent must show the rock really is a rock, i.e. an "authentic" rock, but rather that the proponent must provide testimony supporting the inference *identifying* this rock as the murder weapon. Unfortunately, one often finds accounts in which the general authentication requirement is stated in terms of showing that an exhibit is what "*it* purports to be." *See, e.g.*, United States v. Holmquist, 36 F.3d 154, 167–68 (1st Cir. 1994) (emphasis supplied).

6 *See* 5 CHRISTOPHER B. MUELLER & LAIRD C. KIRKPATRICK, FEDERAL EVIDENCE § 9.2 (4th ed. 2013).

7 *See* FED. R. EVID. 901(a) advisory committee note.

8 *See* **§ 12.11**.

9 *See* **§ 12.07**.

by testimony), and testimony demonstrating that various processes produce accurate results.

Authentication Distinguished from a Determination of Authenticity

The authentication required for an item to be admitted into evidence is distinct from a determination that the item is actually authentic or is otherwise what its proponent claims it to be. The difference between the process of authentication to admit evidence and a finding that the item is authentic relates to who decides and the level of proof required. Under Rule 104(b)'s division of labor the judge decides whether the proponent has made a prima facie case that the item is what that party claims it to be, so that it may be admitted into evidence,[10] and the jury decides—if necessary—whether the thing presented is what its proponent claims it to be and, any event, what weight to give it.[11]

Authentication—the judge's screening process—requires only enough extrinsic evidence to establish a prima facie case that the item is what the proponent claims it to be. If the judge believes that a reasonable jury could find the item to be what the proponent claims, the item is sufficiently authenticated, even if the judge personally believes that it is not.[12] As a practical matter, the judge usually looks only to the proponent's evidence. Assume, for example, that a witness testifies to familiarity with the defendant's handwriting and that the handwriting on a letter offered into evidence is the defendant's. The judge likely will find the letter has been authenticated, even though the defendant's expert testifies that the handwriting is not the defendant's, the defendant testifies that the letter is a forgery, and the judge believes the defendant's evidence on this point is more persuasive.[13] The easy threshold of Rule 104(b) has been met and the jury will see the letter and decide if it is what its proponent claims it to be and how much weight to afford it.

---

[10] *See* United States v. Thomas, 294 F.3d 899, 904 (7th Cir. 2002); United States v. Tropeano, 252 F.3d 653, 661 (2d Cir. 2001) ("The burden of authentication does not require the proponent of the evidence to rule out all possibilities inconsistent with authenticity, or to prove beyond any doubt that the evidence is what it purports to be. Rather, the standard for authentication, and hence for admissibility, is one of reasonable likelihood."). The judge's ruling on an authentication question can only be reversed if the reviewing court finds it was an abuse of discretion. *See, e.g.*, United States v. Hemphill, 40 F. App'x 809, 810 (4th Cir. 2002); United States v. Thomas, 294 F.3d 899, 904 (7th Cir. 2002); United States v. Mirelez, 59 F. App'x 286, 287 (10th Cir. 2003).

[11] *See* Reeves v. Sanderson Plumbing Prods., Inc., 530 U.S. 133, 153 (2000); United States v. Alicea-Cardoza, 132 F.3d 1, 4 (1st Cir. 1997) ("Generally, if the district court is satisfied that the evidence is sufficient to allow a reasonable person to believe the evidence is what it purports to be, Rule 901(a) is satisfied and the jury may decide what weight it will give the evidence."); United States v. Beidler, 110 F.3d 1064, 1067 (4th Cir. 1997) ("The jury, not the reviewing court, weighs the credibility of the evidence and resolves any conflicts in the evidence presented.") (internal quotations omitted).

[12] As compared to the Rule 104(a) determinations made with regard to most other admissibility rules, the judge's 901(a)/104(b) determination must be based on admissible evidence, indeed on evidence that has been or will be admitted, because only evidence that is admitted can be part of what is "sufficient to support a finding" by the fact-finder.

[13] *See* CHRISTOPHER B. MUELLER & LAIRD C. KIRKPATRICK, FEDERAL EVIDENCE § 9:2 at 335 (4th ed. 2013) (footnote omitted):

> Ordinarily such counterproof does not result in exclusion of the evidence, for the question of authenticity is to be determined by the jury, but of course the judge may exclude evidence for failure of the authentication requirement if the counterproof is so cogent and compelling that a reasonable jury could not find the matter to be authentic.

Authentication as Purpose Dependent

The demand of the authentication requirement is primarily determined by the inference that the proponent offers the evidence to support, or, in the language of Rule 901(a), "what the proponent claims it is." The same physical object will require a different authentication if offered for one purpose than if offered for another. Thus, if the proponent offers a letter, which purports to be signed by one Natasha Green, the authentication requirement will depend on whether, for example, the proponent's theory of the case depends on the letter actually being signed by Natasha Green or, rather, on a party merely believing that it was signed by Natasha Green, even if that belief was mistaken. In the former case, the proponent would be required to present evidence sufficient to support a finding that Natasha Green signed the latter, whereas in the latter case the proponent would be required only to present evidence sufficient to support a finding that the party believed Natasha Green signed the latter.[14]

Even though the authentication requirement explicitly depends on what the proponent claims a thing to be, the law is unclear about the extent of the proponent's control over what is claimed about the object. For example, in a murder case, where it is uncontested that the victim was killed with a knife, if the prosecution wants to introduce as evidence a knife the police found in the defendant's possession, there are several possibilities about what exactly the prosecution might claim the knife to be. If, as part of its theory of the case, the prosecution claims that (a) this is a knife found on the defendant when he was arrested, (b) this is a knife of which the defendant had control at the time of the murder, and (c) this is the knife used to kill the victim, then there are three claimed facts about the knife that must be shown to the requisite standard—"sufficient to support a finding"—as a condition on admitting the knife into evidence. But the prosecution is not required to make such a robust claim. While the prosecution is contemplating that the fact-finder will infer that the defendant used that knife to kill the victim, the prosecution is not required to prove that this is so, nor is the prosecution required to prove any other specific theory of the case. The prosecution should win on the merits so long as the evidence shows beyond reasonable doubt that the defendant murdered the victim, even if (for example) the defendant used a different knife, one not found by the police.[15] Consequently, it would seem that the prosecution is free to argue, "We claim only that this is a knife found on the defendant." It will be relatively easy to provide evidence "sufficient to support a finding" that this more modest claim is true. Case law does not seem to address directly the limits on the proponent's control of the authentication claim in this manner. At the least, it would seem that the prosecution must also commit to the claim that it is *possible* that this knife was in the defendant's possession at the time of the murder and that this knife is the murder weapon, for if either of these facts is not possible then the evidence of the knife is irrelevant.[16] Still, it

[14] *See, e.g.*, Selman v. State, 411 P.2d 217 (Alaska 1966) (explaining that a power of attorney might be relevant either as a valid power or as a power, whether valid or invalid, upon which the defendant nonetheless reasonably relied, and discussing how authentication depends on the specific mode of relevance suggested by the proponent).

[15] The jury is not even required to agree on which knife was used. *See generally* 6 WAYNE R. LAFAVE, ET AL., SUBSTANTIVE CRIMINAL LAW § 24.10(c) (4th ed. 2015).

[16] To be sure, if it is possible that this knife was the murder weapon but impossible that it was in defendant's possession at the time of the murder, then the evidence about the knife would still be relevant, but it would be exculpatory. In that case, the evidence of the knife would probably be offered by the defense, and the matter of authentication would need to be addressed from the point of view of the defendant's theory of the

is much easier to present evidence sufficient to support a finding that it is possible these facts are true than to present evidence sufficient to support a finding that these facts are true.[17]

Rationales for the Requirement

The drafters of the Federal Rules explained the authentication requirement as an example of conditional relevance.[18] However, this rationale does not withstand scrutiny. Consider a breach of contract case in which the defendant denies entering into the contract. If the plaintiff offers a typed document that purports to be a contract for the very subject matter of the complaint signed by the parties to the litigation but does not present an authenticating witness, the document would still be relevant.[19] Jurors might well be skeptical, just as they should be skeptical of any evidence presented by an advocate. They might desire additional proof before concluding that it is more likely than not that the document is authentic. And most importantly, jurors would want to know what the defendant has to say about the document (which they will not hear if the document is excluded). But none of those concerns or desires plausibly renders the evidence irrelevant.[20]

Or, assume that in a murder case the only dispute is over which of two persons, Jack or Jill, committed the murder. (All other possible perpetrators have been ruled out.) The prosecution has brought Jack to trial for the crime and wants to introduce a handwritten letter, signed "Jack." It is also undisputed that the letter was *not* signed by Jill. The letter is full of invectives indicating hostility toward the murder victim. The fact-finder would need to consider several possibilities, including: (1) the defendant wrote the letter; (2) someone else named Jack wrote the letter (but did not kill the victim); (3) someone else not named Jack, who did not kill the victim, wrote the letter and signed it Jack to disguise the source of the letter or to frame the defendant. The prosecution endorses the purported authorship as indeed that of defendant, to suggest his motive, and so must authenticate the letter by introducing evidence "sufficient to support a finding" that the letter was signed by the defendant. This requirement makes

---

case, but that theory would not necessarily commit the defendant to the proposition that this knife was the murder weapon.

[17] The complexities involved here cannot be fully resolved without confronting the problems inherent in the doctrine of conditional relevance. *See* **§ 3.11**.

[18] *See* FED. R. EVID. 901(a) advisory committee note.

[19] *See* 9 WIGMORE ON EVIDENCE § 2529 (Chadbourn rev. 1981) (noting that, in regard to the idea of presuming an *"identity of person" from an "identity of name,"* . . . "[a] concordance in name alone is *always some evidence* of identity, and it is not correct to say with the books that, besides proof of the facts in relation to the person named, their identity must be shown, implying that the agreement of name goes for nothing; whereas it is always a considerable step towards that conclusion.") (citation omitted).

[20] If nothing more were forthcoming from the plaintiff on the point, it might be appropriate for the court to direct a verdict at the end of the plaintiff's case on the ground that no reasonable fact-finder could conclude the document is authentic without some additional supporting evidence, at least if there is no other evidence of the existence of a contract. But even if so, that would be a sufficiency-of-the-evidence ruling, not an admissibility ruling. *See* **§ 2.06**. Wigmore's brief discussion of the matter initially suggests that the authentication requirement should apply only when the connection that is suggested by the proponent must itself be found to be true in order for the claim or defense to succeed, which would mean that the authentication requirement is a kind of early directed verdict motion targeted at a particular element of the proof. *See* 7 WIGMORE ON EVIDENCE § 2129 at 695–704 (Chadbourn rev. 1978). But both practice and his description of the rule extend the requirement to situations in which the proponent does not bear the burden of proof and to situations where the proponent, while bearing the burden of proof, can establish the necessary elements of the claim or defense without the fact-finder concluding (by whatever standard of proof) that the object is what its proponent claims it to be.

sense as an implication of the requirement of relevance, however, only if the letter is irrelevant if the fact-finder concludes that it is more likely than not that it was authored by someone other than defendant. This is incorrect. The fact-finder might think it likely that someone other than the defendant wrote the letter and yet take a relatively small, but non-trivial probability that defendant wrote it as tending to incriminate the defendant, because it cannot incriminate Jill and there is no other potential perpetrator. In that case, the letter is some, albeit weak evidence of defendant's dislike of the victim. In other words, the letter is relevant even though the fact-finder would be unable to make the "finding" contemplated by the authentication requirement.[21] Again, the concept of conditional relevance, at least as it is typically understood, does not fit the authentication requirement.

Over the years, commentators have offered other explanations for the authentication requirement. One traditional explanation, articulated by Wigmore long before the Federal Rules, is that authentication counteracts "a general mental tendency, when a corporal object is produced as proving something, to assume, on sight of the object, all else that is implied in the case about it. The sight of it seems to prove all the rest."[22] Whether this is a viable rationale for authentication requirments depends on how one assesses fact-finders' capacities[23] and on the alternatives that exist, by argument of counsel or even counter-proof, for bringing the issues of fraud and mistake to the fact-finder's attention. One of Wigmore's contemporaries asserted simply, "If spurious evidence is admitted, its authenticity can generally be met by a direct denial, and the jury has an uncanny instinct for apprehending the truth in these matters."[24]

---

[21] Unlike the previous contract example, no such "finding" that the defendant wrote the letter is necessary to the prosecution's murder case, because defendant could be the murderer even if he did not author the letter. Indeed, that it is more likely than not that he did not author the letter would not necessarily require a directed verdict of acquittal; the appropriate ruling on a motion for such a directed verdict would depend on what other evidence of defendant's guilt was presented.

[22] *See* 7 WIGMORE ON EVIDENCE § 2129 at 704 (Chadbourn rev. 1978).

[23] Wigmore cites literature, but no social science. He supports his claim of a "tendency deeply rooted in all persons, even the most intelligent and reflective" by noting its satire by Shakespeare

> in his scene with Jack Cade's mob, where their leader proclaims himself, to the questioning magistrate, as the descendant of Earl Mortimer, whose son
>
> > "Was by a beggar woman stol'n away,
> > And, ignorant of his birth and parentage,
> > Became a bricklayer when he came of age,
> > His son am I! deny it if you can!"
>
> to which his follower, Smith the Weaver, adds vehemently the following strong confirmation:
>
> > "Sir, he made a chimney in my father's house; and the bricks are alive at this day to testify it; therefore, deny it not!"

Id. (*quoting* Henry VI, pt. 2, act 4, sec. 2).

[24] *Cf.* Manfred W. Ehrich, *Unnecessary Difficulties of Proof,* 32 YALE L.J. 436, 451 (1923). (To be sure, Professor Ehrich also opined without the support of empirical social science.) Moreover, another obstacle to Wigmore's theory, or any theory based on the assumption of a credulous fact-finder, is that it somehow must be reconciled with the "sufficient to support a finding" language in Rule 901(a), a standard that is usually chosen—instead of the Rule 104(a) criterion that would leave the issue entirely to the court—precisely because the issue is one that can be trusted to the fact-finder to resolve. *See* **§ 3.11**. Sometimes, the risk of fraud or mistake is identified as a concern separate from fact-finder credulity regarding such risk. *See* John William Strong, *Liberalizing the Authentication of Private Writings,* 52 CORNELL. L.Q. 284, 285–86 (1967). The difficulty with such risks, standing alone, as justification for the rule, is that it proves too much: the same risks are present in testimonial evidence. What is to be explained in this context is the special need for this rule respecting tangible evidence, and Wigmore's suggestion of fact-finder gullibility at least provides a superficially plausible (though not particularly convincing) reason to think those risks differentially attend tangible evidence.

Another explanation of the authentication rule rejects the credulous fact-finder theory without embracing the conditional relevance idea. It argues that tangible evidence is particularly likely to be ambiguous and unhelpful in the absence of testimony indicating how the object is connected to the case. This explanation understands the authentication requirement as a specialized application of Rule 403 (rather than an application of Rule 402, as is the case with "conditional relevance"). It posits that, without supporting testimony, tangible evidence is generally insufficiently probative not to be outweighed by its ambiguity and tendency to confuse or waste the time of the fact-finder.[25]

A distinct, but related argument is that the requirement of a sponsoring witness assures the court that it is informed of the basis for the claim of a connection between the thing and the case, which the proponent must be able to provide if its claim is not wholly fictional. At the same time, the opponent is provided with someone who can be cross-examined about that connection. The rule thus serves to force the proponent to divulge useful information, and a source of that information, that might otherwise not be revealed but that should be disclosed before the case proceeds.[26]

§ 12.02 Handling Exhibits in the Courtroom

Exhibits present special visual opportunities in what is an otherwise heavily oral environment. Most lawyers strive to achieve maximum persuasive advantage from the process of authenticating and offering an exhibit. Whatever the nature of the exhibit—document, photograph, diagram, model, etc.—or the particular persuasive approach employed, a lawyer offering an exhibit must follow a basic procedural pattern.[27] The pattern may vary slightly from courtroom to courtroom, but the underlying requirements remain. Pretrial marking of exhibits or informality of practice sometimes allows exhibits to be offered and received into evidence without going through each of the proper steps. Nevertheless, a lawyer must understand the process for those times when an exhibit must be marked and offered in a courtroom in which the judge expects exhibits to be handled in the formal fashion.

1. *Ask the court's permission to have the clerk, the court reporter, or the bailiff (whoever marks exhibits in the particular courtroom) mark the exhibit for identification.*

Exhibits are numbered or lettered in sequence. In many jurisdictions, the plaintiff's or prosecution's exhibits are numbered and the defendant's exhibits are lettered.

2. *Show the exhibit to the opposing lawyer.*

More often than not, the lawyer will have seen the item during discovery, but it is nevertheless important to show the lawyer the exhibit in court. The lawyer who is

---

[25] *See* Dale A. Nance, *Conditional Relevance Reinterpreted*, 70 B.U. L. REV. 447, 474–75 (1990). *See also* Richard D. Friedman, *Conditional Probative Value: Neoclassicism Without Myth*, 93 MICH. L. REV. 439 (1994). Not surprisingly, other Rule 403 concerns—especially the potential for unfair prejudice—come into decisions on the admissibility of some, but not all, tangible exhibits.

[26] *See* Dale A. Nance, *Conditional Relevance Reinterpreted*, 70 B.U. L. REV. 447, 484–97 (1990). This argument is closely related to the one later articulated by the Court in Old Chief v. United States, 519 U.S. 172, 182–84 (1997), because it considers alternative presentations of evidence that may be superior, from the tribunal's perspective, to what a party otherwise chooses to present. *See* **§ 5.03**.

[27] *See* STEVEN H. GOLDBERG, THE FIRST TRIAL: WHERE DO I SIT? WHAT DO I SAY? 26 (1982) (presenting exhibits "By the Numbers").

viewing the prospective exhibit and has seen it during discovery should ascertain that the exhibit is substantially similar to what was viewed during discovery.

While walking around the courtroom with an exhibit that can be identified easily upon sight, such as a photograph or a gun, the attorney should not let the jurors see the exhibit before it is admitted into evidence. If the exhibit is one that ultimately will not be received, exhibition of it to the jurors could result in sanctions against the lawyer and, if the prejudice is sufficiently serious, a mistrial.

Some items may be difficult to handle without exposing them to the jurors during the authentication process. If the exhibit is not seriously contested, or if the item is one that will not cause much prejudice if the jurors see it during the process, opposing counsel may agree or the court may allow it to be within the jurors' view before it has been received in evidence.

3. *Ask the court's permission to approach the witness. Hand the exhibit to the witness and ask whether the witness can identify the exhibit.*

It is important for the lawyer to refer to the item by its identification number so that everyone in the courtroom can keep track and the record is clear for appellate review.

Example

Proponent: I hand you what has been marked Plaintiff's Exhibit No. 1 for identification. Do you recognize it?

Witness: Yes.

Proponent: What is it?

The lawyer must ensure that neither the question nor the answer tells the jurors about the contents or the nature of the exhibit—information that is appropriate only after the exhibit has been received. A question such as, "Mr. Smith, would you examine the shrunken head that has been marked as State's Exhibit No. 1 for identification?" is likely to provoke an objection and could provide the basis for a mistrial.[28]

4. *Ask the witness the questions needed to lay the foundation for the admission of the exhibit into evidence.*

Authenticating questions will vary depending on the exhibit, but all authentication testimony requires the witness to explain why the exhibit is what the proponent claims it to be. Laying the foundation for an exhibit serves two purposes: it authenticates the exhibit so the judge will admit it; and, more importantly, it provides information that will persuade the jurors that the exhibit is authentic and worthy of favorable inferences.

5. *Offer the exhibit into evidence. E.g.: "Your honor, I offer (whatever the item is) that has been marked as Plaintiff's exhibit number one for identification into evidence as Plaintiff's exhibit number one."*

In some jurisdictions, an item is marked originally with a number or letter, without the "for identification" limitation. In such a jurisdiction, the lawyer need not refer to the

[28] *See* Mayer v. Angelica, 790 F.2d 1315, 1338–41 (7th Cir. 1986) (holding that admission of unauthenticated letters was prejudicial, thus requiring new trial).

marked item as an exhibit for identification and might offer the exhibit by saying, "Your honor, I offer plaintiff's exhibit number one (whatever the item is) into evidence."

In jurisdictions in which the original marking is "for identification," the judge will have the court personnel who marked the exhibit strike the "for identification" limitation when the exhibit is received in evidence.

6. *Make sure that the contents or the nature of the exhibit is apparent to the jurors.*

The most important part of having an exhibit admitted into evidence is its influence on the jurors. The lawyer should make sure that the full force of the exhibit is displayed when it is accepted into evidence. Having a witness read a document received in evidence is often the most effective way to present the information to the jury and is proper under most circumstances. Paraphrasing the document, however, misleads and confuses the trier-of-fact and violates Rule 403. Moreover, the witness' paraphrase constitutes an opinion about the author's intended emphasis that, in the absence of some expertise in interpretation, is unlikely to be "helpful" to a jury capable of reading for itself. This can justify an objection, usually phrased as "the document speaks for itself":

Example

Direct examiner:	I'm handing you what has been received in evidence as the plaintiff's exhibit A. Are you familiar with it?
Witness:	Yes.
Direct examiner:	What is it?
Witness:	It's a memorandum telling the marketing department that. . . .
Cross-examiner:	Objection, Your Honor, the document speaks for itself.

Providing copies of a document for distribution to each juror is another way to bring the contents of the document to the jurors' attention. Copies of a diagram might be distributed as well, but often displaying an enlarged version of the diagram on an easel or PowerPoint is more effective and allows the witness to use the exhibit to make the testimony memorable. Photographs also might be enlarged and displayed to the jurors or passed among the jurors. Objects are often passed among the jurors for closer inspection. Whatever method the lawyer chooses for bringing the exhibit to the attention of the jurors, the lawyer should be sure to receive the court's permission.

While such presentation by way of marked exhibits is common, there are other presentations that can satisfy the authentication requirement. Most importantly, demonstrations or reenactments in the courtroom[29] and views taken outside the courtroom[30] do not follow this pattern.

§ 12.03 Laying a Foundation: A Taxonomy of Tangible Evidence

Presenting extrinsic evidence to authenticate an exhibit is usually called "laying the foundation." The foundation can be laid either by direct evidence or by circumstantial evidence. Sometimes a single witness suffices; in other cases, more than one is

[29] *See* **§ 12.08**.

[30] *See* **§ 12.10**.

necessary.[31] In determining what evidence must be offered to lay the foundation for a particular exhibit, the lawyer must determine exactly what the exhibit is offered to prove.[32]

Courts and commentators use various terms to capture the different uses of tangible evidence, but unfortunately the terminology is not entirely consistent. Regardless of terminology, the most important functional distinction is between tangible evidence that is merely used to illustrate a witness's testimony (often called *demonstrative* evidence), and tangible evidence that has probative value beyond the content of any witness's testimony (often called *real* evidence).[33] A typical example of demonstrative evidence is a drawing of an intersection with which a witness explains the location of automobiles during an accident that the witness observed. A typical example of real evidence is a knife claimed to be the murder weapon that has characteristics that allow it to be identified with the defendant. The foundation requirements for these two types of tangible evidence differ significantly.

Confusingly, some authorities call some tangible evidence "demonstrative evidence" even though that evidence has such independent probative value. An example is a surveillance camera video.[34] To clarify the distinction, we call tangible evidence that merely illustrates the testimony of one or more witnesses "illustrative tangible evidence." Illustrative tangible evidence includes maps, summaries, or any other tangible items that a witness uses to explain testimony but for which there is no claim that the item itself conveys any additional information. We call evidence that is offered as having such separate or distinct probative value "substantive tangible evidence."[35] Substantive tangible evidence includes pictures that record information that no witness is reporting from personal knowledge, such as a surveillance video, a category we call "recorded evidence."[36] The category of substantive tangible evidence also includes the demonstration of physical experiments in the courtroom, the results of which the fact-finder observes directly. Also, to prevent confusion, we will follow the more common custom of restricting the term "real evidence" to tangibles that are offered "as playing an actual and direct part in the incident or transaction giving rise to a trial,"[37] such as a murder weapon or a written contract. Thus, there are kinds of substantive tangible evidence that are not real evidence.

---

[31] For a general treatment of foundations for tangible evidence, see EDWARD J. IMWINKELRIED, EVIDENTIARY FOUNDATIONS § 4 (9th ed. 2015).

[32] *See* **§ 12.01** (subsection on "Authentication as Purpose Dependent").

[33] *See, e.g.*, RONALD L. CARLSON, EDWARD J. IMWINKELRIED, JULIE SEAMAN, & ERICA BEECHER-MONAS, EVIDENCE: TEACHING MATERIALS FOR AN AGE OF SCIENCE AND STATUTES ch. 10 (7th ed. 2012).

[34] *See generally* CHRISTOPHER B. MUELLER & LAIRD C. KIRKPATRICK, FEDERAL EVIDENCE § 9:22 (4th ed. 2013).

[35] This is one commonly used term, but it is potentially confusing. Most importantly, the illustrative/substantive distinction used here should not be confused with the credibility/non-credibility distinction used in connection with impeachment of testimony or with the nonhearsay/hearsay distinction. In each of these other contexts, the latter idea is sometimes called "substantive." *See* **§ 19.05**.

[36] Professor Wigmore called this kind of evidence "nonverbal testimony," even when it was merely illustrative. 3 WIGMORE ON EVIDENCE §§ 789 et seq. (Chadbourn rev. 1070). A picture that records events to which no witness testifies could also be real evidence if, for example, it were used to blackmail someone.

[37] *See* 2 MCCORMICK ON EVIDENCE § 213 at 13 (Kenneth S. Broun ed., 7th ed. 2013). By contrast, Wigmore seems to have extended the term "real evidence" to cover all tangible evidence having probative value separate from testimony. *See* 1A WIGMORE ON EVIDENCE § 24 (Tillers rev. 1983), 4 WIGMORE ON EVIDENCE § 1150 et seq. (Chadbourn rev. 1972).

Documents are perhaps the most common form of tangible evidence, especially in civil cases. As a category, documents cut across all the categories described above. Documents in one context may be used as substantive evidence, but in another context they may be purely illustrative. Not only that, when offered substantively, they often have the dual character noted in the first section of this chapter: the proponent claims something about the document and the document makes its own claim because it purports its own source or authorship. The latter claim may or may not be relevant to the use the proponent wants to make of the document.[38] All these considerations affect the necessary foundation for the document.

§ 12.04 Real Evidence

Items that were actually involved in the transaction or occurrence that gave rise to the litigation are usually called real evidence.[39] The stolen goods in a burglary case, the signed agreement in a contract case, and the headlight glass fragments found on the road in a personal injury case are common examples. Often, the purpose of introducing such evidence is to corroborate (not just illustrate) testimony claiming that such objects were found, possessed, and so forth by the parties. In such contexts, real evidence is authenticated by evidence showing that the exhibit in court is the actual item from the transaction or event and that it has not undergone any significant change.[40]

The requirement that the exhibit remain in the same condition that it was at the time of the transaction or event applies only if the change matters in the litigation. If the changes can be explained or understood by the jurors, such change does not bar admission. Therefore, in a counterfeiting trial, the government could authenticate seized counterfeit money as the "real" counterfeit despite a change in the color of the money to blue during government fingerprint analysis of the bills because the identification of the counterfeit money and its relevance to the litigation did not depend upon the color.[41]

Real evidence is frequently authenticated in the manner of Rule 901(b)(4) by referring to its distinctive characteristics. If the condition of the item is unimportant or if the item is distinctive, real evidence often can be authenticated by simple identification. A police officer, who initialed a weapon upon seizing it from a suspect, might authenticate the weapon by recognizing the initials and testifying about the circumstances of the seizure and marking. Money, televisions sets, automobiles, etc., may be authenticated by showing that the witness recorded the item's serial number at the time of the seizure and that it matches the serial number of the proposed exhibit.

When the item of real evidence is not distinctive, or when its condition at the time of testing or trial is crucial, establishing the chain of custody is the most effective way to authenticate the exhibit. A perfect demonstration of the chain of custody would include

---

[38] The special context in which the proponent does endorse a document's internal claim of authorship—authentication in the narrow, traditional sense of that term—is obviously important and recurring. *See* **§ 12.07**.

[39] *See* **§ 12.03**.

[40] United States v. Jones, 56 F. App'x 416, 419 (9th Cir. 2003); United States v. Bokshoven, 258 F. Supp. 2d 397, 400 (E.D. Pa. 2003).

[41] United States v. Skelley, 501 F.2d 447, 451 (7th Cir. 1974) (holding that counterfeit bills were admissible to prove defendant's knowledge that they were counterfeit because they had identical serial numbers and were found on defendant). Counterfeit bills are documents that purport to be the real thing, but the government prosecuting someone for using such bills obviously does not endorse that the item is authentic; indeed, it argues precisely the opposite. So authenticity in the narrow traditional sense—genuineness of purported authorship—is not involved.

testimony about every link in the chain, from the moment the item was retrieved from the scene of the event to the time it is offered into evidence. Each person who touched the exhibit would describe how and from whom it was received, where it was and what happened to it while in the witness's possession, the condition in which it was received, and the delivery to the next link in the chain. The witnesses would describe the precautions taken to ensure there was no change in the condition of the exhibit and no opportunity for someone not in the chain to have possession of the item.

Proof that the chain was perfect is almost impossible and that has never been the standard. Before adoption of the Federal Rules, a chain of custody could be established only if there was reasonable certainty that all the links in the chain were firmly connected. The Rules arguably have made the required showing less onerous.[42] The authentication standard in Rule 901(a) requires only enough evidence to support a finding (by a preponderance of the evidence) that the item is what the proponent claims it to be. Some courts in Federal Rules jurisdictions take the new standard literally and allow greater gaps between the links in a chain of custody.[43] Other courts seem to retain the stricter reasonable certainty standard of the pre-Rules era.[44]

Proponents commonly use chains of custody to demonstrate that a substance seized in one place is the same substance and in the same condition as the substance tested in another place and then returned for use as courtroom evidence. Urine samples, bloody gloves, and trace elements of hair exemplify the myriad objects that might require the showing of a custody chain. However, drugs seized in a drug bust are the most common example.[45] Such an exhibit will have passed through many hands from the point of origin

---

[42] *See* Paul C. Giannelli, *Chain of Custody and the Handling of Real Evidence*, 20 AM. CRIM. L. REV. 527 (1983).

[43] *See, e.g.*, United States v. Smith, 70 F. App'x 359, 362 (7th Cir. 2003) ("[E]vidence kept in official custody is presumed to be authentic absent specific evidence of tampering."); United States v. McGraw, 62 F. App'x 679, 681 (7th Cir. 2003) ("Fed. R. Evid. 901(a) advisory committee notes state that the requirement of proving authenticity falls in the category of relevancy dependent upon fulfillment of a condition of fact and is governed by the procedure set forth in Fed. R. Evid. 104(b). In determining whether there is sufficient evidence to meet the requirements of Rule 104(b), the court neither weighs credibility nor makes a finding that the government has proved the conditional fact by a preponderance of the evidence. The court's role is to examine the evidence to determine whether the jury could reasonably find the conditional fact by a preponderance of the evidence."). Weighing the evidence is traditionally a jury function, and as United States v. Jones, 56 F. App'x 416, 419 (9th Cir. 2003) held, "[a]ny defect in the chain of custody goes to the weight, not the admissibility, of the evidence introduced." *See also* United States v. Myers, 294 F.3d 203, 210 (1st Cir. 2002) ("The links in a chain of custody need not be welded to one another, but, rather, may be more loosely connected. '[T]he prosecution's chain-of-custody evidence must be adequate—not infallible.' To the extent that there were any weak links in the instant chain—notably, the time between the end of the chase and the time when the guns were found—their effect on the authenticity of the evidence was a matter within the exclusive province of the jury.") (internal citations omitted); United States v. Watts, 78 F. App'x 350, 2003 WL 22351968, *1 (5th Cir. 2003) ("The determination of the authenticity of heroin is within the province of the jury.

[44] *See, e.g.*, United States v. Howard-Arias, 679 F.2d 363, 366 (4th Cir.), *cert. denied*, 459 U.S. 874 (1982) ("the ultimate question is whether the authentication testimony [i]s sufficient so as to convince the court that it is improbable that the original item had been exchanged with another or otherwise tampered with."); United States v. Chapman, 345 F.3d 630, 637 (8th Cir. 2003) ("A district court may admit physical evidence if the court believes a reasonable probability exists that the evidence has not been changed or altered. In making this determination, absent a showing of bad faith, ill will, or proof of tampering, the court operates under a presumption of integrity for the physical evidence."); United States v. Diaz-Villasenor, 68 F. App'x 791, 792 (9th Cir. 2003) ("The prosecution may establish chain of custody to lay a proper foundation for admission of physical evidence if it is able to prove that a reasonable juror could find that the evidence is in substantially the same condition as when it was seized and if there is a reasonable probability the evidence has not been changed in important respects.").

[45] An example of acceptable chain of custody shown by government is discussed in United States v. Jackson, 345 F.3d 59 (2d Cir. 2003). "The government established a chain of custody consisting of (i) a videotape that showed Mazyck giving the substance to Redman; (ii) a DEA agent's testimony regarding the government's

to the laboratory to the courtroom, and it also will have been processed or analyzed. The exhibit (and in some courts, the laboratory analysis[46]) will not be admissible unless the proponent can show the chain of custody of the exhibit from the time it was seized to the time it arrives in court.

In the typical drug case, someone associated with the government, often an undercover officer or an informer who made the buy, secures the drugs. The drugs are often transferred to at least one other law enforcement officer and then stored in an evidence locker, sent via some delivery service to a laboratory for testing, stored, handled, tested in the laboratory by at least one technician, and sent via some delivery service back to the law enforcement officer. The proponent can establish the chain of custody without eliciting testimony from every single person who handled the drugs. The habit rule,[47] the business-record hearsay exception,[48] and the public-record hearsay exception[49] allow for using documentary evidence to establish some of the links in the chain.[50] Moreover, courts often accept evidence with imperfect chains and minor gaps. The issue of the weight to be given to the testimony is left to the jury.[51] Despite the flexibility shown when there are minor gaps in the chain, courts will not admit exhibits if the defect in the chain might significantly cloud the identification of the exhibit.[52]

For example, in *Graham v. State*,[53] an informer made a supervised purchase of a substance that was later analyzed as heroin. The break in the chain of custody occurred after the exhibit was deposited in the police property room. The property room records showed that, before the exhibit was analyzed, an officer removed the exhibit from the property room and six days later, another officer returned it. Neither officer testified at trial. There was no evidence of the exhibit's location or who had it during the six days that it was not in the police property room. In holding that it was error to admit the exhibit with the break in the chain of custody, the appellate court emphasized the special

---

surveillance of Redman for most of the time before, during, and after the videotaped transaction; (iii) an agent's testimony regarding the DEA's field-testing and storage of the drugs; and (iv) the testimony of the forensic chemist who subjected the substance to laboratory testing." *Id.* at 65.

[46] *See* **§ 12.11**.

[47] *See* **§ 7.15**.

[48] *See* **§ 16.07**.

[49] *See* **§ 16.09**.

[50] *See, e.g.*, United States v. Lauersen, 348 F.3d 329 (2d Cir. 2003); Hulmes v. Honda Motor Co., 960 F. Supp. 844 (D. N.J. 1997); Judd v. State, 663 So. 2d 690 (La. 1995).

[51] *See, e.g.*, United States v. Turpin, 65 F.3d 1207 (4th Cir. 1995); United States v. Pressley, 978 F.2d 1026, 1028–29 (8th Cir. 1992) (stating that trial court properly admitted substance in package marked by officer at scene of crime when chemist testified she tested substance in same package, and holding that "[t]he government is not required to maintain an eternal vigilance over all evidence in its custody"); United States v. Diaz-Villasenor, 68 F. App'x 791, 792–93 (9th Cir. 2003) ("Merely raising the possibility of tampering, however, is not enough to render evidence inadmissible. Furthermore, a defect in the chain of custody goes to the weight, not the admissibility, of the evidence introduced."); Lee v. State, 689 N.E.2d 435, 439 (Ind. 1997) ("[T]he State need not negate every remote possibility of tampering. It is sufficient if the State presents evidence which strongly suggests the exact whereabouts of the evidence at all times. Once the State has presented such evidence, any gaps in the chain of custody would go to the weight of the evidence and not to the admissibility of the evidence.") (internal quotations and citations omitted); Nimmons v. State, 814 So. 2d 1153, 1154 (Fla. Dist. Ct. App. 2002) ("In order to bar the introduction of relevant evidence due to a gap in the chain of custody, the defendant must show that there was a probability of tampering with the evidence, and a mere possibility of tampering is insufficient.").

[52] *See* Crisco v. State, 943 S.W.2d 582 (Ark. 1997) (excluding methamphetamine test by state due to serious defect in chain of custody); Rabovsky v. Commonwealth, 973 S.W.2d 6 (Ky. 1998) (ruling that blood test results were not admissible in murder trial simply because results had been placed into hospital records where state had failed to show chain of custody sufficient to indicate lack of material tampering).

[53] 255 N.E.2d 652 (Ind. 1970).

nature of substances such as narcotics. The court said that "the danger of tampering, loss, or mistake with respect to an exhibit is greatest where the exhibit is small and is one which has physical characteristics fungible in nature and similar in form to substances familiar to people in their daily lives."[54] It noted the white powder seized could have been heroin, or it could have been sugar or baking powder. The court explained:

> Unless the state can show by producing records or testimony, the continuous whereabouts of the exhibit at least between the time it came into their possession until it was laboratory tested to determine its composition, testimony of the state as to the laboratory's findings is inadmissible.[55]

Courts may also deny admission where the authentication does not match the purpose for which the exhibit was offered. In *Robinson v. Commonwealth*,[56] the victim of a rape identified her underpants and blouse in court, which had been given to the investigating officer shortly after the incident. The evidence would have been sufficient to authenticate the clothing as what she was wearing when she was attacked. The clothing items were offered, however, as the basis of an FBI expert's opinion about the semen stains, bloodstains, and wool fibers found on the clothing—evidence that linked the defendant to the crime. The prosecution did not offer any evidence as to who had handled or what had happened to the items of clothing from the time they were taken from the victim to the time they were given to the local police for storage—the time during which the FBI analysis took place. In reversing the conviction because the chain of custody was inadequate to authenticate the items, the court acknowledged the victim's identification of the clothes and noted that, if "they had been admitted only to establish what the victim was wearing when attacked, then we would agree with the Commonwealth's position."[57] But the clothes had also been admitted "to supply a basis for the opinion testimony of the FBI agents" and "[t]he mere fact the blouse and the panties were identified did not prove the chain of possession necessary to validate the FBI analysis of them."[58]

§ 12.05 Tangible Evidence That Illustrates Testimony

Trial lawyers search for visual aids that will assist them in persuading jurors and tangible evidence that illustrates, clarifies, and amplifies oral testimony (usually called "demonstrative" evidence) can enliven the presentation of evidence. Attorneys use diagrams, models, similar objects, photographs, and drawings to illustrate the ideas to which witnesses testify. The simplest and most common example is an intersection diagram on which a witness illustrates the many simultaneous events that make up the average intersection collision.

The foundation for such tangible evidence, offered only to illustrate testimony, is often simple. The witness must demonstrate familiarity with whatever is depicted and must testify that the exhibit fairly and accurately represents it. Additionally, some courts require that the exhibit assist the witness in explaining the testimony to the jurors. It does not matter whether it is a photograph or a diagram, or even a duplicate

---

[54] *Id.* at 655.

[55] *Id.*

[56] 183 S.E.2d 179 (Va. 1971).

[57] *Id.* at 181.

[58] *Id.*

object. Anyone who knows what the thing depicted looks like can lay the foundation requirement that the exhibit is a fair and accurate representation. The testimony of the photographer or the diagram maker is not required.

Example

Direct examiner: Are you familiar with the intersection of First Avenue and Maple?

Witness: Yes.

Direct examiner: How are you familiar with that intersection?

Witness: I drive through it regularly at least three times a week.

Direct examiner: I'm showing you what has been marked Plaintiff's exhibit number one for identification. Do you recognize it?

Witness: Yes, I do.

Direct examiner: What is it?

Witness: Looks like the intersection of First Avenue and Maple.

Direct examiner: Does Plaintiff's exhibit number one for identification fairly and accurately represent the way the intersection of First Avenue and Maple appeared on (the date of incident?)

Witness: Yes, it does.

Direct examiner: Would the diagram assist you in explaining to the jurors what you saw?

Witness: Yes.

Direct examiner: Your honor, I offer the diagram of First Avenue and Maple into evidence as Plaintiff's exhibit number one.

Opposing attorney: Your honor, I request a limiting instruction be given informing the jurors that the diagram is not drawn to scale.

Judge: Members of the jury. The diagram that has just been received in evidence as Plaintiff's exhibit number one is not drawn to scale. While it is basically accurate as to the intersection of First Avenue and Maple, the distances shown are approximate, and should not be taken by you to necessarily represent the distance relationships on the intersection.[59]

The foundation testimony—that the exhibit fairly and accurately represents whatever it is claimed to represent and that it would assist the witness in testifying—is as sufficient for a complex model or for a hologram as it is for a simple diagram.

---

[59] If a diagram is drawn to scale and is offered to illustrate testimony about precise measurements, the witness must lay a much more complete foundation. Moreover, the witness must be one who can testify from firsthand knowledge about the creation of the diagram. The witness must be able to explain how the measurements were obtained, how they were converted to the diagram, and the scale used. Once a diagram is accepted into evidence as a scale diagram, non-scale marks added to the diagram may destroy the foundation and the exhibit. Markings that show directions might be added because they do not purport to represent distances, but any other marking that reflects a distance must be made to scale with a ruler or placed on an overlay that can be separated from the scale diagram.

The most common objection to demonstrative evidence used for an illustrative purpose is that it is misleading. Diagrams that appear to be to scale, but are not, can mislead the jurors into forgetting that the distances shown are approximate. A photograph taken under lighting conditions different from the event can mislead the jurors into thinking that the lighting shown in the photograph reflects what illuminated the scene at the event in question. Sometimes the problem is handled by an instruction but, if the evidence is sufficiently misleading or prejudicial, the judge may exclude it under Rule 403.

Illustrative tangible evidence is handled differently among jurisdictions and sometimes varies from courtroom to courtroom. Trial courts possess wide discretion in regulating the use of such evidence.[60] Illustrative exhibits are not even marked in some courtrooms, though a lawyer who insists upon having such an exhibit marked to make the record understandable for an appellate court should prevail. Some courts allow the use of demonstrative evidence for illustrative purposes but do not allow the exhibits to be admitted into evidence.[61] In other courts, such evidence is received in evidence, but the jurors are given an instruction that the exhibit is for illustrative purposes only. In some instances, such as when a replica of a gun used in a robbery is admitted for illustrative purposes, it may be error not to give an instruction reminding the jury that the gun is not the actual gun.[62] At one time, demonstrative exhibits were routinely excluded from the jury room during deliberations. The modern tendency is to allow most exhibits to be taken into the jury room,[63] unless they are impractical (bulky items or contraband), too inflammatory,[64] or, in some cases, when they constitute merely testimonial evidence in written form.[65]

Often a diagram is presented when the first witness to the occurrence testifies and remains in front of the jury throughout the trial, for reference or so that other witnesses can write on it.[66] Courts have different preferences about how to handle diagrams. If the

---

60 Carson v. Polley, 689 F.2d 562 (5th Cir. 1982); Ware v. State, 702 A.2d 699 (Md. 1997); State v. Finch, 975 P.2d 967 (Wash. 1999).

61 *See, e.g.*, United States v. Walt, 117 F.3d 1427 (9th Cir. 1997); Standard Jury Instructions—Civil Cases (99–1), 778 So. 2d 264, 265 (Fla. 2000) (providing example of jury instruction regarding demonstrative evidence: "This witness will be using (identify demonstrative or visual aid(s)) to assist in explaining or illustrating [his] [her] testimony. The testimony of the witness is evidence; however, [this] [these] (identify demonstrative or visual aid(s)) [is] [are] not to be considered as evidence in the case unless received in evidence, and should not be used as a substitute for evidence. Only items received in evidence will be available to you for consideration during your deliberations."); Pickren v. State, 500 S.E.2d 566 (Ga.1998).

62 Robinson v. Missouri Pac. R.R., 16 F.3d 1083 (10th Cir. 1994); United States v. Cox, 633 F.2d 871 (9th Cir. 1980); Garrison v. State, 893 S.W.2d 763 (Ark. 1995); Dunlap v. State, 761 N.E.2d 837 (Ind. 2002).

63 2 McCormick on Evidence § 217 (Kenneth S. Broun ed., 7th ed. 2013). *See* United States v. Salerno, 108 F.3d 730, 744 (7th Cir. 1997) ("As long as the district court is evenhanded in its evidentiary rulings, it has wide discretion in determining whether an exhibit will be allowed to go into the jury deliberation room."); People v. Blue, 724 N.E.2d 920 (Ill. 2000).

64 *See* People v. Blue, 724 N.E.2d 920 (Ill. 2000) (holding that trial court erred in allowing state's demonstrative evidence into jury room where that evidence was blood and brain matter splattered on police officer's uniform worn by life size mannequin and where that mannequin was accompanied with rubber gloves, inviting jury to interact with it).

65 *See* State v. Crimi, 665 N.E.2d 230 (Ohio Ct. App. 1995) (stating that jurors are generally entitled to see exhibits received in evidence but that testimonial evidence presents "speaking continuous witness" problem); State v. Monroe, 27 P.3d 1249 (Wash. Ct. App. 2001).

66 When more than one witness marks a diagram, various methods are employed to ensure that the diagram does not become confusing. Using a different colored pen for each witness and creating a legend on the bottom of the diagram is one method. Using a different clear acetate overlay for each witness and ensuring that the acetates are individually marked is another method that provides the lawyer with flexibility.

diagram is one that a witness or a number of witnesses will mark, some judges will not admit the diagram until all of the markings have been completed. Others will allow the diagram to be admitted and then amended as others mark on it. In some courts, diagrams are considered entirely illustrative and are neither admitted in evidence nor allowed in the jury room during deliberations.

Marking diagrams is one way to make sure that the jurors and the appellate court understand the testimony. While the jurors know what a witness means by pointing to a spot on a diagram and saying, "I was standing right here," they may not remember it when they arrive in the jury room. The appellate court will never know what "here" meant. If the witness marks the diagram clearly, the jurors will remember when they take the diagram into the jury room and the appellate court will be able to understand by looking at the diagram.

Models used for illustrative purposes are merely three-dimensional diagrams. Occasionally, courts are less careful about the marking and offering of models used to illustrate testimony than they are about diagrams. For example, a skeleton used by an orthopedic surgeon to show the jurors where the various bones the doctor is talking about are located may often be used without being either marked or admitted. The better practice, however, is to have the model marked and offered. Among other things, it is more likely to be allowed into the jury room if admitted. A model with working parts requires greater foundational detail to ensure that the working parts on the model do not work in a different fashion than the parts represented.

§ 12.06 Recorded Evidence

Photography, sound recordings, and documents are the three major areas in which tangible evidence might have probative value independent of, or at least in addition to, any testimony to which it might relate. A photograph, properly authenticated, may be received as independent evidence of what it shows. A tape recording might be admitted as independent evidence of a conversation. A post on social media may be received as evidence that events described therein occurred. Although a written contract constitutes real evidence, if the contract is ambiguous, one party's memorandum about the contract may be admissible as independent substantive evidence of whether there was a meeting of the minds. If these pieces of evidence (sometimes also called "demonstrative") are to have independent evidentiary value, the foundation must demonstrate that the exhibit should be considered a sufficiently reliable record of the depicted conditions or events.[67]

Photographs: "Pictorial Testimony" and the "Silent Witness"

Photographs, including a still photo, film, digital, or videotape, constitute an important category of recorded evidence. Photographs were initially treated by the courts with suspicion. Earlier twentieth century courts still admitted photographs as "pictorial testimony," merely illustrative of other testimony.[68] Modern courts still accept

---

[67] Authenticating a photograph or other item of recorded evidence does not end the question of admissibility. The exhibit must still pass the hearsay and best evidence hurdles, if those rules apply. *See* FED. R. EVID. 901(b) advisory committee note ("It should be observed that compliance with requirements of authentication or identification by no means assures admission of an item into evidence, as other bars, hearsay for example, may remain."). *See also* Orr v. Bank of Am., NT & SA, 285 F.3d 764, 778 (9th Cir. 2002); United States v. Wadena, 152 F.3d 831 (8th Cir. 1998).

[68] *See generally*, Jennifer L. Mnookin, *The Image of Truth: Photographic Evidence and the Power of Analogy:* 10 YALE J. L. & HUMAN. 1 (1998).

photographs into evidence on this basis upon a showing that, in accord with Rule 901(b)(1), a witness with knowledge has testified that the picture "fairly and accurately" represents what the witness saw.

Example

[Witness has been identified and the photograph has been marked and shown to opposing counsel.]

Direct examiner: Where were you at 3:00 p.m. on November 1, 1997?

Witness: On the southeast corner of First Avenue and Maple.

Direct examiner: What happened while you were on the corner?

Witness: There was a collision between a Ford and a Chevrolet.

Direct examiner: I show you what has been marked the plaintiff's exhibit number one for identification. Do you recognize it?

Witness: Yes.

Direct examiner: What is it?

Witness: It is a picture of the intersection of First Avenue and Maple shortly after the collision.

Direct examiner: Does Plaintiff's exhibit number one fairly and accurately represent the scene at the intersection of First Avenue and Maple on November 1, 1997 as you saw it shortly following the collision between the Ford and the Chevrolet?

Witness: Yes it does.

Direct examiner: Are there any differences between Plaintiff's exhibit number one for identification and the scene at the intersection of First Avenue and Maple as you saw it immediately following the collision?

Witness: Only one that I can see.

Direct examiner: What is that difference?

Witness: The photograph includes a police car parked off to the side that was not there right after the collision. The police officer arrived about five minutes later.

Direct examiner: Other than the police car, is there anything different?

Witness: No.

Direct examiner: Your honor, I offer the picture of the intersection of First Avenue and Maple following the collision into evidence as Plaintiff's exhibit number one.

To bolster the photograph's persuasiveness, the lawyer might expand the examination about what the witness saw. If the witness saw the photographer take the picture, that, too, might be the subject of examination. Neither is necessary, however, to lay the foundation for the photograph.[69] The image produced, even if accurate, must be relevant and not misleading. If the photograph is taken long after the event in question, conditions may have changed too much for the photograph to be helpful.[70] Photographs and the purposes for which they are admitted are uniquely within the trial court's discretion, which will not be overturned unless there is an apparent abuse of discretion.[71]

The modern trend is to accept that photographs inevitably carry their own independent evidentiary value.[72] Many of the details in the photograph will not have been the subjects of the witness's testimony, but the photograph constitutes evidence of everything that it shows, based on judicial notice of the general reliability of the photographic process.[73] Accordingly, the trend is to admit photographs into evidence for whatever they show, as long as there is sufficient foundation,[74] which will vary with the purpose. Authentication is often demonstrated by showing a Rule 901(b)(9) process that produces accurate results.[75]

One of the most commonly recurring issues is the use of photographs to portray the actual conditions found at a crime scene. Aside from the foregoing authentication issues, there are often questions about the inflammatory quality of gruesome photographs. These questions are decided under Rule 403. Courts have been quite liberal in admitting revolting or repulsive pictures even when their probative value on disputed issues is

---

[69] United States v. Stephens, 202 F. Supp. 2d 1361 (N.D. Ga. 2002); Bryant v. State, 810 So. 2d 532 (Fla. Dist. Ct. App. 2002) (stating that witness qualifying photograph need not be photographer or have seen picture taken); Pless v. State, 545 S.E.2d 340 (Ga. Ct. App. 2001).

[70] *See, e.g.*, Truesdell v. Rite Aid of New York Inc., 644 N.Y.S.2d 428, 429 (N.Y. App. Div. 1996) (excluding photographs taken six weeks after plaintiff's fall for which there was no evidence in record to establish that condition at time of plaintiff's fall was substantially as shown in photographs).

[71] *See, e.g.*, ACTONet, Ltd. v. Allou Health & Beauty Care, 219 F.3d 836 (8th Cir. 2000); McCrary-El v. Shaw, 992 F.2d 809, 811, 813 (8th Cir. 1993); State v. Vang, 577 S.E.2d 225 (S.C. App. 2003).

[72] *See, e.g.*, United States v. Holmquist, 36 F.3d 154 (1st Cir. 1994); Bryant v. State, 810 So. 2d 532, 536 (Fla. Dist. Ct. App. 2002) ("Only if a picture is verified as a true representation of the subject about which testimony is offered, is it admissible in evidence.").

[73] United States v. Smith, 27 F. App'x 577 (6th Cir. 2001); United States v. Stephens, 202 F. Supp. 2d 1361 (N.D. Ga. 2002); United States v. Rembert, 863 F.2d 1023 (D.C. Cir. 1988); 1 CHARLES CALVIN SCOTT, PHOTOGRAPHIC EVIDENCE 351–52 (1969).

[74] *See, e.g.*, United States v. Patterson, 277 F.3d 709 (4th Cir. 2002); United States v. Tropeano, 252 F.3d 653 (2d Cir. 2001); United States v. Stearns, 550 F.2d 1167, 1171 (9th Cir. 1977).

[75] Various modern innovations have traveled the authentication trail from a detailed explanation of the entire technology to acceptance by the court by means of judicial notice of the reliability of the process. In discussing still photographs, one court described the journey that each of the photographic technologies has taken:

> When photographs first began finding their way into judicial trials they were viewed with suspicion and received with caution. It was not uncommon to place upon the offering party the burden of producing the negative as well as the photograph itself, and of proving that neither retouching nor other manual or chemical intervention was reflected in the proffered print. That burden has now shifted, and the proponent of a proffered photograph has established a prima facie case for its admissibility when he has shown it to be an accurate representation of the scene in question. The opposing party should then be afforded an opportunity for voir dire to show that the picture is not in fact an accurate representation.

United States v. Hobbs 403 F.2d 977, 978 (6th Cir. 1968).

meager,[76] but the Rule remains a vehicle by which the judge may exclude such evidence, irrespective of its authenticity.[77]

The idea of the "silent witness" first appeared in discussions about whether a photograph was merely illustrative or had independent evidentiary value.[78] Today, however, when most jurisdictions consider all photographs to have some independent evidentiary value,[79] the term "silent witness" is used for those photographs that have no witness to corroborate what is pictured. The picture with no witness has become common with the proliferation of security cameras in public and private spaces. Despite the absence of a witness at the scene or the inability of the proponent to locate such a witness, with the proper foundation pictures of intruders and robbers taken by these silent sentinels have been received in evidence, under the silent witness theory of authentication.[80] While there are myriad circumstances that might, in a particular case, authenticate a picture when no witness is present, a common approach is for the proponent to show the process by which the camera is activated, the scene is recorded, and the film is processed.

The courts' relatively recent comfort with the silent witness theory may be short lived. The risk of alteration of a picture has been considered acceptable because, among other things, alterations were fairly easy to detect. Detection is often impossible, however, if the alteration is done through digital technology. Whether the new world of digital creation and re-creation will also provide a kind of electronic fail-safe remains to be seen. In considering the possibility of federal guidelines related to various criminal-law issues raised by the burgeoning computer technology, The Computer Search and Seizure Working Group, made up of members of various federal agencies, hypothesized the following evidentiary horror story:

> Agents and prosecutors were shown a photograph of a body—twisted on the floor, a gaping wound in the chest. Across the room on the floor was a large

[76] *See, e.g.*, Government of V.I. v. Albert, 241 F.3d 344, 346 (3d Cir. 2001) (holding that "videotape of the crime scene which included a detailed look at [victim's] partially naked body tied to the bed with the neck wound revealed" was properly admitted despite its gruesome depiction); Taylor v. Lafler, 2003 WL 22284561, *5 (E.D. Mich. 2003) ("Petitioner has no right to the writ of habeas corpus on the basis of this claim, because the erroneous admission of gruesome photographs fails to state a constitutional claim."); Simmons v. State, 797 So. 2d 1134 (Ala. Ct. App. 1999) (holding that it was not error to admit pictures of the crime scene, including one showing pieces of victim's intestines in toilet); Newman v. State, 106 S.W.3d 438 (Ark. 2003) (holding that gruesome photos were properly admitted as more probative than prejudicial); Harris v. State, 843 So. 2d 856 (Fla. 2003) (ruling that photos of victim showing maggots around head wounds and short video of body at crime scene were properly admitted, even where they were admittedly gruesome and showed the body in a clear state of decomposition). *See generally* ANDRE A. MOENSSENS ET AL., SCIENTIFIC EVIDENCE IN CRIMINAL CASES § 2.14 (4th ed. 1995).

[77] *See, e.g.*, Spears v. Mullin, 343 F.3d 1215, 1227 (10th Cir. 2003) (determining that admission of photographs depicting numerous post-mortem stab wounds, large gash wounds, exposed intestines, swollen face and black eye rendered trial fundamentally unfair); United States *ex rel.* Gonzalez v. DeTella, 918 F. Supp. 1214 (N.D. Ill. 1996) (holding that close up photos of deceased was improperly admitted but admission not harmful error); Turben v. State, 726 N.E.2d 1245 (Ind. 2000) (stating that admission of autopsy photo was improper but harmless error.

[78] *See, e.g.*, United States v. Bynum, 567 F.2d 1167 (1st Cir. 1978); United States v. Goslee, 389 F. Supp. 490, 493 (W.D. Pa. 1975) ("Under the 'silent witness's theory, when an adequate foundation is provided to assure the accuracy of the process producing a photograph, the photograph can be admitted to speak for itself, even though no witness has vouched for its accuracy."); Fisher v. State, 643 S.W.2d 571 (Ark. Ct. App. 1982) (citing all the cases); Department of Pub. Safety & Corr. Servs. v. Cole, 672 A.2d 1115 (Md. 1996); United States v. Harris, 53 M.J. 514 (N.M. Ct. Crim. App. 2000).

[79] 3 WIGMORE ON EVIDENCE § 792 (James H. Chadbourn rev., 1972).

[80] *See, e.g.*, United States v. Harris, 55 M.J. 433 (C.A.A.F. 2001); Wagner v. State, 707 So. 2d 827 (Fla. Dist. Ct. App. 1998); 2 MCCORMICK ON EVIDENCE § 214 (John William Strong ed., 5th ed. 1999).

> pistol. On the white wall above the victim's body, scrawled in the victim's own blood, were the words, "I'll kill again. You'll never catch me."
>
> [T]his picture was not created with film, but with a digital camera. [L]aw enforcement agents, using commercially available software, started rearranging the digits. They "cleaned" the wall . . . closed the chest wound, choosing instead to have blood trickling from the victim's temple[, and] moved the gun into the victim's hand. The case was now solved: the report would claim, and the photograph would "prove," the victim committed suicide.[81]

Various Medical Imaging Machines

The authentication of x-rays, MRIs, and CAT scans is similar to the procedure developed in the silent witness approach to photographs, depending upon proof that the process produces an accurate result. This Rule 901(b)(9) method of authentication is similar, in many respects, to the showing required before admitting expert scientific opinion testimony.

X-rays have been in use for sufficient time to validate the Advisory Committee's assumption that courts may well take judicial notice of the accuracy of the x-ray process.[82] MRIs and CAT scans may also merit judicial notice of process accuracy. In a court taking judicial notice of the validity of the scientific process by which the device produces a picture of internal portions of the human body not visible to any witness, the foundation focuses on the normal operation of the process and of the proper matching of picture to person. Many hospitals use a lead identification number with each x-ray assembly, making each x-ray picture a separately identifiable item.

The normal foundation, absent stipulation or statutory shortcut involves the testimony of a qualified x-ray technician who can testify:

1. that particular parts of a particular person's body were x-rayed at a particular time,

---

[81] U.S. Dep't of Justice, *Federal Guidelines for Searching and Seizing Computers*, 56 CRIM. L. REP. (BNA) 2023, 2053 (1994). *See* United States v. Harris, 53 M.J. 514, 519 (N.M. Ct. Crim. App. 2000) ("Courts have traditionally taken a strict view towards the admissibility of recordings, recognizing that tapes could be tampered with or distorted. Under the traditional approach, the proponent of the tape was required to account for the custody of the tape. However, with the development of technological means to detect whether a tape has been altered, the foundational standards have been relaxed. If the integrity of the tape is challenged, an expert witness can be called upon to examine the tape. Furthermore, protection against falsification or misrepresentation lies in the requirement of preliminary proof that the picture is an accurate reproduction of the event which it depicts and in the opportunity for cross examination of the witness making such proof."); Bryant v. State, 810 So. 2d 532, 536 (Fla. Dist. Ct. App. 2002) ("If no witness who is available has seen what videotape or a photograph depicts, proof of surrounding circumstances may nevertheless be sufficient for the court to find that the photograph is a fair and accurate representation of a material fact. This approach reflects resort to the so-called 'silent witness's theory which entails proof of foundational facts establishing the reliability of the process that yielded the photographic images, taking into account the following factors: (1) evidence establishing the time and date of the photographic evidence; (2) any evidence of editing or tampering; (3) the operating condition and capability of the equipment producing the photographic evidence as it relates to the accuracy and reliability of the photographic product; (4) the procedure employed as it relates to the preparation, testing, operation, and security of the equipment used to produce the photographic product, including the security of the product itself; and (5) testimony identifying the relevant participants depicted in the photographic evidence.").

[82] The advisory committee note to Rule 901(b)(9) lists the x-ray as a "familiar instance" and states specifically that example 9 "does not foreclose taking judicial notice of the accuracy of the process or system." In addition, some states have passed statutes and rules providing for the easy admission of properly identified x-rays. *See, e.g.*, N.Y. C.P.L.R. 4532–a.

2. that well-maintained and working x-ray equipment was used, and
3. that the operator used the proper procedures in identifying and taking the x-ray.

In addition, the witness should testify to the process for handling and storing the x-ray in the hospital.

Motion Pictures and Videotape

Nothing about authentication of film or videotape differs analytically from still photographs. Because initially the technology was not as familiar, however, courts treated film and videotape differently for many years, requiring more elaborate foundations that described in detail the qualifications of the camera operator and the detail of the film process.[83] Most modern courts accept motion pictures and videotape on a lesser showing.[84] The authentication problems that arise from the introduction of film or videotape are related more to the subject matter than to the technical process. When a tape or film purports to show conditions as they existed at the time of an accident or crime, then, of course, an objection can be interposed that conditions may have changed between the event and the recording.[85]

One of the common uses of videotape is the video diary of the "day in the life" of a personal injury plaintiff. It shows the pain and difficulties the plaintiff suffers as a result of the injury by focusing on the difficulty of things as mundane as moving around the home, performing daily tasks, and interacting with other members of the household. In theory, authentication should not be particularly difficult. The plaintiff, the plaintiff's family, or the filmmaker are all potential witnesses to testify that the film "fairly and accurately represents" an average day in the plaintiff's life. Some courts, however, have taken a very restrictive approach to admission of day-in-the-life films.

In *Bolstridge v. Central Maine Power Co.*,[86] the defendant claimed that the plaintiff's film was unrealistic and slanted. According to the defendant, the film unfairly depicted experiences that the plaintiff would only perform very rarely, such as ordering a wheelchair, and emphasized difficulties instead of giving a true slice of a day's

---

[83] *See, e.g.*, United States v. Gross, 917 F.2d 23 (4th Cir. 1990) (holding that adequate foundation was laid where Agent testified that he had reviewed tape and that it fairly and accurately depicted events he had described); United States v. Roach, 28 F.3d 729, 733 (8th Cir. 1994) ("[There are] seven foundational guidelines for the admission of electronic tape recordings, these guidelines consisting of a showing by the government that: (1) the recording device was capable of recording the events offered in evidence; (2) the operator was competent to operate the device; (3) the recording is authentic and correct; (4) changes, additions, or deletions have not been made in the recording; (5) the recording has been preserved in a manner that is shown to the court; (6) the speakers on the tape are identified; and (7) the conversation elicited was made voluntarily and in good faith, without any kind of inducement [to counter a claim of entrapment].").

[84] *See, e.g.*, Jones v. Los Angeles, 24 Cal.Rptr.2d 528 (Cal. Ct. App. 1993); (holding that authentication standard applicable to photographs is also applicable to motion pictures, film or videotape); Carter v. State, 1995 WL 755918, *1 (Tex. App. 1995) ("The predicate for motion pictures is the same as that for still photographs. Like still photographs, motion pictures may be admitted into evidence where they are properly authenticated, relevant to the issues, and not violative of the rules established for the admissibility of photographs.").

[85] *See, e.g.*, People v. Mayfield, 928 P.2d 485 (Cal. 1997) (holding that videotape was properly admitted, even though it was taken during day and 18 months following crime where lighting and date of recording were irrelevant to show position of fences and walls, which had not changed); State v. Wilson, 637 A.2d 1237 (N.J. 1994).

[86] 621 F. Supp. 1202 (D. Me. 1985).

activities.[87] Without making a specific finding that the film was slanted, the court excluded the film. It said the plaintiff could depict the same difficulties in the courtroom and that physicians and relatives could testify about her handicap. The court expressed concern about the dangers of slanted presentation and the impossibility of cross-examining a videotape. A day-in-the-life film, in the court's view, should be admitted only when the plaintiff could give a specific reason why in-court testimony would not be sufficient to convey the information, and such a showing had not been made in the case before it.[88]

Bannister v. Town of Noble[89] exemplifies those courts that admit day in the life films.[90] Recognizing the benefits as well as the dangers of such evidence, the court noted that the tape, better than words, could illustrate the injury's impact.[91] The trial judge viewed the film before it was shown to the jury and was persuaded the film fairly represented the impact of the injury on the plaintiff's day-to-day activities. The film did not exaggerate the plaintiff's difficulties or include heart-wrenching staged episodes. Moreover, the film's participants were present and available for cross-examination about the accuracy of the film.

In jurisdictions that admit the day-in-the-life film, the objecting party cannot merely assert that in-court testimony would be adequate to depict injuries. Instead, counsel should be prepared to show, with as much specificity as possible, the problems with the film, such as atypicality, exaggeration of difficulties, undue appeals to sympathy, or misleading editing such as reaction shots, especially those not filmed simultaneously with the rest of the film. Defects of this nature can support a Rule 403 objection that the film is prejudicial, misleading, or a waste of time.[92] As a tactical matter, defense counsel may ask to be present at plaintiff's filming of a-day-in-the-life film. If the court grants a formal request, counsel will be in a better position to know if

[87] *Id.* at 1203 & n.1.

[88] *Id.* at 1204.

[89] 812 F.2d 1265 (10th Cir. 1987).

[90] *See, e.g.*, Regalado v. Chicago, 1998 WL 919712 (N.D. Ill. 1998) (noting that case law does not categorically bar a-day-in-the-life videos without a showing of unfair prejudice); Burke v. 12 Rothschild's Liquor Mart, Inc., 568 N.E.2d 80, 84 (Ill. App. 1991) (holding that it was not error to admit day-in-the-life film despite opposing counsel's lack of advance notice and opportunity to be present at filming as long as probative value of film outweighs potential prejudice and there are no demonstrated improprieties in content or production); Wagner v. York Hosp., 608 A.2d 496, 499–501 (Pa. Super. 1992) (holding that day-in-the-life film was properly admitted over objection that it inaccurately depicted reflexive sounds and movements as voluntary and conscious, and holding that video was not misleading despite victim's consciousness of surroundings was disputed); Eckman v. Moore, 2003 WL 22411078 (Miss. 2003); Wal-Mart Stores, Inc. v. Hoke, 2001 WL 931658 (Tex. App. 2001).

[91] *Bannister*, 812 F.2d at 1269.

[92] *See* Cisarik v. Palos Cmty. Hosp., 579 N.E.2d 873, 874–75 (Ill. 1991) ("Because a 'Day-in-the-Life' film is a form of motion picture it is admissible evidence on the same basis as photographs. Consequently, before a 'day-in-the-life' film can become evidence at trial it must first pass a two-prong test. First, someone having personal knowledge of the filmed object must lay a foundation that the film is an accurate portrayal of what it purports to show. Second, the film is only admissible if its probative value is not substantially outweighed by the danger of unfair prejudice. . . . We believe that opposing counsel has no right to intrude into the production of this demonstrative evidence."); Hahn v. Tri-Line Farmers Co-op, 478 N.W.2d 515, 524–25 (Minn. Ct. App. 1991) (holding that under Minn. R. Evid. 403, it was not error to admit film segments in which paraplegic withdraws small amount of money from bank and bends over to pick up newspaper from floor, over objection that segment prejudicially suggested financial hardship and was cumulative and inflammatory; even though injured party, his family, doctors, and vocational experts testified about his rehabilitation). *See generally* Joseph M. Herlihy, *Beyond Words: The Evidentiary Status of "Day in the Life" Films*, 66 B.U. L. REV. 133, 136–41 (1986) (addressing common objections to "day-in-the-life" films based on unfair prejudice and cumulative evidence).

something was left out of the final edited film, redone, or was in some other way at variance with the experience of the day. Even if the court denies a formal request to observe,[93] counsel may be able to argue the unfairness of the process to the jury. Correspondingly, if the plaintiff has a strong case on damages, the plaintiff may want to invite defense counsel to be present at the filming, either to promote settlement or to demonstrate fairness to the tribunal. Any day-in-the-life film that has a voiceover narration or other verbal component is potentially subject to a hearsay objection, on grounds that the film contains statements by an out-of-court declarant offered to prove the truth of what they assert. Moreover, if the film depicts assertive conduct that is the equivalent of a statement by the plaintiff about the nature of a disability, then the defense can interpose a hearsay objection.[94]

Sound Recordings

Authentication of sound recordings, like that of silent witness photographs and videotapes, is, in significant part, about proof of process in the fashion of Rule 901(b)(9).[95] Because of concerns about tampering, courts have developed a relatively demanding list of requirements for authenticating sound recordings. In 1974, the Eighth Circuit, for example, specified that the proponent must show that: (1) the recording device was capable of taking the conversation offered into evidence; (2) the operator of the device was competent to operate the device; (3) the recording is "authentic and correct"; (4) changes, additions, or deletions have not been made; (5) the recording has been preserved in a manner that is shown to the court; (6) the speakers are identified; and (7) the conversation elicited was made voluntarily and in good faith, without any kind of inducement.[96] Depending on how the tape is used, not all of these foundational elements will be germane in every case, and more recent decisions display a willingness to relax the showing accordingly.[97] Nevertheless, courts remain sensitive to the possibility of tampering.[98]

Authentication of sound recordings always includes identifying the participant voices. Rules 901(b)(5) and (6) provide standard means of doing so. Rule 901(b)(5), for example, states that one method of satisfying "the requirement of authenticating or identifying an item of evidence" is:

---

93 Cisarik v. Palos Cmty. Hosp., 579 N.E.2d 873, 874–75 (Ill. 1991) (reversing protective order that would have allowed opposing counsel to be present during day-in-the-life film, to have edited-out footage, and to have copy of completed film). *See* Southern Scrap Material Co. v. Fleming, 2003 WL 22415995 (E.D. La. 2003) (considering surveillance video of plaintiff taken to discredit plaintiff's version of her injuries as work product); Martin v. Intex Recreational Corp., 1994 WL 665742 (D. Kan. 1994) (stating that video made of expert's reenactment was not work product but discoverable expert opinion).

94 *See, e.g.*, People v. Taylor, 732 N.E.2d 120 (Ill. App. Ct. 2000) (ruling that conduct observed on videotape was not hearsay); Marino v. State, 934 P.2d 1321 (Alaska Ct. App. 1997) (ruling that part of videotape of defendant's interview with police was admitted over hearsay objections as non-assertive conduct but defendant was barred from using those portions where defendant protests his innocence because the "verbal conduct" was assertive).

95 Admissibility of sound recordings, like that of documents, is often as much about the best evidence rule, as it is about authentication. *See* **§ 13.01**.

96 United States v. McMillan, 508 F.2d 101, 104 (8th Cir. 1974), *cert. denied*, 421 U.S. 916 (1975).

97 *See, e.g.*, United States v. Buchanan, 70 F.3d 818 (5th Cir. 1995).

98 *See, e.g.*, McAlinney v. Marion Merrell Dow, Inc., 992 F.2d 839 (8th Cir. 1993) (affirming trial court's decision to reject plaintiff's tapes in part because of plaintiff's admitted editing of the tapes).

> An opinion identifying a person's voice—whether heard firsthand or through mechanical or electronic transmission or recording—based on hearing the voice at any time under circumstances that connect it with the alleged speaker.

No extensive familiarity with the person's voice is required, and that familiarity can even be acquired in anticipation of litigation.[99]

A witness who has not previously heard a person's voice nevertheless may sometimes authenticate a recorded telephone conversation with that person. Rule 901(b)(6) provides for authentication of a telephone call by evidence that "a call was made to the number assigned . . . to a particular person" and "circumstances, including self-identification, show the person answering to be the one called." In the case of a business, a call placed to a number assigned to the business can be authenticated, if the conversation "related to business reasonably transacted over the telephone." Although there is no similar authentication illustration for incoming calls, because of the ease of fabrication on the part of the caller, the advent of "Caller ID" may call for a different result.

References to other events or conversations that identify the speaker are common circumstantial methods of identifying a voice sufficiently to authenticate a conversation. Although experts differ on the validity of voiceprints, some courts have ruled that sound spectrography may be used to identify unidentified voices in conversations.[100]

Sound recordings are often used to prosecute organized crime cases, in which wiretaps and bugs are de rigueur. A tape recording may occasionally be authenticated by someone hearing the conversation and testifying that the recording is an accurate rendition,[101] but often the recording is the result of surreptitious recording to which there is no willing witness. When the "silent witness" approach is required, someone must provide the Rule 901(b)(9) testimony about the process that produces an accurate result, in the same fashion as is required for videotape from a surveillance camera. Once again,

---

[99] *See, e.g.*, United States v. Norman, 415 F.3d 466, 473 (5th Cir. 2005) (affirming identification of defendant's voice by DEA agent base on familiarity acquired during one hour interview of defendant); State v. Hill, 630 N.W.2d 276 (Wis. Ct. App. 2001) (concluding that person who has heard only once, and at any time, the voice on a tape may authenticate it for purposes of admissibility).

[100] *See, e.g.*, United States v. Drones, 218 F.3d 496 (5th Cir. 2000) (voiceprints under *Daubert* and pre-*Daubert*). *See generally* PAUL C. GIANNELLI, EDWARD J. IMWINKELRIED, ANDREA ROTH, & JANE CAMPBELL MORIARTY, SCIENTIFIC EVIDENCE § 10.06 (5th ed. 2012).

[101] *See, e.g.*, United States v. Polk, 56 F.3d 613 (5th Cir. 1995) (determining that officer who wired informant and recorded conversation while simultaneously watching defendant and informant speaking properly authenticated the tape and the voices on it); State v. Anderson, 119 Wash. App. 1051 (Wash. Ct. App. 2003) (permitting informant equipped with recording device who witnessed actual conversation to testify to identity of person on tape).

evidence must support the identification of the speakers.[102] A "trace" performed by a telephone company can identify the phone from which a call is made.[103]

§ 12.07 Documents

Documents are the most common trial exhibits. As with all tangible evidence, the required foundation for a document depends on the purpose for which it is offered. Sometimes a document is offered as real evidence—for example, a contract between the parties. Sometimes it is offered as illustrative tangible evidence—for example, a chart or a list of items explained by a witness. And sometimes it is offered as recorded evidence—for example, the transcript of a deposition. The general foundation requirements for such uses described in previous sections apply to documents as well. Most documents are unusual as tangible items of evidence in that they purport to have a source, an author. Usually, the accuracy of this purported authorship or source is important in the case. To be sure, it might not matter, for example, whether the purported authorship is true if the proponent simply wants to show that someone who received a document was aware of its contents.[104] But if the proponent endorses the document's purported authorship or source, that requires an additional element of foundation, traditionally called authentication. This section focuses on this additional foundational element.[105]

A document's appearance, contents, substance, internal patterns, or other distinctive characteristics, considered together with circumstances, can provide sufficient evidence to permit a finding that it is authentic (Rule 901(b)(4)).[106] However, testimony of a person with firsthand knowledge that the document is what it purports to be (Rule 901(b)(1)) or of someone who can identify handwriting (Rule 901(b)(2) & (3)) is the common method for authenticating documents.

---

[102] *See, e.g.*, United States v. Tropeano, 252 F.3d 653, 661 (2d Cir. 2001) ("The government is not required to call as a witness a participant in a recorded conversation in order to authenticate the recording; it may lay the foundation for the recording through the testimony of the technician who actually made it."); United States v. Stephens, 202 F. Supp. 2d 1361, 1367 (N.D. Ga. 2002) ("To determine whether the proponent of electronic surveillance evidence has introduced evidence of its genuineness sufficient to support a finding of authenticity by the jury, within the meaning of Fed. R. Evid. 901(a) and Fed. R. Evid. 104(b), the United States Court of Appeals for the Eleventh Circuit adopts a flexible inquiry. The standard requires the proponent to show, in a criminal case: (1) the competency of the operator of the recording equipment; (2) the fidelity of the recording equipment; (3) the absence of material deletions, additions, or alterations in the relevant part of the tape; and (4) the identification of the relevant speakers."). *See also* EDWARD J. IMWINKELRIED, EVIDENTIARY FOUNDATIONS § 4.05[4] (7th ed., rev. 2008).

[103] *See* Application of U.S. for Order Authorizing Installation of Pen Register, 610 F.2d 1148 (3d Cir. 1979) (discussing court's authority to order phone company to trace calls to a particular phone).

[104] An example that appears in many reported cases is the reliance of an adverse possessor on a document that, while possibly invalid in creating good title in the possessor, nonetheless is sufficient to give the possessor "color of title" sufficient to support adverse possession. 7 WIGMORE ON EVIDENCE § 2132 at 715 (Chadbourn rev. 1978). It is in this context that one must understand statements like the following, still to be found quoted in legal opinions: "When the execution of a document is *not in issue*, but *only the contents* or the fact of the existence of the document of such a tenor, no authentication is necessary." *Id.* at 714 (emphasis in original). Wigmore did not mean by this that no foundation was necessary for such a document.

[105] When authorship matters, the contents of the document will typically matter as well, and this will bring the original recording rule into play. *See* **§ 13.01**. Often, though not always, the importance of the contents may involve the proponent's use of the document to prove that an assertion made by the author in the document is true, and this may bring the hearsay rule into play. *See* **§ 14.05**. Of course, the contents might include matter that would implicate virtually any of the admissibility rules discussed in this text, but the original recording rule and the hearsay rule are the two most commonly encountered.

[106] United States v. Grimmer, 199 F.3d 1324 (2d Cir. 1999) ("Authenticity of a document may be inferred from circumstantial evidence."); United States v. Paulino, 13 F.3d 20, 23 (1st Cir. 1994).

Example

[Witness has been identified and the document has been marked and shown to opposing counsel.]

Direct examiner: I am handing you what has been marked as Plaintiff's exhibit number two. Do you recognize it?

Witness: Yes.

Direct examiner: What is it?

Witness: A letter.

Direct examiner: Have you seen Plaintiff's exhibit number two before?

Witness: Yes.

Direct examiner: Please describe the circumstances.

Witness: I was at Mr. Writer's office about a week ago when he was sending out a series of letters to potential investors. He handed me the pile so that I could see who it was that he hoped would invest in the enterprise.

Direct examiner: Do you recognize Plaintiff's exhibit number two?

Witness: Yes.

Direct examiner: How do you recognize it?

Witness: Well, I went through the letters to check the list and the amounts that the various potential investors were asked for. I remember this letter by the name of the person to whom it was sent and the suggested investment amount.

Direct examiner: Your honor, I offer Plaintiff's exhibit number two for identification into evidence as Plaintiff's exhibit number two.

Example

[Witness has been identified and the document has been marked and shown to opposing counsel.]

Direct examiner: I'm handing you what has been marked as Plaintiff's exhibit number two. Do you recognize it?

Witness: Yes.

Direct examiner: What is it?

Witness: A letter I received on November 5th of this year.

Direct examiner: Is it signed?

Witness: Yes.

Direct examiner: Do you recognize the signature?

Witness: Yes, I do.

Direct examiner: How do you recognize it?

Witness: It is a signature that I have seen many times on letters and occasionally on a check.

Direct examiner: Who signed Plaintiff's exhibit number two for identification?

Witness: Walter Writer.

Direct examiner: Your honor, I offer the letter from Walter Writer to Willie Witness into evidence as Plaintiff's exhibit number two.

Rule 901(b)(3) contemplates authentication of a writing by either expert or juror handwriting comparison of the document in question to a known, authenticated exemplar. Courts have allowed this kind of expert authentication, despite the growing concern that forensic document examination may not be scientifically valid.[107] If the trial judge believes that the handwriting on a document in question is sufficiently similar to the handwriting on a known exemplar so that a reasonable jury could find them to be written by the same person, the judge may admit the document and leave it to the jurors to decide its authenticity.[108]

Documents can be authenticated by circumstantial evidence. For example, the content of a reply can authenticate the source of a letter. The Advisory Committee note to Rule 901(b)(4) incorporates the common-law reply letter doctrine. If one party sends a letter to another, and then receives a letter purporting to be from that person with contents suggesting it is in reply to the first letter, evidence of that is sufficient to authenticate the second letter.[109] Alternatively, the reference in Rule 901(b)(4) to "appearance, content, substance, internal patterns, and other distinctive characteristics" has been understood to embrace analysis of linguistic idiosyncrasies, distinctive vocabulary, average sentence and word length, and so forth.[110]

Rule 901(b)(8), the federal version of the so-called "ancient documents rule," allows that the requirement of authentication can be met by evidence that the document "(A) is in a condition that creates no suspicion about its authenticity; (B) was in a place where, if authentic, it would likely be; and (C) is at least 20 years old when offered."[111] (The common-law period had been 30 years.[112]) The idea is that something meeting condition (B) is likely to be revealed as inauthentic within 20 years. Condition (A) addresses the possibility that there is some indication that a want of authenticity was discovered. These factors, combined with the unavoidability of relying on old records that cannot be authenticated by persons from current memory, warrant receiving the document and leaving challenges to its authenticity to the fact-finder to resolve.[113]

The increasing popularity of email as a common method of communication creates potential authentication problems that have long been resolved for mail that is signed and sent via post. Of course, authenticating that a message is the one received is not difficult when the recipient is available to testify to that effect. The more difficult problem, as with snail mail, is identifying the sender or authenticating that a purported

---

[107] *See* **§ 10.08**.

[108] *See, e.g.*, United States v. Wylie, 919 F.2d 969, 978 (5th Cir. 1990).

[109] United States v. Weinstein, 762 F.2d 1522, 1533 (11th Cir. 1985); FED. R. EVID. 901 advisory committee note.

[110] *See* CHRISTOPHER B. MUELLER & LAIRD C. KIRKPATRICK, FEDERAL EVIDENCE § 9:12 (4th ed. 2013).

[111] The provision has been important, for example, in denaturalization proceedings of persons suspected of having worked with the Nazis during the World War II era. *See, e.g.*, United States v. Stelmokas, 100 F.3d 302 (3d Cir. 1996), *cert. denied,* 520 U.S. 1241 (1997); United States v. Demjanjuk, 367 F.3d 623, 631–32 (6th Cir. 2004).

[112] *See* 7 WIGMORE ON EVIDENCE § 2138 (Chadbourn rev. 1978).

[113] The rule works in coordination with the hearsay exception for ancient documents. *See* **§ 16.13**.

sender is the real sender, when that matters in the litigation.[114] Authentication by circumstantial evidence, such as the reply letter, the content of the message that is unlikely to be known except by a particular person or that uses idiosyncratic linguistic style, or action consistent with the message, suffices in most cases, and in other cases it may suffice to be able to identify the sending device with the claimed or purported sender, using the coded Internet Protocol Address.[115] But there may be instances in which the potential of computers and the Internet to mask identity create unique authentication problems. Cryptography, digital signatures, and other electronic identifying equivalents to the written signature will help to eliminate some of those problems.[116]

Webpages can be important items of evidence. Although governmental websites are probably self-authenticating under Rule 902(5),[117] private websites so far have not been held to fall within the corresponding Rule 902(7) (affixed trade inscriptions) in the list of self-authenticating documents (see below) and so must be authenticated.[118] Likewise, posts to social media can be used in a variety of ways. In some contexts, the content of the post may be recorded evidence regarding earlier events at issue in the trial.[119] In other contexts, posts through social media may constitute real evidence, for example, constituting the means of soliciting illegal acts.[120] In all such cases, either identification or authentication of source, or both, may be disputed and require foundational evidence.

Self-Authenticating Documents [Rule 902]

Rule 902 provides relatively simple and straightforward methods for authenticating various official, public, or acknowledged documents, newspapers, trade inscriptions, commercial paper, and certified business records. It expands and liberalizes the idea of self-authentication, especially regarding business documents.

The exemption from the authentication requirement refers only to authenticity of the source or authorship of the document that appears on it. Thus, a plaintiff who claims injury by using or consuming a product labeled as coming from the X Co. need not show that the X Co. really produced the product as a condition of admitting it in evidence (Rule

---

[114] *See* Devbrow v. Gallegos, 735 F.3d 584, 586–87 (7th Cir. 2013) (excluding email for want of authentication).

[115] *See* Clement v. California Dept. of Corrections, 220 F. Supp. 2d 1098, 1111 (N.D. Cal. 2002), *aff'd*, 364 F.3d 1148 (9th Cir. 2004) (noting that recipient can identify the sender by contacting the service provider).

[116] *See* PAUL R. RICE, ELECTRONIC EVIDENCE 386–91 (2d ed. 2008).

[117] *See, e.g.*, Elliott Assocs., L.P. v. Banco de la Nacion, 194 F.R.D. 116, 121 (S.D.N.Y. 2000) (using interest rates published on Federal Reserve Board's website).

[118] *See, e.g.*, Fraserside IP LLC v. Netvertising Ltd., 902 F. Supp. 2d 1165, 1179 n.2 (N.D. Iowa 2012). *See also* Victaulic Co. v. Tieman, 499 F.3d 227, 236 (3d Cir. 2007) ("it is premature to assume that a webpage is owned by a company merely because its trade name appears in the uniform resource locator."). *Cf.* United States v. Hassan, 742 F.3d 104, 132–34 (4th Cir. 2014) (admitting Facebook pages and YouTube videos as self-authenticating under Rule 902(11) when accompanied by necessary certifications). Of course, information appearing in "chat rooms" is not necessarily attributable to the company that supports the website. *See* EDWARD J. IMWINKELRIED, EVIDENTIARY FOUNDATIONS § 4.03[6] (9th ed. 2015).

[119] *See, e.g.*, Lamb v. State, 246 So.3d 400, 404–10 (Fla. Dist. Ct. App. 2018) (admitting a defendant's Facebook post of a video showing defendants' possession of stolen goods); People v. Goldman, 159 N.E.3d 772, 781–82 (N.Y. 2020) (admitting YouTube video in which of defendant rapping about motive for homicide).

[120] *Compare* United States v. Browne, 834 F.3d 403 (3d Cir. 2016) (admitting a defendant's Facebook messages to prove allegation of child pornography and sexual offenses against minors), *with* United States v. Vayner, 769 F.3d 125 2d Cir. 2014) (holding that trial court abused discretion in admitting profile of owner of social media identifying it as that of defendant in the absence of further evidence connecting the webpage to the defendant).

902(7)), but the plaintiff still must provide the foundation identifying the product as the one he used or consumed.

The advisory committee elaborated on this point in connection with two self-authentication provisions added to the Federal Rules of Evidence in 2017, addressing the increasing use of digitally recorded information.[121] Fed. R. Evid. 902(13) provides that "no extrinsic evidence of authenticity" is required for "a record generated by an electronic process or system that produces an accurate result, as shown by a certification of a qualified person that complies with the certification requirements of Rule 902(11) or (12)."[122] The advisory committee note explains that the new rules permit a certification in place of live testimony for printouts of spreadsheets or webpages, but eliminating the requirement of extrinsic evidence only applies to showing the immediate source of the printout. For example, for a printout of a spreadsheet stored on the hard drive of a computer, the certification avoids the need to have a witness testify that the printout accurately reflects an electronic document that was stored on that particular computer.[123] Any question about the authenticity of the spreadsheet itself—for example, whether it actually is a spreadsheet associated with the company whose name appears at the top of the page—is a separate authentication issue not covered by this self-authentication rule. Similarly, if the proponent claims that it relied on this spreadsheet in making some decision relevant in the case, the spreadsheet would still have to be identified as the one on which the proponent relied, and this will require a testimonial foundation.

Although the exact procedural effect of "self-authentication" is difficult to discern, it is clear that the judge decides whether a document is self-authenticating under the standards of Rule 104(a), not 104(b), and, in this respect, Rule 902 differs significantly from Rule 901. But once the trial court determines to accept the document as self-authenticating, what then? The drafters indicated that the opponent is not foreclosed from challenging authenticity before the fact-finder.[124] But if the matter is thus contested, it is unclear and unresolved what, if anything, the court should instruct the jury about the matter.[125]

The Attesting Witness Rule [Rule 903]

At common law, one way of assuring genuine authorship was to have attesting witnesses sign the document. The primary purpose of such attestation, as well as various statutes requiring such attestation for certain documents (such as wills), was to provide a readily identifiable list of persons to call as witnesses in the event of dispute, including litigation involving the document. But common-law courts took this a step further and developed a rule, applicable to any such attested document, making the use of such witnesses mandatory, not simply optional. That rule required that in order to authenticate the execution of such a document, the proponent must present an attesting

---

121 *See* FED. R. EVID. 902(13) & FED. R. EVID. 902(14).

122 FED. R. EVID. 902(13).

123 *See* FED. R. EVID. 902(13) advisory committee note ("the authentication establishes only that the output came from the computer").

124 FED. R. EVID. 902 advisory committee note ("In no instance is the opposite party foreclosed from disputing authenticity.").

125 *See* CHRISTOPHER B. MUELLER & LAIRD C. KIRKPATRICK, FEDERAL EVIDENCE § 9:29 (4th ed. 2013).

witness to testify to the execution or else show that (all) attesting witnesses are unavailable.[126] The attesters became, in other words, preferred witnesses.

Voluntary attestation is rarely used today, although many states require attestation in certain instances, such as wills. (Documents acknowledged by a notary public are self-authenticating under Rule 902(8).) The inconvenience involved in locating and calling attesters is thought to outweigh any advantage in doing so, and Rule 903 abolishes the common-law preferential principle. The only exception, which will rarely occur in federal courts, is when the law of the jurisdiction that governs validity of the document (such as a will governed by state law) requires authentication by calling these state-mandated attesting witnesses.

§ 12.08 Demonstrations, Reenactments, and Experiments

A common form of tangible evidence in civil cases involves presenting an injured body to the fact-finder.[127] The court has discretion to deny such a demonstration if it would be too inflammatory or indecent, especially if the evidence is cumulative.[128] However, courts are sensitive to the possibility that "the very hideousness of the deformity was a part of the suffering of the victim" relevant in the assessment of damages.[129] Obviously, such evidence cannot become an exhibit that can be marked for identification or entered in the record. But a photograph of the injury could be, and it is better practice to do so in order to make a record for appellate review. Like photographs, a display might be understood as purely illustrative of testimony, but inevitably additional information is conveyed that cannot be captured fully by testimony. Such display evidence occurs in criminal cases as well.[130] Criminal defendants can be required to participate in displays for identification purposes.[131]

Beyond simple display, parties may present the reenactment of events by participating witnesses. Although there may be greater risks of misrepresentation with reenactments than with simple displays, reenactments are generally permitted to illustrate testimony.[132] As with other illustrative tangible evidence, the primary foundation is testimony that the reenactment fairly represents the events described. Because reenactments can become complicated, they are often presented as video-taped versions.[133] This has the advantage of generating an exhibit that can become part of the

---

[126] *See* 4 WIGMORE ON EVIDENCE §§ 1289 et. seq. (Chadbourn rev. 1972).

[127] *See, e.g.*, Olson v. Tyner, 257 N.W. 538, 541 (Iowa 1934) (displaying injured arm); Beal v. Southern Union Gas Co., 349 P.2d 337 (N.M. 1960) (displaying burn wounds).

[128] *See, e.g.*, Hillmon v. Funderburk, 504 A.2d 596, 599 (D.C. 1986) (holding that trial court should have allowed plaintiff's display of injured breast); Bates v. Newman, 264 P.2d 197, 201 (Cal. App. 1953) (concerning display of inability to maintain erection).

[129] Slattery v. Marra Bros., 186 F.2d 134, 138 (2d Cir. 1951).

[130] *See, e.g.*, United States v. Bay, 762 F.2d 1314, 1315 (9th Cir. 1984) (finding error in refusal to allow defendant to display tattooed hands, even though defendant chose not to testify); Simpson v. Portuondo, 2002 WL 31045862, *20–22 (S.D.N.Y. 2002) (holding no error in display of victim's injuries as evidence of intent to kill).

[131] *See, e.g.*, United States v. Emanuele, 51 F.3d 1123, 1133 (3d Cir. 1995) (holding that defendant may be required to make simple alterations in appearance in order to facilitate comparison by jury).

[132] *See, e.g.*, Jones v. Rolls, 187 F.3d 848 (8th Cir. 1999) (reenactment of alleged injury causing act by policeman).

[133] *See, e.g.*, Gregg v. Weeks Marine, Inc., 2000 WL 798493 (E.D. La. 2000) ("Video reenactments may be properly admitted only if they were filmed under conditions substantially similar to those of the actual accident. The conditions do not have to be identical but should be nearly the same in substantial particulars as to afford a fair comparison in respect to the particular issue to which the test is directed. The purpose behind the substantially similar requirement is to avoid the risk of misleading members of the jury who may attach

record on appeal. At the same time, when the tape or film reenacts a crime or accident, opponents of the evidence question whether the reenactment is slanted, misleading, or prejudicial.[134] Opponents may interpose hearsay objections, arguing that the reenactment is an assertion by an out-of-court declarant about how something happened, offered to show the truth of the assertion.[135] Narration accompanying the reenactment may also be the legitimate target of a hearsay objection, and the objecting party may succeed at least in having the tape or film played without its narrative.

A courtroom experiment goes beyond a reenactment because it does more than merely illustrate the testimony of a percipient witness. As one text puts it:

> There is no formal distinction between an in-court demonstration and in in-court experiment, although it might be said that a demonstration becomes an experiment when the witness, particularly an expert witness, attempts to reenact some aspect of an event in order to show a specific result that is at issue in the trial.[136]

Experiments are conducted in court for many purposes, including "to demonstrate scientific principles, to test litigation theories, to measure human, animal, or product capabilities, or to recreate events at issue."[137] Unless the experiment is used to illustrate a general scientific principle, the necessary foundation usually involves showing substantial similarity of conditions between the experiment and the event being litigated. In some contexts, this can be difficult to achieve in the courtroom,[138] necessitating out-of-court experimentation under appropriately controlled conditions,

---

exaggerated significance to the evidence.") (internal citations and quotations omitted); United States v. Beeler, 62 F. Supp. 2d 136 (D. Me. 1999) (admitting time lapse video over objection); State v. Terry, 719 N.E.2d 1046 (Ohio Ct. App. 1998).

[134] *See, e.g.*, Harris v. State, 13 P.3d 489, 495–96 (Okla. Crim. App. 2000) ("In order for a video or computer crime scene reenactment to be seen by a jury, as an aid to illustrate an experts witness's testimony, the court should require (1) that it be authenticated—the trial court should determine that it is a correct representation of the object portrayed, or that it is a fair and accurate representation of the evidence to which it relates, (2) that it is relevant, and (3) that its probative value is not 'substantially outweighed by the danger of unfair prejudice, confusion of the issues, misleading the jury, undue delay, needless presentation of cumulative evidence, or unfair and harmful surprise.'; "[t]he court should give an instruction, contemporaneous with the time the video reenactment evidence is presented, that the exhibition represents only a re-creation of the proponent's version of the event; that it should in no way be viewed as an actual recreation of the crime, and like all evidence, it may be accepted or rejected in whole or in part. The court must also ensure that the other party has prior opportunity to examine the reenactment and underlying data. The trial court should also mark the video reenactment as a court's exhibit so that the record may be preserved."); Wallace v. GMC, 1997 WL 269498 (E.D. La. 1997) (granting motion in limine to exclude evidence of video of left angle barrier tests because video action depicted was not substantially similar to accident in question and because events depicted would tend to confuse jury and any probative value was outweighed by prejudice.); Gorman v. Hunt, 19 S.W.3d 662 (Ky. 2000) (admitting posed photos if authenticated). *See also* Gregory P. Joseph, *Videotape Evidence in the Courts*, 26 S. TEX. L. REV. 453 (1985) (noting that courts carefully scrutinize reenactments because they afford opportunity for confusion, misconception, and manipulation).

[135] *See, e.g.*, Nicholas v. Wal-Mart Stores, Inc., 33 F. App'x 61 (4th Cir. 2002) (action caught on tape was not assertive conduct and hearsay objection overruled); Marino v. State, 934 P.2d 1321 (Alaska Ct. App. 1997) (part of videotape of defendant's interview with police was admitted over hearsay objections as non-assertive conduct but defendant was barred from using those portions where defendant protests his innocence because the "verbal conduct" was not non-assertive); People v. Taylor, 732 N.E.2d 120 (Ill. App. 2000) (conduct observed on videotape was not hearsay).

[136] *See* 2 MCCORMICK ON EVIDENCE § 217 at 51 (Kenneth S. Broun ed., 7th ed. 2013).

[137] 5 CHRISTOPHER B. MUELLER & LAIRD C. KIRKPATRICK, FEDERAL EVIDENCE § 9:27 at 510–11 (4th ed. 2013) (citations omitted).

[138] *See, e.g.*, United States v. Michelena-Orovio, 702 F.2d 496, 499 (5th Cir. 1983) (rejecting defense proposal to let jury smell one of subject bales of marijuana defendant was accused of possessing in order to test whether defendant could have smelled the contraband at time of boarding vessel).

the results of which may be simply reported by an expert witness or else presented as recorded evidence.[139] If presented in court along with expert testimony, the expert who conducted the experiment can authenticate the tape or film. Testimony about out-of-court experiments is subject to the usual rules governing expert evidence.

§ 12.09 The Special Problems of Computer Generated Exhibits

Computers generate evidence that can mere illustrate other testimony as well as evidence that carries its own independent evidentiary value. Business records are the most common example of computer generated records and because they typically have independent evidentiary value in that they are assertive, they usually raise hearsay issues. The necessary foundation for a Rule 803(6) hearsay exception is essentially no different for computer generated evidence than for paper records kept in files, but it raises additional issues about the underlying operating theory and reliability of the computer.

Because computer output is a product of a process that relies upon assumptions that are not immediately apparent to those outside the field, it may be considered a type of scientific evidence. Nevertheless, some courts require almost nothing in addition to the normal business record foundation other than an affirmation that the business has successfully used the computer. They take judicial notice of the operating theory and reliability of computer generated information in the same fashion as they take judicial notice of the validity of radar.[140]

To be sure, some courts have required an affirmation or demonstration that the particular computer or software is reliable,[141] but usually the witness has been able to to make such an affirmation without having any particular knowledge of the workings of the hardware or software.[142] A person who can identify the computer system used can testify to the method by which information is gathered and entered into the computer and can relate the procedures by which the particular record offered in court is produced,

---

[139] *See* **§ 12.06**. Again, if narration occurs in the film or tape, this can result in a film or tape being excluded or the audio being removed. *See, e.g.*, Emerson Elec. Co. v. Superior Court, 946 P.2d 841 (Cal. 1997) (holding that even if video re-creation was admitted, narrative on videotape might still be excluded based on hearsay, authenticity, or other objection); Fields v. Commonwealth, 12 S.W.3d 275 (Ky. 2000) (holding that audio narrative on videotape does not fall within any hearsay exception); State v. Coleman, 756 So. 2d 1218 (La. Ct. App. 2000) (holding that audio narrative on videotape was hearsay, but admission was harmless error).

[140] *See, e.g.*, United States v. Moore, 923 F.2d 910, 915 (1st Cir. 1991) (requiring nothing special for computer generated business record); United States v. Salgado, 250 F.3d 438 (6th Cir. 2001); People v. Huehn, 53 P.3d 733 (Colo. App. 2002); *In re* D. W., 2002 Ohio 5322 (Ohio Ct. App. 2002).

[141] *See, e.g.*, People v. Huehn, 53 P.3d 733 (Colo. App. 2002) ("While presentation of scientific evidence usually requires proof of the validity of the underlying theory and the reliability of the instrument, computers are so widely accepted and used that the proponent of computer evidence need not prove those two elements of the foundation."); Burleson v. State, 802 S.W.2d 429, 441 (Tex. App. 1991). *But see* FDIC v. Carabetta, 739 A.2d 301, 307 (Conn. App. Ct. 1999) ("When computer records are offered as evidence, the proponent must satisfy a two part test. In addition to meeting the three requirements of the business records exception to the hearsay rule, the proponent also must establish that the basic elements of the computer system are reliable.").

[142] *See, e.g.*, United States v. Linn, 880 F.2d 209, 216 (9th Cir. 1989); Midfirst Bank v. C.W. Haynes & Co., 893 F. Supp. 1304, 1311 (D.S.C. 1994) ("Computer records are admissible so long as the requirements of Rule 803(6) are met, and no more is required."); Garden State Bank v. Graef, 775 A.2d 189, 192 (N.J. Super. Ct. App. Div. 2001) ("[C]omputers are universally used and accepted, have become part of everyday life and work and are presumed reliable. There is no reason to believe that a computerized business record is not trustworthy unless the opposing party comes forward with some evidence to question its reliability.") (internal citations and quotations omitted). *But see* FDIC v. Carabetta, 739 A.2d 301, 307 (Conn. App. 1999).

will almost always be a "qualified person" as required by Rule 803(6).[143] Over the years, some commentators have called for a more rigorous foundation for computer generated business records,[144] but few courts have responded. When some computer generated business records have not been received in evidence, the failure has almost always been related to the failure of the normal business record foundation as it relates to computers.[145]

Amendments to the Federal Rules of Evidence have simplified the proess of authenticating computer generated recoreds by adding provisions for the self-authentication of computer generated records and data.[146] Rule 902(13) provides for self-authentication of records generated by a computer using a certificate meeting the same requirements as for self-authenticating private business records under Rule 902(11) or (12). It might be used to certify a record produced showing that a particular USB device was connected to a computer, that a particular server was used to connect to a particular webpage, or that a particular person's cellphone GPS records place the phone a particular place and time.[147] Similarly, Rule 902(14) provides for self-authentication of data copied from one electronic device to another (often important in forensic analyses to preserve unaltered the data on the original device) by a similar certification.[148]

Computer simulations and animations may create both easier and more difficult authentication issues than those presented by computer generated business records. Theoretically, computer animation offered for illustrative purposes is no different from any other diagram or picture offered for the same purpose—it must be a fair and accurate representation of what someone saw or of the oral testimony that it illustrates; for this purpose, it is not necessary to satisfy the standards for the admissibility of scientific evidence.[149] But a computer animation or simulation is not just another diagram. The

143 *See, e.g.*, Dyno Constr. Co. v. McWane, Inc., 198 F.3d 567 (6th Cir. 1999) (Fed Ex operations manager); State v. Hall, 2003 Ohio 2824 (Ohio Ct. App. 2003) (retail help desk specialist); State v. Pannier, 1999 WL 1216327 (Minn. App. 1999) (quality insurance regulatory affairs manager); Fed. R. Evid. 803(6) requires testimony concerning business records by the custodian or some other "qualified fitness."

144 *See, e.g.*, James E. Carbine & Lynn McLain, *Proposed Model Rules Governing the Admissibility Of Computer-Generated Evidence*, 15 SANTA CLARA COMPUTER & HIGH TECH. L.J. 1 (1999); Rudolph J. Peritz, *Computer Data Reliability: A Call for Authentication of Business Records Under the Federal Rules of Evidence*, 80 NW. U. L. REV. 956 (1986). *But see* Fred Galves, *Where the Not-So-Wild Things Are: Computers in the Courtroom, the Federal Rules of Evidence, and the Need for Institutional Reform and More Judicial Acceptance*, 13 HARV. J.L. & TECH. 161 (2000).

145 *See, e.g.*, United States v. Diaz, 176 F.3d 52 (2d Cir. 1999) (concluding that there was foundation problem because witness was unable to testify that computer generated photo was "fair and accurate representation"); United States v. Jackson, 208 F.3d 633 (7th Cir. 2000); United States v. Cestnik, 36 F.3d 904, 910 (10th Cir. 1994) ("A computer printout is admissible under Fed. R. Evid. 803(6), as with any other form of business record, if the offeror establishes a sufficient foundation in the record for its introduction. Computer business records are admissible if (1) they are kept pursuant to a routine procedure designed to assure their accuracy, (2) they are created for motives that tend to assure accuracy, for example, not including those prepared for litigation, and (3) they are not themselves mere accumulations of hearsay."); Baber v. Commonwealth, 2003 WL 1810510 (Va. Ct. App. 2003) (determining that computer records were improperly admitted under business records exception where print outs of information were not provided and foundation therefore was not properly laid).

146 Rules 902(13) and 902(14) were added to the self-authentication provisions of the federal rules, effective December 1, 2017.

147 *See* Report of the Advisory Committee on Evidence Rules, Committee on Rules of Practice and Procedure, Judicial Conference of the United States, May 7, 2016.

148 *Id.*

149 *See, e.g.*, People v. Cauley, 32 P.3d 602 (Colo. App. 2001) (stating that computer animation is demonstrative evidence and that proponent must testify that it fairly and accurately represents testimony it relates to; computer simulation considered scientific evidence and is subject to additional strictures regarding admission of scientific proof); Pierce v. State, 718 So. 2d 806 (Fla. Dist. Ct. App. 1997) (requiring that computer

impact on a jury of a filmed re-creation generated by data in a computer is tremendous, and there is a suspicion in the courts that no instruction minimizing the evidentiary status of the computer simulation can be effective. As a result, many courts require a more substantial foundation for computer animations and simulations.[150] In *Commonwealth v. Serge*,[151] the Pennsylvania Supreme Court considered a computer generated animation used by the prosecution to support a theory of first degree murder, as against the defendant's claim of self-defense. Applying evidence rules essentially equivalent to the federal rules, the court affirmed the defendant's conviction, emphasizing that careful cautionary instructions were given by the trial judge as to the purely illustrative character of the animation, coupled with the avoidance of unnecessary and prejudicial depictions, such as sounds, facial expressions, and blood. "The CGA was devoid of drama so as to prevent the jury from improperly relying on an emotional basis."[152]

Computer simulations are common in airline disaster cases[153] and automobile accident reconstructions.[154] They usually reflect or are the basis for expert testimony. To lay the foundation for the simulation, the expert must lay the same foundation as would be necessary for the expert's testimony,[155] in addition to providing an explanation of how the computer either contributed to or reflects the opinion. Although little case law exists in this rapidly developing area, the foundation described in *Commercial Union v. Boston Edison*,[156] decided in a *Frye* jurisdiction, has been quoted with approval in many jurisdictions. The *Commonwealth Union* court required a showing that (1) the computer was functioning properly, (2) the input and underlying equations were sufficiently complete and accurate (and disclosed to the opposing party so they might be challenged),

---

animation be fair and accurate depiction of that which it purports to be, same foundation that must be established to admit any pictorial representation); People v. McHugh, 476 N.Y.S.2d 721, 722–23 (1984) (concluding that computer reenactment "fairly and accurately" reflected oral testimony that it illustrated).

150 *See, e.g.*, Bray v. Bi-State Dev. Corp., 949 S.W.2d 93 (Mo. App. E.D. 1997) (collecting and discussing cases from various jurisdictions); *see also* State v. Tollardo, 77 P.3d 1023, 1027–28 (N.M. Ct. App. 2003) ("Some courts divide computer-generated exhibits into two categories: computer animations and computer simulations. An 'animation' is a computer-generated exhibit that is used as a visual aid to illustrate an opinion that has been developed without using the computer. On the other hand, a 'simulation' is a computer-generated exhibit created when information is fed into a computer that is programmed to analyze the data and draw a conclusion from it. When the image is used as a visual aid, the courts do not require a showing that the exhibit was produced by a scientifically or technologically valid method. On the other hand, before admitting a simulation, in which the computer has been used to analyze data, the courts require proof of the validity of the scientific principles and data.") *See also* Carole E. Powell, Note, *Computer Generated Visual Evidence: Does* Daubert *Make a Difference?* 12 GA. ST. U. L. REV. 577 (1996) (noting that courts are not always consistent in applying these labels to the particular exhibit at issue).

151 896 A.2d 1170 (Pa. 2006), *cert. denied*, 127 S. Ct. 275 (2006).

152 *Id.* at 1183. The court considered the appellant's argument that challenging the computer generated graphic was beyond the appellant's financial capacity, and the court in dicta stated that this was a factor for the trial court to consider in deciding whether to appoint an expert paid with public funds in order to assist the defense. However, the issue was not presented at trial and was thus held to have been waived. 896 A.2d at 1183–85.

153 *See* Connors v. United States (*In re* Air Crash at Dallas/Fort Worth Airport on August 2, 1985), 720 F. Supp. 1258 (N.D. Tex. 1989); Carlo D'Angelo, *The Snoop Doggy Dogg Trial: A Look at How Computer Animation Will Impact Litigation in the Next Century*, 32 U.S.F. L. REV. 561 (1998); Paul Marcotte, *Animated Evidence: Delta 191 Crash Re-Created Through Computer Simulations at Trial*, A.B.A.J. (Dec. 1989) at 52 (describing competing uses of computer simulations accepted by court as substantive evidence in *In re* Air Crash at Dallas/Fort Worth Airport on August 2, 1985).

154 *See, e.g.*, Smith v. BMW N. Am., Inc., 308 F.3d 913 (8th Cir. 2002); National Union Fire Ins. Co. v. Dowd & Dowd, P.C., 191 F.R.D. 566 (N.D. Ill. 1999); Kudlacek v. Fiat S.p.A., 509 N.W.2d 603 (Neb. 1994).

155 *See* **§ 10.04 & § 10.05**.

156 591 N.E.2d 165 (Mass. 1992).

and (3) the software used is generally accepted in the appropriate community of scientists.[157] Although it would be fair to assume that a more detailed foundation might be required under *Daubert,* the cases have to date offered little guidance.[158]

Unlike the expert witness whose testimony a computer simulation may illustrate, the computer cannot be cross-examined. Some of the expert's assumptions are built into the computer software. This requires the cross-examination of the expert on how the computer is programmed to "decide" what happened in addition to the normal cross-examination concerning the bases and scientific assumptions underlying the expert's testimony.

The use of computer animations, simulations, and conclusions will continue to grow. The more the computer generates the information or conclusion, the more rigorous the courts will be in requiring a complete scientific evidence foundation.

§ 12.10 Views

The preceding sections of this chapter have considered cases where the tangible object is presented in court. Sometimes that may not be practicable. Courts have the authority to permit the fact-finder to go to an object that is not practically presentable in court.[159] This is called a "view" or (in the case of jury trial) a "jury view." Typically, this will be an excursion to the scene of an event, but it may also be to a place where some object rests that is not conveniently movable into the courtroom.[160]

In deciding whether to allow a view, the court must consider various factors, including the time and expense involved in transporting the fact-finder, the extent of the activity involved at the view, and alternatives to taking a view. Regarding alternatives, other forms of recorded evidence, such a maps, photographs, and videotapes, may provide nearly everything that a view provides but at much lower cost.[161] Moreover, using such recorded evidence that is included in the record of trial assures that a reviewing court will have available to it everything that the jury saw.

Parties and counsel attend a jury view, but the trial judge need not. It is usually a wise precaution for the judge to attend, however, to prevent improper party communication with the jury or allegations thereof and to intervene in the event that the foundational conditions turn out not to be met. If, in the unusual case, testimony is to be taken at the scene, then both the trial judge and a court reporter must attend.

Authentication of views operates similarly to in-court authentication. However, an important functional distinction arises between a view that is merely illustrative and one that is substantive. Some courts insist that a view is only illustrative, and not evidence at all.[162] In that case, a view merely assists in understanding other evidence

---

[157] *Id.*

[158] EDWARD J. IMWINKELRIED, EVIDENTIARY FOUNDATIONS § 4.09[5][c](9th ed. 2015) (providing a sample foundation that is likely to be sufficient in courts applying *Daubert* reliability requirements to computer simulations).

[159] Procedures are often governed to some extent by statute or court rule. In California, for example, views are governed by § 651 of the Code of Civil Procedure and § 1119 of the Penal Code.

[160] *See generally* 4 WIGMORE ON EVIDENCE §§ 1162–1164 (Chadbourn rev. 1972).

[161] *See* CHRISTOPHER B. MUELLER & LAIRD C. KIRKPATRICK, FEDERAL EVIDENCE § 9:28 (4th ed. 2013).

[162] *See, e.g.,* Macon County Com'n v. Sanders, 555 So. 2d 1054 (Ala. 1990); Burns v. Janes, 398 A.2d 1125, 1129 (R.I. 1979). This fiction has the supposed virtue of making it easier for an appellate court to review the jury's findings. *See* 2 MCCORMICK ON EVIDENCE § 219 at 73 (Kenneth S. Broun ed., 7th ed. 2013) (noting

presented at trial. Most courts recognize, however, that—even more so than a photograph—a view can have substantive probative value transcending the mere understanding of other evidence. The implications of that might seem to make a view objectionable on the ground that it precludes effective appellate review, but in truth a view does not undermine the ability of an appellate court to conduct its review any more than does the fact-finder's observation of the demeanor of witnesses.[163]

Aside from the pragmatic considerations noted above, the most important foundational showing in support of a proposed view is that the scene has not changed in any material respect that has not been brought to the fact-finder's attention. This requirement is more demanding when the view is accepted as potentially providing substantive evidence, because jurors might draw inferences from very specific aspects of objects or spatial relations at the scene, which must then match—in relevant respects—those of the scene at the time of the litigated incident.[164]

§ 12.11 Authentication of Tangible Objects Discussed in Testimony

Testimony regularly refers to people, places, and events, and often these out-of-court events involve the use of objects—the transfer of documents, the firing of a handgun, and so forth. (This, of course, is true even when the testimony is not the extrinsic evidence offered as foundation for the introduction of tangible evidence.) A question arises whether such testimony invokes a requirement of authentication or identification as to any person or thing discussed, even when that tangible item is not offered in evidence. Given how many persons or things are mentioned in testimony, such a ubiquitous requirement would be profoundly burdensome. Moreover, as noted in the first section of this chapter, the requirement of authentication or identification arose at common law in regard to tangible objects offered in evidence. If it is limited to such tangible evidence, then it would not apply to testimony, and the fact that testimony refers to objects or persons would be insufficient to trigger a requirement of authentication or identification. Some case law supports this view.[165]

On the other hand, it may seem odd that one would be required to authenticate or identify an object that is presented in court for observation but be exempt from the need to do so when the fact-finder cannot even observe the object directly and must rely upon testimony for its description. This paradoxical-sounding element may explain why there are some doctrinal pockets in which authentication or identification is expected for an absent object or person.[166] Of course, the witness's testimony that something was

---

that the problem of the jury having evidence that the reviewing court does not can be circumvented, even when the view is considered substantive evidence, by video-taping the view).

[163] *See* 4 WIGMORE ON EVIDENCE § 1168 (Chadbourn rev. 1972).

[164] *See, e.g.*, United States v. Chiquito, 175 Fed. Appx. 215, 218 (10th Cir. 2006) (noting that a daytime view could be misleading in the context of a shooting that occurred at night).

[165] *See, e.g.*, United States v. Grant, 967 F.2d 81 (2d Cir. 1992) (authentication requirement, and specifically "chain of custody" idea, does not apply when drugs are not offered as tangible evidence and only testimony of expert who tested drugs is presented in court; defects in chain of custody from crime scene to expert might, however, affect the admissibility of the expert's testimony under the rules applicable to such testimony and they can go to the weight of the evidence as a whole).

[166] Some common-law cases apply the "chain of custody" principle in determining the admissibility of expert testimony about a tangible object when the tangible object itself is not presented in court. (There is usually no requirement that the tangible object itself be offered.) *See, e.g.*, United States v. Singer, 43 F. Supp. 863 (E.D.N.Y. 1942) (holding that evidence of expert's analysis can be admissible even if the object is lost or destroyed after the test is conducted). Similarly, something akin to an authentication requirement for a

observed will itself ordinarily constitute evidence sufficient to support a finding that it was observed, in accordance with Rule 901(b)(1). But sometimes courts have held that this is not enough.

The most commonly encountered example is that testimony referring to a voice that the proponent claims to be that of a particular person is inadmissible unless the voice is authenticated or identified. Evidence must be presented sufficient to support a finding that the voice was that of the person the proponent claims it to be.[167] For example, suppose the plaintiff offers W's testimony that W received a phone call from someone identifying himself as Ralph Kramden. If the plaintiff claims that this call was made by the defendant in the case, one Ralph Kramden, then admissibility of the witness's testimony is commonly subject to a requirement that the evidence be sufficient to support a finding that the defendant made the call. This idea finds recognition in pre- and post-Rules case law, in particular in cases stating that mere self-identification by the speaker is not sufficient to authenticate a telephone call as coming from that person.[168] It is explained in the McCormick treatise in the following terms:

> Modern technology makes commonplace the receipt of oral communications from persons who are heard but not seen. The problems of authentication raised by these communications are substantively analogous to the problems of authenticating writings, although no document or other exhibit is necessarily involved.[169]

But is the analogy identified in the treatise excerpt a good one? To make sense of the suggestion that authentication is required of objects or persons that are discussed in testimony, one must return to the rationales of the authentication requirement.[170] If one follows Wigmore's theory—that there is something special about physical objects, so that the typical fact-finder will be unable to remain adequately skeptical of such objects when they are presented in court without authenticating evidence—then there is no obvious basis for extending the requirement to testimony that merely mentions objects or persons, because the psychological propensity that Wigmore posits (correctly or incorrectly) would not seem to be operative; at least it would be highly attenuated when a witness merely mentions some object.

---

document *not* presented is built into the conditions on the admissibility of duplicates in lieu of the original of a document under the original recording rule. *See* **§ 13.02**. *See also* CAL. EVID. CODE § 1401(b) ("Authentication of a writing is required before secondary evidence of its content may be received in evidence.").

[167] *See* 7 WIGMORE ON EVIDENCE §§ 2155, 2157 (Chadbourn rev. 1978). These sections appear in a chapter entitled "Authentication of Documents." Although Wigmore was aware of the apparent anomaly, he did not attempt to explain it. *See id.* § 2156.

[168] *See, e.g.*, People v. Lynes, 49 N.Y.2d 286 (1980) (applying principle to prosecution witness); State v. Valentine, 762 A.2d 1278 (Conn. 2000) (applying principle to defense witness). The idea of authenticating a voice allegedly heard live by a witness seems to be reflected in Rules 901(b)(5) and (6). Rule 901(b)(5), for example, states that one method of satisfying "the requirement of authenticating or identifying an item of evidence" is: "An opinion identifying a person's voice—*whether heard firsthand* or through mechanical or electronic transmission or recording—based on hearing the voice at any time under circumstances that connect it with the alleged speaker." FED. R. EVID. 901(b)(5) (emphasis added). Although the emphasized language could refer only to someone who hears the voice first-hand while a recording is made simultaneously (the recording being the evidence to be authenticated), it also seems to extend to the identification of a voice about which a witness is testifying without the introduction of any tangible evidence. Following common-law precedents, courts have so interpreted it. *See, e.g.*, United States v. Khan, 53 F.3d 507, 516 (2d Cir. 1995) (stating principle in dictum, but rejecting application in particular case because circumstantial evidence pointed to identity of caller).

[169] 2 MCCORMICK ON EVIDENCE § 228 at 112 (Kenneth S. Broun ed., 7th ed. 2013).

[170] *See* § **12.01**.

The conditional relevance rationale of the rule—that the rule provides a quintessential example of conditional relevance—at least seems to be consistent with the extension of the requirement to people or objects discussed in testimony. Testimony about the phone call might seem to be irrelevant unless the person is in fact the one the proponent claims. But that rationale has two serious problems: (1) conditional relevance is largely incoherent on its own terms;[171] and (2) if accepted on its own terms, it yields no stopping point that would prevent its application to every tangible object that is referenced in testimony, not just voices heard in circumstances where the witness cannot see the speaker.[172]

Under the information compulsion theory of the doctrine—that the doctrine serves to compel the proponent of tangible evidence to present a witness to explain why the proponent believes the exhibit is connected to the case and to submit this person for cross-examination about the matter—the extension does not seem to make sense. The indicated goal has been achieved by the very testimony that, based on personal knowledge, mentions the object or person and the submission of that witness to cross-examination. Other evidence might well be necessary to satisfy the proponent's burden of proof, if any, but that is a matter of the sufficiency of the evidence as a whole. Accordingly, such a theory provides no easy justification for application of the authentication requirement in this context.[173] The same is true, though less obviously so, of a reconstruction of conditional relevance that understands it as simply the conditional ruling that certain evidence, without additional support, is not sufficiently probative to avoid exclusion under the principles of Rule 403. Some such self-identifications will be sufficiently probative under Rule 403 and some will not; no blanket rule seems appropriate.

The cases tend to display three features that minimize the effect of this extension of the authentication requirement to purely testimonial evidence. The first feature is illustrated by *United States v. Pool*,[174] reversing a conviction because a DEA agent testified to receiving a call from someone using the same nickname as the defendant but no other evidence confirmed that defendant was the one who made the call, except that evidence tended to show that defendant was one among several persons involved in a conspiracy to import and distribute marijuana to which the questioned phone call

---

[171] *See* **§ 3.11**. In the context of the example in the text, the fact that the caller identifies himself as Ralph Kramden increases the probability that the caller was the defendant, though it is certainly not conclusive evidence.

[172] In accordance with the apparent intent of the Rules' drafters, this rationale is followed by the editors of McCormick. *See* 2 MCCORMICK ON EVIDENCE § 228 at 112 (Kenneth S. Broun ed., 7th ed. 2013) ("It has long been established that if a communication made to or from a disembodied voice is relevant only if it is connected to a particular person, this connection must be proved prior to the admission of any evidence proving the content of the communication."). The editors do not attempt to explain why such a communication is irrelevant if there is a significant possibility that the speaker was the person in question, even if that likelihood is not sufficient to support a finding by a preponderance of the evidence that the speaker was the person in question. Nor do they explain why such a requirement should apply only when the voice is "disembodied." To be fair to the editors, such explanations are also not forthcoming in the judicial opinions upon which the editors rely.

[173] On this theory, it would matter considerably whether a witness (a) testifies that someone called the witness on the phone and "identified himself as Ralph Kramden" or, instead, (b) testifies that "Ralph Kramden called" the witness. The latter, but not the former, would presuppose the witness's ability to give an opinion regarding the identity of the caller, based on voice recognition or otherwise. *See* **§ 10.01** & **§ 10.02**. The case law does not seem to draw this distinction, however, and seems to impose an authentication requirement in both situations. *See, e.g.*, United States v. Hyatt, 565 F.2d 229, 232 (2d Cir. 1977) (rejecting, on authentication grounds, testimony by codefendant's mother that someone who identified himself as "Jimmy" called, looking for defendant, where other evidence in the case indicated the involvement of a person called Jimmy).

[174] 660 F.2d 547 (5th Cir. 1981).

related. What is striking about the decision is that the identification of the speaker was essential to the conviction for illegal use of the telephone system, the specific crime at issue. In other words, the court might just as well have said that this particular evidence is admissible, but that the evidence as a whole, even with the evidence of the call, would be insufficient to support a finding beyond reasonable doubt that the defendant is the one who committed the crime of illegal use of the phones. The authentication doctrine is not actually necessary to achieve the legal result.

Conversely, the second feature is a willingness to find the evidence sufficient to support a finding that an inculpatory or crime-facilitating call was made by the defendant whenever the evidence as a whole, including the call, is sufficient to support a finding that the defendant is guilty.[175] Sufficiency of the evidence to show guilt becomes sufficiency of the evidence to support admission. Again, it looks like the doctrine is really about sufficiency of the evidence as a whole on the issue of identity.

Even in cases that cannot be explained as sufficiency rulings in disguise, another feature minimizes the impact of this extension of the authentication rule. There is a less than rigorous demand in terms of the familiarity required for a witness to identify a voice as belonging to a particular individual.[176] A witness's testimony that a voice heard on the phone is the same as one heard a month later in person has been deemed sufficient for identification, even when there were no other instances of hearing or identifying the voice.[177] In any event, all of the circumstantial methods of authenticating a voice on a recording are available to authenticate a voice heard live by a witness.[178]

175 *See, e.g.*, United States v. Brown, 603 F.2d 1022 (1st Cir. 1979) (call made as part of plan to steal re birds; identification of voice not necessary to conclude that defendant made the call); United States v. insa, 243 F.3d 635, 658–59 (2d Cir. 2001) (threat by self-identified caller sufficient to authenticate identity ere caller needed to self-identify in order to benefit from the threat); United States v. Garrison, 168 F.3d 9, 1092–93 (8th Cir. 1999) (call made as part of attempt to cover up a drug conspiracy; because of his cipation in the conspiracy, voice identification evidence not necessary to conclude that the self-identified was in fact the defendant).

76 *See, e.g.*, Kalola v. Eisenberg, 781 A.2d 77 (N.J. Super. L. 2001) (holding that self-identification ed with "other reliable circumstantial evidence" is sufficient even absent authentication of the voice by ess taking the call).

See, e.g., United States v. Hull, 74 F. App'x 615 (7th Cir. 2003).

See **§ 12.06**.

Chapter 13

THE ORIGINAL RECORDING RULE

Table of Sections

§ 13.01 The Requirement of the Original Recording [FRE 1001, 1002]

The original recording rule—often called the "best evidence" rule—requires that specific tangible evidence be offered in certain situations.[1] The Federal Rules version of this rule, Rule 1002, succinctly states:

> An original writing, recording, or photograph is required in order to prove its content unless these rules or a federal statute provides otherwise.[2]

Rule 1002 does not require a party to prove the content of any record, but if the party chooses to do so (or is required to do so by some other rule), then the rule is triggered.[3]

Sometimes rules of substantive law require proving contents of a record and thus constrain a proponent's choice. For example, a plaintiff seeking to enforce an alleged contract falling within the Statute of Frauds must prove that certain terms are contained in a written contract.[4] Similarly, in a prosecution for exhibiting an obscene movie, the contents of the film must be proved to make the case.[5] These requirements place the contents of the recordings at issue. Because a party must then prove a recording's contents, the original recording requirement applies. As explained further below, however, the scope of the rule is not limited to such situations: even though a party is not legally required to prove the contents of a given document, that party may consider it strategically useful to do so. For example, a contract might be reduced to writing even though no such writing is required by the substantive law as a condition on enforceability of the agreement, and a party seeking to enforce the agreement may well want to evidence the terms of the writing. If so, Rule 1002 will come into play.

---

1 *See generally* 4 WIGMORE ON EVIDENCE § 1177 et. seq. (Chadbourn rev. 1972).

2 FED. R. EVID. 1002.

3 Authentication rules limit the admissibility of tangible evidence that a party offers, whether presenting that tangible thing is optional or required in the context. See **§ 12.01**. The original recording rule, when it applies, precludes a party from avoiding the use of particular tangible evidence.

4 *See* **§ 13.05**.

5 *See* People v. Enskat, 98 Cal. Rptr. 646 (Cal. App. Super. 1971).

When the rule applies, it functions less as a rule of exclusion than as a preference for evidence of a certain kind—the original of the record. Exclusion of "secondary" evidence of the contents (such as testimony describing the contents) merely enforces this preference for the original. Two implications follow from this preferential structure. First, when the original cannot reasonably be produced, or it would be otherwise counterproductive to require its production, the requirement is not enforced. Various rules in Article X (discussed below) articulate when a court may find this to be the case.[6]

Second, once the original is placed in evidence, the preference is satisfied, and there are no further exclusionary implications of this rule. Secondary evidence of the contents may then also be presented, at least as far as this rule is concerned. Such secondary evidence might be a waste of time and excluded as such (under Rule 403), but not always. Common grounds for admitting secondary evidence, once the original has been introduced, include the illegibility or incomprehensibility of the original and the proponent's claim that the original has been doctored and thus no longer accurately presents its original information.[7]

Rationale and Scope of the Rule

Crafted at a time when photographs and tape recordings did not exist, the common-law rule requiring originals applied only to documents,[8] but today information is stored in diverse ways besides what is traditionally called a document. Accordingly, Federal Evidence Rule 1002 applies to writings, recordings, and photographs. Both "writing" and "recording" are defined in terms of "letters, numbers, or their equivalent" set down or recorded in any form."[9] A "photograph" is a "photographic image or its equivalent stored in any form," and includes X-rays, video tapes, and motion pictures.[10]

The principal concern behind the rule is the danger of errors, whether intentional or accidental, in the oral reporting (or human copying) of the informational content of a document or other record.[11] Accordingly, case law has extended the reach of the rule to any tangible record containing communicable information.[12] All of these modalities are covered by the generic term "recording of information," which is why the phrase "original

---

[6] *See* **§ 13.02 & § 13.03.**

[7] *See, e.g.*, United States v. Onori, 535 F.2d 938, 946–9 (5th Cir. 1976) (affirming admission of transcriptions of an admitted tape recording); State v. Ahmadjian, 438 A.2d 1070, 1082–83 n.6 (R.I. 1981) (same). *See* 4 WIGMORE ON EVIDENCE § 1190 (Chadbourn rev. 1972).

[8] *Cf.* Burney v. United States, 339 F.2d 91 (5th Cir. 1964) (holding that best evidence rule applies only to writings); *In re* Reed's Estate, 672 P.2d 829, 834 (Wyo. 1983) (quoting 5 DAVID W. LOUISELL & CHRISTOPHER B. MUELLER, FEDERAL EVIDENCE § 549 (1981)) (stating that modern rule "expand[s] to some extent the common-law tradition, which had sometimes insisted that the doctrine applied only to writings").

[9] FED. R. EVID. 1001(a) & (b).

[10] Fed. R. Evid. 1001(c). *See also* Wagman v. Bradshaw, 739 N.Y.S.2d 421 (N.Y. App. Div. 2002) (holding that where the contents of an x-ray film or MRI are to be proven, original x-ray or MRI must be produced unless unavailability is adequately described and any secondary evidence offered accurately portrays and describes film).

[11] *See* 2 MCCORMICK ON EVIDENCE § 232 (Kenneth S. Broun ed., 7th ed. 2013).

[12] *See, e.g.*, Seiler v. Lucasfilm, Ltd., 808 F.2d 1316 (9th Cir. 1986), *cert. denied*, 484 U.S. 826 (1987) (applying the rule to sketches of a fantasy war machine). Although the court does not make the point in *Lucas*, things like sketches and photographs can be, and routinely are, translated into a digital, numeric form by imaging that creates computer records. The core idea of information is, of course, the basis for an important field of science. *See, e.g.*, JAMES V. STONE, INFORMATION THEORY: A TUTORIAL INTRODUCTION (2016).

recording rule" is used here to represent the full reach of the rule.[13] For the same reason, the required "original," in the case of electronically stored information, includes any printout "if it accurately reflects the information," and the required original of a photograph includes "the negative or a print from it."[14]

Rule 1002 requires the use of the original recording "in order to prove its content." Often it is easy enough to perceive when "proof of content" is involved. The paradigmatic case is proof of contents of a written contract.

Example

Direct examiner: "Why do you claim that your landlord was responsible for maintaining the hallways in a safe condition?"

Witness: "It says so in the lease."

Opponent: "Objection. The terms of the lease must be shown by introduction of the lease itself."

But the rule is not limited to contracts, wills, or other documents that, by their execution, effect a change in legal relations.

Example

Direct examiner: Did your wife communicate with you after that?

Witness: Yes.

Direct examiner: In what way?

Witness: I got a letter from her in the mail.

Direct examiner: When did you receive the letter?

Witness: On July 13, 2019.

Direct examiner: What did the letter say?

Opponent: Objection. Such use of the letter requires the introduction of the original.

The last question asks about the contents of the letter and thereby is attempting to prove those contents. As in the previous example, this will run afoul of the original recording rule unless the proponent of the testimony can: (a) produce the original, (b) produce an alternative, acceptable substitute for the original (discussed below), or (c) demonstrate that the original was lost, destroyed, otherwise unavailable, or concerned with a collateral matter (also discussed below).[15]

"Proof of content" is not involved when a witness testifies about the underlying event based on knowledge from a source other than the recording at issue. In that case, the witness is not trying to prove the contents of the recording, within the meaning of the rule, and there is no requirement that the proponent of the testimony produce the

---

[13] The Federal Rules use the rather ungainly phrase, "Contents of Writings, Recordings, and Photographs," for the title of Article X and simply "Requirement of the Original" for the rule itself. FED. R. EVID. 1002.

[14] FED. R. EVID. 1001(d).

[15] Unlike the first example, the second example might (or might not) also involve a hearsay problem. The document is an out-of-court statement and, if offered to prove the truth of the matter asserted in the letter, it is hearsay. *See* **§ 14.05**.

recording. The rule does not require producing a recording merely because the item happens to exist and records information related to the same subject as testimony.

Examples

If the court reporter who transcribed an earlier hearing at which Walter testified is asked what Walter said at the hearing, the witness may answer. The testimony is about what the witness heard, not what is in the transcript.[16] If the witness is asked what the transcript indicates that Walter said at the hearing then the witness may not answer unless the transcript is produced. By talking about the transcript the witness would be proving the contents of the transcript and that part of his testimony would trigger the original recording rule.

If a witness to an accident that happened to have been videotaped is asked which car entered the intersection first, the witness may answer if the witness has personal knowledge of the event. The testimony is about what the witness saw, not what is on the videotape. If the witness is asked which car the videotape shows entering the intersection first, the witness may not answer. The testimony would be about the contents of the videotape and would trigger the original recording rule.[17]

In a child custody proceeding, one spouse sought to show that the other is unfit by producing evidence that the other spouse was captured in a photograph injecting heroin. If the witness was present during the event and is asked whether her spouse shot up, the witness may answer. But if the witness was not present and was merely shown the photograph, she may not answer the question. The witness has no firsthand knowledge. If the question is rephrased so as to ask about what the witness observed in the photograph, this would trigger the original recording rule.[18]

A very different kind of problem concerns how to prove the "content" of an inscribed physical object when physically presenting that object in court would be unwieldy or absurd. Illustrations include whether a tombstone, a branded cow, an automobile with a VIN number, and the like constitute (very big) writings to which the original recording rule applies. Some commentators favor a balancing approach toward inscribed chattels, taking into account the need for the evidence and the ease or difficulty of production.[19] The problem with this approach is that there is little express basis in the rules for balancing the practical inconvenience of obtaining the original against the need for it.[20]

---

[16] *See, e.g.*, Meyers v. United States, 171 F.2d 800 (D.C. Cir. 1948), *cert. denied*, 336 U.S. 912 (1949) (holding that the transcript is not required, under the best evidence rule, instead of the testimony of a person who heard the testimony).

[17] *See* United States v. Parkins, 7 F. App'x 287, 289 (4th Cir. 2001) ("The best evidence rule does not apply where testimony of detectives is offered to prove the content of the conversations rather than the content of the tapes.").

[18] *See* United States v. Nelson, 38 F. App'x 386 (9th Cir. 2002) (requiring original photo to prove content of photo unless original has been destroyed or otherwise fits within exception to rule, in which case secondary evidence of content may be admissible); Heinz v. Heinz, 165 P.2d 967, 971 (Cal. Ct. App. 1946) (recognizing applicability of best evidence rule to testimony about contents of nude photos, but admits testimony because original photos beyond reach of subpoena power).

[19] *See* 4 WIGMORE ON EVIDENCE § 1182 (Chadbourn rev. 1972); 2 MCCORMICK ON EVIDENCE § 233 at 132–33 (Kenneth S. Broun ed., 7th ed. 2013).

[20] FED. R. EVID. 1004 lists various excuses for not producing the original of a writing, but the physical difficulty of producing an inscribed chattel is not one of the listed excuses. Rule 1004(b), which excuses the

Courts that have been forced to deal with this kind of problem have adopted varying approaches. In *Drummond v. State*,[21] an Alabama court avoided the potential danger of cow dung in the courtroom by fiat: "We conclude it was competent for the witness to testify as to the markings he saw on the cow without producing her in court."[22] The federal courts have engaged in only slightly more sophisticated analyses, often finding Rule 1002 inapplicable to inscribed chattels.[23] There is nothing, however, in the language of the rule that distinguishes between inscribed chattels and other recordings of information.[24] Certainly, it is possible to have a case in which the determinative fact is the precise wording of some complex inscription on a chattel, so that the risks of human transmission error are involved.[25]

Another difficulty arises when, before trial, a person checks a record, usually a list of items, to see if some item is on the list and discovers it is not. Courts disagree about whether testimony that the item was *not* on the list counts as proving the contents of the record. Some common-law decisions have held it does not,[26] and the drafters of the federal rules indicated their agreement.[27] The conclusion is not convincingly explained. The rationale of the rule depends on the importance of precision in reflecting the record accurately, and this can be just as much a problem in testifying about what is not in a record as it is in testifying about what is in the record. The result in many such cases—overruling an objection that would require producing the record in court—might be better justified (when it is justified) in terms of the inconvenience of requiring a voluminous record to be presented in court, a contingency for which there is a specific excusing rule.[28]

"Best Evidence" and the Original Recording Rule

The original recording rule is often called the "best evidence rule." However, the drafters of the Federal Rules avoided that terminology and attorneys should be cautious in their use of that phrase. To understand why, a brief historical digression is necessary.

In the Eighteenth Century, and much of the Nineteenth, at a time when pretrial discovery was very limited, English and American scholars and judges used the phrase

---

production of originals when "an original cannot be obtained through any available judicial process" might be construed to cover such situations, though that was not the contemplated application. *See* FED. R. EVID. 1004 advisory committee note (referring to limits of judicial authority).

[21] 67 So. 2d 280 (Ala. Ct. App. 1953).

[22] *Id.* at 282.

[23] *See* United States v. Yamin, 868 F.2d 130, 134 (5th Cir. 1989) (citing United States v. Duffy, 454 F.2d 809, 812 (5th Cir. 1972)) (noting that in case involving counterfeiting of watches, writing (trademark) on watch makes it counterfeit; however court states that "an object bearing a mark is both a chattel and a writing, and the trial judge has discretion to treat it as a chattel, to which the best evidence rule does not apply.").

[24] One might distinguish between an object the primary use of which is to record information (i.e., a document) and an object the primary use of which is something other than recording information but that also is used to record information (i.e., an inscribed chattel). The problem is that the definitions in the rules draw no such distinction.

[25] A possible solution to this dilemma is for the court to require the objecting party to agree to the use of a photograph of the inscribed chattel or else bear the costs of taking the court to the chattel (a "view"). *See* **§ 12.10**. Another is to invoke Rule 1007, which permits secondary evidence of the contents of "voluminous" records, which by one meaning of that term could embrace even a single record that is very large and heavy. *See* **§ 13.03** (subsection on "Summaries of Voluminous Records").

[26] *See, e.g.*, State v. Nano, 543 P.2d 660 (Ore. 1975).

[27] *See* FED. R. EVID. 1002 advisory committee note ("Nor does the rule apply to testimony that books or records have been examined and found not to contain any reference to a designated matter.").

[28] *See* **§ 13.03** (subsection on "Summaries of Voluminous Records").

"best evidence" in reference to a general requirement of proof. For example, drawing on the work of the philosopher John Locke, Chief Baron Geoffrey Gilbert wrote:

> The first therefore, and most signal Rule, in relation to Evidence, is this, That a Man must have the utmost Evidence, The Nature of the Fact is capable of; For the Design of the Law is to come to rigid Demonstration in Matters of Right, and there can be no Demonstration of a Fact without the best Evidence that the Nature of the Thing is capable of; less Evidence doth create but Opinion and Surmise, and does not leave a Man the entire Satisfaction, that arises from Demonstration.[29]

This "Rule," which actually functions more as a general principle, was used to explain and justify diverse, more specific rules of evidence, including the hearsay rule, the attested document rule, and the original recording rule.[30]

At the end of the Nineteenth Century, however, several scholars, both in the United States and in England, criticized references to this general "best evidence" idea and insisted that the phrase be limited to use in connection with the requirement that a proponent present the original document when trying to prove the contents of a document.[31] For good or ill, that restriction on the use of the phrase "best evidence" has largely stuck.[32] As a consequence, in modern practice a lawyer who objects using the phrase "it's not the best evidence" is likely to be understood by the court as referring to the original recording rule, whether or not that is the lawyer's intention.[33]

In any event, the Federal Rules contain no explicit best evidence requirement similar to that articulated by the Eighteenth Century writers. Broadly speaking, litigation under the Rules primarily relies on the existence of liberal discovery coupled with the parties' incentives to assure the production of the "best evidence" as the result of the parties' competition in the courtroom. As a matter of strategy, however, lawyers try to offer the most persuasive evidence possible, not because evidence law imposes any general hierarchy of evidence, and what is most persuasive from a party's perspective may not be optimal from the fact-finder's perspective. For example, oral testimony about an object that is central to the event in question—such as a knife in a stabbing case—is ordinarily admissible even if the item is not offered, in spite of its being available and capable of authentication.[34] If the broader principle of the common law is to be invoked

---

[29] GEOFFREY GILBERT, THE LAW OF EVIDENCE 3–4 (1st ed. 1754).

[30] *See, e.g.*, SIMON GREENLEAF, A TREATISE ON THE LAW OF EVIDENCE § 82 passim (1st ed. 1842).

[31] *See, e.g.*, JAMES B. THAYER, A PRELIMINARY TREATISE ON EVIDENCE AT THE COMMON LAW 484–507 (1898) (American criticism); J. GULSON, THE PHILOSOPHY OF PROOF 448–54 (1st ed. 1905) (English criticism). For a defense of the importance of the earlier view, see Dale A. Nance, *The Best Evidence Principle*, 73 IOWA L. REV. 227 (1988).

[32] *See* 4 WIGMORE ON EVIDENCE §§ 1173–75 (Chadbourn rev. 1972); 2 MCCORMICK ON EVIDENCE § 230 (Kenneth S. Broun ed., 7th ed. 2013). Occasional decisions diverge from this consensus. *See, e.g.*, State v. Price, 265 P.2d 444, 446 (Ariz. 1954) (allowing the use of the branded hide of a dead calf instead of the deteriorating carcass to prove the loss of the heifer only because the hide was the best available evidence; stating that the best evidence rule, as the court understood it, "requires that the highest degree of proof of which a case is susceptible must be produced, if such proof is accessible").

[33] *See, e.g.*, United States v. Gonzalez-Benitez, 537 F.2d 1051 (9th Cir.), *cert. denied*, 429 U.S. 923 (1976) (summarily rejecting defendants' argument couched in terms of the prosecution's failure to present the "best evidence" in a context where the original recording rule clearly did not apply and without considering any alternative rule that would support defendants' argument).

[34] *See, e.g.*, United States v. Yamin, 868 F.2d 130, 134 (5th Cir. 1989) (holding that best evidence rule does not apply to chattels); People v. Ojeda, 758 F.2d 403, 407 (9th Cir. 1985) (holding that, in burglary case,

by parties or the court as a limitation on admissibility, it must arise from some other particular rule, such as the hearsay rule,[35] the rule of verbal completeness,[36] the original recording rule, or Rule 403.[37] Aside from admissibility rules, there are many doctrinal tools—ranging from instructions to the jury about adverse inferences from the failure of a party to present evidence to directed verdicts for failure of a party to meet its burden of production—that courts use in an effort to make sure the fact-finder is presented the best evidence available.[38]

§ 13.02 Alternative Means of Satisfying the Requirement: Duplicates, Certified Copies, and Admissions

The Federal Rules recognize three alternatives to the production of the original that may be used without the proponent's accounting for the original or excusing its absence.

Mechanically Produced Duplicates [FRE 1003]

The principal concern of the best evidence rule is the danger of errors in the oral reporting (or human copying) of the contents of records of information. Accordingly, mechanically produced copies that are considered generally accurate are admissible in lieu of originals, without any need to explain the absence of the original. The duplication can be the product of a copy machine or a photographic copy of a document,[39] a re-recording of a tape recording,[40] or equivalent techniques that accurately reproduce the original. Handmade or hand-typed material, however, are excluded from this category.[41] Under Rule 1003, mechanically produced duplicates are admissible "to the same extent as the original unless a genuine question is raised about the original's authenticity or the circumstances make it unfair to admit the duplicate." The mere assertion that a duplicate is an inaccurate reproduction is not enough to raise a genuine question.[42] (In the case of public records, the rule permitting the use of duplicates is limited by Rule 1005, discussed below.)

Certified Copies of Public Records [FRE 1005]

The drafters of the Federal Rules explained that "[p]ublic records call for somewhat different treatment. Removing them from their usual place of keeping would be attended

---

it is unnecessary to produce stolen jewelry or excuse for non-production); Byrd v. Bentley, 850 So. 2d 232 (Ala. 2002) (concluding that Alabama's best evidence rule continues to be applicable only to writings).

[35] *See* **§ 14.03**.

[36] *See* **§ 1.12**.

[37] Even Thayer, the eminent legal scholar who led the attack on the phrase "best evidence," acknowledged that the best evidence principle might inform the exercise of exclusionary discretion afforded to trial judges. *See* JAMES B. THAYER, A PRELIMINARY TREATISE ON EVIDENCE AT THE COMMON LAW 495, 505, 507 (1898). Under the Federal Rules, the primary authority through which to apply such a general "best evidence" principle is Rule 403. *See* **§ 5.03**.

[38] *See generally* DALE A. NANCE, THE BURDENS OF PROOF: DISCRIMINATORY POWER, WEIGHT OF EVIDENCE, AND TENACITY OF BELIEF ch.4 (2016).

[39] *See, e.g.*, State v. Brown, 743 A.2d 262 (Md. App. 1999) (introducing photocopy of warrant where there was no question of its authenticity); State v. Andrews, 293 P.3d 1203 (Wash. App. 2013) (admitting photocopy of text message as duplicate).

[40] United States v. Capanelli, 257 F. Supp. 2d 678 (S.D.N.Y. 2003); State v. Fujimoto, 36 P.3d 813 (Haw. 2001); Bryant v. State, 810 So. 2d 532 (Fla. Dist. Ct. App. 2002).

[41] *See* 5 CHRISTOPHER B. MUELLER & LAIRD C. KIRKPATRICK, FEDERAL EVIDENCE § 10:10 (4th ed. 2013).

[42] *See* Colin Miller, *Even Better Than the Real Thing: How Courts Have Been Anything But Liberal in Finding Genuine Questions Raised as to the Authenticity of Originals Under Rule 1003*, 68 MD. L. REV. 160 (2008).

by serious inconvenience to the public and to the custodian."[43] Accordingly, Rule 1005 provides an alternative by which a certified copy or a copy compared with the original by the witness is admissible in lieu of the original record.[44] This rule applies to public records as well as any "document that was lawfully recorded or filed in a public office." The drafters explained that a "blanket dispensation from producing or accounting for the original would open the door to the introduction of every kind of secondary evidence of contents of public records were it not for the preference given [by this rule] to certified or compared copies."[45]

Requiring certified copies of official records presents the only hierarchy of secondary evidence in the federal rules. Rule 1005 states a clear preference for copies that are certified or that are presented through the testimony of a witness who has compared the copy with the original. Other evidence of the contents of an official record is admissible only if the certified or compared copy cannot be obtained by the exercise of due diligence.[46] This limitation, however, does not preclude other evidence of the contents of a document just because the document happens to have been recorded, if the document is relevant apart from the fact of its being recorded. For example, if the contents of a deed are essential to a case, the fact that the deed was recorded does not preclude the use of evidence other than a 1005 copy to prove the content of the deed.[47]

The use of public records sometimes presents a problem that is otherwise rarely encountered in the original recording rule context: the problem of multiple or layered prima facie violations of the rule.[48] For example, if a party were to try to introduce a handwritten copy to prove the contents of a document that is itself a handwritten copy of yet another (original) document, and the point is to prove the contents of the original, then there would be two triggering events for the original recording rule, each of which must be analyzed separately for compliance with Article 7 of the Rules. This makes sense, as the risks of error and fabrication in the two transcriptions each properly invoke the concerns motivating Rule 1002. Similarly, in a case where a prior conviction is to be proved, the original record of conviction does not trigger the rule, but use of a summary tangible public compilation of convictions manually created from information in the original would trigger application of the rule, if it is used to prove the contents of the original record of conviction and thereby establish the fact or nature of the conviction. Moreover, use of evidence of, but distinct from, the original summary tangible public record would present a second prima facie violation of the rule, if it is used to prove the content of the summary compilation and thus the content of the original record of conviction. Because the original record of conviction is a public record, avoiding the first application of the rule would involve showing, pursuant to Rule 1005, that a certified or

---

[43] FED. R. EVID. 1005 advisory committee note.

[44] The rule, like other exceptions to the requirement of an original, does not operate to override other possible objections to the admissibility of the document, such as hearsay. The rule reaffirms this explicitly by specifying that the document must be "otherwise admissible." FED. R. EVID. 1005.

[45] FED. R. EVID. 1005 advisory committee note.

[46] Compliance with Rule 1005 by certification will satisfy both the authentication requirement—showing the copy to be what it purports to be—and the best evidence rule. In order for the record to be admissible under the public records exception to the rule against hearsay, it must also satisfy the requirements of Rule 803(8). A public record that does not describe any of the matters set forth in rule 803(8) does not overcome a hearsay objection merely because it satisfies Rule 1005.

[47] *See* Amoco Production Co. v. United States, 619 F.2d 1383 (10th Cir. 1980) (holding trial court erred in excluding copy of deed that had been recorded, where gravamen of proponent's argument was that original deed was improperly transcribed onto the recorded version).

[48] The problem is more familiar, and better understood, in the hearsay context. *See* **§ 14.07**.

comparison copy of the original record of conviction cannot be obtained by reasonable diligence; this would allow recourse to the secondary evidence that consists of the summary record of convictions.[49] Avoiding the second application of the rule would involve another application of Rule 1005, which expresses a preference for the use of a certified or compared copy of the content of the summary compilation.[50]

Admissions [FRE 1007]

Under Rule 1007, a proponent need not account for the non-production of an original recording if the party against whom the evidence is to be used has admitted what the contents of the recording are. To provide some protection against inaccuracies by the party opponent, the rule is limited to sworn testimony (at trial or in a deposition) or a written admission. Oral extra-judicial admissions may be introduced if secondary evidence becomes generally admissible by virtue of the excuses recognized in Rule 1004.

§ 13.03 Excused Use of "Secondary" Evidence of Contents

Following the common law, the federal rules also permit a proponent to offer certain acceptable excuses for failing to produce an original, thereby authorizing the introduction of "secondary" evidence of the contents of the record.

Originals Lost, Destroyed, Unobtainable, or in the Possession of the Opponent [FRE 1004(a)–(c)]

The original recording rule should rarely prevent a diligent lawyer from introducing testimony about the contents of a writing or other recording. If neither an original nor a duplicate is available, and an admission under Rule 1007 is unavailable, the lawyer should be able to have a witness lay the foundation for oral testimony about (or a handwritten copy of) the contents of a document by establishing that the writing was:

1. Lost or stolen;

2. Destroyed by someone other than the proponent, unless it was destroyed by the proponent's "bad faith" instigation;

3. Destroyed by the proponent, so long as it was not in "bad faith";

4. Found in someone else's possession, and not obtainable by judicial process; or

---

[49] If a certified or comparison copy of the original record of conviction is available, then Rule 1005 would eliminate the need and option of recourse to the summary compilation. In the absence of such a certified or comparison copy of the original record of conviction, the conditions allowing secondary evidence of the contents of that original record of conviction under Rule 1005 must be essentially the same as the conditions excusing the use of an original under Rule 1004. *See* **§ 13.03**. For example, if the government had destroyed the original record of conviction in bad faith, depriving it of the use of Rule 1004(a), it would make no sense to allow the government to invoke the language in Rule 1005 permitting access to "other evidence to prove the content" of the original just because a certified copy cannot now be "obtained by reasonable diligence."

[50] If the summary record of convictions is manually created but digital in form (an increasingly common phenomenon), then the second layer of the problem can be avoided by use of either a printout original satisfying Rule 1001(d) or else a certified or comparison copy under Rule 1005, but neither also addresses the first layer of the problem, which requires a valid excuse for failure to introduce the original record of conviction. While this seems relatively straightforward, courts have had great difficulty with the problem. *See, e.g.*, Hall v. Commonwealth, 817 S.W.2d 228 (Ky. 1991) (presenting striking diversity of judicial opinions), *overruled on other grounds*, Commonwealth v. Ramsey, 920 S.W.2d 526 (Ky. 1996); State v. Waycaster, 846 S.E.2d 688 (N.C. 2020) (same); *In re* Adolph, 243 P.3d 540 (Wash. 2010) (same).

5. Found in the possession of the opponent, and the opponent had notice to produce it, by the pleadings or otherwise.[51]

If lawyers properly prepare their cases, the original recording rule should only exclude evidence when the client is in possession of the original or has destroyed it in bad faith. Bad faith means more than mere negligence, and more than simply intentional destruction for innocent motives; it requires an intent to destroy evidence.[52]

The rules express no preferences among various types of secondary evidence under Rules 1004. That is, there is no "second best evidence" rule requiring the proponent to produce the best available secondary evidence.[53] If the proponent satisfies the judge that the original is missing or that some other valid excuse exists for not producing the original, the proponent can prove the contents of the original either by oral testimony or by producing a handwritten copy. For example, if the original of a hospital record is not available because it is not subject to subpoena, oral testimony about its contents is permitted, even though a machine copy might be obtained easily. A natural extension of the best evidence idea might seem to call for extending the principle of preference beyond simply preferring the original, but the drafters believed that creating a hierarchy of preferences and a procedure for making it effective would be overly complex.[54] The normal motivation of a party to present the most convincing evidence possible will usually achieve the results of an extended scheme of preferences without adding the procedural complexity.

Recordings Related to Collateral Matters [FRE 1004(d)]

The prohibition against proving the contents of a writing, recording, or photograph without presenting the original does not apply when "the writing, recording, or photograph is not closely related to a controlling issue."[55]

Example

Direct examiner: Where were you going?

Witness: I continued down Kirby Avenue.

Direct examiner: You didn't stop?

Witness: No. I was late for an appointment.

Direct examiner: Did you later report that you had seen the accident?

Witness: Yes.

Direct examiner: When?

Witness: The next day.

Direct examiner: Why did you report it the next day?

---

51 FED. R. EVID. 1004(a)–(c).

52 *See, e.g.*, Estate of Gryder v. Commissioner, 705 F.2d 336, 338 (8th Cir. 1983) (holding that negligence does not constitute bad faith); United States v. Workinger, 90 F.3d 1409 (9th Cir. 1996) (holding that destruction in ordinary course of business does not constitute bad faith).

53 FED. R. EVID. 1004 advisory committee note ("The rule recognizes no 'degrees' of secondary evidence"). Rule 1005, requiring use of certified copies of public records, constitutes the only exception. *See* **§ 13.02**.

54 *Id.*

55 FED. R. EVID. 1004(d).

Witness: I read in the newspaper someone had been killed in the accident, and I did not agree with the description of how it all took place.

If the testimony is offered solely for the purpose of explaining why the witness called the police the next day, the contents of the newspaper are collateral and the newspaper itself need not be produced. Although a number of reported decisions apply this exception, they do not explain the concept of "collateralness."[56] A variety of factors may be in play, including the importance of the precise terms of the recording and the implications of error concerning it, as well as the difficulty of presenting the original.[57]

Summaries of Voluminous Records [FRE 1006]

Rule 1006 allows into evidence charts, summaries, or calculations to prove the content of voluminous writings, recordings, or photographs. This exception to the requirement of the original to prove the contents of a document, recording, or photograph is intended to make it more convenient for the trier-of-fact to assimilate the information.[58] The Rule requires the originals to be so "voluminous" that they "cannot conveniently be examined in court" and requires that the originals be made available for other parties to examine at a "reasonable time and place." The source documents, however, must be available to the opposing party before the introduction of the summary,[59] although the summary itself need not be.[60] This requirement is met when the trial judge determines that the underlying documents were made available at a reasonable time and place[61] even if opposing counsel fails to make use of the opportunity to review the documents.[62]

Courts have wide discretion over admission of summaries, which should be guided by whether the summary will be helpful under the circumstances.[63] Court have admitted charts under the Rule 1006 to summarize as few as twenty drug transactions when inspection of various underlying hotel receipts and phone bills would be inconvenient.[64] The need for a summary of voluminous material increases when the material involves hard-to-understand technical data[65] or when the summary clarifies a confusing sequence

---

[56] *See, e.g.*, Farr v. Zoning Bd. of Appeals, 95 A.2d 792, 794 (Conn. 1953) (noting that land ownership relates only to standing to appeal, not to substance of dispute, and is, therefore, collateral, allowing oral testimony); People v. Hamilton, 757 N.Y.S.2d 739 (N.Y. App. Div. 2003) (stating that collateral writings are exempt from best evidence rule); Bickley v. FMC Techs., Inc., 282 F. Supp. 2d 631 (N.D. Ohio 2003).

[57] *See* 5 CHRISTOPHER B. MUELLER & LAIRD C. KIRKPATRICK, FEDERAL EVIDENCE § 10:30 (4th ed. 2013).

[58] FED. R. EVID. 1006 advisory committee note.

[59] *See* Hackett v. Housing Auth. of City of San Antonio, 750 F.2d 1308, 1312 (1985) (concluding that summary was inadmissible under Rule 1006 because proponent party failed to produce underlying documents). *Cf.* United States v. Modena, 302 F.3d 626 (6th Cir. 2002); United States v. Miller, 771 F.2d 1219, 1238 (9th Cir. 1985).

[60] *See* United States v. Stoecker, 215 F.3d 788 (7th Cir. 2000); Coates v. Johnson & Johnson, 756 F.2d 524, 550 (7th Cir. 1985); People v. McDonald, 15 P.3d 788 (Colo. App. 2000).

[61] *See* Air Safety, Inc. v. Roman Catholic Archbishop, 94 F.3d 1 (1st Cir. 1996); Davis & Cox v. Summa Corp., 751 F.2d 1507, 1516 (9th Cir. 1985) (concluding that summaries were inadmissible where underlying documents were not made available to party opponent until just before trial); FED. R. EVID. 1006 advisory committee note.

[62] Frank Music Corp. v. Metro-Goldwyn-Mayer, 772 F.2d 505, 515 n.9 (9th Cir. 1985).

[63] *See, e.g.*, James v. Nico Energy Corp., 838 F.2d 1365, 1373 (5th Cir. 1988); Martin v. Funtime, Inc., 963 F.2d 110 (6th Cir. 1992); Gomez v. Great Lakes Steel Div., 803 F.2d 250, 257 (6th Cir. 1986).

[64] FTC v. Kuykendall, 312 F.3d 1329 (10th Cir. 2002); Martin v. Funtime, Inc., 963 F.2d 110 (6th Cir. 1992); United States v. Possick, 849 F.2d 332, 339 (8th Cir. 1988).

[65] *See* United States v. DeBoer, 966 F.2d 1066 (6th Cir. 1992). *But see* United States v. Taylor, 210 F.3d 311 (5th Cir. 2000) ("Admission of organizational chart in drug conspiracy prosecution was erroneous where it

of events.[66] However, in the circumstances of a given case the court may conclude that the jury ought to consider the source documents in resolving a fact issue and that, on balance, summarization of such evidence would detract from the proper weight or emphasis the evidence deserves.[67] The proponent of a Rule 1006 chart or summary must show that the materials on which it is based are admissible in evidence.[68] Any part of a Rule 1006 summary that is based on inadmissible evidence is itself inadmissible,[69] and the entire chart or summary is inadmissible, unless the admissible portion can be segregated and identified.[70]

Although Rule 1006 is designed to provide an alternative to admitting voluminous records, admission of the underlying records does not prohibit the use of a Rule 1006 chart or summary. If despite their admission into evidence, the records are too voluminous to "conveniently be examined in court," a Rule 1006 chart or summary is admissible as well.[71] Courts have universally agreed that judges have authority to allow summaries in this situation but have disagreed about the status of the summary once introduced. Although some courts talk about Rule 1006 in this circumstance, the language of the rule says that a Rule 1006 summary is conditioned upon the notion that the underlying information "cannot conveniently be examined in court." The better analysis is that admission of a summary not satisfying the condition in 1006 is within the court's discretion under Rule 611(a)—Mode and Order of Interrogation and Presentation.[72]

The difference between admission under Rule 1006 and Rule 611 is the difference between demonstrative evidence that has its own independent value and demonstrative evidence that is merely illustrative.[73] The chart or summary that is admitted under Rule 1006 is itself evidence and not merely an illustration to aid the trier-of-fact in understanding other admitted evidence.[74] Courts have called the summaries of the second kind "pedagogic." One court has suggested that the difference is important in determining whether the summary or chart should go back to the jury room during

---

did not accurately reflect underlying testimony; lines of chart showed that defendant supplied drugs to two persons who testified that they never received drugs from defendant."); United States v. Campbell, 845 F.2d 1374, 1381 (6th Cir. 1988) (admitting summary chart in evidence when "without the chart, the jury would have been forced to review hundreds of pages of technical information which may not have been readily understandable to the lay reader.").

[66] *See* United States v. Meyers, 847 F.2d 1408, 1412 (9th Cir. 1988) (admitting summary chart where underlying FBI surveillance logs for the day in question were admissible and available, but sequence of events was confusing).

[67] United States v. Smyth, 556 F.2d 1179, 1184 n.11 (5th Cir. 1977).

[68] *See, e.g.*, United States v. Hazlewood, 40 F. App'x 347 (9th Cir. 2002); State Office Sys. v. Olivetti Corp., 762 F.2d 843, 845 (10th Cir. 1985); Paddack v. Dave Christensen, Inc., 745 F.2d 1254, 1260 (9th Cir. 1984); Sotavento Corp. v. Morningside, 2001 WL 951329 (Conn. Super. Ct. 2001).

[69] *See* Bergstein v. Jordache Enters., 1996 WL 271910 (S.D.N.Y. 1996); SEC v. Price Waterhouse, 797 F. Supp. 1217 (S.D.N.Y. 1992).

[70] Paddack v. Dave Christensen, Inc., 745 F.2d 1254, 1260–61 (9th Cir. 1984) (excluding audit report based in part on inadmissible hearsay).

[71] United States v. Taylor, 210 F.3d 311 (5th Cir. 2000); Heinzerling v. Goldfarb, 818 A.2d 345 (N.J. Super. L. 2002).

[72] *See, e.g.*, United States v. Pinto, 850 F.2d 927, 935–36 (2d Cir. 1988); United States v. Johnson, 54 F.3d 1150 (4th Cir. 1995); United States v. Scales, 594 F.2d 558, 563–64 (6th Cir. 1979) (alternative holding).

[73] *See* Gomez v. Great Lakes Steel Div., 803 F.2d 250, 257–58 (6th Cir. 1986).

[74] United States v. Smyth, 556 F.2d 1179 (5th Cir. 1977); United States v. Pharis, 2000 WL 1469330 (E.D. Pa. 2000). *But see* United States v. Buck, 324 F.3d 786 (5th Cir. 2003) (using summaries illustratively to clarify or enhance testimony should not be admitted in evidence).

deliberations—allowing the Rule 1006 summary into the jury room, but not the pedagogic summary.[75] Another court has not seemed so concerned about whether the summary goes to the jury room as that the court gives the jury the proper instructions about the lack of evidentiary value in the summary.[76]

Courts' willingness to admit summaries of already examined evidence under Rule 611(a) may encourage undesirable attorney behavior allowing such summaries to become a vehicle for prematurely and unfairly arguing the case to the jury. This happens mostly in criminal cases and almost always to the advantage of the government. In *United States v. Scales*,[77] the court found that a chart was admissible under Rule 1006 because the underlying material, though admitted, could not "conveniently be examined in court." The court also noted that, if the summary had not been admissible under Rule 1006, it would have been admissible under Rule 611(a). It warned, however, that conclusory summaries, or those that presented the evidence from the government's perspective, ought not to be allowed.[78] In *United States v. Johnson*,[79] the Fourth Circuit refused to reverse a conviction where the government offered a summary that reiterated objective information that was before the jury, commented on the credibility of witnesses, and summarized the evidence in a manner most favorable to the government. The summary was not only admitted into evidence but allowed into the jury room. The appellate court held that the procedure was within the court's discretion and noted that the court instructed the jury that the summary was not evidence.[80]

§ 13.04 Preliminary Fact Questions and the Original Recording Rule [FRE 1008]

The usual principles for finding preliminary facts—under Rule 104 in the federal system—also apply to preliminary facts that determine the application of the original recording rule. Most issues are resolved by the court, under the standards stated in Rule 104(a).[81] For example, the court determines (using the preponderance of the evidence standard) whether some item of evidence constitutes a "writing, "recording," or "photograph" for purposes of Rule 1002, whether all originals have been lost or destroyed without bad faith for purposes of Rule 1004(a), whether the originals are "voluminous" for purposes of Rule 1006, and so forth.[82]

However, certain recurring fact patterns raise questions that the drafters of the Federal Rules specifically address in Rule 1008. Suppose, for example, that the plaintiff asserts rights under a document, and the defendant contends that an executed document never existed. The plaintiff offers testimony about the contents of the document, and the defendant objects under the original recording rule, insisting on the production of the original. The defendant's objection does not implicitly concede that the original existed.

---

[75] United States v. Buck, 324 F.3d 786 (5th Cir. 2003); Heinzerling v. Goldfarb, 818 A.2d 345 (N.J. Super. L. 2002).

[76] United States v. Pena, 213 F.3d 634 (4th Cir. 2000).

[77] 594 F.2d 558 (6th Cir. 1979).

[78] *Id.* at 564.

[79] 54 F.3d 1150 (4th Cir. 1995).

[80] *Id.* at 1159. For a sharp criticism of the result as giving the government an extra final argument, *see* Emilia A. Quesada, *Summarizing Prior Witness Testimony: Admissible Evidence, Pedagogical Device, or Violation of the Federal Rules of Evidence?* 24 FLA. ST. U. L. REV. 151 (1996).

[81] *See* **§ 3.11**.

[82] *See* CHRISTOPHER B. MUELLER & LAIRD C. KIRKPATRICK, FEDERAL EVIDENCE § 10:39 (4th ed. 2013).

The defendant may demand its production even as he denies its existence, because the defendant can simultaneously assert that (1) the original never existed, and (2) assuming (favorably to the plaintiff) that it did, the plaintiff must present it or have a valid excuse under the original recording rule for presenting secondary evidence of its contents. The first assertion raises a question that must ultimately be decided by the fact-finder, and need not be decided by the court.[83] The second assertion, however, raises a question under the original recording rule—whether a valid excuse for failing to produce the document has been offered—that must be decided by the court, for which purpose the court will assume that the original once existed, as indeed the plaintiff maintains. If the plaintiff presents an appropriate excuse, so that secondary evidence of the contents is admissible under Rule 1004, then the ultimate questions of whether the original ever existed, and if so, whether the secondary evidence introduced accurately reflects the contents of the original recording are questions for the fact-finder, as specified by Rules 1008(a) and (c).[84]

Rule 1008(b) is a bit more subtle. Suppose the plaintiff offers a document in support of a claim, asserting that it is the original document. And suppose that, instead of denying the existence of an original document under which the plaintiff has asserted claims, the defendant argues instead that there was such an original but what the plaintiff is offering is not that original. If the defendant presents an alternative document that defendant claims to be the original, then the question of which of the two documents is in fact the original is for the fact-finder to determine under Rule 1008(b). It might seem that both plaintiff and defendant could argue that the other party's evidence is barred by the rule, forcing the court to decide the ultimate question concerning which is the original without the fact-finder having an opportunity to reach a different conclusion.[85] The argument is specious: whether the plaintiff or the defendant is correct, the original is before the fact-finder if *both* are admitted, and the original recording rule has served its purpose.[86] To reach the fact-finder, each party's document would have to be authenticated, of course,[87] but then it should be for the jury to decide which document is the original. This is the command of Rule 1008(b). Of course, if the

---

[83] The rule prescribes a "screening" function under Rule 104(b), analogous to sufficiency of the evidence: the court decides merely whether the evidence is sufficient to support a finding that the original once existed. This conditional relevance formulation does no harm when the existence of the contract is an ultimate fact, as to which the court must exercise such a screening function anyway, in the course of monitoring the burden of production. Like all conditional relevance applications, however, requiring the screening function may be pernicious in excluding weakly probative evidence in cases where the existence and terms of the document in question are not determinative of an ultimate fact, but merely one piece of evidence related thereto, as when the document in question is a letter written to the friend of a party acknowledging responsibility for the harm at issue in the litigation.

[84] *See, e.g.*, Seiler v. Lucasfilm, Ltd., 808 F.2d 1316, 1320–21 (9th Cir. 1986), *cert. denied*, 484 U.S. 826 (1987).

[85] For example, the defendant objects to the plaintiff's document as not the original and insists that plaintiff's secondary evidence may not be introduced. During the hearing on that issue, the defense presents what it claims to be the original and then argues that the plaintiff has no valid excuse not to present that original. The defense argues that, if the defendant's document is the original, then the plaintiff's is not, and so the plaintiff's document must be excluded as secondary evidence. The reverse argument might be made by the plaintiff when the defense offers its claimed original.

[86] *See* **§ 13.01**. There is, of course, the possibility that both parties' claims are in error and that neither of the offered documents is the original. In the unlikely event that such a possibility would come to the attention of the court, the court would be called upon to make a Rule 104(a) determination whether at least one of the documents offered by the parties is the original, excluding both parties' evidence if the court finds that the original is neither of the offered documents (and neither party offers a satisfactory excuse for the use of secondary evidence).

[87] *See* **§ 12.01** & **§ 12.07**.

evidence overwhelmingly favors one side or the other, then a directed verdict on the matter might be appropriate as with any other factual question.

But suppose the defendant in such a situation does *not* offer what defendant claims to be the original. How is the court to respond to defendant's objection that the plaintiff's document is not the original, when plaintiff claims that it is? One approach would have the court determine whether the plaintiff's document is the original (as opposed to secondary evidence) as part of determining whether the plaintiff has complied with the original recording rule. Another approach would be to accept, for purposes of the admissibility ruling, the plaintiff's assertion that the plaintiff's (suitably authenticated) document is the original, leaving the ultimate question of whether it is the original to the fact-finder. There is no obvious reason why submitting this issue to a jury should depend on whether the defendant has presented a competing document, as analyzed in the previous paragraph. Although Rule 1008(b) might not be broad enough to authorize giving this question to the jury, the list of jury issues in Rule 1008 is not exclusive, and this solution can be reached by applying Rules 104 and 901. The dispute is ultimately one over the authenticity of the plaintiff's document, not the policy of when to allow secondary evidence.[88]

§ 13.05 The Original Recording Requirement Distinguished from Other Rules

One of the challenges in understanding the original recording rule is that it is easily confused with other rules that also relate to documents. Documents are so central to law and to litigation that several rules exist to regulate their use, both in and out of court. In addition, because the original recording rule serves purposes that are similar to those served by the hearsay rule, it can be confused with that rule, at least when one is dealing with statements in documents.

The Statute of Frauds

The term "statute of frauds" is a generic term for various statutory requirements that certain types of transactions be memorialized by a writing. Wills, conveyances of land, contracts for conveyances of land, and many contracts for the sale of goods are generally subject to such a requirement. Such rules do have an important evidentiary purpose: by requiring the execution of an appropriate writing, they mandate the creation of potential evidence. By the weight of authority, however, the requirement is not a rule of evidence; it does not prescribe that the only way to prove such a transaction is by way of the required writing.[89] Rather, it means that the consequence of a failure to create such a writing, with all the terms specified by statute or interpretive case-law as necessary, is that the transaction cannot be enforced. Thus, the statute of frauds is a substantive rule of law governing validity or enforceability. On the other hand, the original recording rule applies to the proof of the content of any writing, whether or not the substantive law requires that writing to have been created as a condition of validity or enforceability.

---

[88] For a pre-Rules discussion of the issue, see Edmund Morgan, *The Law of Evidence, 1941–1945*, 59 HARV. L. REV. 481, 489–91 (1945).

[89] *See* 9 WIGMORE ON EVIDENCE § 2454 (Chadbourn rev. 1981). To be sure, there is great variety in the statutes, and interpretation is sometimes affected by the particular way that the statute is written. An early, insightful analysis generated by choice-of-law questions, is Ernest G. Lorenzen, *The Statute of Frauds and the Conflict of Laws*, 32 YALE L.J. 311 (1923).

Perhaps the best way to understand the difference between the original recording rule and the statute of frauds is to identify the point in time when each is satisfied (or not). The original recording rule is satisfied (or not) when a proponent presents evidence of the contents of a recording; that is, it is satisfied (or not) at trial. The statute of frauds is satisfied (or not) when the parties create (or fail to create) a writing that memorializes the transaction; that is, it is satisfied (or not) *out of court*, generally when the transaction is (allegedly) attempted, when the parties intend the transaction to have legal effect. Once a satisfactory writing is executed by the parties, the statute of frauds is (forever) satisfied. Of course, proof of that fact will be required at a subsequent trial at which enforceability is an issue. Indeed, the effect of the statute of frauds is to create an additional ultimate material fact that must be proved by a party attempting to enforce the transaction: not only must that party allege and prove, say, an agreement for the sale of land, but that party must allege and prove as well that a writing satisfying the statute of frauds was executed. What proof of that fact will be acceptable is another matter, one that invariably invokes the original recording rule because the contents of the writing are critical. For example, if an appropriate writing is created, but then later destroyed before any duplicates can be made, the use of secondary evidence of its contents at trial is not barred by the statute of frauds; instead, its use is determined by the original recording rule. Secondary evidence will be allowed under that rule if, for example, the proponent can meet the requirements of Rule 1004(a).[90]

The Parol Evidence Rule

Despite its name, this rule is also considered a rule of substantive law, not a rule of evidence. Like the statute of frauds, it does have evidentiary effects, however. The rule generally requires that the terms of certain contracts or other transactions that are reduced to writings that contain an "integration" clause so specifying—may not be varied by recourse to agreements or acts (oral or in writing), not reflected within the writings, that occurred prior to or contemporaneously with the execution of the writings.[91] When this rule applies, courts will treat evidence of such prior or contemporaneous understandings as inadmissible on the question of the parties' obligations under the integrated agreement. Such "extrinsic" evidence is rendered irrelevant by virtue of the parties' agreement with respect to the controlling terms of the transaction, and is thus inadmissible per Rule 402. Of course, a party will often want to prove the terms of the integrated agreement, and doing so is governed by the rules of evidence, including the original recording rule. Testimony that merely purports to describe the contents of the integrated agreement (and thus does not purport to change those terms) is not barred by the parol evidence rule, though it may be barred by the original recording rule.

Interestingly, the question of whether the instrument is integrated, whether the parties intended it to be the exclusive measure of their legal obligations, which is very much a factual question, is generally taken to be a preliminary fact question that

---

[90] *See* 2 FARNSWORTH ON CONTRACTS 160 (3rd ed. 2004); The Uniform Commercial Code's statute of frauds (UCC § 2–201) is ambiguous but compatible with this interpretation. See 1 JAMES J. WHITE, ROBERT S. SUMMERS, & ROBERT H. HILLMAN, UNIFORM COMMERCIAL CODE § 3.6 at 175 (6th ed. 2012). In view of the potential for fraud that the statute is intended to prevent, in most states proof of compliance with the statute by the execution of a qualifying document that was subsequently lost must be made by clear and convincing evidence. 1 CORBIN ON CONTRACTS § 23.10 (Joseph M. Perillo ed. 2015).

[91] 9 WIGMORE ON EVIDENCE § 2400 et seq. (Chadbourn rev. 1981).

determines the relevance of evidence of prior or contemporaneous understandings, and therefore is determined by the judge.[92]

The Hearsay Rule

Both the hearsay rule and the original recording rule operate, to some extent, as rules of preference: the former expresses the law's preference for live testimony by a declarant, while the latter expresses the law's preference for inspection at trial of original records. They are obviously not the same, however. The hearsay rule applies to testimony about out-of-court statements, even where no document or recording is involved. Even when the out-of-court statement is recorded, however, the two rules are not coextensive. The hearsay rule is triggered by evidence that reports an out-of-court assertion when used to prove that the assertion is true.[93] The original recording rule is triggered by secondary evidence of the contents of a recording whenever those contents are relevant, whether or not the relevance of the contents depends on the truth of any assertion contained in the recording.

For example, a writing that memorializes a contract can be introduced without violating the hearsay rule because the out-of-court verbal utterances creating the contract are promissory acts, not assertions of fact, so the proponent's use of the contract ordinarily does not depend on the "truth" of any out-of-court assertion.[94] But secondary evidence—such as testimony—about the contents of such a writing is the paradigmatic case for the application of the original recording rule. Thus, evidence can avoid the hearsay prohibition without avoiding the requirement of the original recording rule. Conversely, evidence can avoid the original recording rule without avoiding the hearsay rule, as when evidence of an out-of-court oral assertion is used to prove that the assertion is true.

Unfortunately, judicial opinions do not always get this right. A few have reasoned, for example, that when an out-of-court written statement is not offered for the truth of the matter asserted, but rather for its effect upon the reader, neither the hearsay rule nor the original document rule applies.[95] This mistakes the conditions that invoke the latter rule: proving what the contents of a document were is not the same as proving that some assertion contained in those contents is true. If the effect of reading a document depends on its contents—as it almost always will—then the specifics of the contents are relevant and proving them triggers the original recording rule, whether or not they are offered for the truth of any assertion made therein. Fortunately, other courts manage to keep this distinction clear.[96]

---

[92] *See* Charles T. McCormick, *The Parol Evidence Rule as a Procedural Device for Control of the Jury*, 41 YALE L.J. 365 (1932).

[93] *See* **§ 15.01**.

[94] *See* **§ 15.03**.

[95] *See, e.g.*, Abulqasim v. Mahmoud, 49 A.3d 828, 837 (D.C. 2012).

[96] *See, e.g.*, Kroh v. Kroh, 567 S.E.2d 760 (N.C. App. 2002). *See generally* Colin Miller, *Contents May Have Shifted: Disentangling the Best Evidence Rule from the Rule Against Hearsay*, 71 WASH. & LEE L. REV. ONLINE 180 (2014).

The Doctrine of Verbal Completeness

The common-law doctrine of verbal completeness complements the original recording rule in the context of proof of the contents of writings or recorded statements.[97] Whether the proponent introduces the original or tangible secondary evidence of its contents, the common-law doctrine of verbal completeness as well as its Federal Rules counterpart, Rule 106, attempt to ensure that the evidence of the contents is not misleadingly incomplete, either because only part of the original is introduced or because only part of the original is revealed by the proponent's secondary evidence. Similarly, when oral evidence of the contents of a document is permitted under Article X, the common-law rule of verbal completeness would work to prevent misleading partial evidence of those contents. Although the federal version of the rule, Rule 106, does not embrace testimony, similar results can be achieved under Rule 611(a).[98]

[97] Whether the principle of verbal completeness can be extended to a principle of "informational" completeness, so as to address photographs, sketches, and other forms of recorded information, is a relatively unexplored issue.

[98] In either context, whether the federal version of the doctrine of verbal completeness provides as much protection as the common-law rule is problematic because of the still unsettled relation between Rule 106 and otherwise applicable exclusionary rules that might bar evidence of the completing portion of the record. The details are discussed elsewhere. *See* **§ 1.12**.

Part VI

HEARSAY AND CONFRONTATION

Chapter 14

THE BASIC PRINCIPLES OF HEARSAY EVIDENCE

Table of Sections

§ 14.01 The Definition of Hearsay and the General Rule of Exclusion [FRE 801, 802]

Although hearsay evidence is inadmissible as a general rule,[1] there are a great many exemptions from and exceptions to this prohibition. In the end, a lot of hearsay is in fact admissible.[2] Still, learning the rule is important, as it does exclude a considerable amount of evidence that is or might be offered. Apart from understanding the various exemptions and exceptions, which are addressed in the following chapters, the initial challenge is defining hearsay evidence.

The definition of hearsay in the Federal Rules of Evidence and most common-law jurisdictions uses an *assertion-oriented* criterion. Under this definition, an out-of-court statement is hearsay if it is an assertion and it is used in court to show the truth of the matter that was asserted out of court.[3] Absent some exception or waiver of objection, a party may not introduce evidence of an assertion made outside of the current trial to convince the trier-of-fact to believe the assertion is true. This hearsay definition requires that the proposition a person (the "declarant") asserts out of court coincide with a proposition that the proponent uses the evidence to prove in court. For example, imagine Wanda (the witness at trial) heard an out-of-court statement from Donald (the out-of-

---

[1] *See, e.g.*, FED. R. EVID. 802.

[2] Noting the steady expansion of the number and breadth of hearsay exceptions, some commentators believe that there is little left of the prohibition. *See, e.g.*, Ronald J. Allen, *The Hearsay Rule as a Rule of Admission Revisited*, 84 FORDHAM L. REV. 1395, 1398–99 (2016) ("Today, . . . , virtually all hearsay that might have probative force is admitted, leaving exclusion primarily for the kinds of evidence that no one would be convinced by anyway (such as the product of the telephone game)").

[3] FED. R. EVID. 801(a)–(c). The phrase "out of court" is commonly used as a shorter way of saying, "not made while testifying at the current trial or hearing." *Id.* Though typically not made in court, such "out of court" statements might actually have been made in a courtroom; if such statements were not made in the "current trial or hearing," they can still qualify as hearsay.

court declarant) stating: "Abigail robbed the bank."[4] If the prosecution attempts to use Wanda's testimony about what Donald stated to show that Abigail robbed the bank, then it is a hearsay use. The proposition that Donald asserted out of court is the very fact the prosecution is attempting to prove with this evidence, and Wanda's testimony is hearsay evidence.[5]

Some jurisdictions have used a *declarant-oriented* criterion of hearsay. That is, an out-of-court statement is hearsay if its use by a trier-of-fact will require relying upon the credibility of the declarant or the accuracy of the declarant's beliefs.[6] The prohibition is invoked when the proponent invites the fact-finder to infer the declarant's belief from the evidence presented and to infer the truth of that belief from the fact that the declarant believed it. A definition using this criterion requires a coincidence between what the proponent claims the declarant believed and what the proponent wants to use the statement to prove. If Wanda testifies and repeats Donald's out-of-court statement to prove the truth of Donald's statement—that Abigail robbed the bank—then the proponent of the evidence is asking the trier-of-fact to infer that Donald believed what he said and that his belief is accurate. Thus, the proponent is relying upon Donald's credibility in making his out-of-court assertion, and the evidence is hearsay evidence.

Usually, the two criteria reach the same result, as the example of Wanda's testimony illustrates. However, they can lead to different results because of differences between what one asserts and what one believes.[7] Suppose that the declarant wrote a letter to his aged cousin describing the writer's visit to Alexandria. The letter was written as if to a person of ordinary understanding. At trial, it is offered to show that the aged cousin was mentally competent, on the theory that, otherwise, the younger cousin would not have written it. Here, one might reach a different result depending on which criterion is applied. The statement is not being used to show that the younger cousin in fact took a trip to Alexandria or anything about that trip, so it is hard to say that the statement is being used to prove that it is true under the assertion-centered criterion. Yet, when the letter is used to show that the person to whom it was written was of sound mind, its value certainly depends on the accuracy of the declarant in believing his cousin to be of sound mind, and hence would be classified as hearsay under the declarant-centered criterion. The value of the letter depends upon the younger cousin's perception and judgment (perhaps he last saw the older cousin years before, or missed signs of senility), and in a sense upon his sincerity (for various reasons, he might have been

---

[4] We are assuming that Wanda has no personal knowledge of what Abigail did in regard to the bank; all she knows is what Donald told her. If Wanda had personal knowledge of what Abigail did, she could testify to that without mentioning Donald's assertion, and no hearsay problem would arise.

[5] Technically, by the Rules' definition, Wanda's testimony is not itself the hearsay in this example; Donald's out-of-court statement is the hearsay. In any event, Wanda's testimony is commonly called "hearsay evidence" and is inadmissible because it *evidences* hearsay. See **§ 14.05**.

[6] *See* Laurence H. Tribe, *Triangulating Hearsay*, 87 HARV. L. REV. 957, 959 (1974). Tribe explains that four factors are usually identified as affecting the declarant's credibility: *perception* (accuracy of declarant's perception of the event); *memory* (accuracy of declarant's recollection of the event); *narration* or *ambiguity* (comprehensibility of declarant's statement about the event); and *sincerity* (honesty of declarant in making the statement). Statement or conduct will be hearsay under a declarant-oriented definition of hearsay if its usefulness to the trier-of-fact is affected by any of these four factors as they relate to the declarant or actor.

[7] *See* Roger C. Park, *McCormick on Evidence and the Concept of Hearsay*, 65 MINN. L. REV. 423 (1981). Park coins the phrases "assertion-oriented" and "declarant-oriented" and discusses the difference between the two criteria. *See also* Roger C. Park, *"I Didn't Tell Them Anything About You": Implied Assertions as Hearsay under the Federal Rules of Evidence,* 74 MINN. L. REV. 783 (1990).

pretending that the older cousin was mentally sound even though he knew that not to be the case).[8]

It would be a mistake to think that one must choose either the assertion-based or the declarant-based definition; these are not the only options. One could define hearsay as any statement that satisfies *either* the assertion-based criterion *or* the declarant-based criterion (which would be a very broad definition, one not in fact encountered), or one could define hearsay as any statement that satisfies *both* criteria (a narrow category). In his pre-Rules distillation of the American common law, for example, Dean Charles McCormick famously wrote:

> Hearsay evidence is testimony in court, or written evidence, of a statement made out of court, the statement being offered as an assertion to show the truth of matters asserted therein, and thus resting for its value upon the credibility of the out-of-court asserter.[9]

The first part of McCormick's definition (up to the word "therein") is assertion-oriented, but the last part is declarant-oriented. McCormick wrote as if the latter follows from the former (using the words, "and thus"), but it is actually a separate limiting condition that the courts routinely applied.[10] As illustrated below, courts following the Federal Rules continue to limit hearsay in this way. Thus, to be within the scope of the hearsay rule, an out-of-court utterance must be used to prove the truth of something asserted *and* its claimed probative value in that regard must rest on the credibility of the out-of-court asserter.

What, then, is an *assertion*?[11] People make assertions when they talk, but do they make assertions when they perspire? When they cry? Does a drug-sniffing dog make an assertion? A breathalyzer? These questions concerning the nature of the "assertion" aspect of the hearsay rule demonstrate its complexity, but probably do not confound the average student, practitioner, or judge and are not discussed at any length here.[12]

---

[8] *See* Wright v. Doe d. Tatham, 7 A. & E. 313, 112 Eng. Rep. 488 (Exch. Ch. 1837), *aff'd*, 5 C. & F. 670, 7 Eng. Rep. 559 (H.L. 1838), a famous case that has traditionally been a rite of passage for evidence students. In *Wright*, the heir at law sued the steward who inherited a large part of the estate and attempted to prove that the deceased was incompetent and under coercive influence when he bequeathed his property to the steward. To demonstrate his master's competence, the steward attempted to introduce letters concerning business matters indicating, though not explicitly stating, that the writers believed that the master was competent to handle the transaction. Baron Parke wrote a famous opinion finding the letters hearsay. Parke went even further, constructing famous hypotheticals concerning nonverbal activities (such as a sea captain inspecting a vessel) and asserting in dicta that even nonverbal, non-assertive conduct may be hearsay.

[9] CHARLES T. MCCORMICK, HANDBOOK OF THE LAW OF EVIDENCE § 225 at 460 (1st ed. 1954).

[10] This is because it is possible for an assertion to be offered to prove the truth of what is asserted *without* relying upon the credibility of the asserter. Examples are presented throughout this chapter.

[11] The Rules use the defined term "statement" rather than "assertion," but the definition of statement is "a person's oral assertion, written assertion, or nonverbal conduct, if the person intended it as an assertion." FED. R. EVID. 801(a). Because oral and written assertions are both verbal conduct, and verbal conduct is either oral or written, another way to say this would be that a statement is "a person's verbal or nonverbal conduct intended as an assertion," or more simply, "a person's conduct intended as an assertion," or even more simply, "an assertion." "Assertion" is not defined in the rules, but lawyers do not understand it to entail any aggressiveness (as in "he was assertive"); it simply means "to say that something is so," to say "that an event happened or a condition existed." 2 MCCORMICK ON EVIDENCE § 246 at 183–84 (Kenneth S. Broun ed., 7th ed. 2013).

[12] Some of these questions might seem to be answered by the Federal Rules definition, which refers only to statements made by a "person" FED. R. EVID. 801(a), (b). This would seem to exclude dog alerts and breathalyzer test results. But are not both of these indicators the result of training or programming *by a person*?

To determine which verbal utterances are hearsay, we must focus on whether an assertion was intended by the utterer and, if so, when such assertion is offered for its truth. As an initial example, imagine that a declarant, trapped in a car after an automobile accident, utters the words, "Help me." Suppose his utterance is offered solely for the purpose of showing that the declarant was alive at the time. In that case, the fact-finder is not being asked to rely upon the truth of any assertion. Nothing is lost by the fact that the out-of-court declarant was not subjected to cross-examination. Instead, it is important simply that the words were uttered. Hence, the utterance would not be considered hearsay at all. The same would be true if the utterance had been the statement, "I'm dead!" The statement is relevant because it was made, rather than because it is truthful. The trier-of-fact is not being asked to believe that the statement is true.

But suppose the declarant had said, "I'm alive," and the proponent is using evidence of the utterance to prove that the declarant was alive at the time. Then, it would seem that the evidence *is* being offered to prove the truth of the matter asserted. Like the previous example, however, the proponent is not relying on the truthfulness of the declarant, so one ought to reach the same conclusion, and most courts would. This result can be explained in two ways. One could argue that the proponent is not *evidencing* the assertion as such, but merely the fact that a verbal utterance was made. Alternatively, this is saved from being considered hearsay under an assertion-oriented criterion by McCormick's addendum to that criterion: though the proponent is offering evidence of the assertion to prove the truth of what was asserted, the proponent is *not* relying on the credibility of the declarant in doing so; the proponent is relying merely on the fact that the declarant spoke. Either way, the evidence is not hearsay.

To give another example, imagine that Dora makes a statement outside the trial in question. The statement can be on a street corner, before a grand jury, or in a prior trial of this very same case; the location does not matter, because all are "out-of-court" for the purpose of the hearsay rule. Dora's statement is: "My, that blue van just drove by very fast!" If Dora's statement is introduced to prove the "truth of the matter asserted," that is to say, to prove that a blue van was speeding, her statement is hearsay. Neither she, nor anyone else can repeat the statement in court before the trier-of-fact. Dora can *testify* as to what she saw (i.e., "I saw the van speeding"), but unless we apply some hearsay exception,[13] no one, including Dora herself, may testify about what Dora said out of court given the stated purpose. However, if the purpose of introducing the statement was quite different—say, to prove that Dora is an English speaker who understood the Miranda warnings she received in English the day before—the analysis is different. Then, Dora's out-of-court statement—"My, that van just drove by very fast!"—is being introduced not to prove what was asserted by Dora in the statement (that the van was speeding), but for another purpose (showing that Dora speaks English). Hence, it is not hearsay.

These examples delineate the contours of the "truth of the matter asserted" part of the hearsay rule, but immediately raise questions of application. How can we determine, for example, the extent of Dora's assertions? Is there some argument that she asserted both that the car was speeding and "impliedly" that she speaks English? The Federal Rules, however, reject the inclusion of this kind of implied assertions as hearsay, drawing a distinction between that which one asserts and that which one knows,

[13] Dora's statement is hearsay, but arguably fits within the exception for present sense impressions. *See* **§ 16.03**.

believes, or assumes (perhaps as the background for what one asserts). Without the intention to assert, it is much less likely the declarant is being insincere; one does not usually lie to oneself.[14] The Rules thus limit hearsay to those words (and gestures) *intended* as assertions.[15] Dora does not intend to assert that she speaks English; she simply speaks English. She does this because she knows how and because she assumes or hopes that the listener will understand English.

To be sure, there are other kinds of assertions plausibly called "implied assertions" that *are* recognized as hearsay under the Federal Rules. For example, if a speaker asserts something but intends to assert something other than what he or she literally says, and a proponent uses the statement to prove what the speaker really intended to assert, then the evidence falls within the hearsay prohibition even under the Federal Rules definition. This is plausibly called an "implied assertion," one in which the content of the assertion is implied by the speaker and inferred by the listener. An obvious example is metaphorical exaggeration, such as the out-of-court statement, "I've driven through that intersection a million times," when offered in court to prove that the speaker was familiar with the intersection.[16] But the same point extends to other ways in which a person intends to assert something other than what is literally said.

Suppose, for example, roommates Mary and Bob go to a party. They agree that, if one of them notices any illegal drugs, that person will say, within the other's earshot, "Oh, no. I think I left the stove on." In fact, Mary and Bob have no stove; by their agreement, this will be understood as a signal for them to leave the party because of the presence of illegal drugs. In subsequent litigation, if a proponent offers the testimony of a witness that, "Mary said to Bob, 'Oh no. I left the stove on,' " and if this testimony is offered to prove that there were drugs at the party, then one might be tempted to think that this is not hearsay because Mary did not explicitly assert, "I see illegal drugs." But in light of the prior understanding between Mary and Bob, her statement was assertive, and she was not really asserting anything about the stove; rather, she was asserting to Bob that drugs were present. What she was asserting, impliedly but intentionally, coincides with what the proponent is using her statement to prove, so this is hearsay, a kind of "implied assertion" that should fall within the hearsay prohibition of the Federal Rules.[17]

These examples indicate that when deciding whether something is hearsay under the Rules, it is essential not to be too caught up in the literal words or the grammatical form of expression. Instead, one should look for the actual intent of the declarant in

---

14 *See* FED. R. EVID. 801(a) advisory committee note.

15 This is the majority interpretation of the Federal Rules. Some argue that implied assertions should be included in a proper definition of hearsay. *See, e.g.*, Eustace Seligman, *An Exception to the Hearsay Rule*, 26 HARV. L. REV. 146, 148–49 & n.6 (1912); Judson F. Falknor, *The 'Hear-Say' Rule as a 'See-Do' Rule: Evidence of Conduct*, 33 ROCKY MT. L. REV. 133, 134–35 (1961); *see also* Olin Guy Wellborn III, *The Definition of Hearsay in the Federal Rules of Evidence*, 61 TEX. L. REV. 49 (1982). Professor Wellborn argues that Federal Rule of Evidence 801 defines hearsay too narrowly and that the rule's treatment of all verbal expressions other than direct verbal assertions as nonhearsay is unsound. Wellborn also argues that Federal Rules of Evidence made a reasonable, if questionable, decision rejecting nonverbal, non-assertive conduct as hearsay but went too far in omitting verbal conduct that is not a direct assertion.

16 *See* GRAHAM C. Lilly, DANIEL J. CAPRA, & STEPHEN A. SALTZBURG, PRINCIPLES OF EVIDENCE 148 (6th ed. 2012).

17 *See* 4 CHRISTOPHER B. MUELLER & LAIRD C. KIRKPATRICK, FEDERAL EVIDENCE § 8:9 (4th ed. 2013) (discussing various kinds of "coded" verbal signals or expressions). A mere hand signal that communicated the same proposition without words to Bob would be understood, uncontroversially, as hearsay of the "nonverbal" variety. *See* **§ 14.02**.

engaging in certain conduct, whether verbal or non-verbal. If that intent is to assert a proposition, whether explicitly expressed in so many words or not, and the proponent of evidence of the declarant's conduct is using that conduct to prove the truth of the proposition the declarant was intending to communicate, then it is hearsay (provided, once again, the proponent is asking the fact-finder to rely on the declarant's credibility). If there is a serious question about the assertive intent of a declarant, as there might be in the Mary and Bob example, a preliminary question of fact is raised: What did Mary actually intend to assert by her statement at the party? Did she really intend to assert that she spotted illegal drugs? To rule on the hearsay objection, the trial court decides this kind of question as it would other preliminary fact questions under Rule 104(a). If it is unable to resolve doubt on the matter, the trial court should rule the evidence not to be hearsay.[18]

Another common confusion arises when the assertion made by the out-of-court statement is different from the ultimate issue the proponent is using it to prove. Hearsay is defined in terms of what the proponent offers the hearsay to prove. Often it happens that the ultimate fact toward which an out-of-court statement is directed is not the truth of the matter asserted but rather some other fact that is inferred from the truth of the matter asserted. This, however, does not avoid the hearsay prohibition. Suppose, for example, in a prosecution for the murder of Ramirez, the only issue is the identity of the perpetrator, and the prosecution offers evidence that, before the death of Ramirez, the wife of the defendant said to the witness, "My husband really hates Ramirez." The prosecution claims that, if this assertion was true, it is evidence of motive, which tends to show that defendant was the perpetrator. The defense objects to this evidence as hearsay, and the prosecution argues in reply, "I'm offering this as evidence that the defendant is the perpetrator, which is not what the defendant's wife asserted. Therefore, it is not hearsay." This response to the hearsay objection is wrong: the prosecution is asking the fact-finder to believe the statement is true. The prosecution wants the fact-finder to infer defendant's hatred of Ramirez from his wife's statement (and possibly other evidence), *and then* to infer the identity of the perpetrator from this hatred (and, presumably, other evidence). That triggers the hearsay rule. So long as this inference process involves using the out-of-court assertion to prove the truth of the matter asserted, the hearsay rule is applicable.[19]

§ 14.02 Nonverbal Conduct as Hearsay

Nonverbal conduct can sometimes amount to a statement offered for the truth of what it asserts. For example, when a person points at another in response to the question "Who did it?" the pointing amounts to an assertion that the other person is the perpetrator. If done out of court and offered in court to show who did the act, that pointing would be non-verbal assertive conduct offered to prove the truth of the matter asserted and thus hearsay.[20]

---

[18] *See* **§ 3.11**. In reference to evidence of conduct, presumably nonverbal, the drafters stated, "The rule is so worded as to place the burden upon the party claiming that the intention existed; ambiguous and doubtful cases will be resolved against him and in favor of admissibility." FED. R. EVID. 801(a) advisory committee note. While it is unclear how the wording of the rule places this burden one way or the other, so placing it is consistent with the general preference of the Rules for admissibility.

[19] *See* GEORGE FISHER, EVIDENCE 397–98 (3d ed. 2013) (calling this a situation of "indirect assertion").

[20] The question—"Who did it?"—is not an assertion in this context, although evidence of posing that question is essential in order to understand the content of the assertion involved in the conduct of pointing:

Under the Federal Rules of Evidence, classifying nonverbal conduct as hearsay depends upon whether it was intended as an assertion, and if so, whether it is being offered to prove the truth of the matter asserted. If nonverbal conduct was not intended as an assertion, then it is not hearsay, even if its use as evidence requires the trier-of-fact to rely upon the credibility of the declarant. If the proponent is using the conduct to prove, for example, what the declarant merely believed to be true or what others might infer to be true, but that the declarant did not intend to assert, then it is not hearsay.

Examples

Hearsay: In the Mary and Bob example of the previous section, if "thumbs down" was the agreed signal to leave the party because illegal drugs were present, then Bob's testimony that Mary gave him the "thumbs down" signal would be hearsay if offered to prove that illegal drugs were present.

Hearsay: In response to a question about who saw the accident, the declarant raises his or her hand. Such hand raising is assertive, and would be hearsay, if offered to show that declarant saw the accident.

Nonhearsay: To prove that it was raining, the proponent offers into evidence testimony that the witness saw pedestrians walking outside with open umbrellas. Because the pedestrians did not intend to make a statement by opening the umbrellas, the evidence of their conduct is not hearsay, even though its value depends upon the assumption that the pedestrians believed it was raining and were correct in that belief.

Nonhearsay: As evidence of innocence, the defendant offers testimony that after the crime a third person fled the jurisdiction. The purpose of the offer is to show that the third person committed the crime. The testimony is not hearsay, because the third person's act of fleeing was not intended as an assertion; the person was merely trying to escape, not to assert or admit guilt. The evidence is categorized as nonhearsay despite the fact that its probative value depends upon inferences about the accuracy of the third person's inferred beliefs.

Regarding the last two examples, one might well think that it would be helpful to put the persons whose beliefs are inferred on the stand to explore the reasons for their conduct, but the rulemakers did not consider this a sufficient reason to classify the conduct as hearsay.[21] They reasoned that, because the fact-finder does not rely upon the *sincerity* of the declarant when drawing inferences from nonassertive conduct, the conduct should be treated as nonhearsay. Under the Federal Rules approach, the existence of other potential dangers to accuracy of inference may affect the weight accorded to the evidence, but they do not render the evidence inadmissible under the hearsay rule.[22]

---

without the question, one does not know what the pointing behavior means. In most contexts, if the hearsay pointing is inadmissible, then the question that elicits it will be irrelevant.

[21] *See* John M. Maguire, *The Hearsay System: Around and Through the Thicket*, 14 VAND. L. REV. 741, 766 (1961). For an argument that such statements should be considered hearsay, see Ted Finman, *Implied Assertions as Hearsay: Some Criticisms of the Uniform Rules of Evidence*, 14 STAN. L. REV. 682, 687–88 (1962).

[22] *See* FED. R. EVID. 801(a) advisory committee note (citing Judson F. Falknor, *The "Hear-Say" Rule as a "See-Do" Rule*, 33 ROCKY MT. L. REV. 133 (1960); *see also* Ted Finman, *Implied Assertions as Hearsay: Some Criticisms of the Uniform Rules of Evidence*, 14 STAN. L. REV. 682, 691–93 (1962) (discussing reliance as a

In the last example above, it is conceivable, though unlikely, that the third person's reason for fleeing was actually to draw suspicion away from someone else. In that case, the conduct would be an assertion that the person fleeing is the guilty party. Where there is a dispute about whether conduct was intended as an assertion, the trial judge decides the question of intent as a preliminary question of fact under Rule 104(a). The opponent of the evidence has the burden of proving that the conduct was intended as an assertion.[23]

§ 14.03 The Rationale of the Rule

The rule excluding hearsay is unique to the Anglo-American trial process.[24] Its origins are in dispute, although its history is closely related to the jury system and to the lawyers' extensive control of the evidence that is presented to the court.

Traditionally, hearsay has been excluded because it is considered inferior evidence, usually lacking four assurances of reliability that apply to live testimony: an in-court oath,[25] the possible prosecution of the declarant for perjury, the ability of the fact-finder to observe the witness's demeanor, and most important, the opportunity for cross-examination. Cross-examination can illuminate problems in the witness's testimony that cannot be addressed adequately if the witness's information comes in by way of another person's in-court report.

Suppose a witness wants to testify that Dora said (out of court), "My, that van just drove by fast." Even if the witness to Dora's declaration is truthful (something that can be at least partially tested on cross-examination because the witness is in court testifying), information could get lost in the translation. Dora could have been joking or lying. Dora might have been sincere but nonetheless expressed herself poorly. There could have been problems with Dora's original perception. It is unclear (at least from Dora's statement) how soon Dora made her remark after the car passed. Her view could have been obstructed or her memory might be deficient. These classical concerns about the declarant's sincerity, perception, memory, and narrative ability form the core of the argument for excluding hearsay.[26]

But recognizing that hearsay has inherent weaknesses, that it is sometimes or even often relatively "unreliable," does not completely justify a rule of exclusion. After all, there are many categories of evidence, such as eyewitness identifications, that often possess dubious reliability, and yet courts routinely admit them.[27] Why the difference?

---

substitute for cross-examination). For criticism of the advisory committee's view, see 2 MICHAEL H. GRAHAM, HANDBOOK OF FEDERAL EVIDENCE § 801.3 (4th ed. 1996).

23 *See* FED. R. EVID. 801(a) advisory committee note.

24 For a discussion of European analogues of the hearsay rule, *see* Mirjan Damaška, *Of Hearsay and Its Analogues*, 76 MINN. L. REV. 425 (1992); Dale A. Nance, *Understanding Responses to Hearsay: An Extension of the Comparative Analysis*, 76 MINN. L. REV. 459 (1992).

25 There is some debate about the efficacy of the oath in an age that has rejected divine retribution. Wigmore argued that the oath was non-essential because out-of-court statements, even when sworn, were not admissible for their hearsay purpose. 5 WIGMORE ON EVIDENCE § 10 (3d ed. 1940). We agree with McCormick, however, that the oath has some vestigial impact by adding to the solemnity and majesty of the proceedings. *See* 2 MCCORMICK ON EVIDENCE § 245 at 179 (Kenneth S. Broun ed., 7th ed. 2013).

26 *See* 2 MCCORMICK ON EVIDENCE § 245 (Kenneth S. Broun ed., 7th ed. 2013) (discussing reasons for the rule against hearsay); Laurence H. Tribe, *Triangulating Hearsay*, 87 HARV. L. REV. 957, 958 (1974).

27 *See, e.g.*, Perry v. New Hampshire, 565 U.S. 228 (2012) (holding that admission of eyewitness identification evidence without preliminary screening for reliability does not violate Due Process Clause in the absence of showing that the identification was procured by the state's use of unnecessarily suggestive circumstances).

It is impossible to discuss the rationale of the hearsay rule without looking to the larger objectives of the evidence rules. A number of competing theories vie to explain the overarching trends of evidence law and, in turn, the hearsay rule and its exceptions.

The most prevalent modern theory is that rules of evidence emanate from the development of the jury system and its shift from a group of neighbors with personal knowledge to an impartial fact-finding group that relies on the parties to present the evidence.[28] A combination of paternalism and distrust of the lay jury led to the exclusion of certain categories of unreliable evidence. With regard to hearsay, out-of-court statements are not only inherently unreliable, but jurors may be too unsophisticated and gullible to weigh such statements appropriately. Of course, the argument must be that jury gullibility is more dangerous in the context of hearsay than in the context of other kinds of evidence that are admissible despite their dubious reliability.

One of the most famous trials in English jurisprudence, the trial of Sir Walter Raleigh, occurred at the beginning of the sixteenth century, before the rule against hearsay had emerged. It illustrates both the problematic nature of the use of hearsay and the interesting assumptions that have been made about jury gullibility. Raleigh was convicted of a conspiracy to commit treason by plotting to dethrone Elizabeth I's successor, James I, and to place a Stuart on the throne.[29] The principal evidence against him came from Lord Cobham, a supposed fellow-conspirator, who apparently had betrayed Raleigh in a sworn pre-trial statement. Cobham himself was in the Tower of London (on the rack, perhaps?), and was not produced at trial.

> Raleigh: "But it is strange to see how you press me still with my Lord Cobham, and yet will not produce him; it is not for gaining of time or prolonging my life that I urge this; he is in the house hard by, and may soon be brought hither; let him be produced, and if he will yet accuse me or avow this confession of his, it shall convict me and ease you of further proof."
>
> Lord Cecil: "Sir Walter Raleigh presseth often that my Lord Cobham should be brought face to face; if he ask a thing of grace and favour, they must come from him only who can give them; but if he ask a matter of law, then, in order that we, who sit here as commissioners, may be satisfied, I desire to hear the opinions of my Lords, the judges, whether it may be done by law."
>
> The Judges all answered, "that in respect it might be a mean to cover many with treasons, and might be prejudicial to the King, therefore, by the law, it was not sufferable."
>
> Popham, CJ: "There must not such a gap be opened for the destruction of the King as would be if we should grant this; you plead hard for yourself, but the laws plead as hard for the King. Where no circumstances agreeing and confirming the accusation in this case, the accuser is not to be produced; for, having first confessed against himself voluntarily, and so charged another person, if we shall now hear him again in person, he may, for favour or fear, retract what formerly he hath said, and the jury may, by that means, be inveigled. . . ."

---

[28] *See* 2 McCormick on Evidence § 244 (Kenneth S. Broun ed., 7th ed. 2013) (discussing relationship between development of the jury and hearsay law); J. Thayer, Preliminary Treatise on Evidence § 519 (1898).

[29] *Raleigh's Case,* 2 How. St. Tr. 1 (1603).

Notice how the modern jury-distrust theory of the hearsay rule turns Justice Popham's reply to Raleigh on its head: Popham had offered the gullibility of the jury as a reason to *credit* hearsay, at least of the sworn kind, over live testimony even when such testimony is possible. In more recent times, at least since the end of the Nineteenth Century, jury gullibility has been used instead as a reason to *reject* hearsay even when live testimony by the declarant is not possible. This difference in judicial attitudes illustrates the malleability of the "jury distrust" theory of excluding evidence, especially when it is devoid of empirical information about how juries actually behave.[30] No one nowadays seems to advance Justice Popham's version of the argument as a general proposition, and empirical evidence about jury behavior, which has been developed only in more recent decades, does little to support the modern version of the jury gullibility argument.[31]

A second theory argues that the general institutional goal of securing the best reasonably obtainable evidence describes the overall function of the rules, and should guide the articulation and interpretation of most rules of admissibility.[32] This notion of best evidence, with origins in the writings of Eighteenth Century courts and commentators, is broader than the so-called "best evidence" rule that prefers the production of the original document.[33] As in the context of the latter rule, "best evidence" here does not mean what might be tactically optimal for the litigant, but rather what would be most useful for the fact-finder.[34] The driving force of this explanation of admissibility rules is distrust of adversarial bias in the selection and presentation of evidence, rather than distrust in the lay jury's ability to process evidence. From this perspective, for example, Raleigh's demand that the government produce Lord Cobham expresses distrust of the motives, competence, or judgment of those who chose not to call him to testify.[35]

Perhaps the most important consideration underlying the exclusion of hearsay is that the out-of-court declarant has not been subjected to the test of cross-examination. According to the jury distrust theory, the absence of cross-examination generally creates an unacceptable danger that the trier-of-fact will not be aware of the flaws of the declarant's hearsay statement and thus will overvalue it. Give the assumption, exceptional situations, when hearsay should be admitted, would be those in which the circumstances surrounding the out-of-court statements are such that the jury safely can

---

30 Perhaps that is why so many lawyers and judges have found the theory congenial: it can be used to support any position.

31 *See, e.g.* Richard F. Rakos, & Stephen Landsman, *Researching the Hearsay Rule: Emerging Findings, General Issues, and Future Directions*, 76 MINN. L. REV. 655 (1992); Peter Meine, Roger Park, & Eugene Borgida, *Juror Decision Making and the Evaluation of Hearsay Evidence*, 76 MINN. L. REV. 683 (1992); Margaret B. Kovera, Roger C. Park, & Steven Penrod, *Jurors' Perceptions of Eyewitness and Hearsay Evidence*, 76 MINN. L. REV. 703 (1992).

32 Dale A. Nance, *The Best Evidence Principle* 73 IOWA L. REV. 227, 233 (1988); *see also* 21 WRIGHT & GRAHAM, FEDERAL PRACTICE AND PROCEDURE § 5001 at 11 (2d ed. 2005) (discussing the best evidence rule as "the keystone of the entire evidentiary edifice" of late Eighteenth Century common-law scholars); Edmund Morgan, *The Jury and Exclusionary Rules of Evidence*, 4 U. CHI. L. REV. 247 (1937) (challenging the view that the admissibility rules are largely attributable to offsetting jury credulity and emphasizing the importance of offsetting lawyers' incentives to distort evidence presented).

33 *See* **§ 13.01**.

34 Dale A. Nance, *The Best Evidence Principle*, 73 IOWA L. REV. 227, 237–39 (1988).

35 The theory depends on the recognition of imperfections in the operation of the adversary system and the system of discovery: if opponents invariably have access to the "best" evidence and can present it without excessive inconvenience to the court, then the court should generally rely on the opponent's self-interest to make that best evidence available to the court. *See id.* at 239–43, 263–70.

be allowed to rely on the hearsay. In contrast, according to the "best evidence" theory the absence of cross-examination means the hearsay is generally less reliable than the declarant's in-court testimony would be, which provides a reason to exclude the hearsay as an inducement to parties to present the declarant in court, whether the fact-finder is a lay jury or a professional judge.[36] According to this theory, exceptions to the hearsay prohibition should cover the occasions where the out-of-court statement nonetheless provides the "epistemically best evidence" that is available for use by the fact-finder.[37]

As different as jury mistrust and best evidence theories may be, they share the premise that an evidence code must regulate the information presented to the trier-of-fact in order to improve its reliability. Thus, the hearsay question is similar for all approaches. What is it about hearsay that would trigger a juror's irrationality or poor judgment? What is it about hearsay that makes it generally not epistemically best? In addition, what is it about the hearsay exceptions that counterbalance juror gullibility and emotion? What makes evidence admitted under a hearsay exception "better" than exclusion or insisting on the requirement of live in-court testimony? We will address potential answers to these questions as we discuss hearsay and its exceptions in this and the following chapters.

Although not identical, the purposes of hearsay and the Confrontation Clause of the Sixth Amendment are closely connected. Certainly, one reason for the hostility to hearsay is the fear of governmental abuse in the presentation of evidence in criminal trials. One of the best solutions to concerns about coerced or manufactured testimony is the requirement that the government's witnesses be produced to testify in court subject to cross-examination.[38]

There are many other explanations and reformulations of the hearsay rule.[39] For example, hearsay can also be understood on efficiency grounds.[40] For every witness who introduces in-court testimony, there are multiple forms of hearsay evidence to prove the same proposition. Hearsay, therefore, takes more valuable court time. Relatedly, the hearsay rule can be seen as a mechanism for protecting criminal defendants or for

---

[36] The idea of a preference for live testimony goes back at least to Second Century Roman law, where a largely adversarial system of *nonjury* trials was used in the provinces. That system included:

> the general principle that a judge might insist on the better form of evidence being produced if it was available. Thus the emperor Hadrian, who was particularly interested in questions of evidence, replies to one of his provincial governors that he declines to allow a prosecutor to adduce written depositions before him instead of oral testimony. He therefore remits the case to the provincial governor in order that the latter should hear the witnesses, who are resident in his province, and form a conclusion as to their credibility. The emperor gives as his reason that he prefers to question witnesses personally.

Tony Honoré, *The Primacy of Oral Evidence?* in CRIME, PROOF, AND PUNISHMENT: ESSAYS IN MEMORY OF SIR RUPERT CROSS 172, 174, 178 (1981).

[37] Dale A. Nance, *The Best Evidence Principle*, 73 IOWA L. REV. 227, 240 (1988). *See also* George F. James, *The Role of Hearsay in a Rational Scheme of Evidence*, 34 ILL. L. REV. 788 (1940); Michael Seigel, *Rationalizing Hearsay: A Proposal for a Best Evidence Hearsay Rule*, 72 B.U. L. REV. 893 (1992).

[38] The Confrontation Clause is discussed in depth in **§§ 20.01 et seq.**

[39] For a critical examination of the standard explanation for excluding hearsay, and a suggestion that other reasons for excluding hearsay may also be important, see Roger C. Park, *A Subject Matter Approach to Hearsay Reform*, 86 MICH. L. REV. 51 (1987). For other analyses of the basis and theory of the hearsay rule, see Craig R. Callen, *Hearsay and Informal Reasoning*, 47 VAND. L. REV. 43 (1994); Richard D. Friedman, *Toward a Partial Economic, Game-Theoretic Analysis of Hearsay*, 76 MINN. L. REV. 723 (1992); Eleanor Swift, *A Foundation Fact Approach to Hearsay*, 75 CAL. L. REV. 1339 (1987); Glen Weissenberger, *Reconstructing the Definition of Hearsay*, 57 OHIO ST. L.J. 1525 (1996).

[40] Dale A. Nance, *The Best Evidence Principle* 73 IOWA L. REV. 227, 284 (1988).

preventing large corporations from manufacturing volumes of documents to deluge smaller opponents.

Finally, whatever the reasons that motivated the creation of the hearsay rule and it many exceptions, hearsay doctrine seems to have its own momentum. As a matter of the anthropology of the legal profession, lawyers who have learned the intricate matrix of hearsay rules, one of the secret handshakes of the legal profession, have little interest in altering the system or reducing its mystique. Importantly, the American Law Institute proposed a fairly radical simplification of the hearsay rule in the 1940s, and it failed in part for this reason.[41]

§ 14.04 Out-of-Court Statements That Are Not Hearsay

Utterances that are not hearsay under the assertion-oriented definition of the Rules generally fall into one of the following four categories:

Statements Offered to Show Their Effect on the Listener or Reader

If a statement is not offered for the truth of what it asserts, but to show its effect upon the hearer or reader of the statement, then it is not hearsay.

Examples

The out-of-court statement, "Do it or I'll kill you," offered to show that the hearer acted under duress.[42]

"Please don't step in that ketchup," to show that the listener had been warned.[43]

"The sponge count came out wrong," to show that the surgeon, upon hearing this statement in the operating room, was put on notice and negligent in not checking for a sponge in the patient's body.[44]

"Dr. Salinsky is incompetent," to show that a hospital was negligent in hiring Dr. Salinsky after being told of Dr. Salinsky's incompetence.[45]

---

41 *See* ALI MODEL CODE OF EVIDENCE Ch. V (1942).

42 *See* United States v. Herrera, 600 F.2d 502, 504 (5th Cir. 1979) (threatening telephone conversation is not hearsay because it was offered to show that criminal defendant acted under duress); United States v. Williams, 952 F.2d 1504 (6th Cir. 1991) (declarants' statement to the alleged victim that suggested adverse economic consequences to the victim if the victim did not cooperate is not hearsay, because it was offered to show effect on victim's state of mind, i.e., victim's fear and the reasonableness of that fear); Martinez v. McCaughtry, 951 F.2d 130 (7th Cir. 1991) (threats and verbal abuse by defendant's brother towards third person is admissible to show why defendant, who was present, shot third person); Subramaniam v. Public Prosecutor, 100 Solicitor's Journal 566 (Privy Council, Federated Malay States, 1956) (threats to show duress).

43 *See* Safeway Stores, Inc. v. Combs, 273 F.2d 295, 296 (5th Cir. 1960). *But cf.* United States v. Sallins, 993 F.2d 344, 346 (3d Cir. 1993) (holding that police radio dispatch call alerting officers to whereabouts of black male suspect wearing black clothes and carrying gun is inadmissible hearsay, even when statement offered to explain officers' reasons for suspecting defendant and not for its truth; officers' conduct could be explained through other nonhearsay testimony, and prosecutor used statement for its truth in closing arguments).

44 *See* Smedra v. Stanek, 187 F.2d 892, 894 (10th Cir. 1951).

45 Johnson v. Misericordia Cmty. Hosp., 294 N.W.2d 501, 515–16 (Wis. Ct. App. 1980); *see also* United States v. Calhoon, 97 F.3d 518, 533–34 (11th Cir. 1996) (holding that corporate outside counsel's advice that defendant's method of collapsing advertising into single account was improper is admissible over hearsay objection because it is not offered to show truth, but merely to show that defendant was on notice that he had reason to question propriety of his action; evidence is relevant to question whether he had knowingly filed false Medicare claims); In the Matter of the Marriage of Fromdahl, 840 P.2d 683, 690 (Or. 1992) (in custody case where mother was alleged to be insane, polygraph examiner's reports that said father had sexually abused

"There's somebody poking around in your neighbor's garage," offered to explain the hearer's reason for checking out the garage of her absent neighbor.

Sometimes both the truth of the matter asserted and the effect on the hearer are relevant to issues in a lawsuit. When a statement has this sort of double relevancy, a limiting instruction should be given to the effect that the statement should not be used for its truth.[46] For example, suppose a mechanic tells a customer, "The brakes on your car are bad." This statement is not hearsay when offered to show that the customer had notice that the brakes were bad, but is hearsay when offered to show that the brakes were, in fact, bad. The court should give a limiting instruction. A limiting instruction is not always sufficient protection when a statement has both a permissible nonhearsay use and a forbidden hearsay use. The trial judge must weigh the statement's probative value for its permitted use against the danger that the jury will use it for the forbidden purpose, and should consider redaction or exclusion if the danger of prejudice is unacceptably high.[47]

Consider the use of statements made to a police officer to explain the officer's subsequent conduct.[48] Very often such explanations are themselves irrelevant at trial: why an investigator did or thought something usually has nothing to do with whether the evidence the officer discovers establishes defendant's guilt.[49] But when such explanations are themselves relevant, as they may be when the defense alleges a frame-up by the police, then statements made to officers that would otherwise be hearsay may not be used to prove the truth of the matter asserted:

1. A houseguest at the mansion of a suspected murderer tells the investigating police officer that he heard thumps on the wall the night before. The investigator looks in the bushes near the wall and finds a bloody glove. The houseguest's statement should be admitted to explain the officer's conduct, at least if the officer is accused of planting the bloody glove. The statement explains why the officer was searching in the bushes, and the need for that explanation outweighs the danger that the jury will misuse the statement by accepting it for the truth of what it asserts.

2. A dispatcher's call tells the officer of a hit-and-run at Larkin and Turk and describes the suspect. The officer proceeds to Larkin and Turk and measures skid marks. The description of the suspect should be excluded

children were found admissible to show that mother's belief in father's abuse was not insane delusion); Rotolo v. Digital Equipment Corp., 150 F.3d 223, 225 (2d Cir. 1998) (admission of videotape of experts discussing danger that keyboards could cause repetitive stress injury to be played at trial, in absence of evidence that defendant should have known about it, to be a reversible error).

46 For a discussion of limited admissibility, *see* **§ 1.05**. For a discussion of the use of limiting instructions, see **§ 3.09**.

47 Of course, the limited admissibility problem disappears if there is an exemption or exception to the hearsay rule that permits the hearsay use as well.

48 The issue is also discussed in **§ 5.04**.

49 *See, e.g.*, United States v. Hernandez, 750 F.2d 1256, 1257 (5th Cir. 1985) (finding reversible error to admit evidence that special agent had been told by United States Customs that defendant was a drug smuggler; agent's state of mind was not at issue); United States v. Dean, 980 F.2d 1286, 1288–89 (9th Cir. 1992) (holding that trial judge committed reversible error in admitting out-of-court statement to police officer that defendant possessed weapon in his mobile home; since probable cause for search was not at issue, evidence had no relevance except for hearsay purpose of showing that defendant did in fact possess weapon); Spencer v. State, 703 N.E.2d 1053, 1056 (Ind. 1999) (murder victim's statements about defendant's threats not admissible either as nonhearsay to show officer's reason for investigating or under state of mind exception to show victim's fear; but error in receiving the evidence was harmless in light of overwhelming evidence of guilt).

because it is not needed to explain the officer's conduct. The officer's conduct can be explained, if an explanation is relevant at all, simply by allowing her to testify that she received a call from the dispatcher and, in response, went to Larkin and Turk. It is not necessary to quote the contents of the call.

3. The officer receives a call from the dispatcher, and then proceeds to the scene to arrest a suspect who meets the description given in the call. A strong case can be made that the contents should be described in order to explain the officer's conduct, at least if the issue is the lawfulness of the arrest, an issue that would arise before trial and be decided by the court. But the better view is that, on the merits at trial, the evidence ordinarily should be excluded because of the danger of misuse.[50]

Legally (or Morally) Operative Language

Legally operative language is language that establishes a new legal relationship by itself or when uttered with a particular intent. It is not considered an assertion and, hence, is not hearsay. It is not offered for what it *says*, but for what it *does*. In essence, the words uttered or written are not a statement about something, but are the thing itself. They create a legal right, duty, power, privilege, or other relationship. Legally operative language is often characterized as a "verbal act"[51] or a "verbal part of an act,"[52] though this text avoids these terms because they are indeterminate and because they might suggest that speech explaining or substituting for conduct is generally not hearsay.[53]

---

50 *See* United States v. Sallins, 993 F.2d 344, 346–47 (3d Cir. 1993) (police radio dispatch call alerting officers to whereabouts of black male suspect wearing black clothes and carrying gun was inadmissible hearsay, even when statement offered to explain officers' reasons for suspecting defendant and not for its truth; officers' conduct could be explained through "testimony that he acted 'upon information received' or words to that effect"). *Compare* Vincelette v. Metropolitan Life Ins. Co., 968 P.2d 275, 277 (Mont. 1998) (holding admission of testimony that officer had received word that plaintiff had fallen on carpet because she was drunk to be prejudicial error; statement about drunkenness not necessary for nonhearsay purpose of showing why engineer investigated fall), *with* United States v. Mancillas, 580 F.2d 1301, 1309–10 (7th Cir. 1978) (excluding statement on grounds of prejudice).

Sometimes evidence that police disregarded statements by out-of-court declarants that incriminated persons other than the accused will be admissible to show the state of mind of the police in "rushing to judgment" and twisting evidence to favor the hypothesis that the defendant was guilty. But where the evidence has only a weak bearing on the state of mind of the investigating officer, and where the most likely use of it would be for the truth of the matter asserted, it may be excluded. In United States v. Sesay, 313 F.3d 591, 598–600 (D.C. Cir. 2002), the defendant wanted to put into evidence a police report that stated that witnesses had claimed someone else had been seen in possession of the gun in question at the time that defendant was later charged with possessing it. The government claimed it had checked with the witnesses and that the police report contained a mistaken rumor. The appellate court upheld the exclusion of the police report, saying that to use the report to support the defense's contention that the police had "lied and manipulated the evidence in a manner designed to strengthen the case against [defendant]" would have required that the jury rely upon the truth of the matter asserted in the report's double hearsay. *Id.* at 600.

51 *See, e.g.*, 2 MICHAEL H. GRAHAM, HANDBOOK OF FEDERAL EVIDENCE § 801.5 (4th ed. 1996).

52 *See* 6 WIGMORE ON EVIDENCE § 1772 (Chadbourn rev. 1976).

53 *See* Roger C. Park, *McCormick on Evidence and the Concept of Hearsay: A Critical Analysis Followed by Suggestions to Law Teachers*, 65 MINN. L. REV. 423, 441–49 (1981).

Examples

"Take this as a gift," offered to show a gift.[54]

"This is a loan," offered to show a loan.

"I offer you $3000 a carload for your widgets," offered to show a contract offer.[55]

"This is my property," offered to show a claim of right sufficient for adverse possession.[56]

"We guarantee the loan," offered to prove a guarantee was made.[57]

The introduction of a slip of paper handed to a bank teller that says "Hand over all the money," offered to demonstrate a criminal act.

The introduction of a defamatory statement by the defendant to prove defamation.

This last example is easily susceptible to the classic analysis: though the defamatory statement was made out of court, the plaintiff who introduces it is not asking the trier-of-fact to believe that the statement is true, just that it was made. In the other cases, the analysis is more difficult. For example, the statement, "We guarantee the loan," does not have what philosophers would call a "truth value;" it does not make sense to say that this utterance is either true or false, but it does make sense to say that it is either effective or ineffective in creating a guarantee.[58] The hearsay rule applies only to assertions. Of an assertion it can always meaningfully be asked, "Is it true or false?", and in the hearsay context the tribunal is being asked to assess the truth of the utterance.

The same is true, though it is even subtler, when legally operative language sets forth the exact proposition to be proved. Thus, "I am making you an offer of $3,000 a carload" is not hearsay when offered to show the making of an offer of $3,000 a carload. On its face, the utterance seems to be a statement offered "to prove the truth of the matter asserted in the statement," falling within the assertion-oriented definition of hearsay.[59] Commentators have reconciled the result with the definition by saying that the statement is not an "assertion" at all, but an "act"; at least it is not offered qua assertion, but rather as an act, and as an act it cannot be false, though it might be ineffective.[60] This makes sense because the speaker's sincerity is not at issue. If the speaker crossed his fingers behind his back and did not intend to make such an offer, it

---

[54] *See* 6 WIGMORE ON EVIDENCE § 1777 (Chadbourn rev. 1976).

[55] *See* Cloverland-Green Spring Dairies, Inc. v. Pennsylvania Milk Mktg. Bd., 298 F.3d 201, 218 n.20 (3d Cir. 2002) (offers to sell milk at a particular price were legally operative and therefore not hearsay); *cf.* California Trucking Assn. v. Brotherhood of Teamsters, 679 F.2d 1275, 1291–92 n.20 (9th Cir. 1981) (evidence of contract rejection was admissible as nonhearsay).

[56] *See* 6 WIGMORE ON EVIDENCE § 1778 (Chadbourn rev. 1976).

[57] *See* NLRB v. H. Koch & Sons, 578 F.2d 1287, 1290–91 (9th Cir. 1978); Ries Biologicals, Inc. v. Bank of Santa Fe, 780 F.2d 888, 890 (10th Cir. 1986). *See generally* 2 MCCORMICK ON EVIDENCE § 249 (Kenneth S. Broun ed., 7th ed. 2013).

[58] A truth value can, of course, be assigned to a different proposition, such as, "Their guarantee of the loan was effective," or "A guarantee of the loan was made," or even "They guaranteed the loan." But none of these is the statement made by the speaker.

[59] *See* FED. R. EVID. 801(c).

[60] *See* Creaghe v. Iowa Home Mut. Cas. Co., 323 F.2d 981 (10th Cir. 1963); JACK H. FRIEDENTHAL & MICHAEL SINGER, THE LAW OF EVIDENCE §§ 83–84 (1985); E. KIMBALL, PROGRAMMED MATERIAL ON PROBLEMS IN EVIDENCE § 273 (1978).

would not affect the result under standard contract theory. What matters—when the question is whether a contract came into being—is that the statement was made, not that the speaker was honest in making it.[61]

Another way to view the problem is to recognize that if the courts were to exclude legally operative language as hearsay, they would render virtually impossible the proof of a great many claims recognized by substantive law. Thus, if the court refuses to allow a party seeking to prove the existence of an oral contract to testify that she said, "I am making you an offer of $3,000 a carload," the only way to prove the contract would be by circumstantial evidence of the behavior of the parties, something that would be very difficult, given that the action itself probably arose because at least one of the parties acted as though there was no contract.[62] Whatever the explanation, the nonhearsay status of legally operative language is established beyond dispute.[63]

Legally operative language is nonhearsay when it is offered to show the legal relationship that it creates or modifies. If it is offered to show something else, then it might be hearsay. For example, language in a pleading (such as a complaint or answer in a civil case) is not hearsay if it is offered only to define the issues in a lawsuit. When used for purposes of defining issues and limiting proof, the language in pleadings is legally operative. Thus, an allegation of negligence in a complaint would not be hearsay when offered to show that the issue of negligence had been properly raised, but would be hearsay when offered to show that the defendant was, in fact, negligent.[64]

It is important to distinguish legally operative language from hearsay that describes a past legal event. The utterance, "Here is the rent money for August," is a legally operative act, and is not hearsay if evidence of it is introduced to prove payment. The out-of-court utterance, "Yesterday, I paid my rent for August," is a statement *asserting* the occurrence of a legally operative event. This latter statement is not part of a legal event; evidence of it is hearsay when offered to prove the payment of the rent.

There is one advantage to the broader term, "verbal act": it is broad enough to include *morally* operative utterances. For example, a promise is not like a description of some state of facts: it undertakes a moral obligation. Some promises are not legally enforceable, so making such a promise is not "legally operative"; evidencing it would not show a change in legal relationships. But evidence of the making of such a promise is not hearsay if used to show the creation of a moral duty that is itself used as evidence of the speaker's (or the recipient's) subsequent behavior. Again, it is not essential to the relevance of such a promise that the speaker was sincere in making it or thought that he would honor it when he made it; the speaker might feel obligated to honor the promise anyway, and the recipient might feel entitled to expect that. In either case, the making of the promise could help explain the subsequent actions of the two persons. This mode

[61] The careful reader will notice, once again, that this explanation does not fit easily within the framework of the nominally assertion-oriented definition of the Federal Rules. While the Federal Rules nominally employ an assertion-based criterion of hearsay, in practice they include a declarant-based limitation as well. *See* **§ 14.01**.

[62] *See* David P. Leonard, *Rules of Evidence and Substantive Policy*, 25 LOY. L.A. L. REV. 797, 804–07 (1992).

[63] *See, e.g.*, United States v. DiMaria, 727 F.2d 265, 270 n.4 (2d Cir. 1984).

[64] It is unlikely that the question of whether an issue of negligence has been raised—as distinct from the question of whether the defendant was negligent—would be an issue for the fact-finder; the former issue will ordinarily be a question for the court, one that might determine the admissibility of other evidence, for example. In that case, the issue is decided under FED. R. EVID. 104(a), and the hearsay rule does not apply anyway. *See* **§ 3.11**.

of relevance is also nonhearsay: it depends on the promisor's sense of duty or the recipient's sense of entitlement, not on the promisor's credibility as a reporter of facts.

Circumstantial (Indirect) Evidence of Declarant's Knowledge or State of Mind

This category includes utterances that are considered not to be hearsay because they can be used to show the declarant's own state of mind without accepting the truth of what is asserted in the utterance.[65] These statements would sometimes be hearsay under a strict application of the declarant-oriented definition—that is, when used to show the truth of the declarant's belief—but they are not hearsay under the assertion-oriented definition.

Examples

"My name is Nancy Reagan," uttered by your evidence professor (who is not Nancy Reagan), offered by the Dean to demonstrate incompetence. When offered to prove incompetence the proponent does not want the finder-of-fact to believe the statement is actually true, just that it was said.

"My wife is trying to poison me," offered to show that the declarant hated his wife. One can believe that declarant hated his wife without believing the truth of the matter asserted, that is, without believing that the wife actually attempted to poison the declarant. In fact, a false accusation might be more persuasive evidence of the declarant's hatred than a true one would be.[66]

"Daddy tried to kill me," to show the declarant's fear of her father, as evidence in a custody dispute that being with the father was not in the best interest of the child, whether or not the father actually tried to kill the child.[67]

The defendant's wife tells police that her husband was with her on the day of the crime, and the prosecution offers her statement in evidence, knowing that it can prove that the alibi is a fabrication. Her statement is not offered to show its truth; indeed, the prosecution's whole theory is based upon the supposition that it is false.[68]

In an apparent application of the principle that circumstantial evidence of the declarant's state of mind is not hearsay under the assertion-centered definition of the Federal Rules of Evidence, a number of cases have admitted drug ledgers into evidence on the theory that they were not being offered for the truth of anything asserted in the

---

[65] *See, e.g.*, Fun-Damental Too, Ltd. v. Gemmy Industries Corp., 111 F.3d 993, 1003–04 (2d Cir. 1997) (that complaints by customers who erroneously thought that one type of product, "currency cans" were same product as "toilet banks" is not hearsay when offered as evidence that defendant's packaging caused declarants to confuse its product with plaintiff's product); *see also* United States v. Newell, 315 F.3d 510, 523 (5th Cir. 2002) (admissible accountant's notes concerning rumors of fake expenses to show reason why accountant confronted defendant).

[66] *Cf.* Loetsch v. New York City Omnibus Corp., 52 N.E.2d 448 (N.Y. 1943) (holding wife's statement in her will accusing husband of cruelty admissible, in husband's wrongful death action to show that wife would not have given husband full comfort and support had she survived).

[67] *Cf.* Betts v. Betts, 473 P.2d 403, 407–09 (Wash. Ct. App. 1970) (admitting, in a custody hearing, child's statements that she was afraid of her stepfather because she believed he had killed her brother).

[68] *See* generally Roger C. Park, *McCormick on Evidence and the Concept of Hearsay: A Critical Analysis Followed by Suggestions to Law Teachers*, 65 MINN. L. REV. 423, 426 (1981) (arguing that statements of this nature do involve some reliance upon credibility of declarant, but that this reliance has generally been ignored); *cf.* Anderson v. United States, 417 U.S. 211, 219–20 (1974);

ledger, but merely to show that drug activity was taking place on the premises.[69] The theory under which this evidence is admitted is arguably wrong, since the ledgers could be viewed as assertions that quantities of drugs or money changed hands. In such a case, ledgers used to show drug activity are offered for the truth of the matter asserted, rather than to show the defendant's state of mind and would be hearsay.

Another example of cases offered as circumstantial evidence of the declarant's state of mind is when evidence of intercepted telephone calls is used to show that the premises were being used for an illegal purpose. Suppose, for example, the police raid a suspected bookmaker and receive calls asking to place bets, or raid a suspected drug dealer and receive calls from persons wanting to buy drugs. Most courts treat these calls as admissible nonhearsay, despite the existence of some conceivable hearsay dangers.[70] Under the assertion-oriented definition of hearsay, a call asking to place a bet does not involve an intention to assert that the place called accepts bets, even though the caller *presupposes* that fact when making the call and the proponent relies on the accuracy of that presupposition.

Verbal utterances that have been received solely as circumstantial evidence of contact or association between two people or between a person and a thing constitute another class of cases. The typical example is where the police, during a search of a person in custody, find the name and telephone number of another person. The evidence then is offered to show that the two are acquainted. Applying the assertion definition, the court is likely to say either that the name and number were not offered to prove what they were asserting (that a certain person had a certain number) or that they were not offered assertively at all, but rather as circumstantial evidence of association.[71]

Thus, the following utterances have been deemed not to be hearsay under the assertion-oriented definition: (1) an address book, when used to show that the holder knew the people listed therein; (2) a receipt for rent or goods, when used to show linkage between a person named in the receipt and the premises or goods; (3) a letter addressed to the defendant at a certain street address, when used to link the defendant with the house at that address; (4) a name mentioned in conversation, when used to show that

---

[69] *See, e.g.*, United States v. Huguez-Ibarra, 954 F.2d 546, 552–53 (9th Cir. 1992) (finding no need for government to lay foundation for admission of drug ledgers as co-conspirator statements because ledgers were only being admitted to show that type of activities charged in indictment were being carried out in residence); People v. Harvey, 233 Cal. App. 3d 1206, 1219–26 (Cal. Ct. App. 1991) (pay/owe sheet is not hearsay when used to show that drug deals had occurred at address); *see also* cases cited in Roger C. Park, *"I Didn't Tell Them Anything About You": Implied Assertions as Hearsay under the Federal Rules of Evidence*, 74 MINN. L. REV. 783, 817 n.220 (1990).

[70] *See* Roger C. Park, *"I Didn't Tell Them Anything About You": Implied Assertions as Hearsay under the Federal Rules of Evidence*, 74 MINN. L. REV. 783, 817 n.220 (1990).

[71] An interesting example of this type of case is United States v. Arteaga, 117 F.3d 388 (9th Cir. 1997). Defendants were charged with involvement in a scheme of drug money laundering. One defendant (Arteaga) allegedly used Western Union to wire drug money from Alaska to another defendant (Arrango-Laverde), who was in California. The prosecution offered evidence of Western Union "to-send-money" forms, used by Western Union on the sending end, and "to-receive-money" forms, issued on the receiving end. Copies of two "to-send-money" forms were found in defendant's apartment. They listed the recipient as "Linda Arce," allegedly an alias of Arrango-Laverde. The trial court instructed the jury that it was not permitted to consider the forms to prove the truth of the matters asserted. On appeal, the court explained the nonhearsay use of the evidence, stating that the piece of paper found in Arteaga's possession was evidence that he had knowledge necessary to commit the criminal acts. "Since the name Linda Arce was an alias, proven by independent evidence to have been used by Laverde in a drug conspiracy, it is unlikely that anyone not involved in that conspiracy would have had knowledge of, or reason to use, that name. In other words, . . . the pieces of paper provided strong circumstantial evidence that the defendant had the knowledge necessary to commit the act, and, therefore, that he likely did commit the act." *Id.* at 398.

the defendant knew the person named; (5) car papers, when used to show a link between the car and those named in the papers. These utterances are not offered for the truth of anything they assert, but to show something else.[72]

Statements by a person who later became a homicide victim that describe threats or abuse by the person later accused of the homicide may also be offered as circumstantial evidence of the declarant's state of mind. The issue often boils down to whether the victim's state of mind is relevant and, if so, whether the relevance of the evidence for the permitted purpose of showing state of mind outweighs any prejudice that may result from use of the statement to show the truth of the matter asserted. The statements are often admitted where:

(1) they are needed to show hostility between the victim and the accused;

(2) the accused advances a defense of self-defense and the victim's fear is used to show that the victim was unlikely to be the first attacker; or

(3) the defense is suicide and the statement shows a will to live.[73]

If the danger that the jury will misuse the statement outweighs the probative value of the statement when used for its limited purpose, then the trial judge may exclude the entire statement under Rule 403.[74] A classic example of a case in which such exclusion would be proper is *Shepard v. United States*.[75] In that case, the defendant was accused of murdering his wife. The trial judge received testimony that shortly before her death,

---

[72] *See* Roger C. Park, *"I Didn't Tell Them Anything About You": Implied Assertions as Hearsay under the Federal Rules of Evidence*, 74 MINN. L. REV. 783, 817–23 n.220 (1990) (collecting cases). For cases taking the concept to its limit, *see* United States v. Alvarez, 960 F.2d 830 (9th Cir. 1992) (inscription "Garnika, Spain" on pistol is not hearsay when offered to prove that pistol came from Spain); United States v. Snow, 517 F.2d 441 (9th Cir. 1975) (finding that red tape on briefcase bearing defendant's name is not hearsay because it is "mechanical trace" and, thus, type of circumstantial evidence designed to show occurrence or non-occurrence of certain act in past); People v. Cox, 70 P.3d 277, 305–306 (Cal. 2003) (admitting as nonhearsay circumstantial evidence of the declarant's knowledge of the murder evidence that another person gave police accurate directions to an area where murder victim's body was found). *But see* United States v. Vigneau, 187 F.3d 70, 74–75 (1st Cir. 1999) (Western Union sender forms listing defendant as sender of money orders are inadmissible hearsay when offered to show that defendant was in fact sender; court indicates result would have been different had Western Union required identification from senders, because then there would have been adequate foundation for admitting the sender form as the admission of a party-opponent); Payne v. Janasz, 711 F.2d 1305, 1313–14 (6th Cir. 1983) (in habeas corpus proceeding the deputy's testimony that, on day after police raid, he saw two pearl-handled pistols in an evidence bag marked with an evidence tag stating "10001 Cedar Avenue" constitutes hearsay because it was offered to show sheriff's possession of pistols and sheriff's office's method of handling guns; however, admission did not violate defendant's confrontation rights).

[73] For full discussion that is still relevant under the Federal Rules of Evidence, see United States v. Brown, 490 F.2d 758, 763–64 (D.C. Cir. 1973). *See also* United States v. Day, 591 F.2d 861 (D.C. Cir. 1978) (not admitting statement that defendant was out to get declarant, but admitting as circumstantial evidence of association declarant's slip of paper containing defendant's phone number). For a case using the hostility theory, see the O.J. Simpson civil case, Rufo v. Simpson, 103 Cal. Rptr. 2d 492 (Cal. Ct. App. 2001) (statements made by victim that defendant abused, stalked, and threatened to kill her were admissible to show her state of mind of fear and hostility toward the defendant, such evidence being valuable because it helped resolve disputed issues about the pre-murder interaction between victim and defendant).

[74] *See* FED. R. EVID. 105 advisory committee note ("A close relationship exists between this rule and Rule 403 which [provides for] exclusion when 'probative value is substantially outweighed by the danger of unfair prejudice, confusion of the issues, or misleading the jury' "). Some commentators have questioned the effectiveness of limiting instructions in any case since a jury may well ignore the limiting instruction and use the admitted statement for an improper purpose. *See, e.g.*, Note, *The Limiting Instruction—Its Effectiveness and Effect*, 51 MINN. L. REV. 264 (1966) (the limiting instructions discussed are different, but the argument is still applicable). Other commentators have argued that all relevant evidence should be admitted and limiting instructions should be preferred over exclusion of evidence in all but the most extreme situations. *See, e.g.*, 1 MCCORMICK ON EVIDENCE § 59 (Kenneth S. Broun ed., 7th ed. 2013).

[75] Shepard v. United States, 290 U.S. 96 (1933).

the wife had said, "Dr. Shepard has poisoned me."[76] On appeal, one of the theories of admission advanced by the prosecution was that the statement tended to negate any suicidal intent on the part of the wife. The Supreme Court recognized the theoretical validity of this ground, but held that the evidence should at any rate have been excluded because "the reverberating clang of those accusatory words would drown all weaker sounds."[77] Of course, such Rule 403-balancing is not necessary when the statement is admissible for the truth of the matter asserted under some hearsay exception, such as the exception for dying declarations.[78]

Prior Statements of a Witness Relevant to Credibility

If a witness says one thing on the stand, but has said something significantly different before trial, the change is usually regarded as relevant to the witness's credibility, regardless of the truth of what was said out-of-court. For this reason, a "prior inconsistent statement" offered solely to impeach a witness is nonhearsay.[79] For example, in an automobile accident case, suppose the plaintiff claims the defendant's light was red, whereas the defendant claims his light was green. If a witness for the defendant testifies that defendant's light was green, that witness may be impeached by a showing that she previously said to an investigator or bystander that the light was yellow. The plaintiff is not using the previous statement to show that the light was yellow, but only to show the witness's change of story.

This is so even if the prior statement happens to coincide with what the impeaching party is trying to prove. Suppose, in the foregoing example, that the prior statement of the witness was that defendant's light was red. This still suggests a change of story and undermines the credibility of the witness, even though, as it happens, the plaintiff is using the prior statement to prove the light was red. (By undermining defendant's evidence that the light was green, the impeachment makes it more likely that the light was red, as the plaintiff claims.) Thus, while the plaintiff is using the prior statement to prove the light was red, the plaintiff is not relying on the credibility of the impeached witness, whether in court or out, to do this.[80]

A limiting instruction regularly accompanies such prior inconsistent statements. One version of the instruction runs as follows:

> The testimony of a witness may be discredited or, as we sometimes say, impeached by showing that he or she previously made statements which are different than or inconsistent with his or her testimony here in court. The earlier inconsistent or contradictory statements are admissible only to discredit or impeach the credibility of the witness and not to establish the truth of these earlier statements made somewhere other than here during this trial. It is the

---

76 *Id.* at 98.

77 *Id.* at 104. *Cf.* United States v. Ingraham, 832 F.2d 229, 231–37 (1st Cir. 1987) (evidence of prior threatening letters and phone calls admissible for purpose of establishing identity of perpetrator, but inadmissible to show defendant's proclivities, where probative value outweighed danger of unfair prejudice).

78 *See* **§ 16.04** (statement of declarant's state of mind), **§ 17.03** (dying declaration).

79 The matter is discussed in detail in **§ 11.05** & **§ 15.03**. The same point applies to impeachment of a hearsay declarant whose statement is admitted pursuant to a hearsay exception. *See* **§ 14.09**.

80 Once again, the careful reader will notice the incorporation of an element of the declarant-oriented criterion so as to limit the category of hearsay. By the language of the Federal Rules, this is hearsay, yet no competent trial judge would exclude it as such. Instead, a judge would rule that this is permissible impeachment, subject to a limiting instruction as explained in the following text.

province of the jury to determine the credibility of a witness who has made prior inconsistent or contradictory statements.[81]

Similar distinctions are made and similar practices employed with regard to prior *consistent* statements use to rehabilitate the witness after impeachment.[82]

Given the foregoing, lawyers sometimes refer to the distinction between using an out-of-court statement for impeachment or rehabilitation purposes and using the statement as "substantive" evidence. That distinction is coherent. Bear in mind, however, that not all substantive uses of out-of-court statements are hearsay, and not all credibility-related uses of out-of-court statements are nonhearsay. That is, "credibility use" and "hearsay use" are not opposites.[83]

§ 14.05 Distinguishing Hearsay from the Evidence of the Hearsay; Relation to Other Objections

Under the Federal Rules formulation, it is the "out-of-court" assertion (an assertion made not while testifying at the instant proceeding) that constitutes the hearsay, provided of course that it is used in court in a particular way, viz., to prove the truth of the matter asserted.[84] This out-of-court assertive conduct—oral, written, or nonverbal—must be distinguished from the evidence of it that is presented in court.[85] That evidence, in turn, can take either of the conventional forms: it can be testimonial, as when a witness reports the hearsay, or it can be tangible, as when a document or tape-recording is introduced that contains the hearsay assertion. Thus, any of the following six situations can occur:

Form of Evidence Presented in Court	Assertive Out-of-Court Conduct		
	Oral	Written	Nonverbal
Testimonial	1	6	3
Tangible	4	2	5

The most common hearsay situations are numbered 1 and 2: either an oral hearsay assertion is repeated in court by a witness (situation 1) or a written hearsay declaration is brought into court (situation 2). Also not uncommon is testimony about nonverbal assertive conduct (situation 3). But the other three situations can also arise. In

[81] 1A KEVIN F. O'MALLEY ET AL., FEDERAL JURY PRACTICE AND INSTRUCTIONS § 15.06 (6th ed. 2008).

[82] *See* **§ 11.13**.

[83] Further discussion of this point appears in **§ 19.05**.

[84] FED. R. EVID. 801(c).

[85] Oddly enough, Rule 802 does not respect this difference, prescribing as it does that the out-of-court assertion is what is assumptively inadmissible, rather than the *evidence of it*. FED. R. EVID. 802. (Only evidence, something presented to the fact-finder, can be either admitted or excluded; something that happens out-of-court cannot be admitted or excluded.) No doubt Rule 802 was meant to convey the idea that *any evidence of* such an assertion is assumptively inadmissible, which is the way the courts read it. *Cf.* CHARLES T. MCCORMICK, HANDBOOK OF THE LAW OF EVIDENCE § 225 at 460 (1st ed. 1954):

> Hearsay evidence is testimony in court, or written evidence, of a statement made out of court, the statement being offered as an assertion to show the truth of matters asserted therein, and thus resting for its value upon the credibility of the out-of-court asserter.

See also ALI MODEL CODE OF EVIDENCE §§ 501(6), 502 (1942) (defining "hearsay evidence" as evidence of a hearsay statement or declaration and stating general rule excluding hearsay evidence).

particular, an oral hearsay assertion or nonverbal assertive conduct might be videotaped and this tangible record provided in court (situations 4 and 5, respectively). Finally, someone might read a written hearsay statement and then testify to what the witness read (situation 6).

Making these distinctions facilitates thinking about the applicability of those rules specifically governing testimonial evidence and those rules relating to tangible evidence. For example, even if an exception to the hearsay prohibition is found, testimonial evidence of hearsay must still come from a competent witness with personal knowledge of the hearsay utterance. Similarly, even if an exception to the hearsay prohibition is found, tangible evidence of it must be suitably authenticated. Of course, even if all such rules are satisfied, hearsay within some exception might still be excluded if it violates some other rule applicable to both testimonial and tangible evidence, such as the rule governing the use of character evidence or the rule governing the use of evidence of subsequent remedial measures.

Situation 6 invites a particular confusion: when testimony repeats a written out-of-court assertion, there is a tendency to think that, because the writing itself is not brought into court, such evidence necessarily adds a level or layer of hearsay (to any hearsay assertion in the document itself).[86] This, however, conflates the hearsay rule with the original recording rule. The latter rule requires that the original recording be used as evidence of its contents, unless a suitable substitute or excuse is offered.[87] That would apply in Situation 6. Confusion can result from not recognizing that the conduct of merely *reading* an out-of-court writing does not *assert* anything. Only when the witness reports the content of the writing is the witness asserting something, and that assertion, because it is made while testifying in the instant proceeding, is not itself hearsay; it is under oath, subject to cross-examination before the present fact-finder. This may or may not be permitted under the original recording rule, but it does not add a layer of hearsay. Similarly, to be admitted, any tangible recording (like a videotape) of a hearsay assertion, whether written or otherwise, must be the original of that recording, absent an appropriate excuse. And in situation 2, unless the recording offered at trial is the original written hearsay, a suitable excuse must be given for that failure to use the original writing. In any event, all this concerns the original recording rule. The number of layers of hearsay depends on the number of layers of *out-of-court* assertions that are made, and neither reading nor mechanically recording something out-of-court is itself an assertion.[88]

As this discussion illustrates, the mere fact that an out-of-court statement satisfies the hearsay rule does not mean that evidence of it satisfies other exclusionary rules, such as the original recording rule, the authentication rules, the rule against character evidence, and the rules of privilege. Conversely, the hearsay ban is not satisfied just because some other evidence rule is satisfied. For example, the fact that evidence is admissible under Rule 404(b)(2) as evidence of motive, plan, etc., does not mean that it can be presented using hearsay without fitting it into some hearsay exception.

---

[86] *See* **§ 14.07** (discussing hearsay within hearsay).

[87] *See* **§§ 13.01 et seq.**

[88] *Transcription* is different. If a person hears or reads a hearsay assertion and (still not while testifying) writes down what she heard or read, that "writing down" can be an assertion about what she heard or read that adds a second level of hearsay, if that writing is then presented in court. Her credibility in making that written assertion about the content of the original hearsay is itself a classic hearsay concern.

§ 14.06 Exceptions to the Hearsay Rule—an Introduction

Under the traditional common-law approach to hearsay, the question whether the hearsay rule barred admission of an out-of-court statement could be reduced to two steps:

1. Was the out-of-court statement being offered for the truth of the matter asserted? If not, the out-of-court statement did not fall within the definition of hearsay, and the hearsay rule posed no obstacle.
2. If the statement was hearsay, did it fall under an exception?

The Federal Rules of Evidence have complicated this system of organization.[89] Instead of treating some prior statements by witnesses and hearsay statements by parties or their co-conspirators as exceptions to the hearsay rule, the Federal Rules of Evidence label them "not hearsay" even though offered to prove the truth of the matter asserted.[90] The Supreme Court of the United States[91] and some commentators have referred to the statements encompassed under Rule 801(d) as "exemptions" from the hearsay rule, as opposed to "exceptions," an approach we adopt here. The Federal Rules have become so pervasive that it makes sense to follow the committee's organizing principles. Under the Federal Rules the following questions should be asked in determining whether an out-of-court statement is barred by the hearsay rule:

1. Is the out-of-court statement offered to prove the truth of the matter asserted? If not, it is not hearsay under the definition of Rule 801(c), and the hearsay rule poses no obstacle to receiving it. As explained above, common not-for-the-truth-of-the-matter-asserted categories include: effect on listener or reader; legally operative fact; circumstantial evidence of state of mind; and impeachment.[92]
2. If the statement is offered to prove the truth of the matter asserted, does it nonetheless fit into one of the special categories of "not hearsay" exemptions described in Rule 801(d), such as statements by parties offered by their opponents or sworn inconsistent statements of witnesses made in prior proceedings?[93] If so, it is likewise admissible for its truth.
3. If the statement is hearsay within the definition of Rule 801(c), and does not fall into any of the special categories of "not hearsay" exemptions of Rule 801(d), does the out-of-court statement nevertheless fit one of the exceptions described in Rules 803, 804, or 807, so that it is admissible even though it is hearsay?[94]

As the organization of the Rules indicates, some exceptions, cataloged under Rule 804, require that the declarant be unavailable before the out-of-court statement will be admissible. For other types of statements, collected under Rule 803, no showing of

---

[89] *See* James W. McElhaney, *Hidden Rules*, 75 A.B.A. J. 92, 92 (1989).

[90] FED. R. EVID. 801(d). For a critical examination of the advisory committee's approach to admissions, and suggested justifications for treating admissions as exceptions to the hearsay rule, see Roger C. Park, *The Rationale of Personal Admissions*, 21 IND. L. REV. 509 (1988).

[91] Bourjaily v. United States, 483 U.S. 171, 186 (1987) (referring to Rule 801(d)(2)(E) as an exemption from the hearsay rule).

[92] *See* **§ 14.04.**

[93] *See* **§§ 15.01 et seq.**

[94] *See* **§§ 16.01 et seq., §§ 17.01 et seq., & § 18.01.**

declarant unavailability is required. The exemptions and exceptions are discussed in detail in subsequent chapters, but for present purposes a few comments suffice.

Hearsay exceptions often reflect a long and tortured common-law history and serve as proof of Oliver Wendell Holmes' famous remark that "a page of history is worth a volume of logic."[95] Although it is sometimes hard to justify the individual hearsay exceptions or their particular applications, some broad general principles explain their origin and rationale. Generally speaking, evidence law admits certain hearsay statements based on an assessment that such out-of-court statements reflect some combination of reliability and necessity.

On the reliability front, something about the context of certain out-of-court statement diminishes traditional concerns about hearsay, at least in comparison to live testimony from the declarant. For instance, looking at Rule 803(4), statements made to doctors tend to be trustworthy because declarants have a strong incentive to get appropriate health care and this can only be achieved by honestly describing symptoms. At the same time, those same persons may be more willing to fabricate when they appear before a court. This policy assessment led to the development of the exception, but does not guarantee that every statement to a doctor is reliable. People can exaggerate symptoms to increase a tort award or because they are hypochondriacs and perceive their symptoms in a distorted fashion. Nevertheless, the categorical exception applies. If a statement falls squarely within a categorical exception, there is usually no specific inquiry into whether the policy of the exception is met in an individual case.

As to necessity, sometimes hearsay is the only practical source of important information. This may be because the declarant is now unavailable to testify, or because they would no longer remember much useful if they did, or because their situation in court would place much greater pressure on the person to distort the truth than was true at the time of the hearsay utterance. In such contexts, the practical need for the evidence trumps other hearsay concerns.

Throughout the chapters on exceptions, it is worth questioning whether the various exceptions to the hearsay rule make sense and whether the rule itself is worth the complexity and confusion it generates. Some reflection on the coherence of the present structure of rules is presented after the exemptions and exceptions have been discussed.[96]

§ 14.07 Hearsay Within Hearsay [FRE 805]

Sometimes the declarant's out-of-court statement will contain another out-of-court statement. For example, a hospital record might contain the patient's story about the cause of the injury. If the entry is offered to prove the cause of injury, the record has hearsay within hearsay. Chronologically, the first level of hearsay is the patient's oral statement to the record-maker about the cause of the injury. The second level is the record-maker's written statement in the hospital record describing what the patient said. Inferentially, however, one goes in reverse chronology: the first question when presented with the hospital record is whether (or more precisely, to what extent) the record-maker's report of the patient's story should be believed, and the second question is whether (or to what extent), assuming the record-maker's report is accurate, the

---

95 New York Trust Co. v. Eisner, 256 U.S. 345, 349 (1921) (Holmes, J.).

96 *See* **§ 17.07**.

patient's story that it reports should be believed. Either way one thinks about it, there are two "levels" or "layers" of hearsay: the patient's (out-of-court) assertion, and the record-maker's (out-of-court) assertion.

Federal Rule of Evidence 805, in accordance with prior law, provides that hearsay within hearsay is admissible if each level of hearsay falls under an exception to the hearsay rule.[97] In the previous example, the patient's assertion must fall within some exemption or exception, and it often will—as a statement of a party opponent, or a statement made for medical diagnosis or treatment, and so forth. But even if the patient's assertion passes the hearsay hurdle, that would authorize the testimony of someone who heard the patient's assertion, but it does not by itself authorize an out-of-court assertion, such as the hospital record, reporting the patient's assertion. So the hospital report must also fit within some exception or exemption—here, the most likely exception being the business record exception.

The late Irving Younger, whose unmatched talent for vivid illustration provided so many evidence students with unforgettable memory aids, used the inferential sequence of analysis explained above and suggested that the hearsay-within-hearsay problem be visualized as follows:[98]

> A trial lawyer who has to deal with this problem every day in the hurly-burly circumstances of the courtroom might want to try the following device, which takes but an instant and is infallible. . . .
>
> You or your opponent is offering a business record that consists of words. First, be satisfied that the business is a business, within the meaning of the business records statute, and that the record was routinely made in the regular course of business. That makes it a business record, which takes care of the first level of hearsay.
>
> Next, in your mind's eye, see the record come to life. Imagine it not as a record, but as the person who wrote the record. It takes the witness stand and it talks. It says from the witness stand whatever is written on it. If a real witness would be permitted to say that from the witness stand, then the record is admissible. If a real person on the stand would not be permitted to say it, then the record is not admissible.

A common example of hearsay within hearsay is the trial or deposition transcript. Chronologically, the first level of hearsay is the witness's statement made at the prior trial or deposition. The second level is the court reporter's statement about what the witness said. Younger's mental exercise starts by checking that the court reporter's assertion (about what was said) falls within the public records exception.[99] If it does, then one imagines the court reporter on the stand testifying about what was said by the witness. Doing so reveals that one must still face the question of whether the witness's (still) out-of-court statement falls within the exception for former testimony.[100]

---

[97] *See* FED. R. EVID. 805 advisory committee note; 2 MCCORMICK ON EVIDENCE § 324.1 (Kenneth S. Broun ed., 7th ed. 2013).

[98] IRVING YOUNGER, HEARSAY: A PRACTICAL GUIDE THROUGH THE THICKET 127–28 (1988).

[99] *See* **§ 16.09**.

[100] *See* **§ 17.02**; *see also* Ramrattan v. Burger King Corp., 656 F. Supp. 522, 527–28 (D. Md. 1987) (deposition properly excluded where, although deponent's statements in deposition would be admissible as

Statements within statements can also be admissible because a hearsay statement that falls within an exception or exemption contains another out-of-court statement that is not hearsay at all. For example, in *Kulick v. Pocono Downs Racing Association*,[101] the plaintiff sought to prove that state officials were behind his ejection from the racetrack. He offered into evidence a statement by a racetrack employee that a state official had said he should be ejected. The court noted that the racetrack employee's statement was admissible as the statement of a party-opponent. The statement-within-a-statement of the state official was admissible because it was not offered for the truth of anything asserted, but only to prove that a state official had made a statement that had the effect of contributing to plaintiff's ejection from the racetrack.[102]

In theory, out-of-court statements can be enclosed within each other, like nesting Russian dolls, ten deep if each statement is either not hearsay or falls under an exception.[103] A hearsay scholar who was extremely precise might point out that a nonhearsay statement contained within an admissible hearsay statement does not need Rule 805 to be admitted at all, since it is not hearsay within hearsay.[104] In any event, it is clear that statements within statements are admissible so long as all statements in the chain are either nonhearsay or admissible under an exception or exemption.[105] Each statement in the chain must be nonhearsay or fall within a hearsay exemption or exception for the chain to be admissible; it is not enough for one statement to fit if another does not.[106]

---

admissions of party, statements included yet a third level of hearsay which did not meet any of the hearsay exceptions).

101 Kulick v. Pocono Downs Racing Ass'n, 816 F.2d 895 (3d Cir. 1987).

102 *Id.* at 897 n.3. *See also* United States v. Basey, 613 F.2d 198, 201 n.1 (9th Cir. 1979) (no double hearsay problem involved where first level statements were admissions or adoptive statements, and second level fell under the business records exception, Rule 803(6)).

103 *See, e.g.*, United States v. Abell, 586 F. Supp. 1414, 1425 (D. Me. 1984) (three levels of statements, all admissible).

104 *See* 2 MCCORMICK ON EVIDENCE § 324.1 at 574 (Kenneth S. Broun ed., 7th ed. 2013); *see also* United States v. Basey, 613 F.2d 198, 201 n.1 (9th Cir. 1979) (no double hearsay problem involved where first level statements were admissions or adoptive admissions, and second level fell under Rule 803(6)).

105 *See* United States v. Diez, 515 F.2d 892, 895–96 n.2 (5th Cir. 1975) (out-of-court statement offered to show declarant's state of mind, and falling under the hearsay exception of Fed. R. Evid. 803(3), admissible when contained within co-conspirator's out-of-court statement, which Rule 801(d)(2)(E) classifies as nonhearsay); Bondie v. Bic Corp., 947 F.2d 1531, 1533–34 (6th Cir. 1991) (social worker's written report that child had told her she had started fire with matches, not cigarette lighter as claimed by plaintiff, admissible as hearsay within hearsay; social worker's report fit the business records exception and child's statement was the statement of a party-opponent).

106 *See* United States v. Sallins, 993 F.2d 344, 347 (3d Cir. 1993) (police computer record detailing contents of a 911 call inadmissible; record itself falls within public records exception, but government failed to show hearsay exception for statements made by person calling 911); Kelly v. Labouisse, 2010 WL 445392 at *1 (5th Cir. 2010) (plaintiffs were injured in a car accident in which a cow in the road was struck, and ownership of the cow was disputed; trial court did not err in refusing to admit statement allegedly made by the defendant that the cow was owned by his farm; the statement was made to a farm hand who then repeated it to person who testified at trial, and the trial court correctly found that the second statement did not fit into a hearsay exception because it was outside the scope of the farm hand's employment); Cedeck v. Hamiltonian Fed. Sav. & Loan Ass'n., 551 F.2d 1136, 1138 (8th Cir. 1977) (where author of statement to supervisor unknown, the statement did not qualify as admission of party-opponent, thus plaintiff's testimony regarding the supervisor's relating that statement was inadmissible double hearsay); Larez v. City of Los Angeles, 946 F.2d 630, 641–44 (9th Cir. 1991) (where police chief was defendant, chief's statements to newspaper reporters were inadmissible hearsay where the reporters did not testify; the chief's statement was an admission, but the reporters' statements about what the chief said were inadmissible hearsay); Boren v. Sable, 887 F.2d 1032 (10th Cir. 1989) (testimony of wife that her deceased husband told her that he had told his plant manager about a dangerous maintenance procedure was properly excluded since the first level of hearsay, the husband's out-of-court statement to his wife, did not fall under one of the hearsay exceptions); *see also* United States v. Reed,

Federal Rule of Evidence 805's liberal attitude toward hearsay within hearsay is in striking contrast to the requirements of trustworthiness that are set forth in many of the exceptions. Common sense tells us that hearsay within hearsay is likely to pose additional problems of reliability even if each statement fits an exception, and studies confirm what common sense tells us about multiple levels of hearsay.[107] Two early psychology researchers, Gordon W. Allport and Leo Postman, developed a series of experiments in which a subject viewed an illustration, and was asked to describe it to another subject, who described it to another subject, and so forth.[108] Allport and Postman noted that about seventy percent of the information depicted in the illustration was lost after five or six mouth-to-mouth transmissions, even when there was virtually no time interval between the statements. The most rapid loss came at the beginning, with the first one or two declarants.[109] The "level" (omission of details) and "sharpening" (selective reporting) effects noted were sometimes startling.[110] As the subjects struggled to assimilate what they had heard from others, they appear also to have added or changed vital details. For example, in more than half of the experiments the subjects erroneously "moved" a weapon (a straight razor blade) from the hand of the white person who held it in the illustration into the hand of a black antagonist during the telling of the story.[111]

Experiments like those performed by Allport and Postman could serve as a basis for arguing that the law should not admit endless levels of hearsay, even if each layer meets an exception. However, one rarely runs into hearsay within hearsay stacked five layers deep in litigation because of the difficulty of fitting each statement into an exception and of showing that each declarant had personal knowledge.[112] Since in practice courts are dealing almost exclusively with one level of hearsay within hearsay, perhaps a rule of thumb that hearsay is admissible if each level fits an exception is the simplest and administrable approach.

§ 14.08 The Requirement That the Hearsay Declarant Have Personal Knowledge

The personal knowledge requirement applies to most out-of-court statements that are admissible despite their hearsay quality.[113] Referring to the long list of exceptions articulated in Rule 803, the drafters of the Federal Rules wrote:

> In a hearsay situation, the declarant is, of course, a witness, and neither this rule nor Rule 804 dispenses with the requirement of firsthand knowledge. It

887 F.2d 1398 (11th Cir. 1989) (multiple hearsay admissible where each level either was nonhearsay or fell under an exception).

[107] *See* GORDON W. ALLPORT & LEO POSTMAN, THE PSYCHOLOGY OF RUMOR 75–76 (1947). *See also* Boren v. Sable, 887 F.2d 1032, 1036–37 (10th Cir. 1989) (discussing dangers of multiple hearsay and exclusion of such evidence under Rule 403); United States v. Daniels, 572 F.2d 535, 539 (5th Cir. 1978) (discussing the special problems double hearsay poses in a criminal trial). *See generally Comment, Hearsay Under the Proposed Federal Rules: A Discretionary Approach*, 15 WAYNE L. REV. 1077, 1231 (1969).

[108] GORDON W. ALLPORT & LEO POSTMAN, THE PSYCHOLOGY OF RUMOR 75–76 (1947).

[109] *Id.*

[110] *Id.* at 75–98.

[111] *Id.* at 111.

[112] Personal knowledge is required for statements offered under most hearsay exceptions. *See* **§ 14.08**.

[113] *Cf.* 2 MCCORMICK ON EVIDENCE § 255 at 265 (Kenneth S. Broun ed., 7th ed. 2013).

may appear from his statement or be inferable from circumstances. See Rule 602.[114]

The first clause of this comment—that a hearsay declarant is, "of course," a witness—cannot be taken literally. For example, witnesses are required to testify under oath, but only a couple of the hearsay exceptions and exemptions involve the declarant being under oath when the hearsay statement was made.[115] Nevertheless, the drafters' statement correctly describes how courts apply the personal knowledge requirement to hearsay assertions.

Suppose that a victim of poisoning tells all to the police just before dying. He says, "I know I am going to die. Dr. Blaeser poisoned me." The foundation for the hearsay exception for dying declarations (Rule 804(b)(2)) may have been satisfied because the declarant has manifested knowledge of the imminence of death. Yet absent additional facts the statement would not be admissible because there is no basis for a conclusion that declarant had personal knowledge.[116] We do not know whether the declarant is merely speculating or whether, perhaps, the declarant is basing his accusation upon another's hearsay statement. An objection should be sustained.[117] The situation would be different, of course, had the declarant been shot in the chest. Then the trier could infer personal knowledge just from the circumstances. Probably the declarant had a view of the assailant, and the fact that the declarant has accused a particular person makes the likelihood even greater that the declarant had the view.[118]

However, the personal knowledge requirement is not required for all admissible hearsay. For example, a statement admissible as the statement of a party-opponent need not have been made on personal knowledge in order to be admissible.[119] If a party says "my wolf bit a little girl" and the statement is offered against the party, then the statement is admissible even if the party can show that she was not present at the time of the alleged biting.[120] In fact, the Advisory Committee specifically noted that

---

114 FED. R. EVID. 803 advisory committee note.

115 Of all the exception in Rules 803 and 804, only one requires the hearsay declaration to have been made under oath. *See* FED. R. EVID. 804(b)(1). Similarly, the restrictions on lay opinion testimony (and other matters of "form") tend to be relaxed in the context of hearsay, for the obvious reason that an out-of-court assertion cannot be restated in order to comply with such rules the way that in-court testimony can. *See* 1 MCCORMICK ON EVIDENCE § 18 (Kenneth S. Broun ed., 7th ed. 2013).

116 *See* Shepard v. United States, 290 U.S. 96, 101 (1933) ("To let the declaration in, the inference must be permissible that there was knowledge or the opportunity for knowledge as to the acts that are declared"). *See generally* 2 MCCORMICK ON EVIDENCE § 313 (Kenneth S. Broun ed., 7th ed. 2013) (noting that personal knowledge requirement applies to dying declarations).

117 *See, e.g.*, Shepard v. United States, 290 U.S. at 101 (statement held inadmissible as a dying declaration on other grounds would almost certainly have failed to meet the personal knowledge requirement as well; the court noted this requirement without deciding whether this statement would meet it).

118 *See, e.g.*, Reese v. Bara, 479 F. Supp. 651, 655–56 (S.D.N.Y. 1979) (woman stabbed in the abdomen would have been "a competent witness as to how she came by her stab wounds").

119 *Id.* at 265–66 (arguing that usually against-interest statements are generally accompanied by adequate investigation to insure high reliability).

120 *See* Mahlandt v. Wild Canid Survival & Research Ctr., Inc., 588 F.2d 626, 630–31 (8th Cir. 1978) (admission by agent that wolf bit child held admissible without requirement of personal knowledge). *See also* Union Mut. Life Ins. Co. v. Chrysler Corp., 793 F.2d 1, 8–9 (1st Cir. 1986) (letter containing admissions that was written by employee held admissible despite lack of personal knowledge); Freda F. Bein, *Parties' Admissions, Agents' Admissions: Hearsay Wolves in Sheep's Clothing*, 12 HOFSTRA L. REV. 393 (1984) (arguing against result in *Mahlandt* case where agent's admissions are involved).

statements by party-opponents rule was free of the personal knowledge requirement.[121] The business records exception is also free of the personal knowledge requirement in the sense that the recording declarant need not have personal knowledge of the transaction recorded, though the information must have been transmitted by a person with such knowledge.[122] Some of the other hearsay exceptions also expressly or implicitly dispense with the requirement that the hearsay declarant have personal knowledge. One such exception is Rule 803(8)(A)(iii), the exception for findings pursuant to investigation, which by its very nature contemplates that sometimes the declarant will make a finding about events that the declarant did not personally observe.[123] For example, in *Beech Aircraft v. Rainey*[124] the Supreme Court held admissible a report of a naval investigator's conclusion about the cause of a fatal air crash. The investigator had not observed the crash nor did the investigator have personal knowledge of the basis for many of the facts and conclusions expressed in his report.[125] Another hearsay exception, the exception for statements of personal and family history in Rule 804(b)(4), expressly eschews any requirement of personal knowledge. It provides that statements concerning the declarant's own birth, adoption, marriage, family relationships, etc. are admissible "even though declarant had no means of acquiring personal knowledge of the matter stated."[126]

Where the hearsay exception requires that the declarant have spoken based on personal knowledge, however, Federal Rule 602 applies. That rule provides that a lay witness "may not testify to a matter unless evidence is introduced sufficient to support a finding that the witness has personal knowledge of the matter." Under this standard, which tracks the standard contained in Rule 104(b) (the so-called "conditional relevancy" rule), the trial court need not be convinced that the declarant had personal knowledge. The court need only find that there is evidence sufficient to support that conclusion (i.e., that it would not be unreasonable for the jury to conclude that the declarant had personal knowledge). Because this is not a very difficult standard to satisfy, the personal knowledge requirement will not often be a significant obstacle to the admission of hearsay under one of the exceptions.

---

[121] FED. R. EVID. 801(d)(2) advisory committee note ("The freedom which admissions have enjoyed . . . from the restrictive influences of the opinion rule and the rule requiring firsthand knowledge. . . call[ ] for generous treatment of this avenue to admissibility").

[122] *See* United States v. Norton, 867 F.2d 1354, 1363 (11th Cir. 1989) (holding memorandum detailing telephone conversation prepared by one officer was admissible as business record through another officer who had no personal knowledge of its contents). *See also* United States v. Iredia, 866 F.2d 114, 119–20 (5th Cir. 1989) ("There is, however, no requirement under Rule 803(6) that the witness laying the foundation be able to attest personally to its accuracy."); 2 MCCORMICK ON EVIDENCE § 290 (Kenneth S. Broun ed., 7th ed. 2013). But note that the person initially gathering the information must have personal knowledge. *See* Meder v. Everest & Jennings, Inc., 637 F.2d 1182, 1186 (8th Cir. 1981) (admission of police accident report was in error where officer could not recall where he had obtained the information).

[123] *See* 2 MCCORMICK ON EVIDENCE § 296 at 466 (Kenneth S. Broun ed., 7th ed. 2013) ("As the name indicates, these reports embody the results of investigations and accordingly are often not the product of the declarant's firsthand knowledge").

[124] Beech Aircraft Corp. v. Rainey, 488 U.S. 153 (1988).

[125] *Id.* at 164–70. *See also* Wolf by Wolf v. Procter & Gamble Co., 555 F. Supp. 613, 625 (D.N.J. 1982) (studies conducted by Centers for Disease Control and state health agencies admissible even if the authors did not have firsthand knowledge of the facts upon which findings were made).

[126] FED. R. EVID. 804(b)(4)(A). *See* **§ 16.4**.

§ 14.09 Attacking and Supporting the Credibility of a Hearsay Declarant [FRE 806]

Another issue that arises regarding the declarant whose hearsay is admitted concerns impeachment and rehabilitation. This is not the impeachment or rehabilitation of a witness in court, who might be called to report the hearsay, but rather the impeachment or rehabilitation of a hearsay declarant. Because the credibility of a hearsay assertion is relevant, Rules 402 and 403 would authorize and regulate the admissibility of such impeachment and rehabilitation even if no other rule existed. Federal Rule of Evidence 806 addresses this question specifically, however, and provides that the credibility of a hearsay declarant can be attacked or supported as if the declarant were a witness.[127] Rule 806 confirms that the same limits are placed on such impeachment and rehabilitation as would apply for live witnesses. However, Rule 806 dispenses with certain foundational requirements for common-law impeachment with prior inconsistent statements.[128] Rule 806 also allows a party to call the declarant as a witness, when this is possible, and to question the declarant as if on cross-examination when that declarant's hearsay statements are used against the party.[129]

To illustrate the operation of Rule 806, suppose that Johnny makes an out-of-court statement, "The light was red!" The statement is received at trial as an excited utterance.[130] Obviously, the opponent ought to be able to put in evidence that at some other time Johnny said, of the same light at the time in question, "The light was green," and the rule provides that this may be done even if the opponent has not given Johnny the opportunity to admit or deny the latter statement. Once Johnny's credibility has been attacked, the proponent may offer any evidence to rehabilitate the declarant that would be admissible if Johnny were a witness.[131]

Now, consider the situation in which Johnny testified at a deposition that the light was red. The opponent has evidence that Johnny had at some other time stated that the light was green. The opponent had an opportunity at the deposition to confront Johnny with the alleged prior statement and ask him to explain or deny the statement. However, the opponent failed to use this opportunity and did not ask Johnny anything about the prior statement during the deposition. Later the deposition is offered as evidence at trial because Johnny has become unavailable to testify.[132] Rule 806 provides that the opponent is not precluded from putting in the declarant's inconsistent statement, even

---

[127] FED. R. EVID. 806. *See generally* 2 MCCORMICK ON EVIDENCE § 324.2 (Kenneth S. Broun ed., 7th ed. 2013).

[128] *See* Smith v. Fairman, 862 F.2d 630, 637–38 (7th Cir. 1988):

> While the general rule is that a witness may be impeached by his prior inconsistent statements only after a proper foundation has been laid . . . that rule has been dispensed with "where the witness is unavailable and hearsay evidence is offered to impeach the previously admitted hearsay evidence of the statements of the absent witness."

[129] FED. R. EVID. 806; *see also* United States v. Inadi, 475 U.S. 387, 397 (1986) ("[I]f the party against whom a co-conspirator statement has been admitted calls the declarant as a witness, 'the party is entitled to examine him on the statement as if under cross-examination.' ").

[130] *See* **§ 16.02**.

[131] *See* United States v. Lechoco, 542 F.2d 84, 88–89 (D.C. Cir. 1976) (error to exclude evidence supporting credibility of out-of-court declarant where credibility has been impeached). Note that the inconsistent statement used to impeach the declarant can occur before or after the admitted hearsay statement. *See* FED. R. EVID. 806 advisory committee note.

[132] *See* **§ 17.02**.

though the opponent failed to lay a foundation for it despite the opportunity to do so?[133] The rule specifically provides that the court "may admit evidence of the evidence of the declarant's inconsistent statement or conduct, regardless of when it occurred or whether the declarant had an opportunity to explain or deny it."[134]

Rule 806 is not limited to impeachment by prior inconsistent statements. The hearsay declarant can be impeached by any method, including impeachment by prior convictions or by a showing of bias.[135]

An interesting question arises concerning the interaction between Rule 806, which provides that the credibility of a hearsay declarant may be attacked by any evidence that would be admissible if declarant had testified as a witness, and Rule 608(b), which bars extrinsic evidence of specific instances of conduct by the witness to attack truthfulness. What if a party seeks to attack the truthfulness of a hearsay declarant by offering specific instances of conduct by the declarant? If the declarant had testified in person, the cross-examiner could have asked the witness about the specific instances on cross-examination, but could not have offered extrinsic evidence to prove those instances. This creates a tension between Rules 806 and 608(b). At least one court has opted to allow impeachment of a hearsay declarant with extrinsic evidence,[136] while another has held that the limitation of Rule 608(b) should be applied literally,[137] and others have limited inquiry into declarant's specific acts to the cross-examination of the witness who reports the hearsay.[138]

Rule 806 also applies to "any statement described in Rules 801(d)(2)(C), (D), or (E)," which are statements admissible against a party because of an agency or conspiratorial relationship between the declarant and the party. The significance of this provision lies in what is not embraced by the Rule, namely statements falling within 801(d)(1) and statements falling within Rules 801(d)(2)(A) and (B). The former are prior statements by a testifying witness, and there is little concern with impeaching the declarant as such when the same person is testifying: as a witness in court, the declarant/witness is obviously subject to the usual impeachment and rehabilitation rules. The exclusion from

---

[133] For the in-court witness, FED. R. EVID. 613(b) provides that "[e]xtrinsic evidence of a witness's prior inconsistent statement is admissible only if the witness is given an opportunity to explain or deny the statement and an adverse party is given an opportunity to examine the witness about it, or if justice so requires."

[134] FED. R. EVID. 806; *see also* Smith v. Fairman, 862 F.2d 630, 637–38 (7th Cir. 1988); Wigmore supported a contrary position. He argued that a foundation should be required whenever an opportunity could have been provided to the declarant to explain or deny the inconsistency. Thus, different hearsay statements would be treated differently. For example, in a dying declaration there would very likely not be such an opportunity, but in prior testimony there would. *See* 3 WIGMORE ON EVIDENCE §§ 1030–1035 (Chadbourn rev., 1970). The Federal Rule treats all hearsay statements in the same way. *See* 5 WEINSTEIN'S FEDERAL EVIDENCE § 806.04[1] (Mark S. Brodin ed., 2d ed. 2015).

[135] *See* United States v. Lawson, 608 F.2d 1129, 1130 (6th Cir. 1979) (court did not err in admitting evidence of out-of-court declarant's felony convictions offered for impeachment purposes); United States v. Becerra, 992 F.2d 960, 965 (9th Cir. 1993) (in criminal case, district court improperly prevented defendant from attacking out-of-court declarant's credibility with evidence of declarant's prior statements, criminal convictions, and compensation as paid police informant); United States v. Bovain, 708 F.2d 606, 613–14 (11th Cir. 1983) (evidence of declarant's prior narcotics and theft convictions held admissible to impeach out-of-court declarant's credibility).

[136] State v. Martisko, 566 S.E.2d 274 (W. Va. 2002) (applying W. VA. R. EVID. 806, but also apparently relying on defendant's constitutional right to confront accuser).

[137] United States v. Saada, 212 F.3d 210, 220 (3d Cir. 2000) ("Fed. R. Evid. 806 does not modify Fed. R. Evid. 608(b)'s ban on extrinsic evidence of prior bad acts in the context of hearsay declarants, even when those declarants are unavailable to testify").

[138] United States v. White, 116 F.3d 903, 920 (D.C. Cir. 1997).

Rule 806 of Rules 801(d)(2)(A) and (B), which covers personal statements (whether express or adoptive) by an opposing party, is harder to understand. The drafters of the Rule provided an unintelligible explanation,[139] but a plausible rationale is readily at hand: if Rule 806 embraced personal statements of a party opponent, then a proponent might be able to "bootstrap" the admission of otherwise inadmissible bad character evidence against an opponent. Suppose, for example, the criminal defendant chooses not to testify. Ordinarily, this would preclude impeachment by a showing of the defendant's general dishonesty.[140] So the prosecutor introduces an out-of-court statement by the defendant that has at least some value on its own to the prosecution but is also somewhat self-serving for the defendant. Then the prosecutor invokes Rule 806 to introduce evidence of the bad character of the defendant-declarant for truthfulness. This strategic ploy might (or might not) be precluded by the defendant's raising a "mere subterfuge" argument.[141] The wording of Rule 806, however, precludes it.

---

[139] A footnote to the Senate Committee report that added the language referring to 801(d)(2) explained this omission on the ground that it was unnecessary to include the personal statements of a party opponent in a rule authorizing impeachment and rehabilitation because "the credibility of the party-opponent is always subject to attack on his credibility." Aside from the redundant grammatical construction, this assertion is off the mark:

> It is of course true that one party may always attack the position taken by his adversary in a lawsuit, and in this broad sense the latter's credibility is always subject to attack. However, the credibility of a party is subject to attack in the manner in which the credibility of witnesses is subject to attack only if the party testifies or, if Rule 806 applies, where his out-of-court statement is admitted in evidence.

5 CHRISTOPHER B. MUELLER & LAIRD C. KIRKPATRICK, FEDERAL EVIDENCE § 8:137 at 256 n.5 (4th ed. 2013). Mueller and Kirkpatrick nonetheless endorse the applicability of impeachment techniques to parties whose personal statements are admitted by an opponent. *Id.* They do not address the bootstrapping problem noted in the text.

[140] *See* **§ 10.06**.

[141] *See* **§ 10.02**.

Chapter 15

HEARSAY "EXEMPTIONS": PRIOR STATEMENTS BY WITNESSES AND STATEMENTS BY PARTY-OPPONENTS

Table of Sections

§ 15.01 Hearsay "Exemptions"

Unlike the common law, the Federal Rules of Evidence include a category of statements that, although used to prove the truth of the matter asserted, are nonetheless called "not hearsay." For the purposes of clarity, we refer to this "not hearsay" category as "exemptions" from the hearsay rule.[1] This category, which appears as Rule 801(d), includes two subclasses: Rule 801(d)(1) admits certain prior statements made by a witness who testifies at trial, while Rule 801(d)(2) admits statements made by a party-opponent or someone appropriately identified with such a party-opponent. Rule 801(d)(1), covering prior statements by testifying witnesses, is largely an innovation of the Federal Rules.[2] In contrast, statements by party-opponents, addressed by Rule 801(d)(2), were long regarded by the common law as within an "exception" to the hearsay prohibition. Indeed, it is one of the most important and commonly encountered kinds of statement that are admissible to prove the truth of the matter asserted.

For practical purposes, exemptions function very much like exceptions: when they apply, the statement is admissible as evidence of the truth of the matter asserted. So we sometimes refer to the use of a statement falling within an exemption in Rule 801(d) as a "hearsay use" because the statement is offered to prove the truth of the matter asserted, just as is the case for a statement falling within an exception in Rules 803, 804, or 807.

---

1 *See* **§ 14.06**.

2 There was only scattered precedent for it in the common law, although reformers had long suggested the liberal admissibility of prior statements of a (testifying) witness *See* ALI MODEL CODE OF EVIDENCE Rule 503(b) (1942).

§ 15.02 Prior Statements of Witnesses—in General [FRE 801(d)(1)]

The mere fact that a person is on the witness stand does not automatically render that person's out-of-court statements free from a hearsay objection. The hearsay rule applies even when the witness and the declarant are the same person. Yet, there are many ways in which the witness/declarant's statement may become admissible. For example, it may not be hearsay at all under the common-law definition; it may be admissible on the theory that it is not offered to prove the truth of the matter asserted, but to establish a legally operative fact or to impeach or rehabilitate the witness. Alternatively, it may fall under one of the traditional hearsay exceptions, embracing such things as excited utterances and business records, exceptions that apply whether or not the declarant testifies or is available to do so.[3] Third, it may be admissible because the witness/declarant is the proponent's party-opponent. And—the present topic—it may be admissible under one of the special categories of "nonhearsay" exemptions created by Rule 801(d)(1) for prior inconsistent statements, prior consistent statements, and prior statements of identification.

Congress vigorously debated the scope of Rule 801(d)(1). The Senate Committee agreed with the advisory committee that all prior statements of a witness should be admitted for their truth, subject only to limitations designed to prevent the use of "prepared testimony."[4] Because the declarant would be present, under oath, and available for cross-examination about the prior statement, the thinking was that there would be no serious danger in admitting any prior statement by the witness. In addition, because a great portion of prior statements of a witness have long been admissible for the theoretically limited purpose of impeachment or rehabilitation of the witness, admitting such statements also for the truth of the matter asserted avoids cumbersome limiting instructions, which may not be effective anyway. Despite these arguments, the advisory committee and Senate's liberal admissibility proposal was modified in Congress as explained below.

§ 15.03 Prior Statements of Witnesses—Prior Inconsistent Statements [FRE 801(d)(1)(A)]

At common-law, courts would generally admit a (testifying) witness's prior inconsistent statement, not made while testifying at the same trial, for impeachment only and not to prove the truth of the matter asserted out-of-court.[5] Under the Federal Rules of Evidence, there are two separate bases for receiving a witness's prior inconsistent statement despite a hearsay objection: impeachment (as at common-law) and Rule 801(d)(1)(A).[6] Rule 801(d)(1)(A) designates a prior out-of-court statement by a witness as "not hearsay," (even though offered, at least in part, to prove the truth of the matter asserted) if:

---

[3] *See* FED. R. EVID. 803, discussed in **§§ 16.01 et seq.**

[4] Prepared testimony refers to the situation when a witness takes the stand and says essentially nothing about the underlying events except to endorse his prior, well-crafted statement.

[5] *See* **§ 11.05**.

[6] Of course, the statement can also be received if it falls under an exception to the hearsay rule. The statement in text applies to prior inconsistent statements that do not fall under any of the enumerated hearsay exceptions.

- the declarant testifies at the current trial or hearing,
- the declarant is subject to cross-examination, at the current trial or hearing, concerning the prior statement,
- the prior statement is inconsistent with the declarant's current testimony,
- the prior statement was given under oath subject to the penalty of perjury, and
- the prior statement was made at a trial, hearing, or other proceeding, or in a deposition.[7]

If the prior inconsistent statement falls under Rule 801(d)(1)(A), then it is admissible as substantive evidence and may be used to prove the truth of the matter asserted.

The House of Representatives Committee desired even more limitations on the substantive use of prior inconsistent statements and attempted to add a requirement that the *prior* statement had been subject to cross-examination. The addition of a cross-examination requirement would have eliminated grand jury testimony from the prior inconsistent statements admissible under 801(d)(1)(A). The compromise reached in Congress and reflected by the current rule does require significant formality for prior statements covered by the rule: they must be under oath, subject to penalty of perjury and made at a deposition, before a grand jury, or at another hearing. Rule 801(d)(1)(A) does not cover casual statements. One benefit of these formal requirements is that the prior statement was probably part of an official record and there can be little debate about what was actually said in the other proceeding.

To be sure, many inconsistent statements are routinely admitted as common-law impeachment even though they do not meet the requirements of Rule 801(d)(1)(A) or any other exception to or exemption from the hearsay prohibition. Under the common-law impeachment theory, the inconsistent statement is offered to demonstrate the unreliability of the witness. The fact that the declarant said different things at different times reflects poorly on the declarant's credibility, whether the original statement was true or not. For example, a witness statement taken by police officer or an insurance investigator is not made under oath or at a "proceeding," and hence does not qualify for admission under Rule 801(d)(1)(A). Such a statement could be received, however, under the traditional common-law theory of impeachment that predated and survived the Federal Rules. Because such a prior inconsistent statement is offered solely to impeach and not offered to prove the truth of the matter asserted, it is not hearsay within the traditional definition stated in Rule 801(c).

In such a case, however, because it is not substantive evidence (i.e., it is not used to prove the truth of the matter asserted), the prior statement may not be used to overcome a motion for a directed verdict. If elements A, B, and C are essential elements of the plaintiff's case, and the only evidence that the plaintiff has on element C is the prior inconsistent statement asserting C, but made by a witness who now testifies in court that C is false, then the defendant is entitled to a directed verdict. The only admissible evidence on the point is the witness's courtroom testimony affirming not-C; the only

---

[7] Not all "proceedings" qualify under this rule. For example, an affidavit taken under oath administered by an IRS special agent in an investigative interview is not a statement made in a "proceeding" within the meaning of this rule. United States v. Williams, 272 F.3d 845 (7th Cir. 2001); *but see* State v. Smith, 651 P.2d 207 (Wash. 1982) (finding under circumstances limited to facts that signed and sworn police interrogation qualified as prior proceeding).

purpose for which the prior statement supporting element C may be used is to impeach the in-court testimony. Therefore, even if the impeachment is fully effective, there is still no evidence affirming C.[8] The rule has an impact even in nonjury trials.[9] If the only evidence to support the verdict in a nonjury trial is evidence of a prior inconsistent statement that can be used only to impeach, then there is no admissible evidence to support the verdict and the trial judge's verdict in favor of the plaintiff must be overturned.

Example

In 2008, on a street corner in Bloomington, Indiana, a blue van hit a red car, killing the driver of the red car. David, a bystander who witnessed the accident, made two statements:

(1) Right after the accident, after he had calmed down, David said to Barbara: "The blue van ran through the red light." Barbara is prepared to testify to David's statement.

(2) In 2009, at the criminal trial for drunk driving of the driver of the blue van, David testified, consistent with his on-the-scene statement, that the blue van ran the red light. The transcripts of that previous trial are available.

Imagine that in a 2010 civil trial for the wrongful death of the driver of the red car, David surprises everyone and testifies that the light was green for the blue van. David's two prior inconsistent statements could be used in the wrongful death suit. The first statement at the scene would not qualify for admission under Rule 801(d)(1)(A) and would not be admissible for its truth (that the blue van ran through a red light). The first statement could, however, be admitted to impeach David, demonstrating that David is an inconsistent and unreliable witness. The second statement made under oath and subject to penalty of perjury at a previous trial fits within Rule 801(d)(1)(A) and is admissible as substantive evidence—that is to say, for its truth. The jury may feel free to disbelieve David's current testimony and instead believe his former testimony.

If only the first statement were available at the 2010 trial for the wrongful death of the driver of the red car, and that statement constituted the only evidence of the blue van's negligence, then the judge would have to grant a judgment as a matter of law in favor of the defendant. The first statement presents no affirmative evidence in the plaintiff's case; it can only be used to impeach the witness.

Another consequence of receiving the prior inconsistent statement under the common-law theory, rather than under Rule 801(d)(1)(A), is that the opponent is entitled to a limiting instruction. The limiting instruction informs the jury that it may use the statement for its bearing on the credibility of the witness, but not as substantive evidence of the truth of the matter asserted. Sometimes evidence of the prior inconsistent statement should be excluded because the limiting instruction would be ineffective or

---

[8] *See* **§ 2.06**.

[9] Normally, the impact of the hearsay rule is minimal in nonjury trials due to the rule that even when the trial judge errs in admitting hearsay, the trial judge's verdict will stand if there is enough admissible evidence to support the verdict. *See* 1 McCormick on Evidence § 60 at 412 (Kenneth S. Broun ed., 7th ed. 2013).

inadequate. If the court takes seriously the theory that the evidence is not received to prove its truth, then the evidence should be excluded under Rule 403 when the danger of its being used for its truth substantially outweighs its probative value for impeachment or the court concludes that it is necessary to deter proponents from inviting improper inferences.

An important illustration is the problem of "mere subterfuge" evidence: the proponent should not be able to put on a witness known to be worthless merely to admit a prior inconsistent statement in hopes that the jury will ignore the limiting instruction and accept the prior statement as true.[10] For example, when a prosecutor knows that the witness will deny any knowledge of a criminal transaction, the prosecutor should not be able to call the witness and introduce a prior statement by that witness incriminating the defendant. The statement cannot possibly help the prosecution if used properly (if the jury believes that the witness is not credible, what does the witness contribute?), and can only be helpful if the jury ignores the limiting instruction and puts the statement to a forbidden use. That is, the statement would only be useful to the prosecution if the jury accepts the statement as true, as substantive evidence of guilt.[11]

§ 15.04 Prior Statements of Witnesses—Prior Consistent Statements [FRE 801(d)(1)(B)]

Federal Rule 801(d)(1)(B) provides that if a witness is currently on the stand, under oath and subject to cross examination that witness's prior out-out-court consistent statements may be admissible "to rebut an express or implied charge that the declarant recently fabricated it or acted from a recent improper influence or motive in so testifying" or "to rehabilitate the declarant's credibility as a witness when attacked on another ground." (The first use, rebutting fabrication and improper motive was part of the Rule from its inception. As explained below, the second way of rehabilitating a witness is the product of the 2014 amendment to the Federal Rules.) Rule 801(d)(1)(B) does not require that the prior statement be made under oath or at a proceeding to qualify as substantive evidence. In this respect, the provision is much broader than Rule 801(d)(1)(A), covering prior inconsistent statements. To understand the current rule, it is necessary to review its history.

Under the common law, prior consistent statements not falling within an exception to the hearsay rule could only be used to rehabilitate the testimony of a witness who had been impeached, and then only if the prior consistent statement logically tended to refute the attempted impeachment. A limiting instruction was necessary to try to explain this difference to the fact-finder.[12] The drafters of the federal rules faced afresh the question of whether to admit all prior consistent statements of a witness for the truth of the matter asserted in view of the fact that the witness is under oath and subject to cross-

---

[10] *See* **§ 11.02**.

[11] *See* United States v. Hogan, 763 F.2d 697 (5th Cir. 1985) (government called witness it knew would testify favorably toward defendants, then offered prior inconsistent statements of witness and called several other witnesses to contradict him; holding that, because none of this impeaching matter was substantively admissible, and because the government's primary purpose in calling witness was to place impeaching matter before jury, the trial court should not have permitted the government to call the witness), *modified*, 771 F.2d 82 (5th Cir. 1985) (modification did not affect issue under consideration here); *see also* Michael H. Graham, *Employing Inconsistent Statements for Impeachment and as Substantive Evidence: A Critical Review and Proposed Amendments of Federal Rules of Evidence 801(d)(1)(A), 613, and 607*, 75 MICH. L. REV. 1565, 1613–15 (1977).

[12] For discussion of rehabilitation using prior consistent statements of a witness, see **§ 11.13**.

examination at the trial, even if he or she was not when the prior statement was made. The primary concern with doing so has been the risk that parties will resort to "prepared statements," written statements carefully crafted with the help of an attorney or other person, which the witness called to the stand could then authenticate and endorse without otherwise testifying on direct.[13] The reasonable compromise was to permit the hearsay use of prior consistent statements only when they are admissible for rehabilitation anyway, thus requiring the witness to testify and be impeached before prior consistent statements would become admissible for the hearsay purpose. By matching the permissible hearsay use with the otherwise existing rehabilitative use, there would be no need for cumbersome limiting instructions of doubtful effectiveness.

Unfortunately, this purpose was (and remains) poorly effectuated by the Rule's wording.[14] Instead of simply saying that the prior statement is admissible for the truth of the matter asserted whenever it is admissible for rehabilitative purposes, the Rule specifies that such use is permitted only when the prior consistent statement is offered to rehabilitate the witness in certain stated ways. Prior to 2015, this problem was relatively acute because of the narrowness of the circumstances authorizing the hearsay use of the prior statement. Until then, to fall within the rule the statement had to be "offered to rebut an express or implied charge against the declarant of recent fabrication or improper influence or motive,"[15] the language that now appears as 801(d)(1)(B)(i). As explained elsewhere, this is not the only way that a prior consistent statement can be relevant to rehabilitate an impeached witness.[16]

The Supreme Court addressed the issue of the admissibility of prior consistent statements in its 1995 decision in *Tome v. United States*.[17] In *Tome*, the defendant was charged with sexual abuse of his four-year-old daughter. He and the child's mother were divorced and had joint custody. The child made out-of-court statements indicating that she had been abused by her father. The defense argued that the statements were concocted to prevent the father from sharing custody. The child, who was six and a half at the time of trial, testified and was cross-examined. For the most part, her direct testimony consisted of one-and two-word answers to a series of leading questions. On cross-examination, the child was reluctant to answer questions, seemed to lose concentration, and sometimes took as long as fifty-five seconds to answer a question.[18] After the child testified, the government called six witnesses who testified to her prior statements describing sexual assaults by her father. A babysitter testified that the child told her she did not want to return to her father because he "gets drunk and thinks I'm his wife."[19] The mother testified to details she overheard the child describe. A social

---

[13] If the witness testifies fully, in a manner that is consistent with the prior statement, then introduction of the prior statement would ordinarily be redundant and excludable on that basis under Rule 403.

[14] By comparison, the Minnesota rule explicitly allows for admission of prior consistent statements that are "helpful to the trier of fact in evaluating the declarant's credibility as a witness." MINN. R. EVID. 801(d)(1)(B).

[15] *See* Gaines v. Walker, 986 F.2d 1438, 1444 (D.C. Cir. 1993) (holding that in civil rights action, plaintiff's cross-examination of defendant police officer regarding supposed omission in latter's police report is implied claim of fabrication; district court abused its discretion in preventing defendant from rebutting fabrication claim by introducing actual police report as evidence of prior consistent statement).

[16] *See* **§ 11.13**.

[17] Tome v. United States, 513 U.S. 150 (1995).

[18] *Id.* at 153.

[19] *Id.* at 154.

worker and three pediatricians also testified about details that the child had told them. The statements were offered by the government as prior consistent statements under Rule 801(d)(1)(B). The trial court admitted the statements and the Tenth Circuit affirmed, accepting the theory that the statements were all admissible under the rule. The United States Supreme Court reversed, holding that the prior consistent statements are only admissible under Rule 801(d)(1)(B) if they were made before the alleged recent fabrication or improper influence or motive arose. The Court held that this requirement was not met under the facts of the *Tome* case.[20] Aside from precedent, the Court offered a policy justification for its holding explaining that "if the Rule were to permit the introduction of prior statements as substantive evidence to rebut every implicit charge that a witness's in-court testimony results from recent fabrication or improper influence or motive, the whole emphasis of the trial would shift to the out-of-court statements, not the in-court ones."[21] The Court suggested that the case before it was an example of this bad result, because the government was permitted to present a "parade of sympathetic and credible witnesses" who repeated the child's out-of-court statements.[22]

For the federal courts, *Tome* settled the question of whether, when a statement is offered under what is now Rule 801(d)(1)(B)(i), the trial judge has discretion to admit post-motive statements. The majority endorsed a per se rule that the statements must be excluded unless they were made before the motive to fabricate or improper influence arose. Note, however, that *Tome* involved statements offered under Rule 801(d)(1)(B), which allows prior consistent statements to be offered not only to bolster credibility, but also as substantive evidence to show the truth of the matter asserted. The Court did not directly address the question whether prior consistent statements might sometimes be admissible on the theory that they fall outside the hearsay ban because they are offered only to show something other than the truth of the matter asserted, such as to rehabilitate the witness. For example, suppose an elderly witness testifies about the details of a transaction and is impeached by cross-examination that touches on memory problems as well as on the witness's motive to help the proponent. The witness's prior statements made soon after the transaction would arguably be admissible to show that the witness's memory was accurate. Just as a prior inconsistent statement might be admitted to challenge the witness's reliability (a purpose other than showing its truth), so might a prior consistent statement be admitted to support reliability (another nonhearsay purpose). If so, then the *Tome* pre-motive requirement might not apply to those consistent statements. *Tome* expressly stated that its "holding is confined to the requirements for admission under Rule 801(d)(1)(B),"[23] so one might infer that the ruling does not cover the use of prior consistent statements to rehabilitate the witness when the proponent does not rely on that rule but instead offers the statement on the theory that it is not being offered to prove the truth. However, there is language elsewhere in *Tome* that suggests that the Court might have believed that Rule 801(d)(1)(B) was the

[20] *Id.* at 165. *Cf.* United States v. Prieto, 232 F.3d 816 (11th Cir. 2000) (government sought to enhance credibility of accomplice, who was cooperating with government, by introducing consistent statements made to police between time accomplice was arrested and month later, when accomplice signed cooperation agreement; court held that whether statements were made before motive to fabricate arose was question of fact for district court and appellate court must defer to district court, which decided to admit evidence; query whether realistic to suppose that accomplice was free of motive to help himself when making statements to police after being arrested, in absence of specific showing otherwise, as was absent here).

[21] Tome v. United States, 513 U.S. 150, 165 (1995).

[22] *Id.*

[23] *Id.* at 167.

only route through which prior consistent statements could be received to combat impeachment. For example, the Court states that "[p]rior consistent statements may not be admitted to counter all forms of impeachment or to bolster the witness merely because she has been discredited."[24] That left matters somewhat confused.

The 2014 amendment resolved this confusion by adding the second basis for substantive admissibility of prior consistent statements, which now appears as Rule 801(d)(1)(B)(ii). It admits as "not hearsay" prior consistent statements "offered" "to rehabilitate the declarant's credibility as a witness when attacked on another ground," that is, a ground other than a charge of recent fabrication or improper influence or motive. The effect of this amendment is to assure that virtually any prior consistent statement that is admissible for rehabilitative purposes is also admissible for the truth of the matter asserted, thus bringing the rule in line with its drafters' original idea.[25] The amendment leaves intact, however, the pre-motive requirement of *Tome* when the rehabilitative relevance of the prior statement is limited to rebutting a charge of recent fabrication. Thus, even if post-motive consistent statements might be relevant to rehabilitate the witness, they will not be substantively admissible.

§ 15.05 Prior Statements of Witnesses—Prior Identification Statements [FRE 801(d)(1)(C)]

Under the Federal Rules of Evidence, a witness's prior statement of identification is "not hearsay" and is admissible for its truth under Rule 801(d)(1)(C).[26] A prior identification is often more reliable than identification made at trial, because it was made closer in time to the event and because at trial the "suggestions of others and the circumstances of the trial may have intervened to create a fancied recognition in the witness's mind."[27] However, there is no specific requirement as to when the prior identification was made: an identification from a photo display or a line-up made several days or weeks after the crime is just as admissible as a victim's identification at the scene of the crime.[28] Moreover, the out-of-court identification statement may be admitted before the witness testifies.

As with other prior witness statements governed by Rule 801(d)(1), prior identification statements are admissible only if the witness testifies in court and is

---

[24] *Id.* at 157. For a full analysis, see Norman M. Garland & Romy Schneider, *Prior Consistent Statements as Evidence in the United States and Canada—A Small Part of the Story of How Sex Crimes Cases Continue to Generate Law Reform*, 2 SW. J. L. & TRADE AM. 451 (1995).

[25] Another problem with the drafting of the Rule was not fixed by the amendment. Instead of stating that a prior consistent statement is exempted from the hearsay rule if it is *admissible* to rehabilitate the witness in the indicated ways, the Rule states merely that prior consistent statements are exempted from the hearsay rule if "offered" to rehabilitate them in the indicated ways. But if it is so offered, it is not within 801(c) in the first place—*see* **§ 14.04** (subsection on "Prior Statements of a Witness Relevant to Credibility")—and no hearsay issue arises. Conversely, if offered for the truth of the matter asserted and not to rehabilitate the witness, then it does not come within the wording of the Rule. Accordingly, in order to be admissible for the hearsay purpose, the proponent must offer the statement for both purposes. This complexity, however, was surely not intended, and cases like *Tomb* illustrate that the courts have had no difficulty reading the Rule as if it conditioned substantive admissibility on whether the statement is admissible for rehabilitation, rather than on whether it is offered for rehabilitation.

[26] *See* People v. Johnson, 701 P.2d 620, 622 (Colo. App. 1985).

[27] Gilbert v. California, 388 U.S. 263, 272 n.3 (1967) (quoting People v. Gould, 354 P.2d 865, 867 (Cal. 1960)); *see also* United States v. Barbati, 284 F. Supp. 409, 413 (E.D.N.Y. 1968) (noting that in-court identifications are generally "an almost worthless formality").

[28] *See* 5 WEINSTEIN'S FEDERAL EVIDENCE § 801.23[1] (Mark S. Brodin ed., 2d ed. 2015).

subject to cross-examination concerning the prior statement.[29] A witness's identification can be admitted at trial either through that witness or through the testimony of another witness who observed the out-of-court identification.[30] For instance, a witness who identified the defendant from a photo display can testify to that fact, and the testimony can be corroborated by the police officer who observed the identification.[31] In addition, testimony about the prior identification will be admissible even though the witness is not able to make an identification in court.[32] Furthermore, if the witness cannot remember, or perhaps even denies, having made the out-of-court identification, another witness can testify to the prior identification.[33]

Admission of an out-of-court identification is independent of the restrictions of Rules 801(d)(1)(A) and 801(d)(1)(B).[34] Thus, if the out-of-court identification is inconsistent with the in-court identification, the former is admissible even though it was not given under oath at a hearing. Likewise, if the out-of-court identification is consistent with the in-court identification, the former is admissible even if the witness's testimony has not been impeached in such a way as to trigger the applicability of 801(d)(1)(B). For this reason, it is important to understand the limits of Rule 801(d)(1)(C), lest it be a vehicle for circumventing the restrictions on the use of prior inconsistent or consistent statements. Most importantly, a prior statement that happens to name someone as the perpetrator of a crime should not be admissible under Rule 801(d)(1)(C) if its relevance is not to establish the identity of the perpetrator but rather to establish what the perpetrator did, as when the identity of the actor is not disputed.[35]

---

[29] *See* United States v. Owens, 484 U.S. 554, 561–64 (1988).

[30] *See* Thomas A. Mauet, *Prior Identification in Criminal Cases: Hearsay and Confrontation Issues*, 24 ARIZ. L. REV. 29, 43–49 (1982).

[31] *See* United States v. Elemy, 656 F.2d 507, 508 (9th Cir. 1981) (at lineup, witness identified someone other than defendant as robber she had seen, but later told officer that she did not think her identification had been correct; officer was allowed to testify about strong resemblance between "stand-in" at lineup and defendant, and about what witness told him after lineup). *See also* United States v. Miller, 381 F.2d 529, 538 (2d Cir. 1967).

[32] *See* United States v. DiTommaso, 817 F.2d 201, 212–14 (2d Cir. 1987) (witness was unable to identify defendant at trial—defendant's appearance had changed "dramatically" since his arrest—but witness's two prior photo identifications of defendant were admissible); United States v. Lewis, 565 F.2d 1248, 1251–52 (2d Cir. 1977) (at trial, witness picked out U.S. Marshal rather than defendant, but her earlier photo identifications of defendant were admissible).

[33] *See* United States v. Owens, 484 U.S. 554, 561–63 (1988) (in prosecution for assault, identifying witness was unable to remember assault because of brain injuries, and he was confused about conversations he had during recovery at hospital; witness's photo identification of defendant was still admissible); United States v. O'Malley, 796 F.2d 891, 899 (7th Cir. 1986); United States v. Jarrad, 754 F.2d 1451, 1456 (9th Cir. 1985).

[34] *See* United States v. Lewis, 565 F.2d 1248, 1251–52 (2d Cir. 1977).

[35] Even if evidence is not excluded by the hearsay rule, there may be another basis for objecting to identification evidence. When the police have used a suggestive identification procedure, defense counsel can challenge the admissibility of the identification on due process grounds. Identifications can also be challenged on grounds that the Sixth Amendment right to counsel was violated because of absence of counsel at a line-up or show-up. Such matters are covered in texts and courses on Criminal Procedure.

§ 15.06 Statements of a Party-Opponent—in General [FRE 801(d)(2)]

The common law recognized an exception to the hearsay prohibition for statements by an opposing party.[36] Federal Rule of Evidence 801(d)(2) calls statements of a party offered by an opponent "not hearsay."[37] As with prior statements by witnesses, it is useful to think of these party-opponent statements as falling within an "exemption" to the hearsay rule.[38] Statements thus exempted from the ban against hearsay include not only the party's explicit statements but also the party's adoptive statements and statements by agents, employees and co-conspirators. These types are discussed in the following sections. This section considers elements that all such types have in common.

As a preliminary matter, one should distinguish between statements by an opposing party that are offered as evidence to prove some fact (the subject of the present discussion) from what are known as "judicial admissions." The latter are binding commitments made by a party in pleadings and as responses to requests to admit during discovery. Judicial admissions narrow the scope of what is to be tried by removing the admitted facts from contention. A party who makes a judicial admission that some fact, X, is true, may not offer evidence at trial to prove that X is false, unless of course the pleading is amended. Other statements, which by way of contrast can be called "evidential admissions," do not bind the declarant-party in this way. A party who admits to a bystander at an accident site that "the light was red" is not foreclosed by that statement from offering evidence at trial that the light was green. (The fact-finder may not believe such a change in story, but that is another matter.) This category of evidential admissions also includes answers to interrogatories and deposition questions, as well as withdrawn or superseded pleadings and even pleadings in separate law suits.[39]

The rationale of admitting statements of a party opponent is difficult to pin down. No one seriously argues that statements are particularly reliable just because they are made by a party, and the best explanation of their admission is the adversarial context in which the parties control the gathering and presentation of proof.[40] Simple fairness dictates that a party should be stuck with his or her own statement. As Professor

---

[36] See 4 WIGMORE ON EVIDENCE § 1048 (Chadbourn rev. 1972); Edmund M. Morgan, *Admissions as an Exception to the Hearsay Rule*, 30 YALE L.J. 355 (1921); John S. Strahorn, *A Reconsideration of the Hearsay Rule and Admissions*, 85 U. PA. L. REV. 484, 493, 569–88 (1937).

[37] The original version of the rule used the section sub-title, "admissions by party-opponents." This terminology is confusing because, as the advisory committee note to the restyled rule explains, "not all statements covered by the exclusion are admissions in the colloquial sense—a statement can be within the exclusion even if it 'admitted' nothing and was not against the party's interest when made." The restyled rules changed the title of the rule from "Admission by party-opponent" to "An opposing party's statement."

[38] The theory that such statements are not hearsay at all, as opposed to saying that they are hearsay that falls within an exception, is rather abstruse. The advisory committee evidently accepted the following line of reasoning: The exceptions to the hearsay rule apply to admit hearsay when surrounding circumstances provide guarantees of reliability. There are no guarantees of reliability in the case of an admission. Therefore, admissions do not qualify for an exception to the hearsay rule. Nevertheless, admissions have been received into evidence since time immemorial. If they do not qualify as an exception, then they must have been received because they are not hearsay at all. *See* FED. R. EVID. 801(d)(2) advisory committee note ("Admissions by a party-opponent are excluded from the category of hearsay on the theory that their admissibility in evidence is the result of the adversary system rather than satisfaction of the conditions of the hearsay rule."); *see also* United States v. United Shoe Machinery Corp., 89 F. Supp. 349, 352 (D. Mass. 1950) (stating that admissions are outside hearsay rule); EDMUND M. MORGAN, BASIC PROBLEMS OF EVIDENCE 265 (1962).

[39] For a discussion of some of the many subtleties involved in this distinction, see CHRISTOPHER B. MUELLER & LAIRD C. KIRKPATRICK, FEDERAL EVIDENCE § 8:51 (4th ed. 2013).

[40] *See, e.g.*, MIRJAN R. DAMASKA, EVIDENCE LAW ADRIFT 79–81 (1997).

Edmund Morgan said, "A party can hardly object that he had no opportunity to cross-examine himself or that he is unworthy of credence save when speaking under sanction of an oath."[41] Moreover, if that party wants to clarify or deny the prior statement or explain the circumstances in which it was made, the party need only take the stand.[42]

There is no requirement that the party's statement be against interest when made or that the declarant be shown to possess personal knowledge.[43] However, these circumstances are usually present, thus providing some assurance of reliability. And the party-declarant's usual presence at trial compensates for lack of opportunity to cross-examine at the time the statement was made.[44]

The general rule against hearsay, combined with an exemption for statements of a party-opponent, has a beneficial effect of encouraging live in-court testimony and not rewarding the generation by a party of multiple out-of-court statements. In the case of statements by parties offered by their opponents, there is not much danger that parties will attempt to manufacture their own out-of-court evidence. There is no incentive for parties to generate multiple out-of-court statements because only those that are detrimental will be introduced by their opponents.

On the other hand, this structure of the rule creates a marked asymmetry: the same item of evidence, an out-of-court statement by a party, is admissible (for the truth of the matter asserted) if offered by one side (the declarant's opponent) but inadmissible (for the truth) if offered by the other side (the party-declarant). This asymmetry occasions a number of difficulties, including:

Incentives to mislead. When only the declarant's opponent may present the out-of-court statement, there is an incentive to distort that statement by presenting only the portions of it that are damaging to the declarant, safe in the belief that the declarant-party will not be able to present the "remainder" of the statement.[45] The doctrine of "verbal completeness," partially codified in Rule 106, addresses this incentive to make sure that the out-of-court statement is not distorted.[46]

Problems of multiple parties on the "same" side. What does it mean for two parties to be "opposing"? Can two parties who are formally defendants have such opposing interests that one defendant can present the out-of-court statement of the other defendant, or is the doctrine limited by one's formal status as a defendant, as to which the only "opponent" is the plaintiff or prosecuting government? The same question can be posed in situations of multiple plaintiffs. The courts have split on these issues,

---

[41] EDMUND M. MORGAN, BASIC PROBLEMS OF EVIDENCE 266 (1962).

[42] *Id.* (noting that, ever since the elimination of incompetency for interest, the party has been able to take the stand to explain or deny a statement attributed to that party). After discussing various theories of why party-opponent admissions do not violate the rule against hearsay, Professor McCormick concludes that "[o]n balance, the most satisfactory justification of the admissibility of admissions is that they are a product of the adversary system, sharing on a lower level the characteristics of admissions in pleadings or stipulations." *See* 1 MCCORMICK ON EVIDENCE § 60 at 261 (Kenneth S. Broun ed., 7th ed. 2013).

[43] *See* FED. R. EVID. 801(d)(2) advisory committee note.

[44] *See* Roger C. Park, *The Rationale of Personal Admissions*, 21 IND. L. REV. 509 (1988).

[45] Attorneys sometimes succumb to the temptation that this presents. *See, e.g.,* United States v. Branch, 91 F.3d 699 (5th Cir. 1996) (in prosecution arising out of federal siege of Branch Davidian compound in Waco, Texas, where prosecutor elicited only inculpatory portions of defendant's post-arrest statement to Texas Ranger, holding on the particular facts that doctrine of verbal completeness did not require trial court to permit defense to introduce exculpatory portions of defendant's statements; strong dissent on this point).

[46] *See* **§ 1.12**.

although formalism appears to dominate so far.[47] When, however, one defendant files a cross-claim against the other (possible only in civil cases), the two defendants are clearly opponents.

The distinction between admissibility and use. Only an opponent may introduce a party's out-of-court statement under this exemption, but that does not settle the question of who may use the statement once it is introduced or how they may use it. For example, if plaintiff introduces the defendant's out-of-court statement under this exemption, may the defendant rely on the truth of that statement to establish an affirmative defense? The little modern authority that exists supports the broader use by both the proponent of the statement and by the declarant party.[48] This seems to accord with the fairness rationale: the party-declarant cannot complain of the other party's use of the declarant's own statement, and—having chosen to introduce this evidence—the party introducing the statement cannot complain of its being used against him or her. However, absent some other exception or exemption, neither the proponent nor the declarant-party may use the admitted statement (for the truth of the matter asserted) against *other* parties—co-defendants or co-plaintiffs—because those individuals neither made the statement nor chose to put it into evidence. Courts should consider limiting instructions in such contexts.[49]

Federal Rule 801(d)(2) breaks down statements of a party-opponent into five categories, providing that a statement is not hearsay if it is "offered against an opposing party" and:

> (A) the statement was made by the opposing party in either an individual or a representative capacity; or
>
> (B) it is a statement that the opposing party manifested that it adopted or believed to be true; or
>
> (C) the statement was made by a person authorized by the opposing party to make a statement concerning the subject, or
>
> (D) the statement was made by the opposing party's agent or servant concerning a matter within the scope of the agency or employment during the existence of the relationship, or

---

[47] *Compare* United States v. Harwood, 998 F.2d 91, 97–98 (2d Cir. 1993), *and* United States v. Gossett, 877 F.2d 901 (11th Cir. 1989) (holding that defendant may not introduce out-of-court statement of co-defendant because only the government can be the party-opponent of a criminal defendant), *with* United States v. Palow, 777 F.2d 52 (1st Cir. 1985) (holding that there was no error in allowing, under 801(d)(2)(A), co-defendant to relate prior statements made by the other). In *Palow*, the court offered the following rationale:

> The requirement of Rule 801(d)(2)(A) that an admission be offered against a party is designed to exclude the introduction of self-serving statements by the party making them. See 4 WIGMORE ON EVIDENCE § 1048, p. 5 (Chadbourn rev. 1972). Rule 801(d)(2)(A) simply requires that the admission at issue be contrary to a party's position at trial. Butler v. Southern Pacific Co., 431 F.2d 77, 80 (5th Cir.1970), cert. denied, 401 U.S. 975, 91 S. Ct. 1196, 28 L.Ed.2d 325 (1971). It does not matter that the admission has been introduced through the testimony of a co-defendant testifying on his own behalf. United States v. Ramirez, 710 F.2d 535, 547 (9th Cir.1983).

Id. at 56.

[48] *See, e.g.*, People v. Dlugash, 363 N.E.2d 1155, 1162 (N.Y. 1977) (affirming fact-finder's freedom to accept substantively the exculpatory portions of a defendant's out-of-court admission). The principle appears to have been well-established in nineteenth century common-law. *See generally* 1 SIMON GREENLEAF, GREENLEAF ON EVIDENCE §§ 201, 218 (16th rev. ed. 1899).

[49] *See* CHRISTOPHER B MUELLER & LAIRD C. KIRKPATRICK, FEDERAL EVIDENCE § 8:44 at 385–87 (4th ed. 2013) (also discussing the constitutional issues arising in criminal cases).

(E) the statement was made by a co-conspirator of an opposing party during the course and in furtherance of the conspiracy.

The first two of these categories involve actual verbal or non-verbal statements by the party-opponent. The last three involve what might be called "vicarious statements," by obvious analogy to principles of vicarious liability in substantive law. Each of those three categories involves statements by someone other than the party-opponent in a situation where such statements are treated for admissibility analysis as if they were made by the party-opponent.[50]

These various categories—addressed in the following sections—cover a great deal of ground. But it is worth noting one category of statements that they do not cover. Suppose D is involved in a transaction or event about which D makes an out-of-court statement. P sues D over the occurrence, but before trial (or even before the suit is brought), D dies, and the suit becomes one between P and D's estate. P wants to use D's statement at trial. A close reading of the five categories of admissions will reveal that D's statement does not fall within them. While a live person may create debts that are binding under substantive law on that person's estate, a live person and that person's estate after death are distinct legal entities, and a declarant cannot be an authorized spokesperson for, or employee of, a legal entity that does not yet exist. In this respect, the Federal Rules are decidedly more restrictive than the common law, which had admitted statements of persons in various forms of legal "privity" with a defendant.[51] Under the Rules, in order to admit the statement of the decedent against the decedent's estate, an opponent must invoke some other exception, such as that for declarations against interest.[52] Sometimes, however, this point has been ignored in the cases, and the common-law principle has been reflexively applied.[53]

§ 15.07 Statements of a Party-Opponent—Personal Statements [FRE 801(d)(2)(A), (B)]

Explicit Statements [FRE 801(d)(2)(A)]

As applied to explicit statements by a party, the Federal Rule is very generous. It means that any statement by a party, offered by an opponent, overcomes the hearsay hurdle. Essentially, anything a party says or does is admissible if offered by the party's opponent. Use of this rule may encounter some other obstacle, such as privilege, but the statement is not hearsay. It does not matter whether the statement was against interest

[50] However, the doctrines of substantive law should not be conflated with the principles of admissibility. In particular, one should not confuse admissibility for the truth of the matter asserted with admissibility to establish a party's substantive liability based on the speaker's verbal acts. Many statements by agents and conspirators are admissible not for the truth but simply to establish a verbal commitment or threat that renders the principal or co-conspirator substantively liable. *See* **§ 14.04** (subsection on "Legally (or Morally) Operative Language").

[51] *See* 2 McCormick on Evidence § 260 at 297–300 (Kenneth S. Broun ed., 7th ed. 2013).

[52] *See* **§ 17.04**.

[53] *See, e.g.*, Savarese v. Agriss, 883 F.2d 1194, 1199–2001 (3d Cir. 1989) (admitting statement of deceased party under 801(d)(2) in a rather confused opinion); Hilao v. Estate of Marcos, 103 F.3d 767, 775 (9th Cir. 1996) (in class action by torture victims against estate of dictator, holding torturer's statements admissible against estate as admission of agents of the defendant; no reference made to the problem that Fed. R. Evid. 801(d)(2) does not provide for such admissions to be used against successors in interest of the principal). For a decision recognizing the problem and using the residual exception to resolve it, see Huff v. White Motor Corp., 609 F.2d 286 (7th Cir. 1979) (statement by plaintiff's decedent not admissible against plaintiff under 801(d)(2), but admissible on the facts under residual exception). For discussion of the residual exception, *see* **§ 18.01**.

when made.[54] Nor does the statement have to be based upon personal knowledge.[55] Furthermore, the opinion rule is no obstacle.[56]

Examples

"It wasn't my fault—the brakes went out." (not against interest when made, but admissible if offered by the opposing party)

"It was all my fault." (opinion, but still admissible)

"My wolf bit a little girl." (admissible even if the speaker has no personal knowledge)[57]

Notice that Rule 801(d)(2)(A) extends to statements made by the party even when made "in a representative capacity." This does not refer to the use of an agent's statement against the principal, which is governed by Rules 801(d)(2)(C) and (D). Thus, if a plaintiff sues a person acting as agent of a principal, but does not sue the principal, the admission of the agent's statement (for the truth of the matter asserted) is authorized by this rule. The agent cannot argue: "But it wasn't really *my* statement. I was just speaking for someone else." If the plaintiff sues both the agent and the principal, admissibility of the agent's statement against the agent is authorized by 801(d)(2)(A), whereas admissibility against the principal is governed by Rule 801(d)(2)(C) & (D).[58]

Custodial statements made by suspects to law enforcement officers are governed by a number of special rules often growing out of constitutional guarantees. For example, custodial confessions generally are not admissible unless they were voluntarily made after the giving of *Miranda* warnings.[59] In recent decades, there has also been a movement to require that custodial statements be recorded and made available at trial, and where such rules have been adopted, admissibility of the defendant's statements is often conditioned on compliance with the recording requirement.[60]

Adoptive Statements [FRE 801(d)(2)(B)]

Sometimes a party makes a statement only by adopting the statement of another person. Suppose, for example, X says to a party-to-be, out of court, "You were at the house that day." And the party replies, "Yes, I was." If an opponent of that party wants to introduce the testimony of a witness who heard this conversation, offered in order to

---

[54] *See* Grace United Methodist Church v. City of Cheyenne, 451 F.3d 643, 665 n.11 (10th Cir. 2006) (comparing Rule 804(b)(3), admissions against interest, and Rule 801(d)(2), statements by party-opponent); People v. Meier, 954 P.2d 1068, 1070 (Colo. 1998) (holding that admission need not be against interest when made to be admissible); 2 McCormick on Evidence § 254 at 263 (Kenneth S. Broun ed., 7th ed. 2013).

[55] *See* United States v. Lindemann, 85 F.3d 1232, 1237–39 (7th Cir. 1996) (holding that it was not necessary to show declarant's personal knowledge as part of foundation for admission of co-conspirator's statement); Mahlandt v. Wild Canid Survival & Research Center, Inc., 588 F.2d 626, 630–31 (8th Cir. 1978) (holding personal knowledge of declarant not necessary in context of statement by agent of party-opponent); *see also* United States v. Haldeman, 559 F.2d 31, 110 (D.C. Cir. 1976) (stating that opinion rule and lack of firsthand knowledge do not bar admissions under co-conspirator exception to hearsay rule).

[56] *See* Russell v. United Parcel Serv., Inc., 666 F.2d 1188, 1190 (8th Cir. 1981); Owens v. Atchison, Topeka & Santa Fe Ry. Co., 393 F.2d 77, 79 (5th Cir. 1968); **§ 10.01** (discussing lay opinion rule).

[57] *See* Mahlandt v. Wild Canid Survival & Research Center, Inc., 588 F.2d 626, 630–31 (8th Cir. 1978) (no requirement of personal knowledge).

[58] *See* **§ 15.08**.

[59] These topics are generally covered in courses on criminal procedure and are not addressed in detail here. *See, e.g.*, 1 McCormick on Evidence §§ 149–57, 162 (Kenneth S. Broun ed., 7th ed. 2013).

[60] *See id.*, § 158; *see also* Alan M. Gershel, *A Review of the Law in Jurisdictions Requiring Electronic Recording of Custodial Interrogations*, 16 Richmond J. Law & Tech. art. 9 (2010).

prove that the party was "at the house that day," testimony about the reply is authorized (as against a hearsay objection) by Rule 801(d)(1)(A). But without testimony of what X said to the party, the meaning of the party's reply ("Yes, I was.") would be unintelligible: the fact-finder would not know to what the party was agreeing. (Presumably, this would render the testimony irrelevant or a waste of time.) So the proponent needs to introduce the witness's account of what X said as well. That problem occasions the need for Rule 801(d)(2)(B), which exempts from the hearsay rule a statement offered against a party that "is one the party manifested that it adopted or believed to be true."[61]

An adoption by silence occurs when a party hears a statement and fails to deny it in circumstances in which a party would naturally deny the statement were it untrue. If the party does not intend to make an assertion by such conduct, then the conduct does not fit the definition of hearsay under Rule 801(c). And if the party does intend to assert something, and that something is affirmation, then Rule 801(d)(2)(B) applies to admit the statement.

Examples

After an accident involving Driver A and Driver B, Driver A accuses Driver B of crossing the centerline. Driver B hangs his head and says nothing. Driver B has adopted Driver A's statement as his own statement, assuming the absence of circumstances (such as severe injury or fear of provoking an attack) that would inhibit him from answering.

Defendant's girlfriend mentions to a visitor, in front of defendant, that they have "sacks" of money in the house. If defendant does not say anything, he has adopted her statement.[62]

Sometimes silence does not fit the rule because the defendant is invoking his Fifth Amendment right to remain silent. The clearest example is when the defendant relies on *Miranda* rights during a custodial interrogation.[63] The principle that invocation of the right to remain silent cannot be used against the defendant applies even to implicit invocations of the right during noncustodial police interrogation.[64] It is permissible,

---

[61] Technically, the report of X's statement ought not to be regarded as hearsay at all, because the proponent is not relying on X's credibility; the proponent is offering the witness's report of what X said merely to show what it was that the party-opponent agreed to. However, because the federal rules adopt a nominally assertion-oriented definition of hearsay rather than a declarant-oriented definition (*see* **§ 14.01**), the witness's report of what X said falls literally within 801(c): the proponent is using X's statement to prove the truth of X's statement. Apparently in an effort to avoid this problem, Rule 801(d)(2)(B) clarifies that the witness's report of X's statement is also exempt, provided of course that the party-opponent adopts it or assents to its truth.

[62] *See* United States v. Hoosier, 542 F.2d 687, 688 (6th Cir. 1976) ("Under the total circumstances, we believe that probable human behavior would have been for appellant promptly to deny [the statement about the sacks of money] if it had not been true. . . ."); *see also* United States v. Schaff, 948 F.2d 501, 505 (9th Cir. 1991) (defendant's sister questioned by police officers in presence of defendant; defendant's failure to contradict her held to be admission by silence of statements she made, such as statement that she made entries in suspicious notebook at defendant's direction).

[63] *See* Miranda v. Arizona, 384 U.S. 436 (1966); *see also* Dickerson v. United States, 530 U.S. 428 (2000) (affirming constitutional status of *Miranda* warnings).

[64] *See* Coppola v. Powell, 878 F.2d 1562, 1567–69 (1st Cir. 1989) (noncustodial statement, "[I]f you think I'm going to confess to you, you're crazy," by street-smart defendant who knew about right against self-incrimination; use of silence in prosecutor's case-in-chief violation of the defendant's Fifth Amendment rights); United States v. Burson, 952 F.2d 1196, 1200–01 (10th Cir. 1991) (defendant's adamant attitude in refusing to answer investigator's questions constituted invocation of right to remain silent, even though defendant did not specifically mention constitutional rights; admission of investigator's testimony about the defendant's silence was plain error). *Cf.* Berghuis v. Thompkins, 560 U.S. 370 (2010) (holding that a suspect who received and understood the *Miranda* warnings and remained silent for the first two hours and forty-five minutes before

however, to use pre-arrest silence as a statement if the defendant would have spoken had he been innocent.[65]

§ 15.08 Statements of a Party-Opponent—Statements by Agents or Employees [FRE 801(d)(2)(C), (D)]

The Federal Rules remove some of the common-law restrictions on the admissibility of statements by agents. In many common-law jurisdictions, the statement of an agent was not admissible against the principal unless the agent was authorized to speak for the principal on the subject of the statement.[66] This rule was sometimes expressed by saying that the agent had to be a "speaking agent." Under the "speaking agent" rule, if a truck driver admitted fault after an accident, the driver's statement was not admissible against the trucking company, because the truck driver was only authorized to drive trucks, not to speak for the company. To be sure, the driver's statement was admissible against the driver, certainly if the driver was named as a party. Authority split on whether this admission against the driver could establish the driver's liability for which the employer would then be liable on the substantive principle of *respondeat superior*.[67]

In contrast to the common law, the Federal Rules provide that an agent's statement is admissible if either (i) the agent was authorized to speak for the principal (Rule 801(d)(2)(C)),[68] or (ii) the agent was speaking about a matter within the scope of his employment during the time of his employment (Rule 801(d)(2)(D)).[69]

---

responding to questions had not invoked his *Miranda* rights and waived the right to remain silent by making an uncoerced statement to the police).

[65] *See* Jenkins v. Anderson, 447 U.S. 231, 235–238 (1980) (holding that it was not violation of Fifth Amendment to cross-examine defendant about pre-arrest silence or to comment on it during closing argument); United States v. Zanabria, 74 F.3d 590, 593 (5th Cir. 1996) (allowing prosecutor to use defendant's pre-arrest silence regarding alleged unidentified third party's threats against defendant's daughter to rebut defendant's duress defense because "silence at issue was neither induced by nor a response to any action by a government agent"); United States v. Oplinger, 150 F.3d 1061, 1065–67 (9th Cir. 1998) (holding that when under no government compulsion to speak, prosecution's use of defendant's noncustodial silence did not violate right against self-incrimination; defendant remained silent during meeting at which employers inquired into defendant's scheme to convert bank funds to his own use); *see also* State v. Kulzer, 979 A.2d 1031, 1035–36 (Vt. 2009) (providing extensive discussion of split among circuit courts and state supreme courts about whether prosecution should be allowed to make substantive use of defendant's pre-arrest silence).

[66] *See* Arber v. American Airlines, Inc., 345 F.2d 130, 131 (1st Cir. 1965) (holding that test pilot who wrote letter about plane crash lacked authority to speak for airline about the cause of the crash); Kelly v. Diesel Constr. Div. of Carl A. Morse, Inc., 315 N.E.2d 751 (N.Y. 1974) (holding that superintendent's statement to inspector that there were 22 men on elevator was not admissible against superintendent's principal because superintendent was not authorized to speak on subject); 4 WIGMORE ON EVIDENCE § 1078 (Chadbourn rev. 1982); *see also* United States v. Sokolow, 91 F.3d 396, 402–03 (3d Cir. 1996) (holding that changes made to documents by insurance company formed by defendant were not made with defendant's consent and thus not admission by agent of party-opponent).

[67] *See* GRAHAM C. LILLY, AN INTRODUCTION TO THE LAW OF EVIDENCE 263 (3d ed. 1996). Even if the principle were invoked in this way, it would not work to render admissible the statement of an employee other than the employee for whose actions the employer would be vicariously liable.

[68] *See* United States v. Reilly, 33 F.3d 1396, 1412–15 (3d Cir. 1994) (in scheme to dump ash into ocean, radio telegram from nonemployee instructing captain of ship to travel to Sri Lanka with 500 tons of ash was admissible against defendant on ground that defendant authorized nonemployee to make statements regarding that particular topic); United States v. Brandon, 50 F.3d 464 (7th Cir. 1995) (attorney responding to subpoena is agent of client "so long as the important policies concerning effective assistance of the counsel of one's choosing are preserved") (citing United States v. Harris, 914 F.2d 927 (7th Cir. 1990)).

[69] A statement of an agent who is not speaking about a matter within the scope of employment can nonetheless be admitted if it is adopted by another agent whose job duties do embrace the subject matter covered by the statement. *See* Sea-Land Serv., Inc. v. Lozen Int'l, LLC., 285 F.3d 808, 821 (9th Cir. 2002)

The Federal Rules thus retain the "speaking agent" theory of admissibility, but it is broader than the common law of many jurisdictions. In particular, the common-law requirement that the agent be authorized to speak for the principal could be construed to mean that statements of the agent to the principal are not admissible against the principal.[70] Thus, if a company authorized one of its officers to conduct an internal investigation, the officer's report of the investigation would not be admissible on this theory.[71] The Federal Rules contain no such restriction on the admissibility of internal reports.[72] Of course, the lawyer attempting to acquire an internal report may encounter work product or privilege objection,[73] but ordinarily the hearsay rule will pose no obstacle to admission.

Moreover, the Federal Rules add a distinct new theory in Rule 801(d)(2)(D). Under this approach, the truck driver's admission of fault hypothesized above would be admissible against the trucking company.[74] Moreover, the rule extends to statements by an observer-employee whose action does not create any liability for the principal, such as a co-driver who at the time of the collision is a passenger in the truck and makes a statement attributing fault to the driver-employee.[75] However, a driver's statement about something outside her job responsibilities, such as a statement about the safety of elevators at the company's main office, would not be admissible against the company.[76]

(employee adopted another employee's statement by forwarding it by email with preface, "Yikes, Pls note the rail screwed us up. . . .") (alternative holding).

[70] *See* EDMUND M. MORGAN, BASIC PROBLEMS OF EVIDENCE 236–37 (1962) ("an agent whose duty is to make statements to the principal or master cannot be said to be representing or speaking for him in performing that duty"; hence, statements to principal are not admissible because of common-law "speaking agent" requirement).

[71] The same point would apply to routine reports and records prepared in the course of business, although these would often be admissible under the business records exception anyway.

[72] As the drafters noted in connection with Rule 801(d)(2)(C), "a party's books or records are usable against him, without regard to any intent to disclose to third persons." FED. R. EVID. 801(d)(2)(C) advisory committee note.

[73] *See* **§§ 4.03 et seq.**

[74] *See* Woodman v. Haemonetics Corp., 51 F.3d 1087, 1093–94 (1st Cir. 1995) (holding in case in which plaintiff claimed to have been terminated because of age, that statement made by plaintiff's supervisor, after supervisor attended management discussion of terminations, that "these damn people" in higher management wanted younger employees, was admissible against company as admission of agent; even if declarant was merely "first-line" supervisor with no authority to make final termination decisions, statement was still within scope of her employment, and it was not necessary that she be acting at instance of her employer for her statement to qualify as agent's admission).

[75] *See* CHRISTOPHER B MUELLER & LAIRD C. KIRKPATRICK, FEDERAL EVIDENCE § 8:54 (4th ed. 2013).

[76] *See, e.g.*, Precision Piping & Instruments, Inc. v. E.I. du Pont de Nemours & Co., 951 F.2d 613, 618–20 (4th Cir. 1991) (in antitrust action, trial court properly excluded statement of employee of rival company, where employee's statement concerned company's decision not to deal with plaintiff and where employee, who was responsible for engineering matters, had influence over which contractors were used but no actual authority to hire or discharge them; it was held that statement was not within scope of employment of employee of opponent); *In re* Air Crash Disaster, 86 F.3d 498, 536 (6th Cir. 1996) (holding that airline maintenance employee's out-of-court statement about what airline vice president said on inspecting crash site was not admissible as agent's admission because it was not part of job of maintenance employees to investigate or report on accidents); Williams v. Pharmacia, Inc., 137 F.3d 944, 949 (7th Cir. 1998) (holding error, though harmless, to allow plaintiff in sex discrimination case to put in evidence that other female employees had complained about boss' conduct and about boss' failure to act on complaints; matter was not within scope of her employment and hence did not qualify as agency admission); Wilkinson v. Carnival Cruise Lines, Inc., 920 F.2d 1560, 1564–67 (11th Cir. 1991) (holding that trial court erred in admitting cruise line steward's statement about condition of sliding doors on passenger deck; statement did not qualify as agent's admission because steward did not have responsibility for doors and was not authorized to be in area where doors were located) (collecting cases).

The drafters of the federal rule provided little insight into this change, except to say that there was dissatisfaction with the loss of valuable information caused by the common-law rule evidenced by a discernible trend in the cases away from the common-law view.[77] Professor McCormick explained the shift, which was appearing in decisions prior to the adoption of the Rules, in the following terms:

> Typically the agent is well informed about acts in the course of the business, the statements are offered against the employer's interest, and while the employment continues, the employee is not likely to make the statements unless they are true. Moreover, if admissions are viewed as arising from the adversary system, responsibility for statements of one's employee is consistent with that theory.[78]

The first component of this rationale speaks to the reliability of the employee's statement, but it is certainly questionable. In particular, think about a statement by our truck driver that attempts to shift the blame for the accident from himself to someone else, a statement like: "I couldn't stop. I told them to get those brakes worked on." Is there not as much reason to distrust this statement as other hearsay?[79] And what about situations in which the agent-declarant is the opponent of the principal or otherwise has opposing interests in anticipated litigation. In such cases, the assumption that the employee will be careful to avoid false statements adversely affecting the employer does not hold. This concern has been taken seriously, with some courts treating such statements as outside the scope of Rule 801(d)(2)(D).[80]

In any event, the primary rationale for the admission of personal statements by an opposing party is the "adversary system" argument in the second component of McCormick's rationale. But recall how Professor Morgan articulated it in the context of a personal admission: "A party can hardly object that he had no opportunity to cross-examine himself or that he is unworthy of credence save when speaking under sanction of an oath."[81] Does this argument really transfer cleanly to an employee-declarant situation? Does an employer have plausible reason to object that he had no opportunity to cross-examine the employee? Does an employer, merely by hiring someone to drive a truck, for example, vouch for the employee's credibility as a witness? With a personal admission, the party-declarant almost always can take the stand to explain or refute the statement imputed to her, and has substantial incentives to do so. How often is this an option with an employee-declarant? What if the employee is not an employee by the time of trial but is dead or has moved to an unknown location, or is now a disgruntled former

---

[77] *See* FED. R. EVID. 801(d)(2)(D) advisory committee note.

[78] *See* 2 MCCORMICK ON EVIDENCE § 259 at 279 (Kenneth S. Broun ed., 7th ed. 2013).

[79] In particular, consider by analogy the limitations on statements against interest that arise when a statement attempts to shift blame. *See* **§ 17.04** (discussing "The Against Interest Element").

[80] *See* SEC v. Geon Industries, Inc., 531 F.2d 39, 43, n.3 (2d Cir. 1976) (excluding agent's statement in light of "conflicting litigating positions" between employee-agent and employer); Young v. James Green Management, Inc., 327 F.3d 616 (7th Cir. 2003) (holding that resignation letter in which employee charged employer with racial discrimination was not statement of agent about matter within scope of employment; policy of rule did not apply because writer was no longer inhibited by relationship with employer from making statements that would harm employer).

[81] EDMUND M. MORGAN, BASIC PROBLEMS OF EVIDENCE 231 (1962). *See also* 4 WIGMORE ON EVIDENCE § 1048 at 4–5 (Chadbourn rev. 1972) ("[The declarant party] cannot complain of lack of opportunity to cross-examine himself . . . ; he now as opponent has the full opportunity to put himself on the stand and explain his former assertion.").

employee?[82] Despite such concerns, case law admits statements of employees who are dead by the time of trial.[83]

Who is an "agent or employee" for the purposes of the rule? The most common approach to answering this question involves looking to the substantive law of agency, borrowing from it distinctions between "agents or employees" and "independent contractors," and treating statements by "independent contractors" as inadmissible.[84] The general rule is that an agent or employee is one "employed by a master to perform service in his affairs whose physical conduct in the performance of the service is controlled or is subject to the right to control by the master."[85] An independent contractor "is a person who contracts with another to do something for him but who is not controlled by the other nor subject to the other's right to control with respect to his physical conduct in the performance of the undertaking."[86]

Some courts have admitted statements by interpreters as statements of agents of the person speaking, even when the person speaking did not hire the interpreter.[87] Thus,

---

[82] These questions suggest that a plausible limitation on 801(d)(2)(D) would be a requirement that the employee still be the agent or employee of the party *at the time of trial*. *See* Michael Siegal, *Rationalizing Hearsay: A Proposal for a Best Evidence Hearsay Rule*, 72 B.U. L. REV. 893, 938 n.142. (1992). While that might create an unfortunate incentive to fire the employee before trial, the more powerful countervailing incentive is that the employer would not wish to create a disgruntled former employee that the opponent could call as a witness. In any event, no such limitation is currently recognized.

[83] *See, e.g.*, Pino v. Protection Maritime Ins. Co., 599 F.2d 10, 13 (1st Cir.), *cert. denied*, 444 U.S. 900 (1979); White v. Honeywell, 141 F.3d 1270, 1274–77 (8th Cir. 1988). Although there is a risk of unfair prejudice in admitting the statement of a deceased employee, the court in *White* held that it was an abuse of discretion to exclude the employee's statement under Rule 403 because of the declarant's unavailability. *Id.* at 1276–77.

[84] This includes statements of outside experts who testified in prior litigation. They are normally considered to be independent contractors whose statements are not admissions of those who employ them. *See* Kirk v. Raymark Indus., Inc., 61 F.3d 147, 163–64 & n.20 (3d Cir. 1995) (holding that testimony of expert witness for party in one case is not admissible in later unrelated case as admission of party because expert is not necessarily either agent "authorized to speak on [the party's] behalf" or agent speaking about matter within scope of employment); Sanford v. Johns-Manville Sales Corp., 923 F.2d 1142, 1149–50 (5th Cir. 1991) (holding that plaintiffs failed to prove that doctor testifying as expert for defendants was agent of defendants since he was merely independent contractor and not under control of defendants); United States v. Wiedyk, 71 F.3d 602, 606 (6th Cir. 1995); *see also* American Eagle Ins. Co. v. Thompson, 85 F.3d 327, 332–33 (8th Cir. 1996) (holding that common-law master-servant doctrine provides definition of "agent" for purposes of FED. R. EVID. 801(d)(2)(D); under facts presented, insurance agent was not "agent" of insurance company for purposes of rule).

For a discussion of what constitutes conduct within the scope of employment for police officers, see Rau v. Roberts, 2010 WL 396223 (D. Minn. 2010). In *Rau*, a uniformed police officer attacked a gas station attendant while off-duty in an area outside the police officer's district and in his personal car. The attendant sued the officer and his employer, the city of Minneapolis. The court granted summary judgment for the city because the officer's conduct was outside the scope of his employment.

[85] RESTATEMENT (SECOND) OF AGENCY § 2(2) (1958).

[86] *Id.* § 2(3). Normally, the question whether a person is an agent is the same as whether the person is an employee. However, the two concepts sometimes differ, as in the case of a person who is an agent for a particular purpose, or the person whose status has technically changed to ex-employee but who continues to perform the same duties under the same restraints. *See* United States v. Chappell, 698 F.2d 308, 311 (7th Cir. 1983) (holding that statement by defendant's accountant, who was no longer on defendant's general payroll but still acting as company's accountant, was admissible under Rule 801(d)(2)(D)). For an example of the opposite situation, deeming a person an early ex-employee for purposes of evidence law, see Young v. James Green Management, Inc., 327 F.3d 616 (7th Cir. 2003) (holding that resignation letter in which employee charged employer with racial discrimination was not statement of agent about matter within scope of employment; policy of rule did not apply because writer was no longer inhibited by relationship with employer from making statements that would harm employer).

[87] For an opinion that simply sweeps away the second layer of hearsay, see Correa v. Superior Court, 40 P.3d 739, 741 (Cal. 2002) (holding that simultaneous translation into English of statement made in another language does not create second level of hearsay because "generally unbiased and adequately skilled translator simply serves as a 'language conduit'.").

when the opposing party spoke through an interpreter, the party's statement was admissible as the personal statement of a party-opponent, while the interpreter's translation was admissible as the statement of an agent.[88] (In many situations, this expansive interpretation of the concept of agency is unnecessary, since the interpreter's statement would be admissible as the interpreter's present sense impression of the statement just made by the opponent.[89])

Courts are split on whether statements by government agents are admissible against the government. Even though Rule 801(d)(2) is silent on the issue and, if literally interpreted, would admit the evidence, some federal authorities follow earlier law and exclude it.[90] The arguments for excluding statements by government employees is generally no stronger than the comparable argument for excluding statements by employees of a large private corporation.[91] At least in one area, the cases are fairly consistent. Government informers may be government agents in one sense, but they do not usually resemble employees of private companies in their degree of reliability or in the extent of the supervision of their conduct by the government. Arguably, even if government employees generally fall within 801(d)(2)(D), most informers may warrant treatment analogous to independent contractors in the private sphere.[92]

By virtue of a 1997 amendment to Federal Rule 801(d)(2),[93] the contents of an agency statement must be considered by the court in deciding whether the agency or employment relationship existed and whether the statement falls within the scope of the agency or employment. However, independent evidence must also be offered on that point to justify the court's finding; the statement alone will not support its own admissibility. This distinguishes the sufficiency of the foundation for admission under Federal Rules 801(d)(2)(C)–(D) from the foundational requirement for other hearsay exceptions. Thus, the judge could find that the foundation has been laid for admitting a statement as an excited utterance by relying solely on the statement itself,[94] whereas in

---

[88] *See, e.g.*, United States v. Nazemian, 948 F.2d 522 (9th Cir. 1991).

[89] *See* FED. R. EVID. 803(1). *See generally* **§ 16.03**. *See, e.g.*, DCS Sanitation Mgmt., Inc. v. Occupational Safety & Health Review Com'n, 82 F.3d 812, 814–16 (8th Cir. 1996) (addressing hearsay-within-hearsay problem in which one level of alleged hearsay is out-of-court translator's rendition of declarant's statements from Spanish to English and describing various approaches to translators' statements and admits evidence).

[90] *Compare* United States v. Yildiz, 355 F.3d 80, 81–82 (2d Cir. 2004) (reaffirming traditional view that statements by government agents are not admissible under this provision), *with* Murrey v. United States, 73 F.3d 1448, 1455 (7th Cir. 1996) (holding statement by Secretary of Veterans Affairs that poor care at VA hospital had contributed to death of patient admissible in malpractice suit by patient's estate against government). *Cf.* United States v. Rioux, 97 F.3d 648, 660–61 (2d Cir. 1996) (holding statements of defendant sheriff's subordinates admissible as agency admissions in prosecution of sheriff for extortion; agency relationship existed even if sheriff did not control daily tasks of declarants).

[91] *See* CHRISTOPHER B. MUELLER & LAIRD C. KIRKPATRICK, FEDERAL EVIDENCE § 8:56 (4th ed. 2013). *See also* Edward J. Imwinkelried, *Of Evidence and Equal Protection: The Unconstitutionality of Excluding Government Agents' Statements Offered as Vicarious Admissions Against the Prosecution*, 71 MINN. L. REV. 269 (1986).

[92] *See* CHRISTOPHER B. MUELLER & LAIRD C. KIRKPATRICK, FEDERAL EVIDENCE § 8:56 at 481–82 (4th ed. 2013).

[93] *See* **§ 15.09**. The purpose of the amendment was to clear up a question left open by Bourjaily v. United States, 483 U.S. 171 (1987), which involved "bootstrapping" in laying the foundation for the co-conspirator exemption. The Advisory Committee decided to apply the clarification to all admissions, however, not merely to co-conspirator statements.

[94] *See* United States v. Campbell, 782 F. Supp. 1258, 1259–61 (N.D. Ill. 1991) (holding call to 911 dispatcher from declarant who stated that he was in store that had "just" been scene of shooting admissible as present sense impression under Rule 803(1) or as excited utterance under Rule 803(2)); Booth v. State, 508 A.2d 976, 981–82 (Md. 1986) (telephonic statement was held to have laid its own foundation).

determining whether a person was an agent for the purpose of the exemption, the judge is to consider the statement, but cannot base a finding of agency on the statement alone.

§ 15.09 Statements of a Party-Opponent—Statements by Co-Conspirators [FRE 801(d)(2)(E)]

Under Rule 801(d)(2)(E), statements of a member of a conspiracy are admissible against the co-conspirators.[95] The co-conspirator rule applies whether or not conspiracy is one of the charged offenses,[96] and applies in both civil and criminal cases.

To qualify under this rule, the statement must be made by someone who was a member of the conspiracy at the time the statement was made; the declarant cannot be an undercover officer or informant, for example.[97] Under Federal Rules of Evidence 801(d)(2)(E), the statements must have been made *in furtherance of* the conspiracy and *during the course of* the conspiracy.[98] To be "in furtherance," a statement must advance the main objectives of the conspiracy.[99] The "in furtherance" requirement means that idle chatter or bragging about the conspiracy, or about its members, is not admissible.[100] Sometimes statements about who is a member of the conspiracy may be in furtherance of the conspiracy, as, for example, when their purpose is to induce another person to participate by showing the range and power of the conspiracy. Although the reliability of such statements may be in question, courts have admitted them.[101]

---

[95] *See, e.g.*, United States v. Abrahamson, 568 F.2d 604, 606 (8th Cir. 1978) (holding that statements made to co-conspirator by unidentified informant not admissible); United States v. Lum, 466 F. Supp. 328, 334 (D. Del. 1979) (pre-conspiracy statements are outside rule). *Cf.* United States v. Monteleone, 257 F.3d 210, 221–22 (2d Cir. 2001) (holding that despite requirement that declarant be member of conspiracy and that statement be in furtherance of conspiracy in order to qualify for admission under rule, statement of informant who was secretly cooperating with government at time of making out-of-court statement was admissible; "the status as a co-conspirator of one who is passing information to the government turns on whether his efforts as an agent of the government supplant his efforts as an agent of his co-conspirators"; in case at bar, declarant was still trying to help conspiracy succeed even though he was exchanging information with government).

[96] United States v. Stratton, 779 F.2d 820, 829 (2d Cir. 1985); Byrd v. State, 187 S.W.3d 436, 440 (Tex. Crim. App. 2005).

[97] Filco v. Amana Refrigeration, Inc., 709 F.2d 1257, 1267 (9th Cir. 1983); SEC v. Tome, 638 F. Supp. 629, 633–36 (S.D.N.Y. 1986) (collecting cases).

[98] *See* United States v. Tombrello, 666 F.2d 485, 490 (11th Cir. 1982).

[99] United States v. Gibbs, 739 F.2d 838, 846 (3d Cir. 1984) (holding that statements to induce continued participation furthered conspiracy); United States v. Hamilton, 689 F.2d 1262, 1269–70 (6th Cir. 1982) ("Rule 801(d)(2)(E) explicitly says statements need be 'in furtherance of the conspiracy,' not that they 'further the conspiracy.' It is enough that they be intended to promote the conspiratorial objectives."); United States v. Watchmaker, 761 F.2d 1459, 1472 (11th Cir. 1985) (recognizing that "[s]tatements made to a non-conspirator in order to induce him to become part of a conspiracy come within the exception as furthering the purposes of the conspiracy").

[100] *See* United States v. Means, 695 F.2d 811, 818 (5th Cir. 1983) (holding that statement was "mere idle conversation" and thus should have been excluded); United States v. Warman, 578 F.3d 320, 338–39 (6th Cir. 2009) (holding that district court erred in admitting co-conspirator's statements bragging about selling drugs and having lot of money); City of Tuscaloosa v. Harcros Chemicals, Inc., 158 F.3d 548, 558–59 (11th Cir. 1998) (holding that statements made over drinks and on golf course that did not solicit participation in or otherwise further conspiracy were not admissible as co-conspirator statements). *Cf.* United States v. Piccolo, 696 F.2d 1162, 1168–69 (6th Cir. 1983) (holding that statement was not "mere conversation"); United States v. Guerro, 693 F.2d 10, 13 (1st Cir. 1982) (holding that comments were not idle and, therefore, conversation was admissible).

[101] *See* United States v. Redd, 2009 WL 348831 at *15 (5th Cir. 2009) ("[S]tatements made by one conspirator to a fellow conspirator identifying yet another conspirator as the ultimate purchaser are statements intended to further a conspiracy."); United States v. Patton, 594 F.2d 444, 447 (5th Cir. 1979) (holding that statements identifying participants could be "intended to affect future dealings between the

The "in furtherance" requirement means that most statements that fall within this exemption will also have a "performative" aspect, that is, such statements constitute legally operative language because they constitute part of the conspiratorial act, which means they may be admitted without regard to the truth of what they assert.[102] But insofar as the relevance of such statements depends on the truth of what is asserted, the proponent will have to rely on and satisfy the requirements of, the hearsay exemption (or some other exemption or exception to the hearsay rule). For example, suppose A and B are accused of robbing a bank together, A driving the getaway car and B doing the work inside the bank. B says to the teller, "I have a gun. Give me the money." Of course, B's statement is admissible, for hearsay and other purposes, against B. This does not involve Rule 801(d)(2)(E). But is B's statement admissible against A? As a threat that constitutes part of the robbery, for which A is responsible as a co-conspirator under substantive criminal law, it is admissible against A without regard to the truth of B's assertion that he has a gun. (The threat might be effective even if B didn't have a gun.) But if, under the substantive law, it matters whether B really had a gun, then B's assertion to that effect is admissible against A to prove that B had a gun only if some hearsay exemption or exception applies. Rule 801(d)(2)(E) is the obvious candidate for this purpose.[103]

The "during the course of" requirement means that the statement must have been made before the conspiracy has terminated.[104] Efforts to conceal a completed crime may be part of an overall conspiracy.[105] Under federal law, however, a conspirator's participation in the conspiracy normally terminates with his or her arrest for the offense,[106] and, therefore, statements made by the arrestee to jailhouse informers are not in the course of the conspiracy and are not admissible against other co-

parties"); United States v. Dorn, 561 F.2d 1252, 1256–57 (7th Cir. 1977), *overruled on other grounds by* United States v. Read, 658 F.2d 1225 (7th Cir. 1981) (holding admissible statement enlisting co-conspirators).

[102] *See* **§ 14.04**.

[103] *See generally* CHRISTOPHER B. MUELLER & LAIRD C. KIRKPATRICK, FEDERAL EVIDENCE § 8:58 at 486–91 (4th ed. 2013). As in the case of agent admissions, one could argue that B's statement does not have to be admissible against A; so long as it is admissible against B, and B is in fact criminally liable, then A is liable under the substantive law. This, however, will not work against A if B is not in fact criminally liable or if B's statement is not what makes B criminally liable.

[104] The termination of a conspiracy is sometimes defined as occurring after the time of the last "overt" act of the conspirators. *See* United States v. Lewis, 759 F.2d 1316, 1347–48 (8th Cir. 1985) (citing Fiswick v. United States, 329 U.S. 211, 216 (1946)); United States v. Barnes, 586 F.2d 1052, 1059 (5th Cir. 1978) (holding that statement made at point when drugs had been confiscated and several co-conspirators had been arrested should not have been admitted under 801(d)(2)(E)); United States v. Sisto, 534 F.2d 616, 622 n.7 (5th Cir. 1976) (holding that conspiracy was terminated by arrest of alleged co-conspirator).

[105] For the federal rule regarding concealment activities, see Grunewald v. United States, 353 U.S. 391, 405–06 (1957) (holding that statements made during concealment phase are admissible under co-conspirator exception if concealment is "done in furtherance of main criminal objectives of the conspiracy"); *see also* Dutton v. Evans, 400 U.S. 74, 81 (1970) (contrasting broader Georgia exception for concealment with federal *Krulewitch* rule); Krulewitch v. United States, 336 U.S. 440 (1949) (rejecting concealment as part of conspiracy). *Cf.* Mares v. United States, 383 F.2d 805, 810 (10th Cir. 1967) (holding that "acting in concert to conceal the crime and to avoid detection" is activity in course of conspiracy).

[106] Wong Sun v. United States, 371 U.S. 471, 490 (1963) ("[O]ut-of-court declaration made after arrest may not be used at trial against one of the declarant's partners in crime."); United States v. Postal, 589 F.2d 862, 888 (5th Cir. 1979). The arrest of some of the co-conspirators does not necessarily end the whole conspiracy. United States v. Ammar, 714 F.2d 238, 253 (3d Cir. 1983). *Cf.* United States v. Gullett, 713 F.2d 1203, 1212–13 (6th Cir. 1983) (finding error in admission of recording from meeting held between two co-conspirators primarily to discuss concealment was not "in course" of conspiracy because two other co-conspirators had already been arrested and others were under grand jury investigation).

conspirators.[107] Statements made after arrest may be admissible in some states if, for instance, their purpose is to cover up the conspiracy;[108] in federal court, statements made after arrest by the person arrested may be admissible if their purpose is to further a continuing conspiracy and not merely to cover up a dead one.[109] Some courts have held that once the defendant is arrested, ending his or her participation in the conspiracy, statements made after the defendant's arrest by other co-conspirators are not admissible against the defendant.[110] Likewise, when a conspirator legitimately withdraws from the conspiracy, his or her post-withdrawal statements are not admissible against the remaining conspirators.[111] On the other hand, the prevailing view appears to be that statements made before the defendant against whom they are offered joined the conspiracy are nonetheless admissible against that defendant.[112]

---

[107] *See* United States v. Alonzo, 991 F.2d 1422, 1427 (8th Cir. 1993) (holding that in narcotics prosecution, trial court committed reversible error by admitting arrested co-conspirator's statement that he still owed defendant, his "source," money); United States v. Taylor, 802 F.2d 1108, 1117 (9th Cir. 1986). *Cf.* United States v. Guerro, 693 F.2d 10, 13 (1st Cir. 1982) (noting that each case is decided on its facts; where defendant, arrested for an unrelated crime, continued to be involved in conspiracy, co-conspirator statement is admissible); United States v. Smith, 578 F.2d 1227, 1233 n.12 (8th Cir. 1978) (holding that statements of arrested co-conspirator acting as informant not admissible); United States v. Williams, 548 F.2d 228, 232 (8th Cir. 1977); United States v. Smith, 623 F.2d 627, 631 (9th Cir. 1980) (conspiracy ended as to co-conspirator when he turned informer).

[108] *See* Reed v. People, 402 P.2d 68, 71 (Colo. 1965) (holding that statements made while trying to cover up crime are admissible); People v. Meagher, 388 N.E.2d 801, 805 (Ill. App. Ct. 1979) (holding that subsequent efforts at concealment are part of conspiracy if proximate in time). *Cf.* Romani v. State, 528 So. 2d 15, 23 (Fla. Dist. Ct. App. 1988) (holding that meetings of conspirators, after the murder, to arrange payments were during the course of the conspiracy); State v. Elam, 328 N.W.2d 314, 319 (Iowa 1982); State v. Clevenger, 733 S.W.2d 782, 784–85 (Mo. Ct. App. 1987).

[109] *See* United States v. Upton, 559 F.3d 3, 13 (1st Cir. 2009) (noting that goal of the conspiracy was money laundering in general and not just money laundering in sale of particular property, and so conspiracy was continuing); United States v. Emuegbunam, 268 F.3d 377 (6th Cir. 2001) (arrested co-conspirator #1 decided to cooperate with authorities and made monitored call to co-conspirator #2, who made statements incriminating co-conspirator #3, defendant against whom statement was later offered in evidence; court held that statement was made in course of and in furtherance of conspiracy because co-conspirators #2 and #3 were still at large and capable of achieving goals of conspiracy).

[110] *See* United States v. Mardian, 546 F.2d 973, 978 n.5 (D.C. Cir. 1976) (stating that if defendant had withdrawn from the conspiracy, "the declarations of co-conspirators uttered after the date of his withdrawal would not be admissible against him"); United States v. Smith, 578 F.2d 1227, 1233 & n.12 (8th Cir. 1978). *But see* United States v. Killian, 639 F.2d 206, 209 (5th Cir. 1981) ("[A] member of a conspiracy continues to be responsible for acts committed by coconspirators even after the former's arrest unless he has withdrawn from the conspiracy."); United States v. Williams, 87 F.3d 249, 253–54 (8th Cir. 1996) (holding that arrest of one conspirator does not end conspiracy where other conspirator continues illegal acts and arrested conspirator's statements were aimed at furthering conspiracy); United States v. Taylor, 802 F.2d 1108, 1117 (9th Cir. 1986) (holding that statements made by unarrested co-conspirator after arrest of conspirator can be introduced against arrested conspirator); United States v. Saavedra, 684 F.2d 1293, 1298–99 (9th Cir. 1982) (holding that defendant's arrest did not terminate conspiracy because co-conspirators were unaware of her arrest and continued their activities); United States v. Marques, 600 F.2d 742, 750 n.4 (9th Cir. 1979); United States v. Wentz, 456 F.2d 634, 637 (9th Cir. 1972) ("An unarrested co-conspirator still operating in furtherance of the conspiracy may say and do things which may be introduced against the arrested one if the conspiracy is still in operation.").

[111] *Cf.* United States v. Smith, 578 F.2d 1227, 1233 (8th Cir. 1978). Legitimate withdrawal requires "affirmative action to defeat or disavow the purpose of the conspiracy . . . '[m]ere cessation of the activity in furtherance of the conspiracy does not constitute withdrawal.' " United States v. Garrett, 720 F.2d 705, 714 (D.C. Cir. 1983) (quoting United States v. Phillips, 664 F.2d 971, 1018 (5th Cir. 1981)); *see also* United States v. Hamilton, 689 F.2d 1262, 1268 (6th Cir. 1982) (holding that without affirmative action to withdraw or terminate it, conspiracy is presumed to continue).

[112] *See* United States v. Goldberg, 105 F.3d 770, 775 (1st Cir. 1997) (holding that late-joining conspirator takes conspiracy as he finds it, and statements admissible against other conspirators are admissible against late joiner even though they were made before he joined; problems with doctrine is acknowledged, but precedent is followed); United States v. United States Gypsum Co., 333 U.S. 364, 393 (1948).

The co-conspirator rule is a powerful tool for the prosecutor. Even if the accused invokes his Fifth Amendment privilege and remains silent, the statements of a co-conspirator can come in as if the accused uttered them himself. Many prosecutions involve testimony of witnesses who made deals with the government for lesser punishment in exchange for their testimony and who might have a motive to lie or exaggerate the role of the accused. Such witnesses are often in a good position to repeat co-conspirator statements, which like all statements under the rule, require no personal knowledge.

To say that the rule is a powerful tool for the prosecutor is not necessarily a commendation. Commentators, and some courts, have expressed concern about the reliability of statements made by a person that the prosecution itself claims to be a criminal. The idea that by joining a conspiracy, each co-conspirator has authorized all statements by the others that further the conspiracy would be quite a stretch. Indeed, many commentators concede that the primary rationale of the rule is necessity, in the sense that conspiracies are hard to prove.[113] But to say that something is hard to prove and, therefore, we will admit even unreliable evidence about it comes close to saying that the goal of the trial is to obtain a conviction rather than an accurate verdict.[114] Perhaps the best thing that can be said for the exemption in its current form is something analogous to the federal exemption for prior statements of a witness: the great majority of statements admitted under the co-conspirator exemption will be admissible anyway, not for the truth of the matter asserted but rather as legally operative language, and allowing their admission for the truth of the matter asserted as well avoids the complications of making subtle distinctions and crafting difficult limiting instructions.

The co-conspirator doctrine has led to some important decisions on complex procedural questions:

The Decisionmaker. In the federal system, the judge decides whether the requirements for the co-conspirator rule have been satisfied.[115] Of course, the prosecutor may request that the out-of-court statements be admitted provisionally, subject to being "linked up" with evidence laying the foundation for the rule. If the linkage evidence is not supplied, then the judge must strike the earlier evidence, or perhaps even grant a mistrial if the prejudice cannot be cured.[116]

Some states allow the jury to decide. Under this approach, the statements are admitted and the jury is instructed to disregard the statements if it fails to find the

---

[113] *See generally* CHRISTOPHER B. MUELLER & LAIRD C. KIRKPATRICK, FEDERAL EVIDENCE § 8:58 at 491–95 (4th ed. 2013).

[114] A different sense of necessity exists, however, because the declarant usually will be unavailable, either because she has not been caught or because she has exercised the privilege against self-incrimination. Under some, but not all, circumstances, this might warrant admission of the hearsay under an application of the "best evidence principle," but this would not depend on any "in furtherance" requirement or any argument that the statements are particularly reliable; it would depend simply on the fact that the only information the tribunal can get from a declarant who cannot or will not testify is what the declarant said out of court. *See* Michael Seigel, *Rationalizing Hearsay: A Proposal for a Best Evidence Hearsay Rule*, 72 B.U. L. REV. 893, 938 n.142. (1992).

[115] Bourjaily v. United States, 483 U.S. 171, 175 (1987) (holding that existence of a conspiracy and defendant's involvement in it are preliminary questions of fact that court must resolve pursuant to Rule 104(a)).

[116] *See* United States v. Grassi, 616 F.2d 1295, 1300–01 (5th Cir. 1980); United States v. Lyles, 593 F.2d 182, 194 (2d Cir. 1979); *see also* 2 MICHAEL H. GRAHAM, HANDBOOK OF FEDERAL EVIDENCE § 801.25 at 336–38 (4th ed. 1996) (discussing order of proof issues). *Cf.* People v. Montoya, 753 P.2d 729, 734 (Colo. 1988) (en banc) (discussing order of proof).

foundational elements (a conspiracy of which defendant was a member, and that the statement was made in the course of and in furtherance of the conspiracy).[117] Even in the states where the jury decides, the judge must exclude the statement if no reasonable jury could decide that the foundational requirement had been met.

The Required Quantum of Proof. In the federal system, the prosecution must show the judge, by a preponderance of the evidence, that the foundational requirements have been met.[118] This accords with the standard generally applied to preliminary fact determinations under Rule 104(a). In some state jurisdictions, a different standard of proof may apply.[119] In states where the jury essentially decides the admissibility of a co-conspirator statement, the judge must simply determine that there is evidence sufficient to support a finding by the jury.

There is a division of authority on whether statements of an alleged co-conspirator may be admitted against the defendant even if the trial court decides to acquit the alleged co-conspirator of the conspiracy charge. The view that they may still be admitted is based on the idea that conviction for conspiracy requires a higher standard of proof (beyond reasonable doubt) than is required in order to admit the statements under 801(d)(2)(E).[120]

"Bootstrapping." Suppose the statement of A is offered against alleged co-conspirator B. In determining whether A's statement is admissible under the co-conspirator rule, may the court consider the statement itself? Before the enactment of the Federal Rules of Evidence and for many years afterwards, many federal courts prohibited relying on the content of the statement itself to determine the foundational questions. They required that the existence of the conspiracy, and B's part in it, be shown

---

[117] *See, e.g.*, CAL. EVID. CODE § 1223 (West 1966); FLA. STAT. ANN. § 90.803(18)(e) (West Supp. 1997); *see also* People v. Smith, 231 Cal. Rptr. 897, 905–06 (Ct. App. 1986) (disapproved of on other grounds by People v. Bacigalupo, 820 P.2d 559 (Cal. 1991)) (noting requirement that jury makes preliminary finding of conspiracy); State v. Morales, 460 So. 2d 410, 413 (Fla. Dist. Ct. App. 1984) (discussing "Apollo instruction" which defense counsel can request to be given to jury "that the conspiracy and each member's participation in it must be established by independent evidence," and noting that despite instruction, trial court has responsibility for determining admissibility of hearsay evidence); Eaton v. State, 438 So. 2d 822, 824 (Fla. 1983) (discussing "Apollo instruction"); Commonwealth v. Beckett, 366 N.E.2d 1252, 1259 (Mass. 1977) (stating that "jury must be instructed that, before they may consider the statements of one coconspirator against another, they must make definite findings on the same questions which the judge must pass on before he may permit the jury to consider whether that evidence may be used against all"); People v. H., 449 N.Y.S.2d 605, 609 n.1 (Sup. Ct. 1982) (indicating that jury must be instructed to make preliminary finding of conspiracy before using co-conspirator's statements); People v. Pontani, 306 N.Y.S.2d 240, 241 (App. Div. 1969) (approving similar charge).

[118] Bourjaily v. United States, 483 U.S. 171, 175–76 (1987); United States v. Chaney, 662 F.2d 1148 1153 (5th Cir. 1981); United States v. Shelton, 669 F.2d 446, 465 (7th Cir. 1982).

[119] *See, e.g.*, State v. Rolon, 201 P.3d 657, 666 (Idaho Ct. App. 2008) (requiring "sufficient evidence from which a trial court may reasonably infer the existence of a conspiracy"); McDowell v. State, 746 P.2d 149, 150 (Nev. 1987) (requiring slight evidence of conspiracy before statement is admitted); State v. Lassiter, 354 S.E.2d 595, 601 (W. Va. 1987) (requiring "fair preponderance of independent evidence"); Burke v. State, 746 P.2d 852, 855 (Wyo. 1987) (requiring prima facie evidence "sufficient . . . to permit the trial court to reasonably infer that a conspiracy existed").

[120] *See* United States v. Peralta, 941 F.2d 1003, 1005–1008 (9th Cir. 1991), *as amended on denial of reh'g*, (Oct. 31, 1991) (collecting cases); *see also* United States v. Lysaith, 2002 WL 31309242 at *1 (4th Cir. 2002) (holding that district court did not err in admitting co-conspirator's statements and acquitting defendant of conspiracy "because the burden of proof for admission of testimony under Rule 801(d)(2)(E) is a mere preponderance rather than the higher standard—beyond a reasonable doubt—that would apply in order to convict him of the conspiracy count").

by "independent evidence," exclusive of the co-conspirator statement, as part of the foundation for the hearsay statement.[121]

The Supreme Court abandoned this requirement in 1987 in *Bourjaily v. United States*,[122] referring to Rule 104(a) and noting that otherwise inadmissible evidence may be used by the judge in making preliminary fact determinations. *Bourjaily* left open the question whether the co-conspirator's statement could be the sole basis for a trial court finding that the defendant was a member of the conspiracy (other evidence pointed to the existence of a conspiracy in *Bourjaily*). A 1997 amendment to Rule 801(d)(2) resolved the issue, clarifying that while the court may consider the contents of the co-conspirator's statement in deciding whether the foundation for the doctrine has been laid, the proponent must also produce independent evidence of conspiracy. The amendment codifies the result reached by most of the circuits.[123] Some states also still embrace the independent evidence requirement, requiring that the trial judge not consider the statement as part of the evidence that the defendant was a member of the conspiracy.[124]

Confrontation Issues. Even if a statement fits under the co-conspirator rule, the defendant may still claim that admission of a co-conspirator's statement violates the Confrontation Clause. This claim is unlikely to succeed in federal court, given prevailing constitutional doctrine, because statements made in furtherance of an on-going conspiracy are unlikely to fall within the concept of "testimonial" statements covered by the Confrontation Clause.[125] A confrontation argument may still be available, however, under state constitution law.[126]

---

[121] *See* United States v. Martorano, 561 F.2d 406, 406 (1st Cir. 1977) (canvassing other circuits); United States v. Lyles, 593 F.2d 182, 194 (2d Cir. 1979); United States v. Simpson, 709 F.2d 903, 909 (5th Cir. 1983); United States v. Dean, 666 F.2d 174, 179 (5th Cir. 1982); United States v. Chaney 662 F.2d 1148, 1153 (5th Cir. 1981); United States v. James, 590 F.2d 575, 581, 588 (5th Cir.) (en banc 1979).

[122] Bourjaily v. United States, 483 U.S. 171, 176–81 (1987).

[123] *See, e.g.*, United States v. Castaneda, 16 F.3d 1504, 1507 (9th Cir. 1994) (holding that foundation for a co-conspirator statement must include "fairly incriminating" independent evidence, aside from proffered statement, showing defendant to be member of conspiracy); *see also* United States v. Sepulveda, 15 F.3d 1161, 1181–82 (1st Cir. 1993); United States v. Daly, 842 F.2d 1380, 1386 (2d Cir. 1988); United States v. Gambino, 926 F.2d 1355, 1361 n.5 (3d Cir. 1991); United States v. Garbett, 867 F.2d 1132, 1134 (8th Cir. 1989); United States v. Silverman, 861 F.2d 571, 577 (9th Cir. 1988); United States v. Zambrana, 841 F.2d 1320, 1344–45 (7th Cir. 1988).

[124] *See, e.g.*, State v. Edwards, 536 So. 2d 288, 294 (Fla. Dist. Ct. App. 1988) (specifically rejecting rule of *Bourjaily* and requiring independent evidence); People v. Woodland Oil Co., 396 N.W.2d 541, 544 (Mich. Ct. App. 1986) (requiring independent evidence); State v. Scanlon, 268 N.W.2d 63, 64 (Minn. 1978) (requiring "independent prima facie proof"); State v. Riggins, 519 N.E.2d 397, 403 (Ohio Ct. App. 1986); *see also* People v. Montoya, 753 P.2d 729, 734–36 (Colo. 1988) (en banc) (holding that statement can be considered in determining admissibility, but "cannot be the sole basis for establishing" admissibility); State v. Florie, 411 N.W.2d 689, 696 (Iowa 1987) (requiring some independent proof in addition to statement); State v. Frederickson, 739 S.W.2d 708, 711 n. 3 (Mo. 1987) (*en banc*) (recognizing *Bourjaily* and noting that Missouri law probably requires some independent evidence in addition to co-conspirator statement).

[125] *See* **§ 20**.

[126] *Cf.* Arnold v. State, 751 P.2d 494, 504–05 (Alaska Ct. App. 1988) (listing four indicators of reliability to be established before hearsay is admitted under co-conspirator doctrine, based on United States and Alaskan constitutions).

Chapter 16

HEARSAY EXCEPTIONS UNDER FEDERAL RULE 803

Table of Sections

§ 16.01 Hearsay Exceptions and Declarant Availability

Based largely on the exceptions that evolved at common law, the Federal Rules of Evidence divide the exceptions to the hearsay rule into two categories: Rule 804 exceptions, which apply only when the declarant is unavailable; and Rule 803 exceptions, which (ostensibly) apply whether or not the declarant is available. In addition to the twenty-three exceptions listed in Rule 803, the hearsay exemptions for statements of a party-opponent, Rule 801(d)(2), apply whether or not the declarant is available to testify, even though the rationale of some of those exemptions rests on the assumption that the declarant is (typically) available.[1]

One might expect a more widespread insistence that the declarant should be called if available.[2] This issue is addressed further in the next chapter.[3] Moreover, the two

---

1 *See* **§ 15.06**.

2 *See generally* I. Daniel Stewart, Jr., *Perception, Memory, and Hearsay: A Criticism of Present Law and the Proposed Federal Rules of Evidence*, 1970 UTAH L. REV. 1

3 *See* **§ 17.01** & **§ 17.07**.

categories of requirements articulated by Rules 803 and 804 do not exhaust the possibilities with respect to conditions of availability. For example, a third category is exceptions that apply only when the declarant testifies, illustrated by the rule for certain prior statements of a witness under Rule 801(d)(1).[4] In any event, the exceptions listed in Rule 803 (with one exception) place no conditions on the availability or unavailability of the declarant: the proponent may offer hearsay falling within one of these exceptions even if the declarant has not testified and is present in the courtroom and willing to testify. This result is considered appropriate because the circumstances surrounding the making of the hearsay statement are such that the hearsay is likely to be relatively reliable.[5]

§ 16.02 Excited Utterances [FRE 803(2)]

Rule 803(2) provides an exception for "a statement relating to a startling event or condition, made while the declarant was under the stress of excitement that it caused."

A core example of an excited utterance is a statement concerning a startling event or condition made while the event or condition is occurring or immediately thereafter. For example, a statement such as "My God! The car is on fire!" made while looking at the burning car and offered to show that the car was on fire, easily fits the exception. The main rationale of this exception is that excited utterances are reliable because excitement suspends the capacity to fabricate. This rationale has been questioned on grounds that excitement, while it suspends fabrication, may also weaken the ability to perceive and report the event accurately. Despite convincing experimental support for this criticism,[6] the rulemakers decided to retain the exception, in part because it was well established in precedent.[7] In addition, because excited utterances typically are made very soon after the startling event, they are usually made before the declarant's memory fades.

A more difficult example is a statement such as, "He's the one who did it!", made upon seeing the person at a later time and offered to prove that the person referred to did the act. In this example, because of the lapse of time between the act to which the statement refers and the statement itself, one must determine whether the excited utterance exception applies even though the declarant was not under the stress of excitement caused by the startling event itself. If the declarant was not suffering the stress of excitement caused by a startling event or condition, the exception obviously should not apply. On the other hand, if the court finds in our example that seeing the person referred to was itself a startling event, and that the declarant spoke while

---

[4] *See* **§§ 15.02 et seq.** There is also one exception in Rule 803 that falls in this category, the exception for past recollection recorded, which appears in Rule 803(5) and is discussed in this chapter. *See* **§ 16.06**. The declarant must testify to establish the foundation for that exception. That, it will be noted, belies the predicate of Rule 803, which states that its exceptions apply "regardless of whether the declarant is available as a witness." The drafters of the Rules evidently had some difficulty finding a home for this exception.

[5] *See* FED. R. EVID. 803 advisory committee note ("The present rule proceeds upon the theory that under appropriate circumstances a hearsay statement may possess circumstantial guarantees of trustworthiness sufficient to justify nonproduction of the declarant in person at the trial even though he may be available.").

[6] *See* Aviva Orenstein, *My God!: A Feminist Critique of the Excited Utterance Exception to the Hearsay Rule,* 85 CALIFORNIA L. REV. 153 (1997); I. Daniel Stewart, Jr., *Perception, Memory, and Hearsay: A Criticism of Present Law and the Proposed Federal Rules of Evidence,* 1970 UTAH L. REV. 1, 27–29, and authorities cited therein; Robert M. Hutchins & Donald Slesinger, *Some Observations on the Law of Evidence: Spontaneous Exclamations,* 28 COLUM. L. REV. 432, 437–39 (1928).

[7] *See* FED. R. EVID. 803(2) advisory committee note.

suffering from the stress of excitement caused by the new event, the excited utterance exception might apply.[8] Nonetheless, the implied (but intended) communication about facts remembered from the first event, presents serious hearsay issues regarding dissipation of memory as well as the opportunity to fabricate, which argue against application of this exception.

The question whether the declarant was under the stress of excitement at the time the utterance was made is a question for the judge to determine under Rule 104(a). In deciding the question, all of the circumstances can be taken into account, including the content of the utterance itself.[9] In other words, the fact that the utterance contains words like "My God!" can be used by the trial judge as evidence on the preliminary determination of fact about excitement. A gap in time between the exciting event and the hearsay utterance does not preclude qualification under this exception, so long as the excitement created by the event continues until the statement is made.[10] As is the case with other preliminary determinations of fact under Rule 104(a), the judge is not bound by the Rules of Evidence (except privilege) in deciding whether a factual foundation has been laid for admission of an utterance under a hearsay exception.[11]

As discussed in an earlier chapter, the use of most hearsay exceptions depends on a showing that the declarant had personal knowledge of the content of the statement.[12] Ordinarily, the requirement that the declarant be under the stress of a startling event will assure that the declarant has personal knowledge, but this is not inevitable. For example, the declarant could simply be told about the startling event by someone else. In accord with the apparent directions from the drafters of the Federal Rules,[13] the trial judge uses the standard of Rule 104(b) and determines simply whether the fact-finder can reasonably infer that the declarant had personal knowledge of the content of the statement.[14]

---

8 *See* United States v. Napier, 518 F.2d 316, 317–18 (9th Cir. 1975) (upholding admission, as an excited utterance, of statement by brain damage victim saying "he killed me!" when shown photograph of defendant long after event). *But cf.* People v. Grubbs, 492 N.Y.S.2d 377, 378–79 (N.Y. App. Div. 1985) (holding inadmissible testimony that claimant recoiled when she first saw defendant in identification lineup offering no explicit hearsay analysis; dissenting opinion cites *Napier,* arguing that evidence should have been admitted as excited utterance).

9 *See* United States v. Brown, 254 F.3d 454, 459–60 (3d Cir. 2001) (holding that court could use excited utterance itself to establish that foundation requirement of startling event was satisfied).

10 *See* United States v. Rivera, 43 F.3d 1291, 1296 (9th Cir. 1995) (not an abuse of discretion for district court to admit, as excited utterance, testimony that victim said at least half an hour after event that the defendant raped and threatened the victim; in determining whether a statement was made under stress of excitement, court should consider not only lapse of time but declarant's age, characteristics of the event, and subject matter of the statements); *see also* Simpson v. Wal-Mart Stores, 744 A.2d 625, 628–29 (N.H. 1999) (neither lapse of time nor fact that statement came in response to question prevents it from qualifying as an excited utterance if excitement persisted).

11 *See* FED. R. EVID. 803(2) advisory committee note; *see also* United States v. Obayagbona, 627 F. Supp. 329, 338–39 (E.D.N.Y. 1985) (determining that statement was an excited utterance by listening to the tape of the statement and evaluating the speaker's tone of voice); United States v. Phelps, 572 F. Supp. 262, 265–66 (E.D. Ky. 1983) (describing the various factors the trial judge considered in a hearing out of the presence of the jury to decide whether a statement was an excited utterance).

12 *See* **§ 14.08**.

13 *See* FED. R. EVID. 803 advisory committee note (referring to Rule 602).

14 *See* United States v. Tocco, 135 F.3d 116, 128 (2d Cir. 1998) (holding evidence sufficient to support a finding that declarant had personal knowledge). When the declarant is an unidentified bystander, courts sometimes do not admit the statement as proof of the event due to insufficient proof of firsthand knowledge. *See* FED. R. EVID. 803(1) advisory committee note; *see also* Garrett v. Howden, 387 P.2d 874, 876–78 (N.M. 1963) (finding no abuse of discretion to reject testimony of unidentified bystander concerning speed of car prior to collision). *But cf.* United States v. Medico, 557 F.2d 309, 315–16 (2d Cir. 1977) (affirming the admission of

§ 16.03 Present Sense Impressions [FRE 803(1)]

Rule 803(1) provides a hearsay exception for a "statement describing or explaining an event or condition, made while or immediately after the declarant perceived it." The statement need not be made exactly at the time of observing the event; substantial contemporaneity is all that is required.[15]

Examples

"I can't seem to turn the wheel," offered to show that the declarant, who was then attempting to do so, could not turn the wheel.[16]

"There's a mouse in the bottle," offered to show that declarant, who was then looking in the bottle, saw a mouse.

"The license number of that car was FJY 644," offered to show that the license number of a car just observed was in fact FJY 644.[17]

The rationale for the present sense impression exception is that: (1) no substantial danger exists that defects in the declarant's memory will diminish the value of the statement; (2) the declarant has very little time to fabricate; and (3) in many cases, the person to whom the statement was addressed would have been in a position to check its accuracy; hence, the declarant would speak with care.

When determining whether to admit a statement as a present sense impression, the trial judge must determine, as a preliminary matter under Rule 104(a), whether the statement was made at the time of the event or immediately afterward. The contents of the statement being offered may be used for this purpose. In other words, it is permissible to "bootstrap" by using the utterance itself to lay its own foundation. This occurs, for instance, in a case where the declarant makes the statement over the telephone and there is no way to corroborate independently whether it was contemporaneous with the event other than examining the contents of the statement itself.[18] The word "immediately" in Rule 803(1) is not defined. One court has held that

---

an unidentified bystander's description of the license plate number of a getaway car under the residual exception created by Rule 804(b)(5) (now Rule 807), noting that the statement fits the requirements of the present sense impression exception, and speculating that Judge Weinstein, the trial judge, may have avoided that exception because of caveats about unidentified bystanders set forth in the advisory committee note to Rule 803(1).).

[15] *See* FED. R. EVID. 803(1) advisory committee note. *See also* United States v. Peacock, 654 F.2d 339, 350 (5th Cir. 1981) (statements made by declarant immediately after phone conversation describing the conversation admissible under 803(1); the underlying conversation was admissible as the statement of a co-conspirator).

[16] *See* Fratzke v. Meyer, 398 N.W.2d 200, 204 (Iowa Ct. App. 1986) (holding statement by boy just before being struck by car, "Hurry up there is a car coming," admissible as present sense impression).

[17] *See* State v. Smith, 285 So. 2d 240, 244–45 (La. 1973) (holding slip of paper on which bystander wrote license number of robbery getaway car offered to prove the license number of the car admissible as present sense impression or excited utterance).

[18] United States v. Campbell, 782 F. Supp. 1258, 1259–61 (N.D. Ill. 1991) (admitting call to 911 dispatcher by declarant who had stated that he was in store that had "just" been scene of shooting as a present sense impression under Rule 803(1) or as an excited utterance under Rule 803(2)); State v. Jones, 532 A.2d 169, 171–72 (Md. 1987) (admitting anonymous citizen's band radio transmissions, purported to be from truck drivers, about their observations of errant police cruiser, making statements such as "Look at Smoky Bear southbound with no lights on," without independent evidence that statements made contemporaneously with witnessing conditions); Booth v. State, 508 A.2d 976, 985 (Md. 1986) (admitting statements about persons present while declarant was talking on telephone as present sense impressions). *See also* United States v. Cain, 587 F.2d 678, 681 (5th Cir. 1979) (holding that citizen's band transmission about identification of persons

the immediacy requirement was satisfied even though the statement might have been made as long as twenty-three minutes after the event.[19] Another has held that a lapse of ten to fifteen minutes was too long.[20] In deciding whether a given period satisfies the requirement of contemporaneity under Rule 803(1), the trial judge should take into account the rationale of Rule 803(1), and decide whether the lapse of time provided an opportunity, under the circumstances, for fabrication or memory loss.[21] It is also relevant whether the lapse of time eliminated the opportunity for the person who heard the declarant's statement to observe what the declarant described. Although independent observation is not an absolute requirement for admission as a present sense impression,[22] one of the justifications for the exception is that the person to whom declarant addressed the statement would often have a chance to check on the validity of the statement by observing the same thing, and therefore the declarant would have a motive to be accurate. Where a lapse of time has removed this opportunity for independent observation by the addressee, the court may consider that fact in deciding whether to find that the statement was made "immediately" after the event.[23]

The rule refers to statements "describing or explaining" an event, and while most statements admitted under this exception involve simple description, an evaluative component is permitted. Like the modern rule regulating lay opinion testimony, description and evaluation are sometimes difficult to distinguish and separate, and the rule wisely makes no attempt to do so. For example, in a medical malpractice case, it was proper to admit the following statement of a consulting physician, made upon examining an X-ray nine months after the operation in question: "He certainly did take a big chunk out of your spine."[24] However, this should not be understood to admit a statement of perception that implicitly contains a reference to some *remembered* event about which the perception statement is intended to communicate. For example, if the declarant witnesses a crime and later happens to see a person the declarant believes to be the perpetrator, declarant's assertion, "That's him," cannot be admitted as a present sense impression, even though there is an immediate description or explanation of a

---

walking near abandoned stolen truck does not satisfy immediacy requirement because circumstantial evidence indicated substantial lapse of time between truck's abandonment and statement).

[19] United States v. Blakey, 607 F.2d 779, 785–86 (7th Cir. 1979), *overruled on other grounds by* Idaho v. Wright, 497 U.S. 805 (1990) (the lapse of time was, at most, twenty-three minutes); *see also* State v. Tucker, 68 P.3d 110, 119 (Ariz. 2003) (noting that trial courts have "some latitude" in deciding whether the immediacy requirement was satisfied). However, most courts interpret the rule as imposing a more literal immediacy requirement. *See* State ex rel. J.A., 949 A.2d 790, 797–99 (N.J. 2008) (collecting cases) (holding that a time lapse of ten minutes meant that a statement did not fit within the present sense impression exception).

[20] United States v. Penney, 576 F.3d 297, 312–13 (6th Cir. 2009), *cert. denied*, 559 U.S. 940 (2010). *See also* Hilyer v. Howat Concrete Co., 578 F.2d 422, 426 n.7 (D.C. Cir. 1978) (suggesting 15 minutes after event is too long).

[21] *See* FED. R. EVID. 803(1) advisory committee note; *see also* Houston Oxygen Co. v. Davis, 161 S.W.2d 474, 476–77 (Tex. Com. App. 1942) (holding that an observer's comment predicting that a car would crash because it was going so fast was admissible as a present sense impression because it was "sufficiently spontaneous to save it from the suspicion of being manufactured evidence").

[22] For discussion of the corroboration issue, see Jon R. Waltz, *The Present Sense Impression Exception to the Rule Against Hearsay: Origins and Attributes*, 66 IOWA L. REV. 869, 898 (1981) (stating that corroboration by an equally percipient witness should not be required, and that the event itself and the circumstances surrounding it will often supply adequate information regarding the accuracy of the statement).

[23] Hall v. De Saussure, 297 S.W.2d 81, 89–90 (Tenn. Ct. App. 1956). For a post-Rules case, see United States v. Ruiz, 249 F.3d 643 (7th Cir. 2001) (whether remote hearer of present sense impression statement was in a position to verify the statement goes to weight of statement but not admissibility).

[24] *See, e.g.*, MCA, Inc. v. Wilson, 425 F. Supp. 443, 450–51 (S.D.N.Y. 1976), *aff'd*, 677 F.2d 180 (2d Cir. 1981) (in intellectual property dispute, admitting report of reactions of audience that a song in a play sounded like the song "Bugle Boy").

perception. Because the explanation identifies the present event with a previous event and is intended to communicate information about the earlier event, such statements involve potential defects in the declarant's perceptions at the *previous* time and potential defects in the declarant's memory about them, unlike the paradigmatic present sense impression.[25]

A statement offered as a present sense impression is not admissible unless the proponent demonstrates that the declarant had personal knowledge. In *Bemis v. Edwards*,[26] the court rejected the argument that statements made in a 911 call were admissible as a present sense impression, stating that the proponent had failed to show that the declarant had firsthand knowledge. The court also stated that the proponent has the burden of proving by a preponderance of the evidence that the declarant had firsthand knowledge. This conclusion is doubtful. What marks off this exception is not the fact that the declarant must have perceived the matters about which he speaks; almost all the hearsay exceptions share this requirement. In the authors' opinion, if the requirement of proof by a "preponderance" is correct in this context—because the exception by its terms requires a preliminary showing that the declarant personally sensed the matter being described—the "preponderance" test cannot be generalized to other instances in which a showing of personal knowledge is required. As to that more general requirement of a showing of firsthand knowledge, the Advisory Committee's Note to Rule 602 indicates that the appropriate standard is whether there is evidence sufficient to support a finding of personal knowledge, not the higher standard of proof by a preponderance of the evidence.[27] In any event, where the challenged statement expressly or implicitly shows that the declarant was speaking from firsthand knowledge, that requirement is satisfied without further proof of personal knowledge.[28]

Present Sense Impressions Compared with Excited Utterances

Although the exception for present sense impressions is akin to the exception for excited utterances, there are, however, three differences between the two exceptions:

Present Sense Impression	Excited Utterance
Must be made while observing the event or "immediately" thereafter.	No specific time limit.
No excitement required	Excitement required
Must "describe or explain" the event."	Utterance need only "relate to" the exciting event.

For example, after a slip and fall accident, the statement by a bystander, "That has been on the floor for a couple of hours," would be admissible under the excited utterance exception even though it does not describe the exciting event (someone falling on the

---

[25] *See* 4 CHRISTOPHER B. MUELLER & LAIRD C. KIRKPATRICK, FEDERAL EVIDENCE § 8:67 at 581–82 (4th ed. 2013).

[26] Bemis v. Edwards, 45 F.3d 1369, 1373–74 (9th Cir. 1995).

[27] *See* **§ 14.08**.

[28] *See* First State Bank of Denton v. Maryland Cas. Co., 918 F.2d 38, 41–42 (5th Cir. 1990) (statement of person answering telephone that it was the Millses' residence but that Mr. Mills was not at home was admissible where declarant apparently looked for Mills before making statement).

substance on the floor). On the other hand, the advisory committee suggests that the quoted statement would not qualify as a present sense impression.[29]

Present Sense Impressions and Double Hearsay

Present sense impressions sometimes arise in contexts presenting issues of hearsay within hearsay.[30] Litigators and judges sometimes overlook the possibility of making a Rule 805 argument for the admission of a present sense impression contained within a present sense impression. Suppose that Declarant A tells Declarant B the license number of a hit-and-run driver. Declarant B then tells Witness X, a police officer, the license number that the first declarant told him. If both statements were made on personal knowledge and were made at or soon after the event, then the joint operation of Rules 805 and 803(1) (the present sense impression exception) would seem to justify admitting the evidence. What Declarant A said ("The license number was 371 CUB") was Declarant A's statement of her present sense impression of the license number, made immediately after the event. What Declarant B said ("Declarant A told me that the license number was 371 CUB") is Declarant B's statement of a present sense impression, from his sense of hearing, made immediately after the relevant event of hearing the other statement.[31]

There are some instances in which the theory outlined would not work because a foundation cannot be laid showing that the hearsay-within-hearsay declarant had personal knowledge. Immediacy is also a requirement of the present sense impression hearsay exception. In the car license hypothetical, suppose that Declarant A told Declarant B the license number over a citizens' band (CB) radio. Neither Declarant B nor the in-court witness has any way of knowing whether Declarant A was reporting on personal knowledge immediately after the event. So, no foundation could be laid showing personal knowledge or immediacy.[32] Suppose, however, that Declarant A said, "I just this second saw the car speeding away and its license plate was 371 CUB," and Declarant B reported the statement to the in-court witness in exactly those words. If a specific claim of seeing the other car had been made, then the trial judge has authority to accept it as sufficient evidence of the existence of personal knowledge.[33] And under Rule 104(a), which provides that in determining preliminary questions about the admissibility of evidence, the trial judge is not bound by the rules of evidence except those of privilege, the trial judge could consider the hearsay itself in determining whether the immediacy requirement was satisfied.[34]

---

[29] *See* FED. R. EVID. 803 advisory committee note.

[30] For a general discussion of hearsay within hearsay, or layered hearsay, see **§ 14.07**.

[31] The courts have recognized a similar possibility where other hearsay exceptions are involved. *See, e.g.*, United States v. Rucker, 586 F.2d 899, 905–06 (2d Cir. 1978) (where both levels of hearsay fell under the exception for admissions of co-conspirators, Rule 801(d)(2)(E), evidence was admissible); United States v. Christian, 786 F.2d 203, 211–12 (6th Cir. 1986) (same).

[32] *See* United States v. Cain, 587 F.2d 678, 681 (5th Cir. 1979), *rev'd on other grounds*, 615 F.2d 380 (5th Cir. 1980) ("The distances and time lapses involved make it impossible to determine whether the declaration by the 'CB'er' was made immediately following the observation or not, but the chances that it was are slim. The exception to the hearsay rule found in Rule 803(1) is, therefore, inapplicable"); *see also* Wolf by Wolf v. Procter & Gamble Co., 555 F. Supp. 613, 620–21 (D.N.J. 1982) (hearsay inadmissible under 803(1) and 803(6) where statements not recorded immediately).

[33] *Cf.* FED. R. EVID. 602 ("Evidence to prove personal knowledge may consist of the witness's own testimony.").

[34] *See* Bourjaily v. United States, 483 U.S. 171, 176–82 (1987) (court could consider the hearsay statements themselves in making Rule 104(a) preliminary fact determination); *see also* FED. R. EVID. 104(a)

There would seem to be no obstacle to accepting the idea that the first level of hearsay, where the declarant reports what another person said immediately after the event, can be a present sense impression. If so, the second level would be admissible if it fit some exception or exemption. Yet this argument seems to have been overlooked in some hotly contested cases. These cases arise from situations in which undercover agents were dealing with declarants through informer-intermediaries. One of the difficulties of drug investigations is that the targets do not want to meet new people, so it is difficult to get the targets to deal directly with undercover agents instead of dealing through persons whom they already know and perhaps trust. In any event, in each of the cases the informer had conversations over the telephone with the target while the agent was standing at the informer's shoulder. For one reason or another, the informer did not testify at trial. The government's case would have benefited had the jury heard what the informer told the agent about what the defendant said over the phone, but the hearsay rule stood as an obstacle. In each case the trial prosecutor sought to solve the problem by putting into evidence the agent's contemporaneous instructions to the informer. The following excerpts from the transcripts illustrate the type of testimony elicited. In *United States v. Check,*[35] the government agent testified, inter alia:

> I instructed William Cali [the informer] that by no means did I intend to front any sum of money to Sandy Check [the defendant]. . . . At that time I told William Cali I didn't particularly care whether or not Check was concerned about rats and not wanting to meet anyone new or about being busted by the man. . . .[36]

In *United States v. Figueroa,*[37] the agent's testimony included the following:

> Mike [the informer] had a conversation [over the telephone after having asked the hotel operator for a co-defendant's room] and Mike asked me, "Would it be all right if we did the two-kilogram deal one pound at a time?" And I told him to tell the people on the other end of the phone that that would be fine, we would deal one pound of cocaine at a time. . . . After Mike had a conversation with the other people on the phone, I told Mike that it would be all right if Leo [the defendant] sent his man down, Tommie, to count the money.[38]

The trial judge in *Figueroa* made clear that the informer's phone call could be used to incriminate the defendant, stating that the informer had called "someone in the apartment who again gave his name as Leo, and they discussed the distribution of cocaine."[39]

In both cases the trial courts admitted the evidence, and in both cases the appellate courts reversed on hearsay grounds.[40] Neither the trial nor appellate courts alluded to

---

advisory committee note (endorsing the view that "the judge should be empowered to hear any relevant evidence, such as affidavits or other reliable hearsay.").

35 United States v. Check, 582 F.2d 668, 671–73 (2d Cir. 1978).

36 *Id.* at 671.

37 United States v. Figueroa, 750 F.2d 232 (2d Cir. 1984).

38 *Id.* at 236.

39 *Id.* at 241.

40 In *Check,* the trial judge seems to have admitted the evidence on the theory that all prior statements of witnesses are admissible. The trial judge apparently accepted the view that if the agent's out-of-court statements were really his own, not merely an artifice to get into evidence another's statements, then they were admissible without limit because the agent was subject to cross-examination. United States v. Check, 582 F.2d 668, 678–79 (2d Cir. 1978). Even under the trial judge's own theory, it appears that some of the

the possible theory that the informer's statement reporting what the target said was admissible as a present sense impression. Had the court agreed with this application of the present sense impression, then admissibility would have been no problem, because each level of hearsay would fit an exception. The target's statements would be admissible as admissions or statements of co-conspirators.

The present sense impression theory that we have outlined would seem to be a better way of getting in the evidence, and the witness could have testified directly about what the informer said the target said without attempting the subterfuge of testifying only about the witness's own statements. However, perhaps the courts would be reluctant to do so because the in-court witness had no way to verify what the informer claimed the target said.[41] Although the drafters of Rule 803(1) did not expressly require that a present sense impression be verified by another equally percipient observer (e.g., by having the person who heard the present sense impression also testify that he or she observed the event about which the declarant spoke), the probative value of the statement would certainly be enhanced were the witness reporting the out-of-court declarant's statement in a position to determine whether the declarant was telling the truth.[42]

§ 16.04 Statements Describing the Declarant's Present State of Mind or Body [FRE 803(3)]

Rule 803(3) excepts from the hearsay rule statements of the declarant's "then existing state of mind," such as motive, intent, or plan, or "emotional, sensory, or physical condition," such as mental feeling, pain, or bodily health. It does not, however, include statements of "memory or belief to prove the fact remembered or believed" unless it relates to the validity or terms of declarant's will.[43]

Examples

"My back hurts" (to show pain).

"I hate him" (to show hatred).

"I'm going to my uncle's house" (to show intent to go to the uncle's house).

---

statements should have been excluded. In *Figueroa*, the trial judge admitted the utterances as "verbal acts" through which the agent gave directions to the informer. United States v. Figueroa, 750 F.2d 232, 238–40 (2d Cir. 1984).

[41] *See* 2 McCormick on Evidence § 271 at 363 (Kenneth S. Broun ed., 7th ed. 2013) (discussing fact that 803(1) does not require corroboration).

[42] *See* Booth v. State, 508 A.2d 976, 983–84 (Md. 1986) (rejecting a requirement of corroboration, though stating it may be used to determine the weight of the evidence).

[43] Fed. R. Evid. 803(3); *see, e.g.*, United States v. DiNome, 954 F.2d 839, 846 (2d Cir. 1992) (admitting murder victim's statement prior to crime that he was going to see a lawyer about his suspicion that his competitor was dealing in stolen cars under Rule 803(3) to show victim-declarant's intent and hence to show competitor's motive to murder declarant to keep him quiet; statement was not made in the presence of competitor, but court evidently assumed that competitor might have heard of statement or of similar conduct by declarant); United States v. Barraza, 576 F.3d 798, 804–05 (8th Cir. 2009) (in a kidnapping and murder prosecution, victim's statements to a friend and in her diary that she was planning to take a trip to Mexico with defendant were admissible under Rule 803(3) to show her state of mind); United States v. Tokars, 95 F.3d 1520, 1535–36 (11th Cir. 1996) (admitting, in prosecution of husband for murdering wife, wife's statements to other persons about her intent to divorce husband and take away his money to show her state of mind, which was probably manifested to him in some way, thus giving him a motive to kill); United States v. Veltmann, 6 F.3d 1483, 1494–95 (11th Cir. 1993) (holding that in arson-murder prosecution, trial court erred by excluding witness's videotaped deposition testimony on prior alleged suicide threats by murder victim; testimony was admissible in light of relevance to defense that victim had committed suicide).

The rationale behind this exception is that the declarant's defects of memory will not affect the validity of the statement, because there has been no lapse of time between the condition being described and the description of it.[44] Also, there is a diminished danger of fabrication because there has been less time to fabricate in many instances—although, of course, in some cases, such as that of a personal injury plaintiff saying "my back hurts," there may be a preexisting motive to fabricate.[45] Certainly some people are unreliable in talking about their feelings, but in terms of necessity, there are only limited ways to know that someone is hurting—physically or emotionally—other than to take his or her word for it.

This very important exception can be invoked in either or both of two ways. First, mental or physical states are sometimes ultimate facts that must be proved under the cause of action, such as a criminal defendant's intent in a murder trial, a civil defendant's maliciousness in a tort claim seeking punitive damages, or a civil plaintiff's pain and suffering as an element of damages. The existence of a mental state, like intent, at one point in time, is circumstantial evidence of its existence at a later point in time. Second, a person's mental or physical condition at one point in time may be an important circumstantial indicator of future actions or events. In the example above, the utterance of the statement, "I'm going to my uncle's house," by manifesting an intent to go to the uncle's house, increases the probability that the speaker actually did so. This is so even if the statement is phrased in a way that does not explicitly assert the intention. For example, the statement, "I'll kill him," taken literally, is a prediction of a future event, not a statement of the declarant's intent. When offered to show an intent to kill, this statement is admissible on one of two theories. Most likely, the statement was uttered in order to communicate the declarant's intent to the listener (what other purpose would it have?), in which case it is hearsay within the present exception. Alternatively, if it really was meant merely as a prediction of a future event, it is nonhearsay (as it is sometimes said, "circumstantial") evidence of the speaker's intent.[46]

However, the exception does not cover statements that are statements of memory or belief offered to show the fact remembered or believed. For example, neither the statement, "I remember that it was Brandon who attacked me yesterday," nor the statement, "I believe that it was Brandon who attacked me yesterday," is permitted by the exception.[47] If the exception were extended to such statements of (present) memory

---

[44] *Cf.* FED. R. EVID. 803(3) advisory committee note (arguably incorporating rationale of present sense impression exception). For an analysis of the concepts underlying the exception, see Glen Weissenberger, *Hearsay Puzzles: An Essay on Federal Evidence Rule 803(3)*, 64 TEMP. L. REV. 145 (1991).

[45] Unlike the Federal Rule, the California rules governing statements of mental or physical state explicitly provide for exclusion "if the statement was made under circumstances such as to indicate its lack of trustworthiness." WEST'S ANN. CAL. EVID. CODE § 1252 (2010). In People v. Smith, 68 P.3d 302, 334–35 (Cal. 2003), a defendant at the penalty phase of a death penalty case sought to admit tape-recorded phone calls he made to his wife soon after he was arrested in order to show that he felt remorse. The California Supreme Court held that trial court did not err in finding that the statements lacked trustworthiness and in refusing to admit the statements because the defendant's primary motivation during the calls was to placate his wife, and so he may not have been sincere.

[46] *See generally* 4 CHRISTOPHER B. MUELLER & LAIRD C. KIRKPATRICK, FEDERAL EVIDENCE §§ 8:71, 8:72 (4th ed. 2013).

[47] *See, e.g.*, Estate of Suskovich v. Anthem Health Plans, 553 F.3d 559, 569 (7th Cir. 2009) (holding decedent's statement that he "felt" that he was defendant's employee, when offered to prove that he was defendant's employee, was a statement of belief offered to prove the fact believed and was thus inadmissible); United States v. Neely, 980 F.2d 1074, 1082 (7th Cir. 1992) (holding trial court properly excluded defendant's letter denying any involvement with fraudulent schemes written two and one-half weeks after defendant received letter from government witness detailing defendant's role in insurance fraud scheme); United States v. Soghanalian, 777 F. Supp. 17 (S.D. Fla. 1991) (holding self-exculpatory statement by defendant who did not

or belief, then that would be an end to the hearsay rule. For these statements are practically indistinguishable from the statement, "Brandon attacked me yesterday," when uttered by someone who asserts that fact based on memory of beliefs formed earlier.

As indicated above, the exception for statements of present state of mind includes statements of present intent to do a future act, offered to show that the declarant did the future act. In the leading pre-Rules case on the subject, *Mutual Life Insurance Co. v. Hillmon*,[48] the declarant's statement that he was going to Colorado with Hillmon was held admissible to show that he had in fact done so. A potential objection arises whenever a statement expressly or implicitly describes the intent of some person other than the declarant, as it also did in *Hillmon*. Suppose, for example, that the statement "I'm going out with Harry" is offered against Harry to prove that the declarant, a murder victim, did go out with Harry, who is charged with her murder. This statement shows the intent of the declarant to go out with Harry, but it also relies upon her memory about what Harry himself said about Harry's plans; the statement would have little evidentiary value (as against Harry) unless Harry had said he was going to go out with her. Extending the exception to allow an inference from the statement to Harry's likely behavior is more doubtful.

During the congressional process, the House Committee on the Judiciary issued a report asserting that Rule 803(3) should be construed "so as to render statements of intent by a declarant admissible only to prove his future conduct, not the future conduct of another person."[49] In a jurisdiction that follows the House Report, a statement like "Amy and I are going to rob a bank" would be inadmissible when offered against Amy to show that Amy participated in the robbery—unless, of course, some other basis for receiving the statement could be found, such as the rule receiving statements of co-conspirators. The statement "I'm going out with Harry" is more problematic. It is arguably admissible even if one accepts the view in the House Report. The theory of admission would be that it is offered not to show Harry's intent, but for the limited purpose of showing declarant's intent to go out with Harry should Harry come. Under this theory, the defense would be entitled to a limiting instruction to the effect that the statement could be used to show that the declarant was planning to go out with Harry but not that Harry was planning to go out with the declarant. Courts have generally favored the reception of these statements despite the danger that the jury would use them to show another's intent.[50]

---

testify at trial, made hours after plane arrived in Iraq with illegal cargo, that arms in cargo were supposed to have been off-loaded in Switzerland, was not admissible under Rule 803(3) because it was a statement of memory or belief offered to prove the fact remembered or believed).

[48] Mutual Life Ins. Co. v. Hillmon, 145 U.S. 285, 295–300 (1892).

[49] FED. R. EVID. 803(3) advisory committee note.

[50] *See* United States v. Astorga-Torres, 682 F.2d 1331 (9th Cir. 1982) (holding that statement by inmate that he intended to bring two guards to site of drug transaction; "was properly admitted not as proof that in fact he did bring guards with him to Tulare . . . but as evidence that he had the intent to do so, from which evidence inferences could properly be drawn by the jury"; admitting the statement against defendants other than declarant and issuing limiting instruction); United States v. Pheaster, 544 F.2d 353, 374–80 (9th Cir. 1976) (canvassing arguments, and deciding in favor of admission; trial court gave limiting instruction; Federal Rules were not applicable to case); United States v. Houlihan, 871 F. Supp. 1495 (D. Mass. 1994) (applying expansive interpretation of Rule 803(3) and allowing admission of murder victim's statement on the evening of the murder that he was going out to meet defendant as circumstantial evidence of the meeting). For a leading case from a non-Rules jurisdiction, see People v. Alcalde, 148 P.2d 627 (Cal. 1944) (decedent's statement that she was going out with a certain person admitted in that person's murder trial; however, court gave limiting

Moreover, one can argue that the House Report does not set forth the proper way to interpret Rule 803(3). To accept the House Report's view would be to reject the common-law foundation for Rule 803(3). The *Hillmon* case involved a declarant who spoke not only about the declarant's own intent but also about the intent of another (though the statement was admitted solely to prove the intentions of the declarant).[51] The advisory committee noted the *Hillmon* case favorably.[52] Though the House Report suggests a different legislative intent,[53] it is only the report of one House Committee, not a statute adopted by Congress, and courts that have given a generous scope to the exception cannot be said to be ignoring any clear statement of uniform legislative intent.[54] Some courts attempt a compromise whereby the declarant's statement is admissible as evidence of the non-declarant's conduct only if other evidence confirms the other person's conduct.[55]

The special provision in the rule regarding wills is, for practical purposes, a separate exception to the hearsay rule that permits temporally "backward-looking" statements, statements about past remembered intentions and events that relate to "the validity or terms of the declarant's will." It is grounded in the necessity arising from the death of the testator as well as the centrality of the testator's intent in the interpretation of wills.[56] Arguably, similar policies should apply to the interpretation of various will

instruction "that the evidence was admitted for the limited purpose of showing the decedent's intention"). The California Supreme Court reaffirmed the *Alcalde* rule in People v. Jones, 917 P.2d 1165, 1173–74 (Cal. 1996) (admitting murder victim's statement to her daughter that she was going to another city with defendant, and that the daughter should call her aunt if declarant did not return; holding that Cal. Evid. Code § 1250 (state of mind exception) was intended in part to codify *Alcalde* rule). For a narrow interpretation of FED. R. EVID. 803(3), see United States v. Jenkins, 579 F.2d 840, 843 (4th Cir. 1978) stating in dicta that "Congress directed only that [Rule 803(3)] be construed to confine the doctrine in *Hillmon* so that statements of intent by declarant would be admissible only to prove the Declarant's future conduct, not the future conduct of others"). *See generally* Diane Kiesel, Comment, *One Person's Thoughts, Another Person's Acts: How the Federal Circuit Courts Interpret the* Hillmon *Doctrine*, 33 CATH. U. L. REV. 699 (1984).

51 Mutual Life Ins. Co. v. Hillmon, 145 U.S. 285, 288 & 295–300 (1892) (admitting statement "I expect to leave Wichita on or about March the 5th, with a certain Mr. Hillmon" for the truth of the matter asserted).

52 *See* FED. R. EVID. 803(3) advisory committee note.

53 *See* House Comm. on the Judiciary, H.R. REP. NO. 93–650 at 5 (1973).

54 Nevertheless, it is worth noting that the party in *Hillmon* against whom the evidence was offered, though objecting to the statement's admission for any purpose, would not have objected to the statement being used to prove Hillmon's intentions once the statement was found admissible to prove the declarant's intention. The issue was whether a body found at Crooked Creek was that of Hillmon. To the extent the statement was offered to show the body might have been that of Walters, the declarant, it also increases the likelihood that the body was that of Hillmon. Thus, once Walters's statement was admitted, the opponent logically would have *wanted* the reference to Hillmon to be heard by the jury. The same would not be true in the case of the person who announces that she intends to go out with Harry. It is unlikely that there would be any real issue as to the declarant's having gone out; the real question would be with whom. To the extent the statement mentions the defendant, defendant will obviously object to its admission to prove his intention to go out with the declarant.

55 *See, e.g.*, United States v. Best, 219 F.3d 192, 197–99 (2d Cir. 2000). This can perhaps best be understood as accepting the House Report's limitation and rejecting admission subject to a limiting instruction because of the risk of misuse by the jury unless independent evidence confirms the other's act. *See* 4 CHRISTOPHER B. MUELLER & LAIRD C. KIRKPATRICK, FEDERAL EVIDENCE § 8:72 at 651–52 (4th ed. 2013).

56 The provision rarely arises in federal court because federal courts do not have probate jurisdiction. But it is commonly employed in state courts. *See, e.g.*, Montgomery v. Montgomery, 205 P.3d 650, 658 (Idaho 2009) (holding that testator's statements were admissible to show that he intended his wife to receive only the minimal devise stated in the will).

substitutes, such inter-vivos trusts and designations of at-death beneficiaries for retirement funds and life insurance, though the rule does not say as much.[57]

Present-state-of-mind statements often arise where hearsay is embedded within hearsay, but it is nonetheless admissible to show the declarant's state of mind, contained within an out-of-court statement by a co-conspirator. For example, suppose that the co-conspirator made an out-of-court statement to an undercover agent who was pretending to be part of the conspiracy. In the out-of-court statement, the co-conspirator said that a parking lot attendant told him she was planning to close the gates at 10:00. The co-conspirator is now dead. The statement of the dead co-conspirator is offered in evidence through the testimony of the undercover agent. The purpose of the testimony is to prove that the gates were closed at 10:00. Using Professor Younger's method, described in an earlier section,[58] once the foundation for the co-conspirator exception has been laid, we imagine the co-conspirator has come alive and appeared on the witness stand to testify against the other conspirators. As a live witness, could he testify that the parking lot attendant told him that she was going to close the gates at 10:00? Yes, because under Rule 803(3) the statement of intent to do a future act is admissible as evidence that the future act was done. Each statement fits within an exception or exclusion to the hearsay rule and the evidence is admissible.

United States v. Diez provides another illustration.[59] The *Diez* court approved the admission of a statement of intent contained within a co-conspirator statement. The co-conspirator had given the agent an account of something that an IRS agent had told the co-conspirator. The court noted that the co-conspirator's statement was admissible under Rule 801(d)(2), and then noted:

> The fact that [co-conspirator] DeGuzman's statement, like numerous others introduced at trial, relied on a statement by another person does not render the testimony inadmissible. [Internal Revenue Service] Agent Hunting's statement, reported to Agent Brock [the witness] by DeGuzman, was a statement of his intention to classify Palori as a dealer in real estate. The statement was received not to prove that Palori was or had been classified as a dealer, but rather to prove that Agent Hunting intended to regard him as one. The statement was thus a "statement of the declarant's then existing state of mind, emotion, sensation, or physical condition (such as intent, plan, motive, design, mental feeling, pain and bodily health)" and falls under the well-established exception to the hearsay rule for such statements. Fed. R. Evid. Rule 803(3).[60]

§ 16.05 Statements for Medical Diagnosis or Treatment [FRE 803(4)]

Rule 803(4) creates an exception for statements made for and reasonably pertinent to medical diagnosis or treatment. The statements must describe medical history, past or present symptoms, when or why the symptoms started, or their general cause. The

---

[57] *See, e.g.*, Primerica Life Ins. Co. v. Watson, 207 S.W.3d 443, 447–48 (Ark. 2004) (in a dispute between ex-wife and widow over life insurance proceeds, holding admissible statements of decedent-insured to third parties describing his belief that he had changed the beneficiary designation to his current spouse).

[58] *See* **§ 14.07**.

[59] United States v. Diez, 515 F.2d 892 (5th Cir. 1975).

[60] *Id.* 895–96 n.2.

exception is grounded in an obvious assumption that patients have a strong incentive to be truthful when making such statements.[61]

The most important restriction on this exception is that the statement must be relevant to medical diagnosis. A statement that "I was hit by a car that went through a red light" would not be admissible in full because the statement about the red light is not pertinent to diagnosis or treatment.[62] A statement such as "I slipped on a banana peel" is problematic; the fact that the patient slipped on a banana peel arguably tends to rebut the theory that the patient had a balance disorder or was intoxicated, and hence is relevant to diagnosis and treatment. Arguably, the statement should be redacted so that only the portion saying that the declarant "slipped" is admissible.[63]

Rule 803(4) creates a relatively broad exception:

1. The Rule does not require that the statement be made to a physician. As long as it is made for purposes of obtaining diagnosis or treatment, it could be made to anyone—an ambulance attendant, a nurse, or even, in the right circumstances, a family member.[64]

2. The statement need not be made by the person who was injured or who suffers from the condition being treated or diagnosed. For example, if a mother brings in a child and describes the child's accident from her firsthand knowledge, her statement falls under the Rule.[65]

---

61 *See* FED. R. EVID. 803(4) advisory committee note (noting the "patient's strong motivation to be truthful").

62 *Id.*; *see also* Merrow v. Bofferding, 581 N.W.2d 696, 701–03 (Mich. 1998) (excluding hospital record stating that plaintiff put his arm through plate glass window after "fight with his girlfriend"; though hospital record fits business record exception, hearsay-within-hearsay in record must be shown to fit another exception; reference to fight with girlfriend had no medical relevance and was not admissible under Rule 803(4); statement also not admissible to impeach or as admission of a party because of inadequate foundation showing that plaintiff was the person who made the statement); *cf.* Cook v. Hoppin, 783 F.2d 684, 689–90 (7th Cir. 1986). (finding reversible error in trial court's admission of a statement in a hospital record that an injury had been caused by a "shoving or wrestling match;." the anonymous source of the statement was not under any business duty to make it, so Rule 803(6) did not apply to it; Rule 803(4) could not be used as a basis for receiving the evidence because Rule 803(4) does not apply to "statements relating to fault which are not relevant to diagnosis or treatment."). *See also* Brown v. St. Paul City Ry. Co., 62 N.W.2d 688, 695–96 (Minn. 1954) (holding inadmissible statement in hospital record that plaintiff's injury occurred when she fell from a step after streetcar door "was closed suddenly in her face").

63 *See* United States v. Pollard, 790 F.2d 1309, 1312–14 (7th Cir. 1986), *overruled on other grounds by* United States v. Sblendorio, 830 F.2d 1382 (7th Cir. 1987) (finding reversible error to exclude portion of medical record relating to cause, though portion relating to fault clearly inadmissible); Roberts v. Hollocher, 664 F.2d 200, 204–05 (8th Cir. 1981) (excluding portion of hospital report, based on patient's statements, that said patient's injuries were "consistent with excessive force" because statement was a "a conclusion going to fault rather than the cause of the condition and does not serve to promote diagnosis or treatment"). Statements regarding identity of individual responsible for injuries or condition are seldom pertinent to treatment or diagnosis. *See* United States v. Iron Shell, 633 F.2d 77, 84 (8th Cir. 1980).

64 FED. R. EVID. 803(4) advisory committee note; *see also* Davignon v. Clemmey, 322 F.3d 1, 8 (1st Cir. 2003) (holding that statement to social worker in effort to enlist help in addressing mental health issues fell under medical treatment exception); United States v. Armstrong, 36 M.J. 311, 313–14 (C.M.A. 1993) (holding that statements made by child sex abuse victim during interview with psychologist and trial counsel were inadmissible because statements were made by victim to trial counsel in preparation for trial, not by victim to doctor for purposes of medical treatment).

65 *See* Lovejoy v. United States, 92 F.3d 628, 631–32 (8th Cir. 1996) (holding that mother's statement to care provider on behalf of handicapped child describing abuse of child witnessed by mother admissible under exception); United States v. Yazzie, 59 F.3d 807, 812 (9th Cir. 1995) (parent's note declaring that "Step-dad brain-washed" victim and "I ask help, please" deemed admissible in child sex abuse case because the statements were apparently made to aid medical treatment of child). Weinstein explains that as the relationship between the affected person and the declarant becomes less close, the statement will be less

3. The Rule is not limited to statements of present symptoms. If made for purposes of medical diagnosis or treatment, statements of past symptoms ("My back has been hurting for three years") are admissible. So are statements about the cause of an injury ("I drank a beer that had a mouse in it") if reasonably pertinent to diagnosis or treatment.

4. Most controversially, the Rule does not require that the statement be made to someone who is going to provide treatment. For example, statements made to expert physicians whose only function is to provide testimony fall within the ambit of the Rule because of the Rule's intentionally inclusive reference to "diagnosis *or* treatment." This result seems inconsistent with the rationale of the exception that persons who make statements for treatment will be careful to be accurate, since their health depends upon it. However, the advisory committee reasoned that courts would have allowed a non-treating expert to describe the patient's statements anyway, in order to show a basis for the diagnosis. The theory was that the statements are admissible not for their truth but to show that the doctor was diligent in forming the diagnosis. If admissible under this theory, then a limiting instruction would be appropriate. As the advisory committee pointed out, however, such a limiting instruction would be rather difficult to follow.[66] One could handle this problem by deciding that this type of credibility bolstering is not permissible because the jury could not follow the limiting instruction. Instead, the advisory committee elected to remove the need for the limiting instruction by providing that the statements made to the forensic expert are admissible without limit, on the same basis as statements made to a treating physician.[67] Nevertheless, the statement must have had a nonspurious diagnostic purpose.[68]

Some courts have used Rule 803(4) to admit the statements of sexual assault victims to physicians who have examined them after the assault, including statements identifying the perpetrator or describing the details of the incident. One justification has been that the physician must treat the whole patient, psychologically as well as physically, and that what the perpetrator said to the victim and the identity of the perpetrator can be relevant to treatment in the broader sense.[69]

---

reliable and courts might exclude it under the Rule 403 balancing test. 5 WEINSTEIN'S FEDERAL EVIDENCE § 803.06[5] (Mark S. Brodin ed., 2d ed. 2015).

[66] FED. R. EVID. 803(4) advisory committee note. In 2000, Rule 703 was amended to make less likely the limited admissibility upon which the advisory committee extended the hearsay exception to statements made to non-treating physicians, but Rule 803(4) was left unchanged. *See* **§ 10.05**.

[67] *See, e.g.*, United States v. Whitted, 994 F.2d 444, 446–47 (8th Cir. 1993), *reh'g granted and opinion vacated on other grounds*, 11 F.3d 782 (8th Cir. 1993) (holding that trial court acted within its discretion by allowing government doctor retained solely as a trial witness to repeat statements made by alleged child victim of sex abuse).

[68] *Cf.* United States v. Armstrong, 36 M.J. 311, 313–14 (C.M.A. 1993) (ruling statements made by child sex abuse victim during interview with psychologist and trial counsel inadmissible because statements were made by victim to trial counsel in preparation for trial, not by victim to doctor for purposes of medical treatment).

[69] *See* United States v. Cherry, 938 F.2d 748, 756–57 (7th Cir. 1991) (holding that, in case arising from sexual abuse on military base, district court did not abuse discretion in admitting statements of victim to doctor in which victim said to doctor, "He held my arms so I couldn't do anything. He laid me on the floor and had intercourse with me. He said not to tell anyone."); United States v. Renville, 779 F.2d 430, 436–38 (8th Cir.

Statements made for diagnosis or treatment are often also admissible under other exceptions. For example, the statement, "my leg hurts" is probably admissible under Rule 803(3) as a statement of then existing physical condition and (if made under the stress of excitement caused by a startling event) under Rule 803(2) as an excited utterance.

Patients' statements described in hospital records raise the special problem of hearsay within hearsay. To be admissible under the Rules, each statement in the chain must fall within an exception to the hearsay rule.[70] The patient's statement may be admissible under Rule 803(4), and the statement of the person who records the patient's statement may be admissible under the business records exception.[71]

Doctor-to-patient statements generally are not covered by this rule,[72] though they often may be admissible under another exception, such as the business record rule.

§ 16.06 Past Recollection Recorded [FRE 803(5)]

Rule 803(5) provides a hearsay exception when a witness once had knowledge but now cannot remember it well enough "to testify fully and accurately." The exception permits the introduction of a record "made or adopted by the witness when the matter was fresh in the witness's memory" that "accurately reflect the witness's knowledge" at the time. If the record is admitted, it can be read into evidence. The rationale for Rule 803(5) is threefold: (1) *necessity*—the witness has insufficient memory to testify fully and accurately; (2) *trustworthiness*—the memorandum or report was made while the matter was fresh in the witness's memory and was embodied in a writing or recording; and (3) *opportunity for cross-examination of the witness*—a witness who made or adopted the

1985) (admitting statements by child abuse victim that abuser is member of victim's immediate household are reasonably pertinent to treatment because of the need for psychological treatment); United States v. Norman T., 129 F.3d 1099, 1105–06 (10th Cir. 1997) (applying Rule 803(4) to statements of five-year-old to physician and nurse accusing defendant of digital penetration considered reasonably pertinent to diagnosis or treatment, rejecting defense argument that a child that young does not understand the need for accuracy in reporting to medical personnel); United States v. Moreno, 36 M.J. 107, 120 (C.M.A. 1992) (admitting statement of teenager hospitalized for suicide attempt, that depression was partly due to sexual activity with his stepfather, admissible under exception); Eleanor Swift, *The Hearsay Rule at Work: Has It Been Abolished De Facto by Judicial Decision?*, 76 MINN. L. REV. 473, 498 (1992) (describing permissive decisions which use exceptions such as excited utterances, statement for diagnosis or treatment, and residual hearsay exception to admit out-of-court statements made by child victims of sexual abuse); *cf.* State v. Haslam, 663 A.2d 902, 908 (R.I. 1995) (holding that a prior statement by a counselor, who testified that a minor patient had previously identified the defendant as her molester, was inadmissible as a prior consistent statement under Rule 801(d)(1)(B) because the prior statement was not made before the motive to lie arose; apparently proceeding on the assumption that identity of the perpetrator would not be within the scope of 803(4)). For an especially expansive interpretation of the medical treatment exception in sex abuse cases, see United States v. Yazzie, 59 F.3d 807, 812 (9th Cir. 1995) (holding that, although statements assigning blame for an injury are not normally admissible under the medical treatment exception, they are admissible in sexual abuse cases because the physician must treat emotional as well as physical injuries, and a parent's note declaring "Step-dad brain-washed" victim and "I ask help, please" was apparently made to aid medical treatment of child). *See also* United States v. Tome, 61 F.3d 1446 (10th Cir. 1995) (10th Circuit decision following Supreme Court reversal and remand) (holding that sexual abuse victim's out-of-court statements to three pediatricians identifying her father as her abuser were properly admitted under Rule 803(4) as reasonably pertinent to the victim's treatment or diagnosis).

[70] FED. R. EVID. 805.

[71] *See* FED. R. EVID. 803(6).

[72] Bombard v. Fort Wayne Newspapers, Inc., 92 F.3d 560, 564 (7th Cir. 1996) (holding doctor's statement to patient recommending course of treatment inadmissible under Rule 803(4), which was not designed to cover statements by the person providing the medical attention).

memorandum will be available for testimony, notwithstanding the acknowledged memory deficit.[73]

Establishing the Foundation for a Past Recollection Recorded

The foundational requirements of the past recollection recorded exception must be satisfied before a writing or recording may be received as substantive evidence.[74] Rule 803(5) requires that:

1. The witness once had sufficient personal knowledge of the underlying events to meet the personal knowledge requirement of Rule 602 if the witness were testifying about these matters;
2. The witness "made or adopted" the record.[75] The "made or adopted" requirement of Rule 803(5) would seem to require that the person whose recollection has been recorded either make the record or examine and approve it. However, that interpretation of the rule has not been universal;[76]
3. The record was made or adopted when the matter was fresh in the witness's memory;
4. The record accurately reflects the witness's knowledge;[77] and

---

[73] See 4 CHRISTOPHER B. MUELLER & LAIRD C. KIRKPATRICK, FEDERAL EVIDENCE § 8:76 at 696 (4th ed. 2013). A record that fails to meet the trustworthiness requirement of the business records exception, Rule 803(6), can be admitted under the recorded recollection exception. *See* Parker v. Reda, 327 F.3d 211 (2d Cir. 2003) (holding that record made by prison official about use-of-force incident in which he was involved was admissible under recorded recollection exception even though not sufficiently reliable to be admitted as a business record; difference in treatment justified because person making the record is available for cross-examination in case of recorded recollection).

[74] *See, e.g.*, United States v. Riccardi, 174 F.2d 883 (3d Cir. 1949). The Third Circuit stated:

> Whether the record is directly admitted into evidence, or indirectly by the permissive parroting of the witness, it is nevertheless a substitute for his memory and is offered for the truth of its contents. It assumes a distinct significance as an independent probative force, and is therefore ordinarily required to meet certain standards. These requirements are [necessary because] the court is . . . determining whether the writing may be safely received as a substitute for the witness's memory and for the truth of the matter asserted.

Id. at 887–88 (footnotes omitted).

[75] The witness does not have to make the record. A record adopted while the matter was fresh in the witness's mind may be admissible under Rule 803(5). Moreover, the advisory comments to Rule 803(5) state that multiple person involvement in the process of observing and recording is entirely consistent with the exception. FED. R. EVID. 803(5) advisory committee note.

[76] Boehmer v. LeBoeuf, 650 A.2d 1336 (Me. 1994), in interpreting a Maine rule identical in wording to FED. R. EVID. 803(5), stated that a person whose recollection is recorded by another in a "jointly produced past recollection recorded" need not have physically adopted or verified the record in order for the exception to apply. Under the facts of the case before it, however, the court held that the trial court did not abuse its discretion in excluding an investigator's notes of a child witness's recollection of the accident made two months after the accident, because it was reasonable for the court to find that there had not been a sufficient showing that the notes were accurate when made.

[77] *See* United States v. Edwards, 539 F.2d 689, 692 (9th Cir. 1976) (concluding that declarant's intoxication at time he made statement bears heavily on weight to be given statement, but not on its admissibility where declarant testified that he believed the statement accurately reflected his recollection at the time it was made, statement was signed and acknowledged by declarant, and government agent who was present at the interview testified that declarant's answers were "fairly detailed narrations"); *cf.* United States v. Porter, 986 F.2d 1014, 1017 (6th Cir. 1993) (admitting girlfriend's repudiated prior statement implicating defendant, claiming she was confused and on drugs when statement was made because, among other things, witness signed and made corrections to statement immediately after events giving rise to prosecution).

5. The witness cannot testify "fully and accurately" from present memory[78] about the facts recorded in the record (counsel must lay the foundation showing lack of present memory because if the witness has a present memory of the facts recited in the record, the witness's memory is considered superior to the hearsay record).[79]

Requirements (2) through (4), attempt to ensure that the witness accurately recorded his knowledge when the witness remembered what he perceived.[80]

Once counsel establishes its foundation under Rule 803(5), a document may be read into evidence but cannot be received as an exhibit or sent to the jury unless offered by the opposing party.[81] The rationale for this limitation is that the memorandum is a substitute for oral testimony, and offering the memorandum into evidence may encourage the jury to give it undue emphasis in relation to other oral testimony.[82]

Example

Imagine a case in which counsel's witness is expected to testify about the contents of a warehouse, but on the stand the witness cannot remember everything that was in the warehouse. Counsel attempts to proceed as follows with a list of what was in the warehouse:

Q: I show you plaintiff's Exhibit 1. What is it?

A: A list of the items in the warehouse.

Q: Now, please tell us what was in the warehouse.

A: [Witness reads list]

This procedure is objectionable and the witness should not be permitted to read from the list because the foundational requirements of Rule 803(5) have not been satisfied. To present the testimony in admissible form:

1. After showing the witness the list, the witness must testify that the witness's memory is not refreshed. Although the witness's recollection must be impaired, it need not be wholly exhausted before the record is

---

78 *See, e.g.*, United States v. Judon, 567 F.2d 1289, 1294 (5th Cir. 1978) (finding error in admitting statement under Rule 803(5) where there was no showing of witness's insufficient recollection); United States v. Felix-Jerez, 667 F.2d 1297, 1300 (9th Cir. 1982) (finding error in admitting marshal's written statement based on his notes of an interview with defendant where there was no showing marshal had insufficient recollection to testify). Thus, the proponent of a recorded recollection must show that the witness's memory was not refreshed by the record.

79 *See* Meder v. Everest & Jennings, Inc., 637 F.2d 1182, 1185–86 (8th Cir. 1981) (holding that police report that contained information officer did not personally know but obtained from someone else constituted hearsay within hearsay and was not admissible under Rule 803(5)).

80 5 WEINSTEIN'S FEDERAL EVIDENCE § 803.07[1] (Mark S. Brodin ed., 2d ed. 2015). A witness who does not remember the facts recorded cannot be cross-examined about his or her perception and, thus, direct testimony about what the witness perceived cannot be obtained. If offered against the accused in a criminal case, this may raise an issue under the confrontation clause if the witness has no recollection about the underlying event because the witness's perception cannot adequately be tested by cross-examination.

81 *See, e.g.*, United States v. Ray, 768 F.2d 991, 995 (8th Cir. 1985) (recognizing transcript of defendant's prior attorney's statement was properly admitted under Rule 803(5), but holding admission of transcript as an exhibit constituted reversible error where the statement was the only evidence on a crucial element of the charged offense).

82 *See* Jack R. Jelsema, William S. Murphy, William B. Nichols & Sanford Tannenbaum, Comment, *Hearsay Under the Proposed Federal Rules: A Discretionary Approach*, 15 WAYNE L. REV. 1077, 1139 (1969).

admissible as evidence.[83] If the witness's memory has been refreshed, counsel should retrieve the list and resume questioning the witness about the items in the warehouse. Because the witness is testifying from present memory and the document merely refreshed that memory, the use of the list is not a hearsay use; counsel is not putting the contents of a hearsay record into evidence, and hence not trying to prove its truth.

2. After showing the witness the list, the witness should testify:

   a. The witness made or adopted the list; and

   b. Such creation or adoption occurred when the witness's memory of the warehouse's contents was fresh. Many factors affect whether the matter was sufficiently fresh, including: the time when list was made, the quality of memory in the list, and whether the list was made before litigation commenced. Under Rule 803(5), courts have discretion to interpret the concept of "freshness" broadly;[84] and

   c. The list was accurate when made or adopted; and

   d. The witness does not now fully remember what was in the warehouse. Although the witness cannot remember the warehouse's contents, the witness can remember being careful in making the list of items. The witness must testify either that the witness recalls making an accurate list or that, although the witness does not specifically recollect the witness's state of mind when making the list, the witness would not have made or adopted it unless it were correct.[85]

Now, the list may be read into evidence, but it will not be received as an exhibit unless offered by the adverse party.

Refreshed Memory Distinguished

The technique of refreshing a witness's memory is sometimes confused with the hearsay exception for past recollection recorded. The Third Circuit described the distinction between refreshing memory and past recollection recorded in *United States v. Riccardi*:[86]

[83] A judge should admit pertinent portions of a recorded recollection that fail to refresh the witness's present memory. *See, e.g.*, United States v. Williams, 571 F.2d 344 (6th Cir. 1978) (admitting statement made to government agent with where witness's memory sufficient to testify generally about his conversations with defendant but did not recall whether defendant told him how the defendant acquired the forged government checks); United States v. Senak, 527 F.2d 129, 137–38 (7th Cir. 1975) (admitting statement made to FBI agent where witness told part of conversation and cannot remember the rest); Fortier v. Dona Anna Plaza Partners, 747 F.2d 1324, 1332 (10th Cir. 1984) (admitting subsurface report referred to by an expert witness in a negligent construction case as the recorded recollection of an expert witness as it enabled the expert to testify fully and accurately).

[84] *See, e.g.*, United States v. Patterson, 678 F.2d 774, 778 (9th Cir. 1982) (trial judge's finding, that witness's memory was fresh at the time he testified before grand jury about his conversation with defendant although 10 months elapsed between the conversation and grand jury appearance, did not abuse the broad discretion intended by Rule 803(5)); 5 WEINSTEIN'S FEDERAL EVIDENCE § 803.07[3][b] (Mark S. Brodin ed., 2d ed. 2015).

[85] *See, e.g.*, 3 WIGMORE ON EVIDENCE § 747 (Chadbourn rev., 1970) ("[T]he witness must be able now to assert that the record accurately represented (the witness') knowledge at the time . . . the witness [must] affirm that [he] knew it to be true at the time").

[86] United States v. Riccardi, 174 F.2d 883 (3d Cir. 1949).

> The primary difference between the two classifications is the ability of the witness to testify from present knowledge; where the witness's memory is revived, and he presently recollects the facts and swears to them, he is obviously in a different position from the witness who cannot directly state the facts from present memory and who must ask the court to accept a writing for the truth of its contents because he is willing to swear, for one reason or another, that its contents are true.[87]

Under Rule 612, any writing shown to a witness must also be shared with opposing counsel and the judge. Because documents used to refresh memory are not evidence, otherwise inadmissible documents may be used to refresh memory. For example, if a state statute provides that accident reports are inadmissible, counsel can still use the accident report to refresh the memory of a witness on the stand.[88] Because the report is not being used as evidence, and the witness on the stand at the trial or hearing is testifying from (now refreshed) memory, the hearsay rule is not implicated.

The following features of refreshing memory distinguish it from using a writing as past recollection recorded:

1. Counsel may use anything to stimulate or refresh the witness's memory, regardless of whether the thing was prepared by the witness or somebody else. The memory prompt need not be a writing; it may be anything that might help to jog the witness's memory. Professor Faust Rossi is rightfully famous for the following example:

   Q: Where were you on October 10th?

   A: I can't recall.

   Q: Does this plate of fettuccine remind you?

   A: Oh, yes. I was at Alfredo's Restaurant in New York City.[89]

2. The witness's memory must actually be refreshed before the witness can testify; the witness must testify independently from memory because the witness cannot read from a writing on the witness stand without first satisfying Rule 803(5).

3. A writing or recording used to refresh the witness's memory is not admissible unless the opponent offers it.

4. The witness does not have to testify that the document is accurate because the document is only being used to awaken the witness's memory, not as evidence. If counsel uses the witness's notes to refresh memory and the notes differ from the witness's testimony, opposing counsel can use the notes to impeach the witness.

---

[87] *Id.* at 886 (footnote omitted). *See* United States v. Rinke, 778 F.2d 581, 587–88 (10th Cir. 1985) (trial judge properly permitted witness to use notes of telephone conversations with defendants to refresh his memory while testifying).

[88] *See, e.g.*, State v. Schultz, 392 N.W.2d 305, 307 (Minn. Ct. App. 1986) (recognizing that use of accident report to refresh a police officer's memory while testifying to facts within his knowledge permitted although report inadmissible under state statute).

[89] See John J. Capowski, *Evidence and the One-Liner: A Beginning Evidence Professor's Exploration of the Use of Humor in the Law School Classroom*, 35 ARIZ. ST. L. J. 877, 887 (2003) (recounting a variant of Rossi's famous example).

§ 16.07 Business Records [FRE 803(6)]

Rule 803(6) creates a hearsay exception for business records. A business record is a record of an "act, event, condition, opinion, or diagnosis" made "at or near the time" of the event recorded by a person with knowledge, or from information transmitted by someone with knowledge. The record must have been kept "in the course of a regularly conducted" activity of a business or organization, and making such a record must have been the "regular practice" of that business activity. The record may be that of any "business, organization, occupation, or calling, whether or not for-profit." The exception does not apply, however, if the "source of information" or the "method or circumstances of preparation" indicate a "lack of trustworthiness."[90]

The business records exception is justified on the grounds that:

- businesses possess an independent motive to be accurate for the sake of profit and viability;
- regularity breeds habits of precision;
- systematic checking is likely;
- careless employees face the danger of being fired and hence have an incentive to be accurate; and
- it would be impractical, and often uninformative, to have every employee who participated in the creation of a business record testify in court.[91]

By its terms, the exception extends to "opinions" and "diagnoses," language of obvious importance for hospital and other medical records.[92]

Regular Practice of the Regularly Conducted Business

To lay the foundation for a business record the proponent must show that the record was made in the course of a regularly conducted business activity and that it was the regular practice of that business to make the record.[93]

Occasionally, a record made in the course of business will be rejected on the ground that the proponent failed to demonstrate that it was the "regular practice" to make such

---

[90] FED. R. EVID. 803(6).

[91] FED. R. EVID. 803(6) advisory committee note; 2 MCCORMICK ON EVIDENCE § 286 (Kenneth S. Broun ed., 7th ed. 2013); United States v. Snyder, 787 F.2d 1429, 1433–34 (10th Cir. 1986) (describing general rationale for the business records exception).

[92] Despite this language, opinions in business records are sometimes excluded. *See, e.g.*, Vance v. Peters, 97 F.3d 987, 995 (7th Cir. 1996). (excluding the finding of an employee review officer, signed by the warden, that the guard had used excessive force against a prisoner even though the requirements of Rule 803(6) were met; holding that Rule 403 required exclusion because the jury should make up its own mind). The authors believe that decision deprives plaintiff of valuable evidence by persons quite capable of forming a judgment on the subject, and who are unlikely to make such a finding unless it was true. (We also note the possible application of the public records exception (Rule 803(8)) and the statement-by-agents rule (Rule 801(d)(2)(D) in this context).

[93] *See* FED. R. EVID. 803(6)(B) & (C). *See also* 2 MCCORMICK ON EVIDENCE § 288 (Kenneth S. Broun ed., 7th ed. 2013). For examples of records held admissible, see Malek v. Federal Ins. Co., 994 F.2d 49, 53 (2d Cir. 1993) (social worker's case notes admissible); United States v. Versaint, 849 F.2d 827, 831–32 (3d Cir. 1988) (police report admissible); United States v. Chatman, 994 F.2d 1510, 1516 (10th Cir. 1993) (trial court properly admitted records of calls made from cellular phone when records routinely printed for billing purposes); United States v. Catabran, 836 F.2d 453, 457 (9th Cir. 1988) (computer printouts of accounting data admissible); City of Idaho Falls v. Beco Constr. Co., 850 P.2d 165, 172–73 (Idaho 1993) (computer printout summary of labor and equipment costs admissible).

records. For example, in *United States v. Freidin*,[94] the defendant, a tax partner in a large accounting firm, was charged with filing false income tax returns and making a false statement to the IRS in connection with those returns. The defendant received a substantial fee from a client that he allegedly deposited in his personal account at his firm without reporting the fee on his income taxes. During his IRS audit, he claimed to have turned over the fee to his firm. One of the crucial pieces of government evidence was an internal office memorandum of the accounting firm memorializing Freidin's directive to place the fee in his own personal account. The memo, which was prepared by the secretary to the controller, stated that Freidin had given her a check for $22,000 and told her that it was to go into his personal account. There was no testimony at trial that it was the regular practice of the business to make such memoranda. Instead, the testimony was that only the partners' secretaries normally made directives about depositing money in personal accounts, and only at the direction of a partner. Rejecting the argument that the record need not be a routine record if it was made in the regular course of business, the court found this record to be an "isolated document" and held that it should have been excluded on grounds that it was not the regular practice of the business to make this type of record. The court acknowledged that it was taking a narrow view of the "regular practice" requirement and noted the existence of authority taking a broader view.[95]

Authentication with and Without a Testifying Witness

The federal rules allow the custodian or other qualified witness to lay the foundation for a business record.[96] The witness need not have made the record or have custody of it. The witness must, however, be able to testify that:

- the record is made as a regularly conducted business activity;
- it is the practice of that business to make that type of record;
- the source of the information was a person with knowledge; and
- the record was made at or near the time of the event.[97]

Note that the witness need not testify, at least initially, to facts attempting to satisfy part (E) of Rule 803, which places the burden on the opponent to show that the record lacks trustworthiness, as discussed below.

Applying a rule identical to Federal Rule 803(6), the Minnesota Supreme Court has allowed a witness who was not an employee of the business to lay the foundation for a business record. The record in question was a report by a nonprofit quality-assurance organization, Underwriters' Laboratories, and the witness laying the foundation demonstrated that he was familiar with the operations and procedures employed by the

---

94 United States v. Freidin, 849 F.2d 716 (2d Cir. 1988).

95 *See also* United States v. Wells, 262 F.3d 455, 461–63 (5th Cir. 2001) (holding that witness should not have been permitted to testify from memory about the contents of destroyed drug ledgers; foundation elements, such as showing records were kept in course of regularly conducted business, were missing); Pierce v. Atchison Topeka & Santa Fe Ry. Co., 110 F.3d 431, 444 (7th Cir. 1997) (finding no abuse of discretion in excluding memo summarizing corporate executive's discussions with plaintiff about release of ADEA claim where district court concluded that memo was not regular or routine because it recorded an "unusual incident" that had "litigation potential"); United States v. Davis, 571 F.2d 1354, 1359 (5th Cir. 1978) (error to admit form indicating Colt had manufactured and shipped gun to Georgia when Colt did not make such records as a regular practice).

96 *See* FED. R. EVID. 803(6)(D).

97 *See* 2 MCCORMICK ON EVIDENCE § 292 at 447 (Kenneth S. Broun ed., 7th ed. 2013).

organization for product certification.[98] Some courts have gone further, allowing records of a business to be sponsored by outsiders who merely relied on those records in their own separate business.[99]

The amendments to the Federal Rules of Evidence enacted in 2000 allow the proponent to authenticate business records without producing a foundation witness. The proponent may do so by producing an affidavit from a person with knowledge averring that the record was:

- made at or near the time of the occurrence;
- made from information transmitted by a person with knowledge;
- kept in the regular course of business; and
- made by a business whose regular practice it was to make the record.[100]

Personal Knowledge

The business records exception does not require strict personal knowledge. For example, to admit a bookkeeper's ledger, it is not necessary that the bookkeeper have personal knowledge of the underlying transactions represented by the entry. However, the rule does require either personal knowledge or that the information was transmitted by a person with knowledge.[101] Several layers of hearsay may be involved without

---

[98] National Tea Co. v. Tyler Refrigeration Co., 339 N.W.2d 59, 61–62 (Minn. 1983). *But see* Karme v. Commissioner, 673 F.2d 1062, 1064 (9th Cir. 1982) (holding records inadmissible when purported foundation provided by government agent, not a custodian or qualified witness capable of testifying that bank records were kept as regularly conducted business activity).

[99] *See* MRT Const. Inc. v. Hardrives, Inc., 158 F.3d 478, 483 (9th Cir. 1998) (holding that client could lay foundation for bills of law firm if client relied on accuracy of bills in client's own business); United States v. Duncan, 919 F.2d 981, 985–87 (5th Cir. 1990) (holding that insurance company representative could lay foundation for hospital records contained within insurance company records where insurance company routinely relied on hospital records); *see also* Cameron v. Otto Bock Orthopedic Indus., 43 F.3d 14, 16 (1st Cir. 1994) (holding that post-accident "product failure reports" were inadmissible hearsay that did not fall under the business records exception because such reports had been prepared by prosthetists based partly upon reports from patients;. "[w]hile the reports may be part of the business records of Otto Bock in a colloquial sense, that does not render admissible information contained in the records whose source is a non-party to the business. Under Fed. R. Evid. 803(6), the report must be made by a person acting 'in the course of a regularly conducted business activity.' It is quite clear that the prosthetists' patients are not part of Otto Bock's business.") *But see* National Labor Relations Bd. v. First Termite Control Co., 646 F.2d 424 (9th Cir. 1981) (holding freight bill inadmissible under the business records exception because the witness knew nothing about how the carrier prepared the freight bill and the company employing the witness did not rely upon or use the information concerning the lumber's origin).

[100] *See* FED. R. EVID. 803(6), 902(11), and 902(12), as amended effective December 1, 2000. *But see* CALIF. EVID. CODE § 1562 (on laying foundation for business records by affidavit). Even before the federal amendments, Rule 104(a), which allows trial judges to consider otherwise inadmissible hearsay in making preliminary determinations about whether foundation facts have been established, might have been read to allow a trial judge to permit the foundation for a business record to be established by affidavits. At least one court, however, declined to take that route on the facts before it. *See* Kolmes v. World Fibers Corp., 107 F.3d 1534, 1542–43 (Fed. Cir. 1997) (affidavits not sufficient to lay foundation for business record because opponent needed opportunity to cross-examine sponsoring witness; moreover, consultant to business could not sponsor records because of lack of familiarity with record-keeping procedures).

[101] FED. R. EVID. 803(6)(A). For an example of a case in which plaintiff failed to satisfy the rule, see Petrocelli v. Gallison, 679 F.2d 286, 289–91 (1st Cir. 1982). There, the plaintiff offered a hospital record that stated that plaintiff had suffered a severed nerve in earlier surgery at another hospital. The source of knowledge was not apparent from the record and it appeared unlikely that the physician or nurses at the second hospital would have personally observed the injury. The evidence was excluded for failure to show that the information was transmitted by a person with knowledge. *See also* Ricciardi v. Children's Hosp. Med. Ctr., 811 F.2d 18, 21–23 (1st Cir. 1987) (holding handwritten notation, not by doctor with personal knowledge of operation, inadmissible to show what happened during operation).

exceeding the bounds of the exception, so long as the proponent shows that the original source was a person with knowledge. For example, if employee A observes the transaction, reports it in the regular course of business to employee B, who transmits the information to employee C in the regular course, then the record created by C comes from information that has been transmitted by a person with knowledge and is admissible.[102]

Issues involving transmission by a person with knowledge have become more complicated with the advent of computerized record-keeping.[103] Today, businesses of all sizes make extensive use of spreadsheets, databases, and other complex software, and locating the source of a particular item within a record is a considerably more daunting task than doing so with handwritten ledgers. Indeed, even defining a "record" is complicated by the way computers store information and the fact that human input—often by a person with no knowledge of the data's accuracy—is necessary in order to retrieve information in a form that can be interpreted by a factfinder. As a result, while computerized record-keeping can be (and generally is) very accurate, courts must pay attention to how the information has been prepared, entered into the computer's storage system, and retrieved. One should not simply assume that because information was retrieved for trial from a computerized spreadsheet, database, or the like, that it is reliable. The careful lawyer must always remain a skeptic.[104]

Contemporaneity

Rule 803(6)(A) requires that the business record be made "at or near the time" of the event recorded. Thus, for example, where a telex (electronic message) describing bank deposits was made two years after the deposits, it did not satisfy this requirement of substantial contemporaneity.[105]

The Business Duty Requirement

The business duty rule, one of the most important limitations on the business records exception cannot be easily discerned from the language of Rule 803(6) or its statutory predecessors. In the leading pre-Rules case of *Johnson v. Lutz*,[106] the plaintiff in a wrongful death action offered a police officer's report of the accident involved. The police officer, who had not been present at the accident, based his report on bystander statements. The New York business record statute purported to eliminate any requirement of personal knowledge for business records. Nevertheless, the New York

---

[102] *See* 2 MCCORMICK ON EVIDENCE § 290 (Kenneth S. Broun ed., 7th ed. 2013); United States v. Baker, 693 F.2d 183, 188 (D.C. Cir. 1982) (discussing double hearsay problem in employment context).

[103] *See* **§ 12.09** (discussing authentication of computer-generated records).

[104] *See generally* Rudolph J. Peritz, *Computer Data and Reliability: A Call for the Authentication of Business Records Under the Federal Rules of Evidence*, 80 NW. U. L. REV. 956 (1986) (arguing that the party that offers computerized business records should be required to meet a high standard for qualification and discovery because of the special reliability problems created by electronic records); Cooper Offenbecher, *Admitting Computer Record Evidence After In re Vinhnee: A Stricter Standard for the Future?*, 4 SHIDLER J. L., COM. & TECH. 6 (2007).

[105] United States v. Kim, 595 F.2d 755, 760–63 (D.C. Cir. 1979); *cf.* Gulf South Mach., Inc. v. Kearney & Trecker Corp., 756 F.2d 377, 381 (5th Cir. 1985) (admitting logbook of machine malfunctions where similar books kept for other machines and entries logged within 24 hours of problem).

[106] Johnson v. Lutz, 170 N.E. 517 (N.Y. 1930).

court held that the hearsay exception did not apply to third-party hearsay where the source of the information possessed no business duty to report.[107]

The Advisory Committee for the Federal Rules of Evidence reached the same conclusion. *Johnson v. Lutz* was specifically cited and approved by the committee, which wrote that "[i]f . . . the supplier of the information does not act in the regular course [of business], an essential link is broken; the assurance of accuracy does not extend to the information [supplied]."[108] Cases decided under the Rules generally have followed this guidance.[109] Some courts have tended to water down the business duty requirement somewhat by holding that information provided by a customer of the business is admissible if the business made an effort to verify its accuracy.[110] Hotel registration information is a common example.[111] Where there was no such effort, however, the courts have tended to exclude the evidence, at least when offered as proof of the facts reported by the person outside the business.[112]

Of course, if the statement contained within the business record is admissible under another hearsay exception, then the business record exception and the other exception can combine to provide a route of admission.[113] For example, in *Kelly v. Wasserman*,[114] the New York Court of Appeals held that an entry in the records of the welfare

---

[107] For an interesting case excluding testimony based on police records on grounds that the police records contained hearsay from declarants who were under no business duty to report, see People v. Hernandez, 63 Cal.Rptr.2d 769 (Cal. Ct. App. 1997). Defendant was prosecuted for rape of two different victims committed in the same general area within a one-month period. The court allowed the prosecution to present the testimony of a police expert that she had searched the San Diego police department's "Sherlock" database for similar crimes, using search criteria such as "suspect not black" and "stranger rape" to identify similar cases. She reported that the only two rapes for an 18-month period in Beats 125 and 114 that had characteristics like those of the charged rapes were the charged rapes themselves. The prosecutor argued to the jury that the lack of evidence of similar crimes in the area before the defendant moved in or after his arrest pointed to the defendant. The court reversed defendant's conviction on hearsay grounds, saying that the "Sherlock" database did not qualify for the business records exception because it contained information from victims and witnesses who had no official duty to observe and report the relevant facts.

[108] FED. R. EVID. 803(6) advisory committee note.

[109] *See, e.g.*, Ramrattan v. Burger King Corp., 656 F. Supp. 522, 529 (D. Md. 1987) (excluding bystander's statement to police at site of auto accident because bystander was not acting in the regular course of business). *See generally* 4 CHRISTOPHER B. MUELLER & LAIRD C. KIRKPATRICK, FEDERAL EVIDENCE § 8:82 (4th ed. 2013).

[110] *See, e.g.*, United States v. Sokolow, 91 F.3d 396, 403–04 (3d Cir. 1996) (admitting insurance company documents containing unpaid insurance claims under business records exception, even though some of the people documenting the information were not under a business duty, because insurance company had standard practice of verifying information); United States v. Emenogha, 1 F.3d 473, 482 (7th Cir. 1993) (holding that trial court properly admitted Currency Transaction Reports to rebut defendant's claim that an impostor used his name; obtaining identification before commencing transaction was a regular business practice and bank employees testified as eyewitnesses to the transactions with defendant).

[111] *See, e.g.*, Wilson v. Zapata Off-Shore Co., 939 F.2d 260 (5th Cir. 1991) (admitting when hotel managed testified that it was standard practice to verify identity using the patron's driver's license).

[112] *See* United States v. Rogers, 556 F.3d 1130 (10th Cir. 2009) (distinguishing hotel registration information from departure log and excluding latter); United States v. McIntyre, 997 F.2d 687, 700–01 (10th Cir. 1993) (holding motel arrival and departure log inadmissible as business record when guest supplied relevant information, employee only recorded it, and motel had no specific policy asking guests to show identification; however, receiving evidence was not plain error). *See also* United States v. Vigneau, 187 F.3d 70, 74–75 (1st Cir. 1999) (holding Western Union sender forms listing defendant as sender of money orders inadmissible as Western Union business records because sender was under no business duty; Western Union did not require identification from senders); Stahl v. State, 686 N.E.2d 89, 91–92 (Ind. 1997) (holding affidavit executed for bank by customer, in which customer averred that he had not authorized anyone to use his ATM card, inadmissible in prosecution of person who withdrew money because customer under no business duty).

[113] *See* FED. R. EVID. 805 (providing that hearsay within hearsay is admissible if each statement falls within an exception). *See, e.g.*, United States v. Baker, 693 F.2d 183 (D.C. Cir. 1982).

[114] Kelly v. Wasserman, 158 N.E.2d 241 (N.Y. 1959).

department by a caseworker who had talked to one of the parties to a lawsuit was admissible. The entry stated that the defendant had promised to allow the plaintiff to live rent-free in an apartment the plaintiff had conveyed to him. The caseworker's statement was a business record, and the defendant's statement was the statement of a party-opponent.[115]

Lack of Trustworthiness

Rule 803(6)(E) provides that even if hearsay otherwise qualifies as a business record, it may be excluded if the opponent shows "that the source of information or the method or circumstances of preparation indicate a lack of trustworthiness." The burden is on the opponent to convince the trial judge to exclude on this basis, but it does not require a showing that the record is erroneous, merely that is untrustworthy.[116] The mere fact that a business record is self-serving does not mean that it will be excluded as untrustworthy. For example, a record showing that a department store customer owes money on a credit card is, when offered by the department store in a collection action, a self-serving statement. Yet, if it was prepared in the regular course of business, not specifically for litigation, and if the other requirements of the rule are met, it would be admitted routinely.[117] However, occasionally such records are found to lack the requisite trustworthiness.[118]

Probably the most common examples of records excluded for lack of trustworthiness are those that were prepared in anticipation of litigation. In a leading pre-Rules case, *Palmer v. Hoffman*,[119] the United States Supreme Court interpreted the federal business records statute to exclude from evidence a report prepared for a railroad by an engineer describing an accident in which the engineer had been involved. The Court held that statements prepared by parties in anticipation of litigation were not admissible under the exception, even if the business made a regular practice of collecting such reports. Searching for a way to exclude the report, the Court said that the railroad was in the railroad business, not the accident-reporting business, and therefore the accident report was not a business record.

The Advisory Committee for the Federal Rules of Evidence spoke approvingly of *Palmer v. Hoffman* in its note, but it did not adopt the Court's reasoning. Instead, it provided generally that the business records exception would not apply when the circumstances of preparation "indicate lack of trustworthiness." The mere fact that the

---

115 *See also In re* Fleet, 95 Bankr. 319, 330–31 (E.D. Pa. 1989) (holding records admissible since OCA record was business record and statements within record were admissions of party-opponents).

116 Taken literally, the rule *requires* (rather than *permits*) the trial judge to exclude upon a showing of untrustworthiness. But because trustworthiness is a matter of degree and because there is no criterion in the exception that would tell the judge how untrustworthy it too untrustworthy to be admitted, the judge exercises effective discretion in making the ruling.

117 *See* Matador Drilling Co. v. Post, 662 F.2d 1190, 1198–99 (5th Cir. 1981) (plaintiff's daily drilling records admissible despite claim that they were self-serving); Downing v. Overhead Door Corp., 707 P.2d 1027, 1031 (Colo. App. 1985) (error to exclude insurance adjuster's report even though it was claimed to be prejudicial and self-serving).

118 *See* Schaps v. Bally's Park Place, Inc., 58 Bankr. 581, 583–84 (E.D. Pa. 1986), *aff'd*, 815 F.2d 693 (3d Cir. 1987) *and aff'd*, 815 F.2d 695 (3d Cir. 1987) (books and records of debtor inadmissible because they were not submitted by the regular custodian and party admitted that the records were not kept in business-like manner, thus the records were untrustworthy); Pan-Islamic Trade Corp. v. Exxon Corp., 632 F.2d 539, 560 (5th Cir. 1980) (excluding record prepared originally as partisan document for presentation to Algerian oil agency). .

119 Palmer v. Hoffman, 318 U.S. 109, 111–15 (1943).

record was prepared in anticipation of litigation does not always indicate untrustworthiness, though the advisory committee implies that this usually would be the case.[120]

Yates v. Bair Transport, Inc.[121] provides an example of a statement prepared for litigation that nevertheless qualifies as a business record. There, the court admitted reports to an insurance company, prepared by doctors retained by the insurance company, concerning the plaintiff's injuries. The reports were offered by the plaintiff, not the company, and the court found that because they had been prepared for a company whose interests would be harmed if they supported the plaintiff, they were sufficiently trustworthy when offered by the plaintiff. The court, however, did not permit the plaintiff to offer reports prepared by doctors he retained.[122]

Aside from the self-serving nature of a record and whether it was prepared for litigation, case law considers the following factors relevant in determining untrustworthiness:

- the extent to which the business relied on the record in making important (non-litigation) decisions;
- the extent to which third parties or employees not personally at risk in the matter were involved in creating the record;
- the extent to which the record contained simple factual information, an error in which would be difficult to deny, as opposed to arguable value-laden appraisals;
- the extent to which the matter recorded was corroborated by independent sources of evidence; and
- the extent to which the record contained demonstrable errors on matters distinct from that which is relevant to the current suit.[123]

Computerized business records can sometimes present special foundational problems. One should not lose sight of the fact that reports prepared for litigation from computers can be no less self-serving than any other types of records. Both proponents and opponents of such reports should be prepared to consider carefully the foundational issues raised by computer-based records.[124]

Special Problems Regarding Hospital Records

Hospitals are businesses under the business records exception, whether they are for-profit or nonprofit institutions. However, this does not automatically mean that everything in their records is admissible. In particular, sometimes hospital records

---

[120] *See* FED. R. EVID. 803(6) advisory committee note.

[121] Yates v. Bair Transport, Inc., 249 F. Supp. 681, 688–92 (S.D.N.Y. 1965).

[122] *See also* State v. Therriault, 485 A.2d 986, 994–95 (Me. 1984) (police report prepared in anticipation of litigation admissible when offered by other party). *But see* United States v. Blackburn, 992 F.2d 666, 670 (7th Cir. 1993) (report prepared for FBI was not admissible under Rule 803(6) as a record of regularly conducted business activity; report was specially prepared at FBI's behest, with knowledge that any information it supplied would be used in an ongoing criminal investigation).

[123] *See generally* 4 CHRISTOPHER B. MUELLER & LAIRD C. KIRKPATRICK, FEDERAL EVIDENCE § 8:83 (4th ed. 2013).

[124] *See also* **§ 12.07** (discussing authentication of documents).

contain hearsay within hearsay. For example, the hospital record might repeat what the patient told the doctor, nurse, or other hospital employee.

Suppose, for example, that a hospital record contains a statement by the plaintiff describing the plaintiff's symptoms and the cause of his injury. If the record is offered in favor of the plaintiff, then a hearsay within hearsay problem arises because the plaintiff was under no business duty to the hospital, hence the business records exception does not cover the plaintiff's statement. The plaintiff's statement may, however, be covered by another exception, such as the Federal Rule of Evidence 803(4) exception for statements for medical diagnosis or treatment.[125] This exception would apply if the plaintiff's statements repeated within the record were reasonably pertinent to diagnosis or treatment. Statements by the plaintiff that his leg hurt or that he had been hit by a car would fit the exception. A statement by the plaintiff that the car that hit him went through a red light would not qualify because it would not be reasonably pertinent to diagnosis or treatment.

If the record is offered against the plaintiff, then there is no problem with fitting the plaintiff's statement into a hearsay exception—it is the statement of a party-opponent. However, the record that repeats the plaintiff's statement—the out-of-court declaration of the doctor or nurse asserting that the plaintiff made the statement—must also fit within an exception to be admissible. The obvious candidate is the business records exception. That exception will work for statements that are pertinent to diagnosis or treatment, such as statements that the plaintiff's leg hurt or that the plaintiff had been hit by a car, since the foundation showing that it is the regular practice of the hospital to make such records can be laid. However, the foundational requirements might not be met in cases in which the hospital employee-declarant recorded something that had no direct connection with medical treatment, such as a statement that the plaintiff had been hit by a car that went through a red light.[126] Hospitals do not regularly record assessments of whether the patient was the victim of a traffic law violation, and a hospital that did would be creating records that might be excluded under the final "lack of trustworthiness" clause of the business records exception. That the patient was injured by a car violating the law is not closely connected with the hospital's business; the hospital employee has no particular reason to record any such statements accurately. Thus, that part of the record would be excluded for lack of regularity or lack of trustworthiness.

The business records exception specifically applies to "opinions" and "diagnoses" that appear in hospital records. This provision seems to reverse a series of pre-Rule cases excluding hospital records that contained expert opinions on grounds that the expert should be subject to cross-examination and the qualifications should be explored.[127]

---

[125] *See* **§ 16.05**; *see also* Elmer v. Tenneco Resins, Inc., 698 F. Supp. 535, 543–45 (D. Del. 1988) (medical records containing plaintiff's statements regarding surgery admissible).

[126] *See* Williams v. Alexander, 129 N.E.2d 417, 418–20 (N.Y. 1955) (hospital record offered against plaintiff stated that plaintiff said "he was crossing the street and an automobile ran into another automobile that was at a standstill, causing [the standing car] to run into him"; trial court reversed for admitting statement on the grounds that it is not the business of the hospital to determine how the accident occurred); *see also* Wagner v. Thomas J. Obert Enters., 396 N.W.2d 223, 228 (Minn. 1986) (excluding hospital record containing plaintiff's version of accident when offered by defendant on basis that such a record lacks trustworthiness).

[127] For examples of pre-Rules cases excluding medical opinions, see England v. United States, 174 F.2d 466, 468 (5th Cir. 1949) (excluding reports containing doctor's individual opinions about defendant's mental capacity); Mullican v. United States, 252 F.2d 398, 404 (5th Cir. 1958) (hospital records concerning defendant's mental condition ruled expert opinions and excluded due to lack of opportunity to cross-examine). For post-

However, courts have sometimes found another way to exclude diagnoses or opinions in medical records.

For example, in *Fowler v. Carrollton Public Library*,[128] the plaintiff offered hospital records on the issue of damages. The records contained a statement that plaintiff had been hospitalized for three days with a diagnosis of "transient global amnesia." They were offered by plaintiff on the theory that the hospitalization was caused by the stress of mistreatment on the job. The court of appeals reversed on other grounds, and went on to discuss the issue to give guidance on retrial. It wrote that

> The district court here abused its discretion in admitting medical records from Fowler's brief hospital stay with no accompanying expert explanation of their significance. The fact of hospitalization in establishing pain and suffering is equivocal, at best, because no expert witness appeared to support Fowler's subjective belief that her "transient global amnesia" was caused by stress at work. The court sustained an objection preventing Fowler from testifying as a layman to the causal connection. This court as well as the jury remains completely unenlightened by the record evidence as to the cause and nature of transient global amnesia. The records could lead only to unwarranted speculation by the jury and inferences in favor of Fowler, and their prejudicial impact manifestly outweighed the benefit of verifying such uncontested facts as the hospitalization. This court has held, in a § 1983 case, that where a plaintiff attempted to prove that racially motivated harassment proximately caused a fatal heart condition, speculation will not suffice. So should it be on retrial.[129]

Though the court did not make specific reference to Rule 403 in its decision, perhaps this case could be viewed as one in which the record overcame the hearsay ban by reason of Rule 803(6), only to run afoul of Rule 403 because, without the help of an expert to explain it, it was confusing and misleading.[130]

In *Petrocelli v. Gallison*,[131] the plaintiff's medical record, created for his second hernia surgery, contained a statement that in his first hernia surgery, the plaintiff's ilioinguinal nerve had been severed. The plaintiff was suing the physician who had allegedly severed the nerve. It was not clear where the statement in the medical record had come from; the plaintiff himself might have told the record keeper that the nerve had been severed in prior surgery. The court upheld the trial judge's exclusion of the record, noting that there was no foundation showing that the information had been transmitted by a "person with knowledge" as required by Rule 803(6). The court

---

Rules cases admitting diagnosis from hospital records, see Norton v. Colyer, 828 F.2d 384, 386–87 (6th Cir. 1987) (medical records concerning plaintiff's alleged drug abuse as hospital diagnosis admissible under 803(6)); Raycraft v. Duluth, Missabe & Iron Range Ry. Co., 472 F.2d 27, 31 (8th Cir. 1973) (stating that lack of opportunity to cross-examine expert medical witness may indicate lack of trustworthiness); Pieters v. B-Right Trucking, Inc., 669 F. Supp. 1463, 1464–66 (N.D. Ind. 1987) (hospital record of blood alcohol level admissible); Manko v. United States, 636 F. Supp. 1419, 1425 (W.D. Mo. 1986) (medical diagnosis admissible under 803(6)).

[128] Fowler v. Carrollton Pub. Library, 799 F.2d 976, 983 (5th Cir. 1986).

[129] *Id.* at 983 (citing the § 1983 case, Hamilton v. Rodgers, 791 F.2d 439, 444–45 (5th Cir. 1986)).

[130] *See* Lovell v. Beavers, 987 S.W.2d 660 (Ark. 1999) (holding that, because of potential for jury confusion, trial judge has discretion under Rule 403 to exclude unexplained medical records even if the records meet the requirements of the business records exception); Nauni v. State, 670 P.2d 126, 131 (Okla. Crim. App. 1983) (excluding psychiatric opinions and diagnosis in hospital record under Rule 403 when doctors were not available for cross-examination to clarify otherwise speculative and subjective process).

[131] Petrocelli v. Gallison, 679 F.2d 286, 289–91 (1st Cir. 1982).

recognized that the Rule 803(4) theory had not been advanced as a basis for letting in hearsay within hearsay, as the source of information was the patient himself; since the Rule 803(4) theory had not been advanced at trial, it refused to allow it to be used on appeal.[132]

§ 16.08 Absence of Entry in Business Record [FRE 803(7)]

Although business records are most often used to prove that something did happen, sometimes they may be used to prove that something did not happen. Rule 803(7) provides for admission of testimony about the absence of an entry in a business record in order to prove that some matter that could have been recorded did not occur or exist. In many contexts, the absence of an entry in a record is not intended as an assertion, even when it is evidence of the belief of the person or persons who made the extant entries, in which case its use to prove that non-occurrence is not hearsay. The present exception takes care of the situations in which an assertive intent *is* present, with the result that the absence of an entry is admissible (as far as the hearsay rule is concerned) whether or not this use of the record is a hearsay use.[133]

To use this exception, however, the proponent must lay a foundation by showing that:

- the record involved was kept in the regular course of business;
- the record derived from information transmitted by persons with knowledge;
- it was the regular practice of the business to make entries such as the one missing in this case; and
- an adequate search was made for the missing record.

Examples of the use of this provision include testimony about the absence of records of orders for fishing reels, to show that the orders had not been received;[134] the absence of records showing receipt of money, to show that the money was not received;[135] and the absence of any record of an offer to donate property, to show that no such offer was made.[136]

---

[132] *Id.*; *see also* Ricciardi v. Children's Hosp. Med. Ctr., 811 F.2d 18, 21–23 (1st Cir. 1987) (holding handwritten note by doctor with no knowledge of operation inadmissible).

[133] *See* 4 CHRISTOPHER B. MUELLER & LAIRD C. KIRKPATRICK, FEDERAL EVIDENCE § 8:85 (4th ed. 2013). These authors provide the following illustration of the distinction:

> If the question is whether a certain car was in the shop for repairs on Tuesday and the shop records appear to reflect all the cars that were repaired but make no mention of the car in question, it is unlikely in the extreme that those who prepared the records or made the entries intended to assert something about the car in question. . . . On the other hand, if the question is whether something was amiss in one of the cars that underwent regular service in which fluid levels are checked, and deficiencies and corrective measures are indicated, evidence that the record of such services indicated nothing wrong [*sic*, better would be "did not indicate something was wrong"] with the brake or transmission fluid could realistically be viewed as a deliberate indication that these points were checked and nothing was amiss—as an assertion to this effect, which implicates the hearsay doctrine.

Id. at 777–78.

[134] Fury Imps., Inc. v. Shakespeare Co., 554 F.2d 1376, 1381 (5th Cir. 1977).

[135] United States v. Zeidman, 540 F.2d 314, 319 (7th Cir. 1976).

[136] United States v. 34.60 Acres of Land, 642 F.2d 788, 790 (5th Cir. 1981).

§ 16.09 Public Records [FRE 803(8)]

Rule 803(8) provides a hearsay exception for public records. The rationales for the public records exception are: (1) government officials are considered trustworthy; (2) the public servant's legal duty to be accurate provides incentive to be careful; and, (3) the exception is necessary because public officials handle many matters and may not have an active memory of facts memorialized in their records that are important to the determination of the suit.[137]

The public records exception, which applies to criminal and civil cases, is divided into three sections, each of which covers a slightly different type of public record. Part (A)(i) of the rule covers records and statements of a public office setting forth the activities of an office or agency. It applies to both civil and criminal cases. Any party, can use the exception, although its use by the prosecution in a criminal case potentially raises Confrontation Clause issues.[138]

Examples of matters falling under part (A)(i) include payroll documents, personnel records, records of receipts and disbursements, and so forth.[139] More exotic examples include a report of the Department of Commerce about the usual ease of expediting defense deliveries, offered to show approval of a "jawboning" policy that gave defense orders informal priority,[140] and a report of the Center for Disease Control to show the existence of vaccine-induced polio cases,[141] though one might argue that these reports would fit more readily under part (A)(ii) or (A)(iii) of the Rule than part (A)(i).[142]

Part (A)(ii) of the rule covers matters observed pursuant to a duty imposed by law when the public servant has a duty to report. Examples include weather records, maps, a court reporter's transcript, an officer's letter describing the circumstances of a refusal to accept induction, a federal "warrant of deportation," routine INS records, and a police property receipt for a weapon.[143]

This part of the rule contains a limitation, applicable to criminal cases, that excludes matters observed by law enforcement personnel. The goal of this exclusion from the hearsay exception, which was added as an amendment on the floor of the House of Representative and debated there, was to make sure that criminal defendants would not

---

[137] *See* FED. R. EVID. 803(8) advisory committee note; 2 MCCORMICK ON EVIDENCE § 295 at 462–63 (Kenneth S. Broun ed., 7th ed. 2013).

[138] *See* **§§ 20.01 et seq.**

[139] *See, e.g.*, Major v. Treen, 574 F. Supp. 325, 330 n.6 (E.D. La. 1983) (records of joint committee and subcommittee sessions of Louisiana legislature admissible under former 803(8)(A), now 803(8)(A)(i)); Needham v. United States, 564 F. Supp. 419, 421–22 (W.D. Okla. 1983) (IRS computer printout of mailing admissible under former 803(8)(A), now 803(8)(A)(i)).

[140] Eastern Air Lines, Inc. v. McDonnell Douglas Corp., 532 F.2d 957, 983 n.79 (5th Cir. 1976).

[141] Givens v. Lederle, 556 F.2d 1341, 1346 (5th Cir. 1977).

[142] GLEN WEISSENBERGER & JAMES J. DUANE, FEDERAL RULES OF EVIDENCE § 803.42 at 635–36 (7th ed. 2011) ("Where the focus of the particular record is more external to the functioning of the agency, in that it largely concerns the activities and conduct of certain citizens, or events or transactions outside the operation of the agency or office," "[i]t is more properly to be regarded as a record reflecting a matter observed under a legal duty, and it is consequently subject to the limiting aspects of subsection A(ii) . . . .").

[143] *See* FED. R. EVID. 803(8) advisory committee note; United States v. Grady, 544 F.2d 598 (2d Cir. 1976) (holding that police records that routinely log serial numbers of guns recovered in Ireland admissible under former 803(8)(B), now 803(8)(A)(ii)); United States v. Torres, 733 F.2d 449, 455 n.5 (7th Cir. 1984) (admitting tribal rolls establishing defendants as American Indians under former 803(8)(B), now 803(A)(ii)); United States v. Contreras, 63 F.3d 852, 857 (9th Cir. 1995) (warrant of deportation); United States v. Agustino-Hernandez, 14 F.3d 42, 43 (11th Cir. 1994) (routine INS records); United States v. Brown, 9 F.3d 907, 910–11 (11th Cir. 1993) (police property receipt for a weapon).

be convicted by police records. An officer with knowledge actually has to show up. Read literally, it prohibits use by any party in a criminal case, whether government or defense, of police or law enforcement reports. There is case authority, however, which supports the use of 803(8)(A)(ii) reports by a criminal defendant.[144] The rule permits either party in criminal cases to use the public records exception when the report arises from an agency other than law enforcement.[145] And in civil cases, reports falling within Part (A)(ii) of the rule can be offered by either party. However, Part (A)(ii) is subject to the limitation of the "business duty rule" examined in connection with business records: the use of these reports does not extend to admit statement made to public officials by non-officials, those who are not speaking pursuant to a business duty; these statements are admissible for their truth only if some other hearsay exemption or exception applies.[146]

Part (A)(iii) of the Rule excepts from hearsay findings resulting from an investigation made pursuant to legal authority. It applies in both in civil and criminal cases, but only the accused may use the exception in criminal cases. Apparently, the rulemakers believed that in fairness, the government ought not to be able to suppress its own prior findings, but that a criminal defendant cannot be convicted based on governmental reports and is entitled to confront an accuser in a criminal case.[147] Part (A)(iii) is not subject to the business duty rule. Factual findings based on information received from a person who had no duty to the public office are admissible under part (A)(iii) of Rule 803(8). For example, a hearing officer's findings would be admissible even if based on testimony from persons who were not public employees and who had no duty to report.[148]

---

144 *See* United States v. Smith, 521 F.2d 957, 968 n.24 (D.C. Cir. 1975) (permitting defense use of police report despite literal language of former Rule 803(8)(B), now R. 803(8)(A)(ii)).

145 *See* 2 MCCORMICK ON EVIDENCE § 296 (Kenneth S. Broun ed., 7th ed. 2013).

146 United States v. De Peri, 778 F.2d 963 (3d Cir. 1985) (holding trial court correctly excluded FBI reports offered by defense to establish the truth of statements made by video poker machine vendors to FBI agent; this "classic hearsay within hearsay" would require identification of a separate hearsay exception covering the vendors' statements); United States v. Morales, 720 F.3d 1194, 1201–02 (9th Cir. 2013) (holding statements made by smuggled individuals to Border Patrol agents and recorded in field reports inadmissible to prove what they asserted).

147 *See* 2 MCCORMICK ON EVIDENCE § 296 at 467 (Kenneth S. Broun ed., 7th ed. 2013).

148 For a case that could be read as stating broadly that Rule 803(8)(A)(iii) (formerly Rule 803(8)(C)) cannot be a vehicle for findings based upon hearsay from a declarant who was not under a public duty, see Miller v. Field, 35 F.3d 1088 (6th Cir. 1994). *Miller* was a federal civil rights case arising from an alleged prison rape. The court held that public records must contain either factual findings from firsthand knowledge of the report's preparer or conclusions derived from those facts. Hence, it ruled, state police reports setting forth witness statements and conclusions of investigators were inadmissible. While *Miller* may reach the right result on its facts, it goes too far in its statement of the limits on Rule 803(8)(A)(iii). Under that rule, when a public official actually makes "findings" pursuant to an investigation required by law (as opposed to merely recording information without evaluating it), then those findings are admissible unless shown to be untrustworthy. Passages of the *Miller* opinion could be read to say that findings based upon statements from declarants who are not under a public duty are simply inadmissible, whether or not they are shown to be untrustworthy. Under that reasoning, findings by hearing officers conducting administrative hearings would be inadmissible whenever based on hearing testimony by persons not under a public duty, a result that seems clearly inconsistent with the intent of the rule makers and the examples given in the Advisory Committee note. The Sixth Circuit has not expressly overruled *Miller*, but in more recent cases it has followed the rule that it is "not necessary that the person who prepares the report have first-hand knowledge of the events for the report to be admissible pursuant to Rule 803(8)." Nowell v. City of Cincinnati, 2006 WL 2619846 at *4 n.2 (S.D. Ohio Sept. 12, 2006) (recognizing abrogation); *see* Combs v. Wilkinson, 315 F.3d 548, 554–56 (6th Cir. 2002) (finding a report prepared by a prison's Use of Force Committee admissible even though the committee members lacked personal knowledge of the disturbance that was the subject of the report); Hickson Corp. v. Norfolk S. Ry. Co., 124 Fed. App'x 336, 345 (6th Cir. 2005).

Examples of findings falling under Part (A)(iii) include: a Coast Guard report containing conclusions about the causes of the grounding of an oil tanker; a report by state police authorities containing factual information and opinions about certain racial disturbances; administrative findings about sex discrimination or employment discrimination; a Center for Disease Control report concerning tampon use and toxic shock syndrome; and FAA findings about the safety of the plane that injured the plaintiff.[149] Reports of the results of tests conducted by forensic science labs, whether nominally governmental or private, at least when conducted at the request of police or the prosecuting authority, properly fall within Part (A)(iii), but are admissible under Rule 803(8) only if offered by the defense.[150]

Regardless of which of the three subdivisions a proponent invokes, the public records exception, like the business records exception, allows the court to exclude evidence that otherwise satisfies the rule if the opponent shows that "the source of information or other circumstances indicate a lack of trustworthiness."[151] This is an important part of the rule; the opponent of a party offering a public record should be prepared to demonstrate lack of trustworthiness, and the offering party should be prepared to defend the report's trustworthiness.[152] The drafters of the rule offered four non-exclusive factors for consideration in assessing whether an evaluative report is trustworthy: (1) the timeliness of the investigation, (2) the special skill or experience of the official, (3) whether a hearing was held and the level at which conducted, and (4) any possible motivation problems.[153]

Many public records are also business records since the government is a business within the meaning of the business records exception. However, the public records exception serves an important function because it covers matters that are not recorded with regularity and not necessarily made at or near the time the matter upon which the record is made transpired. For example, a civil defense official might only once record

---

[149] *See In re* Complaint of Nautilus Motor Tanker Co., Ltd., 85 F.3d 105, 110–13 (3d Cir. 1996) (Coast Guard report concerning grounding of oil tanker); Clark v. Clabaugh, 20 F.3d 1290, 1294–95 (3d Cir. 1994) (Pennsylvania State Police report about circumstances surrounding certain civil disturbances); Chandler v. Roudebush, 425 U.S. 840, 863 n.39 (1976) (administrative findings regarding claims of discrimination generally admissible under 803(8)(C)); Ellis v. International Playtex, Inc., 745 F.2d 292, 299–305 (4th Cir. 1984) (CDC report on toxic shock syndrome); Melville v. American Home Assurance Co., 443 F. Supp. 1064, 1110–13 (E.D. Pa.1977) (FAA directives concerning safety of plane admissible), *rev'd on other grounds*, 584 F.2d 1306 (3d Cir. 1978).

[150] *See* United States v. Oates, 560 F.2d 45 (2d Cir. 1977). When offered against the accused, admissibility of "testimonial" hearsay statements within a lab report is governed the Confrontation Clause. *See* **§ 20.06**. Prosecutors wanting to offer such lab reports may, of course, present its author to testify and may be able to invoke the exception for past recollection recorded if the witness's memory is incomplete. *See generally* 4 CHRISTOPHER B. MUELLER & LAIRD C. KIRKPATRICK, FEDERAL EVIDENCE § 8:91 (4th ed. 2013).

[151] *See* FED. R. EVID. 803(8)(B).

[152] *See* Ellis v. International Playtex, Inc., 745 F.2d 292, 301 (4th Cir. 1984) "[T]he burden is on the party opposing admission to demonstrate that the report is not reliable. *Compare* Montiel v. City of L.A., 2 F.3d 335, 341 (9th Cir. 1993) (holding that, in § 1983 action, district court erred by failing to presume the trustworthiness of the Report of the Independent Commission on the Los Angeles Police Department (Christopher Commission Report) and by not shifting the burden of establishing the report's untrustworthiness to the defendant city), *with* Curtis v. M & S Petroleum, Inc., 174 F.3d 661, 673 (5th Cir. 1999) (upholding trial judge's Rule 403 exclusion of state agency reports indicating that a refinery was not equipped to handle certain hazardous substances and that it did not have proper permits; there was a danger that the government report would be given too much weight; other evidence on the same point was not available).

[153] *See* FED. R. EVID. 803(8) advisory committee note. *See, e.g., In re* Vallecito Gas, L.L.C., 771 F.3d 929 (5th Cir. 2014) (holding trial court properly excluded letter, offered under Rule 803(8), stating opinion of attorney for the Navajo Nation Department of Justice regarding validity of royalty interests when statement was untrustworthy because it was issued after hearing only proponent's side of the dispute).

observations about nuclear damage, and there might be some time lag between the event and the report, but the recorded observations would be public records.[154]

Finally, the public record has long been admissible without the need of a foundation witness. If it meets the self-authentication requirements of Rule 902 (which makes certified copies and like documents self-authenticating),[155] then the foundation for the public records hearsay exception will usually be adequate, because the record will show on its face that it meets the requirements of Rule 803(8).[156] By contrast, without a stipulation to foundation or self-authentication, it has traditionally been necessary for the proponent of a business record to call a foundation witness. However, with the amendments to the Federal Rules in 2000, it is now possible to sponsor business records with affidavits instead of a live witness,[157] so this difference between public records and business records is a matter of the form of the paperwork supporting the record.

The Concept of "Factual Findings"

Rule 803(8)(A)(iii) (formerly Rule 803(8)(C)) permits the admission, in civil suits and against the government in criminal cases, of reports containing "factual findings" derived from investigations made under authority of law. Before *Beech Aircraft v. Rainey*,[158] federal courts disagreed about whether opinions contained in Rule 803(8)(C) reports were also admissible. For example, the Second Circuit excluded an FDA finding that a drug was dangerous on grounds that it was a medical opinion, not a factual finding.[159] However, the Sixth Circuit admitted a finding by an administrative law judge that a tow boat captain had not been negligent, saying that "[a]lthough a finding that [the captain's] actions were reasonable is somewhat conclusory, we do not believe that such a label is controlling. In our view a finding that amounts to an inference drawn from subsidiary findings is admissible under Rule 803(8)(C)."[160]

Attempts to distinguish "fact" from "opinion" are rarely fruitful or edifying. And in *Beech Aircraft* the United States Supreme Court supported the free admission of opinions. *Beech Aircraft* concerned a wrongful death action against an aircraft manufacturer by the survivors of two naval aviators who had died in a training exercise. A naval investigator had issued a JAG report describing the surrounding facts and also offering the opinion that the most probable cause of the crash was pilot error. The Court held that the opinion was admissible, interpreting Rule 803(8)(C) to include within its

---

[154] *See, e.g.*, United States v. Versaint, 849 F.2d 827, 831 n.9 (3d Cir. 1988) (police report admissible under 803(8), thus not necessary to determine if report would meet 803(6) requirements of reliability and regularity).

[155] *See* **§ 12.07**.

[156] *See* Zambito v. Blair, 610 F.2d 1192, 1198 (4th Cir. 1979) (certified "Order Finding Probable Cause" admissible under Rules 902(1) and 803(8)(A)); United States v. Hart, 673 F. Supp. 932, 934 n.2 (N.D. Ind. 1987) (government exhibit self-authenticating under 902(1) and admissible under 803(8)).

[157] *See* **§ 16.07**.

[158] Beech Aircraft Corp. v. Rainey, 488 U.S. 153 (1988).

[159] Lindsay v. Ortho Pharm. Corp., 637 F.2d 87, 94 (2d Cir. 1980); *see also* Matthews v. Ashland Chem., Inc., 770 F.2d 1303, 1309–10 (5th Cir. 1985) (memo outlining future inquiries into safety measures and offering opinions on expected results inadmissible under 803(8)(C)).

[160] *See* Complaint of Paducah Towing Co., Inc., 692 F.2d 412, 420 (6th Cir. 1982) (citations omitted); *see also* Kehm v. Procter & Gamble Mfg. Co., 724 F.2d 613, 619–20 (8th Cir. 1983) (reports analyzing statistical relationship between tampon use and toxic shock syndrome admissible); Zenith Radio Corp. v. Matsushita Elec. Indus. Co., 505 F. Supp. 1125, 1145 (E.D. Pa. 1980) (factual findings as used in the Rule encompass evaluative reports of public agencies).

scope opinions contained in investigative reports so long as the reports also contain factual findings.[161]

The mere fact that conclusions may be admitted under Rule 803(8)(A)(iii) does not mean that they *must* be. Courts may exclude conclusions if the party objecting to admission demonstrates them to be untrustworthy, prejudicial, confusing, or a waste of time. Exclusion may be grounded either on the trustworthiness proviso of Rule 803(8)(B) or under the general discretion granted by Rule 403.[162] Conversely, even in a jurisdiction that excludes the public record from direct admission because it contains opinions and not findings of fact, the public record still might serve as the basis upon which an expert relies in forming an opinion under Rule 703. Rule 703 allows experts to rely upon data not admissible in evidence.[163]

Because there is no "business duty" requirement in Rule 803(8)(A)(iii), the official making the factual finding may use trustworthy hearsay from persons outside the government. Over-reliance on hearsay, however, may indicate that the entire factual finding is untrustworthy.[164] Nevertheless, this difference between (A)(ii) reports and (A)(iii) reports means that it matters considerably into which category a public record

---

[161] 488 U.S. 153 (1988); *see* Goodman v. Pennsylvania Tpk. Comm'n, 293 F.3d 655 (3d Cir. 2002) (holding Budget and Finance Committee Report criticizing political partisanship in appointments to state office admissible as Rule 803(8)(C) record in case in which plaintiff claimed he had been denied a promotion for political reasons); Distaff, Inc. v. Springfield Contracting Corp., 984 F.2d 108, 111–12 (4th Cir. 1993) (holding report by naval investigator about cause of fire admissible in civil case even though Navy refused to permit him to testify subject to cross-examination).

[162] *See* Cortes v. Maxus Exploration Co., 977 F.2d 195, 201 (5th Cir. 1992) (holding trial judge did not err in excluding conclusory EEOC document containing determination that plaintiff had not been sexually harassed; though government reports are presumptively reliable under Rule 803(8) in the absence of an affirmative showing of untrustworthiness by the opponent, here the danger of prejudice substantially outweighed the probative value, justifying exclusion under Rule 403); United States v. Jackson-Randolph, 282 F.3d 369, 380–81 (6th Cir. 2002) (holding that lack of trustworthiness precluded hearing examiner from relying on accomplice testimony in reaching findings); United States Steel, LLC v. Tieco, Inc., 261 F.3d 1275, 1287 (11th Cir. 2001) (holding that statement of facts in prior judicial opinion, drafted for prior judge by proponent of evidence in self-serving fashion, is inadmissible hearsay not fitting under any exception); Lathem v. Department of Children and Youth Servs., 172 F.3d 786, 791 (11th Cir. 1999) (holding that trial judge had discretion under Rule 403 to exclude EEOC no-cause determination in gender discrimination case after finding that agency had not made a complete investigation); Ake v. General Motors Corp., 942 F. Supp. 869, 879 (W.D.N.Y. 1996) (excluding tentative "findings" of National Highway Traffic Safety Administration under Rule 803(8)'s trustworthiness proviso because findings might have been changed after public hearing); Kemper Architects, P.C. v. McFall, Konkel & Kimball Consulting Engineers, Inc., 843 P.2d 1178, 1187–88 (Wyo. 1992) (holding that trial court properly excluded exhibit prepared by Army Corps of Engineers under state's version of Federal Rule 803(8)(C); exhibit lacked indicia of trustworthiness because it contained multiple hearsay-within-hearsay, impermissible legal conclusions, and appeared to have been prepared with a view toward possible litigation). *But see* Blake v. Pellegrino, 329 F.3d 43 (1st Cir. 2003) (holding that trial judge erred in striking cause of death from death certificate on ground it was inaccurate; trustworthiness proviso of Rule 803(8)(C) does not allow judge to strike hearsay merely because judge finds it unpersuasive; the proviso refers to matters such as manner in which death certificate was completed, the sources of information utilized, and credentials of the person completing it, and how the record was maintained, not to whether the judge found the conclusion credible).

[163] *See* **§ 10.05**; Smith v. Isuzu Motors Ltd., 137 F.3d 859, 862–63 (5th Cir. 1998) (excluding National Highway Traffic Safety Administration staff memos on grounds that the memos did not reflect "factual findings" of the agency, but rather the views of individual staff members, which the agency later declined to adopt).

[164] *Compare* Union Pac. R.R. Co. v. Kirby Inland Marine, Inc., 296 F.3d 671, 678–80 (8th Cir. 2002) (holding that district court did not abuse discretion in admitting a Coast Guard order to alter the bridge; the fact that Coast Guard investigators relied on hearsay did not make the report untrustworthy), *with In re* Japanese Elec. Prod. Antitrust Litig., 723 F.2d 238, 264–65 (3d Cir. 1983), *rev'd on other grounds by* Matsushita Elec. Indus. Co., Ltd. v. Zenith Radio Corp., 475 U.S. 574 (1986) (noting with disfavor trial court's consideration of the extent of the agency's reliance on inadmissible and unreliable evidence).

falls. In particular, controversy surrounds the status of police accident and incident reports.[165] The authors believe that best approach is to assess police reports under (A)(ii)—and thus subject to the business duty limitation—when the report serves as a conduit for the admission of statements by witnesses interviewed by the officer. Police reports may qualify under (A)(iii) only to the extent that the officer draws conclusions that go beyond merely reporting such statements and, perhaps, beyond merely accepting or rejecting the credibility of such witnesses.[166]

There is also some division of authority on the issues whether Rule 803(8)(A)(iii) may be used to admit prior convictions or judicial findings of fact. A persuasive argument can be made that the rule applies only to administrative findings, and that judicial findings are covered by other exceptions specifically worded in terms of judgments.[167] The restrictions on the exceptions specifically relating to judgments would be undermined if judgements were admissible under 803(8).[168]

Police and Other Law Enforcement Records

The public records exception contains specific language prohibiting the use of law enforcement records in most criminal cases.[169] Yet there are some bases for arguing that certain law enforcement records are admissible against the defendant in criminal cases.

First, theoretically, a law enforcement record could be offered not as a public record, but as a business record. There is no doubt that law enforcement agencies are businesses within the meaning of the business records rule. The rule is not restricted to profit-making private activity, but applies to any regularly conducted activity, whether it is public, charitable, or otherwise.[170] However, the legislative intent of the public records exception indicates a strong purpose of preventing the report substituting for the police officer's live testimony. Apparently, in considering the amendment made from the House floor that added the phrase that excludes matters observed by law enforcement in a criminal case, Congress simply overlooked the fact that police reports and other law enforcement records would also qualify as business records. Not surprisingly, prosecutors have attempted to use 803(6) to avoid the restrictions on police records imposed by 803(8), sometimes successfully.[171] Because of the intent to exclude law

---

165 *Compare, e.g.,* Simmons v. Chicago & Northwestern Trans. Co., 993 F.2d 1326, 1327–28 (8th Cir. 1993) (admitting accident report by patrolman who testified that he reached his conclusion based on the physics of the situation and would have reached the same conclusion without talking to eyewitnesses), *with* Hill v. Rolleri, 615 F.2d 886, 889–90 (9th Cir. 1980) (excluding police report used to introduce statement made by truck driver to officer).

166 *See, e.g.,* Dortch v. Fowler, 588 F.3d 396, 402–04 (6th Cir. 2009) (admitting police accident report based on extensive training and experience and observations made at scene). *See generally* 4 CHRISTOPHER B. MUELLER & LAIRD C. KIRKPATRICK, FEDERAL EVIDENCE § 8:89 at 808–10 (4th ed. 2013). Our approach is analogous to our treatment of expert testimony under Rule 703. *See* **§ 10.05**.

167 *See* **§ 16.19**. *See* Nipper v. Snipes, 7 F.3d 415, 417 (4th Cir. 1993) (holding that judicial findings of fact are not "public records" within the meaning of Rule 803(8)).

168 *See generally* 4 CHRISTOPHER B. MUELLER & LAIRD C. KIRKPATRICK, FEDERAL EVIDENCE § 8:89 at 816–20 (4th ed. 2013).

169 *See* FED. R. EVID. 803(8)(A)(ii), (iii).

170 *See* FED. RULES OF EVID. H.R. REP. NO. 93–1597 at 11 (1974) (Conf. Rep.).

171 *See, e.g.,* United States v. Roulette, 75 F.3d 418, 422–23 (8th Cir. 1996) (admitting under Rule 803(6) lab report identifying substance as cocaine). Some courts have also held that where the report author testifies, Rule 803(8)(C)—now 803(A)(iii)—does not require exclusion of reports that satisfy Rule 803(6). *See, e.g.,* United States v. Sokolow, 91 F.3d 396, 404–05 (3d Cir. 1996); United States v. Hayes, 861 F.2d 1225, 1230 (10th Cir. 1988); United States v. King, 613 F.2d 670, 672–73 (7th Cir. 1980). A fairly unpersuasive argument can be made for this approach out of the following two premises: (1) the purpose of the restrictions in 803(8) was to

enforcement records when offered under the public records exception, however, most courts have held that they are likewise not admissible as business records.[172]

Second, past case law has supported the admission of law enforcement records under Rule 803(5), the exception for past recollection recorded. This result has been justified on grounds that Congress, in excluding law enforcement records, was concerned about the danger that the defendant would lose the right to cross-examine the officer who made the report. This danger is not present when the past recollection recorded exception is used, because under that exception the person who made or adopted the record must testify in order to lay the foundation for the admission of the report.[173]

Third, courts have allowed law enforcement records into evidence under other exceptions, including Rule 803(10) (the exception for evidence of absence of a public record),[174] and Rule 803(24) (one of the former residual hearsay exceptions, now contained in Rule 807).[175]

Finally, some courts have created an exception for routine, non-adversarial law enforcement reports. Rule 803(8) does not specifically distinguish between routine reports of objective facts, such as records of serial numbers, or fingerprint records, and reports prepared during an investigation that may incriminate a particular defendant. However, a number of courts do draw this distinction. They have used words such as "routine," "non-adversarial," "ministerial," "objective," and "non-evaluative" to describe law enforcement records deemed admissible against the defendant despite the restrictions of Rule 803(8).[176] Typically, these courts have reasoned that routine non-

---

avoid violating the defendant's constitutional right to confront adverse witnesses; and (2) no such violation occurs when the declarant of the hearsay testifies at trial. *See* **§ 20.01**. The difficulty with such an argument is that it reduces the limitation on 803(6) to nothing more than the constitutional protection that would exist anyway, allowing the prosecution to circumvent the stricter statutory limitations that Congress enacted in 803(8).

[172] One leading case on the subject is United States v. Oates, 560 F.2d 45, 78 (2d Cir. 1977), *on remand* 445 F. Supp. 351 (E.D.N.Y.), *aff'd without opinion*, 591 F.2d 1332 (2d Cir. 1978). The *Oates* court reversed a conviction because the trial judge had admitted a laboratory report identifying a substance as heroin without requiring testimony of the chemist who performed the analysis. The court reasoned that the congressional intent not to allow law enforcement reports to be used against the defendant in criminal cases under Rule 803(8)(B) and (C)—now 803(A)(ii) and (iii)—required that they be excluded when offered as business records under Rule 803(6). *See also* United States v. Ruffin, 575 F.2d 346, 356 (2d Cir. 1978) (error, though harmless, to receive IRS investigator's file note describing phone call by defendant); United States v. Cain, 615 F.2d 380, 382 (5th Cir. 1980) (per curiam) (reversible error to receive prison escape report under 803(6)); United States v. Morales, 720 F.3d 1194, 1201–02 (9th Cir. 2013) (holding it was error, but harmless, to admit under Rule 803(6) field reports prepared by Border Patrol agents in prosecution for illegal entry). In dicta the *Oates* court suggested that law enforcement records are not admissible under any of the other hearsay exceptions. As discussed below, this position has not been accepted generally.

[173] *See* United States v. Picciandra, 788 F.2d 39, 44 (1st Cir. 1986) (holding that DEA agent's report was admissible against criminal defendants under Rule 803(5)); United States v. Sawyer, 607 F.2d 1190, 1193 (7th Cir. 1979) (holding that reports excluded under Rule 803(8)(B) may be received under Rule 803(5)).

[174] *See, e.g.*, United States v. Metzger, 778 F.2d 1195, 1201 (6th Cir. 1985) (holding that certificate that defendant had not registered a destructive device or paid tax on one admissible under 803(10) even if record kept by law enforcement official); United States v. Neff, 615 F.2d 1235, 1241 (9th Cir. 1980) (holding that IRS certificate admissible under 803(10)); United States v. Yakobov, 712 F.2d 20, 25 (2d Cir. 1983) (holding that, upon a proper showing of diligent search, ATF certificate stating that there was no record that defendant had applied for or received a firearms license would be admissible).

[175] *See, e.g.*, United States v. Blackburn, 992 F.2d 666, 672 (7th Cir. 1993) (report prepared for FBI investigation admissible under the residual hearsay exception (now Rule 807), even though not admissible under 803(6)).

[176] *See* United States v. Dowdell, 595 F.3d 50, 70–72 (1st Cir. 2010) (police booking report was admissible because it was a "rote recitation of biographical information"); United States v. Wiley, 979 F.2d 365, 369 (5th Cir. 1992) (in action for passing counterfeit IRS obligations, reports indicating that IRS agents investigated

adversarial reports are not subject to the same dangers of bias and clouded perception as are other police reports.[177] To put it another way, in these cases the cross-examination is most unlikely to yield information that would be helpful to the defendant. In some limited circumstances, routine police activities, such as the recording of serial numbers, might be considered "activities of the office" and hence admissible under part (A)(i).[178]

These interpretations of the hearsay exceptions must be qualified by acknowledging the possibility that use of hearsay against the accused in a criminal case raises potential issues under the Confrontation Clause. Between 2004 and 2012, there was strong reason to think that most, if not all of the statements contained in police and law enforcement records, certainly those within 803(8)(A)(ii) and (A)(iii), would fall within the scope of that Clause, precluding use against the accused unless the declarant testifies or the accused had an earlier opportunity to cross-examine the declarant. A decision by the Supreme Court in 2012, however, muddied these waters considerably. Discussion of this issue requires a full treatment of the implications of the Clause, which is presented elsewhere.[179]

§ 16.10 Records of Vital Statistics; Death Certificates [FRE 803(9)]

Rule 803(9) provides a hearsay exception for records of births, fetal deaths, deaths, or marriages, if such events are reported to a public office pursuant to legal requirements. This exception allows official records of birth, death, and marriage to be received in evidence even if someone other than a public official prepares the records.[180] Thus, a death certificate is admissible whether it is prepared by a private doctor, mortician, or public coroner; a marriage certificate is admissible whether it was prepared by a judge or by a minister. In the absence of Rule 803(9), these records might be considered admissible under an expansive reading of Rule 803(8)(B) (the public records exception), but the present exception resolves any doubt about whether the private status of the record-makers affects admissibility.[181]

---

and froze third-party's account admissible under public records hearsay exception because law enforcement actions occurred within "routine, non-adversarial setting"); United States v. Puente, 826 F.2d 1415, 1417–18 (5th Cir. 1987) (Customs Service records of license plates of cars crossing from Mexico to United States admissible under 803(8), even though Customs officers are law enforcement officers; 803(8)(B) does not apply to routine, objective factual observations); United States v. Weiland, 420 F.3d 1062, 1074–75 (9th Cir. 2005) (fingerprints and photographs contained in a penitentiary file were admissible because they were "the types of routine and unambiguous matters to which the public records hearsay exception in Rule 803(8)(B) is designed to apply"); United States v. Wilmer, 799 F.2d 495, 500–01 (9th Cir. 1986) (calibration certificate for breathalyzer admissible); United States v. Gilbert, 774 F.2d 962, 964–65 (9th Cir. 1985) (report on location of latent print admissible; court notes non-evaluative, routine, nonadversarial nature of report).

[177] *See* United States v. Dowdell, 595 F.3d 50, 72 (1st Cir. 2010) ("The rote recitation of biographical information in a booking sheet ordinarily does not implicate the same potential perception biases that a subjective narrative of an investigation or an alleged offense might. . . . [U]nlike the investigative reports that lie at the heart of the law enforcement exception, booking sheets raise little concern that suspicion of guilt will function as proof of guilt"); United States v. Gilbert, 774 F.2d 962, 965 (9th Cir. 1985).

[178] *Cf.* United States v. Grady, 544 F.2d 598, 604 (2d Cir. 1976) (police records of routine nature, such as recording of serial numbers, are admissible under 803(8); in putting limits on admissibility of police records, Congress did not have this sort of routine function in mind); United States v. Orozco, 590 F.2d 789, 793–94 (9th Cir. 1979) (computer cards recording vehicle license plate numbers admissible under 803(8)).

[179] *See* **§§ 20.01 et seq.**, especially **§ 20.06** & **§ 20.09**.

[180] *See* 5 WEINSTEIN'S FEDERAL EVIDENCE § 803.11[1] (Mark S. Brodin ed., 2d ed. 2015).

[181] Many states have statutes providing for the admission of death certificates. These statutes often provide that death certificates are prima facie evidence of the facts stated in them. *See* Annotation, *Official Death Certificate as Evidence of Cause of Death in Civil or Criminal Action*, 21 A.L.R. 3d 418, 422 n.5 (1968 &

Death certificates have been offered in evidence in a wide variety of situations.[182] These include: the prosecution's offer of a death certificate to show the victim in a murder case died of gunshot wounds;[183] an insurance defense counsel's offer, in a suit to recover on a life insurance policy, of a statement that the cause of death was suicide;[184] the government's offer of death certificates in a tax case to show that the death of two taxpayers was not simultaneous, and therefore one inherited from the other;[185] and a plaintiff's offer, in an asbestosis wrongful death action, of a death certificate to show that plaintiff's decedent died of adenocarcinoma of the lung.[186]

Death certificates may be unreliable. A death certificate may contain assertions based on hearsay or speculation by a record-maker who does not have firsthand knowledge of the facts stated in the certificate. Alternatively, a lay coroner may express a medical opinion in the certificate that only a qualified expert could state with confidence. In these situations, cross-examination of the person who prepared the death certificate would be useful. Counsel faced with an unreliable statement in a death certificate could object on several possible grounds:

1. An objection might assert that the certificate contains statements not based on personal knowledge[187] or contains hearsay within hearsay.[188] Thus, when a death certificate describes something that the coroner clearly did not observe or information obtained from another, an objection should prevent reception of the evidence.[189] At least one eminent authority

---

Supp. 1996). If a narrow state statute predates the adoption of a state version of Rule 803(9), Rule 803(9) supersedes the statute or at least expands the limits of admissibility-provided the state supreme court adopted Rule 803(9) under an enabling act that renders prior inconsistent statutes ineffective after implementation of Rule 803(9).

[182] *See generally id.* (discussing the admissibility of death certificates in wrongful death actions, actions on life insurance policies, will contests, personal injury actions, actions to recover property, and criminal homicide prosecutions).

[183] *See, e.g.*, Stevens v. Bordenkircher, 746 F.2d 342 (6th Cir. 1984).

[184] For cases excluding such statements, *see* Security Life Ins. Co. v. Blitch, 270 S.E.2d 349, 352 (Ga. Ct. App. 1980) (trial court did not err in deleting "homicide" from death certificate before receiving certificate in double indemnity insurance recovery case); Hestad v. Pennsylvania Life Ins. Co., 204 N.W.2d 433, 436 (Minn. 1973) (indicating courts should redact portion of death certificate saying that suicide or accident was cause of death). In *Hestad*, the Minnesota Supreme Court stated:

> [D]eath certificates are not admissible to show the manner in which the death occurs, such as by accident or suicide, but may be admitted only to show the immediate cause of death, which, in this case, was carbon monoxide poisoning. Statements as to the manner of death in a death certificate constitute conclusions and hearsay.

Id. Accord State v. Jurgens, 424 N.W.2d 546, 552 (Minn. Ct. App. 1988) (dictum).

[185] *See, e.g.*, Vaughn v. United States, 536 F. Supp. 498 (W.D. Va. 1982). In *Vaughn*, an assailant shot and killed a father and daughter in their home. *Id.* at 500. According to the death certificate, the father died at home and the daughter died about an hour later at the hospital. *Id.* The court admitted the certificate as evidence that the deaths were not simultaneous, and thus the daughter's estate owed additional taxes because she inherited money from her father upon his death. *Id.* at 501–02.

[186] *See, e.g.*, Burton v. Johns-Manville Corp., 613 F. Supp. 91, 93–95 (W.D. Pa. 1985)(admitting a death certificate stating that the decedent died of adenocarcinoma of the lung was admitted in an asbestos case applying a Pennsylvania statute making a death certificate prima facie evidence of its contents; noting that, in any event, reception of the death certificate did not harm the defendant because a medical expert with firsthand knowledge was cross-examined about the cause of death).

[187] *See* **§ 14.07**.

[188] *See* **§ 14.08**.

[189] *See* Bowman v. Redding & Co., 449 F.2d 956, 961 (D.C. Cir. 1971) (holding statement in death certificate describing how decedent fell inadmissible); State v. Gould, 704 P.2d 20, 29–30 (Mont. 1985) (holding admission of portion of death certificate containing statement that decedent was in a pick-up truck which left roadway and overturned, ejecting decedent, was error because statement was based on hearsay; error harmless

has suggested, however, that, in accordance with prior precedent, courts should admit such statements for what they are worth.[190]

2. Where the death certificate expresses an expert opinion, the opposing party may object that the declarant was not qualified as an expert, or at least that the declarant should be produced for cross-examination about his or her qualifications.[191] When the record maker is not a qualified medical expert and the certificate is admitted, counsel can argue that the medical conclusions are insufficient to get the opponent past a directed verdict.[192]

3. Where the death certificate contains extraneous matter, counsel can argue that Rule 803(9)'s prerequisite that the record be made "pursuant to requirements of law" is not satisfied as to the extraneous matter, because its inclusion is not required by law. Similarly, where the argument for admission rests on a state statute that admits death certificates as prima facie evidence of the "facts" stated in them, some courts have redacted the certificates to exclude matters deemed to be opinion or speculation rather than fact.[193]

Rule 803(9) is not subject to the kind of limitation with regard to criminal cases that appears in Rule 803(8), and its use to admit evidence against criminal defendants has already been mentioned. Such use does, however, potentially raise an issue under the Confrontation Clause if (a) the author of the record does not testify, or (b) the author's record relies on information provided by others. Under the pre-2004 doctrinal regime of *Ohio v. Roberts*,[194] arguably unreliable death certificates raised Confrontation Clause objections.[195] The Confrontation analysis of death certificates under the present

---

under circumstances). *But see* Shell v. Parrish, 448 F.2d 528, 531 (6th Cir. 1971) (holding, in diversity jurisdiction, that trial court erred in excluding statement in death certificate that "victim fell in ditch," despite fact that doctor who signed certificate obtained that information from an investigating officer; in pre-Rules context, court relies on Tennessee statute as well as federal statute favoring admissibility of evidence).

190 *See* 5 WEINSTEIN'S FEDERAL EVIDENCE § 803.11[4] (Mark S. Brodin ed., 2d ed. 2015).

191 *See, e.g.*, Charleston Nat'l Bank v. Hennessy, 404 F.2d 539, 542 (5th Cir. 1968) (lay coroner's opinion that decedent "apparently had heart attack" would not be admissible if offered in live testimony and statement did not become admissible because included in official death certificate).

192 *See* De Courcy v. Trustees of Westminster Presbyterian Church, Inc., 134 N.W.2d 326, 328–29 (Minn. 1965) (death certificate prepared by nonexpert insufficient substitute for expert testimony regarding cause of death, and concluding trial court should have directed verdict for defendant hospital where death allegedly occurred as a result of fracture caused by hospital's negligence).

193 *See* Carswell v. State, 320 S.E.2d 249, 253 (Ga. Ct. App. 1984) (excluding statement that "auto struck pedestrian"); *see also* Lockwood v. Travelers Ins. Co., 498 P.2d 947, 952 (Colo. 1972) (error to admit death certificate containing conclusory statement that death resulted from accident rather than suicide or homicide); People v. Fiddler, 258 N.E.2d 359, 361 (Ill. 1970) (coroner's statement about cause of death not a "fact" within meaning of state statute making facts in death certificates admissible).

194 Ohio v. Roberts, 448 U.S. 56 (1980).

195 *See, e.g.*, Stevens v. Bordenkircher, 746 F.2d 342 (6th Cir. 1984) (holding that admission of death certificate prepared by non-testifying coroner and purporting to be an autopsy that revealed the identity of the body, the cause of death, and the approximate date of death violated defendant's confrontation right). *But see* Manocchio v. Moran, 919 F.2d 770, 772 (1st Cir. 1990). There, the medical examiner's autopsy report contained the following statement: "The decedent was beaten by assailants in a parking lot on Mineral Springs Avenue, North Providence, on November 2, 1980, at approximately 1:00 A.M.—He was taken to Roger Williams General Hospital where he died at 1:47 A.M.—Manner of death: Homicide." The First Circuit accepted the proposition that Rule 803(9) was not a "firmly rooted" hearsay exception and hence that hearsay admitted under it should be subjected to special scrutiny for trustworthiness when challenged on Sixth Amendment grounds. Nevertheless, the court found that the record before it had sufficient indicia of reliability to survive Sixth Amendment scrutiny.

doctrinal regime of *Crawford v. Washington*[196] has not been clearly resolved by the United States Supreme Court, but some case law has found death certificates to be beyond the scope of the Clause.[197] Nevertheless, when a death certificate goes beyond merely recording the medical details of death and records attributions of criminality, arguably 803(9) overlaps with 803(8)(A)(iii), and the investigative finding represented by the certificate should then be subject to the same limitation placed upon such investigative findings by the latter provision.[198]

§ 16.11 Absence of Public Record or Entry [FRE 803(10)]

Rule 803(10)(A) provides a hearsay exception for evidence that data was *not* contained in a public record, provided that certification or testimony shows that a diligent search was made. For this exception, a public record certainly includes those public records embraced by 803(8) and 803(9).[199] This provision assures that the absence of document from a public record may be used to show that "the record or statement does not exist" or that "a matter did not occur or exist, if a public office regularly kept a record or statement for a matter of that kind," whether the preparer of the public record intended such an assertion or not.

Examples of the operation of this exception include reception of a certificate from the IRS reciting its failure to find income tax returns, as evidence of failure to file,[200] and use of a certificate from the Navy reciting failure to find a record of registration, to show that a vehicle was not registered.[201]

At common-law, evidence of a diligent search through public records was admissible to show the absence of a record, but some courts did not allow the search to be established by a certificate from a public official reciting that the diligent search had been made.[202] Rule 803(10)(A) cures that omission. The certification must comply with the requirements for self-authentication under Rule 902, which will entail that the search was conducted by an official. Nevertheless, if the pertinent records are available to the public, someone other than the custodian of the records may conduct the search and testify to the absence of the entry in question, unless such a search itself requires expertise.[203]

The party opposing admissibility can seek to rebut the claim that a diligent search occurred. Because the certification provision allows the substitution of a certificate for the person who did the search, this can be difficult unless the opponent has affirmative

---

[196] Crawford v. Washington, 541 U.S. 36 (2004).

[197] *See, e.g.*, Birkhead v. State, 57 So. 3d 1223 (Miss. 2011) (holding that death certificate offered as proof of time of death was not "testimonial" and thus its admission did not violate defendant's confrontation right). The analysis to be used to address such questions is explained in a later chapter. *See* **§§ 20.01 et seq.**

[198] *See* 4 CHRISTOPHER B. MUELLER & LAIRD C. KIRKPATRICK, FEDERAL EVIDENCE § 8:93 at 875 (4th ed. 2013).

[199] *See* FED. R. EVID. 803(10) advisory committee note.

[200] *See* United States v. Cepeda Penes, 577 F.2d 754, 761 (1st Cir. 1978) (certificate from computer check showing defendant had not filed tax returns admissible under Rule 803(10)).

[201] United States v. Martinez, 700 F.2d 1358, 1364–65 (11th Cir. 1983) (under Rule 803(10), no error to admit naval certificate concluding that vessel was not registered). Several recent cases have admitted certificates of nonexistence of record from the Immigration and Naturalization Service. *See, e.g.*, United States v. Cervantes-Flores, 421 F.3d 825 (9th Cir. 2005).

[202] 5 WIGMORE ON EVIDENCE § 1678 (Chadbourn rev. 1974).

[203] *See* 4 CHRISTOPHER B. MUELLER & LAIRD C. KIRKPATRICK, FEDERAL EVIDENCE § 8:95 at 886–87 (4th ed. 2013).

witnesses. However, in some instances lack of diligence may appear from the face of the certificate, as when the certificate uses incorrect names or contains other mistakes.

The public records exception, Rule 803(8), prohibits use of many police and other law enforcement records as evidence against criminal defendants. Rule 803(10) contains no such prohibition, and there is substantial authority allowing evidence of the absence of a law enforcement record to be used against a criminal defendant.[204] The certification procedure permitted by Rule 803(10), however, by allowing the author of the certificate to avoid testifying, presents a serious issue under the post-2004 constitutional doctrine in regard to the Confrontation Clause, whenever such a search of the records is done specifically in contemplation of trial.[205] To address this, Rule 803(10) was amended in 2013 to provide a form of "notice and demand" procedure, which had been approved by the Supreme Court in 2009.[206] Thus, Rule 803(10)(B) provides, unless the trial judge specifies a different timing, "a prosecutor who intends to offer a certification" must provide "written notice of that intent at least 14 days before trial." If, then, "the defendant does not object in writing within 7 days of receiving the notice," the prosecution may proceed by certificate rather than live testimony. Timely objection by the defense eliminates certification as an alternative to live testimony by the person who conducted the "diligent search."

§ 16.12 Learned Treatises [FRE 803(18)]

Rule 803(18) provides a broad exception for learned treatises and other expert publications. The exception allows the introduction of passages from books, scholarly journals, technical magazines, and other published works on any science or art, once a foundation has been established that the work is a reliable authority.

The exception is based on the theory that most learned publications are reliable enough to be helpful. The author ordinarily has no bias or interest in any particular case. In addition, the author realizes that the work will be read and evaluated by other members of the same profession. Thus, the author is highly motivated to be accurate and complete.[207]

The Common-Law Background

The federal rule substantially changed the common law. Under the common law, learned treatises were admissible solely to impeach experts.[208] In some jurisdictions, the

---

204 *Id.* at 25. *See also* United States v. Provencio-Sandoval, 2008 WL 901182 (10th Cir. 2008) (raising the possibility that admission of such certificates could cause a confrontation problem; decided after the Supreme Court granted *cert* on *Melendez-Diaz* but before the decision came down).

205 If the searcher of the record testifies at trial, there is no hearsay and thus no Confrontation issue. *See* Paul W. Grimm, Jerome E. Deise & John R. Grimm, *The Confrontation Clause and the Hearsay Rule: What Hearsay Exceptions are Testimonial?* 40 U. BALT. L.F. 155, 185–86 (2010) (analyzing analogous hearsay rule in Maryland and concluding that certification of record absences are "unlikely to raise Confrontation Clause issues for the simple reason that they do not involve use of any out-of-court statement offered for its truth. To the contrary, they are offered to prove the nonexistence of a fact or nonoccurrence of an event").

206 *See* Melendez-Diaz v. Massachusetts, 557 U.S. 305, 326 (2009).

207 FED. R. EVID. 803(18) advisory committee note; *see also* Schneider v. Revici, 817 F.2d 987, 991 (2d Cir. 1987).

208 *See, e.g.,* Brown v. United States, 419 F.2d 337, 341 (8th Cir. 1969) (holding that medical treatises may be used in cross-examination "but are not admissible to prove the probative facts of opinions in the treatise"); United States v. One Device, 160 F.2d 194, 198–99 (10th Cir. 1947) (holding that medical books and treatises are not admissible to prove the truth of the statements they contain). Courts refused to recognize such an exception primarily because the author was not subject to cross-examination and was not under oath,

expert could not be impeached with the treatise unless the expert had testified that he or she had relied upon the treatise in preparing his or her expert opinion. This approach reflected the fact that the treatise was not being used for its truth, but only to show that the expert was unreliable. For example, imagine a plaintiff's expert testified that a patient's spleen should be removed only if severely damaged. Suppose also that the defense attorney possessed a treatise stating that the spleen should be removed whenever it has suffered the slightest trauma. The defense attorney could ask the opposing expert whether the expert had relied on the treatise. If the expert claimed reliance on the treatise in preparing the opinion, then the attorney could read the damaging passage to the jury or require the expert to do so.[209] The treatise was not being used to prove the truth of anything that it asserted, but to show that the expert was untrustworthy or careless because the expert claimed to have relied upon a treatise that did not support the expert opinion.

Impeachment of an expert who claims to have relied upon a treatise can be highly impressive. Wellman's classic work on cross-examination contains a compelling example from his own experience. Wellman examined an adverse medical expert and asked the expert whether anyone agreed with the expert's diagnosis. The expert testified that Ericson on the Spine agreed with him. Wellman asked who Ericson was, and the expert answered patronizingly that Ericson was probably one of the most famous surgeons that England has ever produced. Wellman then posed the following question:

> *Wellman*: "Well, how is it that a man, whose time is so much occupied as you have told us yours is, has leisure enough to look up medical authorities to see if they agree with him?"
>
> To which he got the dream answer:
>
> *Doctor* [fairly beaming on counsel]: "Well, Mr. Wellman, to tell you the truth, I have often heard of you, and I half suspected that you would ask me some such foolish question; so this morning after my breakfast, and before starting for court, I took down from my library my copy of Ericson's book, and found that he agreed entirely with my diagnosis in this case."

Wellman then reached under the counsel table and took out his own copy of "Ericson on the Spine" and asked the doctor to find the place at which Ericson agreed with him. The doctor said "I have not time to do it now." Wellman responded "Time!—why, there is all the time in the world." The witness sat in pained silence until excused by the trial judge.[210]

This form of impeachment can still be used under the Federal Rules. If the witness will say that he or she has relied on a treatise, then the impeachment will be very successful if the treatise does not support the witness's position. Undoubtedly there are

---

and because of the difficulty in determining whether the author was an authority in the field. Courts also expressed concern that jurors would become confused and that trials might devolve into conflicts between authors that jurors would not be equipped to resolve fairly. *See* 2 MCCORMICK ON EVIDENCE § 321 (Kenneth S. Broun ed., 7th ed. 2013).

[209] *See* Carter Prods., Inc. v. FTC, 201 F.2d 446, 449 (9th Cir. 1953) (noting that many courts hold that learned treatises cannot be used in cross-examination unless witness has relied on treatise in forming opinion, and citing authority); Ullrich v. Chicago City Ry. Co., 106 N.E. 828, 829 (Ill. 1914) (holding that scientific books are not admissible to impeach witness unless witness has relied upon that particular work in forming opinion); Percoco's Case, 173 N.E. 515, 516 (Mass. 1930) (finding error to admit medical books when expert, though stating he had read the books, was not shown to have relied on them in forming opinion).

[210] FRANCIS L. WELLMAN, THE ART OF CROSS-EXAMINATION 69–70 (1923).

lawyers who encounter such witnesses, just as there are poker players who draw royal flushes. However, most experts will not fall into this trap. They will deny relying upon the contrary treatise, perhaps upon any treatise. The problem with the common-law rule was that the expert could always short-circuit the cross-examination by denying reliance on the treatise in forming the expert opinion.[211]

Some common-law courts allowed broader use of the treatise to impeach. Even if the expert was not willing to testify that the expert had relied upon the treatise, the treatise could be used in evidence if the expert conceded that the treatise was a reliable authority in the field.[212] This approach, however, still allowed the expert witness to block cross-examination simply by refusing to concede that the treatise was authoritative.[213]

The common-law position was not completely uniform. Some courts were far more liberal in allowing cross-examination on treatises. Some allowed it even when the opposing expert neither relied on the work nor recognized it as an authority, on grounds that the cross-examination was still a valuable way to test the expert's knowledge, credibility, and accuracy.[214] But many courts imposed restrictions that severely hampered the use of learned treatises.

Expansion of Treatise Use Under the Federal Rules

The federal rule makers thought that the learned treatise ought to be admissible if its reliability was established by any means, whether or not the opposing expert conceded that it was authoritative. The rule makers said that the testing of professional knowledge was incomplete without exploration of the witness's knowledge of, and attitude toward, established treatises in the field.[215]

Because of the danger that the treatise, even if reliable in itself, might be misleading and confusing without the guidance of an expert, the rule makers did require that an expert be available and that the treatise be shown to the expert on the stand.[216] The

---

[211] *See* Percoco's Case, 173 N.E. 515, 516 (Mass. 1930); De Haan v. Winter, 241 N.W. 923, 925 (Mich. 1932) ("If a medical witness refers to a text-book as his authority, then the book referred to may be used to contradict him.").

[212] *See, e.g.*, Lawrence v. Nutter, 203 F.2d 540, 543 (4th Cir. 1953) (finding error to exclude cross-examination of witnesses from treatise recognized by witnesses as authority); Shaw v. Duncan, 194 F.2d 779, 783 (10th Cir. 1952) (finding error to exclude cross-examination upon treatise when witness testified he had read the treatise in question).

[213] Hastings v. Chrysler Corp., 77 N.Y.S.2d 524, 527 (1948) ("If the expert witness does not concede the authoritativeness of the literature attempted to be resorted to, it may not be used on cross-examination."); *see also* Lawrence v. Nutter, 203 F.2d 540, 543 (4th Cir. 1953).

[214] *See* Atlanta Corp. v. Olesen, 124 F. Supp. 482, 488 (S.D. Cal. 1954) (holding that reading portions of medical texts was proper method to test knowledge, accuracy, and credibility of expert witness, and to determine if expert agreed with the text); Reilly v. Pinkus, 338 U.S. 269, 275–76 (1949) (holding it prejudicial error not to allow cross-examination concerning statements in medical texts to test expert's testimony).

[215] FED. R. EVID. 803(18) advisory committee note. The drafters again suggest a binary notion of reliability—reliable or not reliable—even though reliability is in fact a gradational attribute. *See* **§ 10.04**. Presumably, the preliminary question that the court must determine, under Rule 104(a), is whether the treatise is *reliable enough* to be helpful in the context of the particular case.

[216] *Id. See* Tart v. McGann, 697 F.2d 75, 78 (2d Cir. 1982) (holding medical literature admissible as long as called to the attention of expert witness and established as authoritative); Schneider v. Revici, 817 F.2d 987, 991 (2d Cir. 1987).

expert is not required to actually explain the treatise, but the expert is available if either party wishes to ask questions about it.[217]

Established as reliable authority. Under Rule 803(18) the treatise must be shown to be a "reliable" authority, which can be accomplished in a number of ways.[218] The treatise may be established as reliable authority through the testimony of the proponent's own expert witness.[219] Or, the opposing expert can establish that the work is authoritative when the opponent's expert is willing to concede the point. Even a grudging concession that the treatise is "somewhat" authoritative may be enough to support admission.[220] Alternatively, the treatise can be established as authoritative through judicial notice.[221] It seems that this would rarely be appropriate, but Judge Weinstein suggests that

> in a medical malpractice case . . . if plaintiff cannot get an expert to testify on the standard of care, it is equally unlikely that an expert will testify about authoritative treatises. If defendant's experts refuse to concede the qualifications of a particular work, the trial judge should be liberal in allowing other proof of the treatise's authoritativeness so long as it indicates that the book is recognized by the medical professional. For example, reading lists used in medical school courses or postgraduate seminars might be admissible as market reports or commercial publications and a court might take judicial notice of books admitted in the course of other litigation.[222]

A learned treatise might be admitted conditionally, with the expert laying the foundation after it has already been used in cross-examination.[223] However, if the expert being cross-examined says that the treatise is worthless and if there has been no prior testimony establishing that it is authoritative, the judge ought to be reluctant to admit

---

[217] This also helps reduce the danger of passages of learned treatises being taken out of context or otherwise misleadingly presented or incorrectly interpreted. *See* 5 WEINSTEIN'S FEDERAL EVIDENCE § 803.20[1] (Mark S. Brodin ed., 2d ed. 2015).

[218] *See* FED. R. EVID. 803(18) advisory committee note; *see also* Johnson v. William C. Ellis & Sons Iron Works, 609 F.2d 820, 822 (5th Cir. 1980) (noting that treatises may be established as reliable authority by either testimony or admission of an expert witness, or by other expert testimony, or by judicial notice).

[219] *See* Burgess v. Premier Corp., 727 F.2d 826, 834 (9th Cir. 1984) (holding books on cattle investment offered by proponent's expert witness admissible where expert testified that author was the preeminent industry expert).

[220] *See* Allen v. Safeco Ins. Co., 782 F.2d 1517, 1519–20 (11th Cir. 1986) (opposing expert testified that fire investigation magazine was "somewhat" authoritative and that he had used it himself; authority of magazine sufficiently established; no error by trial judge in admitting evidence); *see also* Dawson v. Chrysler Corp., 630 F.2d 950, 961 (3d Cir. 1980) (holding reports inferentially conceded by opposing experts as authoritative properly established). The trial judge, of course, always has discretion under Rule 403 to exclude prejudicial or confusing evidence. For a decision that, on unusual facts, appears to go beyond the rule by requiring that a testifying expert rely upon the learned treatise, see Conde v. Velsicol Chem. Corp., 804 F. Supp. 972, 990 (S.D. Ohio 1992) (holding, in products liability action, scholarly article alleging manipulation of health data by defendant corporation inadmissible when plaintiffs failed to show any expert relied on it and article author did not testify at trial; however, letter to editor, in medical journal, discrediting study upon which defense relied admissible).

[221] *See* Hemingway v. Ochsner Clinic, 608 F.2d 1040, 1047 (5th Cir. 1979) (holding that medical text written by registered nurses could not be established by judicial notice). *See* **§ 2.14**.

[222] Weinstein notes that the finding of authoritativeness goes only to admissibility; it is up to the jury to decide what weight to give to the treatise. 5 WEINSTEIN'S FEDERAL EVIDENCE § 803.20[2] (Mark S. Brodin ed., 2d ed. 2015) (footnotes omitted).

[223] *Cf.* FED. R. EVID. 104(b). *See* Maggipinto v. Reichman, 481 F. Supp. 547, 550–52 (E.D. Pa. 1979) (holding that treatise used for impeachment purposes properly excluded for substantive purposes where treatise not offered and established as reliable authority).

it conditionally.[224] In any event, when there is a controversy about whether the treatise is a reliable authority, the issue is a preliminary question of fact under Rule 104(a) for the trial judge to resolve in determining whether the evidence is admissible.[225]

Shown to expert. The treatise must be shown to an expert, either one's own expert or the opponent's, on the witness stand. Even if the authoritative nature of the treatise is established by judicial notice, as opposed to expert testimony, for the excerpt from the treatise to be admissible, it is still necessary that an expert witness testify. The reason for this requirement is that the trier ought to have the aid of an expert in interpreting the treatise, however authoritative it may be.[226]

United States v. Norman[227] illustrates a dramatic failure to qualify for the exception. A defendant challenged his conviction on the ground that he was denied the opportunity to cross-examine the DEA surveillance agent who identified the defendant as the man involved in the illegal transaction. The defendant wanted to use a Justice Department manual on eyewitness identification that stated proper procedure for eyewitness identifications involves the use of a photo lineup rather than a single photograph as was used in the case. The appellate court affirmed, noting that the DEA agent was not testifying as an expert and that the defendant did not present the manual through his own expert. Moreover, the manual was not shown to be a reliable authority by the testimony of an expert or the taking of judicial notice.[228]

Treatise not an exhibit. The last sentence of Rule 803(18) provides that, if admitted, the treatise excerpts may be read into evidence but may not be received as exhibits. The advisory committee explained:

> The rule avoids the danger of misunderstanding and misapplication by limiting the use of treatises as substantive evidence to situations in which an expert is on the stand and available to explain and assist in the application of the treatise if desired. The limitation upon receiving the publication itself physically in evidence, contained in the last sentence, is designed to further this policy.[229]

---

[224] *See* Dawsey v. Olin Corp., 782 F.2d 1254, 1263–64 (5th Cir. 1986) (no error in prohibiting use of government publication in cross-examination where no experts testified that publication was reliable authority and one testified that it was unreliable).

[225] *See* **§ 3.11**. As often encountered throughout the Rules, a gradational variable—here, reliability comes in degrees—is treated as if it were a dichotomous attribute—reliable or not reliable—with the court's decision supposedly being determined by the preponderance of the evidence. However, because no criteria are provided to inform the court about *how* reliable is reliable *enough*, the trial court inevitably has considerable discretion in making the ruling.

[226] *See* FED. R. EVID. 803(18) advisory committee note. *See also* 2 MCCORMICK ON EVIDENCE § 321 at 547 (Kenneth S. Broun ed., 7th ed. 2013) (explaining that the restriction is "designed to ensure that materials are used only under the sponsorship of an expert who can assist the fact finder and explain how to apply the materials").

[227] United States v. Norman, 415 F.3d 466 (5th Cir. 2005), *cert. denied,* 546 U.S. 1117 (2006).

[228] *Id.* at 473–74.

[229] FED. R. EVID. 803(18) advisory committee note. *See also* Dartez v. Fibreboard Corp., 765 F.2d 456, 465 (5th Cir. 1985):

> The reason for the Rule's restrictions on the use of learned treatises is to avoid the possibility that the jury will misunderstand and misapply the technical language within such an article if they are allowed to consider the publication itself instead of receiving the information through the testimony of an expert in the field.

Id.

In other words, the lawyer or witness can read a passage from the treatise to the jury once the foundation has been established, but the jurors cannot take the treatise into the jury room and read it themselves.

§ 16.13 Ancient Documents [FRE 803(16)]

Rule 803(16) provides an exception for statements in "ancient" documents. Since its adoption, and until its 2017 amendment, it allowed the reception of documents that had been in existence for a certain period of time—twenty years—and "whose authenticity is established." The common-law ancient documents rule used a thirty-year period, and it is subject to dispute whether that rule was limited to a criterion of authentication, that is, whether there was a common-law ancient document exception to the hearsay rule.[230] Those cases that seem to have recognized a hearsay exception as well contained a requirement that the document be found in a naturally expected place.[231] The Federal Rule simply affirms that the document must be "established" as authentic.[232] Under Rule 901, one way, but not the only way, to authenticate a document that is twenty years old is to show, as specified in Rule 901(b)(8), that it "was in a condition that creates no suspicion about its authenticity," and "was in a place where, if authentic, it would likely be."[233]

Before 2018, courts appear to have admitted evidence of statements under Rule 803(16) as long as the document was properly authenticated under Rule 901(b)(8).[234] It is at least arguable, however, that the burden of proof for admission under 803(16) is different from that for authenticating evidence under 901. Rule 803(16) did not (and still does not) state an exception for any twenty-year-old document that "has been authenticated," i.e., satisfying the requirement of Rule 901, but rather for any such document "whose authenticity is established." Arguably, under Rule 803(16), the document must be shown to be authentic by a preponderance of the evidence;[235] under Rule 901, evidence "sufficient to support a finding" by a preponderance of the evidence is enough to authenticate.[236]

In *Dartez v. Fibreboard Corp.*,[237] the exception did not apply because of problems demonstrating the document's was authenticity. *Dartez* involved intracompany

---

[230] *See, e.g.*, Town of Ninety Six v. Southern Ry. Co., 267 F.2d 579, 583–584 (4th Cir. 1959) (limiting the ancient document rule to authentication). *See generally* 2 MCCORMICK ON EVIDENCE § 323 (Kenneth S. Broun ed., 7th ed. 2013).

[231] *See, e.g.*, Sinkora v. Wlach, 35 N.W.2d 40, 47–48 (Iowa 1948) (66-year-old passport found where expected admissible); Tillman v. Lincoln Warehouse Corp., 423 N.Y.S.2d 151, 153 (App. Div. 1979) (30-year-old inventory shown to have come from proper custody admissible).

[232] FED. R. EVID. 803(16); *see also* United States v. Stelmokas, 100 F.3d 302, 312 (3d Cir. 1996) (admitting Nazi and Soviet records showing defendant's membership in Lithuanian unit that murdered Jews admissible as ancient documents despite allegations of policy of spoliation and forgery by such authorities; Holocaust experts vouched for authenticity of documents).

[233] FED. R. EVID. 901(b)(8).

[234] *See, e.g.*, Dartez v. Fibreboard Corp., 765 F.2d 456, 464 (5th Cir. 1985); DeWeerth v. Baldinger, 658 F. Supp. 688, 695 n.12 (S.D.N.Y. 1987), *rev'd on other grounds* 836 F.2d 103 (2d Cir. 1987); Fulmer v. Connors, 665 F. Supp. 1472 (N.D. Ala. 1987).

[235] Ordinarily, the foundation for any hearsay exception must be shown by a preponderance. *See* Bourjaily v. United States, 483 U.S. 171, 175–76 (1987) (the preliminary facts necessary to establish the foundation for evidence under 801(d)(2)(E) must be proven by a preponderance of the evidence).

[236] *See* FED. R. EVID. 901(a); the requirement of authentication is satisfied by "evidence sufficient to support a finding that the matter in question is what its proponent claims."

[237] Dartez v. Fibreboard Corp., 765 F.2d 456 (5th Cir. 1985).

correspondence about employees possibly injured by exposure to asbestos. The plaintiff failed to introduce evidence that the documents came from the company's records, and the court considered that the requirement of authentication had not been satisfied because the documents were not found in the expected place. While finding the documents in the expected place is not an invariable requirement (they can be authenticated by other means, so long as they are shown to be what they purport to be),[238] the absence of other admissible evidence to authenticate the documents in this case made the failure to make that showing fatal.[239]

The use of an ancient document to prove its truth raises traditional hearsay dangers. The maker of the document might have been insincere or deficient in some other way. However, the age of the document at least provides assurance that it was not prepared in a self-serving manner with the present controversy in mind, though it might have been prepared in anticipation of some other controversy. Also, there exists a special need for the hearsay because memories of people who generated the document over twenty years prior may have faded. It also might be difficult to find other evidence. Finally, the fact that the document is in writing at least removes dangers that the in-court witness might have misunderstood the hearsay statement or manufactured it.[240]

The counterarguments prevailed in 2017 in light of one additional concern—the potentially excessive reliance of litigants on the ancient document exception as a result of modern digital recording and storage of documents irrespective of the documents' reliability. The 2017 amendment changes the exception to cover "a statement in a document that was prepared before January 1, 1998, and whose authenticity is established." Effectively, this means that no new ancient documents can come into existence by the passage of time. The advisory committee hastened to add, however, that most reliable twenty-year-old documents created after 1997 will be admissible under the business records or residual hearsay exception anyway.[241] The advisory committee essentially directs courts and advocates to shift their focus from the use of the ancient document exception to such other exceptions.[242]

§ 16.14 Family History and Related Matters

Law school professors sometimes startle students by asking them whether asking a witness "How old are you?" calls for objectionable hearsay. The witness has no personal knowledge, at least not of the exact date of his or her birth. The witness's knowledge is derived from the statements of others, and those statements are out-of-court statements offered for the truth of the matter asserted. So, the rules requiring personal knowledge and banning hearsay seem to obstruct this everyday testimony.[243]

---

[238] See **§ 12.07**.

[239] Dartez v. Fibreboard Corp., 765 F.2d 456, 464–65 (5th Cir. 1985).

[240] *See* 5 WEINSTEIN'S FEDERAL EVIDENCE § 803.18 (Mark S. Brodin ed., 2d ed. 2015); 2 MCCORMICK ON EVIDENCE § 323 at 555 (Kenneth S. Broun ed., 7th ed. 2013); Roger C. Park, *A Subject Matter Approach to Hearsay Reform*, 86 MICH. L. REV. 51, 71–73 (1987).

[241] FED. R. EVID. 803(16) advisory committee note to 2017 amendment.

[242] This change does not, however, affect the twenty-year safe-harbor rule for authentication stated in Rule 901(b)(8), which was not amended in a corresponding fashion.

[243] For an example of taking this idea to its logical extreme, see Mary Morton, Note, *The Hearsay Rule and Epistemological Suicide*, 74 GEO. L.J. 1301, 1301 (1986) (arguing that, when witness testifies that the witness saw a chair, the testimony is hearsay because the witness only knows what a chair is by having been told by others).

The question is not entirely a silly classroom exercise. Sometimes a fact such as age can be a crucial fact in the litigation. This is the case, for example, when the defendant is accused of a sexual crime that can only be committed against a victim who is underage.[244] Ideally one might want to require the best evidence available, such as a birth certificate or even the testimony of someone present at the birth. However, that degree of strictness has not usually been observed. The testimony of a witness about the witness's own age is admissible in evidence, both at common law[245] and under the Federal Rules of Evidence.[246] The hearsay exceptions governing statements about family history cover not only testimony about name and birthdate, but also about adoption, marriage, divorce, legitimacy, family relationship (by blood, marriage, or adoption), ancestry, and similar facts of personal or family history. They apply not only to testimony by the witness on the stand about the witness's own family history, but also about the family history of others.

The modern family history exceptions are descendants of the common-law pedigree exception. The pedigree exception is one of the first established exceptions to the hearsay rule. Chief Justice John Marshall listed it in 1813 as one of the four exceptions "said to be as old as the [hearsay] rule itself."[247] We have referred to "family history exceptions." The Federal Rules of Evidence actually contain five separate exceptions dealing with family history, reflecting a pragmatic permissiveness in regard to proof of such matters.

---

[244] *See* Government of Virgin Islands v. Joseph, 765 F.2d 394, 397 n.5 (3d Cir. 1985) (holding that victim may testify about her own age over hearsay objection). Of course, where age is a crucial fact, the party seeking to prove the person's age will have an incentive to offer stronger evidence of the victim's age. In cases such as *Joseph*, for example, the jury might well discount the victim's own testimony.

[245] *See* 5 WIGMORE ON EVIDENCE § 1493 (Chadbourn rev., 1974); United States v. Austrew, 202 F. Supp. 816, 822 (D. Md. 1962). However, common-law courts were occasionally quite strict. *See* Pickering v. Peskind, 183 N.E. 301, 305–06 (Ohio Ct. App. 1930) (holding plaintiff not allowed to testify about own birthdate, as told to her by her grandmother); National Aid Life Ass'n v. Wiles, 41 P.2d 655 (Okla. 1935) (holding daughter of insured not allowed to testify to family reputation about insured's age). The latter case can perhaps be explained as a case in which age was crucial, the statements were self-serving, and better evidence should have been available.

[246] *See* Government of Virgin Islands v. Joseph, 765 F.2d 394, 397 n.5 (3d Cir. 1985) (victim may testify about her own age over hearsay objection).

[247] Mima Queen & Child, Petitioners for Freedom v. Hepburn, 11 U.S. (7 Cranch) 290, 296 (1813) (Marshall, J.):

> To this rule there are some exceptions which are said to be as old as the rule itself. These are cases of pedigree, of prescription, of custom, and in some cases of boundary. There are also matters of general and public history, which may be received without that full proof which is necessary for the establishment of a private fact.

Id. Mima Queen involved a petition for freedom by slaves. Chief Justice Marshall refused to extend the pedigree exception to allow reception of evidence that the petitioners' ancestors had been free, holding that hearsay evidence on this subject should be excluded, and stating that "this Court is not inclined to extend the exceptions further than they have already been carried." *Id.* at 297. An able dissent by Justice Duvall argued that hearsay evidence was admissible

> [u]pon the same principle, upon which it is admitted to prove a custom, pedigree and the boundaries of land;—because from the antiquity of the transactions to which these subjects may have reference, it is impossible to produce living testimony. To exclude hearsay in such cases, would leave the party interested without remedy. . . . It appears to me that the reason for admitting hearsay evidence upon a question of freedom is much stronger than in cases of pedigree or in controversies relative to the boundaries of land. It will be universally admitted that the right to freedom is more important than the right of property.

Id. at 298–99.

Reputation [FRE 803(19)]

Rule 803(19) states an exception for reputation about family history. It allows a witness to testify about reputation with regard to marriage, birth, and similar facts of personal or family history. The reputation must be either among the family members, among associates, or in the community. The foundation for the testimony is similar to the foundation laid for reputation as to character.[248] For example, the basic foundation for showing through a witness that Julie Curran is the daughter of James Curran could be laid by the following series of questions:

Did you know James Curran?

How long did you know him?

What was the nature of your association with him?

Do you know Julie Curran?

How long have you known her?

What is the nature of your association with her?

Do you know other persons who have known both James and Julie Curran?

Who are those other persons?

What is their relationship to James and Julie Curran?

[The reputation sources can be members of the family, the community, or other associations, such as co-workers.]

Have you talked to those persons about the family relationship of Julie Curran and James Curran?

Are you familiar with the reputation for family relationship of John Curran and Julie Curran among those persons?

What is that reputation?

When proceeding under this exception, there is no need to show that the declarants (the persons making the statements that collectively make up the reputation) are unavailable. However, it is necessary to show the existence of general reputation. The fact that the witness has been told by one person that Sam was the child of Raphael does not constitute a reputation.

Statement by Family Member [FRE 804(b)(4)]

An exception for statements of family history is recognized by Rule 804(b)(4). This exception covers oral or written statements about birth, marriage, adoption, and the like. It does not require a showing of reputation. The statement of one person is enough. However, either that one person must be the person whose family history is sought to be proven (e.g., the statement of declarant about where she was born)[249] or the statement must be that of someone related by blood or marriage or otherwise "so intimately associated with the other's family as to be likely to have accurate information concerning

---

[248] *See* **§ 7.07**.

[249] For examples of statements involving place of birth, decided under the common-law precursors to the federal exceptions, see 5 WIGMORE ON EVIDENCE § 1501 (Chadbourn rev., 1974).

the matter declared."[250] Moreover, the declarant must be unavailable.[251] In contrast, the reputation-based family history exception, Rule 803(19), does not require any showing of unavailability.

The common-law version of the exception for statements of family history required that the statement be made *ante litem motam*, that is, before the controversy arose. Once the controversy arose, the danger of fabricated evidence was considered to be too great.[252] This requirement was intentionally omitted from the Federal Rule. The advisory committee considered that this and other motives to fabricate should go to weight, not to admissibility.[253]

Certificates [FRE 803(12)]

Rule 803(12) provides an exception for statements of fact contained in marriage, baptismal, or similar certificates. The public records exception, Rule 803(8), covers the same ground when the issuer of the certificate is a public official. However, Rule 803(12) goes further in that it admits records prepared by clergy and other non-public officials who are authorized to perform marriages and similar ceremonies.

Rule 803(9), records of vital statistics, also covers some of the same ground as the present exception. For example, a certification of a marriage made to a public office would be admissible under Rule 803(9) as well as the present exception. However, the present exception covers some matters not covered by Rule 803(9). Records of confirmation in a church, or of baptism, are not required to be reported to a public office, and hence are not admissible under Rule 803(9). They are admissible under the present exception, however.

The present exception differs from Rule 803(11), discussed below, in that it does not require that the certificate be part of the internal record of the religious organization. It can, for example, be a certificate issued by a member of the clergy to the husband and wife after a marriage ceremony.

Family Records [FRE 803(13)]

Rule 803(13) creates an exception for statements of fact concerning personal or family history contained in family Bibles, genealogies, charts, engravings on rings, inscriptions of family portraits, engravings on urns, crypts, tombstones, or the like. Examples of "statements concerning personal or family history" include statements about marriage, birth, death, ancestry, and the like. The exception is an ancient one that was long recognized at common law.[254]

The guarantee of trustworthiness presumed for the exception is (1) the lack of motive to make a false statement, and (2) the likelihood that such statements would be

---

[250] *See* FED. R. EVID. 804(b)(4) and advisory committee note.

[251] While this exception does not appear in Rule 803, we have included its discussion in this chapter because of its obvious relationship to four exceptions appearing in Rule 803.

[252] *See* 5 WIGMORE ON EVIDENCE § 1483 (Chadbourn rev., 1974).

[253] *See* FED. R. EVID. 804(b)(4) advisory committee note.

[254] For an early endorsement of the exception, see Whitelocke v. Baker, 13 Ves. 511, 514 (1804), quoted in 5 WIGMORE ON EVIDENCE § 1482 at 373 (Chadbourn rev., 1974 & Supp. 1996) (noting that statements of family history, including "descriptions upon monuments" and "descriptions in Bibles and registry books," are admitted "upon the principle that they are the natural effusions of a party who must know the truth, and who speaks upon an occasion when his mind stands in an even position, without any temptation to exceed or fall short of the truth").

screened by the family for accuracy. It may not be necessary to make a showing of personal knowledge under the current exception, at least not if the family has accepted the record as valid.[255]

Records of Religious Organizations [FRE 803(11)]

Rule 803(11) creates an exception for regularly kept records of religious organizations. These records may be used to show births, marriages, divorces, deaths, legitimacy, ancestry, relationships by blood or marriage, or other similar facts of personal or family history.

Most of this information would be admissible under the business records exception. A religious organization would be a "business" within the meaning of Rule 803(6), which covers institutions and callings of every kind, whether or not conducted for profit. However, the advisory committee decided to supplement the business records exception with the present exception because the business records exception requires that persons contributing to an entry be part of the business or activity (the "business duty" requirement).[256] Were the business records exception the only exception available, many but not all of the records admissible under the present exception would still be admissible. For example, a baptismal certificate could be used to show the fact of baptism. But the business records exception might not provide a basis for using the baptismal certificate to show the date of birth, since that information would have been contributed by the parents or by someone else not under a "business duty" to the religious organization.[257] The committee's decision to extend the present exception beyond the business records exception was based upon the unlikelihood that false information would be furnished in conjunction with an occasion such as baptism or religious circumcision.[258]

In the 1980s, federal litigation on the exception centered on attempts by taxpayers to use church-issued receipts or contribution statements as evidence of charitable contributions. The problem with using the exception for that purpose is that the offered evidence is not a statement of personal or family history similar to the examples listed in the Rule. Both the Second Circuit and the Ninth Circuit have held that such evidence is not admissible under the present exception, and no courts have since addressed the issue.[259] It is therefore necessary to lay a business record foundation for church records of this nature, showing that it was the regular practice of the church to make such records and that the records were kept in the regular course of the church's activities.

§ 16.15 Market Reports and Commercial Publications [FRE 803(17)]

Rule 803(17) recognizes a hearsay exception for market reports and commercial publications. The exception applies to stock market quotations, telephone directories, business directories, commercial compilations, lists, tabulations, and similar

---

[255] For an extensive discussion of the exception at common law, see 5 WIGMORE ON EVIDENCE §§ 1485–1497 (Chadbourn rev., 1974 & Supp. 1996).

[256] *See* **§ 16.07**.

[257] *See* FED. R. EVID. 803(11) advisory committee note.

[258] *Id.*

[259] *See* Ruberto v. Commissioner, 774 F.2d 61, 63 (2d Cir. 1985); Hall v. Commissioner, 729 F.2d 632, 635 (9th Cir. 1984).

publications. The rule requires that the compilations be published and that they be relied upon by the public or by persons in particular occupations.

The rationale of the exception is that there is ordinarily no motive to deceive in compiling these records and that reliance upon the publications by the public or by business users is an assurance of trustworthiness. In any event, it would usually not be feasible to call all of the people involved in making a compilation, so if the information is to be received at trial at all, it must be received in its published form.[260]

The exception overlaps somewhat with the business records exception. Often the foundation for reception as a business record could be laid in the case of a commercial publication. For example, in *United States v. Grossman*,[261] the defendant was charged with knowingly receiving stolen property. The property in question was 300 stolen Colibri cigarette lighters. At trial, a Colibri catalog was admitted to prove the retail price and to show that the lighters in evidence were the same models as those listed in the invoice of a stolen shipment. The court held that the catalog was admissible under the business records exception. The court believed that the prosecution had established a sufficient foundation through the testimony of a purchasing agent for Colibri Corporation. The court noted that the trial judge could have admitted the catalog as a commercial publication under Rule 803(17), because "the catalog was a published compilation generally used and relied upon by retailers of Colibri lighters."[262] The exception specifically requires both that the report be published and that it be generally relied upon. There is some authority for a third requirement, that the report concern objective facts not requiring interpretation or analysis.[263]

Reports that fail to meet both these requirements may nonetheless be used by experts in forming opinions if they meet the reasonable reliance requirements of Rule 703.[264]

§ 16.16 Documents Affecting an Interest in Property

Two exceptions concern documents that purport to affect an interest in property. Such documents ordinarily are drafted with some care and are relied upon by interested parties. These facts suggest a heightened degree of reliability.

Records of Documents [FRE 803(14)]

Rule 803(14) excepts from the hearsay rule a record of a document purporting to affect an interest in property, when offered as proof of the contents of the original document. The record must be the record of a public office, and a statute must authorize the recording of documents of that kind in that office. This exception operates when a title record is offered to prove the contents of the record, its execution, or delivery. If a local statute authorizes the recording of title records and the recording of data about execution and delivery, then the evidence is admissible. The advisory committee's note indicates that personal knowledge of the recorder is not required:

---

[260] *See* 5 WEINSTEIN'S FEDERAL EVIDENCE § 803.19[1] (Mark S. Brodin ed., 2d ed. 2015).

[261] United States v. Grossman, 614 F.2d 295, 296–97 (1st Cir. 1980).

[262] *Id.* at 297.

[263] *See* White Indus. v. Cessna Aircraft Co., 611 F. Supp. 1049, 1068–69 (W.D. Mo. 1985) (rejecting prospectus filed with SEC as evidence, and noting both publication requirement and requirement that the publication concern objective facts).

[264] *See* **§ 10.05**.

> Under any theory of the admissibility of public records, the records would be receivable as evidence of the contents of the recorded document, else the recording process would be reduced to a nullity. When, however, the record is offered for the further purpose of proving execution and delivery, a problem of lack of first-hand knowledge by the recorder, not present as to contents, is presented.[265]

The statute that authorizes recording need not be a federal statute; state statutes generally govern recording of interests in property.[266]

Statements in Documents [FRE 803(15)]

Rule 803(15) provides an exception for *statements in* documents purporting to affect an interest in property. The statement must have been relevant to the purpose of the document. The exception does not apply if transactions concerning the property, which have occurred since the document was made, are not consistent with the statements in the document.

The exception covers recitals of fact in documents such as deeds. Examples are a recital that the parties granting title to the property constitute all of the heirs of the last record owner[267] or a recital that parties named in the deed are married to one another.[268]

§ 16.17 Reputation Concerning Boundaries, Land Customs, and General History [FRE 803(20)]

Rule 803(20) provides what amounts to two exceptions. The first is an exception for reputation in the community as to boundaries or customs affecting lands. As to this exception, the Rule specifically requires that the reputation exist before the controversy arose, though it does not require that the reputation be ancient.[269]

The second is an exception for reputation in the community as to events of general history. As to this exception, the Rule does not specifically require either that the reputation be ancient or that it arise before the controversy. However, the Rule's reference to general "history" may lead courts to believe that the information must be non-contemporary. For example, in *State ex rel. Abrams v. Ocean Club, Inc.*,[270] the court refused to admit, under the exception, a club's relatively contemporaneous reputation for being anti-Semitic as evidence of discrimination, on the grounds that the reputation should be either ancient or at least not likely to be provable with living witnesses. This interpretation is supported by the advisory committee as a rationale for not requiring, in the second part of the rule, that the reputation arise before the controversy—that "the historical character of the subject matter dispenses with any need that the reputation antedate the controversy with respect to which it is offered."

---

265 FED. R. EVID. 803(14) advisory committee note.

266 *Id.* (noting that state law generally limits recordable documents to "those documents shown by a specified procedure, either acknowledgement or a form of probate, to have been executed and delivered").

267 *See* FED. R. EVID. 803(15) advisory committee note.

268 *See* Compton v. Davis Oil Co., 607 F. Supp. 1221, 1228–29 (D. Wyo. 1985).

269 *See* FED. R. EVID. 803(19)–(21) advisory committee note ("The reputation is required to antedate the controversy, though not to be ancient.").

270 New York by Abrams v. Ocean Club, Inc., 602 F. Supp. 489 (E.D.N.Y. 1984).

Like other reputation evidence, the supposed guarantee of trustworthiness for this type of evidence is that the community will have discussed and scrutinized the matter carefully, so that its conclusion is likely to be reliable.[271]

> To be probative, the reputation must concern such facts as have been of interest to all members of the community as such, and therefore have been so likely to receive general and intelligent discussion and examination by competent persons, so that the community's received opinion on the subject cannot be supposed to have reached the condition of definite decision until the matter had gone, in public relief, beyond the stage of controversy and had become settled with fair finality.[272]

In both parts of the exception, the reputation involved must be community reputation, not merely the word of one person or reputation within a narrow group. *Ute Indian Tribe v. Utah*,[273] held that the reputation in the non-Indian community about tribal boundaries was admissible but noted that it would be given little probative weight in the bench trial because of the adverse attitude of the non-Indian community toward the Indian community.

The "general history" aspect of the exception is little used. Facts of general history are likely to be derived from information that qualifies for another hearsay exception, such as the exceptions for ancient documents, learned treatises, or business records. Alternatively, such general history will be a proper subject for judicial notice.[274] As to most events of history, the "general history" part of the exception is not needed. Most historical events are offered not as adjudicative facts, which relate to the issues of who did what in the particular lawsuit, but as legislative facts, which relate to how to interpret law or what the law should be. Legislative fact issues may be resolved by judicial notice. That is, even if there is a reasonable dispute about the accuracy of a legislative fact, a court may resolve the dispute without taking testimony, by referring to whatever sources the court deems reliable.[275] Even as to adjudicative facts, many historical facts are generally known within the territorial jurisdiction of the trial court or are capable of accurate and ready determination by resort to sources whose accuracy

---

[271] FED. R. EVID. 803(19)–(21) advisory committee note. *See* Ute Indian Tribe v. Utah, 521 F. Supp. 1072, 1149 (D. Utah 1981), *rev'd on other grounds* 773 F.2d 1087 (10th Cir. 1985).

[272] 5 WIGMORE ON EVIDENCE § 1598 at 564–65 (Chadbourn rev., 1974). *See also id.* §§ 1583–1597.

[273] Ute Indian Tribe v. Utah, 521 F. Supp. 1072 (D. Utah 1981), *rev'd on other grounds* 773 F.2d 1087, 1148–50 (10th Cir. 1985).

[274] *See* 5 WEINSTEIN'S FEDERAL EVIDENCE § 803.22[2][c] (Mark S. Brodin ed., 2d ed. 2015) (noting that there has always been a dearth of authority under the exception, and that under the Federal Rules there is probably less need of the exception than before because of the learned treatise exception).

[275] KENNETH C. DAVIS, ADMINISTRATIVE LAW TREATISE 296 (3d ed. 1972):

> The cardinal distinction which more than any other governs the use of extra-record facts by courts and agencies is the distinction between legislative facts and adjudicative facts. When a court or an agency finds facts concerning the immediate parties—who did what, where, when, how and with what motive or intent—the court or agency is performing an adjudicative function, and the facts are conveniently called adjudicative facts. When a court or agency develops law or policy, it is acting legislatively. The courts have created the common-law through judicial legislation, and the facts which inform the tribunal's legislative judgment are called legislative facts. . . . The exceedingly practical difference between legislative and adjudicative facts is that, apart from facts properly noticed, the tribunal's findings of adjudicative facts must be supported by evidence, but findings or assumptions of legislative facts need not be, frequently are not, and sometimes cannot be supported by evidence.

(Footnotes omitted).

cannot reasonably be questioned, and hence are judicially noticeable under Rule 201(b).[276]

The exception was mentioned as one possible basis for receiving evidence, in *Pan American World Airways v. Aetna Casualty & Surety Co.*[277] This case involved insurance claims arising out of the hijacking of a Pan Am jet by persons aligned with the Palestine Liberation Organization. To allocate the insurance liability between the "all risk" and the "war risk" carriers, the court had to consider facts about the nature of the PLO and the Middle East conflict. The Court alluded to the predecessor common-law general history exception, as exemplified by what was then Proposed Rule 803(20), and to judicial notice as possible bases for admitting the evidence.

§ 16.18 Reputation Concerning Character [FRE 803(21)]

When evidence of a trait of character of a person is permitted, one form of evidence sometimes allowed is evidence of the reputation of that person for that trait.[278] Federal Rules 405(a) and 608(a) specifically authorize such evidence in particular circumstances, but those rules function as exceptions to the ban on character evidence. Rule 803(21) is there to prevent a hearsay objection from barring the use of otherwise admissible character evidence; it is not an independent source of authority for the admission of such evidence in the face of a character evidence objection.[279]

§ 16.19 Use of Judgments to Prove Facts Determined Thereby

It is reasonable to suppose that the judgment of a court might be used in later cases to show the facts adjudicated by the earlier judgment.

Examples

1. A judgment of conviction might be offered as circumstantial evidence of another crime that the convicted person is alleged to have committed. For example, suppose that the prior conviction is for distributing cocaine and is offered as evidence in a subsequent case arising from a separate occurrence. In the new case, the defendant is charged with possessing cocaine with intent to distribute. The defendant claims that the cocaine possessed in the second case was for the defendant's own personal use, and that he or she had no intent to distribute.[280]

2. A judgment of conviction might be offered for impeachment of a witness in a civil or criminal case, as an attack on the witness's character for truthfulness.[281]

---

[276] *See* **§ 2.14**.

[277] Pan Am. World Airways, Inc. v. Aetna Cas. & Sur. Co., 368 F. Supp. 1098 (S.D.N.Y. 1973) (alluding to the proposed version of Federal Rule 803(20), although the rule was not in effect at the time).

[278] *See* **§ 7.07** & **§ 11.07**.

[279] *See* FED. R. EVID. 803(21) advisory committee note ("The exception deals only with the hearsay aspect of this kind of evidence.").

[280] Most courts would admit the prior conviction as evidence of a subsequent intent to distribute. *See* **§ 7.09**. For that matter, most would admit evidence of prior sales of cocaine that did not lead to conviction on the same theory. Rule 404(b)(2) arguably permits such evidence because it is being offered for a non-propensity use, not impermissible character evidence under rule 404.

[281] Rule 609 details which judgments used for this purpose are exempted from a character evidence objection under Rule 404. *See* **§ 11.10**.

3. In a personal injury action, to show that defendant was driving under the influence at the time of the accident, a plaintiff might offer evidence that defendant was convicted of driving under the influence and that the conviction arises from the accident that caused the plaintiff's injury.[282]

4. In an action to recover on a fire insurance claim, the defendant insurance company offers evidence that the claimant was convicted of arson in the burning of the property that forms the basis for the claim.[283]

In some situations, the earlier adjudication may be claim preclusive (res judicata) or issue preclusive (collateral estoppel), in which case the facts determined by the earlier judgment cannot be relitigated. But even when a prior judgment does not have preclusive effect, the question remains whether the earlier judgment may at least serve as evidence of the facts determined by the prior case, facts that an opponent is nonetheless permitted to dispute in the subsequent case. If the prior judgment is offered in this latter way, the conviction evidence is arguably hearsay.[284] It can be understood as the uncross-examined statement by the trier-of-fact that the accused committed the crime charged.[285] To determine whether a judgment is admissible to prove the truth of facts thereby determined (adjudicated), one must look to the hearsay exceptions covering judgments, Rules 803(22) and 803(23).[286] But to understand the topic fully, one must place it in the context of the principles of issue preclusion.

Principles of Issue Preclusion and the Prior Conviction

The principles of issue preclusion, also known as collateral estoppel, are distinct from the principles that merely require treating a prior conviction as rebuttable evidence. Take, for example, the case in which a convicted arsonist brings a civil action to recover on a fire insurance policy. If the prior conviction is merely admissible evidence,

---

[282] *See, e.g.*, Scott v. Robertson, 583 P.2d 188 (Alaska 1978) (holding drunken driving conviction admissible in subsequent civil action and conclusive on issue of whether defendant was driving when intoxicated).

[283] *See, e.g.*, Schindler v. Royal Ins. Co., 179 N.E. 711 (N.Y. 1932) (allowing insurer to introduce conviction for making fraudulent insurance claim, not preclusive but admissible as evidence).

[284] There are, of course, many uses of judgments that do not present this particular kind of hearsay problem. For example, in the leading case of Old Chief v. United States, 519 U.S. 172 (1997), discussed in **§ 5.03**, the certified record of judgment of conviction was offered not to prove that Old Chief had committed the acts charged in the prior trial, but simply to prove that he was a convicted felon; that was the material fact that was pertinent to the "felon-in-possession" charge that was the subject of the appeal. To be convicted of such a charge, it need not be the case that the prior conviction was accurate or correct. Even if Old Chief had been innocent of the earlier charge, his conviction for it would subject him to the rules limiting his possession of a firearm.

[285] To be precise, it is double hearsay, because a record of conviction is the out-of-court statement of a judicial official that the conviction occurred. Of course, insofar as the document introduced is itself hearsay evidence of the fact of conviction, that layer of hearsay would fall easily within the public record exception, Rule 803(8), without recourse to the exceptions discussed here.

[286] Regarding the first two examples listed in the text, neither Rule 404(b)(2) nor Rule 609 was intended as providing a hearsay exception. Convictions admitted under Rule 404(b)(2) clearly must satisfy Rule 803(22) as well. But there is inconsistency between the requirements specified in Rule 609 and those specified in Rule 803(22). For example, Rule 803(22)'s provision that only convictions for crimes punishable by more than a year are admissible is plainly incompatible with Rule 609 when the conviction used to impeach is one for a crime of dishonesty within the meaning of Rule 609(a)(2). This was most likely a drafting oversight. In such an instance, even though the conviction is still hearsay and even though it is being offered to prove the truth of the matter asserted, Rule 609 should be construed as creating an exception that supplements the exception created in Rule 803(22). Thus, the use of prior convictions solely to impeach the credibility of a witness is not affected by Rule 803(22). If a prior conviction satisfies the requirements of Rule 609, then it is not required separately to satisfy the requirements of Rule 803(22).

then the plaintiff is entitled to present countervailing evidence and to go to the jury on the issue of whether the fire was caused by the plaintiff's arson. If the prior conviction has preclusive effect, however, then the arson cannot be contested at trial and the insurance company is entitled to summary judgment on the issue.

Traditionally, courts often declined to give preclusive effect to prior convictions because of the doctrine of mutuality. In the arson example, the insurer would not have been bound by a decision in the criminal case in favor of the alleged arsonist because it was not a party.[287] It would not be fair to bind the insurer with the results of a case in which it was not represented. Under the doctrine of mutuality, a person who had not been a party to the prior lawsuit was neither bound by the prior suit nor permitted to take advantage of any determinations made in the prior action.[288] This mutuality rule was based on the notion that it was unfair to allow someone to take advantage of findings in an action in which that person was not a party, since that person was not bound by any adverse determination.[289]

The doctrine's appeal to notions of equal treatment was based on an oversimplification. It treated persons equally when in fact they were in quite different situations. It treated the party who had an opportunity to litigate in the first action in the same way that it treated a nonparty who had no opportunity. Scholars generally rejected the mutuality rule.[290] The modern view is that if a party had a full and fair opportunity to litigate in the first action, then that party ought generally to be bound in subsequent litigation, in the absence of special circumstances.[291] Though the trend in the cases seems to be toward preclusion, there is a good deal of local variation in a field that is in flux.[292]

---

[287] *See, e.g.*, Show-World Ctr. v. Walsh, 438 F. Supp. 642, 648 (S.D.N.Y. 1977); RESTATEMENT (SECOND) OF JUDGMENTS § 34(3) (1980). For exceptions to the rule that nonparties are not bound by a judgment. *See id.* §§ 34–61 (codifying privity exceptions); Teitelbaum Furs, Inc. v. Dominion Ins. Co., 375 P.2d 439 (Cal. 1962) (en banc) (corporations collaterally estopped from recovering alleged insurance loss after president convicted of crimes arising from false insurance claims based on same loss).

[288] GENE R. SHREVE & PETER RAVEN-HANSEN, UNDERSTANDING CIVIL PROCEDURE § 15.08[2] (5th ed. 2013).

[289] This rationale has considerable appeal in the context of *claim* preclusion (res judicata), and in that context the doctrine of mutuality retains considerable force, unlike the liberalization of *issue* preclusion described in the following paragraphs. *See id.* § 15.04.

[290] Such opposition goes back at least to Jeremy Bentham, who said that the rule was more appropriate to the gaming table than the law court. 7 WORKS OF JEREMY BENTHAM 171 (U. Bowring ed. 1843), *as quoted in* Brainerd Currie, *Mutuality of Collateral Estoppel: Limits of the Bernhard Doctrine*, 9 STAN. L. REV. 281, 284 n.6 (1957):

> Another curious rule is, that, as a judgment is not evidence against a stranger, the contrary judgment shall not be evidence for him. If the rule itself is a curious one, the reason given for it is still more so:—"nobody can take benefit by a verdict, who had not been prejudiced by it, had it gone contrary": a maxim which one would suppose to have found its way from the gaming table to the bench.

[291] *See, e.g.*, Parklane Hosiery Co. v. Shore, 439 U.S. 322 (1979) (permitting offensive issue preclusion in favor of plaintiffs seeking to take advantage of determination in prior action, brought by SEC, that defendant had issued a materially misleading and false proxy statement); RESTATEMENT (SECOND) OF JUDGMENTS § 29 (1980); *cf.* Gray v. Genlyte Group, Inc., 289 F.3d 128 (1st Cir. 2002) (misdemeanor conviction for using offensive and disorderly acts or language in accosting or annoying member of opposite sex not admissible in civil sexual harassment trial to prove seriousness of harassing conduct; conviction prejudicial because it would be possible to be convicted under the statute without committing serious harassment).

[292] *See, e.g.*, Brown v. Green, 738 F.2d 202, 206 (7th Cir. 1984) (holding that, where defendant is convicted on the merits at trial, conviction not preclusive, but evidence surrounding prior conviction admissible in subsequent civil proceeding as prima facie evidence of facts on which conviction based; applying Illinois law); *see also* Aetna Cas. & Surety Co. v. Niziolek, 481 N.E.2d 1356 (Mass. 1985) (holding that, under

When considering whether a conviction has preclusive effect, one of the traditional requirements of issue preclusion should be borne in mind. The doctrine of issue preclusion traditionally applies only to issues that were actually litigated and determined in a prior action. This traditional requirement imposes a severe limit upon the preclusive effect of prior convictions. It means not only that prior convictions resulting from a plea of nolo contendere are not preclusive, but also that prior convictions resulting from a guilty plea are not preclusive.

Another limitation on preclusion can arise from differences in the standard of proof involved in the first and second cases. In the arson example offered at the beginning of this section, the insurance company could not be bound by an acquittal of the (now) plaintiff in the former criminal trial. An acquittal is merely a decision that there was a reasonable doubt about whether the defendant committed arson, not a decision, by a preponderance of the evidence, that the accused did not commit arson. When the standard of proof changes from proof beyond a reasonable doubt to some lower requirement, then preclusion does not apply if the party against whom it is sought to be used is the beneficiary of a more favorable standard of proof in the second action.[293]

Use of Convictions as Evidence of Acts Charged [FRE 803(22)]

Even if a prior conviction is not preclusive under the doctrine of collateral estoppel, it might still be admissible as evidence of the facts necessary to support the judgment. Though rebuttable, it is likely to be persuasive. Nonetheless, traditionally courts have not welcomed this use of the prior conviction. Historically, they cited some of the same concerns about lack of mutuality that have impeded acceptance of the prior conviction as collateral estoppel. They have also expressed concern that the evidence would be too powerful, that jurors would tend to treat it as conclusive even if told not to do so.[294] Once again, the prior conviction is a hearsay declaration by the trier-of-fact. Moreover, the trier-of-fact necessarily lacks personal knowledge of the accused's guilt and the case specific facts from which it is inferred.

Rule 803(22) affirms a hearsay exception for certain convictions and implicitly overcomes any personal knowledge objection as well. Although Rule 803(22) technically leaves open the possibility of exclusion of a prior conviction on Rule 403 grounds if the jury is likely to be over-influenced by it, in practice if the prior conviction meets the requirements of Rule 803(22), then it is likely to be admitted. To qualify under the rule, the conviction must have been for a crime punishable by death or imprisonment for more than a year. Rule 803(22), by its express terms, does not apply to guilty verdicts that are the result of pleas of nolo contendere, but only to verdicts that follow a trial or guilty plea. The rule preserves the traditional characteristics of a nolo plea, which was created

---

Massachusetts law, insured who was convicted of burning property to collect insurance proceeds was collaterally estopped from relitigating issues in civil action; but conviction of second defendant of arson, entered on guilty plea, did not collaterally estop that party from litigating issues in later civil action, though conviction was admissible in evidence).

[293] *See* RESTATEMENT (SECOND) OF JUDGMENTS § 28(4) (1980) and cases cited in Reporter's Note thereto.

[294] For a useful discussion of the rationale for the traditional view, by a court that departs from it drastically, see Scott v. Robertson, 583 P.2d 188 (Alaska 1978).

essentially to avoid some of the consequences of an admission of guilt but to allow the case to be resolved without trial.[295]

When a prior conviction results from a guilty plea, the guilty plea may be independently admissible as a statement by a party-opponent.[296] Guilty pleas to very minor offenses, such as traffic offenses, might not be very probative on the issue of guilt, because the defendant might merely have wanted to dispose of the problem without bothersome proceedings. Yet when the defendant had a real chance to contest the proceedings, the willingness to plead guilty seems at least relevant. The defendant can offer his explanations to the trier-of-fact.[297] On the other hand, what would be the point of excluding the prior conviction resulting from the plea of guilty if the guilty plea itself could come in?[298]

Rule 803(22) only covers felonies. Could Rule 803(8), regarding public records and reports admit a misdemeanor conviction? The public records exception contains a provision admitting "factual findings from a legally authorized investigation" if offered in a civil action or against the government in a criminal case.[299] The language of Rule 803(8) seems literally to apply, but the better view is that if the punishment requirement of Rule 803(22) is not satisfied, Rule 803(8) is not available as a backdoor alternative. The rulemakers considered the requirements needed for admission of convictions when drafting the more specific rule, Rule 803(22), and they decided that minor convictions should not be admissible to show the commission of the underlying offense. It would be peculiar to allow the broader rule, Rule 803(8), which was drafted without an eye to the problem of evidentiary use of criminal convictions, to be used as a way of getting around this intended limit. Despite the force of this argument, however, there is a division of authority concerning whether Rule 803(8) may be used to receive misdemeanor convictions.[300]

---

[295] *See* FED. R. EVID. 410 & 803(22) advisory committee notes. This result is consistent with prior decisions under the Clayton Act, to the effect that guilty pleas are admissible in subsequent litigation, but nolo pleas are not. *See, e.g.*, General Elec. Co. v. San Antonio, 334 F.2d 480, 484–87 (5th Cir. 1964).

[296] *See* Hancock v. Dodson, 958 F.2d 1367 (6th Cir. 1992) (admitting guilty plea to misdemeanor as statement of a party-opponent, even though final judgment following guilty plea is not admissible under language of Rule 803(22); court leaves open possibility that plea could be excluded under Rule 403 in case in which plea to misdemeanor was made under conditions that suggest its untrustworthiness); Hiroshi Motomura, *Using Judgments As Evidence*, 70 MINN. L. REV. 979, 990 (1986).

[297] *See* Ando v. Woodberry, 168 N.E.2d 520 (N.Y.1960) (rejecting argument that guilty plea to traffic offense should be inadmissible because people who believe themselves innocent often plead guilty merely to avoid expenditure of time and expense of trial).

[298] *But see* Hinshaw v. Keith, 645 F. Supp. 180 (D. Me. 1986) (expressly disagreeing with Weinstein, and holding that guilty plea to leaving scene of accident was admissible in subsequent civil case); McCormick v. United States, 539 F. Supp. 1179, 1183 (D. Colo. 1982) (guilty plea to traffic light violation admissible in subsequent civil action).

[299] FED. R. EVID. 803(8)(A)(iii).

[300] *See* Stroud v. Cook, 931 F. Supp. 733, 736 (D. Nev. 1996) (holding that misdemeanor conviction that did not qualify under Rule 803(22) is admissible as public record under Rule 803(8)) (alternative holding); *cf.* United States v. Wilson, 690 F.2d 1267, 1275 n.2 (9th Cir. 1982) (stating that Judgment and Commitment Order relating to the conviction for which defendant, now being prosecuted for escape, was being held at time of escape is admissible under public records exception). In authors' opinion, the *Wilson* precedent does not apply to situations in which the conviction is offered to prove the facts necessary to sustain the conviction, because all that was necessary in *Wilson* was to prove that he had been convicted and committed, not that he was actually guilty of the underlying crime of counterfeiting for which he had been committed at the time of the escape). *But cf.* Nipper v. Snipes, 7 F.3d 415, 417–18 (4th Cir. 1993) (Rule 803(8)(C)—predecessor of now Rule 803(8)(A)(iii)—does not apply to judicial findings of fact).

For a thoughtful discussion in the analogous context of civil judgments, see Herrick v. Garvey, 298 F.3d 1184, 1191–93 (10th Cir. 2002). An earlier district court decision found as a fact that a certain corporation had

Rule 803(22) is crafted to avoid conflict with the confrontation rights of the accused in a criminal case. It does this by precluding the use of a conviction to prove the adjudicated facts when offered against the accused and the person previously convicted was someone other than the accused. In that case the present accused will not have had the opportunity to defend against the prior allegations.[301]

The Rule is written, however, to avoid conflicting with the authorized use of convictions merely to impeach a witness, even if that witness is someone other than the accused. But the drafters were not entirely successful in this respect. In particular, a conviction for a misdemeanor crime of dishonesty is admissible under Rule 609 even though it does not meet the requirements of Rule 803(22).[302] To effectuate the scheme of the rules, effectively Rule 609 must operate as a hearsay exception as well as an exception to the character evidence prohibition.[303]

Use of Other Judgments as Evidence of Facts Determined Thereby [FRE 803(23)]

Outside the context of felony convictions, which are addressed by Rule 803(22), the law has been perhaps surprisingly reluctant to allow the use of judgments as evidence of the facts thereby adjudicated. If such judgments do not preclude relitigation in the subsequent action, then they may count for nothing in that later case. Nevertheless, the Rules contain a narrow exception, Rule 803(23), that permits the use of a judgment, whether civil or criminal, as evidence of any fact "essential to the judgment."[304] This exception applies only to judgments offered "to prove a matter of personal, family, or general history, or boundaries" if "the matter could be proved by evidence of reputation."[305] This limiting language clearly refers to the admissibility of hearsay under 803(19)—concerning the use of reputation to prove things like the circumstances of a person's birth, adoption, legitimacy, ancestry, etc.[306]—and under 803(20)—concerning

---

transferred ownership of its aircraft business to another company. The plaintiff offered the prior finding of fact as evidence to prove the truth of the matter. *Herrick* held that the finding was properly excluded as hearsay. Rule 803(8)(C)—now 803(8)(A)(iii)—did not apply for three reasons. First, that rule only applies to "investigations made pursuant to authority granted by law," and a judge is not an investigator. Second, the Advisory Committee Note to Rule 803(8)(C) indicates that the intent of the drafters was to cover findings of fact by executive officers, not by judges. Third, the hearsay exceptions for judgments, Rules 803(22) and 803(23), would be rendered redundant by holding that Rule 803(8)(C) provides a "blanket ground" for admission of prior judgments. *Id.*

[301] FED. R. EVID. 803(22) advisory committee note.

[302] FED. R. EVID. 609(a)(2). *See* Martin v. National R.R. Passenger Corp., 1998 WL 575183 at *2–*5 (S.D.N.Y. 1998) (holding evidence of defendant's prior convictions of the "crimen falsi" misdemeanors of fraudulent accosting and criminal impersonation admissible under Rule 609(b)).

[303] One might be tempted to ground this argument on the language of Rule 609, which states that convictions satisfying its requirements "must be admitted." FED. R. EVID. 609(a)(1). Such an argument proves too much, however, because its force cannot be restricted to overcoming a hearsay objection based on the fact-finder's statement of guilt. Rule 609 simply states that "evidence of a [qualifying] criminal conviction" "must be admitted." If the force of that "must" is not limited to overcoming the character evidence prohibition, to which the rule operates as an exception, then it would require, for example, admitting an ordinary hearsay statement that the witness had been convicted. And if the conviction is evidenced by a document, such a construction of "must be admitted" would nullify any objections based on failure to adequately authenticate the document, Rule 901, or to satisfy the requirement of the original of a document, Rule 1002. None of these implications are accepted by the courts, so the force of the "must be admitted" language should be construed more narrowly as referring to the otherwise applicable character evidence prohibition and the otherwise applicable discretionary exclusion of the evidence under Rule 403.

[304] FED. R. EVID. 803(23)(A).

[305] FED. R. EVID. 803(23)(B).

[306] *See* **§ 16.14**.

the use of reputation to prove land boundaries and matters of general history.[307] Although the origins of this exception are peculiar, its modern justification is based simply on the notion that a judgment ought to be considered at least as reliable as community reputation: if community reputation is admissible to prove some fact, then a judgment that depends on a finding that such fact is true ought also to be admissible.[308] Thus, for example, because a defendant in a criminal case would not be allowed to introduce reputation evidence, under either Rule 803(19) or 803(20), to establish that his failure to pay child support was not willful, accordingly he may not introduce a prior civil judgment of another court based on a finding that his failure was not willful.[309]

---

[307] *See* **§ 16.17**.

[308] *See* FED. R. EVID. 803(23) advisory committee note.

[309] *See* Knowles v. State, 708 So.2d 549, 558 (Miss. 1998).

Chapter 17

HEARSAY EXCEPTIONS UNDER FEDERAL RULE 804

Table of Sections

§ 17.01 Exceptions That Apply Only if Declarant Is Unavailable; Criteria of Unavailability [FRE 804(a)]

The exceptions set forth in Rule 804 of the Federal Rules of Evidence apply only if the declarant is unavailable. If the declarant is available, and the proponent wants to make use of the declarant's information, the proponent must produce the declarant as a live witness instead of introducing evidence of the declarant's out-of-court statements, even if the hearsay statement otherwise fits within an Rule 804 exception.[1] This reflects the law's preference for live testimony over hearsay declarations.

At first blush, the preference for live testimony would seem to be a sensible rule for all instances in which hearsay is offered. Why not always require that the live witness be produced if available? Such a rule would promote using the best possible evidence (live testimony), but would not stand in the way of admission of other evidence when the best was not available. Though superficially attractive, this requirement would be too broad. It would be inefficient and sometimes pointless to require the testimony of every available declarant—for example, every declarant in the chain of information represented by a business record. Also, sometimes hearsay is fully as reliable as in-court testimony. For example, a statement of a present sense impression made at the time of the event is arguably more reliable than a witness's recollection of the same event, recited months afterward and after preparation for litigation.[2] Nevertheless, sometimes the law has decided to insist on the live testimony of the declarant when possible, rather than admit the hearsay. Of course, the proponent can decline to present either.

Rule 804 is much shorter than Rule 803, containing only five hearsay exceptions. Undoubtedly historical accident has played a substantial role in the assignment of

[1] FED. R. EVID. 804(b) advisory committee note.

[2] *See* 2 MCCORMICK ON EVIDENCE § 271 at 358 (Kenneth S. Broun ed., 7th ed. 2013) (memory and sincerity dangers not present). Note, however, that the force of the latter argument rests on the idea—inherent in the structure of Rule 804—of having to choose between the hearsay and the live testimony: it has no force if both the hearsay and the live testimony are admitted. *See* **§ 17.07**.

exceptions to one category or the other.[3] In some cases, the hearsay statements covered by the Rule 804 exceptions are more dangerous as substitutes for in-court testimony than are those covered by the Rule 803 exceptions. In addition, the situations anticipated by Rule 804 are often ones in which it is feasible and useful to produce the witness if the witness is available,[4] as opposed to some of the exceptions under Rule 803 where production of the declarant might be difficult or of little value. We must concede, however, a degree of arbitrariness in the division of exceptions between Rule 803 (unavailability immaterial) and Rule 804 (statement admissible only if witness is unavailable). For example, considered as a new matter, it would be hard to justify granting excited utterances (which are likely to be inaccurate because made under stress) easier admissibility than former testimony (which was subject to all of the safeguards of oath and cross-examination).[5] Yet that is what the Federal Rules of Evidence do.[6]

Criteria of Unavailability

Death and disability are common causes of unavailability, but they are not the only ones.[7] Any cause that, through no fault of the proponent, prevents the witness from attending or testifying, constitutes unavailability.[8] If the witness is beyond the court's subpoena power and no other reasonable way to obtain the witness's testimony exists, the witness is unavailable.[9] If the witness appears but is exempt from testifying because of a claim of privilege, the witness is unavailable.[10] If the witness appears but refuses to testify after being ordered to do so, the witness is unavailable.[11] The witness is also unavailable if the witness appears and testifies that he or she cannot recall the subject matter.[12] Rule 804(a) is broadly designed to accommodate the faultless proponent, and it is only when the proponent has procured the unavailability of the witness or has not made proper efforts to subpoena the witness that the proponent will not be allowed to

---

3 *See* FED. R. EVID. 803, 804 advisory committee notes.

4 FED. R. EVID. 804(b) advisory committee note.

5 *See* Aviva Orenstein, *"My God!": A Feminist Critique of the Excited Utterance Exception to the Hearsay Rule*, 85 CAL. L. REV. 159, 179–82 (1997) (outlining the psychological community's critique of the reliability of excited utterances); Robert M. Hutchins & Donald Slesinger, *Some Observations on the Law of Evidence*, 28 COLUM. L. REV. 432, 437 (1928) (excited utterances unreliable); FED. R. EVID. 804(b)(1) advisory committee note ("it may be argued that former testimony is the strongest hearsay and should be included under Rule 803").

6 *See* FED. R. EVID. 803(2), 804(b)(1).

7 *See* FED. R. EVID. 804(a)(4).

8 *See* FED. R. EVID. 804(a); United States v. McGuire, 307 F.3d 1192, 1205 (9th Cir. 2002) (witness who was seven months pregnant was "unavailable" to testify at trial or deposition within meaning of Rule 804(a) because of dangers that stress of testimony raises for late term pregnancy).

9 FED. R. EVID. 804(a)(5). The mere fact that the witness is beyond the subpoena power is not enough; the Rule states that the proponent must be unable to obtain attendance by process or "other reasonable means." *See, e.g.*, Kirk v. Raymark Indus., Inc., 61 F.3d 147, 165 (3d Cir. 1995) (holding that expert who testified in prior case was not "unavailable" merely because he was beyond subpoena power; proponent should have tried to contact expert and request his attendance at trial). A proponent might have means other than subpoena when, for example, a state could request another state to furnish someone incarcerated in its prison system for testimony. Even if the incarcerated person were technically beyond the subpoena power, the state should make the effort to obtain the testimony by other means. *Cf.* Barber v. Page, 390 U.S. 719, 723–25 (1968) (violation of confrontation clause to use declarant's hearsay statement when state failed to make good faith effort to obtain cooperation of federal authorities in delivering declarant for testimony).

10 FED. R. EVID. 804(a)(1).

11 FED. R. EVID. 804(a)(2).

12 FED. R. EVID. 804(a)(3). This is distinct from the level of forgetting required under Rule 803(5), under which a recorded recollection may be admitted if the witness does not fully remember.

take advantage of the Rule.[13] In fact, when a party has procured the unavailability of a declarant, not only does the procuring party lose access to the first four hearsay exceptions in Rule 804(b), but that party's opponent gains access to the broad hearsay exception for forfeiture by wrongdoing in Rule 804(b)(6).[14]

Unavailability due to temporary illness poses a special problem; in such cases, the trial judge could allow the witness to be heard in person by granting a continuance. Although trial judges have discretion in this area, a continuance should be granted in criminal cases where the witness is vital and the charge is serious.[15]

Requirement of Deposition

If a proponent can foresee that the declarant will not be present at trial, he should depose the declarant, so that the opponent will have a chance for cross-examination during the deposition. When the declarant is not present at trial (as opposed to instances in which the declarant is present, but for some reason cannot or will not testify), the proponent of hearsay testimony attempting to invoke an exception under Rule 804(b)(2)–(4) must show that reasonable efforts were made to obtain the declarant's testimony by deposition.[16] However, this requirement does not apply when the hearsay is in the form of former testimony admissible under Rule 804(b)(1).[17] Then, there is no reason to require a deposition because the opportunity for cross-examination was provided at the prior proceeding during which the former testimony was taken.[18]

Unavailability and Privilege Claims

A claim of privilege, if it is accepted by the court, may be the basis for finding unavailability. But the matter is complicated when the privilege claim is asserted *by the proponent of the hearsay*. When the proponent is also the holder of the privilege, it seems odd to allow the proponent to argue that the declarant is unavailable, because the proponent could make the declarant available by waiving the privilege. Plausibly, the proponent's claim of privilege amounts to the procurement of the unavailability of the declarant for the purpose of Rule 804. A number of courts have so held, principally in the context of the criminal defendant who asserts his privilege not to testify as a basis for invoking one of the hearsay exceptions in Rule 804(b) in order to admit his own prior statements.[19]

---

[13] *See* FED. R. EVID. 804(a).

[14] *See* **§ 17.06**.

[15] *See, e.g.*, United States v. Faison, 679 F.2d 292, 297 (3d Cir. 1982) (trial court abused discretion in finding that key prosecution witness, who could not testify for at least four to five weeks because of surgery, was unavailable in prosecution for wire fraud and transporting stolen securities in interstate commerce). In *Faison*, the Third Circuit stated that

> [i]n exercising discretion a trial judge must consider all relevant circumstances, including: the importance of the absent witness for the case; the nature and extent of cross-examination in the earlier testimony; the nature of the illness; the expected time of recovery; the reliability of the evidence of the probable duration of the illness; and any special circumstances counseling against delay.

Id.

[16] FED. R. EVID. 804(a)(5).

[17] *Id.*

[18] H.R. REP. NO. 650, 93d Cong., 1st Sess. 5 (1973), *reprinted in* 1974 U.S. Code Cong. & Admin. News 7075, 7088.

[19] *See, e.g.*, S.E.C. v. Ficken, 546 F.3d 45, 53 (1st Cir. 2008) (holding defendant not unavailable based on invocation of Fifth Amendment when attempting to introduce his prior testimony under Rule 804(b)(1);

More controversial is the question whether a witness, other than the criminal defendant, who asserts the Fifth Amendment privilege not to testify at trial is unavailable to the prosecution when it wants to invoke Rule 804(b). The argument against such a conclusion is that the government has the power to compel the declarant's testimony by granting use immunity.[20] Failure to do so suggests that the government does not really want to hear the testimony of the witness and would rather go with a hearsay statement falling within Rule 804(b) that is favorable to the government. This also arguably amounts to procuring unavailability to invoke Rule 804(b).[21] Here, however, the courts have generally held in favor of the government on the ground that granting or refusing to grant immunity is a decision for the Executive branch, one that the courts have no authority to review.[22]

§ 17.02 Former Testimony [FRE 804(b)(1)]

Like the other Rule 804 exceptions, the former testimony exception applies only if the witness is unavailable. Common-law jurisdictions also required unavailability.[23] If the declarant testifies at trial, his or her former testimony is often, though not always, admissible under the exemption for out-of-court statements of a testifying witness, per Rule 801(d)(1). Rule 804(b)(1) addresses former testimony by a person who does not testify at the proceeding at which the former testimony is offered or who testifies but is nonetheless "unavailable" by the criteria of Rule 804(a) because of lack of memory, a privilege claim, and so forth.[24]

United States v. Hughes, 535 F.3d 880, 882 (8th Cir. 2008) (holding defendant not unavailable based on invocation of Fifth Amendment when attempting to introduce his prior statements as declarations against interest under Rule 804(b)(3)).

[20] *See* **§ 4.18**. *See* Peter Westen, *The Compulsory Process Clause*, 73 MICH. L. REV. 71, 169 (1974) (noting that use immunity is sufficient to compel testimony, with the result that the government loses nothing by granting it).

[21] One might think, therefore, that the defense would be entitled to a missing witness inference and jury instruction. *See* **§ 5.05** (subsection on "Evidence of a Party's Attempt to Withhold, Destroy, or Fabricate Evidence"). But the judicial response to this suggestion has often treated the government's power to control the witness's privilege as if it were itself a weighty privilege and rejected adverse inferences and associated jury instructions. *See, e.g.*, United States v. Myerson, 18 F.3d 153, 158–59 (2d Cir. 1994).

[22] *See, e.g.*, United States v. Lang, 589 F.2d 92, 95–96 (2d Cir. 1978) (holding declarant unavailable to government, as predicate to invoking declaration against interest exception, when declarant exercised privilege not to testify and government refused to grant use immunity in order to compel testimony). In the authors' view, this is not a sound justification. The claim made by defendants here need not be that the courts should second guess executive decisions about granting use immunity, only that the government must pay a price (the loss of the hearsay) if it wants to withhold such immunity. That is essentially the same thing that is said to a criminal defendant who wants to claim a privilege in order to establish the unavailability of a witness; the assertion of the privilege comes with the cost that the witness will not be considered unavailable to the defense.

Some courts have gone pretty far toward second guessing the government, allowing for the possibility that, in an extreme case, the court would order the immunization of the witness to prevent prosecutorial unfairness, with the result that the witness would be available to both parties and both would lose access to the 804(b) exceptions. *See, e.g.*, United States v. Lord, 711 F.2d 887, 889–92 (9th Cir. 1983); *see generally* Reid H. Weingarten & Brian M. Heberlig, *The Defense Witness Immunity Doctrine: The Time Has Come to Give It Strength to Address Prosecutorial Overreaching*, 43 AM. CRIM. L. REV. 1189 (2006).

[23] *See, e.g.*, School Dist. of Pontiac v. Sachse, 264 N.W. 396, 397 (Mich. 1936) (common-law jurisdiction requiring unavailability).

[24] Wigmore believed that former testimony should also be excluded from the definition of hearsay. His rationale was that since the testimony was subject to cross-examination in the first trial, the primary purpose behind the hearsay rule was satisfied. 5 WIGMORE ON EVIDENCE § 1370 (Chadbourn rev. 1974). Under the Rules, however, former testimony fits the technical definition of hearsay in FED. R. EVID. 801(c), and it cannot fall within the exemption for prior statements under Rule 801(d)(1) when the declarant is not testifying at the current trial.

To qualify under Rule 804(b)(1), former testimony must have been made under oath, subject to penalty for perjury, and the party against whom the former testimony was offered must have had a similar motive and opportunity to cross-examine the witness as would the party against whom the hearsay is offered in the later trial. This "similar motive and opportunity" requirement is more easily satisfied when the parties to the former hearing are the same as the parties to the later hearing. Indeed, a typical instance of the operation of the former testimony exception arises when a case has been reversed on appeal and remanded for a new trial. If a witness at the first trial is unavailable for the second, then that witness's testimony at the first trial is admissible at the second under the exception.[25] As discussed below, the Rule varies discernibly between criminal and civil cases in regard to permitting departures from this "same parties" paradigm.

When the testimony is offered in the form of a transcript of the prior trial, there are two levels of hearsay. First, the transcript is the statement of the court reporter about what was said on the witness stand at the prior trial. The public records exception creates an exception for this statement.[26] Many jurisdictions have statutes that provide specific exceptions for statements of court reporters.[27] Second, the witness's testimony at the prior trial is also hearsay, at least under the federal definition. The present exception applies to allow it to be received.

Again, former testimony often comes in through some route other than this exception. For example, former testimony can be used to impeach a witness with a prior inconsistent statement. When the former testimony is used to impeach the witness who gave it, the former testimony exception is not needed because Rule 801(d)(1)(A) provides the basis for receiving the testimony.[28] Similarly, former testimony of the opposing party is admissible against that party under Rule 801(d)(2) without the need for laying the foundation required by the exception for former testimony.[29] Also, the court can admit deposition testimony under Rule 32 of the Rules of Civil Procedure without relying on this exception.[30] As long as the statements made in the deposition would be admissible

---

25 FED. R. EVID. 804(b)(1).

26 FED. R. EVID. 803(8)(A)(ii). It also qualifies as a present sense impression under Rule 803(1).

27 *See, e.g.*, N.C. GEN. STAT. § 8–85:

> Testimony taken and transcribed by a court reporter and certified by the reporter or by the judge who presided at the trial at which the testimony was given, may be offered in evidence in any court as the deposition of the witness whose testimony is so taken and transcribed, in the manner, and under the rules governing the introduction of depositions in civil actions.

California's Evidence Code provides for a public records exception in CAL. EVID. CODE § 1291. The code also provides an arguably stronger exception for the transcript of a court reporter in CAL. CIV. PROC. CODE § 273. Transcribed and certified reports as prima facie evidence: "The report of the official reporter, or official reporter pro tempore, of any court, duly appointed and sworn, when transcribed and certified as being a correct transcript of the testimony and proceedings in the case, is prima facie evidence of such testimony and proceedings." *Id. See* also FED. R. CIV. P. 80(c) (Stenographic Report or Transcript as Evidence), which provides: "Whenever the testimony of a witness at a trial or hearing which was stenographically reported is admissible in evidence at a later trial, it may be proved by the transcript thereof duly certified by the person who reported the testimony."

28 *See* **§ 15.03**.

29 *See* **§ 15.06**.

30 FED. R. CIV. P. 32(a) provides that at a hearing or trial, all or part of a deposition may be used against a party if the party was present or represented at the taking of the deposition or had reasonable notice of it and it is used to the extent it would be admissible under the Federal Rules of Evidence if the deponent were present and testifying. Rule 32 anticipates that any party may use a deposition to contradict or impeach the testimony given by the deponent as a witness, or for any other purpose allowed by the Federal Rules of Evidence. It defines unavailability in much the same way as does FED. R. EVID. 804(a), adding one criterion that "on motion and notice, that exceptional circumstances make it desirable—in the interest of justice and

under the Rules of Evidence if they had been made by a live witness at the present trial, and provided that the deposition is being used against a party who was present or represented at the deposition (or at least had adequate notice of the deposition to have been present or represented), then the statements made in the deposition can be offered as evidence under Rule 32. As in Federal Rule of Evidence 801(d)(2) concerning a statement by a party-opponent, there is no requirement of witness unavailability when introducing the deposition of a party in the current case. However, Rule 32 requires that the witness be unavailable when a party offers the deposition of a non-party witness. Rule 32 also allows a witness's deposition to be used under "exceptional circumstances" when it is "in the interest of justice." Though this rule potentially could admit a great deal more evidence, even where the unavailability requirements have not been met, the courts have not read this exception broadly and it has had a rather limited effect in admitting otherwise objectionable evidence.[31]

The former testimony exception is based on the theory that cross-examination under oath at a prior proceeding adequately substitutes for cross-examination in the current proceeding.[32] Because the absence of cross-examination is thought to be the principal reason for the exclusion of hearsay, one might expect that former testimony would be freely admissible. However, the exception is encumbered with restrictions, which are discussed in the following subsections.

Requirements on the Identity of Parties

Historically, some common-law courts required that the party *against whom the evidence is offered* be the same in both actions.[33] This rule has been criticized on the ground that it needlessly excludes reliable evidence.[34] For example, in a case in which the issue is whether property was destroyed by arson, the alleged arsonist in a criminal trial who claims the fire was accidentally caused would have every incentive to cross-examine the witness vigorously. But if that witness became unavailable in a subsequent civil case involving another party (say, the person who allegedly benefited from the arson), the testimony would be inadmissible. Yet the testimony has almost all the safeguards of courtroom testimony, and arguably the jury could be trusted enough to treat it as being better than nothing.[35]

With this sort of problem in mind, the federal rulemakers originally proposed that the exception be liberalized to provide that such identity of parties (against whom offered) was not necessary so long as the party in the first action had a similar motive to

---

with due regard to the importance of live testimony in open court—to permit the deposition to be used." It includes notice requirements and protections for parties who, despite diligent efforts, could not obtain legal representation at the deposition. *See* Ueland v. United States, 291 F.3d 993, 996–97 (7th Cir. 2002) (illustrating how Fed. R. Civ. P. 32(a)(3) supplements the former testimony exception of Fed. R. Evid. 804(b)(1) by holding that depositions of witnesses located more than 100 miles from the place of trial, and thus satisfying the former, are admissible even if the witnesses are not unavailable for testimony in the sense of being beyond the court's subpoena power, as required by the latter).

[31] *See* 8A CHARLES A. WRIGHT & ARTHUR R. MILLER, FEDERAL PRACTICE AND PROCEDURE: CIVIL §§ 2142, 2146, 2150 (2d ed. 1994).

[32] *See* FED. R. EVID. 804(b)(1) advisory committee note. *See also* 5 WEINSTEIN'S FEDERAL EVIDENCE § 804.04[1][a] (Mark S. Brodin ed., 2d ed. 2015); 2 MCCORMICK ON EVIDENCE § 301 (Kenneth S. Broun ed., 7th ed. 2013).

[33] *See, e.g.*, Bulk Trans., Inc. v. Louisiana Pub. Serv. Comm'n, 209 So. 2d 4, 6–7 (La. 1968).

[34] *See* 2 MCCORMICK ON EVIDENCE § 303 (Kenneth S. Broun ed., 7th ed. 2013).

[35] *See* Travelers Fire Ins. Co. v. Wright, 322 P.2d 417, 421–22 (Okla. 1958) (admitting former testimony, given at criminal arson trial, in subsequent civil action).

cross-examine as the party in the second action.[36] However, Congress rejected this attempt and the final version of Rule 804(b)(1) requires in criminal cases that the party against whom the evidence is offered be the same in both cases.[37] Thus, if the current action is a criminal prosecution and the government wishes to offer into evidence the testimony of a witness in a prior proceeding to which the accused was not a party, that testimony is not admissible under this exception. The same would be true of prior testimony offered by the criminal defendant against the government if the government was not a party to the prior action.[38]

For civil cases, however, the Rule provides that the party against whom the evidence was previously offered must be either (a) the same party as the one against whom it is now offered or (b) a "predecessor in interest" to the party against whom it is now offered.[39] Where the prior testimony is sought to be admitted against a party not represented in the earlier suit, the definition of "predecessor in interest" is thus crucial.[40] Traditionally, the phrase "predecessor in interest" describes someone who had a prior interest in property that is now subject to litigation or who was otherwise in privity with a party.[41] However, some courts have given the term a more expansive meaning.

---

[36] *See* FED. R. EVID. 804(b)(1) (Supreme Court Proposed Draft 1973), *reprinted in* 2 JAMES F. BAILEY & OSCAR M. TRELLES, THE FEDERAL RULES OF EVIDENCE: LEGISLATIVE HISTORIES AND RELATED DOCUMENTS, Doc. 7 at 33 (1980).

[37] *See* H.R. REP. NO. 650, 93d Cong., 1st Sess., 15 (1973), *reprinted in* 4 JAMES F. BAILEY & OSCAR M. TRELLES, THE FEDERAL RULES OF EVIDENCE: LEGISLATIVE HISTORIES AND RELATED DOCUMENTS, Doc. 13 at 15 (1980).

[38] *See, e.g.*, United States v. Peterson, 100 F.3d 7, 11–12 (2d Cir. 1996) (holding that a federal criminal defendant may not use former testimony exception to introduce earlier state grand jury testimony).

When the prior case was a *civil* case and the case in which the testimony is offered is a *criminal* case, some courts take the view that similarity of interest, rather than identity of parties, is the relevant test, at least where the testimony is offered against the government in the criminal case. *See* United States v. McDonald, 837 F.2d 1287, 1291–93 (5th Cir. 1988) (dictum), and see cases cited therein. Given the language of Rule 804(b)(1), this conclusion is difficult to justify. *See* United States v. Harenberg, 732 F.2d 1507, 1516 (10th Cir. 1984) (holding depositions taken in prior civil action should be excluded in subsequent criminal case because the United States did not have an opportunity to cross-examine declarants in the civil depositions). When the defendant in the two cases is the same, and the testimony from the earlier civil case is offered against the defendant in the criminal case, the party identity requirement is clearly satisfied and the issue then is solely the question whether the defendant had a similar motive to develop the testimony in the two cases. *See, e.g.*, United States v. Vartanian, 245 F.3d 609, 613–14 (6th Cir. 2001).

[39] FED. R. EVID. 804(b)(1)(B).

[40] *See generally* 2 MCCORMICK ON EVIDENCE § 303 (Kenneth S. Broun ed., 7th ed. 2013), where the authors note the "murky" Congressional intent and suggest ways of accommodating the "predecessor in interest" language.

[41] In Lloyd v. American Exp. Lines, Inc., 580 F.2d 1179 (3d Cir. 1978), Judge Stem, who concurred in the result but disagreed with the majority's interpretation of predecessor in interest in Rule 804(b)(1), noted that the commentators had defined predecessor in interest in terms of a privity relationship, and gave the following definition of privity:

> The term 'privity' denotes mutual or successive relationships to the same rights of property, and privies are distributed into several classes, according to the manner of this relationship. Thus, there are privies in estate, as donor and donee, lessor and lessee, and joint tenants; privies in blood, as heir and ancestor, and co-parceners; privies in representation, as executor and testator, administrator and intestate; privies in law, where the law, without privity of blood or estate casts the land upon another, as by escheat.

Id. at 1191. The above passage quotes Metropolitan St. Ry. v. Gumby, 99 F. 192, 198 (2d Cir. 1900), which is also quoted in 11 JAMES A. MOORE, MOORE'S FEDERAL PRACTICE § 807.04[02] (2d ed. 1988). For a similar definition, *see* BLACK'S LAW DICTIONARY 1199 (6th ed. 1990).

For example, in *Lloyd v. American Export Lines*,[42] the plaintiff, Roland Alvarez, brought a Jones Act claim against American Export Lines, Inc. The plaintiff, a merchant mariner, had been involved in a violent encounter with Lloyd, a fellow crew member on board the freighter on which both worked.[43] The plaintiff's theory of recovery was that American Export failed to use due care in protecting him against Lloyd. The plaintiff introduced testimony at trial that Lloyd, who was unavailable at trial, made a vicious, unprovoked attack upon him. In countering the plaintiff's version of events, American Export Lines offered Lloyd's sworn prior testimony in the form of a transcript of a Coast Guard hearing, as well as the report of the hearing examiner. The trial court excluded the evidence but the Third Circuit held that the hearing examiner's report should have been admitted under the public records exception, and that the recorded testimony of Lloyd should have been admitted under Rule 804(b)(1). Finding that Lloyd's unavailability had been sufficiently established, it addressed the "more difficult" question, whether the Coast Guard, which had been a party in the prior hearing, was a "predecessor in interest" of Alvarez for purposes of Rule 804(b)(1).[44] The same alleged misconduct was involved in both the Coast Guard hearing and Alvarez's civil action. The Coast Guard investigating officer at the prior hearing had sought to establish that Lloyd had been intoxicated, that he had started the fight with Alvarez, and that he had harassed Alvarez—all facts that Alvarez sought to establish in the later civil case. The court decided that because the Coast Guard and Alvarez had similar interests in the two cases and a similar motive to cross-examine, the predecessor in interest requirement was satisfied.[45]

The result seems to make the statutory words "predecessor in interest" superfluous and instead returns to the similar motive requirement. The House added the predecessor in interest language. The House Committee on the Judiciary explained that "it is generally unfair to impose upon the party against whom the hearsay evidence is being offered responsibility for the manner in which the witness was previously handled by another party."[46] To read the predecessor in interest requirement to mean nothing more than that the parties have a similar motive renders this action by Congress nearly meaningless.[47] The Senate Committee on the Judiciary recommended approval of the House change, describing the difference between the original version containing only a similar motive requirement and the amended version as "not great."[48] *Lloyd* noted this language and stated, "We, too, fail to see a compelling difference between the two

---

[42] Lloyd v. American Exp. Lines, Inc., 580 F.2d 1179, 1181–87 (3d Cir. 1978); *see also* Athridge v. Aetna Cas. & Sur. Co., 474 F. Supp. 2d 102, 115 (D.D.C. 2007) (recognizing *Lloyd* as the "leading case on application of the predecessor-in-interest requirement").

[43] Lloyd, Alvarez's alleged attacker, brought the ongoing claim. Alvarez was impleaded by defendant. Lloyd then dropped out of the case.

[44] Lloyd v. American Exp. Lines, Inc., 580 F.2d 1179, 1184 (3d Cir. 1978).

[45] *Id.* at 1181–87. *See also* Horne v. Owens-Corning Fiberglas Corp., 4 F.3d 276, 283 (4th Cir. 1993) (holding prior claimant in similar asbestos case predecessor in interest because of similarity of motive to examine witnesses, even though the two parties had no relationship and were not in privity).

[46] H.R. REP. NO. 650, 93d Cong., 1st Sess. 15 (1973), *reprinted in* 4 JAMES F. BAILEY & OSCAR M. TRELLES, THE FEDERAL RULES OF EVIDENCE: LEGISLATIVE HISTORIES AND RELATED DOCUMENTS, Doc. 13 at 15 (1980).

[47] Alternatively, one could interpret Congress's change of language as an unartful attempt to reject the advisory committee's original proposal for criminal cases while retaining that proposal's elimination of an identity-of-parties requirement in civil cases.

[48] S. REP. NO. 1277, 93d Cong., 2d Sess. 28 (1974), *reprinted in* 4 JAMES F. BAILEY & OSCAR M. TRELLES, THE FEDERAL RULES OF EVIDENCE: LEGISLATIVE HISTORIES AND RELATED DOCUMENTS, Doc. 15 at 28 (1980).

approaches."[49] It specifically rejected the idea that "this change in wording signaled a return to the common-law approach to former testimony, requiring privity or a common property interest between the parties."[50]

An intermediate position would understand "predecessor in interest" as signifying some kind of nexus or connection between the parties but without being limited by technical conceptions of privity derived from property and contract law. So far, however, nothing very concrete has emerged to implement this idea.[51]

Opportunity and Similar Motive to Develop Testimony

Rule 804(b)(1) requires that the party against whom the former testimony is being introduced (or, in a civil case, someone qualifying as a "predecessor in interest") had an opportunity and similar motive to develop the testimony by direct, cross, or redirect examination. Such similar motive can be lacking, for example, when the party against whom the former testimony is offered has more to lose than or different goals from the corresponding party in the first action. However, conceptual differences between the two actions, new legal theories, or new strategies for cross-examination cannot prevent admission of the prior testimony if the incentive for developing the testimony was essentially the same.[52] And the specific reference in the rule to previous development of the testimony by direct and redirect examination shows that the party opposing the evidence in the later trial (or its predecessor in interest) need not have been opposing the testimony in the earlier proceeding.

The operation of the similar motive requirement is illustrated by the litigation over the deposition of Dr. Kenneth Wallace Smith, the deceased former medical director of Johns-Manville Corporation.[53] Dr. Smith, a former medical director of a manufacturer of asbestos products with 20 years' experience, was deposed in 1976 in a Pennsylvania state court case. After his death the deposition was offered by plaintiffs in various asbestosis cases on issues such as the state of the art during the 1940s and 1950s. The

---

[49] Lloyd v. American Exp. Lines, 580 F.2d 1179, 1185 (3d Cir. 1978).

[50] *Id.* at 1185 n.5; *see also* New England Mutual Life Ins. Co. v. Anderson, 888 F.2d 646, 651–52 (10th Cir. 1989) (citing *Lloyd* and apparently accepting its approach to predecessor in interest requirement, but holding testimony in prior criminal trial against co-conspirator inadmissible against civil party because, under the circumstances, co-conspirator had no motive or interest in protecting innocence of party against whom testimony now offered).

[51] For in depth discussions of the problem, see 5 CHRISTOPHER B. MUELLER & LAIRD C. KIRKPATRICK, FEDERAL EVIDENCE § 8:122 (4th ed. 2013), and 2 MCCORMICK ON EVIDENCE § 303 (Kenneth S. Broun ed., 7th ed. 2013).

[52] *See* Williams v. Commissioner, 999 F.2d 760, 764–66 (4th Cir. 1993) (holding admissible, in action for tax deficiencies, transcript of testimony by government witness in defendant's prior criminal trial for possession of narcotics where defendant failed to show how motive to cross-examine witness differed from prior trial and where transcript was only used to show commissioner's deficiency calculations were not arbitrary); United States v. Koon, 34 F.3d 1416, 1428 (9th Cir. 1994) (holding that defendants in federal civil rights/police brutality case arising from beating of Rodney King were not deprived of Sixth Amendment right to confrontation by admission of videotaped trial testimony of witness against them in earlier state criminal trial; rule's requirements of similar motive and opportunity were satisfied despite fact that additional ammunition for cross-examination had been developed since first trial); United States v. Miles, 290 F.3d 1341, 1352–53 (11th Cir. 2002) (discerning no abuse of discretion in finding that defendant had similar motive to disprove connection with methamphetamine lab in second case as in first, even though broader conspiracy was alleged in second case).

[53] The Smith deposition has nourished its own nest of cases on the former testimony exception. *See* Dykes v. Raymark Indus., 801 F.2d 810 (6th Cir. 1986); Dartez v. Fibreboard Corp., 765 F.2d 456 (5th Cir. 1985); Murphy v. Owens-Illinois, Inc., 779 F.2d 340 (6th Cir. 1985); Clay v. Johns-Manville Sales Corp., 722 F.2d 1289 (6th Cir. 1983); *In re* Johns-Manville/Asbestosis Cases, 93 F.R.D. 853 (N.D. Ill. 1982).

deposition's reception depended upon the party against whom it was offered and the circumstances of the particular case. For example, in *Murphy v. Owens-Illinois, Inc.*,[54] the court upheld a trial judge's decision to exclude the deposition.[55] The party against whom the deposition was offered at trial had not been a party in the case in which the deposition was taken.[56] The Sixth Circuit held that this in itself was insufficient to support exclusion, since it followed *Lloyd* and took an expansive interpretation of the "predecessor in interest" language. If the prior litigant had a similar motive, then it qualified as a predecessor in interest. In this case the prior litigant did not have a similar motive.[57] The defendant corporations that were represented at the deposition did not have the same motive to prove a primitive state of the art during the 1940s and 1950s that the defendant against whom it was offered in the *Murphy* case did because the present defendant, Owens-Illinois, had stopped manufacturing asbestos-containing products in 1958.[58] In contrast, the parties who took the deposition, Johns-Manville and Raybestos-Manhattan, had continued manufacturing until the 1960s and 1970s. They would possibly have harmed their cases had they shown a primitive state of the art in the 1940s or 1950s, because that would have highlighted how much had been learned since then.[59] Owens-Illinois, on the other hand, would have wished to prove that the state of the art through 1958 was primitive, and had that company been able to examine Smith at his deposition, it would have sought to establish these facts. Therefore, Owens-Illinois would have conducted its examination of Smith much differently than Johns-Manville and Raybestos-Manhattan.[60]

The Supreme Court examined the "similar motive" requirement of the former testimony exception in *United States v. Salerno*,[61] a case in which two witnesses received use immunity to testify before the grand jury and gave testimony that was favorable to the defendant. The prosecution had ample opportunity to develop their testimony before the grand jury. Called by the defense at trial, these grand jury witnesses again claimed the right against self-incrimination and refused to testify. But this time, the prosecution refused to grant immunity. The defense then sought to introduce their grand jury testimony under Rule 804(b)(1). The prosecution objected, arguing that, at the grand jury stage, its motive to cross-examine the witnesses was not similar to what its motive would have been at trial, and therefore the "similar motive" requirement of the hearsay exception was not satisfied.

Justice Thomas, writing for an 8–1 majority concluded that the "plain language" of the rule supported the prosecution's contention of dissimilar motive. The defense had argued that adversarial fairness required that the evidence be admitted, observing that when witnesses testify favorably to the government at the grand jury stage, the

---

54 Murphy v. Owens-Illinois, Inc., 779 F.2d 340 (6th Cir. 1985).

55 *Id.* at 346.

56 *Id.* at 343.

57 *Id.* at 343–44.

58 *Id.*

59 *Id.*

60 In other cases, where the difference in motive was not as pronounced, the Smith deposition has been admitted. *See, e.g.*, Clay v. Johns-Manville Sales Corp., 722 F.2d 1289, 1295 (6th Cir. 1983) (holding deposition admissible where prior and current defendants had similar motive to cross-examine Smith regarding manufacturer's knowledge of hazards of asbestos in products liability cases). *See also* Dykes v. Raymark Indus., 801 F.2d 810, 817 (6th Cir. 1986) (holding deposition admissible where objecting party failed to explain why motive and opportunity to cross-examine Smith differed in the first case).

61 United States v. Salerno, 505 U.S. 317 (1992).

government gives them immunity and obtains their trial testimony, but that when the witnesses testify unfavorably the government refuses to give immunity and objects to receiving their grand jury testimony. Justice Thomas indicated that the concept of adversarial fairness did not justify creating an exception to the plain requirements of Rule 804(b)(1). The Court remanded the case to determine whether the prosecutor did in fact have a similar motive to develop testimony at the grand jury stage.[62] On remand, the Second Circuit held that the government's motive was dissimilar because of the difference in the prosecution's goals in the two proceedings. Before the grand jury, the prosecution, operating in investigatory mode, may seek to avoid disclosure of confidential sources, and need only establish a strong enough case to support an indictment. It would not need to challenge in detail exculpatory testimony that the grand jury would not be inclined to believe anyway. By contrast, at trial, the prosecution must prove guilt beyond reasonable doubt and must challenge adverse testimony aggressively.[63]

Whether the "similar motive" requirement of Rule 804(b)(1) has been satisfied is clearly context-driven. Each case must be examined on its own facts as small changes in legal theory, the line-up of parties, and other factors can affect the outcome. In each case, the parties must be prepared to demonstrate to the court the existence (or nonexistence) of a motive sufficiently similar to satisfy the Rule.

§ 17.03 Dying Declarations [FRE 804(b)(2)]

The traditional theory behind the dying declarations exception, which dates back to old English cases in the seventeenth and eighteenth centuries,[64] is that one would not want to go to one's Maker with a lie upon one's lips. The validity of this exception for modern secular society has been questioned; some might feel freer to lie because they do not accept a worldview that encompasses heavenly retribution for sin. Also, the problems of memory, perception, and narrative mistakes may be amplified when a person is dying, particularly of a violent death. On the other hand, the circumstances under which these statements are made tends to decrease the dangers of calculated fabrication by the declarant, and the dangers of misreporting and improper influence on the declarant associated with police interrogations are diminished.[65] In any event, this time-honored exception, one of the very oldest of hearsay exceptions, shows no signs of mortality itself.

Unavailability

As with all Rule 804 exceptions, the declarant must be unavailable in order to use Rule 804(b)(2) to admit a dying declaration. At common law, many courts only allowed the hearsay if the declarant was dead.[66] Under the Federal Rule, it is possible for the

---

[62] Justice Stevens dissented, saying that the record of the particular case did show that the government had the opportunity and similar motive to develop the witness's testimony at the grand jury proceeding. 505 U.S. at 326 (Stevens, J., dissenting).

[63] *See* United States v. DiNapoli, 8 F.3d 909, 912–914 (2d Cir. 1993). *But see* United States v. Foster, 128 F.3d 949, 954–56 (6th Cir. 1997) (reversing exclusion of defense offer of grand jury testimony and holding that prosecution had same motive to develop the testimony before grand jury as it would at trial.).

[64] *See* Mattox v. United States, 146 U.S. 140, 151–52 (1892) (describing early American and English cases dealing with dying declarations).

[65] *See* Roger C. Park, *A Subject Matter Approach to Hearsay Reform*, 86 MICH. L. REV. 51, 76–77 (1987). *See also* FED. R. EVID. 804(b)(2) advisory committee note; 2 MCCORMICK ON EVIDENCE § 310 (Kenneth S. Broun ed., 7th ed. 2013); 5 WEINSTEIN'S FEDERAL EVIDENCE § 804.05[1] (Mark S. Brodin ed., 2d ed. 2015); Ralph Slovenko, *Deathbed Declarations*, 14 J. PSYCHIATRY & L. 469 (1996).

[66] *See, e.g.*, State v. Carden, 183 S.E. 898, 903 (N.C. 1936) (stating rule that declarant must have died before statement admissible).

declarant to be unavailable for some reason other than death.[67] For example, the declarant might have been shot at the same time and by the same person as the murder victim, named the perpetrator while believing that his own death was imminent, and then have recovered. If the declarant then refuses to testify or is unavailable for some other reason, the requirements of the exception have been met. After all, the need for recourse to the hearsay is just as great when the declarant has suffered permanent memory loss regarding the events in question, for example, as it is when the declarant is dead. The need may not be quite as great just because the declarant is beyond the reach of legal process, because that is something that might be temporary, but the rulemakers determined that any of the various conditions of unavailability specified in Rule 804(a) should suffice.

Belief That Death Is Imminent

"Over the strong objections of the state prosecutors, Lincoln addressed the preacher: 'State whether you were with Greek Crafton shortly before he died and at the time he was expecting death, and if so, state what you heard, if you heard anything.' "[68] Attorney Abraham Lincoln may have been jumping ahead a bit in trying to lay the foundation and get in the evidence itself with one triple question, but his question incorporates a version of the most important element of the modern exception. The declarant must have been "expecting death," or, in the words of the Federal Rule, must have made the statement while believing that death was "imminent." For example, in one murder trial the prosecution introduced a letter left by the victim outlining how his wife and her lover would murder him, but a reviewing court held it was error for the trial court to admit the letter because there was nothing in the letter to suggest that the victim thought his death was imminent.[69]

The victim's own statement about belief in imminent death may be used in laying the foundation, and it is perhaps the most common method.[70] Evidence that the victim

---

[67] *See* FED. R. EVID. 804(b)(2) advisory committee note ("Unavailability is not limited to death").

[68] Herbert Mitgang, *Lincoln as Lawyer: Transcript Tells Murder Story*, N.Y. TIMES, Feb. 10, 1989, at B7, col. 4 (excerpt from then newly discovered Lincoln transcripts).

[69] *See* Commonwealth v. Levanduski, 907 A.2d 3, 8–10, 19 (Pa. Super. Ct. 2006); *see also* United States v. Layton, 549 F. Supp. 903, 918 (N.D. Cal. 1982), *rev'd in part on other grounds* 720 F.2d 548 (9th Cir. 1983) (holding tape-recorded statements of Jim Jones concerning the killing of Congressman Leo Ryan during the mass suicide at Jonestown inadmissible where there was no evidence showing Jones believed his own death was imminent and where statements would have nothing to do with the cause or circumstances of Jones death); *cf.* Boone v. State, 668 S.W.2d 17, 20–21 (Ark. 1984) (where child had vomited blood after beating and asked whether he was going to die, statements made by the child prior to assurances from his mother that he would live were admissible); State v. Penley, 347 S.E.2d 783, 789 (N.C. 1986) (holding videotape of victim admissible where homicide victim's statements showed belief of imminent death).

[70] *See* Shepard v. United States, 290 U.S. 96, 99–100 (1933) (requiring a positive statement from the declarant as to belief of imminent death); State v. Phillips, 277 N.W. 609, 615 (N.D. 1938) (noting that declarant said, "I am very sick. I shall soon be with my mother [whom court notes is deceased]. I shall see Jesus"); People v. Del Vermo, 85 N.E. 690, 696 (N.Y. 1908) (noting that declarant said, "I am going to die. What are my children going to do after this?").

was told of impending death,[71] or occasionally that the injury was so grievous that the imminence of death was obvious,[72] may also be used to lay the foundation.[73]

Statement Concerns the Cause or Circumstances of Death

If a declarant, knowing that death is imminent, makes the statement, "Smith owes me $1000," the exception would not apply. The dying declaration must concern the cause and circumstances of the declarant's expected death.[74] This prevents dying persons from making self-serving statements designed to help their heirs or punish their enemies. The result might be different, however, if the declarant said, "Smith owes me $1000. That's why he did this to me." Thus, while the rule does not bar all such statements, it does bar statements that are irrelevant to the declarant's current predicament.[75] There is obviously some flexibility in characterizing a matter as being about "the cause or circumstances" of the declarant's anticipated death, and a narrow construction of that clause risks depriving the fact-finder of valuable evidence.[76]

A Civil Case or Homicide Prosecution

At common law, the dying declaration exception was limited to homicide prosecutions.[77] The federal rule makers extended it to civil actions, leaving one arena in which the federal exception does not apply—criminal prosecutions for matters other than homicide.[78] This limitation is illogical. The danger of concocting dying declarations about matters other than death would seem to be met by the requirement that the declaration concern the circumstances and cause of the anticipated death. Apparently the limitation

---

71 *See, e.g.*, Commonwealth v. Hebert, 163 N.E. 189, 191 (Mass. 1928) (reporting that doctor stated: "You know you are getting worse, don't you[?]" and "We have been talking it over, and we don't think you are going to get better").

72 *See, e.g.*, People v. Monterroso, 101 P.3d 956, 971 (Cal. 2004) (holding that the requirement of knowledge of impending death was satisfied when the declarant had been shot and severely wounded, expressed fear of dying, lay in a fetal position, and did not utter another word after making his statement); United States v. Mobley, 421 F.2d 345, 347 (5th Cir. 1970) (holding that wounds were so severe that victim must have known death imminent); *see also* Commonwealth v. Peyton, 62 A.2d 37, 40 (Pa. 1948) (holding that severity of wounds indicated consciousness of imminent death). *But see* People v. Stiff, 904 N.E.2d 1174, 1178, 1180 (Ill. App. Ct. 2009) (holding that even though declarant had third-degree burns over 77% percent of his body, but "[t]he record is devoid of evidence that [the declarant] believed that his death was imminent at the time he made the statement").

73 *See* 5 WEINSTEIN'S FEDERAL EVIDENCE § 804.05[4][b] (Mark S. Brodin ed., 2d ed. 2015) ("The declarant's belief in the imminence of death may be shown by the declarant's own statements, or through circumstantial evidence such as the nature of the wounds, opinions of declarant's physicians, the fact that declarant received last rites, and statements made in declarant's presence.") (footnotes omitted).

74 FED. R. EVID. 804(b)(2); 2 MCCORMICK ON EVIDENCE § 311 at 516 (Kenneth S. Broun ed., 7th ed. 2013).

75 *See* FED. R. EVID. 804(b)(2) advisory committee note ("[W]hen the statement deals with matters other than the supposed death, its influence is believed to be sufficiently attenuated to justify the limitation."); United States v. Layton, 549 F. Supp. 903, 918 (N.D. Cal. 1982) (holding statements made by Jim Jones regarding killing of congressman inadmissible because they did not concern the cause or circumstances of Jones's death, and because they were not clearly made with a belief of imminent death); United States v. Sacasas, 381 F.2d 451, 454 (2d Cir. 1967) (holding statement that co-indictee had nothing to do with bank robbery held inadmissible because it had nothing to do with declarant's death and because defendant was not being prosecuted for homicide).

76 5 WEINSTEIN'S FEDERAL EVIDENCE § 804.05[5][b] (Mark S. Brodin ed., 2d ed. 2015) (noting that this requirement can result in keeping out some very helpful evidence and arguing for broad treatment of this requirement where admission of the statement will help the jury in its task).

77 *See* 2 MCCORMICK ON EVIDENCE § 311 (Kenneth S. Broun ed., 7th ed. 2013); *see also* Annotation, *Admissibility of Dying Declarations in Civil Case*, 47 A.L.R.2d 526 (1956).

78 FED. R. EVID. 804(b)(2).

reflects a general distrust of dying declarations, at least where criminal penalties are involved, and the influence of common-law precedents.[79]

Personal Knowledge Required

As with most other hearsay exceptions, the dying declaration is admissible only to the extent that it would be admissible if the declarant were present and testifying.[80] Thus, the declarant who was shot while sleeping, and then states a suspicion about the identity of the shooter, has not made an admissible dying declaration because the declarant lacks personal knowledge.[81]

§ 17.04 Declarations Against Interest [FRE 804(b)(3)]

Rule 804(b)(3) sets out an exception for statements against interest (or as it they are more commonly known, "declarations" against interest) by absent declarants. The exception is based on the theory that reasonable people usually do not make statements against their interest unless the statements are true.[82]

Statements by Party-Opponents Distinguished

This exception is often confused with the exemption for statements of a party opponent. The following table articulates the differences.

---

[79] *See* H.R. REP. NO. 650, 93d Cong., 1st Sess. 15 (1973), *reprinted in* 4 JAMES F. BAILEY & OSCAR M. TRELLES, THE FEDERAL RULES OF EVIDENCE: LEGISLATIVE HISTORIES AND RELATED DOCUMENTS, Doc. 13 at 15–16 (1980):

> The Committee did not consider dying declarations as among the most reliable forms of hearsay. Consequently, it amended the provision to limit their admissibility in criminal cases to homicide prosecutions, where exceptional need for the evidence is present. This is existing law. At the same time, the Committee approved the expansion to civil actions and proceedings where the stakes do not involve possible imprisonment, although noting that this could lead to forum shopping in some instances.

See also 2 MCCORMICK ON EVIDENCE § 311 at 514 (Kenneth S. Broun ed., 7th ed. 2013) ("The subsequent history of the rule is an object lesson in the use of precedents to preserve and fossilize judicial mistake of an earlier generation").

[80] Generally the declarant must have the capacities required of any witness, that is, the declarant must be able to perceive and relate facts, have personal knowledge of the facts testified to, and understand the obligation to tell the truth. *See* Boone v. State, 668 S.W.2d 17, 21 (Ark. 1984) ("In order to qualify as a dying declaration the statement must be made by a witness (1) who was a competent witness"); *see also* Annotation, *Admissibility in Criminal Trial of Dying Declarations Involving an Asserted Opinion or Conclusion*, 86 A.L.R.2d 905 (1962).

[81] *See* FED. R. EVID. 804(b)(2) advisory committee note ("Continuation of a requirement of first-hand knowledge is assured by Rule 602"); *see also* Peter Nicolas, *"I'm Dying to Tell You What Happened": The Admissibility of Testimonial Dying Declarations Post-Crawford*, 37 HASTINGS CONST. L Q. 487 (2010); Shepard v. United States, 290 U.S. 96, 101 (1933) ("To let the declaration in, the inference must be permissible that there was knowledge or the opportunity for knowledge as to the acts that are declared"); United States v. Velentzas, 1993 WL 37339 (E.D.N.Y. 1993) (denying government's motion in limine to admit murder victim's statements, after being shot repeatedly from car with tinted glass, that "Spiros [defendant] had done this to me" and victim's reply of "Spiros Velentzas" to police questions about who shot him; victim was talking to defendant on phone from defendant's travel agency, where victim had agreed to meet defendant, but victim lacked personal knowledge that defendant had him shot).

[82] FED. R. EVID. 804(b)(3) advisory committee note.

Declarations Against Interest	Statements by Party-Opponents[83]
Admissible only if the person making the statement is unavailable in accordance with Rule 804(a).	Admissible whether or not the declarant is available for testimony. The opponent has no obligation to call the party-opponent.
Admissible whether or not the declarant is a party or the agent of a party.	Admissible only when the declarant is a party or the agent of a party, and then, only when offered by the opposing party.
Admissible only if against interest when made.	No requirement that the statement was against interest when made.[84]

Although it is possible for a statement to fit into both categories, the declaration against interest exception is most commonly used when the declarant is not a party. In particular, the declaration against interest has traditionally been used to introduce statements by a predecessor in interest of property owned by a party-opponent.[85]

Types of Interest That Qualify

The declaration against interest exception is limited to certain types of interests. Common-law judges developed a hierarchy of interests, with interests nearer the top of the list having a better chance of qualifying for the exception:

1. Pecuniary and proprietary interest (e.g., statements that admit a debt or concede another's property interest).
2. Tort or contract interest (statements that potentially expose the declarant to civil liability).
3. Penal interest (statements that expose the declarant to criminal liability).
4. Self-respect interest (statements that humiliate the declarant and expose him to ridicule or disapprobation, but not to liability).

Common-law jurisdictions tended to admit statements in the first category, and usually the second, but not the third or fourth.[86] Thus, "I gave my diamond to my eldest daughter," "I owe Jarvik $100," "He has a right of way across my land," or "I am holding this as agent for Hardwick" would all be admissible as against declarant's interest, given the appropriate context (see discussion below). By contrast, the confession, "I am Jack the Ripper" would not have been admissible under the common-law definition of a declaration against interest exception.

This different treatment of statements against pecuniary/proprietary interest and statements against penal interest might seem anomalous, even bizarre. Why should a statement that exposes the declarant to loss of liberty or life be treated as less reliable

---

[83] *See* **§ 15.06**.

[84] If a party made a statement that at the time was self-serving, the opposing party is nonetheless entitled to have that statement received as a party statement at trial, should it turn out to be to the advantage of the opposing party to do so. FED. R. EVID. 801(d)(2) advisory committee note.

[85] *See, e.g.*, Seaboard Coast Line R. Co. v. Carter, 177 S.E.2d 683, 685 (Ga. 1970) (holding it was error to exclude a statement by defendant landowner's predecessor in title to the effect that the declarant did not claim title to the railroads right of way); Egbert v. Egbert, 132 N.E.2d 910, 918 (Ind. 1956) (holding that it was proper to admit against the mortgagee statements made by the previous holder of the note, mortgagee's deceased father, to the effect that the note had been paid).

[86] *See* Donnelly v. United States, 228 U.S. 243, 273 (1913). *See generally* 5 WIGMORE ON EVIDENCE § 1476 (3d ed. 1940).

than a statement that might only lead to loss of property? However, the limitation was not as arbitrary as it might appear. Most importantly, it was not as *broad* as it might appear. First, a statement admitting a criminal act usually also will tend to subject the declarant to civil liability, and on this basis, it would have qualified under the common-law exception, but only when offered in a *civil* trial.[87] Thus, although often stated in terms of the affected interest, the limitation was actually a restriction on the use of this exception *in criminal cases*. Second, if the statement, "I am Jack the Ripper," (or, for that matter, a statement that is only against pecuniary interest) is offered *against the declarant* in a criminal trial, then the exception is not necessary—the prosecutor could simply admit the statement as that of a party opponent. But when the declaration against penal interest was that of a third party and was offered by the defense not simply to implicate the speaker, but also to exonerate the accused, the common-law judges shut the door.

This skeptical attitude was founded on experience with defendant-exonerating statements made by unavailable declarants. Courts believed that criminal defendants would be likely to find someone who would fabricate a confession by a declarant who had conveniently died or disappeared and that gullible juries would be too ready to treat such concoctions as raising a reasonable doubt.[88] Even before the Federal Rules, some dissented from the common-law's skepticism on this score. Wigmore condemned it roundly, saying:

> This is the ancient rusty weapon that has always been brandished to oppose any reform in the rules of Evidence, viz., the argument of danger of abuse. This would be a good argument against admitting any witnesses at all, for it is notorious that some witnesses will lie and that it is difficult to avoid being deceived by their lies.[89]

This limitation persisted stubbornly under the Federal Rules, though in a diminished form. As originally enacted, Rule 804(b)(3) permitted statements against penal interest to be received but required corroborating circumstances if it was used to exonerate an accused. After the Rules were enacted, however, it became clear that prosecutors in multiple-perpetrator cases also used this exception to circumvent limitations on the admissibility of statements of a party-opponent. (Often one person's hearsay statement inculpating both himself and another would not be admissible against the other person without use of the declaration against interest exception.[90]) Since December 2010 an amendment to Rule 804(b)(3) has created parity between prosecution and defense; corroborating circumstances are now also required if the prosecution seeks to admit the declaration against interest for inculpatory purposes.

---

[87] *See, e.g.*, G.M. McKelvey Co. v. General Cas. Co. of America, 142 N.E.2d 854, 856 (Ohio 1957) (holding statements of employees admitting misappropriation of funds admissible in suit by employer against insurance company providing employee fidelity insurance where employees unavailable to testify at trial). *See also* Jamaica Time Petroleum, Inc., Federal Ins. Co., 366 F.2d 156, 158–59 (10th Cir. 1966) (admitting in action on property insurance with defense of arson, hearsay statement of third person who admitted being hired to destroy the property; applying Kansas statute and noting that statement tended to subject declarant to both civil and criminal liability).

[88] *See* FED. R. EVID. 804(b)(3) advisory committee note. For an analysis of the admissibility of statements tending to implicate someone other than the accused, *see* David McCord, *"But Perry Mason Made It Look So Easy!": The Admissibility of Evidence Offered By a Criminal Defendant to Suggest that Someone Else Is Guilty*, 63 TENN. L. REV. 917 (1996).

[89] 5 WIGMORE ON EVIDENCE § 1477 at 288–89 (3d ed. 1940).

[90] *See* 5 CHRISTOPHER B. MUELLER & LAIRD C. KIRKPATRICK, FEDERAL EVIDENCE § 8:129 (4th ed. 2013).

Therefore, if offered in a criminal case as tending to expose the declarant to criminal liability, the declaration against interest must be supported by corroborating circumstances that clearly indicate its trustworthiness.[91]

Even under the Rules, a declaration that merely humiliates the declarant without exposing the declarant to legal liability will not support admission of a declaration against interest. For example, a shamefaced confession that the declarant has a secret vice will not suffice, in the absence of potential civil or criminal liability. The advisory committee originally proposed that self-degrading statements be received as declarations against interest, and the Supreme Court accepted this recommendation when it promulgated the Rules.[92] The House Committee on the Judiciary, however, eliminated the provision governing self-degrading statements, asserting that statements falling into this category lacked sufficient guarantees of reliability.[93] Despite the Federal Rules' rejection of declarations against social interest, some states include them within the exception,[94] and the commentary contains support for this extension of the traditional declaration against interest exception.[95]

The Against Interest Requirement

Assuming the statement implicates one of the types of interest covered by the rule, the proponent must still persuade the court that the statement is "so far contrary" to that interest "that a reasonable person in the declarant's position would not have made the statement unless believing it to be true."[96] The rule, somewhat inelegantly, establishes an objective test. The proponent must demonstrate that a reasonable person would not have made the statement unless that person believed it to be true. Whether the standard is satisfied in a given situation will depend on the context in which the statement was made. An inmate's statement taking responsibility for a stabbing might be highly credible if made while being questioned by prison authorities. The same statement, however, might be less credible if made by a prison inmate to other inmates outside the presence of authorities. In the latter situation, the desire to establish oneself in the inmate hierarchy might motivate a person to take credit for a stabbing even if the person was not responsible.[97]

Reflecting on that difference allows one to formulate an answer to the following puzzle: Why would someone make *any* statement that is against the speaker's interests, whether true or not? In most situations where someone utters a statement that is admissible under this rule, there will be some overriding reason that moves the speaker to make the statement, notwithstanding that is seems to be against the speaker's interest. For example, someone who admits to a friend having stolen a car may have made a declaration against interest in one sense, but that does not gainsay that the

---

[91] Fed. R. Evid. 804(b)(3)(B). In civil cases, declarations against penal interest are admissible without any requirement of corroboration.

[92] H.R. REP. NO. 93–650 at 16 (1973), *reprinted in* 1974 U.S.C.C.A.N. 7075, 7089.

[93] *Id.*

[94] *See, e.g.*, CAL. EVID. CODE § 1230 (2010) (covering statements that "create[ ] . . . a risk of making [declarant] an object of hatred, ridicule, or social disgrace in the community").

[95] *See, e.g.*, Edward J. Imwinkelried, *Declarations Against Social Interest: The (Still) Embarrassingly Neglected Hearsay Exception*, 69 S. CAL. L. REV. 1427 (1996).

[96] FED. R. EVID. 804(b)(3).

[97] *See, e.g.*, United States v. Bigesby, 685 F.3d 1060, 1065 (D.C. Cir. 2012), *cert. denied*, 133 S. Ct. 981 (U.S. 2013) (noting motive to fabricate in refusing admission of statement by father of two of defendant's children declaring sole possession of drugs).

speaker had a reason to make his statement to the friend. It might have been made as a brag, as a display of daring, designed to increase a perverse kind of respect for the speaker. Or, it might have been an attempt at expiation by getting the matter off the speaker's chest. In either case, the value of that overriding reason to the speaker outweighed the accompanying risk to the speaker, or else he would not have spoken. Does the latter fact mean the statement was not "against interest" within the meaning of this rule? After all, on balance it was intended to serve the declarant's interests in a broad sense, at least as he perceived them. There is considerable disagreement among scholars about how to handle such questions. One approach is to ask whether the overriding reason itself suggests a motive to fabricate in the statement. In the case of a brag designed to garner the respect of other criminals, such a motive is probable; whereas in the case of the declarant seeking to unburden his conscience, no such motive is likely.[98] Hence the latter is a better candidate for the exception than the former.[99]

Questions sometimes arise concerning statements that are partly disserving and partly self-serving or neutral. For example, in *United States v. Barrett*,[100] the court examined a case in which a man named Tilley had made an out-of-court statement to some card-playing acquaintances that implicated himself and a man named "Buzzy" in a stamp theft conspiracy. When asked by his acquaintances whether he was referring to "Bucky" (the defendant) or "Buzzy," Tilley said, "No, Bucky wasn't involved. It was Buzzy." Naturally, the defendant wanted to use this out-of-court statement exonerating him. He argued that Tilley had made a statement against interest because it implicated Tilley in crime.[101] The trial court excluded the statement on the ground that the relevant part—the part exonerating Bucky—was not against Tilley's interest. The First Circuit reversed, expressing the view that the whole statement was at least "arguably disserving" to Tilley because knowing exactly who was involved showed an "insider's knowledge" that made Tilley's involvement more likely. The court also noted that the case law, "while far from settled," tended to grant a certain latitude to contextual statements.[102]

As the court in *Barrett* noted, the treatment of neutral passages in otherwise disserving statements has been far from uniform. Many courts, fortified by Wigmore's approval, admitted the entire statement, including the neutral portion as if the utterance of one disserving thought had put the declarant in a truth-telling frame of mind.[103] A contrary view, however, also amply supported, endorsed weeding the garden, separating

---

[98] *See* 2 McCormick on Evidence § 319 at 541 (Kenneth S. Broun ed., 7th ed. 2013) (arguing that exception should not apply if the speaker had some purpose in speaking, "whether of self-interest or otherwise, which was likely to lead to misrepresentation of the facts"). *But see* 5 Wigmore on Evidence § 1464 (Chadbourn rev. 1974) (arguing that the effect of the countervailing reason should go to weight and not admissibility of the hearsay).

[99] That might seem like a perverse result: "if you confess honestly, we'll use it against you, but if you brag dishonestly, we won't." But that reaction mistakes the context. This statement is not being used against the speaker, for the speaker is not a party opponent. If he were, then recourse to this exception would be unnecessary. Instead, the statement is being used for (and against) other persons, as to which our primary concern is not the fairness to the declarant but the truth of what he has asserted.

[100] United States v. Barrett, 539 F.2d 244 (1st Cir. 1976).

[101] *Id.* at 249.

[102] *Id.* at 252 (citing McCormick, Handbook of the Law of Evidence § 279(a) (2d ed. 1972)).

[103] *See, e.g.*, United States v. Goodlow, 500 F.2d 954, 956–57 (8th Cir. 1974) (declarant's statements that he was "good for the crime" and defendant was not "good for it" must be considered together and are admissible); 5 Wigmore on Evidence § 1465 (Chadbourn rev., 1974).

the disserving statements from those that are neutral or self-serving and admitting only the former.[104]

A variation on the problem in *Barrett* appears when the statement of a declarant implicates both the declarant and the accused and is, accordingly, offered by the prosecution rather than the defense. In that situation, the declaration against interest exception is frequently not needed, because the statement will often be admissible as the statement of a co-conspirator.[105] Sometimes, however, the co-conspirator route to admission will not be available, as when the statement was made after the conspiracy ended. Then, the declaration against interest exception would furnish a possible basis for admission under the *Barrett* theory, if the court were willing to exercise "contextual latitude" and admit the statement implicating another person under the umbrella of the other, clearly disserving statement.

Sometimes the very same statement has self-serving and disserving aspects. For example, a statement of income in a tax return is self-serving insofar as it asserts that the declarant's income does not exceed a certain level, but disserving to the extent that it concedes that declarant had income up to a certain level. The sensible way to treat such statements is to receive them when they are offered to show facts that were against the declarant's interest when the statement was made—for example, to show that the income reached up to the level conceded in the return—but judicial treatment has not been uniform.[106]

An important line of cases discusses declarations against interest made while in custody or otherwise under circumstances indicating that a reasonable declarant would expect his words to be used against the accused.[107] In this extensive case law, courts attempt to tease out how much of the declaration against interest is admissible against the accused, with special concern directed to the fact that portions of the declarant's statements inculpating the accused may be designed to shift responsibility and curry favor with officials.[108] It is doubtful that any such testimonial declarations against interest could survive the Court's current interpretation of the Confrontation Clause.[109]

---

[104] *See, e.g.*, United States v. Seyfried, 435 F.2d 696, 698 (7th Cir. 1970) (holding that only the part against interest is admissible where statement is separable and one part is against declarant's interest and one is not); United States v. Marquez, 462 F.2d 893, 895 (2d Cir. 1972) (holding that it is only proper to admit portion of statement against declarant's interest; portion exculpating another inadmissible).

[105] *See* **§ 15.09**.

[106] *See, e.g.*, Ghelin v. Johnson, 243 N.W. 443, 446 (Minn. 1932) (admitting declarant's statement on income tax return that he was unmarried as declaration against interest); Barrera v. Gonzalez, 341 S.W.2d 703, 705–06 (Tex. Civ. App. 1960) (holding that declarant's statement that he owed money not admissible because self-serving under circumstances; statement by declarant that he owed money to creditor amounted to assertion that declarant did not transfer real property to creditor in satisfaction of debt as creditor claimed). *But see, e.g.*, Veach's Adm'r v. Louisville & Interurban Ry. Co., 228 S.W. 35, 36–37 (Ky. 1921) (holding that declarant's statement of income on tax return self-serving, even to prove income not less than amount stated).

[107] Lilly v. Virginia, 527 U.S. 116 (1999); Williamson v. United States, 512 U.S. 594 (1994) (reviewing a drug crime conviction in which the trial court allowed the prosecution to use the post-arrest statements of an accomplice against the defendant and holding that each statement in a narrative must be considered separately).

[108] *See, e.g.*, United States v. Mendoza, 85 F.3d 1347, 1351–52 (8th Cir. 1996) (holding statement by suspect caught with drug money implicating her boyfriend not admissible because she had nothing to lose by making statement and she may have been trying to curry favor).

[109] All such cases involved unavailable declarants (a requisite for this Rule 804 exception) and introduced uncross-examined testimonial statements. *See* **§ 20.02**. *See also* Daniel J. Capra, *Amending the Hearsay Exception for Declarations Against Penal Interest in the Wake of* Crawford, 105 COLUM. R. REV. 2409 (2005).

Nonetheless, there are many examples where the declaration against interest will be "nontestimonial" within the meaning of Confrontation Clause jurisprudence, and thus not within the scope of the protection of that Clause. Consequently, the case law considering how courts should handle statements that are only partially against interest will still be useful.

In addition, such case law remains useful in analyzing similar issues in civil cases. For example, in one case three siblings—Edward, Marvin, and Rita—had inherited a brokerage account as tenants in common, and Edward executed a document transferring his third to Rita as compensation for services provided by her to their parent.[110] A recital in the document stated that Edward and Marvin had agreed to transfer their shares to Rita in settlement of the debt, and there was a place for Marvin's signature on the instrument, but Marvin did not sign. In an action by the executor of Marvin's estate to recover Marvin's one third interest, Rita offered the document signed by Edward. Relying on the Supreme Court's treatment of the issue in a criminal law context, the court held that the trial court had erred in admitting the document under Rule 804(b)(3), because the recital would be a valid declaration against the interest of Edward, but not a valid declaration against the interest of Marvin.[111]

§ 17.05 Statements of Personal or Family History [FRE 804(b)(4)]

The exception in Rule 804(b)(4) is discussed elsewhere in connection with other exceptions relating to personal and family history.[112]

§ 17.06 Forfeiture by Wrongdoing [FRE 804(b)(6)]

In 1997, over twenty-five years after the original promulgation of the Federal Rules of Evidence, Rule 804(b)(6) was added to the list of hearsay exceptions that require the declarant's unavailability. The rule excepts from the hearsay prohibition statements offered against a party who has engaged or acquiesced in wrongdoing that was intended to, and did, procure the unavailability of the declarant as a witness. (A separate, but very similar, analysis must be conducted to determine whether a criminal defendant has forfeited his constitutional rights under the Confrontation Clause.[113])

The exception does not arise from a belief that such statements are likely to be reliable, but rather from an equitable principle that parties should not be able to benefit from the absence of a declarant whom they made unavailable. If a party intentionally deprives the fact-finder of the testimony of a witness by making the witness unavailable, the hearsay comes in. This exception applies most obviously to cases in which a criminal defendant arranges to murder a witness against him or intimidates or bribes that person into refusing to testify. The wrongdoing that invokes forfeiture need not consist of a

---

[110] *See, e.g.*, Silverstein v. Chase, 260 F.3d 142, 143–45 (2d Cir. 2001).

[111] Id. at 146–50 (remanding for the trial court to consider the admissibility of the recital under the residual exception, Fed. R. Evid. 807, and the exception for recitals in documents affecting an interest in property, Fed. R. Evid. 803(15). *See also* American Auto. Accessories, Inc. v. Fishman, 991 F. Supp. 995 (N.D. Ill. 1998) (holding that mere fact that statement by plaintiff's employee was facially self-incriminating was insufficient to demonstrate that it was against interest where statement may have been made as part of effort to curry favor with plaintiff in obtaining negotiated settlement).

[112] *See* **§ 16.14**.

[113] *See* **§ 20.05**.

criminal act.[114] Simple threats are sufficient to trigger forfeiture.[115] A party who engages in such behavior has forfeited—not waived—the protection of the hearsay rule: the party does not voluntarily forgo the exercise of the confrontation right; rather, the Rule withdraws that right because of the party's conduct.

The sensible principle that a party may forfeit the protection of the hearsay rule by procuring the unavailability of an adverse witness was recognized at common law in many jurisdictions, including all federal circuits that had addressed the issue before the enactment of Rule 804(b)(6).[116] As one court stated, arranging the unavailability of a witness who will testify against you "strikes at the heart of the system of justice itself."[117]

The Court of Appeals for the Second Circuit has restated the forfeiture rule as follows:

> . . . the district court may admit hearsay evidence as to statements by an unavailable declarant if it finds by a preponderance of the evidence that (a) the "party against whom the out-of-court statement is offered[ ] was involved in, or responsible for, procuring the unavailability of the declarant through knowledge, complicity, planning or in any other way," and (b) that party "acted with the intent of procuring the declarant's unavailability as an actual or potential witness."[118]

Before evidence of a statement will be admitted under this Rule 804(b)(6), the trial court must make the necessary factual finding pursuant to Rule 104(a). In doing so, the court may consider evidence not otherwise admissible.[119] The proponent of the evidence bears the burden of proof, under the "preponderance of the evidence" standard.[120] Thus, if the question is whether the defendant murdered a missing declarant, the declarant's statement will not be admissible unless the trial court finds, by a preponderance of the evidence, that the defendant is responsible for the murder. Courts should apply the rule cautiously, as its effect is to deprive a party of an important procedural and, in criminal cases, constitutional right. This is particularly true with respect to situations in which

---

114 FED. R. EVID. 804 advisory committee note (1997).

115 *See* United States v. Scott, 284 F.3d 758, 763–64 (7th Cir. 2002) ("applying pressure on a potential witness not to testify, including by threats of harm and suggestions of future retribution, is wrongdoing" that triggers Rule 804(b)(6)); United States v. Zlatogur, 271 F.3d 1025, 1028 (11th Cir. 2001) (holding that verbal threats sufficient).

116 *See, e.g.*, United States v. Houlihan, 92 F.3d 1271, 1278–81 (1st Cir. 1996) (holding that defendant's responsibility for murder of declarant to prevent declarant from "turning state's evidence and/or testifying . . . at trial" waives constitutional rights need only be shown by a preponderance of evidence).

117 United States v. Mastrangelo, 693 F.2d 269, 273 (2d Cir. 1982).

118 United States v. Stewart, 485 F.3d 666, 670–71 (2d Cir. 2007) (quoting United States v. Dhinsa, 243 F.3d 635, 653–54 (2d Cir. 2001)).

119 *See* United States v. White, 116 F.3d 903, 914 (D.C. Cir. 1997) (holding not error for trial judge, acting under Rule 104(a), to rely partly on hearsay in determining that defendants had forfeited hearsay objection by murdering hearsay declarant); United States v. Bolano, 618 F.2d 624 (10th Cir. 1979); Jenkins v. United States, 80 A.3d 978, 994–97 (D.C. 2013); Cotto v. Herbert, 331 F.3d 217, 231–35 (2d Cir. 2003). One state court, however, has held that such hearsay may not be considered in making the determination because of the importance of the right that is forfeited under this doctrine. *See* State v. Poole, 232 P.3d 519, 526 (Utah 2010).

120 *See* Steele v. Taylor, 684 F.2d 1193, 1202 (6th Cir. 1982), *cited with approval in* Beckett v. Ford, 384 Fed.Appx. 435 (6th Cir. 2010); United States v. Zlatogur, 271 F.3d 1025, 1028 (11th Cir. 2001) (noting that common-law forfeiture rule, requiring proof by "clear and convincing evidence," had been replaced by adoption of Rule 804(b)(6)).

the party did not directly procure the absence of the witness, but was only involved indirectly or tangentially.

The case law is relatively undeveloped concerning what qualifies as a defendant's acquiescence in wrongdoing that procured with witness's absence. Is mere knowledge that someone else plans to procure the witness's unavailability sufficient? Is it enough that the party and the person who made the witness unavailable were both participants in a criminal conspiracy about which the witness would have testified? In *United States v. Cherry*,[121] involving five defendants charged with a drug conspiracy, much of the state's evidence was provided by a cooperating witness who was murdered prior to trial. Addressing the question of what constitutes "acquiescence" under Rule 804(b)(6), the court held that an accused defendant waived his hearsay objections if "the wrongful procurement was in furtherance, within the scope, and reasonably foreseeable as a necessary or natural consequence of an ongoing conspiracy."[122] In *United States v. Marchesano*,[123] the military court struggled with the definition of acquiescence in a case where the accused was charged with inappropriately touching his daughter, and the wife of the accused did not produce their daughter, PM, who was subpoenaed, for the trial. The accused claimed that he simply removed himself from any involvement with the German subpoena because of his possible criminal liability; the military judge found that "[t]he accused left the decision whether to produce [PM] for trial with [his wife] and made no attempt to influence her decision."[124] The Court held that the facts of the case did not "sufficiently establish whether appellant's 'tacit acceptance' of his wife's refusal to honor the subpoena for PM's appearance sufficiently demonstrated [the accused's] 'design' to have PM unavailable for trial."[125]

The most important limitation on the forfeiture principle is the specific "intent" requirement: the forfeiting party must have acted with the intent to cause the unavailability of the declarant as a witness. Thus, if the party killed the witness solely out of jealousy, revenge, or anger of the moment, with no intention regarding the declarant's future testimony, then the exception does not apply.[126] People often act with multiple purposes, however, so the question naturally arises whether the exception applies if causing the declarant's unavailability as a witness is one but not the only purpose that the party had. Courts have reasonably concluded that single-mindedness is unnecessary for forfeiture to occur; so long as one of the purposes was to cause the unavailability of the declarant as a witness, the exception may apply, and that purpose need not be the "primary" purpose.[127]

Although the rule requires an intent to cause the unavailability of the declarant as a witness, it does not explicitly require that the intended unavailability pertain to the trial at which the hearsay is offered. Suppose, for example, that X intentionally causes

---

121 United States v. Cherry, 217 F.3d 811 (10th Cir. 2000).

122 *Id.* at 820.

123 United States v. Marchesano, 67 M.J. 535 (Army Ct. Crim. App. 2008).

124 *Id.* at 544 (Army Ct. Crim. App. 2008).

125 *Id.*

126 *See, e.g.*, Render v. State, 347 S.W.3d 905, 918 (Tex. App. 2011) (holding error to admit murder victim's hearsay because no evidence showed an intent to make the murder victim unavailable as a witness); Zanders v. United States, 999 A. 2d 149, 155 (D.C. 2010) (same).

127 *See, e.g.*, United States v. Dhinsa, 243 F.3d 635, 654 (2d Cir. 2001); United States v. Jackson, 706 F.3d 264, 267–70 (4th Cir. 2013); State v. Supanchick, 323 P.3d 231, 239 (Ore. 2014) (specifically rejecting a "primary motive or purpose" test).

D to be unavailable for trial #1, but X's opponent, Y, offers D's hearsay at (unrelated) trial #2, as to which D is also unavailable. The issue now under consideration is whether D's hearsay is admissible at trial #2. A natural reading of the rule would connect the fact that Y must show the declarant to be unavailable at trial #2, which is a requirement for invoking any exception in Rule 804(b), with the requirement that Y show that X intentionally caused D's unavailability. If so, then Y must show that X intended to cause D's unavailability as a witness *at trial #2*. But the language of the rule does not quite say this. By a literal reading of the rule, it suffices if Y shows that X intentionally caused D's unavailability at trial #1, so long as D is in fact unavailable (for any reason coming within Rule 804(a)) at trial #2. This point presents several conundrums that the courts have only partly addressed.[128]

Decisions are consistent in holding that X need not have intended to render D unavailable at trial #2; as far as X's *intent* or *purpose* is concerned, it is sufficient that X's intent be directed to trial #1, or indeed at any potential legal proceedings.[129] But specificity regarding *causation* has not been so clearly addressed.[130] That is, what if the defendant's conduct did not cause the unavailability of the declarant as a witness at trial #2? For example, suppose that, even though X did intentionally render D unavailable for trial #1, the reason that D is in fact unavailable as a witness at trial #2 is that D was involved in an auto accident on her way to court (as to which X bears no responsibility). This, too, would satisfy the "plain meaning" of Rule 804(b)(6). But if forfeiture occurs here, then the doctrine is disconnected from its more plausible rationales. Whether it is based on depriving a wrongdoer of an evidentiary advantage that he attempts to gain, or merely on depriving a wrongdoer of an evidentiary advantage he would otherwise obtain, or even simply depriving a person of a right that he would enjoy but for his own conduct, a forfeiture would still require that X caused (or at least acquiesced in someone else causing) the unavailability of the witness at trial #2.[131] Only a much broader, punitive rationale can explain forfeiture that is disconnected from causation, the idea being that X must be punished and deterred from his actions in regard to trial #1, and depriving him of his right to object to D's hearsay in trial #2 is one such punishment.[132] Of course, so would depriving him of his right to object to *any* hearsay at trial #2, or even

---

[128] This issue also has appeared in the context of forfeiture of the criminal defendant's right to confront adverse witnesses. *See* **§ 20.05**.

[129] *See, e.g.,* United States v. Gray, 405 F.3d 227, 240–43 (4th Cir. 2005) (holding that, where defendant murdered declarant in order to prevent his testimony in various assault trials, defendant forfeits hearsay objection under Rule 804(b)(6) as to declarant's out-of-court statements offered in later mail fraud case based on defendant's claims for life insurance proceeds after murdering declarant); United States v. Johnson, 495 F.3d 951, 971 (8th Cir. 2007) (holding that forfeiture applies "even though [the defendant] had worked to procure the unavailability of potential witnesses against [her boyfriend] rather than herself"); Ward v. United States, 55 A.3d 840, 847–51 (D.C. 2012) (holding that, where defendant murdered declarant to prevent declarant from testifying against another person as to a different crime, declarant's hearsay was admissible under forfeiture exception against defendant in trial for murdering declarant).

[130] *See* 5 CHRISTOPHER B. MUELLER & LAIRD C. KIRKPATRICK, FEDERAL EVIDENCE § 8:134 at 239–40 (4th ed. 2013).

[131] *See* Richard D. Friedman, *Confrontation and the Definition of Chutzpa*, 31 ISRAEL L. REV. 506, 516–21 (1997) (arguing that forfeiture should not require defendant's intent to prevent testimony but only defendant's deliberate actions predictably causing the unavailability of the witness).

[132] Occasionally, courts mention general punishment and deterrence as a rationale for the rule, but it is invariably coupled with a discussion of preventing the party from gaining an evidential advantage. *See, e.g.,* United States v. Thompson, 286 F.3d 950, 961–62 (7th Cir. 2002) (referring to the "primary purpose" of the rule as deterrence, but adding the equitable principle admission of the hearsay statements "at least partially offsets the benefit the defendant obtained by his misconduct").

the right to object to any evidence at all, but no one has suggested such an extreme and Rule 804(b)(6) cannot be so construed.

Suppose, then, that, in order to invoke forfeiture, the courts do require that X caused (or acquiesced in causing) D's unavailability at the trial at which D's hearsay is offered. Once this causal limitation is recognized, a subtle problem arises when trial #2 is for the very act that rendered D unavailable at trial #1, such as murdering D. Did X's intentional act in murdering D, intended to render D unavailable as a witness at trial #1, cause D to be unavailable at trial #2 for the murder of D? Is it the case that, had X not murdered D, D would have been available to testify at trial #2, the trial for murdering D? Only a bizarre counterfactual murder trial could involve the alleged murder victim testifying, and one must conclude that X's conduct did not cause D's unavailability at trial #2 in the ordinary case.[133] Yet the courts admit D's hearsay at that trial under the forfeiture exception.[134] Unless this changes, an exception to the requirement of causation must be recognized when trial #2 is for the act of rendering the witness unavailable in trial #1, though no coherent justification for such an exception has yet been offered.[135]

§ 17.07 Declarant Availability Reconsidered

This section extends the discussion of hearsay exceptions in two ways, the first practical and the second theoretical.

Declarant Availability and the Litigant's Situation

The Rules are structured around categories of admissibility requirements: Rule 803 generally imposes no requirement related to declarant availability, while Rule 804 requires the proponent to show that the declarant is unavailable as a condition on admitting that declarant's hearsay. From a practitioner's perspective, a different and perhaps more illuminating way to think about the matter is to consider not categories of *requirements*, but rather categories of *situations*. Thus, one can distinguish three situations regarding the declarant's availability to a potential proponent that a litigant may encounter and ask which exemptions and exceptions are potentially usable in each

---

[133] One might conclude that X's murder of D rendered D unavailable for the trial of some crime short of murder, such as an aggravated assault that would leave D with testimonial capacity. Had D not been killed, D could have testified to such an assault. *See generally* Richard D. Friedman, *Confrontation and the Definition of Chutzpa*, 31 ISRAEL L. REV. 506, 524 (1997). But that would not yield a forfeiture on the murder charge.

[134] *See, e.g.*, Ward v. United States, 55 A.3d 840, 847–51 (D.C. 2012) (holding that, where defendant murdered declarant to prevent declarant from testifying against another person as to a different crime, declarant's hearsay was admissible under forfeiture exception against defendant in trial for murdering declarant); State v. Supanchick, 323 P.3d 231, 236–41 (Ore. 2014) (holding that, where defendant murdered declarant to prevent declarant from testifying against the defendant for violating a restraining order, her hearsay was admissible under the forfeiture exception against the defendant in the trial for murdering the declarant). There is some evidence in the legislative history to suggest that the exception was intended to be limited to the situation in which the crime charged and the wrongful act that triggers the forfeiture exception are different acts, but so far the courts seem to have ignored it. *See* 5 CHRISTOPHER B. MUELLER & LAIRD C. KIRKPATRICK, FEDERAL EVIDENCE § 8:134 at 226–27 (4th ed. 2013).

[135] When trial #2 is for the misconduct in rendering D unavailable, often D's statements will be admissible, at trial #2, for the nonhearsay purpose of showing X's motive in acting. Many of the results in the cases can be explained on this basis. *Cf.* Bibbs v. State, 371 S.W.3d 564, 569–70 (Tex. App. 2012) (considering such an argument but rejecting it in the context because the prosecution had not advanced a theory of limited admissibility at trial).

context. Under the Federal Rules as presently constructed, the possibilities are the following:[136]

1. *The declarant testifies at trial.* When the declarant testifies at trial, all the exemptions are potentially usable: prior statements of the witness, Rule 801(d)(1), and statements of a party-opponent, Rule 801(d)(2). In addition, all the exceptions listed in Rule 803 are potentially usable. The exceptions listed in Rule 804(b), however, are *not* usable in this situation, unless the declarant testifies to a loss of memory concerning the event in question.[137]

2. *The declarant is available (to the proponent) to testify at trial but does not testify.* In this situation, the exemption for statements of a party-opponent, Rule 801(d)(2), is potentially usable as well as all but one of the exceptions listed in Rule 803. *Not* usable in this situation are the exemptions for prior statements of a witness (Rule 801(d)(1)), the exception for past recollection recorded (Rule 803(5)), and the exceptions listed in Rule 804(b).

3. *The declarant is unavailable (to the proponent) to testify at trial.* In this situation, the exemptions for statements of a party-opponent are potentially usable, as are all the exceptions in Rules 803 and 804(b) except Rule 803(5).[138] Neither the exception for past recollection recorded (Rule 803(5)) nor the exemptions for prior statements of a witness (Rule 801(d)(1)) would be usable in this situation.

This summary prompts the following theoretical discussion.

Declarant Availability and Policy Considerations

The first section of this chapter questioned whether the Rules should broaden the requirement that the proponent of hearsay produce available declarants, placing more exceptions in Rule 804, for which the proponent must show the declarant's unavailability. Such an unavailability requirement could be counterproductive in some cases because the hearsay can be more reliable than the live testimony. By requiring the live testimony of an available declarant, the structure of Rule 804 could prevent the use of the hearsay. As an example, consider the exception for an excited utterance, now appearing as Rule 803(2), and suppose that this exception were moved to Rule 804. In that case, the excited utterance would be inadmissible (under 804) if the declarant is available to testify, even though it might be more reliable than the declarant's in-court testimony.[139] The same point applies with respect to hearsay already falling within an exception in Rule 804.

---

[136] The availability issues that arise with regard to the use of the federal residual exception are discussed elsewhere. *See* **§ 18.01**.

[137] As discussed earlier (**§ 17.01**), a declarant who testifies that he or she can no longer remember what happened with regard to a particular event may be considered functionally "unavailable" for purposes of Rule 804, even though the declarant is obviously available in the physical sense and indeed testifies. *See* FED. R. EVID. 804(a)(3).

[138] Again, Rule 803(5) is hard to categorize. This is because (a) the declarant must testify to establish the foundation for the exception, and thus must be available to testify; but (b) the declarant must testify to a loss of memory, which could satisfy the requirements of Rule 804(a) and thus render the declarant functionally "unavailable." *See* FED. R. EVID. 803(5) advisory committee note.

[139] The excited utterance might be admissible to rehabilitate the witness if the witness is impeached in certain ways, but the opponent might prevent this by its decision about whether and how to impeach. *See* **§ 11.13 & § 15.04**.

From a policy perspective, however, it would be misleading to think of this issue in terms of being required to place a given exception either in Rule 803 or else in Rule 804, using the declarant availability requirements for those rules as they are currently structured. Those requirements are not the only options. Rule 804 could be restructured so that requiring an available declarant to testify does not have the effect of depriving the tribunal of that declarant's useful hearsay. In particular, Rule 804 could have been written so as to admit hearsay falling in the specified categories provided that the declarant is *either* unavailable *or* testifies at trial. The requirement would then serve merely to force a proponent to produce an available declarant. In that case, the live testimony of someone who had made an out-of-court declaration against interest, for example,[140] would not entail the tribunal's loss of the declaration against interest itself.[141] In other words, the fact that the hearsay (by itself) might be less (or more) reliable than live testimony from the declarant (by itself) is not necessarily determinative of whether to admit the hearsay. Indeed, in the ordinary case it is hard to see how the court loses much, besides a bit of court time, by having *both* the live testimony of the witness *and* the earlier hearsay. In most contexts, having both yields a package of evidence that is more reliable than having either one without the other.[142] Of course, sometimes such hearsay will be simply redundant of the live testimony, but Rule 403 could prevent that waste of time.

There is another, quite distinct way in which Rule 804 could have been expanded, admitting additional relevant evidence. It could have been written to admit *any* hearsay uttered by a declarant now unavailable to testify, not just those falling within one of the five categories listed in 804(b). (Rule 803 could still allow much hearsay without such a showing. The suggestion here is not that all hearsay be subject to an unavailability requirement, only that all hearsay be admissible, as against a hearsay objection, upon such a showing of unavailability.) Again, hearsay that is so weakly probative as to be a waste of time—mere rumor, for example—could be excluded on that basis, using Rule 403.[143]

Finally, the foregoing approaches could be combined, admitting almost any hearsay when the declarant is *either* unavailable or testifies.[144] This is analogous to the

---

140 *See* **§ 17.04**.

141 Many prior statements by a testifying declarant are admissible for impeachment (**§ 11.05**) or rehabilitation (**§ 11.13**). Some are even admissible substantively under Rule 801(d)(1), but not all. For example, a declaration against interest made by a person who testifies at trial in a way that is inconsistent with the against-interest declaration is not admissible substantively unless it was either a statement made while testifying under oath at a formal hearing or a statement of identification of a person after perceiving him. *See* **§§ 15.02 et seq.**

142 The usefulness of having both has been emphasized by the Supreme Court. *See* Chambers v. Mississippi, 410 U.S. 284, 301 (1975) ("[I]f there was any question about the truthfulness of the extrajudicial statements, [the declarant] was present in the courtroom and was under oath. He could have been cross-examined by the State, and his demeanor and responses weighed by the jury.") The *Chambers* case is discussed in **§ 18.04**.

143 A not uncommonly expressed concern has to do with "prepared statements," where a potential witness would prepare a written statement, perhaps with the help of a lawyer, in preparation for trial. At trial, for example, the witness might take the stand, authenticate and vouch for the accuracy of the written statement, and say no more on direct-examination. *See* FED. R. EVID. 801(d)(1) advisory committee note (expressing "an unwillingness to countenance the general use of prior prepared statements as substantive evidence"). But more direct restrictions on the use of such statements would be possible, either under Rule 403 or a new separate rule specifically targeted at such.

144 The qualification "almost" is necessary because some constraints might still be needed to preclude a party's use of "prepared statements." *See* **§ 15.04**.

"availability" structure that is used in preferring original recordings under Article X.[145] And, in fact, this ambitious (but unsuccessful) proposal was made for hearsay in the 1940s by the American Law Institute's Model Code of Evidence.[146] With such a rule, all the debates about whether something is a dying declaration or a declaration against interest, and all the debates about what exactly is required for the forfeiture exception disappear: unless those exceptions were moved to Rule 803, they would all be subsumed in a general exception that requires only a showing that the declarant is either testifying or unavailable to do so.[147]

If any such approach were to be adopted, it would warrant a rethinking of the exceptions placed in Rule 803 as well as the necessity of a residual exception, Rule 807.[148] For example, if Rule 804's availability criterion were constructed like the Model Code's proposal, it would be difficult to understand why an excited utterance should not be removed from Rule 803 and placed in Rule 804. In that case, an excited utterance would be excluded only when the declarant is available to testify but not called to do so. In such a case, it makes sense to insist on the testimony of the declarant if that is possible.[149] Once an available declarant testifies, or the court is assured that she will testify, the hearsay—whether an excited utterance or a declaration against interest—would still be admissible under such a hypothetical rule. If the declarant's hearsay and the declarant's testimony seriously diverge, the fact-finder would have the benefits of both in deciding what to believe.[150]

The foregoing suggestions do not take into account the separate, constitutional restrictions on the admissibility of hearsay against the accused in criminal cases. These restrictions, derived largely from the Confrontation Clause, are the subject of much controversy, discussed elsewhere.[151]

---

[145] *See* **§ 13.01**.

[146] *See* ALI MODEL CODE OF EVIDENCE Rule 503 (1942). Such a rule would obviously subsume the existing rule for prior statements of a testifying declarant, Rule 801(d)(1).

[147] Thus, the Model Code drafters decided (1) to subsume dying declarations under the general exception for hearsay from a declarant who is either testifying or unavailable to do so (*see id.* at 232), but (2) to create a separate exception for declarations against interest that would not require any showing regarding availability, which is analogous to placing the exception in Rule 803 of the Federal Rules (*see id.*, Rule 509).

[148] *See* **§ 18.01**.

[149] In United States v. Boyce, 742 F.3d 792 (7th Cir. 2014), defendant was convicted of illegal possession of a firearm based, in part, on the recording of a "911" call made by the mother of defendant's children who indicated he had a gun. In this straightforward application of the present sense impression and excited utterance exceptions, the court affirmed, but it expressed unease about the reliability of statements admitted under these exceptions. In a concurring opinion, Judge Posner enlarged upon the criticism of the exceptions and pointedly commented on the fact that the declarant could have been called by either party, but that each party had a strategic reason for not doing so. *Id.* at 800. Thereafter, Judge Posner suggested collapsing many hearsay exceptions into the residual exception (Rule 807), *id.* at 802, which very likely would have required the testimony of the declarant in this case. *See* **§ 18.01**. Judge Posner's suggestion precipitated a symposium on hearsay reform. *See The Philip D. Reed Lecture Series, Advisory Committee on Evidence Rules*, 84 FORDHAM L. REV. Issue 4 (2016).

[150] Various exceptions might still justifiably remain in Rule 803, subject to no required showing regarding declarant availability. Particularly good candidates would be those exceptions, like routine business and public records, where it is unlikely that the declarant will recall the specific hearsay statement or the basis for it.

[151] *See* **§§ 20.01 et seq.**

Chapter 18

OTHER HEARSAY EXCEPTIONS

Table of Sections

§ 18.01 The Residual Exception [FRE 807]

Federal Rule of Evidence 807 creates a "residual" hearsay exception.[1] The legislative history of the rule is complicated and reflects considerable dispute about its wisdom.[2] Roughly a quarter of the states adopting codes patterned on the Federal Rules have not adopted the residual exception.[3] Moreover, the ambiguities in the rule provide ample room for the expression of varying theories about hearsay.

The purpose of the exception is to "provide for treating new and presently unanticipated situations that demonstrate a trustworthiness within the spirit of the specifically stated exceptions," and to leave room "for growth and development of the law of evidence in the hearsay area."[4] On the other hand, the legislative history indicates that it was intended "that the residual hearsay exceptions will be used very rarely, and only in exceptional circumstances."[5]

The requirements of the residual exceptions were changed significantly at the end of 2019. The current rule states:

---

1 Rule 807 consolidates former Rules 803(24) and 804(b)(5), which created two, essentially identical exceptions. Consolidated and renumbered as Rule 807 in an amendment effective December 1, 1997, the change was purely technical and was not intended to affect the interpretation of the exception. The Rule is sometimes called the "catch-all" exception, as if its purpose or effect were to catch all hearsay not otherwise admissible and thus keep it from being excluded. *See, e.g.*, Myrna S. Raeder, *The Effect of the Catchalls on Criminal Defendants: Little Red Riding Hood Meets the Hearsay Wolf and Is Devoured*, 25 LOY. L.A. L. REV. 925 (1992). As explained in the text, however, that was certainly neither its purpose nor its effect, so we avoid this terminology.

2 For early criticism of the residual exceptions, see Jon R. Waltz & James Beckley, *The Exception for Great Hearsay: Some Concerned Comments*, 1 AM. J. TRIAL ADVOC. 123 (1977). *See generally* 5 WEINSTEIN'S FEDERAL EVIDENCE § 807.03 (Mark S. Brodin ed., 2d ed. 2015); 2 MCCORMICK ON EVIDENCE § 324 (Kenneth S. Broun, ed., 7th ed. 2013).

3 6 WEINSTEIN'S FEDERAL EVIDENCE T-202–T-206 (Mark S. Brodin ed., 2d ed. 2015).

4 Former FED. R. EVID. 803(24) advisory committee note. Kerr v. Clary, 37 P.3d 841, 844 (Okla. 2001) (quoting advisory committee language). The advisory committee further noted that it would "be presumptuous to assume that all possible desirable exceptions to the hearsay rule have been catalogued and to pass the hearsay rule to oncoming generations as a closed system." United States v. Walker, 410 F.3d 754, 757 n.1 (5th Cir. 2005) (explaining Congress' reasoning for creating the residual exception and quoting advisory committee language).

5 Senate Comm. on Judiciary, S. Rep. No. 1277, 93d Cong., 2d Sess., 18–20 (1974).

(a) **In General**. Under the following conditions, a hearsay statement is not excluded by the rule against hearsay even if the statement is not admissible under a hearsay exception in Rule 803 or 804:

(1) the statement is supported by sufficient guarantees of trustworthiness—after considering the totality of circumstances under which it was made and evidence, if any, corroborating the statement; and

(2) it is more probative on the point for which it is offered than any other evidence that the proponent can obtain through reasonable efforts.

(b) **Notice**. The statement is admissible only if the proponent gives an adverse party reasonable notice of the intent to offer the statement—including its substance and the declarant's name—so that the party has a fair opportunity to meet it. The notice must be provided in writing before the trial or hearing—or in any form during the trial or hearing if the court, for good cause, excuses a lack of earlier notice.[6]

By design, rulings based on Rule 807 have no precedential value. Each case must be decided on its own unique facts.[7] "The special facts and circumstances which, in the court's judgment, indicate that the statement has a sufficiently high degree of trustworthiness and necessity to justify its admission should be stated on the record."[8] The standard of review is abuse of discretion.

Aside from the requirements articulated in the rule, reviewing courts sometimes express sensitivity to the question of equality, that is, to the idea that the trial court should apply the requirements no more strictly to one side than to the other. In particular, appellate courts have reversed trial courts that are perceived as more generous in applying the residual exception to hearsay offered by the government in a criminal case than they are to hearsay offered by the accused in the same case.[9]

The Trustworthiness Requirement

Until 2020, the residual exception had required that the hearsay statements have "guarantees of trustworthiness" that are "equivalent" to the established exceptions.[10] This requirement was hard to quantify or otherwise operationalize given the variability in trustworthiness of various exceptions. Does the statement admitted under Rule 807 have to be as reliable as an excited utterance (not very reliable) or as reliable as former testimony (highly reliable because taken under oath and subject to cross-examination)? Does the statement have to be as reliable as a statement made to a nontreating physician

---

6 FED. R. EVID. 807. Prior to 2020, the rule contained two additional requirements. One required that the statement be offered as evidence of a "material" fact. The other required that admission be in the "interests of justice." The former merely restates the rule of relevance. *See, e.g.*, United States v. Muscato, 534 F. Supp. 969, 979 (E.D.N.Y. 1982). The latter also seemed to be redundant and unnecessary. *See* FED. R. EVID. 102 ("These rules should be construed so as to administer every proceeding fairly, eliminate unjustifiable expense and delay, and promote the development of evidence law, to the end of ascertaining the truth and securing a just determination.") In any event, disputes over the applicability of the residual exception have focused on the other requirements, as discussed below. Consequently, the 2019 amendment eliminated these two extra requirements.

7 *See* 5 WEINSTEIN'S FEDERAL EVIDENCE § 807.02[1] (Mark S. Brodin ed., 2d ed. 2015).

8 Senate Comm. on Judiciary, S. Rep. No. 1277, 93d Cong., 2d Sess., 18–20 (1974).

9 *See, e.g.*, Gray v. Klauser, 282 F.3d 633, 646–48 (9th Cir. 2002) (identifying, on habeas corpus review, three ways in which the trial court was stricter in applying Idaho's residual exception to defense proffers than to prosecution proffers).

10 FED. R. EVID. 807(a)(1).

in anticipation of expert testimony at trial (not very reliable) or as reliable as a routine business record not made in anticipation of trial (very reliable)? Although there is nothing suggesting it in the Rule, courts often compared the circumstances surrounding the hearsay utterance to those that would appear to be the "closest" regular hearsay exception.[11] The 2019 amendment was intended to reduce the uncertainty associated with this requirement by changing it to require that: "the statement is supported by sufficient guarantees of trustworthiness—after considering the totality of circumstances under which it was made and evidence, if any, corroborating the statement."[12]

The last clause of the new trustworthiness requirement resolves another issue. Traditionally, the guarantees of trustworthiness that have supported the creation of hearsay exceptions have related to the circumstances in which the statements were made, which might be called "intrinsic" guarantees. For example, former testimony is thought to be reliable because the circumstances (prior cross-examination) make it more reliable. Similarly, the excited utterance exception is deemed reliable in part on the theory that the circumstances limit a declarant's powers of fabrication. However, courts interpreting the residual exception have not always required guarantees of trustworthiness that are intrinsic in this sense. A number have admitted statements that had no such guarantees, but that seemed reliable simply because they were corroborated by other ("extrinsic") evidence.[13] The 2019 amendment confirms this more generous approach.

In terms of intrinsic factors, courts reject hearsay under Rule 807 when they identify specific circumstances that undermine trustworthiness, such as when the declarant had a clear motive to lie or when the statement was made in anticipation of litigation.[14] Other factors courts consider include the degree of spontaneity or lapse of time between an event and the statement, whether the statement was under oath or subject to cross-examination, whether the statement was in writing, and the nature of the relationship between the declarant and the person to whom the statement was made.[15] In keeping with the general theory of hearsay, one factor *not* to be considered is the credibility of the person who testifies in court to report the hearsay.[16]

The 2019 amendment to the trustworthiness requirement leaves an important question unanswered: By what criterion is one to know that a particular degree of

---

[11] See the discussion of "Near Miss" theory, *infra*.

[12] FED. R. EVID. 807(a)(1).

[13] United States v. Blackburn, 992 F.2d 666, 672 (7th Cir. 1993) (computer printouts of electronic lensometer readings for lens of eyeglasses left by bank robber in stolen car are admissible under residual exception because test that produces readings used highly reliable method of analysis; furthermore at time test was conducted, defendant was not even a suspect in the case); United States v. Carlson, 547 F.2d 1346, 1354–55 (8th Cir. 1976) (grand jury testimony of a witness who refused to testify at trial because of threats was sufficiently trustworthy to be admitted where declarant was under oath and never recanted or expressed reservations about the accuracy of the testimony). *See generally* David A. Sonenshein, *The Residual Exceptions to the Federal Hearsay Rule: Two Exceptions in Search of a Rule*, 57 N.Y.U. L. REV. 867 (1982).

[14] *See, e.g.*, Polansky v. CNA Ins. Co., 852 F.2d 626, 631 (1st Cir. 1988) (proper to exclude letter written by representative of proponent which was self-serving and lacked guarantees of trustworthiness); United Tech. Corp. v. Mazer, 556 F.3d 1260, 1279 (11th Cir. 2009) (a statement lacked guarantees of trustworthiness and was not admissible under 807 because the declarant was the target of a criminal investigation and had motivation to implicate others to mitigate his own responsibility).

[15] *See* 2 MCCORMICK ON EVIDENCE § 324 at 561–64 (Kenneth S. Broun ed., 7th ed. 2013) (citing numerous cases).

[16] *See* Huff v. White Motor Corp., 609 F.2d 286, 293 (7th Cir. 1979); State v. Cazares-Mendez, 256 P.3d 104, 112–14 (Ore. 2011).

trustworthiness is "sufficient"? Prior to 2019, this was to be discerned by comparison to what was sufficient to warrant one of the categorical exceptions. That was unworkable, to be sure, but now the standard is simply incomplete. What is sufficient trustworthiness depends on what countervailing considerations are being weighed against the degree of trustworthiness that the hearsay possesses.[17] Of course, if the hearsay is clearly as reliable as that admitted under a categorical exception, and if that categorical exception is understood as designed to admit particularly reliable hearsay, then the comparison is probably still a good benchmark. Absent such circumstances, what is a court to do? One commentator had suggested that the best way to make sense of the trustworthiness requirement, even before the 2019 amendment, was to treat it as a mandate to exclude hearsay offered under the residual unless the proponent shows that the trustworthiness of the statement clearly outweighs the risk of 403-dangers, a "reverse 403" test that places the burden on the proponent.[18] Although the advisory committee did not choose to word the trustworthiness requirement this way under the 2019 amendment, that test remains one way to complete the Rule's otherwise open-ended standard.

The Necessity Requirement

What is now Rule 807(a)(2) requires that the hearsay statement be "more probative on the point for which it is offered than any other evidence that the proponent can obtain through reasonable efforts." This somewhat unusual type of requirement, unchanged by the 2019 amendment, is easily misunderstood. In other contexts, when the rules insist that a proponent seek alternative evidence as a condition precedent to admitting specified evidence, what will suffice for such a search is articulated with some degree of detail. Examples are the excuses that must be established for introducing secondary evidence of the contents of a recording under Rule 1004 and the efforts that must be expended before a hearsay declarant will be considered unavailable under Rule 804(a). Moreover, such rules do not connect the duty to search with any "more probative" condition. This condition is implicit in the assumptions that originals are generally more probative than secondary evidence of their contents and that live testimony is generally more probative than hearsay from the same person.

As a result, a confusion arises in regard to the comparison that is required by the rule's reference to "other evidence that the proponent can obtain through reasonable efforts." Consider, for example, a case in which the question is whether a traffic light was red or green, and the issue is whether hearsay statements about the color of the light are admissible under the residual exception if witnesses with firsthand knowledge about the color of the light exist. If such witnesses are available to be called but have not been called, then the requirement has surely not been met. But what happens if such witnesses have testified? Should the hearsay be excluded under this requirement on the ground that the admitted testimony—under oath, subject to cross-examination, and observed directly by the fact-finder—is more probative than the hearsay statements?

---

[17] This is a replay of the problem associated with discerning how reliable is reliable enough for the admission of expertise under *Daubert* and amended Rule 702. *See* **§ 10.04**.

[18] *See* Dale A. Nance, *The Wisdom of* Dallas County, in EVIDENCE STORIES at 318–22, 327–28 (Richard Lempert ed., 2006) (recounting story of and lessons to be gleaned from the pivotal case that inspired the residual exception).

Some authorities suggest as much by comparing the probative value of the proposed hearsay with other evidence already introduced on the same point.[19]

The language of the requirement, however, suggests that the comparison is to be made to other evidence that has not yet been "obtained," as it takes no effort at all to obtain evidence that is already before the court. Thus, in the posited example, the fact that the eyewitnesses to the color of the light have all testified simply means that the existence of such witnesses no longer poses an obstacle to the introduction of the hearsay. And most courts have made rulings consistent with this approach.[20] This reading is more compatible with *Dallas County v. Commercial Union Assurance Co.*,[21] the leading pre-Rules case on which the residual exception was grounded.[22] It is also more sensible than the opposite conclusion:

> The "more probative" requirement could mean the catchall cannot be invoked unless the statement being offered is more probative than all the other evidence in point. However, if the point in question remains at large (it could be decided either way), surely a statement that otherwise fits the catchall should be admitted if the proponent has nothing better to offer within reasonable reach.[23]

The better interpretation of the requirement is thus as a conditioning rule of production: so long as more probative (or equally probative) evidence on the point can be reasonably obtained and admitted, recourse to the hearsay is not (yet) permitted;[24] once such production efforts are exhausted—either because nothing else at least as probative can be found or because all such evidence has been introduced—the requirement is satisfied, regardless of how probative the evidence already admitted on the point may

---

[19] *See, e.g.*, Fryar v. Bissonette, 185 F. Supp. 2d 87, 92–93 (D. Mass. 2002) (addressing a rather peculiar argument by the defense on a habeas petition, the court stated that, even if the residual exception could have been invoked at trial (it could not, because Massachusetts had no residual exception), that exception would not apply because the declarant testified at trial, albeit in a manner inconsistent with the prior statement; strangely expressing the view that the hearsay confession by the declarant could not be more probative than the live testimony of the declarant denying commission of the crime and making of the confession).

[20] *See, e.g.*, United States v. Curro, 847 F.2d 325, 327–28 (6th Cir. 1988) (rejecting defendant's argument that grand jury testimony of deceased declarant was not more probative than other evidence because it was well corroborated by already admitted evidence; noting that the idea that corroboration by admitted evidence would be fatal to admission under the residual would "fly in the face of the requirement that the statement be found to be trustworthy"); United States v. Iaconetti, 406 F. Supp. 554 (E.D.N.Y. 1976) (holding admissible a hearsay statement offered under the residual exception as more probative than other obtainable evidence to resolve a conflict in testimony between witnesses with first-hand knowledge).

[21] Dallas County v. Commercial Union Assurance Co., 286 F.2d 388 (5th Cir. 1961).

[22] *See* Former FED. R. EVID. 803(24) advisory committee note (relying exclusively on the *Dallas County* case). *See* Dale A. Nance, *The Wisdom of* Dallas County, in EVIDENCE STORIES at 328–29 (Richard Lempert ed., 2006) (observing that the Fifth Circuit's opinion in *Dallas County* paid no attention to the fact that the proponent of the hearsay presented considerable nonhearsay evidence on the very point to which the hearsay was directed; instead, the opinion focused on whether better evidence could yet have been adduced on the point without recourse to the hearsay).

[23] *See* 5 CHRISTOPHER B. MUELLER & LAIRD C. KIRKPATRICK, FEDERAL EVIDENCE § 8:142 at 299 (4th ed. 2013).

[24] It is clear that, for "missing" evidence to constitute an obstacle to admission of the proposed hearsay, the former must itself be admissible, or there would be no reason to demand its presentation. In some cases, such admissibility may require invoking the categorical hearsay exemptions or exceptions. Thus, the advisory committee, in proposing the 2019 amendments, commented:

> The Committee decided to retain the requirement that the proponent must show that the hearsay statement is more probative than any other evidence that the proponent can reasonably obtain. This necessity requirement will continue to serve to prevent the residual exception from being used as a device to erode the categorical exceptions.

FED. R. EVID. 807, committee note (2019 amendments).

be.[25] In particular, the fact that the declarant himself testifies at trial does not necessarily preclude satisfaction of condition 807(a)(2): the hearsay may still be more probative on the point than any other potential evidence that can be reasonably obtained.[26] Conversely, if the declarant is available and competent to testify at trial, but does not, the requirement of 807(a)(2) usually cannot be satisfied.[27] However, the absence of the declarant will not preclude admission if the declarant is unavailable to be called by the hearsay's proponent or the declarant's testimony can be expected, because of lost memory or otherwise, to be less probative than the declarant's hearsay.[28]

Examples of evidence that courts deemed more probative on the point for which it was offered than any other reasonably obtainable evidence include:

- in a bankruptcy proceeding, a declarant's admission in a plea agreement that he had operated a Ponzi scheme with intent to defraud, because it was direct proof of fraudulent intent not otherwise available;[29]
- in an action for filing false tax returns, declarant's grand jury testimony where the declarant, unavailable at trial, was the only person who could establish the link between drafting of supplier checks and their conversion to cash, thus demonstrating defendant's guilt.[30]

Examples of cases where the court held that the requirement was not met include:

- Purchase summaries prepared long after the event by nonparty purchaser of crude oil in response to Conoco's request for information for Department of Energy audit when offered under the residual exception because they were not more probative than other evidence that DOE could procure through reasonable efforts, including the materials from which the summaries were constructed;[31]

---

[25] Of course, a comparison to evidence already admitted may be necessary if the opponent objects to the hearsay as unduly cumulative under Rule 403.

[26] *See, e.g.,* United States v. Shaw, 824 F.2d 601, 609–10 (8th Cir. 1987) (holding that the "more probative" requirement does not render child-victim's prior statements inadmissible just because the child testified); United States v. Iaconetti, 406 F. Supp. 554 (E.D.N.Y. 1976) (holding admissible a hearsay statement offered under the residual exception as more probative than other obtainable evidence to resolve a conflict in testimony between the defendant and another witness who was the hearsay declarant).

[27] *See, e.g.,* United States v. Patrick, 248 F.3d 11, 25 (1st Cir. 2001) (holding affidavit inadmissible under residual exception because officer who conducted the search described in the affidavit was available to testify); Larez v. City of Los Angeles, 946 F.2d 630, 644 (9th Cir. 1991) (holding newspaper articles inadmissible under residual exception because reporters were available to testify).

[28] This was the situation in *Dallas County. See* Dallas County v. Commercial Union Assurance Co., 286 F.2d 388, 396–97 (5th Cir. 1961) (noting the difficulty of finding the reporter who wrote an unsigned newspaper article 58 years before the trial and the unlikelihood that the reporter or anyone who provided the reporter information would have present memory of the events reported). *See also* Huff v. White Motor Corp., 609 F.2d 286, 293 (7th Cir. 1979) (holding statement by truck driver before he died admissible under residual exception where no alternative source of evidence existed as to question of a fire occurring in the cab); United States v. Munoz, 16 F.3d 1116, 1122 (11th Cir. 1994) (admitting deposit slips purportedly signed by defendant, whom the government could not call as its witness, where slips were more probative of the making of the deposits than other available evidence).

[29] *In re* Slatkin, 525 F.3d 805, 812 (9th Cir. 2008).

[30] United States v. Marchini, 797 F.2d 759, 764 (9th Cir. 1986). Today, this case would not survive *Crawford* and would be deemed to violate the Confrontation Clause. *See* **§ 20.02.**

[31] Conoco, Inc. v. Department of Energy, 99 F.3d 387, 392 (Fed. Cir. 1996).

- A letter where proponent made no showing that reasonable efforts would not have brought the writer to court to testify.[32]

The reference in condition 807(a)(2) to "reasonable efforts" clearly contemplates that courts take into account the costs and other difficulties of producing any identifiable alternative source of information.[33]

The Notice Provision

When the residual exception was first proposed, the practicing bar objected to relaxation of the hearsay rule on the ground that, if hearsay became freely admissible, trial lawyers would not know how to prepare for trial. In response to this concern, Congress inserted in the rule language that clearly requires notice of intent to offer the hearsay, so that an opponent may prepare to argue the matter. The 2019 amendment made several changes to the notice requirement.

First, to avoid uncertainty, the amendment requires that the substance of the statement be included in the notice. Second, because it is sometimes pointless to provide the address of the declarant (as when he or she is dead), the amendment eliminated that requirement. Third, to avoid controversies about whether notice was given, the amendment requires that notice be given in writing, which includes electronic notification. Finally, the original rule provided that notice must be given before trial. This, however, could be inconvenient and unfair if the proponent was unaware of the need to invoke the residual exception until after the trial began. As a result, most federal courts that had interpreted the provision had not enforced the pretrial notice requirement literally.[34] The 2019 amendment endorses the courts' treatment by relaxing the notice requirement: notice may be given during the trial and in any form if the court "for good cause, excuses the lack of earlier notice."[35]

The "Near Miss" Theory and Legislative Intent

When evidence almost, but not quite, fits under one of the established exceptions, some courts have been inclined to conclude that Congress did not intend for the evidence

---

32 Noble v. Alabama Dept. of Envtl. Mgmt., 872 F.2d 361, 366 (11th Cir. 1989).

33 *Compare* United States v. Mathis, 559 F2d 294 (5th Cir. 1977) (holding trial court erred in admitting hearsay of wife of defendant under residual when marriage was clearly a sham marriage, privilege claim was invalid, and declarant would have testified if ordered to do so; fact that wife was afraid of defendant insufficient excuse for not producing wife to testify), *and* Stokes v. City of Omaha, 23 F.3d 1362, 1366 (8th Cir. 1994) (holding trial court erred in admitting affidavit of now deceased witness where (a) witness's death was anticipatable so witness could have been deposed, and (b) witness reported actions and attitudes of employee of city who was himself available to be called to testify); *with* United States v. Friedman, 593 F.2d 109, 114, 118–119 (9th Cir. 1979) (admitting summary of official Chilean records of entry into and exit from the country prepared by a high ranking Chilean official who was not the custodian of the records; holding that government did all it could reasonably be expected to do to acquire the original records), *and* FTC v. Figgie Intern., Inc., 994 F.2d 595, 608 (9th Cir. 1993) (holding that it would not be reasonable to require FTC to bring customers to court to testify about prices they paid).

34 *See* Joseph W. Rand, Note, *The Residual Exceptions to the Federal Hearsay Rule: The Futile and Misguided Attempt to Restrain Judicial Discretion*, 80 GEO. L.J. 873, 885–86 (1992) (collecting cases that have interpreted the notice requirement in a relaxed fashion); *see also* United States v. Carlson, 547 F.2d 1346, 1355 (8th Cir. 1976) (court excused government from notice requirement where government's attorney first learned just before trial that its witness would refuse to testify; defendant did not request continuance); United States v. Leslie, 542 F.2d 285, 291 (5th Cir. 1976); Furtado v. Bishop, 604 F.2d 80, 90–93 (1st Cir. 1979). For strict interpretations of the old notice requirement, *see, e.g.*, United States v. Cowley, 720 F.2d 1037, 1044–45 (9th Cir. 1983), and United States v. Ruffin, 575 F.2d 346, 357 (2d Cir. 1978).

35 FED. R. EVID. 807(b).

to be admitted under the residual exception.[36] Until the 2019 amendment, this argument could be supported by the precise wording of the rule, which allowed application of the residual only to hearsay that was "not specifically covered by Rule 803 or 804." The idea was that given hearsay might be "covered" by an exception in Rule 803 or 804 without being *admissible* under that exception.[37]

An example would be a routine police recording of a serial number from a weapon found at a crime scene. Courts have disagreed whether this falls within the "criminal case" limitation of the public records exception in Rule 803(8)(A)(ii), and for those that conclude such hearsay is within that limitation, and thus not admissible under the public records exception, it is arguable that such hearsay should also be excluded if offered under the residual exception because it is "covered" (though not admitted) by the public records exception.[38] Similarly, under the "near miss" concept, an argument can be made that the residual exception should never be applied to admit grand jury testimony offered against the accused; arguably, all former testimony, including grand jury testimony, is "specifically covered" by Rule 804(b)(1). Congress considered the question whether to admit former testimony when enacting that rule and decided not to allow it to be admitted except when the party against whom it is offered had the opportunity to cross-examine. Following this logic, such testimony should not be admitted against the accused under the residual exception.

Despite its seeming plausibility, many (probably most) courts have rejected this reasoning.[39] Judicial resistance suggests that, if the "near miss" argument has any validity, it must be carefully understood. It should not be confused with a different argument, which is a reply to a proponent's argument that, if given hearsay is very nearly within a conventional (non-residual) exception, then that should be sufficient by itself to warrant admission under the residual. Such an argument by proponents is rightly rejected, because it incorrectly assumes that any such hearsay will satisfy the conditions enumerated in the residual. Conversely, rejecting use of the residual cannot be based simply on the fact that particular hearsay falls "very close to but not within" a conventional (non-residual) exception. The fact of proximity, by itself, cannot raise a negative implication: it is ambiguous as to whether the lawmakers' intent was to exclude such hearsay or simply not to admit it *under that exception*. There are, in fact, countless examples of hearsay held inadmissible under one exception but admissible under

---

[36] *See id.* at 762–64.

[37] *See, e.g.*, Fryar v. Bissonette, 185 F. Supp. 2d 87, 93 (D. Mass. 2002) (addressing a rather peculiar argument by the defense on a habeas petition, the court stated that, even if the residual exception could have been invoked at trial (it could not, because Massachusetts had no residual exception), that exception would not apply because, but for the fact that the declarant testified, the hearsay would have been a declaration against interest, so the hearsay was "covered by" that exception but not admissible under it). *See also* State v. Cazares-Mendez, 256 P.3d 104, 115–16 (Ore. 2011) (employing "near miss" thinking in applying Oregon's version of the residual exception).

[38] *See* **§ 16.09** (subsection on "Police and Other Law Enforcement Records").

[39] Despite its endorsement by a prominent judge, *see* United States v. Dent, 984 F.2d 1453, 1465–66 (7th Cir. 1993) (Easterbrook, J., concurring), the "near miss" approach has not achieved general acceptance in its application to grand jury testimony, which has been admitted under the residual exception. *See, e.g.*, United States v. Earles, 113 F.3d 796, 800 (8th Cir. 1997) (holding grand jury testimony may be admitted under residual exception; rejecting near miss theory). For an example outside the grand jury testimony context, see United States v. Laster, 258 F.3d 525, 529–530 (6th Cir. 2001) (holding that absent such legislative indication, evidence not shown to satisfy requirements of a specific hearsay exception might be admissible under the residual exception; when the government failed to lay the proper foundation under the business records exception by not producing a sponsoring witness, the record was admissible under the residual exception; dissenting opinion would have applied the near miss theory).

another.[40] Moreover, it is hard to imagine any hearsay that cannot plausibly be described as almost within, but not within, some conventional exception, because there is no generally applicable metric for measuring such proximity.[41]

In some contexts, moreover, the near miss theory is clearly implausible. In contrast to the foregoing examples, consider the ancient document exception, Rule 803(16). In its current form, it applies to documents that were prepared before January 1, 1998, for which authenticity is established.[42] This cutoff reflects the fact that any document now offered for admission that was created before that date must be at least 20 years old. Legislative intent to admit such hearsay cannot plausibly be construed as an intent to *exclude* otherwise comparable hearsay in an authenticated document that was prepared on, say, January 1, 1998, and satisfies the conditions of some other exception, including Rule 807. Here, at least, we have something like a metric, and a better example of "near miss" would be hard to imagine. Yet this is also an example in which the closer one comes to a conventional exception, the *more* plausible it is as a candidate under Rule 807.

Thus, before the indicated negative implication is invoked, it should be clear from the legislative history that lawmakers intended a failure to qualify within a given exception as precluding admission under any other exception or, at least, under the residual itself. To the extent that this reflects a more nuanced and contextual appreciation of legislative intent, the theory may survive, but there is no reason to think of it as having anything to do with the idea of a "near miss." It is simply the idea that, as a matter of legislative intent, for some particular kinds of hearsay a more limited set of exceptions is available than for hearsay generally.

In one respect, the textual basis for the "near miss" theory has been eliminated by the 2019 amendment, which dropped the "covered by" language. Hearsay is now eligible for admission under the residual "even if the statement is not *admissible* under a hearsay exception in Rule 803 or 804."[43] The committee note explained:

> [The amendment] clarifies that a court assessing guarantees of trustworthiness may consider whether the statement is a "near-miss" of one of the Rule 803 or 804 exceptions. If a court employs a "near-miss" analysis it should—in addition to evaluating all relevant guarantees of trustworthiness—take into account the reasons that the hearsay misses the admissibility requirement of the standard exception.

Presumably, these "reasons" include analysis of legislative purpose.

---

40 For example, putting aside Confrontation Clause issues, the public record of a weapon's serial number mentioned above certainly would be admitted if it met the requirements of the prior recollection recorded exception, Rule 803(5), so public records cannot be understood as exclusively covered by 803(8). Similarly, the grand jury testimony mentioned above certainly would be admitted if it falls within the exception for prior inconsistent statements of a testifying witness, Rule 801(d)(1)(A), or within the exception for declarations against interest made by an unavailable declarant, Rule 804(b)(3), so prior testimony cannot be understood as exclusively covered by 804(b)(1).

41 *Cf.* 5 CHRISTOPHER B. MUELLER & LAIRD C. KIRKPATRICK, FEDERAL EVIDENCE § 8:141 at 284 (4th ed. 2013) ("Excluding statements because they *almost* fit some other exception is a very hard notion to implement: What does 'almost fit' mean, anyway?").

42 The argument presented in this paragraph easily can be adjusted to make the same point under the version of the ancient document exception that existed before December 1, 2017. *See* **§ 16.13**.

43 FED. R. EVID. 807(a).

Impact of Rule 807

Although Congress apparently intended that the residual exceptions be applied only in a limited set of near-unique circumstances, some courts have been willing to apply them to ordinary hearsay that does not fit any other standard exceptions. The consensus of scholarly opinion seems to be that courts construing the residual exceptions have been quite liberal in finding evidence trustworthy enough to be received.[44] Still, the case law surrounding the residual exception shows that courts have not abandoned the hearsay ban entirely.

Certainly, there are some startlingly permissive cases. For example, in some jurisdictions it has become common for federal courts to admit grand jury testimony of absent witnesses, even though they may have had a motive to lie, so long as the testimony is corroborated by other evidence.[45] Extension of this line of cases would seem to allow all grand jury testimony to come in as long as the other evidence against the defendant is good. To be sure, there are decisions of equal status that are less permissive.[46] In any event, the Supreme Court's 2004 decision in *Crawford v. Washington*[47] makes clear that admission of grand jury testimony against a criminal defendant, where the accuser does not testify at trial, violates the Confrontation Clause.[48]

In child sex abuse prosecutions, prosecutors have increasingly turned to the residual exceptions, as well as to special state statutes admitting child hearsay. In *United States v. N.B.*,[49] for example, the court found that guarantees of trustworthiness were sufficient to admit under the residual exception a social worker-witness's testimony concerning the child-declarant's statements inculpating defendant in sexual abuse. The court held that in deciding whether statements are sufficiently trustworthy, a court should consider "the training and experience of the social worker; whether the child was interviewed using open-ended questions; the age of the child and whether the child used 'age-appropriate language' in discussing the abuse; the length of time between the incident of abuse and the making of the hearsay statement; and whether the child repeated the same facts consistently to adults." Such statements are less likely to raise

---

44 *See* Jeffrey Cole, *Residual Exceptions to the Hearsay Rule*, LITIG. MAG., Fall 1989 at 26; Randolph N. Jonakait, *The Subversion of the Hearsay Rule: The Residual Hearsay Exceptions, Circumstantial Guarantees of Trustworthiness, and Grand Jury Testimony*, 36 CASE W. RES. L. REV. 431 (1986); Myrna S. Raeder, *The Effect of the Catchalls on Criminal Defendants: Little Red Riding Hood Meets the Hearsay Wolf and Is Devoured*, 25 LOY. L.A. L. REV. 925, 933 (1992); David A. Sonenshein, *The Residual Exceptions to the Federal Hearsay Rule: Two Exceptions in Search of a Rule*, 57 N.Y.U. L. REV. 867 (1982); Elizabeth DeCoux, *Textual Limits on the Residual Exception to the Hearsay Rule: The "Near Miss" Debate and Beyond*, 35 S.U. L. REV. 99 (2007).

45 *See, e.g.*, United States v. Guinan, 836 F.2d 350 (7th Cir. 1988), *overruling recognized by* United States v. Gomez-Lemos, 939 F.2d 326 (6th Cir. 1991) (grand jury testimony by estranged wife admissible when corroborated by other evidence); Randolph N. Jonakait, *The Supreme Court, Plain Meaning, and the Changed Rules of Evidence*, 68 TEX. L. REV. 745, 762–64 (1990).

46 *See* United States v. Gomez-Lemos, 939 F.2d 326, 332–34 (6th Cir. 1991) (reversing trial judge who admitted grand jury testimony under residual exception, noting that Idaho v. Wright, 497 U.S. 805 (1990), does not allow trustworthiness to be established by extrinsic corroboration); United States v. Fernandez, 892 F.2d 976, 980–84 (11th Cir. 1989) (refusing to admit grand jury testimony under the residual exceptions, and noting that the Eleventh Circuit has never done so).

47 Crawford v. Washington, 541 U.S. 36 (2004).

48 *See* **§ 20.02**.

49 United States v. Juvenile NB, 59 F.3d 771, 776–78 (8th Cir. 1995). The alleged child-victims testified, and the defendant did not challenge the hearsay under the "more probative" requirement of (now) Rule 807(a)(3).

Confrontation Clause concerns where the statements are spontaneous comments to parents, teachers, or doctors. Answers to a forensic interview raise more serious confrontation concerns.[50]

In civil cases, courts have used the residual exception to resolve doubts about the admissibility of surveys of consumer or public opinions as well as industry standards such as safety codes.[51] Some courts have been quite permissive in using the residual exception in civil cases.[52] If followed to the extent of their logic, the permissive residual exception cases could destroy the hearsay rule. Yet often the cases are merely examples of appellate courts upholding district court rulings under an abuse of discretion standard, leaving the district courts free to either admit or exclude, rather than requiring them to admit.

§ 18.02 Miscellaneous Exceptions

Statements of Recent Perception

The version of the Federal Rules of Evidence that was promulgated by the Supreme Court under its rulemaking power in 1973 contained an exception for "statements of recent perception." The Supreme Court's version of the statement of recent perception provided an exception for:

> A statement, not in response to the instigation of a person engaged in investigating, litigating, or settling a claim, which narrates, describes, or explains an event or condition recently perceived by the declarant, made in good faith, not in contemplation of pending or anticipated litigation in which he was interested, and while his recollection was clear.[53]

This was one of the Rule 804 exceptions, which meant that the exception did not apply unless the declarant was unavailable. Congress prevented the Supreme Court's version of the rules from going into effect,[54] and by the time the Federal Rules of Evidence had been enacted as a statute by Congress in 1975, the exception had been removed.[55] Although Congress rejected the recent perception exception, versions of it have been adopted in some states[56] and as an option in the Uniform Rules.[57] The option provided

---

[50] *See* **§ 20.07**.

[51] *See* 5 CHRISTOPHER B. MUELLER & LAIRD C. KIRKPATRICK, FEDERAL EVIDENCE § 8:143 (4th ed. 2013).

[52] *See, e.g.*, Turbyfill v. International Harvester Co., 486 F. Supp. 232, 234–35 (E.D. Mich. 1980) (employee's statement, helpful to employer, admitted against third party under residual exception).

[53] *See* FED. R. EVID. 804(b)(2) (Supreme Court Proposed Draft 1973), *reprinted in* 2 JAMES F. BAILEY & OSCAR M. TRELLES, THE FEDERAL RULES OF EVIDENCE: LEGISLATIVE HISTORIES AND RELATED DOCUMENTS, Doc. 13, at 33 (1980); *see also* 5 WEINSTEIN'S FEDERAL EVIDENCE § 804 App.01[3] (Mark S. Brodin ed., 2d ed. 2015).

[54] *See* **§ 1.04** (describing the legislative history of the Federal Rules of Evidence).

[55] *See* H.R. REP. NO. 93–650 at 6 (1973), *reprinted in* 4 JAMES F. BAILEY & OSCAR M. TRELLES, THE FEDERAL RULES OF EVIDENCE: LEGISLATIVE HISTORIES AND RELATED DOCUMENTS, Doc. 13 at 6 (1980); *see also* 5 WEINSTEIN'S FEDERAL EVIDENCE §§ 804 App.01[3], 804 App.01[4] (Mark S. Brodin ed., 2d ed. 2015).

[56] *See, e.g.*, HAW. R. EVID. 804(b)(5); WIS. STAT. ANN. § 908.045(2). For applications of the Wisconsin Rule, see, e.g., State v. Kutz, 671 N.W.2d 660, 681–83 (Wis. Ct. App. 2003) (holding it was not error for trial court to admit statements made by murder victim that the defendant was following her when the statements were made either the same day or a few days after the events described); Kluever by Gonring v. Evangelical Reformed Immanuels Congregation, 422 N.W.2d 874, 876–78 (Wis. Ct. App. 1988) (holding a statement of an injured worker regarding a fall from ladder admissible even though made eight to ten weeks after the accident); State v. Kreuser, 280 N.W.2d 270, 274 (Wis. 1979) (holding out-of-court statement made within a day of the event reported admissible as recent perception).

[57] *See* UNIF. R. EVID. 803(b)(5).

in Uniform Rule 803(b)(5) is like the federal rule rejected by Congress, except that it applies only to civil cases.[58]

Although much of the hearsay covered by the recent perception exception is also covered by the residual exception or the present sense impression exception, it has a niche of its own. Unlike the residual exception, it allows the evidence to be received without notice, and does not require that it be the best evidence obtainable on the point.[59] Unlike the present sense impression exception, it does not require that the statement be made during or immediately after the event, though the event must be "recent" at the time of the statement.[60] The exception seems a useful supplement to the other hearsay exceptions. Because the declarant is unavailable, the choice is to hear the declarant's story in hearsay form or not at all. The protections of the recent perception exception, such as recency of perception, clarity of recollection, good faith, and unavailability of the declarant, seem sufficient.[61] Nevertheless, most states have not adopted this exception.

Statements of Deceased Persons

Since 1898, Massachusetts has had a statute making statements of decedents broadly admissible in civil actions. The current version of the statute reads as follows:

> In any action or other civil judicial proceeding, a declaration of a deceased person shall not be inadmissible in evidence as hearsay . . . if the court finds that it was made in good faith and upon the personal knowledge of the declarant.[62]

The Massachusetts approach has not spread very widely, though a few states have enacted much more limited statutes for cases involving suits against the estates of decedents.[63] And in 1996, in the wake of the widely publicized murder trial of O.J. Simpson, California adopted a new hearsay exception covering statements of unavailable declarants that "purport[ ] to narrate, describe, or explain the infliction or threat of physical injury upon the declarant."[64] Though the rule contains a number of limitations,[65] it is potentially applicable to many types of civil and criminal cases.

---

58 The Uniform Rules had previously applied the exception to criminal cases as well. This practice was criticized by commentators. *See, e.g.*, Charles W. Quick, *Hearsay, Excitement, Necessity and the Uniform Rules: A Reappraisal of Rule 63(4)*, 6 WAYNE L. REV. 204, 219–24 (1960).

59 *Cf.* FED. R. EVID. 807; *see* **§ 18.01**.

60 *Cf.* FED. R. EVID. 803(1); *see* **§ 16.03**; *see, e.g.*, State v. Kreuser, 280 N.W.2d 270, 274 (Wis. 1979) (out-of-court declarant's statement within one day of event described admissible); Kluever by Gonring v. Evangelical Reformed Immanuels Congregation, 422 N.W.2d 874, 876–78 (Wis. Ct. App. 1988) (declarant's statement made eight to ten weeks after incident held admissible as recent perception).

61 *See* Kenneth E. Kraus, Comment, *The Recent Perception Exception to the Hearsay Rule—A Justifiable Track Record*, 1985 WIS. L. REV. 1525, 1543–44 (arguing for reconsideration of the exception by other jurisdictions).

62 *See* MASS. GEN. LAWS ANN. ch. 233, § 65. For cases applying the Massachusetts rule, see Cusher v. Turner, 495 N.E.2d 311, 316 (Mass. App. Ct. 1986) (holding statements made by decedent in diary and tape recordings admissible); Fire Comm'r v. Joseph, 498 N.E.2d 1368, 1370–71 (Mass. App. Ct. 1986) (finding no error in excluding decedent's statement where it was not made in good faith); O'Connell v. Knight, 2009 WL 3929951 at *4–5 (Mass. Land. Ct. 2009) (holding that 1955 conversation between two deceased persons was admissible).

63 *See, e.g.*, OHIO R. EVID. 804(B)(5). *See generally* 5 WIGMORE ON EVIDENCE § 1576 (Chadbourn rev. 1974 & Supp. 1997).

64 CAL. EVID. CODE § 1370.

65 The statement must have been made at or near the time of the injury or threat; it must have been made under circumstances indicating its trustworthiness; and it must have been in writing, electronically recorded, or made to a law enforcement official. § 1370(a). In addition, the rule contains a provision requiring

Statements by Children Describing Abuse

A number of states have adopted statutory exceptions to the hearsay rule for statements by children about sexual or physical abuse.[66] Some apply only when the child is unavailable to testify[67] or when the child is either testifying or unavailable to do so.[68] Typical definitions of unavailability include such things as the declarant's incompetence to testify.[69] Ohio's rule includes a provision stating that the child's testimony is not reasonably obtainable for purposes of the rule if "[t]he child refuses to testify concerning the subject matter of the statement or claims lack of memory of the subject matter of the statement after a person trusted by the child, in the presence of the court, urges the child to both describe the acts described by the [hearsay] statement and to testify."[70]

---

the proponent to make known its intention to offer the statement and its particulars "sufficiently in advance of the proceedings to provide the adverse party with a fair opportunity to prepare the meet the statement." § 1370(c).

[66] *See generally* Michael H. Graham, *The Confrontation Clause, the Hearsay Rule and Child Sexual Abuse Prosecutions: The State of the Relationship*, 72 MINN. L. REV. 523, 534–38 (1988); Jean L. Kelly, Comment, *Legislative Responses to Child Sexual Abuse Cases: The Hearsay Exception and the Videotape Deposition*, 34 CATH. U. L. REV. 1021, 1035–41 (1985); Judy Yun, Note, *A Comprehensive Approach to Child Hearsay Statements in Sex Abuse Cases*, 83 COLUM. L. REV. 1745 (1983).

[67] *See, e.g.*, OHIO R. EVID. 807.

[68] *See, e.g.*, MINN. STAT. ANN. § 595.02, subd. 3:

> An out-of-court statement made by a child under the age of ten years or a person who is mentally impaired . . . alleging, explaining, denying, or describing any act of sexual contact or penetration performed with or on the child . . . is admissible as substantive evidence if:
>
> (a) the court or person authorized to receive evidence finds, in a hearing conducted outside of the presence of the jury, that the time, content, and circumstances of the statement and the reliability of the person to whom the statement is made provide sufficient indicia of reliability; and
>
> (b) the child . . . either:
>
> (i) testifies at the proceedings; or
>
> (ii) is unavailable as a witness and there is corroborative evidence of the act; and
>
> (c) the proponent of the statement notifies the adverse party of the proponent's intention to offer the statement and the particulars of the statement sufficiently in advance of the proceeding at which the proponent intends to offer the statement into evidence to provide the adverse party with a fair opportunity to prepare to meet the statement. . . .

For applications of this statute, *see* State v. Dana, 422 N.W.2d 246, 248–50 (Minn. 1988) (admissibility hearing sufficient; no error in admitting statements of two abused children); State v. Bellotti, 383 N.W.2d 308, 312–13 (Minn. Ct. App. 1986) (statements of four-year-old sex abuse victim admissible). In Danforth v. State, 761 N.W.2d 493, 495 (Minn. 2009), *on remand from* 552 U.S. 264 (2008), the trial court had admitted an incompetent child's videotaped interview under § 595.02, subd. 3, and the defendant was convicted of criminal sexual conduct. The defendant claimed that his right to confrontation had been violated and asked the court retroactively to apply the rule from Crawford v. Washington. *See* **§ 20.02**. Although the Supreme Court would have allowed Minnesota to apply the rule retroactively, the Minnesota Supreme Court declined to do so and affirmed the conviction.

[69] *See, e.g.*, FED. R. EVID. 804(a)(4) (defining as unavailable a person who "is unable to be present or to testify at the hearing because of death or then existing physical or mental illness or infirmity"); CAL. EVID. CODE § 240(a)(3) (a person is unavailable if he or she is "[d]ead or unable to attend or to testify at the hearing because of then existing physical or mental illness or infirmity"); CAL. EVID. CODE § 240(c) ("Expert testimony which establishes that physical or mental trauma resulting from an alleged crime has caused harm to a witness of sufficient severity that the witness is physically unable to testify or is unable to testify without suffering substantial trauma may constitute a sufficient showing of unavailability . . .").

[70] OHIO R. EVID. 807(B)(1).

Of course, many statements of children are admissible under conventional theories, such as the excited utterance,[71] a statement for medical diagnosis or treatment,[72] or the residual exception.[73] In any event, if the child does not testify, in a criminal case, admitting the child's hearsay testimony implicating the accused can present serious issues under the Confrontation Clause.[74]

§ 18.03 Hearsay Through the Mouth of an Expert

In the hands of a skillful trial lawyer, the expert can become a channel through which important fact evidence flows into the ears of jurors. At least prior to 2000, it was not uncommon for trial lawyers to report that some trial judges would allow experts to quote freely the statements of others, reporting case-specific facts, in support of their opinions. For example, an expert on the causes and origins of fire might testify on the issue of arson. If the expert talked to eyewitnesses in the course of investigation, then the expert might be used as a conduit to put into evidence the narratives of those eyewitnesses without calling them to the stand.[75] Or, the expert might be asked to describe the contents of reports of experiments done by others upon which the expert relied.[76] The supposed justification for this practice was Federal Rule of Evidence 703, which provides that experts may rely for their conclusions on the facts or data not admissible into evidence.[77]

The problem with relying upon this Rule as authority for the proposition that experts can freely give hearsay testimony is that the rule only provides that experts may, within reason, rely upon otherwise inadmissible evidence in forming such opinions. The Rule has never stated that experts may freely repeat hearsay that they have heard while forming opinions. Testifying experts are permitted on direct examination to show that they did a careful job of preparing their opinions. To show diligence, it is often reasonable to allow experts to testify to the fact that a conversation took place, without necessarily revealing the content of the conversation. An expert might be allowed, for example, to state that the expert had conferred with another expert while forming an opinion,

---

[71] *See, e.g.*, United States v. NB, 59 F.3d 771, 776 (8th Cir. 1995); United States v. Farley, 992 F.2d 1122, 1125–26 (10th Cir. 1993) (trial court properly admitted testimony from child victim's mother as to victim's statements the morning after alleged sexual assault occurred when victim was still "under the stress of the event"); United States v. Nick, 604 F.2d 1199, 1204 (9th Cir. 1979) (statements of child admissible as excited utterances in sexual assault case).

[72] Goldade v. State, 674 P.2d 721, 722–28 (Wyo. 1983) (statements of child sex abuse victim to nurse and physician admissible under the "treatment and diagnosis" exception).

[73] *See, e.g.*, Doe v. United States, 976 F.2d 1071, 1074–78 (7th Cir. 1992) (in Federal Torts Claim Act action alleging sexual abuse at government-owned center, three-year-old children's hearsay statements admissible under residual hearsay exception where essence of their story did not change despite the addition of varying details and where statements responded to questions by adults); United States v. Dorian, 803 F.2d 1439, 1446 (8th Cir. 1986) (statement of child victim of sex abuse admissible under the residual hearsay exception).

[74] *See* **§ 20.07**.

[75] *See* Stevens v. Cessna Aircraft, 634 F. Supp. 137, 142–43 (E.D. Pa. 1986), *aff'd*, 806 F.2d 252 (3d Cir. 1986) (expert's testimony regarding statements made to him during course of investigation held admissible); State v. Jones, 368 S.E.2d 844 (N.C. 1988) (expert's testimony as to contents of statements relied upon to form opinion held admissible).

[76] *See* Roger C. Park, *Confining the Expert: Rule 703(b) of the Rules of Evidence*, THE BENCH AND BAR OF MINNESOTA, March 1990, at 33–35.

[77] FED. R. EVID. 703.

without expressly stating the opinion of the other expert.[78] However, when the expert begins to describe the content of conversations with other persons, the expert becomes an inappropriate conduit for hearsay and the testimony is often objectionable.[79] In order to reduce the abuse of this quasi-exception to the hearsay rule, Rule 703 was amended in 2000, adding language that (after the Restyling) reads as follows:

> But if the facts or data would otherwise be inadmissible, the proponent of the opinion may disclose them to the jury only if their probative value in helping the jury evaluate the opinion substantially outweighs their prejudicial effect.[80]

As discussed elsewhere,[81] this language establishes a "presumption against disclosure to the jury of information used as the basis of an expert's opinion and not admissible for any substantive purpose, when that information is offered by the proponent of the expert."[82] And "[i]f the otherwise inadmissible information is admitted under this balancing test, the trial judge must give a limiting instruction upon request, informing the jury that the underlying information must not be used for substantive purposes."[83]

§ 18.04 Hearsay Constitutionally Admissible on Behalf of a Criminal Defendant

The accused's constitutional right to present exculpatory evidence has significant impact in the hearsay context. One of the most important cases in the development of that doctrine, *Chambers v. Mississippi*,[84] involved exculpatory evidence offered by the accused but rejected by the Mississippi courts under the hearsay rule. A considerable body of case law applies this doctrine in the hearsay context; we will not attempt a detailed treatment of the subject here.[85] Instead, this section offers a brief summary of the *Chambers* case followed by comments about its implications.

The Chambers *Case*

Officer Aaron Liberty was murdered when he and several other Mississippi police officers attempted to serve an arrest warrant and were resisted by a hostile crowd. Before Liberty died of his wounds, he fired his weapon in the direction from which he was shot and hit Leon Chambers. Chambers survived and was charged with shooting Liberty. The

---

78 *See, e.g.*, United States v. Rollins, 862 F.2d 1282, 1292–93 (7th Cir. 1988) (expert's testimony that he had conversations with others concerning the meaning of certain code-words used in illegal drug deals admissible where content of these conversations not revealed).

79 *See generally* Ronald L. Carlson, *Collision Course in Expert Testimony: Limitations an Affirmative Introduction of Underlying Data*, 36 U. FLA. L. REV. 234 (1984); Ronald L. Carlson, *Policing the Bases of Modern Expert Testimony*, 39 VAND. L. REV. 577 (1986). *But see* Paul R. Rice, *Inadmissible Evidence as a Basis for Expert Opinion Testimony: A Response to Professor Carlson*, 40 VAND. L. REV. 583 (1987) (arguing that admitting the expert's opinion without its basis is illogical because one cannot accept the truth of an opinion without implicitly accepting the facts upon which the opinion is based, and that depriving the jury of the basis of the opinion leads to undesirable blind deference to the witness; also arguing for adoption of a carefully tailored hearsay exception covering the basis of the expert's opinion).

80 FED. R. EVID. 703.

81 *See* **§ 10.05**.

82 FED. R. EVID. 703 advisory committee note (2000 amendment).

83 *Id.* Regarding the Confrontation Clause implications of this practice, *see* **§ 20.07**.

84 Chambers v. Mississippi, 410 U.S. 284 (1975). For a detailed history of the case, see Stephan Landsman, Chambers v. Mississippi: *A New Justice Meets An Old Style Southern Verdict*, in EVIDENCE STORIES 359 (Richard Lempert ed., 2006).

85 For a systematic treatment, *see* EDWARD J. IMWINKELRIED & NORMAN M. GARLAND, EXCULPATORY EVIDENCE: THE ACCUSED'S CONSTITUTIONAL RIGHT TO INTRODUCE FAVORABLE EVIDENCE ch.14 (3d ed. 2004).

trial included conflicting eyewitness testimony as to whether Chambers was the shooter. Chambers called Gable McDonald to testify because, Chambers claimed, McDonald had made several out-of-court statements admitting that he, not Chambers, had shot Officer Liberty. McDonald, however, had recanted his confessions before the trial of Chambers, and defense counsel no doubt expected McDonald to deny shooting Liberty. At the time, Mississippi followed the common-law voucher rule, according to which the party calling a witness may not impeach him except in unusual circumstances, so the calling party is effectively "stuck" with the answers made by his witness.[86] Consequently, defense counsel did nothing more than have McDonald authenticate a written confession to the shooting that he had signed.[87] After introducing the confession, the witness was turned over to the prosecution, which elicited McDonald's recantation and explanation of the confession, and denial that he shot Liberty. Upon redirect, the defense was barred from impeaching McDonald with questions about his other, oral self-inculpatory statements because of the voucher rule and the inapplicability of the exception to that rule for "adverse" witnesses.[88] The defense then tried to introduce substantively the oral admissions McDonald had made to three other persons. The trial court sustained hearsay objections to all of these statements on the ground that they were statements against penal interest offered to exculpate the accused, which were not admissible in Mississippi at the time.[89]

The Supreme Court held that this combination of restrictions constituted a denial of due process. First, the Court criticized the voucher rule and concluded that McDonald was sufficiently "adverse" to trigger the defendant's right to confront him by meaningful cross-examination, which the application of the voucher rule denied.[90] Second, it noted criticism of the "materialistic" limitation on declarations against interest and the trend away from it but did not hold that it *per se* violated the defendant's right to present a defense. Instead, the Court criticized the resulting declaration against interest exception in Mississippi as under-inclusive when "mechanistically" applied in this case, because (a) the point of the hearsay rule is to exclude hearsay that is too unreliable, whereas (b) the circumstances of these particular hearsay statements "provided considerable assurance of their reliability."[91] The reliability of the out-out court statements arose from four factors:

(1) Each of McDonald's oral confessions "was made spontaneously to a close acquaintance shortly after the murder."

(2) Each was corroborated by some other evidence in the case, including (but not limited to) the other confessions.

(3) Each was "in a very real sense self-incriminatory and unquestionably against interest," because McDonald had nothing to gain by making these confessions.

---

86 *See* **§ 11.02** (discussing modern rejection of voucher rule reflected in FED. R. EVID. 607).

87 410 U.S. at 291.

88 The Court noted that the Mississippi appellate courts had affirmed this holding on the dubious ground that McDonald did not testify that the defendant was the perpetrator, only that he, McDonald, was not the perpetrator. 410 U.S. at 291–92.

89 410 U.S. at 292–93. *See* **§ 17.04**. One of the mysteries of the case is why the state did not object to the admission of the written confession by McDonald on the same ground.

90 410 U.S. at 295–98.

91 410 U.S. at 300.

(4) McDonald testified at the trial and could be questioned about his prior confessions.[92]

Additionally, the Court noted that the introduction of these exculpatory statements was "critical" to the defense.[93]

Implications

The Court made an avowedly contextualized judgment that Chambers was denied Due Process because the combined effect of the application of an outmoded common-law voucher principle and the "mechanistic" application of the hearsay rule excluded highly reliable exculpatory statements offered by the accused. In the aftermath of that decision, an initial question was whether either of these two elements, by itself, could constitute such a violation of the defendant's rights. Of course, the voucher rule has been largely abandoned. And, for our present purposes, the question focuses on the exclusion of hearsay offered by the accused. In *Green v. Georgia*[94] the Court held that the defendant's constitutional rights may be violated solely by an overly restrictive application of the hearsay rule. *Green* also added a factor to the analysis that had not been germane in *Chambers*: it counted in favor of admitting hearsay offered by the accused if the government had invited the fact-finder to rely upon the same hearsay in prosecuting another person, such as a co-defendant.[95]

Given these many factors, it is difficult to discern which particular constellation of facts will constitute an application of the hearsay rule to defense evidence that is too restrictive. *Chambers* was unusual in the number and consistency of hearsay statements by the same declarant, as well as in the fact that other specific testimony could be found to corroborate elements of those admissions. The resulting assurance of reliability was central to the Court's reasoning because it showed that exclusion did not achieve the goals of the hearsay rule itself. Later cases do not always require hearsay that is so obviously credible, but it is unclear just how reliable such evidence has to be in order to override the hearsay rule. Each case must be decided on its unique facts.[96]

---

[92] 410 U.S. at 298–301. The Mississippi courts' handling of the hearsay in *Chambers* is not as anachronistic as one might think. If the same case arose today in a federal district court, McDonald's hearsay confessions would still be inadmissible under the exception for declarations against interest: not because Rule 804(b)(3) is subject to the against-penal-interest limitation—it is not—but because McDonald testified and thus was not unavailable as required by Rule 804(b).

[93] 410 U.S. at 302.

[94] Green v. Georgia, 442 U.S. 95, 97 (1979) (applying principle of *Chambers* to trial court's exclusion of hearsay in sentencing context).

[95] 442 U.S. at 97. Several lower courts have applied this principle. *See, e.g.,* Pettijohn v. Hall, 599 F.2d 476, 481 (1st Cir. 1979); Rivera v. Director, Dep't of Corrections, 915 F.2d 280, 282 (7th Cir. 1990); Woods v. State, 696 P.2d 464, 468 (Nev. 1985); State v. Barts, 362 S.E.2d 235, 241 (N.C. 1987); People v. Tenney, 793 N.E.2d 571 (Ill. 2002).

[96] For example, in Chia v. Cambra, 281 F.3d 1032 (9th Cir. 2002), *cert. granted judgment vacated sub nom.* McGrath v. Chia, 538 U.S. 902 (2003), *reaffirmed on remand,* 360 F.3d 997 (9th Cir. 2004), the defendant challenged his conviction on the ground that the trial court excluded several statements made by his good friend and alleged co-conspirator to the police, in which his friend accepted responsibility and downplayed the defendant's involvement. The statements, offered but rejected under California's version of the declaration-against-interest exception, were not made spontaneously, but under questioning; they were made not to a friend, but to the police; and they were made by a person with a personal interest in protecting his friend, the defendant. Finally, the declarant refused to testify at the defendant's trial, invoking his Fifth Amendment privilege. The other members of the conspiracy were all dead and could not testify to the defendant's role. So, while the hearsay was critical to the defense, reliability-related factors (1) and (4) identified in *Chambers* were not present, yet the ruling by the Ninth Circuit sustained the defendant's constitutional challenge via habeas corpus. The majority disagreed with a strong dissent on the extent of corroboration of the hearsay in the

The fourth factor noted by the Supreme Court in *Chambers* is striking: that the declarant testified and could have been examined and cross-examined concerning his prior statements counted in favor of admitting the hearsay. That is hardly surprising on its face, but it is contrary to the message built into the unavailability requirement of Federal Rule of Evidence 804: for a given item of hearsay that satisfies the conditions of, say, Rule 804(b)(3)—statements against interest—if the declarant testifies, the hearsay is inadmissible, but if the declarant is unavailable, the hearsay is admissible. Thus, under Rule 804, the declarant's testifying counts decisively against admission, whereas under Due Process analysis, the declarant's testifying counts in favor of admission. If, then, the defendant offers hearsay that otherwise satisfies the conditions of an exception listed in Rule 804(b)[97] and the declarant testifies, it is difficult to see how the hearsay can be excluded constitutionally. While it is true that such an exception might be over- as well as under-inclusive, and so the particular hearsay offered by the accused might be unusually unreliable, it makes no sense to exclude such hearsay just because the declarant is testifying when that same hearsay would be admitted if the declarant were unavailable.[98]

Much of the case law, however, has focused on situations in which the declarant does *not* testify. In this context, the Second Circuit announced a two-part test in its 1988 decision, *Rosario v. Kuhlman*.[99] First, to qualify for the constitutional override, the hearsay offered by the accused must be reliable (and, presumably, critical to the defense). Second, the declarant must be unavailable, meaning that the defendant must show a "good faith effort" to bring the declarant before the trial court. The court derived the latter requirement from a notion of parity: the prosecution must show unavailability by that standard in order to satisfy the Confrontation Clause, as it was then interpreted, so the defense should be required to do so when invoking its constitutional right to present evidence.[100] Whether or not one accepts this particular rationale, the idea that the defendant should not be allowed to claim a denial of Due Process when the accused himself fails to produce the hearsay declarant has a certain appeal.[101] Why not require the defendant to show a good faith effort to present the declarant as a condition on

testimony of other witnesses (factor (2) above) and in their assessment of factor (3), the against-interest element. The majority considered the against-interest element to be strong enough, together with corroborating evidence and the fact that one of the statements was made when the declarant's death was a serious possibility (albeit not sufficiently so as to trigger the dying declaration exception), to imbue the exculpatory portions of the statements with adequate reliability to invoke the constitutional override. By contrast, the dissent emphasized the importance of distinguishing the against-interest portions from the portions designed to help a good friend.

[97] Not including the exception for forfeiture, Rule 804(b)(6), which is not based on reliability considerations. *See* **§ 17.06.**

[98] *See* State v. Cazares-Mendez, 256 P.3d 104, 108, 114–19 (Ore. 2011) (invoking *Chambers* to hold that a hearsay statement that would satisfy Oregon's declaration against interest exception if the declarant were unavailable may not be excluded, when offered by the accused, just because the declarant testifies). In arriving at its conclusion, the Oregon Supreme Court stated that the reliability requirements of the Due Process standard are no more onerous than those of the hearsay exception for declarations against interest. To the extent that this point is critical to the reasoning, this might not be true of another exception in Rule 804(b), such as the dying declaration exception.

[99] Rosario v. Kuhlman, 839 F.2d 918 (2d Cir. 1988).

[100] *Id.* at 924–25. On the Confrontation Clause doctrine at the time, *see* **§ 20.01.**

[101] Defendants may plausibly believe otherwise, however, if they think that producing such a declarant will render even more clearly inapplicable the hearsay exception upon which they attempt to rely, such as the declaration against interest exception. But if the previous conclusion—that placing the declarant on the stand will permit a Due Process override of the unavailability requirement for such an exception—becomes clearly accepted, then this concern should dissipate.

introducing any hearsay that would override the usual hearsay rules on constitutional grounds?

An answer to that question lies in the fact that, in many cases, the prosecution is perfectly capable of placing the declarant on the stand. In fact, in a number of cases the defense has successfully raised a *Chambers* argument to introduce otherwise inadmissible hearsay, without making a showing of unavailability, under circumstances indicating that the declarant was readily available to the prosecution anyway.[102] The idea of requiring a defendant to show the unavailability of a non-testifying declarant, as a condition of invoking the *Chambers* override makes most sense when the government can first show that it cannot reasonably procure the declarant's testimony on the subject of the prior statements.[103]

---

[102] *See, e.g.*, State v. Barts, 362 S.E.2d 235 (N.C. 1987) (admitting hearsay of person who had been convicted in relation to same events and was in state prison at time of defendant's trial); State v. Brown, 29 S.W.3d 427 (Tenn. 2000) (admitting alleged victim's hearsay admissions to two individuals about prior sexual conduct; declarant-victim testified, but not regarding her prior statements that tended to exonerate the accused, and prosecution easily could have recalled her to deny or explain her hearsay statements).

[103] In most such cases, the government's showing that it cannot obtain the declarant's testimony, if that were required, will effectively demonstrate that the defendant cannot obtain the declarant's testimony either. Several cases not explicitly applying an unavailability requirement as such nonetheless demonstrate this fact. *See, e.g.*, Chia v. Cambra, 360 F.3d 997, 1002 (9th Cir. 2004) (holding it was error for California trial court to exclude exculpatory hearsay made by another person who exercised his Fifth Amendment privilege and refused to testify at defendant's trial); People v. Tenney, 793 N.E.2d 571, 583–89 (Ill. 2002) (holding trial court erred in excluding testimony from a prior trial of one Lane, in which the witness testified that Lane admitted committing the murder for which the defendant was on trial; observing that Lane was initially convicted but conviction was vacated when the state charged the defendant; not explicitly applying an unavailability test with respect to Lane's declaration against penal interest, but noting that "[t]he defense, with the cooperation of the State, diligently and in good faith attempted to locate Lane and [the witness at the previous trial], without success.").

Chapter 19

SOME PRACTICE TIPS ABOUT FREQUENTLY ENCOUNTERED HEARSAY ARGUMENTS

Table of Sections

This chapter examines several commonly encountered arguments regarding hearsay objections. Often it is difficult to track down the source of these arguments in the statutes, rules, or common-law. Some of them are valid; some, even if familiar, are not. This chapter will examine them and, where they are incorrect, suggest alternatives.

§ 19.01 "Objection. Self-serving."

"Objection, self-serving" is heard in many courtrooms. However, most evidence is "self-serving." The adversary system assumes that each side presents evidence that will serve its purpose and damage the other side's case. Far from being inadmissible, offering self-serving evidence is the whole idea of advocacy. By using the "self-serving" objection, a lawyer might signal to the judge that the lawyer does not really understand the law of evidence. More importantly, the objection might substitute for a proper objection, one that, if made, would preserve a crucial point for appeal, whereas the "self-serving" objection will not.

The temptation to make the "self-serving" objection arises because the self-serving quality of the evidence makes it look less reliable. The objection does not, however, adequately describe a specific admissibility problem. The objecting party must raise the appropriate evidentiary problem in order to inform the trial judge and preserve rights to appeal error.[1]

Example

Two people who shared a house are in a dispute over ownership of a painting that was assumed to be of minimal value when purchased but now is valued at $1,000,000. The plaintiff calls a person who was a regular guest at the house:

---

1 *See* **§ 3.04**.

Plaintiff's lawyer:	Have you ever seen what has been received in evidence as the plaintiff's exhibit #1?
Witness:	Yes.
Plaintiff's lawyer:	Under what circumstances?
Witness:	In the plaintiff's bedroom. I saw it on the wall and asked the plaintiff about it.
Plaintiff's lawyer:	What did the plaintiff say?
Defense lawyer:	Objection, self-serving.
Judge:	Overruled.
Witness:	The plaintiff said: "It's my favorite possession. I paid $20 dollars for it. Now it's worth a million."

The plaintiff's out-of-court statement, offered by the plaintiff to prove that the plaintiff owns the painting, is hearsay.[2] When offered by the other side, it would be admissible, exempted from the hearsay rule as the statement of a party opponent.[3] When the party making the statement offers it, it is indeed "self-serving," but the correct objection is that statement is inadmissible hearsay (not within the exception for the statement of a party-opponent).

Example

Following a collision between a driver's automobile and a company's truck, the automobile driver brings a personal injury action against trucking company. The company requires its drivers to file an accident report with the company after every incident. If the driver is able, the company requires him to make the statement immediately after the accident. The statements are kept in an accident file and are reviewed regularly by the company in assessing the adequacy of its insurance, the progress of its training programs, and the position it should take in any lawsuit resulting from an incident. The report in this particular case includes the driver's recitation of the plaintiff's statement to the driver immediately after the accident: "It was my fault; I wasn't watching." The driver is no longer available to testify, so the company offers the report as a business record.

Defense lawyer:	[After laying the traditional business records foundation through the company record custodian]. Defense offers the report of the same date as the event as Defense exhibit #1.
Plaintiff's lawyer:	Objection, self-serving.
Judge:	Overruled.

The "self-serving" objection will not preserve the matter for appeal. But there is a substantial chance that the hearsay report does not fall within the business records exception to the rule against hearsay because it may not satisfy the trustworthiness

[2] *See* **§ 14.01**.

[3] *See* **§ 15.07**.

requirement of Rule 803(6). While the theory that it fails to fall within the business records exception—because prepared for litigation—is akin to self-serving, objecting to the proffered report as "hearsay" will keep the report from being admitted and preserve the matter for appeal.

§ 19.02 "It's admissible because it was said in the presence of the defendant."

In *response* to a hearsay objection by the defense, plaintiffs or prosecutors often say, "It was said in the presence of the defendant." Defendants often make a similar response when they offer hearsay against plaintiffs: "It's admissible because it was said in the presence of the plaintiff." However, not all statements made in the presence of the adverse party are admissible Most of them are, so the response is acceptable when the situation is right, but it is imprecise. Whether a statement was made in the presence of the adverse party matters in two situations.

First, the statement may be offered to show its effect on the hearer.[4] For example, if it is relevant, the statement may be offered by the plaintiff to show that the defendant had notice or that the defendant had been warned. Such statements are not hearsay because they are not offered to prove the truth of the matter asserted. They are merely offered to show the impact of the statement on the state of mind of the hearer. Of course, when offered for this purpose, its probative value depends on the likelihood that the hearer was present and heard the statement. In any event, in such situations, the proper responsive argument is: "It's offered for it effect on the hearer, not for the truth of the matter asserted."

Second, the statement may be offered as an adoptive admission. For example, suppose that after an accident a bystander said to the defendant, "It was all your fault." If the defendant said nothing in return, and if the circumstances were such that a person who was not responsible would be expected to deny the accusation, the statement would be admissible against the defendant as an adoptive admission—the defendant's silence constitutes an adoption of the bystander's accusation.[5] Here, the proper responsive argument would be something like: "It's admissible as an adoptive admission."

But the mere fact that a defendant is present does not automatically make the statement admissible. Sometimes the grounds for escaping the hearsay ban just described—effect on hearer and adoptive admission—are not applicable. For example, suppose that the bystander told the defendant, "It's all your fault," and the defendant responded, "No, it's not!" The bystander's statement is not admissible on a nonhearsay theory of the effect on the listener because the hearer's state of mind at that time is irrelevant to any of the issues in the personal injury action.[6] The adoptive admission theory does not work, because the defendant denied the accusation. Thus, in the situation described, the statement is inadmissible despite having been made in the presence of the defendant.

---

[4] *See* **§ 14.04** (subsection on "Statements Offered to Show Their Effect on the Listener or Reader").

[5] *See* **§ 15.07** (subsection on "Adoptive Statements").

[6] To the extent that the hearer's state of mind is relevant, it would be probative of the absence of fault of the defendant, but presumably the plaintiff would not offer the defendant's response by which this might be inferred, even though the plaintiff would be entitled to present it as a statement of a party opponent. *See* **§ 15.07** (subsection on "Explicit (Non-adoptive) Statements").

The obverse of this point is that it is no good for the defense to object to the introduction of hearsay by saying, "Objection, not made in the presence of the defendant." Countless hearsay exemptions and exceptions apply to statements not made in the presence of the party against whom they are offered.[7]

§ 19.03 "It's admissible as part of the res gestae."

Proponents sometimes argue that hearsay is admissible because "it's part of the res gestae." Res gestae, from the Latin for "things done," means all circumstances surrounding and connected with a happening. But the term has been criticized for inviting confusion. "The discredited shibboleth res gestae is no longer uttered in polite legal society, and we hope to lay its ghost to rest," said the Maryland Court of Special Appeals in 1988.[8] Indeed, probably no legal term has been the victim of such an intense eradication campaign. Wigmore long advocated that the phrase be put to death:

> The phrase "res gestae" has long been not only entirely useless, but even positively harmful. It is useless, because every rule of Evidence to which it has ever been applied exists as a part of some other well established principle and can be explained in the terms of that principle. It is harmful, because by its ambiguity it invites the confusion of one rule with another and thus creates uncertainty as to the limitations of both. It ought therefore wholly to be repudiated, as a vicious element in our legal phraseology. No rule of Evidence can be created or applied by the mere muttering of a shibboleth. There are words enough to describe the rules of Evidence. Even if there were no accepted name for one or another doctrine, any name would be preferable to an empty phrase so encouraging to looseness of thinking and uncertainty of decision.[9]

Professor Edmund Morgan, Justice Oliver Wendell Holmes Jr., and Judge Learned Hand also had unkind things to say about res gestae.[10]

Suppose an advocate makes a hearsay objection. The proponent of the evidence responds that the evidence is part of the res gestae. What answer should the objecting attorney make? "There's no such thing as a res gestae exception" or "Res gestae doesn't apply under the Federal Rules" are possibilities. If those responses do not work, the advocate should attempt to identify the modern equivalent of the argument being made and respond accordingly. For example, "this is not part of the res gestae because too much time had passed between the event and the statement" is appropriate if the phrase

---

[7] *See* 2 McCORMICK ON EVIDENCE § 246 at 185–86 (Kenneth S. Broun ed., 7th ed. 2013).

[8] Cassidy v. State, 536 A.2d 666, 668 (Md. App. 1988).

[9] 6 WIGMORE ON EVIDENCE § 1767 at 182 (3d ed. 1940).

[10] Edmund Morgan wrote:

> The marvelous capacity of a Latin phrase to serve as a substitute for reasoning, and the confusion of thought inevitably accompanying the use of inaccurate terminology, are nowhere better illustrated than in the decisions dealing with the admissibility of evidence as "res gestae." It is probable that this troublesome expression owes its existence and persistence in our law of evidence to an inclination of judges and lawyers to avoid the toilsome exertion of exact analysis and precise thinking. Certain it is that since its introduction at the close of the eighteenth century, on account of its exasperating indefiniteness it has done nothing but bewilder and perplex.

Edmund M. Morgan, *A Suggested Classification of Utterances Admissible as Res Gestae*, 31 YALE L.J. 229, 229 (1922) (quoted in Cassidy v. State, 536 A.2d 666, 669 (Md. App. 1988)). Holmes is thought to have said that "[t]he man that uses that phrase (res gestae) shows that he has lost temporarily all power of analyzing ideas." Learned Hand stated: "[A]s for 'res gestae,' . . . if it means anything but an unwillingness to think at all, what it covers cannot be put in less intelligible terms." United States v. Matot, 146 F.2d 197, 198 (2d Cir. 1944).

is being used as a stand-in for the present sense impression, or "he wasn't still under the stress of excitement," when the phrase seems to have been used to refer to the excited utterance exception.

§ 19.04 "It's admissible because it shows state of mind."

When a proponent responds to a hearsay objection with the assertion that an out-of-court statement is admissible because it shows state of mind, the response is ambiguous: it can mean either that the statement is offered to show the declarant's own state of mind, or that it is offered to show something about the state of mind of the hearer or reader of the statement.

A statement offered to show the state of mind of the hearer or reader of the statement is generally admissible on grounds that the statement is not being offered to prove the truth of the matter asserted, and hence is not hearsay.[11] An objection should still be sustained when the state of mind of the hearer or reader is not relevant to the case, or when the probative value of the statement in showing state of mind is outweighed by the danger that the jury will use the statement to prove the truth of what it asserts. For example, if the good faith of a police officer in making an investigation of a suspect is a real issue in the case, then evidence that the officer had been told by a reliable source that the suspect committed the crime under investigation is admissible. When, however, the only issue is the guilt of the suspect, not the state of mind of the officer, then what the officer was told about the suspect's guilt is inadmissible hearsay.[12]

An utterance offered to show the state of mind of the declarant is generally admissible under the hearsay exception for statements of present state of mind.[13] An objection should still be sustained, however, if the state of mind of the declarant is irrelevant, or though relevant, its probative value is outweighed by the danger that the jury will use the out-of-court statement for some purpose other than showing the declarant's state of mind. An objection should also be sustained if the purpose of showing the declarant's state of mind is to show something about the past. In that case, the statement does not fit the hearsay exception for statements of present state of mind, because the hearsay exception does not cover statements of memory or belief offered to show the fact remembered or believed.[14]

Occasionally, a party will offer a statement to show a fact remembered or believed by the declarant and assert that the statement is not hearsay at all because it is not offered to prove the truth of the matter asserted, but rather to show state of mind circumstantially. For example, evidence that the declarant told a falsehood might be offered to show the guilty state of mind of the declarant, for purposes of showing that the declarant committed a crime in the past. Often such utterances will be admissible as the statement of a party-opponent.[15] When the declarant is not the party-opponent in the case, their evidentiary status is problematic. Certainly, offering a statement as a falsehood to show a guilty state of mind does not seem to be offering it to prove the truth of what it asserts. On the other hand, the statement relies upon the belief of a person

---

[11] *See* **§ 14.04** (subsection on "Statements Offered to Show Their Effect on the Listener or Reader").

[12] See **§ 14.04** (subsection on "Circumstantial (Indirect) Evidence of Declarant's Knowledge or State of Mind").

[13] *See* FED. R. EVID. 803(3).

[14] *See* **§ 16.04**.

[15] *See* **§ 15.07**.

not subject to cross-examination and has most of the infirmities of hearsay. Courts that have considered the admissibility of such statements under the Federal Rules of Evidence have reached divergent results.[16]

§ 19.05 "It's admissible because it's only being offered to impeach."

The assertion, "It's admissible because it's only being offered to impeach," is often a valid one. When an out-of-court statement is being offered as a prior inconsistent statement to impeach the person who made the statement, then it escapes the hearsay ban.[17] However, the word "impeach" is not a magic word that automatically obviates the hearsay rule. In particular, when the statement of a declarant is used to impeach someone other than the declarant, it typically has no value for impeachment unless the factfinder first accepts the statement as proof of what it asserts.[18]

Examples

Example 1: X testifies in court that "the light was red." X said to an investigator out of court that "the light was green." The investigator's in-court report of the out-of-court statement is admissible to impeach. It has impeachment value whether or not one accepts the truth of what was asserted. The mere fact that the witness said different things at different times reflects poorly on the witness's credibility, without regard to the truth of what was said out of court.

Example 2: X testifies in court for the plaintiff that "the light was red." Y tells an investigator that X is a close personal friend of the plaintiff. The investigator's in-court report of Y's statement is hearsay, even though it is being used to impeach X (in this case, for bias). It tends to show bias only to the extent that the fact-finder believes Y's out-of-court assertion.

Thus, there are actually two different distinctions at work here: hearsay versus nonhearsay use, and credibility versus noncredibility use.[19] These can be put in a table of examples as follows:

Out-of-Court Statement	Credibility Use	Noncredibility Use
Nonhearsay Use	*Example 1*	*Example 3*
Hearsay Use	*Example 2*	*Example 4*

16 For an extended discussion, *see* Roger C. Park, *"I Didn't Tell Them Anything About You": Implied Assertions as Hearsay Under the Federal Rules of Evidence*, 74 MINN. L. REV. 783, 802–10 (1990).

17 *See* **§ 14.04** (subsection on "Prior Statements of a Witness Relevant to Credibility").

18 *See* Bemis v. Edwards, 45 F.3d 1369, 1372 (9th Cir. 1995) (holding statement by another person not admissible to impeach police report of beating incident: "Whereas an inconsistent statement by a testifying witness can be used to impeach that witness's credibility, an inconsistent account by another source is offered to show an alternative view of the truth.").

19 As illustrated throughout the chapter devoted to impeachment and rehabilitation of witnesses (Chapter 11), the term "substantive" is often used to refer to non-credibility uses, to indicate that the evidence is relevant in the case by some inference that is more direct than merely attacking or supporting the credibility of a witness. Accordingly, one could characterize the distinction between a credibility use and a non-credibility use as one between a credibility use and a substantive use. Unfortunately, the term "substantive" is also sometimes used to indicate that the statement is used for a hearsay purpose as opposed to a nonhearsay purpose, so we have used less ambiguous terminology in the table.

To fill out the table, we can add two additional examples:

> *Example 3:* X does not testify; X claims that he has been unable to utter a word ever since the accident. To prove that X is capable of speech, defendant offers Y to testify that X said, out-of-court and after the accident, "The light was green."[20] In this case, X's statement is not being offered to prove the truth of X's assertion, so it is nonhearsay, but it is also not being offered to impeach X. It is a nonhearsay, noncredibility use of X's statement.
>
> *Example 4:* X does not testify. To prove that the light was green, defendant offers Y to testify that X said, out-of-court, "The light was green." (This, of course, is "garden variety" hearsay.)

In some situations, of course, multiple functions are potentially in play:

> *Example 5:* X testifies on the stand that "the light was red." Y said out of court that "the light was green." A report of the out-of-court statement of Y is relevant both to prove directly that the light was green (a non-credibility, hearsay use) and to impeach X by contradiction. Its use to contradict X, however, depends on its being accepted for the truth of the matter asserted by Y out-of-court, so the impeachment use depends on the hearsay use (a credibility, hearsay use). For both purposes, an exemption or exception to the hearsay rule will be required.

The point, then, is that one should not think of hearsay and impeachment as opposites; they are, instead, isolated poles of two different, but related distinctions.

§ 19.06 "The statement is only offered to show that it was made."

When a proponent of evidence reporting an out-of-court statement says, "The statement is only offered to show that it was made," it is an abbreviated way of saying, "The statement is only offered to show that it was made, not to prove the truth of any assertion in it." Of course, this is sometimes a valid point, for example, when the statement is legally operative language or when it is offered to show its effect on the hearer or reader.[21] But the words "only offered to show that it was made" are not a magical incantation that allows anything to come into evidence. If the fact that the statement was made is relevant to the case only if one accepts the truth of the matter asserted in the statement, then the statement is hearsay because it is being offered to show its truth.

§ 19.07 "A question can't possibly be hearsay."

The following excerpt from the transcript of a federal drug case illustrates this response to the hearsay objection. The prosecutor was trying to get the witness, an undercover agent, to describe what happened when the informant, in the presence of the agent, called a target to arrange a drug deal:[22]

---

[20] Y's testimony challenges the credibility of X's *claim* regarding damages, to be sure, but not the credibility of X's testimony, because X did not testify.

[21] *See* **§ 14.04** (subsection on "Statements Offered to Show An Effect on the Listener or Reader").

[22] United States v. Figueroa, 750 F.2d 232, 233 (2d Cir. 1984). The court of appeals reversed on grounds that this line of testimony should have been excluded. However, the particular question that led to the

Q: After this first telephone conversation about which you've just testified, were there any-further telephone conversations?

A: Yes.

Q: Will you explain how those came about?

A: There was a second telephone conversation. Mike [the informant] went to the phone. He dialed the number and he asked for room 638 [the defendant's room].

MR. SACHS [defense attorney]: I object again to anything that Mike said on the grounds of hearsay. It is being offered for the truth of the things said. There is no way around that, your Honor.

THE COURT: No. Go ahead. What I'm interested in, you had the second phone call. What happened then?

THE WITNESS: Mike had a conversation and Mike asked me, "Would it be all right if we did the two-kilogram deal one pound at a time?" And I told him to tell the people on the other end of the phone that that would be fine, we would deal one pound of cocaine at a time.

THE COURT: This was a two-kilo deal, one kilo at a time?

THE WITNESS: One pound, of about four and a half pounds, at a time. So we deliver one pound at a time. And I told Mike to relay the message that that would be fine, that we could do one pound at a time.

THE COURT: All right.

Q: After these two telephone conversations, did there come a third telephone conversation?

A: Yes. The third telephone conversation—

Q: What room did Mike call?

A: He asked for—he called 638.

Q. And did he ask to speak to anybody?

A: Yes. He said "Hello" on the phone again.

Q. And can you describe what you heard—what you instructed him to say on the telephone?

A: I told—after the conversation, I told Mike—Mike asked me—

MR. SACHS: I object to what Mike asked him. That is hearsay once again.

MR. CHERTOFF [the prosecutor]: A question can't possibly be hearsay.

Mr. Chertoff's contention that "a question can't possibly be hearsay" is probably based upon the definition of hearsay as an assertion offered to prove the truth of the matter asserted. If an utterance is not an "assertion," it is not hearsay. The word "assertion" is not defined in the Federal Rules, and has received virtually no treatment in the case law. However, one usually does not think of a question as being an "assertion."

---

assertion that "a question can't possibly be hearsay" was never answered in the trial court, so the court of appeals did not rule specifically on whether a question could ever be hearsay.

There is some support for the position that only declarative sentences can be hearsay, a position that would exclude questions and imperative sentences from the hearsay definition.[23]

However, a blanket assertion that "a question can't possibly be hearsay" does not make sense. A question such as "Why did you go so fast?" offered to show that the addressee was speeding, has no fewer dangers of inaccuracy than the declaration "You were going very fast." The same can be said of an imperative sentence such as "Throw that thief out of here!" when offered to show that the person referred to was a thief. The sentences just quoted contain *implied* assertions that the person was speeding or was a thief—in the sense that the speaker *intended* to make those assertions, even if the words also served additional functions, such as calling for an explanation or insisting on action.[24] Sometimes, such implied assertions are treated as hearsay by the courts, even under the Federal Rules of Evidence, and rightly so.[25]

---

[23] *See* EDWARD J. IMWINKELRIED, PAUL C. GIANNELLI, FRANCIS A. GILLIGAN & FREDERIC I. LEDERER, COURTROOM CRIMINAL EVIDENCE 1003 (3d ed. 1998) ("Because most assertive statements are declarative sentences, many trial judges use a rule of thumb that imperative, interrogative, and exclamatory sentences are not hearsay"; the authors, however, would not follow this rule of thumb in all situations); Olin Guy Wellborn III, *The Definition of Hearsay in the Federal Rules of Evidence*, 61 TEX. L. REV. 49, 71–73 (1982) (suggesting that this is at least a plausible, and perhaps the most plausible, interpretation of the word "assertion" in Rule 801(c)); United States v. Thomas, 453 F.3d 838, 844–45 (7th Cir. 2006) (defendant asked police officer who had just arrived on scene of shooting whether officer was responding to defendant's call; court found that question was not hearsay because it was not statement, but excluding it was harmless error).

[24] *See* **§ 14.01**.

[25] *See* Lyle v. Koehler, 720 F.2d 426, 431–35 (6th Cir. 1983) (Merritt, J.) (holding that proof that X wrote letters to X's friends asking friends to set up false alibi for X and Y is hearsay when offered against Y as evidence of Y's guilt); United States v. Summers, 414 F.3d 1287, 1300 (10th Cir. 2005) holding that (co-defendant's question to police, "How did you guys find us so fast?" was hearsay because declarant was making assertion and not merely seeking information; "[F]airly construed the statement intimated both guilt and wonderment at the ability of the police to apprehend the perpetrators of the crime so quickly").

Chapter 20

CONFRONTATION

Table of Sections

§ 20.01 Introduction to the Confrontation Clause

The Confrontation Clause of the Sixth Amendment applies to federal and state criminal trials.[1] It provides: "In all criminal prosecutions, the accused shall enjoy the right . . . to be confronted with the witnesses against him."[2] The language of the amendment is susceptible to a variety of reasonable interpretations that might impose additional obstacles (besides the hearsay rule itself) to the admission of hearsay against a criminal defendant. As Justice Scalia observed: "One could plausibly read 'witnesses against' a defendant to mean those who actually testify at trial, those whose statements are offered at trial, or something in-between."[3]

Under one possible interpretation, all hearsay declarants whose statements are offered by the prosecution would be considered "witnesses against" the defendant, and therefore the Constitution would require that the defendant be confronted with such declarants at trial.[4] This interpretation could lead to the exclusion of all hearsay by a non-testifying declarant, even hearsay that falls under an exception established at the time of the Sixth Amendment's adoption. If the Confrontation Clause is read to require that the declarant must always be present at trial, then all of the exceptions under Federal Rule of Evidence 804 (where the declarant must be unavailable) and many applications of Rule 803 exceptions (when the declarant is in fact not present in the courtroom) are unconstitutional in criminal cases. This would exclude a great deal of

---

[1] Pointer v. Texas, 380 U.S. 400 (1965) (holding that the introduction of testimony from preliminary hearing at which defendant was not represented, and at which he did not cross-examine witness, violates Sixth Amendment as applied to states); *see also* Barber v. Page, 390 U.S. 719 (1968) (introducing declarant's former testimony against defendant, without sufficient attempt to produce declarant for trial, violates Confrontation Clause).

[2] U.S. CONST. amend. VI.

[3] Crawford v. Washington, 541 U.S. 36, 42–43 (2004) (citations omitted).

[4] *Cf.* Fed. R. Evid. 803 advisory committee note ("In a hearsay situation, the declarant is, of course, a witness . . ."; comment not made in context of Confrontation Clause analysis, but nonetheless revealing).

highly reliable hearsay, even from declarants the prosecution is unable to produce at trial. The Supreme Court has never accepted such severe implications.[5] Wigmore thought that all hearsay declarants are witnesses for this purpose, but he nonetheless thought that the Constitution only required either the usual confrontation—including the opportunity to cross-examine the declarant—or a reasonable substitute therefor that is provided by the evolved exceptions to the hearsay rule. This position turns out to be remarkably similar to the Supreme Court's position as it evolved prior to 2004.

Alternatively, one could interpret the amendment to require merely that the defendant be confronted with whatever witnesses the prosecution chooses to produce at trial. Under this interpretation, trial witnesses could testify about hearsay declarations, and the Confrontation Clause would impose no limits upon the creation of new hearsay exceptions. It would merely require the presence of the defendant and the right to cross-examine when evidence is presented to the trier-of-fact.[6] This reading of the Clause is also implausible. The Clause could not possibly mean that any live witness, even someone repeating hearsay from an out-of-court declarant, could satisfy the constitutional right. Such a reading would render the Clause almost meaningless,[7] except insofar as it placed restrictions on the power of the court to curtail a defendant's ability to face witnesses who testify in court and ask questions of them.[8]

The amendment could also be construed so that "witnesses against" the defendant referred only to declarants who are *available* to testify. To be sure, the Clause does not explicitly qualify the right as applicable only to available declarants. On the other hand, what it guarantees is not the *opportunity* to confront witnesses, but the *right* to do so. As part of a Bill of Rights designed to protect against governmental abuse, arguably it prohibits the state from *depriving* the defendant of an opportunity to confront the witness, which the state can only do when the declarant is available to be presented but is not presented, when the state attempts to *substitute* hearsay for live testimony that would otherwise be possible. Under this interpretation, the prosecution would be required to produce declarants for cross-examination when possible, but the statements of unavailable declarants would be admissible as far as the Clause is concerned. Over the years, there has been some judicial and academic support for some such view.[9]

Finally, one could interpret the Clause to mean that the defendant has the right to confrontation whenever a special kind of hearsay evidence is presented, limiting the protection of the Clause to a subclass of hearsay declarants who can more properly be called "witnesses against" the accused. For this special subclass, the protection could be relatively strict, not permitting exceptions where the defendant does not have the opportunity to cross-examine the declarant. Or it could be relatively weak, permitting

---

[5] *See* 5 WIGMORE ON EVIDENCE §§ 1395–97 (3d ed. 1940).

[6] *See* Dutton v. Evans, 400 U.S. 74, 94 (1970) (Harlan, J., concurring). *Cf.* 5 WIGMORE ON EVIDENCE § 1397 at 127, 131 (3d ed. 1940) (stating that Confrontation Clause should be construed so that it merely requires cross-examination of witnesses who are required to testify in court by the hearsay rules in effect at the time of trial; and opining that nothing in the Clause should be construed to inhibit revision and extension of hearsay exceptions, as long as the hearsay rule is not itself abolished).

[7] *See* White v. Illinois, 502 U.S. 346, 359–60 (1992 (Thomas, J., concurring) (noting that such a construction of the clause, while it is a plausible reading of its plain language, is inconsistent with the history that gave rise to it).

[8] *See* **§ 20.09**.

[9] *See* California v. Green, 399 U.S. 149, 174 (1970) (Harlan, J., concurring); Peter Westen, *The Future of Confrontation*, 77 MICH. L. REV. 1185, 1188–89 (1979); Irving Younger, *Confrontation and Hearsay: A Look Backward, a Peek Forward*, 1 HOFSTRA L. REV. 32 (1973).

some exceptions for presumably good reasons. As explained in the following sections, the Court's most recent confrontation decisions are consistent with this final interpretation, although it is not entirely settled just how broad this subclass is or how strict the protection afforded the accused is when hearsay falls within this subclass.

Historically, the relationship between the hearsay rule and the Confrontation Clause has been uneasy and confused. Both stem from concerns about ensuring the fairness of a trial by insisting on witnesses who testify under oath from personal knowledge and who could be tested by cross-examination. However, there are serious differences in theory, policy, history, and practice between hearsay and confrontation. The goal of the hearsay rule is to promote accuracy and ensure the reliability of the evidence; it applies to civil and criminal cases alike. The Confrontation Clause functionally protects accuracy, but it does more than that. The Confrontation Clause ensures a specific trial court process that has unique social value, although debate continues about what exactly that value is and, accordingly, what specific trial process it requires.[10]

In order to understand current controversies, a brief historical synopsis is useful. Between 1965 (when the Clause was applied to state trials) and 2004 (when *Crawford v. Washington*[11] was decided), the Court operated on the assumption that all hearsay is subject to the Clause. But, as explained below, that did not render all hearsay falling within a hearsay exception inadmissible when offered against a criminal defendant. Although the pre-2004 doctrine has been replaced, at least in one respect it survives intact. Specifically, in *California v. Green*,[12] decided in 1970, the Court held that the introduction of a hearsay declaration made by a person who testifies at trial and is subject to cross-examination at that time does not violate the Clause. The Court explained that no confrontation problem exists in this situation because the defendant is able to cross-examine the witness at trial about both his prior statement and his current testimony. Thus, while prior statements of a testifying declarant were hearsay at common law when offered to prove the truth of the matter asserted, and some such statements remain hearsay even under the Federal Rules,[13] the Confrontation Clause poses no obstacle to liberalization of the hearsay rule when the declarant actually testifies at trial. This principle remains valid today.[14]

Consequently, since 1970 the hotly contested constitutional issue has been the admissibility of hearsay from a *non-testifying* declarant whose hearsay falls within a hearsay exception. For such exceptional hearsay, the Clause presents an additional potential obstacle to admission against a criminal defendant. But it does not inevitably lead to its exclusion.

Under the rule as set forth in 1980 in *Ohio v. Roberts*,[15] the leading case for over two decades, the Confrontation Clause was satisfied in regard to such hearsay if:[16]

---

[10] *See* Eileen A. Scallen, *Constitutional Dimensions of Hearsay Reform: Toward a Three-Dimensional Confrontation Clause*, 76 MINN. L. REV. 623 (1992).

[11] 541 U.S. 36 (2004). *See* **§ 20.02**.

[12] California v. Green, 399 U.S. 149 (1970) (considering constitutionality of a liberalization included in California Evidence Code).

[13] *See* **§§ 15.02 et seq.**

[14] *See* Crawford v. Washington, 541 U.S. 36, 53–56 (2004).

[15] 448 U.S. 56 (1980).

[16] *Id.* at 65–66.

(1) the prosecution showed that the declarant was unavailable to testify; and

(2) the out-of-court statement bore "adequate 'indicia of reliability.'" Such reliability was presumed if the hearsay fell within a "firmly rooted hearsay exception," or the prosecution could show there were "particularized guarantees of trustworthiness."

These twin requirements are clearly related to the two conventional reasons to admit hearsay, necessity and trustworthiness. But the first requirement was considerably more demanding than the necessity requirement attending many traditional hearsay exceptions. For example, the Rule 803 exceptions render hearsay from a non-testifying declarant admissible without any showing that the declarant is unavailable to testify. Applying *Roberts* to ordinary business records might seem to entail costs out of proportion to the benefits of confrontation.[17] In fact, not long after the Court announced this requirement, it began to water it down. In two principal decisions,[18] the Court limited the requirement of a showing of unavailability to the specific context in which *Roberts* was decided, namely, prior in-court testimony, as to which the conventional hearsay exception required a showing of unavailability anyway.[19]

By this narrowing of the *Roberts* holding, the Court took attention away from the decisions being made by the prosecution about what evidence to present at trial. The force of *Roberts* was reduced to the second requirement, that the hearsay from the non-testifying declarant have adequate indicia of reliability, which directs attention to the circumstances of the making of the hearsay statement. During the *Roberts* era, confrontation cases concerned novel variations on traditional hearsay exceptions,[20] and statements that fell under a residual hearsay exceptions[21]—none of which could be deemed "firmly rooted." To a large degree, however, analysis under *Roberts* collapsed the confrontation standard onto the hearsay rules. Satisfying the hearsay rules almost always meant that the Confrontation Clause was also satisfied.

The Court changed the doctrine dramatically in 2004 in a case that is the subject of the next section.

§ 20.02 *Crawford v. Washington* (2004)

In *Crawford v. Washington*,[22] the Court revisited its understanding of the Confrontation Clause, radically rethinking the relationship between hearsay rules and

---

[17] To be sure, the Court in *Roberts* left itself an out by noting that the unavailability requirement need not *always* be imposed. *See id.* at 65 n.7 (stating that a showing of unavailability need not be made when the "utility of trial confrontation" is too "remote").

[18] *See* United States v. Inadi, 475 U.S. 387 (1986) (no showing of unavailability required for hearsay admitted pursuant to co-conspirator's exception); White v. Illinois, 502 U.S. 346 (1992) (no showing of unavailability required for hearsay admitted as spontaneous utterances or statements made to facilitate medical treatment).

[19] *See, e.g.*, FED. R. EVID. 804(b)(1). To be sure, the constitutional standard of unavailability is not necessarily the same as the standard of common-law or statutory hearsay exception. A declarant might be unavailable under hearsay law, as specified in Rule 804(a), and still be constitutionally available. *See* RICHARD D. FRIEDMAN, THE ELEMENTS OF EVIDENCE 361–64 (3d ed. 2004).

[20] *See, e.g.*, California v. Green, 399 U.S. 149 (1970) (decided in the context of California's exception to the hearsay rule that admitted all prior inconsistent statements by witnesses).

[21] *See, e.g.*, Idaho v. Wright, 497 U.S. 805 (1990) (admitting statements by a two-and-a-half year old regarding sexual abuse under the residual hearsay rule).

[22] 541 U.S. 36 (2004).

confrontation, and breathing new life into the Confrontation Clause.[23] Michael Crawford was charged with attempted murder of a man who had allegedly attempted to rape his wife. Crawford claimed self-defense, and his wife, Sylvia, who witnessed the stabbing, did not testify at trial because Michael asserted his adverse spousal testimony privilege under Washington state law.[24] Instead, the prosecution played an audiotape from the police interrogation of Sylvia.[25] Her stationhouse statement was admitted as a declaration against interest because Sylvia potentially implicated herself as well as her husband.[26] Crawford objected that even if Sylvia's statements were admissible under Washington State's rules of evidence, such admission violated his rights under the Confrontation Clause. The Washington state trial court ruled that the taped statement was admissible under *Roberts* because it bore particularized guarantees of trustworthiness. The Washington Court of Appeals reversed (also applying *Roberts,* but with a different result), but the Supreme Court of Washington (also applying *Roberts,* but with yet a different result) reinstated the ruling and admitted Sylvia's statement.

The United States Supreme Court, in an opinion by Justice Scalia, reversed the Washington Supreme Court and crafted a new rule regarding the rights afforded by the Confrontation Clause. *Crawford* rejected the *Roberts* doctrine's dependence on hearsay standards and, more generally, its focus on reliability. Specifically, *Crawford* held that the *Roberts* reliability test was unpredictable, as evidenced by the disparate results in the Washington courts, and in violation of the constitutional command. In particular, it found that the *Roberts* focus on reliability was constitutionally misplaced. "Where testimonial statements are involved, we do not think the Framers meant to leave the Sixth Amendment's protection to the vagaries of the rules of evidence, much less to amorphous notions of 'reliability'."[27] Scalia acknowledged that reliability of testimony is the ultimate concern, but insisted that the Clause itself guaranteed not reliability but rather a particular procedure for assuring it. Scalia wrote, "Dispensing with confrontation because testimony is obviously reliable is akin to dispensing with jury trial because a defendant is obviously guilty."[28] Instead, *Crawford* held that an out-of-court "testimonial" statement may be used against the accused only if (1) the declarant is available for cross-examination at trial,[29] or (2) the declarant is proved unavailable and was previously subject to cross-examination about the statement by the accused.[30] In

---

[23] *See* United States v. Saget, 377 F.3d 223, 226 (2d Cir. 2004) ("Crawford redefines the scope and effect of the Confrontation Clause. . . ."); State v. Grace, 111 P.3d 28. 36 (Haw. Ct. App. 2005) ("[*Crawford* effected] a sea change in our understanding of the Confrontation Clause"); People v. Pantoja, 18 Cal. Rptr.3d 492, 498 (Cal. Ct. App. 2004) ("[*Crawford*] may fairly be characterized as a revolutionary decision in the law of evidence."); People v. Victors, 819 N.E.2d 311, 323 (Ill. App. Ct. 2004) (describing *Crawford* as a "Copernican shift in federal constitutional law").

[24] *Crawford,* 541 U.S. at 40.

[25] Even though her testimony was privileged under Washington state law, her prior statement to police was not. *See* **§ 4.16**.

[26] Sylvia's statement to police largely corroborated her husband's, but differed in several respects, most notably in its weaker support for the self-defense claim because Sylvia's statement suggested that Lee reached for something only after Crawford had stabbed him. *Crawford,* 541 U.S at 39.

[27] *Id.* at 61.

[28] Id. at 62.

[29] The Court thus reaffirmed the holding in California v. Green, 399 U.S. 149 (1970). *See Crawford,* 541 U.S. at 59 n.9.

[30] *Id.* at 53–56, 68. One can certainly understand why live testimony subject to cross in the present proceeding would be preferred to live testimony subject to cross in a previous proceeding, but the *Crawford* framework is otherwise devoid of such excusable preferences. That raises the question why the circumstances of declarant's availability to testify can turn what would have qualified as adequate confrontation (i.e., if the

dicta, the Court allowed for a third possibility: admitting such hearsay if it fell within some other common-law exception recognized circa 1791, such as the dying declaration exception or the forfeiture exception.[31] The Court deemed Sylvia Crawford's statement testimonial and held that its admission violated the Confrontation Clause because the accused was not able to cross-examine the declarant.[32]

Crawford is steeped in history. Writing for a majority of seven, Justice Scalia reviewed the history of confrontation from Roman times to the present. Placing primary emphasis on the state of the common law at the time of the Sixth Amendment's framing, Scalia wrote, "First, the principal evil at which the Confrontation Clause was directed was the civil-law mode of criminal procedure, and particularly its use of *ex parte* examinations as evidence against the accused." He continued, "Leaving the regulation of out-of-court statements to the law of evidence would render the Confrontation Clause powerless to prevent even the most flagrant inquisitorial practices." In crafting a new confrontation standard, Justice Scalia strove to effectuate the original intent of the Sixth Amendment, emulating the common law at the time the amendment was originally written.[33]

Crawford's focus on "testimonial statements" represented an entirely new approach to confrontation.[34] Post-*Crawford,* a crucial confrontation question concerns whether an out-of-court statement is "testimonial" for this purpose. In delineating which statements are testimonial, *Crawford* focused primarily on whether the declarant anticipated that the state would use the statement to prosecute the accused.[35] Because Sylvia's statement to police was so clearly testimonial by anyone's definition (her statement was made to the police during a formal interrogation and she obviously should have realized that what she said to police might be used against her husband), the Court did not have to

---

declarant were unavailable) into what does not (because the declarant is available but not testifying). The Court's apparent answer is historical: that particular excusable preference was well established in 1789.

[31] *Id.* at 56 n.6 (dictum re dying declarations), 62 (dictum re forfeiture for wrongdoing). The forfeiture exception is addressed in **§ 20.04**.

[32] Unfortunately, the Court did not address the obvious question whether Crawford was in fact able to confront and cross-examine the declarant, his wife, simply by calling her to testify or by waiving his spousal privilege and permitting the prosecution to call her. *See id.* at 42 n.1.

[33] *Id.* at 68 (explaining that the Confrontation Clause is "most naturally read as a reference to the right of confrontation at common law, admitting only those exceptions established at the time of the founding."). Scalia's originalist approach has been attacked for its lack of wisdom and its method. *See* Thomas Y. Davies, *Not "The Framers' Design": How The Framing-Era Ban Against Hearsay Evidence Refutes the Crawford-Davis "Testimonial" Formulation of the Scope of the Original Confrontation Clause,* 15 J.L. & POL'Y 349, 350 (2007) ("[T]he originalist claims that have appeared in recent criminal procedure decisions have usually reflected the ideological proclivities of the justices who made them, but have rarely resembled the historical legal doctrines that actually shaped the Framers' understanding.").

[34] The approach was first judicially suggested in a concurrence by Justice Thomas joined only by Justice Scalia. *See* White v. Illinois, 502 U.S. 358 (1992). The focus on testimonial hearsay was promoted by Professor Richard Friedman of Michigan Law School. *See* Richard D. Friedman, *Confrontation: The Search for Basic Principles,* 86 GEO. L.J. 1011 (1998). Professor Friedman hosts the "confrontation blog," an excellent forum for discussing new developments in confrontation law. Richard D. Friedman, The Confrontation Blog, http://confrontationright.blogspot.com.

[35] *Crawford,* 541 U.S. at 51–52 ("[Testimonial statements include] 'extrajudicial statements . . . contained in formalized testimonial materials, such as affidavits, depositions, prior testimony, or confessions.' (quoting White v. Illinois, 502 U.S. 346, 365 (1992) (Thomas, J., dissenting)). Beyond this list of obvious, formal testimonial statements, the Court suggested other "statements that were made under circumstances which would lead an objective witness reasonably to believe that the statement would be available for use at a later trial." *Id.* at 52 (quoting the Brief for National Association of Criminal Defense Lawyers et al. as Amici Curiae). Tellingly, the Court did not attempt to craft a definition of its own, but quoted from the parties and amici. *See id.*

struggle with the definition. Therefore, the *Crawford* case itself is not particularly helpful for defining which statements are testimonial and which are not.

Nevertheless, *Crawford* provided some contours of the definition, stating that testimonial statements included, "at a minimum testimony . . . at a preliminary hearing, before a grand jury, or at a former trial; and . . . police interrogations."[36] It quoted with apparent approval, if not full endorsement, potential definitions of a testimonial statement from various amici. At points in the opinion, Justice Scalia also off-handedly mentioned statements that would *not* be considered testimonial, such as business records[37] or informal statements to friends.[38]

Post-*Crawford*, various lower courts struggled with the definition of "testimonial" and focused on additional factors such as the role of the government in generating the evidence, whether the declarant initiated contact with law enforcement authorities, the context in which the declarant gave the statement to law enforcement agents, and the structure and formality of the questioning.[39] Although there was some initial uncertainty about the matter, it is now clear post-*Crawford* that *non*testimonial statements are subject to no restriction under the Confrontation Clause, and their use in criminal cases is checked, if at all, only by the hearsay rule and, potentially, the more general Due Process Clause.[40]

An unfortunate consequence of this focus on the circumstances surrounding the making of the hearsay statement, a focus that *Crawford* shares with the later interpretation of *Roberts*, is that it takes the focus away from the choices made by the state about what evidence to present at trial. Because hearsay is or is not testimonial based on the circumstances surrounding its utterance, the handling of those that are nontestimonial is subject to strategic manipulation by the state after they are made. That is, under *Crawford* the Confrontation Clause poses no impediment to the government's intentional substitution of nontestimonial hearsay for live testimony by

---

36 *Id.* at 68.

37 *Id.* 56.

38 *Id.* at 51.

39 *See* Gary M. Bishop, *Testimonial Statements, Excited Utterances and the Confrontation Clause: Formulating a Precise Rule After Crawford and Davis*, 54 CLEV. ST. L. REV. 559 (2006); Josephine Ross, *Crawford's Short-Lived Revolution: How Davis v. Washington Reins in Crawford's Reach*, 83 N.D. L. REV. 387 (2007).

40 *See* Davis v. Washington, 547 U.S. 813, 823–24 (2006) (stating that the Confrontation Clause does not apply to nontestimonial hearsay); *see also* Whorting v. Bockting, 549 U.S. 406 (2007). Justice Thomas has at least suggested a role for the Confrontation Clause in restricting the use of nontestimonial statements. *See* **§ 20.05 & § 20.06**.

the declarant. This feature of the *Crawford* doctrine has been criticized.[41] The issue would later surface most clearly in the Court's treatment of forensic laboratory reports.[42]

§ 20.03 Statements to Police: *Davis v. Washington* and *Hammon v. Indiana* (2006)

Almost all of the Supreme Court cases following *Crawford* involve statements made to law enforcement officers or prosecuting authorities.[43] *Davis v. Washington*,[44] and its companion case, *Hammon v. Indiana*, arose two years after *Crawford*, in 2006. These were domestic violence cases. It was thoroughly predictable that domestic-violence cases would present a quandary for *Crawford's* new approach to confrontation. Victims in domestic-violence cases often make statements at the scene of the battery, but, for various reasons, later refuse to testify against the accused.[45] Courts around the country immediately had to determine which, if any, statements made by domestic-violence victims to police at the scene of the incident are testimonial. The stakes are enormous for the prosecution of such cases. If the statements are testimonial, the statements cannot be admitted against the accused unless he had an opportunity to cross-examine, which is almost never the case.[46] Because there are often no other witnesses besides the victim and the accused to the actual battery, without the victim's cooperation, the prosecutor often has no case.[47]

In *Davis*, the accused was charged with violating a protective order and assaulting his girlfriend, McCottry, who called 911. Although the call was disconnected, the 911 operator reversed the call and initiated the following conversation:

911 Operator: Hello.

Complainant: Hello.

911 Operator: What's going on?

Complainant: He's here jumpin' on me again.

---

[41] *See* Dale A. Nance, *Rethinking Confrontation After* Crawford, 2:1 INT'L COMMENT. ON EVIDENCE art. 2 (2004) (arguing, in the wake of *Crawford*, that the Clause should be interpreted to prohibit the state from taking actions (or unreasonable inactions) that deprive the accused of the opportunity to cross-examine a hearsay declarant at trial, a prohibition that should apply to all hearsay statements, whether regarded as "testimonial" or "nontestimonial" when uttered; noting, however, that a category of statements that could be called "testimonial" might trigger a heightened concern about such state action or inaction); Josephine Ross, *After* Crawford *Double-Speak: "Testimony" Does Not Mean Testimony and "Witness' Does Not Mean Witness*, 97 J. CRIM. L. & CRIMINOLOGY 147, 151, 196 (2006) (arguing that reach of the Clause should be governed by "the role testimony had at trial rather than trying to decipher what occurred when the statement was originally uttered out-of-court," so that " '[T]estimonial' should mean statements that function as testimony during the trial."); Mark Spottswood, *Truth, Lies, and the Confrontation Clause*, 89 U. COLO. L. REV. 565 (2018) (arguing that the confrontation clause should require the presentation of an available declarant whose hearsay is offered by the government and should preclude hearsay from an unavailable declarant only when the unavailability is caused by the *witness or* the government).

[42] *See* **§ 20.06** (especially the decision in Williams v. Illinois, 567 U.S. 50 (2012)).

[43] The one exception is discussed *infra*, **§ 20.07**.

[44] 547 U.S. 813 (2006).

[45] These reasons include fear, embarrassment, love, financial entanglement with the perpetrator, and even a sense by the victim that the risk of leaving the perpetrator is greater than that of remaining with him.

[46] There is, however, the possibility that the defendant will forfeit his right to confront the declarant if he threatens her to prevent her from testifying. *See* **§ 20.04**.

[47] *See* Tom Lininger, *Prosecuting Batterers After* Crawford, 91 VA. L. REV. 747 (2005).

911 Operator: Okay. Listen to me carefully. Are you in a house or an apartment?

Complainant: I'm in a house.

911 Operator: Are there any weapons?

Complainant: No. He's usin' his fists.

911 Operator: Okay. Has he been drinking?

Complainant: No.

911 Operator: Okay, sweetie. I've got help started. Stay on the line with me, okay?

Complainant: I'm on the line.

911 Operator: Listen to me carefully. Do you know his last name?

Complainant: It's Davis.

911 Operator: Davis? Okay, what's his first name?

Complainant: Adrian.

911 Operator: What is it?

Complainant: Adrian.

911 Operator: Adrian?

Complainant: Yeah.

911 Operator: Okay. What's his middle initial?

Complainant: Martell. He's runnin' now.[48]

The operator continued to speak with McCottry, learning that Davis had left her house shortly after the operator reversed the call. The operator then told McCottry to "Stop talking and answer my questions," and concentrated on eliciting more information about Davis, including his birthday.[49]

Upon arrival, the police observed the victim's "shaken state," the "fresh injuries on her forearm and face," and her "frantic efforts to gather her belongings and her children so that they could leave the residence."[50] Because McCottry did not appear at Davis' trial despite the prosecution's attempt to secure her in-court testimony, the state's only live in-court witnesses were the two responding officers, neither of whom had witnessed the incident.[51] Over Davis' objections, the trial court admitted the recording of the victim's 911 call and convicted Davis of a felony violation of a domestic no-contact order.[52]

Similarly, *Hammon,* the companion case, involved statements made to law enforcement personnel who responded to a reported domestic disturbance between a married couple. When the officers arrived, they found Amy Hammon on the porch

---

[48] *Davis,* 547 U.S. at 817–818.

[49] *Id.* at 818.

[50] *Id.*

[51] *Id.*

[52] *Id.*

appearing "somewhat frightened," although she told them "nothing was the matter."[53] She allowed the police to enter, and they found evidence of a struggle in the living room. The accused, Hershel Hammon, was in the kitchen.[54] The officers separated Hershel and Amy and again asked Amy what had occurred.[55] Though Hershel attempted to interrupt, Amy eventually described the violent incident, and completed and signed a battery affidavit stating that her husband physically attacked her.[56] Amy received a subpoena to testify, but did not appear at trial. Over Hershel's objections, the state called the officer who questioned Amy to describe what she had told him.[57] Herschel Hammon was convicted on the strength of the affidavit and the testimony of the responding police officers.[58]

The Court explained that, like the wife's statements in *Crawford*, the statements in *Davis* and *Hammon* qualified—at least in some sense—as police interrogation.[59] That fact alone, however, did not necessarily render the statements testimonial for the purposes of the Sixth Amendment. The Court described the distinction between testimonial and nontestimonial statements as follows: "Statements are nontestimonial when made in the course of police interrogation under circumstances objectively indicating that the primary purpose of the interrogation is to enable police assistance to meet an ongoing emergency."[60] The Court observed that "the initial interrogation conducted in connection with a 911 call is ordinarily not designed primarily to 'establis[h] or prov[e]' some past fact, but to describe current circumstances requiring police assistance."[61] By contrast, a statement is testimonial "when the circumstances objectively indicate that there is no such ongoing emergency, and that the primary purpose of the interrogation is to establish or prove past events potentially relevant to later criminal prosecution."[62]

Disclaiming any attempt to "produce an exhaustive classification of all conceivable statements,"[63] the Court concluded that the early portions of the 911 call at issue in *Davis* were nontestimonial, but the statements probably became testimonial after the operator learned that Davis had fled and the operator began interrogating the victim as to Davis' personal characteristics.[64] The Court observed that "any reasonable listener" would recognize that the declarant in *Davis* (as opposed to Sylvia Crawford, who gave her statement while safely ensconced in a police station) was facing an ongoing

---

[53] *Id.* at 819.

[54] *Id.*

[55] *Id.*

[56] *Id.* at 819–20.

[57] *Id.*

[58] *Id.* at 821.

[59] *Id.* at 823.

[60] *Id.* at 822.

[61] *Id.* at 827.

[62] *Id.*

[63] *Id.* at 821.

[64] Although the Court did not draw a bright line as to when the statements became testimonial, it is consistent with the rest of the opinion to speculate that the line should be drawn when the operator directed the victim: "Stop talking and answer my questions." Because little, if any, of this later portion of the 911 call was used to convict Davis, and because the nontestimonial portion of the recording provided ample evidence to secure the conviction, the Court affirmed the judgment of the Washington State Supreme Court, upholding Davis' conviction.

emergency.[65] The victim's interrogation in *Davis* elicited statements that were "necessary to be able to *resolve* the present emergency, rather than simply to learn . . . what had happened in the past."[66] The Court concluded that the victim was "speaking about events *as they were actually happening,* rather than 'describ[ing] past events.' "[67] The Court conceded that "one *might* call 911 to provide a narrative report of a crime absent any imminent danger," but decided that the victim in *Davis* (as opposed to Amy Hammon), was plainly making "a call for help against a bona fide physical threat."[68] The circumstances of the interrogation in *Davis* "objectively indicate its primary purpose was to enable police assistance to meet an ongoing emergency."[69]

By contrast, the Court found that the victim's statements to police in *Hammon* were indeed testimonial. The Court analyzed the scenario and concluded that in *Hammon* there was "no emergency in progress."[70] Instead, the officer questioning Amy Hammon "was not seeking to determine (as in *Davis*) 'what is happening,' but rather 'what happened.' "[71] The Court acknowledged that exigencies surrounding a domestic violence call "may *often* mean that 'initial inquiries' produce nontestimonial statements." But it distinguished *Hammon*, where the declarant's statements "were neither a cry for help nor the provision of information enabling officers immediately to end a threatening situation."[72] Because the Court found that the statements were testimonial and Herschel Hammon had no opportunity to cross-examine the declarant, the victim's statements should have been excluded under the Confrontation Clause.[73]

The Court acknowledged that the stationhouse interrogation in *Crawford,* with its location, *Miranda* warning, and tape-recording, was more formal than the frantic impromptu interview in *Hammon.*[74] The Court made clear, however, that intention, not formality, was the touchstone; the mere fact that the victims' statements were made "at an alleged crime scene and were 'initial inquiries' is immaterial."[75] Instead, the Court focused on the intentions of the victim and the police and the timing of the incident to determine whether the statement was an account of past criminality or a cry for immediate police protection. Justice Scalia noted the functional similarities between Amy's interrogation, which was conducted in a separate room, away from her husband (who tried to intervene), and Sylvia Crawford's statement. Both resembled "civil-law *ex parte* examinations," which prompted the rights embodied in the Confrontation Clause.[76]

---

[65] Davis v. Washington, 547 U.S. 813, 827 (2006).

[66] *Id.* (emphasis in original).

[67] *Id.* (emphasis in original).

[68] *Id.* (emphasis in original).

[69] *Id.* at 828.

[70] *Id.* at 829.

[71] *Id.* at 830. As the Court explained: "Amy's [declarant's] narrative of past events was delivered at some remove in time from the danger she described. And after Amy answered the officer's questions, he had her execute an affidavit, in order, he testified, '[t]o establish events that have occurred previously.' " *Id.* at 832.

[72] *Id.* at 832.

[73] *Id.* at 829–30.

[74] *Id.* at 827 (noting "the difference in the level of formality between the two interviews [in *Davis* and *Crawford* was] striking").

[75] *Id.*

[76] *Id.* at 830 (citations and footnotes omitted). Both declarants were actively separated from the defendant—officers forcibly prevented Hershel from participating in the interrogation. Both statements deliberately recounted, in response to police questioning, how potentially criminal past events began and progressed. And both took place sometime after the events described were over. Justice Scalia explained, "Such

Finally, in *Davis,* Justice Scalia acknowledged that the decision would affect domestic-violence cases, which would be significantly harder to prosecute under the new confrontation regime. He noted with some degree of scorn the concern raised by prosecutors that domestic-violence crimes require "greater flexibility in the use of testimonial evidence" because the victim-witnesses are "notoriously susceptible to intimidation or coercion," and "[w]hen this occurs, the Confrontation Clause gives the criminal a windfall." Justice Scalia provided a two-part answer. First, he stated that such practical prosecutorial concerns are not relevant. "We may not, however, vitiate constitutional guarantees when they have the effect of allowing the guilty to go free."[77] Second, he noted that "when defendants seek to undermine the judicial process by procuring or coercing silence from witnesses and victims, the Sixth Amendment does not require courts to acquiesce." Instead, "where the accused makes the declarant unavailable through intimidation or other means, forfeiture is an option."[78]

In *Davis* and *Hammon,* the Court seemed to extend the inquiry into what is testimonial beyond the reasonable expectation of the declarant to include the expectations of the questioner.[79] Although *Davis* certainly considered the declarant's point of view, noting that the victim was "seeking aid, not telling a story about the past,"[80] the case seems to shift focus, at least in part, to the intent of the investigator—was the police officer trying to gather evidence or deal with an ongoing emergency?[81] While much of the opinion in *Davis* appears to focus on the nature of police interrogation, the Court explained that the form of the answer, not the form of the question, renders a statement testimonial or not.[82] The fact that the statements at issue were the product of police interrogation is significant, however, because statements made during interrogations "in some circumstances tend to generate testimonial responses."[83]

Justice Thomas, in dissent, advocated a narrow, bright-line definition of testimonial statements that requires formality and solemnity. His approach, which no other justice adopted, would deem only "formalized testimonial materials, such as affidavits, depositions, prior testimony, or confessions"[84] to be testimonial statements under the

---

statements under official interrogation are an obvious substitute for live testimony, because they do precisely *what a witness does* on direct examination; they are inherently testimonial." *Id.*

77 Davis v. Washington, 547 U.S. 813, 832–33 (2006) (citations omitted).

78 *Id.* For discussion of forfeiture, *see* **§ 20.04**.

79 *See* Robert P. Mosteller, *Testing the Testimonial Concept and Exceptions to Confrontation: "A Little Child Shall Lead Them,"* 82 IND. L.J. 917, 918–19, 938, 942–43, 947 (2007) (discussing the apparent shift of focus from *Crawford,* where the intent of the speaker was clearly dominant, to *Davis,* which appears to shift the focus to the intent of the questioner).

80 Davis v. Washington, 547 U.S. 813, 831 (2006).

81 Without acknowledging it, the Court seemed to switch its focus from the declarant to the government agent. In *Crawford,* the focus was on what Sylvia Crawford believed would happen with her statement. In *Davis* and *Hammon* the purpose of the police investigator was equally if not more important than the intent of the declarant in ascertaining the testimonial quality of the statement. *See* Ellen Liang Yee, *Confronting the "Ongoing Emergency": A Pragmatic Approach to Hearsay Evidence in the Context of the Sixth Amendment,* 35 FLA. ST. U. L. REV. 729, 767 (2008) ("Notwithstanding the Court's claim that the inquiry is focused on 'the declarant's statements, not the interrogator's questions,' the opinion also repeatedly referred to whether the questioner's conduct can generate or produce testimonial statements.").

82 "[I]t is in the final analysis the declarant's statements, not the interrogator's questions, that the Confrontation Clause requires us to evaluate." Davis v. Washington, 547 U.S. 813, 831 (2006).

83 *Id.* at 822 n.1. "This is not to imply, however, that statements made in the absence of any interrogation are necessarily nontestimonial." *Id.* at 831.

84 *Id.* at 836 (Thomas, J., concurring in the judgment in part and dissenting in part) (quoting from Thomas' opinion in White v. Illinois).

Crawford standard. Thomas argued that the line the majority tried to draw between emergencies and reports of past events, relying on primary motives, is blurry and impossible to apply.[85] He made a persuasive case that Amy Hammon was as much in danger at the moment she made her declaration as the victim in *Davis*.[86] Many scholars have expressed similar concerns that the lines drawn by the Court in *Davis* and *Hammon* are unsound and unworkable.[87] This concern would come to the fore in a case decided five years later.[88]

§ 20.04 Forfeiture by Wrongdoing: *Giles v. California* (2008)

In *Giles v. California*,[89] decided in 2008, two years after *Davis*, Justice Scalia, again writing for the majority, addressed the circumstances of forfeiture, a longstanding equitable principle in Anglo-American jurisprudence.[90] In *Giles*, the accused was charged with murdering his girlfriend, Brenda Avie. Three weeks earlier, Avie had made tearful statements to police responding to a domestic-violence report that Giles had choked her, punched her in the face and head, and threatened to kill her with a knife.[91] In fact, Giles did kill Avie, claiming that he acted in self-defense.[92] At his murder trial, Giles supported his self-defense claim by describing Avie as "jealous, vindictive, aggressive, and violent."[93] To rebut Giles' claim of self-defense, the state introduced evidence of Avie's uncross-examined statements to police describing the earlier assault. The trial court admitted the statement under an unusual state hearsay exception.[94]

---

85 *Id.* at 839–42 (Thomas, J., concurring in the judgment in part and dissenting in part). Justice Thomas described the opinion as ahistorical and unpredictable. *Id.* at 834. He notes that "[n]either the call nor the questioning is itself a formalized dialogue. Nor do any circumstances surrounding the taking of the statements render those statements sufficiently formal to resemble the Marian examinations; the statements were neither Mirandized nor custodial, nor accompanied by any similar indicia of formality. Finally, there is no suggestion that the prosecution attempted to offer the women's hearsay evidence at trial in order to evade confrontation." *Id.* at 840.

86 *Id.* at 841 n.6 (noting that some of the factors on which the Court distinguishes *Davis*, such as the fact that Hammon was separated from her attacker and that the events in *Hammon* were already over, apply equally to *Davis*).

87 *See, e.g.*, Tom Lininger, *Reconceptualizing Confrontation After* Davis, 85 TEX. L. REV. 271, 274 (2006) ("[T]he Davis ruling accomplished a rare feat: it caused consternation among both prosecutors and defense attorneys. Commentators on all sides expressed their disappointment that the Court had not devised a comprehensive, easily administrable set of rules for the confrontation of accusers."); Myrna Raeder, *Domestic Violence Cases After* Davis: *Is the Glass Half Empty or Half Full?* 15 J.L. & POL'Y 759, 762 (2007) ("*Davis*' bright line is illusory and hard to apply.").

88 *See* **§ 20.05** (discussing Michigan v. Bryant, 562 U.S. 344 (2011)).

89 554 U.S. 353 (2008).

90 *See* Reynolds v. United States, 98 U.S. 145, 148–50 (1879) (admitting former testimony of wife where accused had kept his wife away from home so that she could not be subpoenaed to testify).

91 *Giles*, 554 U.S. at 356–57.

92 *Id.* at 356.

93 *Id.* at 381 (Breyer, J., dissenting).

94 *Id.* at 357 (noting trial court's use of CAL. EVID. CODE § 1370, admitting statement describing infliction or threat of physical injury on a declarant when the declarant is unavailable to testify at trial and the prior statement is deemed trustworthy). Such statements are sometimes admissible as excited utterances but do not qualify as dying declarations—it is not even a close question. Even where, as in *Giles*, a declaration anticipates murder days or weeks before a homicide, it fails the strictures of the dying declaration exception, since death is neither certain nor imminent. *See* Aviva Orenstein, *Her Last Words*, 2010 U. ILL. L. REV. 1411.

The Justices all treated Avie's statements as testimonial[95] and focused on the question of forfeiture, examining whether by killing the victim (something the accused acknowledged that he did, allegedly in self-defense), the accused thereby forfeited his right to confront her prior statements. The Court ruled that, to fall within the forfeiture doctrine, the accused must act so as to cause the declarant's absence and intend thereby to prevent the witness from testifying.[96] Reviewing at length the old common-law cases and treatises, the Court determined that the common law at the time the Sixth Amendment was written admitted statements by an absent witness who was "detained" or "kept away" by "means or procurement" of the defendant.[97] The Court pointed out that a broader rule, one that did not require such an intent, would render the dying declaration exception unnecessary. If every murder case had involved a potential forfeiture of the victim's hearsay, why would litigants have bothered arguing over the contours of the dying declaration? The Court further noted that subsequent case law and almost all recent attempts to codify a hearsay exception for forfeiture by wrongdoing also required an intent to prevent the witness from testifying. Thus, not every homicide case automatically opens the door to admitting the victim's former testimonial statements about the accused based simply on a judicial determination, by a preponderance of the evidence, that the accused is guilty. "The notion that judges may strip the defendant of a right that the Constitution deems essential to a fair trial, on the basis of a prior *judicial* assessment that the defendant is guilty as charged, does not sit well with the right to trial by jury."[98]

Finally, in Part II-D-2 a plurality section of the *Giles* opinion in which only Justices Roberts, Thomas, and Alito joined, Justice Scalia castigated the dissent for undervaluing the importance of the confrontation right and for attempting to inject policy concerns to modify a constitutional command.[99] Justice Scalia also disdained the notion of special rules for special victims, questioning: "Is the suggestion that we should have one Confrontation Clause (the one the Framers adopted and that *Crawford* described) for all other crimes, but a special, improvised, Confrontation Clause for those crimes that are frequently directed against women?"[100] He was not, however, entirely dismissive of the problem of intimidation in domestic-violence cases. In one paragraph, Justice Scalia hinted that many cases of domestic violence might meet the *Giles* forfeiture standard:

---

[95] *Giles*, 554 U.S. at 358. Some of the Justices expressed doubts about the testimonial nature of Avie's prior statement, which was made at a crime scene, but for the sake of argument, all nine Justices assumed without deciding that the statement was testimonial because the issue had been conceded below.

[96] *Id.* at 359–73.

[97] For an extensive and persuasive critique of Justice Scalia's legal history, see Thomas Davies, *Not "The Framers' Design": How the Framing-Era Ban Against Hearsay Evidence Refutes the Crawford-Davis "Testimonial" Formulation of the Scope of the Original Confrontation Clause,* 15 BROOKLYN J. L. & POL'Y 349 (2007).

[98] *Giles*, 554 U.S. at 365.

[99] The plurality opinion states:

> [T]he guarantee of confrontation is no guarantee at all if it is subject to whatever exceptions courts from time to time consider "fair." It is not the role of courts to extrapolate from the words of the Sixth Amendment to the values behind it, and then to enforce its guarantees only to the extent they serve (in the courts' views) those underlying values. The Sixth Amendment seeks fairness indeed—but seeks it through very specific means (one of which is confrontation) that were the trial rights of Englishmen.

Id. at 375.

[100] *Id.* at 376.

> Acts of domestic violence often are intended to dissuade a victim from resorting to outside help, and include conduct designed to prevent testimony to police officers or cooperation in criminal prosecutions. Where such an abusive relationship culminates in murder, the evidence may support a finding that the crime expressed the intent to isolate the victim and to stop her from reporting abuse to the authorities or cooperating with a criminal prosecution—rendering her prior statements admissible under the forfeiture doctrine. Earlier abuse, or threats of abuse, intended to dissuade the victim from resorting to outside help would be highly relevant to this inquiry, as would evidence of ongoing criminal proceedings at which the victim would have been expected to testify.[101]

Justice Souter's concurrence refers to Justice Scalia's language above and observes that "the element of intention would normally be satisfied by the intent on the part of the domestic abuser in the classic abusive relationship, which is meant to isolate the victim from outside help, including the aid of law enforcement and the judicial process." Justice Souter continued: "If the evidence for admissibility shows a continuing relationship of this sort, it would make no sense to suggest that the oppressing defendant miraculously abandoned the dynamics of abuse the instant before he killed his victim, say in a fit of anger." If Justice Souter is correct, then courts should increasingly apply forfeiture in domestic-violence cases despite the intent requirement.[102]

The dissent, written by Justice Breyer and joined by Justices Stevens and Kennedy,[103] questioned Justice Scalia's historical account of forfeiture and disdained his exercise of "trying to guess the state of mind of 18th Century lawyers," particularly when applied to a cause of action—domestic battery—that was unheard of two hundred years ago.[104] The dissent questioned the majority's focus on the accused's subjective intent to make the declarant unavailable and instead advocated an objective test focused on what the accused should reasonably expect: whether a reasonable accused would recognize that his actions would render the witness unavailable. The dissent argued that such an objective test would be consonant with the equitable notion of forfeiture.[105] Essentially, the dissent's proposed rule would say to the accused: if you make the witness disappear on purpose, then it does not matter what you were thinking, whether you were trying to prevent the witness's testimony or eliminating her for some other reason. You should not be permitted to benefit from your own wrongdoing by the loss of her testimony. The dissent noted the anomalous results of the majority's subjective-intent requirement. In domestic-violence cases, where the victim has made previous statements incriminating the accused, the majority's rule creates a disturbing incentive system whereby the batterer who strikes in anger (not necessarily to silence his victim in future proceedings) is better off killing his victim, than merely intimidating her into refusing to testify. If he

---

[101] *Id.* at 377.

[102] Professor Tom Lininger has suggested a standard for evaluating when an accused intentionally renders a witness unavailable. He has tailored his practical guidelines to the realities of domestic violence. He proposes that courts find "the requisite intent where the defendant has violated a restraining order, committed any act of violence while judicial proceedings are pending, or engaged in a prolonged pattern of abusing and isolating the victim." Tom Lininger, *The Sound of Silence: Holding Batterers Accountable for Silencing Their Victims*, 87 TEX. L. REV. 857, 865 (2009). Intimidation can take many forms, and courts will need to be aware that not only physical force, but credible threats to harm the victim, harm the victim's children, or separation of the victim from her children, will count as the type of intimidation that should trigger forfeiture.

[103] *Giles*, 554 U.S. at 380 (Breyer, J., dissenting).

[104] *Id.* at 402.

[105] *Id.* at 384–89.

kills her, forfeiture will not apply; if he intentionally prevents her from testifying via threats, forfeiture will apply.[106]

None of the opinions deals adequately with the obvious distinction between earlier assaults, as to which the alleged victim might have testified had she lived, and the crime of murder, as to which (obviously) she could not have testified had she lived. Using the majority's theory, while it is possible for the defendant to have killed the victim to prevent her from testifying at a trial *on the earlier assaults*, it is difficult to make sense of the idea that the abuser kills in order to prevent the victim from testifying *at the murder trial*. Even using the dissent's theory, the distinction is important: while the defendant may have benefited at a trial concerning the earlier assault by his wrongdoing in killing a witness to it, he cannot have benefited in this way at the trial for the murder of the witness. Using either theory, had he not killed her, it is not the case that she would have been available to testify at her murder trial, for there would not have been one.

Thus, at least under the theories advanced by the Justices, causally speaking forfeiture must be "trial specific" (or "claim specific," if two crimes are tried together), that is, one forfeits one's hearsay and confrontation objections at a particular trial by eliminating the declarant as a witness for *that* trial, not by eliminating the declarant as a witness for some other trial.[107] If one does not recognize this distinction, then the doctrine of forfeiture is loosed from its moorings in the principle that the litigant should not be permitted to gain an improper evidentiary advantage in a particular proceeding.[108] This seems to be part of what Justice Scalia was worried about: imposing an additional punishment for murder in the form of the loss of the confrontation right, one imposed by judicial fact-finding without the right of jury trial. But even Scalia would allow that the forfeiture can apply in the trial of the crime by which the defendant caused the witness's unavailability, provided the requisite intent is shown.[109] To be sure,

[106] *Id.* at 403.

[107] The matter may be different when the question is whether defendant's *wrongful intent* is trial-specific. *Cf.* United States v. Gray, 405 F.3d 227 (4th Cir. 2005) (where defendant murdered declarant in order to prevent his testimony in an assault trial, defendant forfeits hearsay objection under Rule 804(b)(6) as to declarant's out-of-court statements offered in later mail fraud case). *See* **§ 17.06**.

[108] To be sure, perhaps it *should* be loosed from such moorings. Other theories of confrontation do not depend on them. *Compare* Richard D. Friedman, *Confrontation and the Definition of Chutzpa*, 31 ISRAEL L. REV. 506 (1997) (arguing that forfeiture should not require defendant's intent to prevent testimony but only defendant's wrongful or deliberate actions causing the unavailability of the witness); *with* Dale A. Nance, *Rethinking Confrontation After* Crawford, 2:1 INT'L COMMENT. ON EVIDENCE art. 2 at 9 (2004) (arguing that the whole problem of forfeiture is avoided if hearsay is constitutionally admissible so long as the *government* is not responsible for the unavailability of the witness).

[109] 554 U.S. at 374 n.6. The dissent passes by the point with remarkable indifference:

> [W]hat greater evidentiary "advantage" could one derive from that wrong than thereby to prevent the witness from testifying, e.g., preventing the witness from describing a history of physical abuse that is not consistent with the defendant's claim that he killed her in self-defense.

Id. at 384 (Breyer, J., dissenting). Indeed, the dissenters then gave themselves the perfect opportunity to recognize the mistake when they articulated the argument in terms of a simple hypothetical example:

> Suppose that a husband, H, knows that after he assaulted his wife, W, she gave statements to the police. Based on the fact that W gave statements to the police, H also knows that it is possible he will be tried for assault. If H then kills W, H cannot avoid responsibility for intentionally preventing W from testifying, not even if H says he killed W because he was angry with her and not to keep her away *from the assault trial. Of course, the trial here is not for assault; it is for murder. But I should think that this fact, because of the nature of the crime, would count as a stronger, not a weaker, reason for applying the forfeiture rule.*

Id. at 386 (emphasis added). Justice Breyer describes this as "elementary legal logic." *Id.* at 387. Compare it to the following hypothetical:

statements of such an alleged victim may be relevant at the murder trial (or at any trial for the wrongdoing that caused the unavailability of the witness at some distinct trial) not to prove their truth, but rather to show the defendant's motive for the murder—to show that the defendant acted (at least in part) to prevent her from testifying at trials regarding the prior crimes. When offered at the murder trial in this fashion, the victim's statements would be admissible *nonhearsay*.[110] Perhaps the analysis in the opinions was affected by the fact that the question of a nonhearsay use was not presented to the Court.[111]

§ 20.05 Statements to Police, Revisited: *Michigan v. Bryant* (2011)

In *Michigan v. Bryant*,[112] the Court revisited the police interrogation question in a context not involving domestic abuse. The case concerned the admissibility of the statements made by a gunshot victim to responding police officers relating the circumstances of the shooting. The victim/declarant, obviously in great pain and anxious about the arrival of medical help, told the police that he had been shot some twenty-five minutes earlier at the back door of the defendant's house, after which he had driven to

---

> Suppose (a) H threatened W into not testifying at his trial for theft of W's personal property; (b) H makes no comparable threat with respect to W testifying at his trial for assaulting W; and (c) W in fact intends to testify against H in the assault case; but (d) before the trial on the assault charges, W is accidentally killed in an auto collision. The government offers evidence of W's hearsay statements regarding the assault, arguing that the defendant wrongfully caused the unavailability of W as a witness with the intent to prevent W from testifying (in the theft trial) and thus forfeited his right to confront her (in the assault trial).

Does Breyer's "elementary legal logic" work here? It seems unlikely that he would seriously argue as follows: "H cannot avoid responsibility for intentionally preventing W from testifying, Of course, the trial here is not for theft; it is for assault. But I should think that this fact, because of the nature of the crime, would count as a stronger, not a weaker, reason for applying the forfeiture rule." *See also* **§ 17.06** (discussing same problem in context of forfeiture hearsay exception).

[110] *See* **§ 14.04**. In *Crawford*, the Court had noted that the Clause poses no barrier to the use of out-of-court statements for a nonhearsay purpose. *Crawford*, 541 U.S. at 59 n.9.

[111] Not surprisingly, given the Supreme Court's opinion, most subsequent courts have not recognized the issue and have admitted the statement as hearsay in the murder trial on forfeiture grounds. *See, e.g.*, State v. Fry, 926 N.E.2d 1239, 1260–64 (Ohio 2010) (holding that defendant forfeited confrontation rights because his killing of the victim was designed "to prevent her from testifying against him in *any* future criminal proceedings") (emphasis added); Parker v. Commonwealth, 291 S.W.3d 647, 664–71 (Ky. 2009), *cert. denied*, 559 U.S. 910 (2010) (holding that defendant forfeited confrontation rights in trial for both shooting of X and murder of Y because he had conspired to kill Y in order to prevent him from testifying against defendant in shooting of X as well as out of revenge; not specifically addressing the significance of the dual intent).

In Bibbs v. State, 371 S.W.3d 564 (Tex. App. 2012), the issue surfaced but was not resolved. The defendant was convicted of murdering his former girlfriend after she gave a statement to police in order to obtain a protective order. Her statement was offered and admitted at trial "for all purposes" and without a limiting instruction. On appeal, the State defended the admission of her statement against hearsay and Confrontation objections by arguing that it was nonhearsay and that part of defendant's motive to kill her was to keep her from testifying before an administrative panel convened to consider revoking defendant's parole. This argument would have made sense, had it been the argument at trial. The appellate court held, however, that (a) the statement could not be considered on this nonhearsay theory because it was admitted generally, and (b) the forfeiture doctrine did not apply because, while part of his motive may have been to prevent her from testifying, the evidence also indicated that the motive was "just as likely tied to appellant's obsession with [the victim] after she decided to terminate their relationship." *Id.* at 569–70. (Given the factual ambiguity, it is odd that the appellate court did not explain why it neither addressed the significance of a dual motive nor deferred to the trial court's implicit finding in favor of waiver, especially because it ostensibly applied a highly deferential standard of review. *Id.* at 569.) In the end, the court found the error harmless and affirmed. *Id.* at 570–71.

[112] 562 U.S. 344, 131 S. Ct. 1143 (2011).

the gas station where the police found him.[113] In his statement to police the victim also identified the accused by his voice based on a conversation through the defendant's back door before the shot. The statement was admitted at trial as an excited utterance.[114]

In a 6-to-2 decision, the Court held the statement was not testimonial and hence not subject to the Confrontation Clause. Justice Scalia wrote in dissent, joined only by Justice Ginsburg. The long majority opinion, authored by Justice Sotomayor, emphasized the context-sensitive nature of the inquiry required by *Davis* and *Hammon*.[115] Whereas those domestic abuse cases involved identified perpetrators who posed a threat only to the declarants, the present case involved an assailant of unknown location, who used a gun, and posed a potential threat to both the police and the public at large. Anticipating the dissent's reaction, the majority opinion rather vaguely tried to indicate that temporal and spatial considerations limit an ongoing emergency:

> This is not to suggest that the emergency continued until Bryant was arrested in California a year after the shooting. . . . We need not decide precisely when the emergency ended because Covington's encounter with the police and all of the statements he made during that interaction occurred within the first few minutes of the police officers' arrival and well before they secured the scene of the shooting—the shooter's last known location.[116]

Also relevant, but not itself determinative, was the medical condition of the declarant, insofar as it affected his ability to form a testimonial purpose and "provides context for first responders to judge the existence and magnitude of a continuing threat to the victim, themselves, and the public."[117] In addition, the Court noted the lack of formality in the interrogation; it occurred in an "exposed, public area, prior to the arrival of emergency medical services, and in a disorganized fashion."[118] Considering all the relevant factors, the Court held that the "objective" primary purpose of the interrogation that elicited the declarant's statements was to meet an ongoing emergency, not to create evidence for potential use at trial.[119]

The dissenting opinions by Justices Scalia and Ginsburg found the majority's characterization to be completely implausible. First, the dissenters explicitly adopted the view that the controlling issue is the declarant's purpose, not that of the interrogators, except insofar as the latter shapes the former. Scalia argued that adding the mixed motives of the police to the analysis of "objective purpose" only complicates the question, with no compensating benefits. With regard to the declarant's situation, he certainly knew that he was no longer in danger of further assault by the defendant, and he must have known that his statements were not being used to provide medical treatment and thus address his medical emergency. As a result, he must have known that "his statements had little value except to ensure the arrest and eventual prosecution" of the defendant.[120] Moreover, even if the purposes of the police were taken

---

[113] 131 S. Ct. at 1150.

[114] The declarant did not survive long, and the prosecution also considered invoking the dying declaration exception. But this was abandoned and not addressed on appeal. *Id.* at 1151 n.1.

[115] *Id.* at 1152–67.

[116] *Id.* at 1165.

[117] *Id.* at 1159.

[118] *Id.* at 1160.

[119] *Id.* at 1166–67.

[120] *Id.* at 1170–71.

into account, none of their actions "indicated that they perceived an imminent threat."[121] With regard to the majority's context-sensitive, consider-all-the-factors exegesis, Scalia saw the vices of *Roberts* reemerging:

> The only virtue of the Court's approach (if it can be misnamed a virtue) is that it leaves judges free to reach the "fairest" result under the totality of the circumstances. If the dastardly police trick a declarant into giving an incriminating statement against a sympathetic defendant, a court can focus on the police's intent and declare the statement testimonial. If the defendant "deserves" to go to jail, then a court can focus on whatever perspective is necessary to declare damning hearsay nontestimonial. And when all else fails, a court can mix-and-match perspectives to reach its desired outcome.[122]

Finally, the majority's expansive conception of ongoing emergency would apply in most contexts of unsolved crimes and would permit the use of evidence that is historically paradigmatic of a Confrontation Clause violation.[123]

The controversies over the peculiar concept of an "objective" purpose of a multi-participant interview and over an expansive conception of "ongoing emergency" were both entirely predictable in the wake of *Davis* and *Hammon*. So perhaps the most noteworthy element of the majority opinion is its use of conventional hearsay exceptions as guidance in deciding whether the primary purpose of a statement was to create evidence. Justice Sotomayor wrote, "In making the primary purpose determination, standard rules of hearsay, designed to identify some statements as reliable, will be relevant."[124] The Court noted that excited utterances were admissible against a hearsay objection because fabrication was unlikely and suggested that this was similar to the reason why statements made to address on ongoing emergency are admissible against a Confrontation Clause objection.[125] This drew a particularly emphatic response from Justice Scalia, who perceived in it a reemergence of the discredited reliability analysis of *Ohio v. Roberts*.[126] He reiterated the *Crawford* message: "Reliability tells us *nothing* about whether a statement is testimonial. Testimonial and nontestimonial statements alike come in varying degrees of reliability."[127] He even questioned whether the majority's purpose was to overrule *Crawford* without saying so.[128]

The concurring opinion by Justice Thomas continued to reject the "primary purpose" test as one that is "disconnected from history" and "yields no predictable results."[129] He

---

121 *Id.* at 1171.

122 *Id.* at 1170.

123 Scalia wrote:

> The 16th- and 17th-century English treason trials that helped inspire the Confrontation Clause show that today's decision is a mistake. . . . Royal officials conducted many of the *ex parte* examinations introduced against Sir Walter Raleigh and Sir John Fenwick while investigating alleged treasonous conspiracies of unknown scope, aimed at killing or overthrowing the King. . . . [S]uch a conspiracy posed the most pressing emergency imaginable. . . . I therefore doubt that under the Court's test English officials acted improperly by denying Raleigh and Fenwick the opportunity to confront their accusers . . . .

Id. at 1173.

124 *Id.* at 1155.

125 *Id.* at 1157.

126 *Id.* at 1174–76.

127 *Id.* at 1175.

128 *Id.*

129 131 S. Ct. at 1167 (Thomas, J., concurring in the judgment).

concurred in the judgment based on the lack of formality and solemnity in the statement, reiterating the narrow category of testimonial statements Thomas has favored since at least 1992.[130]

One other point about Justice Thomas's opinion is worth noting, in light of his role in generating the *Crawford* revolution. It may seem easy to criticize his theory of the Clause on the obvious ground that it invites circumvention by the government: police need only avoid the requisite formality/solemnity in order to make statements constitutionally admissible, no matter how accusatory they may be. Multiple statements could be taken—a first one merely oral and perhaps made at the scene; a second, perhaps written later and signed under oath, if time permits. This would allow the prosecution to choose at a later time whether to use the former statement (admissible substantively under Thomas's test) or to put the witness on the stand and use the latter statement for impeachment purposes in case the witness testifies inconsistently. If the prosecution chooses, for whatever reason, to use the former statement without calling the witness, confrontation can be avoided. Thomas has an answer to this risk of circumvention, which he began in *Davis* and reiterated in *Bryant*. He insists that exclusion may be appropriate when, unlike the situation in *Bryant*, the statements are created or offered at trial "in order to evade confrontation."[131] In other words, what are *nontestimonial* statements can be subject to exclusion, whether that be on Confrontation Clause or Due Process grounds, when the government, by using such statements, is attempting to evade confrontation. This theme, which he has not developed at any length, would require a focus on the choices made by the prosecution (and other state actors) in regard to trial evidence. For example, if the police created two such hearsay interviews and the prosecution chose only to present the oral, informal (and thus nontestimonial) one at trial because an available declarant did not seem prepared to give equally inculpatory live testimony, the question of circumvention would be ripe for consideration.[132]

§ 20.06 Lab Reports and Expert Testimony: *Melendez-Diaz*, *Bullcoming*, and *Williams*

One of the most challenging problems in the application of a confrontation requirement to hearsay statements is the issue of the admissibility of routine business records. The need for such evidence, and the costs involved in imposing a requirement of testimony by the author of the record, caused Justice Harlan to abandon any strict requirement that the government show that the declarant is unavailable before admitting hearsay against the accused.[133] Later, under the *Roberts* regime, routine business records were admitted under the "firmly rooted" hearsay exceptions prong of its reliability requirement. And in *Crawford*, The Court simply noted, "Most of the hearsay exceptions [recognized as admissible at the time the Sixth Amendment was adopted] covered statements that by their nature were not testimonial—for example, business records. . . ."[134] But this idea is problematic when the routine business record is created as part of a criminal investigation by an organization such as a forensic science laboratory. In three decisions, the Court has addressed the application of the *Crawford*

---

[130] *See* White v. Illinois, 502 U.S. 358, 365 (1992) (Thomas, J., concurring).

[131] 131 S. Ct. at 1167.

[132] The issue would surface in a rather different way in Williams v. Illinois, 567 U.S. 50 (2012). *See* **§ 20.06**.

[133] *See* Dutton v. Evans, 400 U.S. 74, 94 (1970) (Harlan, J., concurring).

[134] Crawford v. Washington, 541 U.S. 36, 56 (2004).

test to lab reports authored by forensic scientists and expert testimony that would rely on them.

Melendez-Diaz v. Massachusetts (2009)

In *Melendez-Diaz v. Massachusetts,*[135] the Court held 5–4 that a lab analyst's notarized certificate attesting that a substance was cocaine was testimonial. Because the lab analyst was never called as a witness by the government, the admission of the lab report as a business record violated the accused's right to confrontation. The Court, with Scalia again writing for the majority, found that the case presented "a rather straightforward application of our holding in *Crawford,*"[136] triggering the strict confrontation right. The lab report fell within the "core class of testimonial statements,"[137] because it was prepared for use at trial against the accused. Lab reports were testimonial even though in some respects they resemble ordinary business records that are generally nontestimonial.[138]

The Court refused to distinguish the lab report from the type of testimonial evidence in *Crawford,* resisting the notion that the lab report was somehow different because it was scientific, objective, and a post-crime forensic inquiry by a non-accusatory neutral party who was reporting near-contemporaneous observations (as opposed to a conventional fact-statement by a witness regarding past observed events). The Court observed that government forensic laboratories are not immune from pressure or bias, and the confrontation right "is designed to weed out not only the fraudulent analyst, but the incompetent one as well."[139]

The fact that the accused could have subpoenaed the lab analyst did not solve the confrontation problem. The power to subpoena "is no substitute for the right of confrontation."[140] The burden remains with the prosecution to produce the witness or suffer the adverse consequences of the witness's non-appearance.[141]

The majority was unswayed by predictions of the practical effect of its rulings on the prosecution of cases, insisting that the "sky will not fall."[142] It rejected the prediction that the confrontation requirement would be burdensome, noting that many states already required that technicians be produced and that strategically, "[i]t is unlikely that defense counsel will insist on live testimony whose effect will be merely to highlight rather than cast doubt upon the forensic analysis."[143] Additionally, the Court seemed to approve of notice-and-demand systems that are currently used in some states. Under this procedure, the state gives notice that it will introduce a lab report and the accused

---

135 557 U.S. 305, 129 S. Ct. 2527 (2009).

136 129 S. Ct. at 2533.

137 *Id.* at 2532.

138 *Id.* at 2538.

139 *Id.* at 2537.

140 *Id.* at 2540.

141 *Id.* at 2539.

142 *Id.* at 2540.

143 *Id.* at 2542. The Court also made a less persuasive argument that defense attorneys would not raise *Crawford* issues in order to avoid irritating the judge. The dissent rightfully mocked that argument as entirely at odds with defense counsel's ethical and professional obligations. *Id.* at 2556–57 (Breyer, J. dissenting).

must object to the admission of the evidence absent the analyst's live in-court appearance.[144]

Even if the holding in *Melendez-Diaz* turns out to be burdensome, the Court concluded it does not matter. Justice Scalia explained, "The Confrontation Clause may make the prosecution of criminals more burdensome, but that is equally true of the right to trial by jury and the privilege against self-incrimination. The Confrontation Clause—like those other constitutional provisions—is binding, and we may not disregard it at our convenience."[145] He stated further, "Respondent and the dissent may be right that there are other ways—and in some cases better ways—to challenge or verify the results of a forensic test. But the Constitution guarantees one way: confrontation. We do not have license to suspend the Confrontation Clause when a preferable trial strategy is available."[146]

Justice Kennedy, writing in dissent, was joined by Chief Justice Roberts, Justice Breyer and Justice Alito. The dissent charged that *Melendez-Diaz* "sweeps away an accepted rule governing the admission of scientific evidence." For "at least 90 years" according to the dissent, "scientific analysis could be introduced into evidence without testimony from the "analyst" who produced it. This dissent noted sarcastically that "[w]e learn now that we have misinterpreted the Confrontation Clause—hardly an arcane or seldom-used provision of the Constitution—for the first 218 years of its existence."[147]

The dissent argued that there are "real differences between laboratory analysts who perform scientific tests and other, more conventional witnesses," and that laboratory analysts are not witnesses against the accused within the meaning of the Sixth Amendment.[148] It criticized the majority for leaving important questions unanswered, most notably, failing to clarify who, among the many scientists, technicians and engineers who generate a positive-for-cocaine result, must be available for confrontation.[149]

The dissent further portrayed the entire *Crawford* jurisprudence as devolving into a "body of formalistic and wooden rules, divorced from precedent, common sense, and the underlying purpose of the clause."[150] It censured the majority's "formalistic and pointless" reading of the Confrontation Clause,[151] observing that "the States can only guess what future rules this Court will distill from the sparse constitutional text."[152] Ultimately, the dissent took issue with the focus on testimonial statements, arguing:

> The Court's fundamental mistake is to read the Confrontation Clause as referring to a kind of out-of-court statement—namely, a testimonial

---

144 *Id.* at 2541 (citing the procedures of Georgia, Texas, and Ohio). In light of *Melendez-Diaz,* however, the Supreme Court of Kansas struck down a portion of a state law that required an accused to *state objections* to justify live-witness testimony in place of a forensic report, finding that it violated the Confrontation Clause. State v. Laturner, 218 P.3d 23 (Kan. 2009).

145 129 S. Ct. 2540.

146 *Id.* at 2536 (footnote omitted).

147 *Id.* at 2543 (Kennedy, J., dissenting).

148 *Id.*

149 *Id.* at 2544–46.

150 *Id.* at 2544. At another juncture, the dissent remarked that the Court was "driven by nothing more than a wooden application of the *Crawford* and *Davis* definition of 'testimonial,' " and had abandoned "any guidance from history, precedent, or common sense." *Id.* at 2547.

151 *Id.*

152 *Id.* at 2544 (Kennedy, J., dissenting).

statement—that must be excluded from evidence. The Clause does not refer to kinds of statements. Nor does the Clause contain the word "testimonial." The text, instead, refers to kinds of persons, namely, to "witnesses against" the defendant. Laboratory analysts are not "witnesses against" the defendant as those words would have been understood at the framing. There is simply no authority for this proposition.[153]

Bullcoming v. New Mexico (2011)

In *Bullcoming v. New Mexico*,[154] the Court extended its holding in *Melendez-Diaz,* with the same 5-to-4 vote margin, by holding that the technician who authored the forensics report must be produced even if another technician testifies, one who is familiar with the procedures followed and the equipment used. In her opinion for the Court, Justice Ginsburg noted skeptically that the prosecutor excused the fact that the analyst who recorded the blood alcohol readings from the gas chromatograph results did not testify because he had been placed on "unpaid leave," for a reason not revealed, and that the technician who did testify had neither observed nor reviewed the other's work.[155] Ginsburg made easy work of rejecting the arguments of the New Mexico Supreme Court to the effect that the missing technician performed merely ministerial functions, like reading and recording the result of a gas chromatograph test, in view of the fact that he also certified "that he received Bullcoming's blood sample intact with the seal unbroken, that he checked to make sure that the forensic report number and the sample number 'correspond[ed],' and that he performed on Bullcoming's sample a particular test, adhering to a precise protocol, and (in effect) that "no 'circumstance or condition . . . affect[ed] the integrity of the sample or the validity of the analysis," all of which assertions were "meet for cross-examination," on subjects about which the substituted technician had no personal knowledge.[156]

In dissent, Justice Kennedy insisted that, under the circumstances, "requiring the State to call the technician who filled out a form and recorded the results of a test is a hollow formality" in light of the alternatives available to the defense to challenge the evidence.[157] He criticized the *Crawford* doctrine itself: "The persistent ambiguities in the Court's approach are symptomatic of a rule not amenable to sensible applications."[158] And, perhaps most importantly, he criticized the majority for giving too little weight to the question of reliability as well as to the costs being imposed on the state by such a rule.[159] In regard to the latter, he wrote:

> From 2008 to 2010, subpoenas rose 71%, to 1,600—or 8 or 9 every workday. . . . In a State that is the Nation's fifth largest by area and that employs just 10 total analysts, each analyst in blood alcohol cases recently received 200 subpoenas per year, ... The analysts now must travel great distances on most working days. The result has been, in the laboratory's words, "chaotic." And if the defense raises an objection and the analyst is tied up in another court

---

153 *Id.* at 2550–51 (Kennedy, J., dissenting).

154 564 U.S. 647, 131 S. Ct. 2705 (2011).

155 131 S. Ct. at 2711–12.

156 *Id.* at 2714–16.

157 131 S. Ct. at 2724–25 (Kennedy, J., dissenting).

158 *Id.* at 2725–26.

159 *Id.* at 2726–28.

> proceeding; or ill; or no longer living, the defense gets a windfall. . . . Scarce state resources could be committed to other urgent needs in the criminal justice system.[160]

The dissent did not, however, go on to answer certain obvious questions: Why does such a State only have 10 analysts? Is the Court required to interpret the Constitution so that the State is not under pressure to have more appropriate staffing? Or should the state be expected to make the difficult choice between increasing resources devoted to proper prosecution or restricting the reach of the criminal sanction?[161]

Williams v. Illinois (2012)

In *Williams v. Illinois*,[162] the Court considered a more complicated fact pattern, generating the most diverse and divided set of opinions so far in the *Crawford* line of cases. When a rape by an unidentified perpetrator was reported, a vaginal swab was tested for the presence of semen, and when semen was found, the swab was sent to a separate lab, Cellmark Diagnostics, for the development of a DNA profile of the perpetrator. An Illinois state forensic biologist, Sandra Lambatos, found that the profile reported by Cellmark matched a DNA profile of a man who had been arrested on another charge. That man, the defendant Williams, was then identified by the victim of the rape, which led to his prosecution. At trial, Lambatos testified to the DNA "match" between the Cellmark profile and the profile resulting from the defendant's arrest on another charge. The Cellmark report was not introduced into evidence itself. The defendant was convicted in a bench trial. The appeal made a Confrontation Clause challenge, based on the failure of the prosecution to call the author of the Cellmark report to testify, subject to cross-examination.

The Supreme Court affirmed the conviction, in a 4-1-4 decision. Justice Alito delivered the judgment in an opinion for himself and Chief Justice Roberts and Justices Kennedy and Breyer. Justice Kagan wrote for the dissent, representing Justices Scalia, Ginsburg, and Sotomayer. This time, Justice Thomas joined those on the Court who denied a violation of the Clause, but again based on a theory shared by no one else on the Court.

Justice Alito offered two reasons to distinguish this case from *Melendez-Diaz* and *Bullcoming*. First, the Cellmark report was not introduced; rather, expert testimony by Lambatos relied in part on its results in giving her opinion that the DNA profile developed from the vaginal swab matched the DNA profile developed from the blood test of the defendant in the other investigation. In this, the prosecution had relied on Illinois's equivalent of Rule 703 of the Federal Rules of Evidence, which permits an expert to rely on evidence that is not admitted, and even evidence not admissible.[163] In theory, an out-of-court statement used in this way is not used to prove the truth of the matter asserted, but only to provide the basis for expert testimony. Accordingly, it is not subject to the Confrontation Clause.[164] Justice Thomas and the four dissenters (i.e., five of the nine

---

160 *Id.* at 2728.

161 *See* Pamela R. Metzger, *Confrontation as a Rule of Production*, 24 WM. & MARY BILL RTS. J. 995 (2016).

162 567 U.S. 50, 132 S. Ct. 2221 (2012).

163 132 S. Ct. at 2231.

164 *Id.* at 2232–41. *See* **§ 10.05**.

justices) rejected this argument as based on a fiction.[165] As Justice Kagan put it, "If the [Cellmark] statement is true, then the conclusion based on it is probably true; if not, not. So to determine the validity of the witness's conclusion, the factfinder must assess the truth of the out-of-court statement on which it relies."[166] Alito's response was that the expert's opinion—the only testimony challenged, did not use the Cellmark report to prove the truth of its assertions about the DNA profile, but rather used them as the premises that she (reasonably) *assumed* to be true for the purpose of giving her opinion about a "match." That this might undermine the adequacy of the evidence to prove the defendant's guilt was, to Alito, not a Confrontation Clause issue:

> If there were no proof that Cellmark produced an accurate profile based on that sample, Lambatos' testimony regarding the match would be irrelevant, but the Confrontation Clause, as interpreted in *Crawford*, does not bar the admission of irrelevant evidence, only testimonial statements by declarants who are not subject to cross-examination.[167]

Justice Kagan responded by noting that there was no indication in the testimony or the trial court's statements that the report was in fact used in such a limited way.

Justice Alito's second argument assumed, arguendo, that the fact-finder relied on the truth of the data in the Cellmark report, a hearsay use. He argued that, even so, the statements were not testimonial, and this for two reasons. First, extending *Bryant*, Alito argued that the statements in the Cellmark report were made in the context of an ongoing emergency, a rapist at large.[168] Again, five of the justices (Thomas agreeing with the dissent) thought this argument strained credulity, in light of the pace of the investigation: the vaginal swab had been frozen for nine months before being sent to Cellmark, which took another four months to complete its report.[169]

As a second reason not to consider the report testimonial, Justice Alito argued that the report was not the kind of statement involved in the historical abuses that led to the Clause:

> The abuses that the Court has identified as prompting the adoption of the Confrontation Clause shared the following two characteristics: (a) they involved out-of-court statements having the primary purpose of accusing a targeted individual of engaging in criminal conduct and b) they involved formalized statements such as affidavits, depositions, prior testimony, or confessions.[170]

The Cellmark report, by contrast, might just as well have exculpated the defendant as inculpated him. In particular, the situation was such that Cellmark had no idea what result the prosecution would find helpful. Unlike cases like *Melendez-Diaz* and

---

[165] Even Justice Breyer, in his concurring opinion, called the nonhearsay use argument "artificial." *Id.* at 2246.

[166] 132 S. Ct. at 2268–69 (Kagan, J., dissenting); *see also* 132 S. Ct. at 2256–69 (Thomas, J., concurring in the judgment).

[167] 132 S. Ct. at 2238. In a footnote, Justice Alito opined that this might raise a Due Process concern, had the defense raised that issue, but that even if such an issue had been raised, it would not have warranted overturning the verdict, as there was sufficient evidence to support it, given the victim's eye-witness identification of the defendant as the perpetrator. *Id.* at n.8.

[168] *Id.* at 2243.

[169] *Id.* at 2262–63, 2274.

[170] *Id.* at 2242.

Bullcoming, Cellmark operated behind what Justice Breyer in a separate concurring opinion called a "veil of ignorance," thus reducing one risk of error, namely bias.[171] Again, five justices rejected this argument, expressing bewilderment at the newly stated restrictions on what counts as "testimonial."[172] Specifically, they rejected the idea that a testimonial statement must be one that accuses a targeted individual. While this factor might tell us something about the reliability of Cellmark's analysis, it does not change the fact that the statement was made for the primary purpose of establishing past events potentially relevant to later criminal prosecution. Justice Kagan's dissenting opinion reinforced the point by detailing a story of the kind of laboratory error that can occur in doing DNA testing, error that may only be discovered by cross-examination of those who conducted the test.

Because five justices rejected each of the theories of Justice Alito's opinion, it is striking that Alito's position prevailed in terms of result. Justice Thomas concurred in the result only because he did not find the Cellmark report to be testimonial. He opined that the report was insufficiently formalized; it was neither notarized nor sworn nor provided as a certificate and thus lacked the solemnity of testimonial statements. No other justice endorsed this opinion. Justice Kagan, in her dissent, could see no real difference when compared to the reports in *Melendez-Diaz* and *Bullcoming*, and warned that any such formal requirements can easily be avoided by prosecutors. Indeed, she called the strategy used in this case a "neat trick"[173] that was used "to circumvent the Confrontation Clause's requirements."[174] As noted above, Justice Thomas has repeatedly invoked the idea that the prosecution may not use even nontestimonial statements when its purpose is to "evade confrontation," but—with no significant explanation—he simply commented that there was no "indication" that such an attempt was involved in this case.[175]

---

[171] *Id.* at 2249 (Breyer, J., concurring). Breyer's interesting concurrence briefly reviewed the abuses that generated the Clause and stated, "The Confrontation Clause prohibits the use of this kind of evidence because allowing it would deprive a defendant of the ability to cross-examine the witness." *Id.* He did not explore the difference that results from focusing on the "deprivation" of the ability to cross-examine and the mere "absence" of the opportunity to cross-examine. The latter is the emphasis in *Crawford*. Instead, he considered the opportunity to cross-examine as merely one means to the end of reliability, one that is not (in Breyer's opinion) as essential in the context of forensic science lab reports and one that, if enforced by a requirement that the state produce lab technicians to testify, may be counterproductive. *Id.* at 2249–52.

[172] One is tempted to ask why Justice Alito did not add additional commonalities, such as: (c) the historical cases of abuse were all recorded using longhand rather than typewriters or computers, or (d) they were all made at a time when forensic science generally, and DNA evidence in particular, did not exist, or even (e) they were all made in England before 1791. Commonalities are important, to be sure, but identifying which commonalities matter and why is critical to legal reasoning. Justice Alito made no attempt to justify his selection of factors. Of course, the same question can be asked about the other formulations of "testimonial" that have been discussed. Ultimately, such questions cannot be sensibly answered without using an approach to interpreting the Clause that is sensitive to the purpose(s) it was intended to serve. *See* Roger C. Park, *Purpose as a Guide to the Interpretation of the Confrontation Clause*, 71 BROOKLYN L.REV. 297, 298 & n.5 (2005) (arguing that "[t]he primary purpose of the Confrontation Clause is to prevent injustice caused by abuse of state power" and to "deal with a particular kind of threat to the truth.").

[173] 132 S. Ct. at 2272.

[174] *Id.* at 2268.

[175] *Id.* at 2260 n.5. Perhaps Thomas thought that this evasion was not intended, that circumvention can only be shown by evidence of "smoking gun" statements by state actors that indicate a specific intent to evade confrontation. Or perhaps he would have recognized an evasion in this case if the prosecution originally had offered the Cellmark report and, upon its being rejected on Confrontation Clause grounds, it had then called the expert witness to give an opinion based on the report.

§ 20.07 Child Declarants and Unofficial Auditors: *Ohio v. Clark* (2015)

In the most recent Supreme Court decision, *Ohio v. Clark*,[176] the Court finally addressed a situation in which the hearsay statement at issue was not made to police officers. The case is also important because it is the first case to reach the Court that did not involve an adult declarant. A three-year-old child, called "L.P." in the opinion, was in the care of the mother's boyfriend, the accused, while the mother was out of town to engage in prostitution. When teachers noticed suspicious marks on his body and questioned the child, the child reported abuse at the hands of the accused.

At a pretrial competency hearing, the judge questioned L.P. (then aged four) and found him incompetent to testify under Ohio's rule regarding child witnesses, which renders incompetent children under the age of ten who "appear incapable of receiving just impressions of the facts and transactions respecting which they are examined, or of relating them truly."[177] But the court rejected the accused's motion *in limine* to exclude L.P.'s hearsay statements. Instead, the trial court ruled such hearsay admissible under Ohio's residual hearsay exception, applicable only to child declarants and written so as to comply with the old *Roberts* criteria. That exception admits hearsay by a child under the age of twelve that describes sexual or physical abuse if the child's testimony is not "reasonably available," there is "independent proof" of the sexual or physical act, and the court finds "particularized guarantees of the trustworthiness" of the hearsay statements.[178]

The Ohio appellate courts reversed the conviction, relying on the Confrontation Clause as interpreted in *Crawford* and subsequent cases. They found that the teachers were functioning much like police in view of the statutory obligation of teachers to report abuse to law enforcement. Applying the primary purpose test from *Davis* and *Bryant*, they held that the primary objective purpose of the questioning was not to deal with an ongoing emergency but rather to establish facts potentially relevant to a prosecution. Thus, the child's statements were testimonial.[179]

The Supreme Court reversed. All nine justices concurred in the result, although there were differences in emphasis and reasoning. Justice Alito wrote the majority opinion, concluding that, under *Bryant*, there was a dominant purpose for the questioning other than establishing facts relevant to prosecution: the teachers, in their spontaneous and informal queries, had to decide whether it was safe to return L.P. into Clark's custody. Moreover, the child was not old enough to form the purpose of creating evidence for future prosecution. The Court, in dicta, made two generalizations: (1) statements made to someone other than law enforcement are less likely to be testimonial, though they are not inevitably nontestimonial; and (2) statements made by very young children are less likely to be testimonial, though they are not inevitably nontestimonial.[180]

Justice Scalia, joined by Justice Ginsburg, agreed that the statements were nontestimonial even if the mandatory reporting requirement rendered the teachers

---

176 Ohio v. Clark, 576 U.S. 237, 135 S. Ct. 2173 (2015).

177 OHIO R. EVID. 601(A).

178 *See* OHIO R. EVID. 807.

179 *See* State v. Clark, 137 Ohio St. 3d 346 (2013).

180 *Clark*, 135 S. Ct. at 2181–82.

equivalent to law enforcement officers.[181] L.P.'s age made it implausible that he was capable of forming the purpose of invoking the coercive machinery of the state.[182] They did not stop to consider (as Scalia had in *Bryant*) the implications of the stated rationale in *Clark* for classic cases of abuse that gave rise to the Clause. The majority states, and the concurrence does not challenge, that "a young child in these circumstances would simply want the abuse to end, would want to protect other victims, or would have no discernible purpose at all."[183] If this precludes the child's statements from being testimonial, then we might be compelled to see Raleigh's case in a very different light.[184]

Justice Thomas concurred, while again rejecting the primary purpose analysis.[185] According to Thomas, the determinative facts were that: (1) L.P.'s statements were not solemn declarations or affidavits made for the purpose of establishing or proving some fact, so the statements were not testimonial; (2) "nor is there any indication that L.P.'s statements were offered at trial to evade confrontation." In regard to the latter, Thomas wrote only that, "the record suggests that the prosecution would have produced L.P. to testify had he been deemed competent to do so."[186] That kind of analysis puts the focus on the prosecutor's choices about what to present at trial, much like the theory of the Clause advanced by Justice Harlan in *California v. Green*,[187] and the "unavailability" requirement in the original *Roberts* test.[188] Unfortunately, Thomas did not pause to consider the possibility that the substitution of hearsay for live testimony could be effected not by the prosecution's decisions but rather by those of the legislature (as in this case) or even the courts. For example, if a legislature passed a statute barring the defendant from cross-examining any witness called by the prosecution, no one would say that the fact that the prosecution would have been willing in a given case to allow such cross-examination eliminates the Confrontation Clause problem. Nor did Justice Thomas address the question whether statutory competence to testify for the prosecution is constitutionally equivalent to competence to take the stand and be cross-examined by the accused.[189]

---

181 *Id.* at 2183–84 (Scalia, J., concurring).

182 Scalia cited approvingly an article for the proposition that at common law, children were generally considered incompetent to take oaths and thus unavailable as witnesses. *Id.* at 2184 (citing Thomas D. Lyon & Raymond LaMagna, *The History of Children's Hearsay: From Old Bailey to Post*-Davis, 82 Ind. L.J. 1029 (2007)). Although Scalia did not mention it, the same article demonstrates that hearsay statements from such incompetent-to-testify child-declarants were routinely admitted at common law, but not on the theory that the child could not form the intent (or purpose or expectation) that her statements would or could be used as evidence at a trial. Rather embarrassingly, for Justice Scalia's view of the Clause, a major point of that article is that unconfronted hearsay from an incompetent-to-testify child was routinely admitted at common-law as the *best available evidence*, even if the child's statements would be characterized as "testimonial" under *Crawford*. *See* Lyon & Lamagna, 82 Ind. L.J. at 1055–56. That is an important difference.

183 135 S. Ct. at 2182.

184 It is quite plausible that Lord Cobham's statement was obtained by torture, and he may have been unable to form any purpose other than to make the pain stop. Yet no one has ever suggested that, in order to perceive in that case the governmental abuse that necessitated a Confrontation Clause, we need to know more about the circumstances under which Lord Cobham made his statement implicating Raleigh. The problem was that Cobham could have been produced in court but was not.

185 *Id.* at 2185–86 (Thomas, J., concurring).

186 *Id.* at 2186.

187 *See* California v. Green, 399 U.S. 149, 174 (Harlan, J., concurring).

188 *See* **§ 20.01**.

189 By way of comparison, an article cited approvingly by Justice Scalia (mentioned in a previous note) includes a discussion of the 18th century influence of Sir Matthew Hale, whose *The History of Pleas of the Crown*, published in 1736, included the eminently sensible suggestion that, if the child was incompetent to

§ 20.08 Established Principles Post-*Crawford*; Remaining Open Questions

*What We Know Post-*Crawford

The *Crawford* line of cases raises many questions. Before addressing the remaining open questions, however, it is useful to review established principles from *Crawford* and its progeny.

First, the admissibility of out-of-court statements offered for a purpose other than proving the truth of the matter asserted (i.e., offered for a "nonhearsay purpose") is not regulated by the Confrontation Clause.[190]

Second, if an out-of-court (hearsay) statement is testimonial, then in order for it to be constitutionally admissible, ordinarily either (a) the witness must be available for cross-examination at trial or (b) the witness must be unavailable at trial and the accused must have had an opportunity to cross-examine the declarant about the statement at another time. Admitting an out-of-court, testimonial statement from a nontestifying declarant who was not subject to cross by the present accused when the statement was made, presumptively violates the Confrontation Clause, even if the declarant is unavailable at trial without any fault of the government.[191]

Third, the only formal exception to the previous principle that the Supreme Court has considered extensively is forfeiture. To forfeit the confrontation right, the accused must have made the witness unavailable with the intent of preventing the witness's testimony.[192] Outright threats, bribes, and one-way tickets out of town issuing from the accused to the witness would forfeit the right to cross-examine. Questions remain, however, particularly in the domestic-violence context, concerning what constitutes purposely making a witness unavailable and the extent to which forfeiture is trial or claim specific.

Fourth, as a guiding principle, testimonial statements are those "made under circumstances that would lead an objective witness reasonably to believe that the statement would be available for use at a later trial."[193] Although open questions remain concerning the application of this principle, it is possible to generate a list of statements that are clearly testimonial. They include:

- Affidavits[194]
- *Ex parte* in-court testimony[195]
- Depositions and other prior sworn testimony[196]
- Formal stationhouse statements or other custodial examinations[197]

---

take an oath, she should be allowed to testify unsworn. *See* Thomas D. Lyon & Raymond LaMagna, *The History of Children's Hearsay: From Old Bailey to Post-*Davis, 82 Ind. L.J. 1029, 1034–35 (2007).

190 Crawford v. Washington, 541 U.S. 36, 59 n.9 (2004).

191 *See* **§ 20.02**.

192 *See* **§ 20.04**.

193 Crawford v. Washington, 541 U.S. 36, 52 (2004).

194 *Id.* at 51.

195 *Id.*

196 *Id.*

197 This reflects the facts of the *Crawford* case; *see* **§ 20.02**.

- Statements made at the scene of a crime after the emergency has passed.[198]

The Court also indicated that some statements are clearly nontestimonial, and hence outside constitutional protection—excluded, if at all, by hearsay rules, at least when they are not used, as Justice Thomas explains, "to evade confrontation." The Court has indicated, albeit sometimes in dicta, that such nontestimonial statements include:

- Statements made (even to police officers) during an emergency to secure assistance[199]
- Casual remarks made to friends[200]
- Statements of co-conspirators in furtherance of a conspiracy[201]
- Medical reports prepared for treatment purposes[202]
- Regularly kept business records[203] (other than those prepared in anticipation of litigation)[204]
- A clerk's certification that a copy is a true and complete copy of an original on file in the clerk's office[205]
- Documents prepared in the regular course of maintaining and calibrating laboratory equipment[206]
- Statements made by persons too young or otherwise too limited in their mental capacity to form the purpose of creating evidence for potential use in a criminal prosecution.[207]

Remaining Open Questions

The new Confrontation Clause jurisprudence, as laid out in *Crawford*, *Davis*, *Williams*, *Bryant*, and *Clark*, has been fairly criticized for its lack of consistency on what constitutes "testimonial" statements and its focus on purpose, motive, or expectations in

---

198 *See* **§ 20.03**. *See also* Ramirez v. Tegels, 413 F. Supp. 3d 808, 820 (W.D. Wis. 2019) (distinguishing *Clark* in that declarants in present case were eight and five years old and made statements in response to police questioning after any emergency was past).

199 Davis v. Washington, 547 U.S. 813, 828 (2006); Michigan v. Bryant, 562 U.S. 344 (2011); Ohio v. Clark, 576 U.S. 237 (2015).

200 Crawford v. Washington, 541 U.S. 36, 51 (2004). ("An accuser who makes a formal statement to government officers bears testimony in a sense that a person who makes a casual remark to an acquaintance does not."). Generally, statements made to parents, family members, or friends are treated as nontestimonial because their purpose is primarily to obtain help and treatment, rather than for purposes of litigation. *See, e.g.*, State v. Shafer, 128 P.3d 87 (Wash. 2006) (concluding that unprompted statements made by child to mother morning after abuse were nontestimonial); State v. Brigman, 615 S.E.2d 21 (N.C. Ct. App. 2005) (involving statements spontaneously made to foster mother after she saw child engaged in sexual play nontestimonial); *see also* Herrera-Vega v. State, 888 So. 2d 66 (Fla. Dist. Ct. App. 2004) (concluding that spontaneous statement to mother and later repetition to father were nontestimonial because court concluded that there was no intention to use statements in criminal trial).

201 Melendez-Diaz v. Massachusetts, 557 U.S. 305, 129 S. Ct. 2527, 2539–40 (2009).

202 *Id.* at 2533 n.2.

203 Crawford v. Washington, 541 U.S. 36, 56 (2004) ("Most of the hearsay exceptions [recognized as admissible at the time the Sixth Amendment was adopted] covered statements that by their nature were not testimonial-for example, business records. . . .").

204 Melendez-Diaz v. Massachusetts, 557 U.S. 305, 129 S. Ct. 2527, 2538 (2009).

205 *Id.* at 2539.

206 *Id.* at 2532 n.1.

207 Ohio v. Clark, 576 U.S. 237 (2015).

making such statements, which are always difficult to ascertain, especially when such mental states are attributed not to a person but to an event, such as an "interrogation."

Many of the questions that remain regarding the definition of testimonial statements arise when courts struggle to draw the line between nontestimonial statements whose primary purpose is seeking assistance and testimonial statements used to assist the investigation and prosecution of a crime. This task has only been made more difficult by the expansive notion of "ongoing emergency" endorsed in *Bryant* and *Clark*. A similar question arises when a specially trained nurse or counselor may have the dual role of providing needed medical or psychological assistance and collecting forensic evidence and recording statements.[208]

Post-*Williams*, the rules regarding the use of reports of results from forensic science tests are in considerable disarray, owing in no small part to the fact that there was no one rationale supporting the result in *Williams* upon which a majority of the justices could agree.[209] One might hazard the guess that tests conducted in a manner such that the analyst does not know whether the prosecution would be favored by a positive or a negative result on the test, or where it is impossible to characterize a result as inculpatory or exculpatory on its own, may be protected from Constitutional scrutiny under the Clause, especially if the report is not sworn or notarized. Moreover, insofar as an inadmissible report is used as merely one basis for the giving of an expert opinion, it may also withstand scrutiny under the Clause, provided the report is either not made known to the fact-finder or, if it is, a plausibly effective limiting instruction is given.[210]

Questions inevitably have arisen regarding whether autopsy reports are testimonial. Such reports are made knowing full well that they might be pertinent to a potential criminal prosecution, and they are solemn declarations. As compared to other investigative forensics testing, however, autopsies are more likely to be conducted before the government has even concluded that a crime has been committed. In the *Crawford* era, both the pre- and post-*Williams* case law has numerically favored a nontestimonial characterization.[211]

With regard to statements not made to police, *Crawford* itself suggested that casual remarks to a friend are paradigmatically nontestimonial.[212] The question is how far this category will be extended. The opinion in *Clark* gave broader, but less concrete guidance

---

[208] *See* People v. Vargas, 100 Cal.Rptr.3d 578 (Cal. Ct. App. 2009) (holding testimonial victim's statements to a forensic rape nurse whose job was to conduct a separate medical exam to search for evidence of assault).

[209] *See* 4 CHRISTOPHER B. MUELLER & LAIRD C. KIRKPATRICK, FEDERAL EVIDENCE § 8:91 (4th ed. 2013).

[210] *Compare* State v. Ortiz-Zape, 743 S.E.2d 156 (N.C. 2013) (admitting expert testimony based on report of test for presence of cocaine conducted by another analyst who did not testify); *and* Commonwealth v. Greineder, 984 N.E.2d 804 (Mass. 2013) (admitting expert testimony based on report of DNA test conducted by nontestifying analyst; harmless error to allow expert to testify to contents of report itself); *with* Young v. United States, 63 A.3d 1033 (D.C. 2013) (holding that it was error to allow expert to testify based on results of DNA test conducted by another).

[211] Holding autopsy report testimonial: United States v. Moore, 651 F.3d 30 (D.C. 2011); United States v. Ignasiak, 667 F.3d 1217 (11th Cir. 2012); Commonwealth v. Reavis, 992 N.E.2d 304 (Mass. 2013); State v. Locklear, 681 S.E.2d 293, 304–05 (N.C. 2009).

Holding autopsy report nontestimonial: United States v. De La Cruz, 514 F.3d 121, 128 (1st Cir. 2008); United States v. James, 712 F.3d 79 (2d Cir. 2013); Mitchell v. Kelly, 520 F. App'x. 329 (6th Cir. 2013); McNeiece v. Latimore, 501 F. App'x 634 (9th Cir. 2012); People v. Dungo, 286 P.3d 442 (Cal. 2012); People v. Leach, 980 N.E. 2d 570, 590 (Ill. 2012); State v. Maxwell, 9 N.E.3d 930 (Ohio 2014).

[212] *Crawford,* 541 U.S. at 51 ("An accuser who makes a formal statement to government officers bears testimony in a sense that a person who makes a casual remark to an acquaintance does not.").

with its two predictive generalizations: (1) statements made to someone other than law enforcement are less likely to be testimonial, though they are not inevitably nontestimonial; and (2) statements made by very young children are less likely to be testimonial, though they are not inevitably nontestimonial.[213] Not surprisingly, statements made by young children to parents, family members, or friends are generally treated as nontestimonial because their purpose is primarily to obtain help and treatment, rather than for purposes of litigation.[214] On the other hand, and illustrating how the courts inevitably take into account the purposes of the interrogators, even a young child's statement to someone (like a psychologist) who is tasked to report the declarant's statements to the police may well be adjudged testimonial.[215]

A case that fits the first *Clark* characteristic—i.e., the statement was not made to police—but not the second—i.e., the statement was made by an adult—has been addressed several times by the Supreme Court of Wisconsin, the first time a few years after *Crawford* was decided,[216] and the most recent in 2021, after the decisions in *Bryant* and *Clark*.[217] In the most recent decision, the court reaffirmed its earlier holding that a woman's letter given to a neighbor, indicating that she believed her husband was planning to kill her and explaining why, with instructions to give the letter to the police if anything should happen to her, was testimonial.[218] The state had argued that the intervening decisions in *Bryant* and *Clark*, by narrowing the scope of what is testimonial, changed the outcome, and a concurring opinion—citing sixteen contextual factors identified by case law as affecting the determination—was inclined to agree.[219]

Crawford and the cases that followed it have left open other important questions besides the definition of what is "testimonial." One question is the potential breadth of the idea of forfeiture. *Giles* addressed one type of forfeiture: when the defendant's conduct makes it impossible for him to confront the declarant. But there are others. One conspicuous possibility is the accused's introduction of a misleadingly incomplete portion of a third party's hearsay statement, thus triggering the doctrine of verbal completeness.[220] Quite arguably, the accused forfeits the right to confront the declarant when the prosecution invokes the doctrine in order to introduce the whole of the third party's statement.[221] More controversial are the broader notions of "curative admissibility" and "opening the door" by improper defense trial tactics.[222] Here, one

---

213 *Clark*, 135 S. Ct. at 2181–82.

214 *See, e.g.*, State v. Shafer, 128 P.3d 87 (Wash. 2006) (concluding that unprompted statements made by child to mother morning after abuse were nontestimonial); State v. Brigman, 615 S.E.2d 21 (N.C. Ct. App. 2005) (involving statements spontaneously made to foster mother after she saw child engaged in sexual play nontestimonial); *see also* Herrera-Vega v. State, 888 So. 2d 66 (Fla. Dist. Ct. App. 2004) (concluding that spontaneous statement to mother and later repetition to father were nontestimonial because court concluded that there was no intention to use statements in criminal trial).

215 *See, e.g.*, McCarley v. Kelly, 759 F.3d 535 (6th Cir. 2014) (holding testimonial the statement of a three-and-a-half year old child of murder victim to psychologist reporting to law enforcement), *vacated on other grounds*, 135 S. Ct. 2887 (2015) (remanding to reconsider issue of harmless error).

216 State v. Jensen, 727 N.W.2d 518 (Wis. 2007).

217 State v. Jensen, 957 N.W.2d 244 (Wis. 2021).

218 See *Jensen*, 727 N.W.2d at 521–22.

219 *Jensen*, 957 N.W.2d at 255–61.

220 *See* **§ 1.12**.

221 *Cf.* State v. Mallar, 508 A.2d 1070, 1071–72 (N.H. 1986) (permitting the prosecutor to introduce completing portion of third party's declaration against interest; the confrontation issue, then governed by the *Ohio v. Roberts* framework, was noted but not resolved on the merits).

222 *See* **§ 1.11.**

would think that the prosecution usually has adequate protection from improper defense tactics by objecting to inadmissible evidence and making motions to strike improper arguments.[223]

Another unresolved question concerns the admissibility of dying declarations. In dicta—both in *Crawford*[224] and even more explicitly in *Giles*[225]—the Court has indicated that, because dying declarations constituted an exception at the time of the founders, they will be admissible even if testimonial.[226] Because it would stand in sharp contrast with the principles *Crawford* articulated, Scalia acknowledged that, "[i]f this exception must be accepted on historical grounds, it is sui generis."[227] In her dissenting opinion in *Bryant*, Justice Ginsburg made a point of her interest in resolving this question, though she gave no indication about how she would resolve it.[228] Meanwhile, the Court's dictum in *Crawford* has been embraced by lower courts, which have regularly rejected constitutional challenges to dying declarations.[229]

The most important open question is whether the Court will continue to hold to the basic doctrinal structure of *Crawford* itself. While the *Clark* case was unanimous in result, that unanimity conceals deep disagreement about the proper analysis, including in particular, disagreements about the scope of ongoing emergencies that can undermine the conclusion that an out-of-court statement is testimonial and about the role of reliability factors in making that determination. These differences were more conspicuous in the opinions in *Williams*. It is difficult to predict where the Court will go, but among the most likely possibilities are:

1. A nominal continuation of the *Crawford* doctrine subject to continuing expansion of the scope of the ongoing emergency idea and a corresponding narrowing of the range of the Confrontation Clause, ultimately perhaps leaving little more than its application to formalized testimonial materials, akin to what Justice Thomas has long advocated, or even a narrower category;

2. Adoption of a version of *Crawford* that uses the two-part test consistently advocate by Justice Thomas, one that places strict constraints on the use of a narrowly defined category of testimonial statements, but also monitors governmental efforts to circumvent those constraints;

3. The replacement of *Crawford* with some new doctrinal formulation that emphasizes the reliability of the offered statement, not unlike the final

[223] The issue has surfaced in a New York case in which the defense indicated in opening statement that it would introduce certain evidence suggesting an alternative perpetrator, and the prosecution, arguing that the evidence would be misleading, responded by introducing a hearsay statement that would otherwise be inadmissible under *Crawford*. The New York courts affirmed the defendant's conviction, rejecting a Confrontation Clause challenge, but the Supreme Court took up the case, which was pending when this treatise went to press. People v. Hemphill, 150 N.E.3d 356 (N.Y. 2020), *cert. granted*, 141 S. Ct. 2510 (2021).

[224] Crawford v. Washington, 541 U.S. 36, 56 n.6 (2004).

[225] Giles v. California, 554 U.S. 353, 358–59 (2008) (citations omitted).

[226] *See* Peter Nicolas, *'I'm Dying to Tell You What Happened': The Admissibility of Testimonial Dying Declarations Post-Crawford*, 37 HASTINGS CONST. L.Q. 487 (2010); Aviva Orenstein, *Her Last Words: Dying Declarations and Modern Confrontation Jurisprudence*, 2010 U. ILL. L. REV. 1411.

[227] *Crawford*, 541 U.S. at 56 n.6.

[228] Michigan v. Bryant, 562 U.S. 344, 395 (2011) (Ginsburg, J., dissenting).

[229] *See, e.g.*, People v. Monterroso, 101 P.3d 956, 972 (Cal. 2005); Davis v. State, 207 So.3d 177, 198–205 (Fla. 2016); Commonwealth v. Nesbitt, 892 N.E.2d 299, 310–12 (Mass. 2008); State v. Martin, 695 N.W.2d 578, 583 (Minn. 2005); Harkins v. State, 143 P.3d 706, 709–11 (Nev. 2006).

form of *Ohio v. Roberts,* though possibly limited to a narrow category of testimonial statements;

4. The replacement of *Crawford* with a still different doctrine focused on monitoring the state's attempts to substitute hearsay for available live testimony; or
5. An ad hoc, balance-all-the-factors jurisprudence that provides maximal flexibility for the judiciary and minimal predictability for the practicing bar.

Finally, Justice Scalia's focus on history and the original practice of the Founders seemed to have profoundly altered how the Confrontation Clause is understood and applied. Justice Scalia analyzed confrontation as an essentially misunderstood and neglected constitutional demand and used the *Crawford* line of cases as a vehicle for espousing his theory of constitutional interpretation generally. Scalia signaled that policy arguments and practical issues have little or no place in Confrontation Clause analysis.[230] Although he would sometimes debate the real-world consequences of *Crawford,* he ultimately found them irrelevant; they could not defeat what would otherwise be the demand of the Sixth Amendment confrontation right.[231] Most of the rest of the Court's members have indicated some discomfort with the banishment of reliability analysis and other considerations of policy from Confrontation Clause jurisprudence. Even Justice Thomas is consequentialist insofar as he is willing to consider enforcing barriers against the ability of police and prosecutors to circumvent constitutional limitations. This portends change, as Justice Scalia clearly recognized in his later concurring opinions, but the exact direction of that change is difficult to anticipate.

§ 20.09 Adequacy of Confrontation

Most of this chapter addresses when the prosecution's introduction of hearsay triggers the protection of the Confrontation Clause. For this purpose, the opportunity to cross-examine the declarant has been taken as the principal guarantee that results from such protection. But the Clause entails other protections for the accused. This section examines the adequacy of the procedures used when confrontation is constitutionally required and the opportunities the defense must be afforded in confronting a witness. In the paradigmatically adequate procedure, the witness testifies in open court before the accused and the fact-finder and is required to respond to legitimate cross-examination by the defense. We consider variations on that paradigm arising in three situations: (1) when the witness testifies at trial and no hearsay from that witness is at issue; (2) when the witness testifies at trial and the witness's prior statements are admitted to prove the truth of the matter asserted under some hearsay exception; and, (3) when the witness

---

230 *Cf.* Maryland v. Craig, 497 U.S. 836, 869–70 (1990) (Scalia, J., dissenting) ("I have no need to defend the value of confrontation, because the Court has no authority to question it."). Justice's Scalia's preference for rules rather than mushy policy-based standards is evident throughout his jurisprudence. *See, e.g.,* Burnham v. Superior Court, 495 U.S. 604, 623 (1990) (bemoaning the "subjectivity, and hence inadequacy" of a "subjective assessment of what is fair and just" and advocating instead a reliance on tradition for assessing due process in personal jurisdiction).

231 Melendez-Diaz v. Massachusetts, 557 U.S. 305, 129 S. Ct. 2527, 2540–41 (2009) ("The Confrontation Clause may make the prosecution of criminals more burdensome, but that is equally true of the right to trial by jury and the privilege against self-incrimination. The Confrontation Clause—like those other constitutional provisions—is binding, and we may not disregard it at our convenience.").

does not testify at trial and the issue is the adequacy of confrontation that occurred on a previous occasion with respect to hearsay that is admitted.

The Testifying Witness; Hearsay Not at Issue

To what extent may the trial court use a divergent procedure for taking testimony at trial? This question arises most poignantly where a child-witness is a victim of a crime and cannot face the stress of looking the accused in the eye. Courts have struggled with whether alternative physical arrangements can substitute for face-to-face interaction.[232]

In 1988, in *Coy v. Iowa*,[233] the Court struck down the conviction of an accused where a screen had been erected between the defendant and the witness stand. The accused could dimly see the witnesses; the witnesses (two thirteen-year-old girls complaining of a sexual attack) were entirely shielded from the accused.[234] In remanding the conviction, the Court relied on "the irreducible literal meaning of the Clause," which guaranteed the "right to meet face to face all those who appear and give evidence at trial."[235] Reasoning that it is harder to lie to someone's face, the Court held that the face-to-face component of confrontation, like the right to cross examine, ensures "the integrity of the fact-finding process."[236]

Just two years later, however, in *Maryland v. Craig,* the Court permitted the use of one-way, closed-circuit television to display a witness's testimony despite the absence of eye contact between the witness and the accused.[237] The *Craig* Court found that the child-witness testifying about abuse by her teacher would suffer trauma if she had to look at the accused. The six-year-old girl testified in a room with only the prosecutor, defense attorney, camera operators, and a person to provide moral support for the child. The judge and the accused were in the courtroom watching the testimony on television. In explaining the apparent retreat from *Coy*, the *Craig* Court declared that the right of the accused to face-to-face confrontation is not absolute.[238] Writing for the majority, Justice O'Connor explained: "The central concern of the Confrontation Clause is to ensure the reliability of the evidence against a criminal defendant by subjecting it to rigorous testing in the context of an adversary proceeding before the trier of fact."[239] Arguing from this policy of reliability (an entirely plausible approach under the pre-*Crawford* regime of *Ohio v. Roberts*[240]), Justice O'Connor held that the purposes of the Confrontation Clause were satisfied by the witness's physical presence, the taking of an oath, subjection to cross-examination, and by the availability of demeanor evidence.[241] The Sixth Amendment established a *preference* for face-to-face confrontation at trial;[242]

---

232 A related issue concerns whether a witness, fearing for his or her safety, may testify in disguise. *See* Marc C. McAllister, *The Disguised Witness and* Crawford's *Uneasy Tension with* Craig: *Bringing Uniformity to the Supreme Court's Confrontation Jurisprudence,* 58 DRAKE L. REV. 481 (2010).

233 487 U.S. 1012 (1988).

234 *Id.* at 1014–15.

235 *Id.* at 1020–21.

236 *Id.* at 1020 (citations omitted).

237 497 U.S. 836 (1990).

238 *Id.* at 844.

239 *Id.* at 845.

240 *See* **§ 11.01**.

241 Maryland v. Craig, 497 U.S. 836, 846 (1990).

242 *Id.* at 849 (emphasis added) (quoting Ohio v. Roberts, 448 U.S. 56 (1980)).

however, this preference "must occasionally give way to considerations of public policy and the necessities of the case."[243]

Justice Scalia authored a strong dissent in *Craig*, joined by the liberal wing of the Court, Justices Brennan, Marshall, and Stevens, stating, "Seldom has this Court failed so conspicuously to sustain a categorical guarantee of the Constitution against the tide of prevailing current opinion."[244] Given the facts that Justice Scalia authored *Crawford*, that *Crawford* rejects judicial determinations of reliability in the context of the constitutional admissibility of hearsay, and that *Crawford* is unwavering in what it perceives to be the dictates of the Sixth Amendment right to confrontation, there is legitimate question about the continued viability of *Craig*.[245] So far, however, lower courts continue to apply *Craig*'s rule that nonstandard courtroom arrangements for testimony that do not involve fact-to-face confrontation be allowed when (a) "denial of such confrontation is necessary to further an important public policy" and (b) "the reliability of the testimony is otherwise assured."[246]

Deferred Confrontation of the Testifying Hearsay Declarant

When the witness takes the stand at trial, there are many hearsay exemptions and exceptions that would permit the introduction of hearsay statements previously made by the now testifying declarant.[247] If the hearsay statement was not subject to confrontation (cross-examination, and so forth) at the time it was made, the question arises whether the defendant's right to confront the witness later, at trial, suffices to allow the admission of the hearsay. The argument for the defense is that such "deferred" confrontation is inherently inadequate because it does not occur immediately after the hearsay utterance. In the intervening time, the witness may have the opportunity to come up with a good explanation of any weaknesses in his or her original statement.

As indicated earlier, the general answer to this question, ever since the Court's decision in *California v. Green*,[248] is that such deferred confrontation is, or at least can be, constitutionally adequate.[249] The fact that the direct testimony does not touch upon the hearsay at issue does not preclude its admission, because the defense is free to address the matter on cross.[250] Potential problems arise when the witness simply denies making the prior statement, claims (sincerely or not) to have lost memory, or refuses (or is unable) to respond meaningfully to cross-examination. In such situations, the cross-examination may be relatively ineffectual, and the issue is whether this undermines the logic of *Green* that the witness can be fully cross-examined about both the earlier

---

[243] *Id.* (citation omitted).

[244] *Id.* at 860 (Scalia, J., dissenting).

[245] *See* David M. Wagner, *The End of the "Virtually Constitutional"? The Confrontation Right and* Crawford v. Washington *as a Prelude to Reversal of* Maryland v. Craig, 19 REGENT U. L. REV. 469, 470 (2007) ("*Crawford v. Washington* contains dicta incompatible with *Maryland v. Craig* and portends that aberrant decision's downfall.").

[246] *Craig*, 497 U.S. at 840–41. *See, e.g.*, State v. Thomas, 376 P.3d 184, 193–95 (N.M. 2016) (holding *Craig* still good law after *Crawford* but applying *Craig* to disapprove of prosecution's use of "Skype" testimony by out-of-state forensic scientist; mere inconvenience of appearing in person to testify not important enough public policy reason to dispense with face-to-face confrontation).

[247] For a summary, see **§ 17.07**.

[248] California v. Green, 399 U.S. 149 (1970).

[249] The point was confirmed in *Crawford*. See Crawford v. Washington, 541 U.S. 36, 53–56 (2004).

[250] *See, e.g.*, United States v. Pursley, 577 F.3d 1204, 1224–25 (10th Cir. 2009), *cert. denied*, 558 U.S. 1130 (2010) (admitting hearsay where declarant testified at trial but did not recount making of hearsay statement).

statement and any present testimony. Defendants naturally argue that this is confrontation is name only. Prosecutors naturally argue that they have done all that can be expected of them by placing the witness on the stand and that defendants may invite the fact-finder to infer that any denial or claim of memory loss is feigned.

The case law since *Green* has been remarkably consistent in favoring the prosecution on this issue. Whether the witness asserts loss of memory only about the making of the hearsay statement or only about the underlying events, the courts have held that the confrontation was adequate and thus rejected confrontation challenges to the admissibility of the hearsay.[251] The Supreme Court itself, in the (pre-*Crawford*) leading case of *United States v. Owens*,[252] held that admission of a prior statement by a victim identifying the defendant as his attacker did not violate the Confrontation Clause even though the victim testified that he was (at the time of trial) unable to remember "seeing his assailant." He was able to describe some of the attack, and he remembered naming the defendant Owens as his assailant when interviewed three weeks after the attack. The Court stated that the opportunity to cross-examine can be constitutionally adequate even though it is unsuccessful in undermining the credibility of the prior statement.[253] In an oft-quoted passage drawn from an earlier decision, the Court stated, "[T]he Confrontation Clause guarantees only an *opportunity* for effective cross-examination, not cross-examination that is effective in whatever way, and to whatever extent, the defense might wish."[254]

Nevertheless, the occasional court does find the "opportunity" inadequate, at least when the declarant lacks memory of both the events and the earlier statement. For example, in one post-*Crawford* case,[255] a witness to and participant in the alleged improper sexual conduct of a teacher with one of her students gave a signed statement to the police about the event. Before trial, he was injured in an automobile accident and he could no longer remember the events, the parties, or his prior statement. The only positive testimony he could give was that he recognized his signature on the statement. Rightly or wrongly, the trial court admitted the statement as a prior recollection recorded. The Supreme Court of Mississippi reversed on the ground that there was no opportunity for effective cross-examination, so that admission of the statement violated the Confrontation Clause.[256]

Similarly, some courts have found Confrontation Clause violations when the declarant appears at trial but does not respond meaningfully to interrogation. The most frequently encountered examples are child witnesses. Post-*Crawford*, some courts have found unresponsive children to be unavailable for Confrontation Clause purposes,[257] while others have held that unresponsive children are testifying in the sense required

---

[251] *See* 4 CHRISTOPHER B. MUELLER & LAIRD C. KIRKPATRICK, FEDERAL EVIDENCE § 8:29 (4th ed. 2013).

[252] United States v. Owens, 484 U.S. 554 (1988).

[253] *Id* at 559–60.

[254] *Id.* at 559 (quoting Delaware v. Fensterer, 474 U.S. 15, 20 (1985) (emphasis in original).

[255] Goforth v. State, 70 So.3d 174 (Miss. 2011).

[256] *Id.* at 182–87.

[257] *See In re* T.T., 892 N.E.2d 1163, 1174 (Ill. App. Ct. 2008) (involving child victim who had identified the defendant in court and explained why she was in his home; child stopped answering when the questions became more specific about the alleged assault; the court declared her unavailable and ruled that her prior statements were not admissible); Howard v. State, 816 N.E.2d 948 (Ind. Ct. App. 2004) (concluding that twelve-year-old's refusal to testify due to embarrassment rendered her "unavailable").

by *Green* in order to support the constitutional admission of hearsay.[258] As discussed elsewhere, however, if the hearsay statements are determined to be nontestimonial, they may be constitutionally admissible even if the child is entirely unresponsive on the stand.[259]

Prior Confrontation of a Nontestifying Hearsay Declarant

Under most constitutional standards, including both the *Roberts* and *Crawford* tests, situations arise in which an unavailable declarant's hearsay is constitutionally admissible at trial because it was testimony given at a prior trial or hearing, subject to confrontation at that time. Confrontation at the earlier time is not the equivalent of later confrontation at trial, especially in the common absence of a video-tape of the prior examination. Typically, a written transcript of the earlier hearing is introduced, and the fact-finder at trial cannot perceive the absent witness's demeanor. Nevertheless, both *Roberts* and *Crawford* clearly hold prior Confrontation can be sufficient. The accused may challenge the conditions under which the testimony was given at the earlier hearing, and the opportunities available to the defense at that time must have complied with the rules in *Coy* and *Craig*.[260] Beyond that, two additional issues arise.

First, in the case of testimony given *at a preliminary hearing*, as a matter of strategy the defense may forego rigorous cross-examination of a witness until trial, and the question arises whether this foregone opportunity to confront the witness will satisfy the requirements of the Clause. Older case law held that such a choice does not constitute a waiver of the right to confront the witness at trial.[261] But that may not be the end of the matter, given the Court's recurring emphasis on the existence of an opportunity, however well utilized.[262]

Second, a question arises concerning out-of-court statements made outside the context of the earlier hearing at which confrontation was allowed. For example, often an alleged victim will have made statements implicating the defendant before the preliminary hearing takes place. If these statements were "testimonial" and thus within the scope of the Clause under *Crawford*, then the question arises whether an adequate opportunity to confront the witness at the preliminary hearing will satisfy the Clause so as to permit as well the introduction of the out-of-court statements when the declarant is unavailable to testify at trial. Although the issue does not appear to have been decided, a good argument can be made within the *Crawford* framework for the proposition that

---

[258] *See, e.g.,* United States v. Kappell, 418 F.3d 550, 554 (6th Cir. 2005), *cert. denied,* 547 U.S. 1056 (2006) (admitting hearsay of children aged three and six describing sexual abuse despite their becoming unresponsive and inarticulate during cross-examination).

[259] *See* **§ 20.08**.

[260] *See, e.g.,* People v. Gonzales, 281 P.3d 834, 859–64 (Cal. 2012), *cert. denied,* 133 S. Ct. 876 (2013) (rejecting challenge to the admissibility of the video-tape of a child's preliminary hearing testimony, subject to cross-examination, on grounds of denial of face-to-face confrontation at the earlier hearing because of child's fear of defendant; *Craig* standards endorsed in this context, even after the Supreme Court's decision in *Crawford*).

[261] *See* Barber v. Page, 390 U.S. 719, 725 (1968) (in context where witness providing preliminary hearing testimony ended up in prison and was not called by the prosecution, holding that defendant did not waive right to confront the witness at trial, because the defendant could not be expected to assume that the witness would not be called at trial.).

[262] An interesting parallel here is the situation of the prosecution in regard to grand jury testimony and preliminary hearing testimony when the question is whether the prosecution had a "similar motive and opportunity" to develop the testimony as they would at trial, an issue that can arise when the defendant wants to offer the grand jury testimony of a declarant who is not available to testify at trial. *See* **§ 17.02** (subsection on "Similar Motive to Develop Testimony").

the out-of-court statement is not admissible unless it was introduced at the earlier hearing and thus subject to confrontation at that time.[263]

§ 20.10 Confrontation and the Special Rule of *Bruton*

One well-established subcategory of the confrontation doctrine is the rule about co-defendant confessions created by *Bruton v. United States*.[264] In *Bruton* two co-defendants were tried together. The confession of one, implicating both, was admitted by the trial judge, with instructions to the jury not to use it against the nonconfessing co-defendant. The Supreme Court held that this procedure violated the Confrontation Clause. The limiting instruction was not sufficient to eliminate the danger that the jury would use the instruction against both defendants. The danger that the defendant would be convicted by the statement of someone he could not cross-examine could have been avoided by severing the trials.

A redacted confession of a co-defendant that does not mention the defendant by name, and that has only an indirect, inferential incriminating effect, may be received in a joint trial without violating the Confrontation Clause.[265] A purely mechanical redaction of names does not, however, always solve the *Bruton* problem. In *Gray v. Maryland*,[266] the Supreme Court held that redacting the confession of a nontestifying co-defendant by blanking out the name in a written exhibit, or substituting the word "deletion" in oral testimony, did not satisfy the requirements of *Bruton* because the jury would realize that the confession referred to the defendant.

A number of courts have refused to apply *Bruton* to statements that do not fit within *Crawford's* definition of testimonial statements.[267] This result has been criticized.[268] Moreover, even if the Confrontation Clause may not apply because the statements involved are nontestimonial, a constitutional argument based on the Due Process Clause may serve to limit admission of confessions by co-defendants in the same trial. If the co-defendant's confession is inadmissible hearsay against the accused, then even if it is nontestimonial, Due Process may require severing the trials of the two defendants.

---

[263] *See* 4 CHRISTOPHER B. MUELLER & LAIRD C. KIRKPATRICK, FEDERAL EVIDENCE § 8:28 at 251–53. (4th ed. 2013).

[264] 391 U.S. 123 (1968). Despite *Bruton*, confessions of co-defendants were sometimes admitted as declarations against interest when the statement implicating the defendant was against the declarant's interest. *See* **§ 17.04**. Post-*Crawford* any such statements that qualify as testimonial will be inadmissible.

[265] Richardson v. Marsh, 481 U.S. 200 (1987); *see* United States v. Washington, 952 F.2d 1402, 1406–07 (D.C. Cir. 1991) (holding that "where—as here—all references to the defendant in a codefendant's statement are replaced with indefinite pronouns or other general terms, the Confrontation Clause is not violated by the redacted statement's admission if, when viewed together with other evidence, the statement does not create an inevitable association with the defendant, and a proper limiting instruction is given.").

[266] 523 U.S. 185 (1998). For fuller discussion of the implications of *Gray*, see DAVID P. LEONARD, THE NEW WIGMORE: A TREATISE ON EVIDENCE: SELECTED RULES OF LIMITED ADMISSIBILITY § 1.10 (rev. ed. 2002).

[267] *See* United States v. Dale, 614 F.3d 942, 956 (8th Cir. 2010) ("Whereas in *Bruton* the incriminating statement was the product of a formal interrogation and therefore testimonial, the incriminating statements made by Dale here were made unwittingly, and not in anticipation by Dale of future use of the statements at trial. Under our present understanding of the confrontation right, governed by *Crawford,* the introduction of Dale's out of court statements did not violate Johnson's confrontation right."); United States v. Castro-Davis, 612 F.3d 53, 65–66 (1st Cir.2010) (finding defendant's recorded telephone statements to his mother nontestimonial and holding that "the *Bruton* rule does not apply to nontestimonial hearsay statements. Since we have determined that the recorded conversation was nontestimonial, *Bruton* is not implicated.") (citations omitted); United States v. Smalls, 605 F.3d 765, 768 n.2 (10th Cir. 2010); *but see* United States v. Williams, 2010 WL 3909480 at *3 (E.D. Va. 2010) (arguing that applying *Crawford* to *Bruton* would render it a nullity).

[268] *See, e.g.,* Colin Miller, *Avoiding a Confrontation? How Courts Have Erred in Finding That Nontestimonial Hearsay is Beyond the Scope of the* Bruton *Doctrine*, 77 BROOKLYN L. REV. 625 (2016).

Furthermore, even if the argument does not rise to the level of a constitutional right, Rule 403 should apply to preclude the immense unfair prejudice of allowing the jury to hear the confession.

Appendix

FEDERAL RULES OF EVIDENCE FOR UNITED STATES COURTS

Effective July 1, 1975, as amended through September 1, 2021.

SUMMARY OF RULES

ARTICLE I. GENERAL PROVISIONS

Rule 101. Scope; Definitions

(a) **Scope.** These rules apply to proceedings in United States courts. The specific courts and proceedings to which the rules apply, along with exceptions, are set out in Rule 1101.

(b) **Definitions.** In these rules:

(1) "civil case" means a civil action or proceeding;

(2) "criminal case" includes a criminal proceeding;

(3) "public office" includes a public agency;

(4) "record" includes a memorandum, report, or data compilation;

(5) a "rule prescribed by the Supreme Court" means a rule adopted by the Supreme Court under statutory authority; and

(6) a reference to any kind of written material or any other medium includes electronically stored information.

Rule 102. Purpose

These rules should be construed so as to administer every proceeding fairly, eliminate unjustifiable expense and delay, and promote the development of evidence law, to the end of ascertaining the truth and securing a just determination.

Rule 103. Rulings on Evidence

(a) **Preserving a Claim of Error.** A party may claim error in a ruling to admit or exclude evidence only if the error affects a substantial right of the party and:

   (1) if the ruling admits evidence, a party, on the record:

      (A) timely objects or moves to strike; and

      (B) states the specific ground, unless it was apparent from the context; or

   (2) if the ruling excludes evidence, a party informs the court of its substance by an offer of proof, unless the substance was apparent from the context.

(b) **Not Needing to Renew an Objection or Offer of Proof.** Once the court rules definitively on the record—either before or at trial—a party need not renew an objection or offer of proof to preserve a claim of error for appeal.

(c) **Court's Statement About the Ruling; Directing an Offer of Proof.** The court may make any statement about the character or form of the evidence, the objection made, and the ruling. The court may direct that an offer of proof be made in question and-answer form.

(d) **Preventing the Jury from Hearing Inadmissible Evidence.** To the extent practicable, the court must conduct a jury trial so that inadmissible evidence is not suggested to the jury by any means.

(e) **Taking Notice of Plain Error.** A court may take notice of a plain error affecting a substantial right, even if the claim of error was not properly preserved.

Rule 104. Preliminary Questions

(a) **In General.** The court must decide any preliminary question about whether a witness is qualified, a privilege exists, or evidence is admissible. In so deciding, the court is not bound by evidence rules, except those on privilege.

(b) **Relevance That Depends on a Fact.** When the relevance of evidence depends on whether a fact exists, proof must be introduced sufficient to support a finding that the fact does exist. The court may admit the proposed evidence on the condition that the proof be introduced later.

(c) **Conducting a Hearing So That the Jury Cannot Hear It.** The court must conduct any hearing on a preliminary question so that the jury cannot hear it if:

   (1) the hearing involves the admissibility of a confession;

   (2) a defendant in a criminal case is a witness and so requests; or

   (3) justice so requires.

(d) **Cross-Examining a Defendant in a Criminal Case.** By testifying on a preliminary question, a defendant in a criminal case does not become subject to cross-examination on other issues in the case.

(e) **Evidence Relevant to Weight and Credibility.** This rule does not limit a party's right to introduce before the jury evidence that is relevant to the weight or credibility of other evidence.

Rule 105. Limiting Evidence That Is Not Admissible Against Other Parties or for Other Purposes

If the court admits evidence that is admissible against a party or for a purpose—but not against another party or for another purpose—the court, on timely request, must restrict the evidence to its proper scope and instruct the jury accordingly.

Rule 106. Remainder of or Related Writings or Recorded Statements

If a party introduces all or part of a writing or recorded statement, an adverse party may require the introduction, at that time, of any other part—or any other writing or recorded statement—that in fairness ought to be considered at the same time.

ARTICLE II. JUDICIAL NOTICE

Rule 201. Judicial Notice of Adjudicative Facts

(a) **Scope.** This rule governs judicial notice of an adjudicative fact only, not a legislative fact.

(b) **Kinds of Facts That May Be Judicially Noticed.** The court may judicially notice a fact that is not subject to reasonable dispute because it:

  (1) is generally known within the trial court's territorial jurisdiction; or

  (2) can be accurately and readily determined from sources whose accuracy cannot reasonably be questioned.

(c) **Taking Notice.** The court:

  (1) may take judicial notice on its own; or

  (2) must take judicial notice if a party requests it and the court is supplied with the necessary information.

(d) **Timing.** The court may take judicial notice at any stage of the proceeding.

(e) **Opportunity to Be Heard.** On timely request, a party is entitled to be heard on the propriety of taking judicial notice and the nature of the fact to be noticed. If the court takes judicial notice before notifying a party, the party, on request, is still entitled to be heard.

(f) **Instructing the Jury.** In a civil case, the court must instruct the jury to accept the noticed fact as conclusive. In a criminal case, the court must instruct the jury that it may or may not accept the noticed fact as conclusive.

ARTICLE III. PRESUMPTIONS IN CIVIL CASES

Rule 301. Presumptions in Civil Cases Generally

In a civil case, unless a federal statute or these rules provide otherwise, the party against whom a presumption is directed has the burden of producing evidence to rebut the presumption. But this rule does not shift the burden of persuasion, which remains on the party who had it originally.

Rule 302. Applying State Law to Presumptions in Civil Cases

In a civil case, state law governs the effect of a presumption regarding a claim or defense for which state law supplies the rule of decision.

ARTICLE IV. RELEVANCE AND ITS LIMITS

Rule 401. Test for Relevant Evidence

Evidence is relevant if:

(a) it has any tendency to make a fact more or less probable than it would be without the evidence; and

(b) the fact is of consequence in determining the action.

Rule 402. General Admissibility of Relevant Evidence

Relevant evidence is admissible unless any of the following provides otherwise:

- the United States Constitution;
- a federal statute;
- these rules; or
- other rules prescribed by the Supreme Court.

Irrelevant evidence is not admissible.

Rule 403. Excluding Relevant Evidence for Prejudice, Confusion, Waste of Time, or Other Reasons

The court may exclude relevant evidence if its probative value is substantially outweighed by a danger of one or more of the following: unfair prejudice, confusing the issues, misleading the jury, undue delay, wasting time, or needlessly presenting cumulative evidence.

Rule 404. Character Evidence; Crimes or Other Acts

(a) **Character Evidence.**

(1) *Prohibited Uses.* Evidence of a person's character or character trait is not admissible to prove that on a particular occasion the person acted in accordance with the character or trait.

(2) *Exceptions for a Defendant or Victim in a Criminal Case.* The following exceptions apply in a criminal case:

(A) a defendant may offer evidence of the defendant's pertinent trait, and if the evidence is admitted, the prosecutor may offer evidence to rebut it;

(B) subject to the limitations in Rule 412, a defendant may offer evidence of an alleged victim's pertinent trait, and if the evidence is admitted, the prosecutor may:

(i) offer evidence to rebut it; and

(ii) offer evidence of the defendant's same trait; and

(C) in a homicide case, the prosecutor may offer evidence of the alleged victim's trait of peacefulness to rebut evidence that the victim was the first aggressor.

(3) *Exceptions for a Witness.* Evidence of a witness's character may be admitted under Rules 607, 608, and 609.

(b) **Other Crimes, Wrongs, or Acts.**

(1) *Prohibited Uses.* Evidence of a crime, wrong, or other act is not admissible to prove a person's character in order to show that on a particular occasion the person acted in accordance with the character.

(2) *Permitted Uses.* This evidence may be admissible for another purpose, such as proving motive, opportunity, intent, preparation, plan, knowledge, identity, absence of mistake, or lack of accident.

(3) *Notice in a Criminal Case.* In a criminal case, the prosecutor must:

(A) provide reasonable notice of any such evidence that the prosecutor intends to offer at trial;

(B) articulate in the notice the permitted purpose for which the prosecutor intends to offer the evidence and the reasoning that supports the purpose; and

(C) do so in writing before trial—or in any form during trial if the court, for good cause, excuses lack of pretrial notice.

Rule 405. Methods of Proving Character

(a) **By Reputation or Opinion.** When evidence of a person's character or character trait is admissible, it may be proved by testimony about the person's reputation or by testimony in the form of an opinion. On cross-examination of the character witness, the court may allow an inquiry into relevant specific instances of the person's conduct.

(b) **By Specific Instances of Conduct.** When a person's character or character trait is an essential element of a charge, claim, or defense, the character or trait may also be proved by relevant specific instances of the person's conduct.

Rule 406. Habit; Routine Practice

Evidence of a person's habit or an organization's routine practice may be admitted to prove that on a particular occasion the person or organization acted in accordance with the habit or routine practice. The court may admit this evidence regardless of whether it is corroborated or whether there was an eyewitness.

Rule 407. Subsequent Remedial Measures

When measures are taken that would have made an earlier injury or harm less likely to occur, evidence of the subsequent measures is not admissible to prove:

- negligence;
- culpable conduct;
- a defect in a product or its design; or
- a need for a warning or instruction.

But the court may admit this evidence for another purpose, such as impeachment or—if disputed—proving ownership, control, or the feasibility of precautionary measures.

Rule 408. Compromise Offers and Negotiations

(a) **Prohibited Uses.** Evidence of the following is not admissible—on behalf of any party—either to prove or disprove the validity or amount of a disputed claim or to impeach by a prior inconsistent statement or a contradiction:

(1) furnishing, promising, or offering—or accepting, promising to accept, or offering to accept—a valuable consideration in compromising or attempting to compromise the claim; and

(2) conduct or a statement made during compromise negotiations about the claim—except when offered in a criminal case and when the negotiations related to a claim by a public office in the exercise of its regulatory, investigative, or enforcement authority.

(b) **Exceptions.** The court may admit this evidence for another purpose, such as proving a witness's bias or prejudice, negating a contention of undue delay, or proving an effort to obstruct a criminal investigation or prosecution.

Rule 409. Offers to Pay Medical and Similar Expenses

Evidence of furnishing, promising to pay, or offering to pay medical, hospital, or similar expenses resulting from an injury is not admissible to prove liability for the injury.

Rule 410. Pleas, Plea Discussions, and Related Statements

(a) **Prohibited Uses.** In a civil or criminal case, evidence of the following is not admissible against the defendant who made the plea or participated in the plea discussions:

(1) a guilty plea that was later withdrawn;

(2) a nolo contendere plea;

(3) a statement made during a proceeding on either of those pleas under Federal Rule of Criminal Procedure 11 or a comparable state procedure; or

(4) a statement made during plea discussions with an attorney for the prosecuting authority if the discussions did not result in a guilty plea or they resulted in a later-withdrawn guilty plea.

(b) **Exceptions.** The court may admit a statement described in Rule 410(a)(3) or (4):

(1) in any proceeding in which another statement made during the same plea or plea discussions has been introduced, if in fairness the statements ought to be considered together; or

(2) in a criminal proceeding for perjury or false statement, if the defendant made the statement under oath, on the record, and with counsel present.

Rule 411. Liability Insurance

Evidence that a person was or was not insured against liability is not admissible to prove whether the person acted negligently or otherwise wrongfully. But the court may admit this evidence for another purpose, such as proving a witness's bias or prejudice or proving agency, ownership, or control.

Rule 412. Sex-Offense Cases: The Victim's Sexual Behavior or Pre-disposition

(a) **Prohibited Uses.** The following evidence is not admissible in a civil or criminal proceeding involving alleged sexual misconduct:

(1) evidence offered to prove that a victim engaged in other sexual behavior; or

(2) evidence offered to prove a victim's sexual predisposition.

(b) **Exceptions.**

(1) ***Criminal Cases.*** The court may admit the following evidence in a criminal case:

(A) evidence of specific instances of a victim's sexual behavior, if offered to prove that someone other than the defendant was the source of semen, injury, or other physical evidence;

(B) evidence of specific instances of a victim's sexual behavior with respect to the person accused of the sexual misconduct, if offered by the defendant to prove consent or if offered by the prosecutor; and

(C) evidence whose exclusion would violate the defendant's constitutional rights.

(2) ***Civil Cases.*** In a civil case, the court may admit evidence offered to prove a victim's sexual behavior or sexual predisposition if its probative value substantially outweighs the danger of harm to any victim and of unfair prejudice to any party. The court may admit evidence of a victim's reputation only if the victim has placed it in controversy.

(c) **Procedure to Determine Admissibility.**

(1) *Motion.* If a party intends to offer evidence under Rule 412(b), the party must:

(A) file a motion that specifically describes the evidence and states the purpose for which it is to be offered;

(B) do so at least 14 days before trial unless the court, for good cause, sets a different time;

(C) serve the motion on all parties; and

(D) notify the victim or, when appropriate, the victim's guardian or representative.

(2) *Hearing.* Before admitting evidence under this rule, the court must conduct an in camera hearing and give the victim and parties a right to attend and be heard. Unless the court orders otherwise, the motion, related materials, and the record of the hearing must be and remain sealed.

(d) **Definition of "Victim."** In this rule, "victim" includes an alleged victim.

Rule 413. Similar Crimes in Sexual-Assault Cases

(a) **Permitted Uses.** In a criminal case in which a defendant is accused of a sexual assault, the court may admit evidence that the defendant committed any other sexual assault. The evidence may be considered on any matter to which it is relevant.

(b) **Disclosure to the Defendant.** If the prosecutor intends to offer this evidence, the prosecutor must disclose it to the defendant, including witnesses' statements or a summary of the expected testimony. The prosecutor must do so at least 15 days before trial or at a later time that the court allows for good cause.

(c) **Effect on Other Rules.** This rule does not limit the admission or consideration of evidence under any other rule.

(d) **Definition of "Sexual Assault."** In this rule and Rule 415, "sexual assault" means a crime under federal law or under state law (as "state" is defined in 18 U.S.C. § 513) involving:

(1) any conduct prohibited by 18 U.S.C. chapter 109A;

(2) contact, without consent, between any part of the defendant's body—or an object—and another person's genitals or anus;

(3) contact, without consent, between the defendant's genitals or anus and any part of another person's body;

(4) deriving sexual pleasure or gratification from inflicting death, bodily injury, or physical pain on another person; or

(5) an attempt or conspiracy to engage in conduct described in subparagraphs (1)–(4).

Rule 414. Similar Crimes in Child-Molestation Cases

(a) **Permitted Uses.** In a criminal case in which a defendant is accused of child molestation, the court may admit evidence that the defendant committed any other child molestation. The evidence may be considered on any matter to which it is relevant.

(b) **Disclosure to the Defendant.** If the prosecutor intends to offer this evidence, the prosecutor must disclose it to the defendant, including witnesses' statements or a summary of the expected testimony. The prosecutor must do so at least 15 days before trial or at a later time that the court allows for good cause.

(c) **Effect on Other Rules.** This rule does not limit the admission or consideration of evidence under any other rule.

(d) **Definition of "Child" and "Child Molestation."** In this rule and Rule 415:

(1) "child" means a person below the age of 14; and

(2) "child molestation" means a crime under federal law or under state law (as "state" is defined in 18 U.S.C. § 513) involving:

(A) any conduct prohibited by 18 U.S.C. chapter 109A and committed with a child;

(B) any conduct prohibited by 18 U.S.C. chapter 110;

(C) contact between any part of the defendant's body—or an object—and a child's genitals or anus;

(D) contact between the defendant's genitals or anus and any part of a child's body;

(E) deriving sexual pleasure or gratification from inflicting death, bodily injury, or physical pain on a child; or

(F) an attempt or conspiracy to engage in conduct described in subparagraphs (A)–(E).

Rule 415. Similar Acts in Civil Cases Involving Sexual Assault or Child Molestation

(a) **Permitted Uses.** In a civil case involving a claim for relief based on a party's alleged sexual assault or child molestation, the court may admit evidence that the party committed any other sexual assault or child molestation. The evidence may be considered as provided in Rules 413 and 414.

(b) **Disclosure to the Opponent.** If a party intends to offer this evidence, the party must disclose it to the party against whom it will be offered, including witnesses' statements or a summary of the expected testimony. The party must do so at least 15 days before trial or at a later time that the court allows for good cause.

(c) **Effect on Other Rules.** This rule does not limit the admission or consideration of evidence under any other rule.

ARTICLE V. PRIVILEGES

Rule 501. Privilege in General

The common law—as interpreted by United States courts in the light of reason and experience—governs a claim of privilege unless any of the following provides otherwise:

- the United States Constitution;
- a federal statute; or
- rules prescribed by the Supreme Court.

But in a civil case, state law governs privilege regarding a claim or defense for which state law supplies the rule of decision.

Rule 502. Attorney-Client Privilege and Work Product; Limitations on Waiver

The following provisions apply, in the circumstances set out, to disclosure of a communication or information covered by the attorney-client privilege or work-product protection.

(a) **Disclosure Made in a Federal Proceeding or to a Federal Office or Agency; Scope of a Waiver.** When the disclosure is made in a federal proceeding or to a federal office or agency and waives the attorney-client privilege or work-product protection, the waiver extends to an undisclosed communication or information in a federal or state proceeding only if:

(1) the waiver is intentional;

(2) the disclosed and undisclosed communications or information concern the same subject matter; and

(3) they ought in fairness to be considered together.

(b) **Inadvertent Disclosure.** When made in a federal proceeding or to a federal office or agency, the disclosure does not operate as a waiver in a federal or state proceeding if:

(1) the disclosure is inadvertent;

(2) the holder of the privilege or protection took reasonable steps to prevent disclosure; and

(3) the holder promptly took reasonable steps to rectify the error, including (if applicable) following Federal Rule of Civil Procedure 26(b)(5)(B).

(c) **Disclosure Made in a State Proceeding.** When the disclosure is made in a state proceeding and is not the subject of a state-court order concerning waiver, the disclosure does not operate as a waiver in a federal proceeding if the disclosure:

(1) would not be a waiver under this rule if it had been made in a federal proceeding; or

(2) is not a waiver under the law of the state where the disclosure occurred.

(d) **Controlling Effect of a Court Order.** A federal court may order that the privilege or protection is not waived by disclosure connected with the litigation pending before the court—in which event the disclosure is also not a waiver in any other federal or state proceeding.

(e) **Controlling Effect of a Party Agreement.** An agreement on the effect of disclosure in a federal proceeding is binding only on the parties to the agreement, unless it is incorporated into a court order.

(f) **Controlling Effect of this Rule.** Notwithstanding Rules 101 and 1101, this rule applies to state proceedings and to federal court-annexed and federal court-mandated arbitration proceedings, in the circumstances set out in the rule. And notwithstanding Rule 501, this rule applies even if state law provides the rule of decision.

(g) **Definitions.** In this rule:

(1) "attorney-client privilege" means the protection that applicable law provides for confidential attorney-client communications; and

(2) "work-product protection" means the protection that applicable law provides for tangible material (or its intangible equivalent) prepared in anticipation of litigation or for trial.

ARTICLE VI. WITNESSES

Rule 601. Competency to Testify in General

Every person is competent to be a witness unless these rules provide otherwise. But in a civil case, state law governs the witness's competency regarding a claim or defense for which state law supplies the rule of decision.

Rule 602. Need for Personal Knowledge

A witness may testify to a matter only if evidence is introduced sufficient to support a finding that the witness has personal knowledge of the matter. Evidence to prove personal knowledge may consist of the witness's own testimony. This rule does not apply to a witness's expert testimony under Rule 703.

Rule 603. Oath or Affirmation to Testify Truthfully

Before testifying, a witness must give an oath or affirmation to testify truthfully. It must be in a form designed to impress that duty on the witness's conscience.

Rule 604. Interpreter

An interpreter must be qualified and must give an oath or affirmation to make a true translation.

Rule 605. Judge's Competency as a Witness

The presiding judge may not testify as a witness at the trial. A party need not object to preserve the issue.

Rule 606. Juror's Competency as a Witness

(a) **At the Trial.** A juror may not testify as a witness before the other jurors at the trial. If a juror is called to testify, the court must give a party an opportunity to object outside the jury's presence.

(b) **During an Inquiry into the Validity of a Verdict or Indictment.**

(1) ***Prohibited Testimony or Other Evidence.*** During an inquiry into the validity of a verdict or indictment, a juror may not testify about any statement made or incident that occurred during the jury's deliberations; the effect of anything on that juror's or another juror's vote; or any juror's mental processes concerning the verdict or indictment. The court may not receive a juror's affidavit or evidence of a juror's statement on these matters.

(2) ***Exceptions.*** A juror may testify about whether:

(A) extraneous prejudicial information was improperly brought to the jury's attention;

(B) an outside influence was improperly brought to bear on any juror; or

(C) a mistake was made in entering the verdict on the verdict form.

Rule 607. Who May Impeach a Witness

Any party, including the party that called the witness, may attack the witness's credibility.

Rule 608. A Witness's Character for Truthfulness or Untruthfulness

(a) **Reputation or Opinion Evidence.** A witness's credibility may be attacked or supported by testimony about the witness's reputation for having a character for truthfulness or untruthfulness, or by testimony in the form of an opinion about that character. But evidence of truthful character is admissible only after the witness's character for truthfulness has been attacked.

(b) **Specific Instances of Conduct.** Except for a criminal conviction under Rule 609, extrinsic evidence is not admissible to prove specific instances of a witness's conduct in order to attack or support the witness's character for truthfulness. But the court may, on cross-examination, allow them to be inquired into if they are probative of the character for truthfulness or untruthfulness of:

(1) the witness; or

(2) another witness whose character the witness being cross-examined has testified about.

By testifying on another matter, a witness does not waive any privilege against self-incrimination for testimony that relates only to the witness's character for truthfulness.

Rule 609. Impeachment by Evidence of a Criminal Conviction

(a) **In General.** The following rules apply to attacking a witness's character for truthfulness by evidence of a criminal conviction:

(1) for a crime that, in the convicting jurisdiction, was punishable by death or by imprisonment for more than one year, the evidence:

(A) must be admitted, subject to Rule 403, in a civil case or in a criminal case in which the witness is not a defendant; and

(B) must be admitted in a criminal case in which the witness is a defendant, if the probative value of the evidence outweighs its prejudicial effect to that defendant; and

(2) for any crime regardless of the punishment, the evidence must be admitted if the court can readily determine that establishing the elements of the crime required proving—or the witness's admitting—a dishonest act or false statement.

(b) **Limit on Using the Evidence After 10 Years.** This subdivision (b) applies if more than 10 years have passed since the witness's conviction or release from confinement for it, whichever is later. Evidence of the conviction is admissible only if:

(1) its probative value, supported by specific facts and circumstances, substantially outweighs its prejudicial effect; and

(2) the proponent gives an adverse party reasonable written notice of the intent to use it so that the party has a fair opportunity to contest its use.

(c) **Effect of a Pardon, Annulment, or Certificate of Rehabilitation.** Evidence of a conviction is not admissible if:

(1) the conviction has been the subject of a pardon, annulment, certificate of rehabilitation, or other equivalent procedure based on a finding that the person has been rehabilitated, and the person has not been convicted of a later crime punishable by death or by imprisonment for more than one year; or

(2) the conviction has been the subject of a pardon, annulment, or other equivalent procedure based on a finding of innocence.

(d) **Juvenile Adjudications.** Evidence of a juvenile adjudication is admissible under this rule only if:

(1) it is offered in a criminal case;

(2) the adjudication was of a witness other than the defendant;

(3) an adult's conviction for that offense would be admissible to attack the adult's credibility; and

(4) admitting the evidence is necessary to fairly determine guilt or innocence.

(e) **Pendency of an Appeal.** A conviction that satisfies this rule is admissible even if an appeal is pending. Evidence of the pendency is also admissible.

Rule 610. Religious Beliefs or Opinions

Evidence of a witness's religious beliefs or opinions is not admissible to attack or support the witness's credibility.

Rule 611. Mode and Order of Examining Witnesses and Presenting Evidence

(a) **Control by the Court; Purposes.** The court should exercise reasonable control over the mode and order of examining witnesses and presenting evidence so as to:

(1) make those procedures effective for determining the truth;

(2) avoid wasting time; and

(3) protect witnesses from harassment or undue embarrassment.

(b) **Scope of Cross-Examination.** Cross-examination should not go beyond the subject matter of the direct examination and matters affecting the witness's credibility. The court may allow inquiry into additional matters as if on direct examination.

(c) **Leading Questions.** Leading questions should not be used on direct examination except as necessary to develop the witness's testimony. Ordinarily, the court should allow leading questions:

(1) on cross-examination; and

(2) when a party calls a hostile witness, an adverse party, or a witness identified with an adverse party.

Rule 612. Writing Used to Refresh a Witness's Memory

(a) **Scope.** This rule gives an adverse party certain options when a witness uses a writing to refresh memory:

(1) while testifying; or

(2) before testifying, if the court decides that justice requires the party to have those options.

(b) **Adverse Party's Options; Deleting Unrelated Matter.** Unless 18 U.S.C. § 3500 provides otherwise in a criminal case, an adverse party is entitled to have the writing produced at the hearing, to inspect it, to cross-examine the witness about it, and to introduce in evidence any portion that relates to the witness's testimony. If the producing party claims that the writing includes unrelated matter, the court must examine the writing in camera, delete any unrelated portion, and order that the rest be delivered to the adverse party. Any portion deleted over objection must be preserved for the record.

(c) **Failure to Produce or Deliver the Writing.** If a writing is not produced or is not delivered as ordered, the court may issue any appropriate order. But if the prosecution does not comply in a criminal case, the court must strike the witness's testimony or—if justice so requires—declare a mistrial.

Rule 613. Witness's Prior Statement

(a) **Showing or Disclosing the Statement During Examination.** When examining a witness about the witness's prior statement, a party need not show it or disclose its contents to the witness. But the party must, on request, show it or disclose its contents to an adverse party's attorney.

(b) **Extrinsic Evidence of a Prior Inconsistent Statement.** Extrinsic evidence of a witness's prior inconsistent statement is admissible only if the witness is given an opportunity to explain or deny the statement and an adverse party is given an opportunity to examine the witness about it, or if justice so requires. This subdivision (b) does not apply to an opposing party's statement under Rule 801(d)(2).

Rule 614. Court's Calling or Examining a Witness

(a) **Calling.** The court may call a witness on its own or at a party's request. Each party is entitled to cross-examine the witness.

(b) **Examining.** The court may examine a witness regardless of who calls the witness.

(c) **Objections.** A party may object to the court's calling or examining a witness either at that time or at the next opportunity when the jury is not present.

Rule 615. Excluding Witnesses

At a party's request, the court must order witnesses excluded so that they cannot hear other witnesses' testimony. Or the court may do so on its own. But this rule does not authorize excluding:

(a) a party who is a natural person;

(b) an officer or employee of a party that is not a natural person, after being designated as the party's representative by its attorney;

(c) a person whose presence a party shows to be essential to presenting the party's claim or defense; or

(d) a person authorized by statute to be present.

ARTICLE VII. OPINIONS AND EXPERT TESTIMONY

Rule 701. Opinion Testimony by Lay Witnesses

If a witness is not testifying as an expert, testimony in the form of an opinion is limited to one that is:

(a) rationally based on the witness's perception;

(b) helpful to clearly understanding the witness's testimony or to determining a fact in issue; and

(c) not based on scientific, technical, or other specialized knowledge within the scope of Rule 702.

Rule 702. Testimony by Expert Witnesses

A witness who is qualified as an expert by knowledge, skill, experience, training, or education may testify in the form of an opinion or otherwise if:

(a) the expert's scientific, technical, or other specialized knowledge will help the trier of fact to understand the evidence or to determine a fact in issue;

(b) the testimony is based on sufficient facts or data;

(c) the testimony is the product of reliable principles and methods; and

(d) the expert has reliably applied the principles and methods to the facts of the case.

Rule 703. Bases of an Expert's Opinion Testimony

An expert may base an opinion on facts or data in the case that the expert has been made aware of or personally observed. If experts in the particular field would reasonably rely on those kinds of facts or data in forming an opinion on the subject, they need not be admissible for the opinion to be admitted. But if the facts or data would otherwise be inadmissible, the proponent of the opinion may disclose them to the jury only if their probative value in helping the jury evaluate the opinion substantially outweighs their prejudicial effect.

Rule 704. Opinion on an Ultimate Issue

(a) **In General—Not Automatically Objectionable.** An opinion is not objectionable just because it embraces an ultimate issue.

(b) **Exception.** In a criminal case, an expert witness must not state an opinion about whether the defendant did or did not have a mental state or condition that constitutes an element of the crime charged or of a defense. Those matters are for the trier of fact alone.

Rule 705. Disclosing the Facts or Data Underlying an Expert's Opinion

Unless the court orders otherwise, an expert may state an opinion—and give the reasons for it—without first testifying to the underlying facts or data. But the expert may be required to disclose those facts or data on cross-examination.

Rule 706. Court-Appointed Expert Witnesses

(a) **Appointment Process.** On a party's motion or on its own, the court may order the parties to show cause why expert witnesses should not be appointed and may ask the parties to submit nominations. The court may appoint any expert that the parties agree on and any of its own choosing. But the court may only appoint someone who consents to act.

(b) **Expert's Role.** The court must inform the expert of the expert's duties. The court may do so in writing and have a copy filed with the clerk or may do so orally at a conference in which the parties have an opportunity to participate. The expert:

(1) must advise the parties of any findings the expert makes;

(2) may be deposed by any party;

(3) may be called to testify by the court or any party; and

(4) may be cross-examined by any party, including the party that called the expert.

(c) **Compensation.** The expert is entitled to a reasonable compensation, as set by the court. The compensation is payable as follows:

(1) in a criminal case or in a civil case involving just compensation under the Fifth Amendment, from any funds that are provided by law; and

(2) in any other civil case, by the parties in the proportion and at the time that the court directs—and the compensation is then charged like other costs.

(d) **Disclosing the Appointment to the Jury.** The court may authorize disclosure to the jury that the court appointed the expert.

(e) **Parties' Choice of Their Own Experts.** This rule does not limit a party in calling its own experts.

ARTICLE VIII. HEARSAY

Rule 801. Definitions That Apply to This Article; Exclusions from Hearsay

(a) **Statement.** "Statement" means a person's oral assertion, written assertion, or nonverbal conduct, if the person intended it as an assertion.

(b) **Declarant.** "Declarant" means the person who made the statement.

(c) **Hearsay.** "Hearsay" means a statement that:

(1) the declarant does not make while testifying at the current trial or hearing; and

(2) a party offers in evidence to prove the truth of the matter asserted in the statement.

(d) **Statements That Are Not Hearsay.** A statement that meets the following conditions is not hearsay:

(1) ***A Declarant-Witness's Prior Statement.*** The declarant testifies and is subject to cross-examination about a prior statement, and the statement:

(A) is inconsistent with the declarant's testimony and was given under penalty of perjury at a trial, hearing, or other proceeding or in a deposition;

(B) is consistent with the declarant's testimony and is offered:

(i) to rebut an express or implied charge that the declarant recently fabricated it or acted from a recent improper influence or motive in so testifying; or

(ii) to rehabilitate the declarant's credibility as a witness when attacked on another ground; or

(C) identifies a person as someone the declarant perceived earlier.

(2) ***An Opposing Party's Statement.*** The statement is offered against an opposing party and:

(A) was made by the party in an individual or representative capacity;

(B) is one the party manifested that it adopted or believed to be true;

(C) was made by a person whom the party authorized to make a statement on the subject;

(D) was made by the party's agent or employee on a matter within the scope of that relationship and while it existed; or

(E) was made by the party's coconspirator during and in furtherance of the conspiracy.

The statement must be considered but does not by itself establish the declarant's authority under (C); the existence or scope of the relationship under (D); or the existence of the conspiracy or participation in it under (E).

Rule 802. The Rule Against Hearsay

Hearsay is not admissible unless any of the following provides otherwise:

- a federal statute;
- these rules; or
- other rules prescribed by the Supreme Court.

Rule 803. Exceptions to the Rule Against Hearsay—Regardless of Whether the Declarant Is Available as a Witness

The following are not excluded by the rule against hearsay, regardless of whether the declarant is available as a witness:

(1) ***Present Sense Impression.*** A statement describing or explaining an event or condition, made while or immediately after the declarant perceived it.

(2) ***Excited Utterance.*** A statement relating to a startling event or condition, made while the declarant was under the stress of excitement that it caused.

(3) ***Then-Existing Mental, Emotional, or Physical Condition.*** A statement of the declarant's then-existing state of mind (such as motive, intent, or plan) or emotional, sensory, or physical condition (such as mental feeling, pain, or bodily health), but not including a statement of memory or belief to prove the fact remembered or believed unless it relates to the validity or terms of the declarant's will.

(4) ***Statement Made for Medical Diagnosis or Treatment.*** A statement that:

(A) is made for—and is reasonably pertinent to—medical diagnosis or treatment; and

(B) describes medical history; past or present symptoms or sensations; their inception; or their general cause.

(5) ***Recorded Recollection.*** A record that:

(A) is on a matter the witness once knew about but now cannot recall well enough to testify fully and accurately;

(B) was made or adopted by the witness when the matter was fresh in the witness's memory; and

(C) accurately reflects the witness's knowledge.

If admitted, the record may be read into evidence but may be received as an exhibit only if offered by an adverse party.

(6) ***Records of a Regularly Conducted Activity.*** A record of an act, event, condition, opinion, or diagnosis if:

(A) the record was made at or near the time by—or from information transmitted by—someone with knowledge;

(B) the record was kept in the course of a regularly conducted activity of a business, organization, occupation, or calling, whether or not for profit;

(C) making the record was a regular practice of that activity;

(D) all these conditions are shown by the testimony of the custodian or another qualified witness, or by a certification that complies with Rule 902(11) or (12) or with a statute permitting certification; and

(E) the opponent does not show that the source of information or the method or circumstances of preparation indicate a lack of trustworthiness.

(7) ***Absence of a Record of a Regularly Conducted Activity.*** Evidence that a matter is not included in a record described in paragraph (6) if:

(A) the evidence is admitted to prove that the matter did not occur or exist;

(B) a record was regularly kept for a matter of that kind; and

(C) the opponent does not show that the possible source of the information or other circumstances indicate a lack of trustworthiness.

(8) ***Public Records.*** A record or statement of a public office if:

(A) it sets out:

(i) the office's activities;

(ii) a matter observed while under a legal duty to report, but not including, in a criminal case, a matter observed by law-enforcement personnel; or

(iii) in a civil case or against the government in a criminal case, factual findings from a legally authorized investigation; and

(B) the opponent does not show that the source of information or other circumstances indicate a lack of trustworthiness.

(9) ***Public Records of Vital Statistics.*** A record of a birth, death, or marriage, if reported to a public office in accordance with a legal duty.

(10) ***Absence of a Public Record.*** Testimony—or a certification under Rule 902—that a diligent search failed to disclose a public record or statement if:

(A) the testimony or certification is admitted to prove that

(i) the record or statement does not exist; or

(ii) a matter did not occur or exist, if a public office regularly kept a record or statement for a matter of that kind; and

(B) in a criminal case, a prosecutor who intends to offer a certification provides written notice of that intent at least 14 days before trial, and the defendant does not object in writing within 7 days of receiving the notice—unless the court sets a different time for the notice or the objection.

(11) ***Records of Religious Organizations Concerning Personal or Family History.*** A statement of birth, legitimacy, ancestry, marriage, divorce, death, relationship by blood or marriage, or similar facts of personal or family history, contained in a regularly kept record of a religious organization.

(12) ***Certificates of Marriage, Baptism, and Similar Ceremonies.*** A statement of fact contained in a certificate:

(A) made by a person who is authorized by a religious organization or by law to perform the act certified;

(B) attesting that the person performed a marriage or similar ceremony or administered a sacrament; and

(C) purporting to have been issued at the time of the act or within a reasonable time after it.

(13) ***Family Records.*** A statement of fact about personal or family history contained in a family record, such as a Bible, genealogy, chart, engraving on a ring, inscription on a portrait, or engraving on an urn or burial marker.

(14) ***Records of Documents That Affect an Interest in Property.*** *The record of a document that purports to establish or affect an interest in property if:*

(A) the record is admitted to prove the content of the original recorded document, along with its signing and its delivery by each person who purports to have signed it;

(B) the record is kept in a public office; and

(C) a statute authorizes recording documents of that kind in that office.

(15) ***Statements in Documents That Affect an Interest in Property.*** A statement contained in a document that purports to establish or affect an interest in property if the matter stated was relevant to the document's purpose—unless later dealings with the property are inconsistent with the truth of the statement or the purport of the document.

(16) ***Statements in Ancient Documents.*** A statement in a document that was prepared before January 1, 1998, and whose authenticity is established.

(17) ***Market Reports and Similar Commercial Publications.*** Market quotations, lists, directories, or other compilations that are generally relied on by the public or by persons in particular occupations.

(18) ***Statements in Learned Treatises, Periodicals, or Pamphlets.*** A statement contained in a treatise, periodical, or pamphlet if:

(A) the statement is called to the attention of an expert witness on cross-examination or relied on by the expert on direct examination; and

(B) the publication is established as a reliable authority by the expert's admission or testimony, by another expert's testimony, or by judicial notice.

If admitted, the statement may be read into evidence but not received as an exhibit.

(19) ***Reputation Concerning Personal or Family History.*** A reputation among a person's family by blood, adoption, or marriage—or among a person's associates or in the community—concerning the person's birth, adoption, legitimacy, ancestry, marriage, divorce, death, relationship by blood, adoption, or marriage, or similar facts of personal or family history.

(20) ***Reputation Concerning Boundaries or General History.*** A reputation in a community—arising before the controversy—concerning boundaries of land in the community or customs that affect the land, or concerning general historical events important to that community, state, or nation.

(21) ***Reputation Concerning Character.*** A reputation among a person's associates or in the community concerning the person's character.

(22) ***Judgment of a Previous Conviction.*** Evidence of a final judgment of conviction if:

(A) the judgment was entered after a trial or guilty plea, but not a nolo contendere plea;

(B) the conviction was for a crime punishable by death or by imprisonment for more than a year;

(C) the evidence is admitted to prove any fact essential to the judgment; and

(D) when offered by the prosecutor in a criminal case for a purpose other than impeachment, the judgment was against the defendant.

The pendency of an appeal may be shown but does not affect admissibility.

(23) ***Judgments Involving Personal, Family, or General History, or a Boundary.*** A judgment that is admitted to prove a matter of personal, family, or general history, or boundaries, if the matter:

(A) was essential to the judgment; and

(B) could be proved by evidence of reputation.

(24) [**Other Exceptions.**] [Transferred to Rule 807.]

Rule 804. Exceptions to the Rule Against Hearsay—When the Declarant Is Unavailable as a Witness

(a) **Criteria for Being Unavailable.** A declarant is considered to be unavailable as a witness if the declarant:

(1) is exempted from testifying about the subject matter of the declarant's statement because the court rules that a privilege applies;

(2) refuses to testify about the subject matter despite a court order to do so;

(3) testifies to not remembering the subject matter;

(4) cannot be present or testify at the trial or hearing because of death or a then-existing infirmity, physical illness, or mental illness; or

(5) is absent from the trial or hearing and the statement's proponent has not been able, by process or other reasonable means, to procure:

(A) the declarant's attendance, in the case of a hearsay exception under Rule 804(b)(1) or (6); or

(B) the declarant's attendance or testimony, in the case of a hearsay exception under Rule 804(b)(2), (3), or (4).

But this subdivision (a) does not apply if the statement's proponent procured or wrongfully caused the declarant's unavailability as a witness in order to prevent the declarant from attending or testifying.

(b) **The Exceptions.** The following are not excluded by the rule against hearsay if the declarant is unavailable as a witness:

(1) ***Former Testimony.*** Testimony that:

(A) was given as a witness at a trial, hearing, or lawful deposition, whether given during the current proceeding or a different one; and

(B) is now offered against a party who had—or, in a civil case, whose predecessor in interest had—an opportunity and similar motive to develop it by direct, cross-, or redirect examination.

(2) ***Statement Under the Belief of Imminent Death.*** In a prosecution for homicide or in a civil case, a statement that the declarant, while believing the declarant's death to be imminent, made about its cause or circumstances.

(3) ***Statement Against Interest.*** A statement that:

(A) a reasonable person in the declarant's position would have made only if the person believed it to be true because, when made, it was so contrary to the declarant's proprietary or pecuniary interest or had so great a tendency to invalidate the declarant's claim against someone else or to expose the declarant to civil or criminal liability; and

(B) is supported by corroborating circumstances that clearly indicate its trustworthiness, if it is offered in a criminal case as one that tends to expose the declarant to criminal liability.

(4) ***Statement of Personal or Family History.*** A statement about:

(A) the declarant's own birth, adoption, legitimacy, ancestry, marriage, divorce, relationship by blood, adoption, or marriage, or similar facts of personal or family history, even though the declarant had no way of acquiring personal knowledge about that fact; or

(B) another person concerning any of these facts, as well as death, if the declarant was related to the person by blood, adoption, or marriage or was so intimately associated with the person's family that the declarant's information is likely to be accurate.

(5) [**Other Exceptions.**] [Transferred to Rule 807.]

(6) ***Statement Offered Against a Party That Wrongfully Caused the Declarant's Unavailability.*** A statement offered against a party that wrongfully caused—or acquiesced in wrongfully causing—the declarant's unavailability as a witness, and did so intending that result.

Rule 805. Hearsay Within Hearsay

Hearsay within hearsay is not excluded by the rule against hearsay if each part of the combined statements conforms with an exception to the rule.

Rule 806. Attacking and Supporting the Declarant's Credibility

When a hearsay statement—or a statement described in Rule 801(d)(2)(C), (D), or (E)—has been admitted in evidence, the declarant's credibility may be attacked, and then supported, by any evidence that would be admissible for those purposes if the declarant had testified as a witness. The court may admit evidence of the declarant's inconsistent statement or conduct, regardless of when it occurred or whether the declarant had an opportunity to explain or deny it. If the party against whom the statement was admitted calls the declarant as a witness, the party may examine the declarant on the statement as if on cross-examination.

Rule 807. Residual Exception

(a) **In General.** Under the following conditions, a hearsay statement is not excluded by the rule against hearsay even if the statement is not admissible under a hearsay exception in Rule 803 or 804:

 (1) the statement is supported by sufficient guarantees of trustworthiness—after considering the totality of circumstances under which it was made and evidence, if any, corroborating the statement; and

 (2) it is more probative on the point for which it is offered than any other evidence that the proponent can obtain through reasonable efforts.

(b) **Notice.** The statement is admissible only if the proponent gives an adverse party reasonable notice of the intent to offer the statement—including its substance and the declarant's name—so that the party has a fair opportunity to meet it. The notice must be provided in writing before the trial or hearing—or in any form during the trial or hearing if the court, for good cause, excuses a lack of earlier notice.

ARTICLE IX. AUTHENTICATION AND IDENTIFICATION

Rule 901. Authenticating or Identifying Evidence

(a) **In General.** To satisfy the requirement of authenticating or identifying an item of evidence, the proponent must produce evidence sufficient to support a finding that the item is what the proponent claims it is.

(b) **Examples.** The following are examples only—not a complete list—of evidence that satisfies the requirement:

 (1) ***Testimony of a Witness with Knowledge.*** Testimony that an item is what it is claimed to be.

 (2) ***Nonexpert Opinion About Handwriting.*** A nonexpert's opinion that handwriting is genuine, based on a familiarity with it that was not acquired for the current litigation.

 (3) ***Comparison by an Expert Witness or the Trier of Fact.*** A comparison with an authenticated specimen by an expert witness or the trier of fact.

(4) ***Distinctive Characteristics and the Like.*** The appearance, contents, substance, internal patterns, or other distinctive characteristics of the item, taken together with all the circumstances.

(5) ***Opinion About a Voice.*** An opinion identifying a person's voice—whether heard firsthand or through mechanical or electronic transmission or recording—based on hearing the voice at any time under circumstances that connect it with the alleged speaker.

(6) ***Evidence About a Telephone Conversation.*** For a telephone conversation, evidence that a call was made to the number assigned at the time to:

(A) a particular person, if circumstances, including self-identification, show that the person answering was the one called; or

(B) a particular business, if the call was made to a business and the call related to business reasonably transacted over the telephone.

(7) ***Evidence About Public Records.*** Evidence that:

(A) a document was recorded or filed in a public office as authorized by law; or

(B) a purported public record or statement is from the office where items of this kind are kept.

(8) ***Evidence About Ancient Documents or Data Compilations.*** For a document or data compilation, evidence that it:

(A) is in a condition that creates no suspicion about its authenticity;

(B) was in a place where, if authentic, it would likely be; and

(C) is at least 20 years old when offered.

(9) ***Evidence About a Process or System.*** Evidence describing a process or system and showing that it produces an accurate result.

(10) ***Methods Provided by a Statute or Rule.*** Any method of authentication or identification allowed by a federal statute or a rule prescribed by the Supreme Court.

Rule 902. Evidence That Is Self-Authenticating

The following items of evidence are self-authenticating; they require no extrinsic evidence of authenticity in order to be admitted:

(1) ***Domestic Public Documents That Are Sealed and Signed.*** A document that bears:

(A) a seal purporting to be that of the United States; any state, district, commonwealth, territory, or insular possession of the United States; the former Panama Canal Zone; the Trust Territory of the Pacific Islands; a political subdivision of any of these entities; or a department, agency, or officer of any entity named above; and

(B) a signature purporting to be an execution or attestation.

(2) ***Domestic Public Documents That Are Not Sealed but Are Signed and Certified.*** A document that bears no seal if:

(A) it bears the signature of an officer or employee of an entity named in Rule 902(1)(A); and

(B) another public officer who has a seal and official duties within that same entity certifies under seal—or its equivalent—that the signer has the official capacity and that the signature is genuine.

(3) ***Foreign Public Documents.*** A document that purports to be signed or attested by a person who is authorized by a foreign country's law to do so. The document must be accompanied by a final certification that certifies the genuineness of the signature and official position of the signer or attester—or of any foreign official whose certificate of genuineness relates to the signature or attestation or is in a chain of certificates of genuineness relating to the signature or attestation. The certification may be made by a secretary of a United States embassy or legation; by a consul general, vice consul, or consular agent of the United States; or by a diplomatic or consular official of the foreign country assigned or accredited to the United States. If all parties have been given a reasonable opportunity to investigate the document's authenticity and accuracy, the court may, for good cause, either:

(A) order that it be treated as presumptively authentic without final certification; or

(B) allow it to be evidenced by an attested summary with or without final certification.

(4) ***Certified Copies of Public Records.*** A copy of an official record—or a copy of a document that was recorded or filed in a public office as authorized by law—if the copy is certified as correct by:

(A) the custodian or another person authorized to make the certification; or

(B) a certificate that complies with Rule 902(1), (2), or (3), a federal statute, or a rule prescribed by the Supreme Court.

(5) ***Official Publications.*** A book, pamphlet, or other publication purporting to be issued by a public authority.

(6) ***Newspapers and Periodicals.*** Printed material purporting to be a newspaper or periodical.

(7) ***Trade Inscriptions and the Like.*** An inscription, sign, tag, or label purporting to have been affixed in the course of business and indicating origin, ownership, or control.

(8) ***Acknowledged Documents.*** A document accompanied by a certificate of acknowledgment that is lawfully executed by a notary public or another officer who is authorized to take acknowledgments.

(9) ***Commercial Paper and Related Documents.*** Commercial paper, a signature on it, and related documents, to the extent allowed by general commercial law.

(10) ***Presumptions Under a Federal Statute.*** A signature, document, or anything else that a federal statute declares to be presumptively or prima facie genuine or authentic.

(11) ***Certified Domestic Records of a Regularly Conducted Activity.*** The original or a copy of a domestic record that meets the requirements of Rule 803(6)(A)–(C), as shown by a certification of the custodian or another qualified person that complies with a federal statute or a rule prescribed by the Supreme Court. Before the trial or hearing, the proponent must give an adverse party reasonable written notice of the intent to offer the record—and must make the record and certification available for inspection—so that the party has a fair opportunity to challenge them.

(12) ***Certified Foreign Records of a Regularly Conducted Activity.*** In a civil case, the original or a copy of a foreign record that meets the requirements of Rule 902(11), modified as follows: the certification, rather than complying with a federal statute or Supreme Court rule, must be signed in a manner that, if falsely made, would subject the maker to a criminal penalty in the country where the certification is signed. The proponent must also meet the notice requirements of Rule 902(11).

(13) ***Certified Records Generated by an Electronic Process or System.*** A record generated by an electronic process of system that produces an accurate result, as shown by a certification of a qualified person that complies with the certification requirements of Rule 902(11) or (12). The proponent must also meet the notice requirement of Rule 902(11).

(14) ***Certified Data Copied from an Electronic Device, Storage Medium, or File.*** Data copied from an electronic device, storage medium, or file, if authenticated by a process of digital identification, as shown by a certification of a qualified person that complies with the certification requirements of Rule 902(11) or (12). The proponent also must meet the notice requirements of rule 902(11).

Rule 903. Subscribing Witness's Testimony

A subscribing witness's testimony is necessary to authenticate a writing only if required by the law of the jurisdiction that governs its validity.

ARTICLE X. CONTENTS OF WRITINGS, RECORDINGS, AND PHOTOGRAPHS

Rule 1001. Definitions That Apply to This Article

In this article:

(a) A "writing" consists of letters, words, numbers, or their equivalent set down in any form.

(b) A "recording" consists of letters, words, numbers, or their equivalent recorded in any manner.

(c) A "photograph" means a photographic image or its equivalent stored in any form.

(d) An "original" of a writing or recording means the writing or recording itself or any counterpart intended to have the same effect by the person who executed or issued it. For electronically stored information, "original" means any printout—or other output readable by sight—if it accurately reflects the information. An "original" of a photograph includes the negative or a print from it.

(e) A "duplicate" means a counterpart produced by a mechanical, photographic, chemical, electronic, or other equivalent process or technique that accurately reproduces the original.

Rule 1002. Requirement of the Original

An original writing, recording, or photograph is required in order to prove its content unless these rules or a federal statute provides otherwise.

Rule 1003. Admissibility of Duplicates

A duplicate is admissible to the same extent as the original unless a genuine question is raised about the original's authenticity or the circumstances make it unfair to admit the duplicate.

Rule 1004. Admissibility of Other Evidence of Content

An original is not required and other evidence of the content of a writing, recording, or photograph is admissible if:

(a) all the originals are lost or destroyed, and not by the proponent acting in bad faith;

(b) an original cannot be obtained by any available judicial process;

(c) the party against whom the original would be offered had control of the original; was at that time put on notice, by pleadings or otherwise, that the original would be a subject of proof at the trial or hearing; and fails to produce it at the trial or hearing; or

(d) the writing, recording, or photograph is not closely related to a controlling issue.

Rule 1005. Copies of Public Records to Prove Content

The proponent may use a copy to prove the content of an official record—or of a document that was recorded or filed in a public office as authorized by law—if these conditions are met: the record or document is otherwise admissible; and the copy is certified as correct in accordance with Rule 902(4) or is testified to be correct by a witness who has compared it with the original. If no such copy can be obtained by reasonable diligence, then the proponent may use other evidence to prove the content.

Rule 1006. Summaries to Prove Content

The proponent may use a summary, chart, or calculation to prove the content of voluminous writings, recordings, or photographs that cannot be conveniently examined in court. The proponent must make the originals or duplicates available for examination or copying, or both, by other parties at a reasonable time and place. And the court may order the proponent to produce them in court.

Rule 1007. Testimony or Statement of a Party to Prove Content

The proponent may prove the content of a writing, recording, or photograph by the testimony, deposition, or written statement of the party against whom the evidence is offered. The proponent need not account for the original.

Rule 1008. Functions of the Court and Jury

Ordinarily, the court determines whether the proponent has fulfilled the factual conditions for admitting other evidence of the content of a writing, recording, or photograph under Rule 1004 or 1005. But in a jury trial, the jury determines—in accordance with Rule 104(b)—any issue about whether:

(a) an asserted writing, recording, or photograph ever existed;

(b) another one produced at the trial or hearing is the original; or

(c) other evidence of content accurately reflects the content.

ARTICLE XI. MISCELLANEOUS RULES

Rule 1101. Applicability of the Rules

(a) **To Courts and Judges.** These rules apply to proceedings before:

- United States district courts;
- United States bankruptcy and magistrate judges;
- United States courts of appeals;
- the United States Court of Federal Claims; and
- the district courts of Guam, the Virgin Islands, and the Northern Mariana Islands.

(b) **To Cases and Proceedings.** These rules apply in:

- civil cases and proceedings, including bankruptcy, admiralty, and maritime cases;
- criminal cases and proceedings; and
- contempt proceedings, except those in which the court may act summarily.

(c) **Rules on Privilege.** The rules on privilege apply to all stages of a case or proceeding.

(d) **Exceptions.** These rules—except for those on privilege—do not apply to the following:

(1) the court's determination, under Rule 104(a), on a preliminary question of fact governing admissibility;

(2) grand-jury proceedings; and

(3) miscellaneous proceedings such as:

- extradition or rendition;
- issuing an arrest warrant, criminal summons, or search warrant;
- a preliminary examination in a criminal case;
- sentencing;
- granting or revoking probation or supervised release; and
- considering whether to release on bail or otherwise.

(e) **Other Statutes and Rules.** A federal statute or a rule prescribed by the Supreme Court may provide for admitting or excluding evidence independently from these rules.

Rule 1102. Amendments

These rules may be amended as provided in 28 U.S.C. § 2072.

Rule 1103. Title

These rules may be cited as the Federal Rules of Evidence.

Table of Cases

Table of Statutes

Table of Rules

Index

References are to Sections

TRUSTWORTHINESS